THE BUILDINGS OF ENGLAND

Hampshire

AN

D1496739

★

PENGUIN BOOKS

Penguin Books Ltd, Harmondsworth, Middlesex, England
Penguin Books Inc., 3300 Clipper Mill Road, Baltimore, Md. 21211, U.S.A.
Penguin Books Pty Ltd, Ringwood, Victoria, Australia

—

First published 1967

—

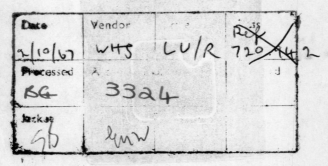

Made and printed in Great Britain
by William Clowes and Sons, Limited, London and Beccles
Gravure plates by Harrison & Sons Ltd
Set in Monotype Plantin

To
the Ministry of Housing and Local Government,
whose lists of buildings of architectural
or historic interest
are one of the finest tools
we have

CONTENTS

FOREWORD 11

INTRODUCTION 15

THE BUILDINGS OF HAMPSHIRE BY NIKOLAUS PEVSNER 15

PREHISTORY BY DEREK SIMPSON 62

ROMAN HAMPSHIRE BY BARRY CUNLIFFE 68

GEOLOGY BY TERENCE MILLER 70

HAMPSHIRE 73

THE ISLE OF WIGHT 729

GLOSSARY 779

INDEX OF PLATES 801

INDEX OF ARTISTS 805

INDEX OF PLACES 817

ADDENDA 826

Map References

★

The numbers printed in italic type in the margin against the place names in the gazetteer of the book indicate the position of the place in question on the index map (pages 2–3), which is divided into sections by the 10-kilometre reference lines of the National Grid. The reference given here omits the two initial letters (formerly numbers) which in a full grid reference refer to the 100-kilometre squares into which the country is divided. The first two numbers indicate the *western* boundary, and the last two the *southern* boundary, of the 10–kilometre square in which the place in question is situated. For example Winchester (reference 4020) will be found in the 10–kilometre square bounded by grid lines 40 and 50 on the *west* and 20 and 30 on the *south*: Bramdean (reference 6020) in the square bounded by grid lines 60 and 70 on the *west* and 20 and 30 on the *south.*

The map contains all those places, whether towns, villages, or isolated buildings, which are the subject of separate entries in the text.

FOREWORD

This volume, like Surrey, Lincolnshire, Sussex, and Warwickshire, is a joint enterprise. Mr David Lloyd has described Southampton and Portsmouth and the towns and villages between and around them, altogether above seventy places. As it would be difficult to set down here the exact boundary between his territory and mine we have marked his places with a DL *in the margin. Even without these initials his way of characterizing villages and towns stands out from my scanty remarks on that important topic. However, I partly rewrote, with Mr Lloyd's agreement, one or two of his descriptions of churches, and the account of Grove Place Nursling is mine.*

The preparation for his and my work was of course enormously helped by the existence of the more than three topographical volumes of the Victoria County History. *On the other hand it suffered from two assistants leaving after only having been able to do part of the work. It was most unfortunate, and the results would have suffered worse had not Miss Jennifer Sherwood in the end completed the job and pulled it all together. Prehistory was more straightforward. As in several of the more recent volumes, Mr Derek Simpson wrote the introduction and the gazetteer entries. For Roman material I welcome Professor Barry Cunliffe. He wrote introduction and entries, and I am flattered by his willingness to do so. Mr Terence Miller, familiar to readers of previous volumes, provided the introduction to Geology.*

So there is little danger of inadequacies in those fields. There is much more in what I have written. I ought to point out for instance that worth-while interiors of houses, especially smaller ones, might easily have been missed. If we did not know their value or importance beforehand, we would not try to penetrate and so no doubt have left out many good and interesting things. Another snag has been Bournemouth, where the boundary between Hampshire and Dorset cuts right through what is now all one town. Yet, because Dorset has not yet been prepared for the future volume of The Buildings of England, *the buildings of the Dorset part of the town just could not be included. As for other shortcomings, it can safely be left to reviewers to spot them.*

The list of thanks for this volume is specially, gratifyingly, long.

In the first place there is my secretary, Mrs Cryer (then Miss Wendy Martin, who never lost her temper, in the second Miss Dorothy Dorn, who typed my hideous manuscript faultlessly, in the third all those incumbents who have answered questions I had put to them, and all those owners of houses who put up with my visits, extended hospitality to us, and again consented to reply to intricate questions or questionnaires. I owe it to all of them to point out that inclusion of a house in the gazetteer does not necessarily mean that it is open to the public. For hospitality very special thanks are due to Mrs Camilla Bagg, then at Bucklebury Slade, and to Sir Allen and Lady Lane at Priory Farm, Beech Hill. The hospitality was extended to Mr John Newman, who had consented to drive me through the whole county and – what is more – seemed to enjoy it.

Now for those thanks which it is a pleasure to repeat in each volume. The Ministry of Housing and Local Government (here abbreviated MHLG*) allowed me the use of their duplicated lists of buildings of architectural or historic interest. The National Buildings Record, now re-christened National Monuments Record (and hence here abbreviated* NMR*), were as helpful as ever. For Victorian churches my own material was greatly increased by Mr Peter Ferriday's Index of Restorations which he most generously gave on permanent loan to* The Buildings of England *(abbreviated* PF*), and Mr Geoffrey Spain offered a large number of amendments from the Victorian technical journals* (GS). *Sir Thomas Kendrick's Index of Stained Glass I have, thanks to his kindness, also had access to (abbreviated* TK*).*

Of others I wish to thank first some librarians in Hampshire and the Isle of Wight. Where, to repeat what I have often said before, would I be without them? Specially helpful were (in alphabetical order of libraries) Mr W. E. French of Aldershot, Mr H. E. Radford of Bournemouth, Mr F. S. Green of Newport, and Mr A. Bullen of Winchester.

In addition I received particularly valuable help from (in roughly alphabetical order) Mr Martin Biddle, who wrote the report on his Winchester excavations; Mr Jack Blakiston, Mr P. J. Gwyn, and Mr R. O. Hall, who gave additional information on Winchester College, and Mr John Harvey, also about Winchester College; the Rev. Basil Clarke; the late Rupert Gunnis, author of the indispensable dictionary of English sculptors from 1660 to 1851 and the most generous of men; John Harris of the R.I.B.A., the great expert on architectural drawings; Rodney Hubbuck (RH)*, who read and commented on the whole of my typescript; Mr R. L. P. Jowitt* *who read all the proofs, Father Paul Meyvaert, who took us round Quarr Abbey; Mr A. C. Sewter of Manchester, author of a yet unpublished catalogue of all Morris glass; Mr E. A. Sibbick, who took us all over Osborne; Mr J. G. Stone, who conducted us all over Winchester College; Nicholas Taylor* (NT) *of* The Architectural Review, *omniscient in Victorian Bournemouth matters, who read all we have written and went on mercilessly improving our entries to the very end; and Mr W. J. Carpenter Turner, architect to Winchester Cathedral, and Mrs Carpenter Turner, Winchester-in-general expert. Mr David Lloyd's list of thanks is as long: the Defence Land Agent (Army) and the Defence Lands Office (Navy), the Admiral Superintendent, Portsmouth Dockyard, Mr R. Sutherland Horne of the Ministry of Public Building and Works, Mr J. P. Halliwell of Southampton University, the City Librarians of Southampton and Portsmouth (Mr H. Sargeant and Mr E. A Clough), the Librarians of Gosport, Havant and Fareham (Miss M. I. Dingle, Mr R. M. Shimmon, and Mr J. B. Homan), Mr J. Pallister of the Southampton Museum, Mr A. Corney of the Portsmouth Museum, the City Architect's Department Southampton, and (in alphabetical order) Mr John Harris, Mr Rodney Hubbuck, Mr George McHardy, Miss E. M. Sandell, who read and commented on the section on Southampton, Mr A. C. Sewter, Mr Nicholas Taylor, Dr Paul Thompson, and Mr Stephen Weeks, as well as innumerable owners, custodians, and others in country houses, service establishments, and, of course, incumbents of churches, any one of whom it would be invidious to single out. Many were extremely hospitable and helpful.*

The gazetteer to this volume is divided into Hampshire and, beginning on p. 729, the Isle of Wight. The principles on which entries are based are the same as in the preceding thirty-one volumes. We have both seen everything we describe. Where this is not the case, the information obtained is placed in brackets. Information ought to be as complete as the space of the volume permits for churches prior to c.*1830 and all town houses, manor houses, and country houses of more than purely local interest. Movable furnishings are not included in secular buildings, though they are in churches. Exceptions to the latter rule are bells, hatchments, chests, chairs, plain fonts, and altar tables. Royal arms, coffin lids with foliate crosses, and brasses of post-Reformation date are mentioned occasionally, church plate of after 1830 only rarely. Village and churchyard crosses are omitted where only a plain base or a stump of the shaft survives. As for churches and chapels of after 1830, we had to make a selection, and this is dictated by architectural value or by significance otherwise in the light of architectural history. The same applies to secular buildings of the* C19 *and* C20.

Finally, as in all previous volumes, it is necessary to end the Foreword to this with an appeal to all users to draw my attention to errors and omissions.

INTRODUCTION

HAMPSHIRE with the Isle of Wight is eighth in size among English counties. In population it comes eleventh. It has two large cities: Southampton with *c.* 205,000 inhabitants (1961) and Portsmouth with *c.* 215,000. The two are getting alarmingly near to becoming one conurbation.* Bournemouth has *c.* 154,000, 3
but otherwise there is no town larger than Aldershot and Farnborough, each with *c.* 31,000, and Winchester, Lymington, Christchurch, and Basingstoke, each with a little under 30,000. So, as one travels through Hampshire by car, it is still a rural county, though travelling by train one sees how suburban housing tends to spread along the line all the way from Surrey to Basingstoke and beyond.

Hampshire is not only a rural county, it is a county with some of the finest scenery in the south of England, and a remarkable variety, from the sandy heath of the Surrey border and around Aldershot to the New Forest with its protected expanses of wood 1
and heathland and to the downs in the middle and the south of the county and, most unspoilt, on the Isle of Wight. But what is perhaps the most impressive landscape feature of Hampshire, is the majestic single conifers and groups of conifers one sees in so many places, enormous yew trees, cedar trees, macrocarpa, Scotch firs, or Wellingtonias. The dependence of this aspect of the flora of Hampshire on the geology of the county needs no emphasis, and geology is being treated separately in an appendix to this introduction on p. 70.

Geology also, and even more directly, tells of building materials, and here, for the purposes of a survey of Hampshire buildings, it is enough to say that Hampshire lies entirely outside the ribbon of England's best building stone, the oölitic limestone of, say, Dorset and Wiltshire, to mention only two adjoining counties. Instead there is flint and chalk (or malm), and on the Isle of Wight some good limestone such as those of Binstead and Quarr, and of course brick, and of course flint,

* Havant *c.* 75,000, Gosport *c.* 62,000, Fareham *c.* 58,000, Eastleigh *c.* 37,000. That makes, without the villages, about 650,000. But there are still surprisingly unspoiled places in between the two large cities – e.g. Botley, Titchfield, Wickham, and the older part of Fareham. *See* p. 827

the most widespread and most ancient material, used in prehistoric tools and in Roman buildings.

Prehistory and Roman architecture have, like geology, been taken out of this introduction. There are special surveys of them, and they will be found on pages 62 to 69.

So here we begin with the ANGLO-SAXON PERIOD.
Quantitatively Hampshire, compared with some other counties,
has not much to contribute, but qualitatively the recent excavations at Winchester and Breamore alone establish the county as
one not to be left out of an Anglo-Saxon pilgrimage, and for
Anglo-Saxon stone sculpture no county has as much to offer as
p. 660 ours. The Winchester excavations refer to the late C10 cathedral.
The results obtained so far are unexpected and thrilling. They
comprise a complex E end of a kind not met with in Anglo-
Saxon England before, with an E apse and odd N and S apses,
7 and one piece of a large figure frieze. This also is something
that is up-to-date without Anglo-Saxon parallel. Of the
New Minster, N of the cathedral, the most interesting find so
far is a small oval building, also of the C10. Breamore belongs to
about 1000, and as a cruciform church with a crossing or an
attempt at a crossing it is one of very few. Dover is the nearest,
Stow in Lincolnshire a superior attempt, Great Paxton in
Huntingdonshire the most perfect. One must speak of attempts,
as the Romanesque crossing proper implied a sense of imposed
order absent in the Anglo-Saxons. The Romanesque crossing is a
real crossing, i.e. the square space where nave, chancel, and transepts, all of identical width and height, meet, and moreover a
space opened to the four arms entirely except for the responds.
Breamore is not like that. The transepts are much narrower and
lower than nave and tower, and the openings are as narrow as
those to the traditional Anglo-Saxon *porticus*. Breamore has
long-and-short quoins and lesenes, motifs which occur in a few
other churches as well, i.e. Boarhunt, Corhampton, Fareham,
Hambledon, Hannington, Headbourne Worthy, Hinton Amp-
9 ner, and Little Somborne. Boarhunt is altogether a Saxon
church – of the simplest two-cell type. Only two more Hampshire churches need a reference, both for towers: Titchfield,
where, as e.g. at Monkwearmouth, an earlier W porch was later
converted into a tower, and Warblington, where there may also
have been a W porch, but W of the present central tower, which
has upper doorway openings to former wooden galleries.

Stone SCULPTURE on a large scale up to the early C11 is a great rarity on the Continent as well as in England. The Hamp-

shire group is perhaps the most important anywhere. There was apparently a tradition in Anglo-Saxon England which Hampshire followed; for at Monkwearmouth there are traces of an over-life-size externally placed figure of Christ of as early a date as the late C7. The external stone figures and groups of Hampshire seem to belong to the first half of the C11: they are the piece from a frieze at Winchester already mentioned, the famous Romsey Rood, and the Crucifixion groups with the Virgin and St John at Headbourne Worthy and Breamore. The latter two alas exist as shadows only, since all that was relief was hacked off by fanatics. The Breamore Crucifixion is the most interesting, because of the way the body of Christ and especially the arms seem warped in agony.* Small-scale stone reliefs of the Crucifixion are at Romsey and of the Crucifixus at New Alresford, sundials with a little leaf decoration at Corhampton and Warnford, a very interesting gravestone in the form of a Roman altar with the demi-figure of Christ at Whit- 6
church, and parts of cross-shafts – assigned by Sir Thomas Kendrick to the late C9, i.e. earlier than any of the other monuments – at Winchester (Prior's Barton) and Steventon.

Of the other monuments, dating as they do from the C11, one or two, and especially the Romsey Rood, have been given by some scholars to the decades after the Conquest. That an overlap existed goes without saying. When the NORMANS came, they did not slaughter all Saxon workmen, nor did they bring with them shiploads of their own. Stylistically the difference between Late Saxon and Early Norman is very marked all the same. It is most patent in illuminated manuscripts: the freedom and verve of the Saxons, the rigidity of the Normans. The modelling of the Romsey Rood belongs to the Saxon side. It is soft and indistinct. If you want to see on the highest level of SCULPTURE the contrast to the style the Normans brought in and favoured, you must take the Tournai fonts, of which Hampshire has four: Winchester Cathedral, East Meon, St Michael 15
Southampton, and St Mary Bourne. In the whole country there are ten. They seem to date from about 1140 or 1150, and their style of ornamental decoration, and even more figure-work, especially the scenes from the legend of St Nicholas at

* Comparable sculpture in other counties are the Bibury Rood in Gloucestershire, the roods of Langford in Oxon and Bitton in Gloucestershire, both with a Christ in a long robe, the angels at Bradford-on-Avon in Wiltshire, no doubt originally also part of a rood, and the head of Christ at Barton-on-Humber in Lincolnshire. They are in all probability of before 1000.

Winchester Cathedral, is resolutely organized and leaves nothing to accident.

Tournai marble had a short fashion in England. From about 1170 it was replaced by a local material, the conglomerate known as Purbeck marble. This is greyer or more greenish, and much of what the quarry so amply produced was just turned shafts. In other fields also the Purbeck marblers tended to prefer the standardized product to individual initiative. The prime proof of that is the Purbeck FONTS, of table-top type, as the Tournai ones had been, but decorated with nothing but very shallow blank arches or simple, if sometimes impressive flat leaves, circles, rosettes, etc.* Of these – which are mostly in the N part of the county – there are over twenty, and in addition six octagonal ones. Of fonts made of other stone the best is that at Portchester, with a broad band of 'inhabited' scrolls above blank intersecting arcading. Architectural sculpture is confined to TYMPANA, and even of these there is hardly anything worth mentioning. Damerham has a slayer on horseback, Whippingham, Isle of Wight, a Tree of Life and two quadrupeds. The others are content with all-over patterns of fish-scales or sunk triangles or small chip-carved motifs no less simple. The best ARCHITECTURAL SCULPTURE in the county is beyond any doubt the capitals from Hyde Abbey now at St Bartholomew, Winchester, with their animals in roundels and their stylized foliage. Similar ones are among the display of sculpture on the balcony of the S transept in the cathedral. They date from about 1140–50.

Now for NORMAN ARCHITECTURE proper. At the beginning
P. 662 of course stands Walkelin's work at the cathedral, begun in 1079 and carried on quickly. The chancel is not preserved, but the groin-vaulted crypt beneath it is. This and the transepts and
10 also the surviving entrance to the chapter house can safely be assumed to date from before 1100. The piers are sturdy, capitals confined to the block shape or large single, double, or triple scallops, vaulting to groin-vaults.‡ Arches are unmoulded, and inside at least there is no ornament whatever. Outside the windows have just a thin band of chip-carving and hood-moulds of billet. That is all. It is the most impressive display in England

* The latter especially at Kingsclere. Only at Christchurch are scenes, and at Minstead is a Christ with the cross and a lamb and cross.

‡ The rib-vaults of a very simple C11 profile (half-roll between half-hollows) are a replacement of after 1107. The same profile was still used in the one surviving room at St Cross Winchester which dates from the foundation time. Henry of Blois established the hospital in 1136.

of architecture of the first generation after the Conquest. At
Christchurch work also began before 1100 (under Flambard).
Again the crypts, plainly tunnel-vaulted here, survive.* Christchurch went on into the middle of the C12. The transepts and p. 168
the crossing are of about 1110–15. The N transept front is a
showpiece of fully decorated Norman, and yet seems to be no 14
later than 1125 or 1130. The transepts inside had upper storeys
all the way through and open to the crossing, just as at Jumièges
and Bayeux. At Romsey work started about 1120 and went on 12 & 13
steadily, except for a change in the system of elevation which was p. 479
made just W of the crossing and then again given up. Whereas
until then Romsey, like Winchester and Christchurch, had had
arcade, gallery, and clerestory – even if the gallery has the
curious anomaly of twin openings with the tympanum not filled
in at all and shafts in its middle instead – the new system was
one of arcade and gallery both comprised within a giant arcade
of round piers carrying blank arches. The arcade arches thus die
awkwardly against the round piers, and the gallery arches are
just inside the blank arches. It is the system used under influence
from Romsey at Jedburgh and also somewhat later at St Frides-
wide (the present cathedral) at Oxford. But apart from this
disturbance work proceeded at Romsey without any major
changes until, towards the W and in the clerestory, Norman gives
way to E.E.

Other churches with major Norman elements are Portchester, 16
a complete cruciform building of *c.*1135, hardly altered, then
Petersfield, East Meon, Pamber Priory, and St Michael Southampton with crossing towers, that of East Meon specially fine,
and quite a large number with chancel arches or doorways. Of
all these the ones most worthy of inclusion in this survey are the
sumptuous doorways of Fawley, Hartley Mauditt, Portchester,
and Titchfield.

The peak of architectural activity in Hampshire was the years between about 1180 and about 1220. No-one has yet explained why. To find an arcade of these years in a church is almost a standard experience. The years are those of the TRANSITION from Norman to E.E., and often in Hampshire not of an organic transition, but of elements of the old style standing side by side with elements of the new. St Cross at

* At Chilton Candover the village church has a tunnel-vaulted crypt too; all that remains of that church. Another tunnel-vaulted undercroft is beneath a house in St Thomas's Street at Winchester and several more under houses, largely ruined, at Southampton. On these *see* p. 23.

20 Winchester is the principal representative of this situation. We
p. 708 have no dates, but the years covered by its erection must be from the 1170s to perhaps the 1230s. The start is with exuberant zigzag, but pointed arches enter into the design soon and the vault, even of the E end, is entirely French Gothic.* The details of the development cannot here be summarized. Smaller in scale, but happily dateable, is Warnford built by Adam de Port, who held the manor from 1171 till he died in 1213. The church has a W tower with round bell-openings, a Norfolk motif (Norwich) occurring also at Pamber Priory. Otherwise there are lancet windows and pointed arches, with only slight chamfers. This is a *Leitmotiv* of the group of churches of the Transition. Others are round piers, often still with the archaic square abacus, or otherwise with a square abacus with nicked corners or an octagonal abacus, capitals first with many small scallops, then very often with trumpet scallops, and occasionally waterleaf or flat plain or fluted upright leaves, changing gradually to stiff-leaf and crockets, and arches ranging in morphological order from round and single-step to round with slight chamfers and pointed. But early and late features are found in any kind of combination. Churches to see this situation particularly well in are Bighton, Binsted, Catherington, Crondall, Nether Wallop, Selborne, St Julian, at Southampton, the latter with a memorable chancel arch, and, on the Isle of Wight, Brading and
17 Carisbrooke. Winchfield has decorative details so raw and ferocious that one would place them without hesitation in the first third of the century, yet the context is one not possible before 1170. How late this Transitional was still accepted even for major buildings is brought out by Mottisfont Priory founded in 1201. What went up then still has round arches and capitals with decorated trumpet scallops, even if up in the clerestory they are replaced by crockets. At Whitwell on the Isle of Wight the relation of Norman to *c.*1200 is topographically different. Here a Norman church of St Radegund – a rare dedication and one of the very few rare dedications in Hampshire – about 1200 received a second nave, not an aisle; for it has its own dedication to the Virgin.

The EARLY ENGLISH style appears for the first time without
19 any Transitional hangover in the chancel of Portsmouth Cathedral, a close parallel to the retrochoir of Chichester and like Chichester of before 1200 (consecrations 1188 and 1196). Also connected with Chichester are the S arcade and the odd W

* A rib-vaulted late C12 chancel and apse is at Easton.

arch of the Anglo-Saxon central tower at Warblington with their
detached Purbeck shafts. Only a few years, if at all, later than
Portsmouth is the retrochoir of Winchester Cathedral begun p. 669
by Bishop de Lucy (1189–1204) before 1202, but not long before.
This is a 'hall' in the sense of nave and aisles of equal height,
and it has tall lancet windows, wonderfully slender Purbeck
piers, and finely detailed ribs. The motif of the hall-retrochoir
was taken over from Winchester at Salisbury. The Lady Chapel
and the nave vault were completed after de Lucy's death and a
change in plan. The Lady Chapel has elaborate plate tracery,
and that cannot be attributed to before *c.*1225–30. Almost the
same tracery appears in the impressive porch to the Winchester 26
Deanery, where the ribs are also exactly like those of the retrochoir 'nave'. In this porch apparently the Ecclesia (or Synagogue) was found, the finest piece of sculpture of its date 24
(*c.*1230) in England and closely dependent on (and worthy
of) Chartres. For the dating of plate tracery in Hampshire
Henry III's Great Hall in Winchester Castle is invaluable. It 22
is known from documents that the hall was built between 1222
and 1236. It is, next to Westminster Hall, the finest medieval
hall in England, with powerful clustered Purbeck piers, doorways in the end bay, as was the English custom, a raised dais
platform, and close to it the ornate doorway to the solar. It is
in its dimensions a double cube: 110 by 55 by 55 ft. The windows with their plate tracery are tall and have a transom.
Just one window with plate tracery was set in a special place
in the exquisitely beautiful refectory of Beaulieu Abbey, now
the parish church. All other windows are lancets. The one two-
light window gives light to the finest feature of Beaulieu, the
reading pulpit with its access.

Beaulieu was an abbey, Henry III's hall belonged to a castle. 23
So this is perhaps the place to interrupt the consideration of
parish churches and sum up MONASTIC BUILDINGS in
Hampshire and on the Isle of Wight and secular buildings. As
regards abbeys and priories, Mottisfont, founded in 1201, has
already been referred to. It was Augustinian. So was St Denys
outside Southampton, founded in 1127, of which hardly anything is left. So was Portchester, founded in 1133 and moved to
Southwick in 1145. The church at Portchester is a first-class
Norman monument, Southwick offers hardly more than St
Denys. Augustinian also was Christchurch (from 1150 onward);
so was Selborne, founded in 1233 and of which excavations
are now beginning to provide us with a picture. Of Christchurch

nothing monastic is preserved. Hyde Abbey, Winchester, also mentioned because of its capitals, was Benedictine. It was the successor of New Minster Winchester, which in its turn had been founded in 901. It moved to Hyde in 1110. All that exists of buildings on the site is the C15 gatehouse. At Mottisfont it is, as we have seen, chiefly the (aisleless) church of which parts are recognizable. Of the monastic buildings only part of the vaulted cellarium and a few elements of the chapter house remain. There is no other Augustinian house in the county. Benedictines also served Winchester Cathedral, and
p. 686 here, apart from the chapter house already mentioned and the Deanery, once the Prior's Lodgings (where also the C15 hall survives), the vaulted C13 undercroft to an upper hall, probably the Guest Hall, and a mid C14 hall, usually called the Pilgrims'
34 Hall, can still be seen. The Pilgrims' Hall has the earliest hammerbeam roof so far identified. There are also a gatehouse and a great deal of precinct wall preserved. Of other Benedictine houses nothing monastic survives at Romsey. At Pamber Priory the crossing tower and a very fine E.E. lancet chancel stand up. Andwell Priory belonged to the rare Order of Tiron. No more exists here than some flint walling.

Beaulieu was Cistercian. It was founded in 1204. The plan of the church is known from excavations. It was the most mature C13 plan type of the order, that of Clairvaux III, with an ambulatory and a ring of radiating chapels one immediately adjoining the next. Apart from the refectory there is an interesting gate-
30 house of the C14, now Palace House. This of a most unusual design, a tripartite outer porch and a tripartite gatehouse, both vaulted with rich displays of tiercerons. Moreover, on the upper floor were two chapels side by side. Quarr Abbey on the Isle of Wight started under the order of Savignac but soon turned Cistercian. The ruins are extensive but confusing. They would deserve more research. Of Premonstratensian Titchfield, founded in 1232, mainly the chapter-house entrance remains. Cistercian again is Netley Abbey, founded in 1239. What
27 remains here is of the second half of the century, i.e. with bar tracery – four lights and three foiled circles, as in the Westminster Abbey Chapter House and the Salisbury Chapter House* – and later on, in the nave, even with pointed-trefoiled window lights and Y-tracery. But for such symptoms of the

* Henry III was patron of the establishment, and so the King's Mason may have designed the church and given it bar tracery as early as at Westminster Abbey.

ending C13 this survey is not yet ready, let alone for an account of monastic building activity in the most recent sixty or seventy years. The buildings in question are the abbey and the sumptuous mausoleum at Farnborough (St Michael's Abbey) and the splendid new church and monastic quarters at Quarr Abbey, Isle of Wight, begun in 1908. To these we shall return when the right moment has come.

Meanwhile SECULAR BUILDINGS of the C12 and C13. Hampshire is not a castle county, but it has three major monuments and one group of minor ones amounting in the aggregate
to a major impact. They are first the keep and curtain wall of 11
Portchester Castle, built in the SW corner of the Roman camp walls (*see* p. 69). The keep and the curtain wall date from the first third of the C12, but the keep was heightened in the second to look from a distance now – it is no good denying it – like another tower-block of flats joining those of Portsmouth and Gosport. Second are the ruins of Wolvesey Palace, the castle of the bishops of Winchester. They consist of a N range, a keep, and another tower of *c.*1130–40, and the traces of a tremendous great hall of *c.*1170, i.e. of Henry of Blois – 140 ft long and on the upper floor. There is also an outer wall, adjoining the cathedral precinct wall, as that adjoins the town wall. At Bishops Waltham the situation is similar. Again the palace was Henry of Blois', the late C12 evidence being – exactly as at Wolvesey – blind arcading of one short wall of the hall, a hall 65 ft long. To these three monuments must be added the Norman (and C13) remains of merchants' houses at Southampton. Only two of them are fairly well preserved, but others are known, and more vaulted storerooms have been revealed by wartime bombing. The best preserved houses are Canute's and the Norman House, both with upper two-light windows, the Norman House standing immediately against the later Southampton City Walls on their most spectacular, W, side.

These walls are without any doubt among the two or three p. 534
finest in England. Especially the long rows of arched recesses are 35
impressive. There are also several of the gates still in existence, Bargate being of course the most monumental. The walls and gates of Winchester (with the exception of the Westgate) cannot compare with those of Southampton, though of the walls also much stands. The Westgate has a C13 aspect to the E, a more impressive late C14 aspect to the W. The principal castle on the Isle of Wight is Carisbrooke. Much here is C19, and the most prominent piece, the Barbican, is of *c.*1335–6, but the doorway

inside this belongs to the C13, the great hall essentially to the late C12, the chapel to the late C13, and the chamber range attached to it to the late C14. The keep on its mound, however, was built *c.*1140–50. Other Hampshire castles include Christchurch, where of the keep only two walls partly stand, but where the
18 hall is still instructive. It must be of about 1170 or so, with its zigzag at r. angles to the wall. It has a fireplace with a high round chimney. Odiham Castle is interesting as having the only octagonal keep in England. It dates from the late C12, and nothing else of the castle is recognizable. At Basing the earthworks are Early Norman, but the remains of buildings are mostly post-Reformation. Of Southampton Castle much of the waterside defence work survives (but not the keep); these remains now appear as part of the (otherwise later) city defences.

Unfortified domestic building is of course rare, but one can point out at least, apart from the Norman and C13 houses at Southampton, King John's House at Warnford of the early C13, with an aisled hall, its 25 ft piers not carrying arches, King John's Hunting Box at Romsey, a small upper-floor hall of *c.*1230, Manor Farm Hambledon, also of the early C13, fragments of the C13 and C14 at Rockbourne Manor House, and fragments of the late C12 and the late C13 at Swainston on the Isle of Wight. With the Court House at East Meon and its fine hall with tall two-light windows we move to beyond 1300, and that is too early.

A postscript to mention the evidence of medieval TOWN PLANNING in Hampshire. The form of the early growth of Southampton is complex and still not quite certain, but it is likely that the area around St Michael's Square is a regular late C11 layout. Old Portsmouth is a planned town of the very end of the C12, with three parallel and slightly curving streets and only a few narrow cross-thoroughfares. The bishops of Winchester may have planned Bishops Waltham in the C12, with its specially intricate plan (possibly partly the result of later accretions); they certainly founded New Towns (or enlarged old villages) in the C13 at New Alresford and Overton (and, only just over the Wiltshire border, Downton), very minor in size and essentially one broad main street. They were founded principally to get the bishop money rents instead of rent in kind from the tenants who took up sites. The splendid elongated square at Wickham (where William of Wykeham happens to have been born) was obviously planned, probably to accommodate a medieval fair, and mention must also be made of small

towns like Fareham and Titchfield, although no direct evidence 4
exists for the deliberate planning of these.

This ends the digression made in the middle of the account
of E.E. CHURCHES. A few more must now be introduced to
complete the C13. Havant and the Garrison Church at Ports- 21
mouth have rib-vaulted chancels, Hayling Island is an all-round
mid C13 job, with the rare motif of arches dying against vertical
pieces rising above the abaci of the piers,* and more dates from
the late C13. Winchester does not help for those decades. The
most characteristic feature occurs at Christchurch: bar tracery
with unfoiled circles. But Christchurch has also, due to the
particular mason directing work there, a number of charming
minor vaulting conceits, and, incidentally, that very mason's 28
drawing office or *trasura*, i.e. tracing room – a unique survival.
The N porch is the finest individual E.E. part of Christchurch,
characteristically later than the equally fine N porch of St Cross
Winchester, with which building there terminated. Freshwater
on the Isle of Wight has an interesting late C13 W tower where W
doorway and W window are set back in a giant arched recess. If
a source for this can be found, it is not in Hampshire (cf. e.g.
Cowthorpe in Yorkshire, W.R.). Immediately influenced by the
Christchurch tracery is that of Milford-on-Sea, near by, a
church almost entirely of the late C13. And in the following of
Christchurch is no doubt also Arreton on the Isle of Wight,
where this particular kind of tracery can with some probability
be assigned to a date shortly after 1289. Perhaps the most beautiful
geometrical tracery in Hampshire is that of the E window of
Chalton. Arreton also has a good later C13 Christ in Majesty,
perhaps from a tympanum. This and the Winchester Ecclesia
are the best sculpture of the C13, unless FUNERARY MONU-
MENTS are included. If so, the mid C13 Purbeck relief in
Winchester Cathedral to mark the heart burial of a bishop is
up to the best standard. Of Purbeck marble also are the
early C13 effigy of a bishop with a low tiara and a short stylized
beard and the effigy of a lady at Romsey and the interesting
coffin lid with a foliated cross at Pamber Priory. The earliest
effigy of a knight is at Thruxton and may well go back to the
early C13.

A tally of C13 CHURCH FURNISHINGS AND DECORATION to
finish this chapter. Wall and vault painting must have first place;
for the Chapel of the Holy Sepulchre and the Chapel of the
Guardian Angels, both in Winchester Cathedral, have some of

* This pattern is also found at Wymering, Portsmouth.

the best C13 work in England, the first of *c.*1230, the second of
*c.*1240. In the former are just roundels with busts of angels in
the vault; the latter has a number of scenes, painted with marked
Byzantine inspiration. Some end-of-the-C12 wall painting is at
Farnborough, some early C13 painting at Portsmouth Cathedral,
and Stoke Charity and East Wellow too, some at Bramley, and
the dim four medallions with stylized drapery below in Romsey
29 Abbey, and so, with Soberton and with Idsworth, into
the early C14. Stained glass of the C13 in Hampshire is rare, and
what there is is not local, but it is all of exquisite beauty: the
panels in the chapel of Winchester College, at Grateley (from
25 Salisbury Cathedral), and at Headley, and the small figures
of saints at East Tytherley. Of C13 furnishings no more can be
reported than two items in Winchester Cathedral: the iron
grille between S transept and S chancel aisle and the twelve-foot
bench in the S transept, which may actually be older than 1200.
Finally church plate, represented by one mid C13 silver-gilt
Paten at St Matthew, Weeke, Winchester, one of the earliest
three or four in the country, and one pewter Coffin Chalice
and Paten at Sparsholt.

In the FOURTEENTH CENTURY the numbers of church
furnishings and monuments increase, the number of churches
decreases. It is astonishing how scarce Dec ARCHITECTURE is
in Hampshire. Hardly more than one or two large windows
(St Cross, Winchester, W), and also hardly any really enterprising flowing tracery Amport is Dec throughout but largely
by *Slater & Carpenter*, Godshill on the Isle of Wight, a
two-naved church, is now late Perp, but must have been like
that already in the early C14, and Fawley church has simple
but well-shaped Early Dec arcades. As for dating, Binsted has
windows with pointed-trefoiled lights and bar tracery, i.e. a
late C13 character, and yet the chantry to which they belong was
established only in 1332. What then will be the date of the one
outstanding piece of Dec CHURCH FURNISHING in the county,
32 the reredos of Christchurch, as enjoyable architecturally as it is
sculpturally? About 1350 is the best guess, but who knows – it
may be yet later. Of other outstanding Dec church furnishings
the Winchester stalls, early C14, even if not as firmly dated as
one usually reads, are the finest, with their slim detached shafts
and their foliage in the spandrels, already nobbly in the C14 way.
The misericords of the seats are varied and of high quality too.
The stalls of Headbourne Worthy are no doubt work of someone
of the cathedral team. A wooden screen of Dec details is in St

John, Winchester, and one of the stone screens in the cathedral is Dec also, with reticulation units. But far finer than this is the blank screen or blank arcading at the foot of the cathedral feretory facing the retrochoir. This, with its ogee arches and ample crocketing, is the most ornate piece of Dec in the county. The best early C14 wall paintings are at Idsworth and at Hurstbourne Tarrant (The Quick and the Dead and a Wheel of
Sins), the best mid C14 ones at Catherington. The only panel 31
painting, dateable to *c*.1325–30, on the other hand, the lid of a Reliquary in Winchester Cathedral, is of poor, provincial quality. The best MONUMENT of these years is also in the cathedral, that of Arnold of Gaveston, of which the front of the tomb-chest is in one place, the effigy with the usual crossed legs in another. Other cross-legged Knights are at Binsted, St Mary Bourne, Gatcombe on the Isle of Wight, and (7 ft long) Pamber Priory, the latter two of oak. Four monuments are of the type with the coffin lid kept as a plain lid except for a sunk shape at the top, where the head or bust of the deceased appears. They are at Silchester (two), East Worldham, and East Tisted. The latter has a dog at the feet of the effigy.

If Dec is thus poor in Hampshire, PERPENDICULAR is rich, but not in the parish churches. There is nothing like the grandeur of East Anglia or Somerset or the Cotswolds. In fact of major Perp parish churches there are no more than Basing and Basingstoke and Alton, and the monumental W towers of Barton Stacey and of Carisbrooke, Isle of Wight. Basingstoke dates from *c*.1450–1540, Basing, mostly brick, from the early C16. Of brick also is the Holy Trinity Guild Chapel at Basingstoke, now in ruins. This was built by Lord Sandys of The Vyne in 1524 and has half-hexagonal W and E ends. Add to this the W tower and splendid early C16 chancel and Lady Chapel of Christchurch Priory, the latter with its curious library high up above the vault, and you have named everything Perp of major interest outside Winchester.

But at Winchester Perp is richer and more instructive than perhaps anywhere else in England. This is due to three causes: the rebuilding of large parts of the cathedral, the foundation and early development of the College, and the six major chantry chapels in the cathedral. Together they present us with a chronological framework as firm as any scholar might desire. Yet owing to the relative immutability of Perp, the lesson is not as valuable as one might expect. Take the beginning as an example. Bishop Edington began the rebuilding of the

36 nave at its W end about 1360, and William of Wykeham con-
38 tinued at greater speed, essentially from *c.* 1394 onwards, and the
differences between their work can easily be seen; but they are
not stylistically a development at all. Edington's and Wykeham's
works are both Perp and essentially the same (panel tracery,
blank panelling round the windows, lierne-vaulting). In Eding-
37 ton's Chantry on the other hand (he died in 1366) there are still
a few Dec elements, the doorway mouldings in particular, and
they derive from the Gloucester S transept of the 1330s, which is
the first complete piece of Perp architecture we have but has also
minor Dec features still. At Edington in Wiltshire in 1351–61
there are Dec and Perp features side by side with more emphasis
on Dec than on Perp.

From Wykeham onwards it is impossible to divide ecclesiastical
from SECULAR ARCHITECTURE, and so it might be useful first
to get secular architecture out of the way. There are first two
35 buildings other than houses, foremost the magnificent Arcades
p. 534 of Southampton, i.e. the C14 strengthening of the town walls
with their blank giant pointed arches, and also the Gates:
Bargate, originally late C12, but added to in the late C13 and
about 1400, God's House Gate and the adjoining tower of
*c.*1300 and *c.*1400, West Gate *c.*1350, and what is left of Watergate of the C14 and C15. Then, still to continue with secular but
not domestic building, there are the C14 lighthouse on St Catherine's Down, Isle of Wight, and the once extremely long Barn of
St Leonard's Grange near Beaulieu (Bucklers Hard). Its
original length was 216 ft, its height 60 ft.* Of houses the great
hall and the adjoining apartments at Portchester Castle were
remodelled in the late C14, and they make a very impressive
group. At Bishops Waltham Palace Bishop Langton *c.*1500
remodelled the great hall too, Chale Abbey, Isle of Wight,
incorporates a C14 hall, Wonston is a late C14 hall house, once
with an open roof, and Hall Farm, Bentworth, has a C14 porch.
C15 Warblington Castle must have been on a monumental
scale. Its brick gatehouse – the first brick building on such a
scale in Hampshire – stands up only partly, but to a prodigious
height. With this we are moving on to the decades of Henry VII
and Henry VIII. The most spectacular display is at Highcliffe,
45 but there the elaborately decorated features in their gorgeous

* But inside Portchester Castle stood a barn about 250 ft long. As a note to this footnote it might be added that the Great Coxwell Barn in Berkshire, probably the most famous barn in England, also belonged to a grange of Beaulieu.

Flamboyant are French. They were taken over and re-used from
Les Andelys by Lord Stuart de Rothesay about the year 1830.
Indigenous work on a large scale, even if far from lavish in
exterior details, is The Vyne, built of brick by Lord Sandys
about 1520–40. It is of the type with a recessed centre and long
projecting wings and has a chapel and a long gallery with
excellent and intricate linenfold panelling inside. The furnish- 46
ings and fitments of the chapel will be dealt with in another
context. Of brick also is the early C16 tower built by Archbishop Warham at Malshanger House, Oakley, part of a larger
building not surviving. The Priory, Odiham, has a brick porch of
about 1530, of a type familiar from Norfolk. Finally of the early
C16 is the remaining original range of Steventon Manor with
mullioned and transomed windows, their lights arched and
uncusped – a typical Henry VIII motif. On that account the
first Earl of Southampton's majestic gatehouse built right 48
across the nave of Titchfield Abbey must be post-Henrician,
though the earl died in 1550. The windows here have assumed
the standard Elizabethan form. The abbey buildings had been
given to the Earl by Henry VIII shortly after 1537.

But Henry VIII's own contribution to Hampshire's architecture was not houses but castles in defence against the French. They belong to the same enterprise as the Kent and Sussex chain and St Mawes and Pendennis in Cornwall. They are Calshot, Hurst, Netley, and Southsea, facing the Solent and Sandown, Yarmouth, and Cowes on the Isle of Wight. They all date from round about 1538–40 and are characterized by low walling, bastions, a low main tower, and in fact everything for defence by guns and cannon. Only Yarmouth forms an exception, as it received its one bastion only *c.*1547, one of the earliest arrowhead-shaped bastions in Northern Europe. Hurst is the most complete and impressive of the Henrician castles of Hampshire. Sandown (Isle of Wight) was square with four towers, Southsea square in a square diagonally set enclosure.

Southsea is now part of Portsmouth; so this is the place to say something of the earlier defences of Portsmouth. The Round Tower was built *c.*1415, but only the footings can be that old. The ground floor is *temp.* Henry VIII, the rest C19. In 1494 the Square Tower was built, but this is also mostly C19. A dry dock was built by Sir Reginald Bray (of Windsor fame) in 1495. Henry VIII in 1538–40 was occupied with the defences of Portsmouth as well.

In a county so poor in good building stone, it is odd that

no major use was made of TIMBER. There are no really interesting timber-framed houses at all.* Yet it is likely that they
did exist; for some bold and impressive timber-work can be
seen in churches, mostly near the Berkshire border: Yateley,
33 Hartley Wespall, Mattingley, and Rotherwick. Mattingley and
Rotherwick were originally entirely timber-framed. In addition
Crawley has wooden posts instead of arcade piers, and Fordingbridge a chapel with a fine, elaborate hammerbeam roof. That
34 the Pilgrims' Hall in the Winchester Close has the earliest known
hammerbeam roof has already been said. Otherwise there is only
the former stables in the Close worth mentioning, with timber-
framing and a timber-roof.

So we are back in Winchester. William of Wykeham with his
38 master mason *William de Wynford* completed the nave of the
cathedral, a remodelling job of the Norman nave, not a rebuilding. The high lierne-vault is one of the most convincing in
England. His chantry chapel in the nave (he died in 1404) is
much higher than Edington's and started the scale of the Winchester chantry chapels to come. In 1387 Wykeham laid the
foundation stone of Winchester College, the largest and most
consistently and intelligently planned school or college of the
time anywhere in Europe. Building went on very quickly, and in
1394 the school and the foundation (with its warden, fellows,
chaplains, etc.) began to function. It consists of an outer court
and then Chamber Court with the sets and dormitories and hall
and chapel. The inner and outer gatehouses are both on a monu-
39 mental scale, and hall and chapel lie in the S range of Chamber
Court and in line, though the chapel is of course on the ground
floor, whereas the hall is on the upper floor. S of Chamber
Court and not axial is the cloister, built as the college graveyard. After 1420 in the middle of the cloister the Fromond
Chantry was built (with an upper library like the – later –
Lady Chapel at Christchurch Priory), and the Thurbern
Chantry with its high tower S of the college chapel was begun
in 1473–4.

Meanwhile during his last years Cardinal Beaufort, Bishop
of Winchester, stimulated no doubt by the College, had rebuilt
40 completely the hospital accommodation of St Cross Hospital.
The work belongs to the forties – the Cardinal died in 1447.
Here again a hall was provided. The kitchen lies in the same
relation to it as at the College, and the gatehouse is almost a

* The most interesting one is perhaps Tudor House at Southampton which has a hall of *c.*1400, but is otherwise of *c.*1500.

copy of Inner Gate. The most interesting part of the buildings is the range for the brethren, two-storeyed and planned so that there is access to four flats from one staircase, and that each four flats have one chimney. Cardinal Beaufort's Chantry is far more ornate than Wykeham's had been. It has a fan-vault (the first in Hampshire) and ends in a thicket of closely detailed canopies. This motif was taken up in the chantry built for Bishop Waynflete († 1486), but not the fan-vaulting.

At the end of the century Bishop Courtenay partly rebuilt and partly remodelled the Lady Chapel and his successor, Bishop Langton, the early C13 SE chapel as a chantry for himself. Both have complex lierne-vaults and both have elaborate reredoses, as they were also an integral part of the chantries, from Edington's onwards. The large reredos in Winchester College Chapel dates from *c.*1470, but the largest of all is that in the cathedral chancel. This is of the early C16. The chancel must have been in a muddled state then. W of Bishop de Lucy's retrochoir, some time in the first half of the C14 the Norman chancel had been replaced by Dec work. The piers are still there, but all above was rebuilt by Bishop Fox before he died in 1528. This is again sumptuous work, though the vault is
of wood, a vault exceptionally richly studded with figured 42
bosses. Bishop Fox's Chantry is still Late Perp, like Beaufort's 43
and Waynflete's. His date of death would make one expect details *all'antica*, but there is no more than a certain Renaissance mood in some of them. Yet in decoration and furnishings and in other monuments earlier Renaissance motifs exist in Hampshire. However, even for the later Gothic period we have not yet examined decoration, furnishings, and monuments.

PAINTING first. The wall paintings in the Lady Chapel of Winchester Cathedral date from *c.*1500 and are strongly influenced by those of Eton College Chapel. There is, as at Eton, a whole cycle on the N and S walls of the chapel, and the style is wholly dependent on that of Flanders. In addition, there is the
exquisite Christ on a foliated cross at Godshill (Isle of Wight), 41
St Christophers of the familiar size and type (Bramley, Shorwell Isle of Wight, Tufton), and at Romsey is an early C16 painted reredos on a wood panel, a rare thing, but bad. For STAINED GLASS the situation is much better. The parts left in their original state of the glass for the E window of the Winchester College Chapel made by Master *Thomas* of Oxford in 1393 are among the most characteristic of their date in England.

From the C15 and earlier C16 there is less of interest (St Cross Winchester, Mottisfont, Basingstoke), but the glass in the chapel of The Vyne, dateable to some time between 1518 and 1527, is side by side with the glass of King's College Chapel the most important in the country. It is Netherlandish and Early Renaissance, and so its discussion must still be delayed. Next SCREENS. The cathedral has several Perp stone screens, and they culminate again in a job over the Renaissance border: the screens N and S of the chancel and the wooden tomb-chests which they support. So to WOODWORK. Wooden screens are of no interest – except perhaps the screen with five-light divisions at Bramley. In the Lady Chapel at Winchester and at South Warnborough rood-lofts or their parapets are preserved. Dummer has a rood canopy. Concerning stalls, Christchurch has some C15 misericords, but most of them, and the stalls themselves, are of about 1525–30, and again the Renaissance is on its way in them. For panelling the before and after is illustrated in Winchester Cathedral by that in the Langton Chapel, very sumptuous, and the much simpler in the S transept. This, with its incipient Renaissance motifs, is of before 1524. For TEXTILES nothing demands comment except the two early C16 Flemish tapestries in Winchester College Chapel, and for METALWORK all we have is the excellent Flemish early C15 eagle lectern for Holy Rood, now at St Michael Southampton, and some PLATE, namely a C15 Spoon at Winchester College, a silver-gilt Italian C15 Chalice at St Alban Portsmouth, an English C15 Thurible in the same church, Chalices or Cups of the late C15(?) at Kimpton, of 1525 in the Portsmouth Guildhall, and of *c.*1540 (secular) at Gatcombe (Isle of Wight), Patens of *c.*1500 at Bishops Sutton, Fawley, and Wield, a parcel-gilt secular Standing Cup of *c.*1500 at Fareham, and the silver-gilt Election Cup at Winchester College which is of *c.*1520. This is quite a lot compared with other counties.

Late Gothic MONUMENTS deserve a little more attention. We start with brasses, of which there are in Hampshire relatively few and very few in any way remarkable. The earliest are at Crondall of the 1380s and at Calbourne on the Isle of Wight also of before 1400, and the finest is at St Cross, Winchester, with the date of death 1410. Another excellent brass, of as late
p. 148 as *c.*1520, is at Brown Candover. The incised slab at Brading, Isle of Wight († 1441) must once have been quite splendid. The most ambitious stone monuments – leaving aside of course the chantries in the cathedral – are those placed between chancel and

a chancel chapel and open to both. To them belong monuments at Basing – four of them, starting *c.*1520 and moving from Gothic to Renaissance – at Thruxton also of *c.*1520, and at Godshill, Isle of Wight. The date of death here is 1529. The effigies are of alabaster and remarkably unemotional. Another alabaster couple, again of *c.*1520, is at Oakley, but the earliest alabaster effigy in Hampshire is Bishop Edington in the cathedral († 1366). Otherwise the effigies of the bishops in their chantries are nothing special, except for Beaufort, who is a late C17 copy. Another monument of the type of Brading and Godshill is at Sherborne St John, and here again just a little of the Renaissance is in evidence.

A type of monument not quite as large as those just discussed but at least as elaborate in decoration is one issuing from Purbeck and sent to many English counties. They stand against the wall and have a tomb-chest and above it an arch, panelled inside and on the side pieces, and a top cresting. The arches always are flat and can even be replaced by a horizontal on curved springers. Such monuments we have in Hampshire at Christchurch (three of them), at Crondall (as late as the 1560s, unless re-appropriated), and in other places. A variant of stone, not Purbeck marble, most familiar in Sussex, is represented by the Wadham Monument at Carisbrooke, Isle of Wight. The distinguishing feature is that, whereas the effigies on the Purbeck monuments are usually brasses against the back wall, they are here carved in relief, and augmented by Saints. This monument also is of *c.*1520. Cadavers or corpses in decomposition instead of, or in addition to, effigies were originally a conception of France of about 1400. They appeared in England some thirty or forty years later (Lincoln, Bishop Fleming † 1435) and then soon became a favourite theme. In Hampshire we have only two cases, both very late: Bishop Fox † 1528 and Bishop Gardener † 1555, both in the cathedral. With Bishop Fox we have touched the incoming Renaissance again, with Bishop Gardener we are already on the border between its first and second phase.

So now we can turn our full attention to the ADVENT OF THE RENAISSANCE. All that is required is to summarize what has already been mentioned and add to it here and there. The Vyne is the most important place. Here there is stained glass designed probably by *Dirk Vellert* and made in the Netherlands and hence much more opulent in its architectural features than anything made in England would be. The stained glass of Sherborne 44

St John is similar and at least as opulent.* At The Vyne also there is that one mysterious large roundel with the representation of the Emperor Probus which is terracotta, purely Tuscan, and in all probability the work of *Giovanni da Majano*, who did the Hampton Court roundels and others as well, and here there are also stalls, of English make, it looks, and Early Renaissance in a more conventional way. All this can be assigned with certainty to the years between 1518 and 1527. Only one fitment in a Hampshire church is as early: the stall-work in the S transept of Winchester Cathedral with the initials of Prior Silkstede, who died in 1524. This has already been referred to. The next date in the cathedral refers to the stone screens and the wooden tomb-chests of the chancel, and that date is 1525. The structural parts such as the four-light windows are purely Gothic, but friezes and inscription tablets are Renaissance. Then follow the Fox
43 Chantry at Winchester († 1528), and the Draper Chantry at Christchurch (1529) with only minor Renaissance details.‡ The brick porch of Sherborne St John comes next, which is of 1533 and also Renaissance only in a few bits. But by then a good deal of other work was probably complete for which dates are lacking, such as the stalls at Christchurch, the stalls at St Cross Winchester with their typical profile heads in medallions, and the de Lisle Monument at Thruxton. Some Renaissance decoration is found on slightly later monuments as well: Michelmersh † 1538,
47 East Tisted *c.*1540, and the Basing group of Paulets of after 1520 and before 1560. The Countess of Salisbury Chantry at Christchurch, erected no doubt shortly after her execution in 1541, is still at the stage of the Winchester chancel screen, i.e. a side-by-side of purely Gothic (the fan-vault!) and purely Renaissance motifs. The same seems at first to be true of the Gardener Chantry, although Bishop Gardener died in 1555. But while the Gothic screen windows and the Early Renaissance pilasters and friezes are as they had been for the last thirty years,§ the reredos
49 inside has – admittedly on a very small scale – columns instead of pilasters and shell niches and also two statuettes, and they

* From the Netherlands also came the several painted Flemish TRIPTYCHS which, by chance, have found their way into Hampshire churches. They date from *c.*1520 and are at St Cross Winchester, Selborne, and Rockbourne. The panel at Broughton is a little earlier and Dutch, the triptych at Basingstoke somewhat later in its centre and of 1649 in its wings.

‡ The Harys Chantry (1525), also at Christchurch, has no Renaissance details.

§ A monument in Southwick church with the date of death 1567 still has a purely Gothic tomb-chest, though Renaissance forms in the superstructure.

are all derived from the Italo-French Cinquecento and no longer the Early Renaissance. Of this change they are among the earliest documents in England.*

The ELIZABETHAN STYLE, however, did not follow up these Cinquecento discoveries as the mature style of the C16 did in France. It was diverted by the influx of craftsmen from the Netherlands and also by the strength of the indigenous English tradition. The former appears most widely in monuments and furnishings, the latter in domestic architecture. New ecclesiastical building was almost absent right down to the later C17, and what there is in Hampshire is Gothic Survival, i.e. an unselfconscious carrying on in the late medieval style (Southwick of 1566, Bishops Waltham tower 1584–9, and even still N aisle 1637 and S aisle 1652, Droxford W tower 1599, North Stoneham).‡ As for furnishings and equipment, they are absent too, at least as long as we confine ourselves to dated pieces and pieces of before 1600. The one exception is PLATE. Here the Elizabethan Settlement brought a sudden imperative need for replacements of Communion Cups and Covers, and the result – in the whole of England – was the boom of all time. It is ununderstandable how silversmiths could cope with it. In Hampshire and the Isle of Wight the score is this: 1551 2,§ 1552 1, 1554 1 (secular), *c.*1560 1 (secular), 1562 3 (one of them secular), 1563 1, 1564 1, 1566 1, 1567 3, 1568 17, 1569 12, 1570 3, *c.*1570 3, 1571 2, 1572 2.||

Concerning church furnishings it is only when one takes in the Jacobean years and even the Laudian years, to use the most appropriate term, that they proliferated. To start with woodwork, there are ten dated PULPITS between 1620 and 1660 (Basing 1622, Whitwell, Isle of Wight, 1623, Bishops Waltham 1626, Durley 1630, Sherborne St John 1634, Winchfield 1634, Newport, Isle of Wight, 1636, Silchester 1639, Tadley 1650, Carisbrooke, Isle of Wight, 1658) and quite a number of undated ones, including so spectacular a piece as that at Alton. The pulpit at Newport has the Seven Liberal Arts and the Seven Cardinal Virtues, a very rare thing in England. Of dated SCREENS there

* The earliest is at Wing in Bucks of 1552. After that there is work at Framlingham in Suffolk of *c.*1560.

‡ The Jesus Chapel at Peartree Green of 1620 has nothing left of any eloquence.

§ A silver-gilt Tazza Cup with chased figures at Deane, and a silver-gilt Chalice at St Michael Southampton.

|| For the purpose of this tally a Cup and Cover together count one, although a Cup by itself and a Cover by itself also count one.

are three (North Baddesley 1602, Empshott 1624, Herriard 1635), of dated FONT COVERS two (Bentworth 1605, Empshott 1624). The most interesting COMMUNION RAILS are those of the Lady Chapel at Winchester and St Cross at Winchester, both not with the usual balusters but with openwork ovals and spurs arranged in a cruciform way. From comparison with dated staircases one can assume a date *c.*1635.* Of FONTS, to conclude with, the most interesting one is that at Tangley, of the early C17, because it is of made lead. All the stone fonts are unremarkable. Three of them have dates. Carisbrooke, Isle of Wight, of 1602 has just mouldings still of a medieval kind. Upper Clatford of 1629 has an octagonal baluster stem and a chalice-like bowl. Newport, Isle of Wight, of 1633 has long and clumsy scrolls or volutes up the stem.

MONUMENTS between the mid C16 and the mid C17 are far more copious, and also more spectacular – a change of mind noticeable all over England. The Elizabethan Age was the first age of monster monuments, e.g. in Westminster Abbey. Hampshire has none of these, but, even so, plenty to show ambition and pride. The evidence is best arranged by types. Two new types appeared about the middle of the C16. One has no figures at all, but classical ornament and strapwork, usually rather large and often very good. This type is represented in Hampshire and the Isle of Wight by Wherwell († 1551), Rowner (1559), Winchester Cathedral (Masson † 1559), Godshill († 1565), Boarhunt (1577) and – a latecomer – Easton (1595). The other new type is that with detached kneeling figures (kneeling brass effigies had of course been quite usual). This appears in Hampshire astonishingly early in the Funtleroy Monument at Michelmersh with date of death 1538. This is followed by Godshill, Isle of Wight († 1557), East Tisted († before 1564), East Tytherley († 1568), Mottisfont (1584), Highclere, and –
55 again latecomers – Andover († 1621), Ibsley († 1627), Chalton († 1632), and some minor ones. But at Andover and Ibsley something significant is taking place. At Andover the effigy of the husband is seated frontally, and only the others kneel, and at Ibsley two kneeling figures hold on to a vine, and the vine has not only produced grapes but also their children, placed radially as heads and busts. This inventiveness, the wish to get away from old-established types and to produce something ingenious as a conceit, is characteristic of the Nicholas Stone period and

* The staircase in the Winchester Deanery is not dated, but it fits the case entirely and so must also be of *c.*1635 or only a little later.

especially the second quarter of the century.* We can see the
same happen in the most conventional of all types of monuments,
that with a recumbent effigy. This now usually occurs with
flanking columns, perhaps a back arch, often strapwork on
the back wall, and as a rule a top achievement with some
strapwork. All this is entirely of Flemish origin, and the craftsmen were often Netherlanders. The most splendid of them
all, the monument to the first and second Earls of Southampton 50
of 1594 at Titchfield, is indeed by Netherlanders: *Gerard
Johnson* and his son *Nicholas Johnson*. It is a free-standing piece
with four large corner obelisks. Other examples of the type in
our county are Hurstbourne Priors († 1574), Newport, Isle of
Wight († 1582, alabaster, and much better), Farley Chamberlayne († 1600), Nursling († 1613), North Stoneham († 1613),
Wickham († 1615), Wield († 1617, his effigy behind and above
hers), Tichborne (alabaster, † 1621; sculpturally very good),
Warnford (alabaster, † 1621; equally good), Catherington
(† 1631) and Greatham († 1632). Oddities of the type are the
two Oglanders at Brading († 1608 and † 1655) and a Lady at
Thruxton, because they are of oak, a material then right out of
use for monuments, and the second of the Oglanders also 58
because his attitude – crossed legs, shield, and sword – is
a curiously archaistic one, a Dec Revival, and the way he is
propped up on a half-rolled-up mat is typically Elizabethan
(i.e. initially Netherlandish) and also so much out of date by the
1650s that this may here even be a case of an Elizabethan
Revival. Other less remarkable variants of the Elizabethan
standard are at Laverstoke († 1614), where the effigy is recumbent but awkwardly rolled on its side, and at Stratfield Saye,
where in 1640 the *Christmas* Brothers made two semi-reclining
alabaster effigies, he behind and above her, and then two grilles
in the tomb-chest with the gruesome sight of crowded bones
behind them.

The variety displayed by the monuments is far greater than
that in ELIZABETHAN AND JACOBEAN HOUSES. Here Hampshire has not much to offer anyway, just one of what Sir John
Summerson calls the prodigy houses, and all the rest minor.
The prodigy house is of course Bramshill, built in 1605–12 to a 53
plan which is unique; for behind the stately façade on the
usual E-plan the building extends in depth much beyond what
the length of the façade is. Moreover it has the relatively rare
motif of open loggias (on the N side), and the façade is a

* On Stone, *see* p. 40.

combination of almost blunt plainness with a fantastic display of the Dietterlin kind in the porch, i.e. the middle frontispiece. This combination is typically Jacobean. We find it in the façade of Charlton House, Greenwich, and in the contrast between the two façades at Hatfield. Greater readiness to experiment in plan is also Jacobean or Late Elizabethan as against the earlier Elizabethan decades. These are best represented in Hampshire by Grove Place, Nursling, of between *c.*1561 and *c.*1576. The plan here is still that of The Vyne, with the long wings. The turrets in the re-entrant angles are a motif paralleled e.g. at Stiffkey in Norfolk a little later. Grove Place has thin-ribbed plaster ceilings, Bramshill broad bands instead. Altogether Bramshill has preserved quite a number of the principal interiors. But the most sumptuous interiors are in Lutyens's New
54 Place, Shedfield, and they were transferred from a house at Bristol. They date from about 1625, and include a chimney-
51 piece. Others are of course at Bramshill, Hursley Park, and Breamore House. Among the early or mid-Elizabethan houses in Hampshire are Moberley's, Kingsgate Street, Winchester of 1571, the charming miniature gatehouse of brick at Bramshott Place of *c.*1575 with its shaped gable, and Pittleworth Manor Bossington, noteworthy not architecturally but for its decorative as well as figural wall paintings dated 1580. The standard E- and H-plans are represented by such homelier yet stately houses as Yaverland Manor and Wolverton Manor, Shorwell, both on the Isle of Wight. At Wolverton the porch still has the thin buttress shafts of the earlier C16. Also on the Isle of Wight is Arreton Manor, as late as 1639, yet still entirely Jacobean, as is the Winchester College Sick House even in 1656.

The REACTION AGAINST THE JACOBEAN STYLE came in two forms. One is *Inigo Jones*'s, and he appears in Hampshire only as the designer about 1638 of the former rood screen of Winchester Cathedral. This was an entirely classical job, as the fragments in the Cambridge Museum of Archeology show, and the sculpture, to which we shall revert soon, was as un-Jacobean too. But the radical purity of Jones's classicism was during his lifetime only for the few. It makes its entry in Hampshire in the remodelling of The Vyne between 1653 and 1659 by Jones's closest assistant and follower *John Webb*. He designed
60 the monumental four-column portico, the earliest actually realized for a domestic purpose in England, but due to him also
59 are a number of fireplaces, and they are not classical but a sign

of a curiously capricious playing with classical materials typical of the mid C17 outside the immediate court circle and called by Sir John Summerson Artisan Mannerism.* This trend is much in evidence in Hampshire, not in stone but in brick building. In brick, the Jones innovation had been what the Victorians scathingly called the brick box, the plain, sensible, unornamented house with a hipped roof, and this also has one representative in Hampshire, Moyles Court, Ellingham. But against this there may be a dozen houses with raised brick quoins, moulded brick friezes, superimposed or giant brick pilasters with terracotta capitals, sometimes shaped or Dutch gables, often raised brick window surrounds, and brick door surrounds, again with pilasters. There is little evidence as to date, but the long gallery range of the Winchester Deanery with just such a surround (with bulgy rustication) is known to have been built *c.*1670–5. This range has stone windows with a mullion and transom cross. These cross windows were universal before sashing came in in the late C17, but they are as a rule of brick. Other good examples of Hampshire Artisan Mannerism are the oldest parts of Stratfield Saye with superimposed pilasters and Dutch gables, Dome Alley in the Winchester Close, originally with shaped gables, Hyde House Winchester with a big Dutch gable, Queen's Lodge Wickham, Old Lodge Titchfield, and No. 8 Church Street Basingstoke, the most notable house in that architecturally lean town. This style was abandoned only for the often loosely and not correctly called domestic Wren style in the eighties.

Secular but not domestic are the monumental defences of p. 420
Portsmouth devised *c.*1665–90 by the Netherlander *Sir Bernard de Gomme* for Charles II. There was little in England to emulate them. As this introduction proceeds naval and military works will become more and more prominent. At Portsmouth de Gomme was preceded by Elizabethan engineers *c.*1560–90. Their work in its own day must have been as interesting as the contemporary walls and bastions of Berwick. But little of it remains, though the Saluting Battery of 1568 is in a reasonably good state. Nor is alas as much of de Gomme's time preserved as one would wish. The best preserved stretch is the Long Curtain, but this, facing the sea, is much simpler in design than the vanished landside defences. By de Gomme also was the Dockyard Round Tower of 1683 and Frederick's Battery of 1688. Both were rebuilt in 1870, but remain at least as shades

* Another such fireplace is at Farleigh House.

of their former existence. The earliest of Portsmouth's surviving town gates, the King James Gate (not *in situ*), dates from 1687; the Landport, still *in situ*, was rebuilt in 1760.*

In the ecclesiastical field the whole development from Jones and Webb to Wren is unrepresented. All that can be found is brick towers, that at Crondall e.g. of the 1660s, but they do not change materially, even between the C17 and the C18. Nor are there any events in church furnishing prior to the eighties. So it is only MONUMENTS where we can look for something parallel to what has been described in houses. There the chief innovation is the replacement of the recumbent or reclining effigy by the bust, or novel conceits doing without effigies. The earliest bust is on *Nicholas Stone*'s monument to Sir Thomas Cornwallis, † 1618, at Portchester. This is in a circular surround. The earliest of the novel conceits is convincingly attributed to
Nicholas Stone as well. It is the monument to the assassinated
56 Duke of Buckingham in Portsmouth Cathedral. He died in 1628,
and the monument has a large, extremely elongated white urn in
a black niche and allegorical figures. Influenced no doubt by
this is the monument to Sir Richard Ryvves at Yateley, a short
column with an oddly organically shaped urn also in a recess.
He died in 1671. Busts as well as a beautiful recumbent effigy
of the traditional kind, but in bronze, characterize *Le Sueur*'s
57 strikingly classical Portland Monument of 1634 at Winchester
Cathedral. For the traditional forms of effigies were not entirely abandoned. At Kingsclere in 1670 there are also still recumbent effigies, and they are remarkably well done, and at Chawton, with a date of death 1679, the semi-reclining effigy has an up-to-date, rather Dutch representative. Busts are placed in an arched niche (Romsey, 1650s), or more often an oval recess (Sherborne St John † 1635, Boldre † 1652, Priors Dean † 1653 and † 1657) or just once at the top of a composition with an open scrolly pediment (Compton † 1661). But that type once again points forward to the eighties and beyond.

THE EIGHTIES appear with as much splendour in Hampshire as in any English county, but less in architecture than in WOODWORK. What has been preserved at Hackwood Park of garlands etc. and was made for Abbotstone is worthy of *Gibbons* himself,
and the screen, reredos, and wall panelling of the Winchester
62 College Chapel provided by Warden Nicholas in 1680–3 and
now displayed in a new envelope, the Communion Rail in

* The Lion Gate and the Unicorn Gate, both now re-set in the Dockyard, were town gates of Portsea and date from *c.*1778.

Winchester Cathedral,* and the staircase in No. 11 The Close Winchester are all of the very first order. Warden Nicholas also remodelled his Lodging, and its E façade is of the 'Wren' style. College, built in 1683–7, has even been attributed to Wren himself. This is of brick, with stone dressings including excellently carved garlands, and has a hipped roof. The stucco work of the ceiling is similar to that over a small staircase in the Pilgrims' School. During the same years (completed in 1684) the Bishop of Winchester built himself a new house close 63
to the ruins of the medieval Wolvesey Palace. This is of substantial size and of stone and has a hipped roof. Much larger was the Royal Palace which *Wren* designed for Charles II in 1683 and which was built on Castle Hill, until work was interrupted in 1685. What was complete became barracks later and was destroyed by fire in 1894. If it had been erected in its totality, it would have been the earliest document of Wren's change from the classical style of his middle years to the ENGLISH BAROQUE.

This is quite prominent in Hampshire and on the Isle of Wight, and it may be best understood by comparing its examples with those of the domestic Classical which preceded it. Such classical houses are Shawford House of 1685 and Abbey House Itchen Abbas of 1693, apart from College and Wolvesey. Shawford House is of stone, Abbey House of brick. Both are plain – at Abbey House any fun with bricks is scorned‡ – and both make use of pediments. The English Baroque was not satisfied with so little in the way of enrichment, but no doubt found the enrichments of Artisan Mannerism finicky. So giant pilasters returned, but they are now robust, and Wren even had giant columns in a key position at the King's House. The masterpiece of the English Baroque in our county is the palatial Appuldurcombe on the Isle of Wight, gravely damaged in its aesthetic appeal by being ruinous. There are, no-one in England could deny it, picturesque ruins, but Appuldurcombe is alas not one of them. With its fine ashlar work, its square centre and lower angle pavilions, its array of giant pilasters and its dramatic twin chimneys on the four corners it is Baroque in the English sense without any doubt, but it is highly personal and has not

* Another Communion Rail with lush openwork acanthus and putti is at Brown Candover, but this is probably Flemish, and in any case not English. As to the woodwork of the College, it is worth noting that *Edward Pierce* worked for the College in the pertinent years.

‡ But chequer work of red and blue, i.e. vitrified, brick seems to have become the fashion in the late C17. The earliest dated examples are Avebury House of 1690 and No. 1 The Close of 1699, both at Winchester.

so far been attached convincingly to any architect's *œuvre*. It dates from *c.*1701 to 1712, the very years of the emergence of Hawksmoor and Vanbrugh.

See p. 827 Neither of these two is represented in Hampshire, but
Archer is. He had a country house at Hale, where it is controversial how much of the house can be his, but he remodelled
the church in 1717, and there much, and especially the two
65 transept doorways, is highly archerish. The church is cruciform
and has bulgy giant angle pilasters and a segmental vault.
Archer made a drawing for the Earl of Plymouth for Hurstbourne Priors, and the surviving Andover Lodge there could
64 well be his. He ought to be considered also for Serle's House,
Southgate Street, Winchester, with its curved centre projection and giant pilasters. There are other early C18 brick houses in Southgate Street (Southgate Hotel, 1715) and other streets in Winchester. In fact the town, and indeed the county, are exceptionally rich in them. If one tries to summarize their features, they are segment-headed windows, narrow windows l. and r. of the doorway or upper middle window, emphasis on this middle window by giving it a round arch, and giant angle pilasters. Examples of the early C18 complying more or less with this scheme are among houses in the county Herriard House of 1704 (now demolished) and Avington Park. But Avington Park has a recessed centre with a wooden giant portico, and has consequently been attributed to *John James*. He also had his country house in Hampshire, at Eversley, and Warbrook House which dates from 1724 has a very strange portico with pilaster strips continued horizontally so as to form a framework. A point of special interest at Warbrook House is the fact that on the top of the house a room with a segmentally vaulted ceiling runs across from front to back and that this was James's studio. James has been suggested as the architect of Eversley church too, which has a date 1724 on the porch and a date 1735 on the tower. For Hursley Park, much enlarged in the C20, but with an original pedimented portico of Doric pilasters, James has been proposed as the designer too. In this context Hinton Park of 1720 ought to be considered also. It has a centre of giant Composite pilasters carrying a pediment and, at r. angles to the façade, wings which were originally detached.*

There now only remain some churches to be mentioned. At the beginning of course must be placed the nave of Portsmouth Cathedral with its high Tuscan columns. This dates from

* Such wings also occur at Hale and (not detached) at Hackwood Park.

1683–93. Lymington of 1720 has three galleries with columns in two tiers and a segmental plaster-vault, i.e. basically a Wren theme. St George's Portsmouth is as late as 1754, i.e. ought to be introduced much later, but its façade, strikingly American-Colonial as an ensemble, harks back to the William and Mary period, and its plan is directly derived from Wren's St Anne and St Agnes. Holy Trinity Gosport on the other hand, though of 1696, is not Wrenian. The pattern for its long arcades of giant unfluted Ionic columns (of oak) and plaster tunnel-vault is the Charles Church at Falmouth. Finally a telling comparison of two village churches. Wolverton of 1717 has a remarkably powerful W tower and shaped and stepped gables as a 'revivalist' feature in the Vanbrugh–Hawksmoor sense, and inside arched screens between centre and transepts in a rhythm small–large–small, but with the second small bent at an angle to allow for diagonal doorways to pulpit and lectern, this also a Vanbrughian conceit. Quarley, on the other hand, in 1723 has a purely Palladian or Inigo-Jonesian E window of the Venetian type, and this is inscribed as a present from two squires on adjoining Wiltshire estates who were connected with the earliest Palladianism or Jonesism in England: William Benson of Wilbury, whose own house of 1710 starts the Jones Revival, and Henry Hoare, Lord of the Manor of Quarley and son of Henry Hoare of Stourhead, who employed Colen Campbell there as early as 1721. The window at Quarley, being dated 1723, is the appropriate beginning for a summary of the GEORGIAN STYLE in the county.

ARCHITECTURE must take precedence. So we have to watch now the development from the defeat of the Baroque and the advent of Palladianism – i.e. in Hampshire the year 1723, as we have seen – to about 1800, remembering, however, all the while, that the brick box in its 'Wren' form remained the accepted pattern for the town house and the country house of moderate size and moderate ambition. Among the latter are West Green House with its pretty busts in round recesses, Dogmersfield Park of 1728, what is left of Farleigh House of 1731, and the S façade of Mottisfont Abbey of *c.*1740. The finest interiors of these years are at Dogmersfield. Others of note are the staircases of South Stoneham House, Southampton and Lainston House.

Moving on beyond the middle of the century we come to the
climax of Hampshire interiors, *John Chute*'s remodelling of The 67
Vyne in the sixties. The staircase with the adjoining rooms opening into it at two levels is the most ingenious and imaginative of

its date in England. In the Gothic field, however keen John Chute, a close friend of Horace Walpole's, was on the Gothic, he was very much less successful. The only entertaining Gothickery at The Vyne is the illusionist paintings of fan-vaults at odd angles which were originally in the chapel above the stalls. They are by *Spiridone Roma* and date from the 1770s.* From the same decade are the pretty interiors of Foxlease, Lyndhurst.

During this quarter of the C18 the only planned village in the county was built, and owing to circumstances it remained small. This is Bucklers Hard near Beaulieu, built by the second Duke of Montagu and intended as a harbour. It became instead a ship-building centre, but only for a short time. It is no more than one wide street running down to the river. And while planning and not architecture is under discussion, an earlier Georgian job of much more central interest must be recorded: Spring Wood, the wood adjoining Hackwood Park which, before the year 1728, was laid out with radiating avenues meeting at a centre in the middle. The layout is in all probability *James Gibbs*'s; for Gibbs illustrates in his *Book of Architecture* two of the buildings adorning the wood. Among them are a temple and a rotunda (of which only the outer colonnade remains). There is one other place in Hampshire with a temple and a rotunda: Highclere. Here the temple came from the grounds of Devonshire House (i.e. at the time Berkeley House), Piccadilly, and must be of *c.*1730. The rotunda and an arch on top of a hill are about ten or twelve years later. But the earliest garden house is
61 at The Vyne. It is very probably by *Webb* and of the 1650s. It is of brick, quite high, round and domed, and has four crosswise projections. At Hackwood Park also there is another kind of ornament in the grounds, an equestrian lead statue of George I given in 1722 by the King to the second Duke of Bolton. The sculptor is unknown. Hampshire has one more equestrian statue – which is remarkable, as in England such monumental memorials are rare. This came from Petersfield House and now
66 stands in the market-place at Petersfield. It represents William of Orange, is of lead, and was made in 1757, probably by *John Cheere*. John was the brother of the better-known *Sir Henry Cheere*, and he did one of the noteworthy MONUMENTS of the years between about 1680 and 1780, that to Bishop Willis † 1734, in Winchester Cathedral. He is shown reclining against a reredos

* He also did an oval ceiling painting for East India House which is dated 1778 and now kept in the Commonwealth Relations (formerly India) Office. Spiridone Roma died in London in 1787.

background. The same attitude is assumed in the monument to Thomas Archer, the architect, at Hale. This dates from 1739, and to his l. and r. stand his two wives. The earliest standing figures on funerary monuments are of John Clobery † 1687 in Winchester Cathedral and of Sir Robert Holmes † 1692 at Yarmouth on the Isle of Wight. The former, by *Sir W. Wilson*, is decidedly clumsy, the latter has a strikingly accomplished figure, the reason being that this is a French statue, probably Louis XIV, captured *en route* to some town where it would have been erected in a public square. Only the head is Holmes's. Standing figures, very unemotional, are also on a monument at East Woodhay († 1724; the wife † 1732). Among the leading mid C18 sculptors both Rysbrack and Roubiliac are represented, but both in a minor way: *Rysbrack* at Eling († 1741 and † 1753) and Lymington († 1747), *Roubiliac* at Highclere († 1740; designed by the amateur architect *Sir Charles Frederick*) and at Wootton St Lawrence (1750s; semi-reclining effigy). *Scheemakers* did a monument at Soberton († 1747), and the Worsley Monument of *c.*1750 († 1747) at Godshill, Isle of Wight, with its two busts on a sarcophagus is at least near in style to him. Busts of course had been a usual element of monuments ever since the 1630s. Now, however, they always appear free-standing and on a pedestal.* Other examples are at Wootton St Lawrence † 1733, Crofton † 1733, and Owslebury † 1749. The best of the anonymous monuments of these years is that to Mrs Rodney † 1757 at Old Alresford, splendidly done in various marbles and with two seated allegorical figures. Old Alresford had its church rebuilt during just these years, the body in 1753, the tower in 1769. It is not a specially interesting job, but the GEORGIAN CHURCHES as such are of little interest in the county. The only one to be remembered for architectural reasons is (apart from St George Portsmouth, on which *see* above, p. 43) Stratfield Saye of 1754–8, which is on a Greek cross plan. Two others up to 1775, Avington of 1768–71 and Crux Easton of 1775, are worth a visit, but not for architectural reasons. What distinguishes them is their FURNISHINGS, which are uncommonly well preserved. This applies to other Hampshire churches as well. Minstead is picturesquely crowded almost as cheerfully as Whitby; so is Stoke Charity, and Bramley, Southwick, Sherborne St John, and Ellingham also have much of their pre-C19 52
furnishings, including in the case of Ellingham a plaster

* This had been the case at Sherborne St John in the 1630s and Compton in the 1660s.

tympanum. At Holy Trinity Fareham is late C18 stained glass after Reynolds's influential New College designs. Portsmouth Cathedral has a charming wind vane of 1710, apart from a pulpit of 1693 and an organ front of 1718. Other furnishings need in no case be singled out.*

Before moving on to the last quarter of the C18, which represents a new and important phase in Hampshire, a paragraph must be devoted to the C18 in NAVAL AND MILITARY ARCHITECTURE. For much happened in the C18 in the Naval Dockyard, and much also outside. The Dockyard received its brick wall in 1704–11. Of 1717 is one row of normal houses inside (and of 1787 another). The handsome former Royal Naval Academy was built in 1729–32, though its pretty cupola dates only from 1808. The size of building increased spectacularly in the second
68 half of the century. The former Ropery of 1770 is 1100 ft long, and many other severely utilitarian and for that reason most impressive buildings are on a similar scale, e.g. the Stores Nos 9–11 of 1778. Also startlingly large is the Royal Naval Hospital at Haslar, Gosport, of 1746–62, with its chapel of 1756. The Dockyard church, St Ann, is of 1785–6, i.e. the same years as the fine Admiralty House by *Samuel Wyatt*, the most elegant building in the Dockyard, a country house to all intents and purposes, and typical of that last quarter of the C18 which we can now examine.‡

In the years immediately after 1775 events in architecture begin to gather momentum. In Hampshire late C18 at its very best is Broadlands of 1788 by *Holland*, with its loggia of giant
70 columns and its fine interiors, starting with an octagonal lobby. Another loggia of giant columns is at Newtown Park, South Baddesley, and this seems to be of *c.*1792. At the same moment *Holland* remodelled Hale, so that the major part of what we now see must be by him and not by Archer. *Bonomi* in 1796–8 rebuilt Laverstoke House, with its portico of attenuated columns. Again in the same years *Samuel Wyatt* (of the Admiralty House)

* Brass CHANDELIERS should perhaps be an exception. There are twelve dated ones in Hampshire, either of the type with a ball as the centre, or with a more Baroquely shaped centre. There is no development from the early to the late C18. The examples are Kingsclere given in 1713, Froyle 1716, Ringwood 1727, Winchester College 1730, Yateley 1738, Winchester Cathedral 1756 (two), Avington 1771, Alton 1780, Winchester St John 1791, Knight's Enham 1798, and Brading (Isle of Wight) also 1798.

‡ Purely defensive but also very impressive is Fort Cumberland of 1786 etc. In the 1770s the Duke of Richmond remodelled the defences of Portsmouth in several places.

was busy at Somerley, though the predominant impression of
the house is now Victorian. His nephew *Lewis Wyatt* remodelled
Hackwood Park, grand, with giant Tuscan porticoes on both
main fronts, but rendered and hence without splendour. The
greatest member of the family, *James Wyatt*, built Norris
Castle, East Cowes, on the Isle of Wight in 1799, after *Nash* had
built for himself East Cowes Castle in 1798,* both castellated
medievalizing jobs of considerable *panache*. At Norris Castle the
vast farm buildings, enclosed by an embattled wall, are particu- 73
larly impressive.‡ These were the years when the Isle of Wight
was becoming fashionable, and we shall hear more of it soon.
Soane built Sydney Lodge, Hamble, in 1789 etc. and did a
minor medievalizing job, the Brocas Chapel at Bramley, dated
1801. The plaster vault, four-centred, is decorated with thin
Gothic arches across and thinner fancy ribs, innocent of
archaeology. The only other work by Soane in the county is still
less important: a house at Hyde, Winchester, renowned as a
private school. This is of 1795. On the other hand Soane's
master *George Dance the Younger* has some of his best work in
Hampshire. Cranbury Park is an amazing house, baffling outside
and spatially daring and quite grandiose inside. It was built by
Dance for his sister, and the accurate date is not known. Dance's
passion for coffered apses, the motif dominating Cranbury Park, 72
is of French derivation, or rather was revived by the French
Academy in the third quarter of the century, from Imperial
Roman baths, palaces, and temples. Dance did Stratton Park,
East Stratton, too. This is 1803 and its extremely impressive Tuscan portico (again of French – Ledoux – derivation) 75
is all that remains of it. One year later *Wilkins* began The
Grange, a large sensational house in the form of a Greek Doric 76
temple.

Dance was responsible also for one ecclesiastical job in Hampshire, the brick octagon serving as the nave of Micheldever
church. This, remarkably sheer outside, was done in 1808.
Nash's church work on the Isle of Wight is as interesting and
even more unexpected. It is the tower of Cowes church, dating 79
from 1816, so uncompromisingly bare and so bold in his use of
very short Greek Doric columns *in antis* in the bell-openings
that one may well at first think of the early C20 in Central
Europe rather than the early C19 in England – and Nash at

* Since demolished.

‡ Of about 1780 must be the super-folly tower at Eaglehurst.

that.* Nash also did, again Greek Doric, the lodge for Northwood House, Cowes,‡ and he may well have designed the FONT in the guise of a Greek Doric column in Whippingham church only a few miles from Cowes. More familiar, within Nash's *œuvre*, is a house only attributed to him, Houghton
74 Lodge on the mainland, a delightful *cottage orné* with steep gables and ornamental bargeboards. The parallel to this revival of Ye Olde English and to the Gothic Revival continuing lustily – the best Gothick church in Hampshire is as late as 1818, Deane, with its pointed plaster vault, its thin chancel screen, and its elaborate altar surround – is the Tudor Revival which got into its stride in the course of the twenties. Hampshire here is particularly early in the field. Marwell Hall is of *c.*1816, Awbridge Danes of 1825. King John's Hunting Lodge near
71 Odiham on the other hand is Jacobean Revival and probably earlier, but then it is a piece of garden furnishing and hence a less responsible job.

How the Elizabethan and Jacobean Revival blossomed with the coming of the Victorian Age, we shall see as soon as we have rounded up the LATE GEORGIAN MONUMENTS. The essential change is that from Baroque and Rococo to Classicism, from Roubiliac to Wilton and then Flaxman. But *Wilton* in Hampshire is not the classicist at once. The monument in Winchester Cathedral to Bishop Hoadly who died in 1761 is a Rococo composition. That at Hale with a date of death only seven years later, on the other hand, helped to establish a type which was repeated *ad nauseam* down to 1830 and beyond, that of a female figure, standing thoughtfully or mournfully by an urn on a high base. An exceedingly fine example of the type is that by *John Bacon Sen.* at Lymington († 1795). The two outstanding funerary monuments of the last quarter of the C18 – one of them really a memorial, not a funerary monument – are also still close to the Baroque: Speaker Chute at The Vyne,
69 1775–81 by *Thomas Carter*, and Bernard Brocas † 1777 at

* An interesting earlier Georgian church at Cowes is the Catholic one, of 1796, with giant Doric pilasters framing the altar. Otherwise no Georgian churches other than those of the Church of England need be mentioned. The earliest surviving NONCONFORMIST CHAPEL is that at Havant of 1718. Other early ones are very small and modest, e.g. that of the Unitarians at Ringwood of 1727 and that of the Countess of Huntingdon's Connexion at Mortimer West End of 1798 (or 1818).

‡ The house itself is a mystery. It seems now largely in the form given it in 1840 by *George Mair*, but *William Cubitt* and the years 1830–1 are also mentioned. The plan is very strange indeed, and so are certain internal details.

Bramley, probably by the same. Both are entirely free-standing without any back wall. Speaker Chute is represented semi-reclining in a wonderfully easy posture, Bernard Brocas is sinking back into the arms of a young woman. By Carter also is an exquisite allegorical roundel on a monument at Romsey († 1769). No wonder, he started as a carver of chimneypieces. Both Wilton and Carter were born in the early 1720s, Wilton for certain, Carter most probably. Of the familiar later Georgian sculptors represented in Hampshire, next in order of birth is *Nollekens*, born in 1737, but what there is of his is not of particular value (Twyford † 1788, Dogmersfield † 1808). After that *Van Gelder* (born 1739, monuments at Havant † 1786 and North Stoneham † 1802) and *J. F. Moore* (born *c.*1740–5, monument at North Stoneham † 1781), and then – at an interval of ten to fifteen years – follows *Flaxman*. He was certainly successful in Hampshire. Thirteen of his monuments are in Hampshire churches* and some of them are among his most beautiful, some among his most interesting works. Of the greatest beauty is the Dr Warton in Winchester Cathedral (1801), an exquisitely set-out composition and at the same time full of that tender sympathy Flaxman had for children, in this case Winchester College boys. As beautiful and again as tender in the rendering of children is Viscountess Fitzharris († 1815) at Christchurch, a 78
free-standing group. The Flaxman at Lyndhurst (1798) is a mourning woman by a broken column, the Flaxman at Petersfield (1801) two mourners standing by an urn, the Flaxman at Romsey two genii composed into a lintel. At Micheldever, between 1801 and 1813, Flaxman did three reliefs of intricate, crowded composition; strangely Baroque for their date. *Sir Richard Westmacott*, again twenty years younger than Flaxman, is represented with five monuments of which the finest is that at Weyhill († 1803) with two youths contemplating a broken column. The earlier of the two monuments at Arreton, Isle of Wight († 1811), is as Baroque as Flaxman's Micheldever monuments, that at Hale († 1796) was designed by *James Wyatt* and has no figures. It is just an urn on a base. Far more monumental as a figureless monument is the anonymous one to Sir Richard Worsley, the traveller and collector who died in 1805, at Godshill, Isle of Wight. This is just an enormous free-standing sarcophagus.‡ Westmacott's son *Richard Westmacott Jun.* has his *magnum opus* at Northington, with two seated

* And one, at Fareham, made from his design by *Regnart*.

‡ The fifth Westmacott is at Fareham († 1811).

allegorical figures above an elaborately portrayed entry to a vault. The conception goes back to Canova, but the date is 1848. He also did the monument to Bishop Tomline † 1827 in Winchester Cathedral. To return to the date order of birth of the sculptors for the few remaining notes, *John Bacon Jun.* has three monuments, none noteworthy, and so we come to Chantrey and Theed, both in their works entirely of the C19. *Chantrey*'s Bishop North of 1825 in Winchester Cathedral is a dignified portrait. He kneels in profile, a composition Chantrey used for other bishops as well. Other monuments by him are at North Stoneham († 1812), Titchfield († 1832), and Peartree Green, Southampton († 1831 and † 1835). *Theed* was a favourite of the Prince Consort and the Queen, worked for them at Osborne, and therefore is the appropriate stepping stone into their age. His monument to Sir Eyre Coote at Rockbourne is an early work.

Except for the sixty years between 1170 and 1230, the sixty-five years of the VICTORIAN AGE are the richest in the history of art and architecture in Hampshire and on the Isle of Wight. Three major mansions of national, not just county, significance went up in the twenty years between 1830 and 1850: the romantic Highcliffe by *Donthorne* (1830–4) for Lord Stuart – who significantly adopted as his title Stuart de Rothesay – made
45 memorable by the transferred Late Gothic parts of the mansion
81 of Les Andelys in Normandy, the enormous Highclere by *Barry*, built on the pattern of Elizabethan Wollaton in 1839–42 but characteristically in lower relief and rather the shallow all-over decoration which Barry's Houses of Parliament display at the
84 same time in Gothic terms,* and the lavishly spreading Osborne, Isle of Wight, by *Thomas Cubitt*, the builder, and *Prince Albert* himself, built in 1845 etc. as a powerfully magnificent Italian villa with Cinquecento motifs and asymmetrically placed towers. The pattern was again Barry, whose Mount Felix, Walton-on-Thames, was built in 1835–9, *Barry* who also built, by the lake below Highclere, the wonderful one-storeyed Lake House, and this is Italianate too. On the Osborne estate there are several Italianate houses along the fringe, and also a genuine (imported) Swiss Cottage and a faithful copy of a Jacobean house, Barton Manor (*c.*1846).

The Isle of Wight, thanks largely to Osborne, rose to be a favourite place for affluent English families to spend seaside holidays. Ryde evidently came first. There are here still quite a number of stuccoed Regency-looking houses and at least one

* The interiors are by *Thomas Allom*, as late as 1860 etc.

attempt at the Brighton scale: Brigstocke Terrace of *c.*1832,* and the churches date significantly from 1827, 1827–8, 1843, 1844, 1845, whereas at Ventnor, Shanklin, and Sandown the 2
corresponding dates are 1837, 1845, 1850, 1860, 1869, 1876, 1880. Hence the houses of Ventnor, Shanklin, and Sandown are entirely Victorian too, the earliest with bargeboarded gables. In the end the Isle of Wight resorts were outdone by the spectacular growth in genteel popularity, in population, and in building activity of Bournemouth. There again the dates of the churches are telling: 1841 (mostly 1860–4), 1868, 1871, 1873, 1876, 1881, 1893, and a number of smaller ones. So, as one walks through Bournemouth, the few remaining early houses are late classical (Royal Bath Hotel of 1838) or again bargeboarded and of the forties, but the bulk is after 1860, its architectural poverty relieved by the generous planting with conifers.

Urban domestic architecture from Regency to Victorian is best seen at Southampton, though without highlights. Carlton Crescent is the best composition. The name is telling as are the surrounding Brunswick, Cumberland, Portland.

It is more profitable to revert to the mansions. *Decimus Burton* built Bay House, Alverstoke, Gosport in 1844 as a marine villa in the Tudor style. *William Burn*, most mysterious of Victorian architects, did Redrice House, Upper Clatford, in 1844, in an odd Latest Classical, but with such a French motif as banded rustication, and Idsworth House in 1852 and Amport House in 1857 in a much more ordinary Elizabethan or Jacobean. *Henry Clutton*'s large Minley Manor of 1858–60 is in a rich *château* style,‡ his Melchet Park of 1863 and 1875 etc. Jacobean.§ *Teulon* built two houses for Lord Calthorpe, Elvetham Hall 87
in 1859–60, and Woodlands outside Ryde in 1870–1. They have the powerful porch tower and the variety of shapes of bay windows in common. Elvetham is the weirder of the two, Frenchy in style. Farnborough Hill, the Empress Eugenie's house, was built before her time, *c.*1862 by *H. E. Kendall Jun.*, and was a monster chalet. Mixed Franco-English C16 is Coldhayes, Steep, by *Waterhouse* of 1869, a house curiously wild

* The only other attempts at competing with Brighton are the Crescents at Alverstoke (Gosport) begun in 1826 and on Hayling Island begun *c.*1830, and the latter was never completed.

‡ But *Devey*, as mysterious as Burn, added elements of William and Mary and Venetian Renaissance in 1886–7.

§ Inside some of the Italian Renaissance features by *Alfred Stevens* and *L. W. Collmann* are left, and the Jacobean was carried on and oddly modified by *Darcy Braddell c.*1912–14.

for so disciplined an architect. Much more reasonably Tudor is Waterhouse's Blackmoor House of 1869–73 and 1882. *F. P. Cockerell*'s disjointed Crawley Court of 1877 is Free Elizabethan, and Tudor Gothic (with Flamboyant touches) *cum* Elizabethan or Jacobean went on to Rhinefield Lodge, Brockenhurst, by *Romaine Walker & Tanner*, 1889–90, and to Tylney Hall, Rotherwick, by *R. Selden Wornum* of 1899–1901, but they were utterly out of date then.

The change in domestic architecture was due to *Norman Shaw* and established itself in the seventies. His Boldre Grange of 1873–4 is nothing very special, his Convent at Bournemouth of the same years is more characteristic, though not as fine as
See p. 827 *J. D. Sedding*'s adjoining Vicarage of St Clement, Bournemouth, of 1873.* Shaw in his early years was in partnership with *Eden Nesfield*, and Nesfield certainly has a share in the establishment of the informal Shavian idiom with its happy borrowings from local English traditions. Nesfield's Lodge for Broadlands is as early as 1870 and has timber-framing and tile-hanging and picturesque high chimneys. *W. R. Lethaby* was perhaps Shaw's
93 most brilliant follower. Avon Tyrrell is his first independent building. It was begun in 1891, and while it is obviously Shaw-school, the sensitively contrived asymmetry of the main façade and the beautiful principal chimneypiece inside are highly original and, within their own idioms, perfect. *Lutyens* started from the same premises, as is proved by Berrydown, Ashe, of 1897, Marsh Court, King's Somborne, begun in 1901, and New Place, Shedfield, begun in 1906, all three Tudor, freely com-
See p. 827 posed. His late development is unrepresented in Hampshire, and so having reached the new century we break off and repeat the survey of the Victorian decades in terms of public buildings and then of churches.

The harvest in public buildings would be poor, if it were not for the BUILDINGS FOR THE SERVICES. But the Army and the Navy have built more – and more of outstanding interest – in Hampshire during the C19 than in any other county. At Aldershot the early Army buildings, mid C19 in date, have mostly disappeared and go on disappearing. But the Naval Dockyard at Portsmouth continued to grow and produce buildings of interest. Some, e.g. the former Pay Office of 1798 (by *Sir*
83 *Samuel Bentham*), No. 6 Boat House of 1843, the Fire Station of the same year, No. 3 Ship Shop of 1849 (?), and No. 1

* Netley Castle, remodelled in 1885–90, though much grander, is far less interesting.

Smithery of 1852, are highly interesting because of their iron construction, others because of their Vanbrughian style. This – a masculine, powerful vernacular – went on nearly throughout the whole C19 (No. 2 Ship Shop 1849, Iron Foundry 1854, No. 1 Ship Shop 1896). The scale of some of the buildings also continued to be impressive.* For scale Netley Military Hospital of 1856–63 deserves first place (the façade is 1,424 ft long), though not for architectural merit. At Gosport on the other hand barracks of 1847 and 1857 as well as the Victualling Yard of 1828 etc. with the Granary of 1853 are impressive or interesting. From the same years, to conclude buildings for the services, date the Palmerston Forts, built *c.* 1860 as a defence against attack of an invader coming from the N. They form a chain N of Portsmouth and N of Gosport.

After this strong group of naval and military buildings, what Hampshire has to offer in the field of Victorian PUBLIC BUILDINGS proper is minor. But as public buildings have up to now been left entirely out of this survey, we must start as far back as 1713 with the Winchester Guildhall with its statue of Queen Anne and its succulent clock bracket reaching out over the street. To the later C18 belong the odd town hall without a town at Newtown, Isle of Wight, and the Yarmouth Town Hall, also Isle of Wight. After that the chief buildings are at Winchester, though Stockbridge has a town hall of 1810, Newport, the county-town of the Isle of Wight, has a town hall by *Nash* of 1816 and a guildhall by the same of 1819, and the much more interesting House of Industry of shortly after 1770, an early workhouse on a vast scale. The centre range is 300 ft long, the r. wing 170, the l. wing was never built.‡ The Andover Town Hall is Greek Doric of 1825, the Whitchurch Town Hall is Grecian too, Ryde Town Hall (Isle of Wight) more summarily classical of 1830, and the Basingstoke Town Hall, classical on the verge of Italianate, of 1832. After that come the Victorian market hall of Botley (1848) and town hall of Christchurch (1859), but still classical, the solidly Italianate court house at Southampton (1851–3) – and so on to the large, proud, and showy Guildhall of Portsmouth by *William Hill* of Leeds. This is of 1886–90. In these small towns another building of dignity is usually the hotel. This applies e.g. to the Star and Garter at Andover, the

* The former School of Naval Architecture of 1815–17 is seventeen bays long.

‡ One early factory deserves a note: the silk mill at Whitchurch of 1815, not large, of brick, with a clock turret.

White Hart at Whitchurch, and the White Hart at Stockbridge. A roll-call of public buildings at Winchester would look like this: The Old Gaol of 1805 by *G. Moneypenny* in Jewry Street is among the most impressive of the kind in the country, even though it survives only in façade fragments: it has vermiculated rustication to demonstrate how impregnable it is. The Corn
80 Exchange (now Library) is by *O. B. Carter*, of 1836–8, and a first-class example to show the step from severe Classical to Italianate. The portico with its Tuscan columns is derived from Inigo Jones, but such sturdy Tuscan columns had also been the favourite order of the architects in France about 1800. The far-projecting eaves, however, and the square tower altogether are of Italian villa derivation.* Winchester Town Hall by *Jeffery & Skiller*, 1871–3, is High Victorian-High Gothic (i.e. Second Pointed – *see* below), on the pattern of Godwin's Northampton Town Hall, but with a Frenchy steep pavilion roof. The best secular neo-Gothic building at Winchester, however, is the County Hospital by *Butterfield*, 1864, brick with blue-brick diapers, where asymmetry is ingeniously planned. Butterfield's contributions to Winchester College are much weaker. At the College the best Victorian building is *Basil Champneys*'s Museum of 1893, in an enterprising, resourceful, and jolly English Baroque. *Sir Herbert Baker*'s War Memorial Cloister, though as late as 1923–4, also belongs in this context; for it is skilfully historicist and not noticeably filtered through the British events of the Arts and Crafts and after.

For VICTORIAN CHURCHES Hampshire is a bumper county. The stages of development can be documented as fully as one could wish. At the start still stand the pre-archaeological buildings, the churches of the Commissioners' type with their thin lancet windows and thin buttresses, such as Chilworth of
77 1812 (with its surprising plaster vaults), Waterlooville, 1830, and, quite a climax, Holy Trinity Fareham of 1834–7, with stone spire and cast-iron piers and traceried beams. All Saints, Landport, Portsmouth of 1827–8 has cast-iron elements too. Characteristic of the forties is the Neo-Norman fashion. This is represented by Emsworth (1839–40); Elvetham (1840–1); St James Portsmouth by *Livesay* (1841; replaced); Cove (1844); St Paul Newport Isle of Wight (1844); St Peter Southampton by *O. B. Carter* (1845); Swanmore (1846) and St

* À propos the change from classical to Italianate, *Tite*'s railway stations
82 must not be forgotten, chiefly Gosport, opened in 1842, with its long Tuscan colonnade.

Boniface Bonchurch, Isle of Wight (1847–8) by *Ferrey*; Newnham (1847); St Mary Magdalene, Widley, Portsmouth by *Colson* (1849; demolished); with odd latecomers or individualists in the sixties. They are chiefly three. Whippingham Isle of Wight is by *Humbert*, the architect of Sandringham and the 85
two Mausolea at Windsor. It dates from 1854 and 1861 and is Italian Romanesque rather than Norman, and that only partly, the rest being E.E.* Hawkley by *Teulon* 1865, Easton by *Woodyer* also in the sixties, and Itchen Abbas 1867 are Norman too. Swanmore and St Boniface, Bonchurch, are, as has been said, by *Ferrey*. Yet Ferrey, a fellow pupil with Pugin, was among the first in England to turn to Second Pointed, recommended in the same years by the *Ecclesiologist*, and to treat it archaeologically accurately. Second Pointed means the period from about 1250 to the early C14, with plate tracery and bar tracery and details freeing themselves gradually from the standard Geometrical motifs, but stopping short of the ogee arch and flowing tracery. The earliest examples of this turn in Hampshire belong to the years 1843–5, but before they are named, two slightly earlier churches deserve record as special and remarkable cases: Newtown on the Isle of Wight and Andover. Newtown is of 1835, Andover of 1840–6. Newtown is by *A. F. Livesay*, Andover by the same, with more than co-operation from the incumbent *Dr Goddard*, former headmaster of Winchester College. Newtown is E.E., but not in the meaningless Commissioners' lancet tradition. It is handled as knowledgeably as only Edward Garbett had until then handled it: at Theale, Berkshire, in 1820–2.‡ Andover is also E.E., but much more majestically. Andover is indeed a church one does not forget, lofty, with an apse two-storeyed to the outside, and screened inside against the chancel by a screen of slender shafts. Here, though in different forms, the respect for the architectural past, as it really was, is as patent as in the four churches of 1843–5 from which this necessary digression has led us. They are Dogmersfield and Baughurst by *Ferrey*, St Thomas Winchester, much grander, by the otherwise little known *E. W. Elmslie*, and West Meon by *Scott*.

Scott is the first of the big High Victorian names to appear in this survey. He did other churches as well, the biggest being

* Completely Romanesque as against Norman, and also of Italian derivation, is Holy Trinity, Bournemouth, by *Cory & Ferguson*, 1868–9.

‡ Edward Garbett must not be confused with William Garbett of Winchester.

Ryde, Isle of Wight, of 1868–72 and Highclere of 1869–70. They are competent, undeniably impressive, but neither very personal nor very sensitive. The leading church architects of the High Victorian decades can be divided into those who believed in the authority of real Gothic buildings, and followed them faithfully, with no more than minor personal comments, and those who took Second Pointed or even not Second Pointed materials, shook them well, and served them with generous seasoning of their own. These latter, the individualists, the hards, the believers in self-expression, are even now, after a hundred years, less easily appreciated than the others who admittedly produced more accomplished work. *Burges* was an individualist, but his church at Fleet of 1861–2 is remarkably restrained and yet very powerful with its transverse brick arches. The *Francis* brothers as a rule did run-of-the-mill stuff, but their Ringwood of 1853–5, unfussy, but with a splendid chancel, amply deserves a place in this summary. *R. J. Jones* will be known to only very few, but his St Michael, Ryde, Isle of Wight, of 1861–3 is serious and impressive and his church at Clanfield with its brick polychromy inside has the same qualities. So has the aisleless Itchen Stoke, 1866, by a relation of its vicar, *H. Conybeare*. *John Johnson*, somewhat better known, but also not in the top flight, produced his *chef d'œuvre* at South Tidworth (1879–80), large and proud, with a wilful exterior, but a noble and yet sumptuous interior. *Sir Arthur Blomfield*, whom books would put among the top flight, did several churches in Hampshire, two of them of some interest: St Mary, Portsmouth, of 1887 etc. for sheer size and Gothic elaboration and the external remodelling of Holy Trinity Gosport of 1887–9, because it is Italian Romanesque with a dominating brick campanile.* The climax of churches in the respectful and
89 sensitive archaeological vein is *Pearson*'s St Stephen at Bournemouth, of 1881 etc., fully E.E., fully stone-vaulted, and yet – as so often in the case of Pearson – not at all without original motifs. The same attitude as in Pearson we find in Scott's sons. By *John Oldrid* is St John, Boscombe, Bournemouth, built in 1893–5. Bournemouth was flourishing in these years, as we have seen. The list of the dates of her churches has already been given. The earliest, St Peter, is by *Street*, but grew by several steps to its present size.‡

* The type had been anticipated, it will be remembered, at Holy Trinity Bournemouth.

‡ By *Street* also the excellent small churches of East Parley (1862–3) and

Now for the individualists, the rogues, as Goodhart-Rendel called them. The centre of that group was *Butterfield*, but there is no church by him in Hampshire as good as his Winchester Hospital. *Woodyer* did Holy Trinity Millbrook, Southampton with its assertively picturesque exterior (1873–80), and *William White* left his *magnum opus* to Hampshire, the Lyndhurst parish 88
church of 1858–70, decidedly unconventional, and with much figure carving. White is as idiosyncratic at Smannell and Hatherden as well, and his are also St Mark Woolston, Southampton, of 1863 etc. and Christ Church Freemantle, Southampton, of 1865–6. But the most roguish of churches in Hampshire is by an architect usually much more conventional: *J. A. Hansom.* His Catholic church at Ryde, Isle of Wight, of 1844–6 has a fiercely asymmetrical exterior and the most curious arcade arches, imitated – strange to report – by *T. H. Wyatt* at Woolton Hill in 1849. An anonymous rogue was the restorer of the church of Thruxton (1869).

The turn from High to Late Victorian in domestic architecture is, as we have seen, closely linked with *Norman Shaw*, and, though his St Michael at Bournemouth of 1873–6 is comparatively conventional, his St Swithun in the same town and begun in the latter year, with its wide barn-like nave and its enormous w window with flowing tracery, is unmistakably anti-High-Victorian. Dec also is *Bodley & Garner*'s fine and quiet Ecchinswell of 1886. Bodley of course, in his attitude, belongs to Pearson and not the aggressive innovators. While at Ecchinswell he is Dec in order not to be Second Pointed, he was also instrumental in bringing about a new appreciation of Perp which, immediately after the Houses of Parliament and after Pugin in his writings had branded it as decadent, had lost all support. In Hampshire Perp appears remarkably early in *T. H. Wyatt*'s not otherwise remarkable Oakley (1869). It was then used by *Sir Thomas Jackson* in his two churches for the Barings: East Stratton of 1878 etc. and the much bigger Northington of 1887–90 with its Somerset tower, and also by *Waterhouse* at Twyford in 1876–7.* Among the best neo-Perp work in the county is a Nonconformist job: *Bonella & Paull*'s Congregational Church at Romsey, of 1887–8, which, thanks to ingenious

Farlington, Portsmouth (1872–5), and the steeple of St Mary Southampton (designed in 1878). The parsonage by Street at Laverstoke (1858) is domestic 86
Street at his best.

* Waterhouse's large aisleless church at Blackmoor of 1868 is stylistically less determinate.

grouping (with the tower astride a street), holds its own close to the abbey church. In connexion with the popularity of the Late Gothic in these years, a completely exceptional building
91 might here find its place: the mausoleum church for Napoleon III and Eugenie built by her at Farnborough, close to the abbey she had founded.* The architect she commissioned was *Destailleur* (of Waddesdon fame), the date of the start 1887, the style chosen French Flamboyant, though the dome and the crypt are both conceits distant from that style.

The Farnborough Mausoleum did not apparently inspire any English architect, yet at the moment when – out of William Morris's teachings and workshop – the Arts and Crafts evolved, one could imagine that the intricate Flamboyant leafage might have been found congenial. The nearest in Hampshire to Arts and Crafts architecture is *Henry Wilson*'s tower added to his master *Sedding*'s church of St Clement at Bournemouth. The church is of 1871–3 the tower of 1890–3.‡ *Morris* GLASS is represented in Hampshire and on the Isle of Wight from Lyndhurst of 1862–3 and Gatcombe of 1865–6 to Yateley of 1876, Heckfield of 1884, and beyond. *Kempe* glass, starting as early as 1874,§ is more fully represented than is good for Kempe.|| Other CHURCH DECORATION is best represented at Lyndhurst, in White's church. The Gothic monument to the donor †1863 is by *Street*, and wall paintings were done by *Mrs*(?) *Pollen* and – above the altar, as a spectacular reredos – by *Lord Leighton* in 1864. A generation later, in the full Arts and Crafts style, indeed so fantastical as to result in an English Art Nouveau, is *Alfred Gilbert*'s grille at Whippingham, Isle of Wight (1897). Alfred Gilbert also did, in the same year, the grand bronze monument to Queen Victoria, now ignominiously pushed into a corner of the Great Hall in Winchester Castle. The queen is seated and crowned by two angels with a fabulously intricate crown.

The overture to the TWENTIETH CENTURY could not be
95 more splendid. *Dom Paul Bellot*'s Quarr Abbey and especially its church is on the highest international level. It was begun in 1908, is of brick and in a Gothic treated so freely that it is

* The abbey building itself, modelled on Solesmes, towering and forbidding, is as alien to Hampshire as the mausoleum. It is mostly by *Fr. Benedict Williamson* and dates from 1900–12.

‡ Two other Sedding churches are Netley of 1886 and Bursledon of 1888.

§ Froyle 1874 and 1878, Ashe 1878.

|| For early C19 glass one must go to Winchester College where *David Evans* of Shrewsbury did a lot (and a lot of damage) from 1825-8 to the middle of the century.

already halfway to Expressionism. One could compare it with the – some years later – Grundtvig Church in Copenhagen by Klint. The plan of the church also is novel and ingenious with the low nave and the high, towering, brick-vaulted monks' choir. The three-dimensional play with bricks is reminiscent of Gaudí, and Bellot's historical sources were indeed partly in Catalonia (Poblet), partly in Moorish Andalusia. From the planning point of view *Comper*'s Cosham near Portsmouth of 1936 is important too, at least for England. The altar here with a baldacchino stands well forward of the E end* – the start of the 'worship-in-the-round' trend so powerful today. Architecturally Cosham is all more civilized and much more genteel than Quarr: outside blocky brick in a Gothic reduced to fundamentals, but inside Italian, as Comper a little perversely liked it. Blocky brick also characterizes *Sir Giles Scott*'s early Annunciation at Bournemouth (1906). A complete contrast is the neo-Baroque of Thorney Hill by *Detmar Blow*, designed in 1906. But that was not a style which could be successful in England. The most interesting English initiative of the time about 1900 is represented by work in an Early Christian or Byzantine style, the style of Bentley's Westminster Cathedral. This is excellently handled in *J. H. Ball*'s St Agatha, Landport, 92
Portsmouth, of 1893–5 with its superb decoration by *Heywood Sumner* and in *G. Drysdale*'s St Joseph Aldershot of 1912–13. But the most typical English work right down to the thirties still remained attached to the Gothic style, such work as that of several of *Sir Charles Nicholson*'s churches.‡

No church in the C20 idiom need be referred to, but the excellent stained glass by *Patrick Reyntiens* at Hound, and – to go back again some twenty years – sculpture by *Eric Gill* at Dogmersfield in the chapel and at Liss. *Stanley Spencer*'s wall paintings at Burghclere are a war memorial and what was 96
built to house them is a chapel. Yet they are not Christian in any conventional sense. Christ appears on only one of them, and very small and distant. Nor are they a war memorial in any conventional sense. There is no fighting here, nor any showy heroism. It is nearly all everyday scenes, and much is hospital routine, but seen and rendered with a deep sense of human fate and of mute endurance. The Burghclere paintings are

* This was preceded by the cruciform Gothic St Alban Southampton by *Cachemaille-Day* two or three years earlier, with a central altar under the crossing.

‡ And his seamen's home at Medstead.

England's prime contribution to European Expressionism and
ought to be visited by foreigners and Englishmen alike.

With Lutyens the summary of SECULAR ARCHITECTURE has
already entered the C20 some pages back. Still to the same Arts
and Crafts climate as his Hampshire buildings belong *Ernest*
94 *Gimson*'s hall and library at Bedales School. As to the rest of
noteworthy secular architecture we have to move straight away
into the last ten years, and for them there is much to report.
To proceed from the small to the large and from the private to
99 the public *Sir Basil Spence*'s cottage outside Beaulieu, built for
himself, is quite simple yet with one or two motifs which at
once single it out. *Stephen Gardiner & Christopher Knight* have
75 recently built a house at Stratton Park, East Stratton, to replace
Dance's mansion and have kept the grand Tuscan portico and
combined it by means of a formal pool with the house in one
composition. By *Stirling & Gowan* is a house at Cowes. For
large-scale housing the City of Southampton (city architect *L.
Berger*) has recently done extremely well. An estate like that at
Northam is as good as anything in any other English city. Some
Southampton work by private architects is commendable too
(Castle House, by *Eric Lyons*). At Portsmouth the best new
building to date is private too (a commercial building at Landport by *Owen Luder*). The municipal housing is on the whole
architecturally poor. But Gosport deserves praise for the boldness of its new tower blocks on the water's edge in the very hub
of the town.

With modern PUBLIC BUILDINGS Hampshire is well
provided. The best are the new buildings of Southampton
98 University, including *Sir Basil Spence*'s dramatic Theatre, and
the Wessex Hotel at Winchester by *Feilden & Mawson* which
offers the much needed proof that a completely up-to-date C20
building can stand perfectly happily next to a medieval cathedral.
Peter Shepheard in his new hall at Winchester College has, alas,
not had the same courage, and the attempt at conformity with
the past strikes one as negative or at least neutral rather than
positive. Gosport has had the enterprise of a brand-new town
hall (by *W. H. Saunders & Son*, 1964), and the Warsash School
97 of Navigation is gradually rebuilding on a large scale and
extremely well (*Richard Sheppard, Robson & Partners*). Add to
this the Marchwood and Fawley Power Stations by *Farmer &
Dark* (1952–9 and 1965 etc.), the best of the new English power
stations, and this survey can close – except that a preliminary
reference must be appended to the plans for new town centres

for Basingstoke and Andover, not yet beyond the model stage at the time of writing, but both very promising.

FURTHER READING

By far the most important work is the Victoria County History, complete for the county and the Isle of Wight in five volumes (1903–14). The architectural descriptions in these volumes are far more detailed than those in the following gazetteer. As supplementary reading one may choose the volumes of the Little Guides (by J. C. Cox, and G. Clinch, both 1904), revised after the war by R. L. P. Jowitt, and the Shell Guide to Hampshire by John Rayner (1937). The county archaeological magazine is the *Proceedings of the Hampshire Field Club and Archaeological Society*. Too late for this book is the report of the 1966 Summer Meeting of the Royal Archaeological Institute published in the volume for 1967 of the *Archaeological Journal*.

PREHISTORY

BY DEREK SIMPSON

THE earliest evidence of human settlement in the region is provided by a series of Lower Palaeolithic hand axes of Acheulean type found in the gravel terraces of the Avon and Test (with particular concentrations at Dunbridge and Timsbury) and the raised beaches E of Portsmouth belonging to the second interglacial and third glacial periods. For the Upper Palaeolithic one again has to rely on flint tools. The most important site is that at Hengistbury Head, Southbourne, where a working floor was found containing tanged and shouldered points for arrow-tips, scrapers for skin dressing, and burins for bone and antler working. Similar material has been found on Long Island, Langstone Harbour, Portsmouth. The remains of these hunters probably date to *c.*11,000–10,000 B.C. and are related to similar finds from Germany (it should be remembered that at this date the English Channel did not exist as a barrier to the free movement of peoples from the continental land mass). With the retreat of the ice at the end of the last glaciation and the increasingly warm conditions, there was a gradual encroachment of forests, first of birch and later pine and mixed oak, with corresponding changes in the wild fauna upon which the hunters were largely dependent. These changes in their natural environment led to an alteration in their hunting economy, settlement pattern, and material equipment. Settlement now tended to be coastal (e.g. Hengistbury Head) or lakeside (e.g. Woolmer, Bramshott) and on the greensands, which would have supported only light forest cover. An important site of these Mesolithic hunters lies in Oakhanger parish near Selborne, where over 8,000 flint implements, microliths for arrowpoints and fish-spears, scrapers, saws, and axes, siltstone rubbers, and a sarsen mace-head with hourglass perforation have been found. A radio-carbon determination suggests a date for the settlement in the second half of the fifth millennium B.C. No dwellings have been found in association with any of this material in the county. Most of the sites appear to represent temporary encampments or flint-knapping areas occupied only sporadically by groups following herds of game.

The first settlers to have left any visible field monuments

in the county were farmers of the Windmill Hill Culture, who arrived in Britain in the latter part of the fourth millennium. These newcomers practised a mixed farming economy, one element of which was the hilltop causewayed camps known from neighbouring counties (*see The Buildings of England: Wiltshire* and *Sussex*) but as yet undiscovered in Hampshire. With the introduction of a Neolithic economy, it was possible to produce a sufficient surplus of food to allow for the emergence of specialists not directly involved in the production of and search for food – the flint miners. A group of their mine-shafts occurs at Martin's Clump on the Hampshire–Wiltshire border. The chief product of such mines appears to have been the axe, which reflects the generally forested conditions prevailing during this period and the need to clear tracts of land for cultivation and grazing. Flint was augmented by the importing of axes of Cornish stone into the area, and this trade was to develop even more extensively in the Later Neolithic period. The most numerous surviving monuments of these farmers are their long barrows, over three dozen of which are known from the county, all (with one exception) occurring on the chalk downs. These consist of elongated earthen mounds, up to 320 ft in length (Knap Barrow, Rockbourne), with flanking quarry ditches from which the material of the mound was obtained. A peculiar form confined to the Cranborne Chase area has the side ditches prolonged around one end of the mound, producing a U-shaped plan (e.g. Holdenhurst – now destroyed). The mounds have a generally E–W orientation, the E end being the broader and higher, and it is beneath this portion of the mound that the interments are encountered. The normal rite was that of collective inhumation, the corpses lying on the old land surface beneath the mound or in a pit, in some cases covered by a primary mound of turf or stone (Holdenhurst). Beneath the barrows at Holdenhurst and Nutbane, Penton Mewsey, were enclosures, of turf in the former case and wood in the latter, which appear to have served as store houses where bodies might accumulate until there were sufficient to warrant the erection of a barrow over them. This feature has been noted beneath long barrows elsewhere in southern Britain.

The Nutbane excavations also revealed the complexity of funerary ritual and structure included in this pre-barrow phase in the disposal of the dead. Only three of the Hampshire long barrows have been excavated, and in none have grave goods been found in direct association with the burials. Sherds of the round-based, baggy vessels of the culture have been found however incorporated in the mound and on the old land surface or in the primary silt of the ditch. Other aspects of their material culture such as leaf-shaped arrowheads, scrapers, and axes of flint, and stone axes are represented only by stray finds. For the Later Neolithic the local evidence is even more scanty. The coarse, cord-impressed Peterborough ware has been found in a secondary position in the long barrows of Holdenhurst, Nutbane, and Nether Wallop, and sherds of Rinyo Clacton ware in the ditch of the Holdenhurst barrow. Possible settlement sites of the period have been found beneath a number of later round barrows (e.g. Arreton and Niton on the Isle of Wight), but the main evidence for the activities of these groups comes from the stray finds of their characteristic flint implements, which owe much to Mesolithic traditions, and from the axes of igneous rock. Axes from the factories of Cornwall, Graig Llwyd, North Wales, Whin Sill, Northumberland, Prescelly, Pembroke, and Great Langdale, Westmorland, and jadeite axes from an as yet unlocated continental source reflect the widespread commercial links established at this period. Some of these axes of foreign stone, notably those from Prescelly, were probably imported by the final Neolithic group to settle in the region from *c.*2000 B.C., the Beaker folk, named after the characteristic S-shaped drinking cups which they placed in graves with their dead. Elsewhere in Wessex the normal form of Beaker interment was that of a crouched inhumation beneath a round barrow. In Hampshire, however, the grave was generally unmarked by a covering mound (e.g. Stockbridge Down, Lymington, and Winchester). These flat graves show a noticeable concentration in the Christchurch region. The evidence of these groups comes again almost entirely from graves; no permanent settlements have been found, although occupation debris on some sites suggests the temporary encampments of semi-nomadic pastoralists (e.g. Broom Hill, Michelmersh).

Over a thousand round barrows are known from the county. The majority are concentrated on the chalk downs, and many of these, from their contents, may be ascribed to the period 1650–1400 B.C. The population during this period represents the continuance of Late Neolithic groups, attested by such features as the cord-ornamented collared urns representing a survival of Neolithic ceramic traditions and the rite of cremation itself beneath a round barrow. Overlying these Neolithic elements are new traditions, introduced probably by fresh immigrants from the Rhineland who settled in the Wessex region athwart the important trade route from the copper and gold deposits of Ireland to the Continent, and adjacent to the equally valuable tin ores of Cornwall. The objects which these immigrants placed in graves with their dead characterize the Early Bronze Age Wessex Culture. The exotic forms of round barrow – bell generally covering male burials and disc and saucer female – have, in Hampshire, generally produced grave goods of the indigenous element in this culture rather than the elaborate weapons and ornaments of bronze, gold, and amber found in the princely graves of Wiltshire. The burials of warriors accompanied by their grooved daggers have been found beneath barrows on Arreton Down on the Isle of Wight, Ibworth, Hannington, and Penton Mewsey, and a rich group found with an urned cremation beneath a barrow on Hengistbury Head, Southbourne, included amber beads, gold buttons, and a miniature gold pendant copying the metal-shafted halberds current at this period in central Europe. Again one is dependent almost entirely on the evidence from burials. A figure-of-eight-shaped pit on Stockbridge Down which produced collared urn sherds, flints, and part of a saddle quern has been interpreted as the encampment of semi-nomadic pastoralists and is the only non-sepulchral site in the county. The objects of gold, amber, and bronze which characterize the Wessex chieftains ceased to be deposited in graves after *c.*1400 B.C. The native peasantry continue to be represented however in the deposition of cremations in urns, now frequently of biconical form, in bowl or pond barrows, the latter again related to Late Neolithic ceremonial monuments of the henge type.

The last major population movement into southern Britain in the Bronze Age took place *c.*1200 B.C. These new immigrants, whose material remains mark the Deverel–Rimbury Culture, were to set an economic pattern which was to remain virtually unchanged until the Roman conquest. Native traditions can still be discerned in their pottery alongside new ceramic forms, but the most important innovation was that of settled agriculture based on some established form of land tenure, crop rotation, and the traction plough. Cattle were penned in winter in embanked enclosures (e.g. Martin Down, Brockley Warren, and Ladle Hill), probably to enable dung to be collected and spread on the adjacent fields. These 'Celtic' fields consist of groups of small embanked fields of $\frac{1}{2}$–$1\frac{1}{2}$ acres in area generally occurring on the southward-facing slopes of the downs (e.g.

Great Litchfield Down and Martin Down). In some cases they are associated with larger enclosures and linear earthworks (e.g. Grim's Ditch, Ladle Hill, and Quarley Hill) which have been interpreted as tribal and ranch boundaries. The dead continued to be cremated, the remains being placed in urns which were inserted into existing mounds (e.g. Latch Farm), or in low, scraped-up round barrows or flat cemeteries (e.g. Dummer, Pokesdown, and Kinson). The latter part of the Bronze Age is also marked by a great increase in the volume of metal in circulation, and there is evidence to suggest a reorganization in the metal trade during this period. Few of these objects are found in direct association with any settlement site, normally occurring as stray finds or in hoards. A bronze shaft-hole axe of Mediterranean type found off Hengistbury Head, Southbourne, and brooches of Italian form reflect the long-distance trade contacts enjoyed by the inhabitants during this period. In the C6 square-mouthed socketed bronze axes of Breton type from Hampshire attest cross-Channel trade; the frequently high lead content and standardized size of such axes might indicate their use as a primitive form of currency rather than as tools.

The introduction of iron into the area and the appearance of immigrants from the continent marking the first Iron Age (A) Culture do not appear to have changed the existing settlement pattern or economy. The pottery of these Iron Age A groups in Hampshire suggests a French origin for them, and the settlement behind the Double Dykes at Hengistbury Head must mark a landfall in the spread of these communities into Wessex. The social unit was still the isolated farmstead (e.g. Worthy Down, Kings Worthy, and Stanmore), with its associated group of Celtic fields. Grain was stored in pits, and seed corn in silos supported on four posts. The only burial of the period recorded from the county was beneath a small round barrow on Beaulieu Heath (now destroyed). The primary inhumation burial had not been preserved in the acid soil conditions, but there remained fragments of wood and metal fittings probably representing a funerary cart – an association unique in Britain, although such cart burials are well attested among related groups on the Continent. A growing land hunger and increasingly unsettled conditions are reflected in the construction of hillforts. The earliest forts are generally univallate and in some cases occupy the sites of earlier Iron Age A open or palisaded settlements (e.g. Quarley Hill and Winklebury Camp). The unfinished site on Ladle Hill has been of considerable value in throwing light on the techniques adopted in the construction of such hillforts. Some of this fort building was probably due to an external threat of invasion by Iron Age B groups who settled in the area in the C2. A number of existing hillforts were remodelled by these newcomers (e.g. Bury Hill fort), who added additional lines of defences, and new multivallate forts were constructed (e.g. Danebury Down, Nether Wallop, and Buckland Rings). These forts with multiple defences and complex entrance works are concentrated in the western part of the county and belong to a series of similar forts in the neighbouring county of Dorset, best represented at Maiden Castle. This mixed A/B culture of west Hampshire may be identified with the tribe of the Durotriges, whose territory also embraced Dorset and south Wiltshire. The eastern area lay within the province of the Belgic tribe of the Atrebates, who had fled to Britain under their king Commius after the great revolt in Gaul in the middle of the C1. This tribe, with their neighbours the Catuvellauni to the NE, were the most culturally and socially advanced peoples of Iron Age Britain. Among the innovations which they introduced were wheel-turned pottery and coinage, both adopted from them by the Durotriges to the W. From a study of this coinage some of the political events in the immediately pre-Roman period may be discerned. Tincommius, Commius's successor, began to produce coins which imitate Roman forms, reflecting the increasing contacts between southern Britain and the Roman world. His position was usurped however by his brothers Eppillus and Verica, and Tincommius fled to Rome for aid. Even closer links, however, appear to have been established between Augustus and the Atrebatic rulers: Verica now included the title REX on his coinage, suggesting some treaty relationship with Rome. The name Calleva on coins of Eppillus also indicates the pre-Roman foundation of the later Roman administrative centre at Silchester. The inner earthwork at the latter site, in part overlain by the later Roman town wall, which echoes its polygonal plan, is Belgic in character but may not be of pre-Conquest construction. Atrebatic control of this northern part of Hampshire appears to have been short-lived, and by the time of the Roman invasion it had come under the sway of their powerful Catuvellaunian neighbours.

ROMAN HAMPSHIRE

BY BARRY CUNLIFFE

HAMPSHIRE'S first contact with the Roman armies would have come in 43, or early in 44, at the time when the second legion under the command of Vespasian was given the task of conquering the West of England. Vespasian's initial supply-base may well have been at Fishbourne (Sussex), near Chichester, in the territory ruled by the friendly king Cogidubnus, who was well rewarded by the Romans for his loyalty. To what extent the whole of the old Atrebatic kingdom was controlled by Cogidubnus, and was therefore pro-Roman, is unknown, but the absence of the anti-Roman fortification of hillforts and the complete lack of Roman camps or forts in the area E of the Itchen suggest that this territory at least did not oppose the Roman advance. Even beyond there is no positive trace of military intervention. It seems likely, therefore, that after the subjugation of the Isle of Wight Vespasian's forces passed quickly through Hampshire to the more exacting problem of the destruction of Durotrigian power in Dorset.

Hampshire in the Roman period was above all an agricultural area – an area intensively farmed by its scattered population, living in all types of buildings from peasant huts to large mansions. Of the seventy or more villas at present known in the county, most are comfortable if unpretentious and many are known to have had such luxuries as heated rooms, bath suites, and simple patterned mosaics. Only a small proportion, among them Brading, Bramdean, and Thruxton, with their fine figured mosaics, can be described as at all luxurious. This essentially rural population was dependent upon two towns: Winchester, in the centre of the county, and Silchester, on its northern fringe. Both would have served as market centres and in both the more prosperous villa owners would have built their town houses. Winchester, lying astride an important thoroughfare, is the hub of the road system, with six main routes radiating out from it; some, for example the roads to Silchester and Mildenhall (Wilts), are still followed for long stretches by modern roads. A high percentage of Hampshire villas lie within 15 miles of the town – a maximum convenient distance for a day's visit to market. Much the same can be said of Silchester, but its hinterland lies more outside the county than in.

The site of Silchester had little attraction for Saxon and p. 503
Norman settlers and, unlike Winchester, remained virtually uninhabited after the C5. This fortunate accident preserved for the archaeologist an entire Roman town which was eagerly, if somewhat inadequately, excavated during the last century and the beginning of this, providing us with a complete plan of the masonry buildings contained within the defences. From it we are able to build up a vivid picture of urban life: the market place in the centre, the temples, the public baths, the hotel for travellers and the houses and shops of the inhabitants, all regularly contained within a grid of streets. But whereas modern techniques of excavation would have told us of growth and development, Victorian method has limited us to the bare plan.

The southern part of the county differs from the inland area in that its sands and clays were not conducive to intensive farming. It is not surprising, therefore, that the population was much less dense and that the economy shows signs of specialization, such as pottery production in the New Forest and in the Shedfield region, and salt extraction along the estuaries of the coastal fringe. Only one port is known, at Bitterne (Clausentum), on the shore of the Itchen estuary, and even here development does not seem to have been particularly vigorous.

But the sea came into its own when, towards the end of the C3, Saxon and Frankish pirates began to raid the Channel coasts. At this time Carausius, who was responsible for coastal defence, erected a large fort in the upper reaches of Portsmouth Harbour at Portchester, a site which is now the best preserved Roman monument in Southern Britain. It may have been in this period that the puzzling fort at Carisbrooke was built. In 367 a concerted barbarian attack caused chaos in the province, and order was not fully restored until Count Theodosius arrived, a year or two later. It was probably as part of the Theodosian policy that Portchester was abandoned and the old port of Clausentum fortified to take its place, only to be abandoned in turn in the early years of the C5.

GEOLOGY

BY TERENCE MILLER

LIKE its neighbour, Wiltshire, Hampshire may be described as a county founded mainly on the Upper Cretaceous Chalk formation. But while in Wiltshire one-third of the ground is in fact based on rocks older than the Chalk, in Hampshire the reverse is the case, and in both the northern and the southern parts, rocks younger than the Chalk appear at the surface.

The Hampshire Chalk country is an eastward continuation of Salisbury Plain. It occupies a rough rectangle whose upper and lower sides run approximately WNW–ESE, from Highclere to Farnham, and from the Tytherleys, between Salisbury and Winchester, to Hambledon, Blendworth, and the Forest of Bere respectively.

Along the N side of the rectangle the country reaches and exceeds 800 ft in the Hampshire Downs, where the Chalk tilts up slightly before plunging down below the younger Tertiary rocks of the Kennet and Thames valleys. Along the E side, about Alton, the ground rises, again reflecting an upward tilt, but here there is no corresponding downward plunge; so the sandy pre-Chalk rocks, Upper Greensand, Gault Clay, and Lower Greensand, come to the surface E, NE, and SE of Selborne, forming a gradual slope down to Woolmer Forest and the edge of the Weald. The S side of the rectangle repeats, S of Winchester, the plunge below Tertiary strata, as a gentle slide, but without the preliminary upward tilt. The country is more subdued and lower. However a sudden upward wrinkle does occur within the Tertiary cover N of Portsmouth, where a long whale-back of grass-covered Chalk emerges as the Portsdown ridge.

Although much of the Chalk country is virtually bare rock, with only a thin, flinty soil, both in north-west Hampshire and over the E part of the Chalk outcrop there are considerable spreads of a brownish clayey or sandy deposit with many flints, and occasional boulder-like masses of hard grey sandstone, the famous 'sarsens' or 'grey wethers'.

Romsey is the N apex of a triangle of soft sandy and clayey post-Chalk Tertiary rocks whose base is a line from Poole Bay through the Isle of Wight to Selsey Bill in Sussex. Within this triangle the Chalk is deep below ground, indeed beneath the Solent many thousands of feet down. The countryside, especially in the New Forest and the Forest of Bere on either side of Southampton Water, forms a strong contrast with the rolling Chalk downlands, and recalls the geologically equivalent ground in the NE part of the county, between Highclere and Aldershot. On both sides of the Chalk 'centre' the younger rocks produce a more 'crowded' countryside, with more trees (and different – oak and pine instead of beech), more villages, more valleys and streams, and flat expanses of sandy heath. It is however impossible in many places to see true bedrock, for just as the Chalk is sometimes masked by 'clay-with-flints', so the soft Tertiary rocks often carry a superficial covering of even younger sands and gravels. This is especially true in the heaths and commons N of Bournemouth and Christchurch, along the N shore of the Solent, and in the low ground about Portsmouth, between Spithead and Portsdown.

Below the Solent and Spithead the Chalk, as we have seen, lies deeply buried. But it turns suddenly upwards, bringing its Tertiary cover with it, and at the W tip of the Isle of Wight appears in the Needles, and the parti-coloured cliffs of Alum Bay, where the strata stand almost vertically. This up-and-down rib of Chalk runs right across the island to Culver Cliff. For most of its course the near-vertical attitude is maintained, and the outcrop of the whole Chalk formation, 1700 ft thick, is little more than half a mile wide, but between Calbourne and Carisbrooke the whole formation leans over to the S (the strata thus 'dipping' N) and forms a patch of typical Chalk downland – Newbarn Down, Rowborough Down, Westridge Down, Bowcombe Down. In the S part of the island this southerly 'lean' takes the Chalk, as it were, into the air. The great upward aerial fold flattens out and slopes down to ground level again in the hills above Ventnor from St Catherine's Down to Shanklin Down. Central Wight is thus formed of rocks exposed *below* the Chalk. These, mainly brown or yellow sandstones, but with clay layers to E and W around Sandown and Brighstone, produce irregular but interesting, more compact scenery across the island from Freshwater Bay and Chale Bay, to Sandown Bay, quite distinct from the higher Chalk patches to N and S.

The commonest stone in all Hampshire is flint, which occurs both in its original position within the Chalk, and also in huge quantities in the various superficial deposits spread over the ground in general and along the sea-beaches. Because of their irregular shapes, however, flint nodules do not make a satisfactory building material by themselves, and are generally used in combination with stone or brick, or brick and timber. Probably the finest example of flintwork is the Roman walled part of Portchester Castle. Here the Norman keep, by contrast, is of imported Caen stone. The Chalk itself, as elsewhere in England, is too soft for building. But in Hampshire occur some of the very few cases of its extensive use, both internal, as in the church at Bentley St Mary, and external, as at Marsh Court. The variety in both instances is a harder stone than the general run of Chalk.

The pre-Chalk Upper Greensand, better known in Surrey as Mersham and Bargate Stone, occurs in East Hampshire, near Farringdon, where it is known as Malmstone. It is a pale buff or middling grey stone, according to whether it is more siliceous or more calcareous, and has been used fairly widely both for interior carved work and for external walling.

In post-Chalk rocks a limestone of the Tertiary strata was formerly quarried on the Isle of Wight at Binstead, west of Ryde, and at Quarr, near by. It can be seen both in local buildings, and farther afield but still in Hampshire, in Winchester Cathedral. It is interesting and unusual among limestones in containing a rich assembage of fossilized *freshwater* organisms. Most – in fact virtually all – other British limestones are of marine origin.

HAMPSHIRE

★

ABBOTTS ANN 3040

ST MARY. 1716. (Built by Thomas 'Diamond' Pitt, East India merchant and Lord Chatham's grandfather. RH) Light brick and stone. The W tower has Victorian pinnacles. Also the easternmost of the round-arched windows have minimum Victorian tracery, just enough to make an honest church of Abbotts Ann. W doorway with a bold segmental hood. W window and bell-openings segment-headed. Inside, a coved ceiling and plenty of original furnishings. – FONT. Polygonal wooden baluster and bowl. It looks like a chalice, i.e. more *c.*1800 than 1716. – PULPIT, BOX PEWS, WEST GALLERY on sturdy Tuscan columns. – More MAIDEN GARLANDS than in any other church. They were funerary memorials hung up at the death of maidens.

RECTORY. Probably also of *c.*1716. Five bays, two storeys, chequer brick, hipped roof. The Victorian porch hides the fact that l. and r. of the original doorway were the typical narrow windows of the Queen Anne style.

ADHURST ST MARY *see* SHEET

ALDERSHOT 8050

The army descended on Aldershot in 1854. It created miles of great dreariness. The dreariness is being remedied now. Plans are for a whole new town S of Queen's Avenue to house and keep busy 25,000, including over 2,000 families. The master plan is by *George Grenfell Baines* of the *Building Design Partnership*, who was appointed in 1960. The final scheme was published in 1965, at the same time as a master plan for the civilian town by the same firm, who are also doing a civic centre for the local authority. By 1965 nearly £7,000,000 had been spent. The old Aldershot of before the army is SE of the station and needs some looking out for. The town S of the army area has nothing to recommend it.

ST MICHAEL, Church Hill. A Perp chancel with a nave of 1865, now the S chapel and S aisle, a new nave and N aisle of 1910–11, by *Sir T. G. Jackson* (NT), and a fine SW tower, built of Bagshot conglomerate and brick. This is of the C17. – MONUMENTS. Two tablets with kneeling ladies, † 1606 and † 1620.

ALDERSHOT MANOR, by the church. Three-storeyed, square, of brick, late C17. Front of five bays: two-one-two.

ALDERSHOT LODGE, Church Lane. White, three-storeyed, C18, with some Venetian windows.

In the CAMP the WELLINGTON LINES, long, classical, and red, of 1854, have recently been demolished. The BEAUMONT BARRACKS of 1854–9 are still there, yellow brick. They are also still classical. As for the work of the last few years, whole areas are already modern and deserve to be looked at. First, on the hill, where the Royal Pavilion was, i.e. W of the Beaumont Barracks and SW of All Saints, is the new TRAINING SCHOOL for the Royal Army Nursing Corps by the *Building Design Partnership* (completion 1966). A system of large precast concrete units is used with skill and imagination. Residential blocks step down, with open terraces, from the central plateau. Windows project, with broad splays inside. New barracks, also by the *Building Design Partnership*, stand N of the destroyed Wellington Lines, i.e. S of Knollys Road, and – the largest area – along the Farnborough Road, cut in half by Hope Grant's Road, MONTGOMERY LINES, by the *Building Design Partnership*, SE of this, and N of Wellington Avenue, TALAVERA PARK (by the *M.P.B. & W.*), E of this and S of Cambridge Hospital WATERLOO PARK (by the *M.P.B. & W.*). Much further N, i.e. between Farnborough Road and Queen's Avenue, S of Hammersley Road, is HAMMERSLEY (by the *M.P.B. & W.*). More jobs were started in 1965. They include the ARMY CATERING COLLEGE in Thornhill Road, to the E, and GIBRALTAR BARRACKS for the Parachute Regiment, reached from Queen's Avenue, opposite St George's, both by the *Building Design Partnership*. Some use the Intergrid and G80 systems of precast concrete, with faceted facing slabs. The quality of all this work is of course not even, but as a sign of a changed attitude to the soldier's day-to-day life these areas are very gratifying indeed.

See p. 827

The principal military churches are as follows:

ALL SAINTS, W of Farnborough Road. By *P. C. Hardwick*, 1863. Brick, with bar tracery and a prominent NE tower. The main view is in fact from the E. The tower has a steep pyramid roof with lucarnes. Nave and aisles, wooden roof with dormers. – MONUMENT. Sir James Yorke Scarlett † 1871. Bust and two standing soldiers, an early C19 pattern.

Just N of the church on a bluff is the WELLINGTON MONUMENT, a bronze equestrian statue on a high pink stone base. By *Matthew Cotes Wyatt*, 1838–46. It was originally placed on top of Constitution Arch in London, but taken down in 1883 and brought here. The horse stands still, the Duke half-raises one arm, and his hat is much in prominence.

ST GEORGE, Queen's Avenue. 1892 by *Major Pitt & Lt. Michie*. Large, reasonable, and dull. W tower with spire. Red brick. Spacious yellow-brick interior.

ST ANDREW, opposite the former. 1927 by *Sir Robert Lorimer*. Blue and red brick, with arched windows. No tower. Much affinity with Lutyens.

In the town little of note.

(ST JOSEPH (R.C.), Queen's Road. 1912–13, by *George Drysdale*, Leonard Stokes's former pupil and future partner. One of the most impressive churches of its date, brilliantly planned on a triangular site, steeply sloping down to the central belfry and the apse on the E apex. The wide W end has a baptistery between two apsidal chapels N and S. The nave of four bays has windowless aisles which taper sharply inwards to the choir and apse with steps down to the E vestries – on the model of St Augustin in Paris (except that the tapering there is to the W). Even at the W end an extra aisle tapers from N to S. After such virtuosity the detailing is disappointingly coarse, in a polychrome Italian basilican mode. Outside, the almost Butterfieldian striping of scarlet and dark red on the windowless drum contrasts strangely with the Lutyenesque grey and dark red of the clerestory. Inside, changes are rung on purple brick (arcades), yellow brick (upper pilasters), terracotta (cornice), and green-blue mottled and glazed tiles (spandrels). NT)

HOLY TRINITY, Albert Road. 1875–9 by *Sidney Stapley* of Farnham. Yellow stone. No tower. Bar tracery.

More interesting, if not architecturally better, are some NONCONFORMIST CHAPELS, especially the PRESBYTERIANS, Victoria Road, 1863, yellow brick, grim, with two short square towers and round arches, and the METHODISTS, Queen's Road, 1874, fully Gothic, with an asymmetrically placed tower, the only prominent tower of Aldershot town.

TOWN HALL, Grosvenor Road. 1904 by *C. E. Hutchinson*. Very typical of its date, and quite attractive.

POST OFFICE, Station Road. 1902 by *Oldrieve* (Board of Works). Of the same type, and attractive too, as its neighbour, the former MASONIC LODGE, 1902 by *Coggin & Wallis*. In STATION ROAD also WELLINGTON HOUSE, a new office building by *Carl Fisher & Associates*, a curtain-wall block on a podium.

ST AUGUSTINE, North Lane, in a residential district. By *Sir T. G. Jackson*, 1907. Red brick, with a timber-framed porch and dormers. Dec tracery. Unfinished to the W.

See p. 827

ALRESFORD *see* OLD ALRESFORD *and* NEW ALRESFORD

7030

ALTON

ST LAURENCE. A Perp town church built round a Norman crossing tower. All four Norman arches are still there. Their big decorated capitals and their arches with one step and one thick roll are emphatically Early Norman, say about 1100. The tower now stands in the S aisle; for in the C15 a new nave and chancel were built N of the previous church.* At the same time the former nave was rebuilt. In the former chancel alterations were also made, and a new S vestry and N chapel built. The exterior is C15 throughout, except for the Victorian broach-spire. Three-light windows with panel tracery under segmental arches. W window of four lights and below it a doorway still with C14 mouldings. The church is essentially a parallelepiped. The S aisle is as wide as the nave. The arcades are the same all the way: octagonal piers, hollow-chamfered arches. Lively busts to support the roof. – PULPIT. An outstanding mid C17 piece. The panels with simple geometrical arrangements, but in addition detached ornamented columns, carrying arches. – STALLS. C15 with plain MISERICORDS. – PAINTINGS. On the N face of the second pier from the W three C15 paintings of saints. – STAINED GLASS. E window, 1870, probably by *Capronnier*. The figures alone are preserved. – (CHANDELIER. Of brass, dated 1780. NMR) – PLATE.

* This original church had a S arcade added to it *c.*1140. There are faint traces of this arcade inside, i.e. remains of the pier imposts with a band of ornament.

Silver-gilt Flagon given in 1711; silver-gilt Flagon left in 1721; silver-gilt Almsdish given in 1722.

ALL SAINTS, Winchester Road. 1873–4 by *F. C. Dyer*. With a SW steeple and bar tracery.

ST MARY'S HOME. The CHAPEL is by *W. D. Caröe*, 1910. Low, with a shingled central tower. Pebbledash, and more than a touch of the cottage.

LORD MAYOR TRELOAR HOSPITAL, ½ m. SW. A vast institution for cripples. 1928 etc. by *Henry C. Smart*.

In CHURCH STREET N of the church the humble FRIENDS' MEETING HOUSE, with attached cottage. It is probably of 1672. Also in Church Street, nearer its S end, where it meets the main street, ALMSHOUSES of 1653, a block of four, brick, two-storeyed with mullioned windows.

The main street ought to be walked. Starting from the E end, it is first ANSTEY ROAD. Here the GRAMMAR SCHOOL, founded in 1638. The old building is symmetrical, of brick, with two big gables and mullioned and transomed five-light windows. Additions of 1880. Then the INFIRMARY, established in 1793, a thirteen-bay range of brick with a three-bay pediment enriched by an oval in it. Mansard roof. After that the street becomes NORMANDY STREET. The CONGREGATIONAL CHAPEL is of 1835, stuccoed, of three bays, with Gothic windows with four-centred heads.

The HIGH STREET starts handsomely. No. 1, on the S side, has an elegant Adamish porch, Nos 4 and 6 opposite are red, of five bays, C18. No. 6 is quite stately and must be early C18. Three storeys, segment-headed windows. The Venetian windows on the ground floor must be a later alteration. Again opposite them the CURTIS MUSEUM etc., red brick, entirely undistinguished except that in the W range a shaped gable looks genuine C17. The buildings date from 1869–80 and are by *Chas. E. Barry*. After these a stretch of no interest. Then No. 74, the MIDLAND BANK, C18, five bays with a pedimented three-bay projection. The pediment is nicely decorated. Doorway with Tuscan columns and pediment. The COUNCIL OFFICES are C18 too, five bays too, but there are two and a half storeys and the doorway has Ionic columns. (Staircase with thin turned and twisted balusters. NMR) On the other side the WESLEYAN CHAPEL of 1846, with a pediment across, and arched windows in rusticated surrounds, i.e. on the way to the Italianate.

BONHAM'S FARM. *See* Froyle.

(NEELHALL FARM. Georgian, of five bays, with hipped roof. Staircase with iron railing. NMR)

ALTON ABBEY *see* MEDSTEAD

ALVERSTOKE *see* GOSPORT, pp. 240, 252, 256

4020

AMPFIELD

ST MARK. 1838–41 by *Carter* of Winchester in collaboration with *W. C. Yonge* (cf. Otterbourne).* Blue brick, lancet windows. Polygonal bell-turret with spire, set diagonally. Short chancel. One must assume that the E window, which is 'Second Pointed', was an alteration of *c.*1855 (cf. below) and this must apply to the upper window and the doorway of the porch as well. Is the whole porch an addition? – STAINED GLASS. Keble Memorial Window, designed by *Butterfield* and made by *Wailes*. – E and W windows by *Wailes*, 1855.

AMPFIELD HOUSE. Built *c.*1760. Brick, two storeys, seven bays, the first and last projecting. Parapet and recessed hipped roof. Doorway with broken pediment. A later addition on the l.

2040

AMPORT

ST MARY. Much of the church is due to *Slater & Carpenter*'s restoration of 1866–7, but it was a conscientious and tactful restoration, and the result is something almost unique in Hampshire: a Dec church. The church is cruciform, with aisleless nave and transepts. The N transept was rebuilt by the restorers and the ruinous nave was reinstated. What one would like to be sure of is that the Kentish tracery – which e.g. occurs on the S transept – is really authentic. The crossing arches are of two chamfers and die into the imposts. The bell-openings are small two-light windows. SEDILIA and PISCINA are in good order, the sedilia with poorly crocketed ogee arches. – SCULPTURE. C15 alabaster panel of familiar subjects. Head of St John Baptist surrounded by saints, Christ rising from the tomb below, angels above. No structural divisions at all. – STAINED GLASS. Much glass by *Holiday* for *Powell*; 1872. The Pre-Raphaelite influence is patent, yet the glass is very different from Morris's. – Also earlier Powell glass, designed by *Casolani* (Noli me tangere, Woman at the Well, etc.). –

* Information received from Anthony Symondson.

PLATE. Chalice, 1798. – MONUMENTS. Good tablets † 1743, † 1753.

AMPORT HOUSE. 1857 by *William Burn*. Nothing special. Yellow brick, Elizabethan, with gables. Symmetrical S front. Two gables and canted bay window for the end bays. Centre with cross windows and dormers. The terraces below are by *Lutyens*, 1923, who also designed the GATEPIERS. If you don't want to believe that an architect can be monumental and whimsical at the same moment, here is proof, especially in the concavely tapering-away bases of his piers. The vertical stone slabs up to the urns are curious too.

ALMSHOUSES, W of the gatepiers. 1815–16. Two-storeyed, of eight bays, with a pediment.

Amport is a village with a green and many nice cottages.

ANDOVER 3040

The architectural interest of Andover is very limited – limited to two buildings, indeed. The Greater London Council plan of increasing its size from the present 16,000 to 48,000 and of building a completely new centre ought to give Andover precisely what is lacking. The plan is concerned with the area N of the town hall and SW of the church. It does not foresee anything competing in height with the church, and its centre is pedestrian and spacious.

ST MARY. Built at the expense of *Dr Goddard*, who retired from the headmastership of Winchester College in 1809 to live at Andover. He died in 1845, aged eighty-eight, just before his church had been completed. It is a very remarkable building, and one which for several reasons strikes one as possibly designed or conceived or outlined by the client himself. It was begun in 1840, opened in 1844, and completed, including the tower, in 1846. Goddard's architect was *Augustus F. Livesay* of Portsmouth, the architect of Holy Trinity at Trowbridge. However, the building turned out to be structurally unsafe, and so it was handed over to *Sydney Smirke*. One would like to know more of the early vicissitudes of this extraordinary and really quite brilliant design. The building first of all is excellently placed on a hill a little above the town. Second it is consistently E.E., which was not what was fashionable in 1840, though it had been done by Edward Garbett at Theale in Berkshire as early as 1820. Garbett went to Salisbury for inspiration. So did Dr Goddard. The building is of knapped flint and stone. Tall W tower, very sheer, with no buttress set-offs, tall lancet bell-openings and blank lancets, high pinnacles. Tall aisles with pairs of lancets, clerestory, transepts, one with three stepped lancets in the end wall, the other with five of equal height. The apse appears externally to be of the full height of the building. Lower windows with geometrical tracery (three unfoiled circles). The exterior is impressive enough, the interior is sensational. Very high nave with a plaster rib-vault. Tall piers with six attached shafts with shaft-rings and rich stiff-leaf capitals. The tower arch is high, but below is a strainer arch, its lower part a normal arch, its upper part curving upward. The E end of the nave is higher than the apse appears inside and has a stepped five-light window leading into the space behind the upper apse windows. The transepts are only as high as the aisles. Transepts and aisles have rib-vaults as well. The wall shafts of aisles and transepts start from twisted or knotted corbels. The apse – a stroke of genius – is separated from the rest of the church by a screen of three arches on immensely long round shafts. The apse itself has double tracery, i.e. tracery in two layers, the climax of this ingenious and fervent design. – FONT. Plain, octagonal Perp. – SCREEN. Stone, with small figures of angels.* – STAINED GLASS. (In the apse windows good patterned glass, coeval with the church. RH) – S transept S by *Mayer* of Munich, 1883. – PLATE. Silver-gilt Chalice and Paten Cover, 1611; Silver-gilt Chalice and Paten Cover, 1632. – MONUMENTS. Richard Kentish † 1611 and family. Small figures. He seated frontally holding a skull, the others kneeling. Columns l. and r. – Richard Venables † 1621 and wife. The usual kneelers facing one another. Large figures.

ST MICHAEL, Weyhill Road. 1962–4 by *R. A. P. Pinckney*. Brick, with a central spike. Shallow pitch of the roofs. Nave and wall passages. Folded ceiling like a complicated groin-vault.

See p. 827 PERAMBULATION. The obvious start is the HIGH STREET. Its S part is wide like a market place and has indeed across its N end the TOWN HALL, an excellent Grecian building of 1825. Ashlar, five bays. Rusticated arches below, an attached portico of Greek Doric columns above with a pediment. Wreaths in the frieze. Pilasters are used on the sides. At the S end of this wide part of the High Street is the STAR AND GARTER HOTEL, of about the same date. It has a spacious stuccoed

* Later than the church, says Mr Hubbuck.

front. Five bays, three storeys. Bays one and five have shallow, wide bows. Broad Tuscan porch. Otherwise, in this broad part of the High Street only No. 19 deserves a word, again of the same time. This has giant upper pilasters, and also wreaths in the frieze. Barclays Bank and Lloyds Bank are of course imitation. The High Street narrows towards the church. At the start of this narrow part the BAPTIST CHURCH, by *C. C. Searle*, 1866, very heavy-handed. Yellow and red brick, with a vast rose window in plate tracery and some incised decoration. Pedimental gable of somehow Italian Romanesque memory. Shortly before the church a NORMAN ARCH from the old church. Two orders of columns with decorated scallops. Zigzag in the arch, all at r. angles to the wall.

To the E, S of the church, NEWBURY STREET branches off. The OLD VICARAGE must be Early Georgian. Five bays, two storeys, stuccoed. Three-bay pediment with an arched window in it. The other windows segment-headed. Ionic porch. The house actually faces NEW STREET, and here, E of the church, is the OLD GRAMMAR SCHOOL. The buildings are Victorian, but the N end is a three-bay Georgian house of red brick. From the end of Newbury Street S runs EAST STREET. Close to its N end is the CONGREGATIONAL CHURCH of about 1830. Three bays, one-bay pediment. Broad Tuscan doorway, and a Venetian window over. Then No. 54, early C18, chequer brick, rubbed lintels, four bays, modillion frieze under the eaves. Nos 38–9 is also early C18, but finer. It has a moulded brick frieze above the ground floor, and one window has a raised brick surround. Six bays, two storeys.

Back to the High Street, and for a moment W into CHANTRY STREET. Nos 9–15 are timber-framed with overhang. No. 17 has two nice Georgian shop windows l. and r. of the doorway. Then the N continuation of the High Street, MARLBOROUGH STREET. The building at the NW corner of the churchyard was the Industrial School for Girls, founded in 1849. It is now the CHURCH INSTITUTE. It is of flint, Gothic, with a small turret. Then the ALMSHOUSES, founded in 1686, but only the chimneys of the l. part of that time. The façades are of 1872.

Little else. E of the Star and Garter, in LONDON STREET, is SAVOY CHAMBERS, white, of three bays with two bows and a curved Tuscan porch with a Venetian window over, both in a giant segmental arch. W of the Star and Garter in BRIDGE STREET the WHITE HART HOTEL, probably of *c.*1850, red brick, three bays, two and a half storeys. The STATION

HOTEL is white and low, three bays, with a Tuscan porch. From the W end of Bridge Street N runs JUNCTION ROAD, and here is the former WORKHOUSE (St John's Hospital), whose centre, still classical, is dated 1836. Nine bays, two storeys, red brick, rendered for the ground floor. Three-bay pedimental gable.

6050 ANDWELL

ANDWELL PRIORY. Founded early in the C12 by Adam de Port for monks of the order of Tiron. The premises were very small. Not much remains, and less that is telling. The garden of the house was the cloister. To its N lay the church, less than 55 ft long internally. Only flint walling of the N, W, and E walls remains. The chapter house, dormitory, and refectory were in the customary positions. Of the W range at least two C14 doorways are *in situ*, quite modest.

3040 APPLESHAW

CHURCH. 1830–1 by *T. M. Shurmur*. Stunted W turret with pinnacles. Aisleless nave, lower transepts, long chancel as high as the nave. The exterior at present pebbledashed. Attractive interior with shallowly segmental plaster tunnel-vault all along nave and chancel and pointed tunnel-vaults for the transepts. – PLATE. Paten probably of 1679; Chalice and Paten Cover of 1742.

OLD VICARAGE, $\frac{1}{4}$ m. S. Seven bays, the middle one with a steepish pediment. Is the curved Tuscan porch original, and the Venetian window above it?

HILL HOUSE, $\frac{3}{8}$ m. S. Red brick, five bays with a three-bay pediment. In it an oval window. Segment-headed windows with keystones painted white. Pretty doorcase. All presumably late C18.

APPLESHAW HOUSE, $\frac{5}{8}$ m. SSE. Five bays, two storeys, red brick. The windows arranged 2–1–2. Curved Tuscan porch. Hipped roof.

REMENHAM HOUSE, $\frac{5}{8}$ m. WNW. A very stately ashlar-faced house of about 1830. Five by seven bays, two storeys. Porch of two pairs of rather heavy unfluted Ionic columns.

5050 ASHE

HOLY TRINITY AND ST ANDREW. 1877–9 by *G. G. Scott Jun.*

Small, with a thin bell-turret with spire. Flint and stone. Dec style. – STAINED GLASS. The E window by *Kempe*, as early as 1878. – PLATE. Chalice and Paten Cover, 1671. – MONUMENT. The Rev. Isaac P. G. Lefroy † 1806. Tablet with an urn. By *Gibbs* of Basingstoke.

ASHE HOUSE, S of the church. Georgian, of brick. Five bays, two storeys, one-bay pediment. Doorway with segmental fanlight.

BERRYDOWN, ⅝ m. SW. By *Lutyens*, 1897. Highly characteristic the high walls to the road, pebbledashed and silent about what lies behind. A doorway with rounded angles, as if they were trying to be turrets, leads into a square walled forecourt, and at its end is the house. It is Tudor in character, with a middle porch. The windows l. and r. are deliberately different. On the r. is a big mullioned and transomed one. The porch is deep, tunnel-vaulted and pebbledashed like a grotto.*

ASHLETT *see* FAWLEY

ASHLEY 3030

ST MARY. Nave and chancel and Victorian bell-gable. Small Norman nave N window, Norman chancel N window, two chancel S windows. The chancel arch is Norman too, but the two round-headed openings l. and r. are later. – PAINTING. In the jamb of a chancel S window a young figure (female or male ?) under a crocketed gable. C13 or a little later. – ALMS-BOX. An impressively rough job cut out of a post, it seems. – PLATE. Chalice and Cover, early C17. – MONUMENTS. Thomas Hobbs † 1698, with volutes and garlands l. and r. of the inscription. – Abraham Weekes † 1755. By *T. Baker* of London. Inscription, two columns, open pediment.

ASHLEY *see* RINGWOOD

ASHMANSWORTH 4050

ST JAMES. Nave and chancel and bell-turret. Brick S porch of 1694. The chancel is of the C13 (see the lancet windows), but the brick E wall is dated 1745. Nicely unrestored interior.

* The garden side I was not allowed to see when I called, and it is not illustrated in Butler & Hussey's Lutyens volumes.

Plain Norman chancel arch. To its l. and r. WALL PAINTINGS of the late C12, almost entirely unrecognizable. But they are said to have represented in large medallions l. of the arch the Harrowing of Hell, r. of the arch the Resurrection (?) and the Pentecost. The paintings above the chancel arch surrounding a former rood are C15. – PULPIT with tester, C18, simple. – MONUMENT. Stone 'In Memoriam Gerald Finzi' † 1956. By *Reynolds Stone*.

ASHTON *see* BISHOPS WALTHAM

5030

AVINGTON

ST MARY. 1768–71. Built of brick. Embattled W tower, three-bay body with battlements also and with a Venetian E window. The other windows are arched. Doorways with rustication of alternating sizes. It all looks earlier than *c*.1770. The furnishings are extremely well preserved. – Marble baluster FONT. – Three-decker PULPIT. – BOX PEWS and FAMILY PEWS. – HAT PEGS along the walls. – The REREDOS with an open segmental pediment in the middle again looks decidedly earlier. – COMMUNION RAIL. Of metal (is it lead? *see* below). – WEST GALLERY with the date 1771. – On it a BARREL ORGAN, the case Gothick; early C19. – (CHANDELIER. Of brass; 1771. NMR) – PLATE. Set of 1829. – MONUMENTS. George Bridges † 1751. Yellow, grey, and pink marble. Two columns support a broken pediment. Sarcophagus and urn in the middle. – Marchioness of Carnarvon † 1768. It was she who had the church built. Pink and white marble with a long inscription, an obelisk, and two urns. – Mrs Peel † 1865. An angel carries her up – a Flaxman motif, but the treatment Victorian. – John Shelley † 1866. In the Renaissance style. Pilasters, pediment, and bust.

AVINGTON PARK. The centre of the house and probably wings less wide than the present ones date from the time of John Clerk († 1587) or Edmund Clerk († 1617). Of this, apart from the thick walls just alluded to, there are only two octagonal chimneys and a big chimneybreast at the back, N of the Library. In 1665 the estate came to George Rodney Brydges. He died in 1713. So it is just possible that the house, as we see it today, is his. Its style is decidedly that of, say, 1705–15. The W front is telling, and the two wings especially establish the date. Mr John Harris attributes this work to *John James*. The wings are four bays wide and two-storeyed, of brick and rubbed brick, with three giant pilasters on the front and segment-headed windows, those on the first floor with aprons. Panelled parapet. The balustrades are later and spoil the relation of wings to centre. This centre is recessed and entirely filled by a giant portico of wood. Four mighty Tuscan columns and a pediment. The pattern is St Paul Covent Garden by Inigo Jones. The three fine lead statues on the pediment are of the mid C18. The sides of the wings are a late C18 alteration, dating from the time of the third Duke of Chandos, who was a Brydges too, came into the property in 1751, and died in 1789. To the S four bays, widely spaced, with a two-bay pediment. This feature was intended to be repeated further E in another wing which was never built. The N side of the other of the wings of about 1710 also has a pediment. The Library, on the S front towards the E, is probably a later C18 addition. It has a gently bowed front. Its continuation is the C19 Conservatory. It is not known where the colonnade in its centre came from: local tradition says from a banqueting hall on the site. Burke's *Seats* (1853) adds: 'Fair flowers having succeeded to fair faces, and the quiet license of nature to the colours of the wine cup'. The Entrance Hall has screens of columns l. and r. and was painted late in the C18, probably by French artists. Trellis pattern on the wall, the sky on the ceiling. The Staircase has a lead balustrade with the balusters as vertical chains, the links filled with honeysuckle. In the centre on the upper floor is the Ballroom, with gilded late C18 decoration but late C17 ceiling paintings. In the Library is Pompeian wall painting. The Drawing Room also has such motifs, but the figures from the Waverley Novels in period costumes must be mid C19. The chronology of Avington Park altogether cannot yet be regarded as established.

STABLES. Late C18. Red brick. Nine bays, with blank arches round the windows. In the centre a bigger arch and a pediment.

BRIDGE. Cast iron, of about 1800. With a handsome parapet of circles.

COTTAGES. A row of seven. Flint and brick. One-bay pediment.

AVON CASTLE *see* RINGWOOD

1000 AVON TYRRELL

Built for Lord Manners by *Lethaby* in 1891. It was his first job, and the job had been offered to Norman Shaw, whose chief assistant and, as Muthesius, an intelligent contemporary, wrote, undoubtedly best pupil he was. Shaw secured the job for young Lethaby, and the result is one of the finest houses of the date in England, Shaw-school, yet already very personal,
93 and subtle and sensitive in the details. The main front faces s and a beautiful wide view. From l. to r. there is first an ingenious canted bay window under a gable, canted forward in two steps with a total of thirteen lights and one transom. Then follows immediately a seven-light window with two transoms. This bay and the three following have four gables to themselves, but there is all the time a slight shifting of axis. The three bays have the Norman-Shaw Ipswich motifs, but with segmental not round arches, and the third has a higher sill zone between ground floor and first floor. Finally a broad chimney bay with some flint and brick chequer. Otherwise the house is red brick with stone trim and much tile-hanging. The entrance side is less completely composed, but the part where the entrance itself is again makes a convincing picture. The doorway has an almost semicircular hood; on the first floor are two stone windows of the Venetian type, but with segmental arches. They project slightly, like oriels. On top two vaguely curved gables with peacocks on top of them. The interior is as original and successful. The walls and ceilings are all white. The plasterwork, more Elizabethan than Lethaby would have been later, was done by *Ernest Gimson*. Only in the principal room the interlocked coffering is wholly original, and in one other room the thin ribs are not like Elizabethan thin ribs, and the flowers in the panels derive from tiles or embroidery rather than from plasterwork. The masterpiece of the interior is the chimneypiece in the principal room. This has no historic connotation any longer. It is basically a chequer of grey and black Derbyshire marble with masses of fossils, but the pattern is much more complex than just a chequer. The large painting of '*L'Amor che muove*' is by *Burne-Jones*.

3020 AWBRIDGE

ALL SAINTS. 1876 by *Colson*. Stone, w tower, nave, and chancel. Bar tracery.

AWBRIDGE DANES. A charming, though quite large house of 1825, between neo-Gothic and neo-Tudor. Rendered. The three-bay part of the front with the date is Tudor, with barge-boarded gables and windows with hood-moulds, but round the corner is a larger front whose centre is a thin Gothic bay window with a funny minimum veranda round its foot. (Romantically sited by Awbridge Danes Water is a BOAT-HOUSE, with a loggia over three rusticated arches. The loggia is rebuilt, but the whole was originally designed *c.*1822 by *Garbett*. John Harris)

BADDESLEY *see* NORTH BADDESLEY *and* SOUTH BADDESLEY

BARTON STACEY 4040

ALL SAINTS. As so often, the architectural history starts with the N arcade. Its W end is of *c.*1200. Round pier, round abaci, capitals of flat, broad, upright leaves, arches with one slight chamfer. The corresponding S part has moulded capitals. Then followed, in the mid C13, the continuation eastward on both sides with octagonal piers and much dogtooth. The odd thing is that from the third pier not only the next arch springs to the E, but also the chancel arch and an arch across the aisle. So there is a chancel arch, but it has no structurally emphasized supports. Externally a few of the mid C13 windows are original, but most of the exterior is of 1877. Fine, ashlar-faced Perp W tower with higher stair-turret and pinnacles. It was built into the nave early in the C16, as the straight-headed uncusped bell-openings indicate. – FONT. Square, of Purbeck marble. Each side has eight of the usual flat blank arches. – FONT COVER. A flat board made up of nine quatrefoiled panels from the screen of Longparish church. – PLATE. Chalice and Paten Cover of 1569; undated Paten; early C19 Flagon. – MONUMENT. Inscription on the outer sill of a S aisle window: 'Hic iacet humatus/Ihon Pann Civellia natus.'

LONG BARROW, 1 m. S, $\frac{1}{3}$ m. E of Moody's Down Farm. The mound is 220 ft long, 75 ft wide, and 4 ft high. The quarry ditch, 27 ft wide, can be clearly seen. A single sherd of Windmill Hill pottery was found on the surface of the mound.

LONG BARROW, $\frac{1}{4}$ m. W of Moody's Down Farm and just S of the road to Wherwell. The barrow has been considerably spread by ploughing and now presents the appearance of a low oval mound, 125 ft long, 90 ft wide, and 4 ft high. No ditches are visible.

LONG BARROW, 2 m. SW of Chilbolton and ¼ m. SW of Middlebarn Farm. This barrow has been considerably reduced by ploughing and is now 150 ft long and 90 ft wide. It has a maximum height of 4 ft. No ditches are visible.

6050

BASING

BASING HOUSE. Basing Castle was a motte-and-bailey castle originally, built probably by Hugh de Port. Basing was the chief estate of the fifty-five he held of the Conqueror. The motte is of an unusual type, comparing with normal mottes as a shell-keep compares with normal keeps, i.e. it consists of a rough enclosure about 300 ft in diameter and a ditch. The entrance is from the N, where a bailey lies. A second bailey is on the E of the first. Inside the enclosure foundations of a few medieval stone walls survive, but most of the walls are of brick and belong to the mid C16. The castle had gone by inheritance to the Paulets in 1428. Sir William Paulet, first Marquess of Winchester, was responsible for the extensive rebuilding and also the erection of the new house E of the enclosure. He received licence to crenellate in 1531 and died in 1572. In illustrations of *c.*1645 the house has four or five broad towers, all with angle turrets, i.e. a general appearance decidedly Early Tudor and not Elizabethan. On the other hand Dr Girouard has drawn attention to the fact that two French mason-carvers who worked at Longleat had very probably been employed at Basing up to *c.*1565. A date 1561 survives on a stone in the little museum at Basing, and a carved coat of arms looks similar to the early work at Longleat. Most easily recognizable now of the buildings is the gatehouse to the old house, on its N side. It had four round towers, the outer ones being detached. The great hall lay SW of it and N of the medieval masonry. W of the N end of the hall is the hexagonal kitchen. More of what the buildings were like can be taken from Smithson's drawing.

On the W side of the bailey was its gatehouse, also with four towers, and outside this to the W the garden. Along its W wall is an octagonal summer house and an octagonal dovecote. N of the garden is GRANGE FARM, late C17, gabled, with an excellent brick BARN. Two tiers of collar-beams, arched braces, and two tiers of wind-braces in the roof. SE of Grange

Farm and N of the NE corner of the castle garden is a polygonal tower of red brick with blue brick diapering. An outer gatehouse is in the village street E of Grange Farm, with a stone arch and arms above. The houses opposite have early brickwork, perhaps re-used. Basing House was besieged in 1645, finally stormed by Cromwell, and destroyed. Among the prisoners taken was Inigo Jones. We know nothing of building activity during his time or in his style, but in the museum are large mid or later C17 capitals.

ST MARY. Within sight of the castle. A big Late Perp church, with much major repair work after 1645. The church is nearly entirely of brick. A date is indicated by an inscription at the E end of the N aisle, referring to John Paulet and the building of *hoc opus* in 1519. The church was drastically restored by *T. H. Wyatt* in 1874. The centre of the building is the crossing tower, and this is basically Norman, see the N and S arches inside. The other arches are Perp and go with the big three-bay arcades. Octagonal piers, clumsily moulded four-centred arches. The exterior is just a rectangle, three gables to the E, three gables to the W. The W doorway is flat and classical, probably mid C17. Above it a Perp image niche. The Perp tracery of the N chapel is of wood. The N and S chapels are the most interesting parts of the church. They are separated from the chancel by pairs of MONUMENTS, open to N and S, each pair with a doorway between. The monuments have panelled depressed arches. They are to Paulets as follows: John and wife (NE) † 1492, but no doubt after 1520 – see the Roman lettering towards the chapel. – John and wife, dates of death not recorded (NW). – William, first Marquess, *c.*1545–60 (SE). – Second Marquess (?) (SW). The latter two monuments have Renaissance details, the former have not. – Good figured corbels for the roofs, especially in the N chapel. – It now only remains to mention two earlier pieces *ex situ*, the small C13 N doorway, not well preserved, and the small late C13(?) S doorway to the coal hole with three continuous chamfers. – FONT. Octagonal, Perp, with quatrefoils. – PULPIT. Brought from Basingstoke. Made in 1622. Of a type used in the villages around as well. Two tiers of panels, the upper ones with flowers in vases under basket arches, the lower rectangular with strapwork. – ROYAL ARMS. 1660. Naïvely painted, with a black and white perspective floor. – HELMS etc. in the N chapel. – PLATE. Chalice and Paten Cover, 1688; Flagon, 1788. – MONUMENT. Sixth Duke of Bolton † 1794, by

Flaxman. White marble. Seated mourning young woman below a circular recess with bust.

CHURCH LANE HOUSE, by the church. The former WORKHOUSE. Built in 1836, but with Tudor brick from Basing House.

PARKER'S FARMHOUSE, Hatch Lane, $\frac{1}{4}$ m. SE. Brick, C17, with a stepped gable up to the chimney and a polygonal stair projection in the middle of the S side.

DANESHILL, 1 m. NW. By *Lutyens,* 1903. Brick, Tudor and conventional.

6050

BASINGSTOKE

ST MICHAEL. W tower, nave and aisles, chancel and chapels. Essentially Perp, but too drastically restored. The W tower has polygonal buttresses, pinnacles, a higher stair-turret, and a Perp doorway, the S porch is two-storeyed and its upper window has uncusped lights. The porch was indeed under construction as late as 1539. The nave and aisles seem to belong to *c.*1500. Large four-light windows. Arcades of four bays. Piers with four shafts and four diagonal hollows. Two-centred arches. The clerestory windows are of three lights under four-centred arches. The E parts of the church are older. The chancel was being built in 1465, and the S chapel looks yet older. The arches are of two hollow chamfers dying into the imposts, and the NE respond is semicircular. All this makes the early C14 likely. When the nave and aisles were built, the intention was indeed to pull down the chapel, cf. the arch higher up, ready for a new chapel. The chancel arch also is relatively small and low. The chancel N wall, with a dainty priest's doorway and three-light windows, is now inside the building, as in 1920 *Sir Charles Nicholson* added a War Memorial N chapel. Flint and stone chequer. – PAINTING. In the N chapel Antwerp Adoration of the Child of *c.*1550 with wings with donors dated 1649. – STAINED GLASS. Early C16 parts from the Holy Ghost Chapel in S aisle and S chapel windows. – The glass in the N chapel is by *Christopher Webb,* 1950. – PLATE. Chalice of 1726; Bowl of 1730; Paten of 1811; Flagon of 1819. *See* p. 827

HOLY GHOST CHAPEL, Chapel Hill, in the cemetery, just N of the station. The term is really wrong. The ruins are of two buildings. Of the Holy Ghost Chapel no more survives than part of the C13 W tower. Flint, with C15 doorway and W window. The chapel had a half-hexagonal apse, and attached to the S side of its chancel Lord Sandys of The Vyne built a Guild Chapel of HOLY TRINITY. This was done in 1524. The building is of brick, with large windows with four-centred heads, a half-hexagonal apse, and a half-hexagonal W end against which stands diagonally a hexagonal SW turret of chalk with angle tabernacles for statuettes.

HOLY GHOST (R.C.), Chapel Hill. 1902 by Canon *A. J. Scoles*. Flint, with a turret by the E end of the nave. N transept and apse. Lancets and plate tracery. Painted nave wagon roof.

ALL SAINTS, Victoria Street. 1915 by *Temple Moore*. A noble building, ashlar-faced. SE tower. Behind the battlements a kind of shingled bell-turret. Simple Dec tracery, except for the large E window with a display of the curvilinear. Much bare wall. Inside, piers without any capitals and giant arches embracing the clerestory. The nave arcades are of four bays, the chancel arcades of three are lower and the upper windows much larger.

ST MARY, Eastrop Lane. High, short nave of 1912 by *Sir T. G. Jackson*, never continued to the E. Lower chancel and brick E end. They were the nave and chancel, of indeterminate date, of the old hamlet chapel. Shingled bell-turret.

ST PETER, South Ham Estate. *See* p. 93.

CONGREGATIONAL CHURCH, London Street. The brick sides with the round-arched windows are of 1800, the grand façade with giant Tuscan columns *in antis* is 1860.

METHODIST CHURCH, Church Street. 1906 by *Gordon & Gunton*. A good front, modelled in its elements on the front of Winchester Cathedral. Knapped flint and stone. Fancy Perp tracery.

If Basingstoke really receives the new centre designed by *Llewelyn-Davies, Weeks & Partners* with *Ian Fraser & Associates*, it will get something worth looking at. At present, for its size, the town is singularly devoid of architectural pleasures. There are a few houses within a hundred yards of the parish church, and that is about all. In CHURCH STREET No. 50 has a stately Greek Doric porch, and QUEEN ANNE HOUSE a recessed front with wings, but no original details. No. 8, N of the church, however, is really enjoyable. It is late C17, what Sir John Summerson calls Artisan Mannerism. Brick, with brick giant pilasters and brick Ionic capitals and a big moulded brick frieze. Raised brick window surrounds, and in the gable a very odd flat aedicule with broken pediment. A little further N in BROOK STREET one house with two big bows, grey headers and red dressings, and another, E of the Church Street corner, with a one-bay pediment, also grey headers and red dressings. It is sad that one has to add to this roll-call of the best houses of Basingstoke that, according to the published plans of the new centre, it would involve the demolition of every one of them. Maybe the price is not too high. As for what would remain, there is so little there that one has to pick them out where they happen to occur. At the W end of the HIGH STREET is WINTON HOUSE of five bays with a porch of pairs of Tuscan columns. Behind it is a recent Government building, quite large and a sensible design. Halfway down the High Street, lying back a little, is the TOWN HALL of 1832. Five bays, rendered, classical going Italianate. From the Town Hall Church Street runs down to the church and parallel to it is WOTE STREET, where the CORN EXCHANGE is the most prominent building. It is Italianate, of seven bays, with big arched windows. The interior has cast-iron details. Galleries above the aisles. The building dates from 1864 and is by *Salter & Wyatt*. Continuing in the direction of the High Street follows LONDON STREET, with the WESTMINSTER BANK by *F. Chancellor*, 1864, three-storeyed, of yellow brick, in the palazzo style, and then the DEANE ALMSHOUSES, founded in 1607. Row of eight with a centre with steep pedimental gable. Yet a little further on the MUNICIPAL OFFICES in a Georgian house with a Doric doorway and two Venetian windows.

ST THOMAS'S HOUSE, Darlington Road. 1874–8 by *A. R. Barker*. The chapel 1885 by *Woodyer*.

(The joint LCC-Hampshire town expansion scheme is administered by the Basingstoke Development Group. The 1963 plan for an increase from 25,000 to 80,000 people over fifteen years was prepared under *Alan G. McCulloch* and is being executed (unless otherwise stated) under his successor, *R. A. Stevens*, group architect. The following anti-clockwise perambulation (or motor tour) will give a sample of the high promise of what is being built – much of it in industrialized or 'rationalized traditional' building.

To the NE, off Reading Road, is OAKRIDGE 1, 1965–6, two-storey terraces in brick with prefabricated timber panels. To the N, off Sherborne Road, is OAKRIDGE 3, 1964–6, similar high density, low rise housing, this time in the Hallamshire system of total prefabrication within load-bearing brick cross walls. Opposite is a small SCHOOL of 1951 by *Richard Sheppard*, with a recent extension in the SCOLA system by the *Hampshire County Architect*. South of this is the INDUSTRIAL ESTATE, which stretches from LILLEY'S prewar modernistic temple (good low extension of 1960–1 by *A. G. Porri & Partners*) to a new group in Houndmills Road, all of 1963–4: CROOKES LABORATORIES, by *H. G. Huckle & Partners*, with the conventional slab block; MACMILLAN'S by *Charles Pike & Partners*, with an undistinguished warehouse block from which an office tower rises in a remarkably successful combination of deep concrete framing and timber cladding; and SAINSBURY'S by *Scott, Brownrigg & Turner*, Basingstoke's most imposing new building, in which the black-and-white glazing of the canteen block (Nottingham Theatre influence) is raised to first-floor level, against a backcloth of giant grey sheds for the food processing and distribution departments. NW of Crookes is CHARLES, SKIPPER & EAST, *c.*1960, by *F. S. Eales* of Nottingham. W of the Industrial Estate is WINKLEBURY 1, 1964–6, an excellent housing area of single-aspect brick terraces of LCC Haverhill type, with a *Hampshire County Architect* SCOLA SCHOOL.

S of the railway, off Worting Road, is WEST HAM CLOSE, in the Hallamshire system (1965–6), blue brick and white weather-boarding, with a FIRE STATION by the *Hampshire County Architect*, and SOUTH HAM EXTENSION, similar to Winklebury 1 (1963–4), with another SCOLA SCHOOL. On the corner of Western Way and Pinkerton Road is ST ANDREW'S METHODIST CHURCH, 1964–5 by *C. G. Lelliott*, and in Pinkerton Road is ST PETER, 1964–5 by *Ronald Sims* of Bournemouth. S of Western Way, close to the bypass, is VAN MOPPES, a good earlier factory of *c.*1955 by *Moiret & Wood*.

Back in the centre, in WOTE STREET, are twenty-four shops of 1965–6 by *Llewelyn-Davies, Weeks & Partners* and *Ian Fraser & Associates*, erected to accommodate traders displaced from the site of the main shopping centre, on which work was due to start late in 1966. Finally, to the E, there is the RIVERDENE ESTATE, begun in 1964, by *Roy Chamberlain*, again high density, two-storey housing. Such housing has an attractive tightness of cluster compared with the early New Towns, but there is no sign that the lack of vertical accents will ultimately be any less depressing. Landscaping is everywhere excellent. NT) *See* p. 827

WINKLEBURY CAMP, 1½ m. WNW. This univallate earthwork

encloses a roughly oval area of 19 acres. The rampart is badly damaged but still stands to a height of 5 ft on the E. The ditch is still 15 ft deep on its S sector. Excavations in 1959 revealed a palisade enclosure as the primary structure on the site, later covered by the rampart, which was subsequently enlarged. The ditch yielded evidence of four periods of occupation from the C4–1 B.C.

BASSETT *see* SOUTHAMPTON, pp. 571, 581, 584

5050

BAUGHURST

ST STEPHEN. 1845 by *Ferrey*, and for that date remarkably 'archaeological', i.e. tending to historical accuracy in the Second Pointed (i.e. lancets and plate tracery), and no longer fanciful or of the papery Commissioners' kind. Ferrey was a fellow-pupil of Pugin in Pugin's father's office. Nave and chancel, S porch tower with octagonal bell-stage and stone spire. The W doorway is genuine Transitional work. One order of thin shafts. The date may be about 1210. – FONT. Octagonal, Perp, with quatrefoils, drastically re-cut. – SCREEN. Perp. One-light divisions. Only parts are old, and some old tracery has been re-used in the STALLS on the N side. – STAINED GLASS. E window by *Mayer & Co.* of Munich and 'Holles St. 10'. Pictorial, and in a facile way romantic still. – PLATE. Chalice and Paten Cover, 1569; Flagon, 1762; Paten, 1780.

NEWBIES, 1¾ m. N. By *Ernest Newton*, 1902. White with asymmetrically contrived gables. Typical porch with segmental hood.

BEACON HILL *see* BURGHCLERE

3000

BEAULIEU

BEAULIEU ABBEY (*Bellus Locus*) was founded by King John in 1204 for Cistercian monks. They took possession of the church in 1227, and it was consecrated in 1246 in the presence of Henry III.

Of the buildings the most perfectly preserved is the refectory, which is now the Beaulieu parish church, but in connexion with the abbey it may be better to start with the CHURCH. This lay near the N end of the precinct and was 336 ft long. The plan with the ambulatory and the radiating chapels forming a solid ring round the ambulatory and only divided from one another by radial walls is the latest Cistercian plan, that of Clairvaux III of *c.*1155–74. It is laid out on the ground, as is the rest of the building. All that stands up is the S aisle wall with the two usual doorways into the cloister, and part of the S transept W wall. The doorways have three and two orders of shafts and arches of many mouldings to the cloister, and to the church one has a segmental arch and stiff-leaf capitals. Towards the cloister this wall has a series of large niches, supposed to have been simply the spaces between flat buttresses, as it were. In the thickness of the S transept wall ran the monks' night stair from the dormitory to the church.

Of the CLOISTER E range the tripartite chapter-house entrance is at once recognizable. The chapter house was square and had four piers. To the N was a recess for keeping things in. It had its own little rib-vault on shafts, and it is interesting as a counter-argument against Viollet-le-Duc's theory about how rib-vaults were built that three of the four ribs have fallen off without doing any damage to the vault, which is in fact a self-supporting groin-vault.

In the S range there is first the day stair and then a shadow of the monks' lavatorium, i.e. the hand-washing basins close to the refectory door. The W corner shows that there must here have been a very strange meeting of arches or half-arches. Then the refectory doorway with fine mouldings. Above, three widely spaced stepped lancets. On the interior *see* below.

The W range, which contained store-rooms and the lay brothers' quarters, is now partly a restaurant. Some of the upper windows are still the narrow oblong ones of the lay brothers' dormitory. Others are Elizabethan cross-windows. Inside, part of the vaulted undercroft remains, with single-chamfered ribs on corbels. There is also the barn-like roof with tie-beams. The range goes much further S than the house, but that part is supposed not to be original. In it, however, is a re-set round-headed doorway. This comes from St Leonard's. Between the cloister W walk and this W range ran a lane, leading to the one doorway into the church. The lane was the lay brothers' cloister, as it were, and the doorway was their access to the church.

Excavations have shown the reredorter or lavatories of the monks at r. angles to the S end of the dormitory, and also the infirmary E of the chapter house etc. and not in axis with them. All this is as was usual.

N of the church stands a stone building with one window of the early C13 and a mutilated large E window. The building was supposedly the winepress. Of the walls of the abbey many parts have survived, one E of the winepress, others nearer the main buildings.

BLESSED VIRGIN AND CHILD, the church of Beaulieu, and the former abbey REFECTORY. This is a noble room, 125 ft long, with lancet windows. It seems to date from *c.*1230. Only the mighty S buttress tells of a late rescue action. The tall, even lancets with their thin continuous roll-moulding are interrupted in one place by a group of three smaller ones and a two-light window with plate tracery. That detracts from the beauty of the exterior, but the exterior of a refectory was not for seeing, and inside this irregularity has its joyful justification. Behind the small lancets in the wall the staircase runs up
23 to the reading pulpit. It runs behind a screen of Purbeck shafts, set two in depth. The window with plate tracery connects with the pulpit. There is even a small rib-vaulted lobby here with pretty bosses and a doorway to the pulpit with dogtooth decoration. The pulpit itself unfortunately does not survive, but its over-large bracket does, conical and decorated with large, heavy individual stiff-leaf sprays. The S end of the room has shafting to the windows. – PLATE. Chalice of 1734. – MONUMENT. Mary Do † 1651. Stone. Recumbent between two Tuscan columns and under an open pediment. It is a monument without any fire.

30 PALACE HOUSE. This was the abbey GATEHOUSE. It was built in the early or mid C14. It is unusually large, and unusual in other ways as well. It consists of two storeys and is two bays deep. The outer bay was a porch, the inner bay, which extends a little further E, the gatehouse proper. On the upper floor – this is very strange – there were two chapels side by side. PISCINAS prove that chapels they were. They are connected by two pointed arches. The N half has an E window with flowing tracery. One of the chapels was probably for those outside the abbey, the others for those having access to its outer yard. On the ground floor of the gatehouse the carriage entrance was in the middle and a small pedestrian entrance to its l. The same arrangement still exists complete in the partition wall. The N carriageway into the abbey yard also exists. The arches have sunk quadrant mouldings. The puzzling

thing is the vaults, tierceron star vaults in three bays in the S half and the same again in the N half. Can that be original? *Arthur Blomfield* built Palace House in 1872, and the VCH calls the vaults 'a modern restoration'. It, i.e. Sir Harold Brakspear, apparently also felt uncomfortable about them. Yet they exist in early C19 drawings kept in the house. The picturesque round towers at the angles of a wall S of the house are supposed to date from 1722, when the second Duke of Montagu was worried about a possible French invasion. Further S is a late C13 OUTER GATEHOUSE, much simpler in design. Segment-headed archway. On the l. of the outer gatehouse was the MILL, C13 also. The S wall remains.

Beaulieu is a village very pleasant to look at. The MONTAGU ARMS was built by *W. H. Mitchell* in 1888.

CONDUIT HOUSE. Small and overgrown at the time of writing. It lies $\frac{3}{4}$ m. NE of the abbey, immediately W of Hilltop House, and is vaulted inside.

SPENCE COTTAGE, Dock Lane, $1\frac{1}{4}$ m. SE. By *Sir Basil Spence*. 99
Small, but powerful and resourceful. Timber, except for two brick walls. The first floor is all timber with a deep cantilever along the whole river front, partly balcony, partly living room. The bedrooms are behind. Dramatic approach to this upper floor by means of an outer stair with a high brick parapet towards the river, with two slashing cuts interrupting the parapet so as to allow glimpses of the water. The house was built in 1960–1.

BEAUREPAIRE *see* BRAMLEY

BEAUWORTH

5020

ST JAMES. 1838. Nave and chancel in one. Rendered. Small slated bell-turret. Lancets. A typical feature is the placing of the S porch in the middle, not near the W end. The bell-turret stands on two tiers of wooden columns. Blank Gothic panels along the walls. – FONT. A miniature white majolica vessel.

BEDALES

7020

BEDALES SCHOOL was founded by J. H. Badley in 1893. It moved to Hampshire in 1900. The main building is by *E. P. Warren*, and was completed by 1907. It is large, in a free Tudor style, mixed with William-and-Mary elements, three-storeyed, of nine bays with a projecting porch with shaped

gable. The hall is distinguished outside by four-transomed windows. The S range has two more gabled brick passages, the rest and the whole fifteen-bay W front are William and Mary, rendered. Inside this building is a cloister of brick with round arches on the ground floor. The cloister is now glazed. In 1911 *Ernest Gimson* added the HALL and MEMORIAL LIBRARY, connected to the older building by a very heavily timbered passageway. The two halls are heavily timbered inside too; that is their *forte*. The exterior of this L-shaped group is less interesting, brick, rather in the Garden City style. The library has two canted bay windows. Then a gabled porch projects and above the passageway appears the bigger gable of the hall. The hall has a massive timber roof. The library is arranged in
94 the college way with bays l. and r. There is a gallery, and the bays repeat. But the 'nave' has a steep open timber roof. It is an impressive interior. The building was supervised by *Alfred Powell*. The furniture is by Gimson too.*

6000 [DL] BEDHAMPTON

The old village centre is an oasis to the S of the Portsmouth–Havant road, a loose cluster of substantial old houses, a little recent low-density infilling, and plenty of old trees.

ST THOMAS A BECKET. Too much gone over in Victorian times (chancel restored 1870 by *E. A. Gruning*; nave restored and N aisle added 1878) to be really attractive; the interior recently chastened with whitewash. The best feature is the chancel arch of *c.*1140, fairly lofty and wide, with a slightly depressed arch, of square section except for a thick roll-moulding on the W side, and two outer bands of flat relief decoration, one in double lozenge pattern, the other with two bands of sawtooth pattern. The responds have on the W angles inset shafts with scalloped capitals. The nave has a low wide lancet at the E end of the S wall and a square-headed window (evidently lighting a former loft) above; the other two side windows are big Early Perp, of three lights to the E and two to the W; re-placed in the W wall of the aisle is a similar window of three lights, evidently from the original N wall. The W window is

* Of the other buildings I cannot report architects and dates, as the Bursar, Mr Walesby, on inquiry replied: 'Neither time nor clerical assistance make it possible to prepare the information'. Mr Hubbuck e.g. tells me that STEEPHURST is very picturesque with its tower crowned by a steep cap. The architect is not known to him, but must of course be recorded in the school papers.

of three stepped cusped lights, early C14.* The chancel was probably rebuilt in the early C14; the S wall comes further out than the S nave wall. The SW window is of two shoulder-headed lights (of the Caernarvon pattern, such as appear in certain medieval buildings at Southampton). The SE window is two-light Perp; the tall E window is Victorian, but may represent an older window of the same shape; in the C19 N vestry is a replaced trefoiled lancet. Cinquefoiled C15 PISCINA, with shelf. The open W bellcote of 1878, uncharacteristic of Hampshire, replaced a wooden belfry. – MONUMENTS. Wall-monument in the chancel to the Rev. St John Alder, † 1864; two angels in relief, holding an unfurled banner with the inscription, all in a well-moulded trefoiled recess. – Two attractive tablets of *c.*1780 and *c.*1800 high on the W chancel wall, above the arch, with pediments, urns, and other embellishments. – Some good TOMBSTONES.

Opposite the church, the OLD RECTORY has a straightforward two-storeyed Georgian façade, with an outsize early C19 enclosed porch, its outer door between Doric columns under a flat segmental hood, with a semicircular recess above the hood, containing a small rounded fanlight and radiating fluted mouldings. BIDBURY HOUSE, facing E across fields, with its side to the church, has an unusual three-storeyed late C18 brick façade, with two canted bay windows on the second storey, the S one continued down to a similar bay window on the ground storey, the N one resting on two free-standing columns to form a porch to the main entrance to the house.

The gem of Bedhampton is THE ELMS, at the W end of the old village, a house of perhaps the C17 (or possibly earlier) which was weirdly gothicized in the C18. It has a stuccoed E façade of three storeys, the second storey having two Venetian windows with the tops of the centre lights twisted into ogee shapes and the outlines of pseudo-keystones incised in the stucco above the points, and a similar single-light window in between. The ground storey has the same arrangement but with the entrance in the middle; the upper storey has three low ogee-headed windows. The owner, Sir Theophilus Lee, added a large room in a new projecting wing to the N after Waterloo to entertain the Duke of Wellington; this has at its angle a delightful three-storeyed stuccoed castellated tower in a Gothick style of later vintage than that of the main part of the

* It is a little awkwardly shaped, and the VCH suggests that it has been re-set.

house, with niches under hoods having foliated bosses on the top storey, panels in the shape of hollow-sided lozenges on the second, and pointed recesses (one of them over a doorway) with tracery like that of two-light Gothic windows on the ground floor.

7040

BENTLEY

ST MARY. The story begins inside the church. The chancel must be Early Norman, as already in the mid C12 a N chapel of two bays was added. Round pier, multi-scallop capitals, square abaci. The arches are C13. They die into vertical pieces above the abaci. The S chapel followed in the C13. Round pier, round abaci, double-chamfered arches. Two low stone screen walls in the W bays N and S. The tower arch is of *c.*1200, pointed, with two slight chamfers. The tower top of brick is a replacement of the C18. The nave aisles are essentially of 1890. Fine views from the church to the E. – FONT. Of the table type. Purbeck marble, each side with four flat round arches. – COMMUNION RAIL. Jacobean, with stubby fat balusters. – STAINED GLASS. In one chancel S window many fragments. – PLATE. Flagon, 1789; Cup, 1790.

BENTLEY HOUSE, ¼ m. SW. Early C18, much enlarged and restored. The best preserved front is to the street. Brick, with hipped roof. Ten bays, the leftmost ones still with the original wooden cross-windows. A gorgeous cedar tree close to this front.

MARELANDS, ¾ m. SE, has a fine aisled BARN.

COLDREY HOUSE, 1 m. SW. Although the front is Georgian, the survival inside of a small stone fireplace and huge brick kitchen fireplace prove that the house is of *c.*1560 or so. (More C16 details given in the MHLG list.)

6040

BENTWORTH

ST MARY. Essentially early C13. The most consistent impression is inside, where the four-bay arcades, just as at Crondall, look so much earlier. They have thick round piers with multi-scalloped capitals and square abaci, i.e. a mid C12 form, but pointed arches with a slight chamfer and a hood-mould of C13 moulding. The chancel arch also has a slight chamfer. Then the chancel lancets, the priest's doorway with one order of shafts, the round-arched N doorway, the re-set bits of another doorway, now inside, and the lower part of the W tower with its lancets. Only the chancel E window seems later C13 – see the fine shafts inside. And what is the date of the chancel PISCINA? It has a trefoiled head with dogtooth. Perp tower arch. Several re-used pieces outside. Nice Victorian tower top. – FONT. Of table type, but not early. Early C16 cusped arches along the sides. – Rustic pyramidal FONT COVER, dated 1605. – MONUMENTS. Small kneeler, † 1606. – Very naïve cartouche, † 1671.

HALL FARM, SW of the church. The house has an early C14 porch. The mouldings of the doorway inside the porch are especially characteristic. A separate building on the r. (now a dairy) is supposed to have been the chapel. Large blocked E window.

MULBERRY HOUSE (former Rectory), E of the church. White, early C19 three-bay house with a handsome porch of two Tuscan columns *in antis*. Decorated frieze.

LOOM FIELD, ½ m. NE, on the Lasham Road. By *Gore, Gibberd & Saunders*, 1962–3. One-storeyed, of brick, with the typical 1960 motif of the window frames reaching the level of the top of the flat wooden roof and the brick pillars between carried up a little higher, just to break the evenness of the roof-line.

BENTWORTH HALL, 1 m. S. Flint, Tudor, built in 1830 (Burke's *Seats*). Symmetrical three-bay arrangements with mullioned windows. A wing of *c.*1850 (Burke's *Seats* too) does not seem to remain.

BERRYDOWN *see* ASHE

BIGHTON

6030

ALL SAINTS. The chancel is Early Norman, see the one S window. Late C12 two-bay arcades, typically Hampshire. Short round piers, spurs on the bases, square abaci, but pointed arches with one slight chamfer. The S capitals multi-scalloped, the N capitals with trumpet-scallops developing into a wavy fringe, i.e. a little later. Genuine E chapels of both aisles, of the date of the arcades, but the S chapel lengthened later. The exterior shows an E lancet for the S aisle. Low W tower, the upper part weatherboarded. – PILLAR PISCINA. The leaf capital goes well with the N arcade. – FONT. Of Purbeck marble, table type, but the sides slightly tapered. Four of the *See* p. 828

flat blank arches to each side. – SCREEN. 1899 by *Comper*. By the same no doubt the decoration of the roofs. It is Bodley-inspired. – PLATE. Paten, 1696; Cup, Paten, and Flagon 1757. – MONUMENTS. Cartouche tablets, † 1695 and † 1735.

MANOR HOUSE, by the church. The façade must be of *c.*1675. Five bays, brick. One-bay projection with a big shaped gable and l. and r. of doorway and middle window vertically set ovals, a typical motif of that date. Raised brick quoins at the angles and the angles of the middle projection.

BIGHTON HOUSE, 1¼ m. NE. Yellow brick. Dated 1844 by the VCH. The S side may well be of that date. The details of the windows are indeed just past Georgian. But the entrance side is so purely Grecian that 1830 seems the latest permissible date. Three widely spaced bays. In the middle a porch with Greek Doric columns *in antis*. The side windows set in giant blank arches. – Very pretty LODGE, thatched and with a tree-trunk veranda.

7040

BINSTED

HOLY CROSS. Externally this is a C13 to C14 church. W tower with lancets and a later recessed spire. Both aisles have small lancets. So has the clerestory. In the chancel is a long lancet too. The S doorway with three hollow chamfers is evidently an addition. The big N transept has pointed-trefoiled window lights and bar tracery. One would call that 1300. But it is known that it is of after 1332, when Richard de la Bere founded a chantry here. His MONUMENT, cross-legged, with two angels by his pillow, originally apparently very good, is still in the transept. So the window tracery is thirty years out. This lesson must be remembered as one enters the church. It is an impressive interior, but it poses a puzzle. The nave is wide and has arcades of four bays l. and r. which one would date 1160 at the latest. Short, sturdy round piers, multi-scallop capitals (and parts of two with stylized leaves), square abaci. How does that fit in with the exterior? On the piers are pointed arches with a thin angle roll. The aisle and the clerestory windows are lancets. Then the tower arch, which is pointed and has one step and one chamfer, and the chancel chapel arcades of two bays, with round piers and round abaci and now round arches of one step and one hollow chamfer. One capital has decorated trumpet scallops; one a nice variation on the trumpet motif.* How does it all fit together? Did they start with the aisles at a preposterously late date, say in 1175, and then by *c.*1190 turn to the pointed arches and lancets? – STAINED GLASS. E window by *Capronnier*, 1875, so different from English glass.

ISINGTON MILL, dating probably from the C18, is an excellent recent conversion job, including the oast-houses.

BISHOPS SUTTON 6030

ST NICHOLAS. Nave and chancel and weatherboarded bell-turret. Flint. Norman nave, see the two doorways, both with beak-heads, and some Norman N and S windows. Internally the nave is remarkably wide. The timbers of the bell-turret stand at its W end. The chancel arch is again Norman and also very wide. The chancel is of the late C13, see the N lancet with pointed-trefoiled head and the E window with three stepped such lancets under one arch. Originally there was a N chapel (an anchorite's cell?) on the N side, cf. the squint and the PISCINA. The W windows of the nave are of *c.*1300 or a little later. – FONT. A clumsy C18 stone baluster. – COMMUNION RAIL. Of slim vertically symmetrical balusters. Probably *c.*1630. – PLATE. Paten with IHS, *c.*1500; Cup, 1678; Almsdish, 1751. – BRASS. Knight and Lady, 17½ in. figures, *c.*1500 (chancel floor).

MANOR HOUSE, W of the church. Of about 1700. Five bays, two storeys, hipped roof. Later doorway with Doric pilasters and broken pediment and later Venetian window.

BISHOPSTOKE [DL] 4010

A strangely mixed-up place. Old riverside village with early C19 villas in expansive grounds; late C19 railway workers' housing; C20 suburban development, kept separate from Eastleigh by the Itchen and its bordering fields.

ST MARY. 1890–1 by *E. P. Warren*. Flint and stone; neo-Dec. Nave, S aisle, chancel, and rectangular W tower completed 1909. Not very lively except for the iron CHANCEL SCREEN, 1903 by *Bainbridge Reynolds*, which succeeds in getting something of the feel of a medieval rood screen in the unfamiliar medium. Open panel pattern with thin vertical members in the

* In the S chapel a low tomb recess of *c.* 1300. The recess of the de la Bere tomb is also low and has fine mouldings.

lower part; twirly openwork tracery in the middle part; upper beam forged into a moulded pattern, surmounted by an open-work cross. – STAINED GLASS. E window by *Kempe*, 1895. – PULPIT. Evidently from the old church. Octagonal, with a pre-Victorian flavour; stairway with tall balustrade. – PLATE. Set of 1749.

The old church stood close to the river. Its TOWER of 1825 survived till 1965; brick and flint, a notable landmark, demolished because it was unsafe. The stump survives in the tidied-up churchyard. Around the church site are houses in ample riverside gardens. The MANOR HOUSE, actually on an island, is early C19, plain and stuccoed, but ITCHEN HOUSE, *c.*1840, has a delightful roofscape: low gables with widely cusped bargeboards and big curving corbels at the angles. The OLD RECTORY (on the road from the old church site towards the new) is plain Late Georgian with a concave-roofed veranda on its S front. Nos 75–77 SPRING LANE is a pair of cottages, timber-framed and thatched, the genuine article.

5010 [DL]

BISHOPS WALTHAM

The town developed alongside the palace established by Bishop Henry of Blois in the C12 (although there was an episcopal manor house before that). It has a tightly-knit plan of parallel and cross streets, and the atmosphere of a half-stranded market town in, say, Shropshire rather than of a place easily accessible from C20 Southampton and Portsmouth.

ST PETER. A minster is recorded at Waltham in early Saxon times. Nothing visible in the present structure is earlier than *c.*1200, but if the proportions of the wide nave represent those of Norman times, it must have then been a building of fairly considerable scale. Many alterations from the C15 to the C17; heavy restorations in the C19 (1849, 1868, and, especially, in 1894–7 by *Sir Thomas Jackson*).

The N arcade of *c.*1200 has slightly double-chamfered arches with round responds, but the piers are C19 renewals. By the pulpit lie loose fragments of the late C12, and among them are two trumpet-scalloped capitals with chamfered abaci. These may come from the original S arcade, which was destroyed in the early C19. The present S arcade is a copy of the N by *Jackson*, whose is also the chancel arch. The chancel is in the main C15, with three-light E window and two-light side windows. The church is most interesting for its post-Reformation alterations, the SW tower rebuilt in 1584–9, the N aisle in 1637, and the S aisle in 1652. All are in Gothic Survival, the aisle side windows square-headed and cusped and the E windows of the aisles straightforward Perp with upper tracery. But what gives away the late date of the N aisle is the window arrangement at the W end, where there are uncusped three-light windows in two storeys, the upper to light a gallery. The tower is low and quite massive, with square-headed Tudor-type windows. From the stairway rises a tall and prominent rounded turret, decorated with quatrefoils and large crosses; it is of C17 origin but must have been altered since. The W end of the nave was rebuilt in 1849. The external texture of the church is varied; much of the old walling is in flint, but most of that of the C17 is in ashlar, except at the E end of the S aisle, where there is chequered stone and flintwork.

FURNISHINGS. FONT. Norman or possibly Saxon, square at the base of the bowl, going over into a rounded shape with rounded angle projections; rough and weathered. – GALLERY. The main W gallery is of 1773, with original BOX PEWS. – PULPIT. A splendid piece, given by Bishop Andrewes in 1626. Panels with strapwork arches under steep little pediments. Elaborate C19 sounding board, matching well. – COMMUNION RAIL. Of *c.*1600; turned balusters, panelled end posts (cf. Droxford). – PLATE. Cup, Elizabethan; Flagon, 1629; Standing Almsdish, 1669; Paten and Flagon, 1747. – MONUMENTS. Miniature wall-monument to Thomas Ashton † 1629. In the N aisle. Bust in ruff, in surround with Tuscan columns and flat entablature. – Ann Cruys † 1624, in the chancel. – Mary Kerby † 1716, with coats of arms and engraved emblems. – Richard Biggs † 1749, in the S aisle gallery. – Jane Wright † 1753, pedimented tablet, with separate small stone signed *James Stubington*. This is one of the few instances of the name being known of one of the local craftsmen who carried out so much fine small-scale work on monuments in south-east Hampshire between the late C17 and the early C19. Mrs Esdaile suggested that he executed some of the TOMBSTONES in the churchyard too.

BISHOP'S PALACE. First built *c.*1135 by Bishop Henry of Blois on the site of a cemetery. Reconstruction on an ambitious scale seems to have taken place *c.* 1160–80. There were various alterations in the next two centuries, and extensive rebuilding in the C15, especially during the episcopate of Bishop Langton (1493–1501). The palace was still occupied by bishops in the early C17, but it was damaged in the Civil War and subsequently allowed to fall into complete ruin. The remains have recently come into the hands of the Ministry of Public Building and Works; part of the site and the principal ruins have been tidied up and made open to the public, but some of the remains have yet to be fully investigated and restored. Little survives above ground level but broken flint-built walls with no traces of their original surface coverings and not much of the stonework dressings of arches, doorways, or windows; parts of the palace can be traced only in foundations. The significance of some of the more fragmentary parts is not at all clear either on the ground or from the accounts available, and the subsequent description is confined to the features of architectural note.

The palace was contained in a rectangular site surrounded by a MOAT, stretches of which are still visible, partly filled with water, especially on the W side. Entrance now is on the site of the GATEHOUSE, of which only a fragment is left. The principal palace buildings were along the W and S sides of the rectangle, and much remains of the W range, facing, over the moat, the present main road to Winchester. The GREAT HALL occupies the centre part of the range; the hall of *c.*1160–80 was built at first-floor level on an undercroft, but in the late C15 the undercroft was removed, the space it had occupied partly filled with earth, and a new hall floor constructed on a level between that of the previous floor and the original ground level. Remains of a C12 arcade in the S wall indicate the level of the previous floor. The W wall of the hall substantially remains, with the openings and part of the stonework of tall transomed two-light Perp windows. N of the hall are the very ruinous KITCHEN and service rooms; immediately to the S is a room retaining a C12 window in its W wall. This connects with the TOWER at the SW corner of the palace, essentially of *c.*1160–80 and remaining to its full height of three storeys on its S and W sides. It contains the remains of C12 and C15 windows as well as of fireplaces. Of the S range, in which were the bishop's private apartments, hardly anything is left above foundation level except the first stretch of outer wall adjoining the tower. At the S end of the S range are the foundations and crypt of the apsidal CHAPEL, a survival of the first palace of Bishop de Blois, not yet fully investigated at the time of writing.

Detached from the ruins of the main buildings, to the NE, is the fairly complete shell of the EAST RANGE, an austere early C14 two-storey building, altered in the late C16, with small square-headed window openings and plain doorways. Next to this is a building externally largely of brick, though partly of stone, containing medieval timber framework, which is being restored at the time of writing.

The curtilage of the palace, including ground to the S and E, was enclosed with a red-brick wall by Bishop Langton. Much of this remains, bordering existing roads, including an octagonal brick turret, pyramidally roofed, at the NE angle, and the lower part of another turret at the SW angle. The SW part of this walled enclosure is now occupied by a brick C17 and C18 house called PLACE HOUSE.

THE TOWN. The focal point of Bishops Waltham is GEORGE SQUARE, a vaguely rectangular space, from which three parallel streets run N – Brook Street, High Street, and Houchin Street – with another, Basingwell Street, parallel to the S and entering George Square at a bend. Across the top of these streets, running N–S, is Bank Street, and there are small intermediate cross-lanes. All this suggests a deliberate medieval grid-plan laid out by some early bishop. But the streets, apart from High Street, are very narrow, and many of the inner plots very small. Could it be that the whole area between Brook and Houchin Streets and between Bank Street and the S side of George Square was once a great rectangular space like that of Wickham and that the shallow island blocks represent consolidated encroachments by market stalls, as has happened to some extent at Wickham and Fareham? This would certainly explain the cramped nature of the plots bordering High Street, so unlike the long burgage plots which bordered the main streets of most medieval planned towns. If this surmise is correct, the houses on the E side of Brook Street and the W side of Houchin Street represent those facing the original square, and Basingwell Street must have originated as a back-lane.

Neither in terms of individual buildings nor in terms of townscape does Bishops Waltham match up architecturally to Botley or Titchfield, let alone Wickham or Fareham. In BROOK STREET very little: minor C18 and later cottages and commercial buildings. It continues as LOWER LANE with the CONGREGATIONAL CHURCH, 1862, with massive pilasters, tall, thickly detailed round-headed windows, and an oddly shaped pediment, in yellow and red brick. On the corner of BANK STREET an attractive brick Victorian GRANARY with elliptical-headed arches. Then back down HIGH STREET, which funnels slightly outwards at its S end; a few plain Georgian fronts of patterned brick and BARCLAYS BANK, a plain Georgian three-storeyed house flanked by Victorian wings with a sort of chequered surface pattern in relief, all stuccoed over. Facing up High Street is the pleasantest group of houses in the town centre, on the S side of the square, including a C17 house with a three-gabled roof-line, an C18 house of grey and red brick, and a long, low C18 pub, stuccoed over. In HOUCHIN STREET the first house, facing along the square, is plain and stuccoed, but has a stone stairway, flanked by heavy outward-curving balustrades, leading to the front door. Along the street were very humble Georgian cottages, now half-cleared. Houchin Street brings one back into Bank Street, and leading off on the opposite side is ST PETER'S STREET, a moderately attractive cul-de-sac ending at the churchyard. The houses in it are individually disappointing; HOPE HOUSE, Georgian, has lost its character through whitewashing, and NORTH HOUSE, long, low, and pleasing in its proportion, is covered in cement.

Through the churchyard, past the RECTORY, exceedingly plain Georgian but with a remarkable doorway, flanked by glass panels and surmounted by an outsize fanlight with radiating pane pattern, and into FREE STREET, which joins Bank Street at its far eastern end. Around the junction of the streets one gets the feeling that one is in a subsidiary village centre, well away from the confined streets of the inner town. C17 and C18 brick houses and a Georgian pub, pleasant as a group. Back along Bank Street there is a short stretch of memorable townscape: there are two blocks of timber-framed cottages, the first set back, the other forward on the street line; a tree projects beyond the latter and the street slopes and bends round intimately. Opposite is COURT HOUSE, a charming two-storey house of grey and red brick, then a large rambling early C19 block in stucco and yellow brick, with no special features but good in the townscape. Then a demolition gap breaks the continuity, and Bank Street, back towards the town centre, no longer has any special character. Turning into BASINGWELL STREET, there is still on the l. an almost continuous line of Georgian and earlier cottages and houses, but many look in a bad way. Nos 9–13 are two C17 blocks with curving eaves, which look as if they would be worth restoring. Basingwell Street enters George Square with a curve.

Much of Bishops Waltham gives one the impression that decay is incipient, if not imminent; whole stretches of street frontage look as if they will not last much longer, and there is less evidence than in some other South Hampshire towns and villages of the restoration of old houses (mainly no doubt by outsiders) which has helped to preserve the visual character of such places. And the traffic problem, thanks to the extreme narrowness of many of the streets and the frequency of right-angle corners, seems even more acute than usual, and makes a walk round parts of the town especially perilous. The planning authority has imminent problems in Bishops Waltham; the town has, belatedly, to come to terms with the C20.

OUTLYING HOUSES

NORTHBROOK HOUSE, now the offices of the Droxford R.D.C. Two-storeyed, Georgian, cemented.

WALTHAM CHASE MILL, 1 m. along the Fareham road. Three-storey, five-bay Georgian grey and red brick façade. Fine doorcase with open rounded pediment and fluted columns.

VERNON HILL, 1 m. N. Said to have been built by Admiral Vernon after the battle of Porto Bello, fought in 1739. But the N façade is much older in origin, probably C17; long, low, two-storeyed; some of the windows have flat-arched hood-moulds and others have quoined frames with keystones. There is an early C19 Gothick porch. The S façade is basically Georgian but altered and stuccoed; two canted bays and, between them, a long early C19 porch with inset Tuscan columns and a nice balustraded parapet. Victorian additions to the E. Inside is a finely fitted mid C18 upstairs drawing room and a staircase with elegant iron balusters with Baroque detailing. In the garden much STATUARY from Lyme Park, Cheshire.

In the hamlet of ASHTON are ASHTON FARM, with a fine group of farm buildings in brick, flint, and boarding, some thatched, and LITTLE MANOR, a T-shaped C17 or earlier timber-framed house with a bland Georgian front, and neo-Georgian features.

BISTERNE 1000

ST PAUL. 1842 by *G. Evans*. Yellow brick, lancets, thin corner pinnacles, bell-turret. Short lower chancel.

BISTERNE. An Elizabethan house with later alterations. But what was done at what time? The general impression of the house, rendered as it is, is *c.*1840. The first problem is the W façade. Recessed centre and two gabled projecting wings. Mullioned windows. In the inner angles are two porches, an un-Elizabethan motif. The l. one must be the original, not only because the r. one has a date 1652, but also because the plan of the house shows clearly that the l. porch gave access to the screens passage of the Elizabethan hall. A second problem is a mullioned window, the only one not at all interfered with, which is in the W wall of the centre core of the house. This core, immediately E of the hall, must have been a courtyard originally, and the window gave on to it. Then, along the W, i.e. hall, range is a spacious rib-vaulted cellar. Is this Elizabethan or even older, i.e. was the Elizabethan work also only a rebuilding? The huge fireplace in the NE corner, obviously part of the former kitchen, also could be pre-Elizabethan.* Of other interiors there is S of the former kitchen a Jacobean or somewhat later subsidiary staircase. The principal staircase of the late C17 has balusters typical of that time.

BITTERNE *see* SOUTHAMPTON, pp. 589, 590, 592, 595, 596, 597

BLACKFIELD *see* FAWLEY

7030 BLACKMOOR

ST MATTHEW. 1868 by *Waterhouse* for Sir Roundell Palmer, first Earl of Selborne. Nave and chancel and a large W tower with steep pyramid roof and an attached stair-turret with its own spirelet. In the chancel ambitious bar tracery. That in the nave is less archaeologically convincing. Plate tracery. Tiny triangular lucarnes in the tiled roof. Large aisleless interior. (Most of the windows still have Waterhouse's characteristic abstract glass in mauve and grey. NT)

(Close to the church the WAR MEMORIAL CLOISTER by *Sir Herbert Baker* – timber piers and stone slate roof – and the SCHOOL, almost certainly by *Waterhouse.*)

(BLACKMOOR HOUSE. 1869–73 by *Waterhouse* for Roundell Palmer. Stone-built, in the Tudor style. Picturesque entrance side with a Gothic porch. The garden side was originally

* Mr Mills pleads on the strength of the history of ownership for a date early in the C16.

symmetrical, but Waterhouse, in 1882, made an addition. The main rooms inside are all large: hall 28 by 22 ft, library 28 by 18 ft, study (of 1882) 26 by 20 ft, dining room 26 by 20 ft. The cost of the house in 1870–3 was £25,000. Information from Mr Stuart Smith.)

BLACKWATER *see* HAWLEY

BLENDWORTH [DL] *7010*

HOLY TRINITY. 1851–2 by *W. G. & E. Habershon.** Neo-Dec with prominent S spire, marked by sharp little gables where it rises from the tower. Set against trees near a few cottages, just removed from the village of Horndean, which it serves. – PLATE. Chalice, 1681; Paten, 1718; Flagon, 1720.

The old, small, largely Georgian church of ST GILES has been pulled down. It stood in the loose cluster of old houses to the E, which composed the original hamlet of Blendworth.

BOARHUNT [DL] *6000*

Boarhunt church lies in a fold of the N slope of Portsdown Hill. All around it is completely rural; there is no village, only two farms with long barns of brick and boarding, and a single flint-built house beside the churchyard. To the N is a vast view over country apparently more wooded than cultivated, and with only thinly scattered houses visible. Yet Portsmouth is just over the brow to the S.

ST NICHOLAS. A small Saxon church, nearly complete struc- 9
turally, for which A. R. Green has suggested a date as precise as *c.*1064. Nave and chancel, with no later structural additions except a C19 open bell-turret. All the windows are, however, later than Saxon except the former N window of the chancel, now blocked. This has a double-splayed frame with the actual window opening out of a solid stone slab set in the middle of the thickness of the wall, with rough cable moulding round it on the outside. The Saxon N and S doors are blocked. Across the base of the chancel E gable is a stone string course, and a stone lesene rises from it to the angle of the gable. The chancel arch is Saxon and is the dominating feature of the interior; it is a plain unmoulded arch with abaci consisting of flat slabs of even length, and with a square raised band

*The church tender was £1,878, that for the RECTORY £1,400 (GS).

running round the outside of the arch on its W face. This band probably continued down to the ground on either side, but was at some time cut off at the level of the abaci. The masonry of the nave walls shows evidence (not now readily visible, since the walls are plastered) of a cross wall having existed towards the W end of the church, indicating that the W part of the present nave was once a separate chamber. Most of the present windows are C13 lancets, including the E window, those in the S chancel wall, those at the W ends of the nave side-walls, and the window in the W gable (the last with restored stonework). There are curious segment-headed recesses, probably dating from the C13, in the wall spaces immediately N and S of the chancel arch, related to similar recesses in the N and S nave walls (that to the S partly cut away by a Tudor window); these may have been constructed to give space for side-altars. (There are other examples of this arrangement in Sussex.)

All the FURNISHINGS, in plain pitch pine, are obviously Early Victorian (presumably from the restoration recorded in 1853), yet they include a three-decker PULPIT, boxed SQUIRE'S PEW, WEST GALLERY, and simple COMMUNION RAIL which, though in pitch pine, seems more puritan than Victorian in character. These suggest an immunity, in this remote place, from the influence of the ecclesiological revival which had by then penetrated almost everywhere else. The present treatment of the walls and roofs probably dates from this conservative Victorian restoration; the walls are roughly plastered, and the roofs are simply ceiled in the Georgian manner, only the cross beams and trusses of the nave being visible. – FONT. Massive tapering stone bowl; probably Saxon. – SCULPTURE. Norman head in the chancel E wall. – PAINTING. In the S doorway arch minor scroll painting. – PLATE. Cup of *c.*1570, Elizabethan type, with a wide engraved band on the bowl. – MONUMENTS. On the N chancel wall monument to the Henslowe family, dated 1577 and showing a typical Elizabethan blend of sophistication and naïvety. Four small Corinthian columns, fluted and with delicately carved capitals, support the large entablature, on which are three little pediments, the middle one segmental, surmounted by statuettes, now sadly mutilated, representing Faith, Hope, and Charity. There are coats of arms in strapwork surrounds between the columns. No effigy. The monument is not in its original position and may have suffered some rearrangement on removal. – Against the S nave wall is the base of a former marble monument to Robert Eddowes, 'Store keeper of the Ordnance at Portsmouth', † 1765.

BOLDRE

3090

ST JOHN. The S arcade comes first, say *c.*1175: the piers are simply chunks of wall, slightly chamfered, and the arches are round, also with a slight chamfer. The N arcade follows. Round piers of Purbeck marble, round abaci, triple-chamfered arches. This arcade goes with the N lancet windows. The date is the earlier C13, and the aisle is remarkably wide for such a date. The E window is not original, but the internal shafting is. In the W wall of the aisle is a doorway, bonded in with the W respond of the arcade. It must have led to some annexe. In the later C13 the S aisle, and the nave of course as well, were considerably lengthened. Octagonal piers, double-chamfered arches. Late C13, one would say, is the W wall, at the end presumably of this operation: doorway with continuous triple-chamfers. The short SE tower is in its lower stage of about 1300: pointed-trefoiled heads to the window lights and a quatrefoil over. The upper stage is of brick and dated 1697. The arch from tower to chancel has no features. – PULPIT. By *Norman Shaw* (*see* below), 1876. Panels with big stiff-leaf configurations, not done with Shaw's usual zest. – STAINED GLASS. By whom are the three large, strongly coloured figures in the E window? – PLATE. Paten, 1669; Chalice, late C17; Flagon, 1830. – MONUMENTS. John Kempe † 1652. Alabaster tablet with demi-figure in an oval recess. Black columns l. and r. – William Gilpin, rector of Boldre from 1777 till his death in 1804, and the most influential of all writers on picturesque travelling, telling his readers what to look for, how to look, and how to create picturesque landscape effects. The monument is by *M. W. Johnson* of New Road, London. Simple tablet with an urn, a laurel branch, and a book. – (In the churchyard the CANTELUPE MEMORIAL FOUNTAIN. This is of 1920 and has Gilbertian detail.)

OLD MANSION (Heywood Manor), ¼ m. WSW. Neo-Georgian, by *Sir Reginald Blomfield*, about 1920–5.

BOLDRE GRANGE, ¾ m. WSW. By *R. Norman Shaw*, 1873–4. Quite a large house, with all the Shaw features, asymmetrical façades, timber-framed gables, some mullioned and transomed windows, high chimneys, brick laid in English bond, yet in this case not resulting in a unified and completely convincing architectural composition. The best view is diagonally towards the entrance from the l., so that the low corridor with its long window bands and its own roof appears below the small window band of the upper corridor and the large upper staircase window.

BONHAMS *see* FROYLE

BORDON CAMP *see* HEADLEY

BOSCOMBE *see* BOURNEMOUTH, pp. 118, 120, 121, 122, 124, 128, 131 ff.

3030

BOSSINGTON

ST JAMES. 1839. Small, of flint, nave and short chancel, and a bellcote on the E end of the nave.

BOSSINGTON HOUSE. 1834 by *John Davies*. Yellow brick, with shaped gables. Symmetrical main façade. Many tall chimney-stacks.

See p. 828 HOUGHTON MILL, ¼ m. NE. Three storeys, red brick. Five-bay front with three-bay pediment. Bays one and five have their windows set in giant four-centred arches. Gothic glazing bars.

PITTLEWORTH MANOR, 1 m. SW. In one room Elizabethan wall paintings. On one wall one of the familiar large-scale damask or brocade motifs in dark red, on another gay and naïve (and not well preserved) scenes of sports and merry-making. Both walls are dated 1580.

5010 [DL]

BOTLEY

Botley is a surprisingly unspoiled place to find at the meeting of main roads 7 m. from the centre of Southampton. William Cobbett had a farm there from 1806 till about 1826, and it still seems the sort of place one would have expected him to have chosen to live in, even though the two most prominent buildings date from after his time.

ALL SAINTS. Originally a plain Gothic unaisled yellow-brick church of 1836, by *J. W. Wild*, with flanking NW tower, a landmark from the main street, effective with its well-shaped buttresses and prominent pinnacles. New chancel, also of yellow brick, and other alterations by *J. Colson*, 1859. Much work by *Sir Thomas Jackson*: N aisle of stone in neo-Perp with decorative parapet, 1892; new nave roof with three dormers; narthex, 1895, with typically Late Victorian triangular wall-shafts. Jackson's N arcade is of square wooden pillars with Tudor-shaped arches, and an intricate series of aisle roof supports is visible from the nave, an engaging piece of elaborate rusticity typical of the architect. – FONT. Circular bowl, C12, with rough arched panels, zigzag and cable moulding; impressive in an earthy way. – STAINED GLASS. E and W windows and one of the S windows (W) by *Clayton & Bell*. – PLATE. Set of 1772. – MONUMENT. C14 ogee tomb canopy, cinquefoiled and crocketed, reset from the old church, containing a fine effigy of a man in tunic and gown, with an expressive clean-shaven face and hair ending at the side in curls; feet and hands damaged.

ST BARTHOLOMEW. The old parish church, among farm buildings nearly 1 m. to the S. Only the chancel is left: C13 with lancets, Perp windows, and a partly late C12 doorway roughly reset in the W wall. – Inside a series of TABLETS and tomb slabs, late C17 to early C19, with good lettering; one is signed *Elderton* of Southampton.

Botley is by tradition a very small town rather than a village (first market charter 1267), and the dominant building in the High Street is the MARKET HALL of 1848, with four Tuscan columns, a rather heavy pediment, and a little turret of 1897, all projecting effectively forward of the adjoining buildings. The street is first-rate small-scale townscape, wide and fairly straight for a stretch, then markedly narrowing and curving out of sight at the W end. The buildings are mostly quite homely, but, as at Wickham, there are just enough larger ones in prominent places to give an urban feeling to the whole, such as the three-storey DOLPHIN HOTEL and the plainer BUGLE HOTEL opposite, both with projecting porches. Other notable buildings are a well-restored timber-framed house (Nos 13–15) near the Market Hall, with some ogee-curved braces and herringbone brickwork, a Georgian house (No. 23) with projecting porch with fluted pillars, and BOTLEY HOUSE, a rather naïve five-bay Georgian house with pediment over the middle three bays, central round-headed window on the first floor, and doorway approached by a flight of steps; it is of the rich red brick baked locally from the C16 to the early C20, the tone hardly changing over all that period. Botley House is where the street narrows and turns; the wall of an adjoining garden, backed by trees, is prominent in perspective in the westward view, as is the succeeding row of Early Victorian cottages with steep little gables, behind which the church tower rises to form the final punctuation to the street scene.

In the opposite direction the townscape is ended more definitely by a group of three cottages facing up the street, dating probably from the early C18 and built of red brick mottled with grey, with tiles of much the same tone, looking more sombre than other brick buildings in Botley. The windows are C19 alterations. These cottages, backed by tall trees, are of disproportionate importance because of their position. They are to be restored.

WINCHESTER STREET leads N from the E end of High Street. No. 8 is a fine timber-framed house with oversailing upper storey and moulded brackets, one of them dated 1610. There are several pleasant small C18 and C19 houses in broken lines along the street. FAREHAM ROAD is the inconspicuous E continuation of High Street. The last house on the S side has a splendid Georgian doorcase with the representation of a masked face and garlands under its pediment. The road crosses the River Hamble at the head of its tidal estuary, where BOTLEY MILL is an agglomeration of functional buildings of various dates. The original early C19 block is two-storeyed of seven bays, the middle bay brought forward with a strong segment-headed doorway on the ground floor. Windows are long and low, and the cornice has a curious pattern with yellow bricks placed in threes alternating with stretches of red brickwork laid horizontally. The MILL HOUSE is older, with grey and red brick façade and pedimented door-hood.

CHURCH LANE, leading S, is the only quiet road in Botley, the others being choked with traffic. It leads past a few pleasant brick houses into open country. STEEPLE COURT is a many-gabled brick house, C17, altered in the C18, and with diamond-leaded lattice windows of the local early C19 type. Beyond Steeple Court is the old parish church, near which is a pleasant pair of old timber-framed cottages, well restored, and a medley of farm buildings, old and new.

BOURNEMOUTH 0090

INTRODUCTION*

Bournemouth has now *c.*154,000 inhabitants, i.e. here is a sizeable 3
town with its shopping streets like anywhere else. Outside the centre however the health resort still dominates, even if the architecture of the great years is getting less, and the new domestic architecture has so far been consistently undistinguished. What gives Bournemouth its character is the scale of the C19 expansion, the hilliness throughout, the chines down to the sea, the gardens and patches of forest streaking through the built-up areas, and – more than anything else – the ubiquitous pines. Even streets are pine-lined.

Bournemouth is only partly in Hampshire. Branksome, Canford Cliffs, and Parkstone are in Dorset. To present a complete picture they ought to have been included, and if they are not it is the fault of the way *The Buildings of England* develop. To have the necessary information on this corner of Dorset would mean collecting all the information on all Dorset, and that, as it happens, has not yet been done. Holdenhurst, Kinson, and Southbourne are within the borough but are treated separately on pp. 295, 313, and 600.

Bournemouth was started as a seaside resort after Lewis Tregonwell had built himself a house in 1810 on the edge of the heathland valley. This is still in existence, though nearly unrecognizable (*see* below). But the real development was due to Sir George Tapps-Gervis, who commissioned *Ferrey*‡ in 1836 to design the WESTOVER ESTATE. Of Ferrey's work virtually nothing is left (the villas went in 1906–29). St Peter's was begun in 1841 as the spiritual centre of the estate. From 1845 to 1859 the Gervis family employed *Decimus Burton*. His main contribution was the fir plantation along Westover Road, which formed the beginning of the extensive system of Pleasure Gardens. In 1859 *Christopher Crabbe Creeke*, one of the founders of the Architectural Association, became the first appointed Surveyor to the Town Commissioners, and he went on to 1879. These were the years which imprinted their character on Bournemouth, the character described at the start of this introduction. As an

*I owe a very great deal to Mr Nicholas Taylor's guidebook for St Peter's (*see* p. 118), his notes prepared for the Victorian Society in 1964, and in addition notes he wrote out for me specially. Whole passages and paragraphs were altered and re-written by him.

‡ On his local connexions with Christchurch *see* p. 169n.

architect, unfortunately, Creeke was not talented, and architecturally indeed, the villas and hotels, with one exception, have little value.

The architectural importance of Bournemouth lies entirely in its churches. Some of them would have to appear in any history of English architecture in the C19. They all date from the second half of the C19, i.e. the time when Alexander Morden Bennett was vicar of St Peter's. He came as a young man, wealthy, and an ardent Tractarian. His zeal was paired with a somewhat forbidding 'austerity of manner and aspect', and it was not surprising that he had to fight much opposition against his alleged popery. On one occasion his effigy was burnt in the street, and Holy Trinity was begun in 1868 as an Evangelical counterblast against his series of Anglo-Catholic outposts. As early as 1853 *Street* designed the new St Peter for Bennett, in which nothing of the old church of 1841–3 was left. He also designed St James Pokesdown in 1857, St Michael in 1866 (since replaced), St Barnabas, East Parley in 1862 (*see* p. 202), and St John Moordown in 1873. Then, in Bennett's last years, followed larger churches, nearer the centre: St Clement by *Sedding*, 1873, and St Swithun and the new St Michael, both by *Shaw* and both building in 1876. St Stephen by *Pearson* was begun in Bennett's memory in 1881, and the series ends with St Aldhelm Branksome (Dorset) by *Bodley*, 1892 etc. and St Ambrose Westbourne by *Hodgson Fowler*, 1898 etc. St John Boscombe by *Oldrid Scott*, 1893–5, much cooler, was another Evangelical counterblast.

CHURCHES*

ST PETER, Hinton Road. A large church, but not one which can convey a sense of unity. This is due to the piecemeal way in which it was built. The church was in the centre of the Gervis Estate, and its predecessor was built in 1841–3 by *John Tulloch* of Wimborne. To it in 1851 a S aisle was added by *Edmund Pearce*. In 1845 Bennett had become perpetual curate (*see* Introduction to Bournemouth). In 1853 he decided that a church for 1,200 was needed, or rather would be needed; for the population was still only 2,000. He engaged *G. E. Street* as his architect and started. The financing was done from small donations. Street, then aged twenty-nine, had made a name among the Tractarians by his designs at Wantage

*N, W, E, and S are here always understood ritually.

and for the Sisters of Mary at East Grinstead, the latter for Mason Neale, one of the founders of the Ecclesiological Movement. *The Ecclesiologist*, while not being uncritical, indeed called St Peter at Bournemouth 'one of the very best [churches] of our time'. Street left Pearce's S aisle intact and first, in 1854–9, added nave and N aisle. The nave is dull, but the clerestory is extremely interesting in its mixture of stones, and the N aisle is one of the finest features of the church. With its very close fenestration, it admirably conveys the functional meaning of the aisle as a passageway. The E end followed in 1860–4. Here, as of course customary, the detail is much more sumptuous; also the sanctuary bay is rib-vaulted. To the l. and r. are arcades of alabaster and marble. The capitals have naturalistic foliage. In 1869 the tower was begun, and when it received its spire in 1879, the church was complete. The spire is externally the best part of the church without question. It rises to a height of 202 ft and is recessed behind a parapet with pinnacles, but has broaches as well. The three tiers of lucarnes are East Midland in origin, certainly not Hampshire. Against the pinnacles stand statues. These are by *Frank Redfern* and were made for the porch of Bristol Cathedral. But before the spire was put on, a W transept was built, between tower and nave. This, though it has a precedent in Butterfield's St Alban Holborn, is the most distinctive feature of the church – an ante-church as it were, like the ante-chapels of Oxford colleges (Street had lived at Oxford in 1854–5). The arch between W transept and nave is of the strainer-arch variety (with which Street was familiar from Bristol Cathedral, enlarged by him from 1868 onwards).

FURNISHINGS. REREDOS by *T. W. Earp*, re-coloured by *Comper* in 1929. – Also by *Comper* the COMMUNION DESKS; 1915. – The TILING l. and r. of the altar is by *Powell's*; 1899. – PAINTINGS on the sanctuary walls by *Clayton & Bell*, 1886 and 1899. – The charming painting of the roof is recognizably *Bodley*'s, 1891. – STAINED GLASS. The E window is by *Clayton & Bell*; 1866. – The E window of the small chapel N of the sanctuary is by *Comper*; 1915. – SCREENS. The parclose screens are very typical *Street* designs (*c.*1867; made by *Leaver*). Also by him the GATES of the rood screen. – By *Sir Thomas G. Jackson* however and instructively different the SCREEN of 1906 between S transept (Keble Chapel) and S aisle. – The REREDOS and PAINTINGS in the S transept and the S chapel are by *Heaton, Butler & Bayne*, 1907–8. – In the

S wall of the S chapel, half-hidden, the finest STAINED GLASS of the church: by *Morris* and *Burne-Jones*, 1864. – In the N transept the SCREEN is by *Comper*; neo-Georgian, and of 1915. – The STAINED GLASS of the N window again *Clayton & Bell*, 1874. – In the nave against the E wall and on the side-walls PAINTINGS by *Clayton & Bell*, 1873 and 1877. – PULPIT. Designed by *Street* and carved by *Earp*. This was exhibited at the Great Exhibition of 1862 and is eminently typical of both men. – The WAR MEMORIAL under the W arch of the N aisle is by *Comper*; 1917. – By the same the RAILING of the lectern (1915). – FONT. Designed by *Street*. The earliest piece of furnishing by Street in the church. It was presented in 1855. – The RAILINGS of the font are *Comper*; doing a Jacobean turn (1915). – STAINED GLASS. SW transept W by *Clayton & Bell*, 1874; tower W by the same, 1880; tower S by the same, designed by *Street*, in memory of Bennett (1881); NW transept N again *Clayton & Bell* (1880). – The S aisle windows have their original stained glass of 1852–7. This is by *Wailes*; Clayton & Bell were introduced by Street.

In the CHURCHYARD is a CROSS, 22 ft high. This was designed by *Street* and carved by *Earp* in 1871. – The RESURRECTION CHAPEL was built in 1925–6 by Comper as a War Memorial and mortuary chapel. It is on a central plan in a simplified Gothic outside, but inside classical, with white pillars and a blue plaster vault – characteristic later Comper.

ST ALBAN, Charminster Road. 1907–9 by *Fellowes Prynne*. An impressive church, the E end facing the street with a window which is placed, due to the fall of the ground, remarkably high up, with vestries beneath. Rockfaced walls, Dec details. Bell-cote at the E end of the nave. Double-cross-gabled transept and a two-storeyed S attachment. Nave and low aisles, seven-light W window. Porches and baptistery beneath it. Interior brick-faced with stone bands. Piers with triangular faces. Segmental aisle arches in giant arches comprising the clerestory. The aisle arches die against the pier. – FONT. A kneeling alabaster angel; life size.

ST AMBROSE, West Cliff Road. 1898–1900 by *C. Hodgson Fowler*. Of yellow stone, smooth outside, and spacious and competent inside. NW tower of 1907 with nicely decorated bell-stage. Eight pinnacles. – STAINED GLASS. E window by *Burlison & Grylls*.

ST ANDREW, Florence Road, Boscombe. By *J. Oldrid Scott & Sons* and *C. T. Miles*, 1907–8. With three separate roofs. No tower. The style is that of *c.*1300. Bellcote at the E end of the S aisle with an odd curved outline.

ST ANDREW, Malmesbury Park. 1891–1900 by *J. A. Chatwin & Son* of Birmingham (GR). Towerless, Dec, one of the few buildings by Chatwin outside Birmingham. *Sidney Tugwell* of Bournemouth was joint architect. Rock-faced outside with a tall apsidal baptistery; disappointing interior of white brick with red brick dressings.

ANNUNCIATION, Charminster Road (R.C.). By *Sir Giles Gilbert Scott*, 1906, when he was only twenty-six years old. Brick, remarkably blocky. The wholly original central effect is the central tower, not really a tower, but a part of the building raised high up like the stage-house of a theatre. Very tall windows and a cyclopean bellcote. The short chancel is lower, but only by a little, whereas the nave and aisles are kept demonstratively low. The aisles are no more than narrow arched passages through the internal buttresses. In the chancel high up on the N and S are two-bay arcades to a gallery or passage. In the W wall of the tower is a small corbelled-out balcony towards the inside. The nave roof is the least satisfactory feature.

ST AUGUSTINE, Wimborne Road. 1891–2 by *Butterfield*. His last church. Rockfaced walling. Geometrical tracery. Polygonal bell-turret partly on a W buttress, square and so big that it appears like the bottom parts of an unusually thin tower. The bell-turret then corbels out and is square, but near the top octagonal. Interior whitened in the 1930s. Arcades with square piers with only a slight chamfer. The arches die into them. The W pair is bigger than the others, because of the bell-turret. Roof with typically Butterfieldian thin scissor-bracing. – STAINED GLASS. E window apparently by *Gibbs*.

CHRIST CHURCH, Alumhurst Road, Westbourne. 1913 by *E. H. Lingen Barker*. Grey and yellow stone. No tower. Bar tracery. Entirely conventional. The CHURCH HALL (of St Ambrose) next door was the first St Ambrose, 1880, by *Cole Adams & Horner*. This also is architecturally insignificant.

ST CLEMENT, St Clement's Road, Boscombe. By *J. D. Sedding*, 1871–3, the tower added 1890–3. In the latter *Henry Wilson* was involved. Mr Molesworth Roberts says: 'a prophetic church', and that is true, though externally the most striking feature is the W front of the tower with the wide segmental arch like that of a fireplace above the doorway and the strikingly original and Art Nouveau flowing tracery in the window above, with the statue by *F. W. Pomeroy* over.* The rest of the exterior is quite unpretentious. The N aisle front with its battlements is perhaps flatter and smoother than one would expect, except for the far-projecting lead spout-heads on graceful brackets. The N chapel by contrast has closely set buttresses and lancet windows. It is the arcade inside which is prophetic: thin, angularly stepped piers with only the slightest abaci to separate them from the arches. The chancel E window is set high up so as to allow for the rich REREDOS of 1882–3, carved by *G. W. Seale*. The stylistic motifs are Perp. – (The FURNISHINGS are exceptionally harmonious, because the first vicar, the Rev. *G. D. Tinling*, whose sister Sedding married, was himself trained as an architect under Scott. The brass LECTERN was designed by *Sedding* and made by *Barkentin & Krall*, 1876. – STAINED GLASS. Lady Chapel scheme designed by *Sedding* and made by *Westlake*, who also did the E window, 1883. Windows in the nave by *Tower*, *Bryans*, *Whall*. Much the best is the W window by *Henry Holiday* for *Powell's*. – CHURCHYARD CROSS. 1908 by *Farmer & Brindley*, with trailing vines on the stem. – GRAVESTONES. In the SE corner of the beautifully planted churchyard, next to the vicarage, are three gravestones designed by *Sedding*: to Tinling † 1880, his mother † 1876, and his curate, Robert Scurfield, † 1880. They use various materials in a freely detailed classicism. The Rev. William Purton † 1891 is similar, by *Farmer & Brindley*. NT) – The church has vestries and a pretty ORATORY to its SE. This is attached by a covered way, brick and wood painted white, to the VICARAGE, which must be Sedding's too. It is very early for 1873 too; for it is entirely of the school of Norman Shaw – so much so that one might well misattribute it. Especially the elaborate oriel window on the entrance side is characteristic. Equally characteristic is the excellent treatment of the chimneys, breasts and stacks.‡

CORPUS CHRISTI (R.C.), off Christchurch Road, Boscombe. By *J. W. Lunn* of Great Malvern, erected in 1887–9, but the W tower of 1932 with its octagonal top by *Wilfred C. Mangan*. Brick. Nave and aisles, clerestory, apse. The brick is exposed

*This is by Sedding, writes Mr Taylor, but the bell stage was re-designed by Wilson.

‡ The postscript to this is that the vicarage and oratory were demolished in 1965, being replaced by an ordinary suburban villa, not even linked properly to Sedding's covered way. A major loss to Hampshire's architecture seems to have passed unnoticed, because it was not 'listed' and church buildings are exempt from normal planning controls (NT).

inside. – (The PAINTING of the English Martyrs on the S wall of the S chapel, with its crowded iconography and oddly adolescent figures, looks as though it might be by *Frederick Rolfe* (cf. Christchurch, p. 177). NT)

HOLY EPIPHANY, Castle Lane West. 1953 by *Ronald Phillips*. Brick with round-arched windows and a square campanile.

ST FRANCIS, Charminster Road. By *J. Harold Gibbons*, 1929–30. Rendered. The exterior Romanesque. Rather German NW tower. Low two-light mullioned aisle windows. Plain arched windows above. The motif of the absolutely plain arches dominates the roughcast interior: the passage aisles e.g. have such arches. Crossing and narrow high chancel. Tunnel-vaulted-looking boarded roofs. Baldacchino altar. The S doorway has carving in a belated Arts and Crafts style. As one approaches the church from the S, there are Hall and Parsonage at r. angles to the church, part of the composition.

ST JAMES, Christchurch Road, Pokesdown. By *Street*, 1857–8. The N aisle of 1870 (GR). The original work stone with ironstone bands. Apse. Plate tracery. The interior has a strange irregularity in the N arcade: the two W bays with their pier differ from the more normal E bays with round piers and square abaci, and the E respond suddenly has two polished granite shafts. All this is connected with alterations of 1931, when the building was lengthened to the W, the N aisle enlarged, the Lady Chapel built, and the organ chamber made. Street's parts have good wooden roofs and foliage capitals. – (STAINED GLASS. Four apse windows of 1858. – Immediately W of the S door, 1863, *Clayton & Bell*. – W window 1884, *Mayer* of Munich. – The adjoining grey stone SCHOOLS of 1860 are also by *Street*, though no one would guess it. NT)

(ST JOHN BAPTIST, Wimborne Road, Moordown. 1873–4 by *Street*, but not an inspired work. SW tower with short pyramid spire, E.E. detail. Chancel 1886–7 by *Blomfield*. All rock-faced, with plate tracery and lancets in the nave, bar tracery in the chancel. Big wheel window at the W end. The original church of 1853, a humble job, survives on the other side of the road as Old St John's Buildings. NT)

ST JOHN EVANGELIST, Surrey Road. 1889 by *T. Stevens*. The chancel 1898 by *E. Greenleaves*. The NE steeple 1906. E.E., with a consistent use of lancets except for two windows with Dec tracery and the W window, which is a group of three lancets but has big detached tracery inside, an original motif. Piers of unusual shape, naturalistic foliage capitals. Vaulting shafts but no vault. Tall clerestory of pairs of lancets. The baptistery at the W end of the nave is separated by a screen of three arches.

ST JOHN EVANGELIST, Christchurch Road, Boscombe. 1893–5 by *J. Oldrid Scott* and *C. T. Miles* (of Bournemouth). A large church, of flint and stone, the NW porch tower never built. Flèche on the E end of the nave. Dec tracery. Tall and wide, very spacious interior. The arcade piers with thick Dec capitals. Wide bays, so that the clerestory has two twin openings to each bay. – (PULPIT. By *Harry Hems*. NT)

ST LUKE, Wimborne Road, Winton. 1898 by *Creeke, Gifford & Oakley* (NT). Large, of brick, without a tower. W end completed in 1913.

(ST MARK, Wallisdown Road, Talbot Village. 1868–70 by *Evans & Fletcher* of Wimborne. The serious conclusion of a charmingly picturesque model village (*see* p. 130). Aisleless, with transepts, in a correct Middle Pointed. Dull interior. The best part is the tower, E.E. in detail, but in four stages, i.e. Perp proportions. Behind, with views to open country, is a very large and beautifully planted churchyard, with CROSSES to Miss Georgina Charlotte Talbot † 1860 and her sister Marianne, who completed the village. NT)

ST MARY, Holdenhurst Road, Springbourne. By *Sir Charles Nicholson*, 1926–34. Brick, Perp, with no tower, but a bellcote set diagonally. Three separate gables to W and E. Interior white with five-bay arcades, the first and last piers without capitals and with the arches dying into them, the others normal. Prettily painted tie-beams below the boarded roof. Nicholson liked this effect.

ST MICHAEL, Poole Road. By *Norman Shaw*, 1873–6, but the beautiful and commanding SE tower by *John Oldrid Scott*, 1900–1, and the W narthex by *W. D. Caröe*, 1930. White and yellow stone. E.E. This is not a church in which one would recognize Norman Shaw. Nave and low aisles. Tall clerestory with coupled lancets. Four W lancets. Inside, the familiar round piers and round abaci. The chancel painted conventionally by *Cox Sons, Buckley & Co.* under the supervision of the architect *R. G. Pinder*. War Memorial Chapel by *Sir T. G. Jackson*, 1920, with STATUE of Fortitude by *Sir George Frampton*. – REREDOS. 1884. Stone and alabaster. – PULPIT. 1889. – STAINED GLASS. The E window by *Mayer & Co.* of Munich, 1882.

PAUL, St Paul's Road. By *A. H. Parken*, 1881–7. The central tower, which Goodhart Rendel calls 'indescribably idiotic', originally had a pavilion roof. The present spire* is by *Sidney Tugwell*, 1901–3.

SACRED HEART (R.C.), Richmond Hill. 1872–4 by *Clutton*, 'considerably enlarged' in 1896–8 by *A. J. Pilkington* (GR). One sees the difference externally, but inside all seems Pilkington.

(ST SAVIOUR, Holdenhurst Avenue, Iford. 1934–5 by *Frederic W. Lawrence*. Decent brick Romanesque with a low bell-tower. Whitewashed interior, irregularly spaced arches. NT)

ST STEPHEN, St Stephen's Road. The finest church in Bournemouth. By *Pearson*, 1881–98. The tower of 1907–8 was supervised by his son, *F. L. Pearson*. The church is a memorial to A. M. Bennett (*see* p. 118) and cost £30,000. White and yellow stone. E.E. in style. NW tower, W of the N aisle. Very tall bell-openings. The intended spire was never built. Nave front with lancets and angle turrets. Flèche over the crossing. Turrets E of the N and S transepts. Altogether, the E view is very complex. The church ends in an apse, and the N transept has a semicircular E chapel. The interior has a high nave with a tall clerestory and Pearson's unmistakable quadripartite rib-vaults. A wall-passage runs below the clerestory windows. It has a quatrefoiled parapet. The aisles are rib-vaulted too, and there are lower outer aisles. Even the W gallery rests on rib-vaults. The E bay of the nave cants inward towards the crossing, probably for perspective reasons. (The motif had been introduced by Street at St Philip and St James in Oxford. NT) The chancel ends in a polygonal apse with a very 89
narrow ambulatory. This has the quatrefoiled parapet, but not a real wall-passage. The apse windows are groups of three stepped lancet lights. The transepts differ one from the other. The S transept has the organ gallery above a chapel with a seven-rib vault, the N transept is open and ends in a rose window. All these details are unconventional, yet the total effect is restful. Pearson never put a foot wrong. But no-one would call him conventional or academic. – STAINED GLASS. A complete scheme by *Clayton & Bell*.

ST SWITHUN, Gervis Road East. By *Norman Shaw*, begun in 1876. Externally not of special interest. The N tower is incomplete. The only motif one may remember is the aisle windows with depressed blank arches which run from buttress to buttress. Low W baptistery. But inside there is the very wide

* Taken down in 1966.

aisleless nave, barn-like, as it were, with a panelled pointed roof and lit by an enormous eleven-light W window with flowing tracery. The side windows are as high up almost as if they represented a clerestory. The motifs appear a little *recherché*, as if Shaw had aimed at the unexpected.* – FURNISHINGS. In the N chapel by *Comper*. – STAINED GLASS. In the chancel by *Burlison & Grylls*.

HOLY TRINITY, Old Christchurch Road. 1868–9 by *Cory & Ferguson* of Carlisle. Red brick with blue bands. The style is something between Early Christian and Italian Romanesque. Separate campanile of 1878 which lost its saddleback roof recently. It is joined to the church by a low W narthex with Romanesque colonnettes with apsed baptistery.‡ Apsed chancel, round clerestory windows. Interior yellow and red brick. Four bays and transepts. – REREDOS. 1910 by *Sir Arthur Blomfield & Sons*. – ALTAR in the Lady Chapel by *W. H. Randoll Blacking*, 1931. – STAINED GLASS. E windows by *A. K. Nicholson*, 1923.

(WIMBORNE ROAD CEMETERY. Spiky Gothic chapel, 1877–8 by *Creeke*. NT)

NONCONFORMIST CHAPELS

Instead of a list, a running commentary is presented on a number of chapels in their historical position. There is not an early one worth looking at. Early Victorian in intent, but as late in fact as 1879, is the EAST CLIFF CONGREGATIONAL CHURCH in Holdenhurst Road, yellow brick, with a NW tower with cupola, windows with Venetian tracery, but also intersecting arches, in fact anything that wiil do *Rundbogen* service, in order to be different from the Church of England.§ But that attitude had already changed by 1875, and the turn at Bournemouth to churchy chapels is marked by two Congregational churches and one Presbyterian church of the 1890s. RICHMOND HILL CONGREGATIONAL CHURCH. 1890–1 by *Lawson & Donkin*. A group with school and house. Perp of all kinds. Ignorant, i.e. incorrect, yet not truly original,

* This nave was built only in 1891, and the foundations for an aisled building were already there and were used (NT).

‡ Mr Hubbuck comments that for 1878 this was a very unusual position. Later of course it became quite a favourite.

§ The architects were *Kemp Welch & Pinder*; the top of the cupola, the apse, lecture hall, schools, and minister's house are even later, 1888–9 by *Lawson & Donkin* (NT).

tower. The WESTBOURNE CONGREGATIONAL CHURCH Poole Road, 1897–8 by *T. Stevens,* is effectively grouped and competently detailed. SW tower with higher turret pinnacle. The W front is canted in representation of the centrally planned interior. Large Perp windows. On the S side cross gables. ST ANDREW'S PRESBYTERIAN CHURCH, Exeter Road, 1887–8 by *Campbell Douglas & Sellars* of Glasgow, is of white and yellow stone, with a SE tower and lancets and plate tracery. After 1900 the Nonconformists liked a free Gothic, influenced by the Arts and Crafts. This stage is represented by the large and lively CONGREGATIONAL CHURCH in the Charminster Road, 1904–5 by *Lawson & Reynolds,* red brick with very typical Arts and Crafts touches. Symmetrical façade at an angle. At the same stage is the METHODIST CHAPEL in Holdenhurst Road, 1907–8, also by *Lawson & Reynolds.* Tudor elements are made use of here. Finally the recent decades. The KINSON METHODIST CHURCH, Wimborne *See* p. 828 Road, 1956, is small, simple, and fresh. The PUNSHON MEMORIAL CHURCH in Exeter Road, 1954–8 by *Ronald H. Sims,* has a tall spike, and is spiky also in other ways typical of church designing today.

PUBLIC BUILDINGS

TOWN HALL, St Stephen's Road. Not a real town hall. Bournemouth has not got one. This was MONT DORE, 'an establishment for the reception of invalids, visitors and residents'. It was built in 1880 and designed by *Alfred Bedborough.* The tender was over £30,000 (GS), and it hardly deserves a glance. It is high, curves round a corner, has a tower, and displays relatively quiet classical to Italianate forms. But the tower top is Frenchy.

MUNICIPAL COLLEGE AND CENTRAL LIBRARY, Lansdowne. 1911–14 by *F. W. Lacey.* Red brick and stone. Baroque. With a high tower.

RUSSELL-COTES MUSEUM, Russell-Cotes Road. Built as a private house by Sir Merton Russell-Cotes. It was called East Cliff Hall. The architect was *J. Fogerty,* and Sir Merton presented the completed building to his wife in 1901. It is of yellow brick and thoroughly debased, i.e. not cognizant of any of the then respectable or enterprising trends. To the seaside verandas, two short towers with conical roofs, and a pavilion roof in the middle. Skylit hall and staircase. The objects collected are in keeping. Russell-Cotes was the owner of the Royal Bath Hotel and rose to be Mayor.

ROYAL NATIONAL HOSPITAL, St Stephen's Road. Founded in 1855. Designed by *E. B. Lamb*, yet quite innocent, in an undistinguished semi-classical idiom. Enlargements 1863 and later. – The CHAPEL is by *Street*, 1865–7. It is small and unimportant architecturally. Grey and brown stone. E.E. Relief of the Good Samaritan in the REREDOS.

CONVENT OF THE SISTERS OF BETHANY, St Clement's Road, Boscombe. 1874–5 by *Shaw*. A wing was added in the 1880s. Brick. In his Wealden tile-hung manner. Gabled. Back with four dramatic chimneybreasts, with long strips of dormer windows, like a clerestory, between them – a motif which looks forward to Voysey. The join of various tile-hung walls at a diagonal in the NW corner is very typical of Shaw's relaxed, non-conventual approach. His sister was a Sister. The corridors had concrete floors. An infirmary was added in 1897, a chapel in 1928–9 by *William G. Newton & Partners*. The latter now contains furnishings from *Ernest Newton*'s chapel of 1892 at the former Mother House at Clerkenwell, London.

HERBERT MEMORIAL CONVALESCENT HOME, Alumhurst Road, Westbourne, 1865–7 by *T. H. Wyatt* (cf. Wilton, where he also built for the Herberts). Stone and red brick bands. Small porch tower, mullioned and transomed windows. More like a Gothic convent than an Elizabethan mansion.

(CLINIC, Christchurch Road, Pokesdown. 1896, an extreme oddity for its date, with red and blue brick and some very free classicism in the style of *c.*1865. NT)

(CENTRAL STATION, Holdenhurst Road. An odd design of 1885. Massively buttressed brick flanks support a system of open girders. NT)

(THE PAVILION, Westover Road. 1925–9 by *G. Wyville Home & Shirley Knight*. Bournemouth's attempt at a grand public building. A lumpish design, brick with stone dressings, portico of square Corinthian columns *in antis*. Modernistic inside. NT)

(TALBOT HEATH SCHOOL FOR GIRLS, off Rothesay Road. 1933–5 by *Sir Hubert Worthington*. Surprisingly acceptable, considering its architect. Above the front door of each of the boarding houses is a painted lunette by *Eric Gill*. NT)

THE TOWN*

The fragments of the earliest Bournemouth have to be picked up in scattered places in the centre. The following may be named: No. 38 Richmond Hill, just one pre-Victorian-looking villa of three bays with giant pilasters, a recessed tripartite entrance, and a recessed tripartite middle window. It dates from 1838 and was designed by an architect called *Shepherd*. Then the MAPLE TREE RESTAURANT in CRANBORNE ROAD, just off Exeter Road, a cottage with steep barge-boarded gables, two and a smaller one for the entrance in the middle. This might be Sidmouth about 1820, but probably dates from the 1840s. The ROYAL EXETER HOTEL in Exeter Road has as its core Lewis Tregonwell's house, but is now more than twice the size it originally was. It looks 1840s, but is in fact of 1876 and 1886. The original building of 1811–12 is the SW part, again with bargeboarded gables. A stylistically more mixed affair is at the start of BATH ROAD: bargeboards appear again, but also Ionic pilasters. Near by, at the corner of Bath Road and Russell-Cotes Road is a yellow brick villa with Jacobean shaped gables. The rather tiredly classical

*As the information on the town is arranged in what seemed to me the most informative way, which, in the particular case of Bournemouth, was not in the form of a PERAMBULATION, I add here the route a perambulation would have to take to include all public and private buildings mentioned in the text.

Start in The Square. To the N Norfolk Hotel, Richmond Hill and No. 38 Richmond Hill. – To the NW Town Hall and Royal National Hospital in St Stephen's Road. – To the W Pembroke Hotel, Poole Hill, and Westbourne Arcade, Poole Road. – From here towards Branksome to see Branksome Dene, Alumhurst Road, and the Herbert Convalescent Home. – To the S in Exeter Road the Exeter Hotel and Maple Tree Restaurant, Cranborne Road. – From the S end of Exeter Road up Bath Road, with No. 10, the Royal Bath Hotel, the large block of flats of 1936, and, off in Russell-Cotes Road, the Museum. – Now from the Square E. In Old Christchurch Road Messrs Bright and The Arcade. Off to the N the Dean Park Estate. In the circus called Lansdowne the College and Library. To their E, in Christchurch Road, Bowmaker House. – At the corner of Derby Road the Manor Heath Hotel. – So to Boscombe. N of Christchurch Road in Knole Road The Knole, S of Christchurch Road in Boscombe Spa Road the Chine Hotel and in Owls Road the Burlington Hotel. – From here E and in Buckland Avenue Boscombe Manor (Technical College), in College Road Wentworth Lodge. – Then N, back to Christchurch Road and back, along it, W to see the Hippodrome and the Arcade. – Finally off N along Walpole Road and W along St Clement's Road for the Sisters of Bethany and St Clement's vicarage and schools.

Outlying items: The Transport Garage, Castle Lane, 1¼ m. due N of Bethany, and Max Factor's, 3½ m. NW.

of *c*.1850 comes in at the E end of POOLE HILL, on the N side a successful rounded front with the arcaded shop windows arranged symmetrically round the bend and opposite the PEMBROKE HOTEL, articulated by rusticated pilasters.

(Of Early Victorian character but quite unconnected with the seaside is TALBOT VILLAGE, Wallisdown Road, a model village in the pinewoods which still has open heaths and farmland to its N and S. Miss Georgina Charlotte Talbot, with wealthy estates in Surrey, began the village in 1835. She spent twenty-five years 'giving up time and fortune to bettering the condition of the poorer classes, seeking to minister to their temporal and spiritual welfare, and erecting habitations suitable to their position in life', as her gravestone puts it. These habitations are straight from the Loudon pattern book, and each has a standard plot of vegetable garden. Brick yellow or red in colouring, patterned tiles, chimneys set diagonally, porches placed often across the angle of an L-shaped cottage. There are twelve along the main road E of the church and several more, as well as larger farms, along tracks to the N. Here can be found the SCHOOLS, 1860, and ALMSHOUSES, 1862, both by *C. C. Creeke*, which are in a wild and ignorant white-brick Rundbogenstil, with diamond quarries in the spandrels of two-light windows. On the church, *see* p. 124. Closer to Bournemouth, now within suburbia, is the TALBOT MANOR BOYS HOME for crippled children, Talbot Avenue, 1890 by *Reynolds & Tamblin*, large and plain, like a manor house. NT)

The Italianate mode is best represented by the ROYAL BATH HOTEL, Bath Road, and the buildings adjoining it on the l. (CASINO CLUB). They are stuccoed white, have pedimented windows and other classical trim, but also such typical later features as angle pavilion-roofs. The date is obscure. The first building of the hotel, according to Mr Taylor, was of 1837–8 by *Ferrey*, and it survives as the five bays in the centre, with triangular and segmental pediments to the windows. The date when wings were added, i.e. 1878–80, by *Creeke*, seems too late for the present building at first sight, but Creeke was a reactionary architect.

DEAN PARK was laid out picturesquely by *Crabbe Creeke*. The coniferous part of the estate is admirable. The villas have little architectural merit. They are mostly yellow brick with red brick trim. The majority have bargeboarded gables. Some have asymmetrically placed towers. But there is nowhere much principle or conviction. The sixties of course are plentifully represented in other parts of Bournemouth as well. (A purposeful piece of roguery is the porch to ASTNEY LODGE (now Public Health Department), St Stephen's Road, opposite Lamb's hospital. It is dated 1866. In CHRISTCHURCH ROAD, No. 57 is a memorable horror, with bright red moulded bricks and a tower.* NT) William Morris in 1883 called the architecture of the wealthy villas of Bournemouth 'simply blackguardly' and only suitable for 'ignorant purse-proud digesting machines'.

Of major private mansions of that moment *Lamb*'s BRANKSOME DENE (Convalescent Home), Alumhurst Road, is of 1860. It is mildly Italianate and only in details, especially of the service wing, Lambish. BOSCOMBE MANOR (now part of the Technical College), Beechwood Avenue, corner of Chesil Avenue, Boscombe, was the house of Sir Percy Shelley. It is very much altered and now really of no interest. To the S it appears in the Georgian tradition; the irregular back has mid-C19 features. The paired cast-iron brackets of the door canopy are the best detail. According to Mr Taylor it is 1850s plus 1873 and by *Creeke*. Lord Portman's Boscombe villa, WENTWORTH LODGE, College Road, is of *c.*1873 entirely and in the details of the garden front shockingly debased Italianate. Especially the bow window could make one despair of the mid-Victorian years. (Yet it has its importance as one of the first large houses constructed in concrete, by the pioneering contractor, *Charles Drake*. The architect was one *James Baker Green*. NT)

But one recovers one's faith in looking at a few other buildings of the same years, those in which the Norman Shaw style makes its appearance, first in the excellent Vicarage and Schools of St Clement (*see* p. 121) by *Sedding* and then in *Sedding*'s THE KNOLE, of 1872–3. This is of red brick, and has a kind of Tudor gatehouse with polygonal angle buttresses as its entrance, mullioned and transomed windows, and a varied skyline. But it is not a masterpiece. The Vicarage of St Clement nearly was, though it was almost too Shavian. The School, mostly of 1876–7, is one-storeyed, symmetrical, with

*By the same hand probably that outsize shocker in Old Christchurch Road, DALKEITH BUILDINGS (incorporating the Dalkeith Hotel), excessively tall Gothic, with two tiers of projecting half-timber bays on top. Yet its date is 1893.

shaped gables and very elongated, segment-headed windows, also a typical Shaw motif. Two cottages alongside are also by Sedding, 1877. These buildings form a leafy group with Shaw's own Convent (*see* p. 128) of the same years. Shavian also – in a more summary way – is the MANOR HEATH HOTEL in Derby Road, 1878; brick ground floor, half-timbered gables, also tile-hanging. This was Lily Langtry's house; she built the smaller LANGTRY HOUSE near by for her mother.

A larger hotel with tile-hung gables is the CHINE HOTEL, Boscombe Spa Road, in a splendid elevated position above Boscombe Chine. It was built for Sir Henry Drummond Wolff as the Boscombe Spa Hotel by *R. W. Edis* in 1873. Drummond Wolff was the developer of Boscombe; his own house, BOSCOMBE TOWER, of 1868 survives in the grounds of the Burlington Hotel. The Chine has been added to and altered a great deal. The only outstandingly good hotel in Bournemouth is the BURLINGTON itself, Owls Road, Boscombe, 1893 by *Collcutt*. It is large, of brick, and symmetrical, with angle tourelles, a raised centre with short columns just in the raised part, and friezes of pargetting. The ground-floor windows are set under deep arches which stand on corbels.

The commercial late C19 is most characteristically shown by THE ARCADE and the former HIPPODROME, both in Christchurch Road, Boscombe. They are both of brick with stone dressings, and both by *Lawson & Donkin*; the former dates from 1891, the latter from 1894. The façade of The Arcade is a free-for-all, with motifs ranging from an E.E. foiled circle (seven foils!) to the curly open pediments of 1700. The Hippodrome is less careless and yet more original. Five bays with shaped gables. The fenestration is of three quite different systems: one, two-three, four-five-six. (Much more cultured is the restrained Arts and Crafts of Nos 628–652 near by. Unchamfered mullions and transoms à la Stokes, chunks of modillion cornice, excellent iron balconies of a Baroque shape. By the same hand evidently Nos 189–205 Old Christchurch Road. NT) Arcades were a feature not new to Bournemouth. THE ARCADE, originally Gervis Arcade, between Old Christchurch Road and Gervis Place is of 1866–73. The architect was *Henry Joy*, builder, and he managed to let the flanking, bow-shaped façades appear Regency in style – survival rather than revival. The arcade itself has a glass tunnel-vault. Much of the detailing is now alas modernistic (the arcade adjoins Messrs Bright – *see* below).*

(An amusing freak is Nos 216–226 OLD CHRISTCHURCH ROAD, a plain Italianate terrace, but with the sly bearded profile of its builder, *Joseph Cutler*, emblazoned (where it survives) on the piers between shops, in green and black tiling. NT)

Art Nouveau stakes its claim in the verandas of the NORFOLK HOTEL in Richmond Hill, built in 1897. The principal local Arts and Crafts architect was *Sidney Tugwell* (1869–1938), a pupil of E. J. May, who did many small houses.

The street of the large shops and stores is OLD CHRISTCHURCH ROAD. BRIGHT'S represents the jazzy Modernistic of the twenties.‡ PLUMMER RODDIS and WILLIAMS & HOPKINS are similar. The MIDLAND BANK is Lutyenesque, by *Whinney, Son & Austen Hall*. In WESTOVER ROAD is the back part of Bright's, iron and glass of *c.*1890 in four storeys (fifth added). Further up Westover Road, opposite the Pavilion, a choice selection of the early thirties: PALACE COURT HOTEL, white and Mendelsohnian, 1935§; GAUMONT CINEMA, with full-dress Quattrocento loggia; and WESTOVER ICE RINK, with indescribably stepped window arches, 1930.

Next in order of time and style the enormous blocks of flats called BATH HILL COURT in BATH ROAD, with classical detail, especially high up – all rather American. It is of 1935–6 and was designed by *F. S. M. Green*.** Even more American, super-Italian with shimmering tiles round the windows, is the complementary block overlooking Boscombe Chine, SAN REMO TOWERS.‡‡ It is a sign of the times that the horrendous courtyard, entered from Michelgrove Road, is built over a car park. In Bath Road again is PINE GRANGE, a vast and ill-advised attempt at multi-storey Tudor.

Of today the best is the BUS GARAGE in CASTLE LANE by *Jackson & Greenen*. The older part is 1950–3, the new part of

*In the mid eighties the same *Henry Joy* also built the WESTBOURNE ARCADE, Poole Road.

‡ The remaining lines of this paragraph are due to Mr Taylor.

§ The architects were *A. J. Seal & Partners*, who used the same idiom, surprisingly early, in THEATRE CHAMBERS, Hinton Road, 1932–3, and also, less successfully, in the BOURNEMOUTH DAILY ECHO, Richmond Hill, 1933–4, and the GAS BOARD offices, Christchurch Road, Boscombe, 1935–6.

** It is said that *S. Beverley* of Verity & Beverley was consulted.

‡‡ The architect was *Hector O. Hamilton* of Hamilton & Green, 1936–8.

1964–5. Prestressed concrete roof spanning 150 ft. In CHRISTCHURCH ROAD, also by *Jackson & Greenen*, is BOWMAKER HOUSE, 1960–1. A dignified ground floor, curtain walling above. Opposite are ROYAL LONDON HOUSE, 1960 by *H. Bramhill*, mosaic panels whizzing round a corner; BRACKEN HOUSE, 1965–6 by *Patrick Holden & Associates*, a high slab rising at r. angles behind a row of shops with precast concrete facings; and a GARAGE, also 1965–6, by *Morgan & Carn*. BEALES, in Old Christchurch Road, is an ambitious but unsuccessful attempt at a new department store. Long bands of window, pink brick, and some patterned tiling. BEALESONS, Commercial Road, 1962, with its windowless louvred façade, is marginally better.

The main feature of recent Bournemouth has been the replacement of Victorian villas by large blocks of so-called 'luxury flats'. In three places the planning authorities have allowed the skyline of the cliffs to be overshadowed. The first and best was TOWER COURT, West Cliff Road, by *Ansell & Bailey*, 1961–2, a plain tower with a well-detailed lower block. In the same road is ADMIRAL'S WALK, 1962–4 by *R. Mountford Pigott & Partners*, a tall L-shaped slab with the fashionable clichés – precast facing slabs, restlessly cantilevered balconies, virtuoso spiral escape stairs – all done with a certain seaside gaiety. Grim by contrast, its seventeen storeys dominating the East Cliff, is THE ALBANY, Manor Road, also 1962–4, by *Ivor Shaw*, a giant block of flats in a double-Y shape. Its facing of grey reconstructed stone has not stood up to the atmosphere and has been mainly rendered over. All details utilitarian. Of the smaller blocks of flats, two of 1962–3 by *Patrick Holden* are worth a glance: CADOGAN COURT, Christchurch Road, and CARLINFORD, Boscombe Cliff Road, the latter with nice polygonal glazed lanterns over the stairs. In Bath Road, AMBERLEY COURT is another tall block of flats, 1963–4 by *W. H. Saunders & Son*.

See p. 828

Factory for MAX FACTOR & CO., Francis Avenue, West Howe. By *Farmer & Dark*, 1959–60. The raised central core with its folded roof houses stores. The offices go round the perimeter. Clear and simple plan and elevation.

6040

BRADLEY

ALL SAINTS. 1877 by *J. Colson*. Nave and chancel and small diagonally set bell-turret. The windows with pointed-trefoiled heads. Re-used medieval parts are small lancets in the chancel and the three-bay late C13 arcade with octagonal piers and double-chamfered arches dying into vertical pieces above the abaci. – PULPIT. Of the 1930s, a delightful amateur piece with tree-trunks at the angles and stories between them. The style is still derived from 1900.

BRAISHFIELD 3020

ALL SAINTS. 1855 by *W. Butterfield* (RH). Brick, laid in English bond. Big roof. No division of chancel from nave. Plate tracery.

BRAISHFIELD MANOR. An Early Georgian five-bay brick house, considerably heightened in its effect by the recent addition of projecting two-bay wings. The old part has segment-headed windows, including the characteristic narrow windows l. and r. of the doorway. On the upper floor niches instead. Hipped roof.

BRAMDEAN 6020

ST SIMON AND ST JUDE. A rather shabby-looking church at the time of writing, and mostly C19. Late C12 plain N doorway and chancel and nave lancets. The chancel arch is better. Two orders with capitals still decidedly Norman and a pointed arch with two slight chamfers. – FONT. High Victorian, with symmetrical stiff-leaf motifs. – PLATE. Flagons of 1706 and 1721.

BRAMDEAN MANOR, by the church. Dated by the MHLG 1740, but the main front with the two canted bay windows and the doorway with broken pediment must be later.

BRAMDEAN HOUSE, on the A-road, opposite the church turn. Early C18. Grey headers and red dressings. Parapet. Doorway with carved brackets carrying a big semicircular hood.

WOODCOTE MANOR, 1 m. E. Built of brick. The gabled W front is dated 1630 (rainwater head). Three gables, the gabled porch between the second and third. The windows sashed. Only in the gables is the original mullioned form still echoed. The S and E sides by *Sir Reginald Blomfield* for Seymour Haden (RH), 1911, the E side with the four little roofs an example of architectural wit.

LONG BARROW. *See* Hinton Ampner.

A ROMAN VILLA more than $\frac{3}{4}$ acre in extent was partly excavated here in 1823 and has since been reburied. It seems to have been of courtyard type, with most of its rooms floored with plain red tesserae. Two, however, contained fine polychrome mosaics: one had a central panel showing a fight between Hercules and Antaeus surrounded by four panels containing heads; the other bore a central Medusa head surrounded by pictures of the deities who presided over the days of the ancient week.

6050 BRAMLEY

ST JAMES. This is one of the most fully furnished churches in Hampshire. The church itself is quite plain, especially internally, where there is no division at all between nave and chancel – except for the ceilure or rood canopy, i.e. that part of the roof which was above the rood screen. This is ceiled and has bosses in the junctions between the square panels. It was made in 1529–31. Externally the church has as its interesting features one complete, one renewed, and one fragmentary Norman window. They are all provided inside with a continuous roll. Then there are the Perp chancel E window, an Elizabethan window in the nave, the squat W tower of brick, dateable to 1636, with a (re-set?) W window and bell-openings like the Elizabethan nave window, the late C18 S porch, and the S transept (Brocas Chapel) which is by *Soane* and was built in 1801. It has a depressed pointed tunnel-vault of plaster with thin transverse ribs and diagonal ribs and additional ribs of tierceron resemblance but archaeologically completely misunderstood. – PILLAR PISCINA. The capital may be Norman, but the pillar with shaft-ring looks highly suspicious. – PULPIT. Plain C18. – SCREEN. Perp. Much restored, but the basic formula of five-light divisions (unique in Hampshire) apparently genuine. – WEST GALLERY. Early C18. On fluted Ionic columns. (On it ORGAN CASE by *Temple Moore*. RH) – COMMUNION RAIL. Early C18. With thin twisted balusters. – BENCH ENDS. Straight-headed, with buttresses. Mentioned in accounts for 1535–6. – PAINTING. In the nave Murder of Becket, C13. Over-restored. To its r. another scene. More scenes were below. – Opposite the nave S door St Christopher, huge, C15. – In the chancel C13 masonry pattern with addorsed flowers on stalks. Also, N of the altar, large over-restored St James, and S of the altar, lower down, a faded Virgin. Above her a quatrefoil. – The altarpiece behind the altar, a triptych, is by *Victor Milner* and was painted in 1885. In its style it is 1850, i.e. romantically inspired by, say, Schongauer or Dürer engravings. – STAINED GLASS. In a N window original fragments, including seven small, partly original, very accomplished mid C14 figures. – In the S transept sixteen largish panes of early C16 Swiss glass. – PLATE. Two Patens, 1708; Chalice, Paten Cover, and Flagon, 1713; Almsdish, 1728. – MONUMENTS. Brass to Gwen Chelford † 1504 (a 2 ft 5 in. figure). – Richard Carter † 1529 and wife (15½ in. figures). Both in the S transept. – Bernard Brocas † 1777. White marble. A fat, stately man expiring in 69 the arms of a kneeling young woman. Completely detached figures, visible all round. Large base. On one short side relief of Charity giving alms and grapes from a cornucopia, Justice, and Fortitude, on the other Bellona defeating an enemy, and fame writing down the events. The monument has been attributed to more than one sculptor. Dr Whinney suggests *Thomas Carter* (cf. The Vyne).

OLD MANOR HOUSE, by the Post Office. Timber-framed, with closely set studs on both floors. The house is of the hall-house type with a recessed centre, the doorway close to one end and two projecting gabled wings. Star chimney.

In the churchyard the SCHOOL. The oldest part with pretty glazing bars is of 1848. Somewhat later the equally pretty Brocas estate housing. Gables, standard pattern of glazing bars, much tile-hanging.

BEAUREPAIRE, 1 m. SW. What is left of the house is of little architectural interest. An early C19 service wing of brick, three-storeyed, with hood-moulds over the windows, and an end feature with two square towers, built in 1964 (architect *T. A. Bird*). But the house, which was the mansion of the Brocas family, still has its moat, and it is crossed by bridges with gatepiers and quite excellent wrought-iron GATES.

BULLSDOWN HILLFORT. *See* Sherfield-on-Loddon.

BRAMSHAW

2010

ST PETER, N of the village. Brick, 1829 by *John Peniston*. But the S tower is early C13 below, and the nave is of stone and C13 also – see the doorway and the three stepped W lancets. – PLATE. Chalice of 1669.

WARRENS. Probably designed by *Nash c.*1805. Two low-pitched gables with deep eaves. The ground-floor windows arched and set in blank arched recesses.

A number of Roman POTTERY KILNS have been found in the forest 4 m. to the W, at Islands Thorns Inclosure, Amberwood Inclosure, Sloden Inclosure, Linwood, and Pitt's Wood. These were the centre of an important industry which originated in the C2, and by the C4 was producing good quality table-ware for much of Southern England.

7050 BRAMSHILL HOUSE

Bramshill was built by Lord Zouche in 1605–12. It is one of the largest Jacobean houses. It is also distinguished by a plan quite exceptional in an age of standard plans. What Bramshill has in common with the other grandest Jacobean houses – Hatfield, Audley End, Holland House, Charlton House Greenwich – is the concentration on a piece of really spectacular display with few decorative embellishments otherwise.

There had been an older house on the site, but of this no more remains than the thicker walling in the E wing of the S front and one or two minor items to which reference will be made in their places. The S front, which is at the end of the present approach, looks normal enough in plan, and would appear yet more so if the wings had not been cut short in 1703 (rainwater heads). At that time the house belonged to Sir John Cope, who had bought the estate in 1700.

53 The façade (and the whole house) is of brick. It is three storeys in height and has mullioned and transomed windows. Square bays project in the angles between centre and wings. The grand display is the central frontispiece. On the ground floor it is an arcade of three bays set in front of the façade. It has rusticated details and an openwork parapet designed in a Gothic and strapwork mixture. The centre part of this then rises to the top on the principle of such frontispieces as those of Burghley or Hatfield. The centre has three tiers of paired superimposed pilasters, all tapering and all decorated, each tier with a different pattern. The capitals bulge out or curve in without rhyme or reason. It is among the most fanciful pieces of Jacobean design in the country. The source is Vredeman de Vries and perhaps Dietterlin. On the first floor in the middle is a bow-fronted oriel. The second floor is blank. The top, standing against the sky, is strapwork of a coarse kind. The rest of the front has an openwork parapet. The entrance to the great hall was originally in the l. bay of the three-bay arcade. The interior proves that.

But while this façade and the position of the hall are entirely standard, the rest of the place has no parallel. The main extension of the house is not that of this façade, but runs back behind it and at r. angles to it. There is here a long and narrow, really rather unsightly courtyard, and to its r., i.e. to the E, another show front, to the N the original entrance.

This N side is deliberately simple, but also grand. It is two storeys in height, long, even, and only punctuated by three canted bays. The middle one projects further than the others, and in it is the round-arched entrance into the courtyard, wide enough for coaches. The DOOR is original, with lozenge panels. The centre is crowned by a shaped gable with an ogee top and in a niche a statue of Lord Zouche(?). The gable is flanked by obelisks.

The E side is the longest side of the house. As the S and N fronts are somewhat wider than the rest of the house, the E side has projecting wings of two bays. These are treated to the inside as loggias with decorated pillars, spandrels, and arches. Above the loggias are no windows at all. Such loggias – see the centre of the S side and see e.g. Holland House and Hatfield House – were a fashion of the early C17. The long recessed part has four canted bays and between each time two long, slender cross windows, not a usual thing in those years. The range, like the N range, is of two storeys. Both have the pierced parapet. The W side is irregular. It also of course has two projecting wings. It is the only one to be gabled. This range was much altered in the C18. The most drastic of these alterations was that a mezzanine was put in.

The INTERIOR culminates in the Great Hall. The present doorway is a fine piece of classical design, probably of *c.*1703. Segmental pediment. The stone screen of course is Jacobean. Its principal decoration is a plethora of shields. The hall is lit only by an E window. The chimneypiece is original and not specially spectacular. To the N of the high-table end is the staircase. This was brought in from Eversley Manor House and, with its alternation of twisted balusters with normal, Jacobean, vertically symmetrical balusters, is probably of the mid C17. Along the E front are the former Dining Room, with a black and white marble chimneypiece, and other rooms. One of these has an Early Georgian chimneypiece. A N room has the fireplace in an angle. The chimneypiece comes from Moore Place Farm (*see* below) and is Jacobean and quite ornate. In a small room next to the N archway is an early C16 doorway, and it may well be that at that time the gatehouse was here.

In the W range is a charming early C18 staircase to the newly made mezzanine.

More rooms of interest on the first floor. Above the hall is the so-called Chapel Drawing Room. The ceiling has plaster decoration with thin ribs and small pendants. Above the fire-place a decorated lintel with Early Renaissance decoration. The Chapel lies in the E wing of the S front. It must originally have been larger, and it is highly likely that the obviously interfered-with window in the S wall of the courtyard (called 'of the former chapel') is the re-set main window of the chapel. It is very large, with three transoms and four-centred heads to all lights. That may at first seem a much earlier motif, but the Hatfield Chapel has it very similar. The ceiling of the chapel in its present form has broad bands in geometrical patterns. – REREDOS of four painted Saints. It looks *c.*1840. – Along the E side several rooms with plaster ceilings and chimneypieces. Especially good the marble chimneypiece in the room above the former dining room, with two orders of flanking columns and a broad-banded ceiling with small pendants. A similar chimneypiece in the former Library. The range of rooms culminates in the Long Gallery along the whole length of the N front: 126½ ft long, with another broad-banded stucco ceiling and an elaborate wooden chimneypiece.

N of the N front the former GATEWAY, a middle arch and two low side arches, all members again studded with decoration.

From the S the house is approached by a long, straight avenue and a GATEHOUSE, probably of the C18. Two three-storeyed turrets with caps and a battlemented centre.

MOORE PLACE FARM, ¾ m. NW. The big central chimney with three diagonally placed stacks and moulded top is the most impressive feature. It must be C16. In addition two big chimneybreasts, also with moulded tops.

8030

BRAMSHOTT

ST MARY. Cruciform and no doubt a C13 building, though nave and aisles are of 1872 (by *S. C. Capes*). Of the C13 the chancel E lancets, a stepped group of three, the N lancets (the S windows are Perp), and the heavy, rather clumsy N and S arches.

The W and E arches are Victorian. So is the shingled broach-spire. The N and S transepts themselves have Early Perp fenestration. Two prominent squints from the transepts into the chancel. – STAINED GLASS. In a chancel N window mediæval bits. – In the N aisle W window good *Holiday* glass of 1895, very much influenced by Burne-Jones. – PLATE. Paten, *c.*1630; Chalice, 1641. – MONUMENTS. John Weston and wife, brass with long scrolls upward from their mouths. C15. The figures are 17½ in. long. – Sir James Macdonald † 1832 and his son † 1831 aged ten. By *Westmacott Jun.* Relief of St James, as a pilgrim, and the little boy.

IMMACULATE CONCEPTION (R.C.), on the Liphook–Headley Road. 1911. Perp; no tower. Turret in the corner of the nave and a S appendix. By Canon *Scoles & G. Raymond.*

BRAMSHOTT MANOR, S of the church. The ground floor is of stone and has big-shaped though not very large C14 to C15 windows, to the S one of two lights, to the W a pair of such set so closely that the hood-mould stops become two little heads under one hood. The upper floor is tile-hung and supposed to be of the C15. (The VCH mentions original roof timbers.)

BRAMSHOTT PLACE. To the l. of the drive to the house is a miniature brick Tudor gatehouse of *c.*1575. The gateway has a four-centred head. The angles have polygonal buttress shafts, two with a trellis pattern, two encrusted with closely set blobs. Small upper windows. To the N a tiny oriel. Big, shaped (i.e. ogee) gables. The gatehouse probably led into the front garden of a house (cf. e.g. Stutton Hall, Suffolk).

BRAMSHOTT VALE, ½ m. W. Early Georgian. The front is now of 2 + 1 + 2 windows, but originally had the typical very narrow early C18 windows l. and r. of the centre. The present porch is Later Georgian, but round the corner is what must have been the original doorway, with the characteristic lintel coming up by curves to a point in the middle.

WOOLMER LODGE, ¾ m. N. Now a Carmelite monastery. Plain C19 Tudor house, but of what date? It was built for Sir James Macdonald by *P. F. Robinson* in 1827–8, but looks mid C19. (Inside an excellent early C18 staircase with carved tread-ends.) The stables are Elizabethan or Jacobean.

PASSFIELD LABORATORIES (Metal Containers Ltd), off Hollywater Road, Passfield Common. 1959–61 by the *Architects' Co-partnership*. Offices as well as laboratories. The building is grouped round a turfed courtyard with the canteen on one short side. Workshops etc. make up a separate building.

This is faced with cedar slatting. The main group is white brick and black steel frame. A well-planned and visually very successful group.

1090 BRANSGORE

ST MARY. 1822 by *J. Hannaford*, the chancel of 1873 (by *Ferrey*). Brick. W tower with later recessed spire. Lancets with wooden Y-tracery. Wide, aisleless nave. Apsed chancel. – FONT. Perp, octagonal. The bowl is moulded and has a small frieze of quatrefoils and encircled shields, and a yet smaller fleuron frieze. The font is supposed to have come from Christchurch. STAINED GLASS. In the apse by *Powell*, 1874 (the design by *Burrow*).

1010 BREAMORE

ST MARY. Breamore is by far the most important and interesting Anglo-Saxon monument in Hampshire. There are no documentary indications of its date, but *c.*1000 is likely. The church is what one would call in a Romanesque, i.e. in England a Norman, church cruciform, but the Anglo-Saxon mason was not aware of the order which in a true Romanesque church the square of the crossing imposes on the rest. At Breamore the crossing is a square, and the nave is of the same width, but neither the chancel nor the transepts are. Of the chancel only the W ends of N and S walls are Anglo-Saxon, but the S transept survives complete, and that is considerably smaller and lower than the nave, a characteristic of Early Christian (Milan) and early medieval churches on the Continent as well – as against Romanesque ones. Moreover, the surviving arch from the crossing to the S transept is narrow, thereby destroying the spatial unity which is implied in the cruciform Romanesque plan, and the original chancel arch was comparatively narrow too.

Now what of Anglo-Saxon features is actually preserved, and what do they look like? Nothing in the chancel, the long-and-short quoins of the central tower, the S transept in its entire masonry (but the E doorway is Norman) and with the complete arch to the crossing, the roof-line of the chancel, the roof-line of the former N transept and one jamb of the arch between N transept and crossing, in the nave two lesenes made up of stones on the long-and-short principle, one N and one S, and the foot of another, and finally two N windows, one

S window (blocked by the porch), all double-splayed and high up, three altered windows in the tower, and two in the S transept (E and – altered – S). The W quoins have gone. The S transept arch has a square capital-cum-abacus with a rope motif along top and bottom and an inscription round the unmoulded arch reading: HER SPUTELAD SEO GECPYDRAEDNEC DE (Here the covenant is explained to thee). Above and not in axis one of the mysterious upper doorways so often leading nowhere in Anglo-Saxon churches. It has been presumed that the tower must have had an upper chamber, but there may just as well have been some wooden gallery. Above the chancel arch is a remnant of another inscription (DES).

The chancel arch and the W arch of the crossing tower are four-centred and probably late C14. They have much decoration with large nobbly leaves. The chancel itself is over-restored, but the reticulated tracery of the E window indicates an early C14 date. Finally in the nave the S doorway is Norman (one order of shafts, capitals with several scallops, arch with roll). So is the porch entrance, but here one may assume that the entrance is re-set, especially as the C13 arch above, on the upper floor of the porch, is clearly not *in situ*.

SCULPTURE. Above the S doorway, i.e. in the porch, is a monumental Saxon ROOD in relief. The figures are all laboriously hacked off, but it is clear that we have here exactly the same kind of rood as at Headbourne Worthy, only that the Christ here, as against both Headbourne and Romsey, is bent by suffering in a way which anticipates the Gothic. Especially the arms, raised like wings, are unforgettable, though the bent body is even more like the C13 or early C14. – Also above the S doorway is a small Norman medallion with the Lamb and Cross. – PAINTING. Behind the rood are traces of landscape and buildings. On the W wall of the porch Judas hanged. What is the date? – PLATE. Set of 1745.

BREAMORE HOUSE. A large Late Elizabethan brick house, reduced in its architectural interest by a fire in 1856 and the rebuilding after. The S façade is as it was, on an E-plan so shallow that the wings project no more than the porch. The porch, the wings, and the recessed parts all have plain, straight gables, and the whole front is indeed, with its even three- and four-light transomed windows, plain and sensible. The doorway is an insertion of 1670. Untouched by the fire was the wing projecting E on the N side. On its first floor, in one room, is a simple, attractive Elizabethan fireplace. The staircase in this wing is of vertically symmetrical balusters, halved some time later to make them go a longer way. In the main range of the house are two gorgeous chimneypieces. The one in the hall has bulgy tapering pilasters, a lintel with fruit, and an overmantel with statuettes and much strapwork. The dining room chimneypiece has two strapping termini girls l. and r., placed frontally, and in the overmantel a fine cartouche.

C18 STABLES of nine bays with a three-bay pediment on four Doric pilasters.

Victorian CLOCK TOWER, octagonal, three-storeyed, with cupola.

RECTORY. Probably of *c.*1830. Three bays with three steep gables.

NORTH CHARFORD MANOR, 1 m. NE. Is this Early Georgian (cf. e.g. West Hanney, Berkshire of 1727)? Red brick, three bays, tripartite windows, the centre bay raised to three storeys, with curved sides to connect it with the rest of the house, a Venetian window, and a small semicircular fancy pediment.

MIZMAZE, on Breamore Down above Breamore House.* The maze is of turf and chalk and surrounded by young yew-trees.

GIANT'S GRAVE LONG BARROW, on Breamore Down, $1\frac{3}{4}$ m. NW of Breamore. The mound has been badly damaged by cultivation and now has a length of 180 ft. It is 84 ft wide at its broader E end, where it stands 11 ft high. The flanking quarry ditches are clearly visible.

BRIDGEMARY *see* ROWNER

BROADHALFPENNY DOWN *see* HAMBLEDON

3020

BROADLANDS

1 m. S of Romsey

Broadlands when Celia Fiennes saw it was 'halfe a Roman H', i.e. one range of rooms and two projecting wings. They projected to the E. All this still exists, though the space between the wings is filled in and the main, i.e. W, range has a whole second range parallel to it now forming the E façade. These alterations are the work of the second Viscount Palmerston. They were done *c.*1767–8 by *Lancelot Brown* (Capability Brown), and further important alterations were made by

*A description of how to find it was given by Mr Geoffrey Grigson in *C. L.*, vol. 132, p. 604.

Holland in 1788. The house as it now is is faced with yellow brick, a material made fashionable in the middle of the C18, and has, on the entrance (E) side, nine bays and a three-bay recessed loggia of very slender pink giant Ionic columns and on the garden (W) side the same number of bays but a giant three-bay portico with pediment. This centrepiece is rendered to appear stone. Some of the principal windows on both sides are pedimented too. The main features of the exterior can be attributed to Holland, for reasons of style. The loggia is followed by one of Holland's characteristic lobbies, octagonal with a skylight, and then by an entrance hall with a N aisle of three bays, the l. and r. bays domed. This is Holland again, but the entrance hall itself is no doubt of 1766. It is equipped for statuary. The main staircase is on the l. It has an iron balustrade of simple lyre-shapes and runs on through two storeys. In the S wing are two rooms with fine, very dainty stucco ceilings, the second of them at the SW corner starting the W suite. The climax is the saloon in the centre of the W 70 front. The stucco is what can be safely called Adamish and presumably of *c.*1788. Drawing room and saloon are connected by an arch. The arch opposite in the saloon holds a mirror. Both arches are a C20 alteration. The room also has stucco wall panels. In the library at the NW corner only two pedimented bookcases are left. The subsidiary staircase is still in its C17 form, and on the first floor is one room with late C17 wood panelling and Gibbonsish details.

In the grounds the ORANGERY with a portico and pediment at one short end. The portico has Ionic columns, but at the corners Ionic pillars instead. In the GROUNDS are genuine Greek altars with reliefs.

The STABLES were mentioned by Celia Fiennes, and they are indeed clearly of the later C17, with wooden cross-windows, vertically placed oval windows on the upper floor, and a hipped roof. The *ensemble* would probably be assigned to about 1675.

The LODGE to Broadlands is by *Nesfield* and was built in 1870. It is very characteristic of his smaller works: of red brick, with half-timbering and tile-hung gables. There is also patterned pargetting, and Nesfield's high chimneys are in evidence too.

RANVILLE'S FARMHOUSE, 1 m. SW. C16, much restored. Timber-framed with brick nogging. The best feature is the gabled dormer with a canted oriel.

3000

BROCKENHURST

ST PETER. Brick W tower of 1761. Still with raised brick quoins The tower has a shingled spire rising from an odd shingled domical base. N aisle of 1832 with arched windows and iron columns inside. Nave and chancel are medieval, the nave Norman – see the doorway with scalloped capitals and, in the arch, zigzag at r. angles to the wall. The chancel is late C13 – see the intersecting and Y-tracery of the windows. – In the chancel a RECESS, cinquecusped and still without ogees. – FONT. Purbeck marble, of the table type. The decoration mostly the familiar flat arches. – COMMUNION RAIL. C18. – WEST GALLERY. Through nave and aisle. – STAINED GLASS. In the chancel side windows naturalistic vine, passion-flower, lily, and sunflowers. There was a restoration in 1896. – PLATE. Set of 1735. – In the churchyard is one of the enormous Hampshire yew trees.

ST SAVIOUR. 1903 by *Romaine-Walker & Besant.* Grey (Swanage) stone, big, without a tower. The details Dec. Nave and aisles. The chancel with striking galleries l. and r., the one distinguishing motif of the church. All the projected ornamental carving – even cusps – was left undone.

RHINEFIELD LODGE, 3 m. NW. By *Romaine-Walker & Tanner,* for Lionel Walker Munro. 1888–90. Estimate for 'completing the carcase and finishing' over £18,000 (GS). Large, Tudor, i.e. Elizabethan, mixed with Flamboyant and Gothic motifs. The building is composed with panache. (The house has a great hall of 67 by 25 ft with a hammerbeam roof and stylistically a mixture of Gothic and Jacobean. 'The principal cellar has a capacity of 1,000 dozen.' *Builder,* 17 August 1889)

WOODPECKERS, Sway Road. By *Paul Phipps, c.*1923–4. Tudor, rendered, with gables but a Georgian doorway. Phipps is not an architect one meets often.

(LITTLE WEIRS. By *Paul Phipps, c.*1922–3. *C.L.*)

BROCKHURST *see* GOSPORT, pp. 243, 247, 249, 253

3030

BROUGHTON

ST MARY. As usual, the interior is more interesting than the exterior. N arcade of, say, *c.*1200. Three bays, round piers, multi-scallop capitals, round abaci, pointed arches with two slight chamfers. S arcade of *c.*1210. The capitals are now moulded. Then the nave was extended to the W, cf. the one N and one S lancet and the W doorway (with dogtooth in the arch) which is now re-set in the Perp W tower. Other external motifs are Perp too. – PILLAR PISCINA. Large and Perp. The pillar was originally attached to the wall. – PAINTING. The Descent from the Cross. Small, and made up as the centre of a triptych. Dutch, early C16; excellent. – STAINED GLASS. E window by *Kempe*, 1904. – PLATE. Chalice and Paten of 1731. – In the churchyard a circular brick DOVECOTE with a conical roof and a little lantern; C17.

Several good timber-framed as well as Georgian brick houses. As examples of the latter e.g. OLD CHURCH FARM with an apsidal door-hood, and THE LINDENS with a graceful late C18 door surround with thin Tuscan columns carrying a broken segmental pediment.

ROUND BARROWS, in Whiteshoot Plantation, on the S edge of Broughton Down. The most conspicuous monument is a fine bell barrow 60 ft in diameter and 6 ft high with low saucer barrows to the E and W. The large mound has a central depression suggestive of robbing.

LONG BARROW. *See* Nether Wallop.

BROWN CANDOVER

5030

ST PETER. 1845 by *Thomas Henry Wyatt*. Coursed knapped flint and stone. SW tower with lead broach-spire. Big nave and short chancel. Tiled roofs. Perp features. Cold interior. – COMMUNION RAIL. From Northington church. Pierced panels of lush acanthus and, mixed up with them, putti with Christian symbols. Said to be Italian, but more probably Flemish. – MONUMENT. Brass to a husband and wife; *c*.1520. They stand praying, but arm in arm, and are cut out of one brass plate. A flower grows behind and between them. The figures are 19 in. long.

BUCKLERS HARD

4000

The late C18 street, wide and with broad grass verges running down to the Beaulieu River, looks odd, almost entirely on its own. Cottages l. and r., as one solid terrace. Top r. has a date 1774, bottom l. is a little more formal, with an enriched doorcase. The reason for this curious display is that the second Duke of Montagu intended to make Bucklers Hard into a port and that, although his plan miscarried, it became for a while

Brown Candover, brass to a husband and wife, *c.*1520

a centre of shipbuilding. Henry Adam started it in 1749. Many warships of Nelson's time were built here.

ST LEONARD'S GRANGE, 1¼ m. S. A grange of Beaulieu Abbey. The house with the raised brick window surrounds looks *c.*1700, but next to it stands the ruin of a chapel of about 1300. The large E and W windows are still recognizable, though of the tracery one can only say that it seems to have been pre-ogee. In its completed form this plain parallelepiped must have been beautiful.

BARN. Of the enormous grange barn the E gable and part of the W gable survive and show with unforgettable force what a mighty building such a monastic collecting-point could be. The barn was 216 ft long and 60 ft high.

BULLINGTON

4040

ST MICHAEL. Nave and chancel in one. The nave is Norman, see the blocked N doorway, one N window, and one S window. The chancel is E.E., see the one S lancet and the lancet re-set in the vestry. Victorian W tower of flint and brick. Is it of 1871, when the church was restored? Re-set early C14 W window.

BULLSDOWN HILLFORT *see* SHERFIELD-ON-LODDON

BURGHCLERE

4060

ALL SAINTS, Old Burghclere, 2 m. S of the new church. Large, of flint, with a low bell-turret. The nave has two Norman doorways. The N doorway is Early Norman. One order of columns, plain capitals with a volute. Billet in the arch. The S doorway has a tympanum with fish-scale pattern and may be later. C13 chancel with priest's doorway and lancets, all over-restored. C13 also the W doorway, with two orders of shafts, stiff-leaf capitals, and several rolls in the arch. One of the orders of shafts has fillets. N transept of *c.*1300, cf. the inter-sected tracery of the E and N windows. The nave inside is long and shapeless. N transept arch dying into the imposts – which goes with the date of the windows. The chancel arch is the same. – PLATE. Paten of 1664; Chalice of 1837; undated Chalice. – MONUMENTS. Many; e.g. Anne Eyre † 1745, a standing monument without figures. Strange section through a sarcophagus, if that is what it is meant to be. – Herbert family of Highclere, made up of tiles. To 1862. – Edward H. C. Herbert, 1872. Gothic almond-shape, with dogtooth.

ASCENSION. 1838 by *G. Guillaume* (GR). The church was remodelled in 1875 by *W. G. Adey* of Reading under the supervision of *Norman Shaw*. The chancel is theirs and of no particular interest. Is the tower-top with two-light mullioned windows theirs as well? The church of 1838 is aisleless, with transepts, low pitched roofs with thin timber-work, and E.E. details. – PLATE. Chalice, illegibly dated; Set of 1837.

SANDHAM MEMORIAL CHAPEL, next to the former station. The first quarter of the C20 was the heroic age of modern painting. Today everything is possible and will find enthusiastic journalists and a patron. The development from Kandinsky, Klee, Duchamp, and Schwitters to 1960–5 is negligible. The step from Impressionism to Cubism, Expressionism, and abstraction was into unknown and dangerous territory. France created Cubism, Germany's strength was Expressionism, both reached abstraction. England was peripheral, and her contributions were inspired by one or another French trend. The only exception is *Stanley Spencer*, whose Expressionism came to full fruition after the first world war and is essentially original. The Burghclere Chapel is thus the outstanding English monument to painting of the pioneering years.

The chapel was commissioned by Mr and Mrs J. L. Behrend to allow Stanley Spencer to paint the cycle he was working on, and also to be a war memorial and more specifically a memorial to Lieut. H. W. Sandham, who had died in 1919 from an illness contracted in the war in Macedonia. The chapel was designed by *Lionel Pearson*. It is an oblong block of brick with stone dressings, and l. and r. of it low three-bay neo-Georgian cottages. The chapel itself, while not strictly imitative, suffers from the very conventionality which Stanley Spencer abhorred. All he wanted was a 'holy box'. He painted the interior from 1927 to 1932, but based his work on sketches made immediately after the war. It was these that gave the Behrends the idea of commissioning him. He was twenty-seven in 1919 and thirty-six, and at the summit of his art, when he started in the chapel. He had spent part of the war as an orderly in a Bristol hospital and later went to Macedonia.

There are nineteen paintings in the chapel, and they are arranged as follows:

E WALL

Resurrection of the dead soldiers

N WALL

Morning in the camp at Kavasuli

The arrival of a convoy of wounded at the hospital	Hospital washroom	Kit inspection	Dug-out Salonika
Scrubbing the floor	Moving kit-bags	Sorting laundry	Filling tea-urns

S WALL

Soldiers in the river-bed at Todorovo

Shaving under mosquito nets	Convoy of wounded filling water-bottles	Officer and his men map-reading	Making a fire-belt
Ward with frost-bitten soldier	Tea in the ward	Bed-making	Washing lockers

In looking at the titles of the paintings the essential quality of Spencer's war recording is at once patent. There is no battle, no sword-rattling, no shining heroism. A war is not fought but undergone. It needs endurance day after day. The headline stuff is no business of other ranks.

The E wall is entirely filled by the Resurrection of the Dead, exactly as in Michelangelo's Sistine Chapel. But there is no Christ in Judgement. Christ is a small, white, distant figure, lovable and pathetic, and His role is not to elevate to Heaven and condemn to Hell. He is there just to receive the crosses which the soldiers hand in. In the foreground they rise, from under the thicket of tumbled crosses, shake hands, and clamber up in confusion. The pattern of all the crosses is disturbing. So is the pair of pink mules, large in the middle, with hieratically long necks turning l. and r. The men are not a variety of types, but mostly one and the same type, with flat, fat impassive faces and round limbs. We are looking at all this at an odd angle, as if from the air. This device to combat everyday normality was familiar to the Mannerists of the C16, and so was the device of placing the most important figure far away and high up, and also the stylizing of the human figures into enforced inertia. Yet no one in England in 1932, let alone 1919, knew about Mannerism. On the other hand there are also parallels with Casorati and even de Chirico, and also the German *Neue Sachlichkeit*. On the N wall, bottom l., is a shell-shocked soldier scrubbing the hospital floor, violently prostrate, and alone in his tragedy with the others stepping by him and over him. This scene is exceptional in alluding so directly to tragedy. In the Moving of Kitbags, bottom two, the man on the l. shows particularly clearly how Spencer's figures are stylized into sack-like shapes so as to limit their freedom of action. Bruegel is the Mannerist who did that before, and Bruegel Spencer must have known and admired. Bottom three is a battle with laundry, and it is again typical how the r. hand soldier is nearly hidden by the geometrical shape of the towel – a sugar-loaf man. On the extreme r. is the only woman. Never is an episode told in a workaday way. Spencer intensifies and removes the stories from reality. At the bottom r. it is the huge tea-urns which provide the geometry.

The larger pictures of the second tier are upright and arched. In the Arrival of the Convoy Spencer's Mannerist trick of the view down at an angle is specially effective. The slings of the wounded are white triangles, the big hats are straight from Bruegel. Spencer's vegetation is dappled and flat. Background space must not be too true to nature and
96 perspective either. In the washroom the soap-sud helmets are Bruegelish again. i.e. a lifting of the person out of what one would normally see about him. The soldier whose wound is being treated with iodine stands fat and inert. Kit inspection seems to move up a hill steeply. The gaiters must have pleased Spencer, converting human into insect legs. In the trench scene the principal figure, an exceptionally cool and courageous sergeant, is dressed up with fern to conceal him. The belts, taken off because the trench was so tight, form a pattern as unexpected as that of the crosses. The background is clouds of barbed wire. The top picture is not easily seen, and it spreads out in episodes. In front of one of the two rows of tents – dominant geometry again – stands the one really martial figure. But his sword is a stick to pick up litter, and his shield is a bag.

On the S side the first picture of the bottom row is a ward with soldiers in night-shirts and blankets all as baggy shapes, and the wire frame for the treatment of frostbite offering a view into a grotesque cave. There is horror, but also compassion in these hospital glimpses, and never sentimentality. Tea in the Ward: Here in particular the identity of the mask-like faces is baffling. Number three has pin-ups on the wall, some of them private records of Stanley Spencer. The man on the l. in his bolder of bed-clothes ought to be noted. He is sitting in a chair while his bed is being made. The Washing of Lockers is the most abstract picture of the series. The men play a minor part between curved baths and angular lockers.

Above, first l. is again full Mannerism, Tintoretto in the encasing of men in transparent abstract shapes and the others lining the margin. Only brushwork and modelling are of course utterly different from Tintoretto. The next scene could almost be a Mannerist painting of the C16, with the men in their ground-sheets converging and looking like strange angels in some incomprehensible glory. The topees also contribute to making the scene belong to a distant age. Large in the foreground two pink mules. In the map-reading scene the centre is the only officer in the whole cycle. That also is telling. He is sitting on a horse, but the map almost hides that. The men around form a radiating pattern. The view down at an angle is as before. So is the dappled leaf background, counteracting the funnelling foreshortening of the front parts. Making a fire-belt has connotations of Vulcan's Smithy. The ropes of the tent and the absurdly over-foreshortened long tube are worth looking for. Finally the top episode, looser than the rest, which was unavoidable in such a sprawling shape. The soldiers on the l. are playing housey-housey, in the middle they are washing clothes.

In the whole of the cycle there is no red, nor a strong blue or yellow. What one remembers is grey, browns, beiges, and silvery greens.

The chapel had already been dedicated in 1927. There was no special celebration for the finishing of the paintings. In fact one must be grateful to the church authorities for having tolerated a cycle as silent about organized religion as about the glories of a won war.

SILVER BIRCHES, $\frac{3}{8}$ m. W of the new church. By *Colin Lucas*, 1927. Still pre-Corbusian, but already with a sense of formality and of unbroken wall surfaces. Colin Lucas was twenty-one when he designed the house, and it is no longer as it was then. In fact, the *Architectural Association Journal* calls it 'altered out of recognition'.

BEACON HILL, 2 m. SW. The fort is of univallate construction, with a well preserved bank 7 ft high and ditch 10 ft deep enclosing an area of 12 acres. The entrance on the S is a complicated one, with the bank and ditch inturned and additional outworks to provide further protection for this weak point in the defences. Within the fort numerous small circular grass-grown mounds mark the position of huts 20–30 ft in diameter.

SEVEN BARROWS. *See* Litchfield.

7020

BURITON

ST MARY. Immediately below the Downs, culminating in Butser Hill, the highest elevation of Hampshire (888 ft). The church is of ironstone. Externally the chancel of the later C13 is the only noteworthy element. Bar tracery with an uncusped circle in the side window. Also priest's doorway. Three stepped SEDILIA with pointed-trefoiled arches and PISCINA of the same date. The interior is exceptionally fine. Four-bay arcades of the late C12. Round piers, multi-scalloped capitals, Greek-cross abaci (i.e. square with nicked corners), round, single-step arches. The tower arch is a great surprise. It has semicircular responds of enormous heaviness, and they stand on stone tables, projecting towards the centre so as to leave only a passage free. What can they have been meant for? Seats? A screen open in the middle? The feature is clearly C13. The tower* has otherwise nothing of interest. – FONT. Purbeck marble, of table type, on five supports. Badly preserved. – PLATE. Cup and Cover Paten, 1669; Paten on foot, 1702; Flagon, given 1740. – MONUMENT. Engraved polished black marble plate with kneeling figures. To Thomas Hanbury † 1617. – (Thomas Bilson † 1695. Tomb-chest and good wall tablet. In the vestry. RH)

MANOR HOUSE. The house of Edward Gibbon's father. A singularly felicitous composition of the Early Georgian years. The house is brick-faced and has to the garden a façade of five bays and three storeys. Grey headers and red dressings. Windows with one white keystone. Round the corner the house is part of the square yard. It has a big canted bay window here and is continued by a lower (older) house with two symmetrical porches. This is of malm and brick, as are the farm buildings. It has a large BARN opposite and the stables on the r.

*Rebuilt in 1714 (RH).

The former has two cart entrances with basket arches reaching up into a broken pediment. The STABLES have a steep central pediment. Gibbon in his Autobiography wrote of the house: 'An old mansion in a state of decay has been converted into the fashion and convenience of a modern house . . ., and if strangers had nothing to see, the inhabitants had little to desire.' (Elegant and spacious staircase with three slender balusters to the tread. *C.L.*)

NURSTED HOUSE, 1 m. NE. Late C17, malm and brick. Seven bays, with a pedimented three-bay projection. The windows have raised surrounds with lugs, the angles raised brick quoins. The doorway with Tuscan columns and a triglyph frieze looks *c.*1760. Outbuilding of malm and brick.

OLD DITCHAM FARM, 1¼ m. E. The farm has a BARN which is truly amazing. It is of malm and brick, and the window details point to a date in the early C18. But inside are a series of enormous pointed malmstone arches, completely unmoulded, carrying the roof, instead of the normal timbers. Can this be of the same time as the barn? The arches do not seem bonded in. They look like Lethaby *c.*1900. Could they be Gothic of *c.*1800? For *c.*1720 they are almost unbelievable.

BURLEY 2000

ST JOHN BAPTIST. 1839 by *Charles Underwood* (GR). Brick, with lancets. *Butterfield* added the chancel in 1886–7, and probably the W front too. It is remarkable how willingly he kept to the lancets and how he kept his own personality under control.

BURSLEDON [DL] 4000

Subtopia on the Southampton–Portsmouth road, except where it sweeps across the Hamble estuary; a secluded village, elusively disposed about a network of side roads, to the S. Warships built in the C17 and C18; yachts in the C20; for long a centre of brickmaking.

ST LEONARD. Away both from old and newer Bursledon, reached from the old village by a wooded path. Essentially by *Sedding*, who in 1888 remodelled a church which had suffered large-scale alterations in 1828. All features of 1828 were expurgated, but medieval ones were conserved, notably the fine C13 chancel arch of two orders, double-chamfered, the inner order resting on short shafts which end with corbels carved with realistic faces. The chancel has restored lancets N and S, and a neo-Perp E window of Sedding's, containing colourful glass which makes an effective termination to the eastward view. The transepts, wholly of 1888, have W aisles. The nave has medieval walling, and a small blocked C13 doorway on the S side. Sedding's most elaborate treatment is at the W end. Here the centre part of the W wall is brought out in a square bay, surmounted by a half-timbered, tile-topped belfry, and a colonnaded wooden porch, full of twirly-rustic detailing, spans the W front. All this is apt in the church's picturesque setting on a slope, beside a wood-filled hollow. – FONT. Massive round C12 bowl, with intersecting arcade pattern on about a third of the circumference, including miniature pilasters and capitals with elementary triangular incisions. The rest of the circumference has the same pattern of pilasters and capitals, similarly spaced, but there are only narrow pointed arches, not intersecting. The base is C19. – WALL PAINTING. 1892. The three Maries round the tomb, above the W door. Faded now, but in keeping with Sedding's architecture. – PLATE. Elizabethan Cup. – MONUMENTS. Tablet to Philemon Ewer, shipbuilder, † 1794, by *J. Nutcher* of Swaythling, with a representation in relief of a man o'war below. – On the external N wall of the nave a cartouche to John Champion † 1773, with a good Rococo surround. – Next to it a tablet to John Taylor † 1691, with representations of brickmakers' tools in the surround.

Bursledon's houses are disposed with a casualness that is at first disconcerting, in loose groups of seldom more than four or five at a time, so that one never seems to get into the heart of the place. This elusiveness in time becomes endearing. The village looks as if it was prettified as a whole at some time early in the C20; evidence of this is in the widespread repetition of walls composed of semicircular tiles in openwork, and in the distinctively Edwardian features added to many older buildings. Individual houses scarcely need mentioning: there are timber-framed survivals (e.g. THE DOLPHIN, formerly an inn, at the S end of the village, with upper-storeyed porch, restored but not overwhelmingly), late C17 and C18 houses in local grey brick tempered with red (e.g. GREYWELL, *c.*1700, with segmental keystoned window-heads), and plain-and-fancy Victorian ones. The most intriguing group in the village is of single-storey buildings, probably of mid C19 origin, but embellished in the early C20, round an open irregular courtyard, formally laid out with a massive circular feature in the middle, against which are crouching lions; there are lion corbels on the buildings around the courtyard, as well as a striking symmetrical array of tall well-corbelled chimneys; stepways have the characteristic semicircular tile pattern. But the village's real gem, quite unsuspected, lies at the back of a big bland Victorian house (now split up) to which it is physically attached.

CHAPEL OF OUR LADY OF THE ROSARY (R.C.). Built in 1906 by a local leading light, Mrs Shawe-Storey (was she responsible for the general prettification of the village?) and furnished to embarrassing richness with Continental fittings, mostly wooden, mostly Baroque, mostly German. Nothing precise, alas, seems to be known of their origin. Only a brief and selective catalogue is possible; all the features mentioned are wooden. – COMMUNION RAIL. Semicircular, on a grand scale; balustraded. – ALTARPIECE. Carved panel of the Last Supper. – REREDOS. Exuberant Baroque. Twisted columns, rounded recessed centrepiece with unsophisticated statue of Our Lady and representations of a monk and a priest on either side, broken pediment, and a cherub on top holding a golden ball. – PANELLING. Round the apse beside the altar; very delicate and detailed carved representations of biblical scenes in medallions. – STATUES. Good Shepherd, carrying sheep. – Virgin and Child, in a shell-hooded recess in the altarpiece of the S chapel, with outstretched arms. – Figure in relief of St Peter, with tears descending; moving. – The aisles are entered through wide square-headed recesses, two on each side, each of them with massive twisted columns set against each side; similar columns support a large entablature against the W wall. Many lesser features. The building itself is almost negative architecturally, except for an elaborate Gothic bellcote over the E end.

Finally the river. Strangely, Old Bursledon lies mainly aloof from it, on higher ground (the separation is strengthened by the railway), but there are repeated sudden views over watery expanses. By the riverside itself is the JOLLY SAILOR, a pleasant C18 inn in grey and red brick, placed on the N side of a peninsula, from which there is a view past corrugated iron boathouses, not unpleasing in aggregate, to the openwork concrete inter-war bridge.

1090 BURTON

ST LUKE. 1874–5 by *Benjamin & Edmund B. Ferrey*. Red brick, E.E., bellcote on a thin buttress. Two-light windows l. and r. No aisles. Plate tracery. The chancel must originally have had a W as well as an E arch.

BURTON HALL. Of *c.*1750. Red brick, two and a half storeys. Seven bays, the middle three slightly projecting. In this projection the narrow windows of Queen Anne's time flank the middle window. Doorway with Corinthian columns, pediment, and a decorated frieze.

BURY *see* GOSPORT, p. 257

BURY HILL *see* UPPER CLATFORD

BUTSER HILL *see* PETERSFIELD

CALLEVA ATREBATUM *see* SILCHESTER

4000 CALSHOT CASTLE

One of Henry VIII's castles to defend the south coast against Francis I. Round stone tower, low, with parapet. No proper study has yet been made of the castle.

CAMS HALL *see* FAREHAM

CASTLE MALWOOD *see* MINSTEAD

7010 CATHERINGTON [DL]

The outer tentacles of Greater Portsmouth's suburban development have stretched along the London road nearly to Clanfield and up the Lovedean valley to the W but, in between, Catherington remains unspoilt, a loosely scattered place where the rural background is more in evidence than the buildings themselves.

ALL SAINTS. Stands at the head of a spur of chalkland, with an enormous view southward (best seen in a misty atmosphere, when the details of the suburban spread are blurred). A medium-sized church, almost all of the later C12, except for the details which date from the thorough restoration of 1883 (by *Edmund Ferrey*). Nave and chancel of the same width and with no structural division between them, N and S aisles under lean-to roofs, large N chapel under separately pitched roof,

and SW tower. The S arcade is of three bays, with fairly slender round columns and simple scalloped capitals; the round arches, of two orders, have deeply incised mouldings and are later in character than the piers. The N arcade has a W respond similar to the piers of the S arcade, and similarly moulded arches, but the piers are different, alternately round and octagonal and with simply moulded capitals. Possibly there was some cessation of building for a time after the piers of the S arcade and the W respond of the N arcade were built. The N arcade continues without a break into an E bay opening from chancel to chapel and ends, very curiously, in a further bay of about half the width of the others and correspondingly lower, although the details are similar. The aisle windows are all Victorian restoration. The S door is of two orders, chamfered, the outer order having engaged shafts. The tower has small round-headed Norman lights on its ground and first storeys, and a plain C18 battlemented top. Opening from tower to nave is a pointed arch of two orders with simple capitals; a similar smaller arch opens from tower to S aisle. The W nave window arrangement, with two lancets and a round window above, is C19. The E chancel window has a C13 surround, with thin internal mouldings and shafts (cf. Hambledon, South Hayling), but a small standard Perp window has been inserted within the frame. Finally the large N chapel, with two widely spaced lancets in its E wall and a circular window in the gable above them, and a N window frame like that of the chancel E window but with a two-light Tudor window inserted. The roof of the nave, possibly C14, is an impressive piece of carpentry; the tie-beams are slightly moulded and rest on small rounded brackets, and some of the upper members make pronounced curves. – FURNISHINGS. Mostly from the 1883 restoration. – SCULPTURE. The shaft and part of the head of a former churchyard cross preserved in the N aisle, with the badly weathered remains of the Crucifixus between St Mary and St John; C14 style. – WALL PAINTINGS. A restored representation of St Michael weighing souls on the N nave wall. Little 31
suggestion of colour is left, but the delineation is very clear – obviously much restored, but giving a better impression of the original design than unrestored faded fragments. The archangel is in active posture, with wings outstretched, holding an upraised sword in one hand and a scale in the other. From one end of the scale a bundle of souls is suspended, and a demon with curly tail is trying to weigh down the beam to

condemn them to damnation. But the Virgin Mary is standing near the other end of the beam, holding it to save the souls from being weighed down, and carrying another soul ready for assessment. Professor Tristram assigns the painting to *c.*1350. On the frame of the rounded upper window of the E wall of the N chapel are traces of patterning. – PLATE. Cup, given in 1660; Paten, given in 1663. – MONUMENT. In the N chapel the canopied tomb of Sir Nicholas Hyde † 1631 and his wife. Two life-sized effigies on a table tomb, hers behind and on a slightly raised level; heads on pillows; hands in prayer. Shallow rounded canopy with panelled underside, scrolls, and cartouches in the spandrels. Entablature and broken pediment with large coat of arms at the top. Prominent columns of marble with Corinthian capitals to either side. Small childlike figures of Time and Death are shown, among other decorative features, at the back of the canopy, and larger figures, representing Justice and Wisdom, rise from the top of the monument, above the columns. Ten children are represented on the front of the table tomb itself. A fine monument of the period, with sophisticated but not over-elaborate decoration.

THE VILLAGE. There is nothing compact about Catherington village. The houses are widely and unevenly spaced along a sloping road, much of which is bounded by old garden walls of flint and brick, overhung by trees. Most of the buildings are pleasantly simple in local brick or flint, but one row of cottages is timber-framed with brick infilling, the upper storey oversailing a little, the roof thatched.

CATHERINGTON HOUSE, at the corner of the road to Horndean, was built by Admiral Hood in the later C18. Main façade of four bays and three storeys, in grey brick dressed with red; large asymmetrical Tuscan porch. Lower later wing.

HINTON DAUBNAY, 1¼ m. W. The former house of the Hyde family; rebuilt in 1868 by *Ewan Christian.* Flint and brick; two-storey façade with plain sashes and two massive ground-floor windows; low slate roof. Not at all impressive.

CATISFIELD *see* FAREHAM, p. 227

CHALTON [DL]

7010

A village probably no larger than it was in the Middle Ages, and perhaps a little smaller. The few houses are strung loosely round a small rough green on a slope, and for short distances along the diverging roads; the country round is chalkland of miniature grandeur, seemingly far in feeling from the traffic and suburban sprawl of the near-by A3.

ST MICHAEL. A small but seemingly stately church, with nave, slightly narrower (and impressively proportioned) chancel, S chapel to the nave, and W tower. The chancel is C13, with very tall slender lancets in the side walls and a splendid geometrical window (presumably an insertion a little later than the chancel itself), of four cuspless lancet lights of even height, with a quatrefoiled circle above each pair of lights, and a larger cinquefoiled circle in the apex of the window. A large hood-mould contains the whole of the arch of the window, and a smaller hood contains each pair of lights with the quatrefoiled circle above them; the smaller hoods meet in the middle of the window, just as the larger and one of the smaller hoods meet on each side of the frame. Head-stops mask the endings of the hoods. There is a fine double trefoiled PISCINA, with incised rounded moulding. The chancel arch has been removed at some time. The nave has a variety of windows, of late C13 to early C14 types, the S wall having a tall ogee-headed W lancet, and a two-light trefoiled window with trefoiled circle to the E; the N wall has two tall ogee-headed lancets and, at the E end, a double window of similar style, with a quatrefoil above. The transeptal S chapel has an arch of two hollow-chamfered orders (the only arch in the church), a two-light ogee-headed E window similar in style to those of the nave, and a two-light reticulated S window. The tower is a little small and thinly proportioned in relation to the rest of the church; it is lit by very small lancets and was patched in brick, with the addition of battlements, in Georgian times. The N porch is partly a Victorian restoration but retains some medieval woodwork, especially in the outer four-centred arch with incised spandrels, and the external bargeboard with its much-worn cusp decoration. – FURNISHINGS. FONT. Octagonal; quatrefoil panels with shields and emblems at their centres (cf. Clanfield and Idsworth). – STAINED GLASS. A few fragments of medieval to Georgian date jumbled up within a Victorian framework in the SE chancel window, SW nave window, and a small light in the porch. – PLATE. Cup and Paten dated 1568, the Cup with two bands of incised ornament; Saucer of 1662, with embossed ornament; Cup of 1725; small Paten of 1794. – MONUMENTS. Richard Ball, rector, † 1632, in the chancel. Small kneeling figure in the gown of Bachelor of Divinity at Oxford, with Corinthian columns, canopy, and entablature. – Tablet to Edward Heberden † 1716, with pediment. – In the churchyard MAUSOLEUM to the Jervoise family (of Idsworth), shrine-like and E.E., probably built shortly after 1852.

Chalton's two notable domestic buildings are close to the church. The former Rectory, now called THE PRIORY, is an irregular building of apparently medieval or at least Tudor origin (walls partly of stone, old stone quoins), but with a handsome frontage of flint with red brick dressings added about the middle of the C18; much plain reconstruction in the C19. The RED LION, across the green from the church, is one of the best pre-Georgian pubs in the county, a two-storeyed timber-framed structure with the outer parts of the upper storey over-sailing but the middle part recessed behind curved brackets (i.e. the Wealden arrangement, very common in Kent), probably C16, possibly earlier. The roof is thatched. No fussing or faking – just a genuine old house simply treated: an example for other brewers. Solid Early to Mid Victorian Idsworth Estate cottages in and around the village.

CHALTON WINDMILL. On a splendid site, at the top of a hill which slopes quite sheerly on the Chalton side, and with bold curves when seen from the A3. Only the stumps of the sails are there, and the building is ruinous. Because of its position, the restoration of this mill to a semblance of working order would be especially worth while.

4020

CHANDLER'S FORD [DL]

A suburban district N of Southampton.

ST BONIFACE. 1904 by *Bodley*, chancel 1929–30. A simple church with a dignified interior. Nave with timber tunnel roof; three-light neo-Perp windows within arched recesses continuing downwards to the ground; chancel with somewhat heavier details (e.g. the thick shafts supporting the roof beams). Blocked arches and external stump-walls to intended transepts. Brick exterior with pretty stone bellcote on the W gable.

ST EDWARD THE CONFESSOR (R.C.), Winchester Road, Fryern Hill. 1938 by *Randoll Blacking*. Simple rough-plastered exterior with square-headed mullioned windows; flanking tower surmounted by a broad boarded belfry and spire in traditional Hampshire or Essex style.

Pretty boarded rural STATION, Mid-Victorian.

(At Fryern Hill a SHOPPING CENTRE is shortly to be built to the design of *Julian Keable & Partners*. Three-sided precinct, with gaily fashionable detail. NT)

CHARLTON

3040

½ m. NW of Andover

ST THOMAS. This is the nave and chancel of Foxcott church rebuilt. Foxcott is less than a mile away. The church was built about 1830, but all the details are clearly Victorian. The low W baptistery of course cannot be 1830 either. The church is faced with squared coursed flint. (The canopy of a niche in the N wall is C15. VCH)

CHAWTON

7030

ST NICHOLAS. By *Sir Arthur Blomfield*, 1871. Old masonry only in the chancel. Flint, with a big SW tower. Three cross-gables to the N. The exterior looks 1850 rather than 1870, and the interior is somewhat stolid. – COMMUNION RAIL. Early C18; pretty. – (ORGAN CASE. This and the SCREEN look as if they might be by *Bodley*. RH) – PAINTING. Crucifixion, by a Netherlander, probably *c*.1600. – STAINED GLASS. Much by *Kempe*, the earliest two Saints of 1896–7. – PLATE. Flagon, 1641; Chalice and small Paten, 1667; large Paten, 1726. – MONUMENTS. Sir Richard Knight † 1679. Good standing marble monument. Semi-reclining figure in armour. Big back display with trophies. The whole remarkably Dutch. – Tablets without figures of † 1723, † 1737.

CHAWTON HOUSE. The best thing is the STABLES, two storeys, with two projecting wings. Flint. They are dated 1591. The house belonged already then to the Knight family. They rebuilt the house at about the same time, but its details are now so much restored that it is no longer a pleasure to look at. The W side has the porch close to the S end, and a broad projecting wing coming out at the N end. The S front is brick-faced with three gables and dates from *c*.1630. The windows are irregular in the middle, because behind them is the staircase.* Nice outbuildings to the NE.

JANE AUSTEN'S HOUSE. A modest two-storeyed brick house, informal in its fenestration. She wrote her later novels here.

*The present state of the interior could not be ascertained. The house was illustrated in *Country Life* in 1945 (vol. XCVII).

The house lies at the corner of the Winchester and Alton roads. What were the traffic and the noise like then?

5020 CHERITON

ST MICHAEL. The S porch entrance is C13, re-set. It prepares for the three-bay arcades, with round piers, round abaci, and double-chamfered arches dying into rounded vertical pieces. The chancel arch goes with the arcade, and the tower arch is basically C13 too. Perp chancel end, with a four-light E window and a good N, a good S window, differing in design. These windows must be an alteration, unless the C13 PISCINA (trefoiled top) has been re-set. However, the aesthetically most satisfactory part of the church is the two mysterious blank spherical triangles with tracery l. and r. of the porch entrance. They must be early C14, and what can they have belonged to? It is said that the church was much altered after a fire in 1744. Of that time probably the flint and brick mixture of tower and parts of the aisles. – PLATE. Cup of 1621; Paten of 1698.

RECTORY. Late C17. Five bays, two storeys, hipped roof. Raised brick quoins and, on the entrance side, also raised brick window surrounds. Some wooden cross-windows. On the garden side the windows are sashed. Entrance and garden doorways have straight hoods on carved brackets. Staircase with bulgy balusters.

CHERITON HOUSE. Five bays, two storeys, grey brick and red dressings. The centre bay has giant pilasters carrying a broken pediment. A tall arched window reaches up into it. The front is a replica of that of a house at New Alresford.

3030 CHILBOLTON

ST MARY. The church started as an aisleless Norman building, cf. the one window inside the nave above the S arcade. C13 chancel. The aisles early C14. The arcades are of two bays only and standard elements. The chancel arch fits the arcades better than it fits the chancel lancets. Victorian SW tower. – PULPIT. Jacobean, with brackets for the book-rest. – STAINED GLASS. The W window is signed by *Wailes*. – PLATE. Elizabethan Cup and Cover Paten; secular two-handled Posset-Cup, 1659.

RECTORY. Five bays, two storeys, chequer brick, hipped roof, *c.*1700.

LONG BARROW. *See* Barton Stacey.

CHILCOMB 5020

ST ANDREW. Away from the village, under the downs. The church is Norman, see the windows in nave and chancel and their inner appearance. See also the two plain doorways and the chancel arch with its unmoulded arch. On the imposts incised zigzag.* – PILLAR PISCINA. Norman, with flat leaves. – FONT. An octagonal pillar with a kind of shaft-ring. It is Gothic in an approximate way and may be C18. – (SCREEN. Perhaps early C17. RH) – TILES. Many in the chancel. – PLATE. Cup and Cover Paten, 1569; Paten, 1683.

ALL SAINTS. *See* Winchester, p. 691.

CHILTON CANDOVER 5040

$1\frac{3}{8}$ m. SW of Preston Candover

ST NICHOLAS. The church was demolished in 1878, but the then incumbent in 1925 excavated the Norman CRYPT. This consists of an apse and a rectangular, tunnel-vaulted room, longer originally than it is now. Its original length was 32 ft. The chancel arch is entirely unmoulded. The crypt was not wholly sunk. Small windows allowed some daylight in. – FONT. Of Purbeck marble. Table-top type with six of the usual flat blank arches per side.

RECTORY, S of the church. Stuccoed. Of five widely spaced bays. Two storeys high. The centre bay has a pedimental gable into which rises a round-arched window. The end bays have Venetian windows on both floors. Unusually fine door-surround with carved brackets and a laurel-frieze below the pediment. 1760–70 may be a likely date.

CHILWORTH [DL] 4010

Southampton's richest fringe, with large houses, Surrey-like, in birchy gardens, giving way to rhododendron-planted woodlands and then open country.

ST DENYS. 1812, stuccoed, with little transepts and a low embattled W tower, set against a wooded hillside. The exterior is

*Above the altar is the iron hook from which the PYX was suspended.

77 pretty, the interior an enlivening surprise; it is all plaster-vaulted, with closely spaced ribs, traceried panel patterns, a series of medieval-looking foliated bosses, and face-corbels at the ends of the vaulting ribs, brought out attractively in pastel colours with silver paint on the bosses and corbels. The windows are all lancets except the E, which is five-light simplified Perp with thin tracery; beside it are the original text boards with engaging little cherubs, in groups of three, looking down from the top. – Delicate iron COMMUNION RAIL in simple Gothic pattern. – Open PEWS (not box), contemporary with the church, with Gothic panels on the pew ends. – The FONT is Norman; square-panelled bowl cut down at the top, on a modern base. – BELLS are not usually mentioned in *The Buildings of England*, but those of Chilworth are said to be C12 and the oldest in the South of England. – PLATE. Set given in 1812. – MONUMENT. Marble medallion with the profile of the sculptor *R. C. Lucas* (1800–83), carved by himself in 1840. He built for himself a house at Chilworth called the Tower of the Winds (later Chilworth Court) in 1854; it was demolished a century later, and suburban houses stand on the site. Not much sculptural work known to be by him seems to survive, but what there is is good – cf. the Watts statue in Southampton (p. 558) and a monument at North Stoneham (p. 359).

The original hamlet of Chilworth is tucked in a hollow to the S of the church. A primitive cluster of thatched cottages till lately; now they are mostly tiled and augmented by a few new ones.

CHILWORTH MANOR (University of Southampton, Hall of Residence). A crummy house of *c.*1900*; a proliferation of bits and pieces in yellow brick and stone, with twirly-headed windows and big-boned segmental archways with widely spaced rustication. In the middle a big hall rises two and a half storeys (the top part a clerestory). It contains a series of small rectangular wooden plaques carved in German Baroque manner with crowded scenes, and some charming Art-Nouveau electroliers, each in the form of a winged creature projecting from the wall with two cone-shaped bulbs at the end of inter-twirling stems. The GARDEN is more remarkable than the house. In front of a wide grass terrace is a varied series of urns, obviously from elsewhere, and indications of many others that have been lost. A straight path leads between box hedges

*On stylistic grounds, an attribution to *Mitchell, Son & Gutteridge* is suggested.

past a former fountain to a pair of stunted columns, also re-used, with fine Ionic capitals surmounted by big balls, beyond which is a contrived wilderness. The ground sweeps down to the r. of the path, romantically landscaped with roughage and rhododendrons, with a small pond, and a background of a huge view over miles of rolling countryside. Other classical bits and pieces re-used as garden furniture elsewhere, some of them crumbling.*

CHRISTCHURCH 1090

CHRISTCHURCH PRIORY. Christchurch became an Augustinian priory only in 1150, but it was an important church quite a long time before, as in Domesday we are told of twenty-four canons resident in the minster church. William Rufus granted town and church to Ranulph Flambard, who destroyed the old church and gradually abolished canonries, but began the building of the church as it now stands. He was banished in 1100, and somewhat later Henry I gave town and church to Richard de Redvers. The dates of importance, besides 1150, are 1195 for the consecration of the high altar and other altars and 1214 and 1221 for more altars. One of the altars of 1214 was the nave altar.

EXTERIOR. The broadside view of the priory from the N is impressive in its length and height, but it is disjointed. The parts will not make up into a whole, as they do inside. A method of describing the exterior will therefore be used different from the usual.

The first question is to be: What can one still see of the Norman work, and what did the C13 alter and add? The E end can therefore at this stage be left out of consideration, although it is known from excavation that the chancel had aisles and that the aisles ended straight, but the chancel in an apse. So what is visible externally of Norman work, first on the N side, is the small gallery windows. The aisle windows themselves are E.E. with enriched quatrefoils. The buttresses of course are E.E. too. The clerestory has flat buttresses still, but the windows are again E.E. (Y-tracery with a solid tympanum).

The N transept is the showpiece of Christchurch. The 14
heavy angle-shafting remains, the large intersecting arcading

*Possibly from *Hopper*'s house at North Stoneham (p. 359), as Chilworth was built by the Flemings, who owned North Stoneham.

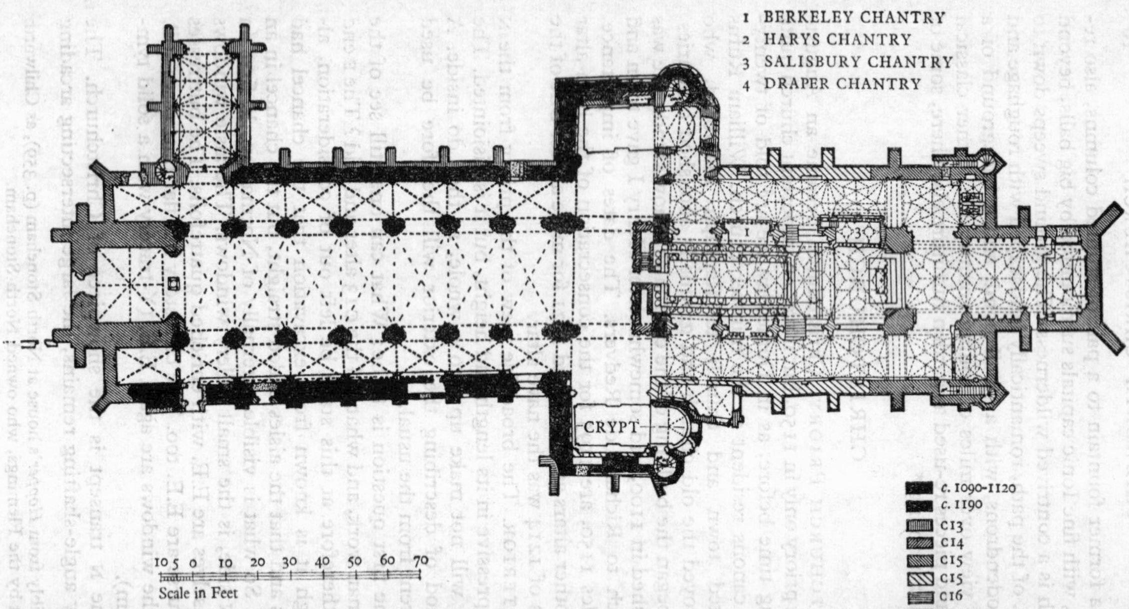

Christchurch Priory, plan

(much of it C19, but the tympana etc. with a fish-scale pattern original), one W window with a blank twin next to it, traces of N windows (but the large present window is Perp), and then the celebrated stair-turret, with a sequence from the bottom upward of intersecting arcade, blank arcade with twin colonnettes, a very bold trellis pattern, and blank arcade with single colonnettes. The stair-turret merges into the former transept E chapel, but this part was altered by E.E. work again with quatrefoiled and cinquefoiled circles.*

The original arrangement comes out much more clearly on the S side. Here the transept E chapel makes its statement. Angle-shafting, E window, also upper windows. The stair-turret exists on the S as on the N side, but is octagonal and much plainer here. The S wall of the transept has two blocked upper windows, and on the W side is one window, later lengthened. What is the date of these transept fronts, especially that on the N side? It looks in its profuse decoration mid C12 or even later. But evidence inside does not bear that out, and so one must assume an exceptionally early indulgence in elaborate ornamentation.

The nave gallery above the aisle has its small windows here too, but in addition there are three doorways, all connected with the monastic parts. The first and richest led into the corner of the N and E walks of the cloister. It is of *c.* 1200 and has a round arch with fine mouldings nearly all over-restored. The second led into the NW corner. This is full C13: pointed and of two continuous chamfers. The third is not medieval. One aisle window is complete. The others are all later C13 in style, but by *Ferrey*.‡ The N walk of the cloister had Norman blank arcading.

But this is not yet all the E.E. work; for the splendid N porch also belongs to the later C13. It is considerably higher than the aisle. The entry arch is on a monumental scale, but also largely new. Four orders of shafts. The arches rise from a plain rounded vertical piece. The buttresses flanking it are chamfered and have set-offs of the Salisbury type. Above is much bare wall, and the upper room has only small, plain, twin windows with triangle heads. The interior of the porch is vaulted in two bays. The vaults (with ridge-ribs and

*The small Norman basement windows belong to the crypt – *see* p. 171.

‡Ferrey's father was Mayor of Christchurch, and Ferrey, with E. W. Brayley, published in 1834 *The Antiquities of the Priory of Christchurch*, an early example of the new archaeological approach to medieval buildings (NT).

tiercerons) are of the restoration of 1862 by *Ferrey* (RH). The wall of each bay is filled by one large blank two-light window with a cinquefoiled circle. The inner doorway is again largely Victorian. It has six orders, and also the curious rounded vertical pieces into which the arch mouldings die. The doorway has a *trumeau* or middle post. The two entries have cinque-cusped arches, and in the tympanum is the most curious of quatrefoils. Three foils are normal, except that colonnettes close the side arms off from the centre. But the top foil is replaced by a three-dimensional pointed arch under a gable. Originally there was of course a figure in the quatrefoil.

There is nothing more of early work here, except for the two W bays of the aisles. The doorway to the N, however, is not ancient, and the rest of the problem can only be recognized inside.

The later work at Christchurch is all Perp. The Dec style, as so often in Hampshire, is not represented. The Perp can be firmly dated only at its end and in one place (*see* below). Activity, however, took place in three. There is first the W tower. The W doorway has shields in tracery in the spandrels. The W window has two transoms, and all the lights are uncusped except those at the very top. Higher up a niche with an original figure. Bell-openings two tall twins with transom. Battlements with quatrefoils, pinnacles on thin shafts. It is a fine, balanced, rich yet restrained composition.

The E parts are much more swagger. They consist of the Lady Chapel and the chancel. The Lady Chapel has very large four-light windows. The grouping of the lights is 2+2. The arches are two-centred. Above the Lady Chapel – a surprising and aesthetically questionable motif – is an upper storey of domestic scale. It is entirely unknown what this was built for. Later it was used for the Grammar School. It has small two-light transomed windows and a three-light E window. Top parapet with openwork quatrefoils and pinnacles. The chancel has windows similar to the large ones of the Lady Chapel, only higher up, and hence this whole upper part is supported by flying buttresses. The chancel aisles are low, and the windows have depressed four-centred heads. No tracery. Parapet with openwork quatrefoils and pinnacles. The aisles at their E ends, where they become an access ambulatory to the Lady Chapel, conflict with the Lady Chapel windows. The Lady Chapel E window is of five lights.

INTERIOR. Here also we start from the earliest work. Inside, this is the three CRYPTS. One is below the choir just E of the stalls and consists of a tunnel-vaulted bay and an arch now blank but originally leading to the apse, which helps to locate the main apse above. The capitals are of the elementary block type. So here we are certainly before 1100. The same is probably true of the two identical, apsed crypts below the outer bays of the transepts. They are also tunnel-vaulted. The apses have thick rolls as ribs and no keystones yet. Flambard no doubt also started above ground. Of the E end, however, we know nothing of elevation or details. So the story starts in the crossing and transepts.

The CROSSING has plain strong shafting and high plain arches. The capitals have big scallops. That might be pre-1100, but there is very small zigzag over the N and S arches, and that is more probably early C12. It is the same with the arches in the TRANSEPT towards the chancel aisle (N), the nave aisle (N), and the nave galleries (N and S). They are all entirely unmoulded. On the other hand heavy and powerful elementary foliage capitals appear, and they look rather 1110–20 than 1090–1100. Of other details the S transept has in its W wall plain blank arcading, unrestored and badly preserved. The E chapel has the foliated capitals just referred to, blank arcading, and the same fat rolls as ribs as the crypts. But the later C13 intervened nicely, adding a bit of its own vaulting, especially a quadripartite bay to connect with a new window of three stepped lancet lights. Naturalistic foliage on the boss. Single-chamfered ribs. Between the chapel and the S chancel aisle the space was filled in later in the C13 by a chapel which extends further E. Four rib-vaulted bays awkwardly but attractively squeezed in. The N transept has in its W wall a remarkable and at first surprising feature: a twin shaft with capitals of the same early and bold foliage as the others in these early parts. But these capitals are placed so low that one must assume that the whole of the transept was two-storeyed (as e.g. at Jumièges and Bayeux). The shafts are identical in style with those in the same wall communicating with the N aisle. More evidence of this gallery filling the transept is one respond, again with a foliage capital, by the arch from transept to chancel aisle, and also the fact observed by Sir Charles Peers (VCH) that the twin shafts of the NW crossing pier are interrupted by lengths of plaster just where the vault supporting the gallery would have been.

The E side of the transept was radically altered in the later

C13. Of the Norman arrangement only part of the blank arch to the former chapel remains. Instead a chapel was created and a second small skew entry made into the area between the former Norman E chapel and the chancel aisle wall. The skew entry is foliated. It makes a charming, quite irregular pattern of dainty rib-vaults with stiff-leaf and naturalistic bosses. Nothing seems to meet quite according to plan, but all somehow comes off. Above this double chapel is a room which has been identified as the master mason's tracing house (*trasura*). On the wall is set out a Gothic arch, and there is also a large area squared up into six times sixteen nine-inch squares (VCH).

The NAVE gives us at least an idea of the original chancel elevation as well; for the style changes so little from the earliest existing details to the W end of the nave that one is inclined to believe that no change of system of elevation took place either. The capitals at the W end do not look later than those at the E end. So *c.*1130 is probably the latest possible date for the completion of the ground stage of the nave. The nave is seven bays long. How it ended to the W is unknown and, as we shall see, poses a problem. The arcade has compound piers with strong shafts to the nave and twin shafts to the arches. Spandrels with a surface pattern of small triangles. Gallery of big broad twins. The columns separating them are mostly plain, but some – apparently without system – are decorated. Only the first bay on the N side has a decorated tympanum. Afterwards all the tympana are plain. The Norman clerestory does not survive. It was replaced by the two-light E.E. windows, which have straight-sided rere-arches. The convincing nave vault is by *Garbett*, 1819 (RH). He also designed the rather thin vault of the tower, 1820.

At the same time the aisles were remodelled. They received plain E.E. rib-vaults of single-chamfered ribs. Most but not all the wall shafts were renewed. Norman wall arcading also remained in the S aisle. In the N aisle the new windows were given little rib-vaults between window and rere-arch, again a charming motif and much in accordance with what this master otherwise did with his vaulting. The window rere-arches incidentally have the same odd rounded vertical pieces for the arches to die against which we have met in the porch. So the porch and the remodelling of the N aisle were probably one job.

A problem is the W bays of the aisles, which more than half

overlap the Perp tower. The VCH simply calls them late C15. But that is wrong. Their details are unmistakably those of the C13 aisles – the same capitals and the same ribs. What did they then embrace? Something that was there at their time. A westwork?

The EAST PARTS are a unified job internally. The chancel is four bays long. It is covered by a lierne-vault forming broad stars, i.e. Greek crosses with triangular ends. From initials this vault can be attributed to the time of William Eyre, prior from 1502 to 1530, and also the nicely decorated arch from the S transept into the chancel aisle. So even this arch, at ground level, cannot have been done before 1502. The motif of the purely decorative pendants close to the wall at the springing of each bay of vaulting is derived from Oxford Cathedral. Below the large windows is bald blank panelling. The arcades are low and have depressed four-centred arches. There is here the same lack of harmony as between the windows of the chancel and the aisles as seen from outside. The Lady Chapel is of three bays and has almost the same vault as the chancel. Only between the W and the two older bays is a broader arch, and therefore pairs of pendants appear. This shows that the architect of the Lady Chapel considered the W bay as something extra, an ante-room, and this is significant, as will be seen presently. The rere-arches of the windows are more ornate than those of the chancel, and there is splendid tall blank arcading with crocketed ogee arches and above it long plain Perp panels. It is likely that the Lady Chapel was built earlier than the chancel, outside the Norman building. The trouble with this beautifully unified composition is the aisles. They go one bay beyond the chancel so as to give access to the Lady Chapel W bay, i.e. the ante-room, as it has just been called. But these aisle E bays are low, and ought to be continued beyond the chancel reredos by a low ambulatory. Instead the Lady Chapel starts at once at full height. Moreover the aisles were given added E chapels. Hence a complete 28
muddle outside. The aisle E bays and E chapels cut into the Lady Chapel in a way only possible if all this was not foreseen. Can it be assumed that the Lady Chapel was ready, that then for chancel and chancel aisles the Norman work was pulled down, and that finally the two were joined by the aisle E bays as best they could be? The aisles and E chapels have lierne-vaults too.

FITTINGS AND FURNISHINGS. LADY CHAPEL. REREDOS.

Perp. Three large and many small niches. No figures left at all. – STAINED GLASS. E window by *O'Connor*. – MONUMENTS. On the N side a Purbeck marble monument of the early C16. Tomb-chest with cusped lozenges and shields. The recess screened by shafts carrying two four-centred arches. There are two five-light screens. Panelled end walls and ceiling. Top cresting. – Opposite another Purbeck tomb-chest. Recess with a very depressed four-centred arch, cusped and sub-cusped. Again panelled end walls and ceiling. Again cresting. But not the screen of shafts.

AMBULATORY. Panelled platform with two 'bastions' behind the reredos. – MONUMENTS. Charles Brander † 1745. Very large hanging monument. Obelisk, urn, no figures. – Sir G. Penleaze † 1819. Excellent large tablet of mottled grey marble by *William Hiscock* of Christchurch. Against it a circular white plaque, within which is Penleaze's jet-black profile, sharp-featured, like the silhouettes so popular at the time.

NORTH CHANCEL AISLE. Excellent PISCINA. – STAINED GLASS. E window by *Lavers & Barraud* (TK). – MONUMENTS. In the E chapel two recumbent alabaster effigies of the mid C15, badly preserved. – Salisbury Chantry *see* chancel. – John Barnes † 1815. By *Chantrey*. Mourning woman and child face a second woman across the sarcophagus. – Early C16 stone recess of the Purbeck type of the Lady Chapel. The Elizabethan achievement on the back wall is a replacement. – Berkeley Chantry, *c*.1486. Very humble, compared with the Countess of Salisbury's. Some PAINTING of red and white roses and white carnations. – On the floor in front of the Berkeley Chantry a black marble slab with a small Gothic brass, exquisitely lettered, to Anne † 1832, wife of *Augustus Welby Northmore de Pugin* (*sic*). – FONT. Purbeck marble, of the table type, C12, with excellent, though badly preserved scenes in intersecting roundels. The scenes are on three sides; on the fourth quatrefoils (i.e. C13). The scenes represent Noah's Ark, Samson and the Lion, Moses striking the rock, the Coronation of the Virgin, the Burial of the Virgin, Pentecost, and three figures in quatrefoils. – SCULPTURE. Many fragments, including two C15 scenes in stone of the type and style familiar from alabaster work. Probably from a reredos. – REREDOS. C18 painted figures of Moses and Aaron.

SOUTH CHANCEL AISLE. MONUMENTS. Draper Chantry. Dated 1529, and the first monument at Christchurch where

Gothic and Renaissance meet. Four-light openings with four-centred arches, doorway with a niche over. But Renaissance friezes and other details. The situation is like that at Winchester Cathedral in the same years. The chapel has Perp windows with two-centred arches to E and S. Inside is a PISCINA like that in the N transept E chapel, i.e. dating from before the chantry was made. – The Harys Chantry is of 1525, and here there is no Renaissance detail yet. Three-light windows with four-centred heads. Broad side pieces and broad centre piece, the latter with the doorway, all three with a big niche. – SCREEN. To the choir. Stone. Row of Perp panels. Frieze with angel-busts. – In the C13 chapel (now vestry) adjoining the chancel aisle plenty of medieval TILES on the floor.

CHANCEL. REREDOS. This, perhaps just because it is forceful rather than refined, is one of the most monumental survivals of Dec sculpture in England. It probably dates from *c.*1350. It rises to the full height of the chancel walls, or rather to the springing-point of the vault. The cresting alone is Perp. It must – and this gives food for thought – have been re-erected piece for piece when the chancel was built early in the C16. It is built up in three tiers and five vertical strips, framed and separated by six thin posts, four of which have small statuettes set in one on top of the other. The lowest of the three tiers has two outer doorways, very narrow, then seated figures of Daniel l. and Solomon r., and in the middle, 32
crossed by two thin extra posts, the reclining figure of Jesse. In the tier above, in the middle, is the Adoration of the Magi. The four niches l. and r. have lost their statues. In the third tier no sculpture is left at all. Top cresting. – STALLS.* Made *c.*1525–30. Two tiers. The wall panels with coarse Renaissance motifs. The top cresting re-made in lead in the C19. The ends with decorative foliage and tracery, all Gothic, and also figures and animals. However, putti and vases and profiles in medallions also appear, and they are *all'antica*. The arms between the seats are decorated too. Full set of MISERICORDS, not all of the same date. Two are of the C13: lower row, S, no. 2 from the E (foliage) and lower row, N, no. 8 from the E (two dragons and foliage). Two are of *c.*1400: Lion of St Mark, Angel of St Matthew, lower row, N, nos 1 and 2 from the E. The rest are early C16. The variety of motifs and stories is great, e.g. lower

* There is a detailed guide to the Stalls by K. F. Wiltshire. They were restored by *Garbett* in 1820.

row, N: rabbit warren, bat, ape, tumbler, jester, lean greyhound. – Lower row, S: eagle, man with an axe, bust of a fat child. – Upper row, N: laughing man, kneeling man, another jester, two more tumblers, king, fox wearing a cowl, yet another jester. – Upper row, S: two profiles, king, *signum triciput*, several griffins, pair of fishes. – HIGH ALTAR. 'This table was made and presented to this Church by *Augustus Welby Pugin* A.D. 1831', says the inscription. Here indeed is a major piece of his early furniture. He was aged nineteen. Quite small oak table with symmetrical five-bay front, the bays of three different widths being filled with Flamboyant openwork vine trails and other writhing shapes. Elaborate corbels and pendants to the projecting table top. Not only is the inscription still Protestant ('table' indeed) but, as his friend and intermediary Ferrey wrote, 'though admirable as a piece of carving, it was wanting in ecclesiastical expression, and too much resembled the richly carved cabinets of the sixteenth century'.*

MONUMENTS. Chantry of the Countess of Salisbury, beheaded in 1541. This is the most ambitious monument in the church. It stands in the N aisle, but is raised so that its main front is towards the high chancel. It is of two large bays of four lights with four-centred heads. Tiers of niches l. and r., buttress-shafts with Renaissance panels and candelabra etc. Very high cresting with two fantastic finials, part round, then suddenly coming out in a star-shape. They rise to clerestory level. To the aisle also there is the juxtaposition of Gothic and Renaissance motifs, quatrefoils, cusped lozenges, niches with nodding ogee arches, etc., on the one hand, friezes and the candelabra shapes on buttress-shafts on the other. Inside on the E wall three canopies. Fan-vault with bosses. Small windows to E and W into the aisles, to W into the choir. – Corisande Countess of Malmesbury † 1876. Recumbent effigy on a tomb-chest. By *A. Trentanove*. – Viscountess
78 Fitzharris † 1815. By *Flaxman*. Free-standing group on a block with (worthwhile) inscription. She is seated on a Grecian chair, her youngest child in her lap, the older boys standing. Very domesticated, and very feelingly carved.

CROSSING. PULPITUM. A splendid late C14 piece, unfortunately nearly entirely *Ferrey*'s work of 1848.

TRANSEPTS. Two large PAINTINGS by *Millais*: The Widow's Mite and The Rich Young Ruler. The latter is of

* The description of the high altar is by NT.

1847. Both show the Nazarene influence on the young Millais.

WEST TOWER. MONUMENT. Shelley, the poet. By *Weekes*, See p. 828 1854. White marble. He lies dead with his head in the lap of a girl. Intended for St Peter, Bournemouth, where his heart is buried (NT).

PORCH. In the W wall a C13 RECESS, much restored.

PLATE. Chalice, given 1618; Chalice, given 1627 and re-made 1812; Paten, 1628; three secular Salvers, 1744, 1752, 1812; Flagon, 1813.

See p. 828

IMMACULATE CONCEPTION AND ST JOSEPH, Purewell. 1866. Red brick and lancet windows. Modest. But inside above the altar fresco PAINTING by *Frederick Rolfe* (Baron Corvo), who lived at Christchurch in 1891–2. It is very competently done in the Italian Renaissance style of the early C16, Venetian rather than Raphaelesque, and with certain betrayingly naturalistic details. The technique Corvo used is typical of the man. There is an element of cheating in the competence. He is said to have photographed models in the appropriate attitudes, made lantern slides from the negatives, and projected them direct on to the wall, where he could then trace the outlines. – (FONT. Of the Purbeck table-type, C12, with four blank arches on each side. Where is it from? NT)

CONGREGATIONAL CHURCH, Millhams Street. Yellow brick with a NW tower. A pattern building of debased E.E., plus round arches, plus Venetian tracery. The dates are 1867 (church) and 1888 (hall). By *Kemp Welch & Pinder*. (The interest lies only in the impressive row of eight TABLE TOMBS to a single design lined up in front of the hall. The first date is 1819. NT)

CASTLE, N of the priory. Built for the Redvers family. Of the keep, built on an artificial motte, only two walls remain, E and W. The keep was oblong, and the angles were bevelled, which is very unusual. There are still indications where windows and doorway were. The hall is in a much better state of preservation. It is by the river, oblong, 67 by 23 ft, running N–S. It is built of rough Purbeck-marble blocks, a highly remarkable material to use, and consisted of a basement and a main floor. In the S wall is one circular top window, in the N wall a two-light window with zigzag to the outside, at r. angles to the wall. In the long E and W walls are more such two-light windows, and the E wall has in addition a garderobe tower 18
which rose to the full height of the building and a fireplace

with a proper flue and a circular chimneystack, a very rare survival at such an early date. The date is evidently the late C12.

(CEMETERY, Jumpers Road. Two chapels and arched gateway. *Ferrey* at his best: solid and severe Gothic construction in grey stone with no gimmicks. NT)

(TWYNHAM SECONDARY SCHOOL and FURTHER EDUCATION CENTRE, Soper's Lane. Excellent new work of 1964–5 by the Hampshire County Architect, *H. Benson Ansell*. NT)

(MILITARY ENGINEERING ESTABLISHMENT, Barrack Road. Insignificant recent buildings (apart from one good group of exhaust vents), but the pretty GUARDROOM, with its white cupola and seven slim Tuscan columns, presumably survives from the Artillery Barracks of 1792. NT)

(BRIDGES. To the E of the castle, first a two-arch bridge renewed, then five good stone arches with triangular breakers, and finally the WATERLOO BRIDGE, 1816–17, five heavily rusticated arches by the local mason *William Hiscock*, with a well-lettered inscription tablet. To the NW of the town, IFORD BRIDGE now runs parallel to the old structure: the latter is a motley succession of old arches, with four of stone in the centre and others of brick. NT)

There is little to Christchurch as a town. The KING'S HEAD HOTEL, opposite the castle, is probably the most attractive building, Latest Georgian, yellow brick, of five bays, with a Tuscan porch and a pedimented tripartite window above. From the hotel E, out of the town, in BRIDGE STREET, is TWYNEHAM HOUSE, early C18 basically, it seems, with its projecting wings and hipped roof. The Tuscan porch has a triglyph frieze, and this is nicely repeated above the l. and r. windows. (Also in Bridge Street No. 23, with a two-storey Gothick bay window, the HENGISTBURY HOUSE HOTEL, C18 with a Tuscan porch set back from the street, and a fiery former chapel in terracotta of 1890. NT) From the hotel to the centre nothing, in the HIGH STREET nothing, until, a little further out, some red brick houses on the W side. The TOWN HALL on the E side is classical, with a cupola, red brick and stone dressings, and yet of 1859.* Finally, immediately by the churchyard, in CHURCH STREET, N of the church, a good five-bay brick house with raised brick quoins and again an (added) Tuscan porch. NW

* Its upper floor and cupola are a reproduction of its predecessor of 1746 (on another site).

of the church the RED HOUSE, formerly the parish workhouse, early C18, red brick, an irregular front with wooden mullioned windows with segmental heads and also a cross-window. Door-hood with open scrolly pediment. The building is now a museum.

CHURCH CROOKHAM

8050

CHRIST CHURCH. 1841. Of brick, in the lancet style, by *James Harding*. The chancel of 1876–7 by *Woodyer*. Brown stone and typical of him inside, with much incised decoration and figure-work. The bellcote is no doubt also Woodyer's. (SGRAFFITO DECORATION over the chancel arcades. 1893, by *Heywood Sumner* (cf. St Agatha Landport, p. 433). – STAINED GLASS. Two W lancets, exquisite angels, clearly by the same hand. NT)

CLANFIELD

[DL] 6010

Clanfield is at the terminus of the long sprawl of inter- and post-war development which runs along and to the W of the line of the London road out of Portsmouth. The bungalows and semis end at the outskirts of the village; the village itself remains relatively unspoiled, with fine rolling chalkland to the W, N, and NE.

ST JAMES. 1875 by *R. J. Jones* of Ryde, a satisfying building by a little-known architect. Externally of flint, with tiled roofs and a prominent double open bellcote, deliberately oversized to be a landmark in the village. Internally the walls are faced wholly with brick, red up to one course below the level of the nave sills, mainly yellow above, but with black and red stripes at intervals. The side windows are little trefoiled lancets the splays of which rise higher, within the thicknesses of the walls, than the arches of their outer frames (an exaggeration of a local C13 tradition). The chancel arch, recessed in four stages, is all of yellow brick except for a patterning of upright red and yellow bricks, in alternate threes, forming a frame to the arch. The E window is a trio of lancets of even height, the splays finished upwards in the same assertive manner as those in the nave lancets. The W window is from the old church, two-light Perp. The whole interior is surprisingly harmonious in its varied detailing and colouring. – CHANCEL SCREEN, open, traceried, and COMMUNION RAIL, both of iron. – FONT. C14, octagonal, with quatrefoiled panels on the bowl and arched panels on the stem – a simpler version of the fonts at Idsworth and Chalton. – PLATE. Cup, 1672.

Clanfield is a loosely disposed chalkland village, completely different from the large, urbane villages of the clayey plain to the SW. But it has definite form because the houses are set along a number of roads which converge near the village centre, marked, most unhappily, by the RISING SUN, erected out of prefabricated materials in 1960 in place of the old pub – interesting constructionally but glaringly out of place. The other buildings are in a happy variety of materials and manners – old red brick, flint, timber-framing, tiling, thatch; softly olde-worlde, blandly Georgian, assertively Victorian. Only the pub doesn't fit in. Suburban Clanfield comes as a shock – it sprawls over downland slopes and hollows for miles to the S and, although planning control forbids any extension of the messed-up area, it is allowing a good deal of intensification. This means that big well-grown gardens (which did soften the impact of the whole a little when seen from higher ground) are being broken up and odd intermediate spaces filled. Except for an enclave at Catherington, there will soon be solid development all the way to Waterlooville – which means all the way to Southsea.

CLANVILLE HOUSE *see* WEYHILL

6040

CLIDDESDEN

ST LEONARD. Almost entirely of 1889. By *W. S. Hicks* of Newcastle. Only on the N side a plain Norman doorway, blocked. Nave and chancel and bellcote. – STAINED GLASS. Most of the windows by *Kempe*, 1896. – PLATE. Silver-gilt Chalice, made at Nuremberg, early C17; Paten, 1702.

RECTORY, to the SW, on the B-road. Later Georgian. Brick. Five bays, two storeys, with a three-bay pediment. In it a round window. Doorway with broken pediment.

3010

COLBURY [DL]

A stretch of half-forest country forming a buffer between Totton and the forest proper. No village, only scattered houses.

CHRIST CHURCH. 1870 by *B. Ferrey*. Quite an arty W front, with three buttresses rising from a gabled projection containing the W door; tapering gable bellcote with open traceried timbering and spirelet with four shingled pinnacles. Pleasant interior, the windows Geometrical, the chancel, with tiling and motley colourful E window, retaining its Victorian atmosphere. – (The VICARAGE is also by *Ferrey*. NT)

COLDEN COMMON

4020

HOLY TRINITY. 1844 by *G. Guillaume* (GR). Nave and chancel; bellcote. Flint and lancet windows. Short chancel and built into it – when? – a polygonal apse with windows with detached shafts and plate tracery. – MONUMENT. J. T. Waddington † 1865. By *Newman* of Winchester. In spite of the date still completely Georgian. Standing allegorical woman.

COLDHAYES *see* STEEP

COLDREY HOUSE *see* BENTLEY

COLEMORE

7030

ST PETER AD VINCULA. Nave and chancel in one. Victorian bell-turret with spire (by *John Colson*; RH), instead of a former W tower. In the nave on the N side a small lancet. The chancel was rebuilt in 1874. But the main interest of the church is the N transept. A small E window proves it to be Norman, and inside the arch indeed survives which once separated it from a crossing. It has simple imposts and an unmoulded arch. In the W wall a blocked doorway (which is unusual). Of the former S transept the jambs of the arch still show outside. – FONT. Purbeck marble, Norman, of table type. Five supports. Two sides of the top of five flat arches each, the other sides with ornament. – SCREEN. The doorway bay is original. – PLATE. Chalice, 1568; Paten, 1719.

COMPTON

4020

ALL SAINTS. Nave and chancel are Norman. Only the bell-turret and the S aisle and S chapel are not (1905 for £3,500; GS). Simple Norman S doorway and more elaborate N doorway with one order of columns and zigzag, also meeting at rounded angles to form lozenges. – FONT. Norman, plain, with four lugs at the upper corners. – PULPIT. With re-used long Jacobean balusters. – SEAT. Made up of two late C15 or early C16 bench ends, very rustically carved. – PAINTING.

In the jamb of a chancel N window Bishop with crozier. The arch under which he stands is C13. But is he? – PLATE. Chalice with flat foot, 1674; Flagon, 1717. – MONUMENT. John Harris † 1661. Tablet with scrolly open pediment and high above it a bust.

COPNOR *see* PORTSMOUTH, pp. 434, 437, 440, 463

COPYTHORNE

3010

ST MARY. 1834 by *Thomas Benham*. Chancel and alterations by *Butterfield*, 1891–2. One of his last works. Red brick. Lancets. W tower with clumsy pinnacles. Butterfield's chancel goes on with lancets, which is a remarkable case of conformity. Did Butterfield also insert the plate tracery in the E bay of the nave? Inside, the nave is typically pre-Victorian, the aisles divided from the nave by very thin columns, said to be of a very hard cast stone. W gallery on iron columns. The chancel is higher inside than the nave and also narrower, an effective way of distinction.

CORHAMPTON

6020

CHURCH. Less than ¼ m. from Meonstoke church. Corhampton is a Saxon church essentially, even though the E wall which faces the road is C19 brick. The long-and-short quoins are as unmistakable as the thin lesenes, and nothing could be more typical than the broad and high surround of the former N doorway with the plain blocks instead of capitals and abaci and the outer accompaniment of the former doorway arch by a lesene bent round semicircularly. The chancel arch has the same motifs. Even the fact that one lesene starts on the apex of the bend round the former doorway arch is telling – telling of the completely unstructural way in which the Anglo-Saxon masons designed. – To the r. of the porch a Saxon SUNDIAL, with tripartite leaves reaching out into the four corners of the square panel. – FONT. Circular, Norman, with a rope band. – WALL PAINTINGS. In the chancel, C13, large lower area of stylized drapery with circles in squares and in the circles addorsed birds; scenes above, e.g. a standing woman in front of a seated priest. – PLATE. Cup of *c.*1570; Paten on foot of 1791. – A yew tree of 26 ft girth grows in the churchyard.

COSHAM *see* PORTSMOUTH, p. 464

COVE

8050

1½ m. W of Farnborough parish church

ST JOHN BAPTIST, St John's Road. 1844 by *G. Alexander*. Neo-Norman with a low crossing tower, standing inside on four arches with semicircular responds.

ST CHRISTOPHER, Cove Road, ¾ m. SE. By *W. Curtis Green*, begun in 1934. Brick, without a tower but with a very big roof in which on both sides a long band of dormer windows appears as a clerestory inside. The interior timberwork is ingenious and original, with all timbers straight, nothing arched. Nave and narrow aisle passages. To E and W one long lancet. – ORGAN CASE. Made up of C17 and early C18 woodwork.

E of St Christopher the modern developments of Farnborough Park (*see* p. 229).

CRANBURY PARK

4020

1¾ m. SE of Hursley

Cranbury Park is a fascinating and internally a very beautiful house. It was built probably in the 1790s for Lady Dance-Holland, i.e. the wife of Sir Nathaniel Dance-Holland, the painter brother of the younger *George Dance*. So it was in all probability designed by him. The style of the interior in fact triumphantly vindicates the attribution. But how much of the exterior can be his? The house is of red brick with stone dressings. The S front has a very generously spaced three-bay centre with, in the middle, a deep porte-cochère. This can be safely exempted at once from Dance's work. On the l. and r. are large windows with columns set in, solid tympana, and round the tympana arches of the Gibbs type. In the tympana are relief-roundels, and a third is above the porte-cochère. That is an unlikely arrangement. To the l. and r. of the three-bay centre are two-bay wings. They are two-storeyed, whereas the centre is of one storey only. The wings have Venetian windows only, on both floors, and giant pilasters, and the centre is flanked by giant pilasters too. On top of the centre is a parapet, with urns, balustraded except in the middle, where it is solid and raised.

Round the corner, on the S side, the system is much simpler, but the articulation by giant pilasters goes on. The front is of thirteen bays here and of three storeys. The N side is the result of the recent demolition of a Victorian addition.

The interior of Cranbury Park is an unforgettable experience. One enters by a minute lobby and has to negotiate a ninety-degree turn to reach the entrance hall, which rises with its coffered tunnel-vaults to the full height of the house. In the end wall two pairs of scagliola columns, the pairs placed in depth. They correspond to the columns set inside and outside the window, which is the r. one of the two large windows with the solid tympana, an ingenious correspondence of exterior and interior, specially palatable to the C20. Behind the scagliola columns is an exedra lit by a circular skylight. In the exedra one ought to turn l. One passes through another small cabinet and reaches a more complex companion-piece to the exedra. This one has the same circular skylight, but the pairs of columns not only to the S but also the N, and smaller apses or exedras to the E and W. On the S is the ballroom, on the N is the organ recess. The ballroom is the climax
72 of the house. It lies behind the other grand window, and so its scagliola columns again correspond to those set in the window. The ballroom has its own two large exedras l. and r. and in the square centre a groin-vault, patently heralding the work of Dance's greatest pupil, Sir John Soane. Dance's passion for exedras and coffering must be traced back to inspiration from Roman baths. Dance had lived for years in Rome about 1770. The style is remarkably similar to that of the progressive pupils of the Paris Academy in the same years, especially those able to spend time at the French Academy in Rome.

The other rooms have good, but more conventional stucco. They are of course more normal in their proportions too. At the SE corner is the Tent Room, with a tent-like ceiling of silk. This, influenced by French Empire work, dates from about 1830, i.e. the time when *J. B. Papworth* worked at Cranbury Park. Was he perhaps responsible for the alterations to the S front too?*

In the grounds, SE of the house, some fragments of NETLEY ABBEY have been re-erected. They were transferred to Cranbury in the 1760s. The tower feature of course is essentially *c.*1770. The windows are typical of such a date. But bits to the N are medieval, especially a number of Perp bosses. In front of the tower is part of the N transept. It is not easy to identify anything precisely under the ivy. But the

* The drawing room W of the ballroom has doorcases etc. of *c.*1740. But are they *in situ*?

fragment seems to consist of two polygonal piers with angle shafts, pushed together.

Also in the grounds is an odd SUMMER HOUSE, quite plain but with two quadrant colonnades, all on a very small scale. This may well have been designed by *Dance*.

CRAWLEY

4030

ST MARY. Nave and chancel and a thin W tower. Some Perp windows with good head-stops at the ends of the hood-moulds. In the N vestry parts of two lancets. The interior is surprising. Instead of arcades there are rough wooden posts with longitudinal arched braces. Also tie-beams on arched braces. The chancel arch has Norman responds and a C13 arch. On the E side of the arch bits of the zigzag of the original Norman arch. To the l. of the chancel arch a squint. The wooden posts must have been put up when the squint already existed. – PLATE. Silver-gilt Chalice, Paten, and Cruet given in 1824.

CRAWLEY COURT. 1877 by *F. P. Cockerell*. In an undisciplined free Elizabethan, large and grand, of flint, brick, and red terracotta.

DOWER HOUSE. Neo-Gothic brick house with a detached brick tower and a series of cottages with timber-framed gables along the village street.

CROFTON AND STUBBINGTON [DL]

5000

Stubbington is an old village caught in the northward spread of Lee-on-Solent; Crofton a straggle of houses towards Titchfield, in the still rural Lower Meon Valley enclave. They are taken together because the present Crofton parish church is in Stubbington, built in the C19 to supersede the still surviving ancient chapel in Crofton proper.

HOLY ROOD, Stubbington. 1878 by *T. Goodchild*. Conventional neo-Dec with clerestory and aisles. Bare yellow brickwork on the inside wall surfaces. Painted TILES on the chancel walls depicting Saints, 1889–92. The NW tower was intended to have a spire, which was never built; instead the tower was finished off in an arty way in 1928. – STAINED GLASS. E window, 1948 by *Hugh Easton*.

HOLY ROOD, Crofton, about $\frac{3}{4}$ m. NW of the village centre of Stubbington. The ancient chapel is an accumulation of homely architecture of several centuries. Wide nave probably C15, chancel and little S chapel perhaps C14; stumpy N transept certainly C14; bellcote of uncertain date; W wall in Georgian brick; big S transept of the early C19. The nave has square-headed windows of C15 type, a large Gothic window with wooden tracery in the W wall, and an attractive old queen-post roof of which the massive cross-beams look as if they are re-used; possibly ships' timbers. The axis of the chancel is well to the N of that of the nave. The chancel arch and the arch from chancel to chapel are simple C14, of two orders dying into square jambs; in the wall space to the S of the chancel arch is a half-arch leading into the chapel, which has a C14 E window. The N transept has a C14 curvilinear N window of three lights; the windows of the S transept are 'churchwarden' Gothick.* – PULPIT. Small, part octagonal, oak panels; late C17 or early C18. – MONUMENTS. In the S transept a large and rather unusual marble wall-monument to Thomas Missing † 1733. Large pedimented tablet with inscription, in front of a sarcophagus whose projecting ends are decorated by diagonal fluting and surmounted by urns. Bust above the tablet set in front of a tapering slab, and coat of arms at the top. – Several wall tablets.

STUBBINGTON. The village centre of Stubbington, with a small green, is still recognizable, but most of the buildings are now of C20 suburban character. The older ones that survive are mostly Georgian cottages. STUBBINGTON HOUSE (Crofton Community Association) has a central part with a mid Georgian façade of five bays and three storeys, in grey brick with red dressings, with an open pedimented porch. Plainer two-bay Georgian wings and considerable later additions.

CROFTON. The MANOR HOUSE next to the church is an old brick building with altered windows. It groups well with the adjoining farmyard, dominated by a round silo tower, and the church. CROFTON HOUSE, set back to the W of the Titchfield road, is a five-bay, three-storey, yellow brick mansion of *c.*1800. The three centre bays project slightly and are surmounted by a pediment, with fretted brickwork pattern under the cornices and slopes of the pediment (a local mannerism). A delicately composed building, unfortunately derelict at the

* The Rev. Basil Clarke (*The Building of Eighteenth Century Churches*) says that the church was considerably enlarged on the S side, *c.*1725, at the expense of Thomas Missing.

time of writing. HOLLAM HOUSE, at the Titchfield end of Crofton, is a three-bay, two-storey, red-brick Georgian house with pedimented porch.

CRONDALL 7040

ALL SAINTS. A puzzle church and a very powerful one, especially inside. Externally the most prominent feature is the high C17 brick W tower with clasping buttresses and arched bell-openings. The date must be shortly after 1659, when complaints were made that the medieval crossing tower endangered the walls. So the crossing tower does not exist any longer, but its NE stair-turret remains. The C17 tower cost £428. A walk round the outside of the church is confusing. It tells in odd places that this is a Norman church and that neo-Norman work was carried out to make it more Norman (in 1847),* but that chancel as well as clerestory and also some other details are E.E., or early C13. Norman a blocked N aisle window, Norman a fragmentarily preserved string course, also the S doorway of *c.*1200 with a roll-moulding, and the W doorway (*ex situ*) of *c.*1200 with a richly moulded arch and a head at the top. The N doorway must be nearly all of 1847. The interior is much more consistent, except that the two E bays of the nave suffer from ill-defined interference probably of *c.*1655, i.e. before the decision was taken to take down the tower. Nave and aisles, four-bay arcades, chancel. The E bay of the nave was the crossing, and the transepts are preserved. The arches from aisles to transepts (two slight chamfers) and the details of the responds here and by the chancel arch are still entirely Norman, without transitional elements. Semicircular responds, multi-scallop capitals, square abaci. The two W bays of the arcade follow. Same details, but one capital with water-leaf and the arches many-moulded. The E bays are the ones tampered with: how is not clear, in spite of the VCH. The second pair of piers from the W anyway were piers originally and not responds. The clerestory windows are tall, pointed, and shafted, i.e. after 1200. So is the splendid rib-vaulted chancel. Two bays, ribs with dogtooth. Crocket capitals, two bosses, one with the Lamb, one with leaves. The E fenestration is by *Scott*, 1871. The W fenestration had already replaced a Perp window in 1847. The chancel arch has Norman-looking responds still,

* By *Ferrey* (NT).

but is pointed and has side by side with zigzag also dogtooth. – PLATE. Cup probably of 1568; undated Paten. – MONUMENTS. Brass to Nicholas de Kaerment, rector 1361–81. A fine brass figure, 58 in. long (chancel floor). – Sir George Paulet † 1532. Recess with depressed, straight-sided arch. Buttress-shafts. Tomb-chest under the arch (chancel N). – John Gyfford † 1563. Purbeck marble with depressed arch and cresting. Against the back wall kneeling figure (chancel S). – Brass to John Eggar † 1641. Small plate with skeleton in shroud. – Tablets of † 1657 and of the C18.

Several good houses in CHURCH STREET.

4050 CRUX EASTON

ST MICHAEL. Built in 1775. Small, of brick, with a nave of three bays (arched windows) and an apse with one large arched window. The apse arch is semi-elliptical, and the apse itself is semi-elliptical too, and preceded by a short straight piece of chancel. Fine radial marble pavement in the apse and fine PANELLING round the altar with pilasters and oval paterae. – Of *c.*1775 also the PULPIT, the LECTERN with a wooden angel, the FONT, an Italian marble bowl on a stone baluster carved with a religious scene (Continental too ?), and the CHURCHYARD GATES. – PLATE. Set of 1707.

CURBRIDGE *see* CURDRIDGE

5010 CURDRIDGE [DL]

On the edge of the fruit-growing country; scattered cottages on smallholdings, rural Victorian villas in well-treed grounds, and a small amount of recent infilling.

ST PETER. 1887–8, tower 1894, by *Sir Thomas Jackson*. Quite a large unaisled church, basically simple, but with too much fussy detailing. Flint, stone. Massive half-timbered porch. Tower to a Dorset-like design but with East-Anglian-style flushwork. Lively gargoyles, including one of a horse. Roomy interior with elaborate roof.

At CURBRIDGE, 1½ m. S of Curdridge church, is a small brick neo-E.E. CHAPEL, 1892 by *Ewan Christian*.

1010 DAMERHAM

ST GEORGE. A complicated story. It begins oddly enough with the arch from the S tower to the N. This is a single-step

Norman arch of alternating brown and white stone. The tower remained short. Its further details are C17, and the top peters out weatherboarded. Was this a tower arch originally or a transept arch? Norman also the three-bay N arcade. The responds and the arches are in order. Two of the arches have fat rolls. The piers themselves are a much later replacement. Then late C12 the N chapel, since demolished. This had a round pier with a trumpet-scallop capital, a round abacus, and arches with rolls. On the respond capitals a kind of small crockets. After that followed the S chancel chapel, also demolished. The remains point to the C13. C13 also the S arcade. Two bays, pier of Greek-cross shape with canted corners. Double-chamfered arches. The arch to the S tower also belongs here. The chancel itself is now Perp, see the large E window and the two large three-light N windows. Big Perp S porch. Big five-light Perp W window. Nice wagon roofs in chancel, nave, and S porch. – SCULPTURE. In the porch a Norman tympanum. A slayer on horseback and his adversary on the ground. – Above the porch entrance small E.E. Christ in Majesty in a mandorla. – PLATE. Chalice and Paten Cover, 1577; Paten, 1719; Flagon, 1755.

COURT FARM. Georgian front of five bays, brick, with a three-bay pediment. But in the centre on the ground floor three early C14 arches and early C14 two-light windows. Big buttressed BARN.

EARTHWORK, at Soldiers Rings, 2 m. NW. A polygonal earthwork of Roman date, thought to be a Late Roman cattle enclosure.

DANESBURY DOWN *see* NETHER WALLOP

DANESHILL *see* BASING

DEANE 5050

ALL SAINTS. Built in 1818. The architect seems unrecorded – which is a pity, as this is the most complete and successful early C19 Gothic church in the county. W tower, nave, and chancel, cement-rendered. Perp tracery, in the E window of iron, battlements, and elaborate pinnacles. Pretty S porch, vaulted inside, with a fine frieze of the kind familiar from Perp screens. Inside, the tower arch, tower gallery, a tripartite chancel screen, a pointed tunnel-vault decorated over the altar (ceilure-wise), the elaborate altar surround, and all the rest is as it was in 1818.* – STAINED GLASS. In the porch windows early C16. – In the E window Crucifixus typical of the early C19, but the surround apparently of *c.*1870 or 1880. – PLATE. Tazza Cup of 1551, chased, with a helmeted figure in the centre, formerly secular; Chalice, 1569, and Paten Cover, 1570; Flagon given in 1694. – MONUMENTS. George Wither † 1666. Oval plate with garland. On the l. and r. black pilasters. Good. – Charles Wither † 1731. White tablet without figures. – Wither Bramston (at whose expense the church was built) † 1832. Gothic tablet, by *Croggan* of London, 1834. – Many more tablets.

DEANE HOUSE. Brick, large and irregular. To the S a five-bay front of two storeys, with a square porch. The upper window has a raised brick surround, and the other windows probably have them too. That would date this side of the house late C17. L. addition and recent complete r. wing. (Inside two C17 overmantels and a Georgian staircase with thin turned balusters. VCH)

6010

DENMEAD [DL]

Once a widely scattered village in the former forest country behind Portsmouth, now extensively infilled and suburban in feeling.

ALL SAINTS. 1880 by *C. R. Pink & S. Fowler*.‡ Flint with stone and brick dressings. – FONT. C14 or C15; octagonal with quatrefoils in panels. From Hambledon.

(At WORLD'S END, to the W of Denmead, is a letter box of 1859, surely one of the earliest in England. S. Weeks)

ROOKWOOD FARM (formerly Denmead Farm), 1¾ m. NW. Apparently altered from a medieval chapel, with Tudor extensions to E and S in timber framing and brick. Remains of round-headed windows in the N and S walls.

See p. 828

4000

DIBDEN [DL]

Fields and woods across the water form the precious, still rural backcloth to Southampton's central quays and waterfront; an interlude between the recently industrialized areas of Fawley and Marchwood. They ought to be kept that way.

* Mr Colvin informed the Rev. Basil Clarke that many of the details are of *Coade* Stone.

‡ Mr Nicholas Taylor says that C. R. Pink was President of the Architectural Association in 1885. Great things were expected of him but he died young, in 1889.

ALL SAINTS. Bombed in 1940, restored by *Pinckney & Gott* and re-opened in 1955. The church now has a late C13 chancel, C20 nave, and tower of 1884. The ruined aisles were demolished and new nave walls built along the lines of the arcades; the new work is Gothic and unexceptionable. The internal stonework of the chancel is worn through calcination and subsequent exposure to the weather, but the effect is visually good and a telling testimony to the tragedy of war. Chancel arch C13, of two chamfered orders, dying into the walls without capitals. The chancel is lofty and well-proportioned, flanked by decorative blank arcading, chamfered and with rounded shafts – an unusual embellishment for a small church. The W arch on the S side has a trefoil shape, perhaps originally to accommodate a window which was larger than the others. The present windows are all later; the two on the N side two-light trefoiled (one of them ogee), C14; the two on the S side to a rather playful design with two cinquefoiled lights under a round arch within a square-headed frame, with tiny triangular openings in the spandrels; possibly late C14. The tall three-light E window is to a Victorian geometrical design within a medieval frame. The tower is pleasantly proportioned; broad, low, and battlemented. – FONT. C12, damaged but well restored. Square Purbeck marble bowl with arched recesses; typical base with stem and detached shafts. – PLATE. Chalice and Paten Cover, Elizabethan type; Paten, 1696. – STAINED GLASS. E window by *Derek Wilson*, *c*.1955. Christ Triumphant, rising from burial. Deep, rich colours, very effective as the climax of the eastward view, blue, blue-grey, and purple.

The houses of Dibden are few and scattered and melt into the rolling park-like landscape; there are splendid views across to the funnels and cranes, chimneys, spires, and towers of Southampton.

DOGMERSFIELD 7050

ALL SAINTS. 1843 by *B. Ferrey*. Of chalk, W tower, nave, and chancel. Modest dimensions. E.E. style. – FONT. Of white marble, baluster stem and small bowl, Georgian. – PLATE. Paten Cover, 1569; Chalice, 1572; Paten, 1677; Flagon, 1711. – MONUMENTS. Brass to Anne Sutton † 1590. Tablet with kneeling figure (nave E). – Large tablet to Sir Henry St J. Mildmay † 1808. By *Nollekens*. White; no figures. – Lady St

J. Mildmay. 1840 by *B. Cacciatori* of Milan. Weeping young woman with a baby by an urn. Good.

OLD CHURCH. The predecessor church was built in 1806 and lies close to the drive to the college. Brick. W tower with battlements. No separate chancel. The nave is only two bays long. Pointed windows.

DOGMERSFIELD PARK (College of the De La Salle Brothers). Built in 1728 for Martha Goodyer and her husband Ellis St John (the later Paulet St John Mildmay family). Large, red brick, and plain. The entrance side of three storeys, the garden side round the corner of two. Both have a central pediment. The interest of the house is wholly inside. Two rooms have sumptuous plaster ceilings with acanthus, shells, etc., and also good cornices. Two rooms also have good fireplaces. One of the two is outstanding, with two diagonally placed young termini maidens.

The new CHAPEL of the college is by *Max Cross*, somewhat modernistic. But in it *Eric Gill*'s late STATIONS OF THE CROSS, exquisitely incised wooden tablets.

The grounds were laid out by *Emes* (Burke's *Seats*).

DRAYTON *see* PORTSMOUTH, p. 466

6010 DROXFORD [DL]

A fairly large village in the Meon Valley, near the border of the chalklands and the clay-and-sand country of south-east Hampshire. It has less positive shape than other prominent old villages in this part of the county, such as Botley or Wickham, and so is less memorable as a whole, even though it is full of pleasant minor domestic architecture.

ST MARY AND ALL SAINTS. A medium-sized, typically Hampshire village church, with work of many periods. Norman nave, chancel arch, and re-set side doorways. N aisle and chapel added in the late C12, and S aisle and chapel in the early C13. Chapels rebuilt in the C14 and aisles in the C15. W tower dated 1599. Chancel roof altered in Georgian times. Victorian restorations did not alter the fabric but resulted in the church being entirely refitted. The steep nave roof slopes down continuously over the aisles in Sussex 'catslide' fashion, broken only by C19 dormers on the S side, but the clerestoried chancel has a distinctive roof-line, with Georgian coved cornice and boldly projecting eaves, in the manner characteristic of some of the early C18 domestic architecture of the district.* The tower, like the rest of the church, is built of flint, with a curious square stair-turret projecting diagonally from the NW corner and later brick battlements. The church's Norman features are straightforward but strong in their detailing. The chancel arch, evidently altered, has a thick roll moulding to its outer order and a thinner one to its inner order, with simple zigzag ornament round its outside and shafts with simply carved capitals to its responds. The N and S doorways, re-set in the later aisles, have much the same elements, except that their outer arches have tooth moulding. The Norman N and S walls of the original nave substantially remain, but pierced by three arches on either side, not forming continuous arcades but separated by stretches of the original walling in between them. All the arches are pointed, those on the N side dating from the late C12 with just a slight chamfer. Only the E bay has a thin angle roll like the chancel arch. The S arcade is early C13, with semicircular, deeply moulded corbels to the inner of their two orders. The arches from the chancel into the N and S chapels are similar to the corresponding ones in the nave, but wider, i.e. the N arch is like the E arch of the N arcade, the S arch is double-chamfered. It rests not on corbels but on two busts in style early C14 like the chapel windows (*see* below). Parts of the splays of two blocked Norman windows above the arch into the S chapel show that this arch, like those in the nave, was pierced through a pre-existing Norman wall. The E window is three-light Perp; the windows of the N and S chapels are early C14, with cusped Y-tracery and one cusped-intersecting. This window has a wide niche, originally much elaborated but now mutilated, in the wall space immediately to the N, with miniature ribbed vaulting under its canopy. The windows of the aisles are Perp. – FURNISHINGS. COMMUNION RAIL. A fine piece of C17 craftsmanship, the thick rail supported on a series of balusters with turned shafts, with end posts crowned by large finials (cf. Bishops Waltham). These were turned out at a Victorian restoration but replaced in 1903, when the present SANCTUARY PANELLING was designed to match them. – SCREEN, from N aisle to chapel. Neo-Jacobean, by *Sir Charles Nicholson*, 1935. – PLATE. Cup, Paten, and Flagon, 1632; Cup and Paten, 1737. – MONUMENTS. In the S chapel

* However, the nave roof inside is hidden by a plaster vault, and the heavy cornice of this shows it to be Georgian.

the recumbent effigy of a lady, late C13, a fine piece of formalized sculpture. Said to have been discovered buried in a near-by meadow in the early C19. – Two wall-tablets at the W end of the N aisle with good lettering; one is a cartouche with simple Baroque decoration on its surround, to Francis Morley † 1690, the other to Charles Morley, 1697.

THE VILLAGE. Many of Droxford's houses are Georgian, humble to moderate in scale, and built in local brick, either all in red or in grey patterned with red. Unfortunately too many are whitewashed, so that the attractive local colour and texture of their brickwork is lost. A few have simple classical doorcases or porches. There is some surviving pre-Georgian timber-framing and a limited use of flint, especially in boundary walls. Roofs are almost all of local tiles, with only a very few humble cottages under thatch, such as are common in the villages of the chalklands further N. The RECTORY next to the church is externally the finest house in the village. It is Early Georgian with a main N front of five bays, the centre three slightly projecting, faced in the characteristic local pattern of grey and red brick, with a hipped roof, tall sashes on the two main storeys, and dormers lighting the attic. The main entrance has a doorcase with entablature and Tuscan demi-columns. There is also a fine five-bay E front. The MANOR HOUSE, also close to the church, is a brick house evidently of C17 origin, with a two-gabled main W façade and gables on other frontages; the windows were altered in Georgian times and afterwards. At the N end of the village street, set back on the E side, is a Georgian house with two canted bays and a pedimented doorcase. Opposite a plain but nicely proportioned five-bay house with a porch. At the S end of the village street is another pleasant group of old houses, the most striking of which is a five-bay Georgian house in grey and red brick with pedimented doorcase. Further S still is BEACON HOUSE, 1928, with a thatched roof, and a garden laid out by *Gertrude Jekyll*.

Outside the village, at the crossing of the main road and the by-road from Soberton, a C17 brick FARMHOUSE with an older timber-framed wing. Near by is MIDLINGTON HOUSE, set in a small park, a tall three-storey mansion of five bays, the middle three brought forward and plainly pedimented. The house is built almost entirely of the local grey brick, the customary red brick dressings being limited to the window heads and the angular quoins – giving a striking visual effect.

DUCK'S NEST LONG BARROW *see* ROCKBOURNE

DUMMER

5040

ALL SAINTS. Nave and chancel and bell-turret. The chancel is of *c.*1200, see the lancets and the chancel arch with one slight chamfer. To the N of the chancel arch is a C14 niche for the reredos of a lay altar. To the S a squint, round-headed from the E. What is its date? In the nave a low tomb recess. – PULPIT. Of wood, Perp, with simple tracery at the top of the panels. – Deep WEST GALLERY. – ROOD CANOPY. Of wood, coved, four by two panels with big square bosses. – COMMUNION RAIL. Late C17, with strong, twisted balusters. – STAINED GLASS. By *Kempe* the E window (1895) and one chancel S window (1898). – PLATE. Cup and Cover Paten, 1570.

PARSONAGE, ¼ m. S. By *W. J. Donthorne*, 1850. Coursed, knapped flint and stone; Tudor style. Symmetrical front with two gables and a smaller middle porch gable. Windows with mullions and transoms. Decorated chimneys of moulded yellow bricks.

DUMMER HOUSE, ¼ m. S. Stuccoed, of eleven bays in a 3–5–3 rhythm. Five-bay pediment, and under it the five first-floor windows all arched. In the pediment a big Palladian tripartite lunette window.

DUMMER GRANGE, 1¼ m. S. Of this impressive brick front on a compact E-plan only the l. wing and the back wall l. and r. of the porch are original. Their date must be the later C17. Giant Ionic angle pilasters with brick capitals. Also a moulded brick frieze. Gable. The porch is dated 1921.

DURLEY

[DL] *5010*

A widely scattered village, mainly of C19 and C20 houses, but with a few older cottages and farms. As so often in the Hampshire claylands, the church stands away from most of the population it serves.

HOLY CROSS. A pleasing hamlet church with a regular plan: nave, chancel, shallow transepts, and W gable bell-turret. Apparently built *c.*1300, but restored in 1879 by *Colson*, and again in 1884, when the exterior was roughcast and (probably) the nave dormers were put in. Chancel and transept windows are *c.*1300 in style and mostly original, those in the chancel trefoiled (three-light E window and two-light side windows), the single-light E transept windows similar, but the N and S transept windows two-light with Y-tracery. S nave doorway a simple chamfered arch without capitals. Chancel arch of 1879. There are no arches into the transepts; their entrances are simply spanned by the lengthwise beams carrying the nave roof. The bell-turret externally has boarded sides and shingled spirelet; the timber substructure is open to the nave, and the central upper beams are curved to an ogee-arched shape, with engaging effect. – PULPIT. Dated 1630, a fine piece; octagonal, with tall round-arched panels, carved with strapwork, and smaller panels above. Sounding-board with panelling underneath, and shallow hood with pointed finials at the angles. – PLATE. Cup and Paten, 1721. – WALL PAINTING. Traces of the painting of a ship with a man in the rigging, on the splay of the E window of the N transept, probably C14. – MONUMENT. A wide, empty C14 tomb recess in the S transept.

4000

EAGLEHURST [DL]

2 m. SE of Fawley

An estate on the woody shore of the Solent, secluded even now. There are two buildings, LUTTRELL'S TOWER, a super-folly built in the mid or later C18 by Temple Simon Luttrell, and a spreading, mainly single-storeyed house with castellated wings. The tower stands near the edge of the low sandy cliff. It is faced with yellow brick and roughcast, and rises through three storeys of unequal height, the middle storey being the lowest of the three and the top storey the tallest and most important. There are mildly Gothick windows to each floor on the seaward and landward façades, those on the top floor brought out in shallow bays, and a sharp central bay on the E (side) façade, flanked by niches on the two lower storeys, those on the middle storey containing urns. The W side of the tower contains the circular stair-turret, which rises for a further three stages and ends, like the main tower, in a castellated top – the dominant feature of the exterior. Inside there is a single handsome room on each floor, that on the top floor specially memorable, with a frieze of Gothick traceried baskets alternating with shells, and a very fine wooden fireplace of *c.*1700 or before, brought in from elsewhere. There is a substantial cellar (containing another very handsome imported fireplace, also probably late C17), from which a passageway leads directly on to the beach;

it seems that it really was designed and used for high-class smuggling. A fine stepway with diverging curves leads up from the beach to the base of the tower.

The house proper is set back across a lawn from the tower. Its centrepiece is one-storeyed, with three low bays, very simply pedimented, the central bay projecting on a slight segmental curve, and aligned directly on the axis of the tower. These are flanked by one further bay each side, similar in outline and proportion, slightly canted forward and linked with the end castellated wings which rise to two storeys. The landward façade of the house is much more simple, with plain Tuscan columns flanking the entrance. The three chief rooms are behind the central bays of the main façade, with boldly coved ceilings in two tiers, each room containing a plaque over the fireplace showing a lively classical scene in plasterwork relief, finely executed. Some of the fireplaces are original (notably that of the central room, with Ionic columns, and that of the hall, Gothick); others have been brought in, such as that probably of Elizabethan date, with a Tudor-shaped arch and strapwork decoration, in the room to the E of the hall.

In the grounds is a simple TEMPLE with four Tuscan columns at the end of a long hedged axis on the line of the entrance of the main house. The whole layout comes into its own when seen from the top of Luttrell's Tower, with the tower, the centre of the main house, and the temple on a single axis.

EAST BOLDRE 3000

ST PAUL. 1839 by *J. Tulloch.* Red brick, lancets, bell-turret a little corbelled out. – WEST GALLERY on iron columns.

EAST DEAN 2020

CHURCH. Nave and chancel and a small bell-turret. One Norman chancel N window. The rest is mostly Victorian, but to the S of the Victorian chancel arch is a blank arch which must have been the arch of a reredos for a lay altar next to the original narrower chancel arch. The N doorway is built of heavy timbers. The interior of the church is unrestored and very attractive in its mood. – WEST GALLERY. – FONT. C18; the stem is the shaft of a fluted column.

4010 ## EASTLEIGH [DL]

A railway town. The station was built in open country in 1839 it became 'Bishopstoke Junction' when the line to Gosport, serving Portsmouth, was opened in 1842 (followed by that t Salisbury in 1847). A mid-Victorian village of railway worker grew up, taking its name from a near-by farm. Town growt came with the removal of the L. & S. W. R. carriage works fron Nine Elms in 1891, which was followed by engine repair shed (from Southampton) in 1903 and locomotive workshops (fron Nine Elms) in 1910. Other industries have developed since th First World War. Modern Eastleigh is a grid pattern of late C1 and early C20 streets, with ordinary suburban fringes, kep physically separate from Southampton only through the stric maintenance of a green belt. The borough (population 36,577 i 1961) includes Bishopstoke, Chandler's Ford, and Nort Stoneham, all of which are described separately.

RAILWAY STATION. *Tite*'s rectangular block of 1840 stil survives amid large-scale later additions; simple Italianat classical, with his favourite ranges of chimneystacks, joine at the tops, the intermediate spaces below formed into roun arches. The same chimney pattern is seen at the faintl Gothic RAILWAY HOTEL, another survival from the days o Bishopstoke Junction.

CHURCH OF THE RESURRECTION. A small church for railway-men was built by *Street* in 1868, with nave, chancel, and S tran-sept. A N aisle was added by *Pearson* in 1884, and a big nev nave, chancel, and S aisle built by *Sir Arthur Blomfield* i 1899–1905, to which the old nave and chancel have become N aisle and chapel. They look relatively humble now, bu pleasantly proportioned, Street's Geometrical E window an chancel arch being in the style of *c.*1300 and Pearson's aisle with low arcades of two orders and octagonal piers, in that o *c.*1320. Nicely shaped arch-braced roofs to old nave and chan-cel. – The REREDOS, with a carving of the Resurrection, an the FONT, circular with trefoiled panels, are from Street' original church. Blomfield's church is big rather than impres-sive, but at its SW corner is the re-erected bell-turret fron Street's church, formerly at the angle of chancel and transept it is circular, with an upper range of open traceried bell openings and a conical tiled cap.

The adjoining SCHOOL, a pleasant many-gabled composi

tion in brick, 1870 (with later additions), looks as if it might be by *Street*.

ALL SAINTS, Derby Road. 1909–10 by *J. B. Colson & Nesbitt*. Nave and chancel with polygonal apse, aisles, and wider chapels, in a sort of neo-Perp style. The most remarkable feature of the church is the BAPTISTERY, a semicircular marble tank designed for total immersion (like those used in Baptist churches), put in at the request of the principal beneficiary of the church and said never to have been used. A conventional font is placed near by.

PARISH HALL, Grantham Road. Built in 1891 as a mission church, the predecessor of All Saints. By *J. H. Ball*, the architect of St Agatha, Portsmouth. A small but distinguished building with inventive brickwork patterning in red against drabber brown, and a slated roof, sweeping over the lean-to aisles at lower pitch. Triple lancets between buttresses in the aisles; the W front with a single buttress, stepped back well below the gable, with a cross brought out in brickwork on the upper part, and a pretty gable turret at the top.

Eastleigh has plenty of public buildings, churches, etc., of the period 1890–1910, but none are architecturally memorable. The RAILWAY INSTITUTE of 1891 is in drab brick with neo-Jacobean details, the COUNCIL OFFICES of 1898–9, in redder brick, have heavy neo-Renaissance motifs. Both are by *Mitchell, Son & Gutteridge*.

EAST MEON 6020

ALL SAINTS. The church, one of the most thrilling village churches in Hampshire, lies immediately below a perfect South Downs hill, smooth turf and no trees. So close does the church come to the hill that it could not have a N aisle. It is a cruciform church commanded by a splendid Norman tower of *c*.1150. This is ashlar-faced, has nook-shafts at the angles, and on each side three bell-openings richly shafted. The capitals have several scallops, the arches much zigzag. A thin zigzag frieze separates this stage from the top stage, which has circular openings. The lead-covered broach-spire fits very well. Norman also is the W doorway. Two orders of shafts. Fluted and primitive leaf capitals. Zigzag at r. angles to the wall, i.e. later than the tower. The (re-set) S doorway is a little simpler than the W doorway but goes with it in date. Externally otherwise there is one Norman N window in the nave, and there are two in the S transept. The western one shows that the S aisle came after the transept. The curious N window of two lights with straight diagonals instead of an arch and equally straightened Y-tracery must be Dec. The S aisle windows are late C13 (plate tracery), though the nook-shafted SW quoin looks suspiciously earlier. The W window is shafted in an early C14 way. The rest of it is C19. The E window also has shafting, but inside. It looks late C13. But the window itself is in the Perp style by *Comper* (RH). Perp S chapel window. These alterations have the arms of Prior Hinton, i.e. must date from between 1470 and 1498.

Inside the church the interest is of course concentrated on the crossing. The E and W arches go with the tower. Tripartite responds. Decorated scallop capitals. But what has happened to the N and S arches? Were they originally left uncarved and then, much later, tidied up in a summary way? The chancel is separated from the S chapel by an early C13 arcade. Sturdy round pier, round capitals and abacus, big hollow chamfers in the arch. The S aisle arcade is different, but in date only a little later. Very short octagonal piers. Arches with one chamfer and one thin roll. This may just match the window plate tracery. The aisle is connected with the transept by a half-arch. – FONT. Of black Tournai marble. Table-top type. Splendid bold, vigorous carving of *c.*1130–40 (cf. Winchester Cathedral). On the N side Creation of Adam, Creation of Eve,
15 and Temptation. On the E side Expulsion from Paradise and the Angel showing Adam how to dig. On the other sides arcading and above this a frieze with affronted dragons, birds, and animals. On the top in the corners foliage and affronted birds. The font is one of a group, the others in Hampshire being Winchester Cathedral, St Mary Bourne, and St Michael Southampton. – PULPIT. 1706. From Holy Trinity, Minories, London. With modest inlay. – (By *Comper* the REREDOS in the Lady Chapel, the SCREEN between chancel and chapel, and the STAINED GLASS of the E window. RH) PLATE. Silver-gilt Cup and Paten, 1747; Paten, 1751.

COURT HOUSE, E of the church. The house and the manor belonged to the Bishops of Winchester. The house was built about 1400 or a little later. The original part consists of the hall running N–S and with two tall transomed straight-headed two-light windows to the W and E. At the N end of the hall, facing W, big doorway with two continuous chamfers. In the N wall two doorways. This and the entrance indicate that this was the screens passage end and that the offices lay in the N wing, which is preserved. The S wing has disappeared. It must have contained the main living room. The small doorway to the former staircase up to the solar can still be seen. In the hall this then was the high-table end. The hall now ends to the S with a big fireplace of *c.*1500. Shields in quatrefoils in the lintel. The hall roof has tie-beams on arched braces and thin long kingposts and four-way struts. The arched braces start from excellent head corbels. In the N wing on the upper floor two two-light windows. On the ground floor were no doubt buttery and pantry, and there are indications that a small entirely separate room was connected with the garderobe shoot.*

The VILLAGE has a very pretty HIGH STREET, with a stream running in its middle. On the N side the finest house, GLENTHORNE, *c.*1690, of brick, in red and blue chequer. Five bays with a bold middle projection. In it the doorway with a big brick pediment and the window above with lugs and tiny volutes. Raised brick quoins at the angles of the house. Pretty closure of the picture looking E. At the N end of the axis, in THE SQUARE is TUDOR HOUSE, with closely set timber studs on the upper floor.

WESTBURY HOUSE, 1½ m. NW. The house is of 1906. In front the ruin of the chapel of ST NICHOLAS, nave and chancel, with hardly any recognizable features left. The STABLES of the house are Early Georgian. Red brick. Seven bays with blank arches and a middle archway, and, in addition, at the ends low towers with pyramid roofs and also with archways.

EASTNEY *see* PORTSMOUTH, pp. 428, 429, 436, 440, 443, 463

EASTON 5030

ST MARY. Entirely of *c.*1200, and made more showily Norman in the 1860s by *Woodyer*. The picturesquely outlandish W tower with its shingled top parts must be his, except for the lower parts, including the arch towards the nave, which takes us to *c.*1200: unmoulded pointed arch. Above it round-arched doorway into the former nave roof. But these motifs will hardly be noticed, so strong is the impact of the chancel. It consists of a rib-vaulted square bay and a rib-vaulted apse. Finely moulded ribs, simple bosses. Between chancel and apse an

* The house was restored by *Morley Horder*, who lived in it and died in it in 1944 (RH).

arch of four orders of slender shafts with typically late C12 capitals. Zigzag in the arch. The chancel has in addition a W arch. This has daintily shafted responds including some keeling and capitals with decorated waterleaf. The arch with keeled rolls has rather caved in. The nave has a S doorway with Norman decoration (e.g. three shaft-rings round the shafts), nearly entirely Victorian, and a simpler N doorway. The position of the doorways midway down the nave is unusual. Also two Norman N windows, small outside, but large and provided with a continuous keeled roll inside. – PULPIT. Jacobean, with arabesque panels above panels with small double-arches. Much over-cleaned. – MONUMENT. Agatha Barlow. Dated 1595. Inscription, two unfluted Ionic columns, and a small ogee-curved gable with the date.

See p. 828

1090

EAST PARLEY

(ST BARNABAS. 1862–3 by *G. E. Street*. The only one of Morden Bennett's foundations (*see* Bournemouth, p. 118) not to be surrounded now by an urban population. A simple brick chapel, an excellent example of Street's versatility on a small budget. Clear-cut geometry: shingled bellcote, low buttresses, English-bond brickwork, Middle-Pointed windows ranging from three-light E and W to a sexfoiled circle on the chancel S. Total cost £900. – STAINED GLASS. E window by *Powell's*, 1918. NT)

5030

EAST STRATTON

ALL SAINTS. Designed by *Sir Thomas G. Jackson* and built in 1885–90. Nave and chancel, small N aisle, and N tower with shingled broach-spire. Knapped flint. Timber porch. Perp windows. A little brother of Northington, and also a Baring job. – PLATE. Silver-gilt Cup and Paten, 1709.

In the village five pairs of ESTATE COTTAGES, brick, each one bay, two storeys, and a side porch. By *Dance*.

STRATTON PARK. By *George Dance* the Younger, 1803. Of the
75 house only the portico survives, with its mighty Tuscan columns and its pediment. Dance must have been fully aware of the Ledoux style in Paris. The portico has been made wonderfully resourcefully into a piece of scenery of a house built in 1963–5 to the design of *Stephen Gardiner & Christopher Knight*. The axis of the portico is continued in an oblong pond, and then the lush conservatory of the house, which has

to the l. of the conservatory most of its rooms, to the r. on the ground floor guest rooms, on the first floor the main living room. The staircase to this rises in the conservatory. The conservatory is steel-framed, the rest brick. The brick is brown, and with the African-mahogany framing makes the house look from a distance a rather sombre hue. Pretty Victorian LODGE on the NW with bargeboarded gable.

LONDON LODGE, 1⅛ m. NNE. Two classical lodges, but a castellated archway with four polygonal turrets, and again, in spite of this, a classical frieze and in the centre a palmette.

EAST TISTED 7030

ST JAMES. 1846, except for the lower part of the tower and one part of the S doorway, which must be early C14. The tower has a stair-turret, an open parapet, and pinnacles. The aisles are given pinnacles too. The tracery is Perp. All this is still pre-ecclesiological in style, yet no longer as carefree as the early Gothic Revival or as matter-of-fact as the Commissioners' type of Gothic church. – REREDOS. Parts of the Gothick reredos now in the S aisle. – PLATE. Cup, Paten, and Almsdish, 1702. – MONUMENTS. In the S aisle on the floor a slab with a cross in whose head a sunk bust. At the foot a dog. – Richard Norton † 1556 and wife. Erected about 1540. The 47
tomb-chest already has Renaissance decoration round the shields, but above is the usual pre-Reformation recess with side pieces and depressed arch plainly traceried inside and a straight cornice. Against the back wall kneeling figures looking from l. and r. to a Resurrection. Scrolls above the figures. – John Norton † before 1564. Early Elizabethan, of stone. Two small kneeling figures facing one another across a prayer-desk. Oblong strapwork cartouche behind. Intricate strapwork and wreaths in the panels on the tomb-chest below. L. and r. Ionic columns. The top is a kind of flat-topped concave-sided gable. – Sir John Norton † 1686. Very bad semi-reclining marble figure on a sarcophagus. – Also busts of Scotts † 1855 and † 1873.

ROTHERFIELD PARK. Rotherfield Park was built for James Scott in 1815–21 by *J. T. Parkinson.* This house survives only in outline. It was Gothic in the sense that it was castellated and had a big SW corner tower and a thinner SE turret. But the windows were normal sashes, and the walls were stuccoed. The latter disadvantage was remedied on the garden side in the 1860s, when this side was more radically gothicized as well, and in 1893, when the other two main sides were elizabethanized. Next to the house, through a gatehouse of 1891 one meets a very mighty twin tower with stair-turret. This is a water tower, and it dates most probably from the 1860s. Next to this are the stables, their proportionate cupola raised in the 1890s as a tower to an excessive height. Inside the house the finest room is the staircase, starting in one arm and returning in two. It fills the space of the courtyard preceding the present house. It is mildly Gothic and has skylighting. This must be of *c.*1820, even if the details here and indeed in the other rooms are of the sixties. The position of Rotherfield Park is superb. The LODGES on the E are unaltered 1820s.

In the village many enterprising and entertaining ESTATE COTTAGES from the 1820s on. They have bargeboards and fancy glazing bars and appear in groups and singles.

VICARAGE. Probably mid C19. According to the Rev. Basil Clarke by *T. E. Owen.* Tudor with steep gables.

2020

EAST TYTHERLEY

ST PETER. Nicely compact, and huddling together. Externally mostly Victorian. The N tower was built in 1897–8. The chancel is E.E., and the side lancets, the priest's doorway, and the chancel arch are all original, though over-restored. – STAINED GLASS. Three small figures of saints, C13 – a rarity. – PLATE. Two Chalices and two Patens, 1705. – MONUMENT. Richard Gifford † 1568 and family. Now badly displayed at the W end. It stood against the nave S wall near its E end. That is the reason why of the small kneeling figures the women look steadfastly ahead, but the man turns his head to look back, and two of his sons turn it at least so far as to be seen frontally. Two big tapering pillars with fancy detail à la Vredeman de Vries. Complete gable with achievement.

SCHOOL, ¼ m. SSE. Founded in 1736. Red brick, five bays, two storeys, wooden mullioned windows of two lights, hipped roof. The doorway is later.

HILDON HALL, 1¾ m. NE, by *Sir Aston Webb*, 1898, has been demolished. Only the water tower is still there.

3020

EAST WELLOW

ST MARGARET. The chancel first. Its stepped C13 E lancets are placed under a slightly chamfered round arch, i.e. an arch of c.1180 or so. In the S wall the priest's doorway and one lancet have double voussoirs. Here also earlier openings must be assumed. The roundel with a quatrefoil in the E gable is of course C13, the low-side window has an ogee head, i.e. must be an earlier C14 insertion, or rather alteration. The nave has an early C13 S doorway with a slight chamfer. The N doorway is the same, but restored almost out of existence. In the N wall a lancet, in the S side in the roof two cosy dormers. – PULPIT. Jacobean, with back panel and tester. – STALLS. With some Jacobean panels. – More in the ALTAR SURROUND. – COMMUNION RAIL. With flat, cut-out balusters; Jacobean. – PAINTING. A remarkable amount of wall painting, probably of the early C13. Ashlar patterns, absolutely square, which deprives it of any reality, with little rosettes on nave and chancel walls. Then above, on the nave N wall, on the l. a castle, then St Christopher holding the child in his arms, not carrying it on his shoulder. Then a smaller figure spinning and a Knight facing her. Also in the jamb of a chancel N window a crowned figure, and on the S chancel wall close to its E end the murder of Thomas Becket. This is much too badly preserved to produce any aesthetic reactions, and this applies to a certain extent even to the scenes on the nave N wall. – An Icon of two Saints, bought in the C20 at Istanbul. – PLATE. Paten of 1714; Chalice of 1733; Almsdish of 1829.

EMBLEY PARK, 1¼ m. ENE. Large, brick, Elizabethan-Victorian. Built mostly just after 1895.

EAST WOODHAY

4060

ST MARTIN. 1823 by *Billing & Son*. Brick. The W tower with its pointed windows is still Georgian. The long and high nave with its characteristically many and thin buttresses has had Victorian geometrical tracery put in. The flint chancel in the Early Dec style is of 1849, the S porch of 1887. Inside, the nave is very typical of the 1820s, wide and not high, with a complicated timber roof of relatively thin timbers. Basically the system is scissor-bracing, and there is plenty of cusping to enrich the effect. – STAINED GLASS. Mrs Stanton knows of a *Pugin* window here. It may well be the one in the S wall of the chancel. – PLATE. Chalice, 1631; Paten, 1696; Flagon, 1718. – MONUMENT. Edward Goddard † 1724 and his wife † 1732. Large standing monument. Husband and wife in their everyday clothes stand l. and r. of an urn. Reredos background with coupled pilasters. The monument lacks swagger and flourishes. Is it meant to represent his 'sober life and conversation'?

See p. 828 HOLLINGTON FARMHOUSE, 1¼ m. SW of Highclere church. Georgian, of brick. Three widely spaced bays. One-bay projection with pediment. This centre has blue headers and red dressings, the side parts are all red. In the side parts Venetian windows with segmental instead of semicircular arches.

7030 EAST WORLDHAM

ST MARY. Early C13 all. Nave and chancel and formerly an apse. Lancet windows, internally with fine continuous roll mouldings. Almost identical S and N doorways of two orders of colonnettes with waterleaf capitals, pointed, richly moulded arches, and dogtooth in the hood-mould. The priest's doorway is contemporary too, though it has fully developed stiff-leaf capitals. The W side has three widely spaced lancets, shafted inside and outside. The corresponding feature on the E side looks Victorian. *David Brandon* did much in 1865. – SCULPTURE. White miniature copy of Thorwaldsen's tympanum of the Frue Church at Copenhagen. – Large architectural fragment with zigzag and dogtooth. Was it a boss or a jambstone, and where would it come from? – PLATE. Early Georgian Chalice and Flagon; two Patens, 1829 and 1843. – MONUMENT. Lady, early C14; only the bust appears in a recess, the rest of the slab is left flat and unworked.

SCHOOL, to the SE, on the B-road. By *Brandon*, 1862–4. Nothing special.

5050 ECCHINSWELL

ST LAURENCE. By *Bodley & Garner*, 1886, and recognizably theirs. Knapped flint; nave and chancel in one; SW porch tower with shingled spire. Ashlar-faced stair projection to the W. The windows mostly Dec. The E window is placed high up to allow for a reredos, as Bodley liked it. This gives an odd rhythm to the E wall, as the S chapel window is at a normal height. The S windows of the S chapel are small and straight-headed, of 3, 3, 2 lights. The interior strikes one as uncommonly high and yet peaceful. The arcades are of only two bays, and there is no chancel arch. Fine ceilure over the altar, i.e. a decorated canopy. – SCREEN. High and combined with the rood-beam high up carrying a rood without Crucifixus. – ORGAN CASE. Also by *Bodley*. – PLATE. Chalice and Paten Cover, 1570.

EFFORD PARK *see* MILFORD-ON-SEA

EGBURY GRANGE *see* ST MARY BOURNE

ELDON *see* UPPER ELDON

ELING [DL] 3010

Eling is an old small port on a creek off the head of Southampton Water. In the C18 it developed N into TOTTON, at the estuary bridgehead. Today Totton is an appalling confusion of C19 and C20 housing along and between main roads which radiate from the bridge; no place in Hampshire is more in need of drastic planning. Eling proper is now a backwater, protected by a toll bridge from through-traffic.

ST MARY. Originally the only church in a huge district, from which several C19 parishes were formed; it is still the parish church of Totton. A many-gabled building with a harsh Victorian texture outside, thanks to a ruthlessly thorough restoration by *Benjamin Ferrey* in 1863–5. Inside still basically medieval, with a complex history made more confusing by Ferrey. Nave, aisles, chancel, chapels, NW tower. The VCH suggests that there was a Saxon church with a N transept and NE chapel, of which the plain round-headed arch from the present aisle to the chapel might be a relic – but it could well be of later date (a fairly similar arch in a corresponding S position is certainly later). More likely to be Saxon are a narrow window, with monolithic jambs and arch of radiating stones, built far to the E in the N wall of the chancel, and a tiny opening, pierced in a single stone and with a continuous shallow moulding, looking like the inner frame of a former double-splayed window and now high in the S nave wall near its W end. Neither can be in its original position; they were presumably discovered in the fabric during the C19 restoration. The nave has a three-bay S arcade of two chamfered orders, with octagonal piers and bell-shaped capitals with varying stiff-leaf foliage; late C12, the carved details all renewed. Large, fanciful Victorian base spurs. Irregular N arcade, the former W bay cut into by the insertion of the tower; the centre bay with octagonal piers, and an arch with slight chamfers, probably C13, and the E bay (separated by a short stretch of wall) probably later. The S aisle was rebuilt and widened by Ferrey. The N aisle has two Perp square-headed windows, and the only medieval external stonework on the church. The late C13 chancel arch is the finest feature in the church, as wide and as tall as possible; of three orders, each with complex keeled mouldings, thick round shafts, and round capitals. The outer two orders are squared off vertically for a little distance above the springing of the arch, to fit into the space available. Ferrey suggested that this arch was a re-insertion from elsewhere. The N chancel arcade is of two bays, the western C13, the eastern C19; the two-bay S arcade is C14. The N chapel was extended in the C19 and the Perp E window re-inserted. The S chapel was rebuilt by Ferrey with flamboyant windows. He was sharply criticized for his restoration in the *Gentlemen's Magazine* of 1867, the allegedly unnecessary renewal of the E window of this chapel being specifically mentioned, but he claimed that the old one had been decayed and the new was a faithful copy; if so, it is a remarkable C14 design, of three lights, the central one shorter than the others, with elongated quatrefoils above, making a flower pattern. The tower is Tudor or possibly early C17; ashlar, three storeys with plain square-headed lights, battlements, and angular buttresses dying above the second storey. The Victorian parts of the church exterior are of flint and stonework pattern.

FURNISHINGS. PAINTING of the Last Supper, Venetian, mid C16. Nothing is known of its history; it may have come from Lord Sandys of The Vyne, who was patron of the church. It was the altarpiece until replaced by a Victorian sculptured reredos of the Nativity; this has in its turn been banished to the W wall of the nave and the painting restored as the altarpiece. – PLATE. Set, 1693; Almsdish, 1707. – MONUMENTS. Many wall-monuments. In the chancel Catherine Mill † 1587; tablet with serif lettering. – In the N aisle Gilbert Serle † 1720. Large tablet of segmental section, with fluted Corinthian columns supporting a broken pediment. – In the nave Elizabeth Serle † 1741, by *Rysbrack*. Tablet with fine detailing; medallion portrait in relief against pyramid above; cherubs below. – In the N chapel Susanna Serle † 1753, also by *Rysbrack*. Large tablet surmounted by a bust. – Also in the N chapel Richard Pawlet † 1737, large tablet with pediment. –

In the S chapel Sir Charles Mill † 1835, allegorical figures, with cross, in relief. – Also some homely C18 tablets with vernacular Roman and Italic lettering and symbols, and two TOMBSTONES in the same tradition brought into the church; one to Thomas Warwick † 1764, with a figure of a ship against a sphere, presumably representing the globe, the other to Mary Bethell † 1765, with very naïve portraits of her and her husband, a heart emblem above them and a ship at sea to one side.

The dominating building by Eling Creek is a WAREHOUSE,* originally of four storeys, of stone with thick brick surrounds to the small arched windows; it must have been quite a handsome functional building until a three-storey tower was added over its middle part, of similar materials, making it simply ungainly. More homely and pleasing is the C18 red-brick former TIDE MILL at the head of the creek. The church and a few houses are hidden behind trees up a steep slope to the S. THE GRANGE, N of the church, has a rounded wing on its E frontage with a delicate Late Georgian veranda, and the OLD RECTORY further S has two massive rounded bays running through three storeys, with a delicately detailed segmental portico between them. Both these buildings turn their backs on the village street and have their best fronts looking over the water; it must once have been a fair scene and still is in part, with green fields sloping down to unreclaimed mudflats on the near shore. But it is precisely opposite here that the recently projected extension to Southampton Docks will take place, with the new deep-water channel coming close in to the Eling coastline. With the shoreline transformed, there is bound to be pressure to urbanize the now rural hinterland of Eling, S of the fringes of Totton.

ELLINGHAM

1000

ST MARY. The brick S porch is dated 1720, the W façade 1747. Originally it probably went up as a tower. The doorway has rustication of alternating sizes. Arched window above. Early C13 N doorway, blocked. C13 chancel, but mostly Victorian. (The restoration by *Sir T. G. Jackson* went on from 1869 into the eighties. NT) The church is very fully furnished. – 52
SCREEN. Perp; simple, single-light divisions. Attached to it an HOURGLASS. – Above it a plaster TYMPANUM with texts. –

* Burnt out in 1966.

PULPIT. Jacobean, on short legs like those of a stool. – REREDOS. A beautiful piece of *c.* 1700, now at the W end. Doric pilasters, grouped. Open pediment with a dove in the middle. Two putto heads below the pediment. Palm-fronds at the foot. In the centre a pedimented panel in which a PAINTING by a Dutch (or German?) Mannerist of *c.*1600. – FAMILY PEW. Jacobean(?), but the foliage spandrels not original. – ORGAN CASE. By *Jackson*, florid Gothic. – STAINED GLASS. By *Kempe*, S side 1896, chancel S 1902. – PLATE. Chalice of 1652; Flagon and Almsdish of 1742.

MOYLES COURT, 1 m. E. A mid C17 brick house of the type which was to dominate English architecture from the late C17. Brick, two storeys, five-bay centre with two-bay projecting wings, heavy eaves moulding, hipped roof, raised brick quoins, chimneystacks with blank arches. The brickwork all still English bond. The back is not so easily understood, and the chimneybreast on one side tells of an earlier house. Fine staircase with three turned balusters for one tread, a pierced board of foliage for the next. Carved tread-ends. – The STABLES have mullioned windows with arched lights, and above oval windows set horizontally. Central doorway. How should one date this?

ELLINGHAM COTTAGE *see* SHERFIELD ENGLISH

6040

ELLISFIELD

ST MARTIN. 1870, and the W tower 1884. The architect of the latter, according to the Rev. Basil Clarke, *J. S. Paull*. However, in the chancel a blocked C13 lancet, in the nave the outline of a Norman S doorway.

MANOR FARMHOUSE. Early C18. Hipped roof. To the N four, to the E three bays. Doorway with segmental pediment on scrolled brackets. To the S much remodelled.

7050

ELVETHAM

87 ELVETHAM HALL. By *S. S. Teulon*, 1859–60, for the fourth Lord Calthorpe.* A major house of his, but not one anybody would praise for beauty. Red brick, very red, with black brick bands. The style is faintly French, the composition as varied as possible in the grouping, but not in the motifs. Porch tower with a mansard-pyramid roof and a tourelle added to

* The bound volume of contract drawings is at the house.

one corner. The porch was open until, in 1901, in a deceivingly Teulonian style, a porte-cochère was added. Another addition, also deceiving, is yet later: the dining room of 1911. The windows of the house are mostly of one type. Ornamentally incised motifs are characteristic, and many-stepped brick modillions. Against the front of the stables, also with a tourelle, the relief originally above the porch entrance. Typical, again French, half-hipped dormers. Inside much original STAINED GLASS, largely yellow, and all telling stories. Good romantic ceiling PAINTINGS in the entrance hall. The staircase has much wood carving, inspired by Gothic to Jacobean, and again stained glass. The principal living rooms all have bays of different sorts. The best chimneypiece is in the drawing room. On the lintel and mantelshelf relief of Queen Elizabeth I visiting Lord Hertford and much naturalistic foliage. Also by *Teulon* the massive WATER TOWER, the estate COTTAGES beside it, and the SCHOOL round the corner.

ST MARY. 1840–1 by *Henry Roberts*. Flint and stone dressings, neo-Norman. But can the spire with its big angel gargoyles and the Signs of the Evangelists on short shafts on the low broaches be Roberts's or indeed part of the scheme of 1840? Must it not be a *Teulon* addendum? Nave and chancel under one slate roof. Plain interior. – MONUMENTS. Reynolds Calthorpe † 1714 and his wife. Twin monuments. Fluted pilasters, wide open pediment with, in the middle, a looped-up baldacchino. In the centre a rather flattened bust. The two monuments are by *James Hardy*.

See p. 828

EMBLEY PARK *see* EAST WELLOW

EMERY DOWN 2000

1 m. W of Lyndhurst

CHRIST CHURCH. 1864 by *Butterfield*. Nave and chancel and bellcote. The windows with pointed trefoiled heads. Red brick with blue diapers, ingeniously detailed. Roof with thin scissor-bracing and the principals cusped above it. – STAINED GLASS. All by the same deplorable artist.

EMPSHOTT 7030

HOLY ROOD. A complete early C13 church. The arcades are of four bays, their piers round, octagonal, round. The arches have two slight chamfers and are pointed. All have dogtooth hood-moulds (much renewed). The capitals have trumpet-scallops or are moulded on the S side, but have rich crockets on the N side. So S is probably older than N. The NE respond is tripartite, the NW respond, with a head, looks a little older than the rest. The chancel arch corresponds to the N arcade.* Externally much is of the same period, but pride of place must be given to the charming Victorian bell-turret with its glazed upper stage, below the spire (1884). The chancel has in its E wall three stepped lancets (roll-moulded inside). On the N it had a one-bay chapel of the same date. To the inside the blocked opening has a dogtooth hood-mould like the arcade. The aisles have small lancets, but the walls are far too close to the arcade to be possible as original C13 work. The VCH suggests that they were rebuilt so tightly in the C17, and that the W porch is C17 too. In the porch two re-set Norman windows. – FONT. Of table type; Purbeck marble. Each side with five flat arches. – FONT COVER. 1624. With openwork ogee volutes and a decorated centre baluster. – SCREEN. 1624. Now under the tower. The top of bold pierced strapwork. – BENCHES. With straight, moulded tops; C15 or C16. – READING DESK. One Jacobean panel, probably from the pulpit. – COMMUNION RAIL. Jacobean. – PLATE. Cup and Paten, 1620; Paten, 1829.

HILL PLACE, E of the church. The pleasure of the house is the brick porch, with its big moulded-brick pediment, and one room inside with stucco decoration on the beams, and between them four panels with round flower and fruit wreaths and a stylized motif in the middle. It is rustic work but very lovable. The date must be about 1670.

7000 EMSWORTH [DL]

An old port at the head of a channel of Chichester Harbour. The town proper is on a blunt peninsula between two small creeks, with an intricate pattern of streets and alleyways leading to different parts of the waterside. It was especially prosperous in the C18, declined in the C19, and still had an atmosphere of staid decay up to a few years ago. Now it is a yachting centre and looks rather chic.

ST JAMES. 1839–40 by *John Elliott*; S aisle 1857 by *Colson*; N aisle and chancel 1892 by *Blomfield*. There was no medieval

* The richness of the details probably due to Empshott belonging to Southwick Priory near Portsmouth. This is Mr Hubbuck's suggestion.

church at Emsworth – it was part of the parish of Warblington. Elliott's work is in the weirdest neo-Norman style, and his W front with attenuated gable, big round-headed window, and staircases flanking the entrance, leading behind vaguely Lombardic colonnades into side turrets which are decorated with arrow-slits (to emerge eventually into the gallery), defies – and does not deserve – serious analysis. Colson's aisle is lanky neo-Norman; Blomfield copied it in the other aisle and designed his chancel in the same vein with an E window of three rounded lights grouped in a wide arched frame – an adaptation of his favourite form of principal window treatment. So the naïve Elliott's neo-Normanism is echoed all through the later enlargements, High and Late Victorian.

PERAMBULATION. This starts at the bridge over the creek on the border of Sussex. QUEEN STREET leads into the town, narrow and traffic-ridden and at first architecturally scrappy. Messrs LEIGH'S MILL of 1897 is the first building of character: plain brick with a wooden gantry in the gable; straightforward and pleasing small-town industrial building. Then the beginning of a Georgian group on the l., simple, mainly two-storeyed houses in Hampshire brick, either all red or grey dressed in red; the best is No. 23 with Venetian upper windows and shallow ground-floor bays. On the N side NEWNHAM HOUSE stands out; three-storey red brick, with several pleasing quirks in its design. Pilastered and fanlit doorway set in a recess, where quoins of imitation-rusticated stonework alternate with brickwork. Shallow ground-floor bow windows set in arched recesses, and string courses at each floor level.

Queen Street leads diagonally into KING STREET; the traffic turns r., and sharp l. is a quiet cul-de-sac which epitomizes Emsworth. First, two severe Early Victorian houses in yellow brick, one with its ground-floor windows in arched recesses. Then a miscellany of pleasant minor houses, mainly Georgian, on individual alignments, some set back in slight gardens, and with a few spaces and trees between houses. No. 19 is weatherboarded, not in the usual Surrey or Essex 'overhung' manner but with flush boards, and has a charming façade with a fanlit doorway under a pediment (fanlights are an Emsworth speciality). Then the character of the street changes; there are workaday cottages as yet unconverted, the entrance into a busy boatyard, and, on the l., maisonettes that might be at Twickenham, on the sites of demolished warehouses. The street ends casually on the harbour's edge, with miles of mud flat at low tide and water up to the walls of shorefront buildings at high tide. Hulks of old barges lie stranded; yachts and boats are moored. Old warehouses, small boatyards with slipways, and the wall of the garden of a Georgian mansion line the waterfront; further along are the jetty and old tide mill and waterside houses at the end of South Street, to be reached at the end of the perambulation. At high tide it is impossible to get there along the shore, so one retraces one's steps through King Street.

Back into the traffic and then, quite unexpectedly, is the most delicious inland backwater in Emsworth, TOWER STREET, a cul-de-sac with a few Georgian houses. TRENTHAM COTTAGE has upper side windows under segmental tympana decorated in stucco fan pattern, a circular central window, and a doorway with a distinctive fanlight. TRENTHAM HOUSE, whose garden half-closes the lane, is a bigger, plainer, stuccoed house with bay windows and delicate iron balconies. SAXTED HOUSE opposite is Early Georgian in grey brick with red dressings and with another fanlit pedimented doorway. Tower Street is continued inconspicuously by a footway, beside the long garden of Trentham House, to emerge on the waterside.

Back to the traffic once more and into HIGH STREET, which widens at its S end into Emsworth's former market place. This could have been a very pleasant urban space; the buildings round are grouped in haphazard harmony and the streets leading off – South Street and King Street – from the two S apexes and the narrowing High Street to the N are effectively closed in perspective. But there is too much fussy treatment; self-conscious pastelling of buildings to different shades and too much street furniture. The most effective building fronting the space is the least self-conscious, the METHODIST CHURCH of 1877 with unashamed red, black, and white brickwork round sharply pointed openings. In the narrower part of High Street the CROWN HOTEL has a good scale, with a pillared porch. Opposite the WESTMINSTER BANK occupies part of a dignified three-storeyed building of grey and red brick, with an Ionic pilastered doorway surviving between the altered ground frontages.

SOUTH STREET leads back to the quayside, its buildings mostly basically simple but recently rather overlaid. The quayside here is dominated by a former TIDE MILL, an ordinary functional building partly in old red brick, placed against the jetty with splendid pictorial effect. Another old TIDE MILL, again quite functional, almost equally effective, is built partly on piles on the side of the creek which laps the W side of the town.

ENHAM ALAMEIN *see* KNIGHT'S ENHAM

EVERSLEY 7060

ST MARY. An C18 brick church and quite probably by *John James*, who lived at Warbrook House. The date 1724 renewed over the porch, the date 1735 on the tower. Handsome nave of blue brick headers with red brick dressings. Arched windows. The W tower has brick battlements and pinnacles. The N aisle is of 1876* but replaces an original earlier one, see the original five-bay arcade of square piers with plain square abaci and unmoulded arches. Only the short chancel is medieval (early C16?). – PULPIT. Plain; C18. – FONT COVER. Nice, plain, conical, with a big knob; C17. – STAINED GLASS. In a S window French *c.*1870 (whom by?). – In a N window by *H. Holiday*, made by *Powell*, 1905. – PLATE. Cup and Paten, 1705; Flagon, 1730. – MONUMENTS. Many tablets, illuminating to compare, especially † 1664, 1666, 1782, 1783, 1784. – Dame Marianne Cope † 1862. Recumbent alabaster effigy; unsigned.

BRICK HOUSE FARMHOUSE, SE of the church. Late C16 or early C17. Brick, with good chimneys and small mullioned brick windows.

GLASTON HILL HOUSE, $\frac{1}{4}$ m. NE. Blue brick headers and red brick dressings. The main part is of five bays. The original doorway is blocked. Three windows have frilly brick lintels. Much addition *c.*1920.

FIR GROVE, $1\frac{3}{8}$ m. ESE. The back with a big hipped roof is probably of *c.*1700. Refronted in 1736. Nine bays, the three and three side bays are canted bay windows. They end in balustrades. The centre has a fine doorway with Ionic columns and a pediment. The three middle bays of the house are raised by a half-storey and crowned by a pediment. A competent, handsome façade, and a quiet one. (Elegant staircase with thin balusters.)

* It was built as a memorial to Charles Kingsley, vicar from 1834 to 1875.

WARBROOK HOUSE, ¾ m. NW. Built by *John James* for himself in 1724. An impressive, remarkably individual house – not large. Brick. The centre is of three bays with a three-bay pediment rising only partly above a parapet. On the end walls of this block four groups of identical chimneys, a pair with an arch between (à la Vanbrugh) and one *à part*. The façade is treated as a giant portico of broad raised rendered pilaster strips connected at the top by an equally flat band or frieze. This motif is repeated on the garden side. The treatment altogether is the same. In the front and back pediment is a Venetian window, and between them right across the house runs a segmentally tunnel-vaulted room said to have been the architect's office. Otherwise the house has lower l. and r. wings with one-bay pediments and segment-headed windows. The staircase branches off the entrance hall to the r. and is the finest room in the house. Walls with pedimented stucco panels and stucco ceiling. The railing one column and one twisted baluster per step. Moulded undersides to the steps, carved tread-ends. The two main rooms on the garden side have been made into one by *Richardson & Gill*, *c.* 1920. Some leaf stucco. At the foot of the garden a straight sheet of water or broad canal à la Versailles. (NT)

5050 EWHURST

The house has been replaced by something neo-Georgian. The CHURCH (1873–4 by *Smith* of Reading, small, of flint, with bellcote and transepts) has hardly space to exist between it and the impressive Late Georgian STABLES of the old house. Three ranges, the middle one with coupled pilasters, a steep pediment with a blank lunette, and a mansard roof, the wings with broken pediments into which arched openings reach up. The three buildings have circular windows on the upper floor and are connected by archways.

8040 EWSHOT

ST MARY. 1873. Brown stone. Nave and chancel and bellcote. Lancets and plate tracery.

4000 EXBURY

ST CATHERINE. 1907 by *J. Oldrid Scott & Son*. Still Gothic in the C19 tradition; not a touch of the Arts and Crafts. But a serious building, the details Dec to Perp. Under the NW tower and in the apse added to it a memorial chapel. – (FONT. Of Purbeck marble. From the old church at Lower Exbury. RH) – PLATE. Cup of *c.*1600. – MONUMENT. John and Alfred Forster, killed in the First World War. A soldier's effigy on a tomb-chest, with tall bronze candlesticks. By *Cecil Thomas*.

(HOUSE, for Mr Leopold de Rothschild, built on the site of the kitchen garden of Exbury House, 1964–5 by *Law & Dunbar-Nasmith* of Edinburgh. One of the largest post-war private houses (cf. the Barings at Stratton, p. 202), though the buff bricks, pitched roofs, and dormers do not immediately establish the scale. The building is L-shaped, one wing being raised over garage and service rooms. The heart of the house is the two-storey MUSIC ROOM, with concert platform, which projects as a lean-to. Its timber-slatted roof rises above the first-floor gallery leading to the bedrooms. External walls are seen through tall windows, where they are prolonged into the landscape as garden walls. – TAPESTRY by *Sax Shaw*; sculptural details by *Ann Henderson* and *Helen Weir*. NT)

EXTON

6020

ST PETER AND ST PAUL. Nave and chancel and bell-turret. Flint. Lancets, and in the chancel E wall a pair of them with a quatrefoil over. Also a PISCINA with trefoiled top. All this is C13, though over-restored. The S doorway Norman in its outline. – FONT. Victorian–E.E. Is it of *Coade* stone? – STAINED GLASS. In the E window, of 1891. Very remarkable Arts and Crafts design, mostly of leaves, but also abstract. – MONUMENT. Gravestone from the churchyard, now in the church. Father Time invades the study of an ailing gentleman. No date.

FACCOMBE

3050

ST BARNABAS. 1866 by *G. B. Mussellwhite*.* Flint. W tower, nave, and chancel. Bar tracery. The bell-openings are Dec. – FONT. Norman, of drum-shape, with tapering sides. One band of zigzag, one of rope, one of two zigzags. – PLATE. Paten of 1720; undated Chalice. – MONUMENT. Anne Reade

* Or was he a builder? (RH)

† 1624. A slate panel, and on it the kneeling lady with her kneeling children.

FACCOMBE MANOR. Mostly of 1936, i.e. neo-Georgian, but the entrance side genuine Early Georgian, except for the doorcase. Five bays, two storeys, brick, the upper middle window with a broad raised brick surround, the ground-floor windows with frills to the rubbed lintels and the string course between ground floor and first floor climbing over their keystones.

4010

FAIR OAK [DL]

A scrappy village on the outskirts of Eastleigh.

ST THOMAS. By *Colson*, 1863. Flint and stone; lancets, apse, turret.

WYVERN SECONDARY SCHOOL. Being built 1965. Promises to be a satisfying group of buildings in frame and panel construction of one to three storeys. By *H. Benson Ansell*, the County Architect.

5000

FAREHAM [DL]

Fareham from the Middle Ages to Victorian times was a market town and small port at the head of an inlet of Portsmouth Harbour. Senior naval officers found it favourable for retirement in Georgian times. Today it is expanding fast, and many motorists who try to get through it on the South Coast trunk road probably think of it as a suburbanized place of little attraction. If so, they do not know the old High Street, leading N from the present main thoroughfare, which is largely unspoiled and one of the best country-town streets in the South of England.

ST PETER AND ST PAUL. The medieval church was a fairly small building, to which a N tower was added in 1742. In 1812 the nave was rebuilt and enlarged, and fitted in a manner which must have been reminiscent of the unrestored church of Whitby in Yorkshire. Late in the C19 *Sir Arthur Blomfield* was commissioned to transform the whole church into a Gothic building, but achieved no more than the building of a new chancel in 1888 (retaining the medieval chancel as a N chapel). In 1930–1 the parts built in 1812 were entirely reconstructed by *Sir Charles Nicholson*. He kept little more than parts of the red brick outer walls, and formed a new spacious nave with aisles. The church is now an amalgam of medieval, Georgian, Victorian, and inter-war architecture, and the various parts are best described chronologically.

NORTH CHAPEL, the chancel of the medieval church. The lower courses of part of the N wall are said to be Saxon.* The E window is a plain trio of slender, widely spaced lancets, the centre one higher, like the E terminations of many small churches in Sussex. A lancet and traces of two more also survive in the N wall, and two more opposite in the old S wall, part of which was retained by Blomfield as a division between the old and new chancels. Other windows are square-headed Perp. The W arch of the chapel (former chancel arch) is Late Norman, pointed with only a slight chamfer, and with round responds and one plain capital, the other multi-scalloped. Square abaci.

TOWER. Built against the N side of the original nave at its E end in 1742, by *James Norris* of Gosport. A big, remarkable, homely piece of local blue-grey brick with generous red-brick dressings. Round-headed archways to the ground storey, a circular N window on the first floor, and windows of crude Venetian shape at the bell-stage, brought out strongly, like many other of the decorative features, by red brick courses in slight relief. The tower is crowned by a pleasant cupola.

CHANCEL. Blomfield's chancel is not inspired. E window of three lancets contained internally within a single arched recessed frame – a favourite Blomfield motif.

NAVE AND AISLES. Nicholson's work is externally in rich red local brick, the new walling being of almost exactly the same colour as the surviving Georgian stretches. He designed what is basically a clerestoried nave with a very low-pitched roof, lower S and inner N aisles, and a second N aisle ending against the tower at its E end. The window styles vary: a Venetian design appears in the outer N aisle, in obvious reference to the bell-openings of the tower; elsewhere there are lancets and square-headed mullioned windows, probably allusions to the medieval windows in the old chancel. Partly because of the fussy effect imparted by the various window designs, and partly because of the rather ungainly rectilinearity of the outline of the building, especially at the W end, the remodelled parts do not make a very attractive composition outside. Inside the first impression is of lightness and

* Long-and-short work is visible on the lower part of the NE angle.

spreading space and simplicity of detailing. The four-bay nave arcades are of simplified Gothic design in smooth buff stone, with no capitals, the octagonal piers simply breaking into moulded arches of two orders. The arches into the outer N aisle are round and plain in a whitened wall surface. Altogether the remodelled church suffers internally from much the same faults as it does externally: it is too diffuse, especially laterally, and the presence of the outer aisle detracts from the clarity of the E–W axis. A more powerful E termination than Blomfield's might have helped to remedy this last defect.

FURNISHINGS. REREDOS. Formerly in the chancel; now N aisle E end. Six panels, simply traceried, under coving. Probably C 15, but much patched with later woodwork. – PLATE. Secular standing covered Cup, parcel-gilt, English, probably *c.*1500; standing Paten, 1718; Flagon, 1720; Almsdishes, 1723 and 1734; two Communion Cups, 1830. – MONUMENTS. Many wall-tablets, few of any special note. The oldest are to Ralph Riggs † 1647, Margaret Riggs †1649, and Thomas Player † 1721, the last in a Baroque cartouche. All these are in the N chapel. – Another, at the W end of the S aisle, is to Captain Newman † 1811, by *Sir Richard Westmacott*, showing a female figure resting on a rock, watching H.M.S. Hero sinking. Also signed *Westmacott* a tablet in the outer N aisle to the Rev. T. A. Woolis, 1790. Garlanded urn above tablet. The signature refers to Richard, Sir Richard's father.

ST COLUMBA, Highlands Road. By *Bailey & Piper*, 1961–3. A rectangular church, the roof supported on transverse arch-frames of laminated wood. But the S wall is glazed and set back from the upright parts of the frames, making a sort of useless veranda outside and an awkward asymmetry inside. Spencey bell-tower with open framework, the bells behind open honeycombed walling and the top of the framework sloping. Long, thin-pillared covered way linking the tower with the entrance to the church.

ST JOHN THE EVANGELIST, Redlands Lane. By *R. P. Thomas*, 1962–4. An ecclesiastical folly, with trapezoidal roof, blue tiled, triangular chancel arch, skylon-like steeple, and other blatantly fashion-conscious features.

HOLY TRINITY. A successful church of the 'Commissioners'' type, standing at what was the W end of the town but is now near the heart of the shopping centre. The date is 1834–7, the architect *Jacob Owen*, whose All Saints in Portsmouth has a strong affinity. Nave, aisles chancel, W tower, all of local yellow brick with a few stone dressings, the tower surmounted by a short stone spire. There is a greater degree of solidity than in most local churches of the period. Obviously more money than usual was available here; the church was in fact paid for by the Rev. Sir Henry Thompson, the first incumbent. The aisle windows are tall, of two lights with transoms and not too incorrect neo-1300 tracery; brick buttresses between them. Large N and S porches. The NW tower is given visual strength by buttresses in three tiers, two of them ending in stone gablets curving to a spearhead point. Chancel rebuilt in 1915 in the same brick as the rest of the church. Internally the architectural effect is enhanced by the present decoration in white, blue, and gold by *S. E. Dykes Bower*. There are seven-bay arcades of cast iron, plastered over, with very thin clustered piers and four-centred arches. Ironwork shafts continue upwards from the piers to support flat cross-beams with rounded brackets, open-traceried. The aisles have similar iron cross-beams, transmitting the weight of the roofs to the external buttresses. The chancel has a neo- Perp E window and two plain arches on the S side filled with rough brickwork, intended to give entrance to a S chapel which was never erected. Formerly galleried all round but now only across the W bay, occupies the W projecting forward a further bay in the aisles, fronted with a Gothic panel pattern, and reached by staircases within the porches. – FURNISHINGS. PAINTED GLASS. Figures of Faith, Hope, and Charity in the three-light W window, above the gallery (and formerly in the E window). It was painted by *Thomas Jeavons* of Windsor, *c.*1770–90, after Reynolds's New College windows and restored by *J. A. Edwards* in 1835, when it was given to the church by the Rev. Sir Henry Thompson. The colouring is deep and rich. Above the figures is gilded Gothic tracery patterning in perspective. In the upper tracery of the window are heraldic and other patterns, the work of *Edwards*. – MONUMENTS. Several large wall-tablets, including one to Admiral Thompson († 1799), presumably removed from the old parish church, executed by *Flaxman* in 1800. L. and r. of the inscription standing figures in uniform with rope and sextant. – Jane Thompson † 1833. By *T. Butler* of London. The same composition, but with a young boy and a young girl, both with books. – Sophia Dickson † 1846, by *E. H. Baily*. She died in childbirth and is shown having the Sacrament administered to her while her child is borne up to heaven by angels. – E. A. Stephens † 1837, by *Flaxman*. She is being carried to heaven – a familiar Flaxman composition, but here not carried out by him but by *Thomas Denman*.

CONGREGATIONAL CHURCH. *See* Perambulation, p. 225.

BISHOPSFIELD SECONDARY SCHOOL, Titchfield Road. 1965 by *H. Benson Ansell*, the County Architect.

RAILWAY STATION. *Tite*'s original small station building of 1841 still largely survives at one corner of the present larger building; of rough stone, simple classical proportions, and typical Tite chimney groupings.

The VIADUCT at the E end of the town, 1848, is impressive. One skew arch.

(H.M.S. COLLINGWOOD. Several recent buildings by the *Ministry of Public Building & Works (Navy Works)*.)

THE TOWN. Fareham's centre of gravity has moved W during the last hundred years, so that High Street is now a commercial backwater, with many Georgian house fronts and even some Georgian shop fronts intact, while West Street, originally a lesser street, is now the main shopping thoroughfare. The town was a centre of the Georgian brickmaking industry, and many of the C18 houses are built of the richly coloured bricks called 'Fareham Reds'. Others are partly in a local variety of grey-blue 'salt-glazed' brick, which, in combination with red-brick dressings, can be very attractive. In the early C19 a more austere 'white' (i.e. yellow) brick came into fashion. Bow windows are common, as in other south-coast towns, and the Georgian doorcases and porches of Fareham and its neighbourhood would be worth a special study.

PERAMBULATION. This starts at the junction of West Street and High Street, with the rapidly changing modern town centre in one direction and the unspoiled old centre in another.

4 HIGH STREET was in the Middle Ages widest at its S end, to accommodate the market place, and funnelled towards the N. As in so many old towns, part of the original market place has been encroached upon by an island block of buildings. Since there are so many good buildings in the street, and part of it is wide, the perambulation will first go up the E side and then return down the W. This means actually starting with UNION STREET, the narrow thoroughfare between the island block at the S end of High Street and the original street frontage on

the E. The corner to East Street is nicely taken by a three-storeyed Early Victorian stuccoed building, with broad windows and a prominent cornice, visible down the length of West Street and so of great importance in Fareham's townscape. Then the height of the buildings drops to two storeys. Nos 8 and 9 are coeval with the corner block, with original shop fronts and fascia board. No. 4 is a timber-framed cottage with Georgian windows and an arched passageway. Then simple Georgian and Early Victorian house and shop fronts, facing the unremarkable frontages of the island block. At the end of the block one emerges on to High Street proper. It narrows, climbs, and curves gracefully out of sight, many of the grandest buildings being happily on the outside of the slight curve, fronted by a few trees. In this stretch houses of three storeys predominate, and even those of two storeys are of generous scale. Nos 70, 69, and 68 are all typical of Fareham in different ways. The KINTYRE HOTEL (No. 70), 1756 has a façade of three storeys in five bays, in blue-grey brick with wide red-brick dressings, and a splendid porch with fluted Ionic columns and pilasters, supporting an open segmental hood. Then WYKEHAM HOUSE (No. 69), Georgian with brown mathematical tiles, stone quoins and window heads, the latter with keystones, and a semicircular porch with detached columns as well as pilasters. The COUNTY CLUB (No. 68) is of two storeys with very bold bows containing, on each storey, three normal-sized windows with wall spaces in between them. The porch has a broken pedimented hood with a high entablature and free-standing Tuscan columns. The WYKEHAM HOUSE JUNIOR SCHOOL (No. 67) is more severe, in brown brick, with pedimented doorcase and elegant little balconies on the first floor. After this is a nondescript piece of neo-Georgian design, then No. 64, Early Victorian, stuccoed, with a heavier cornice and heavier detailing generally than on the Georgian houses; unusual doorcase with scrolled brackets supporting the pediment. Just past No. 64 a path leads between the walls of back gardens and straight into open country, showing how close the countryside was, and still is, to the urbane frontages of inner Fareham. No. 63 is unremarkable Victorian, No. 61 plain Georgian. Then the scale suddenly changes to cottage level, as the street finally narrows and curves out of the inner town. Nos 60, 59, and 58 have a series of Georgian shop fronts, bowed and angular; No. 57 is half-way back to the scale of the middle part of the street, two-storeyed Early Victorian with a segmental porch with Tuscan columns; then a range of very humble cottages, pleasant as part of the whole street scene. LYSSES (No. 51) is set back, two-storeyed, stuccoed, *c.*1840, with a square porch with Ionic columns *in antis*. Nos 50 back to 46 are relatively plain but individually pleasant houses, Georgian and Early Victorian, No. 44 is plain three-storeyed Georgian, and, finally, not part of the old street itself but a detached house just beyond its end, the OLD MANOR HOUSE. This is a specially impressive medium-sized early C18 house, with three-storey five-bay façade in red and grey brick, with segmental window heads and sumptuous porch with open round pedimented hood and richly detailed Corinthian columns and pilasters. Inside are a fine staircase, ceilings, and other decorative features and a strange large staircase window, wooden-framed, like a paraphrase of Gothic: round-headed and containing two pairs of rounded lights, each pair having an intermediate rounded frame. Surely the designer had some local Geometrical window in mind.

The return into the town is along the W side of HIGH STREET. First the parish church, set back in a churchyard full of yew bushes (this is typical of Hampshire). A row of old houses fronts the street, backing on to the churchyard; of these No. 33 has a pleasant Ionic doorcase and No. 30A a Georgian shop front. Then the only real eyesore in the High Street, an asbestos and brick storage building; such an intrusion really hurts here. Then comes the widening of the street, and the group of stately houses on the E side. On the whole the buildings on the W side are less remarkable than those opposite, but the following deserve mention. Nos 25–23 are a timber-framed survival with oversailing upper storey. No. 20 is of *c.*1840–50, with another of the segmental or nearly semi-circular porches that are a repeated feature of Fareham, this one with two slender columns. No. 18 has a single prominent bow window in the upper storey; Nos 17–15 are in grey and red brick with pleasant round-pedimented doorcases; No. 12 has a porch with Roman Doric columns and a well-detailed broken pedimental hood; Nos 11 and 7 are plain three-storeyed Georgian brick houses. Then, opposite the island block, the street begins to acquire something of the workaday commercial character of West Street just round the corner. The preservation of the street up to 1939 was accidental; since 1945 it has depended to a large extent on control by the planning authority, not only by securing the preservation of individual 'listed' buildings, but also in the control of uses to which premises are put.*

West Street is continued E by EAST STREET, in which is a short stretch of pleasant Georgian houses, none calling for special mention except perhaps the RED LION, refronted 1819, with another segmental portico and bow windows. WEST STREET is very wide but of little distinction. The old façades that remain over the modern shop fronts are mostly of humble former houses, seldom more than two storeys high, and the frequent recent rebuildings have nowhere added positively to the character of the street. The width and the importance of the street call for decent buildings of some scale; why, with the present scramble to rebuild so many of the commercial premises fronting the street, cannot a C20 character be imparted that is as memorable in its way as the C18 character of High Street? Just a few odd buildings need mention. On the S side, the CONGREGATIONAL CHURCH, 1836, neo-Perp with a simple gabled W front, of yellow brick, with an attractive pattern of leaded glazing. Probably by *Jacob Owen* because of the stylistic similarities to Holy Trinity. Next the former CORN EXCHANGE, with a handsome upper storey with nine attached Ionic columns set back, tall windows between them, and a severe entablature. The E part is of *c.* 1835, extended to the W in harmony, 1860.‡

Further W is WESTBURY MANOR, a Late Georgian house, now the council offices, then Holy Trinity, the station (p. 222), and finally, on the S side of the main road W of the railway bridge (and well out of the town centre), BISHOPSWOOD, a delicious enlarged *cottage orné*, the history of which is not very clear, but which seems to have been a house of moderate size of about 1800 (possibly altered from an earlier farmhouse), greatly enlarged at some time in the early C20, probably in the twenties. The earlier part has thatched roofs continuing over verandas on the N and E sides which rise the height of both storeys and which have massive, self-consciously rough and slightly crooked tree trunks supporting

* The Hampshire County Council has published a plan for a new civic and shopping development in the angle between High Street and West Street, and for the eventual conversion of High Street and part of West Street into a pedestrian precinct.

‡ Information from Mr J. G. Draper.

the roof. The windows behind are three-light Gothick on the ground floor, with intersecting upper tracery and amusing cusping, all constructed in wood, and broad, round-headed but still Gothick windows on the upper floors, round which the thatch curves in broad 'eyebrows'. The S front of the original portion has no veranda to shade it, but a shallow rounded bay in its central part, behind which the old principal room of the house is oval in shape. To the W is a long wing, also thatched, and roughcast like the rest, but looking as if it were either a completely new C20 addition, or else a drastic alteration of an older wing. This has a series of French windows at ground level, mostly round-headed and distinctive, and a bowed Venetian window above. Inside is a beautifully proportioned neo-Georgian drawing room with white panelling and an impeccable fireplace with detached columns. Another C20 addition is the great hall to the N, thatched and homely outside, but quite stately within, with an enormous neo-Tudor fireplace. The GARDEN must be mentioned, if only for the long straight pathway thrusting deliberately on the axis of the bow window of the original *cottage orné* into a wild piece of woodland underplanted with rhododendrons, off which informal paths wander into the wilderness. Whoever was the C20 enlarger of the house had a stroke of genius and the architect of the original *cottage* had an unerring aptitude for the picturesque. Bishopswood was originally called Blackbrook, and is now the residence of the Bishops of Portsmouth.

QUAYSIDE, about ½ m. S of West Street. There are two groups of quays with a stretch of foreshore in between, the N one used for coal-loading and boat-building, and with no buildings of interest, the S one partly used by commercial barges and partly by pleasure boats. Small C19 warehouses* and Late Georgian grain stores (the latter converted to boathouses) on or near the waterside make a pleasant overall picture, together with the rough stone- and brick-fronted quay wall and a few old houses just behind, notably PROSPECT HOUSE, three-storeyed, of yellow brick, with a segmental portico, and an adjoining older house with several gables.

In the outer parts of Fareham are the following. In OSBORN ROAD several gabled Early Victorian villas built of flint, one

* Mostly demolished in 1965–6. Mr Stephen Weeks says that the present furniture store was a flour mill, with interesting cast-iron columns supporting the first floor.

having neo-Dutch gables, patterned roof tiles, and a large segmental hood over a first-floor bay window – an extraordinary composition. UPLANDS, further N, now an Old People's Home, is a Late Georgian brown-brick mansion with a main (S) front of nine bays and two storeys, and low slate roof with eaves; on the N façade is a massive porch with coupled Tuscan columns. In Wickham Road, ST CHRISTOPHER'S HOSPITAL was built as the Union Workhouse in 1836; it has a pleasant three-storeyed main block of five bays, the lower storey stuccoed with simulated horizontal coursing, and a single-storey wing, similarly treated, to the S.

CAMS HALL, E of the town, adjoining Fareham Creek, S of the Portsmouth Road. Built in 1771 by *Jacob Leroux* for John Delmé, the owner of Place House, Titchfield (p. 627), many of the materials of which were re-used in the construction of Cams Hall. At the time of writing empty and derelict, and in very bad condition. Main (N) front of ashlar, three storeys and five bays, the centre three bays with rusticated round-arched recesses on the ground storey and engaged Ionic columns, supporting a pediment, on the upper two storeys. The S front is of brick, with a bold central bow rising to a greater height than the main part of the façade. One- to two-storeyed wings. There used to be some very fine interiors, but they are now probably past hope. But the house can undoubtedly still be saved.

CATISFIELD, a former hamlet on the W outskirts of the town. CATISFIELD COTTAGE, an C18 house of red and grey brick, has unusually shaped bay windows, rising through both storeys, the windows themselves in canted form but projecting from what begin as semicircular bows, with short stretches of curved brickwork between the façade and the start of the windows; segmental porch with free-standing columns. CATISFIELD HOUSE, overlooking the Meon, almost in Titchfield, is early C18, but unattractively cemented.

FORT FAREHAM, 1 m. S. One of Palmerston's forts, the only one of a projected second line across the Gosport peninsula (p. 248) ever built. Now a council store; overgrown but substantially intact.

ROCHE COURT, *see* p. 475.

FARLEIGH WALLOP

6040

ST ANDREW. Mostly of 1871–2; of the church of *c.*1750 hardly any traces. Perp style. Greek cross plan. – COMMUNION

RAIL. Early C18, with twisted balusters. – SCULPTURE. On the W wall a very handsome Grinling-Gibbonsish garland of wood, of course *ex situ*. – MONUMENTS. First Earl of Portsmouth † 1762 and the Countess † 1738. Twin tablets, large with pilasters and pediment. No figures. His must have been copied from hers. – Second Earl † 1797. Signed *Coo*[*ke*] London. Seated woman by an urn and weeping willow. Much smaller.

FARLEIGH HOUSE. Built by the first Earl of Portsmouth (then Viscount Lymington) in 1731, but the entrance side entirely or almost entirely by *H. S. Goodhart-Rendel*, 1935–7. Squared flint with grey stone dressings, arched ground-floor windows, hipped roof. Central projection carried up tower-like and ending with the coat of arms against the sky.* Classical, with Early Georgian (Gibbs) alterations, but quite free. The garden side is of 1731. It has a large central canted bay with openings with Gibbs surrounds. Behind the bay a good octagonal room with some original doorcases and a fine chimneypiece. In one room inside is an extremely interesting mid C17 chimneypiece. The vertically halved pilasters carrying big ears or lugs are as characteristic as the big broadly decorated volutes in which the feet of the pilasters disappear. On the GATEPIERS two Mermaids, apparently of *Coade* stone.‡

3020

FARLEY CHAMBERLAYNE

ST JOHN. On its own, but by the traces of a deserted village. Nave and chancel and bell-turret. Norman S doorway, the hood-mould on two oversized radially placed faces. The windows mostly C18. Good timbers supporting the bell-turret. Rough nave roof with tie-beams and kingposts. – Early C18 PULPIT with tester, COMMUNION RAIL. – The FONT is C18; a stone baluster, rather stolid. – PLATE. Chalice of 1636; undated Paten. – MONUMENT. William St John † 1600. Stone, of good quality. Recumbent effigy in an oblong recess with solid side walls and a middle column. Ceiling with geometrical patterns. Tomb-chest with fine broad strapwork. Achievement panel at the top. – John St John † 1627. At the foot two small kneeling figures and between them a baby in a forward-tipped basket.

* This comes from one of the park gates of Hurstbourne House.

‡ They also come from Hurstbourne.

OBELISK, on Farley Down, 1 m. NNE. Erected by Sir Paulet St John *c.*1740 to record the leap into a chalk pit 25 ft deep of a horse during fox-hunting. The horse had his mount on his back. The obelisk is 30 ft high and really more like a spire than a genuine obelisk. At the foot four porches like the lucarnes of a spire.

FARLINGTON *see* PORTSMOUTH, p. 466

FARNBOROUGH 8050

Farnborough is a village, grown by much additional housing and industry, an Army Camp, and the Empress Eugenie.

ST PETER. The N and S doorways are of *c.*1200, one with decorated trumpet-scallop capitals and a hood-mould with dogtooth, the other with billet in the hood-mould. The wooden N porch is Perp, the spacious E end of 1901 (*Sir Arthur Blomfield & Sons*). Weatherboarded timber W tower, undated (C17?). – SCREEN (now in the N transept). Jacobean. With big, tall balusters. – WEST GALLERY. On odd polygonal pillars. Square balusters to the parapet. – WALL PAINTING, on the N wall of the nave W of the doorway. Upper parts of three female Saints, including one rare in England: St Eugenia.* All *c.*1190. – STAINED GLASS. The E window by *Kempe*.

Near to the church FARNBOROUGH PLACE. White, of seven bays, with a hipped roof. Inside an early C17 staircase. Some distance NE, at the corner of Rectory Road and HIGHGATE LANE, an old FARMHOUSE, timber-framed, C17.

Quite close to the church, to the NW, is a centre of present-day Farnborough. KINGSHEAD HOUSE, 1964–5 by *Campbell-Jones & Partners* (*Alec Shickle*). Very good, unfussy, on pilotis, well grouped. To its W QUEENSMEAD, a successful shopping street, 1958–60 by *George Davies & Webb*, slightly winding, with identical three-storeyed terraces.

In VICTORIA ROAD is the SOLARTRON works, by *Raglan Squire & Partners*, 1960–1. An extension is being added (1966) by *Eric Firmin & Partners* (NT).

1½ m. NW of the church, in Fernhill Road, BROOMHILL, a timber-framed, restored and enlarged farmhouse.)

m. N of the church is the territory of the Empress Eugenie. She bought FARNBOROUGH HILL (now a convent school) in

* A curious coincidence in this place.

See p. 828 1881 and lived there to her death in 1920. The house had bee built about 1862 for T. G. Longman by *H. E. Kendall Jun* and is an outrageously outsized chalet with entrance tower an a lot of bargeboarding. The entrance side is a letter L Large staircase starting in one arm and returning in twc The Empress added to the house in its own style, and sinc then for the school large additions have been made b *Adrian Gilbert Scott*, including an apsed chapel.

In 1887 the Empress built a MAUSOLEUM for her husband her son, and herself. It was designed by *Destailleur*, th architect of Waddesdon Manor, but much more restrainedly It is in the French Flamboyant, quite convincing, excep for the dome. Below the dome, underground, is the vaulte crypt with the three plain and impassive sarcophagi. It i reached by a palatial curved staircase. The heavy rib-vault stand on short Early Gothic columns. The mausoleum i
91 cruciform, of Bath stone, the arches all with continuou mouldings, the vaults with complicated rib-patterns an pendants. Rich foliage details. The inspiration came from L Ferté Bernard. – The ORGAN is by *Cavaillé-Coll*.

The Empress also built an abbey to serve the mausoleum The whole group is called ST MICHAEL'S ABBEY. It consist of a featureless brick centre of 1886 with a fancy flèche, b *Destailleur*, and to its l. and especially r. dramatic stone part in a style between Romanesque and Early Gothic. They wer modelled on Solesmes and are a fragment of a much large scheme by *Fr. Benedict Williamson*, 1900–12.

The NORTH CAMP, N of Aldershot, though S of Farnborough is featureless.* The church of ST MARK, Alexandra Road, i of 1881–93, E.E., brick, with no tower, and a spacious interio By *J. E. K. & J. P. Cutts*. The TOWN HALL, also in Alex andra Road, is of 1897, in the Tudor-cum-1700 style the current. The architect was *George Sherrin*.

The military miles of Farnborough and Aldershot merg imperceptibly into each other.

FARRINGDON

7030

ALL SAINTS. C13 W tower with lancets below and most unusu bell-openings in the form of small pointed quatrefoils.‡ Th

* But recently the research team of the War Office under *Sir Dona Gibson* (now absorbed in the Ministry of Public Building and Works) ha developed the NE corner of the site, S of Lynchford Road.

‡ Mr Hubbuck's comment is: cf. South Harting, Sussex.

arch towards the nave has one continuous chamfer. The nave has two good Perp windows separated by a brick porch with a pedimented entrance of 1634 and C18 sides. The chancel, in the opinion of the Rev. Basil Clarke, by *Woodyer*. Mr Hubbuck finds the Lychgate to be in Woodyer's style. The inside of the church is strong stuff. N arcade of three exceedingly wide bays with completely unmoulded round arches. The W bay consists of two Norman responds, semicircular, with multi-scallop capitals and square abaci. The W respond has spurs on the base. The responds are far too far from each other to make sense about 1200. The E respond was a little later converted into a round pier by adding a W respond for the next two bays, which are, with their plainly moulded capitals and round abaci, a little later. The VCH has no explanation. Must one assume that some time, say in the C17, the arcade showed signs of failing, that two piers or maybe one was removed and the arches made so absurdly wide? – FONT. The stem is a strange C13 capital or rather a block carved into four capitals. What did it belong to? – TILES. Exceptionally many in the chancel, forming whole patterns. – PLATE. Chalice and Paten Cover, undated.

The church and the whole village are eclipsed by the VILLAGE HALL and SCHOOL, a building very substantial indeed and of fiery red brick and terracotta. There are for example two different towers, the taller with a shaped-gable-saddleback-roof. In another place an oversized semicircular gable. All windows with French basket arches to each light. The terracotta panels are of the kind one could buy from catalogues about 1875–80. The building was indeed begun in 1870. It became known as Massey's Folly; for *T. H. Massey*, the then rector, designed it and built it with one labourer and one carpenter. He was busy on it for thirty years. In the end it had seventeen bedrooms. Massey died in 1939, having been rector for sixty-two years.*

FAWLEY [DL] 4000

ALL SAINTS. A good village church, long, low, and rectangular, with three gables and a strong, fairly tall and happily proportioned tower placed unusually in the middle of the S side between aisle and chancel chapel. Pleasant external texture: rubble walls and tiled roofs. The interior has long, simply

* Information kindly supplied by Mrs S. Kavanagh.

ceiled tunnel roofs, yellow-washed plastered walls, and stonework of a whitish texture; the décor is due to *Randoll Blacking*, who restored the church in 1954, following bomb damage to the chancel and N chapel.* The late C12 church was quite substantial, with aisled nave, S tower, chancel, and N chapel; of this the chancel arch, much of the tower, the W door, and parts of the N chancel arcade survive. Most of this dates from *c.*1170–80, but the chancel arch is probably slightly earlier, as it is humbler than the rest and seems to have belonged originally to a church of small proportions; it is low and rounded, of a single squared order, thinly chamfered, with shallow moulded abaci. The lowest stage of the tower is *c.*1170–80, with a single tall round-headed light on the external (S) wall. The tower rises altogether in three stages of unequal height marked with strong string-courses, and the upper two stages are probably much later; there are small square-headed trefoil windows to N and E on the second stage (probably C15), small two-light square-headed bell-openings, and an even parapet. Of the three massive arches from the tower into the body of the church the narrow one into the S chapel is wholly C19 and those into the nave and S aisle are much renewed, but the capitals of the latter two are all at least partly original and interestingly carved, mainly in variations of scallop decoration with diagonal or sawtooth patterning on the faces of the abaci; the S capital of the W tower arch has a specially effective design resembling wheatsheaves going up and down alternately. The two-bay N chancel arcade has pointed arches of one chamfered order, round piers, and capitals similar in style to those of the tower arches; it is largely a rebuilding after bombing, but the W respond is original, with scalloped capitals and a band of diagonal patterning on the face of the abacus. The W door is a fine piece, with a plain inner order, and an outer arch with thick roll-moulding, springing from nook-shafts with scalloped capitals. The arch has thick zigzag moulding between an inner band of intersecting diagonal pattern on the underside and an outer border of fleuron moulding. About 1300 the chancel was lengthened a little; the E window, blown out by the bomb but skilfully reconstructed, is a tentative, rather naïve Geometrical design with three pointed, cuspless lights, a circle

* He found in the fabric the framing of a small, supposedly Saxon, round-headed window, cut out of a single piece of stone. This has been inserted in the external E wall under the E window.

above, and awkwardly shaped spaces between them and the curves of the arch. Very soon afterwards the present aisles and simple but rather graceful four-bay arcades were built; the arches are of one chamfered order, the piers circular, and the moulded capitals of square section, chamfered at the angles, in their upper and of rounded section in their lower parts. The aisles are lit by short, wide trefoiled lancets, some restored but many original. The rather unusual three-bay S chancel arcade has affinities with the nave arcades and must be early C14. (The VCH says *c.*1200, but this cannot be so, since the recent restoration has revealed the blockings of the tops of widely splayed lancet windows in the walling above the arches; these must be C13). The S chapel is indeed early C14, and so is the almost identical N chapel (on the site of an earlier one): both have fine three-light reticulated E windows and two-light square-headed windows with reticulated tracery on each of the side walls. The only significant C19 alterations to the fabric were a three-light neo-Perp window high in the W wall to light a former W gallery and a neo-Norman porch to protect the W door; the latter and perhaps the former are of 1844. – PULPIT. Excellent Jacobean work in its upper part, with panels patterned with arches shown, unusually, in perspective; graceful scrolled brackets supporting the reading shelf. – PLATE. Paten, *c.*1500*; Communion Cup, 1562; Flagon, 1834. – The STAINED GLASS was destroyed in the bombing.

ESSO REFINERY. Opened 1951, a huge enlargement of a small refinery which had existed since before the Second World War. The refinery spreads over the site of the mansion and grounds of CADLAND HOUSE,‡ both designed by *Capability Brown*. There is a very different landscape now, exciting and impressive in its way, dominating views across Southampton Water from the other side but having strangely little apparent impact on its own immediate hinterland, thanks to the conservation of existing trees round the fringes of the site, supplemented by newly growing ones. The OFFICE BLOCK quite close to the church is by *Lanchester & Lodge*, 1950, not a memorable piece of architecture. The refinery goes on growing.

FAWLEY POWER STATION. Being built in 1965 by *Farmer & Dark*. Much bigger than Marchwood, the same architects'

* Now in the British Museum.

‡ There is a modern house called Cadland on Stanswood Bay, 2 m. S.

earlier power station, but, for scenic reasons, to be built partly underground. It will therefore probably be less prominent than Marchwood.

The village and even its immediate surroundings are still countrified in feeling. The centre is the irregular SQUARE, set off by the FALCON HOTEL, naïve Early Victorian, with massive yellow-brick pilasters and oddly stepped pediment around a largely red-brick front. Opposite is a typical Early Victorian Cadland estate COTTAGE, with steep bargeboards, hooded square-headed windows, and strong quoin pattern, all in yellow brick; other examples survive elsewhere, e.g. by the former entrance to the estate at Hardley. For the rest, the village consists of unassuming Georgian and Victorian cottages. The old creek-quay at ASHLETT, ½ m. away, has an impressive TIDE MILL AND GRANARY, dated 1818, three-storeyed, brick with stone bands at each floor level, and a mansard roof, making a telling contrast to the refinery and power station. It is now used by the Esso Recreational Club.

HOLBURY, BLACKFIELD, and LANGLEY are scrappily developed districts W of Fawley proper, without much coherence or sense of place. Unlike Fawley itself, they are no longer rural in feeling yet are not part of any town.

EAGLEHURST, *see* p. 196.

FIR GROVE *see* EVERSLEY

8050
FLEET

Although Fleet looks quite substantial on the map, it has no shape nor character nor notable buildings, except one.

ALL SAINTS, Church Road. By *Burges*, 1861–2, lengthened to the W in 1934 by *A. J. Stedman*. Lady Chapel of 1958 by *John Purser*. The original W end was an open narthex. The church is of red brick and externally astonishingly restrained. Good steep bellcote over the E end of the nave. Lower chancel and apse. Lancets and plate tracery all of brick. The interior is impressive by the great height of the nave, with the square brick pillars and the steep pointed transverse brick arches. Between them the vault is boarded. Much painted-on decoration of blue brick bands and geometrical ornamental motifs. The apse has very small windows and ought to appear dark, not white. The church cost £3,323. – MONUMENT. C. E. Lefroy † 1861 and wife. They were the donors of the church. It was originally on the N side of the chancel. Recumbent effigies under an arch with large carved angels. Watch for the two dogs by the feet of the effigies. – SCULPTURE. Tympana of Transfiguration over the N door (originally at the W) and of Christ in Majesty over the S door. Like the Lefroy monument, probably by *Thomas Nicholls*. – PLATE. Two Italian Candlesticks; C18.

CALTHORPE PARK ESTATE, Reading Road North. Good group of detached houses, 1962–3 by *Clifford Culpin & Partners*.

FONTLEY *see* FUNTLEY

FORDINGBRIDGE

1010

ST MARY. Much of the church is E.E., i.e. the chancel with its three E stepped lancet lights, the l. and r. ones depressed two-centred on vertical pieces, the side lancets, the fine hood-moulds on leaf-stops inside, the four-bay arcades with round piers, feeble capitals, round abaci, and double-chamfered arches, and the arch from the nave to the N tower. For the church has a N tower, with a slightly higher stair-turret. The N chapel has an arcade of three bays to the chancel, and this, with its quatrefoil piers, looks later C13. In fact there is even some difference between bays one and two and bay three. In the place of the latter there was originally a chancel lancet. The date of the chapel is confirmed by the windows with bar tracery, provided these can be trusted. It is recognizable that they take the place of other windows preceding them. The chancel arch is the same as the chapel arcade, so there is perhaps not much difference between the two phases. Perp S aisle, five-light Perp W window with a transom. Two-storeyed Perp N porch. In the N chapel a splendid hammerbeam roof with angels against the hammers. Tie-beams and queen-posts. Tracery above the hammers, and cusping of the arches between wall and hammer. The whole thing looks East Anglian but is in fact quite similar to Bere Regis in Dorset.* – PAINTINGS. Three Saints from the dado of a screen, also as in East Anglia. The quality is not high. – MONUMENTS. In the chapel See p. 829 N wall an outer recess; Perp. Did it originally have sculpture against the back wall? – John Bulkeley Coventry Bulkeley † 1801. A tablet of very high craftsmanship.

Few houses at Fordingbridge need comment. From the church by Church Street and Provost Street to the MARKET PLACE with the TOWN HALL of 1877, three bays with a turret but

* The church was exemplarily restored in 1901–3 by *C. E. Ponting* (NT).

without any merit. In the HIGH STREET a seven-bay Late Georgian brick house, the first bay representing the carriage entrance. Next to this ST IVES with, on the first floor, two-light mullioned windows with recessed frames. It looks later C17, though there is no authority for the date 1679.* From the end of the High Street to the BRIDGE. Medieval, of seven depressed-pointed arches. Widened in the style of the original in 1841. The street N out of the town is SALISBURY STREET. The OLD MANOR standing across the end is much pulled about, but the two bay windows and the horizontally placed oval window are probably all right and suggest a date 1660–70. At the N exit is BURGATE HOUSE, externally all early C19 Gothic. Towards the river a big castellated bow and set in it two genuine shallow Perp recesses with gables. Towards the entrance two gables and an embattled porch. The house itself is older, cf. the big chimneys with blank arches.

FRYERN COURT, Upper Burgate, *Augustus John*'s house. The façade of *c.*1800, behind C17. Good eight-bay C17 BARN.

FORTON *see* GOSPORT, pp. 240, 243

FOURACRE *see* WEST GREEN HOUSE

6030

FOUR MARKS

GOOD SHEPHERD. By *Felix Lander*, 1953–4. Brick, with a N tower.

3040

FOXCOTT

2 m. NW of Andover

CHURCH. Of the church built *c.*1830 the SW porch tower remains. The rest was taken to Charlton, less than a mile away. But all the details are obviously Victorian. So is the conception of the SW porch tower. A date 1855 is recorded for the addition of a vestry to the church of *c.*1830.

FOXLEASE *see* LYNDHURST

FRATTON *see* PORTSMOUTH, pp. 449, 463

FREEFOLK *see* LAVERSTOKE

FREEMANTLE *see* SOUTHAMPTON, p. 566

*So Mr Paul Hewitt tells me.

FROXFIELD

7020

ST PETER-ON-THE-GREEN. Built on the site of the medieval church (demolished in 1862) in 1887. Small, of nave and chancel, with a bell-turret. On the l. of the path to the church an C18 GRAVESTONE with two cherubs blowing the last trump.

ST PETER. *See* High Cross.

SCHOOL HOUSE. On Froxfield Green. Built in 1733. Five bays, two storeys, red brick, hipped roof. The windows still with wooden mullion-and-transom crosses.

FROYLE

7040

ASSUMPTION. A fine late C13 chancel with characteristic chancel arch and windows with pointed-trefoiled lights and bar tracery (e.g. a spherical triangle). But the E window is a generation later, an ambitious replacement. Five lights, reticulated tracery. The nave is of brick, with two-storeyed windows and porch projections N and S. It is of 1812, by *James Harding*, and the date makes it necessary to assume that the windows are a Victorian improvement. Brick W tower of 1722. Segment-headed windows. – COMMUNION RAIL. Jacobean. – CHANDELIER. Of brass, a gorgeous piece. Dated 1716. – STAINED GLASS. Splendid shields in the reticulation units of the E window. – Many fragments in nave N windows. – By *Kempe* chancel N, 1874 and 1878, and chancel S 1897. – HELM in the chancel. – MONUMENTS. Low tomb recess in the chancel. Segmental arch.

FROYLE PLACE. This is a medieval house, as some five years ago blocked arcading was found in the hall (MHLG). The look of the building however is Jacobean, Georgian, and Victorian. The main front has three steep gables with mullioned windows. Otherwise sash-windows. Towards the garden dominantly Victorian additions (1867). The house is built of clunch.

FROYLE MANOR, just W of Froyle Place, has an irregular exterior, but a fine Early Georgian staircase with slim twisted balusters.

BONHAMS, 1 m. SW of the church. Square, of brick, two-storeyed, with a hipped roof. The front looks Early Georgian, but the back with the two wings and the narrow courtyard between and mullioned and transomed windows must be later C17.

COLDREY HOUSE, 1⅛ m. NE of the church, *see* Bentley.

HUSSEY'S FARM, Lower Froyle, is basically timber-framed, but has an C18 brick front in two parts. Behind, a splendid group of four OASTHOUSES.

SILVESTER'S FARM, also Lower Froyle. Dated 1674, and this date fits the N side with the broad cross-windows.

FRYERN HILL *see* CHANDLER'S FORD

5000

FUNTLEY [DL]

1½ m. NW of Fareham

ST FRANCIS. Minute stuccoed chapel of 1836, T-shaped, with traceried windows, hoods, and bargeboards, probably by *Jacob Owen* (cf. Holy Trinity, Fareham) – STAINED GLASS. E window by *John Ruskin*,* formerly at Duntisbourne Abbots, Glos. In a two-light traceried frame. Small-scale representations of the Nativity and Ascension; richly detailed delineation, deep colouring; smaller medallions of angels above; the background a pattern of deep blue and red. The Duntisbourne Abbots windows were lower than those at Funtley; hence the upper part of the window is filled with pastel-shaded glass.

(IRON MILLS. Off Titchfield Lane a small track, cobbled with iron slag, leads down to the Iron Mills. This was the main working place of the ironmaster *Henry Cort*, who invented the reverbatory furnace and the rolling mill in 1783–4. The remains of the two mill races, slots for the gears with wrought-iron lintels, and the dry mill-pond bounded with a long bank of slag can be seen straddling the river Meon. Near to this is the MILL MASTER'S HOUSE which has a timber-framed W half, bricked over in the early C18, and a large E extension by Cort of about 1779. The half-hipped roof and long wooden lintels typify Cort's millwright's style, probably from Portsmouth Dockyard. Overlooking this on the west side of the valley stood Samuel Jellicoe's (Cort's partner's) house, which is now the farmhouse. This corresponds to the mill master's house in style. Further up the valley side is IRON MILL COTTAGE, once two ironworkers' cottages of the C18. Excavations have uncovered Cort's buildings as well as finding the foundations of an earlier works, attached to Titchfield Abbey before 1536. Waterworks and drains con-

*Information given by Mr R. Hubbuck.

trolling the mill flow spread for 1 m. N and S of the site on the river.)*

GREAT FUNTLEY FARM. An attractive two-storeyed timber-framed house with long regular frontage, the upper storey slightly oversailing. The MHLG says it is C15.

(KNOWLE HOSPITAL. Original building of 1830, erected as the County Lunatic Asylum by *J. Harris*. The tender was for £33,786 (GS). Many additions.)

FYFIELD 2040

ST NICHOLAS. Mostly Victorian. Nave and chancel and bell-cote. Genuine Perp E window. The chancel S window probably C17.

GIANT'S GRAVE *see* BREAMORE

GODSFIELD 6030

2¼ m. NNE of Old Alresford

CHAPEL, on an estate of the Hospitallers. Built in the late C14 probably. Attached is the priest's house. The E part is the chapel. Blocked E window, single-chamfered N doorway, three single-light S windows with cusped heads. To the priest's house a doorway next to that of the chapel. One room below, one room above. The staircase projects a little on the N and has a slit window. Attached on the W to the upper room a garderobe. From this room a small window allows a view of the altar.

GOLEIGH MANOR *see* PRIORS DEAN

GOODWORTH CLATFORD 3040

ST PETER. The W tower is of stone and Dec; yet it is still un-buttressed. The rest of the church is of flint. It is of no interest externally. A few Norman fragments built into the tower. Internally there is much more interest. The arcades are of four bays, but they are by no means a homogeneous job. First come the two W bays of the S side. Round pier, square abacus, trumpet-scallop capitals with some decoration. Spurs on the base. Pointed arches with one slight chamfer. That

* I owe this description to Mr Stephen Weeks, who excavated the site in 1964.

indicates *c.*1190. At the same time or perhaps a few years before, the transept arch, i.e. evidence of a cruciform church, planned – according to how one's dating goes – before, or at the same time as, the S aisle. Then, early C13, the third S arch, connecting arcade and transept. This has a hood-mould of dogtooth. Only after that the N arcade: two bays plus the former transept. Round piers, octagonal abaci, arches with one chamfer and one hollow chamfer. The W respond and even more the E arch have good figural decoration of the early C14. Dec details also in the N aisle E wall. – FONT. Purbeck marble, of table type. Six flat arches on one side. Also other motifs. All extremely over-restored. – PAINTING. Christ and the Woman taken in Adultery. Large, English, *c.*1800.

6000

GOSPORT [DL]

INTRODUCTION

Gosport is on the W side of Portsmouth Harbour, on a flat site indented by two inlets, the many-branching Haslar Creek and the lesser Forton Creek, with the shingly shore of the Solent itself to the SW. The old town is immediately opposite Old Portsmouth and Portsea across the harbour mouth. It was not of much consequence until the C17, when it grew to small-town size and was enclosed within defensive ramparts like Portsmouth itself. The first Anglican chapel in the town proper dates from 1696.* The original parochial centre is at ALVERSTOKE, 1½ m. W, at the head of Haslar Creek, which grew of its own account as a small select resort and place of residence (particularly for naval officers) in the early C19. Gosport sprawled loosely far beyond its enclosing ramparts after about 1830, but the outward growth was checked by the line of forts built by Palmerston from Elson on the harbour to Gomer on the coast in 1850–60. Since the Second World War development has stretched much further. It is now a spread-out town, pleasantly leafy in its better parts, scrappy in its less attractive parts, in marked contrast to the close and crowded development on Portsea Island.

CHURCHES

ST MARY. The parish church of Alverstoke and the mother church of the borough. By *Henry Woodyer*, chancel 1865,

* Though Mr Stephen Weeks points out that Leland mentions a 'profained chapell' in the C16.

nave 1885, the tower built, not to Woodyer's design, in 1906. Nothing is left of the medieval church. Big, pretentious; a major work of Woodyer, an architect who could sometimes be very good (cf. his spire at Dorking and his little church at Hascombe in Surrey) but who was often dull or clumsy. At Alverstoke he was obviously trying hard after original and striking effect. The church consists of a clerestoried nave with aisles and a chancel with chapels. The main windows are elaborately neo-Dec, the clerestory windows sharp lancets, the roofs steep and tall, the W tower rather lanky and an ineffective climax to the main part of the building, with its bombast and upward thrust. Impressive, spacious interior. The nave arcades are of five bays with piers of four shafts and four hollows, the capitals towards nave and aisles being raised *above* those towards the arches; the resulting restless rhythm is Woodyer not quite succeeding. The capitals show a rich and interesting variety of leaf carving, and the E arch of each arcade is treated more elaborately than the rest. The chancel arch has a panelled underside with a curious pattern of tracery interlocking with rings, and a flat outer hood with tracery, all brought out effectively in dark red and gilt in a recent sensitive redecoration of the interior,* which has combined a certain amount of un-Victorian whitewashing of wall surfaces with intensive coloration of details such as this. – The REREDOS is a curious and effective design, basically a rectangular composition, but with the central part set back behind a cusped arch, the whole of its surface encrusted with decoration in tracery, emblems and foliage, within which the outline of a cross is brought out in pale bluish stonework against the darker yellow stonework of the rest of the composition. The cross is the culmination of the eastward view and is Woodyer's ultimate triumph, a piece of originality that comes off. – STAINED GLASS. Nothing of any note, but providing a background of deep glowing colour which is just right for this High Victorian interior. – PLATE. Paten, 1702; Cup, 1783. – MONUMENTS. Many tablets, the oldest dated 1703. One is by *Nollekens* (S. Weeks).

HOLY TRINITY. The parish church of Gosport proper, built as a chapel of ease to Alverstoke in 1696, enlarged in 1734 and *c.*1835, and completely restored by *Blomfield* in 1887, with a campanile added by him in 1889. The present external appearance is due to Blomfield, who turned the old plain building

* By *Campbell-Smith & Co.* (NT).

with its low-pitched nave, tall, steep-pitched aisles, and apsidal chancel into a rather crude and simplified version of a Lombard basilica. The interior is a complete surprise. The nave is still that of 1696, with two rows of seven Ionic columns, each fashioned out of a single oak trunk, supporting heavy entablatures, and a tunnel roof with flat shallow transverse arches at each bay. The culmination is the apse, dating in its original form from 1734, with panelled semi-dome, windows facing NE and SE, flat pilasters between them, and the REREDOS, a Victorian three-gabled panelled frame containing a (supposedly) C18 Florentine painting of the Nativity and, in the side panels, figures of the Apostles, surmounting the marble and mosaic HIGH ALTAR by *J. H. Ball* and *Heywood Sumner* from St Agatha at Landport (p. 432). The vista is now unbroken to the altar – the CHANCEL SCREEN, a pleasant piece of metalwork by *Blomfield*, having been moved to the W end – and the recent redecoration, mainly in white, but with blue and gold in significant places, is effective. – FONT and PULPIT, of coloured marble and alabaster designed by *Blomfield* and executed by *Earp*. – The great treasure of the church is the ORGAN on which Handel played; it was originally at Canons Park, Stanmore, where Handel was organist to the Duke of Chandos, and brought to Gosport in the mid C18. The façade and original pipes are by *Abraham Jordan*. It has since been altered and enlarged, but retains much of its Baroque case. – Many TABLETS with good lettering, including a Baroque cartouche to John Chapman † 1705.

The CAMPANILE is a notable landmark of Gosport, most especially after the complete redevelopment of the surrounding area, with the church as the central feature of the new layout, overtopped but not overwhelmed by the new flats and still seen set against them or between them from many fairly distant viewpoints. It is a successful design by *Blomfield* in brick of a colour slightly darker than that of the church itself, in three stages, the lowest a short, slightly battered base, the second rising through three storeys with thin panel patterns, the upper tier with *trifore*, i.e. three-light arched bell-openings, and surmounted by four pinnacles and a stumpy spire finished in an attractive scaled tile pattern.

CHRIST CHURCH, Stoke Road. 1865 by *Woodyer*. A bulky church, with no tower. Four-bay arcades, wide and thrusting; clerestory of little trefoiled lights between shafts. Wide chancel arch with no capitals but an inner order ending in a concave curve (is this another Woodyer quirk, or is it a piece of simplification by *Sir Charles Nicholson*, who restored the church in the 1930s ?). Wooden chancel roof in imitation-vaulting pattern. E window with elaborate Geometrical tracery behind a cusped outer arch. Woodyer again is trying to make his work noticeable, and it is indeed quite interesting.

OUR LADY OF THE SACRED HEART (R. C.), High Street. Behind an uninspired W front to the street is a surprising interior. It is of 1855–8, by one *Phillips* (D. Evinson), but the W front is 1897. Nave with six-bay S arcade of depressed arches, and a balancing blank arcade on the N side, under big clerestory windows. The wide S aisle has a smaller-scale version of the arcade in low arched recesses on its S wall. N and S chapels with oddly treated polygonal ends. Curious panelled ceilings. – TABLET in memory of Maria Francisca, wife of Carlos V of Spain, who died in 1834 at Alverstoke.

ST FRANCIS (Garrison Church), Brockhurst. 1872. Tin church with clerestory and aisles and wood-framed Gothic windows. Most of the internal framework is wooden, but the nave is spanned by slender iron arched braces.

ST JOHN THE EVANGELIST, Forton. 1907 by *A. Blomfield & Sons*, replacing a church of 1831. Looms large over a dispiriting district of Gosport. Aisled and clerestoried, almost entirely of red brick, except for a few stone dressings, inside and out. Strong lancet windows. Tall W gable surmounted by an assertive flèche. No stained glass left.

ST LUKE (Haslar Hospital Chapel), *see* p. 245.

ST MARY. The medieval parish church of Rowner, *see* p. 490.

CONGREGATIONAL CHURCH, Bury Road. 1957 by *L. F. Kimber*. Octagonal, mostly of brick. E and W sides of glass and vitreous panels between vertical ribs. Projecting two-storeyed vestibule towards the street. The church replaces a Georgian chapel in the old town which was bombed.

NAVAL AND MILITARY BUILDINGS

ROYAL NAVAL HOSPITAL, Haslar. Begun in 1746, opened in 1754, completed in 1762. The original design was for buildings round a very large square, a central block and long wings on each side. Only three sides of the projected square were built, and the central parts of the side blocks were considerably modified in scale.

The buildings are in fairly austere Georgian style in dun brick. The principal range, facing NE, is the only one to be completed according to the original design. The main part of the central block is of three bays, rising to four storeys under a pediment, the windows in the second and third storeys being contained within stone frames which run through both storeys and are round-headed inside but square-headed outside. The pediment contains elaborate sculpture in Portland stone by *Thomas Pierce*, 1752, with the Royal Arms in the centre and figures and emblems depicting Navigation and Commerce to l. and r. Haslar was intended originally for both sailors on service and civilian seamen. In the ground storey are three round-headed arches of brick, opening into groin-vaulted passageways which lead through into the courtyard. Flanking the main part of the central block are sections of façade of two bays, rising to three storeys, under sloping fascias which appear, so to speak, as if they were the ends of a wide pediment which would span the whole seven bays of the central block above third-storey level, if the middle three bays did not rise an extra storey. The wings on either side of the central block have straightforward three-storey façades of ten bays each with stone string courses at first-floor and cornice level and simple receding brick parapets. These wings are in fact of less than half the width of the main central block, and are paralleled by other similar wings facing the courtyard, with long narrow spaces in between. The inner façade of the principal range, towards the courtyard, is similar to the outer except that the central pediment is plain, without sculpture, and the ground storeys of the inner wings were originally entirely open, with round-arched colonnades. The ground storey of the NW inner wing has been filled in and the arches blocked, but that of the SW inner wing has been left partly open, preserving the original effect. The other two ranges were similar to the principal range on the courtyard side except that the central blocks were to a much simplified design, rising to two storeys only under pediments and linked to adjoining blocks by two-bay open colonnades. The centrepiece survives only on the NW side, that on the SE having been bombed and not rebuilt. The ground storeys of all the inner wings on the NW and SE ranges have been filled in and the external arcades blocked. Except for this, and the bombing of the SE centrepiece, the C18 external appearance of the hospital remains remarkably intact.

Beyond the open side of the courtyard is a garden with a short avenue leading to the CHAPEL OF ST LUKE, on the axis of the central block of the main range, built in 1756 (the date 1762 on the clock relates to the clock only) and renovated in 1963 by *Thomas Makins*. A simple rectangle, with pedimented W front surmounted by a little clock turret; W door with entablature and Tuscan columns; round-headed windows. – WEST GALLERY. Reduced from its original extent (it previously extended round the sides of the nave). Panelled front. – BALDACCHINO of 1918–20, with octagonal Corinthian columns, set against what may have been the frame of the original REREDOS, with the top of a wide rounded pediment and fluted Ionic demi-columns. – COMMUNION RAIL. Recently fashioned from part of the balustrade of a staircase in the hospital; effective. – PAINTING of the Restoration of Sight to Bartimaeus, 1928 by *G. Haywood Hardy*; realistic landscape and figures. – PLATE. Set of 1756; Bowl, probably C18 (a recent gift).

Behind the chapel, along another short avenue, is the TERRACE of 1790, consisting of the Medical Officer in Charge's house on the main axis, stuccoed, three-storeyed, with tall windows, and a range of four three-storeyed houses on either side. The C19 and C20 buildings on the hospital do not call for comment, except for the WATER TOWER of 1885, in the powerful Navy style of the second half of the C19; brick with elephantine stone dressings; pyramid roof with a smaller pyramid-topped upper stage, the chief feature of Haslar seen from central Gosport across the creek.

ROYAL CLARENCE VICTUALLING YARD, Weevil Lane. Set up under its present title in 1828, when the whole Victualling Department of the Navy was transferred here. But there was already a sizeable establishment on the site, dating back at least to the early C18. The stuccoed ENTRANCE from Weevil Lane is of 1828. Central round archway, flanked by pairs of pilasters and surmounted by a plain entablature, with the Royal Arms on top; two small side doors for pedestrians and two wings, curving inwards, with five-bay Doric colonnades on the inner side. Two-storeyed houses of the same date, for senior officials of the Yard, just within the entrance, two on the l. and one remaining on the r. The most impressive building is the former GRANARY, close to the harbour's edge, originally used also as a Mill and Bakery for ship's biscuits but now put to general storage use. It is of 1853, said to have been designed by the younger *Rennie*, very conservative in external design for the date, though not in internal structure. The main block is of four storeys with an attic, the ground floor open except for supporting iron piers, the other floors brick-faced, with stone string courses and regular fenestration, ten bays on the longer sides, seven bays on the end, where the second and sixth bays are taken by hoists. The main internal supporting columns are of iron, the subsidiary structural framework of timber. Long three-storey N wing (the balancing S wing was destroyed by bombing) of fifteen bays, with the sixth to eighth bays under a pediment and further emphasized by round-headed arches rising from the ground storey to contain the windows on the second storey. Within the present area of the Yard is part of the former ROYAL RAILWAY STATION, once reached by a special branch line and used by Queen Victoria to embark for the Isle of Wight. A long, narrow curving building with glazing in the low-pitched roof (the upper part of which is slightly raised for ventilation) and the original brick external wall on the outside of the curve, with round-headed windows having iron mullions and transoms. The present wall on the inside of the curve is of recent construction, and all traces of the track and platform arrangement have gone.

H.M.S. ST VINCENT (BARRACKS), Forton Road. Built in 1847 as the Royal Marine Barracks by *Captain James* of the Royal Engineers. An impressive frontage to the road: central entrance feature with rusticated archway, and a complex superstructure ending in a wooden cupola. Symmetrical composition of low, coarsely detailed buildings and linking walls on either side, terminating in single-storey blocks, their façades each originally of eleven bays, but subsequently lengthened outwards, the three central bays of the original eleven projecting slightly with the windows set back in arched recesses. All this is in harsh red brick with stone cornice. Inside, around the large barrack square, are symmetrically disposed three-storey blocks linked, on the side facing the entrance, with a colonnade of brick arches. The whole is a forceful, ordered composition in a debased classical style, the sort of design one would expect from an Early Victorian sapper-surveyor.

ST GEORGE BARRACKS. Built in 1857–9, reputedly to a design intended for barracks in the Far East, the barracks designed for Gosport having been erected out there. Long main block of two storeys, the lower storey a semi-basement, with verandas on both levels for the whole length – more suitable, one would think, for a climate hotter than Gosport's. Yellow brick, flat-roofed behind parapets, the upper veranda with fifty-seven iron columns resting on thicker piers which form the colonnade of the lower veranda. Stepways descend every five bays from the upper level to the ground, and both these and the upper veranda have ironwork balustrades with repeated diagonal cross-pattern. Quite a handsome, functional building. The railings fronting Clarence Road and elsewhere are original, with entrances under elliptical ironwork arches, with an open tracery pattern of diminishing circles. The Guard Room, on the other side of Forton Road, is a simple, massive square building, originally with a colonnade of seven brick arches, the ones at the ends now blocked, and surmounted by a clock turret with crude Italianate detailing. Along Weevil Lane is a series of several blocks in a simplified version of the main block facing Clarence Road, but the verandas are omitted and instead there are tall rectangular windows with massive flat-hooded doorways every five bays and stone staircases, with concave undersides, climbing to each.

(H.M.S. SULTAN, Brockhurst, and H.M.S. DOLPHIN, Haslar. Pleasant recent work by the *Ministry of Public Building and Works* (*Navy Works*) among stodgier stuff of a decade or so ago.)

DEFENSIVE WORKS

RAMPARTS. It is difficult to discover when the various parts of the once elaborate fortifications of Gosport were constructed. A map of 1668 shows works, with salients and moats, on the W side of the town, corresponding to *de Gomme*'s more elaborate fortifications around Portsmouth (p. 419) – but this does not necessarily indicate that they were then complete; they may have been intended or under construction (de Gomme's Portsmouth works were not begun until 1665). Fortifications on the S side of the town (i.e. S of Trinity church) appear on a map of 1725, but on later C18 maps (i.e. of 1775) this part of the defences is shown more lightly than the rest, suggesting that either it was still under construction or was less substantial than the rest – an unfortunate piece of uncertainty, since this is the most considerable part of the fortifications now remaining. By 1770 a large-scale elaboration of the defences on the W side had been carried out, consisting of a second line with separate moats, salients, and ravelins running from Haslar Creek just W of the original ramparts, N to Forton Creek (the original line of defences had turned E well to the S of Forton Creek, ending on the harbour shore). So by the end of the C18 Gosport was a strongly walled town, like Portsmouth and Portsea, with massive brick gateways at the principal entrances. The Gosport fortifications were never systematically demolished, as were those of Portsmouth; the gates were removed in the C19, but large parts of the ramparts remained well into the C20; as recently as 1965 a section to the S of High Street was obliterated by the borough council, the earth being used to fill the adjoining moat. What survives is a stretch of the C18 outer defences in the military area N of Forton Road, not easily accessible, and a section S of Trinity church which is probably of C18 origin (*see* above). It is a continuous flat-topped earthen mound in the form of a large four-sided salient, together with a short stretch from the W corner of the salient to the site of the former gateway which spanned Haslar Street. Within the earthwork are remains of C18 and C19 brick-lined gun emplacements and magazines. Part of the moat outside the salient survives, together with the lock-gate controlling its connexion with the harbour, beside which is a separate gun emplacement of Palmerston's time, elliptically vaulted inside. A new low block of flats, called WATERGATE, is built against the E side of the salient, and bridges connect it at first-floor level with the rampart. The interior of the salient is now a wilderness, but the borough council intend to develop it with flats linked to the rampart, which will be preserved as a historic feature – all the more valuable now that most of the rest of Gosport's defences have gone. Within the open side of the salient, facing the town, is the former GOVERNOR'S HOUSE, now the RECTORY, a severe three-storeyed building of 1801 all in local grey brick, flanked by high C19 brick walls across the rest of the inner side of the salient.

PALMERSTON'S FORTS. In the 1850s there was serious threat of French invasion. Portsmouth would have been an obvious first objective; the city itself might well have been impregnable, but, with the artillery of the time, any force which could gain control of the Gosport side of the harbour or of Portsdown Hill to the N would have been able to harass the harbour effectively and probably put it out of action. An attempted landing on the Solent coast somewhere near Titchfield, followed by an attack on Gosport together with a thrust to Portsdown Hill, was thought to be the most likely enemy strategy. So a series of forts guarding the Gosport peninsula, together with another series on Portsdown Hill (p. 387), was planned.*

Before they were finished the political situation had changed and there was an *entente cordiale*, but they were maintained for future eventualities. For the Gosport peninsula two lines were originally proposed; of the forts in the outer line, which was to have run from Lee-on-the-Solent to Fareham, only Fort Fareham (p. 227) was ever built. The inner line, of five forts, extended from Gomer W of Alverstoke to Elson on Portsmouth Harbour. The Palmerstonian forts are the last major works in Britain in the tradition that began with the Roman forts and continued with the medieval castles and then with the complicated defences of Elizabethan to Georgian times which are exemplified at Portsmouth (p. 418) and ended with the advent of aerial bombing and mechanical traction. In basic principle they are not essentially different from Portchester Castle with its keep and *enceinte*; in more detailed terms they differed in little but scale from the defences initiated by de Gomme at Portsmouth. It was about 1914 that the history of military architecture of the traditional sort ended.

Of the Gosport forts FORT GOMER has been demolished; FORT GRANGE is in naval occupation and has been much modified; FORT ROWNER is also in Service occupation but is more or less intact – like Fort Grange, it is very similar to FORT BROCKHURST, the next fort in the series, which is completed by FORT ELSON, smaller than the others and occupied by the Navy. Fort Brockhurst has survived, very little altered, and has been designated an Ancient Monument; the Ministry of Public Building and Works are restoring it to its original condition. This means clearing away a great deal of vegetation, to the aesthetic detriment of the fort; for the effect of tall trees, much undergrown with scrub, overhanging the half-filled moat, and huge brick-faced ramparts topped by thickets of scrub, is highly romantic.‡ All this cannot be

* As well as the four island fortresses on Spithead, p. 421. Most of the forts were built *c.*1860, but Fort Gomer, now demolished (*see* below), dated from 1853–8 (S. Weeks).

‡ Mr Weeks points out that some of the vegetation was allowed to grow deliberately for camouflage. In fact all the forts, both in the Gosport area and on Portsdown Hill, are remarkably well concealed from their hinterland by earthworks and vegetation.

left, but possibly some might be (provided enough of the fort is restored to mint condition to make quite clear what it all looked like) so that in the end the restored fort is still, in some measure, aesthetically pleasing as well as historically instructive.

Fort Brockhurst is a hollow space surrounded by ramparts in the form of an irregular elongated hexagon, with two sides at a very wide angle to each other facing roughly W (the direction from which an attack would have come), short (roughly) N and S sides at rather more than ninety degrees to the W sides, and two (roughly) E sides at a wide angle to each other, with a large circular keep between them. A large caponnier makes a long salient between the two W sides, and smaller caponniers face (roughly) N and S at the NW and SW corners of the *enceinte*. The whole is surrounded by a wide moat, and beyond the moat, except on part of the E side, are extensive earthworks or glacis (now very overgrown). The keep is a large hollow circle, about half its circumference projecting outside the *enceinte* and into the moat, across which a bridge leads to the main entrance, neo-Norman of three orders, the outer two orders with inset shafts and stylized scalloped capitals. All the forts have these convincing neo-Norman entrances,* in stone, but much in keeping with the massive brick structures in which they are set. Projecting from the outside of the moat, at regular intervals, are short square salients, with two tiers of rifle slits. Between the salients the outer wall of the keep has a lower tier of gunports, segment-headed and framed in granite (like other gunports in the fort), and an upper tier of rifle slits. The part of the keep facing the inside of the fort is of wider external radius and also has gunports and similar salients, for the keep was intended as a place of final defence if the rest of the fort should be over-run. It is guarded by an inner moat crossed by a bridge to a round arch (of brick and simpler than the neo-Norman one at the outside entrance) which gives entrance to the inner circular courtyard of the keep. From this courtyard it can be seen that the keep is in fact a circular rampart, with chambers in its thickness from which the gunports and rifle slits open (used as quarters for the defending forces) and a thick top layer of earth,‡ be-

* Except Fort Gomer, which had classical detailing around the entrance (S. Weeks).

‡ The earth, of course, provided protection from artillery shells at high projections.

hind retaining walls but embanked above the levels of their parapets. The W-facing ramparts are fairly straightforward, with outer retaining wall rising from the moat, very wide embanked earthworks rising considerably higher, gun emplacements on the top of them, and a series of tunnel-vaulted chambers opening from the inside of the fort and extending back for about half the thickness of the rampart, providing space for mens' quarters and store rooms.* A passage leads through to the W caponnier, which is square-ended and has three gunports in round-arched recesses facing N and S (two over the moat, the inner one over the bank of the rampart) with rifle slits above; inside it is impressively tunnel-vaulted in brick, in three bays transversely.

The N and S ramparts are higher and more complex, with gunports at the end of brick-tunnelled casemates. A bomb dropped on one of these casemates, demolishing most of it but revealing the thickness of the construction of the tunnel-vault, with eight courses of brickwork. Inside the enclosure a brick barrack block of the late C19 and after. The fort was in military occupation until fairly recently.

The Palmerstonian scheme also included FORT MONCKTON, of C18 origin and now in naval occupation, and FORT BLOCKHOUSE, opposite the harbour mouth from the Round Tower, where a wooden fortification was established in the C15, a gun platform in the C17, and a fort in the early C18 (now incorporated into H.M.S. Dolphin).

PUBLIC BUILDINGS

TOWN HALL. By *W. H. Saunders & Son*, opened in 1964. Five-storeyed rectangular block, curtain-walled with white vitreous panels between black vertical ribs, with slated fascia and partly open ground storey. There is a shorter two-storey block at r. angles to the main block which, with a surviving part of the undistinguished Late Victorian town hall,‡ makes up a pleasant three-sided courtyard open to High Street, with a vista through the open base of the main block. The Council Chamber is a distinct structure projecting from the W end of the main block at upper-floor level and resting on piers; the

*They connect inwards with passages running lengthwise through the thickness of the ramparts. Each has a fireplace, with the chimney rising oddly from the earthen banks above.

‡ Now demolished and replaced by a new building on the same site completing the composition.

E wall is segmental, and affixed to it is an aluminium representation of the borough coat of arms and a medieval ship. – ENGRAVED GLASS by *J. C. Cooper* and historical mural PAINTING inside by *E. Talbot*.

POST OFFICE. *See* Perambulations, p. 255.

PUBLIC LIBRARY. 1902 by *A. W. S. Cross** of London, with a large plaster frieze by *Schneck*. Two storeys, the ground floor faced mainly in brick and the upper storey mainly in white-washed roughcast. The roof is low and slated, with boldly projecting eaves; at the end of the main frontage is a wide tower rising to three storeys, the lower two of brick but the upper one (above the eaves level of the main building) slate-hung, capped with a low slated pyramid spire. At the corner is a round turret ending in a flat little copper dome. Windows are studiedly haphazard. Massive wooden porch with columns resting on base walls tapering upwards. The whole building has a quirky Voyseyish–Art Nouveau feeling; the most endearing Art Nouveau-ish touch is in the design of a series of diagonal brackets projecting from the wall surface a little below the eaves and apparently supporting the gutters, but continuing above them and ending in slender twists. The frieze occupies a large horizontal panel on the first floor, depicting historical or legendary local scenes (Lady Alwara of Alverstoke, Bishop Henry of Blois landing at Gosport in 1158, Henry Cort experimenting with the smelting of iron‡) in low relief, brought out well in the late horizontal sun. Attached to the Library behind is the many-angled HIGH SCHOOL, similar in manner but simpler.

GOSPORT GRAMMAR SCHOOL. At Bay House, Alverstoke, enlarged from a marine villa built in 1844§ by *Decimus Burton* for Lord Ashburton. It is an asymmetrical Tudor composition in stone, three-storeyed, with a central gable to the main façade, and a turret on one side. Entrance is through a broad projecting porch with a flat rounded arch, into a hall with coved ribbed ceiling and a Tudor-arched recess opposite the entrance. The present LIBRARY was the principal room of the house, with a large square bay window giving a view of the sea at one end, and a plaster-vaulted recess at the other. Externally the bay window is surmounted by a charming veranda at first-floor level, with a tent roof supported by extremely thin iron pillars.

* He was a specialist in designing swimming pools (NT).

‡ See Funtley.

§ According to Colvin. Kelly says 1838.

The neo-Elizabethan chimneystacks are a prominent feature. The new school buildings, which are by *Louis de Soissons, Peacock, Hodges & Robertson*, are sympathetic to Bay House and to its splendid, mature, enveloping foliage (which does, however, cut off the view, enjoyed in Early Victorian times, of the sea). They are in modernized Georgian, and pleasant in their way. Fine ENTRANCE GATES from Burton's time in scrolled ironwork, set in a stretch of wall recessed from the main road frontage, with a small lodge inconspicuously set in the angle.

BRUNE PARK COUNTY HIGH SCHOOL, Brockhurst. 1965 by *Louis de Soissons, Peacock, Hodges, Robertson & Fraser*. A complex of buildings of different height in dun brick, with low-pitched roofs. Quite pleasant; not without neo-Georgian reminiscences, but functional in planning and massing.

NATIONAL CHILDREN'S HOME. *See* Perambulations, p. 256.

RAILWAY STATION. By *Sir William Tite*, opened in 1842, the original terminus for the important Gosport branch of the London & Southampton Railway (which left the main line at Bishopstoke Junction, now Eastleigh), serving Portsmouth until the city obtained its own railway connexion in 1847. Passenger services finally ceased in the 1950s, shortly after which the station was severely damaged by fire; goods traffic also ceased in 1966. The fire left intact Tite's splendid fourteen-bay Tuscan colonnade of Portland stone on the S 82
(side) façade, together with the shell of the stuccoed SE angle pavilion with three rusticated arches on each external façade, separated by flat pilasters which are represented above the cornices by projections on the tall parapets, ending in low pedimented turrets. The whole of the S façade (with its Piranesian background of wild undergrowth in the ruined station) is one of the finest pieces of external station architecture surviving from the beginning of the railway age. The RAILINGS and pediment-topped stone posts fronting the road may be coeval with the station or later, and, to complete the period atmosphere, there is a Victorian pillar box by the entrance, octagonal with ogee top capped by a ball (cf. Bournemouth, p. 829). From the station a siding runs, through a surviving stretch of the ramparts, by a tunnel, originally terminating at the former ROYAL STATION now in the Royal Clarence Victualling Yard (p. 246).

PERAMBULATIONS

(A) The Inner Town

Gosport is reached from Portsmouth across the harbour mouth. It looks impressive as one approaches, chiefly because of the two sixteen-storey blocks of flats which adjoin the waterside, with twelve-storey blocks behind, and the Victorian campanile of Holy Trinity (p. 242) asserting itself between them. When one lands there is an anti-climax, for in front is some distressingly banal recent development (1964–6) at the entrance to High Street.

The old town of Gosport was hemmed in behind its ramparts and was quite congested by the early C19. There were three roughly parallel main streets (High Street the central one), a few interconnecting alleys, and an intricate network of narrow thoroughfares around Holy Trinity, limited by the S rampart. The fabric, till 1940, was still largely Georgian, very mixed and very decayed. Bombing shattered the old town but did not flatten it, and even in 1948 there were still ninety buildings within the area of the ramparts, nearly all C18 or early C19, good enough to be included in the MHLG's provisional list. Few indeed are left now; those in the far N part of the old town have gone to make way for the extension of industry, and the whole of the once close-built area around Holy Trinity has been cleared. The old waterfront, which was a hotchpotch without much charm, has completely gone, and a new promenade has been built S from the ferry landing on reclaimed land. Between this and Holy Trinity is the ambitious new HOUSING scheme, begun in 1961 and incomplete at the time of writing. It was designed by *J. E. Tyrrell*, Chief Architectural Assistant to the borough council. The centrepieces are two sixteen-storey blocks, each a stepped rectangle, the ground storey used for servicing (with a projecting platform on the S side), the long façades with separate rectangular windows and intermediate roughcast facing (with strips of yellow brickwork just within the angle of the stepping), the end façades decorated with striking, almost jarring, abstract mosaic murals (by *J. E. Tyrrell* and *K. Barton*), each in three colours: black, white, and red on the S façade of the N block and the N façade of the S block; black, white, and blue on the other two façades (so that whichever the direction from which one looks the visible panel with red is always in the foreground, that with blue in the background). The S façades of the ground-floor platforms have similar mosaics. The flats are impressive in bulk, and their relative grouping is seen most effectively when one walks towards them N along the promenade, even though the irregular five-storey block which will fill the space between them has not yet (1965) been erected. Further W are two eleven-storey blocks which are not intended to be as eye-catching as the taller blocks but which group well with them. Around and between the tall blocks is a somewhat confusing pattern of two- to five-storey housing, still incomplete; when the whole scheme is finished there will be tightly enclosed spaces around Holy Trinity (whose spire is an effective landmark, topping the lower buildings and holding its own against the taller ones), with the ramparts to the S. From points to the W, especially near the shore of Haslar Creek, there are very exciting views of the church steeple and the tall blocks clustering behind the rough earthen ramparts, which set off the buildings behind and enhance their grandeur. This is one of the more interesting and exciting pieces of recent housing redevelopment in Hampshire, making good use of a first-rate site; it is more sophisticated than anything done by 1965 in Portsmouth, though not at all up to the best Southampton standards.

Back to HIGH STREET, which is fairly wide and curving and still moderately pleasant but with very few individual buildings deserving mention. LLOYDS BANK, 1920 by *G. E. Smith*, is prominent on the outside of a curve, with bold Ionic pilasters between round-headed windows of double-storey height; beyond it THE BELL, also prominent, has a nice ebullient pub front of *c.*1900, of the type common in Portsmouth, with simple Georgian upper storeys in mottled brick. The POST OFFICE, 1963, is a simple design with strong horizontal lines in smooth-faced panels at fascia and inter-floor level, the space between glazed except at the E end of the façade, where there is a void (over the recessed entrance), to good effect. Other near-by recent buildings look commonplace or fussy by comparison. Opposite the Town Hall (p. 251), at the end of the street, is the best group of old houses in the town proper, modest enough, but valuable as survivors from a once much more numerous collection. No. 2 is three-storeyed, of red brick, with a pedimented Doric columned porch; No. 3 is similar but plainer, and in red-grey brick; No. 4 is a more pretentious Early Victorian version of the same theme, of similar height but wider, with stone-framed windows, round-headed on the first floor, and exaggerated pedimented doorcase. Beyond is the Library (p. 252). The perambulation then can continue r. along Clarence Road past St George Barracks (p. 246) and then l. to the Railway Station (p. 253), and possibly on to H.M.S. St Vincent (p. 246) and Forton church (p. 243), or else can continue along the uninteresting Stoke Road into Bury Road (p. 257) and Alverstoke.

(B) ALVERSTOKE

The original village of Alverstoke was tightly clustered at what was the head of Haslar Creek, which has now receded a little. The church is dominant, with the former RECTORY near, a three-storey building with Georgian fenestration but walls partly of stone and originally medieval.* The heart of the old village is just W of the church, where narrow streets lead into a tiny 'square' of a vaguely triangular shape, the buildings varied and homely, including a minute almshouse with a single small gable and, most improbably, a genuine old thatched cottage. An old tree, frequently pruned, is the centrepiece of the 'square', and the top of the church tower is visible in the background. It is a splendid piece of townscape in miniature, and ought to be preserved. Something of the same tight-knit quality survives in the brief tangle of streets to the S, but almost immediately in every direction there begin low-density sylvan suburbs which are, in some places, being insensitively redeveloped.

For the major surprise of Alverstoke one needs to walk S along Anglesea Road, past the NATIONAL CHILDREN'S HOME, which is composed of nondescript neo-Georgian buildings. The Home also occupies ANGLESEA HOUSE, opposite, a seaside villa of *c.*1830, altered, but still with a delicate veranda on the first floor of its seaward façade. An insignificant turning l. leads into the CRESCENT, Alverstoke's architectural *tour de force*. It was begun in 1826 (and probably took a few years to finish) and was intended to be the centrepiece of a new marine town (called Anglesea, after its promoter, the Marquis of Anglesey), of which nothing much else was ever built, until the remaining spaces were filled with ordinary suburban development. It is a nineteen-bay composition, only slightly curved, three-storeyed (apart from the end bays), the centre bay given prominence by a colonnade of four Ionic columns in

* Mr Weeks refers to a blocked C13 arch.

front of the two upper storeys, a Doric colonnade running for the whole length of the crescent on the ground storey between the two projecting end bays, which have rustication and round-headed arches at ground level and Ionic demi-columns on the two storeys above. The end bays also have an extra floor over the cornice, topped by a low, twirly, almost Gothick gable between blunt pinnacles. As a piece of grand urban planning of the early C19 this is unsurpassed in Hampshire – but then Hampshire has no Brighton or Cheltenham.

The few adjoining houses which are roughly contemporary with the Crescent call for little comment; there is an odd assortment to the W, one pair of stuccoed houses looking almost modern, with long horizontal ranges of windows and shutters from wall to wall, cutting even through pilasters. These and the Crescent used to face over a private garden, with the sea visible beyond (at least from upper storeys), but modern development intrudes, and the Crescent now has no apparent connexion with the sea. The perambulation can end on the somewhat bleak foreshore, or else continue N along St Mark's Road, at the far end of which is the PUMPHOUSE, a little single-storeyed stuccoed building with recessed Doric columns flanking its entrance. Near by used to be the GILKICKER TOWER, a landmark for ships, built in 1669 and heightened in the C18, the original part in stone, the later additions in brick, ending in an oddly placed pediment, brought out in several delicate orders of moulding. The intermediate part was a most attractive medley of dark red brick and silver stone. The tower was wantonly destroyed in 1965, despite local protest, in order to widen the road.

About ½ m. N of Alverstoke church is the former hamlet of BURY, a well-to-do place in Georgian times, with several old houses surviving amid later suburban ones. BURY COTTAGE (No. 79 BURY ROAD) is simple Georgian, BURY LODGE (No. 77) is a small mansion in yellow brick, with a pediment enlivened by toothwork brick pattern, wide windows, and a projecting porch with flat hood and round pillars, and BURY HOUSE, now occupied by the Gosport Community Association, remains the best C18 house in the borough. It has a three-storey, five-bay façade, the centre bay brought slightly forward, with tall windows on the ground and first floors and lower ones on the top floor, and a plain panelled doorway; it is built mainly of red-brown brick with brighter brickwork in window dressings and panels below the windows. Further into Gosport,

Bury Road becomes more continuously leafy, and there is a whole row on the N side (Nos 16–40) of agreeable stuccoed Early Victorian villas, mostly with shutters. Then comes BALLARD COURT, a pleasant piece of small-scale recent redevelopment with private flats round a three-sided courtyard, by *Bailey & Piper*, and beyond that drearier townscape. Haslar Creek lies beyond a few dismal streets to the S, but all development hereabouts simply turned its back to it until a recent example was set by the Borough Council on a small redevelopment site, with two pleasant four-storey blocks of flats (architect *J. E. Tyrrell*) prominently placed by the creek so that they enhance it. More redevelopment such as this, taking full account of Gosport's capacious stretches of water, could bring out the special qualities of the town's site which are too frequently ignored.

ROWNER. *See* p. 490.

5030

THE GRANGE

$\frac{3}{4}$ m. SW of Northington

What makes the Grange a national architectural monument is
76 *Wilkins*'s work. He designed The Grange for Henry Drummond in 1804, and it was completed in 1809. In 1817 it went to the Barings (Lord Ashburton † 1835). Wilkins encased a C17 house, and it is not known whether it was of the first or entirely of the second half. In any case *William Samwell* worked here for Sir Robert Henley, and his activity belongs to the third quarter. But of his work nothing survives except a few garlands on the upper gallery of the entrance hall and a rusticated doorway, once external, but now in an internal passage. Wilkins added to his encased house a Parthenon portico of tremendous pathos: six Greek Doric columns wide and two deep, facing E and overlooking the lake. This was one of the first determined *credos* in the coming Grecian mode, highly exacting and far from domestic. Wilkins's sides are of nine bays with giant pilasters and a centre to the N of square piers. Wreaths in the frieze of the piers and the E portico. Unfortunately all this is not stone, but rendered brick.

Additions to this house were made by *S. P. Cockerell* in 1823–5 (or apparently C.R., under his aged father's name) and then by *C. R. Cockerell*, the son, in 1852, and it is not known nor always easy to determine which are which. There are two long wings, both running W. The N wing has two attached

Ionic columns and on the l. and r. a recess for a statue, and then six plain bays. This – *see* below – is C.R.'s work of *c.*1823. The S wing is of seven bays with coupled pilasters. At its end a continuation turns S and forms a link to the ORANGERY, which has six bays. The E front of the orangery is made monumental by an Ionic four-column portico which could well be Wilkins's. Finally, again towards the W, the eight-bay Bachelors' Wing. The terraces steep down in front of the S façade are supposed to date back to the C17.

The INTERIOR is mysterious. The entrance hall and the staircase are both in their C17 positions. The entrance hall has giant pilasters and a gallery in its end wall. Of what date is that, and of what date are the little gallery lantern and the pedimented doorcases? Can they be of Samwell's time? Though Horace Walpole saw the 'small vestibule with a cupola', the details of the foliage look unmistakably 1850. After that much was done anyway in the whole house about 1880, and that date certainly fits the marbling. The staircase is of no interest, but it has another lantern, and this is decorated in the richest English Baroque. This even more makes one think of C. R. Cockerell, with his known Wren sympathies. The chimneypiece in the entrance hall is from Bologna and probably of *c.*1600. Another chimneypiece was given to Lord Ashburton by Napoleon and has a frieze of portrait medallions of the Bonaparte family. Yet other chimneypieces are mid-Georgian English. The dining room in the N wing is the finest room in the house. It has a screen of Ionic columns and wall columns and a coffered segmental vault. On the lintel of the chimneypiece is a Grecian relief. This room is by *C. R. Cockerell*, as the RIBA has a drawing for it on paper watermarked 1821. The orangery was converted into a picture gallery about 1880.

GRANGE FARM *see* ROWNER

GRANS BARROW *see* ROCKBOURNE

GRATELEY 2040

ST LEONARD. Norman one nave N window and the plain S doorway. The N doorway is pointed, while the S doorway is round-headed, but in Hampshire that need not prove a difference of date. Broad C13 N tower with small lancets. C13 chancel with three stepped E lancets. The church is of flint and over-restored (1851). – STAINED GLASS. In a S window a beautiful piece of stained glass representing the Stoning of St Stephen. It comes from Salisbury Cathedral, and must according to style have been done for somewhere close to the E end, where work was ready for receiving glass from *c.*1225 onwards. In the heads of the E windows also C13 glass, including the upper half of a small figure. – TILES. Some, in front of the communion rail. – HOURGLASS STAND. Against the nave N wall. – PLATE. Undated Chalice and Paten.

8030

GRAYSHOTT

ST LUKE. 1901 by *I'Anson & Son*. E.E. with a SE tower surmounted by an exaggeratedly broached shingled spire.

ST JOSEPH (R.C.), ½ m. N. 1911 by *F. A. Walters*. Gothic, with a bell-turret over the E end of the nave. Nothing particular architecturally.

Grayshott is very near Hindhead. So there are hundreds of smallish houses and bungalows about, and larger houses hidden in the foliage.

GRAYSHOTT HALL. Large, with a tower. 1887 by *J. H. Christian*, Ewan's cousin (NT). Wing of 1907 by *E. B. I'Anson*.* Alterations 1939.

7030

GREATHAM

ST JOHN BAPTIST. 1875. SE tower with a shingled broach-spire. Bar tracery.

OLD CHURCH, S of the new. The chancel is roofed, the nave ruinous. In the chancel two lancets. C18 chancel arch, the arch of the basket type. – MONUMENT. Dame Margery Caryll † 1632. Alabaster and touch. Recumbent effigy. Against the back wall an aedicule with columns and inscription.

GREATHAM MILL, ½ m. W. Late C17 miller's house. To its N the mill itself. Early C17, and with the machinery in full working order.

GOLEIGH FARM, ⅜ m. SE. Ironstone, with a big brick chimney on the S side, a broad brick staircase projection, dated 1685, on the N side. The mullioned windows Elizabethan or Jacobean.

7050

GREYWELL

ST MARY. Nave of *c.*1200, cf. the doorways, that to the N (cf. Upnately) with a round arch and dogtooth. The charming

*Whose family lived here (RH).

semicircular projection for the rood-stair is of course later, probably C15. Of *c.*1200 again the tower arch and the chancel arch, pointed arches on simple imposts. The chancel is of 1870–1 (by *Ewan Christian*). – FONT. Octagonal, Perp, with quatrefoils. – SCREEN. Of veranda type, i.e. with a W front, and a ceiling to carry the loft and cover the space between screen and chancel arch. Single-light divisions. – PLATE. Chalice and Paten Cover, 1569; silver-gilt Spoon, undated.

A series of pleasant brick houses mostly along the N side of the village street. On the S side, behind The Forge, the BASINGSTOKE CANAL enters its tunnel. The tunnel is nearly ¾ m. long. The act for the canal is of 1778.

GRIM'S DITCH *see* MARTIN

GROVE PLACE *see* NURSLING

HACKWOOD PARK 6040

Hackwood Park was built by the first Duke of Bolton in 1683–7. It was, to judge from illustrations, a plain hip-roofed house of thirteen bays with wings at r. angles. This is the arrangement still, and it is likely that the masonry of house and wings is that of the 1680s. However, no motif survives.* All the motifs and features are of *c.*1800–13, when *Lewis Wyatt* remodelled the house for the first and second Lords Bolton. He shortened the wings by filling in between part of them, i.e. he pushed the entrance front forward by 24 ft. Until then the centre room on the garden side had been the hall, in the Tudor sense, and represented the whole thickness of the house.

Hackwood Park is grand in scale, but unfortunately all cement-rendered. N front of nine bays and two storeys with a giant portico of Tuscan columns and a pediment. The five-bay wings are connected with the house by somewhat clumsy two-storeyed quadrants, and the wings now end in a handsome blank composition of a giant tripartite opening under an arch. Fine iron railings, and on the axis of the entrance the equestrian lead STATUE of George I, 1722, given by the King to the third Duke of Bolton. The King appears as a Roman emperor.

The S front has an attached giant portico without pediment. The first and last bays have a tripartite window with a blank segmental arch over. Round the corner to the E is a temple front of unfluted Ionic columns and a pediment.

*Except the twisted balusters of the service stairs.

As regards the interior, the hall on the S side went through both floors down to the time of the fifth duke, i.e. 1760–5. In the entrance hall on the N side the first of a large number of *Gibbonsish* carvings from Abbotstone, a Bolton house near Alresford, brought to Hackwood by the fifth duke. In the entrance hall there are hanging trophies. In other rooms are lengths of frieze and garlands. The horizontal panel in the library with two figures and a lace cravat is specially fine. The library ceiling is a C19 imitation of the style of 1680, and some of the woodwork probably also is. High Victorian craftsmen could be uncannily good at imitating Gibbons. The best room in the house is the dining room, with a shallow segmental vault and a shallow apse. The apse is decorated with many thin transverse ribs. The spacious E part of the room is screened and has four niches in the diagonals. At the E end of the S front is the ballroom, with a segment-apsed E end.

STABLES. Rendered. Of nine bays. Centre with turret, and courtyard with, in the far range, the riding school.

But the most interesting feature of Hackwood is SPRING WOOD, laid out probably by *James Gibbs* or at least furnished by him with temples etc. Two are illustrated in his *Book of Architecture* in 1728. It is a formal layout with a centre and eight radiating avenues, the N–S one called Twelve-o'clock Walk, the E–W consisting entirely of yew trees. The most formal composition is the TERRACE with the lily pond in front. It has a portico of two Ionic columns between two pillars, a pediment, and a hipped roof. At the far end of this composition to the l. and r. THE CUBS, two small pavilions with pairs of Doric pilasters and a pediment. Close to them is the TEA HOUSE, also with pairs of Doric pilasters and a pediment. The same repeated at the back. The most impressive feature must have been the ROTUNDA, illustrated by Gibbs, as it was and no longer is. All that remains is eight columns. Originally there were more, and they stood round a centre with drum and dome. Of the other pavilion illustrated by Gibbs, a building of Greek cross shape, there is no trace.

1010

HALE

Hale was *Thomas Archer*'s country house. He re-designed the church, which is all unmistakably Archerish. But what did he design of the house? First of all there was a house in existence, the house designed by *John Webb* for Mr Penruddock. This we know from a drawing at the RIBA, and so we can safely say that no visible evidence remains of it. The present house is seven bays wide and two storeys high. It has a giant three-bay portico of Ionic columns with rich and free capitals and a pediment. The capitals have fluting below the volutes. Is this Archer's house? We have no records what it was like. The portico looks in fact late, not early C18, and it is known that *c.*1792 remodelling went on under *Holland*. In this quandary it becomes important that, visible by the area windows of the front, are the stumps of former giant pilasters which started from the ground, and a ground lower than that of the present house. As the house for Mr Penruddock had no such giant pilasters, this must be Archer's house, and so the whole rest must be Holland's. However, one is not quite happy with this solution either; for the façades of the house have giant angle pilasters and an entablature really far too broad and coarse for Holland. Again, the opposite side of the house has a broad canted bay window in the middle, and in this is a doorcase, possible for Archer but not for Holland. The keystone of the doorway helps to carry the straight hood. Yet, when one compares the doorway with those by Archer in the transepts of the church (*see* below), one is again doubtful. The doorway is reached by a staircase starting in two arms and turning 90 degrees into one middle arm. Canted bay windows of course were not yet usual in the early C18. Yet Archer himself did one for the parsonage of St Paul Deptford.* The house has two separate wings at r. angles to the front. They are of one and a half storeys, seven bays long with a three-bay pediment, and rendered. The lower windows are set in blank arches. The wings are connected to the house by quadrant balustrades. In fact they are sunk quadrant passages. To the back they have oval windows placed horizontally. These passages must be Archer's, especially as in level they correspond to the giant pilasters in the area. The interior of the house is late C18, especially the staircase with a single iron handrail and a circular skylight.‡

ST MARY. Rebuilt in 1717 by *Archer*, but the nave and chancel masonry of the first half of the C17 was kept. Archer added transepts, and so made the church cruciform. Each main end

*Mr John Newman reminded me of this.

‡Mr John Harris draws my attention to a LODGE with a Delos-type Doric portico. He connects this with *Revett*, who used this order at Trafalgar House in Wilts., not far away.

wall has very bulging Doric angle pilasters. Otherwise rectangular and arched openings. Unfortunately Victorian Gothic arched lights have been put into a number of windows, and the roof is Victorian outside and inside. There are a number of true Archer motifs, especially the extraordinary section of the door jambs of the transepts. The N transept doorway also has
65 excessively curled volutes, the S transept doorway a keystone helping to carry the straight hood. The W front has a round window above the plain doorway. Inside, the crossing arches are shallow semi-elliptical. – STAINED GLASS. In the chancel l. and r. by *Mayer* of Munich. – PLATE. Chalice, 1589; two Patens, 1695; Flagon, 1702; Chalice, 1713; Flagon Cover, 1725. – MONUMENTS. Three outstanding ones: Thomas Archer himself, erected in 1739. Comfortably semi-reclining figure in Roman dress. He has settled down on a sarcophagus. L. and r. two female figures, his wives. The background is a grey obelisk. The sculptor is unknown. – Henry Archer † 1768. By *Wilton*, and worthy of this too little known sculptor. Thoughtful standing woman by an urn on a high plinth on which the portrait medallion. The feeling is genuine, and the execution sensitive. – Joseph May † 1796. Designed by *James Wyatt* and carved by *Sir Richard Westmacott*. Urn of a slender, quite individual form on a square base with small rams' heads at the corners.

HALL PLACE *see* WEST MEON

4000 HAMBLE [DL]

Hamble should be approached by water. The ferry from Warsash lands on a rough hard, amid a fleet of boats, and the old village centre is approached by a waterside walk. In its older parts it is an intricate, engaging place, surprisingly unselfconscious, considering that it has been a yachting centre for decades. The approach from Southampton leads into a very different-looking Hamble, a place more concerned with aviation than sailing; with aircraft factories and mid C20 housing. The presence of both the College of Air Training and the training ship Mercury symbolizes the duality of Hamble's character and interests.

ST ANDREW. The small priory of Hamble-le-Rice was founded before 1128 as a cell to Tiron in France. The church consisted of a parochial nave and monastic chancel of about equal size. Both survived at the Dissolution. The architectural evidence of the present church is extremely confusing, and can probably be understood only on the assumption of much re-using of parts. The W tower appears Norman. It is unbuttressed and slender for its height and has two billet string courses and a large W window which is shafted and has two early capitals, one of them with primitive volutes and a head between. The small bell-openings are later. The N wall is the most puzzling part. It has a lavish Late Norman doorway with one order of columns, capitals, one with a kind of concave fluting and the other similar, and an arch with zigzag set diagonally. However, this doorway seems to be re-set in a much larger blocked pointed arch as if of an arcade. Further E in the same wall is a Norman window and then, by the E end of the wall, a blank Norman arch and, again as if of a doorway and under it, but not axial, a small Norman doorway. This has its exact opposite number in the S wall. The N one has zigzag inside. Moreover, this E part of the N wall ended with a wall running N, but below the evidence of that is the springing of an arch as if into a chapel E of an E aisle, and corresponding to this a little further W is the springing of another arch, Norman, with zigzag, but standing on a C14 or C15 respond. In the S wall are paired early C13 lancet windows, the two E pairs beautifully shafted inside and provided with round, only slightly chamfered rere-arches, but allowing the Norman doorway to reach up beyond the sill. A pair of simpler lancets in the W wall. Good later C13 chancel windows and an E window of mature Geometrical tracery: three lights, stepped, and three circles over, the two lower ones quatrefoiled, the large top one septfoiled. This is the finest feature of the church. In the chancel S wall is a contemporary DOUBLE PISCINA, pointed-cinquefoiled with a pointed-cinquefoiled hood-mould. Against the S wall of the chancel is the organ chamber by *Woodyer*, 1880. – PLATE. Cup, 1681; Standing Paten, 1710. – MONUMENTS. Many minor wall tablets, especially a series to the Bratby family, 1769–*c*.1810, one signed by *N. Chase* of Titchfield. – Tablet to Sir Edwin Alliott Verdon-Roe, the first Englishman to fly, † 1958. Black egg-shaped tablet of great sensitivity, with exquisite lettering, by *H. R. Allen*.*

PERAMBULATION. Start at the quayside. The quay wall used to run close to the waterfront houses, with only a narrow road

*Mr George McHardy drew my attention to this.

in between; now a wide stretch has been reclaimed as promenade and car-park with a consequent reduction of the intimate relationship between buildings and water which still pervades places like Emsworth and Langstone. The heart of Hamble is where a row of low brick cottages, with a tablet inscribed 'August 1818', runs at r. angles to the shore and, facing the river, is a bland Georgian three-bay façade of grey and red brick with especially large windows for its size. Here ROPE WALK leads off, between tall brick buildings of any date, and tall functional sheds of corrugated iron and plate glass, all humming with maritime activity, to end again on the foreshore. Private jetties of innumerable clubs project at frequent intervals, and big boathouses loom a little further up the river. Returning to the quayside, the main street of Hamble winds up the hill. It is rather like a Devon or Cornish fishing village without any fussing up, but of course in Hampshire brick. It rises; turns to the r.; continues to climb, with a gentle l.-hand curve, between simple, mainly Georgian houses and pubs, and emerges on to the SQUARE, which once, no doubt, was an intimate hemmed-in space but which now has been wholly cleared on one side to form a car park – by the local council, who ought to know better. Still facing the car park is an attractive timber-framed building, brick-infilled, and, along a side road, a pleasant row of small Georgian cottages. The main street continues with a few more pleasant houses, e.g. HENVILLE HOUSE, strong Victorian, round-windowed, two-storeyed with a three-storeyed tower, and GUN HOUSE, long and low in C17 brick, unfortunately whitewashed, with a projecting porch bay in the centre. SCHOOL LANE passes a recent private housing development which is of little distinction but which needs mentioning because of its important position in the framework of the village. Two-storey houses and three-storey blocks of flats are grouped loosely round a large space, the flats standing lumpily, at variance with the scale and feeling of the village, when seen from the quayside or across the river from Warsash. Something lower, closer, and more intimate would have been more appropriate at Hamble. Finally one emerges on the GREEN, just what a big village green ought to be, not too tidy, not too rough, with scattered trees and only a sprinkling of houses round it (it could take more). Behind one corner of it is MERE HOUSE, by *Baillie Scott*, neo-Georgian, with a polygonal bay and high parapets without cornice. From the Green the estuary is visible over the roofs and chimneys of intervening cottages, and one returns to the waterside, where in Hamble everything ought to start and finish.

SYDNEY LODGE. Built in 1789–98 by *Sir John Soane*. Now used as offices by Hawker Siddeley Aviation Ltd, at the centre of a complex of industrial buildings covering the former grounds which sloped down to the Solent shore (and which provided facilities for the launching of early types of seaplane which were developed at Hamble). Not a major work of Soane's, but valuable because the exterior and the core of the interior are largely unaltered. The house is two-storeyed, nearly square, the N and W sides of yellow brick (from Beaulieu) – at that time just coming into fashion locally – the S and E sides faced with mathematical tiles sembling brick (because of the relative exposure of these sides to inshore winds). There is a stone cornice of distinctive shape, set back a little above its base and then receding upwards; below it a delicate dentillation with bricks arranged in T-patterns; a stone string course runs at first-floor level. The S front is of five bays, the centre three very slightly recessed, the windows taller on the lower storey, all contained within round-arched frames slightly wider than the windows themselves, leaving blank tympana above. There was formerly a veranda (? a later feature) to the ground floor on this side. The E front has a large semicircular three-windowed bay in the centre, rising through both storeys, with first-floor balcony and veranda still extant, the balcony with delicate twisting ironwork decoration; the centre window on the ground floor is a French window, and up to it there leads an external staircase of five steps, flanked by open balustrades; narrower staircases lead l. and r. from the platform in front of the window, each balustraded, to delightful composite effect. The plane of the E façade is slightly recessed a short distance from each corner, giving the subtle effect of double angles. A Victorian conservatory projects from the S end of the E façade. The W façade, which contains the entrance, has the same angle treatment as the E; it is of only three bays, widely spaced, the windows treated as on the S façade.

Entrance is through a grand stone segmental porch, its entablature triglyphed, supported by two Greek Doric columns. This leads into a lobby with short wide tunnel-vault, a prelude to the great STAIRCASE HALL which is the showpiece of the house. This is basically in the shape of an elongated D, the curved end towards the entrance (W), the staircase beginning on the N side of the D, curving round, and then continuing on the S side, to end in a gallery which runs across the straight E side. It has thin iron balusters with intermediate patterns of diamonds enclosing crosses, with bosses at the intersections. There is a band of swags at the level of the first floor, in front of the gallery and around the wall above the staircase. At the top is a frieze in repeated diminishing square pattern, and a tall oval lantern rises from the ceiling, itself ceiled. The ceilings at both levels retain their original painted decoration (which elsewhere in the house has been covered over) with garlands and swags. The E wall of the hall at ground-floor level, under the gallery, is curved inwards, to intriguing effect, and in its centre is a doorway with fluted Composite pilasters and semicircular arch (similar smaller doors lead off the hall l. and r.). This leads into the former DRAWING ROOM, oval in shape, contained at its E end within the semicircular bay, but without any original decoration save a marble fireplace. The corresponding room upstairs is D-shaped, and retains a delicate frieze. The STABLES, much added to and adapted, adjoin the house on the N side; the additions virtually obliterate the N front. S and E of the house is a well maintained formal garden, probably early C20, with low walls in openwork semicircular tile patterns. In local architectural history Sydney Lodge is specially interesting because many of its external features and characteristics – its general austerity and simplified classical detail, its use of drab brick, the big semicircular bay, the round-arched frames to windows, and the segmental porch – were locally specially fashionable in the current and ensuing period.*

HAMBLECLIFF HOUSE (also occupied by Hawker Siddeley). A Gothick house of 1809 with gimcrack details, but with some stone Gothic windows which are almost certainly medieval ones re-used. Set in the centre of the main central projecting bay on the upper floor is a two-light window of lively C14 design, with a cross of quatrefoils, the lower one elongated, in the tracery. Other windows have plain intersecting tracery under four-centred arches. The likely source for these would be Netley Abbey, but there are no extant windows there to these designs. The house stands on an unrivalled site overlooking the Solent. The GARDENS are laid out to an intricate romantic pattern with winding paths, and are well main-

* In Southampton architecture of two or three decades later one detects Soanic characteristics, albeit debased.

tained. The STABLES are Later Victorian Gothic, with steep gables and a low steeple.

HAMBLEDON [DL] *6010*

Hambledon lies in a shallow valley of the chalkland foothills. It combines some of the characteristics of the loose-built chalkland villages and the compact, more urbane settlements of the coastal plain such as Titchfield or Botley. A market town in the Middle Ages, it declined to the status of a large village by the C18, and in the C20 has remained clear of Portsmouth's outward sprawl. Its atmosphere now is that of a self-consciously preserved village.

ST PETER AND ST PAUL. A large and complex building, almost like a text-book of medieval parish church architecture. At first there was a small nave and chancel to which narrow aisles were added, first on the N and then on the S, in the C12. Early in the C13 a new longer chancel was built to which, after a short interval, a N chapel was added. A little later in the same century a major enlargement took place. The old nave and chancel together became a new lengthened nave, and a new chancel was built further E. Almost simultaneously a S aisle was added to what had previously been the chancel, the aisles to the original nave were widened, and a tower was built at the W end. In the C15 a large two-storeyed S porch and a two-storeyed vestry S of the tower were added. The tower was largely rebuilt after a fire in 1794 and the church was fairly conservatively restored in 1876, the chancel by *Ewan Christian*, the rest by *James Foster* of Southampton. So now we have a long nave with N and S aisles, chancel, S porch, and W tower with vestry attached. What makes the form of the church highly unusual, and confusing at first sight, is the retention of the early C13 chancel arch in its original position, now simply dividing the original W part of the nave from its E extension, which was formerly the chancel. It is flanked by two smaller arches which separate the W from the E parts of the aisles.

Because of its complexity, the church is described strictly from W to E. TOWER. In its present form the tower dates from 1794, and is built of mixed flint and rubble, with brick dressings. Unfortunately all the details, including the windows and W door, are harsh Gothic from the 1876 restoration. Part of the S wall is still medieval masonry, and against this is built the C15 VESTRY, of two storeys, with square-headed Tudor windows. – PORCH. A nice piece of Perp, with plain massive outer doorway and a more elaborate inner doorway, with square hood and traceried spandrels. There is now a single space inside. – ORIGINAL NAVE. The evidence of Saxon origin is in the remains of formerly external lesenes above the arcading on both sides (cf. Corhampton). The N arcade is perhaps of *c.*1180, of two bays, with round pier, multi-scallop capitals, square abaci, slightly pointed arches, and – an unusual embellishment – hood-moulds with alternate stretches of stellar (almost dogtooth) and rose ornament. The S arcade, evidently a little later, has slenderer piers, round scalloped capitals, round abaci, and arches with two slight chamfers and with hood-moulds decorated entirely with big dogtooth. The original chancel arch is a fine piece of early C13 work, of two orders, with deep round mouldings and engaged shafts to the responds. – AISLES TO THE ORIGINAL NAVE. Small Norman lights survive in the W walls of the aisles, that in the N aisle having been clearly re-set further N at or after the widening of the aisle. Both aisles have C15 three-light windows in the side walls, the N aisle also an elaborate C19 window. – EASTERN PART OF NAVE. The N wall of the Saxon chancel partly survives – the evidence is a section of string course high up on the formerly external side. This wall is pierced by a single flat-sided pointed arch. Further E is a two-bay arcade of plain round piers and capitals, and arches of two chamfered orders. The S arcade is three-bay, with octagonal piers and capitals, and arches of two chamfered orders; it seems slightly later than the corresponding N arcade. – EASTERN PART OF N AISLE. Two lancets of what had been the N chapel survive in the N wall, with a Perp window in between. The E window of the aisle has thin graceful mouldings and engaged shafts, a pattern repeated in two windows at Catherington (where however the windows themselves have been renewed later) and elsewhere in south-east Hampshire. The window itself is a remarkable and handsome design, with three lancets of equal height and solid stonework in the arch above them, pierced by an octofoiled circular window – a pattern transitional between plate tracery and fully developed geometrical tracery. – EASTERN PART OF SOUTH AISLE. The E window of the S aisle has a frame like that in the N aisle, but the filling (three lancets, the central one rising to the apex of the arch) is Victorian. The S wall has two pairs of double lancets and a Perp window in between. – CHANCEL.

The chancel arch is of two orders, thickly chamfered, the outer order dying into the wall, the inner with thin octagonal capitals and pilaster shafts. The chancel is a beautiful piece of C13 design, not altered at all in its structure except for the restoration of the E window and the heightening of the walls to take the late medieval, nearly flat, panelled roof. There are three two-light windows on either side, each consisting of a simple pair of wide lancets in a thinly moulded frame under a hood-mould which is linked with a string course which continues, with some changes of level, all round the chancel. The E window has an original moulded frame, but the three-light tracery within it is Victorian restoration. The ROOFS are mainly medieval. They have tie-beams and collar-beams and the odd thing is that, on the walls of the nave, posts were erected without infilling. They are connected by big diagonal struts and carry a long longitudinal beam on which the nave roof proper starts. The beams of the aisle roofs rise at a lower pitch and meet those of the nave by the big longitudinal beam.

FURNISHINGS. PULPIT. Late medieval, with traceried panels, very much restored. – STAINED GLASS. The following windows are by *Ward & Hughes*; S aisle W end, 1888; N aisle E end, 1888; N aisle W end 1895, with a near-by one by *H. Hughes*, 1874. The S aisle E window is by *Mayer & Co.* (G. McHardy). – MONUMENTS. A series of small, well designed wall-tablets dating from the early C18 onwards. One is signed by *F. Brewer* of Petersfield. – The tradition of good design is carried on in the Later Georgian tombs in the churchyard.

THE VILLAGE. The main thoroughfare, stragglingly built, runs along the floor of the valley, but the heart of the village is a short wide street leading N, its upper end partly open to the churchyard, allowing a glimpse of the tower. Modest, mainly Georgian, houses line the street and close the view at the lower end, where they are backed by the partly wooded S slope of the valley. The feeling here, and for a short distance eastward along the valley thoroughfare, is of small-scale urbanity, with most of the houses built of brick, too often whitewashed, with some surviving half-timbering and a little flintwork. Occasionally doorways are dignified by simple hoods or even porches. Towards the edges of the village the houses are more widely spaced, and there is a gradual thinning out into the open country.

THE RECTORY, W of the church, is essentially a C17 building of brick, with two shaped gables on its S façade and a single-storey porch similarly gabled; pediments at the head of the gables. There are similar gables to the N and W, but the E front is wholly georgianized. All the windows are Georgian sashes.

MANOR FARM. A highly interesting survival: a C13 stone-built house shaped like a church with nave and narrower chancel, but always divided into two storeys, the lower used for storage. The remains of a three-bay arcade on the ground floor are still visible externally on the S side, and there are two remaining square-headed medieval windows to the upper floor, one on the S side and the other on the N side of the 'chancel' wing. The 'chancel' may well have contained a domestic chapel. Other windows are square-headed Tudor insertions. There is a large N wing, probably of Tudor origin; its E façade is half-timbered, but its W façade is Victorian and now forms the main frontage to the house.

Going E out of the village there is a succession of larger houses. First a Regency house with very broad bays and a veranda. Then WHITEDALE, a large but unremarkable Victorian house evidently with earlier parts behind. Long flint and brick estate walls give a distinctive flavour to the grounds.

Finally PARK HOUSE, $\frac{3}{4}$ m. NE. This is a fascinating building, with a main two-storey block of brick and a tall three-storey wing with an end-gable built of flint and brick and partly tile-hung. The windows are all Georgian, but the chimneys and the remains of former window hoods in brickwork indicate that the building as a whole is of C17 origin. As the two-storeyed part has a porch projection also of flint, it is likely that another wing has gone and that the house originally had a façade of the E-type. Attached to the house are a PIGEON LOFT, timber-framed and tiled, and a fine thatched BARN with low boarded side walls.

At the other end of the village, CAMS is a house of probably C17 origin with C18 additions.

BROADHALFPENNY DOWN, where the Hambledon Cricket Club played in the C18, is $2\frac{1}{2}$ m. NE. The BAT AND BALL INN is of more note historically than architecturally.

5050

HANNINGTON

ALL SAINTS. Not everybody will, in this Victorian-looking church, notice the Anglo-Saxon long-and-short work of the NE quoin of the nave. Nothing else tells us of this building. The next period represented is about 1200. To this belongs the S arcade of three bays with round piers (only one old), square abaci, and trumpet-scallop capitals. But the double-chamfered arches are probably a remodelling of about 1300, when the S aisle received its E window with intersecting tracery. Perp chancel. The C19 lengthened the church to the W and put the bell-turret on, with its odd concave-sided piece below the spire. – PULPIT. Jacobean. – PLATE. Undated Chalice; Paten Cover of 1680; Paten of 1714.

HARBRIDGE 1010

ALL SAINTS. 1838 by *G. Evans*. Only the masonry of the W tower is old. It has a higher stair-turret. The tower arch is four-centred. Nave and short chancel. Perp tracery made apparently of artificial stone. – STAINED GLASS. Many Netherlandish roundels, C17 after C16 and C17 engravings. – MONUMENT. Countess of Normanton † 1841. Gothic, of the same artificial stone. Is it *Coade* stone?

HAREFIELD *see* SOUTHAMPTON, p. 598

HARTFORD BRIDGE 7050

CHURCH. 1876 by *George Birch*. Weatherboarded, with a bell-turret and no aisles. Wooden window details very fancy.

The hamlet lies along the A30 or the old road inflated into the A30. The WHITE LION is a nice irregular brick group.

HARTLEY MAUDITT 7030

CHURCH. On its own by a large pond. Nave and chancel and a pretty polygonal bell-turret held up partly by an external W buttress, partly by a stepped projection inside. The nave is of the C12, with Norman windows, no longer slits, and a sumptuous S doorway of *c.*1200. The arch is pointed. The hood-mould has dogtooth, the main arch radially placed clasps or horseshoes. The chancel arch seems Earlier Norman. It is low and round and has a single-step arch. Chancel of *c.*1300 or later. Windows with pointed-trefoiled heads, the E window with cusped Y-tracery. – FONT. Octagonal, Perp, with quatrefoils and tracery panels. – TILES. Some, in two strips, in the chancel. – PLATE. Set, undated, C17. – MONUMENTS. Sir Nicholas Stuart, later C17. Large black and white marble. Big open semicircular pediment. In the 'predella' relief of a Crusader ancestor slaying a lion with a club. – Other C17 tablets.

6050 HARTLEY WESPALL

ST MARY. Flint with a tile-hung N tower. The church is mostly by *George Gilbert Scott Jun.*, 1868–9, but it has one quite
33 tremendous original feature, the huge early C14 timbers of the W wall. They form one enormous boldly cusped lozenge cut by a cusped middle post. Smaller cusped timbers in the gable. Originally W of this was a timber-framed tower exactly as at Yateley, and Scott used the formerly recessed bell-stage for his N tower. Original also inside the nave roof, a wagon roof with tie-beams on arched braces which rest on timber wall-posts. Kingposts with four-way struts on the tie-beams. Timber also the N and S doorways. The chancel is entirely Scott's. – PULPIT. Laudian, with wide panels having on the usual two short pilasters a twin instead of a single arch. – PLATE. Cup and Cover Paten, 1706; Paten, 1836. – MONUMENT. Abigail Lady Stowell † 1692. White and grey marble tablet. Two standing putti l. and r. At the top oval medallion with bust in relief. At the foot a gruesomely pally demi-skeleton, leaning forward.

7050 HARTLEY WINTNEY

ST JOHN EVANGELIST. 1869–70 by *E. A. Lansdowne* of Newport (Wales). Chancel enlarged 1897. Red brick and stone, quite big, and really ugly. The style is C13, with plate tracery. The composition is very disjointed, the anticlimax being the polygonal SW turret. Transepts, polygonal apse. Short round stone piers with big insensitive stylized foliage capitals.

ST MARY, ½ m. SSE. Nave and chancel seem to be late C13 to early C14 and tell of a substantial church. The brick transepts and the flint W tower are Victorian, but inside the tower is the good original W doorway of the church. Original also a few minor windows. One is of two lights with a spherical triangle in bar tracery. – (PILLAR PISCINA. Late C12, with a plain foliage capital. VCH) – BOX PEWS. – COMMUNION RAIL. With twisted balusters; early C18. (In the churchyard is the grave of *W. R. Lethaby* † 1931. NT)

VICTORIA HALL. 1898 by *T. E. Collcutt*.

Hartley Wintney HIGH STREET is part of the A30. There is not much to sample. At the NE end the RURAL DISTRICT

OFFICES, a plain, detached late C18 brick house of five bays and two and a half storeys with a Tuscan porch. The BAPTIST CHURCH on the other side has a front with two giant pilasters carrying an arch which sticks into the broken pediment and frames an arched window. Said to date from 1807–8 (MHLG), but looking rather 1830. The MANOR HOUSE, timber-framing and brick and gabled, is mostly C20 and lies on a lane forking off NE from the A30 at the NE end of the village. At the SW end HARTLEY ROW with a few more nice minor Georgian houses. *See p. 829*

WEST GREEN HOUSE, *see* p. 646.

HASLAR *see* GOSPORT, pp. 240, 243, 247

HATHERDEN

3050

CHRIST CHURCH. 1857 by *William White*. Flint and brick bands. Nave and apse in one. That far almost identical with White's church at Smannell close by. Half-hipped double bellcote with chimney attached. It is supported by two buttresses with their set-offs in profile. Plate tracery. Interior wide and low, of yellow brick with red bands. – STAINED GLASS. The E window by *Kempe*, 1885.

SCHOOL, SE of the church. Pretty tablet of 1725 with writing-master's flourishes. The cottage itself looks later.

HAVANT

[DL] *7000*

Havant until Victorian times was a small market-town at a crossroads, famous for parchment, with its own little port at Langstone (*see* p. 315) 1 m. away. Now it is a large satellite of Portsmouth consisting of the town proper, residential fringes to E and W, and, to the N, the sprawling post-war Portsmouth corporation housing estate of LEIGH PARK, started in 1955 and not yet finished. Leigh Park has its own shopping centre, but the town centre of Havant proper has been extended, with new shopping thoroughfares added somewhat awkwardly to the simple cross of streets which formed the basis of the original town.

ST FAITH. Stands by the crossroads at the heart of the old town. Outside it looks a venerable and complex building, with rough rubble-built walls, many gables, and a low central tower with a dominant embattled stair-turret. In fact, nearly all the external detailing is C19. The first impressions one obtains on going inside are confused ones, partly because the entrance leads into (of all places) the W aisle of the N transept and partly because the architecture, internally, is so obviously a mixture of medieval and Victorian. But when one has orientated oneself and sorted out at least the elements of its architectural history, one comes to appreciate that it is a building of fair scale and satisfying proportions and that some at least of the older features have high architectural quality. There was a sizeable late C12 church with a central tower, and of this the crossing arches remain. In the early C13 the chancel was rebuilt ambitiously, with a rib-vault, and in the C15 the transepts were reconstructed, with W aisles added to them. In 1832 the medieval nave was replaced and the chancel altered and mutilated. In 1874 the central tower was found to be unsafe, so it was largely taken down above the arches and rebuilt with the old materials. At the same time the nave of 1832 was replaced by one supposedly on the lines of the original, and the chancel was restored, all by *R. Drew*. So we now have a building whose E parts are medieval but much renewed, and whose W parts are wholly Victorian, possessing two medieval features which are rare in parish churches – a vaulted chancel and aisled transepts.

The architectural description is largely chronological. The crossing is composed of broad arches, relatively low for their width. Each is of two orders, those to N and S with two slight chamfers, those to W and E with one slight chamfer, a keeled roll, and a thinner roll. The N and S responds are rounded with upright leaf capitals, the W and E responds have Purbeck marble shafts with scalloped capitals; the capitals on the W arch are restorations but on the E arch they are partly original. The chancel has a beautiful two-bay quadripartite vault with moulded ribs, broad and low like the crossing and, seen in conjunction with the crossing, very satisfyingly proportioned. The foliated bosses remain in the vault, but the corbels supporting the ribs have been mutilated and the shafts which once supported them have been lost. The only original window remaining in the chancel is the NE one, a broad lancet in a moulded frame, now opening into the vestry, which seems to have been added on the N side of the chancel in the C14 and still has a two-light E window of that date. The NW and SE windows of the chancel are C15, and the E window is a Victorian triple lancet. The distinguishing feature of the N transept is the two-bay W arcade, probably C15, with octagonal piers and arches of two orders. The N and E transept windows are C15 and the W aisle window looks Tudor. The S transept is almost all restored, including the arcade, which is a copy of that in the N transept. In the W aisle are two medieval windows, one C15 but the other a late C12 or early C13 lancet, restored but partly an original feature. This poses an interesting problem; if it is in its original position, it is evidence of the existence of a transept aisle in the C13, but it is more likely to have been replaced here from somewhere else, presumably at the C19 restoration. The nave has aisles and clerestory, all of 1875 but incorporating the E respond shafts and an original Norman scalloped respond capital from which the others are copied. The bell-openings of the tower, simulating late C12 work, are Victorian features, but the prominent stair-turret is mainly original, retained when the rest of the tower was reconstructed. Most of the exterior of the church was faced in random rubble at the restoration, giving it its spuriously venerable look.

FURNISHINGS.* STAINED GLASS. E window by *Clayton & Bell*, 1873. Scenes of the Crucifixion and Resurrection with figures of saints and angels. – PLATE. Cup, 1825. – MONUMENTS. Brass to Thomas Aylward, private secretary to William of Wykeham and rector of Havant, † 1413; the figure, 37 in. long, is shown in a cope, with an inscription on a scroll above and a shield below. – Several Georgian wall-tablets, e.g. Isaac Moody † 1728 (S transept), with Italic lettering; Mary Blackman † 1739(?) (N transept) with a surround of Gibbs or Kent type; Selina Newland † 1786 (S transept), with a standing allegorical angel, garlanding an urn, by *P. M. van Gelder*.

ST FRANCIS, Riders Lane, Leigh Park. 1962 by *T. K. Makins* of Portsmouth. A successful design internally; in plan a rectangle with a large free-standing altar well forward of the eastern wall. The roof is humped from W to E, with continuous clerestory. The E wall is largely occupied by a plain panel in which is a piece of plaster SCULPTURE of the Crucifixion, by *H. Phillips* of Leeds, realistic in posture and expression, the nails prominent and real-looking, the Cross behind of rough wooden planks. Although it was not designed for this setting it is right in proportion, and is the dominant feature of the building. – The only STAINED GLASS is in a series of abstract patterns in deep colours in eight square-headed lights arranged symmetrically in three tiers in the S wall. – The FONT, next to the altar, is an early cast-out from Guildford Cathedral; a slender tub, with slight scallop-like mouldings near the rim. On the

* Mr R. Hubbuck mentions the FONT of 1847, 'elaborately and assuredly carved'. By whom?

whole the church is refreshingly free from discordant details and vain striving after effect; the most irritating mannerism is the chequerwork on the face of the W gallery.

(ST ALBAN, West Leigh. A new church by *D. E. Nye & Partners* is to be started in 1966.)

ST JOSEPH (R.C.). 1875 by *J. Crawley*, flint and stone dressings; neo-Dec.

CONGREGATIONAL CHURCH, *see* Perambulation, p. 279.

Havant has no civic buildings of its own to suggest that it is the administrative centre of an urban district of *c.*80,000 people. The recent CROWN BUILDING (*Ministry of Public Building and Works*) and LAW COURTS (*Hampshire County Council*) stand on adjoining sites in Elmleigh Road. The Crown Building is sensibly designed in a three-storey grid framework, with glass and vitreous panelling and dark brick end-walls; the Law Courts try to look more imposing but succeed in being less so.

OAK PARK SECONDARY SCHOOL, Leigh Road. 1957 by *Yorke, Rosenberg & Mardall*. A large complex of buildings, varying from one to four storeys high, in curtain panel construction; very successful irregular grouping. Enlarged 1962.

PERAMBULATION. The old town had a plan like a smaller Chichester, with four cardinal streets and St Faith prominently to the SW of the crossroads. There is even a Pallant in the NE quarter of the town. But Havant's architecture is hardly a match for that of Chichester. In SOUTH STREET is the oldest house in the town, the OLD HOUSE AT HOME (a pub), a well-preserved timber-framed building, probably C16, with over-sailing upper storey and brick infilling. Further along South Street are brick Georgian cottages and HALL PLACE, a plain yellow-brick Georgian house, with a massive porch of pairs of columns and broad bays on the S frontage. Back to the churchyard, whose S and W sides are bordered with plain Victorian houses of two and three storeys, giving the effect of a miniature close. At the crossroads the dominant buildings are Victorian, of some scale and strongly detailed, especially the WHITE HART, dated 1889, in a debased Norman Shaw style, with terracotta, tile-hanging, and timbering. Along EAST STREET, a Victorian building on the r. has odd Lombardic detailing, little rounded gables and decorative shafts. Nearly opposite, at No. 11, is a cast-iron and plate-glass Victorian shop front, with thin spiral iron pillars, round arches, and openwork decoration in the spandrels. Next to it the Georgian BEAR HOTEL, with a three-storey, five-bay façade in grey brick dressed with red, set off by a plain two-storey annex in the same brick. Further on is MAGNOLIA HOUSE, a three-bay Georgian house also in grey and red brick, with a projecting porch and a GAZEBO in its long back garden, visible from the PALLANT (reached by turning l. off East Street and then l. again), a small square building with an ogee-pointed tiled roof. The Pallant may once have been a charming backwater, to judge from the surviving, small-scale Georgian houses in and just off it (e.g. No. 4 Prince George Street, and ST FAITH'S CHURCH HOUSE, whose porch is double-columned on either side). But the total effect of the Pallant is now bitty. The best building in it is the former CONGREGATIONAL CHURCH of 1718* (now a warehouse), built of red and grey chequered brickwork, with big rounded and keystoned windows and doorway and the strange feature of a blank Venetian window, brought out in moulded brickwork, in the place of a gable over the main frontage.‡ The street leads into NORTH STREET, where the most distinctive building is the CONGREGATIONAL CHURCH which superseded the old one in 1891, its tall neo-Dec street façade in random ragstone having a prominent moulded doorway brought forward under a gable. The architect was *A. E. Stallard.*

The post-war extension to Havant's shopping centre is W of North Street. It is mainly in the form of an irregular three-cornered space, partly given over to pedestrians with fussy fountains and other furnishings, but with traffic swirling along one side and cutting off half the shops; a half-hearted echo of early Crawley or Harlow. The linkage with the old centre is casual, but has been lately improved by a pedestrian arcade, quite good in a simple way. Havant still needs a good deal of re-shaping in the area intermediate to the old focal point and the new; the opportunity seems still to be there for something fairly dramatic to be done without demolishing too many substantial buildings. In particular the church could be made almost as dominating a feature in the enlarged, complex centre as it was in the old, smaller, simply planned town.

LEIGH PARK. The Portsmouth Corporation post-war housing estate, which was started in 1949 and will be finished by about 1970 (when it will house *c.* 40,000 people), begins almost immediately N of the railway. It is a garden-city type layout which

*The date was on a tablet over the door, now painted over.

‡Must this not be later than 1718? (NP)

would have seemed quite good in the thirties. The principal roads nearly all curve; there are generous borders of grass, numerous old trees are preserved, and new ones have been planted everywhere. The architecture nowhere calls for notice, but the grouping of house blocks is sometimes carefully done in relation to the alignment of the roads and topography. The general impression is one of extensive dreariness. At the NE corner a part of the fine parkland of the former mansion has been preserved as a public open space, and beyond, now in farmland, is the BEACON, a Late Georgian circular pavilion with eight Doric columns on a high plinth supporting a domed roof. In 1832 *Vulliamy* designed an octagonal Gothic LIBRARY detached from the mansion of 1863 (by *R. Drew*).

7020

HAWKLEY

ST PETER AND ST PAUL. By *Teulon*, 1865. Neo-Norman, not a popular style among the High Victorians. Chalk, the walls in crazy-paving. W tower with a Sompting top, i.e. Rhenish Romanesque. The room inside is vaulted. The E arch is thickly Anglo-Norman, but the N and S arcades have capitals rather Italian Romanesque than English. Oddly enough, the capitals of the chancel arch have naturalistic leaves instead, and so have the roof corbels. Where the true Teulon comes through is in the aisle roofs and fenestration. The windows are arranged symmetrically l. and r. of a gabled rose window with plate tracery. Anglo-Norman again and richly appointed the entry from the N aisle to the N chapel. – PULPIT. Stone, with an Italian Romanesque middle support, no doubt also by *Teulon*. – SCULPTURE. Small English alabaster panel of Christ's Betrayal. C15.

(HAWKLEYHURST, 1 m. NNE. 1860 by *Teulon*.)

8050

HAWLEY

HOLY TRINITY, Blackwater. Red brick, with an embraced steeple. The result of growth in several stages. Of the original church of 1837 nothing remains visible. Additions 1857 (*J. B. Clacy*) and 1863 (*C. Buckeridge*). By the latter the rib-vaulted chancel and the chancel arch etc. with their naturalistic leaves. Semicircular apse. Chancel and apse are the only remarkable part of the church.* The steeple is of 1882. The details of the church are in the style of 1300.

*Buckeridge knew Street at Oxford, and that is apparent here (NT).

Hawley has become all part of the Farnborough–Camberley 'conurbation'.

HAYLING ISLAND [DL] 7000

Hayling Island before the present century must have looked like the coastal parts of Essex: flat fields, tall hedgerow trees, substantial farmsteads, straggling, rather formless hamlets, the land merging imperceptibly into the tidal mudflats of the much indented E coast bordering Chichester Harbour and the rather more regular W coast alongside Langstone Harbour; much of the centre and N of the island is still like that. The first seaside developments followed the building of a bridge from Havant in 1822–4; a hotel and part of a crescent were built, followed by two or three villas, but such developments were premature. A few rich Edwardian houses were planted behind the breezy beach or alongside navigable creeks, but intensive seaside development came only in the 1930s. Now the southern seaboard looks just what it is – a place to which people come in the hope of carefree holidays. In the early Middle Ages the island was considerably larger. There was a small priory subservient to Jumièges in Normandy whose original buildings were flooded in 1324–5, during the worst of a series of inundations which seem to have taken place all round the island; a great deal of land was lost to Langstone Harbour, some to Chichester Harbour, and some to straightforward erosion from the open sea.

There are two medieval churches on the island – St Mary at South Hayling, impressive and individualistic, and St Peter at North Hayling, homely and likeable. Except for what remains of the abortive early C19 developments, there are no secular buildings that deserve more than the briefest mention.

ST MARY, South Hayling, on the N edge of the C20 seaside development. Built over several decades in the middle part of the C13, presumably at the instigation of Jumièges, and probably to replace an earlier church which was submerged; certainly there is no evidence of an earlier building on the present site. It was fairly unusual at this period for a parish church of such relatively large scale to have been built on a site unencumbered by a previous structure; furthermore its designers were talented and in many ways highly individualistic. Victorian restorations were fairly thorough but conservative (nave restored 1869 by *Street*; another restoration 1892–3 by *Blomfield*). The church comprises nave, aisles, central tower, and chancel. The space under the tower appears as an additional E bay to the nave, because there are no transepts in the accepted sense, only continuations of the aisles of the same width and height, alongside the tower, merely separated from the aisles by arches. The nave has wide three-bay arcades of two chamfered orders, with octagonal piers and foliate capitals. The piers are relatively slender; originally they were of Purbeck marble, but in 1892 they had to be replaced because they were crumbling (cf. the chancel arcades in Portsmouth Cathedral), and the present ones are of granite. The capitals and the lower parts of the arcades were renewed at the same time, but comparison with the responds (which are original) shows that the designs are faithful to what was there before – and very remarkable; for the arches do not begin immediately above the capitals but spring from upright octagonal shafts, like prolongations of the piers (but thicker) for about 2 ft above the capitals.* The clerestory windows, quatrefoiled circles, are set above the piers, reaching below the level of the apexes of the arches. The four wide arches under the tower are like those of the nave arcades, polygonal demi-shafts rising for about 2 ft above the capitals before the arches spring, with complex and intriguing effect. The capitals of the two W piers under the tower have unusual stiff-leaf designs, all different, the leaves mostly having the effect of starting stiffly at their stems but springing into freer, more ebullient forms towards their extremities. The small arches at the E ends of the aisles, flanking the tower, rest on their inward sides on specially remarkable capitals and tapering corbels, decorated with foliage to differing patterns, including one which resembles dogtooth but is made up of leaves, and ending with carved heads. The capitals of the two E piers under the tower are simply moulded. The fenestration of the aisles and aisle extensions is mostly original; the E windows of the latter are of two lights with circles above (trefoiled to the S, quatrefoiled to the N), the tracery internally roll-moulded and the mullions shafted, with miniature foliated capitals. How Street must have admired those windows! He placed similar but simpler windows on the side walls of the tower aisles, each under a dormer gable. The W aisle windows are of two lights with quatrefoils above – almost plate tracery – and the side windows of the aisles are simple lancets. The W window is Victorian neo-Perp

* Something like this arrangement is found in the earlier arcade at Wymering, Portsmouth, p. 469, where, however, the piers and capitals are round.

within a medieval frame. The W door is simple C13, of two chamfered orders. The chancel is a complete E.E. design, presumably the first part of the church to be built, comparable to the one at Hambledon. It has a graceful E window of five lancets, diminishing in width as well as height from the centre, and contained on the inside within a roll-moulded frame (the sort of medieval E window that Blomfield reproduced in many of his churches). The side windows of the chancel, four on each side, are lancets within similarly moulded frames. There is a delicate DOUBLE PISCINA with moulded central shaft. The tower rises externally only about a foot above the apex of the nave roof; it is lit by small lancets and supports a short, massive shingle spire – reminiscent of Sussex, as is indeed the external appearance of the church as a whole. The S porch is a substantial wooden structure of medieval origin, with a moulded outer arch, but has been much repaired. – FONT. Square bowl of Purbeck marble, slightly tapering, with four plain flat blank arches on each side. This pre-dates the present church. Almost certainly, however, the base is contemporary with the church; it has carved faces protruding from two of the four angle columns (which are of Purbeck marble), another touch of the inventiveness of the designers of the church. – STAINED GLASS. E window and possibly other windows by *Herbert Bryans*, a pupil and assistant of Kempe (RH). – Three windows in the aisles by *Kempe*, 1897.

ST PETER, North Hayling. An attractive, irregular church, mostly late C12 or C13. Nave, aisles, chancel, big N transept, and shingled belfry and spirelet, unusually over the E end of the nave. The E wall leans outwards alarmingly but is supported by massive late C17 or C18 buttresses. Triple stepped E lancet; N and S chancel lancets; chancel arch of two chamfered orders, nicely shaped, with rounded responds and capitals to the inner order. Nave arcades of three continuous bays each, with a fourth bay further E separated by short stretches of wall; the arches pointed, of one chamfered order, the piers round, the capitals round on the S side but with square abaci and simple trefoiled leaves on the angles on the N side. The E respond of the S arcade has spade decoration. The N aisle has small original lancet windows; those in the S aisle are restored. The transept has two lancets in its E wall with a wide trefoiled recess, hooded and roll-moulded, between them, and one lancet each in its N and W walls. The bell-turret substructure is half-timbered, and against its W (nave) face is an arched beam across the E bay of the nave with cusped and pierced tracery like a broad bargeboard (cf. the porch at Warblington). The wooden N porch is relatively simple late medieval work, restored. – FONT. Circular, tapering, C13. – Two medieval PEWS with mutilated or restored poppyheads. – PLATE. Cup and Cover Paten, 1569. Also slightly larger copies, made later. – MONUMENTS. George Rogers † 1806. Oval tablet with draped urn. – Sarah Rogers † 1812 (a child). Oval with urn and well-carved floral garlands. – Members of the Bannister family, with garlanding and a Rococo-like cherub. – A splendid range of TOMBSTONES, with cherubs, garlands, etc., many in a somewhat Rococo manner. Several show wheatsheaves, and one a miniature representation of a man in a top hat and a weeping lady looking at a coffin on a table, with a cherub ascending. They are all late C18 and early C19.

See p. 829
THE CRESCENT was projected about 1825*; a map of 1833–4 shows a small section of the middle part built, together with the present ROYAL HOTEL to the E, a few odd villas, the outline of a square with villas round it to the N called 'Victoria Square (Projected)', and also two projected terraces to the W, of which a fragment of the easternmost seems to have been built. Nothing more seems ever to have come of this abortive scheme except for the E part of The Crescent, which must have been built soon after the map was published. The house which forms the E end-piece of The Crescent is the most elaborate, of three storeys and an attic, with four wide Corinthian pilasters, the lines of which are continued upwards above the cornice to end in rounded finials above the parapet. The earlier centrepiece of The Crescent is a little simpler and more attenuated; the houses in between have rounded ground-floor windows and a continuous iron balcony at first-floor level. Only one house W of the centrepiece was built; a pity, for The Crescent, if completed, would have been a grand composition, comparable with the much less sharply curved Crescent at Alverstoke (p. 256). The Royal Hotel is a plain three-storeyed building with a pleasant veranda.

There is no recognizable centre to the spreading development on the island. The old straggling hamlets of MENGHAM and WEST TOWN have been all but swamped, but in both, surprisingly, are preserved fine boarded and thatched BARNS.

* Mr F. A. J. Emery-Wallis tells me that the crescent was begun in 1825 from plans prepared by *R. Abraham* of Torrington Street, London.

Among the detached houses in SINAH LANE is a richly detailed Gothic villa of *c.*1850 and, near by, a group of houses in the Cubist style of the thirties, equally wilful in their very different treatment of windows and in their asymmetrical massing. The MANOR HOUSE, near the centre of the island, has a plain but handsome five-bay Georgian front in grey and red brick, the centre three bays brought slightly forward under a brick-dentilled pediment. (The DOVECOTE of the former grange of the priory remains in the grounds, as well as a fine timbered BARN.) NORTH HAYLING was a loosely straggling hamlet where the gaps between the old houses have been filled with suburban-type development; there are still some pleasant cottages in timber-framing and Georgian brick and (uncommonly in these parts) one which is weatherboarded. *See* p. 829

HEADBOURNE WORTHY

4030

ST SWITHUN. A Saxon church with one treasure of international value. Saxon in the chancel the long-and-short quoins and one lesene, in the nave also long-and-short and three lesenes and the re-set tower arch which was the S doorway. Narrow and high, with jambs and arch accompanied in a typical way by lesenes and an arched band of the same width. The VCH attributes the W attachment to the C16, but the quoins surely have fragmentary long-and-short work. The dating of the attachment is important, because in it on its E wall, i.e. the outer W wall of the church, is an overwhelming ROOD in relief: Christ, the Virgin, and St John. Unfortunately they have been totally chiselled off by ill-advised fanatics, so that only silhouettes remain. But they show that these were well over life-size figures, that the grouping was the same as at Breamore, and that Christ resembled the Christ of Romsey, and that above him – and this one part is intact – is the hand of God appearing out of a cloud, exactly as at Romsey. The Continent about the year 1000 has nothing that can compare with this monumental three-figure group. In the C13 the church received a SW tower. Of the C13 also the pretty PISCINA in the nave. – READING DESK. This incorporates a piece of the STALLS of *c.*1300, almost identical with those of Winchester Cathedral. Two lights, shaft with shaft-ring, pointed-trefoiled cusping, in the tympanum a pointed cinquefoil in a circle. In all spandrels foliage, and all this in openwork. – STAINED GLASS. An Angel in the W attachment S window. – MONUMENT. Brass to John Kent † 1434. Scroll thrown up above his head. A 12 in. figure.

5060

HEADLEY

3 m. W of Grayshott

ALL SAINTS. 1859 by *Flockton* of Sheffield. The unbuttressed W tower is Perp and only half the width of the nave. The VCH points out that the tie-beams and other roof timbers of the wide nave are C16. But can the nave be that old? Is it not more likely that they were pieces bought for re-use by Flockton? – PAINTINGS. Moses and Aaron, C18, from a reredos, quite good. – STAINED GLASS. An exquisite oblong
25 piece of the decapitation of a female saint. C13 and supposedly found in the late C19. – Good TABLETS of the mid to late C18.

RECTORY, to the N. Early C18. Five bays, two storeys, hipped roof.

(BENIFOLD, formerly Pinehurst. By *Sir Reginald Blomfield.* Pleasantly informal, in a Norman Shaw manner. RH)

(At BORDON CAMP, 1½ m. W, two promising new housing schemes, both on the main Portsmouth Road, by *Kenneth*
See p. 829 *Scott Associates* in the 12M-Jespersen prefabricated system and by *Scott, Brownrigg & Turner* in load-bearing brick. NT)

8030

HEADLEY

2 m. N of Kingsclere

ST PETER. 1867–8 by *Edwin Dolby*. Brick. Nave and chancel in one; no bellcote. The tender for this church amounted to £456 (GS).

5060

HEATH END

ST MARY. 1874. Red brick.

7060

HECKFIELD

ST MICHAEL. Much of the church looks Victorian, but the W tower is medieval and well preserved. It is of brown conglomerate on a Sarsen base and has brick-dressed buttresses and a brick arch to the nave. Doorway and windows with four-centred arches. All this is C16. So is the brick window in the E gable of the N chapel. There is in fact an inscription from the brass to John Creswell who died in 1518 and who was 'lord of this towne at the tyme of byldyng of this stepyle and the new yle'. The Victorian work is *Butterfield*'s of 1876. – FONT. Perp, octagonal, of Purbeck marble, with diagonally set pointed quatrefoils. – STAINED GLASS. The easternmost window in the nave, on the S side, is of 1884 by *Burne Jones*, i.e. *Morris & Co.* Charity and Faith and green and blue foliage. – HELM, gauntlets, etc. – PLATE. Cup and Cover Paten, 1568. – MONUMENTS. Brass to Mrs Hall † 1514 (19 in. figure; N chapel). – Small alabaster monuments with kneeling figures facing one another, † 1607, 1608, 1609. – General Sir William Augustus Pitt † 1809 and his wife † 1819. By *John Bacon Jun.* and *S. Manning*. Large white tablet. Big inscription. Above it very big obelisk. At its foot a blank arch and in front of it a disconsolate woman lying over two caskets. Quite moving. – Charles Shaw Lefevre † 1823. By *J. Brown*, 1836. Marble tablet without figures.

HEDGE END [DL] *4010*

A village on former heathland reclaimed in the mid C19. Straight roads, brick cots, a bit of the old heath kept and tamed as a recreation ground, fruit holdings in the foreground, tree-shaded villas in the higher background, multiplying bungalows in the form of infilling and controlled compact expansion – such might be a description of up to twenty other villages of similar history in southern Hampshire.

ST JOHN THE EVANGELIST. 1874 by *J. Colson*. Purbeck stone; neo-Dec. Polygonal apse; flanking it a stone spire. A lot of Colsonian heads and bunches of foliage dotted about the building.

HENGISTBURY HEAD *see* SOUTHBOURNE

HERRIARD *6040*

ST MARY. The chancel is C13 with the lancets enriched inside by their continuous roll mouldings. The E window is Perp. The chancel arch is mostly Victorian,* but parts of the rich mouldings and the hood-mould with dogtooth are original. In date this goes with the re-set tower S doorway, which has the same kind of hood-mould. The tower itself is Victorian. In the nave on the S side two more lancets and also Perp

* 1876 by *Colson*, who at the same time added the N aisle (RH).

windows. – SCREEN. 1635. With basket arches and geometrical ornament in the frieze. – STAINED GLASS. St Margaret and small fragments in a chancel S window. – PLATE. Cup of 1562, an early date.

HERRIARD HOUSE, Herriard Park. Recently demolished. The house was dated 1704 (rainwater heads). It was stuccoed, which somewhat spoiled its appearance. It was a block of nine by five bays, two and a half storeys high and punctuated by giant Doric pilasters, each carrying a piece of entablature complete with a triglyph, a motif found very similarly at Cound in Shropshire, also of 1704. The main fronts had them at the angles and after bays three and six – there was a three-bay pediment. The side had the rhythm 1–3–1. The house was, according to Mr Harris, by *John James*, but *Talman* had been consulted.

In the hamlet some nice classical brick cottages with arched entrances, dated 1827 and 1828.

4060

HIGHCLERE

ST MICHAEL. 1869–70 by *Sir George Gilbert Scott*. Flint and stone with a NE steeple carrying a broach-spire. Lancets and plate tracery. Low and dark interior with a S arcade. The chancel has a rose window in the E wall and shafted N and S windows, the shafts being detached. The altar composition seems entirely part of it, but dates from 1894. The PAINTING after Fra Angelico was done by *Fairfax Murray*. – PLATE. Chalice of 1828. – MONUMENTS. Richard Kingsmill, Elizabethan; undated. A very long standing monument. Recumbent effigy and to his l. two kneeling figures, probably his daughter and her husband. Columns l. and r. Open top. Against the tomb-chest the kneeling children. – Robert Sawyer † 1692. Black and white marble. Reredos type. Draperies looped up to reveal a singularly small curved base and on it a skull with a laurel wreath. Top urn with garlands. – Thomas Milles, Bishop of Waterford, † 1740. Signed *Charles Frederick* inv^{t} and *L. F. Roubiliac* Sculp^{t}. Sir Charles Frederick was Surveyor General of the Ordnance. Hanging monument with a big black urn and to its l. a white genius extinguishing a torch. On the r. two books, one of them Cyrilli Opera. Not one of Roubiliac's masterpieces.

81 HIGHCLERE CASTLE. Highclere Castle is the largest mansion in Hampshire. It lies in a perfect park, the work of *Capability*

Brown during 1774–7. Henry Herbert, for whom Brown worked, paid him about £5,000. Henry Herbert became Earl of Carnarvon in 1793. At that time the house in the park was a big square classical mansion built for Henry Herbert's uncle Robert Herbert, second son of the Earl of Pembroke, who had died in 1769. It was three storeys high with a façade nine bays wide and an attached giant portico. Of this nothing is visible any longer, though Robert Herbert's time survives in the garden temples. The house was remodelled and all but rebuilt by *Sir Charles Barry* for the third earl in 1839–42. It is in the Elizabethan style, a style in this elaboration still unexpected about 1840, although it must be remembered that for the competition to build the Houses of Parliament held in 1835 Elizabethan was explicitly permitted as an alternative to Gothic. The pattern for Highclere was evidently Wollaton, but Barry's design is far from imitative. The allusions to Wollaton are restricted to the angle turrets and the big central tower which, as will be noticed, is not even strictly central.

The house is ashlar-faced, of three storeys with an additional storey in the accentuated parts. They are e.g. on the entrance, i.e. N, side, apart from the corner turrets, the three-bay centre of the eleven-bay front. The windows are of the mullion-and-transom-cross type, with the transoms higher up than in genuine Elizabethan houses. At the top is a strapwork balustrade. The front is much flatter than an Elizabethan front would be. There is in fact very little decoration – just ornamented pilasters in stressed places. The W side is the office side. The S side of thirteen bays is still flatter than the side opposite. It is the E front where Barry went more opulent. Eleven bays arranged in an ingenious rhythm. Here, apart from the angle turrets, there are yet smaller turrets framing the middle five bays, themselves set in a one–three–one pattern. These smaller turrets are windowless and have arched niches instead. Moreover the bays between them and the angle turrets, while they are boldly recessed from the latter, are flush with the former. So here there is some degree of relief that could be compared with Wollaton.

But there is another difference between Wollaton and Highclere too. The fenestration on the whole, especially on the N and S sides, is strictly even – Georgian, that is, rather than Tudor. Here also lies the difference between Highclere and a High Victorian descendant of Wollaton, the Rothschild mansion of Mentmore. Mentmore with its thick relief and boisterous decoration is much more in the spirit of the late C16 than Highclere, which eventually remains Early Victorian emphatically, i.e. closer to the Gothic Houses of Parliament, with its even window grid and its shallow all-over decoration, than to Wollaton.

The E side is also the only side where the tower appears really central. It cannot be central from the N and S, because the centre of the house is a great hall with a partially glazed roof. To the W of this is the Grand Staircase, and it is this which is heightened into the tower.

The Great Hall, 70 by 24 ft, is reached by an aisled, purely Gothic, Entrance Hall, a rather low and confined room, with its thickly bossed rib-vault. The Hall itself is Gothic too, but only in its motifs, such as the four-centred arches, not at all as an *ensemble*. A gallery runs round on first-floor level, and the roof is pitched and Perpendicularly panelled, where it is not glazed. The Gothic of these two rooms is not Barry's. Indeed there is no Barry inside Highclere. The fourth Earl from 1860 employed *Thomas Allom*, an architect not without interest, and too little known today. He was famous as a draughtsman and had done drawings for Barry's Houses of Parliament. The Grand Staircase is Jacobean and feeble in its details, but the large window is Gothic again. It gives on an inner court. On the E front are the Library (33 by 23 ft) and North Library. They are separated by a screen of two columns, and the style here – which is very remarkable – is that of the interior of the old house, i.e. that of Kent. So Allom works in a different kind of historicism from Barry. The wish to let every room have a different style is High Victorian rather than Early Victorian. The Music Room in the SE corner has genuine C18 ceiling paintings, and part of the Pompeian wall decoration is genuine too. The Rococo ceiling of the Drawing Room on the S side on the other hand is of *c.*1900.

In the grounds the time of Robert Herbert comes to life. To the E of the house is the TEMPLE, a strange structure, re-erected before 1743 somehow from a site belonging to Devonshire House in Piccadilly, i.e. at that time still Hugh May's Berkeley House, replaced by Kent's Devonshire House after 1733. Only the Corinthian columns are said to come from Piccadilly. There are six in the front and six at the back of the odd oblong structure, which ends on the short sides internally in two apses. To the NE is the large ROTUNDA, altered by *Barry*, who added the drum and altered the dome. The columns are Ionic, unfluted, and stand on a rusticated ground stage with small windows. The LONDON GATES, to the NE, on the A34 road, are a flat, rendered archway with a straight top and paired pilasters. One-storeyed ashlar-faced lodges l. and r. The keystone of the arch is a bearded head, and on the straight top stands a vase. On Sidown Hill, to the S, in the woods stands another archway, called HEAVEN'S GATE. It is triple, and derelict, with now exposed brickwork.

N of the house is the FUNERAL CHAPEL of the third earl; by *Allom*. It is a small Gothic chapel of flint, with an elaborate bellcote and ornate iron GATES. Big W doorway. The monument is simply a slab on the floor. The STALLS are copied from those of the Certosa di Pavia.

LAKE HOUSE, by Milford Lake. A summer house or fishing pavilion by *Barry*, one-storeyed throughout but with a higher centre and spreading out lower links and wings. The whole is humbly of yellow brick with blue brick trim. Much brick rustication. The centre has a doorway and two large arched windows. The parapet curves up to the centre. The links are of three bays and the wings of one with a pediment. The house faces the lake immediately, and if the modish term can ever be used meaningfully, it is out of this world. Inside, the centre room and others have parts from the old house at Highclere, entirely in the *William Kent* style, and, stylistically speaking, very probably by him – an eagle table, overdoors with an eagle and swags, a splendid doorcase, and an equally splendid chimneypiece with two termini caryatids and an open scrolly top pediment.

HIGHCLIFFE

2090

ST MARK. 1843, paid for by Lord Stuart (*see* below). Stone, in ornamental tooling. Nave and chancel, transepts, bellcote. – STAINED GLASS. E window 1935.

HIGHCLIFFE CASTLE. Highcliffe Castle (now the main Claretian Missionary Seminary) is the replacement of a house for which *Robert Adam* had made designs in a summarily medievalizing style in 1773. The actual house Lady Waterford called very ordinary, with two bow windows and two rooms between. This house was enlarged out of all recognition by

Donthorne in 1830–4 for Charles Stuart of the family of the Marquesses of Bute. He was an experienced diplomat, with posts at St Petersburg, Paris, and for a short time Rio. When he received a barony he chose the title Lord Stuart de Rothesay, a telling title, with the *de* as irresistibly ancient and chivalric as his vast house. The house stretches out in all directions, on a varied and completely irregular plan, and the elevations are Gothic throughout. But the Gothic is clearly of two idioms and two qualities, one that of Donthorne, the other French and of the first class. No wonder; for Lord Stuart in 1830 had bought the 'Grande Maison des Andelys' in Normandy and transferred the best parts to his house to
45 adorn it with.* So the splendid oriel window above the porch on the S front, the window details to the r. of this, some parts of a former chimneypiece(?) in the E tower arch, and the doorway under the giant N porch are French Flamboyant and the roundels etc. of the same N porch French Early Renaissance. Recently fragments from Jumièges have also been traced at Highcliffe. They are a Romanesque arch from the Grand Cellier now in the side (E) entrance of the great N portico, and three early C16 bosses from the cloister now corbels in the N portico. Donthorne's contribution must not, however, be forgotten over the early C16 parts. His giant porch with its rib-vault high up and the tremendous staircase hall into which it used to lead are worthy of Fonthill.‡ The hall has now unfortunately been converted into a Catholic chapel. The composition of the S front is almost as felicitous. The interior, alas, has suffered from the change of use. But the very French Drawing Room and the Octagon with its original *boiseries* remain. To return to the outside, it is interesting to compare in one's mind the detail of such a French piece as the oriel with what a contemporary oriel would be like if designed by an English mason. It might be almost as ornate, but it would not have the statuettes in tiers against the angles nor the lacy foliage of the arches. The shapes of the French window and doorway heads (apart from the windows of the oriel) are also different from English usage. – In the CHAPEL relief of God in clouds. This is early C14. The wooden panels

* An illustration of the house under demolition is in Taylor and Nodier's *Voyage Romantique* of 1824.

‡ Lord Stuart's daughter, Ruskin's friend Louisa, Marchioness of Waterford, wrote later that Donthorne had 'a silly desire to build a house that would emulate Fonthill or Ashridge' (NT).

with stories from the Gospels against the W wall are late C15 or early C16. See p. 829

HIGH COXLEASE *see* LYNDHURST

HIGH CROSS 7020

⅝ m. NE of Froxfield

ST PETER. 1862 by *E. H. Martineau*. Nave and chancel and SW steeple. Plate tracery and pointed-trefoiled lancets. Five-bay N arcade. Of this the W part of three bays is actually of the late C12 and was transferred from St Peter at Froxfield Green. Round piers, trumpet-scallop capitals, and one with small pellets on a kind of shovel shapes. Unmoulded round arches. – STAINED GLASS. By *Kempe*, 1901 (S aisle). – PLATE. Paten, given in 1712; Cup and Cover Paten, undated.

HIGHFIELD *see* SOUTHAMPTON, pp. 571, 584

HILDON HALL *see* EAST TYTHERLEY

HILSEA *see* PORTSMOUTH, pp. 430, 437, 442, 463

HINTON ADMIRAL 2090

ST MICHAEL. C18 brick tower. The N wall is C18 too, but the windows here and everywhere else are Victorian.* Red brick nave and chancel. – PLATE. Silver-gilt Chalice, 1595; two Patens, 1747.

HINTON PARK. Built for Sir Peter Mews in 1720. The house then consisted of the unmistakable middle block and two two-storeyed service wings at r. angles, each with a thirteen-bay ground-floor arcade. The wings were connected with the house by quadrant colonnades. The centre is of seven bays and has a stone-faced centre of three, with giant composite pilasters and a pediment. The windows in this centre are, in the Vanbrughian way, all arched. The house was badly damaged by fire in 1777, although we cannot see any traces of repairs. Yet a foundation stone was laid in that year. Would that refer to the two wings continuing the centre? They have a very large tripartite window as their centre. (Much re-modelling by *Harold Peto*, *c.*1905, including the

* By *G. E. Street*, 1875–83 (NT).

servants' wing, the billiard room, the garden terrace, and the rich Frenchy ballroom. NT)

J020

HINTON AMPNER

ALL SAINTS. A Saxon church, even if the Saxon work is a little less obvious than the similar work at Corhampton. Long-and-short NE quoin, lesenes W of it and in the corresponding position on the S side. The doorway now into the N vestry has straight jambs too. In the chancel also re-done C13 lancets, including a low-side one. The W tower has a rather French-looking top of 1879 by *C. N. Tripp*. – PULPIT. C17. The panels with geometrical fields. – PANELLING. By the altar, Jacobean, re-used. – DOOR. Dated 1643. – PLATE. Flagon, *c.*1704; Almsdish, 1740; Cup, 1745. – MONUMENTS (from Laverstoke church). Thomas Stewkley † 1601, aged ten days. Baby on his side. – Another Stewkley boy † 1638. Small recumbent effigy. Columns l. and r. At the top angels in naïve clouds. The monument gives no name. It just refers to *florem in primo vere decerptum*. – Sir J. Trott † 1672. Big grey and white tablet with garlands etc. – Lady Stewkley † 1679. Bust in a recess under a baldacchino. Curiously shaped white urns l. and r. Quite good. – Another cartouche tablet is † 1719. – Henry B. Legge † 1764. Fine large tablet with Ionic columns and a pediment. Trophy in the 'predella'.

HINTON AMPNER HOUSE. Of the house built *c.*1800 only cellars remain. The neo-Georgian house built by *Gerald Wellesley* (the Duke of Wellington) in 1937 with two symmetrically arranged bow windows was severely damaged by fire in 1960. After that the attic storey was taken down and the interior was largely re-equipped. However, the *Adam* ceiling of the Dining Room (from 38 Berkeley Square) survived the fire, though its paintings did not. Also of before the fire is the Library chimneypiece, early C19, allegedly from St Cloud. In the Drawing Room are two beautiful white chimneypieces of the late C18. They were both bought in London.

LONG BARROW, 1 m. N of Hinton House and ¾ m. E of Cheriton. The mound is 200 ft long and 118 ft wide at its broader E end where it is 7 ft high. The site was partially excavated without result at the end of the C19 and again in 1932, when a small sherd of Late Neolithic Peterborough ware was found near the bottom of one of the flanking ditches.

HINTON DAUBNAY *see* CATHERINGTON

HOLBURY *see* FAWLEY

HOLDENHURST 1090

ST JOHN EVANGELIST. 1834 by *G. Evans* of Wimborne (RH), but altered and chancel added 1873 by *Ferrey* (RH). Stone, with open, hexagonal, projecting bellcote. Aisleless nave. The Perp tracery is probably of 1873. – STAINED GLASS. One N window by *Kempe*, 1898. – PLATE. Chalice of 1578; Paten of 1701. – (In the churchyard GRAVESTONES to Gerald Peel † 1910 and Gerald Grahame Peel † 1937 by *Eric Gill*. NT)

NEW HOUSE. Late C17, brick, five bays and two storeys. Wooden casement windows.

HOLLINGTON FARMHOUSE *see* EAST WOODHAY

HOLYBOURNE 7040

HOLY ROOD. Norman W tower with a C19 shingled broach-spire.* E.E. chancel with lancets. Perp N arcade with octagonal piers and arches with two hollow chamfers. N wall of 1879. Good stone corbels of *c.*1400 for the nave roof.

The church has the village pond immediately to its S. To the NE of the church a late C17 house of five bays with wooden cross-windows and a hipped roof.

Of the same type is the FREE SCHOOL, founded in 1719 and built in 1721–30. The windows, however, are not wooden crosses, as they must have been. The school lies on the A road, ⅜ m. SW of the church.

HOLYWELL HOUSE [DL] 5010

1½ m. SE of Swanmore

A house of *c.*1780, unusual in form. Two storeys, red brick, with two very large rounded bays on the S side, and another on the E, each bay with a tall central round-headed window and smaller flanking windows on the ground floor. The roofing comes over the bays in rounded hips, to strange effect. The main entrance, approached by a tapering staircase in the centre of the S side, was altered in the inter-war years. Long

* Part of a Norman respond built into a chancel N window. Also in the nave S wall a length of dogtooth of *c.*1200. Both of course are *ex situ*.

straight cut through an oak wood on the axis of the main front.

HOOK

7050

ST JOHN EVANGELIST. 1937–8 by *Sir Edward Maufe*. Brick, with a N tower, stylistically easily recognizable. The tower has a steep hipped roof, the church windows are long and segment-arched. Only the W window has a typical (Östbergian) fancy arch.

The WHITE HART HOTEL, W of the church, is a nice Georgian group, all rendered, of a low three-bay part with pediment, and a higher part with the carriageway under a canted bay carried on columns. In the bay (which is weatherboarded) a Venetian window.

E of the church, also on the A30, OLD RAVEN HOUSE, dated 1653, but a typical timber-framed house with brick-nogging and two symmetrical gables, i.e. of an earlier type. Further E, N of the Crooked Billet, the highly picturesque OLD MILL HOUSE, timber and brick.

(In architectural history, Hook's permanent, if unseen, importance is that it was the site of the L.C.C.'s abortive New Town, squashed by the Conservative Government during the unfortunate lull before New Towns became all-party policy. The plan, published posthumously in 1960, was by the *L.C.C. Architect's Department* (the team included *Graeme Shankland, Oliver Cox, John Craig, Jack Whittle*, and *Hugh Morris*). The most influential urban planning document of its generation, transforming the dispersed, low-density polynuclear forms of the first New Towns into the concentrated, high-density linear forms since adopted elsewhere. Basingstoke and Andover are being expanded instead. NT)

HOOK-WITH-WARSASH *see* WARSASH

HORDLE

2090

ALL SAINTS. 1872 by *Giles*. Hard red brick, and slate roof. Unfinished SW tower. The style is E.E. No aisles. – PULPIT. With *pietra dura* decoration. – REREDOS. With *Salviati* mosaic – a typically High Victorian piece. – PLATE. Chalice of 1650 and Paten of 1651.

HORNDEAN [DL] 7010

A narrow village street hemmed in a hollow of the downs, through which the traffic from London to Portsmouth almost impossibly passes. GALE'S BREWERY is the dominant building, with a wide, solid brick tower surmounted by a tall chimney-stack. Sprawling development, which has been steadily intensified since the war, now covers much of the surrounding land, but to the E and in places to the W there is still fine downland.

The GOOD INTENT, up the hill to the S of the village centre, has a nice arty early C20 façade. Symmetrical, with plain pilasters slightly receding towards the top, almost like shallow buttresses. Mullioned windows with thick stone frames, coarse roughcast wall surfaces, and heavily hooded doors. The Art-Nouveauish sign is contained within a near-circular iron frame designed like a twirling hop-bine with clusters of hops. MERCHISTOUN HALL (Horndean Community Association), mid C18, has a pleasant ground-floor colonnade, but the effect of the façade has been ruined by the alteration of the windows.

HOUGHTON 3030

ALL SAINTS. Low, with a shingled bell-turret carrying a small broach-spire. No interesting external features, but some interest in the interior. S arcade of three bays with round piers and round abaci. Moulded capitals of minimum section. Pointed arches with two slight chamfers. The N arcade is of two bays divided by a piece of wall. The W arch is late C13, but the E arch, like the S arcade, *c.*1200. Was this a transept arch? C13 chancel PISCINA. – Several ARCHITECTURAL FRAGMENTS. – PLATE. Set of 1796.

RECTORY, NE of the church. Five bays, with a three-bay pediment. Red brick. Hipped roof.

HOUGHTON LODGE. A Gothick *cottage orné*, built shortly 74 before 1801 in a beautiful position by the river Test. The architect is not known. One would guess *Nash*, but the date is a little early. In fact the house looks rather 1810 or 1820 than 1800. It has pointed windows, small steeply gabled dormer windows, big cosy roofs (originally thatched), and high, decorated brick chimneys. On the E side there is a big bow with a Victorian iron veranda. The iron glazing bars of the French window of the bow, however, are original. In the bow is the circular Drawing Room with a sky painted light blue with white clouds and a blue-John chimneypiece. Several good classical chimneypieces. Curious steeply pointed or broadly trefoiled doorways and arches. The gateway to the road is an artificial ruin.

HOUGHTON MILL. *See* Bossington.

4000

HOUND [DL]

Little more than a farm and a church in the brief interlude between Netley and Hamble.

ST MARY. A complete E.E. hamlet church. Nave with wide lancets, all C19 renewals except for a pair on the S side; chancel with smaller lancets, all original, the stepped E trio contained internally within a round-arched recess; chancel arch of two chamfered orders, the outer plain, the inner with semicircular responds. W bell-turret, boarded, on simple substructure within the nave. The church escaped late C19 enlargement because in 1886 it was superseded as the parish church by St Edward at Netley (p. 348). – FONT. Octagonal, broad, with pointed arch panels on each face, all probably coeval with the church, but all re-tooled. – PLATE. *See* Netley, p. 348. – STAINED GLASS. In the E window a representation of the Virgin and Child, with angels in the side lancets, 1959 by *Patrick Reyntiens*. A compelling composition, in large panes with little leading, but with lines and shading represented on the glass. Rich colouring, mostly blue, purple, and yellow-green, with a little yellow, a very little orange, and specks of red. The colouring bears only a partial relationship to the figures and is to a large extent composed as if the design were abstract. But the figures are strongly representational, with firm facial expressions and delicately composed hands and robes. This simple interior, with its finely proportioned chancel arch framing the superb window, is one of the most memorable in Hampshire.

4030

HUNTON

ST JAMES. Nave and small chancel. Recent bell-turret. The nave S wall is of C18 brick with random chequering. – MONUMENT. The frieze of small panels with quatrefoils, leaves, the initials of the Virgin and Christ, etc., cannot have been part of a tomb-chest, though it may have belonged to a cresting.

HUNTON HOUSE, N of the church. Red brick. The centre of

five bays and basement and two storeys. Three-bay pediment; hipped roof. Added to this are projecting two-bay wings. The cupolas on them are probably recent, as are other details.

HURN COURT 1090

3½ m. NW of Christchurch

An Elizabethan house, but altered *c.*1806 by *Garbett* of Southampton and again *c.*1840. The Elizabethan house was two-storeyed with outbuildings on W and E. Garbett removed the E outbuilding to make a picturesque outline. In *c.*1840 a third storey was added to the main block and an extra W wing.

HURSLEY 4020

ALL SAINTS. 1846–8 by *J. P. Harrison* of Oxford for John Keble, the pioneer leader of the Oxford Movement. He was vicar here 1836–66. Harrison was the leading light of the Oxford Architectural Society, a follower of Pugin and Carpenter who died early. The church cost £6,000 and was built from the royalties of Keble's *The Christian Year* and of his second collection, *Lyra Innocentium*, published specially for the purpose. It is a big building of grey stone with early C14 details. The idea to choose Dec came probably from the one remaining medieval feature, the W tower with its (restored) Dec bell-opening. Harrison's spire has recently been replaced by a tiled cap. The W doorway (with quatrefoils in the spandrel) and the W window, however, are Perp. The church has nave and aisles, the aisles under separate roofs, which enabled Harrison to give his main roof dormers unnoticed from outside. The interior layout is based closely on Neale's and Webb's 1843 edition of Durandus's *On the Symbolism of Churches and Church Ornaments*, the bible of Ecclesiology. It is otherwise uneventful, except for the fact that all the original STAINED GLASS is still in the windows. It is by *William Wailes* to a scheme prepared by *William Butterfield*. May it never be replaced. The scheme is based on that of Keble's childhood home, Fairford. The W window is of 1858. The E window is the result of characteristically Butterfieldian determination. Keble himself decided the iconography, and part of a window designed by him, in collaboration with his artist friends, *Dyce*, *Richmond*, and *Copley Fielding*, was inserted. Butterfield arrived, condemned it, and commissioned Wailes, whose fourth attempt at a cartoon he accepted.

– MONUMENT. Mrs Cromwell † 1731. Large, chaste aedicule; small sarcophagus in it; no figures. Signed *G. Sampson*, architect, *John Huntingdon* fecit. – MAUSOLEUM. Of the Heathcote Family, 1797. Brick with a doorway with rustication of alternating sizes, a lunette window over, and round the corner a blank window with inscription. – BRASS to John Keble † 1866. Foliated cross with surrounding inscription. Designed by *Butterfield* and made by *Waller*. – Sir William Heathcote † 1881, Keble's patron. Tablet designed by *Butterfield*.

The LYCH GATE, SCHOOLS, and SCHOOLMASTER'S HOUSE are also by *Harrison*.*

HURSLEY PARK, now I.B.M. LABORATORIES. As one approaches the mansion, one is at first convinced that this is Edwardian, and it is indeed true that Sir George Cooper had the wings built, and the porte-cochère and the ample, domed conservatory. His architect was *A. Marshall Mackenzie* of Aberdeen (cf. Australia House and the Waldorf Hotel in Aldwych, London). But the centre of eleven bays and two storeys plus basement is clearly early C18 and has been attributed by Prosser to *John James*. Portico of four giant Doric pilasters and pediment. Oblong windows, sunk panels above them. The interior is mostly Edwardian. But in one room is an imported Elizabethan chimneypiece which is something spectacular. The overmantel is of wood, richly carved, but below it is stone. A term atlas and a term caryatid imprisoned in strap-
51 work and a lintel with the four parts of the world most entertainingly portrayed and provided with a multitude of animals.‡

Behind the mansion *Farmer & Dark* in 1962–4 built LABORATORIES and OFFICES for I.B.M., who now own the estate. I.B.M.'s own designer-architect *Eliot Noyes* was consultant. The job consists of an eight-storey block of curtain-walling with glass fins and a one-storey range at r. angles with flint walling. More new buildings are planned.

Nice Tudor ESTATE COTTAGES with lattice glazing.

4040 HURSTBOURNE PRIORS

ST ANDREW. Neo-Norman W tower of yellow brick, built deplorably late, in 1870. The architects were *Clark &*

* I owe much of this description to NT and Mr Anthony Symondson.

‡ The most spectacular fitments of Hursley, the late C17 woodwork of the Winchester College Chapel, have gone back to Winchester.

Holland. But the W doorway is original. One order of colonnettes, two-scallop capitals. Arch with zigzag and rosettes in shallow relief. To the same predecessor building belongs the arch now to the N chapel, but originally no doubt fron nave to chancel. It has exactly the same ornamental motifs. Early C13 chancel with lancets and priest's doorway. N chapel Elizabethan with straight-headed windows (of five lights to E and W), but with arched lights. C18 S chapel of brick. – PLATE. Paten, 1682; Flagon, 1692; Chalice, date illegible. – MONUMENT. Robert Oxenbridge † 1574, between chancel and N chapel, and open to both. The arch and the jambs are patterned with the simplest geometrical motifs. Two recumbent effigies of stone, not good. Tomb-chest with kneeling children on both sides. Also detached Doric colonnettes at the angles. Above them the Ionic columns l. and r. of the arch for the effigies. Top achievement.

HURSTBOURNE PARK, the mansion of the Earls of Portsmouth, was demolished in 1965. It had been built in 1894 by *Beeston & Burmester*. What remains is two things only, but both interesting. N of the drive from Whitchurch a curious MONUMENT, the statue of a Roman emperor on a structure of flint looking like wild rustication. The structure is domed and has four niches lined with blackish blue brick. No date is recorded. Secondly the ANDOVER LODGE. This is a tower-like building of grey headers and red brick dressings with tall arches, some blank, some with windows on two floors set in, and a parapet with circular windows over which the top of the parapet rises. It is what one vaguely calls Vanbrughian, and it should perhaps be remembered that in 1712 *Archer* designed a plan of a house for Mr Wallop at Hurstborne, i.e. Lord Portsmouth. It is not known whether that house was built. The house replaced by Beeston & Burmester's had been by *James Wyatt* and was burnt down in 1870.

HURSTBOURNE TARRANT 3050

ST PETER. Of flint, low, with a C17 clerestory and a three-stage, weatherboarded bell-turret with broach-spire. The church has a Late Norman S doorway with one order of columns, their capitals just turning stiff-leaf, the arch pointed, with a slight chamfer and zigzag at r. angles to the wall. At the start and end of the arch monster-heads, one of them a beakhead biting in the wrong direction. Next in order of time comes the chancel, though it looks all Victorian (1890). It has lancet windows and a chancel arch of two chamfers, treated rather roughly. The arcades must be of about 1230. Three bays, round piers, round abaci, double-chamfered arches. The aisle walls on the other hand look *c.*1300. On the N side a fine three-light window with cusped intersected tracery. Early in the C14 the W bays were added to the arcades, and the W doorway (two continuous chamfers) was made. In the C15 the bell-turret was decided upon and the fine strong timber substructure put up. – BENCH ENDS. A number of Perp ones, straight-topped and quite plain. – COMMUNION RAIL. Of *c.*1700. Now in the nave and part of it used for the pulpit stairs. – TILES. Round the font. – PAINTINGS. In the N aisle the three Quick and the three Dead, early C14, and uncommonly well recognizable and unrestored and hence enjoyable. To the l. of this traces of a Wheel of the Seven Deadly Sins. Also areas of all-over ornament. – PLATE. Flagon (secular), 1746; Salver (secular), 1775; Chalice, 1797. – MONUMENT. Sarah Debary † 1823, by *W. Gibbs* of Basingstoke. Standing woman by a sarcophagus. The attitude is unhackneyed.

DALTON HOUSE, by the church. White. Three wide bays articulated by pairs of pilasters and single pilasters. The windows in the end bays are of the Venetian type, but with segmental arches.

CONGREGATIONAL CHAPEL (former), at the NW end of the village. 1840. With segment-headed windows.

Hurstbourne Tarrant is one of the most picturesque villages in Hampshire.

3080

HURST CASTLE

Hurst belongs to the chain of castles which Henry VIII quickly built after a conciliation had taken place between Francis I and the Emperor Charles V. Francis was now free to invade England. So castles arose from Kent to Cornwall, from Deal to Pendennis and St Mawes. In Hampshire Calshot, Southsea, and Netley were built, on the Isle Yarmouth and Cowes. Hurst dates from 1541–4. The mason was in all probability *Thomas Bertie* (*see* Winchester Cathedral, p. 674), made captain of the castle in 1550.* But whether he also designed it is far from certain. *Stephan von Haschenberg* of Moravia was the

* As he appears in the Winchester College papers as Bartu, he may have been French.

king's chief designer of castles. Most of them are characterized by a feature also prominent at Hurst: a geometrical pattern for the plan. At Hurst it is a nine-sided polygon of which three sides are larger than the others and have semicircular bastions. In the centre is a twelve-sided tower. The bastions are low, and this was done in accordance with the new concept of defence by mounted cannon, a concept which originated in Italy in the C15. The entry is from the W. The doorway has a double-chamfered four-centred arch. The portcullis groove is preserved. Above the doorway is a plaque with Quattrocento pilasters l. and r. In the tower in the middle the openings have low-pitched triangular heads. The ground floor is lower than the curtain wall. Inside, the tower is circular and now brick-faced. A garderobe is on the E wall on the ground floor. The first floor has a rebuilt brick vault. There are small cabinets in the thickness of the wall, one of them again a garderobe. Doorways must have opened to wooden bridges to the bastions. The battlements on the top had the odd section of one vertical side and one in a shallow convex curve. This is the same in the case of the bastions. The curved side is the outer side. The bastions have or had a large room on the first floor below the roof.

Henry VIII's castle is now framed by two wings of 1873. They are of brick with impressively plain stone fronts.

HYDE 1010

1½ m. SE of Fordingbridge

HOLY ASCENSION. 1855 by *Woodyer*, but not of any interest. Red brick, nave and chancel. Big double bellcote. The brick is laid English bond, and blue bricks are introduced almost as a chequer. Geometrical tracery, including in the five-light E window Kentish tracery.

HYDE ABBEY *see* WINCHESTER, p. 716

HYTHE [DL] 4000

The ferry to Hythe provides the best means of viewing the Southampton docks and shore-side from the water. It lands at a PIER of 1879, 700 yards long, with a simple iron substructure (and an electric railway of early C20 vintage). The village looks most appealing when one leaves the pier, with the DRUMMOND ARMS as the dominant building, yellow brick, three-storeyed, the Southampton style of *c.*1840. The central three of the five bays are slightly projecting. Thin stone cornice, pilasters with rudimentary stone capitals, and rusticated stonework on the ground storey. All the rest is much humbler – an irregular row of C18 and early C19 cottages (PROSPECT PLACE) ending opposite open shoreland in the process of reclamation, a narrow and cheerfully decorated HIGH STREET, predominantly small-scale Georgian over the shops, and, further SE, ST JOHN'S STREET, another predominantly C18 hotchpotch, petering out among shoreside factories, beyond which are an unreclaimed stretch of water frontage, a view of Netley, and a surprising bit of half-forest country. The near-by Fawley industrial complex is quite hidden.

ST JOHN. 1874 by *John Scott*,* on the site of a church of 1823. Brick, with big-boned stone dressings. Nave, N aisle with arcade à la South Hayling, and short chancel. Stepped lancets grouped in arched surrounds. Quite a powerful E frontage to St John's Street, with a hefty open bellcote over the E gable of the nave, and big stone angular pinnacles.

The hinterland is a disjointed series of private housing estates amid the remains of the landscaping of early C19 estates and the tree-grown gardens of big early C20 houses – the result of a 'planned' post-war expansion of Hythe into a fairly sizeable town in association with the Fawley industries. Maybe some (by no means all) of the housing estates are not in themselves unpleasantly designed, but together they make a distressing hotchpotch.

FOREST LODGE, by the Fawley road. Originally built in 1730, it now has a pleasant early C19 appearance, with stuccoed walls and low slate roofs. The grounds were very romantically landscaped in the early C19 and the landscape is still largely intact. They had a PAGODA, Chinese BRIDGE and BOATHOUSE, and an OBSERVATORY. The boathouse survives, amid a tangle of vegetation a little way from the receded lake, a small wooden building with Chinese roofs in two stages, and veranda on the ground floor. The bridge, which recently collapsed, is said to have had Chinese detailing.

See p. 829

IBSLEY

1000

ST MARTIN. 1832 by *John Peniston* of Salisbury. Red brick, nave and chancel in one. Bellcote. Lancets. – PLATE. Chalice

* Probably John Oldrid Scott.

and Paten, probably late C16. – MONUMENT. Sir John Constable † 1627. Two large kneeling figures with hardly enough 55
space between two columns, and under a wide open pediment. The two both hold on to a vine which has brought forth not only grapes but also their five children, their heads and busts arranged fanwise.

IBSLEY BRIDGE. A fine Georgian bridge of ashlar. Three arches, two segmental, the middle one semi-elliptical.

VENARDS, 1¼ m. NE. A brick house of about 1700–10. Five bays, two storeys, hipped roof. The centre bay has a doorway with a steep pediment, pilasters l. and r. of the upper middle window, and a fully rounded top pediment. Chimneys with blank arches.

ROUND BARROWS. A number of isolated round barrows occur on Ibsley Common, including a fine saucer barrow which produced an Early Bronze Age collared urn.

IBTHORPE 3050

¾ m. NW of Hurstbourne Tarrant

One of the prettiest villages in Hampshire.

IBTHORPE HOUSE. Georgian. Chequer brick. Five bays, two storeys, hipped roof. Dainty dentil frieze.

IBTHORPE MANOR FARMHOUSE. Georgian. Chequer brick. Seven bays, unusually slender windows.

IDSWORTH [DL] 7010

Idsworth is not a village, but a wide stretch of downland on the Sussex border. The church stands alone in a field; the site of the old manor house is in a hollow below, with part of its former stables converted into a cottage, and a great double avenue of lime trees climbing up a hillside to nowhere. The railway from London to Portsmouth runs along the valley, and its construction caused the C19 owner of the old manor house to abandon its site and build a new mansion on higher ground well to the W. Today the line is electrified, and the frequent whine-clatter of the trains is the only disturbing feature in the otherwise deep solitude of the church's setting.

ST HUBERT (this was not the original dedication, which was to St Peter and St Paul). A simple chapel of C12 origin; nave and chancel only, with boarded bell-turret over the E end of the nave. It stood disused through the late C19 and so entirely escaped Victorian restoration, but in 1912 the kindly hand of *H. S. Goodhart-Rendel*, then aged twenty-five, was laid upon it. He preserved some of the Georgian and older fittings and re-arranged others, and added new fittings which are almost indistinguishable from the old ones, so that the interior has at first sight a deceptively unrestored appearance. In fact it is a model of self-conscious restoration. The evidence for the Norman origin of the church is a single round-headed light in the centre of the N nave wall and a mysterious blocked doorway in the same wall a good deal further E, too far E for a nave doorway, but possible as a priest's doorway only if the Norman chancel had been as wide as the nave, which is unlikely. The other windows in the N wall are what used to be called derisively 'churchwarden': simple pairs of pointed lights in wooden frames. The nave was evidently widened a little on the S side in the C16, and the two double square-headed windows in the S wall date from then. The chancel arch is simple and pointed. The chancel has an E window of weird 'churchwarden' design – a kind of pleasing simple parody of Gothic in wood. Is it Georgian or Goodhart-Rendel? The nave roof is simply ceiled, the space at the E end above the chancel arch being taken by the under-framework of the bellcote, outwardly plastered. The chancel roof is plastered, and embellished with a series of medallions, representing birds, animals, fishes, even a ship, or heraldic devices, set within a framework of diamond panels with ribs in cable pattern. This is the work of Goodhart-Rendel. – Now for the FITTINGS. What of these is original, what restored by Goodhart-Rendel, and what introduced by him, cannot be sorted out with certainty. BOX PEWS fill the E part of the nave. – Set within them, against the S wall, is the PULPIT, genuinely Jacobean and rather unusual, with tall panels cusped at the top in a debased 'Gothic Survival' manner, and broad shelving canted upwards at an acute angle and supported by scrolled brackets. There is a high, simple sounding-board. The pulpit is not in its original position. – The W part of the nave is filled with open PEWS of the customary type with bench ends rising to simple circular finials; some are entirely old, others restored. – The well-detailed WEST GALLERY, supporting the organ, is of 1912. – The COMMUNION RAIL is either C18 or a very good imitation. To add further to the pre-Victorian atmosphere there is a coat of arms on the W face of the bellcote framework, with names and dates of

churchwardens. – The FONT is medieval. It is octagonal
with quatrefoil panels of two patterns alternating, and with
shields and emblems contained within them. Stem with
trefoiled panels. Similar but slightly simpler fonts are at
Clanfield and Chalton.

Finally the WALL PAINTINGS, the most important series
in a Hampshire church, apart from Winchester, dated *c.* 1330
by Professor Tristram. What remains is large parts of a
complex composition on the N wall of the chancel, others in
the splays of the E window, and some vague and almost
unintelligible traces on the E chancel wall. – NORTH CHANCEL
WALL. Two tiers of continuous narrative painting, divided
by a band painted in zigzag pattern. The upper tier depicts a
white horse being ridden to a hunt, in partial preservation;
a hunting scene with a huntsman with bow and several 29
hounds; a saintly figure, with an armed knight behind him,
apparently ministering to a grotesque creature with human
head and hairy animal-like body; and two pairs of opposing
figures making gestures, one with his hand on another's
throat. This series has been taken to represent the life of
St Hubert, largely on the strength of the third scene (he
cured a man suffering from the insane belief that he was a
wolf). Another theory is that it represents part of the life of
St John the Baptist, but in this context the man-animal cannot
be explained. The lower tier is more certainly associated with
the life of the Baptist. The scenes are a gaoler incarcerating
St John, and a long representation of the Feast of Herod,
with Salome dancing with swords in front, and the head of the
Baptist being passed to Herod. The prevalent colours are
reds (of several tones) and ochre. The whole composition is
full of movement, the figures visibly talking or gesticulating,
or performing more vigorous acts, the animals jumping or
running; even the trees in the background of the upper panel
appear to be bent with the wind, and there are marked
emphases on curvature in the representations of the men,
animals, and trees and especially in the contorted body of
Salome. It is a matter for wonder that this, like other important wall paintings, should be in a church of such humble
scale. – On the jambs of the chancel E window, though the
window itself is 'churchwarden', are figures of St Peter and
St Paul, Peter's facial features having become obscure but
Paul's remaining clear. Each is set against an elaborate
painted background representing cusped and crocketed

niches, of C14 curvilinear style. In the soffit of the window are figures of angels.

IDSWORTH HOUSE. Built in 1852 on high ground about $1\frac{1}{4}$ m. SW of Old Idsworth to the design of *William Burn.* About 1912–14 extensive alterations were carried out by *H. S. Goodhart-Rendel.* Burn's house was rather tamely neo-Jacobean, in brick with stone dressings, with plain gables and a not very dominant asymmetrical tower to the main façade; windows were, rather incongruously, sashes and there was a little strapwork ornament to the parapet. Much of this remains, as do most of Burn's principal interiors, rooms weak in detailing but impressive in their spaciousness and full of light from the large plate-glass windows. Goodhart-Rendel created a new frontispiece to the ground floor, with a porte-cochère, all in neo-Jacobean more convincing than Burn's, and, within, a new entrance hall, fairly long and narrow, with a moulded ceiling of simple details, ending with a pair of solidly keyed arches in white at the far end. These lead into a cross passage, made interesting by a series of plaster groin-vaults. He also created an ingenious library, and added a drawing room in a single-storey wing, neo-Georgian but to a scale which the Georgians never conceived; rectangular, with an exceptionally big bay with huge windows in the middle of one side, and a corresponding large recess on the other, and a large circular motif in the centre of the ceiling. As a spatial composition the drawing room does not come off. Goodhart-Rendel's detailing is convincing and his small-scale special compositions are successful, but he did not achieve spatial grandeur; Burn's work shows the opposite qualities – weak detailing and massing, but success in the formation of large-scale spaces.

IFORD *see* BOURNEMOUTH, p. 125

8030

ITCHEN ABBAS

ST JOHN BAPTIST. 1867 (GR 1863, chancel 1867, the rest 1883) by *William Coles.* Neo-Norman; cruciform. Bellcote with roof far-projecting to the E. A re-set genuine Early Norman doorway with one order of columns with single-scallop capitals. Heavy billets in the arch. The chancel arch, also genuine, is almost the same. Only one capital has flat leaves.

ABBEY HOUSE, $\frac{1}{2}$ m. NE, on the B-road. Dated 1693 (MHLG).

Five bays, two storeys, three-bay pediment. Quite plain, i.e. nothing any longer of the ornamental brickwork of 1670 etc.

ITCHEN STOKE

5030

ST MARY. 1866, and quite a remarkable church for its date. Tall, of nave and chancel in one. Brown and grey stone. Steep roof, E bellcote. High lancets all along the sides. W wall with doorway and a large wheel-window over. Polygonal apse with cross-gables and windows with bar tracery. One enters from the W through a vaulted lobby with diapered walls and a doorway with marble and granite columns. The room one enters is decidedly high and has a boarded pointed timber roof. All the walls are diapered below, and, above, all the windows are shafted. The W wall has blank arcading instead, and the apse is vaulted. The building cost £7,000, paid for by the then incumbent the Rev. Charles Conybeare and designed by *Henry Conybeare*. – FONT. Of coloured enamel, gilt bronze and black Californian marble. This combination of materials was based on the tomb of Mary of Burgundy at Bourges (NT). – PULPIT and BENCH ENDS all with set-in cast-iron panels. – PAVEMENT. The apse floor is a 'maze', on the Chartres model. – MONUMENTS. Brass to Mrs Batmanson (19 in.); *c*.1500. – Lady, kneeling, early C16 (11 in.).

ARCHWAY, ESE on the main road. Vermiculated rustication. Round arch reaching into a pedimental gable. Mr John Harris reports that *George Clarke* of Oxford made a design for a house at Itchen Stoke.

(A COTTAGE just SW of the church has facing of exceptionally large flints. RH)

KILMESTON

5020

ST ANDREW. Nave and chancel in one. Victorian bell-turret. Lancets. The S aisle of 1875. – FONT. An early C18 stone baluster. – PLATE. Cup of the late C17(?); Paten on foot of 1700.

KILMESTON MANOR, N of the church. Quite a large early C18 brick house with two later C18 projecting wings. The centre is of two and a half storeys and was heightened to match the height of the two-storeyed wings whose floor heights are so much more. The centre has segment-headed windows with the original glazing bars, a one-bay central projection, and a doorway with Ionic pilasters and pediment. At the back a gabled projection with pilasters in two orders and moulded brick courses – about 1660. The lower course has a frieze of red terracotta vine. In front of the early C18 part a front garden with original gatepiers and iron gates.

KIMPTON

2040

ST PETER AND ST PAUL. The tower is surprising. It is dated 1837, and yet has nothing Georgian, or of the Commissioners' type or indeed Early Victorian. It is of brick and flint, square, unfussy, and Gothic only in so far as it has a big, high brick W lancet and lancets as bell-openings. The chancel is of the C13. Lancet windows. Also an early C14 tomb recess. In the S transept the S window is Dec, the small window below too, but re-set; for it cuts into the back wall of a tomb recess. The S arcade with octagonal piers and double-chamfered arches dying into the imposts is Dec too. Perp NW window. The NE window imitates it, but must be post-Reformation. – STAINED GLASS. E window signed by *Morris & Sons* – adding insult to injury; for not everyone may know the difference between Morris & Sons and Morris & Co. Kelly says it cost over £1,400. Can that refer to the stained glass, or does it cover the glass and the stonework? – PLATE. Silver-gilt Chalice, probably late C15; Paten and Flagon, 1688. – MONUMENT. Robert Thornburgh † 1522. Small Purbeck marble tomb-chest and, against the fragmentary back wall, brasses. Kneeling figures. His brass is 10 in. high.

KING JOHN'S HUNTING LODGE *see* ODIHAM

KINGSCLERE

5050

ST MARY. By *Hellyer* of Ryde (Rev. B. Clarke). 1848–9. This is a more accurate way to describe Kingsclere church than to call it a cruciform Norman building. Genuine Norman work is the nave walls, the small windows high up to a certain extent, the big N doorway with one order of columns and saltire crosses and zigzag in the arch, and the small lower tier of windows in the crossing tower. They were l. and r. of the roofs. But the W doorway, the upper part of the crossing tower, the round stair-turret, and the crossing arches are all 1848. Similarly the chancel is 1848 rather than E.E., though the inside shows some original details. The best preserved part is the S chapel of *c*.1300. Quatrefoil piers, arches of two hollow chamfers, also from the W. To the chancel three bays. – FONT. Of Purbeck marble. Table-top type. The ornamental forms are the familiar flat blank arches, rosettes, arrows, roundels, a four-petalled flower. – PULPIT. Jacobean. In the main panels a kind of tree of life. – CHANDELIER. Of brass, given in 1713. – TILES. Uncommonly many, displayed in the S chapel. – PLATE. Chalices of 1567 and 1568; Flagon of 1670; pairs of Patens of 1703 and 1704; Chalice and Paten Cover of 1707. – MONUMENTS. Brass to Cecily Gobard † 1503 (15 in.). – Brass to William Estwood, priest, † 1519 (17 in.) – Sir Henry and Lady Bridget Kingsmill. Erected in 1670. White and black marble, the recumbent effigies of alabaster. They are unusually well carved, both in the faces and hands and in the draperies. Large tomb-chest. The inscription is followed by a signature *Wf*. Original iron railing.

The best houses of Kingsclere are in SWAN STREET, especially No. 24 of the early C18 and the SWAN HOTEL of the same time. Both are grey brick with red brick dressings. The upper windows of No. 24 have aprons, and the house has a hipped roof. The hotel is more modest. The r. half is a copy of the original building. The ALBERT HALL, red with a kind of Dutch gable, is dated 1886.

(KNOWLE HILL HOUSE. Good BARN. NMR)

(CHEAM SCHOOL. 1911–12 by *Detmar Blow & Billerey*.)*

KINGSCLERE WOODLANDS

5060

3 m. NE of Kingsclere

ST PAUL. 1845 by *Thomas Hellyer*, the NW tower with spire and lucarnes of 1860. Coursed knapped flint. Quite a large church. Five-bay arcades. High roof with hammerbeams. Geometrical tracery.

The PARSONAGE was built in 1847–8. Brick with diaper patterns.

KINGSLEY

7030

ALL SAINTS. 1876. Nave and chancel; bellcote. Chalk, crazy-paving patterns. Windows with plate tracery. Interior with red brick exposed; yellow brick patterns.

ST NICHOLAS, ¾ m. WSW. Brick, 1778. Nave and chancel in one; low. Only E wall and window are older, and the W wall of Bagshot conglomerate may be older. The E window looks

* So the headmaster kindly told me.

1300, but may be 1330 (cf. Binsted). – C18 PULPIT and COMMUNION RAIL. – PLATE. Chalice, inscribed 1569; Chalice, 1576; Paten, probably older than that.

3030 KING'S SOMBORNE

ST PETER AND ST PAUL. Long nave and chancel with the two aisles all under one roof. Bell-turret with the stage below the bell-stage tapered. A few old windows, e.g. the reticulated E window. The arcades inside are of 1886, except for part of the S arcade. This is early C13: round pier, round abacus, pointed arches with a slight chamfer. The chancel arch is partly of the same time. The one-bay N and S chancel chapels are C14 (double-chamfered arches dying into the imposts). – FONT. Purbeck marble, of table type, octagonal. Unusually big. On each side two flat blank arches. – COMMUNION RAIL. Early C18. Charming, with alternatingly columnar and twisted balusters. – PLATE. Paten Ewer, 1624; Paten, 1700; two Chalices, 1801. – MONUMENTS. Effigy of a Priest, under a pointed-trefoiled canopy; very flat; C13. – The RECESS in which this effigy lies is of course, later. It is Dec. – Brasses of two Civilians, Tweedledum and Tweedledee, early C14, 29 in. figures (chancel floor). – Needham Family, 1736. Reredos type with two columns and a segmental pediment. No figures.

On the road to Little Somborne is a CRUCK COTTAGE.

MARSH COURT. Built for Herbert Johnson, a typically Edwardian adventurer, stock jobber and sportsman, as Mr Hussey puts it. The house was designed by *Lutyens* in 1901–4 with an addition of 1926. It lies in a splendid position above the river Test. It is of chalk ashlar with random bits of flint and tile, a whim speculators have taken up here and there and always disastrously. The N front is in the E-form suited to its basically Elizabethan fenestration. The wings have mullioned and transomed windows, the recessed centre just low mullioned windows, the upper ones almost as a continuous band below the high hipped roof. There is a good deal of Voysey in this. The porch has a gable, but inside a tunnel-vault of stone and tile squares. Here the Lutyens of the unexpected oddities and also the Lutyens of the classical future make their appearance. The oddest thing is the entry into the porch with stone tongues curving inward. The S front of the house is in the strongest contrast to the character as well as the motifs of the entrance side. It is as emphatically vertical as the other is horizontal and as emphatically broken up by bay windows, both straight-sided and canted, as the other is smooth, and it is as emphatically irregular – with one projecting wing only – as the other is symmetrical. The windows here also are all vertical and transomed. Behind the wing, in 1926, a ballroom was added by Lutyens. It has windows with three transoms. Along the side exposed they are smaller and placed high up, with oval niches below.

The GARDEN is full of Lutyens faerie, at a multitude of levels.

The STABLES have a self-consciously barn-like entrance, a loggia of brick columns in the yard, and strong, sloping buttresses to the outside.

KINGSTON *see* PORTSMOUTH, pp. 441, 463

KINGS WORTHY 4030

ST MARY. Mostly of 1864, by *J. Colson*. A polygonal vestry is the only feature one may remember. In the S chapel three re-used windows, two Perp, one of *c*.1300. The W tower is probably early C13. It is unbuttressed, and the W doorway has two continuous nook rolls. The arch towards the nave on the other hand (two continuous chamfers dying into the imposts) looks rather *c*.1300. – FONT. Octagonal, C14, with different variations on the theme of the mouchette wheel. – PLATE. Set of 1622. – MONUMENT. Is the tomb-chest in the chancel with four cusped quatrefoils containing shields entirely or not entirely C19?

WORTHY PARK, ¾ m. NE. Yellow brick. The centre a one-storeyed porte-cochère of four fluted Ionic columns. To the l. and r. two short towers. One-storeyed three-bay wings with slender windows with blank arches. On the garden side also two towers and in the centre between three such windows. The house was built shortly before 1829 and designed by *Sir Robert Smirke*. The arched windows look rather five or ten years later.

KINSON 0090

ST ANDREW. Late Norman W tower of ironstone, cf. the small W window and the pointed single-chamfered arch towards the nave. Nave and aisles 1893–5 (NT). Probably of that date also the roof with dormers whose windows are quatrefoiled circles. Medieval chancel masonry, but the E window Victorian. – FONT. Octagonal, Purbeck marble, with four small blank arches to each side. The bowl must be C12 or early C13, but the arches seem to be a recutting of *c.*1300.

KITCOMBE HOUSE *see* NEWTON VALENCE

KNAP BARROW *see* ROCKBOURNE

3040

KNIGHT'S ENHAM

$1\frac{3}{8}$ m. N of Andover

ST MICHAEL. Nave and chancel in one. Small bell-turret. In the chancel lancet windows. The nave originally had a two-bay arcade, also of the C13. – FONT. Norman; defaced. Small, with tapering sides. Frieze of stylized leaves. Trellis below. – ROOD BEAM. Moulded – a rare survival. – CHANDELIER. Of brass, the Baroque type of body. Dated 1798. – (SCULPTURE. Over the vestry N window a C12 head, probably from a rood. It could be earlier still. VCH)

4030

LADLE HILL *see* LITCHFIELD

LAINSTON

LAINSTON HOUSE. A fine brick house of about 1700, with something older and something a little younger. The entrance side is of *c.*1700. Three-bay centre with two-bay projecting wings. Two storeys, hipped roof. In the middle a slight one-bay projection with pediment. The ground-floor entrance feature is not original. Round the corners are façades which must be about twenty years later. Plum-coloured brick and rubbed dressings. Slightly segment-headed windows. Raised brick quoins. The back, i.e. the garden side, is superficially like the entrance side, but must be older. The brickwork is different, the brick quoins are not bonded in, and the inner quoins are of stone. The basement windows are mullioned. So an early C17 house was given first one beauty treatment and then another. The handsome brick arcades flanking the forecourt are probably also of *c.*1720. (Very fine staircase with slim twisted balusters, starting from the hall behind a screen of Corinthian columns. *C.L.*)

ST PETER, SW of the house. In ruins. Only the nave survives, with two plain Norman doorways. The wall where the chancel arch should be is wide open to the view into the landscape.

LANDPORT *see* PORTSMOUTH, pp. 432, 435, 438, 449, 458

LANGLEY *see* FAWLEY

LANGRISH 7020

ST JOHN EVANGELIST. 1869–70 by *Ewan Christian*. Nave and chancel and a small polygonal stone turret. Flint with stone dressings. Plate tracery.

LANGSTONE [DL] 7000

The old port for Havant, on the creek which links Chichester and Langstone Harbours and separates Hayling from the mainland. Now a small, self-conscious, impeccably preserved hamlet, with an intricate relationship between tidal water and buildings. Irregular quay walls of brick and stone; motley buildings, mostly simple Georgian, some with a frontage to the waterside; old boundary walls with flint and brick. A pub, coldly whitewashed, is the focal building; beside it a miniature street leads a short distance inland, with a row of thatched brick cottages and one or two Victorian villas. At the E end of the hamlet is a curious MILL, now converted into a house, but once a combined tide mill (partly on piles over the water) and windmill, the latter having lost its sails and looking like a lighthouse.

LASHAM 6040

ST MARY. 1866 by *Woodyer*. Coursed squared flint. Nave and lower chancel. Very tall E window, massively shafted. Bell-turret with shingled broach-spire. Inside the E and S chancel windows all shafted. The vestry doorway has, hanging from one impost only, the most extraordinary drooping grape of stiff-leaf. The S doorway has a pointed-trefoiled head. These are two personal touches. – PULPIT. The pulpit has a Jacobean sounding-board which was presented and came, it is said, from a private house.

LASHAM HOUSE (the former Rectory), S of the church. Five bays, brick, two storeys, pedimented one-bay projection. The mansard roof is a later alteration.

4040 # LAVERSTOKE

ST MARY. By *J. L. Pearson*, 1896, and not a church to do him much credit. Flint and brown stone, S tower with shingled broach-spire, lancets (nave S), small coupled lancets (N aisle), and plate tracery. Nothing is vaulted, and the only a little more than humdrum feature inside is the wall-passage or detached shafting in the chancel S wall.

ST NICHOLAS, Freefolk, ¼ m. S. Nave and chancel in one, wee bell-turret. Plain oblong without any help in dating. – SCREEN. Perp, of single-light divisions. – REREDOS. Naïve C18 painting of a military Moses and a classical Aaron holding the Commandment Boards. – MONUMENTS. Sir Richard Powlett † 1614. He is represented stiffly recumbent but rolled on his side. On the tomb-chest strapwork, but also, kneeling in a recess, his two wives. Strapwork back panel, and strapwork round his coat of arms. All stone and uncouth. Above the monument his HELM. – Tablet to Thomas Deane † 1686. The inscription is written on drapery which seems pleated with a flat iron. The flowers below have accordingly a herbarium look.

OLD ST MARY, in the grounds of Laverstoke House. The walls remain to a height of about 7 ft, with gravestones leaning against them. No architectural features. The monuments have gone to Hinton Ampner.

LAVERSTOKE HOUSE. Built by *Joseph Bonomi* in 1796–8 for Harry Portal. Yellow brick. The principal front of seven bays with a detached giant portico of very slender unfluted Ionic columns with pronounced entasis. Round the corner porch of two pairs of normal unfluted Ionic columns. The windows are all cut in without any surround.

86 PARSONAGE. 1858 by *Street*, at the expense of Melville Portal. SE of the church, the other side of the river. Brick and flint, with tile-hung gables, a small round turret, and altogether remarkably varied. Shaw could learn a lot from such jobs of Street.

MILL HOUSE, SE of the church. This belongs to the LAVERSTOKE MILL, where Bank of England notes were made for over two hundred years. Henri Portal, a French refugee, had made the first watermarked paper in 1712. The original mill on this site was built in 1719, but it is uncertain if anything now is as old as this. The Mill House is Georgian; that is all that can be said. Red brick. Three bays, steep one-bay pediment.

ALMSHOUSES, S of the church. Very extensive and with thatched roof and half-timbered gables. All a little ridiculous, considering that Lord Portal had these almshouses built in 1939. The architect was *E. T. Mort*.

ROUND BARROWS, ½ m. SW of Roundwood Farm. The group consists of two disc barrows, a bell barrow, and a twin barrow – two mounds surrounded by a common ditch. The disc barrows have been almost obliterated by ploughing and are difficult to detect. The bell barrow, 70 ft in diameter and 9 ft high, was excavated in 1920 and found to cover a central pit containing a cremated male burial. The twin barrow, which was excavated at the same time, proved to have been robbed.

LECKFORD

3030

ST NICHOLAS. Low, with a low, incomplete W tower. Flint, much of it rendered, and much brick repair. The identifiable external features are all Perp. Nice interior, well furnished. Architecturally it is curious that the chancel arch is off centre of the nave. It is likely that an aisle had existed and was at some time removed. – FONT. Of black Purbeck marble, square, with the familiar flat blank arches. – PULPIT. Plain, Jacobean, but the tester with little hanging arches. – STALLS. Given in 1923. Seven and seven. They are Italian. The back panels have fluted Doric pilasters and finely designed panels. Frieze with cherubs' heads. The date may be about 1600. – PLATE. A Set, but undated.

(ABBESS GRANGE. By *Sir Banister Fletcher*. In the Elizabethan style. NT)

LEE

[DL] *3010*

1½ m. S of Romsey

Scattered hamlet on the edge of the Broadlands estate; a few old cottages, and varied estate housing from Lord Palmerston's time onwards.*

CHAPEL (now disused). Built by Palmerston in 1862 to the design of *Professor Donaldson*. Powerful composition in red and yellow brick, three courses of each alternately, with heavy cornice in brickwork pattern and strong patterning round the round-headed windows. Apse; open bellcote. Well seen from the W among the trees.

* Some of the partly timbered cottages, e.g. those opposite the church, might be by *Nesfield*, as he did work at Broadlands (p. 145).

5000 LEE-ON-THE-SOLENT [DL]

A seaside resort which began to grow in the late C19: the pier (long vanished) was built in 1885; the branch railway (long closed) was opened in 1894. The chief asset of Lee is its view across to the Isle of Wight. LEE TOWER is the focal landmark, built on the site of the railway station and pier entrance in 1935 by *Yates, Cook & Darbyshire*, a good piece of second-rate inter-war modernism of the slightly jazzy sort, constructed of concrete when concrete seemed very up-to-date. It is V-shaped, with the apex to the sea, and a tall slender tower in the angle, having incised parallel lines on each face, and glass lantern and viewing platform at the top, rather like an elongated cigarette lighter. The wings have widely spaced pilasters rising above the parapets to rounded ends, and metal-framed windows with horizontal glazing; there are various parabolic protuberances towards the sea at the apex. Nice, elegant vulgarity, partly spoiled lately by artlessly vulgar alterations, including a crude sign with neon-Gothic lettering over the entrance.

ST FAITH. 1933 by *Seely & Paget*. Demure outside, with rose-red brick walls on many planes, white-framed windows, and little open bellcote over the W gable; it might have been designed for a garden city. Inside it is original and impressive. Long nave and chancel, structurally continuous, with a series of tall concrete transverse arches in the shape of sharp parabolas, and subsidiary small arches, similarly shaped, across the aisles. The big stone altar is flanked by tall round-arched recesses, but the curtain in between was surely not intended in the original design, and makes an indeterminate termination to the impressive vista along the church. Strange and slightly jazzy chancel FITTINGS, together with PULPIT and READING DESK, all very low, white-painted on their sides and topped with heavy polished wooden shelves. A wide S chapel, against the middle part of the nave, adds a little spatial complexity. Windows are round-headed, and those of the pseudo-clerestory appear as tall dormers outside, since the wall itself above the aisles is inclined, following the shape of the transverse arches.

FLEET AIR ARM MEMORIAL. By *J. C. Smith* and *L. K. Pallister*, 1952.

LEE BRETON FARM. An odd survival, amid tile-gabled Edwardian villas and post-war gap-filling; a small, two-storeyed farmhouse with rubble walls, tall tiled roof, and two-storeyed central projecting feature, with its upper storey oversailing, timber-framed with herringbone brick infilling. Altogether alluring, and well maintained.

LEIGH PARK *see* HAVANT, pp. 275, 277, 279

LINKENHOLT 3050

ST PETER. 1871 by *William White*.* Nave and chancel and timber-framed bell-turret. Flint and brick bands. Bar tracery. Only one N window and the S doorway are medieval. They must be *c*.1200. The doorway has a round arch with one slight chamfer. Billet in the outer order. – FONT. Of drum shape, with tapering sides. Norman, with bands of zigzag, rope, and small raised triangles. – PLATE. Flagon, 1693; Chalice, 1715.

SCHOOL. The school, next to the church, is also of 1871 and unquestionably more fun.

LIPHOOK 8030

ROYAL ANCHOR HOTEL. Late C17, with a good egg-and-dart frieze below the modillions of the hipped roof.

(Mr Brandon-Jones tells me that *Philip Webb* was paid in 1894 for a COTTAGE and gatehouse at Liphook. Does it still exist?)

COLDHARBOUR HOUSE, on the A3, between Rake village and the turning to St Luke's. By *Collcutt*, with half-timbered gables and high chimneys. Large. Complete by 1895. *See* p. 830

LISS 7020

ST MARY, East Liss. 1891–2 by *Sir A. Blomfield*. Dignified and dull. Stone outside, brick inside. The windows mostly lancets. The interest lies in the W tower and S porch added by *Sir Edward Maufe* in 1930 in a freer and squarer Gothic, the big tower with its rows of square bell-openings an impressive piece, the porch ennobled by a small piece of SCULPTURE of the child Christ by *Eric Gill*. (Under the tower a prettily painted ceiling. RH) – (TRIPTYCH by *Martin Travers*. RH) – STAINED GLASS. By *Kempe* the E window, 1901, and some others. – PLATE. Paten and Flagon, 1761; Paten, 1828.

ST PETER, West Liss. Small, against a fine screen of mixed

* According to the Rev. Basil Clarke.

conifers. C13 chancel, late C13 S doorway with filleted shafts and rolls. The W tower, of course without the weather-boarded top stage and the pyramid roof, is also C13. The S arcade has octagonal piers, their capitals also late C13. The double-chamfered arches die into vertical pieces above the abaci. The S aisle W window is mullioned and transomed and must be C17.* In 1639 a S porch, though not the present one, was built. On the N side of the church a Perp three-light window. – TABLETS. Several of the C18 are worth while.

RECTORY, E of the church on the A road. By *Withers*, 1863. With typical lancets rising into gabled dormers.

LISS PLACE, $\frac{1}{2}$ m. SW of St Peter. A stone range is assigned to the C14. Thin W buttresses, big later S buttresses. An Elizabethan or Jacobean mullioned window.

WEATHAM FARM, $1\frac{1}{2}$ m. SW. The house has two Elizabethan or Jacobean mullioned windows.

See p. 830

4050

LITCHFIELD

ST JAMES. Nave and chancel in one, and bell-turret. Irregular windows, including in the chancel three largish Norman ones not perhaps quite to be trusted, and also including, again in the chancel, two small lancets which are in order. The exterior also tells of a demolished S arcade, but not the whole story. This S arcade originally consisted of two bays with a round pier with a multi-scalloped capital, a square abacus, and pointed arches with a slight chamfer, i.e. work of *c.*1200. The N arcade is quite different. It has three bays with chamfered square piers, and single-chamfered arches. It was probably put in with its E bay when the rebuilding of the chancel had been completed. This is an interesting job. The arch rests on fluted corbels and in the four corners are corbels, three of them with excellent heads. That means vaulting or the intention to vault. But it would have put the Norman windows out of operation – provided they are genuine and *in situ*. Was the S arcade E bay built last, then, to link the old and the new? The trouble is that both these E bays, N and S, look older in their details than the rest. The VCH does not recognize this observation, but it makes another. The NE respond is set in front of a prior respond or jamb from which springs a segmental arch. This is clearly bonded with the chancel. What can have happened then? Was the con-

* Mr Hubbuck points out that a tie-beam in the church is dated 1655.

necting link of chancel and two-bay N arcade at first conceived to have a segmental arch? It seems too improbable. The problem of Litchfield is not yet solved; and it can here only be presented.* – PLATE. Chalice, 1571. – SUNDIAL. On a baluster, E of the church. Dated 1795.

THE SEVEN BARROWS, on Lower Woodcott Down, 2½ m. S of Burghclere and W of the A34. There are in fact ten Bronze Age round barrows in the cemetery. In addition to the group of seven W of the A34 there are two further sites between the road and the railway line and a tenth barrow just E of the railway cutting. Examples of bell and disc barrows as well as the ubiquitous bowl form occur in this group. All the barrows have been considerably reduced by ploughing, but the large bell barrow on the S is still 10 ft high and 150 ft in diameter.

IRON AGE HILLFORT, on Ladle Hill, 2 m. NE. Although the present apparently dilapidated condition of this small, 7-acre univallate fort might appear unattractive to the visitor, its very condition makes it a site of considerable interest and importance. Its appearance is not due entirely to the ravages of time, but to the unfinished state in which the Iron Age builders left it. Because of this it is possible to see some of the steps whereby this and presumably similar Iron Age hillforts were constructed. The first phase consisted of the digging of a small marking-out ditch indicating the line of the later defence ditch. Traces of this small ditch can be seen on the ground in the NE part of the site. Elsewhere it has been largely obliterated by the work which was begun on the main ditch. The interrupted nature of the latter suggests that individual gangs of diggers were responsible for the cutting of each section. The top-soil and turf from the ditch were not piled immediately behind it on the projected line of the rampart, but were carried some distance inside the fort and there dumped – these top-soil dumps can still be seen as irregular mounds. Once the top-soil had been removed, the chalk rubble from the deeper levels in the ditch was dumped behind it to form a solid and stable core for the rampart. It was at this point that the whole work was abandoned. The final phase would have been the capping of this rubble core with the turf and top-soil from the dumps inside the earthwork.

* According to the Rev. Basil Clarke the N aisle was rebuilt by *Woodyer* in 1875.

Three Early Bronze Age ROUND BARROWS also occupy the hilltop. Just N of the fort is a fine DISC BARROW with a low mound 28 ft in diameter and 1 ft high surrounded by a ditch 12 ft wide and 76 ft in diameter and an outer bank. 600 yds SE is a BELL BARROW 56 ft in diameter and 5 ft high, the ditch of which cuts through the bank of an earlier SAUCER BARROW 47 ft in diameter and 1 ft high.

3030

LITTLE SOMBORNE

ALL SAINTS. Nave and chancel in one and bell-turret. The nave is Saxon, see the one lesene on the N side and a small fragment of another on the S side, and also the W quoins of long-and-short work. Plain Late Norman S doorway with one slight continuous chamfer. Traces of a blocked N doorway. Several altered Norman windows. Late Norman also the blocked former chancel arch with trumpet-scallop capitals. Above this low former chancel in the E wall two lancets. To the S of the chancel arch a re-set Norman window or, according to the VCH, an image niche.

ROOKLEY HOUSE, 1 m. E. To an C18 house of five bays an early C19 Gothic façade was added round the corner. The centre is a broad canted bay. Pointed windows, battlements.

4030

LITTLETON

ST CATHERINE. Mostly of 1884–5. Very small, with a bell gable. In the chancel a lancet and a pointed-trefoiled lancet. – FONT. Of table-top type; Purbeck marble. Various simple patterns.

A COTTAGE E of the church has a very large chimneybreast of flint and brick chequer and some timber-work with closely set studs.

2020

LOCKERLEY

ST JOHN EVANGELIST. 1889–90 by *Colson*. SW tower with stone broach-spire. Aisleless, but with transepts. In the W wall of the S transept a tiny Norman window, *ex situ*. It used to stand in the churchyard. The rest of the church has Dec and Perp details. – PLATE. Chalice, 1659; Paten, 1694; Almsdish, 1782.

LOCKERLEY HALL, 1 m. N. Built in 1868 and designed by *Burn & McVicar Anderson*. But can that be the house as it now is? On the road two very large Jacobean GATE LODGES, red brick with stone dressings and shaped gables. They alone look convincingly 1868. High WATER TOWER.

LOCK'S HEATH [DL] *5000*

The heath was enclosed in mid Victorian times – almost the last bit of enclosure of wild country for cultivation anywhere in England. Straight roads; strawberry plots, each with a substantial brick house. Pocket package suburbanization now proceeding piecemeal; there is no need to try to describe the resultant mess.

ST JOHN. 1895 by *Ewan Christian*. Neo-E.E., with open bellcote over the E end of the nave. A carefully considered, effective design.

LONGPARISH *4040*

ST NICHOLAS. Perp W tower of chequer flint and stone, built into the existing nave. This nave received its aisles or was put up with aisles about 1210. The arcades of four bays have round piers with octagonal abaci and capitals, where the decoration of the mouths of trumpet-scallops creates a kind of running frieze (cf. Mottisfont). One of the capitals is actually going stiff-leaf. Pointed arches with two slight chamfers. The priest's doorway could be of the same date. The chancel arch, however, and the details of the N and S windows inside are full C13. Full C13 also the S doorway with rolls, much restored. – FONT. C18. A square, strongly moulded baluster and a round, basin-like bowl with swags. – STAINED GLASS. NE and SE windows by *Wailes*; S windows by *Hardman*; the E window by *Morris & Co.* but as late as 1912; the other chancel windows by *Clayton & Bell*.

LONGSTOCK *3030*

ST MARY. 1880 by *William White*. Flint, with a NW tower, carrying a shingled broach-spire. Of no architectural interest externally. But the chancel inside is a climax. Chancel arch with lily and rose capitals. Chancel roof with East Anglian horizontal angels. – COMMUNION RAIL. C18. – TILES. Some medieval ones behind the altar. – STAINED GLASS. E and chancel SE by *Mayer* of Munich.

A pretty village with many thatched cottages. *See* p. 830

7040

LONG SUTTON

ALL SAINTS. Early C13, with a late C13 S aisle. Nave and chan- cel and a bell-turret E of the nave W bay. The early C13 win- dows are lancets, made to look Norman outside, but witl pointed rere-arches. The S aisle windows have pointed-trefoilec heads. Arcade of one arch. Semicircular responds, double- chamfered arch. In the aisle ogee-headed PISCINA anc niche. – PLATE. Chalice, 1570.

(LORD WANDSWORTH AGRICULTURAL COLLEGE, ¾ m. SE By *Sir Guy Dawber*, 1915 etc. Big, symmetrical, neo-Georgian and uninspired. The farm buildings etc. are by *Sir Reginal* *Blomfield*, *c.*1913. NT)

See p. 830

LOOM FIELD *see* BENTWORTH

LOWER FROYLE *see* FROYLE

3090

LYMINGTON

ST THOMAS. The visual attraction of the church with the cupol on its W tower seen along the High Street is beyond question But there is much architectural interest also. Although th medieval church is at first not noticed, it must have had th same size as the present one. There are a W respond of abou 1200 (base with spurs, round abacus) and a W lancet next to it The chancel shows inside traces of fine tall shafted blanl arcading no doubt to frame and connect lancet windows, anc there is a late C13 N chapel, the N windows with geometrica tracery, the E window with cusped intersecting tracery an shafted inside. Then, in 1670, the SW tower was built. Th cupola looks C18. Of *c.*1670 perhaps also are the W window with their fancy tracery. But the principal impression of th church, inside, is of the C18. The church has three gallerie on Tuscan columns in pairs, one behind the other. This i repeated for a second tier, and on this rests the segmenta plaster vault, dated 1720, and replacing a wagon roof witl bosses.* The pretty decoration of the roof, however, is of th restoration of 1910–11. – FONT. An C18 stone baluster. – STAINED GLASS. N transept N, garish colours, by *Powell* 1865. – PLATE. Chalice and two Patens, 1774. – MONU

* Some BOSSES now in a showcase. Mr Hubbuck gives as the dates: gallery 1792, S gallery 1811, W end 1811. He also refers to White's Director as giving 1756 as the date for a lengthening and for the N aisle. (The preser N windows are of 1868, the S windows of 1871. NT)

MENTS. Charles Colebourn † 1747, by *Rysbrack*. Inscription block and a bust above. Nothing outstanding. – Capt. Josias Rogers † 1795. By *Bacon Sen*. An exquisitely elegant female figure by an urn on a pedestal. – Sir Matthew Blakiston † 1806. By *Benjamin R. Shout*. This is the entirely conventional treatment of the same customary subject.

ALL SAINTS, All Saints Road. 1909 by *Romaine-Walker*. Dec. The N aisle ends a little W of the nave. Turret with spire in this place. Aisles, high-up E windows. Nave with a panelled tunnel-vault. Attached HALL with cross-windows.

OUR LADY OF MERCY AND ST JOSEPH (R.C.), off the High Street. 1859 by *J. A. Hansom*. Brick, nave and chancel. Tracery of *c*.1300 and also plate tracery. The brick shows inside. – STAINED GLASS. The E window is much more medieval in intention than *Mayer & Co.*'s chancel N windows.

CONGREGATIONAL CHURCH, High Street. 1847. Grey brick, gabled front with pinnacles. The (altered) W window is in a giant recess. Otherwise two-light lancets.

PERAMBULATION. The best way of walking Lymington is to come from the ferry, and start by walking up QUAY HILL. This is pedestrian, wide, paved with setts, and has on both sides cheerful cottages with bay windows, a seaside effect. At the top one looks up the HIGH STREET which, seen from here, seems to end at the top of its rise. It is only as one reaches halfway up the hill that St Thomas becomes visible as the ideal *point-de-vue*. As for individual houses, there are plenty to enjoy, though not one is outstanding. No. 1 has a large canted bay window and a nice doorway. Nos 133–4 opposite are a pair, with two doorways, but also have only two widely spaced bays. This is Late Georgian. No. 132 is of five bays. The doorway has very thin Tuscan columns. Then the TOWN HALL, 1913 by *Dexter & Staniland* of Bournemouth. Three bays, brick and much stone. Baroque, with a cupola. The ANGEL HOTEL has five bays and three storeys. Along the first floor a veranda. On the r. the higher, plain Assembly Room. Very thin Ionic columns on the ground floor. Back to the S side. No. 29 is early C19, two bays, stuccoed, with giant pilasters and a pediment across. Pretty honeysuckle balcony. The LONDESBOROUGH HOTEL is Early Victorian and has a typically Victorian-Gothic balcony. The NATIONAL PROVINCIAL BANK is of brick, four bays with giant angle pilasters. Then another four-bay house, but of three and a half storeys, plain, but adorned with Messrs Scats' glorious Victorian cast-iron shop window of five bays with florid spandrels to the arches. No. 48 is the most handsome house in Lymington. It has a front courtyard and low projecting wings. Five bays, three storeys, doorway with Roman Doric pilasters and broken pediment. Then No. 52, early C19, three-storeyed and rendered. Grecian, with two unfluted giant Ionic columns *in antis* on the upper floor. Screen walls l. and r. Back to the N side. No. 73 is inordinately high: three and a half storeys, yellow brick, much bare wall l. and r. of a wide three-windowed bow. No. 68 is of three storeys and only two bays. On the ground floor two Greek Doric columns at the angles, the upper floors with giant pilasters: early C19. By the church on the same side a group of three red-brick houses slightly stepped up towards the church. Opposite another red house, plain, of four bays.

The church stands close to the street. If you turn S along CHURCH LANE, you meet SOUTHEND HOUSE. Early C18. Fine brickwork, giant angle pilasters, the centre projecting and with very narrow windows flanking the middle one. The doorway is later. Then on the W a CRINKLE-CRANKLE WALL, eight bulges, and a little later another on the other side. This belongs to GROVE PLACE, a large early C19 house of yellow brick. Porch of pairs of Tuscan columns. Facing this house and Church Lane is FAIRFIELD, also Late Georgian, seven bays, rendered, with a wooden veranda and a wooden balcony.

Back to the church and continue in the direction of the High Street along ST THOMAS'S STREET. On the S side at once MONMOUTH HOUSE, late C17, low, of five bays, with raised brick quoins, a doorway with rustication of alternating sizes, the window surrounds curiously moulded inwards. On the E side an oval window placed vertically. On the W side garden gate of iron and urns on the piers. QUADRILLE COURT, much restored, is also late C17: ten bays including three-bay slightly projecting wings. Cross-windows of mullions.

2000

LYNDHURST

ST MICHAEL. 1858–70 by *William White*. Steeply above the High Street. Red brick with yellow trim and a NW steeple. E.E. details, but handled wilfully. Not only does the tracery do unauthorized things, but the cross-gables also add a personal note. The W and S doorways are indeed extremely personal, and the iconography of the sculpture deserves notice too. The interior is very large. The exposed brickwork is yellow, white, and two reds. The arches are set with bricks at an angle so as to result in a spiky edge. Piers with eight Purbeck shafts and texts round the shaft-rings. Many varieties of leaves in the capitals.* The aisles have lean-to roofs and half-arches to the transepts. The nave roof is decorated with life-size supporting angels, and there is plenty more figure carving. – PAINTING. The reredos is painted in Gambier Parry's spirit fresco by *Lord Leighton*, 1864. He represented in his idealized yet so realistic figures the Wise and the Foolish Virgins. – Higher up and on the S wall *John H. Pollen*‡ painted figures in a more Pre-Raphaelite style, probably a little earlier. – For the STAINED GLASS by *Morris* is of 1862–3. It fills the E and S transept S windows and is exquisite throughout, among the best of the firm and infinitely superior to anything done by anyone else at that time, or, for that matter, by *Kempe* in 1903 (W window). The E window, including its foliage background, was designed by *Burne-Jones*.§ – The N transept Te Deum window is by *Clayton & Bell*.§ – (Six-light window in the N aisle by *Powell*. NT) – PLATE. Flagon, 1694; Chalice and Paten Cover, 1757. – MONUMENTS. The monument in the chancel N wall which looks like an Easter Sepulchre and might well be by White is in fact by *Street* and commemorates Mr & Mrs Hargreaves, who had the church built. He died in 1863. – Sir Charles P. Jennings. By *Flaxman*, 1798. White marble. Mourning woman leaning over a broken column. – Anne Frances Cockerell. By *S. P. Cockerell Jun.*, 1882. She lies a little precariously on two Quattrocento brackets. Mosaic lunette behind. 88

OUR LADY OF THE ASSUMPTION AND ST EDWARD (R.C.), Empress Road. 1886 by *Sir Arthur Blomfield*. Nave and chancel in one; NW turret. In the chancel Purbeck shafting. – Reredos with fresco PAINTING signed by *Paul Natter*. In a Quattrocento style.

Opposite the church is the CROWN HOTEL, large and typical of its date: 1896. Much half-timber in the gables, much tile-hanging otherwise – Norman Shaw influence, evidently.

W of the church the KING'S HOUSE and QUEEN'S HOUSE. In the former the Verderers' Court was held, and the court room

*They were carved by *G. W. Seale*, who also did the PULPIT and the lower part of the SCREEN (NT).

‡ By Mrs John Pollen, says Kelly.

§ According to Mr Sewter.

is preserved. The architectural history of the house is not easily deciphered. The E porch and the N gables are C17, the former late. Then there are rainwater heads with the date 1712, and to that belong the W doorway with its apsed hood, and the fine S façade with raised brick window surrounds.

NORTHERWOOD, ½ m. NW. Long, white house, with pedimented, slightly-projecting wings and a veranda or colonnade between them.

FOXLEASE, 1 m. S. The exterior, evidently of *c.*1700–30, is unpromising. But inside are a number of Gothic rooms, inspired – it is always said – by Strawberry Hill. They are not up to that level, but they are very charming all the same and the best 'Gothick' in the county. Outside appears the date 1775. – Above a fireplace an Italian C18 RELIEF of scenes from the story of Iphigenia.

(HIGH COXLEASE, 1 m. S, set back in the Forest W of the Brockenhurst Road. A comfortable and characteristic medium-sized house by *W. R. Lethaby*, 1898. Whitewashed brick, tile roof, two-storey H-shaped main block with service wing. J. Brandon-Jones)

MALSHANGER HOUSE *see* OAKLEY

6050

MAPLEDURWELL

ST MARY. Flint. Nave and chancel and a weatherboarded bell-turret. One Norman chancel N window, plain Late Norman W doorway. The nave has lancets, mostly but not all C19. – BRASS. John Canner and wife, † MCV . . . (i.e. early C16); 14 in. figures.

3010

MARCHWOOD [DL]

POWER STATION. Commissioned in 1951, construction begun 1952, generating begun 1955, in full production in 1959. Architects *Farmer & Dark*; Consulting Engineers *Sir William Halcrow & Partners*. One of the best pieces of post-war industrial architecture in Britain. The main building containing the turbines has a framework of encased structural steel members and sawtooth cladding of aluminium and glass, with continuous glass panelling on the upward incline and the aluminium on the downward incline of the sawtooth pattern. The interior of the turbine building is superb, with the transverse stanchions set rhythmically at wider and narrower intervals, and clerestory lighting over the wider and solid flat roofing over the narrower spaces, the huge turbines themselves only rising to about a third of the height, so emphasizing the scale of the space. Outside, the clean clear lines and the splendid mass-proportions of the turbine building are not overwhelmed by the more intricate but carefully arranged detailing of the adjoining parts (even though these rise higher), and its horizontality and solidity are set off by the verticality and slenderness of the two tall chimneys. The station was designed for coal-firing, and indeed the coal gantry, rising at a graceful angle from shore level to the top of the building, is a notable feature of the whole composition; but a decision was made to change to oil-firing (using oil from near-by Fawley) shortly before it started to operate. Marchwood is on the shore of Southampton Water and is far and away the dominant landmark on the W side of the Water above Southampton, balancing Fawley in the downward direction.

Near by, buildings were under construction at the time of writing for the Electricity Research Station. In strange contrast are the small two-storey red-brick barrack block and iron-colonnaded guard rooms of the former MARCHWOOD MAGAZINE, established in the mid C19, just to the N.

The VILLAGE remains an inconsequent straggle of indifferent houses against a rural background, almost the only recent housing being by the *Ministry of Public Building and Works* (for the Royal Engineers), including some newly completed flats, elegant and precise.

Looming over the houses and fields is the extraordinarily lofty bulk of the church of ST JOHN THE APOSTLE, 1843 by *J. Derick,* its style transitional between Commissioners' Lancet Gothic and ecclesiological E.E., its materials yellow brick and stone, its height disproportionate in relation to its other dimensions, as if it had been designed to be lower but had been stretched upwards. Nave, transepts, chancel, S aisle, with S flanking tower just managing to assert itself against the main bulk of the church. Inside the scale is grand but the proportions are awkward, and details such as mouldings and bosses are over-large. – FONT. A partial copy, coeval with the church, of the Tournai-marble font in Winchester Cathedral, executed in ordinary stone and looking strangely like an original work of the nineteen-thirties or early forties. – STAINED GLASS. E window, Christ Triumphant; post-war, quite good.

The former RECTORY, S of the village, is by *Woodyer,* 1846, having 'that peculiar character which ought to distinguish a parsonage' (*Ecclesiologist*). Among tall trees, unoccupied at the time of writing; it has neo-Dec windows and a Gothic arched entrance.

MARELANDS *see* BENTLEY

MARSH COURT *see* KING'S SOMBORNE

0010

MARTIN

ALL SAINTS. On the N side a blocked plain Norman or Transitional doorway. The W tower in its lower parts C13. Perp bell-openings and recessed stone spire. In the S transept the Dec windows seem Victorian, but the arch to the nave, dying into the imposts, is also C14. So is that to the former N transept. Here is a good deal of confusion. The N aisle appears to start from the E. In fact it is the transept plus a two-bay chancel chapel which ceased to be that, owing to a shifting of the chancel arch. The chapel had responds of typical Perp section (four shafts and four hollows). But what is one to make of the bay window, as it were, with its rere-arch of the same section and its five-light window, trustworthy at least inside? Did it hold a tomb-chest? Externally most of the windows of the church are Victorian. – FONT. An C18 baluster. – PLATE. Elizabethan Chalice; Paten, 1743.

GRIM'S DITCH. This great earthwork forms the N boundary of the parish and county and extends into Wiltshire and Dorset. It consists of a pair of banks 50 ft wide with a medial ditch 5–6 ft deep. It can be traced eastwards for 5 m., where it forms part of the N boundaries of Breamore and Rockbourne parishes. Part of its S stretch can be seen in the S of Martin parish and its W edge lies just over the parish and county boundary (at this point marked by Bokerley Dyke). The whole earthwork encloses an area of 16 square m. and probably delimits the holding of a large ranch of the Middle and Late Bronze Age.

Contemporary with this earthwork is a small ENCLOSURE of 2 acres ½ m. ENE of Bokerley Junction and ½ m. SE of the A354. It consists of a slight bank and V-sectioned ditch enclosing a roughly rectangular area. The earthwork is broken by gaps on the NE and SE. Excavations in the C19 produced Middle and Late Bronze Age pottery and also proved the contemporaneity of this cattle enclosure with Grim's Ditch.

MARTYR WORTHY

5030

ST SWITHUN. Nave and chancel with apse. Bell-turret of 1871. The nave is Late Norman, see the doorways. The N doorway has one order of columns and zigzag at r. angles to the wall, the S doorway nutmeg. The Norman-looking apse is of 1865. Perp W window.

MARWELL HALL

5020

1 m. SSW of Owslebury

The house was built *c.*1816 for William Long. Who was the architect? One would like to know; for it is a remarkably early case of Tudor Revival. The garden side will more easily be called 1816 than the entrance side; for although it has a Tudor gable l. and a Tudor gable r. and mullioned and transomed windows under them, the centre is a higher piece of four bays with polygonal angle turrets with caps and a ground-floor display of Gothic windows (with wooden bar tracery). But the entrance side is entirely Tudor. Two gables and battlements between and a middle porch. Handsome rib-vaulted (plaster-vaulted) entrance hall. In the dining room a Jacobean fireplace with tapering pilasters below, but above, in the overmantel, Ionic pilasters tapering outward in an excessive, highly incorrect way. The staircase is early C18 and has twisted balusters.

MATTINGLEY

7050

CHURCH. Timber-framed throughout and late medieval. Nave and aisles, chancel, shingled bell-turret. The aisles are of 1867, and at that time much was restored too. The infilling between the timbers is of brick-nogging. The chancel is in a good state and has a straight-headed five-light E window. The N porch, at the W end of the N aisle, is original too, though partly renewed. Inside, the arcade piers show clearly that they were originally wall-posts of an aisleless nave. In the chancel the wall-posts are in order. Their mouldings are Perp. The roof has tie-beams, collar-beams, and one tier of wind-braces. – PANELLING. In the altar area; C17. – FRONTAL. Embroidered with the letters of God (in Hebrew) and Christ surrounded by rays. Dated 1667. – STAINED GLASS. In a chancel N window some original bits. – PLATE. Chalice and Paten Cover, 1568.

MAYBUSH *see* SOUTHAMPTON, pp. 567, 568

6030 MEDSTEAD

ST ANDREW. Nave and chancel, bar tracery, N aisle under very low roof. Weatherboarded bell-turret. The chancel has lancets, but even so the interior is a surprise. Two-bay N arcade. Short round pier, multi-scalloped capital, square abacus, round, slightly chamfered arches. Hood-mould with a quarter hollow. That must be about 1200. The church was lengthened to the W. The collecting box stands on a fine later C13 tripartite corbel with leaf decoration. – PLATE. Cup of 1563, an early date; Paten of 1680.

ALTON ABBEY, 1½ m. ENE. Of the Order of St Paul for the welfare of seamen. Founded in 1889. The move to Medstead took place in 1895. The original architect was *Percy Green*. The gatehouse is of 1903, of flint and yellow brick, and these are also the materials of the church, begun in 1896 and completed in 1907. The flint and brick appear inside as well as outside. Much chamfering of the bricks characterizes the remarkably personal design. The W portal e.g. is entirely brick. The style is early C13 and very restrained. The interior is determinedly divided by a big flint pulpitum. Behind it rises the crossing tower, high with high N lancets and crowned by a bold roof designed by *Sir Charles Nicholson*. He also designed the Seamen's Home adjoining (1929–36) and his firm a further addition of 1955–6. A pleasantly easy, undogmatic design.

2020 MELCHET PARK

1¼ m. W of Sherfield English

Melchet Park was begun by *Henry Clutton* in 1863 for the second Lord Ashburton. It was much damaged by fire and redone inside in 1875–9. But what is visible now is interspersed with the work of *Darcy Braddell* of about 1912–14 for the first Lord Melchet. Clutton's style is Jacobean, his material brick with ample stone dressings. Braddell's is the same style, e.g. in the GATEHOUSE, and his material is the same too. Clutton's house is large in its scale, not in number of rooms. To the entrance there are two ample bows and a square middle porch. Shaped gables on top, all strictly symmetrical. To the S two canted bay windows and an uncanted one in the middle. That just encases three main rooms to the S and three to the N. The doorway is by Braddell 1914, and Braddell also added the dining room, connecting the house with a lower, L-shaped wing to the E. To the W the former ORANGERY, with under its middle arch an aedicule of rubbed brick and terracotta. Can this be 1875–9?* The interior certainly was remodelled by Braddell. In the interior of the house the most interesting thing is the intervention of Darcy Braddell in playfully classical, rather Swedish ceilings and many other details. Originally *Alfred Stevens* and *L. W. Collmann* had done much, but that was consumed by the fire, except, it is said, the staircase, and the staircase is without any doubt not Italian Renaissance, as one would expect from Stevens, but grandly Wrenish. For the coffered ceiling the Victoria and Albert Museum has the drawings. By Stevens probably is the beautiful grey-marble hall fireplace with putti and foliage. And also by him could be the two wooden overdoors in the present chapel, former dining room. The Jacobean ceiling in this room must again be Braddell's.

MENGHAM *see* HAYLING ISLAND

MEONSTOKE

6010

ST ANDREW. The church is less than ¼ m. from that of Corhampton. W tower with a nice timbered top in the Welsh-border style. Nave and chancel. The aisles are under one roof with the nave. Lancets in tower and chancel, i.e. E.E. Low early C14 tomb recess in the chancel. Good interior of nave and aisles. Four-bay arcades E.E. Alternatingly round and octagonal piers. Double-chamfered arches. Above, now inside too, the former clerestory, the windows quatrefoils in circles. The chancel arch is almost entirely C19. – FONT. Of Purbeck marble. Table type with flat arches. – SCULPTURE. Small North German Baroque carving of Jacob and the Angel. – PLATE. Cup, 1682; Cover Paten, probably 1682.

IRON AGE HILLFORT, on Old Winchester Hill, 2½ m. NE. The hill is crowned by a single rampart 4–5 ft high and a ditch never more than 1–2 ft deep. The defences are broken by inturned entrances on the E and W. Partly enclosed by the ramparts but extending down the slopes of the hill on the E and W are a series of fine BOWL BARROWS.

*Mr M. J. Donovan gave me the date 'between 1880 and 1896'.

4020 MERDON CASTLE

¾ m. NW of Hursley

(Circular earthwork with a deep ditch around. Traces of another bank inside the ditch. On the S a short length of curtain walling with a tower. This is attributed to Bishop Henry of Blois and the year 1138. VCH)

5030 MICHELDEVER

ST MARY. The thrill of the church – more for unexpectedness perhaps than for strictly architectural quality – is *George Dance*'s centre octagon inserted into what had been a normal medieval church. Of that church the W tower remained standing. It is of flint and stone and has a higher stair-turret and four-light bell-openings with a transom. The arches of the lights are uncusped; so it will probably be *temp.* Henry VIII. To mediate between the tower and the octagon Dance introduced a bay of transition of which the sides are the beginning of the medieval arcade, but the E arch may be the re-used chancel arch and E responds. The present chancel is of 1880–1,* and at that time windows with flowing tracery were introduced, not only in the chancel E wall. Dance was ruthless. His octagon, which was built in 1808, is of brick, showing bluntly outside and without any finesses of mouldings for the windows, let alone any stone dressings. The walls are bare below – windows are only on the clerestory level, and they are just arch-heads. The interior is less rigid. Four shallow niches in the diagonals, two deeper ones instead of transepts. All surrounds are of fine continuous mouldings. Plaster star-vault.‡ – PLATE. Cup of 1703. – MONUMENTS. A group of three Baring monuments by *Flaxman*. The Barings resided at The Grange and Stratton Court. They were made between 1801 and 1813. The centre is Thy Will be Done, a resignedly seated praying woman in a mildly Gothic surround. The two side pieces are smaller and each have a square, surprisingly Baroque panel: Thy Kingdom Come, a mother and child carried heavenwards by a tangle of angels, and Deliver us from Evil, a figure battling devils and helped by angels. – Thomas Baring † 1873. By *Sir J. E. Boehm*. Two large kneeling angels.

*Probably by *Colson* who (according to the Rev. Basil Clarke) did the REREDOS in 1883.

‡Dance's London church of St Bartholomew the Less is on a central plan too.

(RAILWAY STATION. By *Tite*, 1840. Called Andover Road till Andover got its own station. Simple flint building with veranda. The TUNNELS to the N and high embankment to the S are part of *Joseph Locke*'s impressive engineering on the London-Southampton line, and from the enormous cutting N of the station (really a cutting enlarged into a quarry) chalk was taken to build the Southampton Docks extensions in the inter-war years. The sidings and sheds within the cutting were built during the Second World War in connexion with military movements. DL) See p. 830

MICHELMERSH

3020

ST MARY. Detached, or at least originally detached, W tower, of timber, weatherboarded. Pyramid roof. Inside the big posts, and tiers of pairs of scissor-bracing on every side. The church is quite large. Plain S doorway of *c*.1200. One fine straight-headed Dec window with reticulation unit. The S façade is of 1847, but the one-bay N and S chapels are again of *c*.1200. Round arches with one slight chamfer. – FONT. C13, stone, circular, with big lilies and four heads at the corners. It must have been re-cut, perhaps about 1500. – STAINED GLASS. In a chancel window two well-preserved C15 heads and further bits. – MONUMENT. Cross-legged Knight, his feet against a stag. Angels l. and r. of his pillow. Early C14. – Trustram Funtleroy † 1538. Small and very unusual tablet. Two small kneeling figures in relief in fields bordering on the l. and r. margins but neither on top nor bottom. All the rest is inscription.

MANOR FARM, ⅜ m. E. Behind the façade is a flint building with two lancets to the E, one each to N and S, one doorway W of the northern one, and another doorway E and at r. angles to the southern one. This may have led to a priest's dwelling. The most likely date is the C13.

MIDANBURY *see* SOUTHAMPTON, pp. 592, 599

MIDLINGTON HOUSE *see* DROXFORD

MILFORD LAKE *see* HIGHCLERE

MILFORD-ON-SEA

2090

On-sea is a development initiated by Col. Cornwallis West about 1887. The sea front is no longer terraces as at Brighton, but single or double houses in gardens. The styles go from Norman-Shavian half-timbered gables and tile-hanging to neo-Georgian. Examples are the SOLENT COURT HOTEL (former Victoria Hotel), Cliff Road, 1889–90 by *W. Charles Evans*, symmetrical with two shaped gables on the angle pavilions and two storeys of verandas between.* Also WESTOVER HOUSE, Park Lane, 1897 by *A. Mitchell*, free late C16 or early C17, with late C17 features. Centre and two different wings. But what the Milford architectural explorers ought to visit chiefly is inland. *See* p. 830

ALL SAINTS. This is a church almost completely E.E., of the later C13, in its style derived from the work of the same moment at Christchurch. The 'almost' refers to the S arcade, which tells of a preceding Late Norman church. The aisle had three bays. The piers are round with base spurs, the capitals of simple, coarse types, the abaci square, the arches round and unmoulded. This church, it is evident, had a crossing tower and transepts. Both transepts have in their end walls small doorways of about 1200. That of the N transept has a trefoiled head. The position is unusual, but not impossible. Some suggest that they are re-set aisle doorways. Then, before 1250, the crossing tower was replaced by a W tower. The crossing tower may well have come to grief. The W tower has to the W a middle buttress and two slender lancets. The bell-openings are twin lancets, and there is a top corbel-frieze. Later short recessed spire. The tower originally opened to the S and N into embracing W bays of aisles. In fact the position of the W lancet of the S aisle indicates probably the width of the Norman aisle. After that all is later C13 – except for the arches from the aisles into the former transepts. They are round and have only a slight chamfer. But aisles that wide cannot be presumed for 1200. May one then assume that, when the later C13 plan of a wide-aisled church taking in the whole depth of the Norman transepts was put into operation, two of the former crossing arches were re-used in this form ? The whole of the arrangement of the former crossing area is a very botched job anyway. The new piers S and N are round with round abaci. The new arches are pointed and double-chamfered. The W bays of the N aisle have octagonal piers instead and narrower arches. Only the chancel is pure late C13. But so also is the exterior. The windows are of two or three or stepped three lights with one or three circles enclosing trefoils, quatrefoils,

*Demolished in 1965.

cinquefoils. Elegant S doorway and contemporary S porch. One more attractive detail is the roof over the former crossing with timbers forming crossing ribs and emphasizing the importance of the position by bosses. This arrangement is of 1640.

EFFORD PARK, $1\frac{5}{8}$ m. NNE. Early C19. White, irregular, but with very pretty iron verandas, one two-storeyed. The VCH says the house was built in 1838.

NEWLANDS MANOR, $\frac{3}{4}$ m. NW. An early C19 Gothic mansion with a symmetrical façade. The Georgian canted bay windows l. and r. have been gothicized and given buttresses and the middle colonnade has turned Gothic too. The house is embattled and has oversized pinnacles, but all is unfortunately rendered. There is also a castellated LODGE, but close to the house is a tower with cupola, brick, and purely Georgian. It must have belonged to the STABLES.

MILLBROOK *see* SOUTHAMPTON, pp. 566, 567, 568, 569

MILTON 2090

ST MARY MAGDALENE. The W tower is attributed by the VCH to the early C17. The church of brick with the Y-tracery was built in 1831 by *William Hiscock*,* but *Sir Howard Robertson* in 1928 and 1958 added the E end and the N aisle, very nicely indeed, in a modernized Georgian (not simply neo-Georgian). The E end e.g. has a low tunnel-vault. – PLATE. Set of 1726. – MONUMENT. Thomas White † 1720. He kneels nearly frontally in a niche which alas does not allow his legs space, and so they have just been left out. This in contrast with the dignity of wig, sword, and armour and the faces of the cherubs results in an irresistably funny *ensemble*. Columns l. and r., gathered-up drapery above him. The sword he is holding is reproduced from a real Italian C17 sword, hanging next to the monument. It is signed by *Andrea Ferrata*.

FERNHILL MANOR, Fernhill Lane, N of the station. Late C17. Five bays, two storeys, wooden cross-windows, hipped roof.

(OXEY CLOSE, New Milton. Handsome group of eleven houses in three units. By *C. H. Elsom & Partners*, 1962–3.)

MILTON *see* PORTSMOUTH, pp. 439, 445, 448, 463

*According to the Rev. Basil Clarke.

MINLEY

8050

MINLEY MANOR. 1858–60 by *Henry Clutton.* A French brick château in the style of Louis XII, very varied in outline, with steep roofs and many dormers. It was built for Raikes Currie, a Catholic banker, and Clutton also gave him a chapel (disused) with a steep copper roof. In 1886–7 *George Devey* made additions. They are evident by their more relaxed style, varying from Venetian Renaissance to Dutch C17 and Wren elements. To his additions belong the gate lodge, the stables, the orangery (a specially fine piece), and connecting links. What he did to the house itself is not recorded.* Finally in 1898 the big wing was added which stands at r. angles to Clutton's entrance side. This is in imitation of Clutton's style. What date are the RELIEFS of St Laurence and St Catherine and the ornamental parts now used in the SE front (with its beautiful view)? The principal room inside is the dining room, with both ends apsed. This looks 1887 and not earlier, but is nothing special. Avenue of Wellingtonias from the NW. The landscapist was *James Veitch II*, the leading Victorian nursery gardener (NT).

ST ANDREW. By *Clutton*, *c.*1871. Small, of flint, with a flèche. Minimum bell-hanging arrangement on the N side.

MINSTEAD

2010

ALL SAINTS. Minstead church is Whitby *en miniature.* As one approaches it, one sees the W tower, which is of brick and was built in 1774, a gabled porch with the date 1683 and other cross-gables, and a variety of windows in wall and roof, all entirely domestic. On the S side a long addition of 1792 sticks out. The medieval evidence is quite swamped by this: remains of a N lancet in the chancel and the N doorway, both C13. The chancel E window is again typically 'Gothick'. Inside, the chancel arch is C13, the rest is, as at Whitby, galleries and attachments – everything to seat as many as possible. – WEST GALLERY. C18. – A more recent upper W gallery in addition. – PEWS in the N attachments, one with a fireplace. The long S attachment is separated from the nave by an iron column. – PULPIT. A three-decker. – FONT. Late C12, square with tapering sides, Purbeck marble. On the W side Christ

* Inside is an equestrian relief signed *M. Hiolle*, 1887. (In the cloister of his chapel is a MEMORIAL to Devey † 1886. Admirable bust by *C. H. Mabey.* A palette is more in evidence than the compasses; for Devey was first trained as a water-colour painter by Cotman. NT)

with the Cross and two assistant figures. On the S side stylized eagles, on the N side two lions with one head, on the E side the Lamb and Cross.* – PLATE. Parcel-gilt Chalice, probably C17; Parcel-gilt Flagon, 1739; Paten with gilt edges, 1836.

CASTLE MALWOOD, 1 m. NW. 1892. Yellow brick. Low, rambling, in a free Jacobean with some Baroque touches. See p. 830

MONK SHERBORNE

6050

ALL SAINTS. This is an Early Norman church, see the herring-bone flint-laying and one chancel window high up. Traces of two more are visible inside. A little later Norman the large N doorway with one order of columns, capitals of two decorated scallops, a roll and a zigzag order in the arch, and a plain tympanum. Of the same time probably the chancel arch with a big semicircular respond and a subsidiary shaft to the W. The former has a multi-scalloped capital with a flat face in the middle ending at the mouth, the latter reeded leaves. There is also evidence of an E arch with shafts and zigzag. Was there then in the C12 a chancel and an apse? The present chancel has one blocked lancet, but the operating windows are of *c.*1300. At the W end the church has a recently tile-hung bell-turret, but also a very large square medieval stair-turret. Was a W tower planned? Big timber N porch of the C14. – PILLAR PISCINA. With broad leaves (vestry). – FONT. Norman, with three C19 supports and three heads sticking out from the underside. Only one of them is original. – PULPIT. Given by a rector who officiated between 1648 and probably 1654. Late Perp, but almost entirely re-tooled. – BENCH ENDS. – (SCREEN and ORGAN CASE. By *Bodley*. RH) – COMMUNION RAIL. Jacobean. Now at the W end. – STAINED GLASS. In the vestry a sweetly inept set of the 1850s, signed *T. Wells*. – PLATE. Elizabethan Chalice, Paten Cover, and Flagon.

MONXTON

3040

ST MARY. 1854 by *Woodyer*. Flint, nave and chancel and somewhat overhanging bellcote. Plate tracery. Big timber S porch. Steep nave roof with collar-beams. The chancel-arch capitals of *c.*1200 were re-used. They are of the trumpet-scallop type. – STAINED GLASS. E window by *Kempe*, 1887.

*The font stands in front of the pulpit, a position more usual in pre-Tractarian times than now (RH).

MOORDOWN *see* BOURNEMOUTH, pp. 118, 123

MOORE PLACE FARM *see* BRAMSHILL HOUSE

5020
MORESTEAD

CHURCH. The cottagey W attachment is of 1833. The brick bellcote must be more recent. Nave and chancel, the details neo-Norman, but the S and N doorway plain genuine Norman. – FONT. Octagonal, of Purbeck marble. On each side two flat arches.

6060
MORTIMER WEST END

ST SAVIOUR. 1856 by *Richard Benyon*. Flint. Nave and chancel, polygonal vestry, bellcote, and a low late W addition. Geometrical tracery, incorrect.

PARSONAGE. 1855. Tudor, big, chequer brick. A good design.

CHAPEL OF THE COUNTESS OF HUNTINGDON'S CONNEXION. 1798 (Betjeman & Piper) or 1818 (Kelly). Chequer brick, with the typical Late Georgian segment-headed windows, wider than high. The chapel has a three-bay front, like a cottage. The manse of four bays and two storeys is attached.

3020
MOTTISFONT

ST ANDREW. Nave and chancel and weatherboarded bell-turret. The *pièce de resistance* is the Norman chancel arch: one order of shafts, zigzag and billet in the arch. Of the same time or a little later perhaps the plain round-arched S doorway. In the chancel early C14 and Perp windows, in the nave N and S lancets and Dec windows. The W window is Perp. Two tomb recesses in the nave, the larger one of them with an ogee tip. – STAINED GLASS. In the chancel more of C15 glass than in any other Hampshire village church. In the E window the larger lower figures are largely the work of the restorer, but the small figures in the tracery heads are almost intact. Fragments in the chancel side windows. – PLATE. Chalice, probably of 1586; Paten of 1707. – MONUMENT. An Elizabethan family. Dated 1584. Small kneeling figures in a row. Below the tomb-chest four panels with excellent strapwork. In the large upper part pilasters l. and r. with candelabra and arabesque motifs, a feature more of 1560 than of 1580. Good decorative friezes also, and on top a small ogee-sided gable similar to those in the monuments of 1564 at East Tisted and 1595 at Easton.

MOTTISFONT ABBEY. Mottisfont was an Augustinian priory, founded in 1201. It is now an inhabited, large and comfortable house, life going on principally in the nave of the church, but at an upper level. The unravelling of the medieval work from that of the C18 and the C20 is fascinating and rewarding, and easy for anybody who can memorize the standard monastic plan. But one must start in the present basement, which is indeed ground level as regards the N and E sides. At the N end of the present house (renewed) N buttresses indicate the N wall of the aisleless church. Inside one enters the nave through a straight-headed doorway made up of moulded medieval pieces. Then one has at once on the r. some C13 blank arcading which was on the nave S wall. Next, and visible only outside from the N, is the arch from the former crossing tower to the N transept. The transept does not exist any longer. The capitals are of fanciful trumpet scallops, the trumpet openings connected by curves and little scrolls. The S transept masonry stands upright, and here the E wall is preserved which led from this transept to a S chancel chapel. This had the same fanciful trumpets. Pointed arch with two slight chamfers. These details fit a date shortly after 1201 well. The chapel, the chancel, and the N chapel have completely gone. If they were there, they would nearly reach the Test, which helps the landscape of Mottisfont so happily, but it is likely that the course of the river has changed somewhat. Of the church a few telling details have also been found on the level of the present main living rooms, namely two shafts with capitals in different rooms which belonged to S windows above the cloister level. The capitals (one with modest crockets) are indeed a little later than the capitals further E. Of the chancel arch also part of the arch has recently been discovered, and one capital.

Of the monastic quarters the following is still in evidence. Externally in the SW corner of the S transept exposed from outside in a corner of the C18 S front and made a showpiece by MOSAIC by *Boris Anrep* is the N jamb of the N window between cloister and chapter house. The chapter house entrance (cf. e.g. Winchester) had a doorway flanked by two windows. Behind this, and accessible only from within, are some of the wall-shafts of the chapter house, which was vaulted in three by three bays. Two more such shafts were found in the garden and are now rather bafflingly displayed in the room W of the arch from S transept to S chancel chapel. They have round capitals and ribs with rolls and hollows.

Then as a cellar the short cellarium, i.e. W range, still exists. It is two-naved with low circular piers, circular capitals, and single-chamfered ribs. The piers were originally *c.*20 in. longer, i.e. the floor level has risen. The cellarium lies of course S of the W end of the nave. All the monastic details are a little later than those of the church, i.e. full C13.

Finally in the church between crossing tower and nave a pulpitum was erected between 1521 and 1536. It had a central archway through, with a fine panelled four-centred arch and a side doorway now largely C19.

At the Dissolution the priory went to Lord Sandys. He lived in the nave but added wings towards the S probably of brick. The only record of this is the canted connecting links which now so much disturb the unity of the C18 work replacing Lord Sandys's. But they are not now as they still were about 1820. They were quite small then, and their enlargement without abandoning their un-Georgian character must be Victorian. The present red-brick house facing S is of about 1740. It has a recessed centre of three bays, all of red headers, the windows in flat surrounds and the whole surmounted by a pediment with a lunette. The Victorian links are of red headers also, and so are the somewhat shapeless brick pieces which follow. The Georgian front ends l. and r. in little more projecting stone-faced wings with canted bay windows and Tuscan doorcases. But the principal living rooms are not in this part, but in the N part, i.e. the church nave. Here are beautiful fireplaces brought in in the C20, and here also, or strictly speaking at the N end of the W range, where it touches the nave, is the Gothic extravaganza of *Rex Whistler*'s drawing room. He did the work in 1938–9.

The STABLES are small, close to the house, of red brick, and a very precise job of 1837. Three sides of a courtyard. The recessed centre of four bays with arched windows and a cupola. The fronts of the wings have pilasters, well set and well balanced.

MOUNDSMERE MANOR *see* NUTLEY

MOYLES COURT *see* ELLINGHAM

MUDEFORD

1090

CHAPEL. 1871. Brick with polygonal apse and a detached wooden bell-frame. By *Pearson* (RH).

SANDHILLS. Derelict at the time of writing and facing caravans rather than the sea. The house is remarkable for its attachment, which has as a veranda a more than semicircular two-storeyed Tuscan colonnade.

See p. 830

NATELY SCURES

6050

ST SWITHIN. Only a farmhouse and a barn are near. Norman, of flint, nave, chancel, and apse in one. The bellcote of *Salvin*'s restoration of 1865. Nice N doorway with a depressed trefoiled head with two big cusps, *c*.1200 probably. Arch with zigzag, one capital with a mermaid. – (PULPIT. By *Salvin*, big and elementary, as though of *c*.1930. NT) – PLATE. Chalice, 1795. – TABLETS. Among the many a curious series looking like diamonds, hearts, and clubs.

NETHERTON

3050

1 m. W of Faccombe

OLD RECTORY. A very fine house of about 1720. Brick. Grey headers and red dressings. Smooth entrance side with cut-in windows without any surround. Five bays, two and a half storeys, only the top windows segment-headed. One-bay pediment. Doorway with pediment on Doric pilasters. The garden side is more interesting. It is of six bays, the middle two having segment-headed first-floor and large round-arched top windows. They represent the staircase inside, which has three slim balusters to the step. The interior has quite a number of the arches characteristic of Queen Anne houses. Low-pitched hipped roof.

NETHER WALLOP

3030

ST ANDREW. Flint W tower of 1704. Much of the N aisle C18 brick. The medieval external features are Perp, except for the Norman N doorway with one order of columns and a simple arch. But the interior contains a complicated architectural story which may have taken place as follows. First, about 1200, an aisleless church was given a S aisle of three bays. The arcade has the usual round piers and round abaci, with capitals of flat, broad, simple leaves. Pointed arches with one step and one slight chamfer. At about the same time the tower arch was made, though the height of the responds cannot be 1200, and so they may be re-used from somewhere else, e.g. the chancel arch, which is not now in its state of 1200. There was a chancel; for the W respond of the present S crossing arch – it looks like four crossing arches, but was not a crossing – was part of the arch into a S chancel chapel. Then the N arcade was built, very soon after. The capitals are now moulded, and the arches have two slight chamfers. This arcade was at once continued by one bay to the E, beyond the line where the original chancel arch had been (hence the thickness of wall). At the same time the S arcade was equally lengthened. Then a N chapel was built opposite the S chapel of 1200, though the date of the N chapel is uncertain. This history is not conclusive, and that of the VCH ought to be looked at as well as a comparison. – WALL PAINTINGS. St George and the Dragon, the tower on the r. To the l. of St George traces of a St Michael with the scales. Early C15. – PLATE. Paten, 1640; Chalice, 1786. – MONUMENTS. Brass to Mary Gore † 1437. A 22½ in. figure. – Pyramidal Mausoleum right opposite and close to the W front of the church. To Dr Francis Douce † 1760.

BERRY COURT, ½ m. SSW. A BARN belonging to the farm is C15 work. Aisles, tie-beams, queen-posts, and four tiers of wind-braces. The hipped sides of the roof have their wind-braces too.

WALLOP HOUSE, ½ m. WNW. Built in 1838. In the Tudor parsonage style. Red brick. Façade with four steep gables. Porch with polygonal buttress shafts. Tall mullioned windows with wooden mullions.

LONG BARROW, on Houghton Down, ¼ m. N of Chattis Hill House. This is a much denuded long barrow now only 1 ft high and having a length of 170 ft. The side ditches can still be traced on the ground. Part of the barrow was excavated in the C19, when a number of crouched inhumation burials without grave goods were found.

DANEBURY HILLFORT, on Danebury Down, ½ m. NNE of Danebury Stables. This is a multivallate hillfort consisting of three lines of ramparts and ditches enclosing an oval area of 13 acres. The lines of defences increase in strength towards the centre of the fort, the innermost being 16 ft high and 60 ft broad. On the E is a complex entrance with elaborate outworks designed to expose the flanks of an attacker. The middle and outer defences are also broken by two further entrances on the SW. The site is unexcavated, but the position of the entrances and its complex plan suggests that the present monument represents several building phases.

LONG BARROWS, ½ m. NW of the fort. The W and larger of this pair of long barrows is 210 ft long and 72 ft wide at its broader E end, where it stands 6 ft high. The flanking quarry ditches, 27 ft wide, are still clearly visible. In a rabbit scrape in the ditch was found a single sherd of Late Neolithic Peterborough pottery. The E barrow is 170 ft long and 70 ft wide and, like its neighbour, is orientated E–W. The silted-up quarry ditches are visible here too.

½ m. NE is a third LONG BARROW, 85 ft long and 70 ft wide.

NETLEY 4000

Netley means three separate things – the Abbey, the Castle, and the Hospital. There was no village till the C19, and most of it grew after the hospital was built and the railway opened.

NETLEY ABBEY. Netley Abbey was a Cistercian house. Monks came from Beaulieu and moved in in 1239. In 1251 Henry III declared himself patron of the abbey, and his name appears on the base of the NE crossing tower. So work no doubt began in the 1240s.

As one approaches the site, the impression is curiously domestic, for reasons which will soon be explained. It is best to walk through at once to the CHURCH at the far end and start in its chancel, since almost without exception building started at the E end of the church in the Middle Ages. Netley has a straight E end with a spectacular E window which must have formerly been of four lights, with three circles above in bar tracery. That is a Westminster Abbey chapter house motif (*c.*1245–53) and seems improbable here as early as in the Abbey. However, Netley was a royal job, and the King's Mason may well have been responsible here as at Westminster. The window has an inner surround which is richly and finely moulded. Otherwise however all the windows are just lancets, and in the aisles even pairs under a round arch. The aisles were rib-vaulted, the ribs being plainly single-chamfered. Above the arcade was a wall-passage, and the clerestory windows were placed considerably above this passage. They are groups of three stepped lancets. The buttressing outside has three bold and very steep set-offs.

All these arrangements can be seen much more vividly in 27

the S transept. The N transept has vanished.* The S transept has an E aisle, and here the rib-vaults have bosses with stiff-leaf. On the other hand a corbel for a vaulting shaft for the S transept 'nave' on the W side already has naturalistic foliage. The pier between 'nave' and E aisle is octagonal with four shafts. The arches are triple-chamfered. In the transept the wall-passage and clerestory arrangement is perfectly clear. On the S wall is a large blank window, probably like the E window: four lights, two quatrefoiled circles and a large sexfoiled circle over. A doorway leads from the transept into the sacristy (*see* below), another, at first-floor level, led to the dormitory. The night staircase from the dormitory down into the nave was probably of wood. A third doorway goes into the cloister. The 'nave' vault was rebuilt late in the Middle Ages – see the rib profiles at the springers, the bosses against the S wall.

Now the nave. Of the arcade piers we have nothing, less even than of the crossing piers, where at least the base tells something of the distribution of responds. The aisle windows on the S side are placed higher up than those on the N, because of the cloister walk. One important change of detail must be noted: the groups of lancets now have pointed-trefoiled heads. Also the aisle W windows have cusped Y-tracery. So the year 1300 must have been reached. Nave and aisles were rib-vaulted.‡ At the top of the S aisle wall brick courses appear, and this is a reminder of the fact that at the Reformation Sir William Paulet, later first Marquis of Winchester, was granted Netley Abbey and converted it into a house. His hall was in the nave, and a typical C16 doorway indeed leads into the nave from the S. The S transept also was inhabited by him. Another doorway from the S to the aisle is original. The W doorway to the nave is of two orders and has a large W window the tracery of which is all broken out. The W doorway to the S aisle is constructed askew. It led to a wooden pentice which must have been the access to the nave for the lay brothers, who in Cistercian houses always lived in the W range.

The ranges round the CLOISTER are fairly well recognizable. The cloister is now lawn. The cloister walks have all gone entirely. Of the W range we have the E wall, one complete apartment at the S end, and to the N of this a C14 entry (ogee-

* But cf. p. 184.

‡ Incidentally, it is interesting to see in some of the vaults that the ribs have fallen off, but the vaults with their groins stand. So these vaults were not built on the skeleton principle.

headed windows) with a C15 porch nearly all gone. The S range is not well preserved either. Here was the KITCHEN (brick chimneys) and then the REFECTORY. This ran N–S in the Cistercian way and is not preserved. Instead we have Sir William's porch. It led into the cloister by another doorway. Sir William must have treated the cloister as his spacious inner courtyard. On the upper floor much remains of his brick remodelling, here and further E. One complete mullioned and transomed window of four lights is preserved. Outside the refectory in the cloister is the LAVATORIUM, i.e. the place where the monks washed their hands before meals. It is a recess in four parts.

The most interesting range is the E range. This was built at the same time as the E parts of the abbey church. On the upper floor here was the DORMITORY, extending all the way N–S and with small, closely set, oblong windows of which quite a number remain, although here also Sir William's brick adjustments interfere. S of the transept was the SACRISTY, three rib-vaulted bays, the ribs single-chamfered. Two E lancets under one arch starting with vertical pieces. Trefoil-headed PISCINA. In the sacristy is a display of TILES. Above the E bay of the sacristy was a small vaulted room, probably a strong room. The CHAPTER HOUSE has the usual doorway flanked by windows. Springers of the vault remain. The three E windows have unencircled sexfoils in plate tracery, i.e. really a form earlier than the bar tracery of the chancel E window. S of the chapter house a passage, and then the DORMITORY UNDERCROFT, two-naved, with circular piers. At its S end, standing across and not at a r. angle, was the REREDORTER or lavatories. This was on the first floor, but the shoots went straight into the stream channelled in below ground. On the ground floor was a vaulted room suggested as the INFIRMARY. It has a large fireplace with hood and was vaulted in four bays with a ridge-rib. E window of two lights with a quatrefoil in plate tracery. To the S of the dormitory undercroft and the W of the so-called infirmary is a room with doorways to both and hatches to both as well. So this was probably a SERVERY and the room to the N the so-called MISERICORD, where certain monks at certain times were allowed to eat meat.

Finally an isolated building to the E, not axially aligned. It is supposed to have been the ABBOT'S LODGING. It is oblong with two wings projecting to the E. Small W doorway with continuous mouldings. The ground floor vaulted in three bays, again with single-chamfered ribs. The S wing to the E was the CHAPEL. It is vaulted in two bays and has a PISCINA.

When Westall recorded Netley Abbey in 1828 the ruins were embedded in trees. It must have been a wonderful site, but the Ministry of Public Works are rightly concerned with making the ruins instructive and their neat, *riant* landscape does that and has its own attraction. It is right and proper to leave Odiham Castle rough and picturesque: at Netley there is too much to learn, and intellectual pleasures have their privileges side by side with visual ones.

[DL] ST EDWARD THE CONFESSOR, close to the abbey. Built in 1886, to the designs of *J. D. Sedding*, and now the parish church of Hound (*see* p. 298). It is full of careful detailing, but leaves no strong impression as a whole. Long nave with short two-bay aisles, like shallow transepts, at its E end, and the tower built on the S side flanking the chancel. So there is a good view as one approaches from the W, along the S side, closed by the tower with the carefully hipped roof of the aisle in its immediate foreground. The tower has deeply set bell-openings, single on the well-seen W façade but double on the S, set in strongly moulded blank panels. Angle buttresses diminish in irregular stages to die below the parapet, which has battlements and slender pinnacles. Buttresses are also a feature of the nave side wall, dying well below eaves level. Slender lancets along the nave walls. The internal effect is rather cold, but this is largely due to recent whitewashing of wall surfaces, against which the texture of the stonework and other decorative details are not strong enough to stand out. Oddly asymmetrical W wall. – Nice iron SCREENS into the space under the tower and S aisle with circle and reticulated patterning and figures of dragons along the top. – Substantial PULPIT with veined marble panels of several colours. – The low CHANCEL SCREEN and the FONT are treated in a similar way. – PLATE (from Hound). Chalice, 1689; Paten, 1724. – MONUMENT. Under the tower part of the tomb of a Knight with crossed legs, in Purbeck marble, later C13, originally from the abbey, re-used in the castle and brought to the church when the castle was restored. The effigy cannot have been longer than 30 in.

NETLEY CASTLE. One of the Solent forts, built in 1542. Garrisoned till 1627, after which it was turned into a residence. Its C19 history is not very clear. Old prints in the house show that *c.*1840 the fort substantially remained, with little enlargement. By 1857 it had been heightened and an asymmetrical Gothic tower built. Between then and 1880 there were further additions, including a large dining room. In 1885–90 the building was transformed and greatly enlarged to the design of *Sedding*. The Henry VIII fort was little more than a single-storeyed oblong structure with archways on the seaward side, and strong battlemented parapet, the battlements curving convexly on their outward face. What the treatment was on the landward façade is not known. By 1840 an oriel window had been built in the centre of the seaward façade, and in the alterations of *c.*1840–60 an upper storey had been formed by continuing the parapet upwards and using the spaces between the battlements as the lower parts of window surrounds. The DINING ROOM at the NW end, of *c.*1860–80, has a complicated roof framework resting on impressive large corbels in carved representation of various types of human figures, all in crouching or kneeling positions visibly represented as if they were holding up their beams either with their arms or backs. Sedding's alterations consisted of adding a further storey to the two-storeyed main block (gabled externally, and rising behind the parapet of the second storey); adding a new wing on the SE side, rising to three storeys, and entirely reconstructing and heightening the TOWER, which had been built on this side *c.*1840–60, with a very prominent stair-turret; and making considerable additions on the SW side, with a fairly prominent stair-turret. The external elevations as they now appear are not very successful asymmetrical compositions (though the effect is better on the seaward side, where there are a few trees as a foil) with a skyline of battlements, small gables, a few chimneys, turret, and very prominent tower, the old symmetrical centrepiece, based on the original fort, standing out clearly.

But Sedding's architecture comes into its own inside. The HALL is a pleasant room, broken into quite homely scale by broad transverse Tudor-shaped arches, one at the end opening from the staircase, one in the middle, and one at the other end, framing a massive neo-Tudor fireplace. The room is contained within the original fort, and the ceilings are quite low. The STAIRCASE is splendid; it leads axially from the hall under the arch, is neo-Jacobean in detailing, and has treads gracefully and effectively curved forwards. At first-landing stage (levels are complicated and varied in the building) is the entrance into the old DRAWING ROOM, intriguingly shaped, since part of it, arch-screened off from the rest, is octagonal, contained within the tower. The staircase continues in the return direction to the higher floor; all the way up a series of large lions and griffins rise from the massive balusters.* There are other rooms pre-dating Sedding with features modified by him.

Finally the ENTRANCE. This is in a projecting bay, a porch beneath and a room above, at the middle of the landward façade of the old fort building. Its external stonework is indistinguishable from Sedding's work, except in the main archway, which is Tudor in form and consists of three massive orders, recessed in between. This doorway looks defensive and may be part of the original Tudor structure.

ROYAL VICTORIA HOSPITAL.‡ A monster of a building, 1,424 ft long, built in 1856–63 as the main military hospital of Great Britain,§ on a site facing Southampton Water on which there was formerly a pier. Three-storeyed, of brick with stone dressings. Two very long ranges extend on either side of a boldly projecting centrepiece, which has an extraordinarily muddled façade with classical and Italianate round-arched motifs, central small pediment, and small cupolas at the forward angles. In the centre of the composition is an attenuated dome. The wings would each make reasonable major buildings in themselves, and are quite impressively composed, each with central tetrastyle pedimented portico rising from first-floor level with quoined round arches underneath, and continuous ranges of round-arched windows on each floor (smaller and closer on the top floor), separated by thick string courses. Bold dentilled parapet. The end five bays are brought forward fairly boldly. In the middle of each wing an attenuated turret with pyramid top; at the end a lower Italianate tower (in the villa sense) with round-arched lights in the top storey and a low pyramid top. Corridors run the whole length of the wings just inside the façades. The wards all had their windows at the back (NE) of the building, overlooking the outhouses. It would be difficult to find a more extreme example of a building where outward grandeur and rigid planning came first, convenience and 'amenity' a very poor second. Florence Nightingale dis-

* These came from the man o'war Lord Warden, scrapped in 1889.

‡ Demolition work started in September 1966 (except for the Royal Chapel).

§ It also until 1907 housed the Army Medical School. The architect was a War Department surveyor named *Mennie* (NT).

approved. But the building is now almost wholly empty, the centrepiece fire-damaged; the only part still in use is the ROYAL CHAPEL at the back of the centrepiece, a strangely astylar building, with a very wide coved roof and galleries on cast-iron pillars and brackets all round. The chancel has tall windows in wider frames with Ionic columns in between. Notable REREDOS, with three wide segmental-headed arches, and STAINED GLASS of the Ascension in the E window, *c.*1875.* Well planted grounds. The present hospital quarters are in wartime buildings behind the original block. From the Hound direction the skyline is distinctly romantic, with the rhythm of towers, turrets, cupolas, and central dome, rising above the trees which hide the main bulk of the buildings. The hospital had its own railway station, which still exists.

The VILLAGE is a Victorian period piece; villas on the low wooded cliff, brick terrace houses behind. The former MARKET HALL, now a warehouse, has a massive broad frontage like a chapel, with an odd pediment. The RAILWAY STATION, 1867, originally a terminus, is typical L. & S.W.R. work of the period, in the Tite tradition, simple Italianate-Classical, seven bays with heavy eaves, the centre three bays recessed and containing three round-arched doorways, under a hooded canopy.

NETLEY MARSH *3010*

ST MATTHEW. 1855 by *J. P. Harrison* of Oxford (cf. Hursley), and a design of some character. Nave and chancel, bell-turret on the W bay of the chancel. Hence inside there are two chancel arches. Their corbels have naturalistic vine, strawberry, oak, and one rather stiff-leafy species. Very narrow aisles. The piers are octagonal, but have a square vertical piece on top into which the single-chamfered arches die. To reach the square from the octagon pointed-trefoiled stop-chamfers are used. It results in a very unexpected junction.

NEW ALRESFORD *5030*

New as against Old, because this is a made little town, founded and laid out by Bishop de Lucy of Winchester in 1200. It is nothing like as elaborate as the French bastides or Winchelsea – just one wide street, running S–N. The reason for the founding

*The chapel was used alternately by different denominations, including the Roman Catholics, till *c.*1920.

of the Winchester new towns was not military but simply to reap advantages from a place where building lots were let against money rents instead of rents in kind. It made procedure simpler and income safer. The most interesting thing about New Alresford, however, is not its plan, but the grand reservoir to its NE, dammed at its W end. The canalizing of the Itchen above Winchester was a useful enterprise, again of Bishop de Lucy's. The pond is now 30 acres in area but was originally 200.

BROAD STREET is the principal street, broad indeed, especially by C13 standards. It runs towards the bridge. It now has two rows of trees, and the houses l. and r. are agreeable without exception. Even the shop windows cannot defeat the claim that this is Hampshire's best village street. Most of the houses are rendered. None stand out. The best are perhaps Nos 1–3 at the corner of West Street, with a broad doorcase with Doric pilasters, and No. 47, not rendered, five bays, with wooden cross-windows. Both are late C17. From the N end of Broad Street one reaches the BRIDGE, medieval on the W side, but small fry, and then the lake and the causeway.

From the S end of Broad Street EAST STREET runs E. No. 6 is another five-bay house. The pretty doorcase is later C18. No. 5 (NATIONAL PROVINCIAL BANK), early C18, grey headers and red dressings, five bays with a central projection framed by giant pilasters and carrying a broken pediment. A tall arched window reaches into it.* Then again nice modest houses l. and r.

WEST STREET has first the dreary but unobtrusive TOWN HALL, yellow brick with red and black brick. Three bays and three-bay pediment. It ought to be rendered. Then No. 9 (LLOYDS BANK), of five bays, with a Later Georgian doorcase with Ionic columns and a broken pediment. The POST OFFICE also has a nice doorcase. At the foot of West Street starts POUND HILL. The METHODIST CHURCH of 1825 lies back. It is not big, of brick, three bays with a three-bay pediment. Its l. neighbour is a three-storeyed early C18 house of five bays, grey brick with red dressings.

ST JOHN BAPTIST. The church lies away to the S from the main T of the streets. It is alas a disappointing church. Flint. Early C14 W tower with a C17 brick top. The rest is mostly by *Sir Arthur Blomfield*, 1898.‡ Only the blocked S doorway is early C14 again, at the W end of the S aisle is a C13 lancet, the

*The façade is a replica of that of Cheriton House.
‡The church replaces one of 1694 (RH).

E window of the N chapel has later C13 shafting, and the N doorway is Perp. – SCULPTURE. On the W wall of the nave fairly high up a Saxon Crucifixus, small figure on a larger cross, but the whole quite small. – PLATE. Cup, 1564; Paten on foot, 1694; large Flagon, 1728; Paten, 1729. – MONUMENTS. Three cartouche tablets in the style of 1690, but dated 1757, 1762, 1763, all three obviously by the same hand.

NEWBIES *see* BAUGHURST

NEWLANDS MANOR *see* MILFORD-ON-SEA

NEW MILTON *see* MILTON

NEWNHAM

7050

ST NICHOLAS. 1847, neo-Norman. Flint, with a NW tower carrying a sort of Rhenish helm (cf. Sompting, Sussex). Original Norman remains are the tower S doorway with a roll-moulding and plain capitals, the nave W doorway with decorated capitals, and the chancel arch with a curious zigzag of 45 degrees only, chip-carved. – PLATE. Set of 1730; Almsdish of 1840.

NEW PLACE *see* SHEDFIELD

NEWTON VALENCE

7030

ST MARY. The W tower is E.E. (one small W lancet), but has a Perp W doorway and a brick top of 1812.* Nave and chancel look Victorian (restoration 1871), but are E.E., cf. the S lancet and in the chancel more lancets, the priest's doorway with inner segmental arch, the E window of three stepped lancets very close together and under one arch, and see also the pointed-trefoiled PISCINA. Mounted in it is a C12 PILLAR PISCINA. Wide N chapel of *c.*1300 attached to the nave. – BELL. C14, with an inscription in English. – PLATE. Set of 1725.

MANOR HOUSE, to the E. A five-bay addition to an older house is supposed to date from 1787. Yellow brick. Round the corner a canted bay window.

PELHAM PLACE, $1\frac{1}{2}$ m. W. A very pretty Gothic villa of *c.*1820. Three gables arranged symmetrically, white wooden oriels

*By *J. Dyer* and *J. Parfect*. According to the Rev. Basil Clarke, the restoration was by *Blomfield*.

under them, and on the ground floor a stone veranda with four-centred heads to the arches. The gables are very heavily detailed. The windows have hood-moulds and some ogee hood-moulds. Porte-cochère round the corner. (Central hall, skylit with spacious staircase. MHLG)

KITCOMBE HOUSE. $1\frac{3}{4}$ m. NW. Brick. Five bays, two storeys, with parapet.

4060

NEWTOWN

1 m. N of Burghclere

ST MARY AND ST JOHN BAPTIST. 1865 by *Woodyer*. Flint, with a N porch tower with shingled broach-spire. The details vaguely in the style of *c.*1300. The E window tracery is fanciful. N arcade of round piers, the round capitals decorated with sprays of wild flowers, including ferns and buttercup. Victorian church architects can be divided into the correct and the fanciful, the archaeologists and the original. Woodyer is certainly one of the latter. – STAINED GLASS. The E and W windows must be by *Hardman*.

SWAN INN. C16. Timber-framed, with closely set studs. Over-restored.

6010

NEWTOWN [DL]

2 m. S of Soberton

HOLY TRINITY. 1848–50 by *Colson*. Lancet windows.

NEWTOWN *see* SOUTHAMPTON, pp. 520, 561

NEWTOWN PARK *see* SOUTH BADDESLEY

NORTHAM *see* SOUTHAMPTON, pp. 519, 561

4020

NORTH BADDESLEY [DL]

Village and church are ages apart. The village is a conglomeration of C20 housing and industry on a former common; the church, together with the few scattered houses of the original hamlet, is in rural seclusion to the N.

ST JOHN. A delightful building, set on a hillbrow with a view over miles of mainly wooded country. Small nave and chancel of equal width, with a slight difference in the roof height between them, the chancel C15, the nave of uncertain earlier origin. Walls of rubble and flint, except at the W end, where they are of C17 brick. Miniature embattled W tower, dated 1674, scarcely rising over the ridge of the nave roof. Timber-framed porch on a stone base, with simple balustraded open sides and brick infilling in the gable. It is altogether a medley of local materials. The porch is probably C17, like the simple S doorway of a debased Tudor type. The E window is of three cinquefoiled lights within a flat-arched frame; the chancel side windows, one in each wall, are two-light cinquefoiled, with tall upper quatrefoils, set in square-headed frames. The nave has an attractive SE window, with two cinquefoiled lights and a sexfoil above, set in an arched frame, with a hood-mould ending with carvings of angels, possibly late C14; the two N nave windows are similar to the chancel side windows, the W one medieval, the E one a copy. Inside there is a slight C17 atmosphere tempered with C20 high churchmanship. – The SCREEN sets the tone, a very attractive, simple design inscribed 'T.F. 1602', with turned balusters and a slightly carved cross-beam, on which stands a C20 rood. It is said to have come from North Stoneham (p. 358n). – The PULPIT looks of a piece with the screen and is probably coeval; it has plain panels and a well-shaped, simply carved sounding-board projecting over only part of the width of the pulpit. – The WEST GALLERY has a C20 panelled front, but may originally have dated from 1822, when the double square-headed 'churchwarden' window lighting it, high in the S wall, was probably put in. The nave has an open timber roof, but the chancel has an attractive barrel roof. The church was restored, clearly with great sensitivity, in 1878–89 by *G. G. Scott* (according to the church handbook); this must refer to the younger Scott.* – FONT. C14, plain, octagonal. – PLATE. Cover and Paten, 1618; Paten on foot, 1716. – MONUMENTS. C15 tomb-chest in the chancel, with quatrefoil panels and Purbeck marble slab. – Also in the chancel, high in the NE angle (but removed at the time of writing for repairs to the wall), a massive wall-monument, framed by Tuscan columns and surmounted by a rounded pediment, to John More † 1620. – The temporary removal of the monument has revealed WALL PAINTING in a simple sparse pattern of a regularly repeated symbol, like an elaborated lower-case 't', with a thick double red line along the bottom of the pattern. Presumably all the

* Mr Taylor says that the Scott in question must be *John Oldrid Scott*.

chancel walls were covered with this design. The wall surfac also contains remains of superimposed later wall painting possibly of the C17, with fragments of inscriptions in Gothi lettering.

BADDESLEY MANOR, opposite the church. The successor of th medieval Preceptory of the Knights Hospitallers, originall a cell of that at Godsfield (p. 239) but after 1365 the head quarters of the Hospitallers in Hampshire. Nothing visibl remains of the Preceptory; the house has a main rectangula block of brick, *c.*1780, but altered in the C19, when a strap work parapet was added. Ancillary parts of the building ar older, with C17 and possibly C16 brickwork. To the W of th church and manor is a C16 or early C17 house with a tile-hun upper storey – unusual for this part of Hampshire.

NORTH CHARFORD MANOR *see* BREAMORE

NORTH END *see* PORTSMOUTH, pp. 441, 446

NORTHERWOOD *see* LYNDHURST

NORTH FORELAND LODGE *see* SHERFIELD-ON-LODDON

NORTH HAYLING *see* HAYLING ISLAND

5030

NORTHINGTON

ST JOHN EVANGELIST. 1887–90 by *Sir T. G. Jackson* for Lor Ashburton of The Grange. A typical estate church proudl provided by the squire. Flint and stone chequer. Also flush work. Big W tower of Somerset type. N aisle. Polygonal aps Perp windows. S porch curiously domestic. What looks like rood-stair turret is access to the pulpit. Disappointing interio – MONUMENTS. Robert Henley, first Earl of Northbrook, 1786. Large inscription plate. Above crying putto in relie and above him obelisk with two roundels with coats of arm and garlands. – Baring Family, 1848 by *Westmacott Jun.*, hi *magnum opus*. Below, the entrance to the vault, complete wit the door rendered in stone – a Baroque to Canova moti Above, two seated figures, one an angel with the key, the othe seated on the ledge. Sentimental, but restrained. – Busts *c.*1875 of the fourth Lord Ashburton and his wife, period pieces.

THE GRANGE. *See* p. 258.

NORTH STONEHAM [DL] *4010*

The church is in rural isolation on the edge of a former park, in the midst of the narrow but effective green belt between Southampton and Eastleigh.

ST NICHOLAS. An intriguing and problematical building, with a three-gabled E termination and a W tower, looking like a Devon church. Nave, chancel, and aisles continuing into chapels; a rectangle except for the tower and N porch. The church was rebuilt at some time between 1590 and about 1610* in an interesting Gothic Survival manner, but incorporating older features (not necessarily from the previous church on the site). It was restored in 1826, and again (by *Bodley*) in the late C19. The tower is of ashlar, in two tall stages, with plain double bell-openings in arched frames on three sides, battlements, and thin crocketed pinnacles; typical work of *c.*1600. But re-set in the W wall is a C13 window of three lancets, the centre one higher, elaborately moulded and shafted within, and contained within an arched internal frame which has been truncated at the sides, indicating that it was once set in a space of greater width. It was probably the E window of a church of some pretension. The aisles are also of ashlar, mainly Perp in character, but the simple round-headed N doorway and the Elizabethan-looking porch give away their true date. The side windows are all square-headed, of three or four lights; they are all cusped now, but the cusping looks original only in the E window on the S side; the other windows are said to have been uncusped before Bodley restored them.‡ The E and W windows of the aisles are all three-light Perp in arched frames, but differing in details and looking, for the most part, authentically medieval; all or some of them are probably re-used. The E wall of the chancel is built of rubble, and is obviously earlier than the ashlar walls of the aisles and chapels; presumably it is part of the medieval church, and the three-light Perp E window is a feature *in situ*. Inside there is no structural division between nave and chancel, except for short stretches of wall between the three-bay nave arcades and two-bay chan-

* Largely at the expense of the incumbent, the Rev. Lewis Alcock, who had been chaplain to the Earl of Southampton.

‡ But cf. the even later Perp windows at Bishops Waltham, p. 105.

cel arcades, against which a chancel screen probably originally rested.* The nave arcades are simple: plain arches of two chamfered orders on octagonal piers, late medieval in character; they could either be surviving features of the earlier church or Gothic Survival. The chancel arcades are altogether different. The capitals, with a series of hollow mouldings rounded above and pointed below, are typical work of *c.*1600; the arches are well moulded; the piers and responds of quatrefoil section with hollows in the diagonals on the N side (but not the S) would by themselves seem to be of early C14 date – it is just possible that they are older features re-used to support the capitals and arches of *c.*1600. The E window is set internally in a frame with wide splays in which are two niches, with traceried panels, pinnacles, and crocketed finials – clearly Gothic Revival work of 1826.

FURNISHINGS. STAINED GLASS. A series of heraldic windows of 1826 illustrating the ancestry of the Fleming family was shattered by bomb blast. Fragments are re-set in the aisle windows; others are at St Michael, Bassett (p. 571). The E window of the same date by *Edwards* of Winchester was completely destroyed. – PULPIT. By *Bodley*. – PLATE. Silver-gilt Cup and Paten, 1702; Paten, 1702; Flagon, given 1713. – MONUMENTS. On the chancel floor is a gravestone inscribed, in Gothic lettering, to Slavonian sailors (members of a Venetian guild) who died at Southampton in 1491. No plausible reason can be suggested, other than the dedication of the church, for these sailors to have been buried as far out as North Stoneham, and it is more likely that their grave was in fact in Southampton, the slab having been moved out to Stoneham at a later date – possibly at the time of the rebuilding of the church. St Mary, Southampton (which had the town's chief medieval graveyard) was largely demolished in 1550, but part of the medieval church is known to have survived longer, and both the slab and some of the re-used materials might have come from there.‡ – Large tomb of Sir

* The screen at North Baddesley (p. 355), dated 1602 and engraved T. F. (which could stand for Sir Thomas Fleming), is said to have come from North Stoneham. If this is so, the pulpit at North Baddesley, which is similar in style, must have come from Stoneham too.

‡ Mr F. Greenhill says that 'the slab is certainly foreign work; the stone looks like Tournai stone, while the inscription is Italian. The very ornate capitals have a rather Lombardic flavour. The shield bears what appears to be the Imperial eagle. The translation appears to be: "The burial place of the guild of the Sclavonians"' (information passed on by Mr G. McHardy).

Thomas Fleming, Lord Chief Justice, † 1613, and his wife; their reclining effigies in tiers. Two obelisks l. and r. Marble rear-piece without much decoration, and two bearded allegorical figures; coats of arms above; kneeling figures of eight children below. – Elaborate wall-monument to Admiral Lord Hawke † 1781, by *J. F. Moore*, in marble of various colours. Representation of a sarcophagus with detailed rendering of the battle of Quiberon Bay in relief, coat of arms, urn, and draped standards above, all contained within a blank arch of Gothic shape, in relief. – Rev. Stephen Sloane † 1812, by *Chantrey*, showing a draped urn on a plinth against which are a chalice, a pelican in her piety, a book, and a spray of flowers. – Tablet to John Fleming † 1802, by *P. M. van Gelder*; half-draped urn. – Tablet to John Fleming † 1844, with portrait in relief in a sunk oval, very elegant and skilful; by *R. C. Lucas* of Chilworth. – Two First World War memorial panels, of lead, in the porch, by *Eric Gill*.

NORTH STONEHAM PARK. The house, by *Hopper*, 1818, has long been demolished,* but the former STABLES remain, converted into a farmhouse (Park Farm): in yellow brick with gabled wings, a square doorway in each wing surmounted by a recessed rounded panel, the brickwork flanking the doorways being brought out in rusticated pattern. Nearer the church TEMPLE LODGE, presumably by *Hopper*, very ruinous at the time of writing; small, simple rectangle with Ionic colonnade and pediment at either end, the W one having been walled up when the temple was converted into a lodge.‡ There is a single window with moulded frame in the N wall.

OLD RECTORY, nearly opposite the church. Large, two-storeyed, yellow brick, *c.*1800, with rusticated doorcase and an expansive bow window on the S front.

WELLINGTON SPORTS GROUND (University of Southampton). Good PAVILION by *Ronald Sims*.

NORTH WALTHAM

5040

ST MICHAEL. 1865–6 by *J. Colson*. Nave and chancel and neat bell-turret with shingled spire. The window details *c.*1300. But inside is a N arcade which, while largely also of 1865–6, has enough original work of *c.*1200 to be regarded as authentic. Round piers, square, chamfered abaci, single-chamfered

*Cf. Chilworth Manor, p. 167n.

‡According to Prosser the temple is a copy of the Temple of Ceres at Eleusis.

pointed arches. Medieval also the PISCINA with its crocketed gable. This of course is Dec. – FONT. Octagonal, Perp, with quatrefoils. – PLATE. Chalice and Paten of secular pattern, 1599; Silver-gilt Paten, 1681.

WHEATSHEAF INN, ¾ m. SW. On the A30. Late Georgian. Front of five bays and two storeys. Red brick. The windows are all set in giant arches which instead of capitals and abaci have a raised block of flint. Also flint keystones.

7050

NORTH WARNBOROUGH

¾ m. NW of Odiham

Administratively North Warnborough is part of Odiham, but visually it has its own existence. It has no church, but a string of pleasant houses, though none outstanding.

Starting from the S there is first, S of the Post Office, THATCH COTTAGE, C15, of cruck construction. The main group is a little further N, CEDAR TREE HOUSE, late C18, of three bays, and RED HOUSE, late C17, of five bays, with wooden cross-windows and a hipped roof. Towards the N end a long row of C15 to C16 timber-framed cottages; restored.

½ m. NE is LODGE FARM HOUSE, with a brick front of *c.*1700. Big shaped central gable. Later Tuscan porch. (But behind the gable the remains of a C15 to C16 great hall originally through two storeys. Above the first floor remains a heavy arched truss. MHLG)

½ m. W is ODIHAM CASTLE, reached by the towpath just N of the canal bridge. Its keep is all that remains, an eminently picturesque object of flint with large shapeless (or shapely) holes for windows. It dates from *c.*1207–12, is octagonal, the only octagonal keep in England, and has thin buttresses (2 in. wide, 4 in. deep). It was three storeys high.

NORTON MANOR HOUSE *see* WONSTON

3010

NURSLING [DL]

Nursling is the site of the monastery from which St Boniface (or St Winfrid) went in the C8 to convert the Germans to the Christian faith, one of the most important acts of evangelization in European history. The Danes destroyed the monastery; O. G. S. Crawford thought that it probably stood in the vicinity of the present church.

ST BONIFACE. Simple, essentially early C14, but retaining evidence of an earlier church; restored, conservatively, by *Street* in 1881 and by *F. W. Kinnear Tarte* in 1890. Nave, chancel, S transept, and shingled steeple over the S porch, the steeple taller and more substantial than the usual Hampshire timber-framed bell-turrets. Almost all the windows are of two lights, C14, with simple cusped tracery, apart from the fine three-light reticulated W window. The double-chamfered chancel arch is tall for its width* and, flanking it on the S, is half a small arch cut off by the nave wall, the blocked S part of which is visible in the masonry of the transept; this was the aisle-chapel arch of the C13 predecessor of the present building. The church, despite its small size, is quite impressively proportioned. – PULPIT. Good standard Jacobean, part hexagonal, with lower round-arched panels and smaller panels with strapwork above. – PLATE. Cup, Paten, and Flagon, 1727. – MONUMENTS. Two in the S transept. Fine canopied tomb to Sir Richard Mille † 1613 and his wife, two life-size figures in tiers, each elbow resting on a pillow, the lady's effigy well executed. Obelisks, strapwork, decoration under the canopy; not overdone. – Large tablet to Thomas Knollys, 1751 by *S. Walldin* of Winchester. Pediment, floral garlands, and other decorative detailing.

Opposite the church is NURSLING HOUSE, the former rectory, 1778, with five-bay red-brick front. The lane that leads past the church ends by a side-stream of the Test, where all seems deeply rural. But turn back, and Southampton is soon imminent, with the twenty-five-storey block of flats at Millbrook dominating the skyline, and pylons threading the landscape everywhere.

GROVE PLACE, ½ m. NE. A typical Early Elizabethan house. Brick, with gables and diagonally set chimneys. The front has two far-projecting wings and polygonal turrets in the inner angles, i.e. the same arrangement as at Stiffkey in Norfolk. The windows are all sashed, except two on the first floor in the recessed centre which have mullions and a transom and the low windows immediately below the tower battlements which are mullioned only. The garden side has as its chief motif four big, nearly symmetrically arranged chimneys.

The house has a number of simple but dainty stone fireplaces. The openings have straight shanks and the spandrels

*Mr G. McHardy suggests that the tall narrow proportions of the chancel may imply a Saxon origin.

a little decoration. There are also plaster ceilings with patterns of thin ribs. The best is in the dining room, which also has a lively frieze. The staircase in one of the towers has balusters of the vertically symmetrical kind, and it is highly unusual to have a wooden handrail for a spiral staircase. At the top of the house a long gallery runs all the way along. It has a tunnel-vault with a minimum of ribbing and penetrations for the windows. That is the Elizabethan remains. As for their date, the only evidence is that James Paget came into the property in 1561 and that in the room above the dining room the date 1576 is scribbled in red next to a funny dragon. The house has, however, also some Georgian features, especially the ceiling and the chimneypiece in the room which is now the chapel and the door surrounds in the library.

NURSTED HOUSE *see* BURITON

6040

NUTLEY

The church has been pulled down.

MANOR FARMHOUSE. It has a date 1814, and so one can see what a small farmhouse was like at that date. Widely spaced horizontal segment-headed windows.

MOUNDSMERE MANOR, 1½ m. SE. The pattern of the sumptuous Edwardian mansion. Built in 1908–9 by *Sir Reginald Blomfield* for Wilfred Buckley. The model for the style was Hampton Court. Two storeys and an attic storey. Brick with ample stone dressings. The entrance side has far-projecting wings. Towards the garden giant pilasters in the centre, round windows with swags in the attic.

5050

OAKLEY

ST LEONARD. 1869 by *T. H. Wyatt*. The cost was *c.*£5,000 (PF). SW tower with much higher stair-turret; nave and chancel. Perp style. Wyatt re-used quite a number of items from the predecessor church: the Perp W doorway and parts of the tower arch, and the W bay of the S aisle with a semicircular respond of *c.*1200 with a capital of very many small scallops and a base with spurs. The arch is pointed and has the usual two slight chamfers. The panelled arch of the E bay is also medieval. It belonged to the Malshanger Chapel, and Malshanger belonged to Archbishop Warham early in the C16. He also built the tower. The most memorable touch of Wyatt's is the internal appearance of the tower stair-turret, with its wildflower corbel and the incised floral decoration higher up. – STAINED GLASS. Inscription below a figure of the Archbishop. – PLATE. Chalice and Paten Cover, 1569; Paten, 1617; Flagon, 1792. – MONUMENTS. Brass to Robert Warham † 1487 and wife, $20\frac{1}{2}$ in. figures. – Knight and Lady *c.*1520. Recumbent effigies of alabaster. At both their pillows pairs of tiny angels. Tomb-chest with shields in quatrefoils.

MALSHANGER HOUSE, $1\frac{1}{2}$ m. N. The house is Late Georgian. It was built after 1806. Stuccoed brick. Entrance side of five bays and two and a half storeys; refaced in the C20, when the porch was added too. Venetian window over. Round the corner two big bows and in between another Venetian window. But what matters most is to the r. of the entrance side: the thin polygonal brick tower remaining of Archbishop Warham's house. It was linked up on the l. to a high wall, probably living quarters, on the r. to a lower wall. The top of the tower is restoration. Traces of blue-brick diapering remain.

OAKLEY PARK, $\frac{5}{8}$ m. SW. Built in 1795, remodelled in 1860. Of 1795 the nine-bay front with two big three-bay bows l. and r. Two and a half storeys; balustrade. The porte-cochère will be of 1860, and also the water tower with its pyramid roof.

ODIHAM 7050

ALL SAINTS. A large flint church, with a brick tower embraced. The tower is of the C17, English bond, with angle pilasters and the bell-openings surrounded by rustication and flanked by pilasters; battlements. The aisles have few and C19 windows. The E end with three gables. The whole a rectangle rather like Basing, but disappointing in all details except for the tower. Perp N porch entrance, pretty Perp N doorway with leaf in the spandrels. The interior shows a more varied history. The two-bay arcades to the chancel chapels are early C13. Round, short piers, octagonal abaci, single-chamfered arches. In the nave W wall the tower arch is early C13, see the imposts and the one slight chamfer. Above the remains of a Dec window. In the chancel E wall is a small doorway, probably to a former E vestry. Both the arcades are high and Late Perp, but they differ considerably. First S, four bays, the slender piers of the often-seen section of four shafts and four diagonal hollows. Moulded arches. Latest Perp the N arcade of three bays with plain octagonal piers, concave-sided capitals, and nearly round double-chamfered arches. – PILLAR PISCINA. Late C12, with a kind of thin crocket capital. – FONT. Round, of chalk, with a black-letter inscription. – PULPIT. 1634. Of the Basingstoke type. Arched upper panels with flower vases, rectangular lower strapwork panels. – SCREEN. Between chancel and N chapel. Single-light divisions. Nothing special. – WEST GALLERIES. 1632, with bulgy columns and sturdy balusters. – COMMUNION RAIL, N chapel. C18. – STAINED GLASS. The three E windows by *Hardman*, 1858 (TK). – PLATE. Silver-gilt Chalice and Paten, 1617, given by the London goldsmith *Robert South*; two Flagons, one of 1680; silver-gilt Paten, 1711. – MONUMENTS. A whole series of brasses, notably a couple of the early C15 (19½ in. figures; nave E). – Mag. William Goode † 1498, priest (17½ in.). – Knight, early C16 (23½ in. to below the knees). – Agnes Chapman † 1522 (18½ in.). – Elizabeth Haydock *c.*1540 (19 in.). – On the S wall of the N chapel Elizabethan tablet with an ogee top. No figures; no inscription. – (CURIOSUM. A HUDD or funeral shelter for the parson to be out of the rain at funeral services. It looks like a sentry box.)

Against the N side of the churchyard STOCKS and WHIPPING POST.

S of the church the ALMSHOUSES, founded in 1623. Brick, one-storeyed, three sides of a courtyard. In the back range three doorways with four-centred heads.

The church stands away to the S of the High Street. Near it a few minor streets, especially THE BURY with some good timber-framed houses.

The HIGH STREET has much of interest and ought to be perambulated properly. Starting from the Winchfield–Aldershot fork, i.e. the E, first on the N side WHITE HOUSE, 1812, with a Greek-Doric porch. Then OLD HOUSE with pretty Venetian ground-floor windows, late C18. Then opposite MARYCOURT, the only splendid house at Odiham, early C18. Dark brick, five bays, with a gorgeous shell-hood on carved brackets above the doorway. Further on DANESHILL SCHOOL with a Tuscan porch, then, after the King Street turn, a charming late C18 shop front with dainty details. Opposite the GEORGE HOTEL. This has a Georgian front with porch, but C16 timber-framing inside and behind. Inside also a wooden Elizabethan chimneypiece said to come from Basing House. On the same side down a lane, through a brick barn to PALACE GATE BUILDINGS, an irregular C17 group of which the major part is a formal three-bay front with projecting centre and raised brick quoins. Then the VICARAGE. 'C15–16, altered' says the VCH. Centre and two gabled wings, the l. one of brick, the r. one timber-framed. Opposite THE CLOSE, C18, white, of five bays with a hipped roof and a pediment with a tall arched window below, and then WESTERN HOUSE, charming, late C18, with tripartite windows with blank segmental arches.

Finally, opposite once more, THE PRIORY, the most interesting house in Odiham. It consists of three ranges. To the S plain, sensible Queen Anne, seven bays, no ornament. To the W some Early Tudor bricks under the W gable of the S range, continued in the W range by a miniature brick porch, of two storeys, *c.*1530 and entirely like such Norfolk buildings as Great Snoring and East Barsham. Polygonal buttress shafts, four-centred doorhead, sweet little central oriel. But the E range is of the C15, two-storeyed, of flint, with cinquefoiled tops to the one-light windows and also similar two- and three-light windows.

ODIHAM CASTLE. *See* North Warnborough.

KING JOHN'S HUNTING LODGE, 1¼ m. NE in the woods. An 71
eye-catcher for Dogmersfield Park. Georgian, but with a pretended Jacobean front, i.e. three gables, the middle one higher, shaped, with steep ogee tops carrying urns. Nothing behind the gables. In front of the house a lake.

OLD ALRESFORD 5030

ST MARY. The church is of 1753, the W tower of 1769. The tower has a doorway with rustication of alternating sizes, twin-arched bell-openings, and a parapet sweeping up at the corners to ball finials. All this looks 1720 rather than 1770. The church is aisleless and has transepts. The materials are flint with brick bands. The interior was thoroughly gothicized and transepts added in 1862 by *J. Colson*. – PLATE. C17 Cup and Paten; Paten on foot, 1679; Flagon, 1717. – MONUMENTS. Mrs Rodney † 1757. A splendid, alas unsigned, monument of white, pink, and black marble with many garlands etc. Two seated allegorical figures with book and anchor on the ledge on which the Rococo sarcophagus stands. Bust in circular recess at the top and above it large broken pediment.* – Mrs

*Mr John Newman assigns the monument convincingly to *Sir Henry Cheere*, on the strength of the allegorical figures being identical on the signed Polehill monument at Otford in Kent († 1755).

Davenport † 1760, friend and servant of Dr Hoadly, rector (*see* below). Small oval, with a doggie guarding the keys. – Esther North † 1823. By *Behnes*. White marble. Large frontal angel with big wings and one arm raised. Below to his l. a pillar with profile bust. – MAUSOLEUM. C.F.G.R. Schwerdt † 1839. Temple front, and inside a large Italian relief of *c*.1500. Seated Virgin suckling the child. Small angels above and below

OLD ALRESFORD PLACE, N of the church. Built as the rectory by Dr Hoadly. The style is Early Georgian. Five bays, two and a half storeys. Red headers and rubbed dressings. Broad angle pilasters (grey headers) in three tiers. Slight middle projection. Parapet. Additions to the N in the same style. The drawing room is said to be of 1817. It is tripartite, but the columns, though original, have only recently been re-erected. The chimneypieces are original.

OLD ALRESFORD HOUSE, E of the church. Built by Sir George Rodney Brydges about 1752. Red brick, two storeys, seven-bay front with projections and one recession. High attic, three-bay pediment. The doorway with Roman Doric columns and a bucrania frieze must be later.

OLD DITCHAM FARM *see* BURITON

OLD WINCHESTER HILL *see* MEONSTOKE

OTTERBOURNE

4020

ST MATTHEW. 1837–9 by *W. C. Yonge*, the squire and Charlotte Yonge's father, with *Owen Carter*.* Blue brick, just as if it were 1965. Nave; low N aisle. Transepts. Polygonal bell-turret. Polygonal apse. Apse and aisle Later Victorian. For the apse we have the date 1875. The architect was *T. H. Wyatt*, and the work was paid for by Charlotte Yonge (Rev. B. Clarke). The roof is the best piece of 1837–9, steep, with very thin timbers and Perp panels with cusped arches. – COMMUNION RAIL. A low balustrade, excellently carved with openwork foliage scrolls and figure work. According to the VCH from an abbey in Flanders. No doubt late C17. It was bought by Yonge in London. – STAINED GLASS. An illuminating comparison can be made between S transept 1847‡ and

* Yonge had studied military engineering in his youth. Mr A. Symondson contributed this interesting piece of information.

‡ By *Evans* of Shrewsbury. Information received from Anthony Symondson.

N transept, no doubt by *Powell* and looking *c.*1875. – PLATE. Paten of 1641.

OLD CHURCH, ½ m. SE, on the main road, by the streams. Chancel only. C13. S lancets, the E window with plate tracery. The chancel arch narrow and with, to its l. and r., shafted niches for reredoses of subsidiary altars.

(SCHOOL. Also by *Yonge*, this time without Carter. It incorporates an E.E. doorway from the old church.)

OVERTON

5040

Overton consists of the old village with church and manor houses on one side of the Test, and a New Town erected by Bishop de Lucy of Winchester in the early C13 on the other side of the river. It has a wide main street, not as straight and impressive as Alresford or Downton (Wilts.), and two streets parallel to it and two across forming an elementary, very imprecise grid.

ST MARY. Externally all is Victorian, the ashlar W tower (rebuilt in 1909)* and the flint nave and chancel. Medieval is no more than the N aisle W lancet, re-set, a chancel N window with plate tracery, and parts of two minor doorways. Internally there is more to keep one occupied. Three-bay N and S arcades of *c.*1200. Round piers, square but chamfered abaci, multi-scalloped capitals, pointed, single-chamfered arches. The next element, in terms of chronology, is the chancel: mid C13 according to the plate tracery (*see* above). The single-frame roof with tie-beams may well be contemporary. The W tower is *c.*1500, and so are the W bays of the two arcades, built to connect the old nave with the new tower. Only the typically Dec arch from the tower to the S was re-set. Where was it originally? – STAINED GLASS. The E window by *Kempe*, *c.*1900–5. – PLATE. Chalice and Paten, 1676; Flagon, 1762; Almsplate, 1764. – MONUMENT. A funerary inscription on the inner sill of the chancel NE window: 'Hic jacet do. Willms Savage quondam rector istius ecclesie' etc.

COURT FARM HOUSE, W of the church. Five bays, two storeys. The middle bay projects a little and carries a broken pediment. Hipped roof.

QUIDHAMPTON FARMHOUSE, ⅜ m. NE. A coal-shed SW of the house is a Norman chapel. Plain rectangle of flint, laid

* By *Cancellor & Hill* (Rev. Basil Clarke).

herringbone-wise. The E wall is missing. Blocked S doorway. Traces of a S and a N window.

POLHAMPTON FARM, 1 m. NE. C17 brick house. On the side and at the back moulded brick cornice and mullioned brick windows of five lights. (A good panelled room inside.)

ROUND BARROW CEMETERY. *See* Steventon.

2030 OVER WALLOP

ST PETER. The chancel rebuilt in 1866 by *Pearson*,* the rest terribly over-restored in 1875. The interior tells its story with a minimum of authentic details. Two-bay N arcade of the late C12: round pier, round abaci, capitals of flat, broad, smooth, upright leaves (cf. Nether Wallop). Round arches of one step and one chamfer. S arcade with moulded capitals, and pointed arches with two slight chamfers, i.e. early C13. (The S aisle E window is authentic and Dec.) N arcade third and fourth bays fully C13. To the earlier part of the N arcade belongs on the outside the re-set N aisle W doorway and the S doorway. The good, plain W tower with its saddleback roof is Pearson's. Its date is not recorded. – FONT. Big, Perp, octagonal. With quatrefoils. – SCREEN. Of wrought iron.

TOWNSEND HOUSE, at the NW end of the village. Five bays, two storeys. Doorway with broken pediment on Doric pilasters.

LONG BARROW, 3½ m. WNW. This is a small example of this class of monument, being only 100 ft long and 50 ft wide at its broader E end, where it stands 5 ft high. The side ditches are clearly visible.

5030 OVINGTON

ST PETER. 1866 by *Colson*. SW porch tower with wooden top. Aisleless, but with transepts, rather an early C19 taste. The windows are Early Dec. – PLATE. Cup of 1807; Paten and Flagon of 1811.

5020 OWSLEBURY

ST ANDREW. The chancel is E.E. S and N lancets and a chancel arch with two slight chamfers. The C17 did a certain amount

* According to Mr Hubbuck, who considers the church characteristic of the transitional years between his early correct Camdenian Middle Pointed and the individual Gothic of his maturity.

to the exterior. The date 1675 is on the W tower. Is the Perp two-light W window of that time? And how about the cross-gabled aisles and their Perp windows? The SE looks original. The VCH calls the others C17. The interior had two cast-iron columns l. and r. They were encased in wood and other wooden pillars added in 1956. – COMMUNION RAIL. C18. – N aisle PANELLING. Made of Jacobean bench ends. – PLATE. Cup of 1552, a remarkably early post-Reformation date; Almsdish of 1680. – MONUMENT. Second Lord Carpenter † 1749. Bust in front of a grey obelisk with garlands. Urns l. and r. The inscription plate curves forward. The monument is a fine piece, and one would like to know the sculptor.

LONGWOOD HOUSE, by *Devey*, 1880, has been pulled down. It was Elizabethan with gables and mullioned and transomed windows. The main façade was quite asymmetrical.

PAMBER END

6050

PAMBER PRIORY. The Benedictine priory of Pamber was founded about 1120–30 by Henry de Port as a cell of Cerisy-la-Forêt. It was dissolved as an alien priory by Henry VI in 1414. The remains of the priory are largely Norman, but not so early. They are exclusively of the church. The crossing tower dominates the scene. It stands on its four arches, but of details only the completely plain imposts and the roll mouldings of the W and E arches remain. The tower itself has inside on each side three tall blank arches with thin continuous rolls. The small windows are set in them. On the NW side there is a square stair-turret. The tower now has a pyramid roof, and probably always has had one, though it is possible that it had one more storey. Standing under the crossing one looks into the majestic and serene chancel, which is preserved completely. It is very long and has first on the N and S depressed, blocked arches which represent the curiously low access to former chapels E of the transepts. Above them, high up, are two circular windows on either side, Norman, and nearly unique in this county (cf. the bell-openings at Warnford), though not infrequent in East Anglia. Then follow four lancets N and four S and the beautiful E wall of three widely spaced very long and slender stepped lancets. They have inside a continuous thin keeled roll moulding, oddly set on bases. Fine PISCINA with a trefoiled head. Of the transepts nothing survives, except a short stump of the SW wall with a small doorway into the cloister, and of the nave only the S wall with traces of two doorways into the cloister, and a short stump of the N wall with one shafted jamb of an upper window. The place where the nave W wall was can still be deciphered. The wall continuing the S wall to the W must represent the N wall of the W range of the cloister. – PLATE. Cup, Paten Cover, and Almsdish, Elizabethan. – MONUMENT. C12 coffin lid with a foliated cross with big leaves also issuing from the shaft and an inscription interesting because so early a case of a familiar tag of the later Middle Ages: 'Si quis eris qui transieris, sta, perlege, plora † Sum quod eris, fueramque quod es; pro me precor hora'. – Oaken effigy of a Knight, early C14, about 7 ft long, crossed legs, praying hands, feet against a lion.

WYFORD FARM, ⅝ m. NW. Later C17. Brick, with gables. The original building was L-shaped. The angles have giant pilasters with brick Ionic capitals. The windows have flat raised surrounds. The mullions of the windows are of brick too, though they are cement-rendered. One side is completely symmetrical, with 3-light–1-light–3-light windows on both floors. The doorway is round the corner, and at the back is one window with a steep pediment. Large C20 addition.

3090 PARK

2¼ m. SE of East Boldre

ST JOHN EVANGELIST. By *Sir H. Brakspear*, 1906, nothing special. Brick; low, with an openwork bell-turret on the E end of the nave.

PARK HOUSE *see* HAMBLEDON

PAULSGROVE *see* PORTSMOUTH, p. 467

PEARTREE GREEN *see* SOUTHAMPTON, pp. 592, 593, 597

PELHAM PLACE *see* NEWTON VALENCE

3090 PENNINGTON

ST MARK. 1859 by *C. E. Giles*. Red and yellow brick and a little black brick, inside as well as out. Aiseless and quite dignified. Plate and bar tracery. Bellcote over the E end of the nave.

PENTON MEWSEY

3040

HOLY TRINITY. Nave and chancel; bellcote. Nearly entirely Victorian (1888), but there are indications that the church was indeed Dec, as the restorer made it. One chancel (N) window is supposed to be basically original. It has flowing tracery with small infillings in a reticulation unit, and the chancel arch (two chamfers dying into the imposts) also suggests the Dec style. The chancel S doorway is made up of old pieces, but they look C13 rather than C14. – FONT. Octagonal, Dec, with two small ogee-headed arches per side. – COMMUNION RAIL. Handsome, of twisted balusters; C18. – STAINED GLASS. In a nave S window bits of medieval glass – C15, it seems. – PLATE. Chalice, 1713; Paten, 1714; Almsplate, 1828.

OLD RECTORY (Penton Close). Grandly Victorian. Flint and yellow brick. Many gables and dormers, elaborate hood-moulds. Can the date given (1833) apply? The cost is said to have been £1,700.

NEOLITHIC LONG BARROW, 300 yds NE of Nutbane farm. The barrow now presents the appearance of a very low mound, 180 ft long and 110 ft broad. Excavation showed the surviving mound to be 170 ft long and 75 ft wide at its broader E end, tapering to 25 ft at the W. Beneath the E end was a complicated timber mortuary building showing several phases of construction and four crouched inhumation burials within a small mortuary enclosure. These wooden structures at the E end had been deliberately burnt down before the erection of the mound over them. The barrow has flanking quarry ditches, but these are no longer visible on the ground.

PETERSFIELD

7020

ST PETER. Here is one of the most interesting Norman churches in Hampshire, interesting especially because of the two phases it represents. It began about 1120 as an extremely lavish cruciform church with a crossing tower. The arch to the E is preserved, and the E responds of the N and S arches. They are tripartite and big, with somewhat elementary capitals with volutes. The upper stage was reached, say, about 1130–40. It has three windows to the E, thickly shafted – to the inside, it must be remembered – and one window in the gable above. The shafting of the N and S sides only just starts. But one more piece of evidence is there: the herringbone laying of the flintwork in what was the transept end walls. Then, towards the end of the C12, the nave received aisles and, probably because the crossing tower was never finished or gave trouble, a W tower was provided, and this – a rarity – is embraced by the aisles. Externally this work is recognizable by flat Norman buttressing, some comparatively trustworthy Norman windows, and much neo-Norman reinforcement. Genuine the N and S doorways, one with one order of columns, the other with two. Typically late C12 capitals, e.g. waterleaf. The tower top is Perp. Perp also are N windows. Inside the four-bay arcades are the principal testimony to the late C12 campaign. They have circular piers and on the S side scalloped capitals and square abaci with nicked corners, on the N side round abaci on capitals with trumpet-scallop or characteristic leaves. The arches are round and single-stepped. The tower arch is wide and also single-stepped. (*Sir Arthur Blomfield* in 1873–4 did a lot to the church. His are the clerestory windows, the steep roof-pitch, nearly all the detail in the chancel, vestry, organ chamber, and the N porch, the latter *c.*1885. He also altered the position of windows and designed most of the FURNISHINGS. RH) – FONT. Octagonal, Perp, panelled. – (SCULPTURE. Small wooden Cross by *Alan Durst*, 1955. – STAINED GLASS. S aisle E, by *Lavers & Barraud*. RH) – PLATE. Cup and Cover Paten, 1568; Cup and Cover Paten, given in 1612; Paten on foot, 1721; Almsdishes, 1757 and 1812. – MONUMENTS. Catherine Jolliffe † 1731. By *Samuel Huskisson*. Large tablet. The Latin ought to be read. – John Jolliffe † 1771. Pink and grey marble with an urn. – George Jolliffe † 1799. In the segmental top allegorical figure with naval implements, in the semicircular bottom part the sea and ships. – John Sainsbury, 1801 by *Flaxman*. White marble. Two standing mourners by an urn on a high pedestal.

ST LAURENCE (R.C.), Station Road. 1890–1 by *Kelly*. A handsome church, purely Italian, if it were not for the red brick, and very restrained. Nave without aisles or chapels, octagonal dome, transepts, and chancel. The nave has a segmental vault, another bow to England.

(CONGREGATIONAL CHURCH, next to the College. By *J. B. Surman*, 1882. Gothic and unfortunate. RH)

METHODIST CHURCH, opposite St Laurence. 1903 by *Gordon & Gunton*. Black flint and red brick, with a SW tower and Perp details, churchy, rather ostentatious and very conservative.

(TOWN HALL, Heath Road. Built *c.*1935 by *Seely & Paget.* Quiet and restrained, with generous fenestration. RH)

PERAMBULATION. Petersfield received its first charter from William Earl of Gloucester in the mid C12. The prosperity of the town was wool and cloth. As in so many other places that trade declined in the C17, and the Petersfield we see now gives the impression of an affluent but not spectacularly rich C18 country town. It was on the main London–Portsmouth road and about 1700 had nine inns. Its best houses are all Georgian, though some timber-framed C16 houses also survive.

The perambulation of course starts in THE SQUARE, which faces the N side of the church. It is ennobled by the beautiful equestrian lead STATUE of William III, originally gilded. 66
This was made, probably by *John Cheere*, in 1757 under the will of Sir William Jolliffe of Petersfield House. It stood in the grounds of that house, which was near the church and was pulled down in 1793. The King appears as a Roman, and with a laurel wreath. The horse is not moving. Round the square are C18 buildings mixed with neo-C18 buildings. On the E side is first a three-bay house of blue and red brick, then nine bays of neo, and then the weeny former CORN EXCHANGE of 1866.* On the N side is a humbler eight-bay house, also blue and red, and in the NW corner LLOYDS BANK, a fine red-brick house of about 1760. Five bays, two and a half storeys, doorway with Tuscan columns and a triglyph frieze. Window above with elegant volutes and a pediment. To its l. a timber-framed house with closely-set studs and flint infill.

From the Square the HIGH STREET runs E. On the N side the WESTMINSTER BANK, 1861, stately and Italianate. Then, further on, on the S side, Nos 17–19, early C17, timber-framed with gable, dated 1613. The apsed hood over the doorway must be of *c.*1700. No. 18 opposite has a Roman Doric porch. The corner of Dragon Street (HIGH SCHOOL FOR GIRLS) was formerly a hotel. Late C18. Two canted bay windows to the High Street. Nice doorway.‡

Turn N from this corner, along COLLEGE STREET. At the start the RED LION HOTEL, low, brick, with pediment. Doorway with Roman Doric columns. At the N end of College Street CHURCHER'S COLLEGE. The house dates from 1729. Five bays, three storeys, red and blue brick chequer. Angle pilasters in tiers. Doorway with straight hood on modestly

* Much altered after the First World War (RH).

‡ Demolished 1965.

carved brackets. Panelled parapet. Fine staircase with dainty columnar and twisted balusters.* Back and continue S along DRAGON STREET. Here DRAGON HOUSE, early C18, grey headers and red dressings. But this is only a refronting, and the E side is Elizabethan and timber-framed. Two gables with mullioned windows. Dragon Street and College Street are ruined by the A3 traffic and the garages etc. engendered by it.

From the S end of Dragon Street S to THE CAUSEWAY. On the r. at once THE GRANGE. Malm, of seven bays, with raised window surrounds and a doorway with Tuscan columns and pediment. The side and back have brick trim and segment-headed windows.

From the S end of Dragon Street W is SUSSEX ROAD. No. 32 is a handsome, white three-bay house with a segmental porch of Tuscan columns and l. and r. tripartite windows with a segmental arch filled by an Adamish fan. From the S end of Dragon Street E, following Hylton Street, one reaches THE SPAIN, where originally markets of the Spanish wool merchants were held. On the N side is a low five-bay house of grey headers and red dressings and to its r. a higher four-bay house with a nice late C18 doorway. Finally NE from The Spain along SHEEP STREET, past a timber-framed C16 house with narrowly spaced upright timbers, back to The Square.

If one leaves The Square at its NW corner and walks straight W, down SWAN STREET, passing SWAN COURT, a deplorable neo-Georgian office building by *Sir John Brown & Henson*, one reaches a recent building of some interest: the factory of U. K. PLASTICS in FRENCHMAN'S ROAD, by *Carter, Salaman, MacIver & Upfold*, 1962–3. It is alas rather gimmicky with its hexagons in plan, its hundreds of horizontal slit-lozenge windows, and its hyperbolic paraboloid roof.

(WINDWARD, Reservoir Lane, Tilmore. By *Barry Parker*, built in 1926–7. Since enlarged twice.)

ROUND BARROWS, on Petersfield Heath, ¾ m. SE. On the heath are twenty-one round barrows, the majority of bowl type, but including two fine bell barrows, one disc, and four saucer barrows.

BUTSER HILL, 2¾ m. SW of Petersfield. On this great flat-topped hill 889 ft above sea level are a number of earthworks. On the spur called Ramsdean Down are three BOWL BAR-

* The present buildings of the College are at the top of Ramshill. They are of 1881, by *G. R. Crickmay* of Weymouth (RH).

ROWS, each approximately 60 ft in diameter and 4 ft high. All have depressions in their centres suggesting previous examination. On the flat top of the hill are two large round barrows set close together. The S example is a BOWL BARROW, badly damaged by rabbits; the N one is a great BELL BARROW, 135 ft in diameter and 8 ft high, which shows signs of having been robbed. Across the ridge on the SW of the hill which links it with an adjoining hill are three lines of BANKS AND DITCHES which effectively block access to the hill at this point. Finally on the S and SE slopes of the hill are a series of CELTIC FIELDS. Romano-British pottery has been found in this area, although the field systems may have been laid out in the Iron Age.

PETERSON'S TOWER *see* SWAY

PITT 4020

CHURCH. Built in 1858 as a school-cum-chapel at the expense of Charlotte Yonge, who used the royalties of her best seller *The Heir of Redclyffe*.* Designed by *Butterfield*. Nave and chancel in one. Hipped bell-gable. Wide interior. Odd timber roof, with arched braces up to collar-beams. Lancets, plate tracery, and pointed-trefoiled lancets.

PITTLEWORTH MANOR *see* BOSSINGTON

PLAITFORD 2020

ST PETER. Flint and stone. Nave and chancel. Bell-turret with thin shingled spire. Mostly Victorian, but early C13 S and N doorways (ironstone with one continuous chamfer) and one small original (re-set) lancet in the vestry S wall (ironstone too). – FONT. A C13 bowl with angle spurs, used upside down, and completely re-tooled. – TILES. Plenty on the chancel S wall.

POKESDOWN *see* BOURNEMOUTH, pp. 118, 123, 128

POLHAMPTON FARM *see* OVERTON

PORTCHESTER [DL] 6000

PORTCHESTER CASTLE. Portchester Castle is built on a low-lying promontory, surrounded on three sides by the sea.

* So Anthony Symondson tells me.

Although traces of C1 occupation have recently been discovered, the main phase of Roman occupation began in the late C3, when a square 9-acre fort was built. The entire defensive wall, 10 ft wide and about 20 ft high, still survives, together with fourteen of its original twenty projecting bastions. Medieval and later refacing has obscured some of the original work, but the Roman masonry, of coursed flint work with horizontal bonding courses of tile and stone at intervals, survives in large stretches.

The projecting bastions are D-shaped and hollow, each with a small tiled drain leading out of the bottom to prevent water-pressure from building up inside. The bastions were originally floored at the top with timber joists which probably supported *ballistae* or other types of defensive light artillery. The fort was entered through four gates: two main gates in the centres of the E and W sides, and two simple posterns in the N and S sides. The main gates each consisted of a 'forecourt' formed by inturning the curtain wall, at the inner end of which was the 10-ft-wide entrance passage flanked by guard houses supporting gate-towers. This type of gate plan is far easier to defend than those usually found on Roman sites. Of the gates nothing is clearly visible above ground, but part of the lower courses of the Westgate can be seen, together with the original back face of the Roman wall, immediately S of the medieval Landgate. Outside the walls the fort was defended by a double ditch system, part of which is still visible. Inside the fort excavation has begun to produce traces of the timber military buildings and of streets.

Archaeological evidence has shown that the fort was constructed in the late C3, possibly by Carausius, and that it was abandoned by about 370. The early abandonment may well be due to a shift from Portchester to Bitterne at this time. The forts on this part of the coast – Portchester, Bitterne, and possibly Carisbrooke – were all part of the 'Saxon Shore' fort system which originated in the latter half of the Roman period to protect the coast against pirate raids.

Recent work has shown that the fort was again occupied in the late C5 or early C6, and that occupation continued sporadically until the Norman period. Several structures belonging to the Saxon period have been found, the best preserved being a timber hall 22 ft by 41 ft, with walls of wattle and daub supported by evenly spaced external buttress posts. Doors lay in the centres of the two long sides, and the

W end of the building was divided into two rooms, one with a hearth. Pottery suggests that the building is of late pre-conquest date and may well be the 'halla' referred to in Domesday.

THE MEDIEVAL CASTLE. The Roman fortress was transformed into a medieval castle in the C12, probably during the middle or later part of the reign of Henry I (1100–35), by the building of a keep and the walling-off of a small inner bailey, with a moat, at the NW corner of the Roman enclosure, the rest of which became a large outer bailey. An Augustinian priory was founded in the castle precinct in 1133, but less than twenty years later this was moved to Southwick (*see* p. 604), probably because the presence of the priory within the castle was inconvenient to both the military and ecclesiastical bodies. The keep was heightened in the mid C12 (historical and documentary evidence suggests before 1175). It was important as a royal fortress in the late C12 and early C13, especially in connexion with military assemblies and embarkations at Portsmouth, which sprang into importance during this period. Later in the C13 the castle was neglected, but in the C14 it came into favour as a royal residence; from *c.*1320 there was a series of alterations and improvements, culminating in large-scale rebuilding of the domestic quarters under Richard II, and making the castle more of a small fortified palace than a capital fortress. In the C15 it again became comparatively neglected; in the C16 it was used to some extent as a base depot associated with Portsmouth and a prison for distinguished captives. Sir Thomas Cornwallis, governor until 1618, carried out some reconstruction. It was sold by the Crown in 1632, but was leased intermittently by private owners for use as a military prison, particularly during the Napoleonic Wars. During the Crimean War there was a serious proposal to turn it into a military hospital, but wiser counsels prevailed, and a new hospital was built at Netley instead. Except for the two outer gateways and the church, all the medieval buildings are contained within the inner bailey.

The KEEP is on the site of the NW angle of the Roman fort, 11
its N and W walls standing slightly forward of the adjoining Roman walls. When first built it had a basement (only a little below ground level), a tall main storey, and high parapet walls which concealed the roof. When it was heightened, two extra storeys were added (the parapet walls becoming the lower parts of the walls of one of the new storeys). It is faced with

fine ashlar, with wide, shallow buttresses on each of the two outward façades (one at each angle and one in the centre of the façade), with impressively stepped footings between the buttresses. The fenestration is best described in relation to the interior. Inside, the whole keep is divided transversely from E to W by a party wall, so that on each floor there were two rooms. The spiral staircase is in the SW angle. Nothing survives of the original floor divisions, since the keep was gutted and entirely refloored when used as a prison; the flooring has been re-arranged and now bears a general relationship to the medieval arrangement. The basement was originally entered only downwards from the first floor; a door was inserted in the E wall of the S compartment in the C14 and renewed with a flat brick frame in the C18. The S compartment has small round-headed windows, two S and one W, which are double-splayed, the inner splays being wider and stepped at the bottom. The N compartment (now inaccessible to the public) is generally similar. The basement was vaulted in the C14; of this the ribs against the walls remain. Access to the main part of the keep is by a stepway (represented by a modern wooden staircase, but on the site of the original one) against the line of the N wall of the fortress, entered through a ruinous round-headed arch and leading to a narrow platform against the E wall of the keep, alongside a complicated fore-building, the ruins of which are described later. A door leads into the S room of the main floor, which has two handsome but somewhat ruinous windows on the S side, roll-moulded and shafted; the E one is now blocked. The W window, a round-headed light, was high in the wall; it was superseded and partly obliterated by a lower window in the C14, but the upper part has been re-opened. The N room, which was the main hall of the keep, has the remains of a fireplace in the middle of the N side, with single-light windows, partly blocked later, to l. and r. There is another single-light window high up in the W wall. At the NE corner of the room is a well-head in a recess, and in the thickness of the W wall (and reached from the S room) is a narrow passageway, recently reinforced with concrete, leading to a garderobe at the NW corner of the keep, lit by small round-headed lights – an unusually well-preserved early medieval sanitary arrangement. The next floor up is on the roof level of the early C12 keep, and the marks of the original valley roofs can still be seen on the E and W walls of each compartment. Underneath the mark of each roof-slope is a small round-headed window, showing that there were garret rooms; there are larger round-headed windows, dating from the time of the heightening of the keep, high in the W wall of each compartment. The topmost floor is lit by two-light windows (two each on the N and S walls of the respective compartments and one in the E wall of each) of a straightforward utilitarian type; the windows themselves are square-headed, but they are contained within round-headed frames, represented outside by recesses of similar shape. These windows are distinctive features of the external elevations. There are single-light square-headed windows in the W walls of the two compartments. The roof is not the original, but may be in a similar position to one inserted in the C14, when the parapets were reconstructed with very low-pitched gables, curiously battlemented, on the E and W sides; the level N and S parapets have no battlements.*

The FOREBUILDING of the keep is very ruinous, and has a complicated history. It was originally coeval with the keep, and had a chapel on an undercroft, built against the S end of the E keep wall; of the chapel only a large recess in the keep wall and parts of the broken S wall, including the jamb of a C12 window and a small C14 doorway which led into the apartments to the S, remain; of the undercroft there is the shell. The chapel was extended to the E, probably in the C13. N of it is a small ruinous late C12 room which was used as a cell, with the remains of an original window high on its E wall and the outline of another in the S wall (blocked when the chapel was extended). N of the cell is the modern stepway on the site of the medieval one, and to the N of that a small room, built over the site of a section of the Roman fortress wall and forward to the line of the N wall of the keep; a sumptuous oriel window, of which the frame survives, was inserted in its outer wall probably in the late C15.

The INNER BAILEY still has its C12 S and E walls more or less intact, with later buildings set against them almost all the way round. It is faced in ashlar (which has worn off in places) and a few later openings pierced in it have been blocked. It is bounded on the outside by a moat (which, however, is irregular in shape, having a marked curve and coming well outside the S wall, suggesting that the moat may have ante-dated the C12 inner bailey, and have been related to a previous defensive work of which there is no other

* The parapets are all in ruins.

evidence). At the SE angle of the bailey is a diagonal square-ended bastion, with small round-headed lights at upper-storey level facing SW and SE, and a ruinous hole where one probably existed facing NE. The INNER GATEHOUSE was originally within a rectangular projection of the S bailey wall, with an upper storey. This is in ruins, with the E and W lights of the upper storey and the inner arch of the doorway, plain and round-headed, remaining. In the early C14 the outer arch of the doorway was replaced by a segmental arch of two orders with thick rounded chamfers, and a beautiful little porch, narrower from N to S than across, was added in front. This has a vault with thick round-chamfered diagonal ribs and thin longitudinal and transverse ridge-ribs, a big and very worn boss in the centre, and very worn angle corbels which look as if they originally had foliage decoration. On the outer face of the porch are three arches, all round-chamfered, of diminishing height inwards, with a portcullis groove between the second and third. In the late C14 another compartment, coarser in character, was built outwards from the earlier porch, with two arches (the outer segmental, and springing from the side walls, without capitals), with another portcullis groove in between. The final addition to the gatehouse came in the C17, and of this there remain the two massive side walls (with no outer arch) with a small sentry's compartment in the thickness of the N wall.

Of the C12 buildings within the inner bailey, other than the keep and its forebuilding, there is very little evidence; fragments of wall arcading in the great hall (described later), and traces of a room over an undercroft (half-underground), set against the Roman N wall of the fortress, which later became the hall of the CONSTABLE'S LODGING, considerably altered by Sir Robert Assheton, Constable of the Castle from 1376 to 1381. The vault of the undercroft was renewed by Assheton; there are only indications of its springing and its E termination against the adjoining walls. The blocking of the hall fireplace is visible against the fortress wall, and there is a small C12 doorway which led from high in the hall to the walkway along the fortress wall.* To the E (and at the NE corner of the bailey) is ASSHETON'S TOWER, of four storeys, built by Assheton and now a substantial shell. On its W side are doorways into the former undercroft, hall, and rampart

* Behind the walkway can be seen the C14 infilling of the inner face of one of the Roman bastions, converted into rooms.

walk (from the first, second, and third storeys), and on its S side are a ruinous arched two-light window in the third storey and a two-light square-headed one in the top storey; the hollow-chamfered cornice is intact.

Between 1366 and 1399 Richard I built his small PALACE, a series of rooms set against the S and W walls of the inner bailey, and the S wall of the keep. This was mostly a new build, but it incorporated Norman fragments, notably parts of two simply moulded arches of a C12 wall-arcade, with shafts and block capitals, on the inside of the N wall of the undercroft of the great hall.* The GREAT HALL was built over a subdivided undercroft in the middle of the S range and was approached through a porch, the shell of which is intact, with a tall, coarsely moulded pointed-arched doorway under a square hood, having trefoiled panels in the spandrels, very much in the Winchester style of the time. There were projecting niches, now very ruinous, for lights on either side of the entrance. The interior of the porch was vaulted (the springings remain), and there was an upper storey (of which the shell survives) reached by a spiral staircase in the SE angle of the porch. A stepway inside the porch (now gone) led to the door into the hall, thickly moulded. Nothing is left of the hall floor, but the N wall remains, with the frames of three tall two-light windows of which only the tops of the tracery are left. A range of small windows and doorways opens into what was the undercroft. E of the hall were the buttery (over) and pantry (under), and farther E the KITCHEN, which was open from floor to roof, all with the remains of various windows facing the courtyard. The W range of the palace included the GREAT CHAMBER, which was larger and more splendid than the great hall, with a range of four tall transomed two-light windows facing the courtyard (their tracery still largely intact except for the S window). Between the middle two is a buttress, and three two-light windows and a doorway open into what was the undercroft. There is an INNER CHAMBER at the SW angle of the palace and, finally, a room used as the EXCHEQUER, with small windows, in the part of the palace against the S wall of the keep (from which the small doorway already noted led into the chapel).

The alterations carried out by Cornwallis in the early C17 were in the E range (S of Assheton's Tower) and in the small

* The MPBW suggests that this may have been on the outside wall of a C12 room which stood to the N.

range against the S bailey wall to the E of the gatehouse; of these there are only the ruined shells. The W wall of the E range had three-light square-headed windows in simplified Perp without cusps (the heads of the lights remain) opening into the main floor and smaller square-headed windows, together with two doorways, one of which is a survival from the C14, which opened into the undercroft. Inside there are the remains of a brick fireplace against the E wall. In the S range, just E of the gatehouse, is a simple C17 doorway with a Tudor-shaped arch, over which is a re-used section of a C12 arch with two orders of V-shaped scale decoration.*

The two gatehouses to the outer bailey both date from the C12, and occupy parts of the areas of the recesses in the Roman E and W walls within which the Roman gates were set. The LAND GATE (Landport) retains its plain C12 inner arch, but the outer arch is early C14, of two round-chamfered orders and segment-headed; the springing of a vault of the late C14, with weathered corbels which appear to represent winged birds, remains inside. The upper storey dates from the late C14, with a small square-headed two-light window facing inwards, a later three-light mullioned and transomed window on the outer face, a thin cornice, parapet, and low pyramid roof. The WATER GATE (Waterport) has a C12 inner arch with light and dark stones alternating, to curious effect.‡ The rest of the Water Gate, like the Land Gate, was altered in the C14, but is much more ruinous. The E part, projecting from the line of the Roman wall, is late C14; part of the early C14 outer arch remains within the gate. In the outer bailey traces have been excavated of a BARN which was one of the largest in England. Its length was about 250 ft and its width about 40 ft.§

ST MARY. An Augustinian priory was founded by Henry I in 1133 within the SE part of the outer bailey, i.e. the Roman enclosure. Almost certainly it took over a pre-existing parish church, and the church remained parochial (as well as being the chapel of the castle) when the priory was moved over Portsdown Hill to Southwick (p. 604) *c.*1144–53. It is an outstanding Romanesque church of moderate size with some details of high quality, and it is fortunate that it is possible to date it within such a relatively narrow margin. There were a

* As in the E arch of the N transept of the parish church (p. 384).
‡ Apparently the earliest Norman work in the castle.
§ Information kindly given us by Mr S. E. Rigold.

long aisleless nave, central tower, transepts, chancel, and N chapel. The E part of the chancel and the S transept have been lost and the N chapel replaced, but otherwise the Norman church remains substantially intact; restorations in 1705 (after a fire, which must have damaged little more than the roof and fittings), 1867 (*Colson*), and 1888 were fairly superficial or conservative. The priory building, of which there is no indication above ground,* stood in the space between the church and the Roman S wall.

The W front is a splendid piece, virtually unmutilated. The 16
W doorway is of three orders, the outer two with thick roll-mouldings and inset shafts, the inner plain, with square-sided jambs, no capitals, and horizontal zigzag moulding on the arch. The shafts all have incised spiral decoration (varying in thickness and spacing), except for the S shaft of the middle order, which has V decoration. The outer face of the arch of the middle order has a series of circles in relief, each with a pattern of segments forming a sexfoil with a small embossed ball in the centre, the outer bands of the circles having miniature ball patterns. The last circles but one on each side are a little larger and contain much-weathered animal figures. The outer order has several bands of zigzag moulding (of varying width and depth) and small cylindrical terminations to the points of the zigzags (a motif repeated in certain internal features), and the label has a series of hollow-sided lozenges contained within small circles. The capitals to the shafts, much worn, have volutes on the N side and simpler decoration on the S. The W window above is within a triple-arch composition, the central arch containing the window being taller and wider than the arches to l. and r., which are blank. The arches are all roll-moulded, with inset shafts, block capitals, and zigzag-moulded surrounds; even the narrow spaces between the shafts of the arches each have two opposing bands of zigzag making diamond patterns. The wall spaces within the blank outer arches are decorated with patterns of quatrefoils within circles. On its inner face, the doorway is of two orders, with roll moulding and shafts set within the angle between the orders; around the outer arch is zigzag with cylindrical ends to the points, as on the outer face.‡

* Except for a range of garderobe drain openings high in the thickness of the S fortress wall at its E end, and the marks of the abutment of the cloister against the S nave wall.

‡ It is obscured by an internal porch.

The nave is of five bays, with widely spaced round-headed windows, which are relatively tall and slender, of two plain square-edged orders externally, their splays stepped at the bases internally (just as are the windows on the S side of the main floor of the keep). There is no window in the centre bay on the N side, which was occupied by a doorway externally surmounted by a high gable, but of which only the blocked arch, visible inside, and the mark of the outside gable remain. The W window on the S side (on to which the W range of the cloister abutted) is blocked, and so are the lower parts of the other four S windows (against which the roof of the N range of the cloister was built). There is also the blocked inner archway to the former W door from nave to cloister and, in the corresponding position at the E end of the S wall, the indications of two blocked doorways overlapping – suggesting an early change in the position of the E door into the cloister. The massive yet elegant tower arches are of two square orders, each with a thick roll moulding in the angle between the orders of the arches, demi-columns with wide capitals to the inner orders and inset shafts to the outer orders of the responds; the inner order of the S arch is filled with the post-Reformation wall erected after the demolition of the transept. The capitals have interesting variations of a few rudimentary forms of decoration; one or two are quite plain and others are simply scalloped, but most have simple incised or fluted stem patterns radiating outwards to varying degrees (some with marked outward curves) leaving, in some cases, the angles clear; in others there are quite elaborate volutes on the angles, sometimes embellished with what look like rudimentary foliage patterns on the undersides of the volutes. One of the smaller capitals has a scale-pattern of inverted V shapes around its angle. All this suggests the earliest, tentative steps towards Gothic foliation, with rudimentary classical reminiscences (in the volutes) which could conceivably have been suggested directly by extant Roman remains. The capitals are comparable to those of the W doorway, and, as often in Norman churches, the disposition of their various designs is apparently quite haphazard. The chancel is only a ghost of its former self; all that is left is one bay of what was evidently a vaulted chamber, of which the intermediate vaulting shafts and capitals (carved with diverging incisions similar to those on the central capitals) survive at the E end. The E wall is of *c.*1600 or a little later, and the E

. *Landscape:* New Forest

2. (above) *Seaside:* Shanklin (I.o.W.)
3. (top right) *Townscape:* Bournemouth, air view
4. (right) *Townscape:* Fareham, High Street

5. (top left) Portchester Castle, Roman walls, late third century
6. (bottom left) Whitchurch church, gravestone, mid ninth century
7. (below) Winchester, part of frieze found in excavations, tenth century

8. (left) Romsey Abbey, rood, eleventh century (first half)

9. (below) Boarhunt church, c.1064(?)

10. (top right) Winchester Cathedral, begun 1079, entrance to chapter house

11. (bottom right) Portchester Castle, keep, twelfth century

12. (below) Romsey Abbey, begun *c.*1120
13. (top right) Romsey Abbey, begun *c.*1120, capital in the chancel aisle, by Robert
14. (bottom right) Christchurch Priory, north transept, *c.*1125–30

15. (top left) East Meon church, font of Tournai marble, *c.*1130–40
16. (bottom left) Portchester church, founded 1133, west front
17. (above) Winchfield church, chancel arch, *c.*1170

18. (top left) Christchurch, castle, hall, late twelfth century

19. (bottom left) Portsmouth Cathedral, chancel, late twelfth century

20. (right) Winchester, St Cross, late twelfth–early thirteenth century

21. (bottom right) Portsmouth, Royal Garrison Church, boss in the chancel, late thirteenth century

22. (top far left) Winchester Castle, great hall, by Stephen, between 1222 and 1236

23. (bottom far left) Beaulieu church (former refectory), reading pulpit, *c.*1230

24. (left) Winchester Cathedral, Ecclesia or Synagogue, *c.*1230

25. (above) Headley, near Grayshott, church, stained glass, thirteenth century

26. Winchester, Deanery, porch, *c.*1230 (*Copyright Country Life*)

27. Netley Abbey, begun 1240s, south transept

28. (top left) Christchurch Priory, south-east chapel, late thirteenth century

29. (bottom left) Idsworth church, wall paintings, *c.*1330

30. (above) Beaulieu, Palace House (former abbey gatehouse), early or mid fourteenth century

31. (right) Catherington church, wall paintings, *c.*1350

32. (above) Christchurch Priory, detail of reredos, *c.*1350
33. (top right) Hartley Wespall church, west end, early fourteenth century
34. (right) Winchester, Pilgrims' Hall, roof, mid fourteenth century
(*Copyright Country Life*)

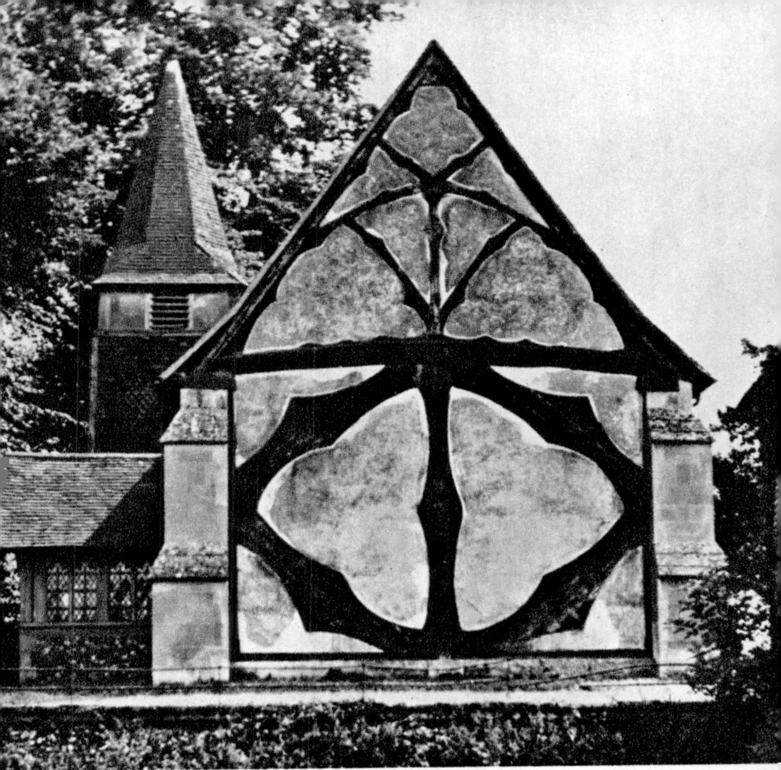

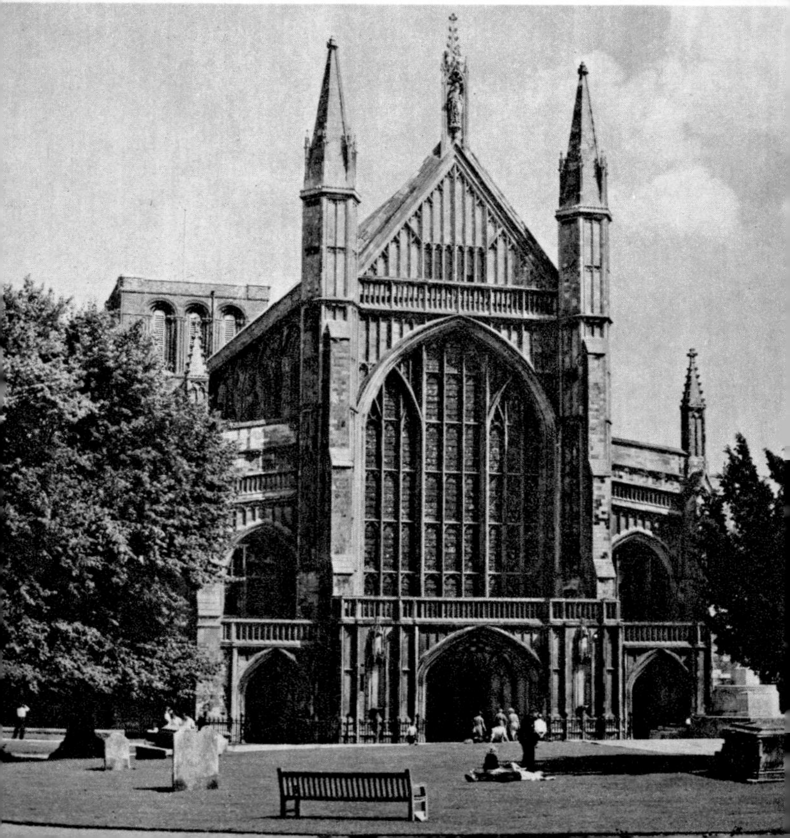

35. (top left) Southampton, walls, *c.*1360/85
36. (left) Winchester Cathedral, west front, *c.*1360–1400
37. (above) Winchester Cathedral, chantry of Bishop Edington †1366

38. (above) Winchester Cathedral, nave, finished by William de Wynford, mostly *c.*1394 onwards
39. (top right) Winchester College, Hall and Chapel, complete by 1404 (*Copyright Country Life*)
40. (right) Winchester, St Cross Hospital, *c.*1445, hall and gatehouse

41. (left) Godshill church (I.o.W.), wall painting, fifteenth–sixteenth century

42. (below) Winchester Cathedral, boss from wooden vault of presbytery, early sixteenth century

43. (right) Winchester Cathedral, chantry of Bishop Fox †1528, roof

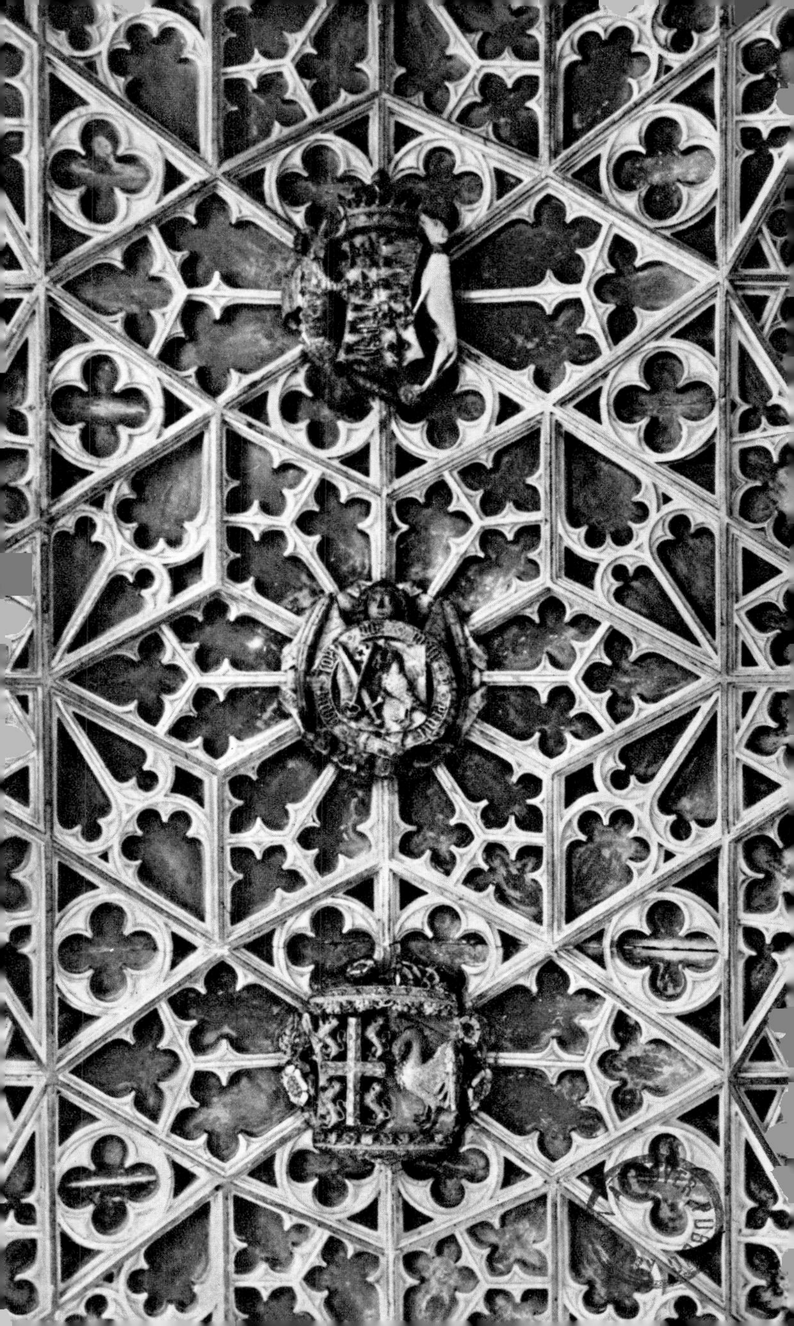

44. (left) Sherborne St John church, stained glass, early sixteenth century
45. (above) Highcliffe Castle, oriel window in the south front from Les Andelys, French Late Gothic (*Copyright Country Life*)

46. (left) The Vyne, long gallery, linenfold panelling, *c*.1525

47. (bottom left) East Tisted church, monument to Richard Norton, *c*.1540

48. (right) Titchfield Abbey, gatehouse, finished by 1542

49. (bottom right) Winchester Cathedral, chantry of Bishop Gardener † 1555

50. (below) Titchfield church, monument to the first and second Earls of Southampton, by Gerard Johnson, 1594
51. (right) Hursley Park, detail of chimneypiece, Elizabethan
52. (bottom right) Ellingham church, screen Perpendicular, family pew Jacobean(?)

53. (top left) Bramshill House, 1605–12 (*Copyright Country Life*)
54. (left) Shedfield, New Place, Bristol Room, *c.*1623–8 (*Copyright Country Life*)
55. (above) Ibsley church, monument to Sir John Constable †1627

56. (left) Portsmouth Cathedral, monument to the Duke of Buckingham †1628, by Nicholas Stone
57. (below) Winchester Cathedral, monument to Lord Portland †1634, effigy by Le Sueur(?)
58. (bottom) Brading church (I.o.W.), monument to Sir John Oglander †1655

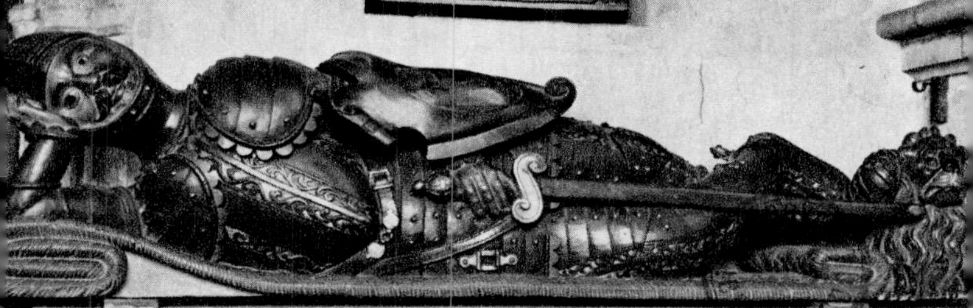

59. (above) The Vyne, long gallery, chimneypiece, by John Webb, *c.*1655
60. (top right) The Vyne, north portico, by John Webb, *c.*1655
61. (right) The Vyne, garden pavilion, by John Webb(?), 1650s

62. (above) Winchester College, New Hall, woodwork, by Edward Pierce(?). 1680–3 (*Copyright Country Life*)
63. (top right) Winchester, Wolvesey Palace, Bishop's House, 1684
64. (right) Winchester, Serle's House, *c.*1710–20

65. (left) Hale church, transept, by Thomas Archer, 1717, doorway
66. (below) Petersfield, statue of William III, by John Cheere(?), 1757

67. The Vyne, staircase, by John Chute, *c.*1760–70

68. (top) Portsmouth, Dockyard, No. 18 Store (former Ropery), 1770, reconstructed 1960

69. (bottom) Bramley church, monument to Bernard Brocas †1777, by Thomas Carter(?)

70. (top left) Broadlands, altered by Henry Holland, 1788, saloon (*Copyright Country Life*)
71. (left) Odiham, King John's Hunting Lodge, Georgian
72. (above) Cranbury Park, by George Dance, 1790s(?), ballroom

73. (top) East Cowes (I.o.W.), Norris Castle, by James Wyatt, 1799, farm buildings
74. (bottom) Houghton Lodge, by John Nash(?), shortly before 1801

75. (top) East Stratton, Stratton Park, portico by George Dance, 1803, house by Stephen Gardiner and Christopher Knight, 1963–5
76. (bottom) The Grange, remodelled by William Wilkins, 1804–9

77. (left) Chilworth church, 1812

78. (bottom left) Christchurch Priory, monument to Viscountess Fitzharris †1815, by John Flaxman

79. (right) Cowes (I.o.W.), St Mary, tower, by John Nash, 1816

80. (top) Winchester, library, by O. B. Carter, 1836–8
81. (bottom) Highclere Castle, remodelled by Sir Charles Barry, 1839–42
(*Copyright Country Life*)

82. (top) Gosport, railway station, by Sir William Tite, opened in 1842
83. (bottom) Portsmouth, Dockyard, fire station, 1843

84. (top) Osborne House (I.o.W.), by Prince Albert and Thomas Cubitt, begun 1845
85. (bottom) Whippingham church (I.o.W.), by A. J. Humbert, 1854–62

86. (top) Laverstoke, parsonage, by G. E. Street, 1858
87. (bottom) Elvetham Hall, by S. S. Teulon, 1859–60

88. Lyndhurst church, by William White, 1858–70

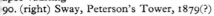

89. (left) Bournemouth, St Stephen, by J. L. Pearson, 1881–98, apse vaulting
90. (right) Sway, Peterson's Tower, 1879(?)

91. (left) Farnborough, mausoleum of the Empress Eugenie, by H.-A.-G.-W. Destailleur, 1887
92. (above) Portsmouth, St Agatha, by J. H. Ball, 1893–5, mosaics by Heywood Sumner

93. (top left) Avon Tyrrell, by W. R. Lethaby, 1891
94. (left) Bedales School, library, by Ernest Gimson, 1911
95. (above) Quarr Abbey (I.o.W.), by Paul Bellot, 1911–12

96. (above) Burghclere, Sandham Memorial Chapel, painting by Stanley Spencer, 1927–32
97. (top right) Warsash, School of Navigation, by Richard Sheppard, Robson & Partners, 1956–61 and 1964–6
98. (right) Southampton University, Nuffield Theatre, by Sir Basil Spence, Bonnington & Collins, 1960–1

99. Beaulieu, Spence Cottage, by Sir Basil Spence, 1960–1

window is simplified Perp, with three cuspless lights and cuspless tracery above.* The chancel had wall arcading with plain arches along the lower parts of its side walls, and of this the arches remain, but not the shafts or capitals. The N transept is now used as a vestry, and its architectural features are partly obscured. It has a large N window with inset shafts and an arch with a curious pattern of radiating line mouldings, the lines in groups of three alternating with recessed spaces, the hood with lozenge pattern. The W window of the transept is similar. Along the lower parts of the W, N, and part of the E walls of the transept were arcades like those of the chancel; these now have shafts and elaborate foliated capitals. The VCH says that the latter are all C19 work, but those in the N wall look tantalizingly medieval, with a worn texture. They could hardly be so, however, since they have sophisticated foliage and pattern designs of *c.*1200; so they must be very good imitation.‡ The arch from S transept to S chapel (the latter now represented by a C19 organ chamber) is now all but obscured from view; it is very similar to the inner arch of the W doorway, with zigzag moulding with cylinders at the points, but it also has a label with two bands of sawtooth ornament. At the S end of the W wall of the transept is a doorway; all the stonework is C19 but it may represent a medieval one (was the S transept, with its comparatively rich treatment, and its own chapel to the E, possibly used specifically as the castle chapel?). The central tower is very low, hardly rising externally above the apexes of the roofs, with two small lancet bell-openings on each face and a low pyramid roof. The exterior of the church is of fine ashlar like that of the castle, with wide, flat buttresses.

FURNISHINGS. FONT. A splendid C12 piece on a base of 1888; a large cylinder with lower patterning of intersecting arches (original above the level of the capitals), the upper part with an almost Celtic or Northumbrian pattern of writhing intersecting stems and varied representations of men, beasts, birds, reptiles, and plants. – COMMUNION

* This clearly goes with Sir Thomas Cornwallis's early C17 work in the castle (pp. 388–2).

‡ It would not however be quite impossible for capitals of this nature to have been inserted in the church *c.*1200, since it remained the castle chapel and still presumably had a connexion with Southwick Priory, which was right in the forefront of architectural development at that time. It would be worth investigating further whether any of these capitals are in fact medieval or whether they are all C19, as the ones on the N and S sides certainly are.

RAIL. Probably early C18; turned balusters and panelled posts; a decent job. – HATCHMENT. An unusually elaborate example, on the N nave wall, commemorating the payment out of Queen Anne's Bounty of a sum towards the restoration of the church after the fire of 1705; very large coat of arms, with cherubs over pedestals to the sides, ornate surround. – MONUMENTS. On the E chancel wall, Sir Thomas Cornwallis † 1618, by *Nicholas Stone*. Bust of a bearded man in plate armour, with a sash across his left shoulder, in a circular frame, surmounted by a coat of arms in a smaller round frame with the inscription underneath. – Pedimented tablet to Thomas Luttman † 1757.

See p. 830

OUTER EARTHWORK. The tip of the promontory upon which the castle stands is crossed by a bank 8 ft high fronted by a silted-up ditch still traceable N and S of the modern road. The defensive circuit has recently been shown to be post-Roman and probably dates from the early C14.

THE VILLAGE. Nineteen-twentieths of Portchester is suburban, spreading thickly over the coastal strip underneath Portsdown Hill, but it is the other twentieth that matters, including not only the castle and its immediate surroundings but also, unexpectedly, an unspoiled village centre to the NE. CASTLE STREET leads S from the A27 fairly unpromisingly, with a thin scatter of Georgian houses amid later development. Beyond White Hart Lane it becomes more interesting, and past three hideous bungalows on the l. is wholly unblemished. It curves gently to the r., widening gradually, and culminates in an irregular wide space, with a small triangle of green shaded by a low spreading tree, from which one narrow way leads diagonally l. to the castle, another diagonally r. to the shore. The houses are mostly C18, all different, varying not only in height and scale but also in alignment; some front the pavements, some are set back behind short gardens, others (especially on the inside of the curve) are placed more amply within walled gardens; some are detached, others are joined to their neighbours. They vary in colour and texture (brick and various renderings); some have canted bay windows and some simple pedimented doorcases. Tall trees top the furthest houses, and the keep tops the trees, its huge scale specially telling. It is a wholly delightful village centre, a modest foil to the great keep, and astonishing in its preservation against such a rabidly suburban hinterland. But there is not a single house in the main group that deserves individual mention.

PORTCHESTER HOUSE, along the lane that leads to the sea, has ogee-headed Venetian windows. The seashore is a rough shingle beach, from which one looks over almost the whole harbour, to the dockyard cranes with the masts of H.M.S. Victory rising among them, and the tall flats of Gosport as dominating landmarks to the r. of the harbour mouth.

PORTSDOWN HILL [DL] *6000*

Portsmouth's natural northern wall of chalk. W of Cosham it rises almost sheer from the developed coastal strip, crowned with the massive Palmerstonian forts and the more conspicuous mid C20 naval installations, with unspoiled country, seemingly more wooded than cultivated, stretching far to the N. From Cosham E the outline is not so clear, as development has spread up the slopes and on to the skyline and for miles beyond, all the way to Horndean and Clanfield (*see* pp. 297 and 179).

PALMERSTON'S FORTS. For the general history of Lord Palmerston's forts *see* p. 248. The Portsdown Hill forts were meant to defend the harbour against land attack from the N. They are six in number, 1½–2 m. apart; from W to E FORT WALLINGTON (close to Fareham), FORT NELSON, FORT SOUTHWICK, FORT WIDLEY, FORT PURBROOK, and FARLINGTON REDOUBT. The first is half-ruined, the second disused, the third and fifth in Service occupation; Widley is owned by Portsmouth Corporation, and Farlington has been partly demolished. They are larger and more massively constructed than the Gosport forts (e.g. Fort Brockhurst), with dry moats, more extensive earthworks, and (unlike the low-lying Gosport forts) extensive chambers and passageways underground. The general layouts are however similar in principle to those at Gosport; there are polygonal enclosures (always slightly irregular, to suit the terrain), longer from E to W than from N to S, with 'keeps' at the centre of the inward side, containing the greater part of the barrack accommodation and designed to be the last bastion of defence, cut off from the rest of the inner enclosure by (dry) moats. At Widley the keep is long and rectangular, projecting forward of the adjoining *enceinte*, and with a forward bastion at each end, the outer face of the bastion inclined at an angle inwards. The keep looks, particularly from across its inward moat, almost like a Romanesque fortress of unusual size in Victorian brick; it is, like Brockhurst, protected by several yards of earth, behind retaining walls, above the barrack rooms and gun emplacements. The entrance here, and in all the other forts, is convincingly neo-Norman, of two orders with scalloped capitals. At Nelson and at Wallington the keep is of triangular shape, projecting between two stretches of rampart which are inwardly (not outwardly) angled, with barrack blocks extending a little further in each direction on the inner side of the rampart. The ramparts, as in the Gosport forts, have gun emplacements on top and tunnel-vaulted chambers, opening into the enclosed area, in their thickness below, caponniers and bastions of varied shape and design, earthen glacis beyond the moats, and (unlike the forts with wet moats) emplacements facing into the moats, reached through a complex system of brick-vaulted tunnels. From the N, the brickwork of the forts is quite hidden by the massive chalk works of the glacis. The scale and romantic quality of some of the forts is emphasized by the wild tangles of foliage that have been allowed to intrude, particularly in the moats.

NELSON'S MONUMENT. On the crest above Portchester.* A tapering column of square section, 120 ft high, with a horizontal cylindrical termination, and a bust of Nelson in the circle facing over the harbour. The base is tapering, moulded on its upper edges and uplifted in strange hook shapes at the angles.

CHRIST CHURCH. *See* Portsmouth Mainland, Widley, p. 468.

PORTSEA *see* PORTSMOUTH, pp. 393, 428, 429, 438, 456

* A design by *J. T. Groves* was exhibited in the Royal Academy in 1807 (Colvin).

PORTSMOUTH

[DL] 6090

Introduction 389
Portsea Island:
Medieval Churches 393
Her Majesty's Dockyard 407
Defensive Works 418
Naval and Military Buildings (outside the Dockyard) 428
Post-medieval Churches 431
Public Buildings 445
Perambulations 450
(a) Old Portsmouth 450
(b) Portsea 456
(c) Landport 458
(d) Southsea 459
(e) The Rest of the Island 463
Portsmouth Mainland:
Cosham 464
Drayton 466
Farlington 466
Paulsgrove 467
Widley 468
Wymering 468

INTRODUCTION

Portsmouth is the only British city on an island site. Portsea Island, about four miles from N to S and two to three miles wide, is separated from the mainland by the narrow Port Creek*; Portsmouth Harbour is to the W, Langstone Harbour to the E, and to the S is the open sea. Its history follows from that of Roman and early medieval Portchester on the N shore of the harbour. There was probably nothing more than agricultural settlement on the island before the late C12 (a reference to 'Portes Mutha' in the Anglo-Saxon Chronicle related to a geographical location, not to a town or village).‡ But by the end of the C12 a flourishing little town had grown up beside the harbour mouth and around a small inlet called the Camber; of its favoured status and its prosperity over a period of a few decades we have plenty of evidence. About 1180 a local magnate, in collaboration with Southwick Priory (the dominant ecclesiastical establishment in this part of Hampshire), founded a chapel on an ambitious scale§; in 1194 Richard I established the

* One of the present roads on to Portsea Island from Cosham runs for the whole way along a causeway, so dividing Port Creek and making the island, technically, into a peninsula. But the two main roads entering the island, as well as the railway, cross the creek by bridges.

‡ Just as, in later times, 'Bourne Mouth' appeared on Hampshire maps before there was any settlement there.

§ Now St Thomas' Cathedral (p. 393).

town as a municipal entity, granting it a charter and probably promoting the layout of new streets and also of burgage plots; a dock was built in 1194 and a 'king's house' in 1197–8. About 1212 a second religious establishment, the Domus Dei, an almshouse and hospice for travellers, was founded, also in association with Southwick Priory, and provided with substantial and architecturally sophisticated buildings. After that the fortunes of the town seem to have flagged; it had some commerce and was the scene of some military movements in connexion with the wars with France, but was less important in both respects than Southampton, which, legally, had control of Portsmouth as an outport. Portsmouth could well have relapsed into the obscurity of a New Romney, a Hythe, or a Winchelsea with little but a fine church to tell of a short period of prodigious prosperity. But in the C15 its potentialities as a naval base were beginning to be realized; the first stone defensive work, the Round Tower, was built (probably) by Henry V in 1418, followed by the Square Tower in 1494. Henry VII built a dry dock; Henry VIII strengthened the defences; Elizabeth I, Charles I, and Cromwell all expended considerable resources on the port and its defences. Under Charles II the harbour definitely became the chief naval base in the country (previously it had been less important in this respect than the Thames and Medway), and so it has remained ever since (though Devonport, obviously, has never been far behind in importance). Ramparts of the most advanced design enclosed the old town by the end of the C16; C18 growth was concentrated in the new town of Portsea (between the old town and the Dockyard), which had its own ramparts by 1780. From Napoleonic times until very recently Portsmouth has been an important garrison town as well as a naval base. C19 growth was prodigious; in the first few decades two new 'towns' – Landport and Southsea – grew up beyond the ramparts of Portsmouth proper and Portsea; later building spread thickly over the island, so that Landport succeeded Old Portsmouth as the focal part of the urban area, while Southsea developed, to some extent, in its own right as a seaside resort. During the C20 the remaining available spaces on the island* have been filled up and the city has sprawled on to the mainland, swamping the old bridgehead village of Cosham and stretching, in effect, for many miles along the roads towards London, Southampton, and Chichester, yet leaving quite unspoiled areas of countryside off the main roads in wide stretches (e.g.

* Much land, of course, is in Service occupation.

around Southwick) or in small pockets (e.g. at Warblington). Portchester, Havant, Waterlooville, and adjoining places are parts of Greater Portsmouth; but the present section is confined to the city within its 1965 boundaries, districts beyond the boundary being treated under their own headings in the gazetteer.

The city suffered terribly from bombing, and large areas were laid waste, but very little boldness or imagination was used in the redevelopment of the bombed areas. In its essentials it has changed less than Southampton; the Navy is not expanding, the military element has almost disappeared, and nothing new of special significance has arisen. Considering how close they are, the cities of Portsmouth and Southampton are astonishingly independent of each other; their hinterlands overlap, but they have so little to do with each other directly that they might be eighty, not eighteen, miles apart.

Apart from the city's two splendid partly medieval churches – the present cathedral and the Garrison Church – and one or two more recent churches, the city's architectural interest is mainly confined to the naval, military, and defensive buildings. Some would say that its architectural heyday was in the C18, and the still abundant storehouses and other buildings of that period in the Dockyard, with their functional elegance, are amongst its best buildings. But the C19 Dockyard architecture is really more exciting, both from the constructional point of view (there are many remarkable early examples of building with iron) and from the more purely architectural standpoint. Some of the storehouses of *c.*1850 onwards, with their Vanbrugh-like style and scale, are as fine examples as any of what can be broadly designated as industrial architecture (pp. 415–17). If more of Portsmouth's C17 and C18 defences had been allowed to survive (they were mostly demolished in 1870–80), the city would have been of unique interest as the only place in Britain with post-medieval defences of the elaborate type common on the Continent during the period; even what survives is interesting and impressive, especially the outlying C18 Cumberland Fort and the complex Southsea Castle. Palmerston's C19 forts must be mentioned in relation to the history of military architecture in the city, even though they are nearly all outside its boundaries (pp. 227, 248, 387). For civilian (apart from ecclesiastical*) architecture Portsmouth is hardly notable. There are still plenty of C18 houses in Old Portsmouth and Portsea, some quite demure with locally characteristic shallow segmental bow windows on

* Post-medieval church architecture is discussed in general on p. 431.

the first floor, so different from the bold, usually semicircular, bows characteristic of Southampton. It is strange that so much of Late Georgian Portsmouth, with its martial traditions, should have looked so Jane Austenish, while peaceable Southampton, then a spa, should have developed a domestic architectural tradition that was much more robust. Early C19 architecture at Portsmouth is disappointing; what is left of early Southsea (mainly from the late thirties and forties) is, architecturally, strangely clumsy. Of the civilian architecture of the last hundred years nothing positive can generally be said, except that geographical limitations have forced a high overall density of development (making a very marked contrast to the much more spacious and often leafy development of Southampton), and that many tall blocks of flats, impressive at least in bulk, have gone up since 1960. In civic architecture Portsmouth made a great flourish with the Guildhall in 1886–90 (in a style characteristic of a few decades before) and employed a very individualistic borough architect, *G. E. Smith*, in the early years of the C20. The city has promoted some very promising new buildings in the 1960s, notably the Teachers' Training College (*Gollins, Melvin, Ward & Partners*) and the latest block of the College of Technology (*Owen Luder*); these and the current Charlotte Street redevelopment (*Owen Luder*), together with *Lionel Brett & Pollen*'s proposals, published in sketch form, for Guildhall Square, suggest that, belatedly, Portsmouth may be catching up, in terms of architecture and town planning, with the times. It has a unique site; a huge amount of redevelopment will need to be done in the next two or three decades, and much land hitherto occupied by the Services will be freed. Land, generally, is short (for Portsmouth to sprawl much more extensively over the adjoining mainland would be unthinkable), but the spaciousness imparted by the surrounding water and undeveloped sea frontages makes a higher-than-average residential density more acceptable on Portsea Island than it would be in many places. Portsmouth in 1965 is, as a whole, muddled and visually squalid; it still has the chance to make itself something very different, and much better, before the end of the C20. *See* p. 831

Because of the special nature of its historical and architectural development, the treatment of Portsmouth does not follow exactly the established pattern for most big cities in the *Buildings of England* series. It seems that the two outstanding medieval churches ought to come first since they were, so to speak, present in the city's infancy; then, obviously, comes the Dockyard, followed by the Defensive Works and the remaining naval and military buildings; then, according to the usual pattern, the rest of the churches and the public buildings in the inner city (i.e. on Portsea Island), followed by Perambulations of the more rewarding parts. Finally, the mainland suburbs within the city boundary are treated in an entirely separate section, each of the old village centres or distinct modern districts, with their churches, being treated under a separate heading.

Population: 1801, 33,226; 1851, 72,096; 1901, 188,095; 1951, 233,545. In 1961 the figure was down to 215,077, but this was due to overspill beyond the city boundaries. If one adds most of the 74,500 people in Havant urban district in 1961 one gets a better idea of the size of Greater Portsmouth.

PORTSEA ISLAND

MEDIEVAL CHURCHES

CATHEDRAL OF ST THOMAS. Made a cathedral in 1927, and a parish church in 1320.* It had been founded *c.*1180 at the instance of John de Gisors, a rich merchant who possibly had interests in London and was lord of the manor of Titchfield. His avowed intent was to build a chapel in honour of the recently martyred Thomas Becket, but he must also have had in mind the needs of the nascent community at the mouth of the harbour. He entrusted the building to the canons of Southwick Priory (p. 604). So the church was something special, a testimonial of piety, a chapel for the needs of a growing port (and those who passed through it), and, in the event, a showpiece for a fairly powerful monastery. It was not particularly big but, in many respects, it had more of the character of a miniature cathedral or monastic church than of a medium-sized parochial church. Architecturally it was always perhaps a little patchy (and parts of it must have been built piecemeal over a few decades), but much of the building was of the first architectural quality, in the mainstream of South English tradition – as exemplified in the late C12 reconstruction of Chichester Cathedral and the somewhat similarly situated (though grander) parish church of New Shoreham.

The central tower suffered damage in the Civil War; it must have been patched for a time, but in 1683–93 the old tower and nave were taken down and replaced by a new nave,

* Till 1320 it was a chapel to the island's parish church of St Mary (p. 441).

aisles, and W tower. C19 restorations did not alter the essential character of the building, but enlargements since 1927 to provide for its new role as the cathedral of a populous diocese and, alas, to try to turn it into something faintly like the traditional idea of a cathedral have deprived it of much of its old character as a medium-sized town church without making it seem in size or in splendour anything even remotely reminiscent of York or Lincoln. But, to be fair, the inter-war enlargements were never finished, and a recently published scheme for completion of the enlarged building in a very different style could result in something exciting.

The description is split into three sections, relating to the surviving medieval parts, the C17 parts, and the C20 enlargements, which corresponds to a description from E to W. The medieval work is so good and so remarkable that it needs detailed description.

MEDIEVAL CHOIR AND TRANSEPTS. One would dearly like to have seen the medieval St Thomas in its entirety, and still more the vanished church of the priory of Southwick (p. 607), of which St Thomas was a protégé. St Thomas was never particularly large, but it was ambitiously conceived and has unusual features, most notably the arrangement of pairs of small arches within the choir arcade contained within larger arched frames, the larger frames representing the width of the vaulting bays of the main space and the smaller arches the widths of the bays of the aisles. Only here and at Boxgrove Priory in Sussex is such an arrangement extant. Portsmouth also has affinities with Chichester and New Shoreham and with numerous lesser churches in Sussex and eastern Hampshire, and, in order to fit it properly into the regional architectural picture of *c.*1150–1250, it is necessary to examine the evidence we have for its dating in relation to the other buildings. There is record that St Thomas was being built in 1185, that part was consecrated in 1188, and that in 1196 the churchyard and two transept altars were also consecrated. It is a reasonable assumption that work started with the choir, which would, at least, be under way by 1185; some of its architectural details support such a presumption. Parts at least of the transepts must have been built by 1196; stylistic evidence suggests that the S transept could have been built by then, but obviously much of the N transept, with its cusped windows and arch, is somewhat later.* So we have a

* The Garrison Church, probably begun *c.*1212, has cusped E lancets.

choir probably of *c*.1180–90, and transepts of *c*.1190–1220; of the medieval nave we have no evidence. This must be set against New Shoreham, where building of the choir probably began about 1170 but continued over several decades; Chichester, where major remodelling followed the fire of 1187 (although some work, e.g. in the Lady Chapel, probably dates from just before); and Boxgrove, where the choir is probably of *c*.1220. Portsmouth then comes fairly early in the regional architectural sequence of the Transitional period; much of the choir probably just pre-dates most of the work at Chichester, and the doubled arcading certainly pre-dates, by a fairly wide margin, the comparable arcading at Boxgrove. The missing link is Southwick Priory, and if we knew more about how that looked, the architectural history of Southern England during this important period might become clearer.

The CHOIR arcades attract attention first. There are only 19
two main bays, each consisting of a broad blank round outer arch containing a pair of smaller, sharply pointed arches. The smaller arches are of two orders, heavily moulded, the moulding thicker and more incisive (and evidently slightly earlier) on the N than on the S, where it is subtler and more undulating. The intermediate piers within each pair of smaller arches are of black marble, dating in their present form from 1904 (the original Purbeck marble piers having crumbled),* with renewed moulded round capitals of stone, except in the SW main bay, where the original moulded capital of Purbeck marble has been preserved. The outer containing arches are of a single moulded order. The piers between the main bays are octagonal, big (out of structural necessity), and with simply moulded capitals. The responds are clustered, and have engaged shafts corresponding to the inner orders of the smaller arches, and slightly slenderer shafts, within square-angled recesses, corresponding to the outer orders of the smaller arches and to the single orders of the containing arches; each shaft has a capital of its own under a moulded square abacus. The W responds form continuous compositions with the adjoining responds of the W arches of the choir aisles, so that there is a continuous series of capitals and shafts (including five in a straight diagonal line) at the W end of each choir arcade, to striking effect. The W arches of the choir arcades are specially notable, of three orders, with beautifully formed mouldings – wide and narrow rolls, deep

* In fact they were replaced by iron supports in 1843.

and shallow incisions, in undulating patterns, much as on the arches of the S arcade. The aisle vaulting is quadripartite, with transverse arches of the same section as the diagonal ribs – thick rolls with hollow sides; the bays are beautifully balanced in their proportions, since each is related to the width of one of the lesser arches of the arcades, roughly equal to the width of the aisles, so that the awkward elongated effect which is obtained, e.g., at Chichester, is avoided. Furthermore the difficulty arising from the difference in the thicknesses of the main and intermediate capitals of the arcades is neatly mastered at Portsmouth by having the ribs springing in bunches from the smaller intermediate capitals but separately from the larger capitals. At Boxgrove the solution to this problem is aesthetically much more clumsy. On the outer sides of the aisles the ribs rise from corbels resting on trefoiled slightly keeled shafts, resembling those at Chichester and New Shoreham but, of course, on a much smaller scale than at Chichester. In the E angles of the aisles the diagonal ribs spring from small corbels resting on single shafts. The capitals and corbels of responds and vaulting-shafts in the aisles are intriguingly but haphazardly varied; some are straightforwardly round and moulded, but others are in varieties of simple, rather primitive, foliage in the preliminary or early stages of development to stiff-leaf; the obviously early date of these lends support to the documentary evidence that the choir was built *c.*1180–90. The most striking array is on the combined W respond of the S arcade and N respond of the W arch of the S aisle, where there are nine shafts in all, each with a capital (some damaged or partly renewed) of distinct Portsmouth types, having spearpoint leaves (i.e. with a straight broadening and then a gradual narrowing to points) with simple incisions usually following the shapes of the leaves, or, in some cases, broadening more roundly into the shape of spades (in the playing-card sense). The leaves have slight convex curves (suggestively anticipating crocket capitals), which seem to echo in miniature those of the vaulting-ribs.* The corresponding pair of responds on the N side has ordinary round capitals and the total effect is not so memorable. The rest of the capitals and corbels are carved as follows. In the S aisle, the S respond of the W arch has spearpoint decoration as on the opposite respond, except for the

* Unbelievably, a loudspeaker has been set against the arch and ribs just above these capitals (1965).

capital of the inner order, which has a contorted foliage pattern, with twirling stems and leaves. The corbel at the end of the first bay has crocket foliage; the next two corbels and the one in the SE corner of the aisle have dagger foliage (i.e. narrow leaves curving to points, without the initial widening from stems characteristic of spearpoint leaves), usually with simple incisions; the capitals of the E respond of the S arcade have crocket foliage. In the N aisle the capitals of the N respond of the W arch, and the corbels at the end of the first two bays and in the NE corner have varieties of dagger and spearpoint foliage, whereas the corbel at the end of the third bay and the capitals of the E respond of the N aisle are plain, round and moulded. These, on the whole, like the differences in the mouldings of the two arcades, suggest a slightly earlier date for the N aisle than for the S.

The medieval vaulting of the choir has disappeared; the present mock-vaulting in plaster is remarkably convincing work of 1843* and probably represents, pretty closely, the appearance of the medieval vault. The original corbels remain, with crocket foliage, with vaulting-shafts of the same trefoiled section as those in the aisles, ending at lower corbels, in the spandrels of the main bays of the arcades, which consist of half-rings of stiff-leaf foliage (the most fully developed in the cathedral) surmounting small brackets carved with grotesque human faces. The choir has a galleried clerestory, tall in relation to the height of the arches underneath, each main bay having an internal screen of three lancet-shaped arches, the centre ones wider and higher, with slender intermediate shafts of Purbeck marble and engaged end-shafts of stone, all with moulded round capitals, the end-shafts also with shaft-rings. The actual clerestory consists of one lancet window only over each bay, behind the central arch of each triple screen (much as at Chichester). The high E window, level with the clerestory, has a similar internal screen, but with rings half-way up the intermediate Purbeck marble shafts as well as on the end-shafts, and with rib-moulding round the arches. The window itself is a triple lancet, repeating the scale and shape of the screen. In its lower storey the choir terminates in a pointed-arched recess, with marble shafts and capitals entirely renewed, and flanked by a pair of miniature trefoiled arches on either side, about five feet up; this again is wholly renewed but may represent a medieval

* Mr R. Hubbuck suggests that it may be by *Livesay*.

feature. Within the arched recess is a single, very slender, lancet window.* In the gable of the E wall a small circular window, visible outside, opens into the space above the vaulting. The aisle side windows were originally very thin lancets, one to each bay; one survives in the N aisle (E bay) and two in the S (two E bays). Other aisle windows are Victorian, including the two-light E windows.

The TRANSEPTS are relatively tall and narrow, the S shallower than the N. The fenestration is in two tiers, corresponding to the two stages of the choir, but windows and other architectural features are rather jumbled, suggesting that the transepts were built in a somewhat piecemeal way, the N transept being, on the whole, later than the S. The S transept has in its E wall a plain chamfered arched recess, containing a small blocked lancet window. Above, but to the N, is a larger lancet. The S wall has two fairly wide lancet windows in the lower tier and a wider one above. At the SW corner of the transept is a stairway leading into the clerestory passage, which continues round the transept and into the choir. The transept was, or was intended to be, vaulted, and the corbels for the vaulting-ribs, together with short lengths of shafts below, remain in the SW and SE corners. The N transept has two arched recesses in its E wall. The northern one is like that in the S transept, but contains a two-light window with quatrefoiled circle above; the southern one is trefoiled and roll-moulded and contains the remains of a WALL PAINTING of Christ in Majesty in a small vesica which is contained within the head of the arch, with a host of angels in the space below. The upper part is fairly distinct (it was touched up by *Tristram*), but the bottom of the painting is completely gone. The vesica suggests that the painting is coeval with the recess: early C13. In the upper stage of the E transept wall are three trefoiled lancets, two paired towards the N and a single one to the S. The N transept wall has in its lower tier a three-light uncusped window in an arched frame, in its present form wholly Victorian, and three stepped trefoiled lancets above. In the gable is a small sexfoiled circle. The W transept wall has a single trefoiled lancet at upper level.‡ Of the medieval CROSSING there survive the two E piers (the chancel arch, above the piers, dates with the vaulting from 1843), with a

* This is a medieval feature, revealed and re-opened in 1920.

‡ Such lancets are found in neighbouring village churches, e.g. Chalton and Soberton.

series of rounded shafts facing diagonally NW and SW into the crossing; the original capitals, simply moulded and of hollow-sided octagonal shape, survive on the N side, but are renewed on the S (1843). The W arches of the choir arcades and the aisles spring from the piers at much lower levels on other sides.

SEVENTEENTH CENTURY NAVE AND TOWER. Although the medieval central tower and nave were damaged in the Civil War they survived till *c.*1683, between when and 1693 they were replaced by a new nave with aisles and W tower. The C17 work, internally, is like a provincial adaptation of Wren's architecture: arcades with fairly slender round piers resting on tall octagonal bases (indicating the height of the original pews); Tuscan capitals; round arches with straightforward mouldings. The nave arcades proper are of three bays; there is a further E bay with wider and taller arches opening into the transepts and preserving something of the feel of the original crossing. Coved plaster ceiling with dentilled cornice, broken by dormer windows; there are other dormers lighting the aisles, and both sets of dormers appear outside, picturesquely, projecting from the tiled 'catslide' roof which sweeps over nave and aisles without a break. A WEST GALLERY was erected in 1706; it was extended along the aisles and into the transepts in 1750. The parts filling the transepts were removed in 1904. In 1938 the rest of the old galleries were removed and a new attenuated gallery, using parts of the fine panelled fronts of the old ones, was erected across the W end of the former nave and aisles a few feet in front of the W wall. It serves as part of the organ loft, and contains an Early Victorian royal HATCHMENT from St Mary, Portsea. – The PEWS of *See* p. 831 the former nave date in their present form from 1904, but it seems that much of the panelling of the C17 pews was re-used in the present much lower ones, especially in the roomy CORPORATION PEW, which is said to date from 1693 but has obviously been reduced in height. – The PULPIT is of 1693, in the same decent, solid, but unostentatious style as the rest of the C17 features of the church; octagonal, with large vertical panels, tapering at the base in ogee curves to a stem; the splendid sounding-board with a gilded angel blowing a trumpet is a replica of 1904 of the original sounding-board cast out *c.*1885 – a very telling example of how an act of iconoclasm can be regretted, and put right at considerable expense, less than a generation later. The former nave from

1904 till the enlargements of the late 1930s must have been very attractive and full of atmosphere, with the galleries wrapping round the aisles (but not then encumbering the transepts), the dark-stained fittings of the C17 and 1904 very much in keeping with the simple Renaissance architecture, and the walls abounding in monuments and wall-tablets; crowded but capacious. Only a little of the pre-cathedral atmosphere can now be savoured.

The aisles of the C17 nave had straightforward three-light square-headed windows, faintly, vestigially, Gothic, now re-set in the C20 outer aisles. The tower, now central in the enlarged cathedral, is almost astylar, with small pairs of round-headed lights to the top storey and parapets slightly raised at the corners to give the suggestion of angle battlements. The unusual size of the attractive wooden cupola, added in 1702–3, is explained by the fact that it was built to take bells. It is octagonal, with louvres on each face, and a domical top with miniature second cupola, open-sided, rising at the top, ending in a tiny ogee spirelet and a golden ball. On the ball is a WEATHER VANE, a replica of one of 1710 which was blown down in 1954 and is now inside the cathedral; a splendid piece of gilded metalwork, with the outline of a sailing ship and the date in openwork figures.

TWENTIETH CENTURY EXTENSIONS. Plans were first drawn out by *Sir Charles Nicholson* in 1935 for the enlargement of the newly-established cathedral, but the large-scale enlargements and alterations took place mostly in 1938–9. Nicholson in his early days designed churches using Gothic and Renaissance motifs which were yet original in general conception and sensitively composed in terms of colour and space; the Ascension, Southampton (p. 590), and St Alban, Portsmouth (p. 434), built in the tens and twenties, indicate this clearly. His restoration of St Peter and St Paul, Fareham, in the early thirties (p. 218) shows a diminution in sensitivity. His work at Portsmouth Cathedral suggests that he had lost almost all feeling for spatial composition and all stylistic conviction. The problem was a difficult one; in fact few parish churches of comparable size could have seemed less suitable for enlargement. Eastward expansion was impossible because of the medieval work; large-scale lateral expansion might have been possible but would have resulted in a weirdly-shaped building; straightforward western expansion would have been relatively easy, if the tower had been demolished – but this was unacceptable for the understandable reason that, with its cupola, it was a familiar and well-liked landmark in the city (more so than now, with the power station and many other tall buildings fairly close). So somehow the church had to be expanded westward while retaining the tower. This was done by making the tower the focal point in the enlarged building, with new transepts and new double-aisled nave, turning the old nave and choir into a roomy choir and sanctuary for the enlarged building. But the tower still proved an obstruction; any opening through it was necessarily fairly narrow and very deep and, although an impressive effect could have been obtained if a tall crossing space had been formed under the tower, this was not done, and instead a two-tiered space was created, the upper tier being taken by the organ and the lower consisting only of a low round arch giving a restricted view from nave to choir. The tower and the space under it, therefore, act as a pulpitum of unusual thickness, cutting the choir off, functionally, from the nave. An attempt was made to reduce the effect of this separation by having wide interconnecting spaces between nave and choir on either side of the tower – from the new nave aisles into the new transepts, from there into new second aisles added beyond the old aisles of the former nave (now choir), and so into the old building. Such a flowing of one space into another provided a splendid challenge to which almost any medieval designer and all the best Victorian architects like Street or Pearson or Scott would have risen – but Nicholson did not rise to it; instead of an exciting series of oblique vistas there are just muddled views through arches of different shapes (or degrees of shapelessness) which simply confuse and do not satisfy. Furthermore the spatial qualities of the old nave have been largely destroyed by the addition of the second aisles. Of Nicholson's new nave and aisles only three bays out of an intended six were completed. The main arcades are in a sort of watered-down Romanesque, with tall circular piers, circular capitals with rounded protuberances and round arches, the roofs tunnel- or groin-vaulted and the arcades of the second aisles small, round and paired in bays (like a parody of the medieval choir arrangement); the windows (forming a kind of double clerestory, one range over the main arcades, one, more prominent, over the subsidiary arcades) in a sort of simplified Tudor style in segmental-arched frames.

The present outer N entrance to the N aisle has an open

round pediment containing representations of skulls and bones, the Portsmouth star and crescent, and the date 1691.

In 1966 plans were published for the completion of the nave by *Seely & Paget* (architect in charge *Anthony New*), with *Pier Luigi Nervi* as consulting engineer. It certainly involves a departure from Nicholson's inert traditionalism. The main space of the new extension will be 76 ft wide (i.e. as wide as the existing incomplete nave and its inner aisles) and will extend W to about the length of the present incomplete nave, with a semicircular W termination. Aisles, as wide and as high as the existing outer nave aisles, will continue round the semicircle and interconnect. The construction will be of reinforced concrete framework, with external curtain glazing to the aisles, aisle roofs with precast concrete panels, and tunnel roof to the nave with arched braces, concrete framing in web patterns, and precast concrete panels, except in the lower parts of the roof, where the web framework will be left open.* Externally the lower parts of the roof will be concealed behind parapet walls, continuing the line of Nicholson's outer clerestory, which will have glazing in concrete framework of a web pattern corresponding to the open parts of the roof framework behind, so giving the effect of a clerestory piercing the lower parts of the tunnel roof. The new roof will be continued E to the tower to cover over Nicholson's existing vaulting, so forming an even external roof-line (although this part of the new roof will be concealed inside). Outside wall surfaces will be faced in stone to match the older parts of the cathedral, and at the junction of the new work and the old will be a polygonal S porch surmounted by a spirelet of gilded fibre glass. The FURNISHINGS will include a nave altar W of the crossing, with seating arranged conventionally over most of the nave space, but with five rising tiers of seating round the perimeter of the nave (continuing round the W semicircle), leaving the aisles as processional spaces. This will allow for a congregation of 1,200 to be seated with uninterrupted view of the altar and pulpit. There is no doubt that internally the effect of the extension will be tremendously exciting, with the immense new space set off by the solidly composed and much subdivided space of the older parts. The old parish church will be treated as a largely separate

* Nervi has constructed roofs to the same principle elsewhere in Europe, but this will be his first work of any sort in Britain. The unsupported span, it is claimed, will exceed that in any other church except St Peter's.

choir, with the high altar moved forward to the entrance to the original chancel, which will become a Lady Chapel. With exquisite small-scale medieval work at one end, daring C20 construction at the other, and a perhaps rather endearing muddle in between, there will be no other cathedral quite like it. It is expected that the work will be finished in 1969.

FURNISHINGS. For the WALL PAINTINGS *see* p. 398; for WEST GALLERY, HATCHMENT, PULPIT, PEWS, and WEATHER VANE pp. 399–400. – The FONT is C15; not very significant; octagonal with quatrefoil panels. – The HIGH ALTAR, 1939 by *Nicholson*, has a suspended tester, effective in itself, but it spoils the spatial effect of the medieval choir. – The ORGAN, in the upper tier of the space under the tower, has an exquisite façade of 1718, by *Abraham Jordan, Jun.*, now facing the new nave. – Against the temporary W nave wall and now looking meaningless is the wooden DOOR SURROUND formerly on the interior of the W door (by *Lewis Allen*; 1694) – two pairs of simple posts supporting a cross-beam surmounted by a royal coat of arms and intricate carving to the sides. – The cathedral's artistic treasure is a majolica PLAQUE of the Virgin and Child, *c.*1500 by *Andrea della Robbia*, the personal gift of Sir Charles Nicholson. – PAINTINGS. S. Filippo Benizi, reputedly by *Carlo Dolci*, C17. – The Miraculous Draught of Fishes, by *W. L. Wyllie* (who lived locally). – STAINED GLASS. A few Victorian windows, many of them by *Clayton & Bell*, survived bomb blast. They are in the N choir aisle, the old N transept, and elsewhere, mostly in small lancets. – PLATE. The TANGIER PLATE is said to have been brought home by the returning Tangier garrison in 1683, having previously been in the church of King Charles the Martyr at Tangier. It seems to have been intended at first as a gift to God's House Chapel (the present Royal Garrison Church), but was given to St Thomas by James II in 1687. It consists of: pair of Flagons, one of 1639, the other a copy given (according to an inscription) to the church of Tangier in 1672; Cup by *Anthony Nelme* of London, second half of the C17; two Standing Patens, 1677; also two Cups, one before 1764, the other a copy with a Cover of 1803; eight Silver Plates, in pairs of four dates, 1708, 1804, 1809, 1812; Strainer, 1805. – MONUMENTS. None except the Buckingham monument of any scale or special interest, but a great many tablets and cartouches of merit, some (probably most) of them by local craftsmen. Only brief mention of a selection can be made.

56 In the S choir aisle: Duke of Buckingham, murdered in a house in High Street (p. 452) in 1628. Rather overloaded, with a large and extremely elongated urn in a black rounded recess, scroll work and military emblems to either side. An open pediment on top with cherubs. Lively allegories, one Fame blowing her trumpet, on either side of the tablet below. By *Nicholas Stone*; originally at the E end of the chancel, now crowded in a bay of the aisle, and probably modified a little on removal. – Cartouches to Thomas Heather † 1696, with cherubs, and John Mellish † 1765. – Oval tablet with unusual surround to Thomas Spearing † 1779. – Wall-slab with heraldry, brightly repainted, to Robert Moulton † 1652 and William Willoughby † 1651. – In the N choir aisle: cartouche to Admiral John Cleland † 1795. – In the old S transept: five cartouches, to William Read † 1790, Thomas Stanyford † 1795, Robert Haswell † 1765, James Gee † 1762, the Hon. John Barrie † 1791. Henry Stanyford † 1735, with a miniature mourning figure. – In the old N transept: recumbent bronze figure in relief to William Thomas Wyllie, the son of W. L. Wyllie, † 1916. – In the new N transept: tablet to Sir Charles Blount † 1600, flanked by free-standing Corinthian columns supporting a hood with miniature kneeling figure on top; military emblems on a coved shelf below. – In the new S transept: tablet to Richard Holford † 1703, draped, the folds and edges of the drapery indicated in a curious way. – Tablet to Philip Varlo † 1749, an elegant triangular composition enlivened by cherubs and garlands.

ROYAL GARRISON CHURCH, Old Portsmouth. Originally part of God's House, Domus Dei or the Hospital of St John and St Nicholas, founded *c.*1212 by Bishop Peter des Roches, to accommodate travellers and sick and aged people, and managed by Southwick Priory. Unlike its Southampton counterpart (p. 551) it did not escape the Dissolution; the buildings were first converted into military stores and then, in the late C16, the residence for the military Governor of Portsmouth. In 1827 all the buildings were demolished except what is now the Garrison Church. Nave and aisles had been the living accommodation for the hospital (just as in the somewhat smaller, unaisled, St Mary's Hospital in Chichester), only a screen (as still at St Mary's) separating them from the chancel, which was the chapel. In 1866 there was an extremely thorough restoration by *G. E. Street*, undoing the alterations and 'improvements' of 1827 and other dates and, of course, trying to get back to the purity of the original design, but inevitably giving it all a Street stamp. Both as a basically medieval building and as a piece of Street restoration the church is first-rate. In the 1940 bombing the nave roof was destroyed and the fittings damaged. Prompt action prevented the fire from gutting the whole building; the chancel was undamaged, but the nave is now a roofless shell, screened off from the still-used chancel by a glazed wall. The Ministry of Public Building and Works have decided not to restore the building for the present; they should think again. For the nave and aisles are, to all appearance, structurally intact except for the roof and glazing; in such a condition they do not make a picturesque ruin and the quality and (when intact) spatial unity of the whole building demand that, for primarily architectural reasons, it be completely restored – the fact that the diminution almost to extinction of the strength of the Army stationed at Portsmouth makes it technically redundant is only a secondary consideration.* The chancel presumably dates from the time of the foundation, i.e. *c.*1212–20; the nave is slightly later.

At some time the nave and aisles lost their medieval W bay; this was built again by Street. His W front has a steeply gabled centre composition, with four-light geometrical window and fine simple W door of three orders. The aisles are pitched less steeply, and their W and side windows (all Street's) are two-light geometrical. The aisles were heightened by Street (their older, steeper, roof-line can be seen inside). The E window of the N aisle is original but blocked, with a trio of stepped lancets in an arched frame, the frame simply chamfered outside, thinly moulded and shafted within (as are several windows of this period or a little later with similar internal frames in south-east Hampshire – e.g. Hambledon, Catherington, Hayling); this window represents the very last stage in the development of grouped lancets before tracery appears. The side wall of the S aisle is very curious; the first seven feet or so are exceptionally thick, but then the wall is set back to a more normal width. The usual explanation for this is that the building was originally intended to be wider, but, when the S aisle wall had been partly built, it was decided to reduce the width so that the wall was thickened inwards. The windows (all Street's, like the S door)

* Actually the chancel is still well used, and grossly over-furnished to accommodate the congregations.

are all above the level of the setback. At the E end of the aisle the wall rises for an extra two feet or so on the outer plane so as to accommodate a shallow recess inside, lit by a small lancet. The E aisle window is an original lancet. In the angle of the S aisle and the chancel is an octagonal stair-turret (giving access to the space above the chancel vault), medieval up to eaves level, the stage above that a very characteristic work of Street, with a small lancet on each face and a spiky spirelet. The S wall of the chancel has a prominent corbel table (the corbels grotesquely carved) and three tall windows in the form of triple lancets within arched frames – the windows entirely the work of Street (who took his cue from the E window of the N aisle), except possibly for the outlines of the frames. The N wall of the chancel is partly abutted on by a large C19 vestry; it has a similar corbel table and windows of only two lights (again Street's) otherwise similar to those on the S. The E window is original; externally it is a trio of widely spaced, stepped lancets without any framing but with significant cusping to form trefoil patterns. In the gable above (ventilating the space over the vaulting) is a tiny lancet, and three miniature round openings arranged in triangular pattern.

Entry to the church is now by a small chamfered priest's door on the S of the chancel. It leads into a beautiful space,
21 with three vaulted bays of mature E.E. design, quadripartite with cross ribs but no ridge ribs (as in the cathedral aisles and at Chichester), the ribs deeply hollowed with keeling on the centre moulding. They spring from moulded capitals, below which trefoiled keeled shafts descend to a string course at sill level, below which are corbels in delicately wrought formal leaf patterns, except in the two E angles, where there are figure corbels. As in the aisles of the cathedral, the whole composition of each foliate corbel, shaft, capital, and springing of the ribs is exquisitely balanced. The lancets of the E window are framed internally with moulded and hooded arches, and side and intermediate shafts and capitals. The SEDILIA are Street renewals, said to be based on the medieval design.

The nave is now, alas, separate and roofless, and the true beauty of its proportions cannot be appreciated properly, either in themselves or in conjunction with those of the more delicately shaped chancel, until the whole church has been restored and re-roofed. The five-bay nave arcades, essentially original apart from Street's W bay (and substantially undamaged except for discoloration), have a quality of noble simplicity, with their octagonal piers, moulded capitals, and arches of two chamfered orders; the wider, now blocked, chancel arch is similar.

FURNISHINGS. The chancel is cluttered, additional furniture having been brought in since the ruination of the nave. Elaborate fittings by *Street*, with *Earp* as craftsman; choir stalls, sanctuary furniture, tiling, perhaps a little too much for the pristine beauty of the building itself. – STAINED GLASS. E window by *Carl Edwards*, 1958. Central figure of Christ Ascendant; a great deal of detail, all richly coloured, a good total effect. – PLATE. Given by Queen Anne.

HER MAJESTY'S DOCKYARD*

Portsmouth's first dock, constructed by Richard I in 1194, stood at the head of a small creek to the N of the old town (where H.M.S. Vernon now is). It was probably improved by King John, but had become ruinous by 1224. The first dry dock in the world, lined with wood, was constructed here in 1495 by Sir Reginald Bray (who had been concerned with the building of Henry VII's Chapel at Westminster and even more St George's Chapel at Windsor) further to the N, very near to where H.M.S. Victory now is. It marked the beginning of the present-day Dockyard.‡ Big developments took place in the C17: during the reign of Charles I, under the Duke of Buckingham (who was murdered in Portsmouth in 1628); during the Civil War and Commonwealth periods (a new dock was built in 1642); and from 1660 under Samuel Pepys, who held the post of Clerk of the Acts and then Secretary to the Admiralty from 1684 until 1689. In 1691 the Great Stone Dock was built.§ By the end of the century the Dockyard had become the chief naval base in the kingdom, with large buildings, at first wholly of timber, for storage and rope-making and facilities for ship building and repairing – many men-o'-war were built at Portsmouth in the late C17 and C18, and others at Bursledon on the Hamble River and at Bucklers Hard on the Beaulieu River, using the

* I am indebted to Mr R. Sutherland Horne for a great deal of information relating to the Dockyard.

‡ The original dry dock was filled in in 1623.

§ Just to the N of the site of Henry VII's dock, where No. 5 Dock now is (p. 415).

plentiful supplies of Hampshire oak. The Dockyard was defended by earthen ramparts forming part of *Sir Bernard de Gomme*'s scheme for fortifying Portsmouth (p. 419), but in 1704–11 these were superseded by a brick wall, of protective rather than defensive character, following the lines of the ramparts. In the C18 brick became the usual material for the dockyard buildings, especially after a spectacular fire of 1760, when the earlier wooden Rope Houses were destroyed. They were replaced by new ones with brick walls and internal timber framing, which were themselves destroyed in 1770;
68 their successors were set on fire (though not gutted) in 1776 by 'Jack the Painter', a Scot who sympathized with the rebel American colonists and who also tried but failed to set fire to the Rope House at Devonport and indulged in further incendiarism in Bristol.* Many decent buildings were erected in the last decades of the C18, in red brick, with solid functional elegance; the contractors for most of them were *Thomas Parlby & Son*. In 1795 Brigadier-General *Sir Samuel Bentham*, brother of Jeremy Bentham, became Inspector-General of Naval Works. He had previously carried out several major engineering works in the Russia of Catherine the Great, including the building of a whole private dockyard for Prince Potemkin, and was an experimenter and innovator of boundless energy. Besides completing or carrying out major operations at Portsmouth Dockyard, including the construction of a large basin and several dry docks, he obtained the collaboration of *Marc Isambard Brunel* in the development of machinery to revolutionize the manufacture of wooden purchase blocks‡ (a basic requirement for the Navy then). Some of Brunel's machinery is still in working order, in a building specially erected by Bentham over a pre-existing basin.§ Dockyard extensions, both outwards over tidal land and inwards towards the town, continued intermittently through the C18 and early C19; there was a big extension in 1843–8 (the Steam Basin), and a very large enlargement was begun in 1864. There have been smaller subsequent extensions up to the present day. Early C19 buildings are usually of yellow brick and austere. The Victorian stylistic breakthrough came with the 1843–8

* He was convicted and hanged on Blockhouse Point.

‡ Previously blocks for the Navy had been supplied by the firm of Taylor, which owned establishments at Redbridge, Swaythling (Woodmill), and Northam, all in the vicinity of Southampton.

§ Bentham also invented recoil-less guns and caisson dock-gates, and built the first steam dredger in 1803.

extensions and the first of a series of buildings with monumental scale and appearance which might almost have been designed by Sir John Vanbrugh. Bold experimentation in the constructional use of iron began with Bentham's Pay Office (now the Royal Naval Film Corporation, p. 411) in 1798, continued with No. 6 Boat House (p. 410) and the present Fire Station (p. 414), both of 1843, and culminated 83
in the great iron-framed No. 3 Ship Shop (p. 415), which may date from 1849; if it is as early as that, it is of outstanding importance in constructional history. Recent development has taken the form mainly of repairs to bombed buildings, and the renovation of some of the other older structures, retaining their walls and external appearance; the most striking wholly post-Second World War building is the multi-storey Office Block of 1965.

The only part of the Dockyard which is regularly accessible to visitors is that on the route between the Main Gate and H.M.S. Victory, passing many of the notable C18 buildings. St Ann, the Dockyard Church, can also be visited by the public. Except on special occasions, such as Navy Days, the rest of the Dockyard is not accessible to the general public. The architectural descriptions are in two sections, the first covering the direct route from the Main Gate to H.M.S. Victory, the second, starting also from the Main Gate, covering the rest of the Dockyard.

(a) *Main Gate to H.M.S. Victory.*

In 1704–11, as a tablet records, the original DOCKYARD WALL was built. It was in red brick, and a section of it still forms part of the boundary of the Dockyard on the S and SE sides, and other stretches, left behind by later extensions, are preserved within the yard. It follows generally the line of Sir Bernard de Gomme's C17 Dockyard defences, which were mainly of earth (p. 408).* The MAIN GATE, with piers of Portland stone (contemporary with the wall), was widened in 1949, when the W pier was re-set. Inside, the POLICE OFFICE, built as the Porter's Lodge in 1708, with a simple two-storeyed domestic façade, now stuccoed over, is the oldest building within the yard. Next, on the r., are NOS 5 AND 7 BOAT HOUSES, timber-framed and boarded, built as

* The line of de Gomme's triangular salient on the E side of the C17 Dockyard is indicated by a projection in the C18 Dockyard Wall behind Short Row (p. 414), now within the later Dockyard extensions.

Mast Houses over parts of the former Mast Pond in 1882 and 1875, belatedly exemplifying the form of construction of most of the buildings in the Dockyard before the mid C18. No. 6 BOAT HOUSE, seen r. across the pond, is much more substantial; it was built as a Mast House in 1843, of three storeys, in yellow brick, with stone string courses, cornice, and pediment and solid round arches to the ground storey. Inside, it is of remarkable cast-iron construction, with substantial round columns supporting floor beams of very wide span, reinforced by underslung trusses.* On the l. NOS 9, 10, AND 11 STORES, all of 1778, are among the grandest of the numerous red-brick structures erected in the period *c.*1760–1800, each a rectangular three-storeyed block, thirteen bays wide with the three central bays projecting slightly and pedimented, the ground storey having rounded keystoned arches and the upper two storeys sash windows. No. 10 was originally more monumental, and had a fine clock tower and cupola, destroyed in the bombing; it is still distinguished from the others by a rusticated stone central archway. Between Nos 9 and 10 one has a glimpse of the SEMAPHORE TOWER of six storeys, attached to a five-storey block, all rebuilt in 1926–9 in a bleak modified neo-Georgian to replace structures mysteriously destroyed by fire in 1913. On the top of the tower is a stone replica of the early C19 semaphore, like a large octagonal cupola with Ionic columns at the angles, the chief landmark of the Dockyard seen from the harbour mouth and Spithead. Built into the base of the tower is the former LION GATE, originally erected in 1778 as one of the town gateways of Portsea (p. 417) and re-erected here in 1929. On its present W (originally outer) front the round central arch is smoothly rusticated and flanked with pairs of pilasters which have intermittent bands of rock-faced masonry; in the pediment is a lion couchant.

68 Opposite No. 10 Store is the end of NO. 18 STORE, the former Ropery, built in 1770, after fire had destroyed the previous building of 1760, which itself had replaced two wooden ones destroyed in that year. The present building is the one which was set on fire by Jack the Painter in 1776, the brick walls being retained in the subsequent reconstruction.‡ It is all but 1,100 feet long, of three storeys, in mottled brick, with low,

* The E part of the building was bombed, and is still in a half-ruined state.

‡ Mr R. S. Horne says that the 1760 building was of two storeys only, and that the present external walls are those of the 1770 rebuilding.

broad, warehouse-like windows, segment-headed in the lower two storeys, square-headed on the top; of uniform width except for the five bays at each extremity, which are brought forward slightly. It was completely reconstructed in 1960, hardly more than the external side walls being kept of the C18 building; even the end elevations were rebuilt – but the original C18 external appearance has been kept.* Beyond the end of the Store are two STATUES, one to William III, originally set up elsewhere in 1717,‡ the other to Captain Scott (of the Antarctic) by his widow *Lady Katherine Scott*. Beyond, on the r., is the SOUTH OFFICE BLOCK (including the Admiral Superintendent's Office), really two two-storeyed pedimented blocks, of 1786–8, in brick with stone dressings, and a three-storeyed linking central block, with a stone rusticated archway, of 1840. The Office Block faces H.M.S. VICTORY, permanently in dry dock (p. 415), the heart-centre of the Dockyard and indeed of Portsmouth, but beyond the scope of this volume, even though she is of great architectural or near-architectural as well as of historical interest. She was launched as early as 1765.

(b) *The rest of the Dockyard.*

The parts of the Dockyard referred to in this section, apart from St Ann's Church, are not generally accessible to the public.

Turning r. inside the Main Gate, with Boat Houses Nos 5 and 7 (p. 409) on the l., the first building on the r. is the former Pay Office, now housing the ROYAL NAVAL FILM CORPORATION. It was built in 1798 of fireproof construction by *Sir Samuel Bentham*; the first storey was burnt in the blitz, but the ground storey was left intact, and the building has been restored without the upper storey. The roof construction is of intersecting tunnel-vaults, resting on cast-iron pillars which broaden out at the tops into the shapes of the springings of the vaults, the actual junctions of iron and brick taking place a little above the beginnings of the curvatures. The exterior has massive round arches with keystones, concealed

* Because of its great length, the Rope House was for long an obstruction to N–S passage, almost dividing the Dockyard into two. Two arched passages were constructed through its lower storey towards its E end, near St Ann's Church, in the early C20, and a third, making a composition of a wide central arch and two narrower side arches, was added *c*.1960.

‡ In front of Long Row (p. 414); it was later moved to a position in front of Admiralty House.

behind verandas with iron pillars which have later been closed by walls of wood framing and glass. Beyond, at the SE corner of the Dockyard, is the STAFF OFFICERS' MESS, built in 1729–32 as the Royal Naval Academy, and remodelled in 1808 as the Royal Naval College (which moved to Greenwich in 1875). It became the School of Navigation (H.M.S. Dryad) in 1906. The building was bomb-damaged in 1941 (when H.M.S. Dryad was transferred to Southwick, pp. 604, 607), and repaired with great ingenuity by *Hodgeman*, an Australian civil engineer, who re-set the central part of the façade, which had leant forward a foot, and re-secured the cupola, which had become dislodged. The exterior largely retains its Early Georgian character, three-storeyed, with symmetrical wings forming a shallow open-fronted courtyard, in dark red brick with brighter brick dressings, stone-painted quoins and string courses, and an open parapet. The windows are round-headed on the ground storey, segment-headed on the upper storey. The main part is of nine bays, the centre three slightly projecting, and the entrance has a handsome pedimented Doric doorcase, with engaged columns and frieze with triglyphs. The dominant feature of the composition is the large octagonal wooden cupola of 1808, surmounted by a ball which was used for the teaching of the sextant.

To the N is ADMIRALTY HOUSE, the residence of the Commander-in-Chief, Portsmouth, 1784–6 by *Samuel Wyatt*, altered and added to in the C19; it was bomb-damaged and subsequently restored, and some of the Victorian accretions have disappeared.* It is of yellow brick, with a central three-storeyed block of five bays (the top storey lower than the other two), low-pitched slate roof, string course at first-floor sill level, and a massive porch of *c.*1900 replacing the original delicate Doric porch. To l. and r. are slightly recessed stretches of single-storey façade each with three windows and balustrades, connecting with wings, which are each of a single tall pedimented storey with one wide window inside an elliptically arched frame. The whole building stands on a plinth several courses high, strengthened visually by a string course at the level of the ground floor. The delicate octagonal cupola, rising from a low square base, and the

* The young *Thomas Telford* was put in charge of the building of the house, having previously worked as a mason at Somerset House. He is also said to have worked on St Ann's Church (p. 436).

shutters on the second and third storeys are not part of Wyatt's original design. Internally the building shows a 'classical lucidity',* reflecting the building's triple function – as a place of residence, administration, and entertaining. There is a vestibule with a half-octagonal end, leading into a wider hall with a fine cornice, extending to the far end of the building. The reception and dining rooms have relatively restrained decoration, but the latter has a delicately enriched semi-domed recess, and both have chimneypieces by *John Bacon*. To the l. of the vestibule is a small library, with one of the original inset bookcases, having a wide central space divided from narrower side spaces by delicate square pillars, still intact; the others have been blocked. The main staircase has fine Victorian balusters; a secondary one, with simpler iron balusters dating from the building of the house, has the very unusual feature of a double handrail, with intermediate iron hoops. The garden (E) front of the main block has three widely spaced bays, but Wyatt's original design for the ground storey has been obliterated or obscured by C19 alterations.

Both Admiralty House and the Staff Officers' Mess face the GREEN, with the SHIP MAINTENANCE AUTHORITY'S OFFICES, originally the School of Naval Architecture and later the Tactical School, on the opposite (W) side, built in 1815–17 by *Edmund Hall*. It is two-storeyed, of yellow brick with stone dressings, its façade of seventeen bays, the three at each end and the three in the centre slightly projecting, the central projection having a pediment and a Doric porch. On the S side of the Green is the bomb-damaged part of NO. 6 BOAT HOUSE (p. 410), and on the N side is NO. 16 STORE, one of a series of three stores (there were originally four, but No. 14, further W, was bombed), which lie parallel to the S side of the very long No. 18 Store, the former Ropery, which is described on p. 410. No. 16 is three-storeyed, austere, of red brick, eighteen bays long with nine rather elegant buttresses rising through one and a half storeys, and 'G. R. 1771' inscribed in brickwork pattern on the E façade. NO. 15 STORE, to the W, is similar, extensively restored after bomb damage; NO. 17 STORE, to the E, 1789, of fourteen bays with seven buttresses, is also similar, but with dentilled brickwork under the eaves. Further E is St Ann's church (p. 436), to the N of which is the eastern

* The phrase is Christopher Hussey's (*Country Life*).

extremity of No. 18 Store (p. 410), linked on its N side by a passageway over three round arches* to No. 19 Store, formerly the Halchling House and the Hemp House, two separate buildings of 1771 later joined, with simple two-storeyed elevations. Part of the upper storey (now a badminton court) was originally the Convicts' Messroom. E of these buildings is Short Row, 1787, a terrace of five three-storeyed houses in brick, with later enclosed porches.‡ Long Row, to the N, is a terrace of nine larger three-storeyed houses, built in 1717 for the principal officers of the Dockyard. In the early C19 their façades were stuccoed and large enclosed porches, with Doric pilasters on the fronts, were added. The southernmost house, the residence of the Admiral Superintendent, was enlarged in the late C18 and C19. To the
83 SW of Long Row is the Fire Station, a very interesting cast-iron structure of 1843,§ built to support a large tank of water, and replacing a wooden structure of similar purpose built by Bentham in 1800. It has two tiers of horizontal girders, flat on top and arched underneath, with open spandrels, spanning between closely spaced cylindrical iron piers. The lower girders rest on the piers, and above them are continuing but separate short sections of piers supporting the upper girders. The tank was removed in 1950, but the structure is now roofed and in continued use. It is a landmark in constructional history. To the W are Nos 25 and 24 Stores, each a rectangle with internal courtyard, the N part of each built in 1782–3, the S part after 1790; of red brick, each originally of two storeys and seventeen bays, the two bays at each end and the three in the middle of each façade projecting slightly, under pediments with oval openings. No. 25 remains unaltered outside, but No. 24 had a third storey added in 1939. They have wide doorways with projecting cornices and scroll brackets, and round arches on the end façades. These two stores were originally called the South-West and South-East Buildings, and were balanced by North-West and North-East Buildings a little distance away; the NE building was bombed, but the NW remains as No. 33 Store,

* The passageway and arches, of C18 origin, were altered in the C19 but were restored in 1960, largely to their original appearance.

‡ Short Row is contained within the triangular projection of the original Dockyard Wall on the line of de Gomme's salient; *see* note on p. 409.

§ This date has recently been established by Mr R. S. Horne, making the building far more remarkable historically than had been hitherto thought. It had been considered previously to be about thirty years later.

of 1783 with some later alterations, of three storeys and a little grander than Nos 24 and 25.

To the W is NO. 1 BASIN, built in 1797–1802 by *Sir Samuel Bentham* as an extension to the Great Ship Basin originally formed in 1698. Four docks open from it to E and SE, the northernmost of them, NO. 5 DOCK, being a reconstruction of the Great Stone Dock of 1691–8. NOS 4 AND 3 DOCKS date from 1772 and 1803 respectively and NO. 2 DOCK, at the SE angle of the basin, now containing H.M.S. Victory (p. 411), from 1802. Of 1801 are NOS 1 AND 6 DOCKS, to the S and N of the Basin respectively. E of NO. 5 Dock are the BLOCK MILLS, built *c.*1800 by *Sir Samuel Bentham* over the site of an old ship basin, which was filled with two tiers of brick vaulting in 1799, the lower encasing a reservoir, connected with the adjoining docks and basin, the upper used for storage. The buildings themselves are a functional agglomeration, internally timber-framed and clad in brickwork, a single-storey block with roof lights standing between two three-storey blocks of which the S has a flat parapet, the N a gable. They were built to house the block-making machinery designed by *Marc Isambard Brunel* under Bentham, much of which is still *in situ* and used; some has, however, recently gone to the Science Museum at South Kensington, and some will be exhibited at Southsea Castle.

Both geographically and historically the Block Mills mark the end of the C18 and early C19 Dockyard – with its domestic-scale buildings mostly straightforwardly constructed of brick and timber, though a few of the later ones incorporated daring experiments in cast-iron construction – and the beginning of the greatly extended later C19 Dockyard, with its buildings of great size and sometimes of external splendour, often adventurous in their construction: the Dockyard of the Age of Steam. One of the most remarkable of the Victorian buildings is NO. 3 SHIP SHOP, said to date from 1849, but not with certainty – if it does date from then, it is of very great interest in constructional history. It consists of two great sheds (originally with open ends and sides, but now wholly clad) which sheltered Building Slips (now filled in), each with a very wide span traversed by unusually slender curved braces springing from upright columns which are in the form of filled flanges, linked lengthwise by lattice girders. The two spans have a relatively narrow space between them, and there is a second row of columns on the outer side of each span. The roof on each section is pitched, and is carried on light metal framework tangential to the arched braces, passing over the girders which link the side columns and ending, on the outward side, above the second row of columns. The inward slopes of the pitches meet in the space between the main spans, the braces of their framework intersecting and ending on the inner columns of the opposite span – altogether an ingeniously economical as well as aesthetically pleasing piece of engineering. The present cladding, including that of the roof, is of galvanized iron; originally, no doubt, the roof was of light timber. Adjoining is NO. 1 SMITHERY, a very large building of 1852, purely industrial in character, square in shape and largely of cast-iron framework construction, but with brick and stone towers at the angles, and a very tall brick chimney rising from the centre. Most of the space is covered by pitched roofs parallel to the four sides, inwardly resting on series of iron columns forming an inner square, above which rises a tall clerestory; the inner square is covered by a separate higher roof spanning from the clerestory to the central chimney. NO. 2 SHIP SHOP, 1849, faces No. 2 Basin. Red brick and stone dressings, very long and narrow, almost Vanbrugh-like in its scale and indeed in its decoration. Two storeys, of which the lower is much taller, and twenty-five bays, grouped in ranges of five, the central bay of each range having an arched recess rusticated in stonework pattern alternating with brick, rising through both storeys, and containing a round-arched doorway to the lower storey with a small semicircular window, in the head of the arch, to the upper storey. The other bays have round-headed windows to the lower storey and semicircular ones to the upper storey. A broad cornice runs the whole length of the building, except over the central bays of the first, third, and fifth ranges of five bays, which have pediments; the corresponding bays of the intermediate ranges have no pediments, so that an alternating rhythm on a grand scale is produced. The short end façades have tall rusticated recesses and very strong pediments. Not far away is the IRON FOUNDRY, 1854, in the same style, and with the same grand scale in the detailing, but not so large. It is three-storeyed on its eleven-bay W façade, with huge rusticated arches, massively keystoned, in two of the bays. The windows in the two lower storeys in the remaining bays are contained within strong round-arched recesses. A thick string course runs at second-floor level, and the windows on the top storey are round-headed. Round the corner, the N façade drops to two storeys, with windows similarly contained in round-arched recesses.

Various other buildings in the NE part of the Dockyard are in this magnificent Victorian style – truly symbolic of the British Navy in the second half of the C19 – e.g. the single-storeyed PAINT SHOP, 1896, with round-headed window recesses, rusticated pilasters flanking the doorways, and a moulded stone string course; NO. 1 PUMPING STATION, 1878, two-storeyed, and strangely mannered, with brick dentillation around the arches and arch-frames, and every fourth course of the brickwork in black brick, set back behind the other courses, giving an odd surface texture; the adjoining GUNNERY EQUIPMENT STORE, 1892, in similar style; and NO. 1 SHIP SHOP, 1896, mainly quite functionally built, but with monumental end elevations, more Vanbrughian even than No. 2 Ship Shop or the Iron Foundry. Each elevation has a huge arch, with brickwork gauged in fanwise fashion, between narrow projecting bays, and a very strong cornice across the top. Also in this part of the Dockyard is the only post-Second World War building of note, the OFFICE BLOCK, 1965 by the *Navy Works Department* of the Admiralty (latterly of the Ministry of Public Building and Works), eight-storeyed, with glazing and grey vitreous panelling between thin vertical members, and a long, heavily flat-roofed porch. In the vestibule is a piece of mural SCULPTURE by *J. D. Lennox*, using varied materials, including wood, stainless steel, and expanded polystyrene.

At the far NE corner of the Dockyard are the re-erected C17 Dockyard Round Tower and Frederick's Battery (p. 425), and further S the ruins of Holy Trinity Church (p. 444). The UNICORN GATE is the entrance to the Dockyard from Flathouse Road. It was one of the two original town gateways to Portsea, built *c.*1778 and moved to its present position in 1868. It is of Portland stone, the arch rusticated and keystoned, with two pilasters on either side, under a heavy entablature which has a pediment containing a representation of a unicorn; to l. and r. are small round-headed footway arches flanked by massive rusticated pilasters with ball finials. The side arches are topped by concave curtains of stonework imparting a strong Baroque touch to the overall design. There were originally similar curved curtains of stone to the side of the Lion Gate (p. 410) and the much earlier King James'

Gate (p. 451), but they have not survived the re-erection of these gates. The DOCKYARD WALL bordering the E part of the Dockyard (i.e. the part constructed in Mid-Victorian times) is of rubble interspersed with brick courses and with brick dressings; at frequent intervals are semicircular projections which look at first like open-air pulpits; but the rifle slits in them indicate their true nature. A similar though later wall with defensive 'pulpits' encloses H.M.S. VERNON, the former Gunwharf, to the S of, but closely associated with, the Dockyard. This has a variant of the massive classical Portsmouth gateway treated with mock-medieval embellishments, together with a square asymmetrical embattled tower, to altogether weird effect.

DEFENSIVE WORKS*

Portsmouth had some sort of rudimentary defences in the early C14 or before, but these were insufficient to keep the French out, and the town was not wealthy enough in the Middle Ages to erect anything comparable to the walls of Southampton. But it was too important strategically to be left to rely on its own resources for defending itself, and in 1386 a royal commission was appointed to investigate its defences. As a result of their recommendations fairly strong earthen ramparts and a moat, supplemented by wooden defensive structures, seem to have been built round the town on its two landward sides (NE and SE) by the end of the C14. Resumption of war with France in 1415 led to further defensive building in Portsmouth, including, probably, the Round Tower by the harbour entrance to the W of the town, the first stone-built defensive structure on Portsea Island. The Square Tower, a little to the SE, dates from 1494. Henry VIII's ambitious scheme of defence along the Solent and elsewhere in 1538–40 included the building of Southsea Castle, on the S shore of Portsea Island, and further strengthening of the town ramparts, including the erection of a large new bastion projecting from the centre of the NE rampart, blocking the original main landward entrance to the town, the Landport,‡ which was re-sited further NW. Between about 1560 and 1590 the fortifications were again greatly improved: a second large bastion was built forward of the middle of the SE rampart, and

* I am indebted to Mr A. Corney for much information relating to the defensive works.

‡ From the Latin *porta*, a gate, not *portus*, a harbour. Town gateways in Scotland were usually called 'ports'.

the older simple round corner bastions were replaced by new ones of advanced arrowhead design; the moat was widened and a new bridge built across it to the re-sited Landport; and a new stone wall was constructed along the NW side of the town bordering the Camber, cutting off the commercial quayside from the town, as the older walls at Southampton had done. These improvements were carried out simultaneously with the building of the still extant fortifications at Berwick-upon-Tweed, and both schemes were financed by a State lottery in 1566–9.

In 1665 Charles II instituted a major programme of reconstruction of the defences which lasted several decades. The work was supervised by *Sir Bernard de Gomme*, Engineer-in-Chief of all the King's Castles in England and Wales, a Dutchman who was in touch with the most advanced Continental ideas on the design of defences, and an advocate for the building of elaborate secondary works beyond the main lines with their moats. His work included remodelling the existing ramparts, reconstructing the bastions, widening the moats, and building the first ravelin, or detached triangular bulwark on an island site beyond the main moat and protected by an outer moat on its own, outside the Landport; three other ravelins were to follow after his time. Beyond the moat he constructed a glacis, or continuous earthwork with its outer scarp angled to deflect shot, its inner face (counterscarp) vertical to protect a walkway beside the moat. De Gomme died in 1685, and some of the works initiated by him were not completed until after his death, particularly in the Point area around the Square and Round Towers. Considerable improvements were carried out on the town defences in the first half of the C18, much of it by *Desmaretz*. The Dockyard, well to the N of the town, was far less strongly defended than the town; it had a relatively simple earthen rampart constructed by *de Gomme*, which was superseded in the early C18 by a brick wall of protective rather than defensive character (p. 408). To the NE of the Dockyard a second Round Tower and a stone-built battery (Frederick's Battery) were built in 1685–8. Other defensive works carried out in the Portsmouth area during the period *c.*1660–1750 were the building of the original ramparts at Gosport, started by de Gomme, the building of Forts James and Charles (long since vanished), also at Gosport, the erection of a battery at the Blockhouse on the Gosport side of Portsmouth Harbour entrance, improvements to Southsea Castle, and, in 1745, the erection of Fort Cumberland to guard the entrance to Langstone Harbour.

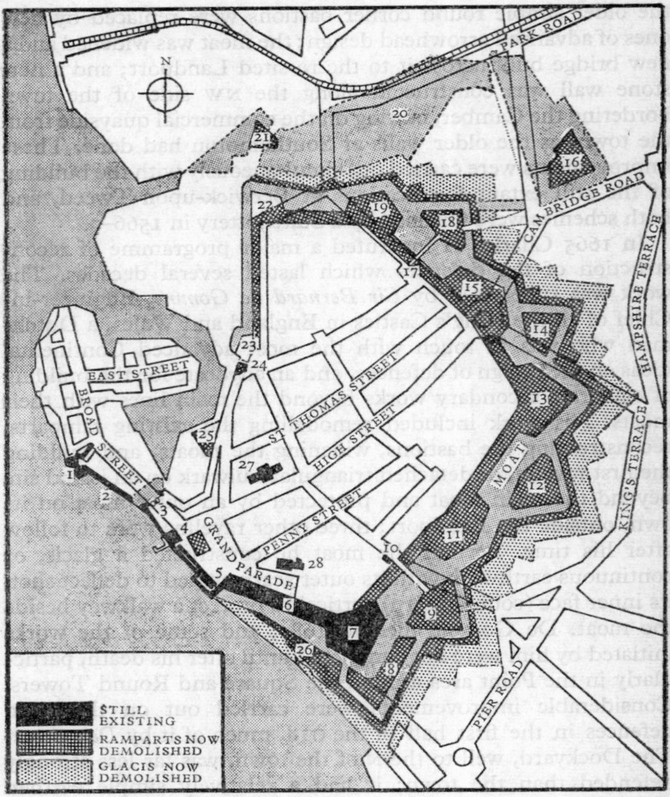

Portsmouth, plan of the defences *c.*1800 (by courtesy of the Libraries and Museums Committee, Portsmouth)

1. *Round Tower*
2. *Eighteen-Gun Battery,* part of Point Battery
3. King James' Gate
4. *Square Tower*
5. *Saluting Platform*
6. *Long Curtain*
7. *King's Bastion*
8. King's Counterguard
9. King's Ravelin
10. King William's Gate
11. Pembroke Bastion
12. Montague Ravelin
13. East Bastion
14. East Ravelin
15. Town Mount Bastion
16. Amhurst's Redoubt
17. *Landport Gate*
18. Landport Ravelin
19. Guy's Bastion
20. Mill Pond
21. Mill Redoubt
22. Beeston's Bastion
23. Legg's Demi-Bastion
24. Quay Gate
25. Camber Bastion
26. Spur Redoubt
27. *St Thomas's Church, Portsmouth Cathedra*
28. *Domus Dei now the Garrison Church*

Italic type indicates fortifications and buildings still existing

The next major series of defensive undertakings began under the Duke of Richmond in 1770, when work started on a second line of ramparts extending from the Old Portsmouth ramparts on their NE side to the harbour shore E of the Dockyard, completely enclosing the dockyard town of Portsea (which had grown up since c.1700, p. 456) and the Dockyard on their landward sides. The new fortifications were very much on the lines of de Gomme's, with bastions, ravelins, moats, and glacis, but generally on a bigger scale and with certain refinements of detail. At the same time the Gosport defences were elaborated (p. 247) – so that at the end of the C18 there were three heavily defended towns bordering the mouth of Portsmouth Harbour, the only post-medieval walled towns in England apart from Berwick, and the only ones which had fortifications to the complicated patterns characteristic of the Continental urban defences of the C17 and C18. In 1789 the Duke of Richmond reconstructed Cumberland Fort (which survives intact, perhaps the most impressive piece of C18 defensive architecture remaining in England), and about the same time there were alterations at Southsea Castle. In 1814 more extensive works were carried out at Southsea, and probably also at the Round Tower. In 1847–50 considerable reconstruction took place in the Point area, and large-scale outworks were built round Southsea Castle (which is almost a microcosm of the history of post-medieval defensive architecture). In 1858 Hilsea Lines, guarding the N shore of Portsea Island alongside the narrow Port Creek, which had existed in some form since at least the early C18, were reconstructed on a massive scale, in earth and brick and with a moat, in a form quite recognizably still in the tradition of de Gomme and his C18 successors.

The culmination of Greater Portsmouth's defensive history came with Lord Palmerston's scheme of 1860 against the threat of French invasion, with the series of forts at Gosport (p. 248) and Fareham, along Portsdown Hill (p. 387), and, most remarkably, in the Solent itself, where four circular island bastions were built, in stone and brick, with great structural ingenuity.* Southsea Castle, Cumberland Fort, the small intermediate Lumps Fort, and Forts Blockhouse and Monckton (the latter a C18 creation) in Gosport, were all included in the Palmerstonian scheme, so that Portsmouth with its harbour, entirely ringed with forts except on the E side (where there was Langstone

* Called Horse Sand, Spit Bank, No Man's Land, and St Helen's Forts; the last is close to the Isle of Wight shore.

Harbour), became, for a time, one of the most strongly defended places in the world. With the construction of the widespread new defences the old town ramparts around Portsmouth and Portsea (beyond which urban development had spread far since *c.*1800) became redundant, and in the 1870s they were demolished, all except the very varied stretch along the harbourside at Old Portsmouth and four of the old town gateways, one (the Landport) remaining *in situ* but in a strangely incongruous setting, the others (King James Gate in Old Portsmouth and the Lion and Unicorn Gates in Portsea) being re-erected elsewhere (pp. 451, 410, 417). The sites of the destroyed ramparts were used for barracks, Service recreation grounds, a public park (Victoria Park, p. 456), and for Dockyard extension. Fortunately, accurate plans of them remain which, together with the surviving structures, make the study of the Portsmouth defences of special interest in the history of military architecture.

The ROUND TOWER stands by the shore just NW of the area of the ramparted town of Old Portsmouth, on the harbour side of the Point, the peninsula between the harbour mouth and the Camber. It is cylindrical, of three storeys separated by string courses. Nothing, except possibly the footings, is visible of the fort probably built in 1415. The ground storey probably dates from the time of Henry VIII (*c.*1538–40), and originally had eight gunports covering two-thirds of the circumference (omitting part of the inward frontage), externally under flat segmental arches. These were later mainly blocked, probably under *de Gomme* (when his adjoining Eighteen Gun Battery was built), leaving three open on the N–NW side, with their segmental heads (probably) renewed at the time. Possibly the upper two storeys date basically from de Gomme's time; more probably they were rebuilt in Napoleonic times, when (almost certainly) the interior was reconstructed with massive brickwork, casemates being formed behind the surviving gunports – work comparable with that on the Martello Towers. In *c.*1847–50 the top was reconstructed, being shortened by six feet and adapted to form gun positions.

SW of the Round Tower is the EIGHTEEN GUN BATTERY, parallel with the shore, and the shorter FLANKING BATTERY at r. angles, backing on to the Round Tower, with which it is linked by another short stretch of rampart parallel with the shore. The Eighteen Gun Battery was originally built as one of the last stages of *de Gomme*'s scheme in the late C17 (possibly on the site of earlier lesser works), but it was reconstructed from 1847 to 1850. De Gomme's battery originally had gunports, with shallow casemates; at the reconstruction the casemates were greatly deepened inwards in brick, and a second tier of three added to the top of the Flanking Battery. The whole was evidently refaced externally in stone and, on the sites of demolished houses in the narrow wedge-shaped space between the Battery and Broad Street, POINT BARRACKS were built. The buildings were all recently acquired by Portsmouth Corporation. Point Barracks were pulled down (except for part of the N range, where tunnel-vaulted chambers were half demolished, leaving the remaining parts to look confusingly like casemates), and the Battery converted into a section of a splendidly sited promenade which runs from the Round Tower along all the surviving ramparts to the King's Bastion.* In the fifth bay from the N on the main battery is the COMMON SALLY PORT, a broad, plain archway which had been constructed in the late C18, in replacement of one of de Gomme's gunports, in order to allow access to the foreshore from Broad Street, was blocked in the 1847–50 reconstruction, and recently reopened.‡ Beyond the S end of Point Battery a moat cut across the peninsula from the Camber from the late C17; it was filled in in the C19 and a connecting stretch of wall built against the site. This moat was the outer protection to the KING JAMES' GATE into Old Portsmouth (p. 455), which was built in 1687 to replace an Elizabethan gate, and removed in the 1870s; the gateway, somewhat reduced, stands re-erected in Burnaby Road (p.451). Part of the abutment on the S side survives, including a tunnel-vaulted recess which was formerly part of a small room, probably used as a cell. Adjoining this on the shoreward side can be seen the lower part of the square bastion of *c.*1560–90 (the upper part is later reconstruction), which marked the harbour end of the wall built along the NW side of the town during that period.

From here to the SE the surviving walls and ramparts are parts of

* Unfortunately including conspicuous railings which, at the time of writing, were painted a lurid blue.

‡ The history of the various Sally Ports is confusing. The original one, at the S end of the Point Battery, was a very narrow passageway, with two angles, constructed in order to allow public access to the Point foreshore; this was replaced by the present Common Sally Port, while the opening now simply called the Sally Port was used by service personnel. They were important because this stretch of foreshore was used for landing merchandise.

the defences of the town proper. The short section from King James' Gate to the Square Tower is also of late C16 origin (though its upper parts are reconstructed); it contains the SALLY PORT, a wide opening probably built, like the Common Sally Port, in the late C18, in order to provide access for the garrison within the walled town directly on to the seashore.* The SQUARE TOWER was originally built in 1494, and it may in the C16 have been used as the residence of the military Governor of Portsmouth.‡ It was transformed into a magazine in the late C16 or early C17, when it was reduced in height; in 1827 it was plainly refaced in stone, and in 1847–50 the tower was included within the remodelled defences and reconstructed internally. Parts of the medieval walls remain behind the outer casings, and on the E front, facing down High Street, is a small circular recess containing a BUST of Charles I, 1635 by *Le Sueur*, and part of a once long inscription (the rest of which was obliterated in 1827).

Southward is the TEN GUN BATTERY, which probably began as a C16 shoreside wall, adapted and thickened by de Gomme to accommodate guns, and raised in 1860 to the level of the SALUTING BATTERY to the S, a rectangular platform projecting slightly seaward from the adjoining ramparts and faced in stone. It was built in 1568 on the site of an earlier installation and remains probably little altered, apart from the upper surfacing and the parapet walls. Then the LONG CURTAIN, extending to the King's Bastion at the southernmost corner of the Old Portsmouth defences, the only section of de Gomme's main scheme of defences surviving in something like its original condition although (like the rest of his Old Portsmouth ramparts) it was modified in the C18. It is, however, not very typical of most of what existed until *c.*1870, since it faces the sea, and the outer defensive arrangements, beyond the main moat, were much smaller in scale than the elaborate system of ravelins, outer moats, and glacis which characterized the landward defences of the town. Moreover there was no stretch of main rampart on the landward sides which extended as far as the Long Curtain without the elaboration of a bastion. It is basically an earthen rampart with inclined inner face, flat top, and stone outward face rising almost vertically from the moat, with a strong rounded

* See note above.

‡ Until the buildings of the Domus Dei (p. 404) were converted into a Governor's residence.

string course at the top of the stonework; above this is a brick parapet bordering a walkway along the outward side of the rampart (an C18 modification of de Gomme's arrangements). On the seaward side of the moat is a rudimentary glacis (now converted into a promenade) with vertical inner face, behind which is a covered passageway* leading to the SPUR, a sort of miniature ravelin projecting out to sea (part of de Gomme's scheme), of which all but the point is now covered by the promenade. The KING'S BASTION is the only one of the C17 or C18 angle bastions surviving. It was originally a small Elizabethan bastion called at first the Green Bulwark, then Wimbledon's Bastion (after Lord Wimbledon, Governor in 1630–8); it obtained its present form in the C18. It is outwardly faced like the Long Curtain, but the moat in the foreground has been filled in to form part of a car park, which also extends over the site of the KING'S COUNTERGUARD, a detached outer salient like an elongated ravelin, which was constructed in the 1730s. NE of the King's Bastion the defensive works have disappeared, apart from the low inner abutment of the main rampart, which borders a footpath alongside Governor's Green (now a football field) to the site of KING WILLIAM'S GATE, across Pembroke Road, which was built in 1834 as a new entrance to the old town from the SE.‡ Entrance into the gate, like that into the Landport and the two Portsea gates, was complicated, first over a subsidiary moat on to the KING'S RAVELIN (an C18 construction), then over the main moat to the gate itself. Clarence and Victoria Barracks (p. 429) occupy the sites of the ramparts further NE.

KING JAMES' GATE, *see* p. 451.

LANDPORT GATE, *see* p. 451.

LION GATE, *see* p. 410.

UNICORN GATE, *see* p. 417.

DOCKYARD ROUND TOWER AND FREDERICK'S BATTERY. A second Round Tower (not to be confused with the original one near the Point) was built in 1683 on the harbour shore well to the N of Old Portsmouth and E of the then existing Dockyard (the site is well within the present area of the Dockyard). In 1688 Frederick's Battery was built alongside,

* The stone covering of this passageway can be seen leading from the lower part of the Saluting Battery and then disappearing under the promenade which covers the former glacis. The stonework is probably late C17.

‡ A small single-storey building survives inside the site of the gate, formerly the Guard Room. It post-dated the gate.

facing NE across an inlet of the harbour. Both were re-erected (the Battery in modified form) in 1870, when the Dockyard was extended, on sites on the new periphery, the Tower close to the new shoreline, the Battery hard against the gasworks. The Tower is of three storeys, the lowest storey tapering, the rest upright, with a string course between the two lower storeys, mock-machicolated underneath, and square-headed windows on the top two storeys. The Battery originally had twelve gunports with casemates in groups of three, separated by towers, of which the tower in the centre was evidently larger. In its present form it consists of a continuous series of six gunports with a tower at each end, that to the E being taller. Each of the gunports is an upright rectangular recess (they are now all blocked) within a casemate with a segment-arched head; above the casemates is a walkway, bounded on the outside of the wall by a parapet. The tower at the E end is of four stages, the lower two tapering, the top two upright, the top stage having intriguing mock-medieval arrow slits in cross pattern, the second and third stages square-headed gun slits, and the ground storey a massive round-headed door. Abutting against this tower to the W is a two-storeyed structure, all tapering and rising no higher than the rampart walk, with gun slits on the upper storey and a round-headed window below. The tower at the W end is in two stages, the lower tapering and rising to the rampart walk, with similar gun slits and window, the upper stage open to the walkway. Even in its truncated state (and it is obvious that much re-assortment of parts has taken place) this is a highly interesting piece, one of the few relics of the once extensive C17 defensive works in Portsmouth; the mock-medievalisms on the Tower and Battery are intriguing.

SOUTHSEA CASTLE. One of Henry VIII's forts, built *c.*1538–40 (cf. Calshot, Hurst, Netley, Cowes (I.o.W.), Yarmouth (I.o.W.)), right on the sea shore. Its original plan was unusual; a square keep within an *enceinte* which was shaped like a diamond (or a larger square at forty-five degrees with the keep) with big rectangular gun platforms at its E and W flanks. The castle has been continuously modified; it was fire-damaged in 1626 and 1640, saw some action in the Civil War, was elaborated in 1683 by *de Gomme*, who provided a glacis and covered way, damaged by explosion in 1759, reconstructed internally *c.*1800, much altered in 1814–16 by *Major-Gen. Sir John Fisher* (when the *enceinte* was partly rebuilt), used as a prison *c.*1844–50, and, in 1850, again altered and contained within a large area of new fortifications, which transformed it into an Early Victorian fortress, with the original castle as the centrepiece – a precursor to Palmerston's forts (*see* p. 248). It remained in military occupation until 1960; Portsmouth Corporation were, at the time of writing, restoring it with great care to its condition in 1850. It will house a Military Museum, and is due to open to the public in 1966. It is a microcosm of the history of defensive building in Portsmouth. The KEEP is basically Henry VIII's. It had three gunports on the S side, at the present first-floor level, doubly splayed with external four-centred arches; they were blocked by *de Gomme*, but one has recently been re-opened. The blockings of the other two can be seen externally, as can the blockings of two other gunports on the E and W walls. In the C18 the keep was a shell, with two small buildings, facing across a rectangular courtyard, within it. The present internal arrangement, with the walls and facings of red brick interspersed with occasional black bricks, dates from the late C18 or very early C19.* There are a basement, ground storey,‡ and tall upper storey divided into two wide tunnel-vaulted compartments interconnected by two elliptically vaulted passageways – a very fine piece of brick engineering, strong enough to support an open gun platform on the roof. The way up to the roof is by a spiral staircase of iron (an interesting construction for *c.*1800) within a cylindrical space in the thickness of the central cross-wall.§ The present fenestration of the castle, with small segment-headed windows, and the stonework of the parapets date from the time of the internal rearrangement.

The ENCEINTE preserves Henry VIII's basic shape. The original E and W gun platforms are still there (though refaced and internally reconstructed); the S part is basically Henry VIII's, although the seaward angle was rounded to a blunt point and the rest has been refaced and heightened. In 1814 the N part of the *enceinte* was built. The original shape was preserved, but new outer walls were built further N, allowing space for internal military quarters against them; similar military quarters were erected (all in brick) within the E and

* There is no written record of this work, but Mr Corney points out that it has a strong affinity to the late C18 work at Cumberland Fort.

‡ Actually a little above the ground level of the *enceinte*, approached up a short flight of steps.

§ The newel posts as well as the steps are all of iron, but the balustrade at the top landing, recently renewed, is of wood.

W parts of the *enceinte*. At the same time the moat* was reconstructed and a covered walkway erected within the counterscarp of the glacis (with musket-holes facing inwards over the moat). This was connected to the basement of the keep by a covered passageway in brick across the bed of the moat. The refacing of the exterior of the older parts of the *enceinte* dates from 1814.

In 1828 a LIGHTHOUSE was built on the N face of the W gun platform, to rather engaging effect.‡ The 1850 alterations included the heightening of the S part of the *enceinte* in brick to provide improved gun platforms. The massive earthworks then constructed in the area around the castle proper are being partly flattened; others are being smoothed over to form parts of the seaside open space – an admirable idea appallingly executed. Imaginative landscaping could have worked wonders with what is left of the mounds of the Victorian fortress.

CUMBERLAND FORT, Eastney. Originally built in 1746 by the Duke of Cumberland in the form of a slightly irregular five-cornered star. Reconstructed in 1786 etc. by the Duke of Richmond, who transformed it into a wide pentagon, with a sharp arrowhead salient at each angle, a glacis beyond a dry moat, and one ravelin. The ramparts are faced externally in stone, with brick parapets and segment-headed gunports, behind which are deep tunnel-vaulted brick chambers superimposed with earth. Within the *enceinte* are a few buildings of C18 and later date. The fort is little altered from its original condition; the main part is still in military occupation and maintained, but the glacis and the ravelin (the only one of its kind still existing in Portsmouth) are crumbling. It is perhaps the best piece of C18 defensive architecture left in Britain and the precursor to the better-known Palmerstonian forts. Its preservation in entirety§ is of the utmost importance.

NAVAL AND MILITARY BUILDINGS

outside the Dockyard

H.M.S. VICTORY BARRACKS (ROYAL NAVAL BARRACKS), Queen Street, Portsea. 1899–1903. Extensive blocks, mainly

* Always a dry moat.

‡ Still used as a lighthouse, and painted black and white.

§ Military use of the fort will probably shortly cease; the Ministry of Public Building and Works are taking a keen interest in it as a historical monument.

three-storeyed, a little more than utilitarian, with faintly Flemish or Scottish outlines. Tower with triple round arches on its upper storey and a stumpy spire; next to it an insipid five-storeyed block by *E. Berry Webber*, *c.*1960. New four-storey block being built 1965, decorous and straightforward, with white fascia, exposed floor ends, windows and vitreous panels in thin white framework, well managed service installations on the roof; typical of the excellent recent architectural work by the *Ministry of Public Building and Works* (*Navy Works*). The GATEWAY into the barracks is in the Portsmouth tradition: rusticated arch, heavy segmental pediment, Ionic pilasters. Across the street is the WARD ROOM, floridly Flemish with a tower central to the façade. Inside is a series of PAINTINGS of naval battles, the two best by *H. Wyllie* (Glorious First of June and Copenhagen).

MILLDAM BARRACKS, Burnaby Road, Portsea. Some quite modest two-storey Late Georgian red brick blocks remain, now used by the Ministry of Public Building and Works.

CAMBRIDGE BARRACKS, High Street. *See* Portsmouth Grammar School, p. 449.

VICTORIA BARRACKS AND CLARENCE BARRACKS, between Alexandra Road and Pembroke Road. Of *c.*1880. Extensive large-scale group in red brick with heavy stone dressings. Assertive Gothic with Butterfieldan or Teulonic derivation and Scots Baronial cross-reference. Skyline with variegated turrets, steeples, gables, looking weird from certain angles. Some of the blocks are bomb-damaged and half-ruined, others empty and derelict; this heightens their romantic appeal. The site adjoins Southsea Common and would offer a wonderful opportunity for imaginative redevelopment.

EASTNEY BARRACKS (Royal Marines). 1862–7. An impressive *ensemble* of mid-Victorian naval-military architecture, mainly arranged round a very long open-sided courtyard facing the sea. The long centre block, with marines' quarters, is austere, in drab brown brick with brighter red dressings, three-storeyed with string courses at the intermediate floor levels, round-headed windows on the ground storey and low slated roof. The façade is articulated by bringing three bays slightly forward at intervals (the forwarded bays slightly narrower than the others) under hipped roofs. To the E a range containing the OFFICERS' MESS in the centre, stone-faced (the rest of the range is in brick) with the main entrance approached up a balustraded staircase on the second storey, which is brought forward with an Italianate round-arched colonnade, balustraded on top. Internally, the DINING ROOM is quite splendid, a large rectangle with a massive coved ceiling, big round-headed plate-glass windows, and a central semicircular bay. Round archways lead into a first-floor gallery. There is also a grand staircase hall. At the W end of the courtyard are blocks with a strong and distinctive character of their own; three-storeyed with attics, in red brick with rusticated yellow brick pilasters at intervals, yellow brick frieze and stone cornice, the windows (round-headed on the ground storey, segment-headed above) all stone-framed. In the background at the W end a WATER TOWER of 1870–1, with a stone frieze, mock-machicolated, below the top storey and a flat pyramid top. – ST ANDREW, *see* p. 436.

HILSEA BARRACKS. The oldest barracks in Portsmouth, although they were far outside the pre-Victorian town, near the N edge of Portsea Island. The first encampment was in 1756, but for a long time the buildings were mainly temporary. Permanent buildings were erected in 1854 and later for the Royal Artillery, who occupied the barracks till 1921. – GATCOMBE HOUSE, a three-storey, five-bay brick Georgian house on an older site, became the Officers' Mess in 1877, and was uninterestingly altered and enlarged; it retains an C18 pedimented doorcase with Ionic engaged columns.* – Also a pleasant plain two-storeyed late C18 brick house which must have been the residence of the Commanding Officer. – ST BARBARA, *see* p. 437.

H.M.S. EXCELLENT. On Whale Island, which was largely created through the dumping of dredged material during the Victorian extensions of the Dockyard – a remarkable achievement. The Island is hump-shaped, with fairly steeply rising edges, and several mature trees grow there. Unremarkable late C19 buildings, but some good recent work by the architects of the *Ministry of Public Building and Works* (*Navy Works*), including the W.R.N.S. BLOCK, 1963. This is three-storeyed and concrete-framed with brick façades and a single-storey E extension, partly enclosing a pleasant small open courtyard. – PETTY OFFICERS' BLOCK, eight-storeyed, concrete and red brick façades, the top storey mainly an open concrete framework enclosing service installations. Big,

* There is said to be a doorway of *c.*1500 in the garden, and the font in St Barbara's Church was dug up there (p. 437).

flat-roofed porches to E and W resting on thin columns. Single-storey projection to the N with green panelling.

H.M.S. VERNON. *See* p. 418.

NAVAL WAR MEMORIAL. *See* p. 462.

POST-MEDIEVAL CHURCHES*

St Mary, more or less in the middle of Portsea Island, was the only church on the island outside Old Portsmouth until the C18, when St George and St John (the latter destroyed) were built in the dockyard town of Portsea, and St Ann in the Dockyard itself. Two quite ambitious churches, All Saints and St Paul (the latter also destroyed), were built in the 1820s, followed by a series of C19 churches of no special interest.‡ St Mary itself was rebuilt on a grand scale in the 1880s. The most interesting period of post-medieval church architecture in Portsmouth began in the 1890s with the building of St Agatha, which, with its austere, impressive Italianate shell and splendid (mainly later) internal embellishments, was one of the great churches of the period. Alas, it is no longer a church, and its future is in doubt. The first four decades of the C20 saw a remarkable outburst of church building in a variety of styles – notably at St Alban, St Cuthbert, St John, St Margaret, the Holy Spirit, and *Comper*'s St Philip, Cosham.

CATHEDRAL OF ST JOHN EVANGELIST (R.C.), Edinburgh Road. 1877–82 by *J. Crawley*; additions by *J. S. Hansom*, 1886 and 1892; W end and porch 1906 by Canon *A.J.C. Scoles*. Not especially impressive outside. Deep red brick with stone dressings. Nave, transepts, and choir with tall roof-lines; apsed sanctuary with strong buttresses; lean-to aisles and chapels. Angle turrets at the W end. The windows are mainly conventionally neo-Dec, except for the conspicuous S transept window with weirdly flowing tracery. Inside, immediately, an impression of moderate grandeur; this does feel like a cathedral (more than the Anglican cathedral does), albeit a modest one, thanks very largely to the exquisite proportions and shapes of the six-bay nave arcades, in Midland High Gothic, with slender tall piers, foliated capitals, and delicately moulded arches, satisfactorily related to the proportions of the nave and the width of the aisles. The sanctuary occupies

* Many of the facts relating to Portsmouth churches were provided by Mr R. Hubbuck.

‡ Not, at least, since the recent demolition of *Butterfield*'s St Michael.

the crossing-space, with a big Gothic BALDACCHINO with massive marble angle columns, behind which most of the structural choir is a shut-off chapel. Thick gilt and dark colour decoration all over the choir and S chapel walls and arches.* – STAINED GLASS. In the N transept three panels, one with a portrait of Pope John XXIII, the glass in shades from deep purple to red and blue, the features realistic and the expression full of strength. The other two panels are heraldic.

BISHOP'S HOUSE. By *Hansom*. Gothic. Restored after bomb damage.

ST AGATHA, off Charlotte Street, Landport.‡ Built 1893–5 in what was a slum district outside the Dockyard, under the inspiration of Father R. R. Dolling, a vigorous Anglo-Catholic priest. It ceased to be a church in 1955, most of the houses in the parish having disappeared through bombing or clearance, without being replaced by residential accommodation. Since then it has been a naval store, and its future is uncertain. It is the *tour de force* of *J. H. Ball*, a pupil of Waterhouse, who practised in Southsea until 1896, when he moved to London. Dolling wanted a capacious and spatially impressive shell which could be beautified internally as time went on and resources became available; Ball provided a church in the Early Christian style which now looks ungainly outside with bare brick walls, most of them never intended to be seen from public roads, since the church was closely hemmed in by houses, the stump of an unfinished SW tower, and a raw brick wall set diagonally across the site of the apse of the Lady Chapel, recently demolished to allow for the widening of Charlotte Street. Inside it is now filled with stored materials, intermediate floors having been inserted, so that only the central space of the nave and the apse of the sanctuary remain clear.§ It had a very broad nave with four-bay arcades, the walls of bare stock brick, the round arches brought out in red brick. The first and third piers of the arcades are of polished red granite, round and relatively slender, the responds and central piers faced in alabaster, square and relatively massive. Thus a rhythm was created which dimin-

* Some of the decoration is by *Westlake* (RH).

‡ Most of the information in this account is taken from Mr Nicholas Taylor's article in the *Architectural Review* (May 1964).

§ The naval authorities have kept the apse clear and are carefully avoiding damage to its decoration.

See p. 831

ished the effect of length and increased that of width* – the width being further emphasized by the cross-beams of the substantial timber roof. Lighting throughout the church was at clerestory level only, because of the houses that hemmed the church in. The main clerestory consisted of groups of small round-arched windows in buff terracotta. The intended N aisle was never built. The S aisle broadened out in its two E bays to form a spacious Lady Chapel, which had an apsed sanctuary. The climax of the building was the semi-domed apse at the E end, behind a round-headed arch.

It was the internal decoration which made the church out- 92
standing artistically. In 1895 Father Dolling commissioned *Heywood Sumner*, a friend and disciple of William Morris, to decorate the semi-dome of the now vanished apse of the Lady Chapel with a MOSAIC of the Virgin (executed by *Powell's*) and a series of scenes from her life in SGRAFFITO – a technique practised in Roman and Renaissance times which involves the incision of lines in coloured plaster before it has set. It produces colours of a bright intensity, stronger than pastel shades, less deep than those of High Victorian stained glass, and clear, straightforward definition of features. In 1901 Sumner began his masterpiece – the decoration of the apse and its semi-dome in sgraffito. Its centrepiece is a great figure of Christ in Majesty in the semi-dome, set in a vesica with a many-lined border, with a representation of the radiant sun in the top of the dome, texts to the sides (in a rather mannered version of Roman lettering), and, below them, six large medallions (three on each side) including Christian symbols. The broad arc of a rainbow rises from the base of the semi-dome, intersects the borders of the vesica, and passes behind the lower part of Christ's body, imparting, with the vesica, a basic curved geometrical pattern which unifies the composition. Along the top of the apse itself is a range of small round-headed clerestory windows (originally filled with stained glass representations of angels and cherubim). Below them is a range of ovals with Christian symbols, and below these seven tall figures of the Evangelists and major Prophets. This part of the composition is unified vertically by wide borders decorated with vine stem and leaf pattern separating the figures, continuing up between the ovals with the symbols

* The neo-Ravennate capitals were carved, to *Heywood Sumner*'s designs, over a period of several years and completed in 1927 by *A. V. Heal*; they were in the first plan blocks of stone.

and curving round the clerestory lights. The dominant colours are red and blue, but others are used, particularly in the patterning and the background, and, of course, in the sun and rainbow. It is one of Portsmouth's few major works of art, and, had it dated from any time before the middle of the C19, people would undoubtedly have gone to great lengths to preserve it. But because it is not yet 'old' nor any longer 'modern' it is simply disregarded and its very existence is in jeopardy. The walling round the arch to the apse is decorated in intriguing geometrical patterns. The lower part of the apse was plainly panelled, and in front of this was the great BALDACCHINO, with short round marble columns standing on the top of tall square bases, supporting a gabled superstructure with round arches and quadripartite vaulting. This was removed to *Butterfield*'s former church of St Michael (near the Guildhall) and ignorantly destroyed when that church was demolished a few years ago. – The not specially impressive ALTAR is now in Holy Trinity, Gosport (p. 242), and the very fine PULPIT is in St John, Rudmore (p. 439).

ST ALBAN, Copnor Road, Copnor. 1914 by *Sir Charles Nicholson*. W end bomb-damaged and rebuilt in 1956. Simplified, angular Gothic. Red brick outside; interior with whitewashed walls, reddish sandstone arcades, and richly coloured fittings. It has a strong affinity to Nicholson's slightly later Ascension, Southampton (p. 590). Five-bay nave arcades with lumpy octagonal piers; tall clerestory of lancets; lancets in the aisles; very low-pitched nave roof; flat aisle and chancel roofs. The chancel is slightly narrower than the nave but similar in height. E window of two tall lancets with square-sided reveals; tall side windows. Low N chapel, with broad arches into it. Triple blocked three-bay arcade on the S side of the S aisle, intended for a chapel, never built. The interior spatial effect is now not satisfactory because of the removal of the SCREEN from the chancel entrance to the W end; in a simplified Jacobean style and brightly coloured, it must have been very effective in its original position. Now there is a long eastward vista culminating ineffectively in the two E lancets, which are filled with STAINED GLASS by *A. K. Nicholson*; intricate detailing in strong, rich colours, but small in scale and not designed to be seen from a distance. No other pre-war glass remains in the body of the church, and the post-war glass (e.g. in the N chapel by *Geoffrey Webb*) is feeble. In the sacristy some C16–18 roundels, Flemish or

German; from Uplands, Fareham (p. 227). Recent re-decoration by *S. Dykes Bower* has included the painting of the roofs in strong colours (to good effect). The intended repainting of the woodwork at the E end may provide the effective E climax so much needed after the removal of the screen. – FONT. Plain, octagonal, C15, from St Mary, Portsea. Sentimentally admired as the font where both Brunel and Dickens were baptized. – PLATE. Italian C15 Chalice in copper-gilt; English C18 Flagon; remarkable set of modern plate presented by Edward Spenser; also a C17 Spanish Processional Cross and a C15 English Thurible.

ALL SAINTS, Commercial Road, Church Street, Landport. 1827–8 by *Jacob Owen*. A remarkably handsome neo-Perp church, externally in stone, but with internal framework of cast-iron piers and plastered vaults, bringing out a specifically early C19 Gothic quality in those materials much more successfully than usual. Externally the church makes a good show with its W front to Commercial Road, the W doorway and the large neo-Perp window above it being contained within a tall, deeply moulded recess, the gable surmounted by a pretty, well-shaped spirelet (a modification of the arrangement on St Helen and St Michael-le-Belfrey, York).* The spirelet, crocketed, rises from a small square base with pinnacles and battlements, and is brought out in golden Bath stone against the silver Dorset stone of most of the ashlar walls. There are other felicitous features, such as an ogee-hooded clock just below the spirelet. Inside, a spacious six-bay nave with thin iron pillars of quatrefoil section supporting ribbed mock-vaults, those in the aisles coming a little lower than those in the nave, the wall spaces between the arches of the arcades (at the height of the aisle vaults) and the nave vault being taken up by delicate plaster patterns including ogee arch-shapes, traceried panels, and portcullises. Filling the aisles and the W bay of the nave are GALLERIES, their undersides shaped to flat transverse-vault patterns and their fronts panelled. The aisle windows, bisected internally by the galleries, are tall, of three lights, in a style transitional between Dec and Perp, their tracery surprisingly convincing. A lively series of bosses and corbels, especially in the aisles, with foliage patterns and expressive faces. The nave space extends

* Mr R. Hubbuck says that a perspective drawing of *c.* 1828 shows a projected tower with open arches, to which the present arrangement must be a reduced alternative.

one bay W from the main space, between side vestibules containing the gallery staircases. The chancel was rebuilt in 1877, and is attributed to *Sir Gilbert Scott*, but in view of the date and, especially, the style, it must have been by *John Oldrid Scott*, his son. It is neo-Perp, especially sensitive, harmonious with the early C19 nave yet asserting its different quality to just the degree that is appropriate to the difference in date. Of fine stone, with a complex, much embossed lierne-vault, the vaulting-shafts ending in a splendid series of caryatid figures, displaying a variety of characterization and detailing. The whole church was recently restored, sensitively and unobtrusively, by *Romilly B. Craze*. – STAINED GLASS. E window by *Terence Randall*, 1950.

ST ANDREW (Garrison Church), Eastney. 1905. One of a series of churches designed for the Admiralty; there are nearly identical ones at Devonport (Keyham) and Chatham. Brick with stone dressings. Eight-bay arcades with stone piers and capitals and moulded brick arches. Lancets. Terracotta panelling round the sanctuary. – STAINED GLASS. E window, three lancets, by *Kempe*.

ST ANN, the Dockyard Church (p. 413). The original chapel was built in 1704, to serve Dockyard officials and staff. Its site was required for the building of Admiralty House (p. 412), and the present church, a little to the NE of the original site, was built in 1785–6. The contractors were Thomas Parlby & Son (who were responsible for most of the major contemporary works in the Dockyard, p. 408), and the design was said to have been by *Marquand*, an Admiralty surveyor who was working under Samuel Wyatt at Admiralty House. *Thomas Telford*, who was in charge of the building of Admiralty House (*see* note on p. 412), is said to have had a hand in the building as well. The W end was bomb-damaged in 1940, and the whole restored in 1955–6 by *A. E. Cogswell & Sons*, the nave being shortened and the W end rebuilt, to the original design, a bay further E. A simple brick church, with wide rectangular nave lit by two ranges of round-headed windows and a reconstructed cupola over the W gable. There is a narrow eastward projection of the nave which is continued, beyond the chancel arch, as the chancel. The nave has a three-sided gallery (reconstructed on the old lines after bombing) curving gracefully inwards short of the last bay. The unsupported ceiling has a large and elegant central rose feature with radiating fluting patterns, embellished with delicate leaf patterns, which was, with great ingenuity, kept *in situ* when the rest of the nave roof was renewed. In the wall-space above the plain chancel arch is a swag pattern in the form of a draped curtain, with representations of urns, brought out in sensitive colouring by *Randoll Blacking*, who recently redecorated the chancel. There is a similar curtain-swag pattern over the E window, a large Venetian composition within an upper semicircular frame, embellished with radiating patterning. – PLATE. Chalice, 1698 by *J. Caumartin* of Paris; Paten and Almsdish, 1705; Silver-gilt Chalice, Paten, and Flagon, 1704. – On the WEST GALLERY (*see* above) a carved composition including a royal coat of arms, a figure of Justice, blindfold, with scales and Fame with trumpet, and dolphins, probably from an early C18 Admiral's Barge. – STAINED GLASS. In the nave windows, *c.*1880 etc.; some of the earliest (e.g. the E window on the N side) of considerable quality. – E window by *Hugh Easton*; Christ Ascendant over the Dockyard, which is depicted realistically as it was after the Second World War. – (TABLET to Admiral Sir John Kelly † 1936 by *Eric Gill*. NT)

ASCENSION, Stubbington Avenue. Of *c.*1917, by *A. E. Cogswell*.

ST BARBARA (Garrison Church), Hilsea (p. 430). A corrugated iron church of 1888 – a form of prefabricated construction more common in later Victorian times than might now be thought; it was often used for garrison churches (cf. St Francis, Gosport, p. 243), colonial churches, and for mission churches in suburbs. St Barbara is quite ambitious, with two-light cusped thin traceried side windows, stepped E triple lancet with cusps, pretty W bell-turret, and aedicular W porch. Wide nave framed internally on arched wooden beams; narrower chancel. The walls are lined with boarding inside. – FONT. Said to have been dug up in the grounds of near-by Gatcombe House. Of light polished marble, unusual shape, and uncertain date. Dodecagonal, with two projecting circular brackets, dying downwards in concave curves (but with semicircular clasping bands just above the downward point). The bowl tapers to the stem with a double curve, but the shape is made irregular by a receding flat surface on one side, suggesting that the font (? originally a stoup) projected from a wall. It is claimed to be medieval.

ST CUTHBERT, Hayling Avenue, Copnor. 1914–15 by *E. Stanley Hall*. An ambitious and in many ways an original design. Red brick outside, with a flanking tower reminiscent of that of Westminster Cathedral, on a much smaller scale. Internal subdivision into three main spaces; the nave of two main bays, each shallow-domed, the chancel tunnel-vaulted, the main spaces separated by very wide brick-faced transverse arches, so that, despite the spatial subdivision, there is a marked W–E axis. Each main bay of the nave has triple round side arches leading into aisles. The chancel has three round-headed windows on either side, their arches cutting into the tunnel-vault. The E end originally had an apse; the present straight E end is a post-war reconstruction after bombing. The total effect is impressive, but the spatial arrangement is not quite satisfactory, being something of a compromise between a basilican and a multi-cellular arrangement. A less negative E end, strengthening the pull of the eastward axis, would give the whole interior a more decisive effect. – STAINED GLASS. Powerful figure of Christ in the small E window by *Osmund Caine*, 1959; Byzantine-looking face. Not large enough for its position; a bigger window of this quality would have made an appropriate termination to the interior.

ST FAITH, Charles Street, Landport. A mission church to St Mary, replacing two bombed churches. 1956 by *Thomas Ford*, in an eclectic style. Brick exterior with gabled nave, round W window, and flat-topped aisles. Slender tower ending in an open balconied cupola with an ogee-pointed top. Interior with broad segmental plastered roof and transverse segmental bays to the aisles. Curious piers of square section with incised bands near the tops and rose emblems above. Big round-headed E window with two small flanking square-headed windows. It really has a good deal of character and is refreshingly unfashionable. – STAINED GLASS. E window by *Clare Dawson*. Figure of the Virgin in a medallion in the centre light; figures of St Faith and St Barnabas filling the smaller side windows. Drawn with conviction. Deep, effective colours and plenty of good detailing.

ST GEORGE, St George's Square, Portsea. Built in 1754, the first Anglican church to serve the new dockyard town of Portsea. Probably designed by a Dockyard surveyor. A homely job as far as details go, but complex and intriguing in form. The plan is a cross contained within a square, like Wren's St Anne and St Agnes. The exterior has a well-managed variety of planes and roof-lines, in grey and red brick, with two tiers of windows round the building, round-headed below and smaller and segment-headed above (to light the galleries), and a tall low-gabled three-bay centrepiece on the W front, with an extra tier of windows above (the outer two 'windows' on the top storey being actually blank frames), and an open-arched bell-turret, with a concave upward curve, ball finial, and weather vane. It must strike American visitors as a greeting from New England. Inside, much of the Georgian atmosphere was dispelled following fairly severe bomb damage and subsequent restoration; not many Georgian fittings survive, and there is rather a bare, over-polished atmosphere. But there are big Tuscan columns surrounding the central space, with galleries set against them, supplementarily supported by slenderer fluted piers, and a nice E end with a big Venetian E window, flanked by text-boards with the texts painted out, and quarter Corinthian columns in the angles of the sanctuary.

ST JAMES, Milton Park Avenue, Milton. 1913 by *J. Oldrid Scott* (replacing a church of 1841 by *Livesay*). Stone with brick dressings; big but not remarkable. – STAINED GLASS. E window by *Sir Ninian Comper*. Saintly figures within a framework of intersecting stems.

ST JOHN, Simpson Road, Rudmore. 1915–16 by *J. D. Coleridge*.* Austere brick basilica, fairly impressive within, due largely to the well-proportioned brick arcades of three orders, with stone capitals that are mostly plain but were all evidently intended to be carved (one of them is). The chancel arch is similar. The sanctuary has an apse, with low open arcade, contained, rather disconcertingly, within an outer square E termination. – MOSAIC on the semi-dome of the sanctuary. Christ on the Cross with St Mary and St John the Evangelist. Completed in 1935 by *Philip Suffolk*; artistically crude but powerful. – STAINED GLASS. In the S chapel; 1918–54. Colourful scenes of the Nativity by *Karl Parsons*, except the E window in the S wall which is by Parsons's successor *Edward Woore*. – Bronze STATUE of St John Baptist by *David Wynne*. – PULPIT. From St Agatha, Landport (p. 432). Designed by *J. H. Ball*, later than 1902, and carved by *Hoare* of Southsea. More sophisticated than anything else in the church. Square, on a narrower base, with Corinthian capitals embellished with diagonal foliage pattern, set in the angles and continuing down to floor level as free-standing columns. Convex cove on each face; decorated with slender vine- and leaf-patterned

* Who had been an assistant of Lutyens (NT).

panels. It has lost its tester.* – PLATE. Also from St Agatha, a C17 Chalice and a Processional Cross, evidently medieval Italian (NT).

ST JOSEPH (R.C.), Tangier Road, Copnor. By Canon *A. J. C. Scoles*, *c.*1911. Red brick with stone dressings, rather mechanical outside. Delicately fashioned arcades make the interior quite impressive.

ST JUDE, Palmerston Road, Southsea. A seaside 'low church', built in 1851 by *Thomas Ellis Owen* in conjunction with the extensive housing development carried out by him at the time (p. 461). Awkward, angular, lofty exterior, rock-faced, with many gables and excrescences, and a tall asymmetrical spire; like an ecclesiastical version of Owen's strange and awkward villas. The interior is full of period atmosphere and hardly altered. Tall, unorthodox arcades and aisle galleries; clerestory. Fairly plausible neo-Dec E window with crudely colourful glass. REREDOS with upper open tracery rising above the base of the window so that one looks through a piece of transparent Gothic screen to brightly coloured glass, with engaging effect. Odd, angular S transept with a roomy gallery resting on a single plain wooden pillar. A Late Georgian builder-architect lived on to learn some of the elementary vocabulary of Early Victorian Gothic, but hardly the correct grammar. The spirit of unorthodoxy continued in the church till later in the century; to the S of the S aisle is a MAUSOLEUM for members of the Lanyon family, *c.*1887–93, with a roof stone-ribbed and embossed as if for stone vaulting – but the 'vaulting' is in glass. VESTRY of 1897 by *J. H. Ball*.

ST LUKE, Greetham Street. 1858–61 by *Thomas Hellyer* of Ryde. Neo-Norman. Quite a pleasing Evangelical interior; five-bay arcades of red and yellow brick with round piers and scalloped capitals, tall chancel arch, apsed sanctuary with big text boards. W bellcote.

ST MARGARET (OF SCOTLAND), Highland Road, Eastney. 1903 by *John T. Lee*. Of plain brick and not very exciting outside, except for flying buttresses against the tall clerestory; the weak W end was built only in 1965. Inside, a church of character, quirky but successfully so, in a more or less Bristolian Perp style. Four-bay nave with transverse arches, the arch and clerestory window of each bay of the arcade being contained within a tall arched recess, the mullions

* The pulpit is a paraphrase in wood of a Ravennate white marble form (NT).

of the clerestory windows being continued downwards to the arch as panel strips. The wide aisles have strainer arches. The treatment of the chancel is very original: it is narrower than the nave by the width of two passageways, and there are double arcades, from chancel to passageway and passageway to side spaces (organ-chamber and a small chapel to N, larger Lady Chapel to S), filled with openwork stone screens. The passageways have tall narrow W arches into the nave (divided about half-way up) which flank the chancel arch, making a triple composition. Spatially the effects, especially when one looks angularly into the S chapel, are intriguing. High, circular E window, making the church seem, as a whole, less Gothic than most of it, in detail, is.

ST MARK, London Road, Derby Road, North End. 1874 by *Sir Arthur Blomfield* (nave, N aisle, flanking tower, and chancel); matching S aisle 1898; two-bay W extension and baptistery 1911, by *Rake & Cogswell*. Big but not impressive inside (as so often Blomfield's churches are); the exterior given interest by its texture of rocky rubble thickly dressed with brick, and its tall lanky tower with pyramid top. – STAINED GLASS. W window of the Crucifixion 1959 by *F. H. Spear*.

ST MARY, Fratton Road, Kingston. Historically the parish church of the whole of Portsea Island until the C14, and of the whole island outside Old Portsmouth until the C19, in an area which was quite rural up to Early Victorian times. The medieval church survived in some measure till 1843, when it was superseded by a building to the design of *T. E. Owen*. This was replaced in 1887–9 by the present church by *Sir Arthur Blomfield*, grand in scale and conception, intended to look and feel like the chief parish church of a great town, and suitably (as a comparable church two or three decades earlier would not have been) in the Perp style. Blomfield, usually so dull, rose to the challenge here and produced a building which is architecturally splendid, if not quite outstanding. Long, tall open interior with six-bay arcades, the piers octagonal and slightly hollow-sided, with delicate little tracery patterns at the head of the hollowing on each face. Capitals with castellated tops, moulded arches, and rolled hood-moulds which twist into little ogees above the arches and continue as shafts up to the roof corbels (alternately with shafts which rise from corbels between the springing of the arches). Neo-Perp aisle windows and clerestory windows;

coved hammerbeam roof, continuing E over the main part of the chancel, which occupies a bay space beyond the nave without any structural division other than a screen, of which only the base remains *in situ*. The sanctuary is narrower and one bay deep, impressively vaulted, with intersecting diagonal ribs. The climax of the long vista down the church (uninterrupted now that the chancel screen has been removed) is the gilt and coloured, many panelled and much traceried REREDOS, set against a panelled wall surface with a striking arched rib intersecting the panel pattern, above which is the seven-light E window. – PULPIT. Octagonal, exceptionally wide, with a substructure embellished like miniature vaulting springing from a stem; grouped with the elaborately decorative ORGAN on the N side of the chancel. – SCREENS. Cast-iron; delicate tracery; the chancel screen banished to the E end but the chapel screens still *in situ*. – STAINED GLASS. In the aisles by *Burlison & Grylls*, *c*.1890–1920. Pre-Raphaelite derivative in rather sickly colours. – MONUMENT. Cartouche in the porch to Thomas Bowerbane † 1761.

Externally the church is faced in flint with stone dressings. It rears magnificently in a spacious, well-treed churchyard, long since largely cleared of its tombstones and partly given over to children's play (very much needed hereabouts), its scale enhanced by the very humble homes all around it. The tall, pinnacled East-Anglian-style tower is a dominant landmark in distant views, though less so now that so many taller buildings have sprung up on Portsea Island.

The CHURCH INSTITUTE, across Fratton Road, 1899 by *Sir R. Blomfield*, is in simple Wrenaissance style, dark red brick, seven bays, with shallow arched panels containing two tiers of windows, and prominent buttresses between them ending in hollowed stone copings. Small stone-quoined wing at the N end. Graceful cupola. A Venetian window high in the N gabled elevation. A neat and ordered design.

ST NICHOLAS, Battenburg Avenue, Hilsea. 1935 by *A. E. Cogswell & Sons*. Artily homely, of brick with a lot of wood. Sweeping roofs with a shingled belfry riding over the E end of the nave. Wood-framed and mullioned windows with quirky tracery. Inside, a series of frames of horizontal and braced beams across the nave, a single bare beam across the chancel entrance supporting a rood. The lower stage of the belfry is open to the interior as a lantern. – STAINED GLASS. E window 1949, by *F. H. Spear*. Strongly drawn and colourful figures of

Christ, St Mark, and St Nicholas, against a background partly plain but with coloured borders. Successful.

ST PATRICK, Eastfield Road, Eastney. 1906 by *G. E. Smith.* Mission church in a strange style, reminiscent of Harrison Townsend. The exterior is of red brick with stone framing. Odd rounded gables. Windows in broad keystoned arches with thin tracery in a curious Art-Nouveau paraphrase of Perp. The doorway flanked by tapering brick pilasters ending in wavily topped copings. The W front (properly visible only from the adjoining gardens) with odd little circular turrets, each domed with four circular shafts ending as blunt pinnacles, like thick pins, and neo-Perp openwork tracery. The interior does not have much character; the fittings are on the whole dull (and probably from elsewhere), but the COMMUNION RAIL has delicate Art-Nouveau metal supports, and in the windows is some STAINED GLASS with arty leaf and stem patterning, including representations of shamrocks.

ST PETER, Somers Road, Southsea. 1883 by *Alfred J. Hudson.* Red brick with meagre stone dressings. Polygonal apse; windows all small lancets, quite effectively arranged on the tall gabled W front; generally solid effect. – Elaborate Gothic REREDOS with figures in brightly coloured mosaic, against a gold background. – STAINED GLASS by *Walter Tower* (of *Kempe*'s firm) in the aisle.

ST SAVIOUR, Jervis Road, Tipner. 1913–14 by *A. E. Cogswell.* Red brick, arty neo-Gothic.

ST SIMON, Waverley Road, Southsea. 1864–6 by *Thomas Hellyer* of Ryde. Another seaside 'low church' (*see* St Jude, p. 440), roomy and quite successful, a mildly unorthodox exercise in spatial planning and brick polychromy. Big tall clerestoried nave with five-bay arcades of three orders patterned in yellow and red brick. Circular panels inscribed with texts in the spandrels of the arcades all the way down the nave. Chancel arch with tall side arches, also all patterned, leading into chapels. Polygonal apse with tall two-light traceried windows and an awful lot of texts jostling one another around the sanctuary. The towerless brick exterior is quite impressive.

HOLY SPIRIT (formerly St Matthew), Fawcett Road, Southsea. 1904–26. Designed by *J. T. Micklethwaite*, completed under *Sir Charles Nicholson.* Burnt by bombing. Restoration by *S. E. Dykes Bower* carried out in 1956–8. Tall austere brick exterior, rearing above the humble homes that hem it in. Beautiful, spacious interior. Aisles as high as the nave, all under panelled barrel roofs, the nave and N aisle roofs continuing over the chancel and N chapel (of which the floor level is raised considerably above that of the rest of the church). Arcades of octagonal section, elongated a little from N to S; no capitals (they were eliminated at the post-war restoration). Curvilinear window tracery. Wall and arch surfaces all whitened; this is set off by the treatment of the roofs, white panels over the nave and aisles separated by strongly coloured ribs, stridently coloured panels over the chancel and N chapel. The chapel is reached up a flight of steps and through the N arch of a triple arched screen. – STAINED GLASS. E window by *Kempe*, from demolished St Bartholomew, Southsea. Windows in the small S chapel effectively made up of *Kempe* fragments from St Bartholomew and St Agnes, Kennington, London, – FURNISHINGS by *Temple Moore*, from St Agnes, Kennington, including a splendid PULPIT with very elaborate Gothic traceried patternwork, and dispersed CHOIR STALLS, some in the chancel, others at the W end. Moore's magnificent SCREEN from St Agnes lies dismantled in the store rooms at the W end of the church, awaiting eventual re-erection. One must have mixed thoughts about this: the interior as it is with its sheer scale, its splendid proportions, the austere simplicity of the whole set off by the colour and elaboration of a few features, is very impressive; erection of the screen would turn it into a different sort of building. Is there another church which could take St Agnes' screen? – (LECTERN by *Bainbridge Reynolds* from St Andrew, Worthing. RH)

HOLY TRINITY. Originally built in 1841 to serve the N part of Portsea; the site became absorbed into the Dockyard with the late C19 extensions, and it became for a time the Royal Naval Church. Bombed and still in ruins. The architect was *Augustus F. Livesay* of Portsea, the designer of Andover church (p. 79), and probably of the plaster vaulting in the choir of St Thomas Cathedral (p. 397).* The ruins have rubble walls with smooth stone facings. Tall lancets. Nave, chancel, and transepts. The church may possibly be restored.

IMMANUEL BAPTIST CHURCH, Victoria Road North, Southsea. 1953–7 by *R. W. Leggatt*. Concrete-framed, glass-walled street front with a slight gable, massive brick flanking tower.

* He also designed a neo-Norman church, St James, Milton, since demolished (p. 439).

VICTORIA ROAD CONGREGATIONAL CHURCH, Southsea. 1911. Arty neo-Perp in brick with profuse stone dressings. Massive battlemented angular tower with elaborate traceried belfry lights, the tracery continued upwards in panel patterning. Big traceried window on the street elevation, with chequerwork in the gable above.

TRINITY METHODIST CHURCH, Albert Road, Southsea. 1901. The slender angle tower of stone-dressed brick is a notable landmark. Double tall panels on each face; string course at the base of the upper storey, which has four round-arched openings on each side and is surmounted by an elongated leaded dome capped by a small cupola. The rest of the church nothing like as elegant as the tower.

MILTON CEMETERY. Chapel by *G. E. Smith*, 1911, in his most felicitous manner. Brick with generous stone dressings; some chequerwork. Neo-Jacobean windows with three tiers of flat-arched lights. Buttresses ending in Smith's characteristic double-curved copings. Heavy stone parapets with urn-shaped finials. Central copper spirelet rising from a dome. – SCULPTURE in flat relief in panels on the main façade with 'Be Ye Also Ready'. – Wiry Art-Nouveauish fruit and stem designs in STAINED GLASS. – GATEPOSTS to the cemetery, with garlands, and metal urns on elaborate metal substructure.

PUBLIC BUILDINGS

GUILDHALL. 1886–90 by *William Hill* of Leeds, much like his town hall at Bolton of about fifteen years earlier (though on a grander scale), the inspiration obviously deriving ultimately from Cuthbert Brodrick's Town Hall at Leeds. One of the grander gestures of Late Victorian municipal pride (there is little or nothing else of the period in provincial England S of the Midlands to compare in scale) but, in its heavy Italianate Classical style, very old-fashioned for the date. Burnt out during the bombing; reconstructed by *E. Berry Webber*, who retained Hill's main (E) and side (N and S) frontages but, alas, simplified his skyline. It is of two main storeys, on a rusticated raised basement, with a spectacular staircase leading up to the main entrance under a hexastyle Corinthian portico which forms the centrepiece of the E façade, its pediment filled with symbolic sculpture and surmounted by a statue of Neptune. The E façade on either side of the centrepiece is recessed behind engaged five-bay colonnades rising to the height of the two storeys, with fairly strong entablature and balustrade; there used to be domed turrets near the corners but Webber removed (or did not restore) them, leaving only the lumpy bases. He spared however the pair of attractive cupolas with small elongated domes rising behind either end of the portico, forming the foreground features to the TOWER, which is of three main stages, the lowest rusticated, rising for several feet above roof level, the next a bell-stage, with round lights, pilasters, and entablature, the uppermost stage containing a clock, recessed behind the plane of the balustrade surmounting the stage below. Above this the composition now ends abruptly with an ugly short octagonal feature, nearly flat-topped – the result of the work of Webber, who never replaced Hill's ultimate cupola. One day, perhaps, Portsmouth will put a replica of it back. The side façades of the two main storeys are recessed behind engaged Corinthian colonnades, the central parts articulated forward. The windows to the upper floor are round-headed and to the lower floor square-headed.*

The space in front of the Guildhall is called GUILDHALL SQUARE; but except for the Guildhall itself and a massive bronze memorial STATUE of Queen Victoria, aged and plump (it was erected in 1904), it is just a formless meeting of roads, with desolately dreary buildings to the S and E, and the railway station and yard to the NE.‡ It is, however, the focal point of the city. Portsmouth Corporation have commissioned *Lionel Brett & Pollen* to prepare a plan for the redevelopment of the Square, with civic buildings on the E side, the square itself becoming a pedestrian precinct. For the first time since it became a big city in the middle of the C19 Portsmouth will obtain a civic heart worthy of its status and importance.

POLICE STATION, Kingston Crescent, North End. 1963 by *Bailey & Piper*, a decent modern design.

CUMBERLAND HOUSE MUSEUM, Eastern Parade, Southsea. A

* PLATE. Cup, 1525–6; Tazza, 1582; three Spoons, 1588–9; Spoons, 1588, 1601, 1618; Silver-gilt Covered Cup with female figure, 1590–1; Silver-gilt Standing Cups and Covers, 1606, 1609; Silver double Salt Cellar and Cover, 1615; Wine Cups, 1617, 1617, 1618; Cups, 1619, 1625; Salver and Ewer, 1637; Silver Salt Cellar, 1665; Tankard, 1679; Flagon, 1681; two Silver-gilt Flagons, 1683, the latter given by the Duchess of Portsmouth, Charles II's mistress.

‡ The WAR MEMORIAL, by *J. S. Gibson*, is not notable as a composition, nor as a feature in the square.

modest Early Victorian stuccoed house in three parts of diminishing height. Thinly rusticated pilasters. Round-arched porch with upper storey. Probably by *Thomas Ellis Owen*. The old museum was housed in the former town hall in High Street, destroyed in the blitz.

CHARLES DICKENS MUSEUM, Commercial Road, Landport. *See* Perambulation, p. 459.

SOUTHSEA CASTLE MUSEUM. *See* Defensive Works, p. 426.

COLLEGE OF TECHNOLOGY (formerly the Portsmouth Municipal College) and PUBLIC LIBRARY. 1903–8 by *G. E. Smith*, the highly individualistic Borough Architect who practised in the early part of the C20. Smith usually designed in an elaborate style which borrowed freely from Jacobean and Dutch or Flemish, but was also evidently influenced by Harrison Townsend and C. R. Mackintosh. The most characteristic of his buildings are in red brick with stone dressings; with the Municipal College and Library he had to be more restrained and conventional, as the building occupies an important site right behind the Guildhall, and is faced in Portland stone. But his individuality comes through. The building is of three main storeys, the lowest a raised basement, on a corner site, facing S and E, with the main entrance to the College at an angle on the corner, and that to the Library further E, both reached by a flight of steps. The College entrance is surmounted by a fairly large cupola of square section, with double-columned angle projections and a broad dome, and flanked by octagonal stair-turrets rising from corbelled bases at the main floor level and ending in small cupolas with open columns, the lower parts of which are treated with massive rustication – an assertive mannerism. Similar cupolas rise from turrets at the far W and N ends of the main façades, and in between is a range of very Smithian neo-Flemish gables with little pediments at their tops. The façades have thick rustication; the windows are generally Jacobean. It is a pity that this moderately grand building is subdued by the bigger block of the adjoining Guildhall.

Two separate post-war blocks have been built for the College of Technology. One, in Anglesea Road, by *F. Mellor* the City Architect was completed in 1952. Three-storeyed, rectangular main block and a large wing with distinctive façade to the road. The upper two storeys have a widely-spaced concrete framework, glass-curtained with some blue vitreous panelling, the thin vertical concrete members receding downwards; the ground storey is open, except for enclosed staircases, on concrete piers. The other block is at the corner of Hampshire Terrace and Cambridge Road, making maximum use, practically and architecturally, of an awkward island site; 1962–3 by *Owen Luder*. Mainly of eleven storeys, the ground floor nearly all open except for the concrete piers and the staircase entrances at either end, and used for car parking. The two main façades (NW and SE) are simply treated, with continuous glazing (separated only by widely spaced thin concrete mullions) alternating with strips of façade faced with grey roughcast panels. At the short NE end is a staircase wing of bare concrete with inclined glazing strips following the rise of each flight. The SW façade is complicated, on two planes with a recess in between, the more projecting part also containing a staircase; the facing here is partly of shuttered concrete and partly of roughcast panels. At this end the building rises to an extra part-storey to accommodate services. Altogether a nice piece of architectural sculpture in concrete.

TEACHERS' TRAINING COLLEGE, Milton. The College proper has an elegant block by *Gollins, Melvin, Ward & Partners*, 1963, four-storeyed, the main façade having, on the upper three floors, a concrete grid framework of vertical rectangular units, the framework relatively slender (especially the vertical members), the infilling partly of green vitreous panelling. The end façades of purply brick between the horizontal floor strips. Further E, at the end of Locksway Road, on an open site beside Langstone Harbour, is QUEEN ELIZABETH THE QUEEN MOTHER HALL, 1963 by *Gollins, Melvin, Ward & Partners*, at the time of writing the best group of modern buildings in Portsmouth. The centrepiece is BARNARD TOWER, of thirteen storeys, quite slender, in sculptural concrete form, with strips alternating with continuous glazing and a very thick fascia. The ground storey is inset on the main frontage, and the position of the staircase on the S façade is indicated by thin double-angled glazing strips. To the N, two three-storeyed residential blocks and a single-storey hall make an informal open courtyard with the tower as the pivot. The blocks have wide fascias and floor-strips painted white and ends faced in grey brick; the hall has a similar strongly treated fascia. Another single-storey building to the S of the tower completes the composition.

PORTSMOUTH GRAMMAR SCHOOL. Founded in 1732. It moved to buildings at the corner of Cambridge Road and St

George's Road (on the site of the ramparts) in 1878, and later occupied the former CAMBRIDGE BARRACKS in High Street near by, built *c.*1855–60. Handsome restrained classical façade in yellow brick. Two-storeyed, forty bays long, with a stone cornice below the parapet, slight dentillation, and a strong frieze. Entrance feature of three round stone-framed arches, the centre wider and higher than the others. The façade is subtly articulated by bringing forward the five bays at each end and also the two which are on either side of the four central ones.

PORTSMOUTH HIGH SCHOOL, Kent Road, Southsea. 1886 by *Osborne Smith* of London. Brick. Elaborate neo-Dutch façade of three bays, separated by chimneystacks treated like pilasters, each bay with a fancy hollow-sided gable, the centre one ending in a little pediment, the end ones in semicircles. Intricate friezes and other embellishments in brick and terracotta.

SOUTHSEA MODERN SCHOOL FOR BOYS, Albert Road. Probably by *G. E. Smith*. Nice intricate neo-Flemish gables in brick and stone; angular octagonal turrets.

NAZARETH HOUSE, Lawrence Road, Southsea. Of red brick in two shades. Jutting chimneys and gables make a fretted skyline, the chimneystacks enlivened with vertical decorative strips of triangular section. Broad pilasters with wavy copings. Tower with cupola, open stage with thin columns supporting a copper-domed top. CHAPEL with elaborated neo-Perp window. The architect was *Leonard Stokes* (NT).

PORTSMOUTH ROYAL HOSPITAL, Commercial Road, Landport. Founded in 1849 and steadily enlarged since. GATEWAY by *A. E. Cogswell*, 1921, carrying on the Portsmouth tradition derived from the old town gates. Elliptical rusticated brick arch with keystone; engaged Ionic pilasters; thick square side pillars and balustrade above. Reminiscent of the Victorian naval architecture in the Dockyard.

ST MARY'S HOSPITAL, Fratton. Probably the Portsea Union House built by *A. F. Livesay* in 1844; since extended, but the original long three-storey red-brick block fronting St Mary's Road remains, with a most oddly awkward centrepiece under a pediment. MATERNITY UNIT and OUT-PATIENTS' DEPARTMENT 1965–6 by *Stewart Kilgour*, architect to the Wessex Regional Hospital Board, in association with *Sydney Greenwood*, the Maternity Unit based on sketch designs by *Lanchester & Lodge*.

PERAMBULATIONS

(a) Old Portsmouth, 450
(b) Portsea, 456
(c) Landport, 458
(d) Southsea, 459
(e) The Rest of the Island, 463

Barrack Street, 453
Bath Square, 455
Bellevue Terrace, 461
Broad Street, 455
Burnaby Road, 451
Cambridge Road, 451
Castle Street, 461
Charlotte Street, 458
Clarence Parade, 462
Clarence Pier, 463
Clarence Promenade, 462
Commercial Road, 458, 459, 460
Common Hard, 458
Conan Road, 464
Grand Parade, 455
Hampshire Terrace, 461
High Street, 452, 454
Highbury Street, 453
Kent Road, 461
King Street, 457
King's Terrace, 461
Landport Terrace, 461
Lion Terrace, 457
Lombard Street, 452
Palmerston Road, 462
Park Road, 451
Pembroke Road, 454
Penny Street, 454
Point, 455
Portland Street, 457
Portland Terrace, 462
Queen Street, 457
St George's Square, 457
St Paul's Road, 460
St Thomas Street, 452
South Parade Pier, 462
Southsea Terrace, 461
Sussex Place, 462
Victoria Park, 456

The Perambulations cover each of the four 'towns' which composed Portsmouth before mid-Victorian times, followed by a brief reference to the rest of Portsea Island. Each of the four main Perambulations starts at Guildhall Square, the heart of the present city, described on p. 446.

(a) *Old Portsmouth*

Old Portsmouth was until the 1870s defined by its ramparts, which were based on a line originally established in the Late Middle Ages (p. 418). The street pattern was probably determined in the late C12 (p. 389); it is fairly regular, with a long, quite wide and gently curving High Street, roughly on a NE–SW axis, narrower parallel streets (St Thomas and Warblington Streets to the NE; Penny and St Nicholas Streets to the SW), and a few cross streets (e.g. Highbury and Lombard Streets). The Camber (the tidal inlet around which the settlement had first sprung up, p. 389) lies to the NW, and the Point, the small peninsula between the Camber and the Harbour entrance, was outside the old town proper and cut off from it from the C16 onwards by a wall and gate across the isthmus. There is no evidence of any stone-built medieval domestic architecture comparable to that in Southampton; some of the oldest surviving houses have inner timber framework of the late C16 or early C17 but, as in most non-stone-bearing districts, brick was generally used in domestic building before the end of the C17.

Most of the houses in the old town were either rebuilt or refronted during the Georgian period, many with the locally characteristic bow windows of shallow segmental form. Canted bay windows are also common, as in other southern towns. Stuccoed houses dating from the first half of the C19 often have bold imitation pointing on the ground storey. By the mid C19 Old Portsmouth had become something of a backwater; Portsea was the dockyard quarter, Landport housed the overflow of the proletariat, Southsea was the fashionable quarter, leaving Old Portsmouth as little more than an appendage to the Camber with its limited maritime trade, and to the adjoining barracks. Even after the ramparts were removed, the new barracks and sports grounds that took their place cut it off from the rest of the greater growing city. It was decayed and picturesque in the 1930s, savagely bombed in the Second World War, and a partial ruin for many years after. Today it has undergone a strange metamorphosis into a fashionable residential quarter; many of the surviving old houses have been discreetly restored and new flats (the architectural standard of which is, almost without exception, deplorable) have risen on most of the bombed sites. In the background, in strange contrast, are the looming bulk of the power station and the industrial and commercial activities of the now busy Camber.

First from Guildhall Square W along PARK ROAD and S along BURNABY ROAD, running between two parts of the United Services Recreation Ground, which was laid out on part of the site of the demolished ramparts *c.*1880. Leading to the field on the l. is what is left of KING JAMES' GATE, originally built in 1687 across Broad Street between Old Portsmouth and the Point (pp. 423, 455), re-erected in the Royal Naval Barracks when the fortifications were demolished, and later moved here. In the successive moves it has been shorn of its Baroque superstructure, with a pediment and the royal coat of arms. What is left is an arch with keystone, flanked with pairs of pilasters and smaller arches (originally for pedestrians); rusticated, and topped by a flat entablature. Right into CAMBRIDGE ROAD. The traffic roundabout at the junction with St George's Road, Alexandra Road, and High Street marks the beginning of Old Portsmouth proper. Here was the original entrance to the old town through the rudimentary late medieval ramparts, blocked by the 'Great Bastion' built by Henry VIII, which caused the entrance to the town to be shifted a little to the N, where the LANDPORT GATE now stands, leading rather forlornly into a football field but the only one of the Portsmouth town gateways left *in situ* when all the rest of the fortifications were demolished. It dates from 1760 and has a rusticated base with segment-headed arch leading into a tunnel-vaulted passage. It is surmounted by a curious circular cupola from which eight buttresses project, ending in a tapering cone with a ball finial. This was the inner gateway into the town, through the ramparts proper; it was preceded by an outer gateway in the ravelin which stood where the sports field now is (p. 425).

Back to HIGH STREET, which begins promisingly with the Grammar School occupying the former Cambridge Barracks (p. 448) on the l., and a series of pleasant houses on both sides, of which the only two deserving special notice are CAMBRIDGE HOUSE (No. 132) on the r., an individualistic Early Victorian design grossly parodying Regency neo-Greek with all the details such as window frames, cornice, and pilasters exaggerated, and BUCKINGHAM HOUSE, famed chiefly as the place where Charles Villiers, Duke of Buckingham (who as adviser to Charles I initiated the C17 development of the Dockyard, p. 407), was murdered in 1628. It is basically a timber-framed house of the C16 or early C17, but altered and refronted in the late C17 or early C18 and now unattractively cemented. The NE part, two-storeyed, is recessed and has windows with round rusticated surrounds; the SW part is three-storeyed and has a doorway with hood supported on well-carved scrolled brackets.

High Street continues, with its gentle curve, but the whole of the middle stretch on the SE side (the outside of the curve) has been rebuilt after bombing, and is now a wretched hotchpotch of buildings that are neither modern nor even decently copyist but just unpleasantly nondescript. LOMBARD STREET leads NW past the E end of the cathedral to the pleasantest series of old houses surviving in Old Portsmouth. They start with the group fronting the cathedral in ST THOMAS STREET. Nos 60–62, facing the W end, are a decent mid C18 three-storeyed red-brick trio with brick dentilled cornice and varying simple doorcases. Then the sickly neo-Georgian CATHEDRAL HOUSE, then a group on the street corner, including Nos 1–5 Lombard Street, middle to late C17, two-storeyed houses with Dutch gables but with their façades stuccoed and simplified in Late Georgian times. Nos 7 and 9 are of the late C18 Portsmouth type, with shallow bow windows (that of No. 7 canted, No. 9 segmental) on the first floor; No. 7 is in grey brick with red dressings and has a nice doorcase with engaged columns and flat hood; No. 9's doorcase is simpler. No. 11 has a shell-patterned semicircular panel over the doorway (another local stylism) and No. 13 a square canopy over its door. The line of houses continues with a pleasant hotchpotch of homely façades, until Lombard Street ends under the monstrous POWER STATION, of pre-war origin but enlarged post-war, lumpy and brick-encased, without anything of either the 'cathedral of power' grandeur of Battersea or the elegant functionalism of Marchwood. It is the biggest building in Portsmouth, obtruding into all sorts of views, none of which does it enhance. More acceptable (but still out of harmony with the domesticity of Old Portsmouth) are the ELECTRICITY GENERATING BOARD'S OFFICES, 1963 by *Philip Hirst and Wyn Jones*, five-storeyed, with a pleasant grid pattern of vertical window panes and yellow brick panels between thin vertical concrete members. This takes up the N angle between Lombard and St Thomas Streets. Facing it, on the SE side of St Thomas Street are more pleasant houses decently restored, No. 51 being especially endearing, with delicate Adamish decoration with urns and swags in the fascia above the shallow segmental first-floor bow window. Are they genuine, or a piece of recent tasteful restoration work? Further NE, St Thomas Street is crossed by HIGHBURY STREET, with a Victorian former BANK* on the W corner, the doorway in the chamfered angle being flanked by massive rusticated pilasters and the parapet balustraded. Most of the other old buildings hereabouts have been cleared by bombing or following decay, and the NE end of St Thomas Street has been redeveloped in a manner more appropriate to say Waterlooville than to Old Portsmouth. One distinguished old building remained, forlorn and decrepit, at the NW end of Lombard Street at the time of writing, the former LITERARY AND PHILOSOPHICAL INSTITUTE, latterly the MASONIC HALL, with an Ionic portico rising the height of two storeys, with fluted columns and strong capitals and supporting a thick, strong entablature without pediment.‡ SE along Highbury Street, across High Street and into BARRACK STREET and another corner of Old Portsmouth with the

* Mr F. A. J. Emery-Wallis tells me that this was the Savings Bank and is by *T. E. Owen*.

‡ Said to be by *Jacob Owen*. Demolished 1966.

usual mixture of preserved old houses and nondescript new development. The best group is on the corner of PENNY STREET, to which there is a handsome three-storey C18 frontage. Another pleasant group, restored, is on the corner of Penny Street and PEMBROKE ROAD, which is the main thoroughfare out of Old Portsmouth south-eastwards. It passed under KING WILLIAM'S GATE, built in 1834, but swept away with the rest of the ramparts (p. 425).

Returning to High Street, opposite the cathedral, the SW extremity of the street retains a fair amount of its pre-C20 urban character. First there is the DOLPHIN HOTEL, three-storeyed, with two canted bays on the first and second floors and a handsome entrance feature, with Doric fluted columns and entablature, then a group of tall, three- or four-storey buildings of which the chief is the Y.M.C.A., formerly the Fountain Inn, converted into a Soldiers' Institute by Miss Sarah Robinson in 1874 (parallel with several sailors' institutes also founded by benevolent Victorian ladies). It is basically a C17 building with a mansard roof parallel with the street but the exterior at present is early C19, stuccoed and recently mutilated. Main five-bay three-storey façade with tall windows on the first floor, showing the marks of hoods that have gone, and rusticated ground storey with arched recesses (a typical Portsmouth pattern). Further SW are two bays of façade of the same height, but with four lower storeys, and further SW again is another stretch of façade similar to the first. With the adjoining buildings the block sets the scale of the far end of High Street and so is of disproportionate value; if it were demolished there would be a risk that High Street would finally cease to be recognizably a distinctive street and would become a C20 hotchpotch with a few remaining old buildings. If – as there is danger – the Y.M.C.A. building is demolished, the building which takes its place must not only be comparable in scale and effectiveness, but must initiate a clean break from the wretched precedent set by the rebuilding of the other parts of High Street.* Next to the Y.M.C.A. is the SALLYPORT HOTEL, with quite a distinguished Late Georgian façade, pairs of canted bay windows going all the way up, and the added embellishments on the first floor of pediments over the central windows of

* At the back of the old building, flanking Penny Street, are extensions to the Y.M.C.A., 1965 by *F. J. Guy*, about the only bit of decent modern building in Old Portsmouth.

each of the bays and over the window between them, immediately over the entrance. Then, on the corner of GRAND PARADE, an Early Victorian block, effective in scale and proportion, though plain except for the rusticated ground storey with tall round arches in the characteristic local pattern. Grand Parade itself is a wide rectangular square at r. angles to High Street, open at the far end to the backs of the surviving ramparts (pp. 423–4). It was formerly used as a military parade ground before and after services at the neighbouring Garrison Church. The row of houses on the NW side offers extreme contrasts in scale in rather an engaging way: one very massive Early Victorian four-storeyed house; next to it some very dinky Regency ones, with quite spirited displays of ironwork (e.g. on No. 5). The SW façade of the Parade is deplorably rebuilt in the post-Second-World-War manner, as are the flats on the NW side of High Street facing down Grand Parade, bad even by Old Portsmouth standards. Here High Street ends, the view closed by the gaunt mass of the SQUARE TOWER as refaced in 1827 but with *Le Sueur*'s bust of Charles I (p. 424). The Perambulation can end satisfactorily with the exploration of the remaining defensive works and ramparts.

But there remains POINT, the district on the peninsula between the harbour mouth and the Camber, beyond the place where King James' Gate (p. 451) spanned High Street, indicated by a tablet. Point was a crowded district inhabited by some of the roughest, toughest Portsmuthians, at least until the later C19, but now it is either thoroughly industrial and commercial (between Broad Street and the Camber) or respectably residential (W of Broad Street and around Bath Square). BROAD STREET itself, though architecturally battered, retains some semblance of its pre-Victorian architectural character with a variety of bow windows on the first floors, but nothing to note individually. The street ends pretty suddenly in a shingle beach descending to the open harbour (now that the century-and-more-old vehicular chain ferry to Gosport has been dismantled) in an endearingly informal way. Facing the harbour are three pubs (the UNION TAVERN, the COAL EXCHANGE, the STILL AND WEST COUNTRY HOUSE), all basically Georgian, all variously battered by eye-catching accretions, but nevertheless still making a nice townscape group, especially when seen from the harbour or even from Gosport. Round the corner is BATH SQUARE which, one can see, was not very long ago a very atmospheric part of the town. Something of the old feel survives, even though all the houses on the NE side have been rebuilt or done up in post-war Old Portsmouth style – for once with quite pleasant aggregate effect. Opposite, and further on, the activities of a boatyard, and those of a British Railways goods landing stage (used by the Isle of Wight boats), give visitors from Southsea at the end of a long walk along the ramparts and people just trying to get the atmosphere of Old Portsmouth a sense of engaging variety and muddle. There is even a bit of open foreshore, and by it QUEBEC HOUSE, a delightful two-storeyed weatherboarded house, right on the water's edge. It was built as a bathing house for sea water bathing by public subscription in 1754 – an early date for that purpose.

(b) *Portsea*

The district between Old Portsmouth and the Dockyard was originally Portsea Common. Urban development had begun by *c.*1700 and soon there was a sizeable town of close-built streets with an open frontage to the Harbour at Common Hard. In 1770–80 ramparts were built to protect town and Dockyard on the landward side, so that Portsea was as hemmed-in as Old Portsmouth, inhabited by dockyard workers, and the keepers of taverns, shops, and brothels that catered for the Navy. Its relationship to Old Portsmouth was comparable to that of Devonport to Plymouth, but it never had the strong individuality, let alone the distinct architectural character (or the municipal independence) that Devonport possessed. It was much decayed before the Second World War, suffered heavy bombing, and has been partly rebuilt in piecemeal fashion, with pieces of the old muddle remaining, and just one or two buildings that are worth looking at.

The way from Guildhall Square is by a passageway under the railway to VICTORIA PARK, laid out *c.*1880 on part of the site of the cleared ramparts, in an intricate pattern, and seemingly more extensive than it is. At the NW extremity is a covey of MONUMENTS. The only ones worth mentioning are to Admiral Napier † 1860, a marble column on a tall base, surmounted by a lion; and an improbable miniature representation of a Chinese temple, with solid stone roof, brown marble columns, and white marble base, commemorating the Far Eastern exploits of H.M.S. Orlando in 1899–1902, and containing a captured bell with a Chinese inscription, the translation of which – 'Come pleasant weather and gentle rain. The Empire happy, at peace again' – is inscribed on a tablet below. Into QUEEN STREET, past H.M.S. Victory Barracks (p. 428), and then l. along LION TERRACE, a hotchpotch of stuccoed houses built *c*.1835–40, two- to four-storeyed, the ground storeys with imitation pointing, the upper ones with rudimentary pilasters and friezes, some with iron balconies on the first floor. The end house has a pedimented porch with Ionic columns round the corner in Portland Street. These houses used to face the inner side of the Portsea ramparts; most of them have long since passed their prime. Turn r. into PORTLAND STREET; in the angle with ST GEORGE'S SQUARE is an irregularly massed late C18 house, impressive because it is almost entirely in grey brick, with a minimal amount of red brick quoining on some of the angles. Next to it is ST GEORGE'S HOUSE (No. 4), a house of *c*.1700 or a little earlier. Three storeys, five bays, cemented over. The centre bay is recessed and has a very fine doorcase, a flat hood with a triglyph frieze and caryatid supports; the door is reached by a short flight of steps. Above the door is a round staircase window. One has the feeling that until quite lately there were plenty more houses like this in Portsea, just as there were at Chatham and Gillingham. The house is now derelict.

St George's Square is a curving and widening space, now mostly tarred, but with an unattractively fenced-off playground at the end, and dismal new flats along its perimeter – minimal visual advantage taken of its promising shape. St George's Church (p. 438) is at the NW corner; N of the church is still some Georgian character. No. 88A is one of the most attractive small houses of its type in Portsmouth. Shallow bow window on the first floor; two windows on the second floor; a shop front on the ground floor with a small doorway to the side, under the pedimented hood of which is a piece of Adamesque decoration with urn and swags. The frieze is decorated with a chain of semicircles of similar delicacy, and the quoins and window surrounds have incised irregular rustication – a mannerism fairly characteristic of Portsmouth. S of the church is MILLGATE HOUSE, an isolated twenty-storey block of flats, 1964 by *F. Mellor*, the City Architect, faced in roughcast panels; impressive in mass, and grouping happily with the church and adjoining small Georgian houses which are a foil to it. Further N in KING STREET is the PORTSEA

REMEDIAL CENTRE, built as the Beneficial School in 1784, of two storeys with a pediment. The tall upper storey contains the former large schoolroom, with a Venetian window contained in a big semicircular surround. Stuccoed ground floor and nice Doric open pedimented porch. Near by is the COMMON HARD, with a collection of tallish buildings (none individually remarkable), with some bomb gaps, facing a muddy piece of foreshore with a glimpse of Gosport opposite. At the end of the Hard is the Main Gate of the Dockyard (p. 409).

(c) *Landport*

Landport in the C18 was a scatter of houses called 'Spring Gardens' outside the ramparts of Portsmouth and Portsea, mainly along the line of the present Commercial Road. Quite a bit of extra-mural development had taken place by *c*.1800, which by *c*.1840 had solidified into what was considered for a time a third 'town', named after the Landport Gate of Old Portsmouth (p. 451). With the further spread of development all over Portsea Island it became the hub of the greater city of Portsmouth, and the stretch of Commercial Road N of the railway developed into the main shopping centre. The building of the Guildhall on the edge of Landport in 1886–90 made it the municipal centre as well.

Few people would guess that the stretch of COMMERCIAL ROAD N of Edinburgh Road, containing the biggest shops, was largely rebuilt after the Second World War; the main clue to the recent date is in the consistent relative cleanness of the Portland stone of the façades, certainly not in the architectural styles. Portland stone (rather than good architecture) was required by the city authorities on all façades fronting Commercial Road, but not on any side façades. So there is at least one place where a big shop occupies a corner site, its frontage to Commercial Road being of stone but that to the side street being of brick. Space is too short to waste on further comment. In CHARLOTTE STREET, leading l., something really exciting is going on (at the time of writing), a sign that Portsmouth is at last catching up with the mid C20. Here a complex of shops, offices, and a great deal else, by *Owen Luder*, in association with *Clayton, Black & Petch*, is being developed; in 1965 it was not far enough on for anything like a final judgement, but it already makes a splendid composition. Everything is in concrete. The form of the whole is highly romantic, with many planes and varied heights and (at least in its incomplete state) a fascinating skyline. The ground storey has massive square piers, boldly corbelled at the top, the second has balconies at different heights, shutter-finished, their undersides with a grid pattern in relief. Other surfaces are finished in smooth concrete, others again with rough panels, so that as much textural variety as possible in the concrete idiom is obtained. Cantilevered spiral car ramps at either end are boldly emphasized features, and there are curious little hemispheres on the skyline. But for the most part the outline is chunky and angular. As the building nears completion, it looks, if anything, more exciting than it did in the earlier years.

Behind All Saints (p. 435), back in Commercial Road, are two eighteen-storey blocks of flats (BARKIS HOUSE and NICKLEBY HOUSE), completed 1965 by *F. Mellor*, the City Architect, with buff roughcast panels, impressive in bulk. Near by is a twelve-storey rectangular block with gay balcony fronts and an eye-catching skyline feature. Portsmouth is by tradition a densely built city (set off by the sea), and it can take, visually, a greater concentration of tall buildings than most places. Further N along Commercial Road is a surviving piece of the tail-end of Late Georgian development; Nos 393–399, two-storeyed, of red brick, with simple pedimented doorways and high parapets; No. 393 is the DICKENS MUSEUM, Dickens's birthplace. No. 391 is more ambitious, with wide bows running up both storeys and an iron balcony.

(d) *Southsea*

Southsea started to develop *c.*1810–20 with a series of terraces fronting the E ramparts of Old Portsmouth, with a few smaller streets behind, and a social centre, the 'King's Room' (of which the present Clarence Pier is a descendant at several removes), on the shore to the SW. It was, as it has remained ever since, partly a residential suburb of Portsmouth and partly a seaside resort in its own right. The coastline is bordered by Southsea Common, originally a morass, reclaimed in the early C19 and gradually transformed into a varied pleasure ground. Across the Common, at the southernmost tip of Portsea Island, is Southsea Castle (p. 426). Extensive developments to the N of the Common, and also, to a lesser extent, well to the E (around the site of the present South Parade Pier), were undertaken *c.*1840–50 by *Thomas Ellis Owen*, a local speculator. Later development was piecemeal; by *c.*1900 almost everything except the Common and the seafront had been built up. Apart from the castle, the Naval War Memorial, and one church on the far N fringe (Holy Spirit, p. 443), there is no architecture whatever of special interest in Southsea, and not much that is worth looking at at all. But a walk through some of the older parts, with a return along the sea front, is, from the architectural point of view, just worth while.

Starting at Guildhall Square, the Perambulation covers what is really the S part of Landport. The southward-leading thoroughfare, confusingly called COMMERCIAL ROAD (but it hardly seems a straightforward extension of the main part of Commercial Road further N, p. 458), still has a strong Victorian character. The PRUDENTIAL ASSURANCE, in brick and red terracotta, is, needless to say, by *Waterhouse*, with its serrated skyline still happily intact. Next to it is the former THEATRE ROYAL (now called the Royal Arena), built in 1884 by *C. J. Phipps*, and largely rebuilt in 1900 by *Frank Matcham*, the stage being then one of the largest in England. It has a charming iron-built frontispiece projecting over the pavement, with a round-arched colonnade supported by pairs of slender Ionic columns of iron, and a closed-in balcony above, with twirly decorated panels and fretwork balustrades. The interior also is fine. Will it be preserved?

Opposite, the PORTSMOUTH WATER COMPANY, of 1883, occupies a prominent site on an acute corner, in stone with marble dressings, with a well-shaped dome over the inset circular entrance feature in the angle, and a complicated façade to Commercial Road with narrow double round-headed windows between pairs of pilasters on the first floor, and dormer windows in wide circular surrounds surmounted by pediments. Next to it CHARTER HOUSE, *c.*1890, is one of the few commercial buildings in Portsmouth of any scale. It is heavily and exuberantly neo-Flemish with a distinctive skyline; a series of small stepped gables ending in ogee finials, with draped urns and open strapwork at each step, and small copper domes set back behind balustrades at the corners. It is an excellent foil to the new block of the College of Technology (p. 447).*

Looming up to the E are two tall blocks off ST PAUL'S ROAD (SOLIHULL HOUSE and LEAMINGTON HOUSE) by *Miall Rhys-Davies & Partners* in association with the City Archi-

* Stylistically it looks like *G. E. Smith* before he became City Architect.

tect's Department.* They have fairly pleasantly ordered façades with roughcast panelling below and between the windows, and black crinkly panelling on the ends. They are seen from many quite distant viewpoints, and their scale is acceptable in this part of the city. Southsea proper begins with HAMPSHIRE TERRACE, started *c.*1820 but developed quite piecemeal, most of the houses having been rebuilt or greatly altered later in the century. No. 7 has a fairly good façade of *c.*1830, with brown brick upper storeys, a rudimentary pediment, and stuccoed ground storey; No. 8 has a projecting enclosed porch, rusticated, of similar date. LANDPORT TERRACE is a similar mixture. No. 24, *c.*1840, has a fine first-floor balcony with geometrical tracery in the curved brackets. Many of the later Victorian façades here and in Hampshire Terrace are worth looking at as oddities, No. 17 Landport Terrace being perhaps the weirdest. KING'S TERRACE, started *c.*1810, was a uniform terrace, of three storeys, but only the centre part survives, including the central house of three bays under a pediment, a two-bay house to the N, and another house to the S rebuilt as a replica; the façades are of brown brick with simple dentil pattern under the cornices, and round-headed ground-floor windows within slightly larger surrounds. BELLEVUE TERRACE is another hotchpotch, but Nos 10–11 have graceful segmental bow windows on ground and first floors. On the corner facing the Common is the WESTON NAVAL HOTEL, built as the Pier Hotel in 1865, bleak and bulky, many-angled, with heavy bay windows on the first floor and iron balcony on the second, a typical mid-Victorian seaside hotel, but patchily altered. SOUTHSEA TERRACE facing the Common, *c.*1860, is graceless, with heavy bay windows rising to three storeys and iron balconies, reached from the third floor, oddly spanning the space between them. Further E is a group of houses some of which, simple Late Georgian, belong to the earliest Southsea. CASTLE STREET, leading inland, has a medley of early and late C19 near-seaside development but is dominated by an extraordinary building of *c.*1900 with a half-timbered clock tower.

KENT ROAD runs E into residential Southsea, with stuccoed villas of the forties or early fifties mostly in short terraces, behind greenery to the N (part of *Thomas Ellis Owen*'s

* They adjoin the site of Southsea's first church, St Paul, 1822 by *Goodwin*, destroyed by bombs.

development) and duller streets, not developed till the sixties or seventies, to the S. Owen's houses are in odd variants of Late Regency or Early Victorian styles. SUSSEX PLACE, to the N of Kent Road, is odder than most, a three-storeyed terrace with first-floor balconies passing over projecting porches and four-storeyed towers, capped with pyramid roofs, at the ends. PORTLAND TERRACE looks a little later; it is marked on a map of *c.*1845 but it may then have been a project.* It is fairly monumental in scale and effective in massing, with projecting ends and slightly forwarded middle part, set back pleasantly behind trees, but with strangely awkward fenestration. St Jude's Church, showing Owen's vagaries in ecclesiastical Gothic dress (p. 440), presides over this area. There is no architectural reason for continuing the walk any further E; a few patches of housing developed *c.*1850–60 are pleasant and leafy, but almost all the rest is very dreary. So the Perambulation turns S along PALMERSTON ROAD, the busy shopping centre of Southsea, extensively bombed and dismally rebuilt, to CLARENCE PARADE facing Southsea Common, a long row of mixed mid-Victorian seaside houses, all individually undistinguished; the only striking façade is that of ST MARTIN'S HOUSE, 1964 by *Scherrer & Hicks*, a ten-storey block of flats with a simple, pleasantly proportioned, concrete-framed grid eight bays wide, the second, third, sixth, and seventh bays having recessed balconies, the other bays with flush glazing and black panels. Additional horizontal emphasis is given at each storey by thick wooden members, marking the bases of the windows or the tops of the balcony balustrades. It is the best recent block of flats in Portsmouth.

One can continue E to SOUTH PARADE PIER, erected in 1908–9 by *C. W. Ball*, which is in a mild Edwardian Baroque, or S to the castle (p. 426) and then NW along CLARENCE PROMENADE, originally laid out in 1847–51 at the instance of Lieutenant-General Lord Fitzclarence. Its most striking feature is the ROYAL NAVAL WAR MEMORIAL (to the First World War), 1920–4 by *Sir Robert Lorimer* (one of the too few structures by him S of the Border), a slightly tapering square column, with a four-stepped base rising from a plinth and a top of four diminishing stages changing to an octagon in the two top stages and ending in a finial with poops of ships, winged figures, and a globe. The plinth has

* It is illustrated in a guidebook of 1849.

pedestals projecting diagonally at the corners, each with a lion carved with strong, simple realism. It is a splendidly balanced composition, standing at the end of a long stretch of greensward a few yards from the beach and a landmark from a considerable distance. The Second World War memorial is a low walled enclosure to the N, ending in wing pavilions with high round-pedimented roofs, and now forming the foreground to the earlier memorial, but the later work lacks the sensitivity of Lorimer's. For the rest, Clarence Promenade has a series of Victorian MONUMENTS of different sizes, interspersed with shack-like seaside structures. The Crimean War Obelisk erected in 1857 by the Portsmouth Debating Society, and the Chesapeake Column, 1862 by *Theodore Phyffers*, are the most interesting. Finally CLARENCE PIER, rebuilt in 1961 by *Everett*; quite an acceptable piece of festive architecture, with gaily coloured curtain panels and a flat circular table motif at the top of the main tower, but spoiled by crude advertising. The walk can continue along the surviving defences of Old Portsmouth (pp. 423-4) or else return to the junction of Pembroke Road and Bellevue Terrace, where there is a MONUMENT to Lieutenant-General Fitzclarence † 1852 by *J. Truefitt*, a tapering octagonal column on a many-stepped base, with a nice Gothic top, an octagonal capital with ogee crocketed tracery on its underside, and a finial with traceried panels and crockets.

(e) *The Rest of the Island*

Almost nothing to mention on Portsea Island outside the older-developed areas, apart from churches and public and Service buildings. The original village and hamlet groups (Kingston, Fratton, Eastney, Milton, Copnor, Hilsea) were formless and straggling, and hardly anything in them survived the outward spread of close-built C19 and early C20 streets; except in a few parts of Southsea there is nothing to compare with the leafy arcadian spaciousness of so much of suburban Southampton. One old house survives in HILSEA, opposite the Barracks, C18, of red and grey brick, two storeys and six bays, with pilasters at the ends and after the second, third, and fifth bays – an odd arrangement. Pedimented pillared porch. Not far off, on the corner of London Road and Torrington Road, an OBELISK, which marked the old boundary of the borough, on a square base with mouldings and a tablet inscribed with the Portsmouth star and crescent and dated 1799. Also in the vicinity, in CONAN ROAD, recent development by Portsmouth Corporation: short four-storeyed blocks thickly tile-hung above the ground storey, with short balconies thinly framed all round in concrete on the first floor (alternating with windows) and similarly treated verandas on the ground floor. End façades of yellow brick. Fussy but stylish, and there is precious little municipal housing in Portsmouth which could be called that.

PORTSMOUTH MAINLAND

COSHAM

Formerly a big village at the mainland bridgehead of Portsmouth, now a suburb crowded between arterial roads. The long main street, by-passed, has become a suburban shopping centre and retains hardly a trace of character. The medieval parish church is at Wymering to the W (p. 468).

ST PHILIP, Hawthorn Crescent, in a dead-end piece of suburbia between the railway line and Port Creek. 1936–8 by *Sir Ninian Comper*, one of his most famous and original churches, achieving (as he claimed) 'unity by inclusion' – i.e. by borrowing from all sorts of styles. The exterior with its brick walls, thin stone dressings, three-light cuspless windows, and small classical cupola on the low W gable recalls, at first sight, an early C19 Gothic church. The interior is a space of ordered complexity, with mostly simple surface treatment set off by a few rich details and dominated by the magnificently ornate BALDACCHINO in a free-standing sanctuary occupying the E part of what is structurally the nave. The church has a four-bay nave with wide aisles, a short structural chancel (forming in practice a chapel partly screened by the altar and baldacchino), and a W projection of the nave which is filled with an organ loft and vestibule beneath. The nave pillars, painted white, have marked entasis; the capitals, also white, are richly detailed with water-leaf, volutes, and flowers with stems. There are similar three-quarter columns set against the aisle walls. The roof is a series of plaster mock-vaults in quadripartite form, without diagonal ribs, but with insignificant flat arches, hardly more than broad ribs, spanning the columns both lengthwise and transversely across nave and aisles. The windows of the aisles are of three lights and sharply pointed, with intersecting cuspless tracery, and embossed roses over the main intersections of the tracery (a motif repeated externally). The pseudo-chancel has similar side windows, but the E window is six-light-Curvilinear, cusped, with large ogee centre light containing STAINED GLASS with a figure of Christ; there are figures of angels in the smaller lights. The rest of the window, and all the other windows, are clear-glazed. – The ORGAN LOFT projects into the W bay of the nave. The frontispiece of the organ is lavishly treated in gilt; the underside of the loft has a ninefold grid pattern on its ceiling, with painted shields in gilded surroundings. – The FONT is plainly octagonal, but with a gilded and painted cover, ogee-pointed and crocketed, on eight simple columns. – Now for the baldacchino (which Comper rightly called the CIBORIUM). This stands in the midst of a square sanctuary with COMMUNION RAILS of simple late C17 or C18 character all round (one of the earliest examples of the now very fashionable centralized planning). The columns of the baldacchino are now painted white (they were originally gilded). The capitals are Corinthian; the superstructure has pointed arches and quadripartite vault and is ornately decorated, mainly in blue and gilt, with four angels against the background of a spangled sky on the underside of the vault and holy figures in the spandrels. Four eagles, perched above the columns, hold the chains of suspended censers. Something of Comper's effect has been lost with the whitening of the baldacchino columns (has any other Comper glitter been puritanically subdued?). But it is still a splendid church, focused absolutely on the baldacchino, but with an effect more subtle than that of straightforward ornateness against a background of simplicity. The background itself is complex; the break-up of the space into many small units helps to emphasize the scale of the baldacchino, and the minor ornate features, themselves set against the relatively simple surface treatment of most of the walls and roofs, act as foils to it. The variations of style achieve total harmony, not discord. Probably, after the lapse of the interval necessary for an objective judgement, this will seem (as indeed it was thought to be at the time when it was built) one of the outstanding pieces of church architecture of the inter-war period.

Beyond the church, in HAWTHORN CRESCENT, some municipal housing, 1965–6 by *Thomas E. Makins*. Three- and four-storeyed, the three-storey blocks with yellow-brick side elevations and party-wall ends, white boarded fascias and windows, and grey panelling in thin white frames, the four-storeyed blocks with bluish-red and yellow patterned brick-work, the façades mostly set back with inset balconies. Pleasantly grouped on a narrow curving site – the best bit of council housing development in the city yet.

On the HAVANT ROAD are two or three solid pre-suburban villas. On the N side, No. 69 (COSHAM HOUSE) is early C19, two-storeyed, with wide-spreading eaves, central curved bay with three windows, and veranda round the bay; No. 91 (EAST COSHAM HOUSE) is probably late C18, with simple two-storeyed façade, shuttered on the upper storey, and with a delicate segment-headed wooden trellis veranda (probably a little later than the house) on the ground storey. Opposite, No. 154 (EAST COURT) is early C19, stuccoed, the N façade with low pedimented gables and flat pilasters (cf. Paulsgrove House, p. 468); there is a big rounded bay to the W.

DRAYTON

CHURCH OF THE RESURRECTION, Lampeter Avenue. 1930 by *Randoll Blacking*. A mixture of folksy simplicity and neo-medievalism. Exterior of brick with stone neo-Perp windows and low SW tower with diminishing upper stages and pyramid top. No internal nave–chancel division. The N and S aisles are oddly unbalanced, the S aisle extending a bay eastward into a chapel, the N aisle ending short of the E end but extending a bay further W opposite the tower. The arcades are simply plain square-sided round arches all rendered in pastel colouring. The chancel FITTINGS are of unstained oak, with neo-Tudor linenfold patterns; the altar has riddel-posts surmounted by angels. Not really very satisfying.

FARLINGTON

ST ANDREW. One of *Street*'s best small village churches, very little known but comparable in quality to Fawley in Berks or Holmbury St Mary in Surrey. The chancel dates from 1872, the nave (not a rebuilding but a very thorough restoration) and N aisle from 1875. At first sight the external effect is rather odd, with the chancel roof rising higher than that of the nave, but this results from the internal spatial arrangement, the chancel being vaulted, the nave not (compare Street's treatment of the restored medieval church at Stone,

Kent). Flint with smooth stone dressings, varied Geometrical windows, pretty but assertive W bell-turret. The W window, an exceptionally big lancet, is a carry-over from the medieval church, with original jambs but renewed head. The nave internally is lofty but relatively narrow, suggesting in its proportions a possible Saxon derivation. The three-bay N arcade has quatrefoiled piers of multi-coloured marble and arches of two chamfered orders. The chancel arch is similarly C13 in style, with the shaft of the inner order in marble. The chancel has a two-bay quadripartite vault, the ribs springing from foliated capitals which rest on marble shafts. The spatial effect is splendid; at least as important aesthetically is the total effect of the colouring. The basic wall surfaces are whitish clunch, but the fine dressings are in rich buff Bath stone; in the vaulting the two materials are combined in a stripwork pattern. So we have creamy white, buff, a little rich marble colouring, together with the darkish browns of the furnishings and, in the background, the rich dark colouring of STAINED GLASS (most of it designed by *Street*) – a fairly ordinary Victorian colour range, very subtly and effectively assembled; nothing harsh in a Butterfield way nor strident in a Teulon way but rich and thick in a way that Street could manage best.* – MONUMENTS. Baroque cartouche to Thomas Smith † 1742. – Laura Richards † 1833. Kneeling woman with two small children. Small, but good.

All that is left of the village (there never was much) is the OLD RECTORY, early C19, austere but handsome; two-storeyed with broadly spaced windows, the centre part brought out slightly under a simple pediment, with a broad bow window and a veranda on the ground floor.

FARLINGTON REDOUBT. *See* Portsdown Hill, p. 387.

PAULSGROVE

An early post-war municipal housing estate under Portsdown Hill.

ST MICHAEL. 1955 by *Thomas Ford*. Unashamedly neo-Georgian outside, in brick with stone dressings, except for the SE tower with an individualistic top. Wide cove-roofed interior with segmental ceiling recesses over the windows. The altar is

* The glass in the N aisle window was given by Street to commemorate his parents' marriage in the medieval church in 1815.

in a segmental recess with an ALTARPIECE painted by *Hans Feibusch*, who also did a celestial PAINTING on the ceiling above. Clear glass windows to l. and r. of the altar, engraved with angelic figures, allow glimpses of the separate spacious Lady Chapel beyond, which has brilliantly colourful STAINED GLASS of the Ascension in the E window.

PAULSGROVE HOUSE, on the Southampton Road (A27). A pleasant early C19 brick villa with an older portion behind; the outer two bays of the three-bay front project slightly with low gable-like pediments.

WIDLEY

A strange place, half a deserted parish and half a suburb of Portsmouth, sprawling down the N slope of Portsdown Hill along the A3. The old centre was away in the country to the W, with a medieval church of ST MARY MAGDALENE rebuilt in 1849 (by *Colson**) and pulled down a few years ago; there is nothing near the site but a single farm, a bare stretch of the slope of Portsdown Hill with the fort on the skyline, and scrubby woods to the N. Yet suburban Widley is only half a mile away, hidden by a fold in the ground.

CHRIST CHURCH, Portsdown, N of the brow of the hill by the A3, just within the city boundary; the parish church of present-day Widley. 1874 by *J. Colson*, supposed to be neo-Norman; of flint and stone with tall, lanky round-headed windows, paired in the aisles, pilaster-buttresses, a sturdy SW tower of Sussex-like outline, and a triple-windowed apse. Lanky round-arched arcades with tall cylindrical piers. – STAINED GLASS. An impressive series in the aisle windows, *c*.1952–61 by *M. Farrar Bell*; varied figures and scenes with strong detailing and deep colours.

FORT WIDLEY. *See* p. 387.

WYMERING

Hemmed in by closest suburbia in a by-passed backwater between arterial roads just W of Cosham, a memorable group remains of church, vicarage, and manor house.

ST PETER AND ST PAUL. Thoroughly gone over by *Street* in 1860–1, so that at first glance it looks all Victorian. In fact the

* The church was neo-Norman. Goodhart-Rendel commented on the sweep of the roof from the nave down over the N aisle almost to the ground, which he called 'bold and in advance of its time'.

outlines are medieval, and so is some of the stonework; all the windows are renewed, though some look as if they are close representations of medieval ones. The pretty shingled W bell-turret, with open arcading all round, is absolutely Streetish. Inside one notices first the four-bay medieval arcades. The N arcade is late C12, plain but well proportioned, of one thinly chamfered order with hood-moulds, square scalloped capitals, and round piers. The early C13 S arcade is the church's engaging oddity. The piers are improbably slender, looking like little more than large round shafts; the moulded capitals broaden boldly; above the capitals are cylinders of stonework rising for two or three feet (considerably wider than the piers) before the arches (of two hollow-chamfered orders) die into them. This extraordinary arrangement is fairly closely paralleled in the somewhat later arcades at South Hayling (p. 282), where, however, the shapes are octagonal. In the S aisle is a nicely moulded PISCINA, trefoiled inside, and a rather elegant tomb recess with segmental arch and vertical jambs, continuously moulded. In the chancel an assortment of SEDILIA, PISCINA, and other recesses look as if they had been restored by Street rather than invented by him. The total effect of the interior as restored by Street is disappointing, partly because the colour pattern has been destroyed through whitewashing. But the effect can never have been anything comparable to that of Farlington. – FONT. Massive, neo-Norman, with intersecting arcading; unlikely to be by Street. – REREDOS. A rich piece; sculptured representations of Crucifixion scenes in three marble Gothic frames.*

The church's restoration was instigated by the vicar, Father Nugée, who founded both a Brotherhood and a Sisterhood at Wymering. The Brothers lived partly in the VICARAGE behind the church, a long, two-storeyed, eight-bay Georgian block of red brick, one of the window spaces in the upper floor being blocked and tile-hung, and partly in an adjoining CLOISTER which was destroyed by a bomb.

WYMERING MANOR, now a Youth Hostel, NW of the church, has medieval masonry, but what is visible is mostly later. A half-H-shaped building with the hollow filled in in the late C19 or C20, the exterior stuccoed and without much character, the gables of the original wings ending in ball finials. Small

* Mr Taylor has drawn my attention to the excellent Victorian glass in the E window – by whom?

C16 or early C17 windows on the S façade and big asymmetrical Late Georgian bow windows on both storeys on the W façade. Inside, the hall occupied the centre of the original three-sided composition; it has Elizabethan or Early Jacobean panelling (is it *in situ*?) with broad flat pilaster patterns, plain on the N side and fluted on the S. Against the W wall is a fireplace which may be of earlier date, but restored. It has a nearly flat top coming to a little ogee in the middle, and a heavily projecting mantelpiece supported on plain corbels, hollowed in their lowest stage. Externally the chimney of this fireplace is rubble-faced. The hall opens through arches into the present entrance hall in the space of the original courtyard, with two curving neo-Jacobean staircases with turned balusters.

PORTSWOOD *see* SOUTHAMPTON, pp. 571n, 572

5020

PRESHAW HOUSE

3 m. W of Warnford

A strange house. It consists of a mid C17 part of characteristic forms, repeated in the C18, which was an unlikely thing to do, and added to on the S side first by *Nash* (Prosser) and then on a much larger scale about 1910. The original house has to the N two gables, a gabled porch between, and a projecting two-bay wing on the r. The façade is articulated by pilasters in two orders, Doric below, Ionic above, and by moulded brick friezes. The porch seems to cut into the arrangement. It is, to repeat it, most surprising that this façade should have been continued and at its l. end provided with a second projecting two-bay wing in the C18. Yet this is what the brickwork tells us. The porch round the corner looks Victorian. Nash's façade is long and flat, also with gables. The only accents are two shallow canted bays placed symmetrically.

6040

PRESTON CANDOVER

ST MARY. 1884–5 by *Sir Arthur Blomfield*. Flint and brick. NW tower with a shingled spire. Freely geometrical tracery. All this is rather coarse for Blomfield; the interior with brick facing and stone dressings is much smoother. – PLATE. Cup and Paten, 1746; Almsdish, 1798.

ST MARY, ⅛ m. SW. This was the old church. Only the chancel survives. In it one lancet.

PRESTON HOUSE. Built about 1720 and much remodelled recently. To the remodelling belong the entrance side and most of the interior. The side towards the garden is in the original state. Seven bays, articulated by giant pilasters, and with a piece of entablature including egg-and-dart. Segment-headed windows. On the stables a very pretty lantern. This comes from the Southampton audit house (*see* Civic Centre, p. 526) and hence is of *c.*1790.

NORTH HALL, WSW of the church. Built in 1769, but recently made to look Queen Anne. Front garden with busts on the piers. Five bays, brick, one-bay projection with broken pediment. Doorway with decorated frieze and segmental pediment. At the back projecting wings. Delightful original staircase with three twisted balusters to each step.

SOUTH HALL, opposite North Hall. A later Georgian brick house, also five bays, also a one-bay projection, also a broken pediment.

PRIORS DEAN

7020

CHURCH. Nave and chancel, rendered, and bell-turret. Norman N doorway, in the abaci saltire crosses. Billet on the hood-mould. E.E. chancel, cf. the S side. – A HELM of *c.*1600. – PLATE. Chalice and Paten Cover, 1609. – MONUMENTS. Elizabeth Tichborne † 1623, with small kneeling figure. Alabaster. – Bridget Stoughton † 1631. Also alabaster, kneeling figure, between two columns. – Sir John Compton † 1653. Two rather flat busts in oval recesses. Surround partly gristly, partly of garlands. – Compton Tichborne † 1657, but quite a lot more classical. Also a bust in an oval recess. – In the churchyard a very large yew-tree.

GOLEIGH MANOR, 1¼ m. NNE. Irregular, ironstone below, perhaps of the C14, timber-framing with narrowly spaced studs above. The latter may date from 1473–4.

PRIVETT

6020

HOLY TRINITY. By *Sir A. Blomfield*, 1876–8. Exceptionally good. Commanding W tower with broach-spire. Three tiers of lucarnes. The total height is 160 ft. Lancets, also in the clerestory. Internally even more than externally this strikes one as a substantial town church. Four-bay arcades. Lofty tower arch. Elaborate altar surround. The church was paid for by W. Nicholson of Basing Park. It cost £22,000. – FONT. Square, with much stiff-leaf. – PULPIT. Round, of stone. – LECTERN. Wrought-iron and most intricate.

6000 PURBROOK [DL]

A suburban village close to Portsmouth.

ST JOHN. 1843 by *J. P. Harrison* of Oxford (cf. Hursley). Like a Sussex village church outside; flinty, with steep roof sweeping over nave and aisle and low square flanking tower with pyramid cap. Quite lofty inside, with tall chancel and two-bay S arcade.

See p. 831 N of the church a three-storey, Late Georgian, brown brick HOUSE with embellished cornice and brickwork quoins, and two fine segmental porches with free-standing columns. A nice recent layout of private housing in the former grounds, preserving trees, by the *Page-Johnson Design Group*, 1963.

PURBROOK PARK COUNTY GRAMMAR SCHOOL. In an early C19 stuccoed mansion, with piecemeal later additions.* The mansion is roughly square, stuccoed, of two storeys, with a boldly projecting, though fairly small, tetrastyle Ionic portico rising through both storeys on the W front. Wide flat pilasters, thin moulded cornice; a general feeling of elegant austerity. S front with big central bay, three-windowed on each floor. N front with the ends slightly projecting and a round-headed staircase window above a hooded doorway in the centre. The interior nearly all remodelled, except for the vestibule, which is rectangular, with a segmental recess at the far end; ceiling with thickly patterned surround and thin cornice. A small oval vestibule under a lantern window upstairs.

SOUTHWICK HOUSE, formerly PURBROOK HEATH HOUSE, 1 m. W of the A3. Elegant, medium-sized, two-storeyed early C19 mansion. Stuccoed. Simple detailing.

FORT PURBROOK, *see* p. 387.

2040 QUARLEY

ST MICHAEL. The nave is C11 and characteristic Saxo-Norman overlap. The N wall shows herringbone laying of the flint. The slate-like thin stones arranged ineffectually as voussoirs

* Built in 1840 (White's Directory) near the site of a house by *Sir Robert Taylor*, demolished in 1829 (information from Mr Marcus Binney).

of the blocked S window and blocked N window (the latter only visible inside) are typically Saxon (cf. Warblington). The splays are single, not double. The N doorway, though not Saxon, has Saxon proportions. The W window is single-splayed and its voussoirs are Norman rather than Saxon. The church has no bell-turret or bellcote. The three bells hang from a wooden frame only a few feet high, standing on the ground N of the church. The E window is a completely different story. It is a Venetian window with square Ionic pillars to outside and inside, and it carries an inscription outside GULIELMUS BENSON & HENRICUS HOARE F. A.D. 1723. The inscription repeats inside, with the names reversed. This is very interesting indeed. *Benson*'s Wilbury House in Wiltshire is only a few miles away. He built it in 1710 and some people call it the first Palladian house in England. It is rather the first of the Inigo-Jones–Webb Revival. But never mind; for *Henry Hoare* Sen., Benson's son-in-law, built Stourhead in 1721–3, and this is indeed among the earliest Palladian buildings in England. His architect was Colen Campbell. Benson was his own architect. Henry Hoare Jun., son of Henry Hoare Sen., was already Lord of the Manor of Quarley in 1719. So he or his father clubbed together with Benson to produce this very early specimen of the Venetian window in England.

QUARLEY HILL. The most conspicuous feature on the hill today is the oval bank and ditch of the Iron Age hillfort enclosing some eight acres. The ramparts are broken by gaps on the N, S, NE, and SW, the latter pair marking the original entrances. Excavations conducted on the site suggested that an earlier Iron Age palisaded enclosure stood on the hilltop before the earthwork was constructed. Earlier still are the Bronze Age BOUNDARY DITCHES which run beneath the rampart N and S of the NE entrance.

QUIDHAMPTON FARMHOUSE *see* OVERTON

RAMSDELL 5050

CHRIST CHURCH. 1867 by *J. Colson* (GR). Small. Of flint and red brick. Tiled roofs. SW tower and spire on a truncated lower part. Not much to recommend it outside or inside. – STAINED GLASS. The E window no doubt by *Hardman*.

RANVILLE'S FARMHOUSE *see* BROADLANDS

REDBRIDGE *see* SOUTHAMPTON, pp. 566, 567n, 569, 570

REDHILL *see* ROWLANDS CASTLE

REDRICE HOUSE *see* UPPER CLATFORD

REMENHAM HOUSE *see* APPLESHAW

RHINEFIELD LODGE *see* BROCKENHURST

1000

RINGWOOD

ST PETER AND ST PAUL. By *F. & H. Francis*, 1853–5. A large, impressively unfussy job, simple in outline and restrained in the motifs. They go from lancet to Early Dec. Central tower with double bell-openings. Four-bay arcades, crossing, and quite a splendid chancel of eight closely set lancets N and eight S. There can be few works of this calibre among the *œuvre* of the Francis brothers.* The PISCINA in the chancel is an original late C13 piece. – (CHANDELIER. Of brass, 1727. NMR) – PLATE. Chalice, late C16; Set of 1664; Chalice, 1836. – MONUMENTS. Brass to John Prophete, Dean of Hereford, † 1416. The figure is 5 ft 3 in. long. – Ann Willis † 1716. An architectural piece. – Henry Compton † 1724. Also purely architectural, but standing and much larger. – Bright family, *c.*1792. A very elegant piece.

The church lies by the MARKET PLACE. Next to the church the VICARAGE, red brick, five bays, parapet, hipped roof, and next to this a stuccoed late C18 house of five bays with a Venetian window as its centre and a crowning one-bay pediment. The CORN EXCHANGE of 1866 (now a cinema) is very undistinguished. Brick and stone, three bays only, Italianate with a big arched middle window.

Off the W end of the Market Place runs WEST STREET. The BRIDGE HOUSE HOTEL is red brick, five bays, with late C18 details. Opposite the OLD COTTAGE: timber-framed, thatched.

Off the E end of the Market Place the High Street, too much altered to be of interest. At its end N runs Southampton Road, E Christchurch Road. Off SOUTHAMPTON ROAD, down Meeting House Lane, is the UNITARIAN CHAPEL of 1727, segment-headed windows with one painful middle mullion.

* Nicholas Taylor finds that the internal harmony is greatly enhanced in the chancel by STAINED GLASS (*Ward & Hughes*, 1857), WALL PAINTINGS of 1870 on the E wall, and the CARPETING of very deep pile, made by parishioners as late as 1905–7.

Plain later doorway set into an original surround with brick pilasters. Tiny top pediment. Half-hipped roof. In Southampton Road itself is the OLD MANOR HOUSE, dated 1737 on a rainwater head. Five bays, two storeys, rendered. The angle quoins are of even length, the quoins of the centre of alternating length. One-bay pediment. Parapet. The STABLES are a lovely job, mid C18, three bays, grey headers and red dressings. The centre bay has an archway with a Gibbs surround and a pediment. The side bays have one Venetian window each. Cupola.

In CHRISTCHURCH ROAD No. 44 is the showpiece among Ringwood houses. Late C18, fine red brick, two and a half storeys, five bays. The centre three bays have extremely elongated giant pilasters with Adamish capitals and carry a pediment. On the other side the CONGREGATIONAL CHURCH of 1866, by *T. H. Hellyer*, yellow brick, and still entirely like a Commissioners' church of about 1830 – see especially the big pinnacles. No. 86 is a handsome low five-bay house of the early C18 with giant angle pilasters and a panelled parapet.

At ASHLEY, ⅝ m. SW, is another five-bay house. The doorway has a stone pediment.

ST IVES HOUSE (Old People's Cottages), 1½ m. SW on the Bournemouth road. 1960–2 by *J. M. Austin-Smith & Partners*. Added to an existing house. Six cottages, on a curved plan, very attractive.

AVON CASTLE, 1¾ m. SSW. Built in 1874–5 for the Earl of Egmont. Symmetrical entrance side with a square middle tower and rounded angle towers. Behind the middle a higher tower with round turret. Mullioned and transomed windows.

ROCHE COURT [DL] *5000*

1 m. N of Fareham

Now the Boundary Oak Preparatory School. A moderately large house with a medieval core, successively enlarged at various periods. The medieval house is represented by a N–S block, with stone walls of great thickness, but with no visible feature earlier than an Elizabethan five-light mullioned and transomed window on the E side. To this was added an E–W wing, probably also Elizabethan. This retains much of its original N façade, with two bays of half-timbering on the first floor, evidently original in the main but with Georgian or later windows. There was a slight C17 lengthening of the medieval block southwards, with a façade of three hipped gables, small windows, and overall tile-hanging – not very common in this part of Hampshire. A long ancillary wing was added eastwards in the C18, brick on the S, tile-hung on the N. About 1900–10 the house was enlarged, turning the medieval and Elizabethan L-shaped house into a rectangle, with a new W and part of a new S façade, in a style based on the older parts; timbered gables and tile-hanging. Further additions have been made since the house became a school. Inside, the upstairs room of the Elizabethan wing has original panelling, with pilasters enlivened with scrolls and strapwork over the former fireplace, and plain square patterns in the panels. The GATEHOUSE, off the Wickham road, is by *Sir Jeffry Wyatville*, 1808, of grey brick, with a high vaulted gateway; two-storeyed keeper's lodge with Gothick windows to the S, under the same roof-line, extended S in harmony at a later date.

1010 ROCKBOURNE

ST ANDREW. That there was a cruciform Early Norman church here is proved by the plain, unmoulded arch into the N transept. The masonry of the transept (now the vestry) in fact also survives, and so does that of the S transept S wall. The nave was as long as it is now, as is proved by the remains of the jambs of the W doorway. In the C13 followed the S aisle with its arcade (octagonal piers, double-chamfered arches) and the insertion of a new nave W window (re-used parts in a Victorian window). The S aisle W and SW windows are original lancets. The bell-turret is of timber, weatherboarded, and carries the date 1613. The church was restored in 1893 by *C. E. Ponting*, and due to him are the ornate S porch and some details outside the chancel, recognizable by their touches of Arts and Crafts Gothic. – PAINTING. Triptych, probably from Antwerp, probably *c.*1520–30. – PLATE. Chalice of 1692. – MONUMENTS to the Coote family of West Park, notably General Sir Eyre Coote † 1823, by *W. Theed*, his earliest work. Sir Eyre Coote is lying on his deathbed. His family is with him and an angel is hovering over him. – Eyre Coote † 1834. By *John Gibson*. An angel is standing by the abandoned family, comforting them.

WEST PARK has been pulled down, but a COLUMN to two members of the Coote family remains, erected in 1827.

MANOR HOUSE, by the church. A baffling assembly of buildings, not in any axial relation. There are three. The centre is an Elizabethan range and attached to it, L-wise, a C13 chapel. This has a doorway with a shallow cinquefoiled head, flanked by lancets, and in the E gable a quatrefoil opening. To the W of this is a small house of the C14, consisting of hall, at r. angles to it another room, and at r. angles to that a square projection. This roughly S-shaped building is attached to a range of the C19 running S–N. Immediately N of the C13 part is a large late C14 BARN with two entrances from the W. The N end of this has windows in two tiers, i.e. was a dwelling. The buildings deserve further examination.

The VILLAGE street of Rockbourne is one of the prettiest in Hampshire.

LONG BARROWS, on Toyd Down, ½ m. W of Down Farm. The SW example, GRANS BARROW, is 190 ft long and 60 ft wide with a maximum height of 9 ft at the S. There are no surface indications of flanking ditches. 200 yds NW is KNAP BARROW, the largest in the county, with a mound 320 ft long by 80 ft wide and 6 ft high. The site has been extensively ploughed and may originally have been larger. No ditches are visible.

DUCK'S NEST LONG BARROW, on Rockbourne Down, just S of the E entrance to Tenantry Farm. This is one of the finest surviving long barrows in the county. The mound measures 130 ft by 75 ft and still stands 15 ft high at its broader E end. The flanking quarry ditches are clearly visible.

ROMAN VILLA, 1 m. SE. More than forty-six rooms have been excavated in recent years. The plan so far recovered consists of two wings, each containing bath suites and several mosaic-floored rooms. The coin series shows that the site was occupied from the middle of the C2 until the end of the Roman period. During this time the building would have been considerably modified and enlarged, the existing plan representing the final stage of this process. The remains are at present laid open, and a small museum has been arranged on the site.

On Rockbourne Down is a polygonal EARTHWORK, possibly a cattle enclosure, and a settlement site of Roman date.

ROMSEY

ROMSEY ABBEY

The first foundation of a nunnery at Romsey dates from 907. It was by Edward the Elder for his daughter Elfleda. A second foundation became necessary in 967. Now the initiative was Aethelwold's and King Edgar's. To their church probably an apse belonged which was found below the floor exactly under the crossing, and possibly part of the S wall below the second to fourth bay from the E of the S arcade. A general rebuilding began about 1120 and continued to about 1230. The stone used was from Chilmark. The length of the church is 256 ft in its present form. At the Dissolution the church was bought by the town, and that has saved it from demolition. All the conventual buildings on the other hand were pulled down (except perhaps for one wall of the refectory inside a house S of the church; VCH).

The architectural history of the church reads as easily outside as inside, and so we may start by circumambulating.

EXTERIOR. The E end is flat and clearly the result of two later alterations. Of the Norman building the chancel aisle E windows remain, with shafts and simple two-scallop and similar capitals. The arches have a big roll, the hood-mould a thin flat zigzag. Corbel-table with heads. Between these two the width of the chancel was continued eastward. But of that externally only two blank arches tell. Inside the situation is clearer. How this Norman chapel, probably the Lady Chapel, ended, we don't know – probably straight. Later, i.e. about 1270–80, this chapel was replaced by a new one. The wall shafts in the corners and the middle remain, but this second chapel has also gone. Its E windows were apparently set back when the chapel was demolished. They are of three lights and three circles over, two quatrefoiled, the top one sexfoiled. At the same time the chancel itself received two very similar but much larger windows, also of three lights, but with two sexfoiled circles and one larger quatrefoiled circle. Up there also large blocked Norman arches appear.

Round the corner, the S chancel aisle has an E bay with two narrow blank arches and then the first window, and then windows like the E window. Corbel-frieze also as on the E wall. The capitals are mostly of two scallops, but also of primitive leaves. The clerestory is arranged in threes, two blanks and one window. Only the window is shafted. All this is the same on the N side, except that the W aisle windows have finer arch mouldings.

The transepts have an E chapel each which curves out apsidally, but instead of curving in again runs lamely against the chancel aisle. The chapels have a blank twin in the middle

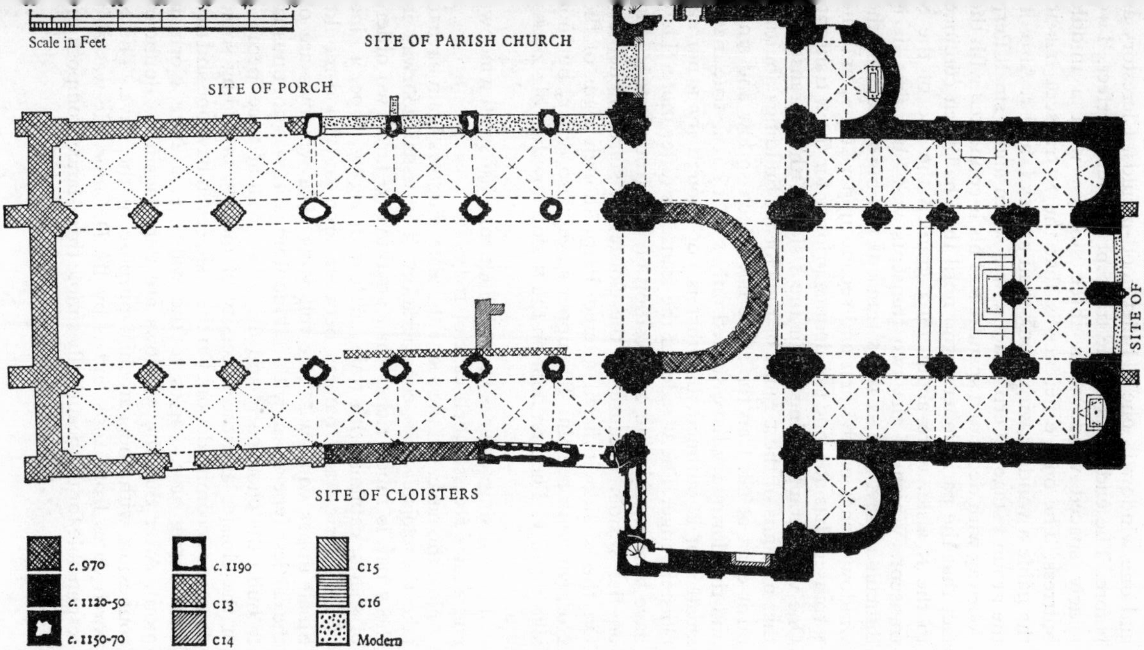

Romsey Abbey, plan

and one window l., one r. Billet hood-moulds. Clerestory as before. The end walls of the transept are very perfect. Two widely spaced windows in three storeys, with a middle buttress. The only difference is that the N transept has in the gable a window with blank twin arches l. and r. Also on the ground stage a Perp window was set in and a small Perp doorway with decorated spandrels. This is connected with the fact that the parishioners, who until then had been confined to the N aisle, were about 1403 granted the use of the N transept. Which of the two transepts was built first, it is difficult to say. But as the S transept has big zigzag for the window arches on the first and second upper stages, and the N transept has not, one can deduce priority for the N transept. One very strange thing about the S side of the S transept is that no signs of the E range of the cloister buildings abutting on it exist at all. Can the slype have been so low and small and the dormitory have started only S of it? It is true that a small roof is outlined, but that is not enough for a normal cloister range. The W sides of the transepts differ more. They have a large tripartite composition on the ground stage. But on the S side, because of the cloister, it starts higher up. On the N side it is all altered Perp, though signs of the Norman work remain. The upper stages also differ, but not significantly. The first floor on the N side now has big zigzag too.

The crossing tower is very uneloquent. Just small windows and a later recessed bell-cage of 1625.

Now the nave. On the S side the aisle windows again have to take the cloister into consideration. The usual doorway in the E bay is much richer than anything so far. Two orders of shafts, capitals with trails, arch with zigzag, rope, a kind of raspberries, and paterae between arch and hood-mould. Small upper window.* The following aisle windows are of the earliest type again, with roll mouldings. It was not unusual to build the choir parts and the S aisle wall at once, because of the cloister and the necessity of quickly providing some domestic accommodation. On the N side even bays one and two have zigzag at r. angles to the wall, i.e. a Late Norman motif. After that the windows are Perp, again no doubt in connexion with the parochial purpose of the nave. The N porch dates from 1908 and is by *W. D. Caröe*. He was also responsible for the beautifully simple three-lancet composition

* This part shows clear signs of a fire.

of the W wall.* The nave clerestory deserves special attention. It is no longer Norman from the very beginning (not quite – see inside). On the S side it has one shafted lancet per bay. The capitals in the E bays however are still of Norman types, and only in the W bays stiff-leaf comes in. There are also different string courses. On the N side work obviously started later (*see* the observation on the aisle windows). Here the whole clerestory has shafted tripartite arcading, with double shafts flanking the actual window. However, for whatever reason, the corbel frieze remains Norman in type. In the W bays, to return to them, even the aisle windows are now pointed and have stiff-leaf shafts. The corbel-table above them here changes to a pointed-trefoiled shape. Finally the doorway from the W bay into the cloister. This again has stiff-leaf capitals, and an arch of many mouldings including a keeled roll and a roll with a fillet. Hood-mould with dogtooth.

So one can see that the S aisle was proceeded with first and that the clerestory also was reached earlier on the S than the N side. One can also see that the W bays are the result not of evolution but of a total change of style. The interior will show all this more fully.

INTERIOR. We start again in the retrochoir or ambulatory. Here it is at once evident that the Norman building went on E two bays wide. Tripartite responds. Capitals some with primitive leaves but others livelier, with trails, animals, and faces at corners. To the W, i.e. the E arcades of the chancel, they have plain big scallop capitals instead. The ambulatory is rib-vaulted, but the ribs lack supports in the form of shafts; so groin-vaults were probably intended at first. The rib profile is a half-roll and two half-hollows (cf. Winchester Cathedral transepts, after 1107). The chancel aisles have four bays, the fourth also belonging to the retrochoir. These fourth bays are extended by apses in the thickness of the wall, i.e. not visible from outside. The apses have broad unmoulded ribs, which is surprising. The walls with tall blank arcading. Chip-carved arches.

The chancel aisles are essentially the same, but in the W bays the ribs do not stand on shafts. Most capitals are of the big-scalloped kind, but one on the N and the corresponding one on the S tell stories. They are of two crowned men and an 13
angel (signed *Robertus* me fecit), of two seated men with a

* Mr Hubbuck doubts this. He suggests that the W window might be genuine and the rest by *Ferrey*.

monster-head between (signed *Robert* tute consule qs.), and of a battle, with a King helped by an angel in a fight with a bearded man. The style is very close to that of the Canterbury crypt. In the S aisle also some decorated capitals. On the arches from the transepts *see* below.

The chancel itself is of three bays with a straight two-bay end. Arcade, gallery, clerestory, no vault, but the main beams supported on mighty mast-like shafts which separate the bays. The arches have big scalloped capitals and zigzag in the arch itself. Above, a billet frieze runs round the masts too. The gallery arcade is very strange. A twin opening per bay; decorated sub-arches, the super-arch with two rolls. The hood-mould again runs round the masts. But the odd thing is that the tympanum of the super-arch is left open, and that here a colonnette stands on the shaft between the two sub-arches. There is no parallel to this. Another odd motif is that on the gallery one can see that the orders of the super-arches towards the gallery have springers for segmental arches never built. They would have about reached the top of the sub-arches. The clerestory is in stepped tripartite groups, but above the low side-pieces are blank arches to the height of the middle arch, and they have pairs of small colonnettes on their side towards the middle arch. The upper E wall is, as we have already seen, of *c.*1270–80. The windows have ample Purbeck-marble shafting, and the arches have big (renewed) stiff-leaf sprays.

The crossing piers have tripartite responds to the N and S arches, to the W all shafts are shaved off, to the E the shafts start high up on brackets with heads etc. These anomalies are probably connected with screen and pulpitum. The crossing arches are in three steps. Inside the tower are shafts up the angles and on each side three twins. The columns between the twins stand on brackets.*

The transepts continue the system of the chancel, though of course varied by the fact that the end walls and the W walls have a different elevation. The arches from transepts to chancel arch have busily decorated capitals. The gallery N bay on the E side of the S transept has big zigzag – the only one so far, but cf. the gallery windows of the S transept externally. Also the same bay has its tympanum solid, which has not occurred before. The upper colonnettes of the S tran-

* The crossing piers have more developed bases than the E end, except that the same form occurs in the W parts of the N chancel aisle.

sept clerestory are a little different. Both chapels have quadripartite rib-vaults, in spite of their semi-apsidal form. The ribs have their proper supports, and the capitals of these stand lower than the tall blank arcading of the walls. Of the end walls little need be said. The clerestory is tripartite, though externally it does not appear so. The walls differ, as we have seen, by the placing of the big stepped tripartite window groups. Below the higher one in the S transept is some blank intersecting arcading.

The Romsey nave continues the system of the E parts. 12
Altogether, with the exception of the Gothic W bay, the building is impressively uniform. Even the motif of the column standing in the gallery tympanum is carried on with. The nave must of course have been begun at once; for otherwise the crossing tower could not be safely built. But at this moment a change of plan occurred in the elevation. The first two bays of the nave are separated by a giant round pier the height of nave and gallery together. This motif must have been thought out as a compromise between the system used so far, which was Franco-Norman and Anglo-Norman standard, and the West and South-West English regional system of detached giant round piers, i.e. the system of Gloucester and Tewkesbury. The piers have round multi-scalloped capitals and round abaci. The way the arcade arches run into the giant pier is bound to be painful, and this is no doubt why the system did not become popular. It only re-appears at Jedburgh in Scotland (and Professor Boase has pointed out the Scottish connexions of Romsey) about 1150, at Oxford Cathedral (then a nunnery like Romsey) about 1175, and at Glastonbury at the end of the C12. Did the motif then originate at Romsey? We have no way of knowing. Anyway, when at Romsey the change of plan had been decided on, the S side was evidently done first; for here alone the arch of the arcade bay still has zigzag. After that it is given up, and moreover the zigzag arch dies awkwardly into the big round pier. On the N side the arch is caught up by a fragmentary multi-scalloped capital that runs round the arcade and aisle sides. The gallery continues the billet frieze at sill level. The sub-arches have zigzag in the first bay, but are plain in the second bay. Also the sill course stops going round the masts. In the clerestory only the very E responds and first piers are still Norman (round S, polygonal N), and the high middle arch is still Norman. Then at once the clerestory

turns Gothic. (The wooden tunnel-vault is by *Ferrey* an very good. RH)

The aisles are entered from the transept by arcade an gallery arches framed by giant shafts, i.e. part of the nev deal, which must have been decided on that early. Th gallery opening on the N side is normal, but on the S side it ha a completely unexpected twin, with a colossally fat shor round pier on a base with spurs. Why was this done? Th tympanum incidentally is solid, like its opposite number o the E side, but unlike anything in the N transept.

The second nave pier is not a giant column but a compoun pier, and no more giant columns follow after that. So the nev plan was given up. What one cannot say is, if it was given u after the first, i.e. if the plan foresaw the system of Jedburgh or if alternation of piers was intended. In any case we can nov see how the building of the nave began. It is Norman in th whole first bay of the arcade (and more). It has zigzag for th sub-arches of the gallery only in the first bay, and the clere story is Norman for even less than one whole bay.

The aisles have the same rib-vaults as the chancel aisles but on the S side bays two and three have more elementar profiles than any before. Does that mean that work here wa undertaken specially early? It is doubtful, especially becaus bay two has some intersecting wall arcading more advanced i detail than that of the S transept. The next bays of the nave i.e. Nos 3 and 4, show development of a very telling kind o the gallery level. Capitals appear with trumpet-scallop an decorated trumpets, which came in only about 1170 or so, an the arches, though still round, are finely moulded: transitio to the E.E.

The fourth bay on the N side is a problem. It is differen from all others. The ribs of the bay have decoration with kind of crenellation motif. The pier at its W end, i.e. betwee bays four and five, has double shafts to all sides. The capita are decorated. The arch has zigzag at r. angles to the wal a Late Norman motif, as we have seen. The wall frieze run round the exceptional pier. The pier ends at the level of th springing of the gallery arches with capitals with trumpets an a square abacus. Why all this display in this one place?

The nave continues Norman only to here. The last thre bays are entirely E.E. But we must remember that at clerestor level the E.E. starts already at half a bay from the crossing and in the gallery at least with the arches of bays three an four. This is again the way medieval buildings proceeded. The last three bays have piers with a triple shaft and two subsidiary shafts to each side. The bases, curiously enough, are of Purbeck marble. The capitals are moulded, except for some stiff-leaf on the N side. The arches are pointed, with a big chamfer and fine mouldings starting vertically. Hood-moulds with stiff-leaf stops. No more billet frieze at gallery sill level. The gallery now has trefoiled sub-arches and a quatrefoil pierced through the tympanum. The blank arches above the low parts of the clerestory triplets change from round to pointed. In the N aisle is a doorway with Purbeck shafts and a depressed pointed arch with much dogtooth. The ribs of the vault are Gothic too. All these things take one to about 1230, and that was the end of the building. A consecration date is not known.

FURNISHINGS. AMBULATORY. WALL PAINTING, S side of N arch. Four medallions from the life of a saint. Bold draperies below. C13. – (STAINED GLASS. By *Clayton & Bell*. RH) – SCULPTURE. Demi-figure of an angel, wood, no doubt from a roof. – MONUMENTS. Mrs Ashley, 1913. A French Salon type in immaculate white marble. She is seen with her two children quite undressed. By *Fuchs*. – Handsome cartouche tablet († 1727). – Tomb-chest of an abbess. Shields in cusped fields. On the top indent of a brass. *See* p. 831

SOUTH CHANCEL AISLE. SCREEN. A piece of a Perp screen is used as the reredos of the SE apse. In it a small, very valuable piece of Anglo-Saxon C10–11 SCULPTURE. Christ crucified with two Angels on the arms of the cross, the Virgin and St John below and Longinus and the Soldier with the sponge yet lower. The composition is typically Saxon in that it is loose and lively, not hieratic like Romanesque pieces. – STAINED GLASS. E by *Kempe & Tower*, 1907. – MONUMENT. Large tablet to John Storke † 1711 with columns and three putto heads in the arched top.

NORTH CHANCEL AISLE. STAINED GLASS. E by *Kempe*, 1897. – ALTAR FRONTAL. Gold embroidery on green velvet; C15. – PAINTING. Board with kneeling figure, *c.* 4 ft high. Early C16. What did it belong to?

CHANCEL. The STALLS have a cresting from a former SCREEN. – ORGAN CASE. Neo-Norman, 1858 by *Christian*. – (STAINED GLASS. E window. By *Powell*.) – HIGH ALTAR with relief of the Virgin by *Martin Travers*.

SOUTH TRANSEPT. MONUMENTS. Purbeck marble effigy

of a slender lady wearing a wimple. Her head under a three-dimensional pointed-trefoil arch. The effigy is C13, as is obvious from the stiff-leaf border. – The CANOPY with its ogee top can therefore not belong to her. Big cusps with leaf motifs and sub-cusps. Crockets on the arch. Early C14. – John St Barbe and wife; 1650s. Two frontal busts in arched recesses. Pillars l. and r., pediment within pediment. Below, the four children kneel, all white. – Original iron RAILING.

NORTH TRANSEPT. PAINTING. This large board is that uncommon survival, a complete REREDOS, bad but rare. Nine upright Saints in the top row. Below Christ rising from his coffin, the soldiers, two censing angels, and the donor, an abbess. The piece is of *c.*1525. – MONUMENT. In the chapel fragmentary standing monument to Robert Brackley † 1628. No figures left.

NAVE. (FONT and PULPIT by *Caröe*. RH) – MONUMENTS. Sir William Petty. Recumbent effigy on a tomb-chest. Erected in 1868. – Against the W wall: Viscount Palmerston † 1802. By *Flaxman*. White. Above the inscription Grecian pedimental lintel with two genii and a wreath. – Viscountess Palmerston † 1769. By *Carter*. Quite exquisite. The only figure is a tiny allegory in a roundel. Otherwise just very precise and dainty ornamental carving. – Sir William Temple † 1856. By *Thomas* of London. A repeat of the Flaxman.

NORTH AISLE. CHEST. A splendid Netherlandish piece. Flamboyant tracery and a fine lock. – MONUMENT. Top of a tapering coffin lid, with the arm of an abbess and her crozier; C13.

PLATE. Chalices of 1568 and 1637; Patens of 1659 and 1741; Flagon, 1727; Almsdish, 1732.

8 OUTSIDE THE BUILDING. SCULPTURE. The famous Romsey Rood is outside the W wall of the S transept. The figure is about 6 ft 9 in. high, and the soft, a little undecided modelling is typically pre-Romanesque, or, in Continental terms, Ottonian. So the most likely date is the first half of the C11. Above Christ's head the hand of God shooting out of a cloud. Is this part somewhat re-cut? – MONUMENT. Waterloo Memorial, 1815, S of the abbey. Designed by 'a young architect of the town'. Obelisk with three rather clumsy ornamented bands. Low, broad urn on the top.

THE TOWN

CONGREGATIONAL CHURCH, The Abbey. 1887–8 by *Bonella & Paull*, designed clearly to hold its own against the abbey.

And this is indeed an outstandingly good job, very freely composed, including a gatehouse with tower through which The Abbey runs. The style is Perp, and the church itself is of nave and aisles, with three-light Perp windows, and an eight-light E window. But inside the Congregational arrangement is kept by three wooden galleries and the seating plan. The building cost £11,000.

TOWN HALL. 1866 by *Bedborough* of Southampton. Three bays, brick, Italianate, insignificant.

CORN EXCHANGE, Cornmarket, now Barclays Bank. 1864. Quite a different proposition. Surprisingly classical for its date. Three bays, giant Corinthian pilasters, pediment with sheaves, a sickle, and a pitchfork. The windows were altered in the 1920s.

MAGISTRATES' COURT, Church Street. 1964–5 by *Fowler, Grove & Heggar* and the County Architect, *H. B. Ansell.*

NATIONAL SCHOOL, Station Road. 1872 by *Nesfield*, and typical of him with its rather heavy-handed picturesqueness. Brick and tile-hung gables. Prominent chimneys, one of them combined with the bellcote.

PERAMBULATION

Romsey has few noteworthy houses, and they are not grouped. So one has to fan out in all directions just for odd houses. The MARKET PLACE is roughly triangular. In the middle STATUE of Palmerston by *Matthew Noble*, 1867. On the E side a good late C18 house, four bays; doorway with Tuscan columns and pediment. Then W first. In THE ABBEY No. 1 is of three bays and two and a half storeys with a one-bay pediment. Pretty doorway. Next to the N. In CHURCH STREET No. 6 has Gothic lancets. Date probably the early C19. Then off to the E, is the medieval house called KING JOHN'S HUNTING BOX. It is a hall house of *c.* 1230 with the hall on the upper floor. The W window has keeled shafts and an odd arch of which just one moulding starts vertically. Hood-mould with dogtooth. To the S of the window was the doorway. A small NW window has the same moulding trick. In the E wall is a plain doorway, perhaps to a former chapel. The staircase is in the SE angle. At the corner of Portersbridge Road a crisp early C19 house of yellow brick. It is linked with Strong's offices in Church Street, with a yellow brick front of five bays and a three-bay pediment.

Porch with Tuscan columns and broken pediment. Turn l. into Horsefair and again r. into CHERVILLE STREET to see the curiously solemn early C19 entrance to a nurseryman's premises. Loggia of square Doric stone piers, reached up steps.

Back to the Market Place and now to the S. In BELL STREET the BAPTIST CHAPEL of 1811. White, three bays, with segment-headed windows below, arched windows above. On into MIDDLE BRIDGE STREET. At the start BROADWATER HOUSE, Late Georgian, brick, five bays, two and a half storeys, with one-bay pediment and pedimented doorway. Then No. 44, three-storeyed, of five bays, with parapet, also brick, also Late Georgian. No. 91, BATH HOUSE, is small, of Bath stone, and decorated with masses of motifs by a maniac or an advertising monumental mason. At the end, on the A-road, MIDDLE BRIDGE, by *Robert Mylne*, 1783. Rebuilt accurately in 1933. One beautiful segmental arch.

Back once more to the Market Place and turn E. In the CORN MARKET the DOLPHIN HOTEL, three bays, white, with two bows on the first floor, and a one-bay l. attachment. On along The Hundred and then first straight into WINCHESTER ROAD for one more pleasant three-bay house of yellow brick. Then turn r. from the end of Ball Street into PALMERSTON STREET. On one side mostly Late Georgian cottages in terraces, on the other No. 9 with an attractive porch with Roman Doric columns and metopes and paterae. No. 19 is timber-framed and has three gables. The r. third is considerably older than the rest – cf. the much heavier timbers.

ROOKLEY HOUSE *see* LITTLE SOMBORNE

ROOKSBURY *see* WICKHAM

ROOKWOOD FARM *see* DENMEAD

6030

ROPLEY

ST PETER. Mostly of 1896, by *John Oldrid Scott* (Rev. B. Clarke), but original in the S tower a re-set plain doorway of *c*.1200, in the chancel the two-bay arcade to the S chapel of *c*.1300 (octagonal pier, double-chamfered arches dying into vertical pieces above the abaci), the Perp S doorway, and the C17 brick porch. Also some windows. – FONT. Octagonal,

Perp; on the underside and the stem some bald decoration. – PLATE. Cup and Cover Paten, 1592; two Flagons, 1714; Paten, 1715. – MONUMENT. Sarah Rodney † 1793. Gothic tablet. In the four-centred head her profile crowned by two putti.

ROPLEY HOUSE, ¾ m. W. Early C18. Five bays, two storeys, parapet. Shaped end gables of parallel roofs. C20 additions.

BOUNTY HOUSE, ½ m. NE. Also early C18, also five bays. Blue brick with red dressings. Between ground floor and first floor a boldly moulded string course.

ROSEBANK *see* SILCHESTER

ROTHERFIELD PARK *see* EAST TISTED

ROTHERWICK 7050

CHURCH. A brick church of the C16 to C17. The nave was originally timber-framed (cf. the interior) and received a brick facing in the C16. The broad W tower – Flemish bond as against the nave's English bond – is probably late C17. Brick windows, basket arches. The chancel is of flint and mostly of 1865. The N aisle and the picturesque N chapel were added in 1876. The roof inside is said to be of the C15. It has remarkably fine, delicate timbers. Arched scissor-braces and two tiers of wind-braces. – BENCHES. Plain, with straight, roll-moulded tops; C16? – PLATE. Chalice, 1568; Paten Cover, 1614; Flagon, 1776. – MONUMENT. Frederick Tylney † 1725. A metropolitan piece. Marble, of reredos type, with Ionic columns and a pediment. Against it pyramid with inscription. Below a small black sarcophagus, heavily moulded. In front of the columns two urns.

TYLNEY HALL, ¾ m. S. Rebuilt in 1878, but now almost entirely of 1899–1901, by *R. Selden Wornum*. Tudor style, brick with stone dressings. Recessed centre, far-projecting wings. Only summarily symmetrical. Porch with big neo-Jacobean frontispiece. The r. wing has the hall or ballroom with three large, canted bay windows à la Bramshill. Varied sides to the gardens. An asymmetrical tower is the only piece whose details look truly 1900; the rest is conservative for its date (except for some Arts and Crafts details added by *R. Weir Schultz* c.1905; NT).

7010 ROWLANDS CASTLE [DL]

A village with a specially attractive plan: a curving, broadening green, like half a crescent moon, fronted by a few Georgian and more Victorian houses.

ST JOHN, Redhill, on the S edge of the village. Originally a cheap cruciform church by *Jacob Owen*,* 1838; aisles added and chancel rebuilt in 1853. Nothing is remarkable except the intricate pattern of roof-timbers at the crossing and the series of stern, almost life-size, carved heads in the spandrels of the arcades.

The green is admirably half-closed at its end by the CONGREGATIONAL CHURCH of 1881, of flint and brick dressings with a flèche; less remarkable in itself than for its effectiveness in its setting. At the other end the green tapers to two RAILWAY ARCHES, through which is glimpsed the foliage of the Stansted estate in Sussex, the entrance to which is just beyond. The STATION is a pleasing design of 1859, with low-pitched, heavily-eaved centrepiece, round-windowed and with low balancing wings. Rowlands Castle grew from a hamlet into a large village following the enclosure of heathland, the opening of the railway, and the development of the local brick industry; the change is symbolized by the RAILWAY INN, originally a simple Georgian house with tile-hung upper storey, to which a heavily gabled third storey and pretentious wing were added in Victorian brick.

STANSTED COLLEGE. Built in 1850–2 as a home for retired gentlefolk. Long main block of warm brick; simple Dutch end-gables and neo-Jacobean windows; smaller asymmetrical wing more domestic in character. Recently converted into a club.

5000 ROWNER [DL]

Till *c.*1950 a quiet rural area with scattered farms; now a vast sprawl of housing estates, mostly Gosport municipal, but with a large area of Service housing to the S. Tall trees have been deliberately preserved around the church, making a real oasis, and a single thatched cottage beside the churchyard gate has been carefully restored.

ST MARY. Small and very appealing, partly through contrast with its setting. Thoroughly restored in 1874 by *F. E. Thicke*, who gave it a completely Victorian rocky-textured exterior,

* Or *T. E. Owen*.

but the medieval origin of the church is evident inside. Originally a nave and chancel with narrow N aisle and wide N chapel; the aisle widened at the restoration to become a new nave with the old N chapel as chancel, the old nave as an aisle, and the old chancel as an organ chamber (restored in 1950 by *Potter & Hare* as a chapel). The two-bay nave arcade is C13, of two orders, the arches chamfered, the central pier round with bell-shaped capitals, the responds flat and chamfered, with demi-shafts and round capitals to the inner order. The old chancel arch is of similar date, the arch of two chamfered orders, the responds with demi-shafts to the inner order. The arches are of pleasantly textured Isle of Wight stone and more than any other features give the interior its character. The arch from chancel to chapel is probably a little later; broad, of two chamfered orders, resting on moulded brackets. The present chancel arch is Victorian. All the windows are renewed, but in the present S chapel is an elegant moulded trefoiled PISCINA with a hood; it had been moved at the restoration of 1874 to the present chancel but got its present position in 1950. – FURNISHINGS. REREDOS by *Blomfield*, 1896. – STAINED GLASS. In the E window of the S chapel an Annunciation by *Hugh Easton*, 1950; also by him the small S chapel window, and the S chancel window. – PLATE. Almsdish, 1677; Flagon, 1726; Cup and Paten, 1728. – MONUMENTS. Curious tomb on the N side of the present chancel to a member of the Brune family, dated 1559. Tomb-chest with four embossed heraldic panels. Canopy in the form of a very thick semicircular arch, its outer face simply decorated with incised radiating lines and slight mouldings on the edges. Surmounted by three massive pedestals, two on the sides and one at the top, with heraldic beasts carrying shields, that on the E broken. In the recess is an elaborate coat of arms. – Several wall-monuments, the most appealing being a small brass tablet to John Castleman of Bridgemary † 1778, delicately lettered and with a swag and representations of angels at the top, in a faintly Rococo pattern; a most unusual type of monument. – Stone tablets to James Henville † 1805, with urn and coat of arms; Philip Henville † 1757, pedimented, inscription in handwriting; John Dash † 1812, thick oval centrepiece, by *J. Stone* of Forton. – Many nicely lettered HEADSTONES in the churchyard. – Work has begun (1965) on a major W extension of the church by *Potter & Hare*,* with new nave,

* Architect in charge, *K. F. Wiltshire*.

hexagonal central space with spire, and adjoining courtyard, the old church becoming the chancel of the enlarged building. Probably this is the best solution in this case to the difficult problem which arises when a small hamlet church suddenly comes to serve a suburban parish; structurally the old church will remain unaltered except for the (uninteresting) W wall, and the historical continuity will be maintained as an alternative to building afresh and retaining the old church as an ancient monument, which always endangers the survival of the old.

(ST MATTHEW, Bridgemary. By *Potter & Hare*.)

The Gosport council housing looks desperately dreary from the main traffic roads, but the later parts (e.g. N of Rowner Road) are not without attractive internal effects: interweaving green spaces, footpaths divorced from traffic roads, trees preserved and planted. THE LEISURE is a pleasant group of one- and two-storeyed old people's dwellings, 1965, by the architectural staff of the borough council. The older Ministry of Defence housing (S of the church) is dismal, but in 1965 a beginning was made on a prefabricated housing scheme further S, by *Farmer & Dark* with the *Ministry of Public Building and Works*' architects, using the 12M-Jespersen system; this is excitingly promising.

GRANGE FARM, about 1 m. S of the church. Brick, late C16 or early C17, gabled, with large brick chimneystack; later sash windows. Not in too good condition at the time of writing.

FORT ROWNER. *See* p. 249.

3010 ROWNHAMS [DL]

A Victorian village amid thick woods and parklands.

ST JOHN EVANGELIST. 1855, designed by an amateur, the *Rev. William Grey*.* Quite a good job. Nave and chancel with neo-Dec windows behind cinquefoiled rere-arches, complex arch-braced roofs, and a fairly low S tower surmounted by a stone spire. Enlarged to the W in harmony in 1885 by *R. Critchlow*. Walling of Plymouth whinstone. – The windows are filled with fifty-two medallions of Flemish STAINED GLASS, presented by the foundress of the church, Mrs Colt of Rownhams House. Nothing is known of their origin. Some are in monochrome, some in browns and yellows, a few in many colours; most represent biblical scenes, but some are

* Cf. St Michael, Swanmore, Ryde, Isle of Wight.

simply pictorial. The Victorian glass framework in which they are set is by *Ward* of London; the chancel N and S windows contain jumbled fragments of other old glass.

ROWNHAMS HOUSE (Victory Transport Ltd). A brick house of *c*.1800 to a strange, austere design. The entrance front altered, but the S front with wide pilasters in each bay, continuing to the parapet without capitals; no cornice; simple panels above the two storeys of windows. The STABLES by comparison are delightfully elaborate: they have a five-arched colonnade, the centre arch higher and wider, with castellated parapet and central tile-hung cupola. Landscaped GROUNDS in the romantic early C19 manner, with tree-shaded lake.

LORD'S HILL. Southampton Corporation are to develop the area to the S of the village as a neighbourhood for 20,000 people. Preliminary designs have been prepared by *Lionel Brett & Pollen.*

RUDMORE *see* PORTSMOUTH, p. 439

ST DENYS *see* SOUTHAMPTON, pp. 572, 584, 588n

ST MARGARET'S *see* TITCHFIELD

ST MARY BOURNE 4050

ST PETER. The church remains in several ways a riddle. There is interesting late C12 work inside, but it will not fall into place. The N arcade seems all of a piece. Square piers, with angle shafts, decorated trumpet-scallop capitals and capitals with upright leaves to the shafts, pointed arches with one slight chamfer. The S arcade is not in line, and only one of its piers belongs evidently to the N arcade. This pier, number two from the W, is in axis, not with the N arcade, but with the W wall of the present (later) S chapel, and this wall is excessively thick. It probably represented a Norman S tower, earlier than the rest. If that is so, then that would explain the arch across from the S pier to the former tower (one slight chamfer), and the S pier would represent an otherwise altered arcade, whereas the N arcade was spaced from the start all the way from E to W. When the W tower was built in the C15 it cut into an arch on the N side, a pier (not a respond) on the S side. The S arcade, except for the one pier discussed, is later than the N arcade, the W bays only a little, the E bays to the fullness of E.E – cf. the bases and the fillets on the shafts. But there are yet more irregularities. The chancel arch is round and unmoulded and has a small ornament of pellets. Is it indeed so early? In fact everything seems to point to its having been radically interfered with. So we can discount it. But the E bay of the N arcade has a respond different from all the others and also a different arch in that it is narrower and has a roll, and this seems *in situ*. Was the aisle started from the E, then, and the arch moulding changed almost at once? In that case the early chancel arch may well, in a different guise, have been where it is now. But where did the enlarging of the earliest building start? By the NE bay, or by the S tower and the S pier? Stylistically one must vote for the former. Actually, if one takes the width of the NE arch and repeats it three times one comes to a position in line with the S pier. Four such N bays would correspond to the present three and a half. Several Dec contributions must now be mentioned, and foremost the S aisle chapel with a wide four-light window with moderate flowing tracery and a tomb-recess with a big ogee arch, and the chancel with reticulated tracery. The W tower has late C16 or early C17 bell-openings. – FONT. One of the most splendid of English Tournai-marble fonts. Of table-top type, very large. On the N and W sides low arches on coupled colonnettes. On the S and E sides two trees of life each with bunches of grapes. On the top a round band of reeded leaves, and in the corners two leaf motifs and two of affronted birds drinking from a vase – an oriental motif. – LECTERN. Late C17. A fine piece with a reading surface to all four sides. – COMMUNION RAIL. Late C17. – TILES. Some by the font. – PLATE. Chalice and Paten Cover, 1588. – MONUMENT. Early C14 Knight with crossed legs, in the recess in the S chapel. Defaced. – (In the churchyard a fine set of C18 and early C19 table-tombs. RH)

ALMSHOUSES, NW of the church. 1862. Flint and brick. Two-storeyed. No wings.

EGBURY GRANGE, 1¾ m. NE. Dated 1778. Five bays, two storeys. The doorway has Doric pilasters and a broken pediment.

1010

SANDLEHEATH

ST ALDHELM. Small, brick, with bell-turret. By *C. E. Ponting*, 1907.

SANDLE MANOR. Elizabethan, but with considerable additions of *c.*1900 and of 1936.

SARISBURY AND SWANWICK [DL] 5000

Fruit holdings with Victorian cottages, villas in small grounds, boatyards by the Hamble, a brickyard behind, and suburban development steadily filling odd spaces; an area that is no longer country but not yet town. The only recognizable focal point is Sarisbury Green.

ST PAUL, well placed at the end of the Green. 1836 by *Jacob Owen**; chancel 1881 by *Fellowes Prynne*, and S chapel, also by Prynne, added in the C20. Purplish brown bricks, stucco dressings. Small W tower with buttresses which end at the second stage, between which and the parapet the angles of the tower are bevelled – a quirk also repeated at the angles of the body of the church. Inside a wide barren nave with transepts and a spindly roof, and a W gallery. Fellowes Prynne's Late Victorian chancel, with low ironwork SCREEN and three stiff E lancets, is an effective antidote to the 'churchwarden' nave. The S chapel is the best part of the church, particularly when seen obliquely from the nave; a simple rectangular space with an apsed sanctuary, lit by lancets.

SARISBURY GREEN originated as a tongue of Titchfield Common which was left when the rest was enclosed. Now mown for cricket, and surrounded by nondescript houses.

Near the Hamble, and visible from Bursledon, is BROOKLANDS, a stuccoed Regency villa heightened later in the C19, with a big bow to the S, enveloped with a Doric colonnade.

(COLDEAST HOSPITAL. Hospital Block and ancillary buildings by *E. M. Galloway & Partners*, 1965.)

A few old houses of the former thinly scattered hamlet of SWANWICK survive, notably YEW TREE FARM, N of the station, dated 1754, in grey and red brick. Elliptical arches, with keystones, above the ground-floor windows give it distinction.

SELBORNE 7030

ST MARY. Impressive Norman arcades of four bays. Round piers, square abaci, multi-scalloped capitals, unmoulded pointed arches. It is a Hampshire problem. How late square abaci, how early pointed arches? The chancel arch, the chancel E wall, and much else is by *William White*, a great-nephew of Gilbert White, 1856. The N transept was once in the style of the late C13 – cf. the fine jamb-shafts inside. The tower arch is Perp. – COMMUNION RAIL. Rustically Jacobean. –

* Or *T. E. Owen.*

READER'S DESK. Panels from rustic bench ends. They must be C15. – SOUTH DOOR. Two valves; yet C13. Good ironwork. – TILES. Many in the chancel floor. – SCULPTURE. Small relief of the Descent from the Cross; Flemish, *c.*1520. – PAINTING. Outstandingly good Flemish triptych of *c.*1520. In the centre the Adoration of the Magi, on the wings donors with St Andrew and St George. The painting has been attributed to *Mostaert*. – PLATE. Cup and Cover Paten, 1638.

A huge yew-tree in the churchyard.

A handsome Green by the church, and not far away, in the main street, THE WAKES, Gilbert White's house (now a museum). It is older than White's time, but White added rooms to it.

PRIORY. Selborne Priory was an Augustinian house founded in 1233 by Bishop des Roches of Winchester. Excavations by Priory Farm, 1¼ m. ENE, in the last ten years have found the shape of the church, with aisleless nave, crossing, transepts, and straight-ended chancel. The total length was 205 ft. There were chapels or other accessories on the E and W sides of the S transept. The cloister lay N of the nave. Among individual finds were vaulting-ribs and a boss belonging to the choir, and a pier with four detached shafts belonging to a screen 23 ft W of the E wall.

SEVEN BARROWS *see* LITCHFIELD

6040

SHALDEN

CHURCH. 1865 by *J. Colson*. Flint. Nave and lower chancel. Open bell-turret. Plate tracery. The chancel arch with stiff-leaf capitals. – FONT. Octagonal, Perp, with quatrefoils.

4020

SHAWFORD

SHAWFORD HOUSE. A beautiful and restful stone house of 1685. Seven-bay front with slightly projecting two-bay wings. Hipped roof. The doorway with its segmental pediment is of 1911–13, when the architect *Jewell* made alterations and added – not at all imitatively – the wing on the r. with its arcade towards the house. Towards the garden of the seven bays the middle three project. The doorway here has a triangular pediment. The wings, like those of the entrance side, have a curious horizontally placed oval recess in the middle of the wall between the two tiers of windows. In the dining room lintel of an Elizabethan chimneypiece. (In the library fine mid-Georgian chimneypiece. Marble, with wooden over-mantel. *C.L.*)

SHEDFIELD

[DL] 5010

A village of Victorian brick cottages and tree-shaded villas around an irregular bit of common which is almost the last surviving fragment of the huge stretches of open heathland which are shown on early C19 maps in the area between the Itchen and the Sussex border S of Bishops Waltham and Hambledon.

ST JOHN. 1875–80 by *Colson & Son*; tower completed in 1887. Outwardly somewhat ungainly: rocky Purbeck stone, big steep roofs, fancy neo-Dec windows, the pinnacled tower awkwardly related to the rest. The interior comes as a surprise. Spacious, well proportioned, almost entirely in brick – light red brick, deep red brick, yellow brick, even patches of black and blue brick; some at least, no doubt, baked locally (for this is traditionally a brick-making district). Stonework in capitals and corbels in rich varied foliage patterns, and other corbels carved as realistic heads. The angles of the brickwork on the arcades are moulded to a simplified dogtooth pattern (cf. Lyndhurst). A much more interesting and original piece than most of Colson's work. At the back of the churchyard the humble brick tower of the preceding church of 1829.

NEW PLACE. Built by *Lutyens* in 1906 for Mrs Franklyn, primarily to accommodate some magnificent fittings from an early C17 house on the Welsh Back in Bristol, which was demolished in that year. The house is built entirely of deep red brick, unrelieved by any other external materials apart from tiling. The style is more or less Jacobean, to accord with the date of the fittings. Entrance from the road is through a pair of iron gates between brick piers, aligned directly on the centre of the symmetrical façade. This is E-shaped, with boldly projecting wings of three storeys, a centrepiece of two storeys with an attic, and a square two-storeyed porch. The wings, gabled, have broad canted bays rising through all three storeys; the windows are brick-mullioned, of two tiers with transoms on the ground and top storeys, of one tier only on the second storey. A group of three tall diagonally set chimneys rises from the inner façade of each wing, which is otherwise simply treated in brickwork. The effect of the wings is one of restrained, almost functional simplicity, with no embellishment except where it expresses the structure. Decoration is concentrated on the centrepiece, with its balustrade of openwork lozenge pattern (partly concealing attic windows) and especially on the porch, which has a balustrade at the same level, a delicate and mannered brickwork pattern in relief on the wall surfaces (rhythmically quoined on the angles), and what amounts to a Norman arch of three recessed orders, in brick, resting perversely on massive brick responds with every few courses incised. A gentle flight of steps leads up to the doorway.

The interior seems at first an anti-climax, as the porch leads into the side of a tunnel-vaulted corridor treated with extreme simplicity with rough whitewashed walls; even the mullioned windows are plainly treated internally in a Voysey-like manner. This is part of Lutyens's artistry; the passageway does not appear to go anywhere special to the r.; the eye is led l., where it ends invitingly in a two-light window opening to the SW. Halfway along the passage in this direction a doorway attracts attention, treated in a manner of magnificence that the simplicity sets off, and one is enticed into the show-
54 piece of the house, the BRISTOL ROOM – filled with the fittings from the state room of the original house. The fittings here and elsewhere in New Place date from *c.*1623–8 (former date on an overmantel; latter date on the state room door) and were commissioned by John Langton, a merchant who was mayor of Bristol in 1628 – so that presumably the state room was fitted in that year to be his showplace during his term of office. The room in the old house was irregular; the Lutyens room is regular, but its basic shape is wholly related to the fittings. The fireplace is a magnificent piece, with double fluted Ionic engaged columns, on strapwork-decorated bases, supporting a mantelpiece with wide frieze, circle-patterned with foliate decoration, the centre part of which is brought forward slightly, and rests on Ionic volutes, which are supported by corbels carved in the form of realistic busts, seemingly of Turks; the space between and beside the corbels, above the fireplace itself, is filled with arabesque decoration. The overmantel, which rises to the ceiling, has a slightly projecting centrepiece with a lively royal coat of arms and flanking caryatid pilasters; to l. and r. are recessed panels with winged mermaids (said to represent Peace and Plenty); at the outer ends the overmantel slightly projects again, with two more caryatid pilasters on each side, directly above the Ionic columns flanking the fireplace. Was this something extra special for Bristol

at that time, or have other fireplaces of comparable magnificence disappeared without trace in what was, at the time, the second richest city in England? Such a question is equally prompted when one looks at the door, which internally has a projecting wooden frame with two composite pillars, inlaid with ivory, ebony and mother-of-pearl, almost free-standing, on tall panelled bases, supporting an architrave with a large panel containing a coat of arms, embellished with side strapwork and broken pediment, and flanked by pierced obelisks; the frieze of the architrave has small carved Turk-like heads. On the sides of the doorcase are formalized figures and thick scrolls. The door itself is of mahogany,* with a profusion of panelling, also inlaid with precious materials, strapwork, and formalized figures, including one representing Justice on the centre panel. Possibly Langton actually went to the East. The panelling on the walls, by comparison, is reticent, with a fairly regular pattern of panels of different sizes and a not very obtrusively decorated frieze, effectively setting off the two show features, and also the ceiling, which has an elaborate (but not too overwhelming) strapwork pattern, widely spaced pendants, and small-scale delicate detailing mostly of formalized foliage designs. There are simpler, though still quite rich, fittings from Bristol in other rooms (including a fireplace with a Tudor-shaped arch and fairly conventional Jacobean overmantel with round arch between demi-columns), but the other really notable Bristol feature is the STAIRCASE, reached unobtrusively through a Tudor-shaped arch from the main passageway opposite the entrance; this has balusters thickly embossed with fruit and foliage, heraldic beasts on top of the newel posts, and the original ceiling, with thickly foliated oval centrepiece and equally heavy (yet elegant) swags, at the top. On the first floor we revert to Lutyens's self-effacing reticence, though here there is something of a transitional stage in what amounts to a long gallery, with three simple transverse Tudor arches, and a side opening into the small space over the porch. In the upper rooms there is Voyseyish simplicity again, especially in the plain treatment of the insides of the mullions; there are also changes of level on the upper floors because the room heights of the centre part of the house are related to those of the Bristol Room and the staircase; those of the wings are different (as is evident on the external elevations).

The SW (garden) front is decidedly awkward, of the same

*A very early example of the use of mahogany in England.

basic pattern as the main front, but the wings are broader and the central recess narrower, its centrepiece a two-storeyed bay shaped as five sides of a dodecagon, with mullioned windows in three tiers below (lighting the Bristol Room) and two tiers above and a top-heavy fascia; chimneystacks flank the wings as in the main façade. A single storey Sun Room, with wood-framed windows, at the W corner is a later addition. The NW frontage is decidedly the back, but it is intriguing; again with tall wings and recessed central part, but here the top two storeys of the central part are under a sweeping roof, pierced with five dormers artily arranged. On the NE side are single-storey outhouses round a small courtyard and an overall asymmetrical effect, with dormers again artfully placed in a sweeping stretch of roof.

(SPENCER PLACE. Timber-framed house with oversailing upper storey and flint and brick infilling, probably C15; MHLG. Also some outlying Georgian houses, e.g. HALL COURT and ROWAN ASH.) SHEDFIELD LODGE, now a Convalescent Home, is a plain, solid three-storeyed Early Victorian yellow-brick house. In front, by the Portsmouth–Southampton road, is a pretty Gothic MONUMENT commemorating the armed forces who marched past during the First World War to embarkation; it might be fifty years older.

7020

SHEET

ST MARY. 1869 by *Sir A. Blomfield*. Rusticated walls, of 1300 style, SE steeple, no aisles. Chancel arch with naturalistic lilies and passion-flowers.

ADHURST ST MARY, ½ m. NE. 1858 by *P. C. Hardwick*. Gabled, with mullioned and transomed windows, but Gothic enrichments. Varied, but not disciplined.

6050

SHERBORNE ST JOHN

ST ANDREW. A church full of a variety of furnishings. The church itself consists of nave and chancel in one with a N aisle of 1834. The W tower is of 1837 and typical of that date with its windows and pinnacles. (Much restoration of 1854 and 1866–84 by *St Aubyn*. Rev. Basil Clarke) Recent recessed spire. In the nave, on the S side, one Dec window

with reticulation. Perp N chapel (Brocas Chapel) windows and small doorway. But the most interesting part of the church is the S porch of brick, dated by an inscription 1533. The entrance has a four-centred head, and in the spandrels is already Early Renaissance decoration. Over the S doorway inside one can see the donors of the porch kneeling, husband and wife. It was an unpedantic or perhaps simply unbookish age in which the donor could appear inside the porch as Iamys Spier and outside as Iames Spyre. – FONT. Purbeck marble, of the table type, but with tapering sides. The sides carry the usual blank arcading, but the arches are not as flat as usual. – PULPIT. 'Mad by *Henri Sly* 1634'. With the familiar short blank arches, but this time diamond-studded. Back panel and tester. – LECTERN. Later C17, with a three-sided reading surface. – COMMUNION RAIL. Late C17; boldly twisted. – TILES. In the N chapel. – SCULPTURE. In the N chapel bits from some Early Renaissance frieze with flowers and leaves. – STAINED GLASS. In the N aisle E window some early C16 and other 44
glass, e.g. one panel dated 1638. The early C16 glass is Netherlandish, in an exuberant Early Renaissance style, and the best of the kind in the county. – PLATE. Chalice and Paten Cover 1669; Flagon 1708; Paten 1806. – MONUMENTS. The principal monument is that to Ralph Perall and his wife. Their dates of death are not recorded. The most likely date is *c.*1525–30 (cf. Thruxton). Large opening between chancel and chapel. Four-centred arch. Two recumbent stone effigies. Both are holding their hearts. The arch is baldly panelled, but there are dainty details above. The large tomb-chest also has some minimum Renaissance decoration. – Two HELMS in the chapel. – Many brasses also in the chapel. Raulin Brocas and wife, demi-figures, 7 in. long, *c.*1350. – John Brocas † 1482, kneeling, a 12½ in. figure. Above a shield and a panel of the Trinity. – Husband and two wives, the children below, 20 in. figures. – Bernard Brocas, *c.*1500. Kneeling figure of 20 in. length. Below he is seen as a skeleton in a shroud. Inscription frame round the whole. – Richard Atkins † 1635. Alabaster bust on a pedestal in an oval recess. The top pediment is segmental, without a base but curled up at the ends. Two reclining putti on it. Finely detailed frame. At the sides not pilasters but guilloche bands without bases or capitals. – George Beverly; 1678. Grey and white marble. A very restrained classical tablet. Garland at the foot. – William Chute † 1824. Gothic tablet of stone. No figures. By *Humphrey Hopper*.

SHERFIELD ENGLISH

2020

ST LEONARD. 1902, by *Fred Bath* of Salisbury (GR). Built very lavishly by Lady Ashburton (of the Baring family) to commemorate her daughter. Red brick and stone, nave with clerestory and lower transepts and chancel. Crossing tower with octagonal bell-stage connected by flying buttresses to four big pinnacles, the motif of Fotheringhay. Spire. Inside even a complete SEDILIA and PISCINA composition. – PULPIT. The pulpit incorporates Mannerist panels (Netherlandish ?) of Temperance, Justice, and Charity, set in much strapwork. – FONT COVER. C18, ogee in outline. – COMMUNION RAIL. C18. – STAINED GLASS. All the subsidiary glass is Art Nouveau.

ELLINGHAM COTTAGE, ½ m. NE. Brick, three bays and two storeys. The upper windows in a wide–narrower–wide rhythm. Low, single-storey wings with hipped roofs.

SHERFIELD-ON-LODDON

6050

ST LEONARD. Nave and chancel and S tower with shingled broach-spire. Nearly entirely 1866 by *Woodman* and 1872 by *J. West Hugall*. Of the former date the chancel, of the latter the steeple. Medieval only some few windows: early C14. – STAINED GLASS. In a N window some of the early C16. – PLATE. Chalice and Paten Cover, 1651.

SHERFIELD COURT. A spacious Georgian centre of seven bays. The middle window Venetian. Big panelled parapet. Porch and additions later.

NORTH FORELAND LODGE, the former Manor House, ⅝ m. NE. 1898. Brick and yellow stone. In the typical Tudor-cum-Baroque of *c*.1900. High Victorian STABLES. Recent CHAPEL by *Playne & Lacey*.

BULLSDOWN HILLFORT, ½ m. SE of Bramley Green. This is a small univallate earthwork of oval plan enclosing an area of 10 acres. At no point do the ramparts stand more than 3 ft high, and the silted-up ditch has a maximum depth of 5 ft.

SHIPTON BELLINGER

2040

ST PETER. Flint and stone, irregularly arranged. Nave and chancel and bellcote. Nearly entirely by *R. J. Withers*, 1879. The S chancel doorway is C13, and the bold stone SCREEN between nave and chancel is said to be based on the existence of the arch springers against the imposts.

SHIRLEY *see* SOUTHAMPTON, pp. 566, 567, 568, 569, 570

SHOLING *see* SOUTHAMPTON, pp. 590, 593

6060

SILCHESTER

The Roman town of CALLEVA ATREBATUM is now deserted apart from a church and a farm. The first pre-Roman defensive circuit, no longer visible, enclosed an area of about 85 acres, largely beneath the C3 town. In the C1 A.D. a new earthwork, defending a polygonal area of 235 acres, was built, and it was in relation to this that the street-grid was laid out in the reign of Hadrian. The town, however, did not develop as fully as was expected, and in the latter half of the C2 a new earthwork was constructed around the urban centre, which at

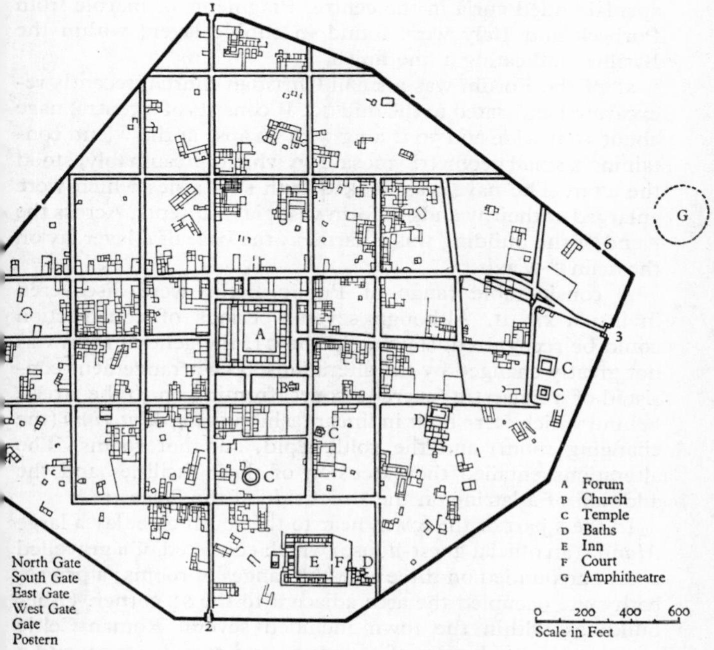

Silchester, plan of Roman town

this stage occupied only 107 acres. Later still, probably in the early C3, the earthwork was strengthened with a flint rubble wall with horizontal limestone bonding courses at intervals. It still survives, in some places to a height of 10–15 ft.

The inside of the town was extensively excavated between 1864 and 1909. In the centre lay the Forum and Basilica, measuring 313 ft by 275 ft. The Forum court was surrounded on the N, E, and S sides by a continuous row of shops and offices, flanked inside and out by porticos of Bath-stone Tuscan columns; the main entrance was in the centre of the E side. Across the W side of the Forum court lay the Basilica – an aisled hall 234 ft long and 58 ft wide with tribunals at each end; it had been partly rebuilt and slightly modified during the latter part of the Roman period. The columns of the main order were Corinthian, standing about 27 ft high. The W side of the Basilica hall was flanked with a range of offices with an apsidal-ended curia in the centre. Fragments of marble from Purbeck and Italy were found in rubble layers within the Basilica, indicating a fine finish.

SE of the Forum was a small Christian church, recently re-excavated and dated to the mid C4. It consists of a central nave about 10 ft wide and 30 ft long with an apse at the W end containing a small geometric mosaic on which, presumably, stood the altar. The nave was flanked with side aisles which were enlarged at their W ends to form vestigial transepts. Across the E end of the building was a narthex; the base of a laver lay on the main E–W axis.

A considerable range of Public Baths were discovered in insula XXXIII. Although several periods of construction could be recognized, starting in the C1, the general form was not greatly changed by the alterations. The arrangement consisted of a Palaestra (exercise court) fronting on to the street, behind which were built in linear fashion the *apodyterium* (the changing room) and the cold, tepid, and hot rooms. The alterations entailed the extension of these facilities and the addition of a latrine on the street side of the Palaestra.

In the S part of the town, near to the south gate, lay a large *Mansio* (an official guest-house) which consisted of a gravelled court surrounded on three sides by ranges of rooms; a private bath suite occupied the area adjacent to the SE corner. Other buildings within the town included several Roman-Celtic temples, private houses of courtyard and corridor type, and a number of shops and workshops which produced a wide range of commodities. Just outside the NE corner of the walled area is an amphitheatre, measuring about 250 ft by 220 ft overall. Although it has never been excavated, its basic form can still be recognized beneath the chicken-farm which now occupies the site. The fine collection of archaeological material from the excavations is now housed in the museum at Reading.

Alas, all this has been covered over, and now there is nothing inside the impressive girdle of the walls but a field cut by what was the two principal Roman streets. At the E end of the town close to the wall is the church.

ST MARY. Nave, aisles, and chancel and the usual bell-turret. The church is pleasantly un-over-restored. At the beginning stands the N arcade of two bays. It has a round pier with a square chamfered abacus, trumpet-scallop capitals, and pointed arches with a slight chamfer. That one would call 1210 at the latest. But the N aisle has not only a W lancet but a doorway with a hood-mould decorated with dogtooth, which indicates *c.*1230, a date which would fit the S arcade better than the N arcade. The capitals here are moulded, and the arches have a proper chamfer. The S aisle wall was rebuilt about 1325–50 with windows with reticulated tracery and an ogee-headed tomb recess with uncommonly big cusps. Again of the early C13 must be the chancel, see its lancet windows and priest's doorway. The E window is Perp. There is no chancel arch. – FONT. Octagonal, C14 probably, with a short moulded stem. – PULPIT. Early C18, but with a fine domed tester dated 1639. – SCREEN. Perp. Of one-light divisions, but with a charming pierced top frieze of angels with spread wings. – PAINTING. In the splays of the chancel lancets masonry pattern with flowers; *c.*1300 or earlier. – PLATE. Cup and Cover Paten, 1572; Flagon, 1635; Paten, 1757. – MONUMENTS. In the tomb recess effigy of a Lady, wearing a wimple, early C14, very slender. – Outside the E end of the church two C14 coffin lids. One has the busts of husband and wife, but below the busts just the lid with a foliated cross, the other has a man's head in a quatrefoil, and also a cross below. – Viscount Ikerrin † 1712. By *James Hardy*. Cartouche with drapery and two putto heads.

(ROSEBANK, 1 m. W. A good house, his own, by *Sir Mervyn Macartney*, *c.*1905. Informal, brick and tile-hanging, with a central polygonal bay window. Prominent single-storey drawing-room gable on the l. Excellent garden. NT)

3040

SMANNELL

CHRIST CHURCH. By *William White*, 1857, and indeed a church of many oddities. Flint with brick bands. Nave and apse in one; N aisle. Brick S porch, but timber-framed roof. The W wall carries the bellcote. It is in two stages, the lower one cross-gabled. The upper is all brick and not really a bellcote but a bell-turret squashed longitudinally so as to be broader than deep. The tracery is of the plate type but not archaeologically correct. The inside is brick-faced. Very low piers, square and chamfered. Absurdly tall impost blocks in which the chamfer fades out so that their top is square. Unmoulded pointed arches.

6010

SOBERTON [DL]

A widespread village in the Meon valley, with an old small core around the church, a straggling village street a little S, and, further S still, Victorian cottages scattered over former heathland.

ST PETER AND ST PAUL. A puzzle church, if ever there was one. The story seems to start with an aisleless Norman building of which nothing but two arches of W windows remain, visible inside the tower. This church about 1180–90 received a two-bay N arcade, starting – why? – some distance E of the W wall so that that part of the Norman N wall remained. The arcade pier is round with a square abacus and very wide pointed arches with just one slight chamfer. A S arcade followed in the early C13, in the same position. At the same time a W tower was built, and this had the extremely odd feature of a tripartite E arch. The octagonal piers are identical with those of the S arcade. Had the tower a tripartite porch inside? For the springers of arches survive from the octagonal piers to the W. But this tower – to anticipate – has nothing to do with the present W tower, which is Late Perp and projects a good deal further W than its predecessor. It is of flint and stone, in irregular chequerwork, and has a Perp doorway and W window and a higher stair-turret. The triple bell-openings have uncusped arches to the lights and Somerset stone screens and look post-Reformation. To continue the history of the building, late in the C13 the aisles were at last lengthened to reach the tower and yet further to embrace the tower. The four new arches needed are identical, rather coarse, with the inner order on corbels. Then, at the end of the C13, the finest part of the church was built, the S transept. It has two long E lancets, with pointed-trefoiled heads and between them a high image niche with shafts and an openwork rounded trefoiled head with one encircled quatrefoil over. At the foot of the recess is a short contemporary shaft on which three excellent human heads carry a shelf. Late C13 also the chancel arch. The responds are short and start somewhat higher up than normal, no doubt because of a stone screen. The chancel itself was rebuilt Dec. Ogee-headed N and S lancets (including one low-side one), and an E window with (renewed) reticulated tracery. In the S aisle in the C15 or early C16 a three-light Perp window was inserted. The N chapel arcade is of two bays. The capitals look post-Reformation and may belong to the tower-top.

WALL PAINTINGS. On the jambs of the two E lancet windows of the S transept are the remains of some very impressive wall paintings. Most traces of colouring have gone, but the black outline of parts of the designs are clear. They depict St Anne, St Catherine, St Margaret, and a fourth unidentified lady. Large parts of the representation of St Anne with the young Virgin beside her are very clear; many curves are apparent in the composition, e.g. in the folds of the drapery and in the postures, particularly in the line of the Virgin's half-raised forearm and hand. St Catherine is largely indistinct, except for the lower part of her drapery and a head, representing that of Emperor Maximinius, at her feet; the outline of her wheel, which she holds up in her hand, can be seen. The lower part of St Margaret's robes is similarly clear, with the dragon being trampled at her feet, and the outline of her upraised hand can be made out. Professor Tristram attributes them to *c.*1300. The liking for curvature and the emphasis on gestures with the arms and hands suggest a relationship with the paintings at Idsworth. There are considerable traces of stone-pointing patterns in red, with rosettes in each of the rectangles so formed, and of a scrolled frieze along the top of the wall.

FITTINGS. The S transept still has a Georgian atmosphere, with a ceiled roof and BOX PEWS. All the rest of the fittings are Victorian, except the COMMUNION RAIL, C17; heavy rails on slender turned balusters; square panelled end posts (cf. Droxford and Bishops Waltham). – PLATE. Set of 1706. – MONUMENTS. In the transept a mutilated Purbeck marble tomb, attributed to John Newport † 1521. Recess with rounded upper corners; trellis pattern underneath the canopy, a frieze of quatrefoils above. The cornice is damaged. Quatrefoils and shields in front of the tomb-chest. – In the N aisle a large wall-monument to Thomas Lewis † 1747, by *Peter Scheemakers.* The centrepiece is a bust standing on a sarcophagus, with a large cherub leaning on each end of the sarcophagus; high above is an open pediment in the form of a canopy, with a coat of arms immediately below it. – Several other wall-tablets, including Walter Curll † 1678, a cartouche in a Baroque surround, set in the medieval recess in the S transept wall, and Barbara Howe † 1698, another Baroque cartouche, with lettering in handwriting style, in the S transept.

SOBERTON TOWERS, N of the church. 1897–1904. Built by *Colonel Charles Brome Bashford* and said to be designed by him. With its battlements, round corner turrets, and mullioned windows, it is impressive at first but soon recognized as the last gasp of Otranto and Fonthill. The plan is utterly unpicturesque, and so are the even four-light windows.

SOLDIERS RINGS *see* DAMERHAM

1000 SOMERLEY

$1\frac{1}{2}$ m. NNW of Ringwood

The centre of the house, yellow brick, of five bays, dates from 1792–5 and is the house designed by *Samuel Wyatt* for David Hobson, a Salford manufacturer. Only the second floor is an addition of 1868 etc., when, as we shall see, *William Burn* did a lot of remodelling. At that time also the porch with its two pairs of unfluted Ionic columns was moved forward. It projects as far as did two wings, built at the same time and recently demolished. The house of 1792–5 has a very regular plan, a grid, three rooms wide and two rooms deep. Along the S side a colonnade of coupled Ionic columns was added. In 1828 the second Earl of Normanton bought the estate. He was a great collector of paintings, and in 1850–1 built a spacious picture gallery. This is still there, but was refaced by Burn. At the same time he added the large drawing room N of the gallery which makes the E side of the house so irregular. Fine terrace towards the Avon. The principal rooms inside are in the shape which Wyatt gave them. The entrance hall has at the end two dark green demi-columns. Straight on from it is the saloon, which goes through two storeys and has a balcony round. This is an alteration of either 1850 or 1868 etc. To the l. of the entrance hall is Wyatt's staircase with an iron hand-rail of simple classical motifs and an oval skylight. To the r. of the hall is the West Library, continued E by the East Library. In the former are fine, again not at all spectacular, bookcases, in the latter a delicate plaster ceiling with circular motifs and an overmantel older than 1790. N of the saloon is the dining room, white and blue, with a good chimneypiece of the 1790s. In 1870 E of the East Library a new drawing room was built. It forms the link between house and picture gallery. It is L-shaped with the two parts divided by a wide opening and two fluted columns set in. The chimneypiece with the two white maidens is by *F. Brown Jun.* of Salisbury. It dates from 1835.* The picture gallery of 1850–1 has an impressive lighting system and ceiling treatment. Coffered coving and a coffered long centre strip along accompanied l. and r. by narrower longitudinal strips of glazing in panels of different lengths. The middle coffering is done diagonally, as the mid C19 liked.‡ It is likely that Lord Normanton was his own designer. The chimneypiece of the gallery is called the Rubens Chimneypiece, and it may well be Flemish. It has two pairs of twisted columns and in the lintel close foliage and putti. *Burn*'s exterior of the gallery is restrained Italianate. Burn was remarkably independent of current fashions and indeed style, always ready to take his cue from the mood of the buildings he found on the site.

SOPLEY

1090

ST MICHAEL. The oldest part is the N transept. Its PISCINA and the string course above it look decidedly C13. The E window on the other hand is early C14, if it can be trusted (three stepped lancets with pointed-trefoiled heads). If so, it would go with the two mighty crossing arches which survive: to N and S. They have mouldings of two sunk waves. The masters active at that time liked SCULPTURE. In the transept E window are two excellent C13 heads, the arch from N aisle to N transept is supported by two late C13 or early C14 heads, and the gable of the transept is supported by two grotesque figures, mid C14 at the earliest. The dating of the two-bay arcades of the nave is not easy. They are so rough that any date might fit. The C14 is the most likely. Small W tower, embraced by the

*So Mr Gunnis says. *C.L.* says: *c.*1770 and possibly from Rathfarnham Castle.

‡The gallery among many other pictures contains twenty-seven paintings by *Reynolds*.

aisles. Is the tower C18? – PULPIT. Jacobean, with simple motifs. – SCREEN. Under the tower, with linenfold panelling. (Some of this also in the STALLS.) – PAINTING. Large Crucifixion, above the chancel arch. By *J. Emms* of London, 1869. – PLATE. Chalice, early C17. – MONUMENTS. Two Purbeck marble effigies of the C13, a Civilian and a Lady. Under three-dimensional trefoiled canopies or gables. Badly preserved. – (War Memorial tablet by *Eric Gill*, 1927. NT)

(SOPLEY PARK. A crude Gothic-cum-Italianate mansion of *c.*1875,* but the apsidal LODGE and GATES are good brick-Gothic of the same period, by another hand. Also the nice patrician touch of a DRINKING FOUNTAIN. NT)

* Mr Taylor suggests *Kemp Welch & Pinder* as the architects.

SOUTHAMPTON

[DL] *4010*

Introduction, 511
Inner Southampton, 516
  Churches, 517
  Public Buildings, 526
  Perambulations, 533
    (a) The Walled Town, 533
    (b) East of the Walled Town, 553
    (c) North of the Walled Town, 555
    (d) Northam and St Mary's, 561
    (e) The Docks, 563
Outer Southampton. For index of places and definition of areas, *see* p. 565.

INTRODUCTION

Southampton's history begins with the establishment of a small Roman settlement at Bitterne, on the E side of the Itchen estuary (p. 596). By the C8 a trading settlement, known in early times as Hamwic, had been established on the W bank of the Itchen, around the site of the present St Mary's church. The name Hamtun occurs as early as the C8 (giving its name to Hamtunscire or Hampshire, first mentioned in 755, though not then necessarily applying to the whole of the present-day county). It has been suggested that Hamtun was a separate settlement, on a more easily defensible site W of Hamwic and close to the Test estuary (around where Portland Street now is), but there is not yet much archaeological evidence in support of this theory. By the C11, possibly before the Norman Conquest and certainly very soon after, urban development had been concentrated in the SW angle of the broad peninsula between the Test and the Itchen, with a curved frontage to the former and a castle at the NW corner, just to the S of the supposed site of Hamtun and well away from that of Hamwic, which, apart from St Mary's church, became largely deserted.

The Normans developed Southampton as a vital link in the connexion between England and Normandy. After Normandy was separated politically from England, the town became periodically an important base for hostile excursions into France, the French retaliating with repeated raids, the most serious in 1338. In more peaceful circumstances it developed a rich trade with northern and western France, as well as with Portugal, and, above all in the later Middle Ages, with the Mediterranean and

Adriatic. Southampton was the terminal for the frequent voyages of ships from Venice and Genoa to England, carrying the riches of the East which were exchanged for the wool and cloth of Southern England. Fortunately for Southampton, the overland route to London, almost all over chalk and Bagshot sand, was a relatively easy one and preferable, under medieval conditions, to the long voyage round Kent and into the Thames.

In later Tudor times Southampton declined. The Venetian and Genoese ships no longer sailed to England; with improvements in the construction of vessels other trade was drawn directly into the Thames rather than by the overland route from Southampton. In the C17 and the C18 the volume of the town's commerce was very small. But from the mid C18 (a spa was discovered in 1750) it developed as a watering place. Ambitious schemes for urban development both within and well beyond the walled town were promoted in the later part of the century but only fragmentarily realized; it was not until after about 1810 that Southampton really reached its heyday as a place of resort and residence, with stucco terraces built extensively outside the walls and villas dotting the surrounding countryside. At the same time the trade of the town, stimulated first by the Napoleonic Wars, was picking up a little.

Modern Southampton dates from 1840, when the railway from London was opened, with the primary purpose of connecting with the new dock then under construction, which was opened in 1842. Other docks followed all through the C19 and early C20 (p. 563), and Southampton's Victorian and Edwardian history was one of continued development as a port, with a concurrent and final eclipse of its older role as a watering place and retreat for retirement. Bournemouth took over this role as Southampton abandoned it. But the port really came into its own in the second to fourth decades of the C20; the White Star Line moved their chief terminal there from Liverpool in 1907, followed by the Cunard Line in 1921, and the enterprising Southern Railway (owners of the Docks) quickened the previous pace of port development after 1929, when the vast New Docks were constructed out of mudland, culminating with the King George V Graving Dock, big enough to take the Queen Mary, in 1933.

In the Second World War Southampton was delivered devastating blows. The whole shopping centre was wrecked, waterside establishments were shattered, and thousands of homes were destroyed or damaged. For several years after the war the town seemed stunned and half-ruined, but since the early fifties it has made a remarkable recovery. It is now bigger in population and bigger in status than it was before the war; it is well on the way to establishing itself as the regional capital of an important part of England, with its university and extensive commercial enterprises, industries (much developed since the war), and, of course, its continued pre-eminence as a passenger port. Further developments, including an extension to the port, seem likely.

Southampton in 1447 obtained the status of a county in its own right (like Bristol, Newcastle, and other important medieval towns), but it did not achieve the honorary title of a city until 1964. Population: 1801, 7,913; 1851, 35,305; 1901, 104,824*; 1951, 178,326; 1961, 204,707; contiguous suburban villages would add several thousand more.

Architecturally, Southampton's interest is primarily in its medieval remains; secondarily in its modern building (i.e. in that done since about 1955); thirdly and fourthly in what remains to tell of its early C19 status as a watering place and of its later C19 development as a port.

In all Britain there are few, if any, examples of medieval 35
urban defences as impressive as those in Southampton. The circuits at York and Conway are more nearly complete, but these are on the whole considerably less variedly interesting than what survives at Southampton. The defended town probably acquired its present shape during the Norman period – it contained the castle, the spinal High Street, and, in the SW quarter (around St Michael's Square and French Street), an area probably laid out for Norman settlers after the Conquest. The original defences on the landward sides (N and E) were banks and ditches; by *c.*1200 two gateways had been built (the core of the present Bargate and the vanished Eastgate). The first stone walls seem to have been built in the early C13 towards the S end of the E side of the town (p. 562), followed by extensive works *c.*1260–90 completing or nearly completing‡ the stone defences on the N and E sides. But on the seaward side of the town – along the curving sweep of the Test estuary – there were no defences before the C14 between where the E and N walls met the shore, with the very important exception of the castle (p. 537), which had a long seaward

* The figure for 1901 includes suburban districts not then within the borough boundaries.

‡ Excavations carried out in 1958 by J. S. Wacher suggest that the part of the E stone wall between the Eastgate and Polymond Tower at the NE corner of the town was not built until the C14.

frontage stone-fortified in the C12. There was a quay outside the castle, another long one (the West Quay) further S, with substantial merchants' houses facing it, and probably some sort of anchorage (which in the later Middle Ages was developed into an important quay, the Town Quay) at the S end of High Street. The havoc wrought by the French on the imperfectly defended town in 1338 shocked the central government (since Southampton was strategically important) into pressing for defences to be constructed along the shore – but it does not seem that very much was done until the period *c.*1360–85, during which the
35 whole of the West, South-West, and South Walls were constructed, the former in two parts N and S of the castle.* For the most part these walls were wholly new-built, but for one long stretch the West Wall incorporated the seaward walls of pre-existing houses, to very interesting effect (p. 537). By 1385 the circuit was probably complete, with five main gates (God's House Gate, Watergate, and Westgate besides the earlier two); large-scale additional works were carried out during the following half-century including God's House Tower, and the impressive N front of the Bargate. So the Southampton defences contain work (and impressive work at that) of many different periods spanning the Middle Ages. Quite a lot has gone – including most of the castle, part of the East Wall with the Eastgate, most of the South and South-West Walls with the arch of the Watergate, and shorter stretches elsewhere. But what remains is very exciting. It is all described in Perambulation (a), p. 533.

Southampton also abounds in remains of stone-built medieval domestic architecture (although unfortunately no single house remains intact or largely unaltered). Among surviving C12 domestic architecture in England the ruins of the so-called King John's House (p. 539) and Canute's Palace (p. 550) and the transplanted Norman chimney (p. 540) are specially important, and there are remains of later stone-built houses. Stone vaults, usually below or partly below ground level, are still numerous (with the original houses above them almost always destroyed or rebuilt); some have been demolished in connexion with post-war development, but a number are carefully preserved. They are usually tunnel-vaulted, pointed or otherwise; except for the

*An order went out in 1360 requiring the blocking of openings in houses fronting the quay, but it may have been many years before that was fully carried out. In 1378–9 *Henry Yevele* and *William Wynford* were commissioned to impress masons for the defences of Southampton.

non-domestic Castle Vault (p. 538), none is certainly earlier than the C13 and the latest are C15 or early C16. These vaults, which are mostly in the S part of High Street, in French Street, and around St Michael's Square, must have been used in connexion with the town's thriving wine trade. Not all are described in this volume (nor have all been visited), but those mentioned are representative. Of medieval commercial buildings the C14 Wool House (p. 542) is a splendid survival. Ecclesiastical remains are less impressive (p. 517), especially as the town's chief medieval church, St Mary, has gone.

Of late medieval timber-framed houses there are two impressive examples, the Red Lion (p. 547) and Tudor House (p. 529). Of C17 and C18 domestic architecture little survives: the Dolphin Hotel is the best C18 building in the town proper, and mention must be made of *Hawksmoor*'s country house at South Stoneham, much altered. From the town's heyday as a watering place a lot remains – though not nearly so much as existed in 1939, let alone 1930 – strangely widespread, since the town extended very loosely beyond its walls in Late Georgian times, partly because the inviolate common fields (turned later into Victorian parks) occupied so much space. Around 1800 houses were usually of red brick; *c.*1820–40 they were generally stuccoed; after about 1840 yellow brick was the favoured material. The names of few local architects of this period are known (*Plaw*,* *T. S. Hack*), but there was a distinctive local tradition (see pp. 527, 556, 560) that produced buildings which might be called elegantly austere. Bow windows, very bold and often semicircular, and canted bay windows were common during this period, and back elevations were often faced with slates from Devon. But Regency and Early Victorian Southampton never had the consistent character of Cheltenham or the grandeur of parts of Brighton; nothing on a really ambitious scale was ever achieved. (The grandest scheme, for twelve houses within a circle at the Polygon, their gardens tapering inwards to a sheet of water in the middle of the circle, designed by *Leroux* in the 1770s, never got beyond three houses; p. 558.)

Victorian architecture in Southampton calls for few general words; not many buildings (South-Western Hotel, p. 553) were

***John Plaw* came to Southampton from London in 1796; he prepared ambitious schemes for residential development at Albion Place and Brunswick Place of which little or none was carried out, and designed the first Barracks (on the site of the present Ordnance Survey Office, p. 528) in 1806. Nothing known to be by him survives, but he must be mentioned in a brief architectural history of the town.

of any great scale, but the medium-scale commercial architecture, of which little survives, often combined the solidity characteristic of the earlier tradition with a greater floridity of detail (usually Italianate). Among Victorian church buildings (p. 518) the only masterpiece is *Street*'s spire of St Mary (not actually built until 1914).

The great inter-war landmark of Southampton is the Civic Centre, impressive for its scale and massing rather than for its style, in the context of the period. Few memorable buildings were built in the town for several years after the war; the town's shopping centre, Above Bar, was largely reconstructed *c.*1950–5 and has the look that the main street of an up-and-coming Middle West town might have had in the early 1930s if there had been planning control and Portland stone. Since about 1955 the city has undergone an architectural revolution. The City Architect's Department under *L. Berger* has produced varied and often distinguished work, the most impressive being the Northam redevelopment, p. 561, and the Swimming Baths, p. 529, and first-class architects from outside have been employed, notably *Eric Lyons* (Castle House, p. 545), *Lyons, Israel & Ellis* (Holy Rood Estate, p. 555; two schools), and *Richard Sheppard, Robson & Partners* (Bitterne Park, p. 595, and two other schools). The University has expanded rapidly under the guidance, and largely
98 to the design, of *Sir Basil Spence*, with an important contribution from *Ronald Sims*. Two good commercial buildings (by *Yorke, Rosenberg & Mardall* and *Oliver Carey*) have relieved the general dreariness of Above Bar (pp. 556, 557). Further exciting developments are on the drawing board. Altogether Southampton has become, more than most provincial cities, a place to come to for modern architecture.

Mention must be made of the excellent restoration (by the *City Architect's Department*) of ancient buildings, notably God's House Tower (p. 551) and the Wool House (p. 542), in recent years, and of the enlightened way in which many lesser monuments are looked after, mainly by the City Council, but in some cases privately. At the same time, archaeological excavations are continually throwing more light on the history of one of Britain's major historic cities.

INNER SOUTHAMPTON

Inner Southampton is bounded on the W and N by the S part of Hill Lane, Archer's Road, Middle Street, and Denzil Avenue.

CHURCHES

St Mary, the mother church of Southampton, is in the area of the Saxon town of Hamwic (p. 511) and retained its pre-eminence in the later Middle Ages even though it was well outside the later walled town. Within the walls were five medieval parish churches, all subservient at first to St Mary. St John (which stood in French Street) disappeared in the C18; All Saints, rebuilt in 1792 by *William Reveley* as a stuccoed classical temple with an engaged Ionic W portico and a vast unsupported internal roof span, was destroyed by bombing; St Lawrence, rebuilt in 1839–42 by *J. W. Wild* (with a spire added in 1861), was demolished in 1926*; Holy Rood was blitzed but the ruins have been preserved; St Michael is the only medieval parish church in the town centre still intact. Of the non-parochial churches St Julian, the chapel of God's House, survives in a much restored state, but nothing is left of the Franciscan friary nor of the chapel of Holy Trinity‡ which stood close to the Itchen near St Mary. The Augustinian priory of St Denys, founded in 1127 at Portswood (p. 572), well outside the walled town but within the medieval borough, was the most important local religious establishment, but only minute fragments are left.

Suburban churches are dealt with mainly in the three sections on Outer Southampton West (p. 566), North (p. 571), and East (p. 590), but it would be appropriate to say a few words about the churches generally in the present area of the city. There were medieval village churches at South Stoneham (p. 573) and Millbrook (the latter entirely gone) and, very interestingly, a chapel built in 1620 at Peartree Green (p. 592). The next wholly new churches were St Paul, 1826 (destroyed), on the edge of the growing town, and Shirley, 1836 (p. 568), in a distant but developing village. Victorian churches were built in great number, both in localities which were urban or suburban from the start, and in villages which later became suburbs. As a group they are not specially remarkable; individually the best are what remains of *Street*'s rebuilding of St Mary; *Woodyer*'s Millbrook (p. 567); *White*'s Christ Church Freemantle (p. 566) and St Mark Woolston (p. 594), and *Scott*'s St Denys (p. 572). A favourite material was Purbeck stone,

*The Ascension, Bitterne Park (p. 590), is in some measure the successor to St Lawrence. The spire of 1861 was by *Hinves & Bedborough*.

‡Parts of the medieval chapel of Holy Trinity were incorporated in Chapel Mill, recently demolished.

shipped from Swanage, which can be roughly worked into rocky texture or used as freestone for fine dressings; it is also very suitable for spires, which are often disproportionate features of Southampton churches. But local brick (yellow at first, red later) was much used. Among C20 churches the chief landmark is *Nicholson*'s Ascension (p. 590); the post-war achievement has been disappointing, apart from one brilliant window by *Gabriel Loire* in All Saints at Millbrook (p. 567).

ST MARY. The mother church of Southampton, descended from the original church of Saxon Hamwic, and sited in what was the rural fringe of the town from the early Middle Ages to the beginning of the C19. It is now a humdrum area largely developed in Early Victorian times and at present being rapidly redeveloped – well to the E of the city centre. A major church in the Middle Ages, probably collegiate; largely destroyed in 1550; rebuilt in the C18 and enlarged in the early C19; entirely rebuilt in 1878–84 to the designs of *G. E. Street*; gutted in the Second World War and rebuilt in 1954–6 by *Romilly B. Craze*, retaining Street's steeple, general ground plan, and some of his outside walls, but not his proportions (for the body of the building was heightened) nor many of his details, for the present arcading and vaulting are in emasculated Gothic bearing no relation in detail to anything Street designed. The proportions are now simply awkward and the interior is just a big main space and a few subsidiary spaces, with no subtle relationships between dimensions or parts, textured uniformly in insipid off-white. No FURNISHINGS deserve mention except, just, the STAINED GLASS in the W window by *Gerald Smith*, with a great deal of detail dispersed among clear glass which spoils the total effect. What an opportunity, so sadly squandered, to build a new mother church worthy of a great city which had played such a significant part in the war in which it had so much suffered; what a failure to use artistic resources of a calibre to meet the challenge. The ghost of *Street*'s building is still dimly seen as one walks around the reconstructed building, looking along the aisles or into the transepts, where windows retaining Street's tracery frequently close the view – they are in early geometrical patterns or simply groups of lancets, with a rose window above two lancets in the S transept. The semicircular vaulted BAPTISTERY, approached through a pair of arches, is Street's, undamaged (containing STAINED GLASS by *Clayton & Bell*) and so is the former REREDOS depicting the Nativity, carved by *Earp*, which also, as if by a miracle, survived the fire, but has now been banished to the S transept. And above all there are the TOWER AND SPIRE, standing at the SW angle of the church, with a lofty internal space lit by two-light geometrical windows over the richly moulded doorway. Externally they make a splendid composition, one of the finest Victorian steeples in England, even though not built till 1914 (posthumously, but to *Street*'s design). There is no special, obvious emphasis on height in relation to breadth, and the design achieves an admirable three-dimensional balance. The buttresses disappear just below the level of the springing. The spire is widely broached, with small pinnacles rising from the broaches; it is not unduly attenuated and finishes in a strong point. The emphasis in the composition is on the bell-openings, which are assertive pairs of tall moulded lancets. The steeple seems wonderfully impressive when seen from a medium distance.

ST AUGUSTINE, Northam Road, Northam. 1881–4 by *Henry Woodyer*. Tall, neo-E.E., with lancet clerestory windows contained within external arched recesses. Apse with range of high lancets like an engrossed version of Woodyer's little church at Hascombe in Surrey. Open bellcote over the E end of the nave. Spacious internally, the nave well proportioned, but the proportions of the chancel not so successful.

ST EDMUND (R.C.), The Avenue, S end. 1889 by *J. W. Lunn*. Brick with stone dressings; neo-Dec; tall clerestoreyed nave; copper flèche.

ST JAMES, Bernard Street. 1956 by *Sutcliffe, Brandt & Partners*, on the site of a bombed Victorian church. Red brick exterior with thin tower, capped by low gables. The interior quite a suprise, with a well-proportioned, broadly tunnel-vaulted main space, and aisles with transverse flat-arched bays vaulted in concrete. The E end is ineffective with a high, circular cross-traceried window.

ST JOSEPH (R.C.), Bugle Street. A puzzling church, the recorded history of which is: original design by *A. W. N. Pugin*, 1843, of which the chancel only was executed; alteration and enlargement 1850 by *J. G. Poole*; alteration and partial rebuilding 1888 by *Leonard Stokes*. Probably the chancel arch with its lesser flanking arches, making a triple composition, is Pugin's, the shell of the nave Poole's, and most of the decoration (including the elaborate neo-Dec windows, the chancel clerestory, and the nave roof) Stokes's. Yellow brick outside, with some stone dressing, fitting unassertively into the street. A W tower was obviously intended, but all there is now is a slate-hung temporary W end. – The buildings of the SCHOOL behind, in part originally by *Stokes*, have been largely reconstructed (*see* also p. 544).

ST JULIAN (the French church), Winkle Street. The chapel of God's House (p. 551), used by French-speaking Protestants regularly from the C16 to 1939 (a service according to the Anglican Prayer Book in French is still held every year). A deceptive building, thoroughly restored in 1861, and looking at first sight as if it dated wholly from then. But the restoration was only skin-deep, and the church is still, basically, that built with the hospital founded *c.*1190. Flat buttresses, largely original, ending in gables with rolls at the apexes. Renewed N door in old shallow gabled projection to the wall, with similar roll at its apex. The windows are all bogus Transitional, those in the side walls merely adaptations from round-headed Georgian ones. The chancel arch is authentic: a beautiful piece, pointed, of two orders, each roll-moulded with broad delicate incisions; rounded inner responds and outer engaged shafts. Both capitals to the outer order on the W face have drooping, almost Rococo foliage (they are damaged, but not sufficient to spoil the general effect); that to the inner order on the S side has weird twirly decoration, and that to the N side has wide fluted decoration. The S capital on the E face has horn-shaped carvings with flower emblems in the ends, and that on the N side has waterleaf decoration. In the chancel are two trefoiled PISCINAS. – BRASS. Headless figure of a priest; robes in good detail. – MONUMENT. Tablet, probably of the early C19, commemorating the execution near by of Richard Plantagenet, Lord Scrope of Masham, and Sir Thomas Gray of Northumberland in 1415 for complicity against Henry V. – PLATE. Chalice, 1711. – The tower is also the entrance to God's House; it was originally gable-roofed but was given a flat top at the restoration. It has a plain rounded inner arch and segment-headed outer arch, both of uncertain date; there is a blocked C15 square-headed doorway which gave entrance from the passageway into the church.

ST LUKE, Onslow Road and Cranbury Avenue, Newtown. Nave and aisles of 1852–3 and 1860 by *J. Elliott* of Chichester. Chancel 1875 by *J. P. St Aubyn*. The W end was restored in 1958 after bomb damage. Straightforward neo-Gothic. –

Mosaic REREDOS by *Salvati*, 1877; draped on the advice of *Comper*. The marble superstructure (uncovered) is later.

ST MARK, Archers Road. 1890–1 by *J. E. K. & J. P. Cutts*. Brick and stone; neo-Dec. Pleasant internal proportions. – It would be a dull church if it were not for the STAINED GLASS of 1909–13 and later by *H. Holiday*. He was commissioned to design glass for the whole church, but the only windows now are in the chancel, S aisle, and S chapel. The big E window is memorable: Christ on the Cross with the thieves on their crosses beside him; a multitude below; the skyline of Jerusalem, a many-coloured sky, and the Heavenly Host above. The figures are realistic, almost Pre-Raphaelite, but their limbs have a muscular, three-dimensional quality, and the scene (especially when seen from fairly well back) has the effect of perspective. There is shading in the colours; and tints unusual in stained glass, such as emerald green and purple, are fairly prominent, especially in the aisle windows.

ST MATTHEW, St Mary's Road. 1870 by *Hinves & Bedborough*. Queer neo-Norman.

ST MICHAEL, St Michael's Square. The only medieval parish church remaining intact in central Southampton. It was probably first built *c.*1066–76 – i.e. at the time of the settlement of Norman immigrants in this quarter of the town (p. 511). The base of the tower of the original cruciform church survives, rather strangely, in the centre of a building which, through a complicated evolutionary history, has become almost rectangular. The round tower arches, built of smooth-faced, irregularly jointed stone, are austere and impressive; they are of a single order, now without any decoration, but they originally had thin impost mouldings (well below the actual springing of the arches), which have been cut back to the planes of the rest of the arches. Above the W arch, facing the nave, are three shallow round-headed recesses, seemingly intended for a rood and saintly figures. The Norman nave was as wide as the present nave – i.e. wider than the tower, the inner faces of its side walls ending against the outer N and S faces of the tower (just as the present-day arcades do). Part of its W wall survives, with flat buttresses which were originally at the angles of the unaisled church. Aisles were added in the late C12, and probably at about the same time the chancel was rebuilt to the size of the present one (its SE angle survives, with an external vertical roll moulding). In the C13 N and S chapels were added, with the existing wide arches, one on each side, of two chamfered orders, the responds of the inner orders resting on diagonal brackets. From this period also are two graceful trefoiled PISCINAS, one in the N chapel, the other against the N wall of the tower in what was originally the transept. In the late C14–15 aisles and chapels were rebuilt and widened, absorbing what had previously been the transepts. This process may have been carried out in stages over a number of decades, and many windows have since been altered. However, four windows in the N aisle and chapel are probably late C14 (though the stonework has been partly renewed): the two to the E with three cinquefoiled lights in low arched frames, and tracery patterns in the small spandrels between the heads of the lights (the westernmost with round quatrefoils, the easternmost with trefoil dagger patterns); the two further W of two lights, in very sharply pointed frames, but the cinquefoiled lights themselves, together with small quatrefoils in the upper spaces between them, contained within tracery arches of much lower pitch, the space between this lower arch and the arch of the window frame being subdivided with more tracery, principally two cinquefoiled lights. There is a similar window with this intriguing pattern opposite the tower arch in the S aisle chapel. The W door is C15; flat-arched in a square frame, the spandrels with diminishing trefoiled panels. Also of the late C14 or C15 is the delicate PISCINA in the chancel, ogee-arched with crockets and pinnacles. About 1500 a chantry chapel was added to the S of the S chapel (later converted to a dwelling), and of this the blocked arch survives. In 1828–9 great alterations took place, primarily to allow galleries to be inserted, to the design of *Francis Goodwin*. The aisles were heightened, the N aisle was extended W level with the nave (it had previously ended one bay short), the medieval nave arcades were replaced, and new low-pitched roofs were constructed. Goodwin's slender, plastered arcades are elegant Commissioners' Perp; they are of two chamfered orders, the inner orders of the arches resting on concave-sided octagonal capitals supported by face-and-foliage capitals (well-executed). Similar capitals and corbels terminate the shafts which rise to support the beam-ends of the spindly roof. The galleries were removed at a restoration of 1872 ('by a committee' – *Builder*), when the plaster was stripped from the walls – to now unfashionable but by no means unpleasing effect. Goodwin's tall and slender arcades, seen against the rough rubble side walls, form a most effective foil to the austere tower arches. The upper part of the tower (which is not at all massive, like most Later Norman towers were) was probably rebuilt later in the Middle Ages and the present small bell-stage lights date from 1877, when the stone spire which had replaced a medieval one in 1732 was reconstructed and heightened 9 ft (to be a more effective landmark for shipping). Now it is beautifully slender, rising rather improbably from the not very substantial tower, a landmark still in many a view of the lower part of the town, though, inevitably, no longer as dominant as it was. – The FURNISHINGS are of surprising quality and interest. FONT. One of the four black Tournai marble fonts in Hampshire (p. 17); *c.*1170. Very big square bowl, with decoration far more elementary than that on the font at Winchester. Of the twelve round panels, eleven are filled with grotesque figures, similar but not identical, with turned heads and gnashing teeth and, in most but not all instances, wings. The twelfth panel has the crude representation of a man. Renewed shafts; old stem and base. – LECTERNS. Two medieval lecterns, one of them perhaps the most beautiful in England, perhaps early C15, Flemish. It came from Holy Rood (p. 524), having been rescued, much damaged, from the blitzed ruins of that church and excellently restored. The eagle's body exquisitely tapering, the wings with separated, gently curving end feathers; the claws set on a globe with a small winged demon between them. Triangular base with lions' heads and front legs as supports. – The other lectern, always at St Michael's, is late C15, of a type found in over thirty places in England and the Continent (Southwell, Coventry, Newcastle, Urbino). The eagle is again set on a globe, and stands on a triangular base with lions at the feet, like the Holy Rood lectern, but uninspired in comparison. – SCREENS. Effective C19 metal screens in the W tower arch and at the entrance to the S chapel. – PLATE. Silver-gilt Chalice of 1551 (the oldest post-Reformation piece in the county); two more Chalices given in 1830; Paten, 1733; Tazza of 1567, a very fine piece of Elizabethan silverware, the bowl externally engraved with beasts, heraldry, fruit, flowers, and strapwork, the stem embossed with similar decorations, the base with a frieze of sea monsters, the interior of the bowl chased and embossed with the story of Isaac and Rebecca. – Also, from Holy Rood, Two Chalices and Patens, 1626; Plate, 1685; two Flagons, 1765; Almsdish, 1765. – MONUMENTS. Tomb, with effigy, to Sir Richard Lyster, who lived at Tudor House (p. 529), 1567; re-erected, incompletely, at the W end of the N aisle. Two sides of the canopy remain, with four fluted columns supporting a convex-sided cornice, bordered with scrollwork decoration and engraved with rudimentary Roman lettering showing exaggerated, yet elegant, serifs. The chest has purely Gothic cusped panels. Altogether an endearing Elizabethan compromise between lingering Gothic and tentative classical. – Many C18 and C19 tablets.*

ST PETER, Commercial Road. 1845–6 by *O. B. Carter*. Neo-Norman, quite impressive outside: shallow buttresses separating each bay, large round-framed windows of two orders, with no capitals, broad polygonal apse. Inside, the church is not a success. It is meant to be divided into a tripartite space, but the two transverse arches are very wide and the whole appears as a single broad space, with an inappropriate hammerbeam roof. NW tower, effective in outline, with a four-gabled Rhenish top like Sompting. Double bell-openings in rounded frames, with large, crowded, carved capitals; a similar large window lower down on the W side.‡ – Pretty former SCHOOLROOM in the churchyard, 1856, with neo-Norman features and a variegated tiled roof. – At the SE corner of the churchyard is the medieval WATERHOUSE (p. 532).

HOLY ROOD, High Street and Bernard Street. Built in 1320 to replace an earlier church which was islanded in High Street, and largely rebuilt in 1849–50 on the old lines, retaining parts of the C14 chancel and aisles and the SW tower and spire. Wrecked in the blitz, when most of the Victorian work was destroyed, but the medieval parts largely survived; the ruins were restored in 1957 (by *L. Berger*) as a memorial to merchant seamen. The shell of the tower is intact, but without the wooden spire which crowned it (and used to pair with St Michael's, when seen in distant views of the town). It is a happily proportioned C14 design, in three stages, with a tall Y-tracery window on the S side at the top of the first stage and two-light cuspless windows, with circular tracery, to the belfry. There are gracefully stepped buttresses, and small-scale corbelling to the shelf of the now vanished parapet. The

*STAINED GLASS. The post-war E window (by *G. S. Kinder*) is of documentary value in showing the five former parish churches of the walled town – St John conjecturally, *Reveley*'s All Saints, the 1861 spire of St Lawrence, Holy Rood with its now lost spire, and St Michael.

‡*G. E. Street* worked in Carter's office until 1844, and Mr Nicholas Taylor considers that he may have had a hand in the design of the tower, which is decidedly better than the rest of the church.

QUARTER JACKS in a recess on the N side, dating probably from the late C17 or C18 and reset in the C19, were damaged in the bombing but have been restored to working order. The arches from tower to nave and S aisle are calcined, but not badly; they are of two orders with rounded chamfering and octagonal responds. Little (parts of the outside walls) is left of the nave or aisles, but the chancel is a substantial shell, with two Perp windows in the S wall, the E of two lights and medieval in origin, the W of three lights and wholly or partly restored, and in the N wall is part of the broken framework of a three-light Early Perp window. The blocked outline of trefoiled SEDILIA can be seen in the S wall. – The Victorian REREDOS has been repaired and replaced to good effect. The layout of the space within the ruin, with a large anchor as a prominent feature, is fairly imaginative. – LECTERN and PLATE, *see* St Michael, p. 523.

CENTRAL BAPTIST CHURCH, Devonshire Road. Built as the Polygon Baptist Church in 1910. The architects were *Baines & Son* of London. Fancy, arty Gothic, in red brick with profuse stone dressings. The main front faces E, with a tower at the NE corner; on the S is an elaborate series of ancillary buildings. The view from the S is an intriguing one, with a variety of slated roofs, turrets, hipped gables, lacy tracery, bevelled angles, and the tower rising to a stepped and pinnacled parapet with an openwork turret in wood, tapering to a graceful point.

JAMES STREET EVANGELICAL CHURCH. 1965 by *Weston, Burnett & Thorne*. Small, but with assertive tent-like outline; copper-roofed; low forebuilding. A good foil to the adjoining redevelopment in Bevois Street (p. 562).

UNITED PRESBYTERIAN AND CONGREGATIONAL CHURCH, Brunswick Place. Built as St Andrew's Presbyterian church in 1852–3 by *W. Hinves & A. Bedborough*. Looks at first sight like a rather fanciful Anglican Commissioners' church of about twenty years before, of yellow brick, with an engaging tower of two stages, the upper one recessed behind four tall pinnacles, and carrying four more similar pinnacles, the tower parapet with an intermediate triangular point on each side, over the prominent bell-openings. The crowded High Gothic detailing of the windows in the tower, with their shafts and capitals, reveals the true date of the building. The body of the church is wide and aisleless, with tall two-light traceried windows.

PUBLIC BUILDINGS

CIVIC CENTRE. 1929–39 by *E. Berry Webber*, winner of a competition in 1928. Perhaps the most ambitious civic building erected in the provinces during the inter-war years, a symbol of Southampton's heyday as a port, prospering while much of the rest of the country was in the darkness of slump. It is really a complex of buildings put to widely varying uses: Municipal Offices, Guildhall, Law Courts, Art Gallery, Public Library, all of which had previously been housed inadequately (the municipal administration was centred on the modest Georgian Audit House in High Street, bombed in the war; the Law Courts were crowded in and around the medieval Bargate Guildhall, p. 535). The site was an open space known as the West Marlands, the only one of the series of medieval common fields around the city centre that had not been landscaped as a park in the C19. Webber designed what approximated to a quadrangle of buildings, with access ways in the middle separating (apart from some bridges at first-floor level) the four main blocks. All the facing is in Portland stone, and the style was probably called 'Free Classical'. Each of the four frontages was designed as a symmetrical composition, with the same basic elements of central grand entrance and flanking wings, the latter in a more or less standardized two-storey pattern with windows of Georgian proportions (though not with Georgian glazing-bars) set in vertical recessed frames rising through both storeys. But because (until Guildhall Square is completed, p. 527) there is no axial approach to any of the frontages, the buildings are almost always seen at some sort of angle, and thus usually give the appearance at first (and quite effectively) of forming an asymmetrical composition – an effect heightened, from most angles, by the position of the tower, the one overwhelmingly dominant feature, well to the W of the centre of the group, on the axis of the frontage to the LAW COURTS (facing Havelock Road). The gabled centrepiece of this front has a tall round-headed recess containing the entrance, and is flanked by fairly long two-storey blocks on the same plane. Behind the entrance rises the TOWER, from a complex structural base at a level well above the top of the centrepiece of the façade. It has a very long, gently tapering stem (punctuated by a series of six small but noticeable staircase lights on each side) with a clock at the top, surmounted by an upright bell-stage, with open side lights (allowing glimpses of the outline of the bell machinery) and a low, pyramidal, copper-sheathed top. It is *the* landmark of Southampton (there was never anything else comparable anywhere near; St Mary's and St Michael's spires are far away), and although purists dislike the idea of a stone-faced metal-framed structure of this height pretending to be of solid stone (which it could not possibly be), there is no doubt that its general form is pleasing, and assertive in just the way in which the architect must have intended.

The MUNICIPAL OFFICES occupy the S part of the Civic Centre, with the most amply composed of the four frontages. Here the centrepiece (containing the entrance within the usual tall round-arched frame) has a broad gable, embellished with a frilly parapet in a manner that is almost suggestive of Portuguese Baroque, and surmounted by a shell-shaped finial. Southampton's coat of arms dominates the façade below. The entrance, flanked by stretches of two-storey façade, faces a shallow open courtyard, the short sides of which end in broad corner turrets surmounted by low pedimented pavilions, from which extend two-storey wings. The whole composition of this frontage is overshadowed by the tower behind it to the NW, so that the total effect is one of asymmetry. The E frontage is centred on the GUILDHALL, a large public hall with a high pedimented roof, with a flat-roofed forebuilding faced with an inset hexastyle Ionic colonnade. This is set behind forward wings, making an open courtyard, the formal effect of which has up to now been largely lost, since it all faced a narrow street (West Marlands Road) with nondescript buildings opposite. But GUILDHALL SQUARE (p. 557) is being constructed at the time of writing, as a formal forecourt to the Guildhall. The N façade of the Civic Centre, facing Watts Park (p. 558), has the PUBLIC LIBRARY in the E wing and the ART GALLERY in the centre. The latter was bomb-damaged, and its façade has been restored (by *Webber*) in a simplified style (the gallery inside is spatially effective, with a main wide tunnel-vaulted space and transverse tunnel-vaulted bays, interlinked with arches to form aisles). In the forecourt a STATUE of Eve, by *Rodin*, made in 1882.*

Because so much is concentrated in the Civic Centre, Southampton does not put up much of a show of civic architecture elsewhere.

COUNTY COURT, Castle Lane. 1851–3. In the best mid C19

* Actually an outdoor exhibit of the Art Gallery.

Southampton tradition of solid Italianate austerity. Tall centrepiece with single-storey wings, basically of yellow brick but with everything massively quoined. Heavy cornices, that at the lower level continued right across the façade of the centrepiece, bisecting a tall round-arched (and, of course, quoined) recess. Rusticated doorways in the wings. The name of the architect is unrecorded, but *T. S. Hack* is known to have prepared plans for temporary accommodation elsewhere, before the present building was erected.

CUSTOM HOUSE, Orchard Lane. 1965 by *E. Bedford*, Chief Architect, Ministry of Public Building and Works. Ten-storeyed, faced in smooth concrete. Strip fenestration with very thin mullions making vertical rectangular panes. More interesting than the main block is the octagonal structure to the W, the upper storey glass-sided and slightly oversailing. For the earlier Custom Houses, *see* Perambulation (*b*), p. 553.

ORDNANCE SURVEY OFFICE, London Road and The Avenue. The Ordnance Survey Office moved to Southampton from the Tower of London in 1841, occupying a site where barracks had been built in the first decade of the C19, converted into an asylum for military orphans in 1816. Many buildings were added in the later C19, but the whole group was severely bomb-damaged in 1940. Several earlier buildings survive, in whole or in part, two-storeyed in yellow brick, some with locally characteristic shell-decorated tympana over the ground-floor windows. They look more like *c.*1840 than earlier. The best surviving individual building, probably the former GOVERNOR'S HOUSE, is on the corner of The Avenue and Rockstone Place. It is almost square, three-storeyed, of drab yellow brick, the Avenue frontage five-bay with tall lower-storey windows topped by shell tympana, the Rockstone Place frontage with three more broadly spaced bays, the centre part of the façade very slightly brought forward, with a rounded stuccoed doorway under a flat shallow hood. Brick cornice and angle pilasters. A nice example of the Southampton domestic architectural tradition of the period.*

TELEPHONE EXCHANGE, Ogle Road. Part of the façade by *Leonard Stokes*, 1900. Three storeys, in two shades of red brick. Windows between wide, shallow pilasters, those on the

*The O.S.O., following the Southampton bombing, is now largely centred at Chessington, Surrey, but will shortly move back to Southampton, to new buildings at Maybush (p. 568).

second storey segment-headed. Semi-basement faced in glazed brick. The roof-line altered.

SWIMMING BATHS, Western Esplanade. 1962 by the City Architect (*L. Berger*). An excellent building. Central space with braced roof in the form of a broad gable with rounded top, end-glazed above the roof of the long flat-roofed forebuilding, which has a tall upper storey framed in smooth concrete, with tall windows between thin vertical members and expanses of grey mottled panel decoration at the ends. The ground-storey façade is recessed.

CASTLE, TOWN WALLS, and GATES. *See* Perambulation (*a*), pp. 533 ff.

TUDOR HOUSE MUSEUM, Bugle Street. A specially interesting late medieval town-house, built in its present form mainly by Sir John Dawtrey M.P. at some time between 1491 and 1518, but incorporating a banqueting hall basically older, perhaps by a century or so. The house was altered in the C18, and had become subdivided into tenements by the C19 (with shops on the ground storey); in the early C20 it was thoroughly but, on the whole, commendably restored and presented to the town council as a museum in 1911. The hall is on the N–S axis parallel to Bugle Street, with N frontage to Blue Anchor Lane, and rises to the height of two of the three storeys of the front part of the house, which faces Bugle Street. The E wall of the hall is timber-framed (restored), but the S wall and the southern part of the W wall (visible from the garden) are of stone. The S wall has a large arched window of five cusped lights, its stonework wholly new; at the end of the W wall is a two-light arched Perp window which looks basically authentic, though restored. A hearth and chimney, externally of brick above the first few feet, project externally from the W wall; the stone fireplace within is renewed. Across the N end of the hall is a screened passage with gallery above, of which the panelled screen, with two doors in four-centred arches with carved spandrels, is at least partly Tudor; the balustrade above is new work. The side walls of the hall show timber framing. The ceiling is wooden and square-panelled. In the E wall is a blocked doorway with four-centred arch and carved spandrels. The hall is probably as authentic-looking as the restorers could make it. It is now filled with period furniture.

The front part of the building contains a fairly narrow room on the ground floor (E of the banqueting hall), significantly wider rooms above (thanks to an oversail), and attic rooms with gable-ends to the street. This part is wholly of Dawtrey's time or later, but presumably stands on the site of the solar to the earlier great hall. The show façade to Bugle Street is in general appearance as Dawtrey built it, but with a great deal of detailed restoration, much of it faithfully copying original features (as comparison with pre-restoration photographs proves), but some of it straightforward neo-Tudor, where the original features had been obliterated (as on the whole of the ground-floor frontage, apart from the two porches). The second storey oversails boldly, with coved under-angle, and there is another, rather smaller, continuous coved oversail just under the sill level of the second-storey windows. The third storey again oversails, the coving this time overhung with eaves of four broad Tudor-shaped arches separated by pendants. The gables are of different sizes, the two centre ones being identical, the S one smaller and the N one larger. At the N end a timber-framed porch, with a very boldly oversailing upper storey (coved twice, similarly though not identically to the main part of the façade) flatly roofed just above second-floor level. The porch itself has carved brackets, outer and inner four-centred doorways with carved spandrels, at least partly original, and low side walls of brick, each surmounted by four small arched openings; the door, with vertical ribs and studs, is original. At the S end of the façade is a recessed porch, of which the outer arched doorway is original. The timber framework of the upper storeys is everywhere exposed, most of the lesser timbers being vertical, between white-plastered strips of wall surface; the main horizontal beams are moulded.* The windows on the second storey are wood-mullioned and transomed within flat-arched frames; they are (from S to N) of three, seven, seven, seven, and five lights (the last in the projection); reference to old illustrations shows that they are original in general design except for the first and last, even though the woodwork of the mullions and transoms seems to have been wholly renewed. There are smaller windows in the centre two gables of the attic, and in

*Old illustrations show that the timbering was mainly plastered over before the C20 restoration. Whether or not individual timber-framed houses were so treated in medieval or Tudor times is often problematical; it depends upon the traditions of particular districts. The timbering of Tudor House was quite probably exposed originally.

the S side of the second-storey projection. The gables are generally renewed, but original in outline.

Internally there are no original features to note on the ground floor outside the banqueting hall, save a massive stone fireplace in the main front room with a Tudor arch. The staircase is wholly new, though fairly convincing. Upstairs, the southernmost room (furnished, rather oddly, as a Victorian period room) has a ceiling coved to a flat Tudor arch, plastered over. The larger room further N has a panelled ceiling very flatly arched. From the N room on the first floor (which includes the projection over the porch) one passes along the gallery over the hall screen into the long N wing, a two-storey build much more humble than the front part of the house, with rough, internal exposed roof-beams and walls partly stone-built, though very much patched; in origin this wing probably predates Dawtrey. Finally, a tall two-storey addition, with canted bay windows, was made in the C18 in the angle between the great hall and the W wing. This is now furnished in Georgian style. From the garden it can be seen how much the Tudor part of the house was altered in the C18. Its rear elevation has varying textures, including some tile-hanging. Under the house are extensive irregular cellars, including a VAULT of flat-arched tunnel shape. The GARDEN contains various features from elsewhere (notably a plain chamfered arch from St Denys Priory, p. 572) and abuts on to KING JOHN'S HOUSE (p. 539).

Other museums are described in the Perambulations: BARGATE GUILDHALL MUSEUM, p. 535; ARCHAEOLOGICAL MUSEUM, God's House Tower, p. 551; MARITIME MUSEUM, Wool House, p. 542; the future MUSEUM OF SCIENCE AND INDUSTRY, French Street, p. 548.

UNIVERSITY OF SOUTHAMPTON. *See* Outer Southampton North, pp. 575 ff.

COLLEGE OF TECHNOLOGY, East Park Terrace. First part 1961 by *L. Berger*, the City Architect. Nine-storey block, eleven bays wide, with very thin external concrete framing, and strips of green vitreous panelling between the glazing. Slightly projecting glazed frontage to the staircase, rising the full height of the building in the fourth bay. Four-storey wing to the N. This is the first instalment of an extensive, ambitious scheme.

ST ANNE'S SCHOOL. *See* Perambulation, p. 560.

ST JOSEPH'S SCHOOL. *See* Perambulation, p. 544.

ROYAL SOUTH HANTS HOSPITAL, Fanshawe Street. Originally built in 1838 and repeatedly added to; the first plain classical block can still be recognized. Later C19 chapel in a mild Royal Chapel Perp.

CENTRAL HEALTH CLINIC AND AMBULANCE STATION, East Park Terrace. 1959–64 by the *City Architect* (*L. Berger*). Smaller but more assertive than the completed part of the College of Technology further s. Five-storeyed with wide concrete framework; mauve mosaic panel surfaces between the glazing; vertical glazed strips lighting the staircases at the ends. Lower buildings behind, extending s to the back of a small courtyard, at the front of which is an attractive glass-sided passageway linking the Clinic with the Ambulance Station, the latter a two-storey building with similar decorative elements to the Clinic.

TERMINUS STATION. 1839–40 by *Sir William Tite*. Only the façade and the shell of the central building are original, but form one of the earliest surviving pieces of railway architecture of any scale in Britain. Three-storeyed stuccoed Italianate block with well detailed cornice and quoin pattern. Attic third-storey windows; second-storey windows with pediments; projecting ground-storey colonnade with rusticated round arches and balustrade. This set the style of local L. & S.W.R. stations into the 1860s (cf. St Denys, p. 584; Netley, p. 351). The station lost its importance when principal trains began to bypass it and go on to Bournemouth, making the present Central Station the main station. The Terminus is now due for closure, but its façade is worth preserving. – RAILWAY SHEDS, *see* Perambulation, p. 554.

WATERHOUSE AND CONDUIT HEAD. In 1290 the Franciscan Friars of Southampton obtained a spring at Colwell (in the grounds of the present NAZARETH HOUSE, Hill Lane) as a water supply, and they erected there the still existing CONDUIT HEAD. From there the water was conducted to the WATERHOUSE (at the corner of modern Commercial Road and Water Lane), a small, engaging early C14 building of rough stone, with stone slated roof, and only a small square-headed doorway, standing now at the corner of the churchyard of the Victorian St Peter's church (p. 524). The water system was transferred to the town council in 1420 – one of the earliest known examples of municipally controlled water supply on this scale.

PERAMBULATIONS

(a) The Walled Town, (b) East of the Walled Town, (c) North of the Walled Town, (d) Northam and St Mary's, (e) The Docks. For definition of area included, *see* p. 516.

Above Bar 555
Andrews Park 558
Arcade 538, 541
Arundel Tower 536
The Avenue 561
Bargate 533
Bedford Place 561
Bernard Street 562
Bevois Street 562
Biddlesgate 538
Blue Anchor Postern 539
Brunswick Place 559
Bugle Street 543
Bugle Tower 541
Canute Road 553
Carlton Crescent 559
Carlton Place 559
Castle 537
Castle Lane 546
Castle Way 546
Catchcold Tower 537
Civic Centre Road 557
Cranbury Avenue 561
Cranbury Place 561
Cumberland Place 558
Denzil Avenue 561
Docks 563
Eastgate 552
East Street 555
French Street 548
God's House Gate 551
Grosvenor Square 558
High Street 546
Hoglands 555
Holy Rood Estate 555
Latimer Street 554
Nicholls Tower 540
Oxford Street 554
Palmerston Park 556
Palmerston Road 556
Polygon 558
Polymond Tower 536
Porters' Lane 550
Portland Street 556
Portland Terrace 556
Queen's Park 553
Queen's Terrace 554
Queen's Way 555
Rockstone Place 561
St Mary Street 562
St Michael's Square 544
Simnel Street 544
Square Tower 541
Terminus Terrace 554
Upper Bugle Street 544
Vyse Lane 543
Walls 533 ff.
Watergate 541, 549
Watts Park 558
Westgate 540
Westgate Street 540
Winkle Street 551
York Buildings 536

(*a*) *The Walled Town.*

The general development of the town's fortifications is outlined on p. 513. This Perambulation covers their entire circuit, and all the notable buildings, medieval or later, within the walled town. It is necessarily a long and intricate walk but can conveniently be split into two parts, the first starting and finishing at the Bargate, the second beginning there (p. 546) and ending at God's House Gate, where the second Perambulation begins.

The BARGATE is probably the finest, and certainly the most complex, town gateway in Britain. Its core is a round-headed archway of *c.*1180–1200, originally of three orders, the arch and responds all round-chamfered with small square abaci, the inner order of the arch cut away. Large drum towers were added on the N side *c.*1280–90. These retain arrow slits, one on each tower just above ground level, facing flankwise, and others at first-floor level facing NW and NE. The embattled parapets have been partly altered and infilled, especially on

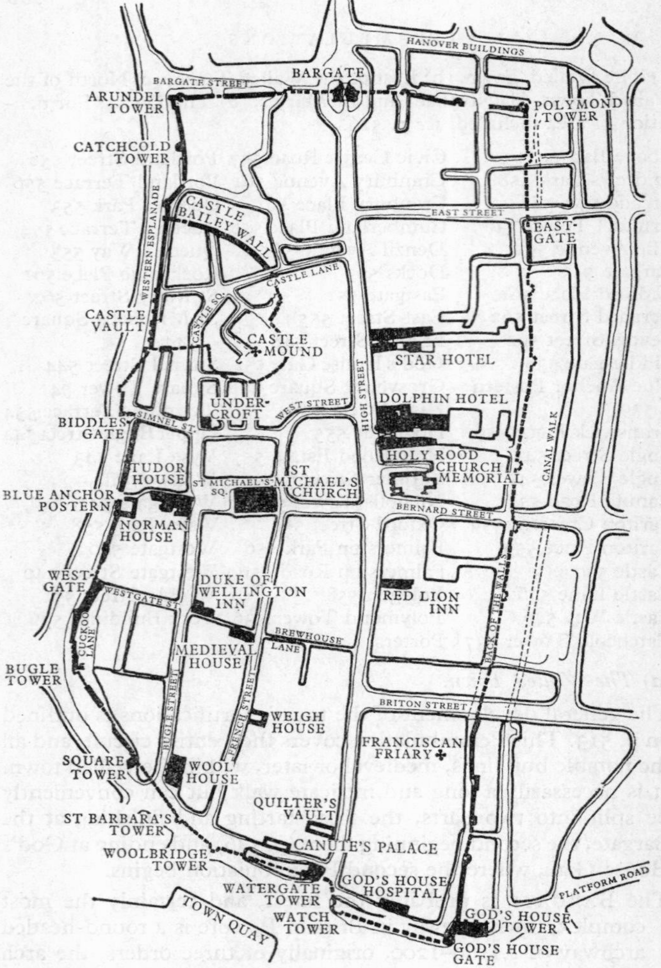

Southampton, plan of the walled town. This map shows the street layout of the medieval town before very recent redevelopment. Castle House (a block of flats) now occupies the site of the castle mound, and a ring road now continues the line of Briton Street W to French Street, and continues N, passing just E of St Michael and the castle site (map courtesy Museums Dept., Southampton City Council)

the E tower, but there is an arrow slit in one of the battlements of the W tower. Perhaps at the same time as the drum towers were built, an imposing new embattled façade of two storeys was added to the S side of the gateway, with a range of four windows lighting an upper-storey room. This façade was much restored in 1864–5,* but the outline and many of the details are medieval. The well-proportioned pointed central arch is of two chamfered orders, with no capitals and a restored hood. The smaller arches immediately to E and W were originally insertions of 1764 and 1774 respectively. The outermost small arches are medieval in origin, that to the W largely original, that to the E restored. The Dec tracery of the windows of the upper storey is Victorian (stylistically a little too late for the date of the façade), but their jambs are medieval, and between the centre two is a trefoiled niche, unrestored, containing a clumsy STATUE to George III, in Roman clothing, which replaced in 1809 a rather unbecoming statue to Queen Anne (now within the Bargate Museum). About 1400 or soon afterwards a large and remarkably handsome N front was added to the Bargate, with canted sides, projecting well in advance of the round towers and with an embattled and machicolated parapet rising well above them. The machicolations are bold and pointed-arched, and project over large corbels rounded in two stages. Two strong square buttresses rise to the parapet, and between them, at first-floor level, is a crossed arrow slit in its original condition, flanked by two vertical slits which are restorations.‡ There are also single arrow slits on each of the canted sides. Above the string course which divides the two storeys is a range of five panels containing painted shields of C18 date. The archway itself is of two substantial orders, each wave-moulded, the outer without capitals, the inner with plain corbel capitals and flat chamfered jambs. The front has the general character of *Wynford*'s and *Yevele*'s work. The passageway inside the projection is flanked by four-centred arches. The medieval GUILDHALL occupies the whole of the upper floor over the Bargate, approached by a long stairway to the E of the gate proper, at the top of which, partly blocked, is a diamond-shaped opening containing a quatrefoil (seen

* The restoration was carried out by *J. G. Poole*, the Borough Surveyor, the window designs in association with *E. Roberts*.

‡ Early C19 prints show a large coat of arms over the central arrow slit, and sash windows to the sides. These may simply have been widenings of the original slits, the inner sides of which may still remain in the restored openings.

externally on the N side). The hall is entered through a doorway of fascinating shape, irregularly cinquefoiled, the upper foil pointed, the two middle foils on the sides rounded. The unusual design of this doorway is not appreciated till one is inside the Guildhall, since a wooden screen with modern door is set against it on the outside – a crass arrangement. The hall itself is now a museum; the roof is C19 and the only internal structural feature of note is a most elegant fireplace N of the entrance, with a wide cinquefoiled arch, thinly hollow-chamfered, with scrolls at the ends of the cusps, and flanking inset shafts, the capital of the N shaft with sprigs of delicate foliage, that to the S plainer. This and the doorway must date from when the Bargate was enlarged in the late C13.

The Bargate of *c.*1200 was a single arch between earthen banks with outside ditches. The NORTH WALL replaced the banks in the late C13. It survived largely intact, although much hidden by houses, until 1932–7, when the parts adjoining the Bargate were demolished to make way for a traffic roundabout, leaving the gate to look like a piece of huge stage scenery, a sort of medieval Arc de Triomphe in an insipid C20 setting. Only the stumps of the walls flanking the gate remain, with the parapet neatly stepped down from the level of the roof of the gateway to that of the walls. To pick up the wall again to the E, one has to go down a passageway between the shops, behind which an impressive stretch begins, and, although the Perambulation proper goes W from the Bargate, it is worth-while to make a short detour in the opposite direction to see this stretch of wall. There are two half-round towers, neither rising to its original height, then a gap at YORK BUILDINGS, where the walls were breached in the C18 and an attractive brick archway built on their line.* At the NE corner of the walled town is the round POLYMOND TOWER, coeval with the wall, but enlarged in the later C14. Only two storeys remain, the third having been demolished in 1828. A small tree grows, apparently quite harmlessly, at the top of the tower, giving this corner of the walls something of the romantic, ruinous, vegetation-covered appearance which they have in early C19 prints.

W of the Bargate the North Wall survives only intermittently; a wide breach was made as recently as 1960 to accommodate a ring road. At the NW corner of the walled town is the ARUNDEL TOWER, a round tower built in the early to mid C13, with another stage added in the later C14 (probably in

*This has recently been demolished.

1377–9, when Sir John Arundel was governor of the castle). It stands against what was originally a natural cliff, with the Test estuary to the W; only the uppermost two stages, ruinous at the top and roofless, rise above the level of the ground on the landward side, their shell entered through a tall round arch. Inside, the lower of these two storeys has the shape of a heptagon, with the space of two of the sides occupied by the entrance arch, and tall arrow slits opening to NW, N, and NE, each with wide inward splays like those of lancet windows. To the W a doorway leads to a small (probably late C14) salient which projects from the line of the town wall like a large buttress, but with a polygonal embattled parapet. A small PUB of 1899, with neo-Tudor gables and prominent brick castellated turret, clings to the N side of the tower; it will soon be demolished, when the tower is restored.

The first stage of the WEST WALL, S of the Arundel Tower, is really a retaining wall, built close against the line of the original cliff (how much the ground behind has been infilled and levelled is not known), and dating from the later C14. On the town side the rampart walk, behind the parapet, is only three or four feet above the level of the ground. But from the outside (i.e. from what was originally tidal estuary), this stretch of wall looks spectacular, with the projecting semicircular CATCHCOLD TOWER as its centrepiece – an early C15 addition, in remarkably good preservation, with a boldly corbelled parapet and low-vaulted upper room opening from which, immediately under the corbels, there are three small gunports. S of Catchcold Tower the FORTY STEPS were built, forward of the line of the wall, in 1850, when the first stage of reclamation of the adjoining foreshore was carried out, and the present road constructed. Old prints show how delightful this stretch of wall was when the tidal water came up to it. The 1850 reclamation did not extend beyond the line of the road, but further reclamations, mainly for industrial use, were carried out from time to time, until finally, in the inter-war years, the whole of this side of the estuary was reclaimed as part of the New Docks scheme (p. 563).

S of the Forty Steps the wall turns slightly SW for a short distance and then resumes its southward line, with a polygonal salient at the second change of direction. Just to the S of this, the late C14 town wall meets the late C12 seaward wall of the CASTLE. The keep and motte were on the higher ground above (p. 545), the bailey was enclosed by a stone wall on the landward side in the late C12 (p. 545), and at the same time the seaward wall was built, in front of the natural cliff, as part of the bailey defences on the lower level. The beginning of the Norman masonry is marked by a flat rectangular buttress, S of which, for some distance, there is an unbroken stretch of finely built wall with a C19 parapet. Then a series of buttresses begins, between two of which is the restored round-headed entrance to the CASTLE VAULT. This is a rectangular tunnel-vaulted chamber, its axis parallel to the wall. The roof originally had tranverse ribs (purely decorative features), but these have all gone, leaving only a few corbels with foliage and figure carvings, mostly mutilated. The vault is lit by a single round-headed window to the S of the entrance, with an inner splay breaking into the S side of the roof tunnel. This was obviously the main storage chamber for merchandise landed at the small Castle Quay which existed alongside the wall. Immediately to the S is the CASTLE WATERGATE, much mutilated, but originally a deeply recessed, segment-headed C14 doorway. It is now blocked; it must have led to a stairway connecting with the main part of the castle above.

The castle wall ends a little S of the Castle Watergate.* The next stretch of the C14 town wall ran SW a little way, then S, and back E for a short distance to the site of BIDDLESGATE, a minor gateway which stood at the end of Simnel Street. This wide salient has completely disappeared, and the roadway runs over its site. The frontage is now occupied by council housing of *c.*1900 (p. 544), and opposite are the new Swimming Baths (p. 529). S of Simnel Street is the long stretch of wall known as the ARCADE. Before the seaward side of the town was forti-
35 fied, there had been a series of stone-built merchants' houses fronting the West Quay. The quayside frontages of these houses were used as far as possible as part of the late C14 defences, doors and windows being blocked and gaps filled. But this did not result in a wall of sufficient thickness at the top, where a rampart walk was needed. So an arcaded screen wall was built against the outside of the adapted domestic walls, forming a series of deep arched recesses, thus giving sufficient additional width at the top to form a parapeted rampart walk, with the added defensive refinement of a series of spaces opening from behind the parapet down into the heads of the

* The Castle Watergate should not be confused with the Town Watergate (p. 549).

arched recesses, forming concealed machicolations. It was an economical and ingenious way of converting existing masonry to effective defensive use. The Arcade has nineteen arches altogether, fairly consistently sized and spaced, but the first from the N is smaller, and the tenth is wider and largely renewed. Within the recesses can be seen various traces of blocked arches and doors to the former houses. In the sixteenth recess is the BLUE ANCHOR POSTERN, a widened medieval postern gate, opening into Blue Anchor Lane (which leads up, past the N side of Tudor House, into St Michael's Square, p. 544). Just S of the postern is the so-called KING JOHN'S HOUSE, one of the most impressive pieces of surviving C12 domestic architecture in Britain (probably from the third quarter of the century). It was a substantial two-storeyed merchant's house, the ground floor used for storage and the upper floor for domestic purposes. Its seaward frontage, like those of the adjoining houses, was used as part of the C14 defences with the Arcade built against it, with the rampart walk above, but the building continued to be used, though altered from time to time, till the early C20, when the upper floor and roof (not the original ones) were removed. However the shell survives, built closely against the rising ground on the E side; three massive retaining arches are built against the S wall. The original windows of the upper storey are of two round-headed lights in round-arched frames, with square jambs and intermediate shafts with block capitals. One remains on the N frontage; the indication of the blocking of another can be seen. The two on the W front were blocked with the building of the Arcade, but they have been re-opened and can be seen high in the recesses of the Arcade – a strange and, to those unaware of the history of the town's defences, confusing sight. The lower storey had archways leading directly on to the quay, blocked but clearly visible – a low, broad C12 round arch to the N and two taller, probably early C14, segment-headed arches further S. Within the infillings of these arches are two vertical defensive slits, with rounded openings at the bottom – obviously designed for guns. These are almost certainly parts of the C14 defences and may be the earliest surviving gunports in Britain.* On the N frontage of the house, opening on to Blue Anchor Lane, is a round-headed archway, possibly inserted in the C14 to allow access to the lower storey after the

*For the historical significance of these gunports, see D. F. Renn's article in *Medieval Archaeology*, vol. VII (1964).

quay had been blocked. Adjoining it, to the N, is a single Norman light, the only window in the lower storey for which there is any surviving evidence. The interior of King John's House can be reached only by going through the grounds of Tudor House (pp. 529, 544). Parts of the original fireplace on the N side of the first floor survive, including both jambs, with inset shafts and scalloped capitals. Re-erected against the E wall is a Late Norman chimney (*c*.1200) which had formed part of No. 79½ High Street, survived the destruction of all around it, and was moved here in 1953. It has a long round stone shaft rising from a square base.

The Arcade ends just S of King John's House, and the next stretch of wall is solid masonry,* with one small rectangular tower (NICHOLLS TOWER) projecting slightly outwards. Here the C14 wall had been built partly across and partly outside the sites of pre-existing merchants' houses, the foundations of which, dating back to the C12, are, at the time of writing, being excavated.‡ A large pointed arch was inserted in the wall in the C18 or early C19, immediately to the S of which is the ROYAL STANDARD, a suave stuccoed early C19 pub, with a castellated parapet, built on the site of a demolished stretch of wall. This adjoins the WESTGATE, probably always the least impressive of the town's five main gateways, even though it provided the principal public access to the West Quay, along which most of Southampton's medieval maritime activity took place. It is mid C14 (i.e. probably the first piece of defensive work on the shore-front other than the Arundel Tower and castle wall), with simple chamfered outer arches, and a pointed tunnel-vault, with two portcullis grooves and a space in the vault on the town side of the inner groove (as a final defensive measure). The two upper storeys have C16 gunports, with wide splays, on the outer face and medieval window frames with Georgian infilling, pointed above and segment-headed below, on the inner face. The parapets are embattled. The arch leads into WESTGATE STREET, largely cleared on the S side (but with the lower courses of walls of medieval houses still visible) and a few pleasant Georgian houses on the N. Immediately S of the gate, and built against the inner face of the wall, is the so-called GUARD ROOM, with

*Immediately to the S of King John's House is a large blocked opening, which looks late medieval, but its significance is obscure.

‡The excavations are being carried out by Mr J. Pallister, of the Southampton Museums Department.

its ground storey partly stone-walled but mostly timber-framed and now faced with boarding (a recent substitute for the original wattle-and-daub). The internal effect of the timber framing in the upper storey is specially good, the cross-beam brackets and posts (in part, clearly, of re-used timber) forming a series of slightly irregular flat arches. This was long supposed to be the C15 guard room, but documentary evidence suggests that the building did not exist before the mid C17 – for which date it would be conservative (but not impossibly so). It was probably a merchant's store. There used to be a space between the upper W wall of the building and the parapet of the town wall, but at a recent restoration the roof was continued down to and over the town wall parapet – a reasonable measure, but one giving a falsifying effect. It also blocks the rampart walk.

The wall S of Westgate is straightforward late C14, with a slight projection S of the Guard Room and a corresponding recession further S. Then comes another stretch of ARCADE, five bays, of which the three N are wholly of 1899–1900 (on the site of a Georgian house, where the wall had been breached) and only the two S are medieval. There was no question here of incorporating the walls of pre-existing houses; the whole structure was built to the arcaded design, incorporating the same hidden machicolations as in the Arcade further N (p. 538).

Here, at the site of the vanished BUGLE TOWER, the nearly continuous stretch of surviving wall ends. The wall originally turned fairly sharply SE at this point, and then gradually curved, with the shoreline, into an easterly direction. But little survives of this stretch: only a few fragments of lower courses as far as the scanty remains of the SQUARE TOWER (W of Bugle Street), then nothing until the WATERGATE (described on p. 549), to which those who simply wish to follow the course of the wall should turn.

The PILGRIM FATHERS' MEMORIAL, 1913 by *R. M. Lucas*, commemorates the sailing of the Mayflower and the Speedwell from the West Quay in 1620. Tall, rough-faced stem, slightly tapering, rising from a base of five slightly stepped stages, ending in a Baroque cupola, with eight fluted Ionic columns supporting a little dome; quite a nice design. Next to it the pretty little STELLA MEMORIAL, commemorating a stewardess of a ship which sank in 1899, octagonal with open rounded arches and a low stepped roof ending in a little ball. Behind the ruins of the town wall can be seen part of the former garden wall of BUGLE HALL, once one of the greatest mansions in the town, built in the C16 and later occupied by the Earls of Southampton (see Titchfield, p. 622) as their local town house, but burnt down in 1791. The garden wall is largely of re-used stone and brick, and the greater parts of two brick piers to a blocked doorway survive.

The former YACHT CLUB (now occupied by the University Air Squadron) at the corner of Bugle Street, 1846 by *T. S. Hack*, is the finest piece of Early Victorian architecture in the city ('anything but hack work'; Hitchcock). Stuccoed Italianate classical, with strong but restrained detailing. Projecting five-bay Tuscan colonnade across the whole of the front of the ground floor. First-floor windows with tympana containing shell decoration. Wide cornice with scrolled brackets in pairs, and the small windows of the second floor between each pair. Two-bay attic rising above the centre of the façade. The five-bay side elevation to Bugle Street is similar, but without the colonnade of the attic elevation, and with a handsome doorway in the centre. The WOOL HOUSE, across Bugle Street from the Yacht Club, is a fine C14 warehouse, stone-built, two-storeyed, the quay front rebuilt in the C18 with segment-headed windows and central door. The side walls are original, but the curious buttresses on the W side, semicircular for most of their height, are later, possibly C16 or C17. The best feature of the building is the arched collar-braced C14 roof, essentially unaltered except for the hipped front part, which was reconstructed in the C18. A warehouse uninterruptedly till a few years ago, it has now been splendidly restored as a Maritime Museum; a graceful curving staircase of laminated wood has been put in, making an exciting and deliberate contrast with the venerable oak beams of the roof. The former gantry-space, in the centre of the front of the first floor, is now filled with plate glass, so that one has a view, while walking among the exhibits, straight on to the modern shipping.

This is an appropriate place to take stock of the townscape. The reclaimed land which intrudes between the W walls and the open estuary ends just to the W, near the pompous neo-Georgian entrance gates to the New Docks, beside which the nine-storey SKYWAY HOTEL, by *W. H. Saunders & Son*, is being built at the time of writing. No industrial area or dockland intrudes between the end of Bugle Street and the waterside, which is here only about a hundred yards further out than it was in medieval times; one looks from public roadway out to water and across to the still unsullied fields and woods of the opposite shore (*see* Dibden, p. 190). This is the only publicly accessible stretch of frontage to Southampton Water, an interlude between the Old and the New Docks, broken by the Royal Pier (bringing something of the feeling of a seaside resort) and the Town Quay (reconstructed in the C19, and catering for small-scale shipping).

BUGLE STREET is the best historic street in Southampton, in fact the only street in the old town with a grouping of mainly domestic or commercial buildings forming memorable townscape. Architecture of medieval to modern times is happily mingled. The transition between the relative grandeur of the Yacht Club and the domesticity of the rest of the street is marked by a pleasant pair of Early Victorian stuccoed houses, next to the club, with recessed rounded doorways. Then a space behind an ugly corrugated fence – specially hurtful here – and beyond that a five-bay Georgian house with plain parapet above the cornice and a fine pedimented Doric doorcase. Then unremarkable buildings on both sides until VYSE LANE FLATS (r.) are reached, a nice piece of infilling by *Lyons, Israel & Ellis*, 1958, for Southampton Corporation. Three-storey block facing Bugle Street (with which it is properly in scale) with concrete fascia, and yellow brick walling, recessed balconies, and vitreous panels within the visible framework of concrete party walls and floors. Behind it (and fronting the parallel French Street) is a similar four-storey block, with a short single-storey block between two medieval buildings forming the third side of an attractive courtyard. One of the medieval buildings is No. 58 French Street (r.), described later in the Perambulation (p. 548), the other (l.) is the DUKE OF WELLINGTON a fine timber-framed early C16 house with a three-storey gabled frontage to Bugle Street, the upper storeys oversailing. The essential timber framework is original (except in the top storey, which was destroyed in the blitz and replaced to the original proportions), but all the infillings and details are spurious, and quite blatantly so.

The interest of Bugle Street now switches to the l. where a long series of mainly three-storeyed houses makes a memorable piece of townscape culminating in Tudor House. No. 43 has a large canted bay window on the first floor; No. 45, though fussily altered, has two attractive Georgian rectangular bays on the upper two storeys; No. 47 is red-brick mid-Georgian with keystones, four-storeyed with an even parapet; No. 49

had two Georgian storeys and a rebuilt upper floor with Dutch gable; No. 51 is small and pretty, stuccoed, with one wide window on each of two storeys and three arched recesses on the tall attic storey, the middle one containing a little window; No. 53 is grand in scale, of yellow brick, severe in a Palladian way, with a semicircular window within the large pediment-gable and a handsome Greek porch with fluted columns; No. 55 is a recent rebuilding; No. 57 is solid ordinary Victorian with canted bay windows, nicely in place; No. 59 is a cottage-like wing of Tudor House (p. 529).

Tudor House fronts ST MICHAEL'S SQUARE, a small regular market-place, the centrepiece of the Norman-French quarter of the town, probably laid out soon after the Conquest, which also included French Street and the parallel Bugle Street. St Michael's church (p. 521) is to the E, pleasant but dilapidated buildings to the N,* and an attractive group to the S, including the former annexe to ST JOSEPH'S SCHOOL, 1870 by *R. Critchlow*, intricately bargeboarded (p. 520), and a Late Georgian house which takes the corner to Bugle Street nicely, with upper-storey canted bays on both frontages. S the view is along Bugle Street to the water; N to the dominating Castle House (p. 545); the only disturbing feature is the disproportionate ST MICHAEL'S HOUSE (1899 by *C. J. Hair*) on the W.‡

To the N the area of UPPER BUGLE STREET and SIMNEL STREET was largely redeveloped as a very early exercise in slum clearance *c.*1899–1900. Many historic and picturesque but insanitary dwellings were destroyed, but the UNDERCROFT was spared, originally the lowest, partly underground, storey of a medieval house, but now with two-storey council flats above. It is a particularly handsome early C14 room with two broad bays of rib-vaulting, which is lit by two two-light windows in the S wall of the E bay and by a single-light window beside the entrance doorway in the W bay. There are a fine range of figure corbels, two splendid bosses at the intersections of the vaulting-ribs, one foliated, the other a sensitively carved head with flowing hair, beard, and even lines on the forehead, and a C14 fireplace at the W end in a fairly good state of preservation. The COUNCIL HOUSING by *C. J. Hair* is mostly terraces of two-storey flats. COUNCIL BUILDINGS

*The N side of St Michael's Square is shortly to be redeveloped by the City Council, with due regard for the townscape effect. A medieval VAULT on a now derelict site will be incorporated into the new development.

‡ To be replaced by new council housing.

facing Simnel Street, 1900, is a five-storey block, with tall gable-ends and octagonal turrets ending in fancy finials, like a lesser, romanticized version of a Scottish tenement block in brick. In telling, powerful contrast, the fourteen-storey CASTLE HOUSE, by *Eric Lyons*, completed in 1963, looms to the N. It stands on the site of the castle keep, a wooden structure on a tall motte in the C11, possibly replaced by a stone keep in the late C12, superseded by a larger round keep in the C14, which was ruinous in the C17; the remains were finally incorporated in a fantastic mock medieval castle built by the Marquis of Lansdowne in 1804, which lasted only until 1818. Then the motte was lowered in height and a chapel was built on it which, latterly secularized, remained till after the Second World War. Castle House occupies the site of the motte (which had previously been thoroughly explored archaeologically),* dominating the old town more surely than the late medieval keep or Lord Lansdowne's castle must have done, and to good visual effect. It is a subtle design, clear in its general framework but intricate in its detailing. The S façade has a rectangular grid of floors and party walls; in each compartment the party walls, largely of glass, are set back behind balconies, the balustrades of which, flush with the façade, have a complex pattern, arranged with studied haphazardness, of vertical black bands and glass panels. The end façades have a rough concrete finish. The two lowest storeys are used for servicing and faced with shiny black brick, except at the E end, where they are open, and the upper storeys are supported impressively on tall concrete piers. The N façade is more complex than the S; the third bay from the E is occupied by the lift shaft, rising to an extra storey; every third storey has a continuous balcony, and the other storeys have flush glazing and vitreous panelling.

The Castle Bailey was an irregular area of about three acres, with the keep at its SE angle, which became covered with houses on an irregular street pattern after the early C17. But part of the curving NE BAILEY WALL remains, with a series of arches (many blocked) like a rough arcade. Most of the masonry which survives was originally hidden behind earthen banks (the construction of the arched openings, rather than solid masonry, behind the earth representing a considerable economy in stone), above which an embattled wall rose several feet higher

*These excavations failed to reveal any conclusive evidence as to whether the castle site had been occupied in pre-Norman times.

than at present. At the E end of CASTLE LANE the bases of the C14 drum towers of the former eastern CASTLE GATE have been recently uncovered and restored. Just inside the site of the gateway is the COUNTY COURT (p. 527) and opposite it a three-storey six-bay late C18 house with a pedimented doorcase. Across the new CASTLE WAY a pedestrian way leads into High Street.

HIGH STREET was considered, up to a century or so ago, to be one of the finest streets in the South of England. Leland praised it in 1546, when it was largely timber-fronted; topographical writers commented favourably on it in the early C19, when it abounded in bow windows. It remained a fairly distinguished thoroughfare until the nineteen-thirties, when the demolition of buildings round the Bargate, creating a traffic circus with the gate in the middle, destroyed the street's coherence at its vital N end. Bombs wrecked much of the rest, and scarcely any of the post-war reconstruction is, alas, of architectural distinction. Yet a few fine buildings remain, and in the wide, slightly wavering section between the Bargate and Holy Rood a little of the atmosphere of the pre-1930 street still lingers. No. 6 is a nicely detailed three-storeyed stucco house of *c.*1840 with strong window frames and hoods on the first floor, and flat pilasters enlivened with garlands; the office front dates from 1964–5, when the whole was sensitively restored. MARTIN'S BANK, *c.*1900, probably by *S. Kelway Pope*, is neo-Burghley, with mullioned windows framed between pilasters of each order successively on three floors, and gay Elizabethan decoration including an open-strapwork balustrade. The MIDLAND BANK, 1900 by *T. B. Whinney*, is more ponderous neo-Baroque but with a lively skyline; little cupolas at the canted corners, a tall balustrade, and a hefty chimneystack. LLOYDS BANK, 1927–8 by *Horace Field*, is a distinguished classical design which stands out in a line of otherwise dead neo-Georgian buildings; in pleasant buff stone with strong but not overdone window detailing and a pretty but purposeless balcony in front of the middle window of the top floor. The STAR HOTEL has a severe four-storey front of seven bays, stuccoed, with a rusticated ground storey and a broad elliptical archway occupying the space of the middle two bays; above it is a large window under a segmental panel with fanwise fluted decoration. The lower three storeys are probably pre-1800, but the fourth storey was added and the whole stuccoed *c.*1830–40; the fine, rather heavy ironwork of the continuous balcony on the first floor looks post-1840. The DOLPHIN HOTEL is the best C18 building in the city proper. It has a mainly red-brick symmetrical façade with a small pediment, and another elliptical archway in a stuccoed rusticated ground storey. Its specially distinctive features are the great bow windows, one each side on the ground and first storeys, among the largest anywhere. There is a lower, yellow brick early C19 N extension, recently heightened a storey. Next to the hotel is WOOLWICH HOUSE, *c.*1850–60, a nice piece of moderate scale mid-Victorian commercial architecture; in yellow brick and stone, with basically classical proportions and thick Italianate details. It takes the corner beside Holy Rood Church (p. 524) in a complex and effective way.* Opposite Holy Rood is the NATIONAL PROVINCIAL BANK, 1867 by *J. Gibson*, the best mid-Victorian commercial building in the city, though on quite a modest scale. Tall lower storey with strongly detailed round-arched windows. Swagger round-arched entrance with engaged Ionic columns supporting a rectangular hood, surmounted by a huge coat of arms. Rusticated angle pilasters, more rustication on the side (St Michael's Street) elevation, and a lively roof-line with pedimented windows of two sizes alternating with stretches of openwork balustrade.

Below Holy Rood the street funnels and changes character; warehouses rather than banks dominate. Beyond the narrowing it has been almost wholly devastated by the blitz and meanly rebuilt. But there is a short transitional stretch with two or three buildings of note. HOLY ROOD CHAMBERS has a lively Waterhousey character: shiny red brick and terracotta with frilly Gothic decoration in orange stone; big central gable and flanking little ones; broad-arched lower storey with heraldic lions on engaged columns. Next to it a long Italianate façade with narrow pairs of round-arched windows on the third storey and twirly little turrets in front of the slated roof. Opposite, the RED LION, behind the blatantly bogus front of which is, amazingly, a late medieval timber-framed house. The front (W) part, with two storeys and a gabled attic, probably represents the original solar; the hall behind, tall for its width, rises through the whole height of the building to the massively framed roof.‡ The hall is altogether three bays long, but a

*Under the QUEEN'S HOTEL is a fine medieval VAULT.

‡The roof is irregular and was probably altered in post-medieval times, perhaps in the C17.

screened passageway with balustraded gallery above at first-floor level runs along the N (long) side for two bays, while the E bay is filled with a wide screened gallery at the same level. A stone fireplace is built into the hall against the S wall of the E bay, facing W, with moulded Tudor arch and rounded tracery patterns in square panels on the front of the over-mantel. The fireplace looks C16, but it and the galleries could have been insertions into the hall, which may be considerably earlier.*

Turn r. along the new ring road into FRENCH STREET, one of the streets of Early Norman origin in the SW quarter of the town (p. 544), with a few interesting buildings but no overall townscape. First, the E façade of the flats by *Lyons, Israel & Ellis* noted in Bugle Street (p. 543) and, to their N, No. 58, a patched-up medieval house, long, rectangular with a VAULT below, a shoulder-headed window of *c.*1300 on each side elevation, and much old timberwork within. It was damaged during the war and has been kept in provisional repair by the Corporation (the façade to French Street is temporary). Further N another block of flats similar to the first, skilfully built over two tunnel VAULTS in a semi-basement position, now open to the E, the N one rubble-faced and possibly late C13 or early C14, the S one ashlar-faced and probably C15. Both have doorways at their W ends opening into blocked spiral staircases. There is an interconnecting arch between the two vaults near their E ends. Back S along French Street. Nos 88–90 on the r. is a four-storey warehouse of 1903, with Art-Nouveau decoration in the panels between the first and second floors: stylized flowers on stems, heart emblems, initials, and date. It is to be converted into a Museum of Science and Industry. Opposite, the WEIGH HOUSE is the shell of a medieval building gutted in the blitz, probably the place where the king's weigh-beam was kept. Simple rectangle of one tall storey, with a C13 window in the N wall, of two trefoiled lights with a quatrefoiled circle in the stonework between their heads, a wide blocked doorway also in the N wall, and a small C13 doorway in the E wall. The four-centred doorway on the street façade is a C15 insertion, cutting into the blocked frame of an earlier window above; the present large W window is C19.‡ The S end of French Street is still partly in a bombed condition, with the

*Below the hall is a medieval VAULT.

‡ Under the playground of ST JOHN'S SCHOOL, N of the Weigh House, a medieval VAULT.

broken lower parts of medieval party walls revealed. To the r. is the Wool House (p. 542) and to the l. a park has recently been created, which will later be extended and will incorporate several interesting medieval survivals (*see* below, p. 550). In front is the open water and the Royal Pier. Facing the Pier is a six-storeyed WAREHOUSE of red brick with grey and yellow dressings, built in two sections, the W one inscribed *D. Geddes*, Surveyor, 1866; right in scale for this position, but eventually to be demolished so as to give the new park an uninterrupted view of the waterfront. Unfortunately this will also make the inward view of downtown Southampton from the water less interesting than it is now. Some large well-designed building on a conspicuous site will be needed, visually, to replace the warehouse, possibly just behind the park (why not over one of the medieval vaults?). Next to the warehouse, SEAWAY HOUSE, also threatened, a nice two-storey Italianate façade of *c.*1860, strong and restrained in the local manner of the date, exemplified also in Woolwich House (p. 547). Seaway House adjoins what is left of the WATERGATE, the S gate of the town, at the end of High Street, giving access to the Town Quay. It was largely demolished in 1804, but parts of the C14 drum tower, and of later additions to the W and N of it, were incorporated into a house, which was bomb-damaged. Now, stripped of later accretions, the medieval remains have been carefully restored. The drum tower remains up to three storeys, and part of the fourth, with three ruinous window-openings on the third storey and one square-headed window (facing SW) on the storey below. A three-storey rectangular tower was added to the W in the early C15 (before 1439); its S façade is largely intact with a central part recessed between buttresses, and below a parapet with bold machicolations resting on three-stepped corbels like those on the Bargate. The SW diagonal buttress of the tower (closely hemmed in by Seaway House) is hollow, and contains the remains of a garderobe on each floor. The tower was built on the seaward side of the earlier town wall, part of the masonry of which, pared down in thickness, forms the lower part of the tower's N wall; the upper part contains a two-light square-headed window. The bottom storey of the rectangular tower was tunnel-vaulted; the vaulting has gone, but the E wall of the vaulted chamber remains, with a four-centred doorway. Another rectangular addition was made to the Watergate, N of the drum tower, possibly in the late C15, and of this the W wall survives, with a two-light square-headed window in the top storey and the ruin of a wider segment-headed window-opening below. A small part of the N wall of this addition also still stands.

On the N side of PORTERS' LANE, which runs behind the line of the town wall, are the remains of CANUTE'S PALACE, the name given by a romantic early C19 antiquary to a once fine late C12 merchant's house, much altered and mutilated before it was bomb-damaged, and now awaiting restoration to be preserved as a ruin. It was very long and narrow, and, before the C14 town wall was built, faced the open quay. A stone wall, probably not the original one, indicates its E extremity; the original gabled W wall survived until 1952, when part of it collapsed. It was rebuilt with the old materials, including a typical Late Norman window of two round-headed lights within a round-headed hooded frame. The long, very much patched S wall has interesting features, including the inner jambs and the beginnings of the arches, thinly chamfered, of what was a pair of tall first-floor lancet windows* and, further W, a roughly infilled round-headed window with a remarkable inner frame; this has a very flat segmental arch and delicate nook-shafts with miniature foliated capitals. The ruinous N wall shows no significant feature. The house was two-storeyed with the principal room upstairs; the lower storey was never vaulted, and the line of the floor can be traced. The ruins of both Canute's Palace and the Watergate will be incorporated into the new park (p. 549).

On the E fringe of the park, facing High Street, are two highly interesting medieval VAULTS of otherwise vanished houses. QUILTER'S VAULT is a long tunnel-vault, half underground, said (like many of the vaults in the city, probably erroneously) to be late C12 – its datable features suggest that it is more likely to be C14. A damaged doorway, retaining its inner segmental arch and its chamfered jambs, leads in from the street, and a flight of seven stone steps, possibly original, descends into the vault. To the S of this door is a single-light square-headed window; at the other end of the vault is a chamfered four-centred doorway and a similar square-headed window. The tunnel-vault actually springs from a chamfered ledge about 2 ft above floor level. On the N side, towards the W, is another entrance, at the end of a short transverse tunnel-vault, the doorway rounded to fit the vaulting but chamfered in a way resembling

*In early C19 prints, these lancets appear largely intact.

the E and W doorways. To the E of this doorway, visible outside, are the remains of a spiral staircase which led into the house above. The vault further N (formerly No. 93 High Street) is wholly underground. It has a flat-arched tunnel-vault with transverse chamfered ribs which make it the most impressive of the Southampton vaults, the vaulting and the ribs springing from a shallow ledge as at Quilter's. The easternmost section is split into two short vaulted spaces of unequal size, the smaller (N) acting as a kind of vestibule inside the entrance, the larger (S) ending with a wall which contains two elegant blocked E.E. lancet windows, roll-moulded, in such a position (the arch of the vault actually overlaps them) as to indicate that they must pre-date the present vault, which is probably C15. At the W end is a small four-centred doorway, hollow-chamfered, with a square-headed window beside it, leading now into a narrow passage (the further wall of which is of recent construction) which ends at a stone-lined WELL-SHAFT adjoining the SW corner of the vault. To the S of the main vault, towards its W end, and at r. angles to it, is a short brick vault, probably Late Tudor, interconnected by a low four-centred archway and a higher window in the side of the main vault.

In WINKLE STREET, off High Street (running behind the line of the S wall, E of the Watergate), is the HOSPITAL OF ST JULIAN or GOD'S HOUSE, founded *c.*1185 by a rich merchant as an almshouse and hostel for travellers. The former function survived the Reformation, but the domestic quarters were rebuilt in 1861; two simple brick blocks forming two sides of a quadrangle, of which the Warden's House, demolished in 1926, formed a third and the chapel (p. 520) the fourth. Winkle Street leads to the early C14 GOD'S HOUSE GATE, facing E, at the SE corner of the walled town, adjoining which is the much larger GOD'S HOUSE TOWER, built in the early C15* to protect the sluice which controlled the flow of water into the extra-mural defensive ditch. Together they form an impressive group, recently converted, most admirably, into an Archaeological Museum. The upper room of the gate is mainly rectangular, but with a S wall of two canted planes meeting at a blunt point, lit by low trefoiled lancet windows, three on the E side, one on each of the canted S faces, and one on the W side over the arch. The archway has the remains of two portcullis grooves and a series of internal transverse

*Before 1424, when there is recorded reference to it.

chamfered arches forming ribs to the pointed tunnel-vault, which rises slightly higher in the W part of the archway than in the E. God's House Tower consists of a three-storey tower proper, built over the site of the sluice, and a two-storey rectangular block connecting it with the line of the E wall just N of God's House Gate, the whole constituting a large defensive salient. The windows are standardized, of two quatrefoiled lights, square-headed and hooded, within inner segment-arched frames; three on the S face of the upper storey of the connecting range, and one to each storey on each of the three outer faces of the tower proper (the topmost on the E side blocked). Gunports flank the windows of the second storey of the tower. The N side of the connecting block has one two-light window, one single-light, and two gunports on its upper floor. The tower has angle buttresses and wide battlements at the end of each side, with lower parapet in between, the tops of the battlements and parapets pitched downwards towards the outside; the connecting block has regular parapets. Nothing remains of the internal subdivision of the tower; there is evidence that the ground storey of the connecting block was vaulted. An original fireplace, with a hollow-chamfered four-centred arch, remains on the upper storey. Modern concrete floors were put in, largely in the positions of the original floors, to excellent effect, in the conversion of the tower to a museum – which was completed in 1960.

The W wall of God's House Tower is at an angle to the rest of the building and clearly follows the line of the older town wall, part of the masonry of which it appears to incorporate. The stretch of EAST WALL to the N is one of the best-preserved free-standing sections in the whole circuit, with the parapet and rampart walk entire. It ends in a well-preserved semicircular hollow tower pierced with arrow slits; *c.*1300. N of this, beyond a gap, is a more ruinous section of the wall, with the remains of two shallowly projecting rectangular turrets. The nature of the stonework suggests that these turrets and the intervening stretch of wall are early C13, and the earliest part of the stone fortifications (apart from gateways) to have been built.

The Perambulation of the walled town ends here, and that of the area to the E begins near by. The only other part of the town wall surviving is a short, very ruinous stretch S of the site of the EASTGATE (demolished 1775), which spanned East Street, to the N of which is Polymond Tower, p. 536.

(*b*) *East of the Walled Town*

The Perambulation begins at God's House Gate. E of this was Porters' Mead, which in the C19 became QUEEN'S PARK, a rather threadbare piece of Victorian municipal landscaping with a grotesque MONUMENT to General Gordon, 1885, in the middle – a marble column ending in a clumsily shaped capital. The area around was hardly developed at all until the 1830s, when what was first a fashionable residential quarter, to the N of Queen's Park, was laid out. This was associated with the town's last years as a residential seaside resort. By 1839 the railway had come to the new terminal station to the E of Queen's Park, and three years later the first of the Docks were opened. Within a few decades the entire shoreline E of God's House Gate, formerly a bathing beach, had disappeared, the sardonically named CANUTE ROAD marking the line of the original shore. By the end of the C19 the area around the Terminus Station and around the Dock entrances was a prosperous business district.

The new CUSTOM HOUSE (p. 528) is on the W side of the park. The older Custom House in Canute Road, still being used as such at the time of writing, is poor neo-Wrenish, 1902 by *Hawke*. Next to it the original Custom House of 1847 by *Alfred Giles* (the engineer to the Dock Company), now UNION CASTLE HOUSE, which was a distinguished building, two-storeyed, in yellow brick, with strongly dentilled eaves, thick-framed windows, brick quoin pattern, and a small cupola on the low-pitched roof; unfortunately it has had a ponderous stone frontispiece added on the lower storey. Opposite is the huge SOUTH WESTERN HOUSE, originally the South Western Hotel, promoted by the London & South Western Railway and opened in 1872. The architect was *John Norton*. Short frontage to Terminus Terrace, a longer one to Canute Road, the corner being taken by a wide curve. Most of it has four main storeys, with two attic storeys, basically of red brick, but overlaid with stone or stucco embellishments, the ground storey being entirely rusticated. The details are French Renaissance, laid on with a heavy hand, the windows elaborately framed and many of them fronted with little balconies with twirly ironwork; the roofs have slated double pitches, mansard fashion, attic dormer windows opening from the lower stage of the roof, and little porthole-shaped windows from the upper stage. The really swagger piece of frontage is at the E end, over the entrance, with an extra main storey and a big rounded pediment, containing a portrait of Queen Victoria within a rosette, winged figures, and small emblematic pieces suggesting railways and the sea. The whole building very nearly convinces; the best part visually (characteristically for Norton) is the complicated roof-line. DOCK HOUSE opposite, completed in 1962, by *C. B. Dromgoole*, is a nice clean piece of C20 austerity, a flat five-storey grid, and panels infilled with glass and vitreous panelling, the end walls, cornice, and string course faced in reconstructed stone, the entrance in a thin projecting rectangular frame of marble blocks, rising to two storeys. Beyond it are the CUNARD OFFICES, a brown brick, stone-dressed building of 1899, almost impeccably Palladian, with a monogram in the pediment showing it was built by the L. & S.W.R. Opposite (i.e. on the landward side) a few decayed relics of the first post-Regency expansion in this direction, culminating in the CANUTE CASTLE HOTEL, an agreeable piece of whimsicality of *c.*1835–40, stuccoed, on a corner site, with the name in fanciful twirly-serif lettering on the frieze below the top storey, and an octagonal balustraded balcony. Above this originally rose an octagonal viewing chamber.

There are no strong architectural reasons for proceeding further E. So we return to South Western House, noticing, perhaps, an eight-gabled brick-faced RAILWAY SHED behind Terminus Station, with a Gothic arched recess with thin stone hood-mould to each bay; it seems to bear the stamp of *Tite* and is probably coeval, or nearly so, with the station itself (p. 532). Turning r. into Terminus Terrace, QUEEN'S TERRACE comes into view, facing S over Queen's Park, a stuccoed terrace of *c.*1830–40 that begins in four storeys and ends in three, the two scales overlapping in an engaging way in the two-bay ORIENTAL HOTEL. The special feature of the terrace is its series of first-floor bow windows, almost semicircular. Similar stuccoed, bow-windowed frontages once lined the adjoining streets (e.g. LATIMER STREET, OXFORD STREET), but piecemeal rebuildings and alterations have left only a few intact. Our route lies along TERMINUS TERRACE, with the façade of the station (p. 532) on the r. and Street's powerful St Mary's spire ahead. Some massive Victorian road works on the r. form the approach to CENTRAL BRIDGE, built over several railway lines and leading to the Floating Bridge across the Itchen to Woolston (p. 590). But our way is l., along BERNARD STREET, with a row of stuccoed houses (Nos 123–

135) on the l., *c.*1840, undistinguished except for their impressive array of nearly semicircular bow windows on the first floors. Past St James church (p. 519) to the HOLY ROOD ESTATE, 1956–62 for Southampton Corporation by *Lyons, Israel & Ellis*. Four- and nine-storey blocks, divided by cement-faced floor ends and topped by tall concrete fascias; brickwork in yellow and grey between the windows and on the end façades; short recessed balconies. The blocks are pleasingly proportioned, and their visual enlivenment is given by the bright red colouring of wall surfaces within the balcony space. The layout is subtle, and best appreciated from QUEEN'S WAY; there are numerous diagonal vistas across series of spaces part-enclosed by the flats. On the edge of the development, a suave early C19 stuccoed pub, THE GLOBE, with big bow windows, has been preserved and provides an excellent foil. Across Queen's Way PALMERSTON HOUSE is a range of shops and flats by *L. Berger*, the City Architect, taller blocks alternating with stretches of lower frontage, all colonnaded, and obviously trying to blend rather than contrast with the Holy Rood flats but not succeeding; it would have been better if it had provided a straightforward contrast. Queen's Way crosses EAST STREET, an old thoroughfare entirely rebuilt in a messy way (p. 552), to emerge on the edge of the HOGLANDS, the southernmost of a series of central parks which were created out of ancient common pastures in the C19 (p. 558). In the middle of the traffic roundabout is the iron GAS COLUMN, originally erected elsewhere in 1829 as a tribute to William Chamberlayne M.P. (p. 597), who had provided a series of columns (of which this is a replica) for the town's first gas street lamps. The column is fluted, standing on a square base and surmounted by a large urn and ball-shaped finial. The road to the l. (Hanover Buildings) leads back to the Bargate; alternatively one can go r. to St Mary's church (p. 518) and the adjoining redevelopment area (p. 562).

(c) *North of the Walled Town*

ABOVE BAR, running N from the Bargate, is the city's main shopping street. It skirts the possible site of Saxon Hamtun (p. 511), which, however, was left outside the later walled town. There was a ribbon of houses for about ¼ m. above the Bargate at least as early as the C17, much extended N by Late Georgian developments. With the huge expansion of the town further N and NW in the C19 the urban centre of gravity moved outside the old walled town, and Above Bar succeeded High Street as the chief commercial thoroughfare. In the 1930s it was a street of shops and cinemas with nothing special to distinguish it from the main street of any other medium-large town; in 1940 it was largely destroyed (the only substantial part to escape destruction being a group of buildings about the middle of the W side). Rebuilding took place mostly *c.*1950–5 – alas, in a thoroughly commonplace manner, in watered-down neo-Georgian or half-hearted modernistic styles, or in compromises of both. There are only two buildings really worth looking at in the whole of Above Bar; fortunately there is also some decent Regency architecture just off it near its S end and beyond its N extremity, so that a walk along it from the Bargate is, visually, just worth while.

PORTLAND STREET (leading l.) was built *c.*1828–30; the S side was destroyed by bombs but the N side is intact. Four-storeyed stuccoed terraces with locally typical simplified classical details – flat pilasters with thin incised lines, rusticated ground storey, broad segmental doorways with twirly traceried fanlights, nice iron balconies to the first floor (not all survive), and just the shape of a pediment over the central house of the terrace. It leads to PORTLAND TERRACE, now part of the ring road, where a terrace of *c.*1835–40 has been preserved, a bit bigger in scale than Portland Street and a bit nearer to Early Victorian in feeling. The second-storey windows have shallow cornice hoods supported on scroll brackets; prominent porches with triglyphs and fluted Doric columns. Back in Above Bar there is nothing to look at until PALMERSTON PARK on the r., with fine trees and a STATUE to Lord Palmerston, 1868 by *Sharpe.* (Across the other side of the park, Nos 30–34 PALMERSTON ROAD make a pleasant Late Georgian group; a three-storeyed house with a pair of convex folds making continuous bow windows up its whole height, a wide two-storeyed house with similar treatment, and, in between, two three-storeyed houses one of which has a self-contained bow window of the more usual Southampton type on the first floor.) Facing the park in Above Bar, the brick and terracotta PRUDENTIAL ASSURANCE is, needless to say, by *Waterhouse*, but with its skyline sawn off. A little N, the first of Above Bar's two really good buildings, MARLANDS HOUSE, 1963 by *Oliver Carey*, with colonnaded shopping on the ground floor, the façades of the two upper storeys being set back behind the black-faced ends of the floor and roof slabs, with small balconies. The glazing is in upright rectangular panes separated by thin divisions in black and white strip pattern. Round the corner in CIVIC CENTRE ROAD the N façade, similarly treated, takes a gentle convex curve. The climax of the composition is a rectangular tower rising for a further five storeys (with a sixth service storey set back) from the W end of the block, pleasantly patterned with upright rectangular panes and white vitreous panelling in black and white framework. The building is exceptionally happy both when seen as part of the general linear composition in Above Bar and (with its tower) as a climactic feature in the widely diffused townscape on the S side of the Civic Centre. The CO-OPERATIVE PERMANENT BUILDING SOCIETY on the r., a reasonably satisfactory building by *W. H. Saunders & Son*, 1964–5, would not be mentioned except to say that it replaced a much pleasanter bow-windowed building of 1841 (MOIRA HOUSE), on which the Southampton Corporation placed a Preservation Order, not confirmed by the Ministry of Housing and Local Government after an enquiry. Further on on the r. is TYRRELL & GREEN, the second really good modern building in Above Bar, 1956–8 by *Yorke, Rosenberg & Mardall*. Three main storeys, ten bays, simple concrete frame with slender vertical divisions between the bays, the frame rising to a fourth storey with a hollow frontage to the street but with the extra storey set back behind it; large windows with green panels below them, three of the windows on the first floor (the second, third, and fourth bays) reaching down to the floor level, effectively asymmetrizing the design. Few post-war department stores, and no others in Southampton, have reached this standard. To the N something unfortunate is happening at the time of writing; a building is being erected corresponding in general framework and proportions, and in some details, to Tyrrell & Green but differing in some marked respects. This is not the way to treat a good building which was designed as an entity in itself; in a street developed piecemeal, buildings should be seen to be different (though harmonious) and not inferior copies of their neighbours.

Opposite, the only piece of imaginative post-war planning in the whole of the Above Bar area is taking shape at the time of writing; part of the narrow strip of land between the street and the Civic Centre, hitherto occupied by temporary shops on the sites of blitzed ones, is being laid out as a civic square, a formal forecourt to the classical façade of the Guildhall

(p. 527), bringing the civic buildings into visual contact with the main street and providing the only relief (apart from parkland) to the long ribbon of commercial frontage.

The shopping area ends abruptly at WATTS PARK, l., and ANDREWS PARK, r. These are parts of the former common pastures of the medieval town, which extended from the Hoglands (p. 555) through Houndwell and Palmerston Parks and also included the West Marlands (where the Civic Centre now is). Most of them were laid out as parks *c.*1850–60, Andrews Park and Watts Park as an Arboretum, with many specimens of trees. Watts Park is centred on the ISAAC WATTS STATUE, 1861 by *R. C. Lucas*, on a tall rectangular base of grey marble, with three panels in light marble depicting events in Watts's life. Life-sized figure with outstretched arms in (presumably) clothes of his time (1674–1748) with some of the jacket buttons undone; realistic and convincing. Lucas lived a life of eccentricity at Chilworth (p. 166); relatively little sculptural work by him is known, but what there is is good. S of the park is the Civic Centre (p. 526); N is a quarter originally developed in Late Georgian times, which keeps a little of its former character; CUMBERLAND PLACE had till recently a consistent four-storey scale, now intruded on by an indifferent eight-storey block (LATIMER HOUSE). Nos 17–15 and 11–5 are all more or less Regency, 7 and 5 being the best, with bland stuccoed fronts, pillared porches, and nice iron-fronted balconies. GROSVENOR SQUARE, to the N, was never completed; now it is nearly all car park and bus garage, but two fine detached stuccoed two-storeyed houses of *c.*1835 remain, with big central segmental bay, three-windowed with intervening flat pilasters on both storeys; typical Southampton simplified Classical features elsewhere. W of Cumberland Place is the POLYGON, where the curvature of the road is the only relic of *Leroux*'s scheme of *c.*1770 (p. 515); the two or three C18 houses which were built have disappeared, and the oldest surviving are a short terrace of *c.*1840, now attached to the Polygon Hotel, with yellow brick façades framed by stone pilasters and frieze.*

We return to Watts's Statue. To the E is the CENOTAPH by *Lutyens*, tall, rectangular, of Portland stone, the narrower side towards the street, ending through a series of irregularly

* At the W end of Cumberland Place, opposite the Polygon Hotel, is QUEEN'S KEEP, a multi-storey office block by *W. H. Saunders & Son*, begun in 1965.

diminishing stages in a sarcophagus. Many-stepped base towards the park; flanking short square pylons surmounted by 'pineapples' on the street side. Across Above Bar, set against the trees of Andrews Park, is the TITANIC MEMORIAL, 1912, a concave neo-Baroque composition, with Paris-Salon type of sculpture: a winged angel and representations of engineer officers (to whom the memorial is dedicated). Andrews Park is a delightful piece of Victorian landscaping, the main paths laid out in formal cross and circular patterns, the subsidiary paths winding about; stretches of lawn flowing between bushes and shrubs (thinned out but fortunately not eliminated); perimeter buildings glimpsed here and there. Even the early C20 rock gardening is quite good of its kind. The centrepiece is the fanciful ANDREWS MEMORIAL, to a councillor and mayor whose statue (by *Brain*, artistically valueless) stands on an extraordinary triangular pedestal of two stages by *Philip Brannon* (who engraved, with embellishments that sometimes exceeded realism, scenes of Early Victorian Southampton, and drew a highly imaginative reconstruction of the town in the Middle Ages). The pedestal has embellishments in all sorts of styles mixed up, and is an engaging piece of Victorian whimsicality amid the rich foliage of the park. On the N fringe of the park, BRUNSWICK PLACE, developed piecemeal from *c.*1820, with modest early houses with pillared porches at the W end, then BRUNSWICK HOUSE, 1963 by *W. H. Saunders & Son*, a twelve-storey block which has a very different effect on Brunswick Place from what Latimer House has on Cumberland Place. In fact the development includes a three-storey podium following the line of the road frontage, respecting the scale of the older buildings, with the tower rising from it (and a good landmark from the park), with glass and brick strips repeated, perhaps a little disconcertingly, like a many-layered sandwich. Next to it a pleasant terrace of *c.*1840, of yellow brick with big bow windows on the first floor. Then the fanciful tower of the United Church (p. 525).

Through architecturally negative King's Park Road and Bellevue Road lead to CARLTON CRESCENT, the most spectacular piece of Regency development in Southampton, evidently started in the late 1820s and probably developed piecemeal over a decade or more. The frontispiece is actually CARLTON PLACE, a short straight street off London Road, with a three-storeyed stuccoed house on the l., the distinguishing feature of which is a slightly projecting rusticated porch, with round arch and iron balcony above, and then a row of four houses with big bow windows on the first floor. Carlton Crescent leads off r., composed in the main of broad three-bay three-storey stuccoed detached houses, mostly sufficiently close to each other for the street, except in a few places, to appear as a piece of unified townscape. The houses vary in detail, but are mostly the same in general composition, typical of Southampton with their elements of classical decoration almost without refinements: flat pilasters; entablature with basic cornice, frieze and architrave; rusticated ground storeys; usually simple square-headed or rounded doorways, but sometimes with pillared porches in front; balcony ironwork in some, but not all, of the houses. Occasionally, where the situation seems to demand it, there is a folding outwards of the façade in a shallow bay. The houses generally give an effect of austere elegance and economy of detail, in a manner that might, perhaps, be more appropriate to a medium such as granite than to stucco. Did the anonymous designers of these and similar houses come from somewhere like Plymouth or Aberdeen? On the inside of the curve, Nos 30–32 make a triple group, the central house set back, but with a slightly projecting three-arched rustic porch with rounded arches, distantly recalling *Tite*'s Terminus Station (p. 532). ALLEYN HOUSE, also fortunately on the inside of the curve, is a harsh post-war intruder on a bombed site. Beyond it is a three-storeyed terrace, very austere, but pleasantly set behind a group of trees. Opposite is an extension to ST ANNE'S SCHOOL, 1961 by *Richard Sheppard, Robson & Partners*, fitting admirably into the three-storeyed stucco townscape. Three long ranges of glazing on each floor, with white mosaic panelling beneath the glazing, projecting slightly like long bays from the plane of the façade; delicate yellow brickwork on the intermediate stretches of façade. On the corner of Bedford Place is CARLTON LODGE, a charming composition, two-storeyed, with more demure detailing than the other houses though it is probably by the same architect. The centre part of the façade projects slightly, with a stepped parapet and an entrance feature with an entablature over the recessed doorway with two flanking niches. Corner pilasters; frieze with rectangular panel pattern. The Bedford Place façade has a two-storeyed bow, and next door is a yellow brick house with a much larger bow – altogether a most engaging corner composition. The Perambulation returns to

Rockstone Place, but BEDFORD PLACE is a street of character, developed mainly *c.*1820–40 in a pleasant piecemeal way, worth a quick detour. Bow windows and iron balconies mixed up with shop fronts. The best unaltered group is Nos 73–77; No. 73, on a corner, has a big bow window on the ground storey, topped by ironwork, the others are a pleasant yellow-brick terrace with segmental bow windows, all well maintained.

ROCKSTONE PLACE, N from Carlton Crescent, has a series of large triple-grouped houses almost forming a continuous terrace, probably *c.*1835. The central house of each group has a strong round-headed doorway with shallow hood, and a diagrammatic pediment on the parapet. Past the former Governor's House of the Ordnance Survey Office (p. 528) and into the foot of THE AVENUE (p. 585), with a strip of leafy parkland. In the park a pretty DRINKING FOUNTAIN, erected in 1866, with little engaged Corinthian capitals and pediment on each side, and a domed top surmounted by an elaborate finial. Well executed but pleasantly weathered sculptured figures in the panels. The drinking bowls are like holy-water stoups.

The Outer Southampton North perambulation begins here, but those who want to follow to the end the remains of the pre-1840 town will find some austere but pleasant houses of *c.*1835 in CRANBURY PLACE and the final splutter of the local Late Georgian tradition in CRANBURY AVENUE and DENZIL AVENUE, around the Victorian St Luke, Newtown.

(*d*) *Northam and St Mary's*

This is not a Perambulation, but a description of two areas of recent redevelopment bordering the central part of the city.

NORTHAM was a farm before the C19, and the farmhouse astonishingly survives as a public house, called appropriately THE OLD FARM HOUSE, built in 1611 (date on wall), of brick and timber-framing. (Inside a CHIMNEYPIECE consisting of a four-centred arch with carved wooden surround and overmantel.) The rest of the area was developed in the mid C19, with shipyards and small industries (some of earlier origin) along the river bank. The GAS WORKS were originally established on the present site in 1819, at what was considered a safe distance from the town proper.

The inner part of Northam, SE of Northam Road, was redeveloped in 1959–65, to the design of *L. Berger*, the City Architect. It is an outstanding piece of urban redevelopment, rivalling Castle House (p. 545) and Holy Rood Estate (p. 555) as the best post-war rehousing scheme in the city. The centrepiece is MILLBANK TOWER, rectangular, of sixteen storeys, faced in purply brown brick with long balcony panels and concrete floor strips. Set against it is a shopping arcade, colonnaded, in a straight three-storey block which leads from Northam Road to the tower. Around are four-storey rectangular blocks with external concrete gridwork pattern, infilled with purply brick and glazing, and transeptal staircase blocks, wholly glazed on one side. The spaces around and between the blocks are laid out with unusual sensitivity, with paved areas and paths of varying shapes and alignments and just perceptible changes in level, and a sunk playground with dwarf surrounding wall. The earlier part of the scheme (nearest to Northam Road) is the best. The lower blocks are all consistent in scale and consistent in materials, but in the later parts of the scheme, further E, there is a fussy variety of external materials, including yellow and even red brick. The scheme appears as a self-contained island in the midst of an otherwise shapelessly developed area; only St Augustine (p. 519) across Northam Road acts to some extent as a foil. Millbank tower appears particularly happily in fairly distant views (e.g. from across the river), landmarking the area without any comparable rival feature near.

ST MARY'S, the area of Anglo-Saxon Hamwic, was agricultural land from the C11 to the C18, apart from St Mary's Church (p. 518), a few buildings around and to the S of it, and a small settlement at CHAPEL by the riverside. It was developed, piecemeal, in Early Victorian times. ST MARY STREET (which as a country lane and then as a built-up street has retained, at least approximately, the alignment of the main street of Hamwic) is a lively small-scale shopping centre without a single building of note, but pleasant in a hodgepodge way – a sort of foil to the more pretentious main shopping centre across the parks to the W. To the E, around BEVOIS STREET, an area is being redeveloped at the time of writing (1965).* Its dominating feature is a sixteen-storey slab block faced with panels surfaced in rough rubble texture ('large-panel construction'), leaving window openings of a repeated inverted L shape. It is harsh without being impressively so; not good enough for its scale or for such a conspicuous site and a sad disappointment after Castle House or Millbank

* By *L. Berger*, the City Architect.

Tower. Around it are five-storey blocks partly faced in dark tiling and small patio houses in semi-terraces (i.e. with two-storey mono-pitch elevations alternating with linking blocks of a single storey) all in harsh yellow brick, approached off intimate footpaths. The latter are satisfying in themselves and in their small-scale grouping, and perpetuate, in better modern form, the character of the homely brick Victorian terraces which have been pulled down. One would wish (as on some of the outer housing estates) that Southampton Corporation would not mix up the scales of its housing – giant, medium, and intimate – so much; a bigger area of this tight small-scale housing just here (with St Mary's great spire looming to the S) would have been quite appropriate, leaving the blocks of the larger scales to be grouped more appropriately elsewhere in the vicinity.

Another area of redevelopment is proposed N of the CENTRAL STATION, largely bomb-devastated. Plans for high-density residential development with a few shops are being prepared at the time of writing by *Lyons, Israel, Ellis & Partners.*

(*e*) *The Docks*

From the late Middle Ages to the early C19 shipping activity was concentrated on the Town Quay (p. 514). The Southampton Dock Company was formed in 1836 to build the first enclosed dock (to be served by the London & Southampton Railway, promoted at about the same time). What is now the OUTER DOCK was completed in 1842, and the INNER DOCK (now filled in) in 1851. More docks or open quays were provided as additional land was reclaimed; the EMPRESS DOCK in 1890 and the OCEAN DOCK in 1911. With the last the general pattern of what is now known as the OLD DOCKS was completed. The London & South Western Railway had acquired the Docks in 1892, and in 1927 their successors, the Southern Railway, began work on the NEW DOCKS, involving the reclamation of a large area of mudflat on the side of the Test estuary, well to the NW of the Old Docks. The New Docks were completed in 1933. The Old Docks and the New Docks are separated by a still partly open stretch of foreshore with the present Town Quay and Royal Pier (p. 543).*

*The term 'Town Quay' probably originally applied to the improved foreshore outside the Watergate, but there was a small jetty by the early C19;

Architectural interest in the Docks is confined to post-Second-World-War buildings. The earliest dock buildings (of which few survive) were of timber or brick; late C19 or early C20 ones were often of corrugated iron, and those built *c.*1930–3 in the New Docks are of no architectural merit. Buildings on the fringe of the Old Docks estate directly or indirectly connected with the Docks, including DOCK HOUSE (the administrative centre), are described in Perambulation (*b*) (p. 553).

OCEAN TERMINAL, adjoining Ocean Dock, Old Docks. Promoted by the Southern Railway before nationalization; completed in 1953, by *C. B. Dromgoole*, architect to the British Transport Commission. When built it was a great innovation, since it provided facilities for ocean passengers on landing to a reasonable standard of comfort (whereas previously they had simply been accommodated in sheds); it set a physical standard for later similar development in Southampton and elsewhere. A very long block of two main storeys, faced in small rectangular precast concrete panels, with windows subdivided into small panes, giving a horizontal emphasis. From the centre part of the short S façade (the show façade, seen as ships sail into the harbour) there projects a wide semicircular bay, with balconies at first- and second-floor level, rising to a third storey, higher than the other two, with prominent small-pane fenestration. The ultimate skyline feature is a vertical service turret embellished with three projecting shelves, holding a flagpole. Passengers land at upper-floor level, the lower floor being used for merchandise or baggage; a long railway platform with continuous concave hood adjoins on the E side.

NOS 38/39 BERTHS, Old Docks. At the tip of the Dockland peninsula. Under construction at the time of writing; completion date 1966. By *Ronald Sims*. Main space with very wide span, with cross-framework of steel girders on two pitches; taller transeptal axis with flat roof-line.

NO. 102 BERTH, New Docks. New building 1956, by *C. B. Dromgoole*. A long structure with a roof-line of low transverse gables. The E end contains a passenger reception hall at ground level, internally a big rectangle with rounded corners, varied wall surfaces, and a ceiling of which the central part, in an irregular rounded shape, is raised to give a two-dimensional roof effect. On the wall a MURAL by *John Hutton* depicting

---

the present Town Quay, a long platform, is the result of a succession of C19 improvements. The Royal Pier was built in 1833 (for shipping trade rather than for pleasure) and rebuilt in 1892. The forebuilding is later.

King Manuel's dream of Vasco de Gama's sailing round the Cape. This part of the building has a three-storeyed elevation to the quayside with broad balcony at second-floor level, concrete-faced second storey, and fenestration of small opaque panes. The rest of the building is mainly brick-faced, but on the N side is a long projecting bay (over a rail siding and crane equipment) clad in two layers of green asbestos sheeting with a continuous layer of glazing in between.

NO. 105 BERTH, New Docks. Partial rebuilding of earlier sheds, 1958 by *C. B. Dromgoole*. Three-storey frontage to the quayside, with balconied upper storey under canopy of shallow segmental transverse arches. Passenger reception hall on the ground storey, with irregularly rounded corners; vertical cedar panelling and some contrasting wall surfaces; abstract MURAL by *Sillock & King*.

Also on the New Docks estate the UNION CASTLE OFFICE, 1963 by *Ronald Ward*, three-storey block with single-storey annexe, all in a simple concrete grid with large vertical glazed panels, pleasantly proportioned; the LONDON AND SOUTHAMPTON STEVEDORING COMPANY, 1962, also by *Ronald Ward*, a simple block of two storeys, similar in design; and STANDARD TELEPHONES AND CABLES, 1961–2 by the company's own Architectural Department, a big irregular range of buildings and naked steel equipment, the buildings clad, with austere impressiveness, in sheer asbestos sheeting and roofed with slight, just perceptible pitches.

OUTER SOUTHAMPTON

Outer Southampton is divided as follows:

West (between the Test and the Common) – Freemantle, Maybush, Millbrook, Redbridge, and Shirley

North (between the Common and the Itchen) – Bassett, Highfield, Portswood, St Denys, South Stoneham, and Swaythling

East (across the Itchen) – Bitterne, Harefield, Midanbury, Peartree Green, Sholing, Thornhill, Weston, and Woolston

The following index includes all the Southampton villages, including those of the area defined as Inner Southampton.

Bassett 571, 581, 584
Bitterne 589, 590, 592, 595, 596, 597
Freemantle 566
Harefield 598
Highfield 571, 584,
Maybush 567, 568
Midanbury 592, 599
Millbrook 566, 567, 568, 569
Newtown 520
Northam 519, 561
Peartree Green 589, 592, 593, 597

Portswood 571n, 572
Redbridge 566, 567n, 569, 570
St Denys 572, 584, 588n
Shirley 566, 567, 568, 569, 570
Sholing 590, 593
South Stoneham 571, 573, 581
Swaythling 571, 573, 574, 581, 583, 584, 588
Thornhill 594, 596, 598
University of Southampton 575
Weston 594, 596, 599
Woolston 590, 594, 595

OUTER SOUTHAMPTON: WEST

For definition of area and index *see* above.

Western Southampton is mostly flattish, except towards the N, and, compared with some other parts of the town, fairly closely built. Until the early 1930s there was a tidal shoreline along the Test estuary, but now the reclaimed area of the New Docks extends to Millbrook Point, and above that further reclamation is now proceeding. Millbrook used to be a long straggling village on the line of Millbrook Road; Redbridge an old small port at the head of the estuary; Old Shirley a hamlet a little inland; Shirley a big Victorian suburban village on the site of a common enclosed in the 1820s; all around were country villas or estates of Georgian or Early Victorian origin. Freemantle was laid out as a residential suburb in 1852, but the open land around Shirley was not wholly developed until the inter-war years. Since the war the big Millbrook estate has covered the former fields to the W. Altogether it is an area of mixed character and very little architectural interest; two Victorian churches and a few bits of post-war housing – that is almost all that is worth looking at. An architectural description is inevitably only a short catalogue of unrelated buildings.

CHURCHES*

CHRIST CHURCH, Waterloo and Paynes Road, Freemantle. 1865–6 by *William White*; spire completed 1875. Well placed at the focal point of a Victorian residential estate. Purbeck rubble and ashlar, with characteristic William-White red-brick hoods over the windows. Tall commanding W tower, with fairly short tapering spire (reduced in height from that originally designed). Internally it shows the individuality one expects from William White, in one of his more ambitious churches, in spatial planning and surface decoration. Three-

* Arranged in alphabetical order of parishes.

bay nave arcades; wider and taller arches to the transepts. Wide chancel arch. The piers square, of red brick, the capitals of stone, with naturalistic foliage, the arches of red and yellow brick with red hoods, the wall surfaces above of yellow, with variegated red patterns. Tall, strongly detailed tower arch also in brick. The windows in the Geometrical style characteristic of White (cf. Lyndhurst, p. 326, St Mark Woolston, p. 594); the four-light W window with a large quatrefoil in the upper tracery looks very effective when seen through the tower arch.

ST PETER, Irving Walk, Maybush. 1956 by *Romilly B. Craze.*

HOLY TRINITY, the parish church of Millbrook. 1873–80 by *Henry Woodyer*, the successor to a medieval church on a different site. A moderately ambitious village church with an assertively picturesque exterior: steep roofs, tall clerestory, seven-light E window copied from Ockham in Surrey, and a flanking NW tower with sharp bell-openings and a mountainous spire. Mild interior: five-bay nave with simple foliage capitals; lancets throughout (paired in the aisles). – Outsize BALDACCHINO probably by *Comper*, who designed the canopied altar in the S chapel after 1918. – STAINED GLASS. Several windows look as if they were by *Clayton & Bell.*

ALL SAINTS, Kendal Avenue, Millbrook.* 1964–5 by *Pinckney & Gott.* A whimsical building with a brick exterior and a tower with a steep gabled roof. Interior centrally planned, but visually focused on the superb STAINED GLASS of the E window, by *Gabriel Loire* of Chartres.‡ Three tall square-headed lights filled with glass mainly in an abstract pattern but with the figure of Christ prominent at the top of the central light, his right arm upraised, and his left hand holding a book inscribed A and Ω. The patterning is in blues and yellows with touches of red, with a preponderance of orange, suggesting the glow of a halo, around Christ's head, which is portrayed in shades of brown and grey.

HOLY FAMILY (R.C.), Redbridge Hill and Wimpson Lane, Millbrook. 1965–6 by *Liam McCormick.*

ST BONIFACE (R.C.), Shirley Road, Shirley. 1927, by *W. C. Mangan.* Expensive neo-Byzantine with heavily-laden brick exterior; slender NW tower ending in a tall octagon with tiled cap; long nave with transverse apsidal bays each heavily tiled;

* Officially All Saints, Redbridge.

‡ Gabriel Loire designed a stunning series of windows in St Richard (R.C.), Chichester, inserted too late to be included in the *Buildings of England: Sussex.*

eastern dome and short apsidal sanctuary. The long complex interior does not really come off spatially.

ST JAMES, Bellemoor and St James' Roads, Shirley. 1836 by *W. Hinves*, a rural-suburban 'Commissioners'' church. Yellow brick with pinnacled W tower. Broad, galleried nave with tall neo-Dec windows. Chancel 1881.

ST JOHN, St James' Road, Shirley. 1960 by *Mrs R. Williams*.

ST JUDE, Warren Avenue, Shirley Warren. 1956 by *Gutteridge & Gutteridge*.

SHIRLEY BAPTIST CHURCH, Church Street. 1914 by *Spalding & Myers*. Art-Nouveau Gothic. Brick tower with stone strips; fancy embattled top and short shingled spire; intermediate circular windows split into three traceried lights, the outer ones in the shape of upturned eyes. The body of the church more straightforward Perp.

PUBLIC BUILDINGS

ORDNANCE SURVEY OFFICE, Romsey Road, Maybush. Of *c*.1964–7 by *L. R. Murphy* of the Ministry of Public Building and Works. New headquarters for the whole Ordnance Survey, replacing the bombed buildings in Southampton (p. 528) and others at Chessington and elsewhere. Large complex of five distinct buildings, all interconnected, the main building in the shape of an E with long stems, of six storeys, the others of different heights. The buildings of reinforced concrete construction, largely faced with light-toned mosaic, apart from the storage building, which will be faced in brick. Not complete at the time of writing.

KING EDWARD VI SCHOOL, Hill Lane and Wilton Avenue, Shirley. 1938 by *E. Berry Webber*. Lumpily modernistic.

WIMPSON SECONDARY SCHOOL, Helvellyn Road, Millbrook. 1953 by *Lyons, Israel & Ellis*. Rectangular three-storeyed main block in yellow brick, with regular pattern of square-framed windows, thinly separated, on the two upper floors; partly transparent lower storey. Complex ancillary buildings in different materials. Three funnel-shaped features on the skyline containing the service equipment, and causing the school to be nicknamed the 'Queen Mary'.

SOUTHAMPTON GENERAL HOSPITAL, Tremona Road, Shirley. WESSEX NEUROLOGICAL CENTRE. 1965 by *Stewart Kilgour*, architect to the Wessex Regional Hospital Board. The main block of four storeys on a raised basement,

T-shaped, with thick horizontal lines made by concrete fascia and floor ends. Brick facing. Grey mosaic panels below the windows. The basement is stone-faced. Extra service storey with concrete fascia and green asbestos facing over the crossing, single-storey ancillary buildings. A strong, assertive design, well set on a gentle rise. To the N a SERVICE AREA with various service buildings and installations, also by *S. Kilgour*; completion 1966.

PERAMBULATION

Of the old straggling village of MILLBROOK hardly anything is left; of REDBRIDGE there is more, in the part of the village street that has been by-passed, with a few pleasant Georgian and earlier brick dwellings, the most striking with a C17 wing embellished with brick pilasters and moulded brick capitals, brick panels beneath the sills, and fluted keystones. It is in a bad way at the time of writing. The N part of the old village street has recently been demolished for the new BRIDGE, the latest addition to an already interesting series. The oldest is C17 (on the site of an earlier one) with five round arches, spanning the main stream of the Test. A single-span bridge of 1793 crosses a side stream. Both these have been widened. A great new bridge, of open-framed concrete construction, was built above and alongside the old ones in 1930. The one now being built (to the S) will duplicate this. Finally there is the low railway viaduct, not visually distinctive, recently rebuilt. Altogether there is something of a Berwick quality. Scattered around the older parts of SHIRLEY are still a few pleasant stuccoed or yellow-brick villas of the 1830s or 1840s, but nothing to mention specially. (At the ROBERT THORNER CHARITY HOMES, Regent's Park Road, there are tablets recording the trustees and details of the benefaction by *Eric Gill*. NT)

HOLLYBROOK ESTATE, Malwood Avenue and Seagarth Lane, Shirley. Small housing scheme by *L. Berger*, the City Architect, 1960. In the style of early Roehampton without the tall blocks. Pleasant two-storeyed houses in staggered terraces; four-storey blocks in lawn settings shaded by old trees.

MILLBROOK ESTATE. The first large housing estate developed by the Southampton Council after the Second World War. In the garden-city tradition, with greens and closes and curving roads, but the earlier housing undistinguished. The central feature now is a very large tree-studded green at one end of which is MILLBROOK TOWER, 1965 by *Ryder & Yates* of Newcastle upon Tyne, twenty-five-storeyed, T-shaped in plan, faced in near-white brick on the end elevations and in dark red brick on the wider side faces. The windows, with big rough concrete panels, make clear vertical lines up the centres of the end elevations, but a more restless pattern on the wider elevations. The ground storey is faced in shiny black mosaic. Why this, the tallest building in Southampton, should have been placed in the middle of a largely two-storeyed estate in an outlandish part of the city's fringes, instead of on some focal or dominating site where it would add tremendously to the townscape of the city, is not easy to explain. Opposite the tower, a NEIGHBOURHOOD CENTRE, with canopied shops and five- and two-storeyed blocks (by *L. Berger*) is being erected at the time of writing. REDBRIDGE TOWER, about ¾ m. away, also by *Ryder & Yates*, 1963, is similar to Millbrook Tower but only fifteen-storeyed; its siting, beside a traffic roundabout at one of the main entrances to the city, makes much more townscape sense. Near by is a small intimate housing scheme, CLOVER NOOK, by *L. Berger*, 1961, with four-storeyed blocks in yellow and red brick and a little modish tile-hanging. It abuts on to the old village street of Redbridge (*see* above).

At REDBRIDGE HILL (NE of the main part of the Millbrook Estate) a fifteen-storeyed slab block, completed in 1966, dominates a neighbourhood. Prefabricated 'large-panel' construction, similar to the block in Bevois Street, St Mary's (p. 562); harsh and not really pleasing, though inevitably impressive in bulk. Adjoining it is four- and two-storeyed housing, the former in pleasant blocks faced in purple brick with broad white fascias, the latter in harsh yellow brick with dark tiling and roofing. Across Redbridge Hill some tame neo-Georgian council housing of 1938 offers an interesting contrast.

At the time of writing redevelopment is taking place in the inner part of Early Victorian SHIRLEY, NE of the shopping centre. The dominating feature will be a sixteen-storeyed block.

OUTER SOUTHAMPTON: NORTH

For definition of area and index *see* p. 565.

This is by far the most rewarding section of suburban Southampton *qua* suburbia. It was rough forest country, partly transformed into luxuriant estates in Late Georgian and Early

Victorian times, and gently developed as suburbia over the last hundred years. Over most parts of the area trees – both forest trees like oaks and landscape trees like big evergreens – abound as the carefully conserved background to late C19 and early C20 housing. To the E, around the head of the Itchen estuary, the country was naturally more fertile, and SWAYTHLING, with the medieval church of South Stoneham, was a substantial pre-Victorian village. In terms of pure architecture, if one excepts the University (and that is a big exception) there is not much to describe – one or two moderately worthwhile churches, a house attributed to *Hawksmoor* but altered (and now part of the University), and some pieces of very good inter-war garden-city development, by a sensitive local architect, at Highfield and Swaythling.

CHURCHES*

ST MICHAEL AND ALL ANGELS, Bassett Avenue, Bassett. 1897–1910 by *E. P. Warren*, an associate of G. F. Bodley. An intriguing and distinguished design internally: six broad rib-vaulted bays, four for the nave, two for the chancel, divided by a rood-screen. The ribs simply converge downwards into points, dying into the walls. The three W bays of the nave have tall shallow arched recesses, with large three-light Perp windows above, and deeper segment-headed recesses below, interconnected by small round-headed openings to form access aisles. The fourth bay is treated similarly, except that the segment-headed arches are higher, that on the S side leading into a wide lean-to one-bay S aisle which is the frontispiece of a S chapel. Other churches by Warren (Bishopstoke, p. 103; Bryanston, Dorset) are not as inventive spatially as this. Brick exterior with stone dressings. – STAINED GLASS. Two pieces of heraldic glass of *c.*1825, from the series damaged by bomb blast at North Stoneham (p. 358), of which this is a daughter church.

CHRIST CHURCH, Highfield Lane and Church Lane, Highfield.‡ Looks picturesque in its leafy setting, with its SE flanking tower and shingled spire. Internally an oddly shapeless building with a complicated history. Originally 1846–7 by *J. A. & R. Brandon*; very wide N aisle added in 1855 by *Elliott &*

*Arranged in alphabetical order of parishes.

‡The official title is Christ Church, Portswood, but it is always called Highfield Church.

Mason; the E part reconstructed in 1878 by *Colson*, who built a new wide chancel on the axis of the N nave arcade, opening with an arch on either side into the original nave and the N aisle, giving an odd two-naves–one-chancel effect (which is paralleled e.g. in the medieval church at Crayford in Kent). To the N and S of the chancel are an organ-chamber and chapel respectively, so that there is altogether a four-bay arcade running N–S, separating the E parts from the body of the church. Further extensions W by *J. Oldrid Scott & Son*, 1915, and more recently. There is nothing lively about the architecture of the church, except perhaps the carvings of the chancel arcades and, especially, the GARGOYLES taking the water from the valleys between the chancel and its flanking chambers; unusually large and mock-fearsome beasts crouching downwards, their necks bent to avoid the buttresses immediately below the gutter outlets. – BRASSES. Mrs Harriet Crabbe † 1848. Demi-figure on stone slab, with surrounding rectangular inscription band. Quite a convincing piece of mock-medievalism. – Large crucifix on slab with inscription to Joshua Arthur Brandon, joint architect of the original church, who died in 1847, before it was completed, aged twenty-five.

IMMACULATE CONCEPTION (R.C.), Portswood Road, Portswood. 1955 by *W. H. Saunders & Son.*

ST DENYS, St Denys Road. Of the Augustinian priory of St Denys, founded in 1127, only a fragment survives in a garden in Priory Road, and a small archway has been re-erected at Tudor House (p. 531). A farm occupied the site till the middle of the C19, when it was developed. The present church, on a near-by site, was built in 1868 by *Sir George Gilbert Scott*, with a nave, N aisle, and apsed chancel; the matching S aisle was added in 1889. A pleasant, relatively inexpensive but not austere neo-E.E. church, mostly of red brick, with some stone. Open bellcote over the E end of the nave. Wide and spacious inside. Ranges of tall lancets in the aisles with inner shafts and mouldings. Arches of brick with intermittent stone. Apse with paired lancets. The S chapel gives asymmetrical complexity to the space. Pleasant colour effect, the warm brick tempered with the buff stone; no stridency; harmonious fittings. – REREDOS by *Powell & Sons*, 1871. Sculptured Ascension in cusped recess, mosaic and gilt underneath. – TILES. Several encaustic tiles from the priory, in a panel in the S chapel; geometrical and floral designs and letters.

ST MARY, the parish church of South Stoneham and the village church of Swaythling. Tucked away in a quiet corner against trees by the river, behind the outward- and upward-expanding Halls of Residence of the University, but not overwhelmed by them. Its parish was once very large, extending beyond what is now suburban Southampton. Lowly W tower, nave with small N and larger S transepts, small chancel. The dominating feature of the interior is the fine late C12 chancel arch of chalk, pointed, of two orders, each roll moulded on the W face; engaged shafts with hollow fluted capitals to the inner order and nook-shafts to the outer order, with similar fluted capitals on the E side and simple waterleaf capitals on the W side. The chancel is of C12 origin, and a single round-headed light remains in the centre of each side wall. The other side windows (two on the N side and one on the S) are larger, later lancets, the E window is three-light Perp. The nave is decidedly nondescript; the windows are of 1854 (restoration by *G. Guillaume*), and the roof simply a covered Georgian ceiling concealing medieval timbering. The uniform whitening of both walls and ceiling gives an odd effect. The S transept is wholly by *Guillaume*; the jambs of the N transept arch and parts of the transept walls are medieval, but it too is largely restored. The tower is late C15 or early C16 (but pre-Reformation, because of the mutilated niche over the W door), with small double uncusped belfry lights, later battlemented parapet, and C19 W doorway. – FURNISHINGS. FONT. Late C12, of Purbeck marble, but more distinguished than the standard type; tapering bowl with four flat-arched panels on each face, each with a wedge-shaped pattern in relief. Victorian stem and shafts, old base. – PLATE. Cup, 1630; Cup and Paten, given 1704; another Cup and Paten, given 1756; Salver, 1828. – MONUMENTS. A varied collection. Chancel: tomb of *c*.1540. Tudor-arched recess with cusped Gothic panelling on its underside; cornice with arabesque decoration; three panels within the recess, the outer ones cartouches, the centre one with strapwork, the initials F.D. and B.D., and a cherub's head. – Small wall-monument to Edmund Clarke † 1632. Miniature effigies of him and his wife kneeling at a desk in a canopy with flat cornice and Corinthian columns; figures of twelve children below. An elegant piece. – Large tablet to Mary Jones † 1828, with a relief representation of her head on the side of a sarcophagus, a distressed looking angel on one side, and mourners on the other. By *Niccolo Bazzanti* of Florence (where, according to an inscription, it was made; cf. Bazzanti's other monument in Jesus Church, Peartree Green (p. 593). – N transept: large baroque monument to Edward Dummer, the builder of South Stoneham House (p. 581), † 1724. Double fluted Corinthian pilasters support a massive rounded open pediment; central medallion with portrait in curtained surround, the ropes tying the curtains realistically depicted. Coat of arms and garlands within and under the pediment which supports an urn. Hollow-sided sarcophagus and inscription below. A masterly piece; could it be by *Hawksmoor*? – Nave: tablet to Sarah Sloane † 1783, wife of Sir Hans Sloane (who owned South Stoneham House). – Tablet to Lieut-Gen. Stibbert † 1809, by *J. Bacon Jun.* Urn and coat of arms. – Tablet to Thomas Wells † 1760, in a frame with a pediment. – Many C19 wall-tablets.

ST ALBAN, Burgess Road, Swaythling. 1933 by *N. Cachemaille-Day*. Big cruciform church with low broad central tower, embattled, with angle turret. Neo-Perp windows and big folksy church hall attached to the S. The interior is spacious and well shaped. Nave with three-bay arcades of four-centred arches to the aisles. Big space under the tower with wide capital-less pointed arches, the symmetry of the space broken by a large tower-stairway cylinder rising from the ground at the NE corner. Centralized ALTAR (an original feature) under the tower space; big sanctuary bounded by low stone walls to N and S and open wooden COMMUNION RAILS to the W. The space behind the altar, in the structural chancel, forms an effective chapel. The nave (though not its aisles) was designed to be much longer, and there is now a temporary boarded W front, but the general proportions of the church, both outside and in, are perfectly satisfactory as they are.

SWAYTHLING METHODIST CHURCH, Burgess Road. Big brick octagon with roof sections curving to a central cupola. Round-headed stone-framed windows. Large fore-structure with rounded doorway flanked with square-headed openings in a 'Venetian' composition.

ST BARNABAS, Lodge Road. 1956 by *Gutteridge & Gutteridge*. Red brick with a gabled tower. Nave arcades and windows triangle-headed. On the site of a bombed Edwardian church.

AVENUE CONGREGATIONAL CHURCH, The Avenue and Alma Road. 1897–8 by *Cubitt & Collinson*. Rich neo-Dec; red brick with stone dressings. Short but strong near-W tower, with small assertive shingled spire and fancy wooden openwork turret over the stairway.

SOUTHAMPTON OLD CEMETERY. Formerly a section of the Common. Laid out in 1846 to the design of *W. H. Rogers*, approved by *Loudon*, with old forest trees preserved and new evergreens planted; there is now an almost Scottish density of tombstone masonry between them. Anglican and Nonconformist chapels and lodge possibly by *J. & J. Francis*, respectively Norman, E.E., and Tudor.

PUBLIC BUILDINGS

UNIVERSITY OF SOUTHAMPTON. The University originated from a bequest made by Henry Robinson Hartley, who died in 1850, and who intended to provide a cultural institution for the benefit of the educated people of the town. Because of delay through litigation (which greatly reduced the money available), the actual opening of the 'Hartley Institute' did not take place until 1862, in a building in the High Street. The Institute gradually developed into an establishment primarily devoted to teaching, and was recognized as a University College in 1902, but its progress continued to be hampered by lack of resources. A small site at Highfield, then on the rural outskirts of the town, was bought, and the first permanent buildings there were finished in 1914 (but not occupied by the College until after the First World War). The University College really got on to its feet in the inter-war years, and new buildings, impressive at least in bulk, were erected in the late 1930s. Full University status came in 1952; at that time it was not thought likely that the number of students would ever grow much above a thousand, and building expansion was on a relatively modest scale to a fairly spacious layout. But since then the 'target' student population has steadily risen; a total of 4,000 by 1967 is being aimed at, and, in the 'post-Robbins' era, the figure may be raised even higher. So, as new development progresses (and the rate has accelerated in the 1960s), the buildings become larger and closer on the restricted land available, and there are already some clashes of scale.

The main university site extends over 32 acres, irregularly bounded by suburban development, except on the W, where there is a thickly wooded part of Southampton Common. Long-term proposals include the extension of the site over some of the land occupied by adjoining houses, but little of this extension can take place for many years. All the teaching and technical accommodation will, if possible, be contained within the main site and its eventual extension, but residential accommodation is provided elsewhere, mainly in two areas at Bassett and Swaythling (pp. 580 ff.). The architects employed have been *Mitchell, Son & Gutteridge* (in 1914); *Gutteridge & Gutteridge* (between the wars and since the Second World War); *Sir Basil Spence & Partners* (Partners in Charge, *Bonnington & Collins*), who prepared an overall plan for the development of the site in 1957 (since repeatedly modified with the changes in the University's programme) and who have designed most of the more recent larger buildings; *Ronald Sims* of Bournemouth; and *Potter & Hare* of Salisbury, who have designed new residential buildings at Swaythling.

The MAIN BUILDING lies E of University Road, 1935 by *Gutteridge & Gutteridge*, in association with *Sir Giles Gilbert Scott*. In the reddest of red brick, with red mullioned windows and red Roman tiles. Two-storeyed, the upper storey tall and containing the library. Long main façade with shallow low-gabled transepts at either end, each with tall windows on the upper storey, the lines of the mullions of which are continued down to those of the windows of the lower storey. The intermediate stretch of façade is recessed towards the top (at the level of the tops of the bookcases), above which is clerestory fenestration. There is thus a horizontal emphasis over most of the façade, offset by the vertical emphasis in the transepts, with fair balance. Central upper window over square-headed entrance, which leads into a spreading entrance hall broken with red brick pillars. Flanking the Main Building, to which they now form wings, are the two original blocks of *c.*1914 (by *Mitchell, Son & Gutteridge*), surprisingly pleasant externally, with red brick in two shades, stone-mullioned windows, carefully designed buttresses with concave stone copings, and prominent entrances with massive moulded segment-arched heads – they have a suggestion of Voysey or even Mackintosh.

At the back of the Main Building a big extension of 1959, also by *Gutteridge*, but in a more up-to-date style. This thrusts to the area where the architectural chaos resulting from the accumulation of temporary buildings and the haphazard siting of permanent ones over many years is gradually being turned into some sort of architectural order, under *Sir Basil Spence*'s plan. The first post-war permanent buildings, by *Gutteridge*, are one- or two-storeyed, square and lumpish, of unrelieved redness, laid out when the University's proposed expansion was quite modest in scale and there seemed to be plenty of space to spare. Around and among them *Spence*'s more recent buildings make an extraordinary contrast in scale and inventiveness.

To the SE is the extension to the CHEMISTRY BUILDING, started in 1960, rectangular, eight storeys plus upper service floor, conspicuously framed by eight pairs of thin rectangular concrete piers linked over the roof by cross-beams. The main walls are set against the inner faces of the piers, and the roof of the service floor touches the undersides of the cross-beams, leaving clear spaces (since the service floor is set back) in the angles of the piers and the cross-beams, to striking effect. The façades of the six main storeys have continuous glazing between long panels faced in grey mosaic; the two lowest storeys, with various doorways and windows (and facing panels of fluted concrete finish, or rubble mosaic), are set back, leaving free-standing the lower parts of the shutter-finished concrete piers, and revealing the ends of the concrete cross-beams at first-floor level, to dramatic effect. At the short ends the six main storeys are boldly cantilevered over the two lower storeys.

Balancing the Chemistry Building at the NE corner of the university site, comparable in scale and finish though different in shape, is the TOWER BUILDING OF ENGINEERING, begun 1960. This is of ten main storeys, of which the top eight form a straightforward tower (with a set-back service storey on top, conspicuous from a distance), square in plan, strip-patterned with glazing and grey mosaic panelling. The two lower storeys are recessed, as if they formed a thick square stem, constructed of a wide grid of thick concrete beams, inter-glazed. The scale of the whole building is emphasized by the small-scale shutter pattern on the concrete surfaces of the underside of the third storey and elsewhere. A delicate glass-sided Spencian bridge links this with the LANCHESTER BUILDING, with a long façade of four storeys, the two upper storeys, strip-glazed and smooth concrete-panelled, projecting far in front of the first floor, which is brick-faced and recessed behind the vertical structural piers of the buildings, revealed at this level in their concrete bareness. The glass-fronted ground storey comes just in front of the bases of the piers. The great feature of the Lanchester Building is the LECTURE THEATRE, projecting at second-floor level, trapezoidal with a convex end, conspicuously supported on two rectangular piers. The scale of the whole is again emphasized by the shutter-pattern on the bare underside surfaces and piers. The Lanchester Building stands in front of earlier utilitarian structures, behind which is Spence's TIZARD BUILDING, of 1959, simple, two-storeyed, with the usual grey mosaic wall-surfacing; no dramatic effects, because it is hidden away, and no gimmickry.

The Lanchester Building and the recently extended Main Building form the N and W sides of what will be a fairly small courtyard with the Engineering Tower rising beyond the NE corner, and Gutteridge's ZOOLOGY BUILDING (recently partly heightened a storey) on the E. On the S side of the area is the elegant long extension by *Spence* (1959) to the older SOCIAL SCIENCES BUILDING – a single storey at first-floor level, mostly glazed (though brick-faced towards the W end), and supported by widely spaced piers. Beyond this will be another small courtyard, less well defined by surrounding buildings, but dominated by the Chemistry Building to the E. Many temporary pre- and post-war structures have to be cleared before the spatial effect can be fully realized.

On the W side of University Road the oldest building is the OLD UNION, 1939 by *Gutteridge*, a smaller version in paler red brick of the Main Building opposite. To this *Spence* has added a single-storey SENIOR COMMON ROOM (1960), mainly on the N side, with two roof levels, partly brick-fronted towards the E, the taller parts with conspicuous copper-sheeted fascias, the lower parts mostly glass-sided. Internally, it is planned round two small courtyards. Further N is the
98 NUFFIELD THEATRE, begun 1961, austere and apparently unfenestrated – in fact the small windows in the lower brick-faced storey are set back in narrow recesses. Its external distinction is due to the shapes of the auditorium and proscenium roofs, generally tapering upwards and round-cornered, the latter taller, all covered with copper sheeting.* Between the S façade of the Theatre and the N façade of the Senior Common Room is a small pleasant courtyard, with an old tree and a sheet of water, in the midst of which is a fountain and a piece of SCULPTURE by *F. E. McWilliam*. Facing the W side of the courtyard is part of the façade of the Arts and Law Building (*see* below); the E side is open to what is now a large and indeterminately shaped space, traversed by University Road, and

*The Nuffield Theatre was designed in consultation with *Dr Richard Southern* of the University.

irregularly bounded by housing (some of it converted to University use) to N and S. It has a few pleasant trees, and its chief architectural accent is the Main Building to the E, and the Old Union, Senior Common Room, and Theatre to the W. This will eventually be shaped – following the closure of University Road, the demolition of some of the adjoining houses, and the erection of more University buildings (especially to the N) – into a central campus, the relative spaciousness of which will offset the inevitable crowdedness of the increasingly intensively developed outer parts of the University area.

W of the Old Union the ground slopes briefly to a stream, with a bit of pretty and effective landscaping (undertaken before the University's sights were raised to their present height and recently curtailed by the encroachment of new buildings), dominated by the return frontage to the Senior Common Room, dramatically cantilevered over the falling ground, with a stage-set external staircase. To the N is the end façade of the ARTS AND LAW BUILDING, begun 1961, one of the simplest but most pleasing of *Spence*'s works at Southampton. Four storeys, smooth concrete finish, perfectly regular fenestration of upright rectangular units on all the storeys, each window unit divided by a transom towards the top. There is an upper service storey, conspicuous on the skyline, towards the N end, sheathed in copper sheeting to match the Nuffield Theatre.

At the NW corner of the University site is the MATHEMATICS BUILDING, by *Ronald Sims*, 1965, a building of striking and attractive shape, complex in planning and elevational detail because of the varied nature of the accommodation required (and the smallness of the site available). Essentially it is in three parts. The lowest, containing laboratories and equipment rooms, is of three storeys, faced in brick, and against it on the E side is a BOILER ROOM, partly underground, with a platform roof. Entrance to the Mathematics Building is made by passing over this platform and then up a short flight of steps into the fourth storey, round which is a cantilevered balcony with thick upper rail. Above this level the building is visually emphasized by two sections, the N section containing mainly lecture rooms in four large storeys, the S section containing six smaller storeys (above the fourth storey in each case). The S part is distinguished by broad concrete vertical slab features which project forward of the S elevation and upward of the roof-line (and end vertically in inclined planes); the elevations of the upper storeys (with strip glazing alternating with concrete facing) are set back between these slab features on the S side and cantilevered out from them on the E and W. The N part has a simpler square outline, but more complicated window patterns. Despite its subdivision, the building is given unity by its consistent concrete facing (apart from the bottom three storeys), much of it incised with a regular vertical fluted pattern (although some parts are left smooth-faced). The whole composition has large-scale sculptural quality, bringing out effectively the textural quality of concrete. At the moment it appears a little isolated, but it has been designed in proper relationship to future buildings by *Sir Basil Spence* (including a GEOGRAPHY BUILDING) between it and the existing Arts and Law Building, on which work was to begin shortly at the time of writing. To the S of the Mathematics Building is the small PEGASUS COMPUTER BUILDING, also by *Ronald Sims*, single-storeyed, partly brick-faced, with a central raised clerestoried part with a distinctive inward-sloping double pitch.

Three buildings are being erected at the time of writing on the S part of the University site, all by *Spence*, generally on a bigger scale than are most of the earlier individual buildings. These include the PHYSICS BUILDING, adjoining the Common, a large rectangular block of four main storeys, with grey mosaic-faced wall surfaces between strips of fenestration, and well placed service structures above the main roof level, giving an interesting skyline; the BOTANY AND GEOLOGY BUILDING further E; and the new UNION BUILDING in a hollow S of the existing Union. Construction of the latter two was not sufficiently far advanced at the time of writing for their final appearance to be properly judged.

Further development will take place mainly to the N, as existing housing is acquired and demolished over the next twenty years. One small structure, the OCEANOGRAPHY BUILDING by *Richard Sheppard, Robson & Partners*, brick-faced, has already been erected (1965) away from the existing main site on the corner of Burgess Road and University Road. From a distance the University has an exciting skyline, particularly when seen from the far slopes of the Itchen valley in the Bitterne Park area; the most conspicuous elements are Spence's Engineering Tower and Chemistry Building, situated on the brow of rising ground, and the thick trees of the Common make an effective backcloth.

HALLS OF RESIDENCE. Chamberlain Hall and Glen Eyre

Hall are off Glen Eyre Road, Bassett (p. 581); South Stoneham House, Connaught Hall, and Montefiore House are off Wessex Lane, Swaythling (pp. 581 ff.), adjoining South Stoneham church (p. 573).

CHAMBERLAIN HALL, Glen Eyre Road, Bassett. 1959 by *Sir Basil Spence*, for women. In the big grounds of a Victorian house. Two blocks of three to four storeys, in yellow-red brick, on axes that converge slightly, linked at their closer ends with a single-storey dining hall, and intermediately by a two-storeyed cross-passageway, thus creating one enclosed and one three-sided courtyard, with the glazed passageway as a transparent screen between them. The hall has an entirely glazed wall facing the courtyard and a distinctive grooved roof. The blocks have students' rooms on their upper floors, and communal rooms on the ground floors, the ground floor of the block on the E side of the courtyard being set back behind a colonnade of cylindrical piers. The original Victorian house, with a pretty gable-ranged roof-line, is preserved.

GLEN EYRE HALL, Bassett. Of various post-war dates, by *Gutteridge & Gutteridge*. Dispersed red brick blocks; a circular common room (1962) is the only lively feature. In the very large grounds of a demolished house, with plenty of mature landscaping.

See p. 831

SOUTH STONEHAM HOUSE, Swaythling. The manor house of South Stoneham, adjoining the medieval church (p. 573). It became a Hall of Residence after the First World War. Built in 1708 (date on drainpipes) almost certainly by *Nicholas Hawksmoor*.* It was much altered *c.*1900 and possibly on one or more occasions before, in a disconcertingly sensitive manner (at least as far as the exterior is concerned) that makes uncertain (in the absence of available documents) exactly how much of Hawksmoor's work survives. Recent large-scale additions by *Potter & Hare*, begun in 1960, including a seventeen-storey tower, have been handled without detriment either to the old house or even to its setting (small-scale luxuriant landscape with lawns and mature trees, and the river flowing near; early C19 in feeling). The house was originally a rectangle of seven bays and three storeys, to which remarkably harmonious additions have been made at either end, elongating

*Information supplied by Mr John Harris, who has found reference to Hawksmoor in documents relating to 'Mr Dummer's house', almost certainly South Stoneham.

the rectangle. A simply moulded, but well projecting stone cornice runs along the top of the second storey; the attic storey is plainly finished except for a small very Hawksmoorish stone pediment rising from the parapet over the central bay, repeated on both sides; it rests on capitals decorated with triglyphs, dentilled underneath, the pediment itself, thinly moulded, being infilled with brick. The walls are largely of dun red brick but a frieze of several courses under the cornice, very slightly planed forward, is in brighter brick, as are also the lintels of the windows which, except on the attic storey, are notably tall for their width. On the N side a large enclosed porch has been added; the S front is less altered, and has a large canted projecting centrepiece rising to two storeys and flat-roofed. The attic storey with the Hawksmoor pediment simply continues above it on the plane of the façade. The projection has three windows, one in the centre and two in the canted sides, on the first floor, and side windows and a central stone doorway at ground level or, strictly, just above ground level; for it is reached by a flight of five steps, shortly but assertively balustraded. This door is the most distinctive feature of the building, thoroughly Hawksmoorish, a big square-framed opening widely hollow-chamfered, with a prominent scrolled keystone embellished with formalized foliage and a wide shell pattern above; flat, fairly shallow hood resting on fluted scrolled brackets which are canted outwards at angles of forty-five degrees. There is an identical doorway on the N side of the house, but now encased within the porch, the roof of which comes to the level of (and obliterates) the hood of the doorway.* The N door was the main entrance to the remodelled house, and leads into an entrance hall which appears to have been formed out of an older, moderate-sized rectangular room, which has been made to open through a screen of two impressive fluted Corinthian columns – can they be Hawksmoorian features replaced from elsewhere? – into the fairly small staircase hall, with its beautiful staircase which in part at least is an original feature but which has almost certainly been remodelled. The straight intermediate and upper flights, at r. angles, are probably original and *in situ*, but the sharply curving lower flight seems suspiciously like a remodelled feature, both carefully re-using features and copying them. The scale of the staircase is not at all massive; there are tall, fairly

*One cannot quite be certain that this N doorway is not a copy of the undoubtedly genuine S one, put in at the remodelling.

delicate, turned balusters, and the stair ends are beautifully carved with scroll, flower, and leaf decoration. The undersides of the stairs are widely hollow-chamfered, giving a graceful effect. The staircase hall opens at ground-floor level into a passageway to the S, with some rather gimcrack columniation which cannot bear any relation to anything Hawksmoor did. The ceiling above the staircase is painted to a classical design with Adamish or Soanish qualities (certainly later than Hawksmoor) with geometrical patterning and delicate foliate detail.

The additions made by *Potter & Hare* are all at the W end of the old house, partly replacing a C19 or early C20 wing. The dominating feature is the tower, well to the NW of the house, square in plan, with all but the lowest two storeys faced in green-grey roughcast panels in two shades and plain concrete panels, giving quite an interesting overall textural and colour effect. The thin concrete floor ends are revealed, and there is a neat but not too assertive rail around the roof-line. From a distance, e.g. down the Itchen valley to the S, this tower is a pleasing landmark, rising on its own from among trees with no competing features near by. At closer view it is kept skilfully away from the old house, yet visibly linked with it with a one-storey connexion. Abutting on to the tower to the S, and on the axis of the house, is the hall, with convex brick E and W walls and an open glazed S frontage facing the grounds. The interconnecting one-storey block which abuts on to the W wall of the hall also has a glazed S frontage under a strongly projecting hood.

CONNAUGHT HALL, Swaythling. 1931 by *Gutteridge & Gutteridge*. A two-storeyed brick enclosed courtyard with neo-Georgian windows and more domesticity than usual in Gutteridge's buildings. Big entrance archways on the axis rising through two storeys and brick-quoined. Sensitive large-scale additions to the N by *Potter & Hare* 1964, two- to four-storeyed.

MONTEFIORE HOUSE, Swaythling. 1964–5 by *Potter & Hare*, opposite South Stoneham and next to Connaught, completing the group. Two parallel rectangular five-storeyed blocks of different length, similarly treated, with thin end-exposed concrete floors and, above the ground storey, brick infilling between widely-spaced (and paired) windows. Two tall chimneys, concrete-faced and quite elegantly shaped, are made the dominating feature at the end of the longer building.

CHILWORTH MANOR (Hall of Residence), *see* p. 166.

SCHOOL OF NAVIGATION, *see* Warsash, p. 643.

WELLINGTON SPORTS GROUND, *see* North Stoneham, p. 359.

GLEN EYRE SECONDARY SCHOOL, Violet Road, Bassett. 1962 by *L. Berger*, the City Architect. A pleasant amalgam of blocks of one to four storeys, the façades partly of brick but mainly with concrete grid framing infilled with glazing and dark panelling.

ST GEORGE R.C. SCHOOL, off Leaside Way, Bassett Green. 1962 by *R. Sheppard, Robson & Partners*. One- to three-storey blocks; big glazing units with thin divisions; stretches of buff brick wall; fairly narrow white fascias. Taking the utmost advantage of a slightly undulating site. Dramatic effect in the NW part; a view flowing through a glazed partition with both external and internal staircase stagily contrived.

TAUNTON'S SCHOOL, Highfield Road, Highfield. 1926 by *Gutteridge & Gutteridge*. Acceptable neo-Wrenaissance. Red brick and generous stone dressings. Two-storeyed, with shallow wings and prominent segmental pillared porch, surmounted by a canted bay window with concave roofing. Round pediments over the centre and wings. Strongly detailed cornices.

ST DENYS STATION. Of 1867, when the branch line to Netley (p. 351) was built. The main block (up) is original and, like Netley, in the Mid Victorian L. & S.W.R. tradition derived from Tite: strong, simple Italianate classical; red brick (not stuccoed).

SWAYTHLING STATION. The platform buildings are humble, but the frontispiece has an elaborate Late Victorian brick façade overlaid with brick and terracotta neo-Flemish motifs. The station was opened in 1883.

PERAMBULATIONS

Two suburban Perambulations are set out:

(a) From the Ordnance Survey Office (at the end of Perambulation (*c*) of Inner Southampton, p. 561) via the Common and Highfield to the University and Bassett.

(b) In Swaythling village.

(a) *The Common, Highfield and Bassett*

This is a long Perambulation and, until the inter-war development at Highfield and then the University are reached, includes no striking pieces of architecture. Its attractions are essentially scenic – suburban scenery at its best – and its interest is mainly in that it covers successive stages of typical low-density middle-class suburban growth.

From the old Ordnance Survey Office (p. 528), THE AVENUE leads N. This is the main northward road out of the town, along which a continuous avenue of mature trees has been maintained since the C18. For about ¼ m. the road is bordered by a strip of parkland (actually old common land landscaped in the C19) and faced with a miscellany of C19 and C20 buildings. Beyond the junction with Lodge Road (r.) The Avenue narrows and curves. To the r. are yellow-brick villas of the 1850s to 1870s, broad, square, and very solid, in unostentatious vaguely Italianate styles (there are few flights of Gothic fancy in mid-Victorian Southampton villas), often with distinctive quoin patterns, and with low slated hipped roofs. Similar villas are found in the other suburbs which were developed during the period (such as Freemantle, the S part of Portswood, and Woolston), but nowhere over sufficiently large areas to give the feeling of extensive low-density mid-Victorian suburbia; there are always closer-built terrace houses near at hand or just round the corner (such occur behind the frontage to The Avenue on the E side).

Past the Avenue Congregational Church (p. 574), SOUTHAMPTON COMMON begins. This is an amazing open space to find within the suburbs of a large city. It was conveyed to the burgesses of Southampton by Nicholas, lord of Shirley in 1228 to be their common pasture, but it has been used mainly for recreation since the C18. Large areas are intensively used for sport, but a great deal is woodland (mainly deciduous) and some of the recesses seem quite wild. The standard of maintenance practised by the Corporation is admirable. To the r. are two parallel roads, WINN ROAD and WESTWOOD ROAD, typical of the last phase of local Victorian suburbia. This was originally a Late Georgian estate (Westwood House) which was sold for building *c.*1880; many of the mature trees were kept in the gardens of the large villas that were afterwards built – mostly gabled, in red brick, with patches of terracotta, tiling or timbering, very different in spirit from the sober mid-Victorian villas further S. (Actually there is a good deal of admixture of later development, due to bombing and infilling.)

The Perambulation continues l. into BROOKVALE ROAD, typical suburbia of *c.*1910–30, with villas in more fancy varieties (though often quite tasteful), still against a background of carefully conserved trees from the pre-existing estates, augmented by planting coeval with the houses. Further along Brookvale Road (towards Highfield Church) is the beginning of the best piece of suburbia in Southampton – an area developed *c.*1920–1939 by *Herbert Collins* in the finest garden-city traditions. The housing is mostly in terraces of four or five, two-storeyed, with low-pitched hipped roofs, broad windows broken into little white-framed panes, with front doors hooded or pedimented or simply shaped in some distinctive way. There are often canted bays on the ground floors, and shutters to upper storeys. Round-arched passageways lead through the blocks to the back gardens of the intermediate houses in the terraces. The feel is neo-Georgian, but not of the copyist sort; the manner is a refinement of that of Georgian cottages with small casement windows rather than that of larger Georgian houses with correctly proportioned sash windows. Some of the oldest terraces face Brookvale Road (date 1922 on one); they are roughcast. HIGHFIELD CLOSE, leading NW, might be in the Hampstead garden suburb; three roughcast blocks facing round a little square, linked at the corner by round-arched connecting walls, the square itself intensely planted (tastefully) with rockeries, roses, and a small pond. UPLANDS WAY, also leading NW off Brookvale Road, is from the later stage (1937 on one terrace). The terraces are red brick and a little more assertively Georgian; the road is widely grass-bordered and the line of the housing is curved on one side, with old trees preserved. This leads into ORCHARDS WAY, the centrepiece of the scheme. The first part to be developed was between Highfield Lane and Uplands Way; terraces dated 1921–4, set back behind high grassy banks which are traversed by brick footpaths. Opposite Uplands Way a large (and deliberately rough) green is preserved, with a stream crossing it, houses backed by trees on two sides, and garages (*c.*1930, not unsightly) on the third; opposite, a small copse is kept. Orchards Way continues SW, behind widening grass borders, curves where old estate trees are preserved as focal landmarks (with the terraces artily set back behind them), and finally comes to an end at a little roundabout, unfortunately faced by a post-war terrace which is poorer than the rest. This is the sort of suburban development which set the pattern in the better council housing estates for about ten years after the Second World War, but the standard here was seldom if ever reached. Back in Highfield Lane, GLEBE COURT is also by *Collins*; three terraces, bigger in scale and more outspokenly Georgian, round a large (and here disconcertingly rough) square green. They are sadly unpleasing in their half-hearted formality after the studied informality of Orchards Way.

There are then two ways of getting to the University; either l. up Highfield Lane to HIGHFIELD VILLAGE, with a little rough Late Georgian to Mid Victorian character (but not much), then r. along Hawthorn Road and Chamberlain Road entering the University, rather impressively, by a back way along a footpath; or else past Highfield Church (p. 571) and up Church Lane to the heart of the University (p. 575). The Perambulation can then end at a thickly wooded part of the Common (entrance from Salisbury Road) or else continue along GLEN EYRE ROAD, past two Halls of Residence (p. 581), near to a school (p. 584) and into BASSETT. Like so many suburbs of Southampton, Bassett was originally rough country, which went through a stage of transition to big ornamental estates before it became purely suburb – but this intermediate stage came, mainly, later in Bassett than in other comparable districts. Much of the basic road pattern was laid out *c.*1853, and a number of super-villas were built between then and the end of the century, parcelling out between them most of the available land into thickly underplanted wooded estates. Since the First World War there has been gradual suburban intensification, but even the recent development is largely at a relatively low density by current standards, and a great deal of Victorian greenery is kept. An exception to the prevalent pattern of detached houses in big gardens is provided by BRAMPTON TOWER in Bassett Avenue, 1962, fourteen-storeyed, faced in brick between thin concrete floor-ends, with wide windows between fluted panels and flint-faced balconies. It is an elegant piece, and quite a landmark from distant viewpoints, especially to the E, rising out of its wooded surroundings. To the E, along BEECHMOUNT ROAD, are terraces of sophisticated three-storey houses, with delicate metal balconies, designed, like the Tower, by *Hubbard Ford & Associates*. There is not much else in Bassett, and the Perambulation proper ends at St Michael's Church (p. 571). But the intrepid explorer can go on to BASSETT GREEN, hemmed in by new development rather more closely built than further S, but remaining a pleasant miniature village green bordered by simple C18 and

C19 brick cottages, some fairly sensitive new development, and ST CHRISTOPHER'S CHURCH, fashioned out of an early C19 schoolroom. From there it is a fairly short walk into Swaythling (*see* below), passing some more development by *Herbert Collins* (e.g. ETHELBURT AVENUE), not so good as Orchards Way (p. 586) but pleasant enough, even if the greenery is untidily maintained.*

(b) *Swaythling*

Swaythling is an old village near the tidal head of the Itchen estuary, adjoining the church and manor house of South Stoneham. E of the railway it retained quite a lot of rural character until recently, but suburbanization (which has been a gentler process here than in many other parts of the city) is now almost complete. It still remains a distinctive area, with the University Halls of Residence in its midst and the river and the newly created riverside park in the background.

A Perambulation of Swaythling ought to begin with South Stoneham Church (p. 573) and the adjoining Halls of Residence (p. 581). WESSEX LANE leads N, still faintly countryfied, past the Station (p. 584) to what was the village centre, where the simple Georgian FLEMING ARMS, distinguished by a pillared porch, stands by a tributary of the Itchen. Further E, SWAYTHLING FARM, C16 to C18, has recently been swept away (although it was listed Grade II by the MHLG), and THE GRANGE opposite (also Grade II) is now doomed; it has a central core (brick-gabled elevation to the road) which is partly at least C17 (according to the MHLG there is a C15 traceried window) and a handsome two-storeyed W frontage of *c.*1800, with five ranges of windows under a pediment and canted bays at the ends, that to the S having the pathetic fragment of a once elaborate tent-roofed veranda. The building is still occupied, but in desperate decay at the time of writing. The Grange and the site of Swaythling Farm adjoin a particularly awkward road junction and, once the obvious road improvements have been carried out, there will be a chance to create a new focal centre to what was the old village. To the E of the junction, WESTFIELD CORNER is a two-storeyed clumsy

* No. 324 PORTSWOOD ROAD is a charming stuccoed castellated building with angle turrets and Gothick decoration. It was formerly the lodge to the St Denys Estate, which covered the site of the priory (p. 572). Recently restored and now used commercially.

neo-Georgian curving terrace of shops and flats by *Herbert Collins* which is effective because of its position on a steep bank. It is the frontispiece to an area of suburban housing developed gradually since 1925 by the Swaythling Housing Society (architects *Herbert Collins* and *J. C. Birkett*) in the garden city manner, not so good as Collins's housing in the Orchards Way area of Highfield (p. 586) but, in its earlier parts, effective. Three closes succeed one another on the N side of Mansbridge Road. PILGRIM PLACE is dated 1925, long, low terraces on three sides of a rectangular green, connected at the angles with round-arched screens; roughcast and Roman-tiled, with simple round-headed doorways and windows of the Georgian cottage type. Three splendid trees on the Green. It might be at Welwyn. CAPON CLOSE, 1926, is similar, but with classical door hoods and plain tiles, and only a small tree on the green. HOWARD CLOSE, 1927, is again slightly different and altogether bleaker because there are no trees. (The name Howard tells whence the inspiration came.) The later development, S of Mansbridge Road, partly of the late 1930s and partly post-war, is pleasant, but altogether more insipid; there are plenty of grass borders and little greens (and notices forbidding one to play on them) but few felicitous general effects, and the simplified designs of the houses lack the conviction of the earlier examples.

Across the River Itchen is the semblance of country, and paths run alongside open spaces (exemplarily laid out by Southampton Corporation in the last few years) to WOODMILL, a pleasant Late Georgian functional brick building (the survivor of once more extensive premises), beyond which there is more attractive riverside walking past further newly created open spaces to Cobden Bridge and the fine churches of St Denys (p. 572) and the Ascension (p. 590).

OUTER SOUTHAMPTON: EAST

For definition of area and index *see* p. 565

What is now the part of Southampton E of the Itchen was largely a wilderness in the early C19. There was the medieval manor house of Bitterne, on the site of Roman Clausentum, within a loop of the river, and a fishing village at Itchen over a mile downstream, served by an Anglican chapel built in 1620 at Peartree Green to the E; the only other village was a very small one at Weston. Gentlemen's estates, mostly created in Late Georgian times, were dispersed along the waterside and on the high ground to the N. In the interior were miles of rough common, sprinkled with a few squatters' holdings, one cluster of which was tellingly called Botany Bay.

The commons were mostly enclosed in the middle part of the last century. A close-built Victorian village grew up on the hill-top at Bitterne, a looser straggle of brick cottages, interspersed with soft-fruit holdings, developed at Sholing, and a sizeable Victorian suburb was established at Woolston, served by the Floating Bridge, a steam chain-ferry, which was opened in 1836. Inter-war speculative housing sprawled over the former country estates and many of the fruit holdings, hardly any of it sensitively related to the hilly terrain with its sudden exciting views, or to the thick mature landscaping of the old estates, much of which was simply destroyed. Post-war housing by Southampton Corporation on the fringes has been much more imaginatively designed, and more effectively related to the topography and the pre-existing landscape. Few people would go to Eastern Southampton today to look at architecture, and the few buildings or features of more than ordinary interest are widely scattered and not related to any others – the church of the Ascension, the medieval fragments at Bitterne Manor, the various monuments in Jesus Church, several post-war schools, some impressive multi-storey flats – all these, and things of milder interest, have to be hunted for in what is now a suburban wilderness; nothing like a Perambulation can be attempted.

CHURCHES

Arranged in alphabetical order of parishes

ASCENSION, Cobden Avenue, Bitterne Park. 1924–6 by *Sir Charles Nicholson*, the most rewarding post-medieval church in Southampton. It is angular and rather bleak externally, with bare brick walls and stumpy W tower (not completed to Nicholson's intended design or height). The church is on a slope, and the nave floor well above ground level at the W end; the entrance is through the tower and up a staircase as if to a gallery. So the spacious, well proportioned interior comes as a surprise. Six bays to the nave arcades, the piers of warm stone; the arches and the wall surfaces above white. Clerestory of square-headed windows. Very low-pitched nave roof (intended to be, but not, coloured); flat panelled chancel roof (nicely coloured). The E window recalls that of St Katherine

Cree, London (though not in detail); it has a circle of twirling lights within a square frame with traceried spandrels. The aisle windows are three-light square-headed neo-Perp. The large N chapel is different in character from the rest of the church. It has two bays of ribbed vaulting and lancet windows, reminiscent of Early Victorian E.E. rather than medieval E.E. – the design of this chapel was in fact influenced by that of J. W. Wild's church of St Lawrence in High Street (p. 517), which was of 1839 and was demolished in 1926, the Ascension being partly paid for from the proceeds of the sale of the site. – The FURNISHINGS have been gradually put in as funds have permitted, many of them since the Second World War. – ALTAR designed by *Nicholson*, decorated by *Randoll Blacking*. Four wooden riddel posts surmounted by angels. – SCREENS. The chancel screen designed by *Blacking*, but executed after his death by *K. F. Wiltshire* of *Potter & Hare*, 1959. Neo-Classical with Corinthian pillars and Roman inscription along the beam; strange for 1959 but wholly in character with the church. The earlier screens enclosing the chapels are more Gothic in character. – STAINED GLASS. All the aisle windows were executed in the inter-war years by *A. K. Nicholson*, brother of Sir Charles, but in close collaboration with *Eric Milner-White*, afterwards Dean of York (who had a close connexion with the parish), and it is likely that much of the inspiration was Milner-White's. The five windows in the S aisle represent the Ascended Christ in heaven; those in the N aisle the work of the Church on earth. Predominantly rich colours, especially on the N side, where almost all the glazing is coloured in some way – the windows on the S side have a higher proportion of clear glass, giving something of the insipid overall effect which characterizes too many early post-war windows where a large amount of clear glazing is interspersed with coloured glass. The earthly figures are realistic and effective; the heavenly figures look wishy-washy, as if they were beyond the designer's comprehension. Small panels include detailed monochrome representations of buildings or scenes (as varied as the temple of Nicaea, Hampton Court, Zanzibar Cathedral, and a fairly idealized view of Southampton in 1930). The E window is also by *A. K. Nicholson*; very good colour effect, with the Ascended Christ as a small figure in the central round panel, against a partly white and partly pale yellow background, with a radiating spectrum of colours – yellow, orange (the dominant colour of the window which first attracts one's attention and sticks in one's memory), red, purple, and so on. Other windows are by *G. E. R. Smith* of the A. K. Nicholson Studios. His W window is a great success in general effect – or seems so when seen from well down the church against the oblique sun: the Ship of the Church, with full-blown sails, against a very blue sky; but it does not bear close detailed comparison with Nicholson's windows in the aisles. – PULPIT. C18 from King's College Chapel. It must have seemed pretty insignificant there, but stands quite well at Bitterne Park; hexagon with plain square panels and simply moulded frieze; clumsy base (the original had a tapering stem). – PLATE. Silver Paten, 1629, from St Lawrence. – MONUMENTS. A few tablets from St Lawrence in the N chapel, notably one to William Reade, a goldsmith, † 1732; italic and Roman lettering.

CHRIST THE KING (R.C.), Bitterne Road, Bitterne Village. 1960 by *E. M. Galloway & Partners*. Impressive, straightforward interior: tall rectangular space with low-pitched roof and lean-to aisles with concrete piers; tall mullioned window on the S side of the sanctuary. The decorative effect is spoiled by poor and conventional representations of the Stations of the Cross over the arcades. Steeple like a firemen's practice tower.

HOLY SAVIOUR, Bursledon Road, Bitterne Village. 1852 by *G. Guillaume*, originally with N aisle and N flanking tower and spire. Identical S aisle added in 1885. Neo-Dec. No internal division between nave and chancel; considerable width in relation to length. The church stands high, and its spire, though not particularly tall, is a far-seen landmark. – STAINED GLASS. In the N window of the chancel a single small light by *Morris & Co.*, 1896. Figure of Christ, Salvator Mundi, in rich red; elaborately folded robe.

ALL HALLOWS, Witts Hill, Midanbury. 1965–6 by *Pinckney & Gott*. Tall, brick, apsidal; windows at clerestory level; whimsical bell-turret to the S.

JESUS CHURCH, Peartree Green. Built as Jesus Chapel in 1620 to serve that part of the old parish of St Mary, Southampton ('St Mary Extra'), which lay across the Itchen. The first chapel, recorded in illustrations, was a simple rectangle with square-headed side windows and a three-light E window which looks as if it had an Early Perp character – either an interesting piece of Gothic Survival or (perhaps more likely) the re-use of an old feature from elsewhere.* A big S transept and a W

* Cf. North Stoneham, p. 357.

porch were added in 1822, by *E. Burrough & J. Ede*, a N aisle built in 1846, an E aisle added to the transept in 1866, and a new chancel and S chapel built in 1883. All that is left of the C17 church is the W extremity, with rough rubble walls, diagonal buttresses, and a small open bell-turret with a low stone pyramidal top. The 1822 additions are in smooth ashlar with flat-headed neo-Tudor windows; the rest is conventional neo-Dec. The interior is oddly shaped, with N nave and E transept arcades, but no arch from the nave into the transept. – PLATE. Chalice, 1620; Paten, probably *c.*1620–30; two Flagons, 1665–6. – MONUMENTS. Plenty all round the walls. The two best are by *Chantrey*. One is to William Chamberlayne of Weston Grove † 1831, with a realistic life-size profile in low relief, showing the short strands of hair and the protuberances of the face in great detail, on a medallion in the upper part of a large tablet; the inscription below is surmounted by a frieze of alternate triglyphs and rosettes. – The other is to his sister Charlotte Chamberlayne † 1835, with a half-size weeping figure in bold relief, again meticulously detailed, but her face hidden by her hands. – George Ede † 1821, by *Henry Westmacott*. Small kneeling figure and child against the garlanded stump of a pillar. – Captain Lewis Shedden † 1844, by *Niccolo Bazzanti* of Florence (and executed there in 1845).* Large tablet with angels in low relief, elaborately detailed, hovering over a helmet, sword, plume of feathers, and other military insignia. – Catherine Scott † 1831, by *J. Bacon*. Wide garlanded urn in low relief. – Robert Scott † 1807, by *R. Tomlinson*. Confused representation of a shipwreck. – Mary Gaulter, and her baby son, † 1819; the pensive husband sits in a chair next to another chair with a shroud across it; no signature.

PEARTREE CONGREGATIONAL CHURCH, Peartree Green. 1838. Gabled front of yellow brick with high neo-Dec window and pretty spirelet.

ST MARY, St Monica Road, Sholing. 1866–7 by *Colson*. Small; odd SW turret with a stem of cross-shaped section, changing in a curious way into a spirelet of octagonal section, with open lancet belfry lights in the angles. Prettily set in a pine-backed churchyard in a strange Victorian rural backwater of suburban Southampton.

ST MARY EXTRA CEMETERY, Portsmouth Road, Sholing. Chapels of 1879 by *W. H. Mitchell*, Anglican and dissenting end-to-end, with central two-arched porch and turret, the

* Cf. Bazzanti's other monument in St Mary, South Stoneham, p. 573.

Anglican one with an apse. Red brick hotted up by black-brick patterning and scaly slated roofs. – ENTRANCE GATES. Rectangular patterned iron gates; iron screens in rectangular stone frames to either side. 1955 by *L. Berger*, the City Architect.

ST CHRISTOPHER, Hinkler Road, Thornhill. 1960 by *Sebastian Comper*. Small brick rectangle with neo-Tudor side windows and E triple lancet. – (PULPIT of 1781.)

HOLY TRINITY, Weston Lane, Weston. 1865 by *A. Bedborough*. Moderate-sized village church with N aisle and N flanking tower and spire: neo-Dec, steep and spiky, superficially picturesque. Internal profusion of foliated and symbolically carved capitals.

ST MARK, Weston Grove Road, Woolston. 1863, enlarged 1866 and 1867, by *William White*. Complex plan: four-bay nave, chancel, narrow N and very wide S aisles, pseudo-transepts (i.e. with high transverse roof-lines and gables, but extending no further than the widths of the aisles), and S chapel with small polygonal apse. A tower and spire at the NW corner were intended, but built only to about aisle height; without this crowning feature the exterior looks rather a muddle of rubble walls, gables, and steep slated roofs. The interior is confused spatially, but the treatment of the wall surfaces is an intriguing exercise in the effect of brick polychromy. The nave arcades have stone quatrefoiled piers and wide stone capitals with varied and profuse foliage; the arches are all of brick, the inner orders brown, the outer red, the spandrels of a motley pattern of brown, red, and blue. Above is a tall clerestory, with four-light geometrical windows (repeated as blank openings into the transepts, the arches into which are simply E continuations of the nave arcades), the wall spaces in between them decorated in strip and motley brick patterns. The chancel arch is of red brick in its inner order, yellow in its outer (the reverse of the colouring in the nave arcades), with brickwork patterning above and a brickwork cross high in the gable. The five-light E window and three-light aisle windows have tracery mostly in complicated geometrical patterns (with brick hoods outside – typical William White motifs). The internal decoration of the chancel was probably similar to that of the nave, but the chancel walls have been recently whitewashed, as have also those of the S chapel apse. High Victorian polychromy like this at Woolston (and, on a much more splendid scale, at Lyndhurst) may still be anathema to some people, but it is crazy to cover it over, perhaps irretrievably, and so make the church into a shapeless agglomeration of whitewashed spaces. No more wall surface ought to be whitened. – STAINED GLASS. In the S chapel apse, their effect somewhat suppressed by the surrounding whitewash, four small lights with figures of the Evangelists, 1887 by *Morris & Co.*

ST PATRICK (R.C.), Portsmouth Road, Woolston. 1938 by *W. C. Mangan*, gutted 1940, restored 1950. Basically a simple brick church with the architectural effect concentrated in the big rectangular W tower, which is covered in modernistic motifs vaguely reminiscent of Gothic.

PRESBYTERIAN CHURCH, Portsmouth Road, Woolston. 1876 by *Barker*. Red brick, High Gothic. The tower is the chief accent in the drab centre of Woolston: octagonal upper storey with tall lancets on the main sides, ending below small gables rising above the parapet of the stumpy spire.

PUBLIC BUILDINGS

POLICE STATION, Bitterne Village. 1965 by *L. Berger*, the City Architect. Two-storeyed, brick; simple ranges of single-paned windows, the sort of design that depends almost entirely on its proportions, which here are good.

PUBLIC LIBRARY, Bitterne Village. 1963 by *L. Berger*. Straightforward. Single glass-fronted storey with slated fascia. Mentioned because it groups well with the church of Christ the King.

ITCHEN GRAMMAR SCHOOL, Middle Road, Bitterne. In three parts; the original 1927 in watery neo-Wrenaissance; a dreadful annexe of 1939 in lumpy brick; and, in between, a sensitively designed block of 1964 by *Richard Sheppard, Robson & Partners*, of three storeys, brick-faced, but with broad continuous glazing on the two upper floors and a boarded fascia; lower storey largely open-sided circulation space; very attractive two-storey link with the original building, with a small glass-fronted room bridging an archway.

BITTERNE PARK SECONDARY SCHOOL, Dimond Road. 1965 by *R. Sheppard, Robson & Partners*. One to three storeys, on a sloping site. Harsh yellow brick. Varied fenestration, mostly in thin strips on the external façades, with thin concrete lintels and widely spaced mullions. Roof-line on varied planes. Courtyard with partly open lower storeys on two sides, cobbled expanses and young trees growing; stepways leading up to another, smaller, more irregular courtyard; glimpses of an immense panorama to the NW, over the woods of North Stoneham to the distant downs. A compelling, sensitively designed building, subtly related to the topography.

HIGHTOWN SECONDARY SCHOOL, off Bursledon Road, Thornhill. 1963 by *L. Berger*. Two to four storeys; brick, glass and vitreous panelling; fairly even skyline. Small courtyard around an ornamental sheet of water, hemmed in by glass-walled classrooms on three sides and with an open lower storey, raised slightly above the level of the pond, on the fourth.

WESTON PARK SECONDARY SCHOOL, The Grove, Weston. Boys' block 1960 by *Lyons, Israel & Ellis*, regular, three-storeyed, with cement-faced fascia and floor ends; thin vertical supports. The patterning of the windows, with fairly small panes and thick framing, is the chief accent. Small low service storey asymmetrically placed. Irregular grouping of buildings to the N, linked by a short glazed corridor. A pleasant, restful but strongly detailed design. The girls' block is by *Howard V. Lobb & Partners*, 1957.

GLENFIELD INFANTS SCHOOL, Rosyth Road, Bitterne. 1952 by *Howard V. Lobb & Partners*. Irregular, lowly, single-storey brick and glazed building, set against half-wild wooded slopes in a suburban backwater.

ITCHEN COMMUNITY CENTRE, Merry Oak Road, Bitterne. By *Martin, Pilch & Harris*, 1964. A pleasant single-storey building in two parts of differing heights, with tall rectangular windows between stretches of brick façades.

CLOCK TOWER, originally built in 1889 by *S. Kelway Pope* at the intersection of Above Bar and New Road in the city centre, removed in 1936 to Bitterne Park Triangle (at the E end of Cobden Bridge), where it looks very effective and right in scale. A reduced and fussed-up version of an E.E. steeple with triple lancets on each face; drinking fountains at ground level.

GENERAL

CLAUSENTUM. Bitterne, Roman Clausentum, was a small port which grew up on a promontory within a bend of the river Itchen. Most of the site is now beneath the modern suburbs of Southampton. Excavation has shown that the settlement flourished in the C1 and C2, but apparently declined during the C3. Towards the end of the C4, probably as a result of the military reorganization of Count

Theodosius, the site was surrounded by a stone wall, built on piles, and a ditch – parts of both can still be seen near the Manor House. At this time the outer earthwork, which cuts off the promontory and was probably already in existence, was increased in size. It is probable that the newly defended site served as one of the 'Saxon Shore' forts, replacing Portchester. The only internal building which has been extensively excavated is a Roman bath block, which lies to the W of the manor house.

BITTERNE MANOR. The site of Clausentum was occupied by a medieval manor house of the Bishops of Winchester. This was largely rebuilt in the C19, bomb-damaged, and reconstructed as a block of flats by *Herbert Collins*, 1951–5. Some medieval walling, including a C13 lancet and square-headed windows of uncertain date, can still be seen. The rest is in a simplified neo-Tudor style, with rubble walls and mullioned windows, not at all bogus in feeling. Set amid carefully preserved trees beside the tidal river, it seems a real oasis in a rather dreary part of the city.

Few of the picturesque country estates which once abounded in this area (and which were described in rich terms in early C19 guide books) survive in any measure. The mansion at MAYFIELD PARK has gone, but the grounds are maintained as an open space, with an attractive Early Victorian LODGE in Weston Lane, two-gabled, with castellated bay windows and porch, and windows glazed in a curious pattern of intersecting eye shapes. In the more open parkland to the S is an OBELISK, erected in 1810 by William Chamberlayne M.P., of Weston Grove near by,* to commemorate Charles James Fox, whom he admired. Tall, plain, on a square base with three steps.

PEARTREE HOUSE, N of Peartree Green. Built by 1617, but refaced *c.*1800. Charming castellated S façade, stuccoed, of two storeys and seven bays, the three centre bays recessed, but with a ground-floor colonnade of five neo-Tudor arches. The short E façade has a central projecting tower with a Gothick window above and a summer-room in the lower storey. The house, hemmed in by suburban development, is well maintained as an old people's home.

*William Chamberlayne is also commemorated in the Gas Column (p. 555), and his monument is in Jesus Church, p. 593. He was a great friend of William Cobbett, who frequently visited Weston Grove (cf. *Rural Rides*); the house stood near the shore S of Woolston, where there is now a Royal Naval depot.

Finally the housing estates (all designed by *L. Berger*, the City Architect).

HAREFIELD ESTATE. Mostly developed 1949–60 in a garden-city manner, to quite pleasant effect, with the usual plenitude of grass strips frequently widening into small greens and, happily, plenty of trees preserved and planted. The NEIGHBOURHOOD CENTRE, 1964, is different in character and impressive; canopied shopping parade with two storeys of flats above; five-storeyed blocks of flats in L-form making, with one end of the shopping parade, a small open courtyard, the flats in the locally favourite brown-purple brick. More similar blocks behind, forming a tight group in a big sloping area of park-like open space with many old trees. Unfortunately, with all the open space about, there do not appear to be many expanses large enough, and not bisected by roads, to be of much real use for recreation.

THORNHILL ESTATE. Mostly built 1955–65. On a hilly site, the housing predominantly of two-storey terraces and blocks of four or five storeys. Generous grass expanses and green wedges giving a superficially garden-city effect, but the densities of the blocks of housing in between the grassed area are evidently fairly tight, and the effect of the whole is rather muddled. It is not pulled together by the NEIGHBOURHOOD CENTRE, 1963, well-placed on a sloping site, with two three-storeyed blocks placed like an L, the shops behind colonnaded canopies.

But what has imprinted the Thornhill Estate on the townscape of eastern Southampton (and on the landscape of a good deal of the adjoining part of Hampshire as well) is the three fifteen-storey blocks of flats of 1964–5 (HIGHTOWN TOWER, MEREDITH TOWER, and DUMBLETON'S TOWER) at the easternmost, highest, part of the estate. They are almost rectangular in shape (each façade has a slight stepping beside the lift-shaft) with sheer, impressive ends, the central vertical ranges of windows flanked by wide expanses of brick façade (yellow brick at Hightown, grey brick on the other two towers); the roof-line is boldly marked by a wide concrete fascia and a thinner concrete rail above a narrow gap. The long façades are faced in asbestos panelling between the gallery recesses; the ground storeys have a mosaic of fragmented grey rubble. The surrounding two- and four-storey development is not happily related to the towers, but the towers undoubtedly have a majestic urban character. But is it visually or socially right to place buildings of such hugely urban scale, with such a concentration of population, far on the suburban fringe?

TOWNHILL PARK ESTATE, Midanbury. 1965–6. In a shallow valley; the usual Southampton mixture of two- and five-storey housing, the groupings of each type satisfactory in themselves, but the mixture muddled. Five-storey housing, some of it in acceptable rectangular blocks in currently fashionable harsh yellow bricks, predominates.

WESTON. A muddle of early post-war housing round the old small village centre, which has been mostly obliterated. Effective NEIGHBOURHOOD CENTRE, 1959. Three-storeyed blocks with shopping colonnades at r. angles (the façades on the outsides of the angles); five-storeyed block making a visual stop to the S. Good management of varying levels and of pedestrian circulation. The Victorian spire of Holy Trinity rises to the N.

In 1965 work started on development at WESTON SHORE, facing Southampton Water, including a twenty-five-storey block (by *Ryder & Yates*, in association with *L. Berger*, the City Architect) and five fourteen-storey blocks (by *L. Berger*). Completion 1967. They will form effective landmarks from the water.

SOUTH BADDESLEY

3090

ST MARY. 1858, but still like a church of 1830. Lancet windows. Transepts, a tiny chancel, and a starved W tower. Round the chancel arch fretwork tracery, rustic and jolly.

NEWTOWN PARK, ½ m. WNW. A splendid façade. Three l. and three r. bays, rendered, and in the middle a recessed giant portico of ashlar. Unfluted Ionic columns and pediment. A date 1792 on a roof-slate is reported.

WALHAMPTON HOUSE. The total impression is neo-Georgian. Five-bay centre and three-bay projecting wings. Raised quoins and panelled parapet.*

NEALE OBELISK. By *George Draper* of Chichester to the memory of Admiral Neale, who died in 1840. The obelisk forms the end of the vista along Lymington High Street.

*But the house was built originally in 1711, and the E wing is by *Norman Shaw*, 1884. The neo-Georgian effect is due to the substantial rebuilding of the C18 portions in 1912–14. With this *T. Mawson* is connected. Fine C18 shell GROTTO in the grounds (Nicholas Plumley).

1090 SOUTHBOURNE*

St Katharine. The church of 1881–2 has a chancel of 1899–1900 by *A. Birt*. E.E.; no tower. Chancel with lancets. Two clerestory lancets over each arcade spandrel. – (MONUMENT. Mary Buxton † 1916. Bronze inscription by the Arts and Crafts artist *Harold Stabler*. NT)

(All Saints, Castlemain Avenue. 1913–14 by *J. Oldrid Scott & Son* and *C. T. Miles*. – Ornate FONT. – STAINED GLASS. E window by *Percy Bacon*. NT)

Immanuel Congregational Church, Southbourne Road. 1930 by *Frederic W. Lawrence*. A good example of its date; blocky brickwork with round-headed windows and a square tower. Churchy interior with tripartite 'Venetian' arches to both choir and sanctuary. Byzantine capitals. – STATUE of St Francis in the forecourt by *Mrs G. F. Watts*.

Douglas House Hospital, Southbourne Road. 1898, and the usual slap-happy mixture of brick, tile-hanging and half-timber, but on the E side, incongruously set in a half-timbered wall, is a delightful surprise: the main entrance of Stourfield House, built *c.*1766, long before any other houses at Southbourne. Corinthian porch with a straight cornice, raised on a rusticated basement and reached by two sweeping flights with iron balustrades. The basement door is round-headed with a big keystone. The STABLES are plain work of the same date.

Southbourne, now part of Bournemouth, began as a separate and select resort, laid out for large mansions from 1857 by *C. C. Creeke*, with its own (long destroyed) pier. In Belle Vue Road is Foxholes (now W. T. A. Guest House), designed in 1874–6 by *F. P. Cockerell* for Henry Reeve, editor of the *Greville Memoirs* and the *Edinburgh Review*. Big graceless stucco villa, almost styleless, except for the bold Shaw-style loggias filling the gables at second-floor level. Near by are four houses in the Voysey manner, obviously by the same hand: No. 257 and (particularly good) No. 108 Belle Vue Road, and No. 38 and the house opposite in St Catherine's Road.

Next to St Katharine's church are two handsome neo-Wren works by *G. A. B. Livesay* (who was killed in the First World War): the Vicarage, 1907–8, and the Parish Hall, 1904–5, the latter with segment-headed window bays rising

* I owe much of the entries on Southbourne to Mr Taylor.

above the eaves. Also by *Livesay* is ST KATHARINE'S HOME, Church Road, 1910–11, tile-hung with Venetian windows. In Dalmeny Road is the derelict MOUNT PLEASANT SCHOOL, *c.*1891–3, Dutch-gabled, with tiled voussoirs to doors and windows.

HENGISTBURY HEAD PROMONTORY FORT. The neck of the promontory is cut off by two lines of banks and ditches. The outer line appears to be the lesser of the two earthworks. Only the bank of this feature, some 5 ft high, is now visible. The inner defences were on a more massive scale, with a bank still 12 ft high in places and a ditch 45 ft wide and 12 ft deep. Excavation within the area enclosed by the ramparts has revealed traces of occupation covering the period from the earliest iron-using cultures in Britain until the Roman occupation. *See p. 831*

Also on the promontory are seven BOWL BARROWS, and on the low ground NW two further bowl barrows. One of the latter covered a cremation burial in an Early Bronze Age collared urn accompanied by an incense cup, beads of gold and amber, and a small gold pendant in the form of a halberd – a miniature copy of the metal shafted weapons of the Central European Bronze Age. The group may be assigned to the first phase of the Wessex Culture (*c.*1650–1500 B.C.).

SOUTH GORLEY [DL] *1010*

1½ m. NE of Ibsley

(CUCKOO HILL. Built in 1902–6 for himself by *Heywood Sumner*, the designer of the sgraffito murals in St Agatha, Portsmouth (p. 433), and also a noted archaeologist. The site is on the edge of a heathy part of the New Forest. Materials were all as local as possible: bricks from Blissford a short distance away, tiles from Creekmoor near Poole, shingle from near-by beaches, and gravel and sand from the site. Homely gabled composition, H-shaped, with simple bargeboards and a strange bow window to each wing. Near by is a COTTAGE, also by *Sumner*, 1905–6.)

SOUTH HAYLING *see* HAYLING ISLAND

SOUTHSEA *see* PORTSMOUTH, pp. 426, 440, 443, 444, 445, 446, 449, 459

SOUTH STONEHAM *see* SOUTHAMPTON, pp. 573, 581

2040 SOUTH TIDWORTH

South Tidworth is two things: mansion and estate church and Tidworth Barracks.

ST MARY. Built at the expense of Sir John Kelk of Tidworth House in 1879–80. The architect was *John Johnson*. Externally the church does not appear very large. It is the interior that is sensational, in scale as in everything else. Also externally it is rather a crotchety church, and the interior has absolutely nothing of that. It is the bell-tower that is so perverse and wilful. Round and thin with a round, extremely elongated spire. And this thin round beacon stands on a mighty, far-projecting mid-buttress. Otherwise the church is of small rock-faced brown stones and has lancets and plate tracery and quite some dogtooth. The S transept is balanced on the N side by the vestry with two very high chimneys, one on the W, the other on the E wall. The S porch prepares for the interior, with its size, its many-columned entrance with much stiff-leaf, and the blank arcading l. and r. with yet more stiff-leaf. The interior consists of a strikingly high, short, sumptuous nave of three bays and a yet more sumptuous chancel. The nave has tall quatrefoil piers of grey, veined marble, stiff-leaf capitals, and upper shafts with stiff-leaf to support the principals of the steeply pointed roof. The aisle bays are marked off one from the other by steep rising half-arches. The chancel arch goes all out with stiff-leaf and dogtooth, and the chancel is marble-shafted with more dogtooth. To the organ chamber and the S chapel are large three-light screens like very large windows. Their tracery is geometrical, but with just one touch of Dec. Surely a church like this is as valid a monument of architecture as any of the Middle Ages or the C17 or C18.

TIDWORTH HOUSE. Built for Thomas Assheton Smith about 1825–30.* Of this the exterior reveals nothing, except perhaps the Georgian-looking service wing at the back, though its archway frontispiece is patently later. Indeed, the building is also said to date from *c.*1860. Of that time probably the central hall. It runs through both floors, has much bare wall and on each side just one motif: a Tuscan aedicule on which there is an upper balcony. On one side the Tuscan columns frame the entrance to the staircase, which runs up between solid walls and under small glass domes. The ashlar façades of the house to the S and the E cannot be earlier than *c.*1850 either. The S side

*'About twenty years ago' (Moody 1846).

is nine bays wide. The centre is an attached portico of freely detailed giant Ionic columns, only their bottom parts fluted. The columns carry a pediment. The three central first-floor windows are arched. The windows in the side parts are quite simple. The E front is yet further removed from the Georgian tradition. The central portico here has no pediment. The ground-floor windows have Gibbs surrounds (is that 1830 ?), the upper-floor windows elaborate, wholly Victorian surrounds. The porch at the back looks later still – of the time of the service frontispiece.

TIDWORTH BARRACKS, the camp, was started in 1903. The older buildings can be easily distinguished from the newer. The camp, as against, say, Aldershot, seems to have been leafy from the beginning.*

ST MICHAEL. 1912 by *Douglas Hoyland*. Really terribly lifeless. All terracotta, smooth and untextured. Perpendicularish windows. Bell-turret over the crossing. Transepts.

ST GEORGE AND ST PATRICK (R.C.). 1912 by *G. L. W. Blount*. Flint, low and long, with a short NE tower. The interior, with its white walls and its complicated thin, black timber roof, reminds one somehow of churches in Africa.

(LLOYDS BANK is a small early work of *Sir Edward Maufe*, *c*.1915. NT)

SOUTH WARNBOROUGH

7040

ST ANDREW. Nave and chancel and bell-turret. Norman N doorway with an order of lozenges broken at an angle. One Norman S window. E.E. chancel with three closely set stepped E lancets. Dec single-light nave N window and Dec S aisle W window, the latter re-used, as the S aisle is by *Street*, 1870. – ROOD SCREEN. The loft alone is preserved; but that is a rare survival. – HELM (chancel E). – (STAINED GLASS. Some C15 and C16 fragments.) – PLATE. Cup and Paten, 1689. – MONUMENTS. Big tomb-chest with shields in quatrefoils. Against the E wall behind it Brass to Robert White, kneeling. He died in 1512. – In the chancel N wall Perp recess of stone, of a type more usual in Purbeck marble. Against the back wall small kneeling figures of Sir Thomas White, wife, and fourteen plus six children.

*A master plan for future development has been drawn up by the *Austin-Smith, Salmon, Lord Partnership*, and work is already in progress on MARRIED QUARTERS to their design. Some three-storey flats, but mainly pleasant two-storey houses in staggered terraces (NT).

He died in 1566. No trace of Renaissance; or was an Easter Sepulchre appropriated? – Above two small Late Elizabethan tablets with kneeling effigies. – In the chancel also, on the E wall, a very ornate Elizabethan bracket. – On the S wall another tablet, this with two kneeling men, Late Elizabethan.

6000 SOUTHWICK [DL]

An engaging, enigmatic place in the lowlands N of Portsdown Hill, less than three miles from the edge of Portsmouth but seemingly far from any city. The Augustinian priory, which had been founded in 1133 within the castle of Portchester (p. 377), was transferred to Southwick *c.*1145–53; it became influential in the vicinity and was instrumental in the foundation of the remarkable church of St Thomas, now the cathedral, in Portsmouth (p. 393) and also in that of the Domus Dei (now the Garrison Church). At the Dissolution, some of the priory buildings were transformed into an important country house, which was burnt in 1750 and replaced by a house on a new site *c.*1812 (Prosser); this in its turn was burnt and replaced by the present house *c.*1841. The estate, with the whole village, remained a unit, free from any suburban development, until the house was taken over during the Second World War to accommodate H.M.S. Dryad (the School of Navigation), transferred from Portsmouth Dockyard (p. 412). In 1944 the house became the headquarters for General Eisenhower as Supreme Allied Commander, and the final orders for the landing in France on D-Day were given there.

ST JAMES. Rebuilt 1566, according to a tablet on the external E gable wall of the chancel, by John Whyte (the Earl of Southampton's servant, to whom the priory had been granted at the Dissolution), and so a rare example of a post-Reformation Tudor church. But part of the S nave wall is medieval, and there are several other medieval features re-set, some at least probably from Southwick Priory rather than from the preceding parish church. But first and foremost the church is remarkable for its FURNISHINGS, and these, exceptionally, shall be described first. Until lately it was one of the best examples of an 'unrestored' church in the South of England, with box pews, three-decker pulpit, gallery, classical reredos, and hardly anything post-Georgian. Alas, in the 1950s the nave pews, having been found to be worm-eaten beyond repair, were cleared away and replaced by polished open pews which are about as incongruous as any seating could be in such a church. Despite this depletion, it remains a delightful interior, still with a pre-Victorian atmosphere. The GALLERY has a simple painted panelled front, supported by twisted wooden posts. – Of the three-decker PULPIT the two lower parts are in the same simple painted panelled pattern as the gallery, but the main part is probably coeval with the church's rebuilding, a half-octagon with three tiers of panelling, the upper tier with simple vertical round-headed incisions. – Two family BOX PEWS, large and comfortable, fill much of the chancel, the southern with internal subdivision. – The COMMUNION RAIL has thin twisted balusters. – The REREDOS is the showpiece of the church, with a central C18 painting of cherubs and doves floating in the sky, and a pair of fluted pilasters, supporting a section of entablature, on either side, the whole composition surmounted by a short, delicately wrought balustrade, with little pedestals supporting urns and an emblematic representation including cherubs and garlands. Much of this is painted to simulate marble, enlivened with gilt. – Plain dark PANELLING lines the sanctuary on either side of the reredos. The delightful, unrestored atmosphere is heightened by the rough texture of the internal walls, painted not in white but in very light grey, and by the plastered ceilings, coved in the nave and chancel, flat in the N aisle. – The FONT is late C12, large, octagonal, with pairs of pointed arched panels on each face, and a C19 base. – PLATE. Silver-gilt Set of 1691. – MONUMENTS. In the N chapel arch the tomb of John Whyte, the rebuilder of the church, † 1567, and his wife † 1548. Tomb-chest with completely Gothic decoration; three panels with cusped quatrefoils containing shields and cusped vertical panels in between. On top are BRASSES of the couple and their children, with shields. Naïve and clumsy classical surround, with central pediment not so wide as the tomb, and columns with marked entasis on either side, each supporting a small pedimented section of entablature. Three small figures with shields surmount the composition of the chancel side. The altar tomb may have come from the priory, or have been conservatively wrought in 1548; the surround certainly does not pre-date the rebuilding of the church. – Pedimented tablet to Edward Wynn, servant to Richard Norton of Southwick House, † 1748, signed *James Stubington* of Bishops Waltham.

Now for the fabric. The N arcade has two wide bays and one much narrower E bay, coarse Late Tudor Gothic with depressed arches of two chamfered orders, and octagonal piers with simple moulded capitals. There is a similar arch from chancel to N chapel, but no chancel arch, the only structural division between the nave and narrower chancel being a cross-beam surmounted by solid walling in the gable (on which is affixed, facing the nave, a text board). The E window is three-light Perp, probably C15 work re-set; one of the two three-light square-headed S chancel windows has the date 1566 inscribed on the stonework. The N aisle and chapel have a continuous N wall and no arch between them, but the chapel is wider than the aisle (because of the chancel being narrower than the nave). The aisle and chapel windows are all of Tudor type with flat-arched cuspless lights in square frames. At the E end of the S wall of the nave is a recess partly accommodating the pulpit and its stairway, framed by moulded stonework forming a flat arch (obviously from the priory) and containing a small re-set two-light cinquefoiled window. Further W is a two-light C14 window with ogee trefoiled tracery (probably *in situ*), and a former S porch, now a vestry and kept locked, is said to contain parts of C13 wall arcades, with Purbeck marble shafts, from the priory. At the W end of the S wall is another two-light ogee trefoiled window, lighting the stairway to the gallery. The tower has a C14 W doorway of two chamfered orders with a hood-mould, and a three-light reticulated W window. But the walling in which these are set is finished in chequerwork pattern, with stone and knapped flints, probably later than the C14 – so that either the doorway and window are re-set or the wall has been refaced. The rest of the tower is wholly of post-medieval date; it is rectangular (the shorter side W–E) and set within the pre-existing nave, leaving narrow spaces between it and the older N and S walls, occupied by gallery staircases. Externally the upper stage of the tower, with square double bell-openings and battlemented parapet, seems to ride on the W extremity of the nave roof like a stone version of a traditional Hampshire wooden bell-turret. It could be of any date from the later C16 to the C18. Finally, in the angle of wall at the junction of the N aisle and N chapel is a pair of CAPITALS, obviously from Southwick Priory, with finely executed crocket foliage and intermediate leaves, of the size to fit on to large shafts; the capitals are joined corner to corner and the adjacent crocketed leaves merge into each other, showing that they had always been joined like that. They must have come from a large pier which had a cluster of shafts around it.

SOUTHWICK PRIORY. Almost a total loss above ground. What survives is a section of wall, much patched in post-medieval times, with the remains of eight semicircular wall shafts surmounted, at no very great height, by round capitals. The easternmost of these (a quarter capital, formerly at the corner of a room) is little damaged and has simple scalloped decoration. These date from the establishment of the priory or soon after, and must have been vaulting-shafts in the undercroft of a relatively long building, possibly the refectory. Between two of the shafts are the remains of a fireplace, probably early C14, with a moulded octagonal capital supporting one end of the mantelpiece; this must have been a tight fit upwards into one of the bays of the vaulted space. There is also a re-set C14 chamfered doorway, in a part of the walling tampered with since the Reformation, and, above it, a fragment of a vaulting-rib, keeled, with hollows to the sides. To the N of the remains is an irregular wooded hollow; to the S and E many suggestive bumps and terracings in the ground, which could indicate foundations of buildings or, possibly, the remains of formal gardens attached to the post-Reformation mansion. Considering the regional importance of the Priory (p. 604), the site ought to be investigated.

H.M.S. DRYAD. The centrepiece is SOUTHWICK HOUSE, which in its present form is by *Sydney Howell*, *c*.1841. But a print of the old house suggests that the present building is largely based on the older one, with a third storey added. The garden (S) front has a central broad bow rising through all three storeys, three bays of windows on either side, and three windows on each floor within the bow. The bow arrangement and window disposition are derived from the earlier house. Along the length of the ground floor is a wide stone veranda curving round with the bow, supported by Ionic columns singly or in pairs, in a rhythm of 1, 2, 2, 1 (angle with the bow), 1, 1, 1 (angle with the bow), 2, 2, 1. A similar veranda, with the exact arrangement of the colonnade, existed in the earlier house, so that the present one is either the same or a replica. The windows have typically Early Victorian moulded frames, with slightly projecting pediments supported on scrolled brackets on the first floor – embellishments not on the house before the fire. The whole building is cemented, with quoin pattern on the angles. The E front is of five bays, the centre part, with three bays projecting slightly and containing the main entrance, protected by a wide porte-cochère resting on a peristyle Ionic colonnade and surmounted by a balustrade – another feature carried over (except the balustrade) from the earlier house. The N front is curious: the centrepiece is a canted bay window rising only to two storeys, there being a gap in the façade above the second storey between the three-storey, three-bay end parts. To the NW, near the stables, is a short Italianate campanile, with tall shallow panels on the sides, double rounded top lights, and a stumpy spire, cemented. Internally the show features are the hall-passage leading from the entrance to the central stair-hall, flanked by free-standing dark egyptianizing marble-coloured columns, and the stair-hall itself. The flying staircase rises through two storeys to a rectangular clerestory lantern, the roof of which is embellished with circular tapering leaf patterns suggesting fan-vaulting.

Around the house a hotchpotch of buildings has accumulated in the last twenty-five years. Among them some seemly new structures are rising at the time of writing: the W.R.N.S. QUARTERS, a rectangular seven-storey block with a five-bay grid pattern of glazing and aluminium panelling, with wide vertical concrete-faced subdivisions, and projecting framed staircases at either end; RATINGS' QUARTERS, two long three-storeyed blocks, with continuous external glazing and vitreous panelling between the concrete floors except on the ends, where there is brick infilling, and with wide white-painted boarded fascias; and the ADMINISTRATION BLOCK, four-storeyed, of concrete floor and round pier construction, the piers set behind the external glazing. All these are by the Architects' Department of the *Ministry of Public Building and Works* (*Naval Works*).

THE VILLAGE. The residential quarters of H.M.S. Dryad are desolately suburban, but fortunately kept separate from Southwick village, which is absolutely unspoiled except for the traffic. No building needs separate mention; it is sufficient to generalize that there are timber-framed cottages, many of them thatched; C18 brick-fronted houses, small and medium-sized; and two or three Early Victorian houses of flint with brown brick dressings and gables (including the SCHOOL, originally of 1845). In the background are black-boarded barns. There seems to be nothing at all later than *c.*1850; and the village remains under a single ownership. There is good townscape in the centre of the village – reached up a brief hill from the S: a short widening street closely built with varied houses, half-ended by the church with the W tower. But most of the other houses are set rather formlessly and intermittently along streets that make a kind of elongated grid; two long, closely parallel ones running E–W and two others, wide apart, running N–S. This form suggests a small medieval planned town, or at least the tentative outline of one which may never have grown to the expected extent. Southwick had a market in the Middle Ages and obviously the priory stimulated its prosperity, but any tendency to develop in more recent times has been restrained by squirarchical ownership.

FORT SOUTHWICK. *See* p. 387.

SPARSHOLT 4030

ST STEPHEN. Much of the church is by *Butterfield*, 1883, e.g. the timbered upper part of the tower. The arch towards the nave is Perp. The N side is all Butterfield and looks rather like part of an Anglican convent or a rather rigid public school. Simple early C13 priest's doorway. S doorway dated 1631, and not discarded by Butterfield. The S arcade is of *c.*1200: round piers, round abaci, round arches with two slight chamfers. – SOUTH DOOR. Also of 1631, and very attractive. – ORGAN SCREEN. Is it late C17? Three widely spaced columns. – SCULPTURE. Three Netherlandish panels of the second quarter of the C16. The Temptation of Christ ought to be looked for. – PLATE. Paten on foot, 1715; Almsdish, 1766; Cup and Cover Paten, 1826. – Also, from Lainston, Cup and Cover Paten, 1628; Paten on foot, 1723. – Also a C13 Pewter Chalice and Paten from the grave of a priest in the church.

(MANOR HOUSE. Gothick façade with angle towers, three bays between, pointed windows and battlements. NMR)

STANBRIDGE EARLS 3020

1½ m. NW of Romsey

Nearly symmetrical C17 ashlar façade with renewed wooden mullioned and transomed windows. Timber-framed gables, large, three smaller, large. The porch is in a characteristic way just out of the middle position. In the gable of the porch the date 1658. However, at the back, on the ground floor, is a length of flint walling with four two-light early C16 windows. Only one of them has cusped lights.

7020
STEEP

ALL SAINTS. The exterior is dominated by the bell-turret of 1875 (*R. W. Edis*), partly tile-hung. The earliest features are the N doorway with two continuous slight chamfers, the N aisle wall with small lancets, and the chancel with S lancets – all this early C13. Early C14 S doorway and nave W window. The story as seen in the church is more interesting. It starts with the S aisle, still as narrow as it was made late in the C12, when the arcade was built. Circular piers, trumpet capitals, circular abaci, round single-chamfered arches. The W arches are a C14 replacement. The N aisle is, as we have seen, early C13. The capitals are now moulded, the arches have two slight chamfers, and the aisle is much wider. – FONT. Late C13, raw, with big pointed-trefoiled arches. – NORTH DOOR. With tracery; Perp. – (Excellent ORGAN CASE by *Edward Barnsley*. RH) – ALTAR CROSS set free of a copper panel with a wild abstract relief. By *Tanya Ashken*, *c.*1962. – PLATE. Cup and Cover Paten, 1568.

COLDHAYES, 1¼ m. NE. By *Waterhouse*, 1869. Oddly free and undisciplined. The motifs are partly English but mostly French. The latter e.g. the basket arches to the window lights and the half-hipped dormers with exposed timbers to carry the eaves. Decorated Tudor brick chimneys.

(BY THE CHURCH, just E, by *W. F. Unsworth*, a Street pupil, for himself, *c.*1900. Genuine C17, L-shaped, brick, tile-hung, with dormers, but Unsworth's loving care has made it an Edwardian fantasy. Big square chimney in the angle. Cf. Unsworth's Woodhambury, Woodton, Surrey, built also for himself. NT)

(THE PLATTS is a typical house dating from *c.*1905 by the same architect (as *Unsworth, Son & Triggs*). Quite large, with brick and tile-hanging in the early Lutyens style. Round-arched central porch and some half-timbering on the garden side. NT)

(There are two pleasant houses near by by the local architects, *Carter, Salaman, MacIver & Upfold*. KETTLEBROOK MEADOWS of 1955 is quite large, flint-faced below, timber clad above. The main cruciform part is joined by a bedroom wing to the projecting studio over the garage. ASHFORD COTTAGE, below Stoner Hill, for Lord Horder, is a split-level villa of brick, the bedroom floor clad in timber. NT)

MILLPONDS COTTAGE. By *Kenneth Claxton*, 1964. On stilts, and nearly all glass-walled.

BEDALES SCHOOL. *See* p. 97.

STEVENTON

5040

ST NICHOLAS. Nave and chancel and bell-turret. Essentially of the early C13, but with a puzzling arrangement at the W end, where the W tower with a W lancet and an early C13 doorway later inserted (it cuts into the sill of the lancet) is embraced by bays which are not W bays of aisles, because there are no aisles. But the arches around here all have just one slight chamfer. So has the chancel arch, and the chancel, with its small lancets, is again no doubt early C13. L. and r. of the chancel arch are flat reredos niches for lay altars. In one of these are remains of WALL PAINTING. The chancel vault looks early C19. It is of plaster with wooden ribs. – SCREEN. Rather flimsy C17 screen, now near the W end. Simple geometrical patterns. – SCULPTURE. Saxon cross-shaft, assigned by Sir Thomas Kendrick to the late C9 and connected with Prior's Barton Winchester and Colerne in Wiltshire. One panel with two intertwined dragons, another with very wild interlace. – PLATE. Chalice and Paten, 1663; Paten, 1722. – MONUMENTS. Anne Austen † 1795, pleasant tablet. – Rev. James Austen † 1819. Gothic, of stone, by *Humphrey Hopper*. – Jane Austen was born at Steventon in 1775.

STEVENTON MANOR. Derelict at the time of writing. By *R. Morrison Marnock*, 1875–6. It cost about £20,000. Flint and stone, with large mullioned and transomed windows. The individual lights are arched and uncusped. This motif was taken from the one wing which remained of the medieval mansion. The wing has a three-storeyed shallow porch with a four-centred head to the entrance and two very large brick chimney-breasts.

ROUND BARROW CEMETERY, in the extreme S of the parish of Overton, just N of the A30 at its junction with a minor road to South Litchfield Grange. This is a linear cemetery of five barrows. The S site is a fine bell barrow 7 ft high and 130 ft in diameter. N of it are first a bowl barrow 118 ft in diameter and 6 ft high and a saucer barrow partly cut through by the building of the former mound and by a second bell barrow. 40 ft N is a further bowl barrow, 90 ft in diameter and 6 ft high.

STOCKBRIDGE

3030

Stockbridge strikes one as a town, with its wide main street and some of the buildings along it. What one does not realize is that there is nothing behind the street either N or S. The street runs W–E across the valley of the river Test.

OLD CHURCH, at the E end of the street. Only the chancel stands. It is of the C13, cf. the chancel arch and the blocked arch to a one-bay S chapel. The W doorway set in the chancel arch is Perp, but there is also, E of the S chapel arch, a round arch with a slight chamfer. This was probably connected with the SEDILIA, and, if so, would date the masonry of the chance late C12 rather than C13.

ST PETER. 1866, the SW steeple 1887. By *Colson*. Some windows of the old church were re-used. The new windows are from plate tracery to Early Dec. Lush N arcade. Tall round piers free Dec foliage. In the transepts and the chancel also large foliage corbels. – FONT. Of the standard Purbeck table-top type, much decayed. – SCULPTURE. Small Crucifixus, C15(?) made up with new parts into a stone cross. – Figural corbels in the vestry. – PLATE. Silver-gilt Chalice and two Patens 1697; Chalices of 1805 and 1813.

Only three buildings require a few words. First the TOWN HALL of 1810, yellow brick, very elementary and without graces Deep eaves and cupola. Then the GROSVENOR HOTEL, also yellow brick, two and a half storeys, five bays, the windows of the first and fifth set in giant arches. Far-projecting porch on (new) Tuscan columns and a whole room above projected with it. Thirdly the WHITE HART, by the old church, whose whole front stands on five thin Tuscan cast-iron columns. The two hotels must also be of the early C19.

ROUND BARROW CEMETERY, 1 m. ESE and just N of the A272. The group consists of fifteen bowl barrows, 25–45 ft in diameter and 6 in.–3 ft in height. One of the group was excavated in 1938. Beneath the centre of the mound was an oval grave containing a crouched inhumation accompanied by a bell beaker and a copper awl. Two cremations were found in the filling of this grave, and a third cremation in a collared urn had been inserted, presumably at a later date, on the periphery of the site. This latter burial was accompanied by a bronze awl and beads of shale, amber, and faience.

WOOLBURY RING, 1¼ m. E. This univallate Iron Age hillfort encloses an oval area of 20 acres. The ramparts have been considerably reduced by ploughing, although they still stand to a height of 10 ft in places. S of the fort on the slope of the hill a length of DITCH is visible – possibly the remains of a Bronze Age boundary ditch.

STOKE CHARITY

4030

ST MICHAEL. The church is of little interest outside, but inside it is chock-a-block with furnishings and especially monuments. Flint; nave and chancel; short bell-turret. What there is of medieval windows is Dec and Perp. On the N side in a doorway re-set zigzag at r. angles to the wall. The church (which is uncommonly well restored and kept) contains to one's surprise a mighty Early Norman N arcade of two bays. The pier is octagonal, but of monstrous girth, and has, like the responds, a capital of many biggish scallops. The arches are round and unmoulded. But what can the small arch mean which opens from the E end of the N aisle to the E? It has one slight chamfer. Is it re-set, or can it be contemporary with the so much more elaborate chancel arch with its zigzag at r. angles to the wall, i.e. can it be Late Norman? The chancel arch is round, and its section is just a single step. The capitals have reeded foliage. And where does the zigzag at r. angles in the outer doorway come from? One of the nave doorways? – PILLAR PISCINA, N aisle. The top of one; C12. – SCULPTURE. Also in the N aisle an almost totally defaced figure, or two parts of two figures. Was it seated? – Mass of St Gregory; late C15. It is rare that in England a stone-carved scene of this kind remained undamaged. But that does not improve the artistic quality of the piece. – WALL PAINTING. Large mid C13 fragment on the N chapel S wall, with much colour preserved and for once not restored. – STAINED GLASS. In the E window very little that is old, in the N chapel windows more fragments. – PLATE. Chalice of 1568. – MONUMENTS. Under the E arch of the N arcade a Purbeck marble tomb-chest with shields in quatrefoils. – In the N chapel plain tomb-chest, but on the lid brasses of Thomas Hampton † 1483, his wife and children. The main figures are 2 ft 8½ in. long. He is in swagger armour. The children on a panel below, a panel of the Trinity at the top. – Also in the chapel tomb-chest with back wall and shallow four-centred arch, all panelled. Cresting on top. This is to John Waller † 1526. – Again in the chapel a plain Jacobean tomb-chest, to Sir Thomas Phelipps † 1626. – In the nave on the S side brass to Thomas Wayte † 1482. The figure, 2 ft 2½ in. long, is almost identical with Thomas Hampton. There was certainly no craving for originality among suppliers of funerary monuments or their customers about 1480. But then, was there about 1780? – In the N aisle at its W end Sir James

Phelypps † 1652. Very elementary tomb-chest and back wall only partially preserved. No figures survive.

6060 STRATFIELD SAYE

STRATFIELD SAYE HOUSE. Stratfield Saye was the first Duke of Wellington's choice, and so it was purchased for him by Parliament after Waterloo in 1817. It was a choice dictated by the excellent state of the farms more than by any special qualities of grandeur or beauty of the house itself. The Duke in fact intended to build a new house on higher ground, the other side of the river. The old house was built by Sir William Pitt, it is said about 1630, but probably ten or fifteen years later. His house was of brick, two-storeyed, long and low. The entrance (W) side had nine bays and two-bay wings projecting by two bays. The façade had as its principal motif two orders of broad pilasters and in the wings raised brick window surrounds of alternating block sizes. The quoins were treated in the same way. The wings end in a big Dutch gable. The heavy Tuscan porch is of 1838, when *Benjamin Wyatt* worked at Stratfield Saye. The character of the columns is still that of Ledoux and his contemporaries in France. Above the porch on the upper floor are thin Ionic columns and a pediment. These are of the date of the façade. The pretty cupola is of 1964, by the present *Duke of Wellington*. The front of the house has in addition two further, outer, wings, and these are of the C18 below, of 1847 above.

The garden (E) side has a longer front. The outer bay with, at the r. angle, its canted bay windows was added by George Pitt, first Lord Rivers, *c.*1775, the conservatory behind the outer l. bay in 1838. It belongs to Wyatt's work.* The rest is again Pitt's. There are two more Dutch gables, and all the windows below them have raised brick surrounds just as on the other side. The centre, in spite of the same windows, is a mid C18 infilling. To it belong the four-column porch and the five-bay pediment.

The entrance hall runs through both floors and has in the lower part attached Ionic columns, continued to support a gallery along the back wall. All this is Lord Rivers's. The ROMAN PAVEMENTS came from Silchester. On the r. of the hall is the library, of the mid C18 (cf. the cornice). The ceiling

*In the conservatory columns collected by the first Duke in France and Italy against his plan to build a new house.

has an uncommon coffering motif. Screen of columns to the S. In the S wing the study with a Rococo ceiling. Rococo also the ceiling of the staircase, though the staircase itself is of the time when the house was built. Square tapering balusters.* In several of the rooms along the garden front more Rococo ceilings. The house also has several rooms decorated with stuck-on prints. The dining room, i.e. the room added by Lord Rivers, has a ceiling copied from Wood's *Palmyra* (cf. Osterley Park and Woburn Abbey).

One room on the upper floor is in the original state of *c.*1640. It is in the l. wing of the W side. The lintel of the fireplace is unmistakable, and behind the door in the panelling is also a fragment of wall painting.

In front of the entrance stands a bronze horse with a dragon. This is by *Matthew Cotes Wyatt* and is all that was done on a commission for a St George given by George IV to Wyatt. When the King died, no more was ready. The second Duke bought the fragment in 1865 and put it into the garden of Apsley House. It went to Stratfield Saye in 1950. The STABLES with thin rows of plain gables belong to Sir William Pitt's time.

ST MARY. In the grounds. Built for the first Lord Rivers in 1754–8. Brick, on a Greek-cross plan, with an octagonal central dome. Arched windows and pediments in the arms. Four small round windows in the drum of the dome. The E window is of the Venetian type. The W side has a three-arched entrance loggia. Disappointing C19 ceiling inside. – FONT. A tapering octagonal pillar and small bowl; *c.*1760 (in the porch).– PLATE. Cup and Cover Paten, 1650; silver-gilt Cup and Paten, 1712; two Flagons, 1712; silver-gilt Paten, undated; Plate, undated. – MONUMENTS. Sir William Pitt † 1636 and wife. Two semi-reclining alabaster effigies, he above and a little behind her. Below in the sarcophagus two feigned grilles behind which jumbled-up feigned bones. The monument is signed by *John and Matthias Christmas*, and dated 1640. – Pitt Family, 1681. Big tablet with urn at top and garlands l. and r. The bottom part characteristically different: an addition for George Pitt † 1734. – Anna Maria Trapp † 1762. Pretty tablet with dainty garlands. – George Lord Rivers † 1803. By *Flaxman*. Large, with two tall standing figures in relief by an urn. – The Hon. and Rev. Gerald Wellesley † 1882. By *George G. Adams*. White, with a bust flattened and nearly in

*The subsidiary staircase has big vertically symmetrical balusters.

profile. – Second Duke of Wellington † 1884. Bust in framing. – Capt. Lord Richard Wellesley † 1914. Tablet by *Eric Gill* (NT).

RECTORY, by the church. Early C19, rendered. With an attached Tuscan four-column porch and a lunette window over. Pediment above this.

WELLINGTON MONUMENT, by the E lodges. 1863 by *Baron Marochetti*. Column on a high plinth. On the top the statue of the Duke, rather too small, though in fact 7 ft high. The monument cost £3,000.

6060

STRATFIELD TURGIS

ALL SAINTS. Nave and chancel and bell-turret. The chancel is of brick, of 1792, plain. The only ancient feature of the church is one late C13 N window (Y-tracery). Homely interior. – PLATE. Cup and Cover Paten, 1662; silver-gilt Plate, secular, 1774.

TURGIS COURT. Brick, five bays, hipped roof, pedimented doorway. The house lies by the church in a moat.

WELLINGTON ARMS, on the A-road, ½ m. NE. Heavy vernacular Grecian, stuccoed. Three-bay centre and one-bay wings, the latter with a pedimented, tripartite window.

THE FISHERY, ½ m. SW. By the river Loddon. Derelict at the time of writing. Partly timber-framing and brick, C16, partly gabled brick, C17.

STRATTON PARK *see* EAST STRATTON

STUBBINGTON *see* CROFTON AND STUBBINGTON

5010

SWANMORE [DL]

On the edge of the Waltham Chase country, where extensive heaths were enclosed in the C19. Mostly Victorian cottages thickly scattered in small plots, with a few dwellings of what had been the older hamlet on the N fringe.

ST BARNABAS. Originally a neo-Norman church of 1846 by *Ferrey*, with a nave and apsidal chancel, to which a Gothic S aisle and N tower with shingled spire were added in 1876–7. Flint and stone; big round-headed windows in the Norman parts, those in the chancel with shafted framework, the nave windows plainer and set between shallow pilasters above string-course level. Ferrey's W front actually has E.E. lancets (a little echo of Romsey) above a neo-Norman door. Better outside than in.

HILL PARK. Square early C19 house of two storeys in yellow brick, with striking open balustraded parapet.

HOLYWELL HOUSE. *See* p. 295.

SWANWICK *see* SARISBURY

SWAY 2090

ST LUKE. 1839. Brick. Nave and chancel and square little bell-turret with spire. Lancets. The W front lancets all have hood-moulds with stops. The stops are all taken from the same mould. The chancel was added in 1888 (by *Kemp Welch & Pinder*; NT), the N aisle in 1907.

PETERSON'S TOWER, $1\frac{1}{4}$ m. S. The tower is 218 ft high, and 90
the remarkable thing about it is that it is of concrete, still a highly unusual material when the tower was built. It is of course not reinforced concrete, but cement blocks rammed into wooden frames.* But when was it built? The date given in *C.L.* in 1952 and 1957 is 1879, and the man who built it was Andrew Peterson, a retired Indian judge. He wanted to be buried under it and to have a permanent strong light at the top in his commemoration. This, however, was not permitted. The tower is square and very slender with a higher polygonal stair-turret and a drum and dome on the top. The windows are mostly pointed, but the general style was intended to be Indian. Mr Peterson built, also of concrete, two more towers and several farm buildings and some smaller buildings.

SWAYTHLING *see* SOUTHAMPTON, pp. 571, 573, 574, 581, 583, 584, 588

SYDMONTON 4050

SYDMONTON COURT. The house seems to present a complicated architectural history. It ought to be unravelled. The two stepped gables must be C16. In front of them is later filling-in.

*Norman Shaw in 1878 designed concrete cottages for W. H. Lascelles, who had taken out a patent for building in concrete blocks, the blocks having iron rods embedded in them. Peterson's tower has been repeatedly called reinforced concrete. So perhaps Lascelles' or a similar system was used.

The wing to the l. with raised brick window surrounds should be early C18. The N side is rendered and probably C18.

ST MARY. The church stands on the lawn in front of the house, and looks more private than most. It was rebuilt in 1853. Flint. Broad W tower with buttresses continued as detached angle pinnacles – the Somerset way. Nave and chancel. Dec details. However, the N and S doorways are genuinely Norman, though sweepingly restored. In the arch chip-carving and a band of small raised triangles. The chancel arch of this Norman church is now the tower arch. It has a broad band of leaf, represented by symmetrical volutes sprouting out of a central stem. Also an order with a big twisted rope. – PILLAR PISCINA. Norman; now outside the N doorway. – STAINED GLASS. E and W windows by *W. Holland* of Warwick. – PLATE. Set of Chalice, Paten Cover, and Paten, 1707; Flagon, 1723.

SYDNEY LODGE *see* HAMBLE

6060

TADLEY

ST PETER. The short brick W tower with a recent pyramid roof is of 1685. The low brick chancel – the brickwork roughly chequered – must be Georgian. The nave is pebbledashed and may be of brick also. Friendly interior. – Big WEST GALLERY with sturdy late C17 balusters (1685?), the balusters alas half-sawn off. – PULPIT. Dated 1650. Back panels round the corner. Sounding board. – BENCHENDS with moulded tops, some Perp, some dated 1765. – PLATE. Chalice and Paten, 1780.

(TADLEY PLACE FARMHOUSE. In the house an Elizabethan stone chimneypiece with pilasters etc. VCH)

TALBOT VILLAGE *see* BOURNEMOUTH, p. 130

3050

TANGLEY

ST THOMAS. Nave and chancel and a low apse. Above the apse, in the chancel E wall, is a Norman twin window with a strong middle pillar. Is this *in situ*? It is an odd place to be in. The apse is of 1875, but built on Norman foundations. The apse arch inside is partly original. It is pointed, with one slight chamfer. The rest of the church is of 1875 too,* except for the

* By *William White* (Rev. Basil Clarke).

ashlar-faced W steeple, which was built in 1898. – FONT. Of lead, drum-shaped. It is decorated with roses, fleurs-de-lis, and thistles, i.e. must be Jacobean or could be early Charles I. It is a very handsome piece in its minor way.

TESTWOOD

[DL] *3010*

Suburban extension to Totton, on the outskirts of Southampton.

ST WINFRID. 1937 by *N. Cachemaille-Day*. An impressive church, with an austere brick exterior and an interior on an unusual plan. Large square space with the altar at the middle of one side and a very wide rounded arch behind it, opening into a chapel at a higher level whose further wall curves into the roof, pierced on the curve by little windows. On either side of the central space are low aisles, each entered through two low, broad rounded arches, and rising to well under half the roof height; above them are galleries open to the main space and each lit by three large round-headed windows.* The ceiling of the main space is flat. All wall surfaces are whitewashed, except in the chapel behind the altar, which is rendered in blue. The planning is adventurous, the shaping bold and clear, the scale fairly grand, but the exercise in spatial planning does not quite come off, perhaps largely because of the lack of a clear (ritual) E–W axis to counteract the N–S axis. Externally the clarity of the all-brick composition, with its rectangular outlines and round-headed windows, is muddled by the angle tower, prominent but not dominant, with a saddleback roofline and a fussy brickwork pattern, overlaid by a cross, on its main façade. – The FONT is very large; rectangular and slightly tapering from bottom to top.

TESTWOOD HOUSE (formerly Little Testwood House), out in the country beyond the edge of development. A modest-sized country house with a pleasant brick façade of *c.*1700, three-storeyed, with central angular bay and ball finials to the parapet. Inside there is plenty of evidence that the house is basically a timber-framed structure, probably of the C16 or early C17. The house is now used and excellently maintained as an office and sherry bottling store, with inconspicuous additions behind.

(WATERWORKS. For Southampton Corporation, 1965–6 by *L. Berger*, the City Architect.)

*The gallery space on the S side has been furnished by *Cachemaille-Day* as the chapel of St Lioba, 1965.

1090 THORNEY HILL

CHRIST CHURCH. 1906 by *Detmar Blow* for Lord Manners of Avon Tyrrell. A remarkable Edwardian performance. W end with doorway and cupola, E end with shallow apse, N side with a second, central, doorway. Otherwise essentially symmetrical with very big semicircular gables and a hipped roof. It is all decidedly Baroque. Inside four Tuscan giant columns. They carry a central groin-vault. – (WALL PAINTINGS by *Phoebe Traquair*, completed in 1922: the Te Deum. Among the worshippers e.g. Lord Salisbury. NT) – (In the church three INSCRIPTIONS by *Eric Gill*. – In front of one of them MONUMENT to John Manners, bronze effigy by *Sir Bertram Mackennal*, 1917.)

THORNHILL *see* SOUTHAMPTON, pp. 594, 596, 598

2040 THRUXTON

ST PETER AND ST PAUL. Who was the Victorian restorer of 1869? What he did to the tomb recess on the chancel S side is outrageous but full of pluck. The shape of the recess is repeated in the four-centred arch of a window, but he wanted a priest's doorway as well, and so the doorway merrily cut off about two-fifths of the arch. Moreover, a normal doorway would have been no fun, and so the l. jamb suddenly develops a niche at an angle, the roll moulding of the jamb splitting for the purpose. The rest of the exterior is of less interest. Short, ashlar-faced W tower of 1801. The chancel of 1869 uses enormous flints. The N aisle is of 1869 too. Inside also no architectural interest, but much in the furnishings. – STAINED GLASS. N and S, also E, also the vestry, by *David & Charles Evans* of Shrewsbury; 1857 (TK). – MONUMENTS. Very defaced early C13 effigy of a Knight (tower). Strictly frontal, shield on breast. – Brass to Sir John de Lisle † 1407, figure nearly 5 ft long. The figure is dull, but the triple canopy is splendid. – Tomb-chest in the chancel S recess (*see* above). Late C15. The recess has a panelled arch. – A Knight of the Lisle family and his wife. On the N side of the chancel. It consisted of a large arch to the N chapel and the smaller arch filled by the monument itself. Both are four-centred. The tomb-chest is of Purbeck marble and of the usual Late Gothic details. The effigies are carved in a fine-grained limestone and alas somewhat re-cut. Their costume dates them to *c.*1520.

Her mantle falls in beautiful folds round her feet. The arches, friezes, and crestings above have plenty of Early Renaissance detail – very early for Hampshire. – Oak effigy of an Elizabethan Lady wearing a ruff. Very late for the use of oak.

MEMORIAL HALL, in the village. Red brick, three bays, two storeys, the arched windows tied together by giant arches. No pediment. Built in 1817 as the Methodist Chapel.

ROMAN VILLA. In 1823 a Roman villa, possibly of basilican type, was discovered. One room contained a fine mosaic, in the centre of which was a circular panel depicting Bacchus seated on his tiger; surrounding this were squares containing heads. The mosaic is unusual in that on two sides of the panel were inscriptions; the one that can still be read mentions Quintus Natalius Natalinus, who may have been the owner of the villa. This mosaic is now in the British Museum.

TICHBORNE 5030

ST ANDREW. The church has an C11 chancel – Saxo-Norman overlap, as it is called – cf. the still Saxon tradition of the double splays of the windows, but the typically Norman flat buttresses. The W tower is of brick, blue and red, and dated 1703. Round-arched doorway. The nave and its two-bay arcades are poor E.E. The N arcade has as its pier a hardly treated chunk of wall and pointed arches with one slight chamfer. The S arcade has the same arches but a thick octagonal pier. In the E gable of the nave two blank arches, probably originally windows to give light to the rood. The S doorway goes with the nave, the plain round-headed N doorway may be older. The chancel has an E window with reticulated tracery. – FONT. Norman, of cauldron shape, with a little bald decoration at the top. – COMMUNION RAIL. Jacobean, good. – BOX PEWS. Jacobean. – STAINED GLASS. In the head of the E window fragments including a St Andrew. – PLATE. Cover Paten of 1567; Cup of 1569. – MONUMENTS. In the N aisle, divided from the rest by Elizabethan(?) iron RAILINGS. This is the Tichborne Chapel, and the monuments are to members of the family. Michael † 1619, aged eighteen months. Baby lying on his side. – Sir Benjamin † 1621. An excellent standing alabaster monument. Two recumbent effigies. Against the tomb-chest outstandingly fine kneeling children. Very good back wall with columns too. – Sir Henry James † 1845. By *J. E. Carew*. White relief of the deceased on his deathbed surrounded by his family. Two angels above, embracing. – Henry Tichborne Doughty † 1835. Tomb-chest, and against the back wall Gothic relief with a boy and his guardian angel.

TICHBORNE HOUSE, in Tichborne Park. Built shortly after 1803. Seven bays, two storeys, white. Good one-storeyed porch of four Tuscan columns with a triglyph frieze.

TIDWORTH HOUSE *see* SOUTH TIDWORTH

3020

TIMSBURY

ST ANDREW. Nave and chancel and small bell-turret. One N lancet. Nicely unrestored interior. – PULPIT. Only the back panel is C17. – SCREEN. One-light divisions. Perp, rustic. – TILES. A few, on a window sill. – STAINED GLASS. C15 bits in the chancel N and S windows. – PLATE. Patens of the early C18 and 1718; Chalice, unmarked.

TIPNER *see* PORTSMOUTH, p. 443

5000

TITCHFIELD [DL]

Titchfield in the Middle Ages was a small port at the head of the Meon estuary, with a Premonstratensian abbey founded in 1232. After the Dissolution the abbey was converted into a mansion by Thomas Wriothesley,* Lord Chancellor of England and first Earl of Southampton. The family lived there for several generations, but by the mid C17 the house had passed out of their hands and was finally dismantled in 1781.

The Meon estuary was drained in the C17, and, though a canal was dug, Titchfield ceased to be a port of any significance. It was henceforth far less important than Fareham, although, to judge from its architecture, it must have had some modest prosperity in the C18. The tide of the C19 bypassed it, and so, almost, has that of the C20; here, midway between Southampton and Portsmouth, is a backwater with a Georgian and earlier atmosphere, set in a stretch of valley which still remains surprisingly rural, even though suburban or subtopian development is only just over the brows of the low slopes on either side.

ST PETER. An amalgam of work of many periods and many degrees of quality. Outside, especially when the church is approached from the village, it is the tower that compels attention. The lower part is Anglo-Saxon, not Anglo-Danish, i.e.

*Pronounced Risly.

of the C9 or perhaps C8. It was not a tower but a W porch, as at Monkwearmouth in the late C7. It stood in front of an aisleless nave. Of all this the following parts survive: the high W entry with a round arch, the quoins of the porch, not sufficiently high up to determine how high the porch was, the traces of a round-arched W window (the heightening to a tower is C13), a bonding course of Roman tiles, and the SW quoins of the nave. The NW quoins are hidden, but the line of the remarkably high nave roof – remarkable, but typically Anglo-Saxon – is preserved S of the tower, and a part of it appears on the N side also above the much later N aisle roof. The tower ends in a low shingled spire. *See* p. 831

The tower still serves as W porch,* and leading into the nave is a well preserved C12 doorway of three orders of zigzag moulding with some small-scale ball and lozenge ornament, with shafted jambs and capitals carved in strange writhing reeded leaf patterns. The present nave retains the proportions of the Saxon original. A S aisle was added in the C12, the chancel was rebuilt in the C13, a S chapel added in the C14, and a spacious N aisle in the C15, when also the chancel was remodelled. In 1867 the Norman S aisle was replaced by an unsatisfactory neo-Dec one (designed by the Rector, the *Rev. J. T. Turner*). The chancel arch is low, wide, and plain, probably early C14 but re-using plain semicircular late C12 responds. Three-bay C19 S arcade in rather unhappy relationship with the splendid C15 N arcade, with lofty slender piers of the four-shafts-and-four-hollows section. The N aisle is spacious, with four side windows and the W window all of the same three-light design, with the central light rising slightly higher than the rest. E window of five lights, stepped, under a segmental head. On either side of the E window are elaborate niches, slightly mutilated but still showing fine details in cusps, crockets, and miniature vaulting pattern. Hampshire can show few examples of Perp architecture as ambitious as this aisle, although it would not be specially notable in the West Country or East Anglia. The chancel has a C19 neo-Perp E window of five lights in an old surround, three C15 N windows of three lights, and damaged niches in two tiers on either side of the E window, simpler than those in the N aisle. Obviously the Perp work in the chancel and aisle was not done at the same time, and that in the chancel is probably later. The inner string

* The GATES under the tower were made at Funtley Ironworks (p. 238) in the C17 (S. Weeks).

course and the SEDILIA, the latter over-restored, are C13 survivals. The two-bay S arcade dates from *c.*1320, when the S chapel was built, and has curious capitals carved with engaging though grotesque winged figures and profuse foliage. It stands on a stone screen wall. In the S chapel three-light E window and two-light S windows, the lights long, slender, and ogee-headed (cf. Soberton, chancel). Also ogee-headed SEDILIA.

FURNISHINGS. FONT. By *Charles Upton*, a pupil of Eric Gill, *c.*1950. Octagonal, with alternate representational and symbolic carvings in relief, the former with plenty of vitality. – SCREEN. Mid Victorian, open tracery, not over-elaborate. – PAINTING. Affixed to the wall over the low chancel arch a representation of the Crucifixion by *Kempe*, 1889; Christ on the Cross is shown against a background painted to represent tapestry. Rich, realistic detailing, dark red and gilt predominating; probably originally a reredos, but seen to good effect in this position. – On the W wall a WALL PAINTING of the Miraculous Draught of Fishes, originally executed *c.*1890, but redone in 1951–2 by art students from Portsmouth School of Art in a style more medieval than the original, with figures slightly stylized but realistic detailing; it has the feeling of folk-art. – MONUMENTS. In the S chapel the magnificent
50 monument to the first Earl and Countess of Southampton († 1550 and 1574) and to the second Earl, who died in 1581 and left money to erect 'two faire monuments' to himself and his parents; only this one with its three effigies was in fact executed. By *Gerard Johnson*, a refugee from Flanders. The contract is dated 1594. A two-tiered structure of marble and alabaster, with an upper table supported by three round open arches decorated in a simple Renaissance manner and resting on a much wider tomb-chest, with four massive obelisks at the corners. The effigy of Lady Southampton rests on the upper tier and the somewhat smaller effigies of her husband and son on the lower tier to either side, with figures of heraldic beasts by their heads and feet. On the side panels of the tomb-chest, between plain pilasters, are small kneeling figures of the family's children, one of whom became the third Earl, patron of Shakespeare. – On the S wall of the chapel a charming monument to Lady Mary Wriothesley, who died in 1615 at the age of four, attributed to *Epiphanius Evesham*. She is shown in miniature effigy, dressed in adult clothes with a ruff, but with a childish expression (not very common in children's effigies).

Small seated angel at the top. – On the N chancel wall a monument to William Chamberlayne † 1608 and his wife, with small kneeling figures, each in a round-headed recess under a flat cornice, with four children below. – On the N wall of the chapel monument to John Hornby † 1832, by *Chantrey*. A sleeping woman and urn above. – Many smaller wall tablets. – Tablet to David Kerr † 1794, by *Nollekens*, with a plain urn (chancel N) and one to Edward Ives † 1783 by *Cooke* of London, with a weeping willow and an allegorical figure (chancel S).

THE VILLAGE. Titchfield's centre is the long and wide High Street, the former market place, running N–S. Narrow streets run W (West Street) and E (Church Street) from the S end of High Street, which itself is continued, much more narrowly, by South Street. From the N end of High Street another narrow street, East Street, leads off at a r. angle. The fairly regular rectilinear pattern of streets, supported by a network of footpaths mostly parallel to one or other of the streets, suggests deliberate planning which must have taken place before the end of the Middle Ages, and probably long before.

Titchfield's street architecture is dominantly Georgian brick, though there is plenty of evidence, especially behind the façades, of timber-frame construction. There are few large houses comparable with the best in Fareham; most of the domestic architecture is homely in scale, but in aggregate very pleasing.

The PERAMBULATION begins at the S end of the High Street, with short excursions along Church, South, and West Streets, then along the High Street and East Street to the abbey. CHURCH STREET is only a short cul-de-sac terminated by the church tower with its Saxon doorway, to which the homely two-storey, mainly Georgian façades along the street act as a foil. Some of the houses are enlivened by simple door-canopies. SOUTH STREET has, in its first part, much the same character, but Nos 28 and 30 are fine timber-framed, brick-infilled houses with slightly oversailing upper storeys. On the opposite side, Nos 37–9 are also timber-framed, but roughcast in front; they retain a pleasant double Georgian shopfront with thin framed small-paned windows. At the street's wider S end, Nos 44–6 are in characteristic Hampshire grey brick with red quoins and dressings, No. 46 having a fine projecting porch with fluted columns.

Back to WEST STREET. The townscape at its entrance is spoiled by a demolition (a site now laid out with a public garden), breaking its contact with South Street and making an unfortunate gap when seen from the High Street. West Street has a varied row of two-storeyed cottages on the N side, climbing a hill; all very simple, but well maintained, and charming in total effect. The HIGH STREET is widest at its S end, funnels slightly northwards, narrows suddenly at a projection of the frontage on the E side, and funnels a little more further N. All this makes for an extremely pleasant total effect. The houses are two- or three-storeyed, with more scale generally than in the narrower streets, and their fronts are mostly Georgian. Of individual buildings only a few need mentioning; the BUGLE HOTEL, with segmental porch supported by two free-standing columns between three-storey polygonal bay windows; No. 33, nearly opposite, with a very large segmental bow window and columned porch; the QUEEN'S HEAD; and, opposite it, No. 8, with another projecting porch. Behind the Queen's Head is the former MARKET HALL, late C16 or C17, re-erected here after removal from the High Street; timber-framed upper storey with brick infilling, the lower storey partly open, with timber columns and braces supporting the superstructure. Now in a bad state, but it is hoped to restore it. The N view along the High Street is closed by a plain but effective bow-windowed Georgian house at the angle with EAST STREET. Beside it a footpath leads N, passing the end façade of OLD LODGE, in decorative C17 brickwork, with a wavy-moulded string-course, dentil-patterned underneath. There is more of this patterning on the long N front, which has however been altered and whitewashed. In East Street no house needs special mention, but the entire N frontage is a typical Titchfield range of small two-storeyed Georgian cottages, some of them with simple canopied or hooded doorways. Here the view is partly closed by a relatively plain Georgian house, marking the corner with Mill Street, which turns off to the N. But traffic finds its way through a narrow gap between it and the house to the S, almost like a town gateway without an upper arch, through which a glimpse is had of the riverside fields. MILL STREET is very homely, but pleasantly so, the scale of its houses gradually fading out till they finally end beside the Southampton–Portsmouth road.

ST MARGARET'S, ½ m. NW. A curious tall brick tower with intermediate string course, few windows, and a plain parapet angled up to a prominent corner turret. Is it Tudor, or later? The N wing, certainly Tudor or very early Stuart, has side gables and regularly arrayed tall brick chimneys. Tall three-storeyed W wing attached to the tower, of similar brick and looking in its present state C18; sash windows and battlements.

TITCHFIELD ABBEY (PLACE HOUSE), ½ m. N of the village. The Premonstratensian abbey was founded in 1232 by Peter des Roches, Bishop of Winchester. It consisted of an aisleless church with central tower and E aisles to the transepts, evidently vaulted throughout. The cloister was on the N side, with, as usual, chapter house to the E and refectory to the N. Alterations subsequent to the time of the foundation were relatively small, and of the parts of the medieval abbey that survive, nothing significant is of later than C13 date. Thomas Wriothesley, Earl of Southampton, converted parts of the buildings into a mansion (known as Place House) very soon after the Dissolution, and his work was finished by 1542. The works were supervised by *Thomas Bertie* (John Harvey). It was lived in till the C18 but largely demolished in 1781. What remains is the substantial ruin of the gatehouse and parts of its flanking wings, fashioned out of the abbey nave, and the much scantier remains of buildings, partly medieval and partly Tudor, round the site of the cloister, which became the courtyard of the mansion.

The shell of the GATEHOUSE is virtually intact. It is a spec- 48
tacular piece of Tudor work, entirely Gothic in general conception and in the principal detailing, but of that peculiarly Tudor variety of Gothic that developed out of the purer Perpendicular, with cuspless square-headed windows, very flat arches, and a paucity of fine decoration. The angle turrets are exceptionally large, rising to four storeys and castellated, with pairs of square-headed windows on the two middle storeys and smaller single lights at the top. The main part of the gatehouse is three-storeyed. The uppermost storey is tall, with a shallow canted oriel window, transomed and mullioned, of four main and two side lights, on each of the upper floors, the two being linked intermediately; top oriel with miniature crenellation, the base of the lower bracketed back to the façade. The four-centred archway has incised mouldings dying into the jambs about half-way down; the original DOORS remain, each door with horizontal and vertical moulded strips dividing it into eight panels, and with strong lattice work on the inner face. Almost the only pieces of ornamentation on the gatehouse, not simply related to the structure, are the grotesque gargoyles on the string courses of the parapets and – among

the most engaging Tudor features at Titchfield – mock arrow-slits on the ground floor of the turrets, cross-shaped on the angular faces, vertical only on the outer faces. These could not possibly have been intended to have any defensive significance and are an extraordinarily early piece of mock 'medievalism' – hardly before the Middle Ages had ended. The two-storey wings E and W of the gatehouse (of which the E is the more ruinous) are simply fashioned out of the E and W parts of the monastic nave, reduced a little in height and castellated (another piece of 'medievalism' of course – but of a much more common sort), with all the original windows obliterated and various square-headed mullioned windows inserted. The upper part of the W front was largely rebuilt in Tudor brick, making a fine composition, with crowstepped gables and a crowning pair of chimneys, standing on octagonal brick bases with cusped panel patterns, one of the stacks ornamented in a zig-zag pattern. Similar, but simpler, chimneys rise from the sides of the gatehouse. Very few details of the medieval nave work are visible – principally one of the shafts (in the SW corner) which supported the corbels from which sprang the vault, parts of the outer jambs of the former triplet of lancets in the W wall, parts of a string course, a section of a blocked doorway in the N wall, and part of the spiral staircase in the W corner turrets (which were encased and heightened with battlemented crowns to be the angle features of the new building). It is known from excavations that the E end of the church had a square chancel, slightly shorter, also square-ended chancel aisles, and pairs of yet shorter, again square-ended chapels E of the transepts – a typical Cistercian (i.e. also Premonstratensian) plan of an ambitious sort.

The best surviving feature of the abbey is what is left of the entrance to the CHAPTER HOUSE. This is seriously ruinous, but sufficient remains to testify to the general character of the design. There was a central moulded doorway, with clustered Purbeck marble jamb shafts and moulded capitals, flanked by similarly treated arched window openings based on sills. The columns flanking the doorway consisted of a central, surprisingly slender, shaft and four detached subsidiary shafts, not much slenderer, under composite moulded capitals; it must have been an exceptionally delicate composition. These remains are incorporated into the surviving, largely Tudor façade of the former range on the E side of the courtyard; everything behind the façade has been demolished. On the N side of the cloister, the refectory was converted into the great hall of Place House, but all that remains there is a low, featureless stretch of wall. The refectory was on the upper floor, accessible by a porch. The present W range facing the courtyard is straightforward Tudor. Several TILES, of the late C13 or early C14, remain *in situ* in the cloister and elsewhere, their designs varying between floral, bestial, heraldic, and simply geometrical patterns. Similar tiles have been found on the site of the monastery at Durford in Sussex (near Petersfield), and there are affinities to the C13 pavements at Halesowen Abbey, Worcs. Both these abbeys were Premonstratensian.

TITHE BARN, SW of the abbey. Probably C15. Hipped tiled roofs on fine timber framework with arched braces; two E entrances under hipped roof projections. The E wall is of boarding, the W of stone.

TOTTON *see* ELING

TUFTON 4040

1 m. S of Whitchurch

ST MARY. Nave and chancel. Stunted bell-turret. In the nave on the N side two small Early Norman windows high up, on the S side a doorway, plain and very tall, with a big lintel, an undecorated tympanum, and an arch with small saltire crosses and a billet hood-mould. The nave has also on either side a big domestic C18 window. Norman also the unmoulded chancel arch. But the chancel is early C13 and has lancet windows set internally in quite a monumental three-bay arcading with proper columns and arches. – PAINTING. A fine, very large early C15 St Christopher with an ornamental frame, but none of the genre details one sees so often. – Also painted fragments above the chancel arch. – The chancel has recently been re-furnished in accordance with the so-called Liturgical Movement. Free-standing altar. Communion rail to N, S, and E. The furnishing is very well done.

TUNWORTH 6040

ALL SAINTS. 1854–5. Is it by *Woodyer*? Flint, nave and chancel and a bell-turret. One small genuine Norman N window in the nave, one small C13 N window in the chancel. The chancel arch is of *c*.1200, pointed, with one slight chamfer. The nave S doorway with two continuous chamfers, probably *c.*1300. – ALMSBOX. C17; funny and very engaging.

4020
TWYFORD

ST MARY. 1876–7 by *Waterhouse*, or rather nearly entirely by him. Inside he re-used the round piers of the preceding church. They are, judging by their capitals, of the late C12: trumpet-scallop, broad leaves, and a kind of diagonal fluting. Waterhouse is hard and precise. Knapped flint and red brick bands. Perp details, rather early for 1876. NW steeple. N and S chapels, higher than the aisles. – FONT. Purbeck marble, octagonal, with two flat blank arches to each side. – PLATE. Paten, 1692. – MONUMENTS. Dulcebella Wells † 1616. Small alabaster tablet, strongly convex. No figures. – Jonathan Shipley † 1788. By *Nollekens*. Grey obelisk with bust in profile and trophy. – Mrs Naylor † 1806. By *Flaxman*. Woman seated on the ground in front of a squat obelisk.

RECTORY, E of the church. Brick. Five bays, two storeys, hipped roof. Doorway with apsidal hood. The date no doubt *c.*1700.

TWYFORD HOUSE, on the main road, E of the rectory. Early C18. Seven-bay front, but the three middle windows very narrow, in the Queen Anne fashion. The other windows are segment-headed. Clumsy Victorian doorway. On the garden side three later C18 bow windows. Panelled parapet. On its centre vases.

(MANOR FARM. The BARN has an extension to the N with a blocked C14 archway and a larger gateway, both perhaps from Marwell Manor Farm. MHLG)

(TWYFORD BRIDGE. Medieval with breakwaters. NMR)

TYLNEY HALL *see* ROTHERWICK

5020
UPHAM

CHURCH. Externally an C18 brick W tower, blue and red chequer, and otherwise all *G. E. Street*, 1881. And internally? The N arcade is certainly his. But did he do a S arcade deliberately different, with so much slenderer piers, or had he evidence? The E respond looks like it. Street re-used one early C13 arch at the E end of his N aisle. Semicircular responds, arch with two slight chamfers. – STAINED GLASS. By *Kempe* S aisle W, 1892, and two in the N aisle, *c.*1895.

UPNATELY

7050

ST STEPHEN. 1844. Flint and brick bands and a thin W tower. The N doorway is of *c*.1200, round arch, a slight chamfer, and dogtooth (cf. Greywell). The chancel arch, much cleaned up, also of *c*.1200. Nave roof C15, with arched braces and scissor-braces above the collars. – PAINTING. An icon of St Thomas, Greek, early C19(?). Presented in 1959. – COMMUNION RAIL. Part in the tower gallery. Of *c*.1700, with twisted balusters. – PLATE. Chalice and Paten Cover, 1681; Flagon, 1788; Almsdish, 1792.

UPPER CLATFORD

3040

ALL SAINTS. The interior is most peculiar. It has a very wide nave divided by a N arcade in 1890, and by wooden posts on the S side, and the chancel arch is double. This arch is in fact a Late Norman two-bay piece, re-set no doubt. Round pier, round abacus, some nailhead decoration. Of about the same time the plain N doorway. In the chancel S wall, said to come from the E wall, a fragmentary Norman window too. W tower of 1578. S porch, brick, probably C17. The VCH, on the strength of some straight-headed windows with round-arched lights, attributes the re-setting of the arcade as a twin chancel arch to the C17. – PILLAR PISCINA. With a decorated scallop capital. – FONT. 1629. Octagonal baluster and semi-globular bowl. – PULPIT. Jacobean. The sounding board with some decoration. – PLATE. Paten of 1631; Paten of 1654; Chalice of 1811.

The WATERLOO IRON WORKS were established in the ANNA VALLEY in 1815. Of the oldest factory parts nothing is preserved but the ironmaster's house, CLATFORD LODGE, with a Roman-Doric doorway and a cast-iron veranda of four bays l. and four bays r. plus a special veranda for the middle window on the upper floor. The LODGES l. and r. of the archway were built as SCHOOLHOUSE and house for the mistress in 1836. They have flint-vermiculated window surrounds. WATERLOO SQUARE, a group of workers' cottages, has been demolished.

REDRICE HOUSE. By *William Burn*, 1844. Classical, of ashlar stone but with French banded rustication on the ground floor, and arched windows on that floor as well. Thirteen bays, the porte-cochère of four Tuscan columns not in the middle. (Inside, the great hall runs up through one and a half storeys and has a coved ceiling. This is of *c.*1911. Also much restoration *c.*1933, when the present stone facing was done and the windows were remodelled.)* On the STABLES still the date 1845.

BURY HILLFORT, ½ m. W. The three lines of bank and ditch which crown the hill have been shown by excavation to represent three distinct phases in the history of the site. The outermost earthwork, built in the C3 B.C. to enclose an area of 22 acres, now stands to a height of 6 ft, and the ditch when excavated was 11 ft deep and 5 ft wide. The entrance to this first fort is on the SE. In the first half of the C1 B.C. the defended area was reduced to 11 acres by building the two inner lines of defences which incorporated part of the earlier work on the E side and had the same entrance. These ramparts still stand over 8 ft high in places, and their V-shaped ditches were found to be 20 ft and 10 ft deep for the inner and outer examples respectively. Finally, in the latter part of the C1 B.C. the defences were remodelled by Belgic groups, who restored the fort to its original size, and finds from this phase suggest intermittent occupation until the end of the C1 A.D.

3020 UPPER ELDON

ST JOHN BAPTIST. Nave and chancel in one, late C12. Two round-headed N windows with continuous rolls, plus one W, one S. The E wall is of brick; early C19.

6040 UPTON GREY

ST MARY. Nave, central tower, the upper parts of brick (*c.*1700?), chancel. In addition a fine N aisle begun in 1715 and also of brick. The bonding is still English. In the W and E gables a blank oval. The W crossing arch is Norman, but evidently much pulled about. Arch with two rows of billet. The much lower and more convincing E arch E.E., single-chamfered. E.E. also the chancel windows. In the E wall two lancets and a detached quatrefoil over. Plain E.E. S doorway. A S aisle has been demolished. The arcading is still visible in the S wall. It was E.E. too, and shows a W respond and a one-bay lengthening W beyond it. The N arcade belongs to the N chapel but is in its details much coarser. Octagonal piers,

* Information kindly given me by the Headmaster of Redrice School.

octagonal capitals. One would like to see Tuscan columns here. – FONT. Small, Perp, octagonal, with quatrefoils. On the underside more rewarding heads and flowers. – PEW RAILING. Late C18, semi-Gothick. – PLATE. Set of 1724. That is probably when the addition was complete. – MONUMENTS. Lady Dorothy Eyre † 1650. Typical mid C17 piece, with a flat, frontal bust in a recess and a swag across. Two pediments inside pediments. Black marble and alabaster. – Other interesting tablets, e.g. John Matthew † 1687 by *Richard Wood* of Oxford. A broad, gristly white cartouche, rather 1665 than 1685 in style. – Another tablet † 1692, and yet another † 1766, white and pink, with ribbons and leaf garlands.

A pleasant village with several good houses up the hill, e.g. UPTON GREY HOUSE, altered and added to by *Ernest Newton* in 1907 for Charles Holme, the editor of *The Studio*. Half-timbered bay window and tile-hanging. But by far the best house lies ½ m. SE, HODDINGTON HOUSE. This must be late C17, with its steep one-bay pediment on a five-bay façade. The windows have stylized faces as keystones, and round the middle window is flat foliage typical of *c.*1660.

VENARDS *see* IBSLEY

VENTA BELGARUM *see* WINCHESTER, p. 658

VERNHAM DEAN 3050

ST MARY. Nave and chancel and bellcote. Medieval masonry in the nave N wall. The W doorway also is genuine, though it may be re-set. It dates from *c.*1220. Two orders of colonnettes, capitals crockets, stiff-leaf, and also turned-in leaves rather like oak. The arch is still round and still has zigzag at r. angles to the wall. But the hood-mould is decorated with dogtooth. The rest of the church is of 1851, by *A. Ashpitel* (GR) or, as *The Builder* says: 'the design of the curate, the Rev. *J. M. Rawlins*.' – STAINED GLASS. In the chancel of *c.*1851, naïve, very lovable, and with some deep blue.

VERNHAM MANOR. Jacobean* with two gables l. and r., their bargeboards original. The façade between the two gables was altered in the C18. Two-storeyed, of brick. Inside, the hall SCREEN remains with Ionic pilasters and boldly profiled

* The core timber-framed (MHLG).

panels. The panelling and chimneypiece of the room also had Ionic pilasters.

VERNON HILL *see* BISHOPS WALTHAM

6050 THE VYNE

The Vyne is one of the most rewarding houses in Hampshire, both visually and historically. The house represents three periods: Henry VIII, the mid C17, and the C18. I.e. the first is the period of Lord Sandys, who succeeded in 1496, received his title in 1523, became Lord Chamberlain in 1526, and died in 1540. Henry VIII visited The Vyne in 1510. Lord Sandys built the house, according to heraldic dates, between 1518 and 1527. Chaloner Chute bought the estate from the sixth Lord Sandys in 1653. He was a barrister, became Speaker in 1659, and died in the same year. John Chute, the friend of Horace Walpole, came into the property in 1754 and died in 1776. Some alterations were made by William Lyde Wiggett Chute after 1837 and before his death in 1879. That is the framework of dates. For the house they mean *c.*1520–5, *c.*1655, *c.*1760–70, and the mid C19.

EXTERIOR. The Tudor house first. It was apparently much larger than the house is now. Leland about 1530 mentions a 'fair base court', and Wiggett Chute found evidence of a courtyard S of the S, i.e. the entrance, front, quite far away, and also N of the N front, only about 30 ft from the lake. The Tudor house, as far as it still stands, is of two storeys, red brick with blue diapers. The only original windows are on the S front on the r. of the middle porch. They are of one and two lights, with uncusped four-centred heads to the lights. The S front otherwise consists of a recessed centre and two gabled wings. Small square projection in the re-entrant angles. There were raised, tower-like eminences on the ends as they now exist only on the N front. On that front the house has as a l. hand appendix the antechapel with Victorian windows in two tiers and the chapel with its polygonal apse to the E and its transomed windows with four-centred heads. The windows have uncusped arches below the transom, but cusped ones at the top. They are actually Victorian, but repeat the original ones of the E apse. Internally the Tudor evidence is spectacular, as will be seen later.

60 The Commonwealth contribution is chiefly the N portico.

This is by *John Webb*. It is of brick, rendered, with giant columns carrying lush Corinthian capitals. There are two columns and two square angle pillars. The pediment is of wood. This portico is the earliest domestic portico in England, although Webb designed one for Durham House in London in 1649 (which was not executed), and the motif, derived from Palladio's Villa Barbaro at Maser, was no doubt among possibilities considered in the Inigo Jones office. The view from the portico to the lake is exquisite. Webb's additions inside will have to wait until some more detailed description of the exterior has been made.

The plan of the house is exceptional in that the centre is a 'double pile', i.e. two rooms deep. The hall was in the middle to the N, and it looks as if the centre to the S must have been an additional entrance hall – to which there would be no parallel. The plan of the S front is that of Barrington Court in Somerset, i.e. an E-plan. Where the porch is now there no doubt always has been a porch. Barrington Court was begun *c.*1514, i.e. just a few years before The Vyne. The centre part of the front is eleven bays wide. The porch doorway with its open pediment must be Webb's, although it is very quiet, much quieter in fact than Webb's side doorways in the square angle projections. The windows all have receding surrounds, all of Webb's time, though the sashing must of course have been done later. There are no Webb windows preserved at all. They no doubt had mullion-and-transom crosses. The wings start to the inside with big chimney-breasts, but the stacks are mid C19. The canted bay windows in the end walls are Georgian.

The W front is all diapered brick, but the r. part is C18, of four widely spaced bays. At the l. (NW) corner is a square projecting tower rising to three storeys. This prepares for the N or portico front. Here the tower repeats at the l. (NE) end. The towers are two bays wide, the rest of the façade including the portico has eleven bays. The battlements are mid C19. The l. attachment, as has already been said, contains the chapel. It is preceded by the antechapel. The two-storeyed Tudor-looking windows here are again Wiggett Chute's, and so are the battlements. The chapel apse has original battlements with shields. To its l., i.e. on the E side of the house, is a canted C18 bay, and behind this is John Chute's tomb chamber.

INTERIOR. The house is normally entered in the r. wing of

the S front, from the W side. The STONE GALLERY here is Wiggett Chute, but in it is a plaster medallion of the Emperor Probus, so much like *Giovanni da Majano*'s medallions at Hampton Court, which were made in 1521, that it must be by the same (Florentine) sculptor and of about the same years. The next two rooms and the DRAWING ROOM, all on the N side, have Rococo ceilings of the John Chute years. But in the drawing room is a wooden chimneypiece by *Webb*, with over-large volutes l. and r., curling askew, and caryatids in relief against the sides, i.e. in profile so that they look forward.

After that follows the VESTIBULE behind the portico. This is all one with the STAIRCASE, and upper adjoining rooms. It is all *John Chute*'s, and apparently really his, also as far as design and detailing go. Horace Walpole appreciated him as a designer. The *ensemble* at The Vyne is indeed the most sensational in the county. Horace Walpole in 1770 called it 'theatric', and that unquestionably it is. It is also the spatially most fascinating staircase composition of the second half of the C18 in England. It has not a touch of the Rococo, although its contemporary equivalents in Central Europe are Rococo in every respect. The composition is hard to describe. You enter through the S porch into what is meant as a tripartite room, though the l. third is stunted. On the r. is a screen of Roman Doric columns, set two-deep and connecting the room with the adjoining apartment, which serves as a passage to the dining room. The ceiling is coffered throughout.

The centre part is again divided in three. The l. and r. parts are low and connect with passages to the N vestibule, i.e. the room one enters from the portico. All ceilings are coffered again. The centrepiece is the staircase itself. It is not wide, and rises first in the vestibule with balusters and then between solid walls. After one straight flight it turns at 90 degrees and disappears out of sight. But this middle piece,
67 where the staircase goes up, is open to the ceiling (coffered of course) of the first floor, and the ceiling at that level runs through uninterrupted to the first-floor room above the portico vestibule, which is visible from the foot of the stairs through a screen of slender fluted Corinthian columns. There are also upper columns on the r., and there again an upper room with a coffered ceiling becomes visible. It is without any question the climax of The Vyne.

On the W of the vestibule is the PRINT ROOM, C18, with a

good chimneypiece and the walls decorated by stuck-on prints. On the E of the portico vestibule is the DINING ROOM. It is thus the counterpiece to the drawing room. It has another *Webb* chimneypiece, this one with termini atlantes looking out of straight-jackets of black blocks. Frieze with two heads and garlands. In the CHAPEL PARLOUR is linenfold panelling of Lord Sandys's time. The chimneypiece here is dated 1601 but evidently not in order.

The walls of the ANTECHAPEL are in a poor *John Chute*-Gothic, but the ribbed ceiling is supposed (VCH) to be original, i.e. of *c.*1520. – In the windows heraldic STAINED GLASS from the Chapel of Holy Trinity at Basingstoke, a chapel built by Lord Sandys. – SCULPTURE. Excellent bearded bust (God the Father ?), stone, early C16, as good as if it were from Champagne. The style is similar to sculpture at Winchester Cathedral.

The CHAPEL of The Vyne is doubtless the best late medieval private chapel in England. The polygonal apse has already been mentioned. It has its counterpart in Lord Sandys's Holy Trinity Chapel at Basingstoke. The ceiling is vaulted in a four-centred section and has wooden ribs. – STALLS. One tier and fronts. Ends with poppy-heads, e.g. three putti, women and jugglers, also openwork decoration. The back panels have fine tracery tops in two tiers. Traceried fronts also. Horizontal canopy, curving forward. The detail is entirely Gothic here as well, but the stress on the top horizontal shows that England was ready for the Renaissance. – TILES. Probably Flemish copies of Italian majolica. Mid C16, but laid in the C19. – STAINED GLASS. In all probability done by itinerant Flemings in 1521.* *Dirk Vellert* as the designer is not acceptable. Resurrection, Crucifixion, Christ carrying the cross, Henry VIII, Catherine of Aragon, Margaret of Scotland with their patrons, all in fantastic, typically Flemish architectural settings. – PANELLING. Round the altar; C18. – PAINTINGS. The only Gothick feature of John Chute's years was paintings above the stall canopies, now on the gallery of the chapel. Perspective plays with fan-vaulting and Gothic tracery, by *Spiridone Roma*, who came to England about 1770 and shows himself inspired here by Italian stage design.

To the S of the chapel is the TOMB CHAMBER, built by

* But the VCH proposes a date before 1503, which is stylistically hardly possible.

John Chute to house the memorial to Chaloner Chute. The panelling is again poor Gothick. The STAINED GLASS is by *John Rowell*, after Rubens. The MONUMENT is by *Thomas Carter*, who received payments between 1775 and 1781. It is one of the finest monuments of its date in England and serves to show what quality could be achieved at that time even by sculptors whom we don't consider in the first flight. The Speaker, looking younger than he was when he died, is lying wonderfully at ease with his head propped up on his elbow. He seems to be musing and all alone. There is no playing to an audience as one finds it so often in the funerary art of Baroque and Rococo. He lies in Speaker's robes on the traditional straw mat, his large hat by his side. High tomb-chest with fluted Ionic colonnettes, the four at the corners detached. The tomb-chest was designed by *John Chute*.

On the upper floor the most important room is the LONG GALLERY, occupying the whole W front. It is perfectly panel-
46 led still, the pattern being a specially intricate linenfold
with devices of Lord Sandys and others. As Cardinal Wolsey is included and as he fell into disgrace in 1528, this gives a *terminus ante quem*. On the other hand the arms of Bishop Tunstall of London give 1522 as *terminus post quem*. The
59 chimneypiece is by *Webb*, but more classical than the others.
It is white with just a dark green panel. Open broken pediment, and fat garlands and a cartouche in the centre.

Of the other rooms only the Library and the Tapestry Room need comment. In the LIBRARY is yet another *Webb* chimneypiece. Two columns clothed by four tiers of upright leaves. Lintel with arms and palm fronds. In the TAPESTRY ROOM large Jacobean chimneypiece of wood from the Chapel Parlour with small figures of Justice and Faith.

In the grounds, near the house and close to the main road,
61 is a GARDEN PAVILION by *Webb*. It is of brick and in the
uncourtly style of Mills. Two storeys; round. Dome with a fishscale pattern, and four projections, each with a round-headed doorway and a round-headed window over. The windows are flanked by brick pilasters. In the diagonals on the upper floor are two small niches, one above the other.

LODGES. They repeat the pattern of the pavilion, a little simplified, and are probably C18 work.

GATEPIERS in front of the house. Low, of stone, rusticated, with a niche. No doubt by *Webb*. They are re-set.

WALTHAM CHASE MILL *see* BISHOPS WALTHAM

WARBLINGTON [DL] *7000*

A stretch of undisturbed farmland between the A27 and the channel that connects Chichester and Langstone Harbours. Tall trees, fields sloping gently to the tidal water, the church beside farm buildings, a spreading cemetery, and very few houses in sight. All this is a bare crow's mile from the busy centre of Havant. Historically it is the parish church of the small town of Emsworth, two miles away over the fields to the E.

ST THOMAS A BECKET. The church is nearly hidden from any distance by the trees that envelop the churchyard and the big barns beside it. Long steep roofs sweep down over the aisles nearly to the ground, but their sweeps are broken by the gables of dormer windows and, on the N side, a porch, so that the whole church has a highly picturesque outline, with tiled roofs at many angles, set off by rough plastered walls. A small stone spire rises from a central tower which is, historically, the core of the church. Its lowest stage was reconstructed in the C13, but the second stage is Anglo-Saxon, with round-headed openings in the N and S walls, constructed of Roman tiles which have no splays and so were undoubtedly doorways. They must have led to wooden galleries, as so many of the same period have recently been proved to have existed. A similar opening on the W face, altered in the C13, can be seen inside the nave. It has been surmised that this was the upper storey of a two-storey W porch of a church the nave of which is represented by the present chancel, rather on the lines of Monkwearmouth or Titchfield (p. 622), though later than either. But if so, how can what appears to be a gable mark on the W face of the tower (seen within the church) be explained; does it represent another early chamber further W (though possibly later than the present tower)?*

The rest of the church is essentially of the very late C12 and the first third of the C13, without much later alteration except in details (restorations 1859 and 1893‡). During that period a three-bay nave and aisles were built to the W of the tower, the lower stage of which was widened N–S, the

* Or does it represent the roof-line of the original porch? It looks more like the mark of a roof formerly abutting to the W.

‡ The latter by *J. H. Ball.*

present long chancel was built (supposedly on the site of the Saxon nave), and the tower heightened a stage (the final stage, with the spirelet, is of 1859). The N arcade has round piers with round abaci and pointed arches with two slight chamfers – i.e. *c*.1200 or earlier. Then followed, in archaic E.E., the S arcade. Here, obviously, is the pattern of the Chichester retrochoir – the arcade piers are octagonal and surrounded by four detached Purbeck marble shafts with stiff-leaf capitals. The responds have moulded capitals and shaft-rings. At the same time the Anglo-Saxon base of the tower was removed and replaced by a wider space, with arches to E and W and a short pointed tunnel-vault between. The responds of the W arch are nearly as in the S arcade, with detached shafts and slightly more elaborate stiff-leaf capitals, but the E arch has thicker engaged shafts to the responds, with hollow chamfers between them, plainer capitals, and rounded chamfering to the arch itself, suggesting a slightly later date. The aisles extend E, parallel with the tower space, to form chapels, ending flush with the E wall of the tower. The E window of the N aisle has simple Geometrical tracery with an encircled trefoil; the W windows of the aisles are wide lancets; the easternmost of the three dormers on the S aisle is old, with simple two-light tracery within an arched surround; all the other dormer windows to N and S are Victorian insertions. The W window is of three simple lights within an arched surround (going with the old dormer in the S aisle). The C13 design of the chancel is still evident. It had a three-light E window (the present tracery is Victorian, the surround medieval); on the S side it has two-light windows E and W with a central single-light window (the two-light windows were replaced in the late C14 or C15, within the old surrounds), and on the N side a two-light window to the W, remaining in its original condition, simply two wide lancets within a surround. All the surrounds have round-chamfered rere-arches, going with the E arch under the tower. The big N vestry looks coeval (cf. Havant). It has a single lancet in its N wall and a restored two-light window in its E wall; inside is a small C14 recess with trefoiled tracery and an ogee-traceried hood with slender pinnacles above it, probably a pyx chamber where the Sacrament was reserved. The N porch has side walls of stone-filled timber framing. The N arch and gable are very good woodwork, probably C14, with sexfoiled barge-board, each main tracery division being subdivided into smaller cusped patterns with fretwork tracery. The actual entrance arch is plain and pointed, but in its way impressive. – PLATE. Cup, 1709; small Paten, 1825; Flagon, 1823. – MONUMENTS. In the N aisle a Civilian, praying, in a recess with segmental arch and a thin filleted roll. Against the back wall in small figures his soul in a napkin, raised to heaven by two angels. Unfortunately it is all very worn, and the face of the effigy is obliterated. – In the S chapel a Lady, in a cinquefoil ogee-headed recess with the remains of crockets and finial, C14. Her body and head slightly inclined outwards, her hands to her sides finely delineated. Unfortunately the effigy is much worn and mutilated, but the face is still expressive. – Brass to Raffe Smalpage, chaplain to the Earl of Southampton, † 1588. Kneeling figure by a reading-desk. Good Roman lettering. – Some fine minor C18 and early C19 monuments; there must have been talented craftsmen in Emsworth or Havant. – Cartouches to Thomas Sone Senior † 1763 and Junior † 1767. With cherubs at the top and curtain hangings at the bottom. – John Lear † 1800. Triangular tablet, with draped curtains wrapped round the heads of expressive cherubs. – Sophia Letherington † 1805. Shield-shaped, with busts of cherubs, in lively postures. – Many TOMBSTONES in the same fine tradition; hosts of cherubs, curtains, urns, ships. One (to the N of the tower) shows H.M.S. Torbay burning in Portsmouth Harbour in 1758. – In the NW and SE corners of the churchyard two small flint-and-brick huts used in the early C19 by watchmen against body-snatchers, who frequented this lonely but well-filled churchyard.

WARBLINGTON CASTLE, N of the church. A large moated house round a courtyard was built, on the site of an older one, by Margaret Pole, Countess of Salisbury,* between 1514 and 1526.‡ It was ruined in the Civil War, and all that survives is the inner S octagonal turret of the gatehouse (preserved no doubt as a navigational landmark), together with part of the abutting wall and the frame of the four-centred outer arch. The turret is of brick with stone quoins, battlements, and dressings, rising for an extra stage above the three storeys of the gatehouse. It rises amid farm buildings, in front of a plain house which is probably of late C17 origin.

* The Blessed Margaret Pole, martyred by Henry VIII. Her empty tomb is in Christchurch Priory (p. 176).

‡ *Thomas Bertie* carried out works at Warblington in 1518 (John Harvey).

WARBROOK HOUSE *see* EVERSLEY

6020

WARNFORD

OUR LADY. For the historian the special importance of the church lies in the two inscriptions, in the S porch and on the N side, which tell us that Wilfrid founded the church, but that Adam de Port renovated it. Now Adam de Port (cf. Basing) held Warnford from 1171 to his death in 1213, and it is quite possible that the tower represents *c.*1175 and the rest *c.*1210. The tower is assertively Norman, broad and sturdy, with clasping buttresses and with the bell-openings as pairs of big circular holes. Nave and chancel (in one, without a chancel arch) have lancets, the S doorway and the priest's doorway are pointed and have slight chamfers, and even the tower arch – a later widening? – is pointed, though it has only a one-step profile. But what does the large blank round arch round the early C14 E window mean? The window is of three lights and has quite enterprising flowing tracery. – FONT. Of table type, on five supports, but the carving rubbed off. – ROOD SCREEN. Partly of *c.*1630. – TOWER SCREEN. With fluted pilasters and large panels geometrically arranged. – BENCHES. Straight-topped moulded ends; early C16. – STALLS (nave W end). Plain; C15(?). – SUNDIAL. In the porch. Is it E.E., see the stiff-leaf spreading into the corners of the square panel? Or can it be Saxon, like that at Corhampton? – MONUMENTS. William Neale † 1601. Standing monument, not large. Alabaster. Two Corinthian columns, fine frame of the inscription. No figures. – Sir Thomas Neale † 1621 with two wives. Alabaster. The three recumbent effigies one behind the other and stepped up. Coffered ceiling as a canopy and behind it coffered arch. Against the tomb-chest the kneeling children. On the top achievement and two allegorical figures.

KING JOHN'S HOUSE. An oblong hall range, not large, but yet monumental. It was built in the early C13 and consists of an aisled hall of three bays and slender circular piers 25 ft high on octagonal bases. They do not seem to have carried any arches. The responds are curiously thin. The E wall is windowless. Of the N and S windows little can be recognized. At the W end of the hall on the S side was the main entrance. It no doubt led into a screens passage. Two doorways lead W from this into the low ground floor of the service end. This has to the W four small oblong windows with inner and outer splays. Of the floor above we know nothing.

WARNFORD PARK has been demolished. (At the edge of the park, S of where the house was, is an early C19 SUMMER HOUSE. Flint. Parapet with blank quatrefoils. Pointed windows. MHLG)

WARSASH

[DL] 4000

Warsash was a very primitive crab-fishing hamlet, with a hinterland of heaths, transformed after the mid C19 into a warren of strawberry holdings. Yachtsmen discovered the Hamble in the early C20, but there was less scope for mooring on the Warsash side than at Hamble proper across the river; even now there are only a few (pleasantly functional) small boathouses at Warsash. A weird clock tower of *c.*1900 with a half-timbered top and a cap shaped like a policeman's helmet gives some identity to a loose straggle of houses at a crossroads, as does a pub of similar vintage to the waterside. What sticks most in one's memory are the spacious vistas out into the Solent, with the strange industrial landscape of Fawley in the background, the more intimate view up the yacht-filled river, with Hamble snug on the other side, and, above all, the School of Navigation.

SCHOOL OF NAVIGATION (UNIVERSITY OF SOUTHAMPTON). The school moved to Warsash in 1946, occupying miscellaneous buildings which had been put to Service and other uses. First stage of the new building 1959–61, second stage 1964–6, all by *Richard Sheppard, Robson & Partners*, and first-rate in design and grouping. The CADETS' BLOCK is rectangular, of five storeys, brick-faced, with a complex but 97
symmetrical pattern of large-scale and small-scale windows, including three big square-sided glazed projections on the first floor. Even roof-line with boarded fascia. The building stands well above irregularly rising lawns, facing W. A wide, open-sided covered passageway (over a basement boiler-room) runs at r. angles from the S end – with an exceedingly well shaped concrete-panel-faced chimney making an apt visual pivot near the angle – and links with the REFECTORY BLOCK, of which the N end is two-storeyed, the glass-sided upper storey (on a level with the passageway, because of the descent of the ground) boldly oversailing the storey below. Round the corner this block has a striking W façade: long continuous glazing at ground level, and slate-faced walling with three,

very gentle, roof-line pitches above. Buildings of the second stage were under construction at the time of writing; they include a three-storey rectangular block with a distinctive façade of alternate strip brickwork and glazing, the fascia boarded, and a central LIBRARY BLOCK, its ground storey recessed, revealing the massive concrete understructure of the first floor, its tall upper storey mostly brick-faced with clerestory lighting, and topped with a strong concrete fascia. Further E is the OFFICERS' BLOCK, from the first stage. Down by the river a nice BOATHOUSE with brick walls within thin metal framework. Each of the buildings has its own distinct architectural character, yet they are harmonized by the consistent range of materials used throughout the scheme and by their very sensitive grouping, spoiled, alas, both in relation to each other and to their setting, by the surviving older utilitarian structures.

ST MARY, Hook-with-Warsash, in an out-of-the-way position between Warsash proper and the Hook estate. 1871 by *Raphael Brandon*, a building with many quirks. Oddly angular W front, with bell-spirelet over the W gable and long polygonal buttress running down from it to the ground. Tall neo-Dec windows on either side. Inside, suave nave arcades and tall clerestory; elaborate angel roof. Chancel arch with inner order springing from profusely foliated corbels. E end polygonal, with broad shafted lights and intermediate shafts rising to an elaborate wooden mock-vaulted roof – a crowded composition. – STAINED GLASS. E window. Crucifixion by *Barton, Kinder & Alderson* of Brighton, 1950. – Assertive LYCHGATE; grim SCHOOL opposite, built in 1872; RECTORY a little away, the whole group no doubt by *Brandon*.

HOOK PARK. The C19 mansion was burnt down; the brick STABLES survive, neo-Georgianized, with many Weybridgey houses around them amid the remains of fine Victorian landscape. Flat fields border the Solent shore itself, which is strangely undeveloped.

6000

WATERLOOVILLE [DL]

A suburban satellite of Portsmouth, of surprisingly early origin, almost as early as the name suggests. There were villas *c.*1830, and they have been multiplying ever since. The shopping centre was Late Victorian in character, but is being rapidly re-developed, with mini-precincts on both sides of the roaring A3.

ST GEORGE. 1830 by *T. E. Owen.** Small, like a Nonconformist chapel of the period, but with an Anglican tower. Wide nave with traceried windows. Big WEST GALLERY with Royal Arms. Tower with diagonal buttresses up to the bottom of the top stage, chamfered angles above that, and lancet bell-openings. Big neo-Tudor door. All stuccoed. Small C20 chancel.

BAPTIST CHURCH. 1884–5 by *G. Rake*. Weird Italianate tower, rough-faced on the lower two stages, the second with circular openings decked with swags and garlands. Swags again on the frieze below the cornice of the second stage; top stage of ashlar with double pilasters on either side of a round-arched recess containing a clock on each face; low pyramid top. The church is the only real landmark in the main street.

SACRED HEART (R.C.) and ST MICHAEL'S CONVENT. The Convent (also a home for girls) was built in 1889 by *Leonard Stokes* and has been added to piecemeal. Stokes's original block has his unmistakable originality, but tempered with monastic austerity. Three-storeyed, the top storey an attic, the second with small windows, the lower with wide brick pilasters (of a brighter brick than the rest of the walls), which die above first-floor level, spanned with wide segmental arches of the same brick, containing the ground-floor windows. The gabled end is white-rendered. New addition to the S, 1965 by *H. Tompsett* and *Elisabeth Holliss*, of gaunt brick with narrow vertical strip-recesses between pilasters, containing three tiers of slender windows. The church, to the W of the convent, by *W. C. Mangan*, *c.*1925, has an extraordinary plan; three naves converge on a single chancel each at forty-five degrees to the next, the central one (aligned geographically W) for the nuns, the N one (aligned SW) for the children, the S one (aligned NW) for the parishioners. The sanctuary has communion rails to each nave; the altar is set in a shallow apse. Alas, the architecture is not so imaginative as the planning; the roof arrangement at the junction is simply awkward and the exterior a mass of round arches in fussy brickwork. ST PETER'S PRIMARY SCHOOL, also in the grounds, by *F. G. Broadbent*, 1964, is more uplifting architecturally; a nice amalgam of cubic shapes of different heights, in light grey brick. No fascias, the windows set in vertical recesses with rough white panelling above and between them; dated but pleasing.

* Or *Jacob Owen*.

The villas fade out northwards fairly pleasantly into what passes for the FOREST OF BERE. There were still wide intermittent stretches of forest (in the old sense of the word – rough country, not necessarily all wooded) between the Meon and Sussex in the early C19; by the end of the century most of it had been enclosed or squatted away, and what remains are mainly Forestry Commission plantations.

WEATHAM FARM *see* LISS

WEEKE *see* WINCHESTER, p. 692

WESTBOURNE *see* BOURNEMOUTH, pp. 121, 127, 128

WESTBURY HOUSE *see* EAST MEON

4010

WEST END [DL]

A Victorian hilltop village near Southampton, being steadily suburbanized.

ST JAMES. 1890 by *Blomfield*, on the site of a church of 1838; big but not inspiring. – Imported C15 FONT, octagonal with traceried panels.

7050

WEST GREEN HOUSE

$1\frac{1}{4}$ m. WSW of Hartley Wintney High Street

West Green House is a delightful house, but it is also a puzzling house. Its architectural history is not really unravelled. All one sees, except the principal staircase, looks *c.*1700–30, but definitely of two distinct phases. Which came first?

The entrance is on the N side. In the middle of the front is a polygonal bay with a porch, and the doorway has a Gibbs surround.* Originally the entrance was not here. So this was a canted bay. On the l. and r. are windows, some with frilly lintels. This and the top battlements would make one suggest *c.*1710–20 – cf. e.g. Biddesden in Wiltshire. But according to the literature the battlements and the porch are an alteration of *c.*1750. Added to this centre are one bay l. and one bay r. with, on the ground floor, a bust in a round recess. This is the preparation for the W front, which has just such busts in roundels on the upper floor. On the ground floor the doorway – the principal doorway originally – has a Gibbs surround.

* Big iron lampholder above.

Five bays, hipped roof with three dormers. If the angle bays of the N front are an addition and the W front belongs to them, then N must precede W. The Gibbs doorway in the N porch may well be re-set. The W side is extended by screen walls with brick arches with Gibbs rustication. The wall on the N side is not original. It dates from 1905. The E side of the house is informal. On the S side are C20 additions.

Inside, behind the N entrance, from the first to the second floor a piece of a very fine staircase with square fluted balusters and skew capitals following the ascent of the stairs and carved tread-ends. That looks earlier than anything else, late C17 rather than early C18. Behind the W front is a large room, *c.*1730 in style, and a small room with an angle fireplace (which is a late C17 to early C18 motif). The main staircase alone is obviously later than the rest. Iron balustrade with S- and honeysuckle motifs, i.e. *c.*1770. But at its top landing there is here also Queen Anne evidence: three arches.

DUTCH HOUSE. Three by three bays with giant pilaster-strips and a mansard roof.

FOURACRE, ½ m. E of West Green House. By *Ernest Newton*, 1901. Brick, symmetrical front with two gables and, as its climax, in the middle a set of three chimneys, belonging to the hall inside.

WEST HOWE *see* BOURNEMOUTH, p. 134

WEST LEIGH *see* HAVANT, p. 278

WEST MEON

6020

ST JOHN EVANGELIST. By *G. G. Scott*, 1843–6. Large, of squared flints, with a prominent tower. 'Second Pointed', i.e. with plate and bar tracery. Five-bay arcades. Not much carved decoration. – ROYAL ARMS. Daintily carved; 1712. – SCULPTURE. Two small Flemish panels of *c.*1600, Annunciation and Nativity.

HALL PLACE, ½ m. E. Late C17 centre of five bays with a doorway with segmental pediment. Two-bay additions l. and r. of *c.*1720. Round the corner one of them has a five-bay front of its own with a steep two-bay pediment. The older windows are oblong, the later segment-headed. The main late C17 doorway has a charming openwork frieze and a segmental pediment.

(DRUIDS' CIRCLE. On the A272 road W of The Hut, near The Dean. A folly.)

WESTON *see* SOUTHAMPTON, pp. 594, 596, 599

6040 WESTON PATRICK

ST LAURENCE. 1868 by *Thomas Henry Wyatt*. Flint; nave and chancel in one, and a funny pagoda bell-turret. The Wyatts owned the manor, and the family paid for the building of the church and still contribute to its upkeep. Some rich foliage carving inside. – The STAINED GLASS of the E window commemorates Thomas Henry's parents. – PLATE. Chalice and Paten Cover, 1568.

(WESTON PATRICK HOUSE. 1956–7 by *Sir Albert Richardson*. Quiet and scholarly neo-Georgian. Brick. The professor at his best. NT)

WESTON CORBETT HOUSE, ¼ m. NW. Nice, brick, C18. Five bays, hipped roof.

6020 WEST TISTED

ST MARY MAGDALEN. Nave and chancel. Small weather-boarded bell-turret. Blocked Norman S window, blocked Norman N doorway. Brick S porch of 1750. The chancel of 1848. – STAINED GLASS. The E window by *Kempe*, 1892. – PLATE. Cup with incised ornament and Cover Paten, 1568; Paten, 1723.

WEST TOWN *see* HAYLING ISLAND

2020 WEST TYTHERLEY

CHURCH. 1833 by *G. Guthrie* (GR); still entirely Georgian. W tower of flint and red and grey brick. S porch the same. But the body of the church all red and grey headers. The Perp window details probably belong to 1877, when the stone chancel was added. – Fine WEST GALLERY on slim clustered Gothick shafts. – FONT. Purbeck marble, of the table type. Against the side square leaf motifs. – PLATE. Chalice of the late C16; Chalice of 1656; Paten of 1741; Cup of gold, recent, by *A. W. Mowbray*. – BRASS to Ann Whitehead † 1480. The figure is 22½ in. long.

It was at West Tytherley that in 1841–2 Robert Owen built his

HARMONY HALL. His architect was *J. A. Hansom.* It was built for 100 adults and 40 children to encourage them to live a rational life.* The building was pulled down in 1903.

NORMAN COURT. The dates given for the house are *c.*1730, *c.*1810, and *c.*1910. The last-named date determines the exterior: neo-Georgian, with angle towers. The two projecting lower wings, however, are of *c.*1730. The side of the house has giant Ionic pilasters. The architectural history needs sorting out, especially since the work of *c.*1810 was by *Dance.*‡

WEST WORLDHAM 7040

ST NICHOLAS. Small. Nave and chancel in one. Simple C13 S and N doorways. Of the same date the jambs of former lancets in the E wall (the present window is Perp) and two small N lancets. The bell recess is probably of 1888. – PLATE. Paten inscribed 1723.

BOWL BARROW, on the SW boundary of Littlewood Copse. The SW edge of the barrow has been ploughed out, the surviving monument being 75 ft in diameter and 6 ft high.

WEYHILL 3040

Weyhill was famous in the past for its Fair, second only to that of Winchester. Piers Plowman knows it in the later C14, Defoe mentions it, Cobbett still writes of it in 1822, and Hardy fictionalizes it in *The Mayor of Casterbridge.*

ST MICHAEL. Mostly of 1864 (by *Hakewill,* according to the Rev. Basil Clarke). Flint and brick bands. Plate tracery. Only the chancel is medieval. Norman chancel arch, round with one slight chamfer. E.E. chancel side lancets. – PLATE. Elizabethan Chalice; Almsplate of 1692(?); Chalice and Paten of 1722. – MONUMENTS. John Gawler † 1803. By *Sir Richard Westmacott.* Two youths in contemplation of the broken-off Corinthian capital of a column whose upper ending is now covered by a branch of weeping willow. – Henry Bosanquet † 1817. Signed *Maddox,* Undertaker, Welbeck Street.

CLANVILLE HOUSE, Clanville, 1¼ m. N. Four bays plus middle doorway and above it round-arched blank window. The real windows are segment-headed. Later doorway. Hipped roof on modillion frieze. The house must be early C18.

* Information kindly given me by Mr Denis Evinson.

‡ I was told about this by Mr John Harris.

WHALE ISLAND *see* PORTSMOUTH, p. 430

WHEATSHEAF INN *see* NORTH WALTHAM

3040 WHERWELL

ST PETER AND HOLY CROSS. 1856–8 by *Woodyer*. Lively, rather Scandinavian bell-turret with spire. The nave roof sweeps down with a break into the aisle roof. On the W front a semicircular stair-turret. The window surrounds in the aisles are deliberately not archaeologically correct, and in the chancel the windows themselves carry no authority. The bell-turret stands inside not on wooden posts but on two slim stone piers which do not try to keep a *modus vivendi* with the arcade piers. – ARCHITECTURAL FRAGMENTS from the old church inside and also in vicarage buildings. The most interesting is a block with Anglo-Saxon interlace and C13 detail: a re-used CROSS SHAFT with part of the cross-head, the VCH suggests. – SCULPTURE. Two small early C14 stone reliefs: the Harrowing of Hell, and Noli me tangere. – STAINED GLASS. E window by *Wailes*, 1858. – PLATE. Chalice and Paten, *c.*1650; Paten, 1662. – MONUMENTS. Nun, early C15, in an ample mantle. – Sir Owen West † 1551. Tomb-chest with sparse strapwork. The inscription is still in black-letter. – MAUSOLEUM of the Iremonger family. Victorian. Large, of shrine-type, and incorporating monster heads from the corbel-table of the medieval church.

THE PRIORY. White, early C19, with a Tuscan porch, a cupola, and on the E side the three middle windows carried up through ground floor and first floor. (Behind is the dining room, which has a coved ceiling. In the dressing room a chimneypiece from Carlton House Terrace. MHLG)

4040 WHITCHURCH

ALL HALLOWS. Externally all of 1866 (by *Ferrey*), except for the lower part of the W tower, which is dated 1716 and has a horizontally placed, keyed-in oval window above the doorway. Plate tracery, also lancets, also bar tracery. The tower carries a shingled broach-spire. The tower arch is probably early C13, but altered. But the S arcade is genuine C13 work. Three bays, round piers, round abaci, single-chamfered arches. The N arcade is patently Perp. The piers have the four-shafts-and-four-hollows section and the arches three

hollow chamfers. The E bays on both sides are of 1866. So is the chancel. – FONT. Octagonal, Perp, with quatrefoils. – PAINTING. A panel, 43½ by 48 in., with the Ten Commandments surrounded by fourteen naïve but lively paintings of appropriate biblical scenes. The date is C18. It is like a broadsheet. – PLATE. Chalice of 1648; Paten of 1713; Flagon of 1730. – MONUMENTS. First of all an extremely interesting Anglo-Saxon gravestone, the front like that of a Roman 6
gravestone of the Legions. Sir Thomas Kendrick dates it mid C9. The stone has an arched top and the front an arched recess in which is the demi-figure of Christ. The inscription runs along the top in Roman letters: Hic Corpus Frithburgae requiescit in pacem sepultum. At the back a symmetrical plant scroll of 'delightful precision and strength'. – Thomas Brooke † 1612. Two recumbent stone effigies. Poor in execution. – John Portal and his wife who died in 1877. A neo-Jacobean tablet of alabaster, interesting for its date. – In the churchyard a tremendous burst yew tree.

TOWN HALL. Georgian. Brick, of three bays, the ground floor with three segmental arches, the upper floor with one monumental arched window. One-bay pediment and cupola. Hipped roof.

WHITE HART HOTEL. At the main street crossing. Brick, limewashed. At the boldly and effectively rounded corner an Ionic porch of rather stocky proportions.

On the way out S in WINCHESTER ROAD the SILK MILL, dated 1815. Red brick, of five widely spaced bays, with broad, segment-headed windows with metal glazing bars. Steep one-bay pediment. Thin cupola.

On the way out to Laverstoke THE GABLES, built as the WORKHOUSE in 1847–8 by *S. O. Foden* for *c.* £3,500 (GS). Flint and brick dressings. Symmetrical gabled centre and symmetrical wings, probably partly later.

WHITSBURY 1010

ST LEONARD. 1878. Brick W tower, with the odd conceit of a square bell-stage but a chamfered stage below. Nave and chancel. – ORGAN, by *Willis's*, recent, and remarkably well designed. – MONUMENT. Cap. E. H. Gage Lambert † 1872. By *Gaffin & Co.* Anchor with the inscription on a piece of cloth hanging over the anchor.

OLD RECTORY. A curious Late Georgian three-bay front with a passion for thin long niches.

WHITSBURY CAMP, ¼ m. NNE of the church. The defences of this oval fort consist of three lines of ramparts and ditches enclosing about 16 acres. The banks increase in size towards the interior, the innermost still standing to a height of over 10 ft. In 1960 part of the interior near the N defences was excavated and the plan of a circular timber house 25 ft in diameter recovered. The associated pottery was of the Iron Age B cultures. Slight traces of Mesolithic and Roman occupation were also found.

5010 WICKHAM [DL]

Wickham is the finest village in Hampshire, and one of the best in the South of England. It is built round a great rectangular 'square' broken only by an island block of buildings at its N end, and along a narrow street, Bridge Street, leading E. Not only the layout but also the scale and disposition of the buildings in relation to the spaces are exceptionally happy. The village was the birthplace of William of Wykeham in 1324.

ST NICHOLAS. A most unfortunate building, so thoroughly restored in 1862 (by *F. & H. Francis* and in 1872–7 that it has lost almost all its medieval interest, without gaining any positive Victorian character. The W tower, with fancy bell-stage and shingled spire, is completely by the Francises, but in it is re-set a restored Norman doorway with original capitals, one having a representation of a centaur with a bow and arrow (Sagittarius?), the other a leaf design. Aisleless nave, transepts, chancel, the S transept externally of brick. The best preserved detail is the E.E. W respond of the arch from chancel to S chapel.* – PLATE. Set of 1639. – MONUMENTS. In the chancel N wall front of a large former tomb-chest. Four cusped fields with shields. – In the S transept canopied alabaster tomb to Sir William Uvedale † 1615 and his wife, not in its original position and possibly rearranged. Deep round coffered canopy, surmounted by a coat of arms

* There has been a recent sensitive restoration internally by *Potter & Hare*, consisting mainly of rearrangement and renewal of fittings, but revealing unsuspected spatial qualities in the church, particularly in the S transept and S chapel, between which there is a very effective stone screen of open traceried panels.

between two lions and flanked by obelisks. The figures lie in half-reclining position on their sides, with kneeling children in front of the tomb-chest. The back of the canopy is crowded with ornament and emblems, including numerous representations of skulls and bones as well as a cadaver; the designer was clearly afflicted with morbidity. – Fragment of a monument to W. Uvedale † 1569. Inscription tablet with restrained strapwork surround in a guilloche frame. No figures at all. At the top coat of arms between two miniature columns. – Also tablet to William Faulkner † 1689, a cartouche with a Baroque surround.

WICKHAM RECTORY, E of the church. Almost a mansion. Early C18. Five bays, two storeys, of red and grey brick with wooden cornice, hipped roof and dormers. Elegant Doric pedimented porch and doorway with semicircular fanlight.

THE VILLAGE. Wickham had a charter for a market and fair in 1268. The market did not survive, but the fair prospered, and it was probably to accommodate it that the Square was laid out. It is perfectly regular, except for the rectangular island block which encroaches on the N end, leaving a fairly wide thoroughfare on the E side and a narrow one on the W. Most of the buildings round the square are quite humble, but there are just enough of the larger scale, some of them most happily placed, and set off by the smaller ones, to give the whole townscape composition a feeling of urbanity.

THE SQUARE, EAST SIDE. The whole range, almost as far as the island block, is of two storeys, humble in pretension, with many shopfronts and upper storeys anything from Georgian to C20 in date. The roof-lines are irregular and mostly old-tiled; these more than the façades make it an interesting composition. Doubtless many of these houses are much older than they look from the front. The range is ended northwards by two Georgian houses which more than any other individual buildings help to make the townscape of Wickham so memorable: the first is of three storeys, Early Georgian, of moderate urban scale; the second is also of three storeys, but to an altogether larger scale. Both are in local grey and red brick. The smaller house has a massive doorcase with segmental pediment, large entablature, and fluted Tuscan columns; the larger house has a simpler doorcase with broken pediment. The special value of these houses is in their relationship to the whole of the composition of the square; the scale of the buildings on the E side is suddenly heightened by the first and then reaches its climax in the second, which is visually the focal point of the whole square. Without these two houses the scale of the buildings round the square would probably seem too small for the expanse.

THE SQUARE, WEST SIDE. At the S end the CURIO SHOP is a two-storeyed timber-framed survival, with overhanging upper storey, now roughcast. The KING'S HEAD has a Georgian brick façade unfortunately painted over, with pedimented porch. The next two houses form a semi-detached pair of Early Georgian urban character, in grey and red brick, with segment-headed windows and string courses, and fine door-cases. EASTWOOD HOUSE, the last house on the W of the square before it is encroached on by the island block, is a charming composition of two storeys, in grey and red brick, with a single canted bay on the upper storey, resting on four free-standing piers.

THE SQUARE, NORTH END. On the E frontage of the island block is a pleasant but homely group of Georgian and Early Victorian buildings. At the end a charming early shopfront, with two small square projecting windows, and an open pitched hood, like an elementary pediment, between them. This stretch of street, and the whole townscape looking N from the square, is closed visually by a small Early Victorian house at the top of Bridge Street, flint with brown brick dressings, a wavy bargeboard over the asymmetrical gable, small windows of intricate leaded panes, and a small second gable over one of the upper-floor windows, the only piece of Gothicism visible in Wickham Square. It is admirable in its position.

THE SQUARE, SOUTH END. Till lately the square was closed southwards simply by trees behind a garden wall, with the main E–W road running in front of it. Now the road is being widened, the wall has gone, and with it most of the trees. The site is to be developed with three-storey terrace housing on two sides of an open courtyard (an existing Georgian house forming the third) which will in effect create a S extension to the square, giving it for the first time an architectural S termination. The design, by *H. Hubbard Ford & Associates*, was exhibited at the Royal Academy in 1965 and looks a little too uniformly urban for Wickham; it would have been better to have created a studiedly informal grouping echoing that in the rest of the square, with most of the houses quite small in scale but one or two noticeably larger. But it is comforting that so much trouble has obviously been taken about the design of houses on this outstandingly important site.

BRIDGE STREET leads E from the prolongation of the square at its N end. It is narrow and homely, curving out of sight with a range of old cottages (THE BARRACKS) on the outside of the curve, with a slightly raised pavement and a touch of greensward in front. The cottages have stretches of exposed timbering on their upper storeys, alternating with brick, and are distinctly arty in feeling. Elsewhere on the S side are pleasant but humble cottages; on the N side are two moderate scaled Georgian houses, WARWICK HOUSE, unfortunately whitewashed, and BLANTON HOUSE, still with its Hampshire grey and red brick uncovered. Then, further E, the most intriguing house in Wickham, QUEEN LODGE. It is of brick and must date from the later C17. Formerly five bays, the middle bay with giant brick pilasters ending in Ionic capitals and supporting an entablature, all in brickwork and rising nearly to the top. Within this frame there is a small pediment to the main door of the house, also in brick. All the rest of the façade has been altered; the windows had raised brick surrounds with scrolly ears. The E façade shows some flintwork and tile-hanging. At the foot of Bridge Street, on the Meon, CHESAPEAKE MILL, 1820, with a three-storey façade with segment-headed windows, and wooden gantry projecting from the gable; essentially functional. The internal woodwork was taken from the former American man o'war Chesapeake, captured by the British in 1813. The adjoining mill house is a little earlier than the mill, with broad bay windows. Opposite, the former WICKHAM BREWERY, buildings of uncertain date grouped around an irregular unenclosed courtyard, with broad wooden-framed windows. Typical rural-industrial building, but dominated by a four-storeyed gabled tower block dated 1887.

ROOKSBURY. 1835 by *C. H. Tatham* in an extensive park; now a girls' school. Square stuccoed two-storeyed block with big-scale details. Wide plain pilasters at the angles and intermediately, widely spaced windows with simple surrounds, those of the lower storey taller and with moulded hoods. Bold segmental bay in the centre of the SE front, rising the whole height of the building with triple windows on each floor; thin but strongly projecting cornice, boldly moulded above a slight frieze. Grand tetrastyle Ionic portico, with cornice and pediment similarly detailed, boldly projecting from the SW façade, with tall, hooded, square-headed doorway underneath. Entrance lobby with segmental end opposite the entrance. Some fine rooms: the former drawing room has an elliptical bay, the former dining room Corinthian pillars simulating granite. The library has similar pillars simulating marble and the original mahogany shelves, light and angular. In the upstairs passageways a series of elliptical arches. STABLES with cupola; sympathetic extensions of 1964 by *K. G. Brooke*. In the grounds a weird TOWER of 1826, also by *Tatham*, octagonal, of three diminishing tiers all castellated; gutted. Stucco LODGE on the Droxford road. (PARK PLACE. C18; now a convent.)

WIDLEY *see* PORTSMOUTH, p. 468

6030 WIELD

ST JAMES. Nave and chancel and weatherboarded bell-turret. Mostly of 1884–5, but the S doorway (one order of columns, single-step arch), the chancel arch (two slight chamfers), and the plain priest's doorway are late C12. – FONT. Of table type, Purbeck marble, with six flat arches to each side. The font was found in a garden in the Close at Winchester. – PLATE. Paten of *c.*1500, with the monogram of Christ; Cup 1569. – MONUMENT. William Walop † 1617. Alabaster. Two recumbent effigies, he behind and above her. Back plate with ribbons and trophies. At the top large coat of arms and two cherubs with symbols of death.

WINCHESTER 4020

Introduction, 657
Roman Winchester, 658
Saxon Winchester, 659
The Cathedral, 661
Crypt, Transepts, and Crossing, 661
Retrochoir and Lady Chapel 668
Nave, 671
The Changes in Lady Chapel, South-East Chapel, and Crossing, 673
Chancel, 674
Furnishings, 675
The Precinct, 685
The Town, 691
Churches, 691
Public Buildings, 694
Perambulation, 713

INTRODUCTION

Winchester with not only the Cathedral but also the College, St Cross, the Royal Hall, and Wolvesey Palace is the richest architecturally of all English bishops' sees. It is also England's second capital, and was still (or again) felt as such in the C17. Winchester was the capital of Wessex and the capital of England from Egbert in 829 to Athelstan, Edgar, Alfred, to Canute who was buried at Winchester, and to William the Conqueror, who had himself crowned at Winchester as well as in London. He is supposed to have built a palace immediately N of the Old Minster (the cathedral) and the New Minster and also built defensive earthworks on the W hill, and Henry III, who was born at Winchester, built there his Royal Hall. By then London had established its primacy. For the Norman period Mr Colvin writes: 'If under the Norman Kings England can be said to have possessed an administrative capital, then Winchester shared that distinction with Westminster. For it was at Winchester that the King kept his treasure, and in the C11 and C12 the King's treasury was the heart of his government.' Domesday Book also was kept at Winchester. And for a much later century it must be recorded that Charles II in 1683 commissioned *Wren* to build him a large palace on the same hill, and that this went up indeed, even if it was never completed. But by that time Winchester was a thriving town in its own right. Out of quarrels between the Kings and the Bishops residing at Wolvesey, and between the town and both or either, Winchester had got its charters. Admittedly in the C18 Winchester was thriving in a much more modest way – a county town not a capital. The bishops resided at Farnham rather than Wolvesey, and many of the ancient monuments were demolished: large parts of Wolvesey, almost the whole of Hyde Abbey, St Mary Magdalen's Hospital, the North Gate, the South Gate, the East Gate.

Winchester lies on the W bank of the river Itchen. A millrace runs parallel from the grounds of Hyde Abbey to N of St Cross. Of the town walls a certain amount is preserved (*see* p. 697), but they ought to be kept separate from the cathedral precinct walls and the walls of the bishop's palace.

ROMAN WINCHESTER

The Roman town of VENTA BELGARUM, which now lies beneath the medieval and modern city, was sited on a spur of gravel which projected into the Itchen valley. The city wall, representing the final limits of the Roman town, encloses an area of 138 acres. Of the original Roman structure practically nothing is now visible, with the exception of a small sector exposed behind a grating in the wall running parallel to the river Itchen, S of the city bridge. The medieval wall, surviving in the SW corner of the city, is largely a re-faced version of its Roman predecessor. The town itself is not well known, but excavations have brought to light traces of the street-grid and of several buildings. In the insula which lies immediately N of the cathedral nave a large public building measuring 340 ft by 280 ft has recently been identified, its position, size, and plan strongly suggesting that it is the forum and basilica. Of the other public buildings no details are at present available; the existence of an Imperial weaving mill is, however, mentioned in the *Notitia Dignitatum* and a fine inscription bearing the letters]NTO[, 12 in. high, found in Middle Brook Street, probably comes from a large public building of C2 or C3 date. Several town houses have been partly examined: when St George Street was widened, remains of large buildings were discovered at the junction of St Peter's Street, Upper Brook Street, and Middle Brook Street; more recently houses have come to light beneath the cathedral car park, and the distribution of remains discovered in the last century suggests that large buildings were numerous, particularly in the S part of the town. To the W of the walled area is an earthwork called Oram's Arbour; it is not yet certain whether this is a Belgic or an Early Roman defence.

SAXON WINCHESTER*

The Saxon cathedral, the Old Minster, was founded in the mid C7. This church, outside the W door of which St Swithun was buried in 862, was rebuilt between 971 and 994. A century later it was demolished to make way for the Norman cathedral. Two hundred years before, in 903, a second church, the New Minster, had been built alongside the Old, so close that the singing in the two churches mingled in confusion. The New Minster, to which in the late C10 a tower perhaps adorned on six storeys with sculptured friezes was added, was abandoned for a new site in 1110. A Nuns' Minster, founded by Alfred and his wife in the late C9, was brought by Edgar (959–75) into a single monastic enclosure together with the Old and New Minsters. As the burial and coronation churches of many of the kings of Wessex and of England, these minsters formed an ecclesiastical group without parallel in this country.

The sites of the Old and New Minsters had long been uncertain when the evidence was rigorously analysed by the late Roger Quirk in 1957 and 1961. He initiated excavations which have located the two minsters and aim at their complete investigation. The Old Minster lies immediately N of the present nave, at a slight angle, so that the W end of the minster is partly below the W end of the cathedral. The New Minster lies N of and parallel to the Old, in places as little as 3 ft away. The Nuns' Minster, S of the Guildhall, has not been precisely located.

Only the E half of the Old Minster has so far been excavated. Before the C10 rebuilding there was an E–W alignment of church, chapels, and crosses. After the rebuilding the church may have been 300 ft long, with apsidal E end, lateral apses to N and S, and high altar raised over a crypt of *confessio*-type contrived in a chapel of the earlier alignment. The external crypt, lateral apses, tower, and the western entrance, as analysed from the documents by Roger Quirk, indicate that the rebuilt minster drew heavily on Carolingian architecture.

The New Minster, little excavated so far, was an aisled church about 68 ft wide with shallow projections for an eastern transept. Once again Carolingian models seem not far away. Within the New Minister precinct various Saxon structures were found (A–D on the plan). The oval building (which was perhaps a mortuary chapel) lay E of a cemetery which probably belongs to the earlier stages of the New Minster, 903–1066. Buildings

* Contributed by Martin Biddle.

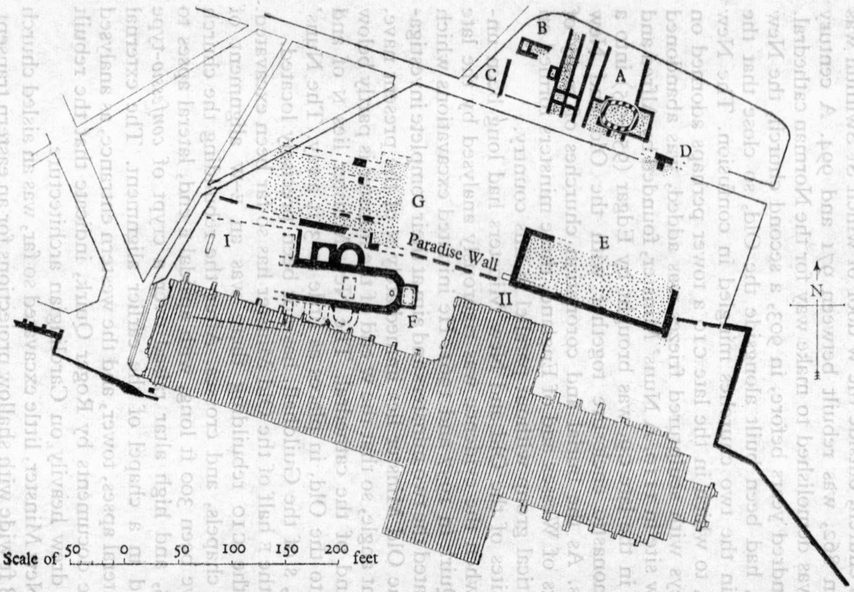

Winchester Cathedral, plan of Saxon church, excavated in 1962–5
(plan by courtesy of Martin Biddle)

A–D were constructed on the site of the cemetery and over the oval building. Buildings A–D are interpreted by Roger Quirk and Mr Biddle as being later domestic building of the New Minster in the period 1066–1110. Group A surrounding a courtyard with a veranda on the W side seems to be an attempt at a claustral layout.

During excavation of the Old Minster in 1965 a stone panel, perhaps from a narrative frieze, was found. The subject may 7
represent an incident from the legend of Sigmund as recorded in the Volsunga Saga. It could occur here as part of a great frieze celebrating the origin and traditional history of the houses of England and Denmark. Cnut, buried in the Old Minster in 1035, could have intended the frieze as a neat demonstration of Anglo-Danish concord. Although this is the only known part of a late Saxon narrative frieze, Roger Quirk's discussion of the New Minster tower shows that sculpture on a comparable scale may have existed within a few feet of the Old Minster. *See* p. 831

THE CATHEDRAL

Winchester town and cathedral lie in a hollow. There are therefore no dramatic distant views – the less so, as the cathedral has no strong vertical accents. It is only in the Close that one realizes its size, and inside the building that its immense length can speak fully.

The cathedral with its 556 ft external length is the longest in England and in Europe. The height of its nave vault is only 78 ft. The building is largely of stone from the Isle of Wight. Its main periods are Walkelin's (1070–98) for the Norman transepts and E range of the cloister, de Lucy's (1189–1204) and des Roches's (1204–38) for the retrochoir and Lady Chapel, Edington's (1345–66) and more Wykeham's (1366–1404) for the total remodelling of the nave, Courtenay's (1486–92) and Langton's (1493–1500) for the remodelling of the Lady Chapel and the chapel S of it, and Fox's (1500–28) for the remodelling of the chancel. It is in this order that the cathedral will be presented. The principal restorations were as follows: *Garbett* 1812–28, *Colson* 1874–91 (£40,000), *Jackson* 1906–10 (£100,000; more a securing than a restoration. It included the complete underpinning of the foundations with concrete).

CRYPT, TRANSEPTS, AND CROSSING

Walkelin, the first Norman bishop, began the cathedral in 1079. In 1093 the relics of St Swithun were transferred to

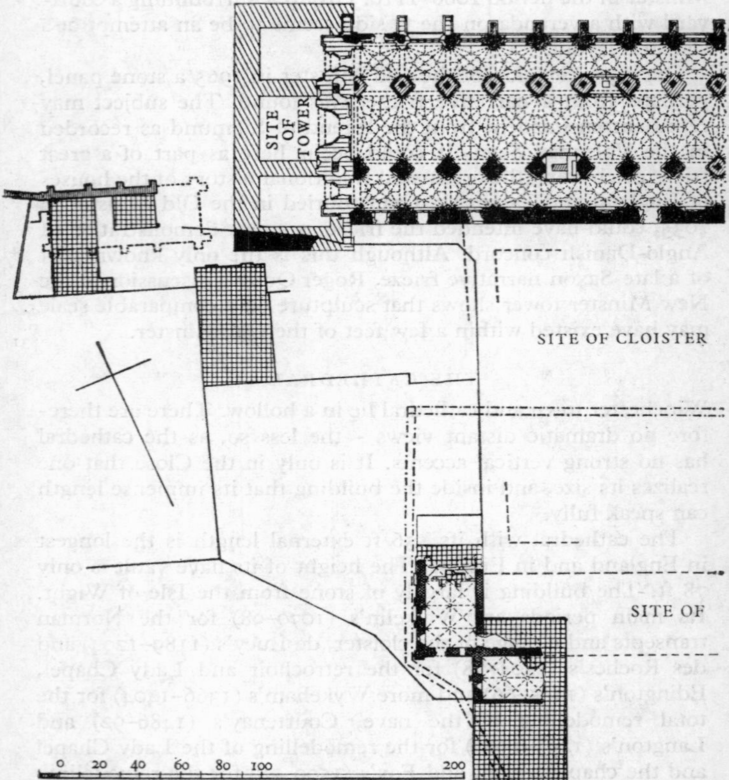
SITE OF TOWER
SITE OF CLOISTER
SITE OF
0 20 40 60 80 100 200
Scale in Feet

Winchester

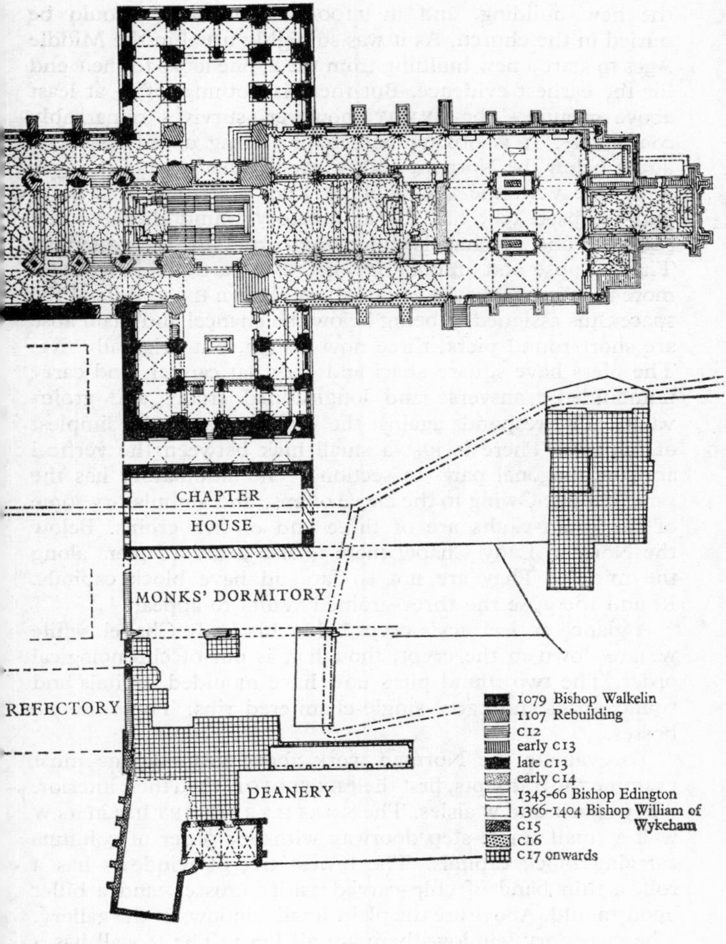

Cathedral, plan

the new building, and in 1100 William Rufus could be buried in the church. As it was so highly usual in the Middle Ages to start a new building from the E, one looks to the E end for the earliest evidence. But there is nothing left – at least above ground. The CRYPT, however, survives remarkably completely. It is oblong with a projecting apsed space no doubt below the Norman Lady Chapel. The E end of the apse is in line with the E end of de Lucy's retrochoir. The W part is apsed too, but the ambulatory round the apse has small NE and SE chapels filling the corners of the rectangle. The big apse and ambulatory of the W part again represent more than probably the layout above. Down the middle of the space thus assigned to being below the chancel and main apse are short round piers, three now visible, but originally five. The piers have square abaci and very flat capitals and carry unmoulded transverse and longitudinal arches and groin-vaults. The responds against the walls have not the simplest of imposts. There is just a small nick between the vertical and the diagonal part (in section). The ambulatory has the same details. Owing to the curve of apse and ambulatory some of the groin-vaults are of three and of five groins. Below the Norman Lady Chapel there is also a row of piers along the middle. They are not so fat and have block capitals. Round the apse the three-groined vaults re-appear.

A glance at de Lucy's crypt below his Lady Chapel, while we are down in the crypt, though it is out of chronological order. The two round piers now have moulded capitals and round abaci and carry single-chamfered ribs. There are no bosses.

To evaluate the Norman work above ground, one must examine the transepts, first their EXTERIOR, then their interior. They have E and W aisles. The NORTH TRANSEPT has in its W wall a small single-step doorway with one order of columns carrying block capitals. The lowest tier of windows has a roll, a thin band of chip-carved saltire crosses, and a billet hood-mould. Above are the plain small windows of the gallery. The clerestory windows here are all Perp. The N wall has a regular three-part composition with five flat buttresses, two at the angles, two at the angles of the 'nave', and one up the middle. The lower windows are as before, except for the easternmost, which was replaced *c.*1300 by one with cusped intersecting tracery. Sill frieze of billets, and another at the sill of the next stage. The windows are the same, only those corresponding to the galleries are blank. The two middle windows are a Perp replacement; so are those of the next stage. In the gable is a tracery rose window whose date it is hard to decide. To the E the Norman ground-stage windows are replaced by Dec ones, two with reticulated tracery and one with three spherical triangles, two of them set diagonally, in the head. This is in style ten or twenty years earlier than reticulation. Above are again the small gallery windows. In the clerestory three windows are like the others, but the fourth, northernmost, is puzzling. It is flatter and altogether different. Moreover just N of it, facing E, at the top of the pitched roof of the gallery, is the start of arcading, probably blank. This can only mean that the E wall of the aisle gallery was intended to be carried up higher. For what other reason can that have been done than for a tower? The odd window would then have been meant to look from such a tower into the transept. Willis, in 1845, observant as always, noticed and explained this, and we shall see when we look at the interior that he had conclusive reasons to assume the plan to build four such towers on the four outer corners of the transepts. The E wall of the N transept ends with a corbel-table with heads, monsters, etc.

The SOUTH TRANSEPT is essentially the same, though on the W and S sides the cloister and the monastic buildings meant some interference. The top corbel-table is preserved here on the W side, which it is not in the N transept. To the S there are two flat turrets without any decoration, whereas on the N side no turrets were built or are preserved. In the gable is blank, flat intersecting arcading and higher up a group of five stepped arches. To the E, at the ground stage, is another window with the same three spherical triangles and also one with reticulation.

The CROSSING TOWER has small windows originally l. and r. of the roofs and, above, three tall arches each side with zigzag on shafts and rolls, which indicates a date after about 1100. That there is reason to assume such a date we shall see presently.

Now the INTERIOR. The crossing piers have to the E and W three shafts, two slender, one a segment of a fat pier. To the N and S there are three of equal girth. The arches are also preserved. They are unmoulded. An uninterrupted shaft rises inside the tower to the top, others inside the transepts to the roof. Even the briefest glance at the adjoining parts of the transepts to which we now turn will show – as Willis was the first to state – that the masonry of the crossing piers and arches and also of the immediately adjoining piers N and S of the crossing piers is more smoothly tooled and more finely jointed than the rest. The reason for this (and the zigzag outside) is that this is a rebuilding after Walkelin's tower had fallen in 1107. Fear of a recurrence of such a calamity is also responsible for the fact that the crossing piers are of a size (in section) unparalleled among English crossing piers. The W and E arches were kept as wide open as probably before, but the N and S arches were narrowed so much that the arches needed a great deal of stilting. Another amendment after the collapse of the tower will have to be referred to presently.

The SOUTH TRANSEPT E side is of four bays separated by the same mast-like shafts. The clerestory sill goes round them. The first bay contains the entrance into the chancel aisle. The arch is stilted and of one step. The capitals here and all round both transepts at all levels are either block capitals or of one, two, or three scallops, all very substantial. The next bays have rib-vaults, the ribs of a profile of a half-roll and two half-hollows. The gallery openings are high, almost as high as the arcade (26 as against 29 ft), and twins. Again all the detail is of the simplest: one-step arches e.g. The clerestory is also very high (23 ft) and has a wall-passage, basically tripartite per bay: low, high, low. This standard English arrangement occurs here for the first time,* and it occurs disarmingly irregularly. In bay one it is high–low, in bay two complete, in bays three and four – owing to the absence of the mast (*see* below) – it is low, high, low, low, high. The S side is different, because there is a S aisle of two bays. To the N it has a fat pier with the same very flat capital as in the crypt, but to the aisle a respond is tacked on to it. Unmoulded arches. The vaults behind are groin-vaults, and so it must be added now that the rib-vaults, where they occur, are replacements of groin-vaults after the tower had fallen. Against the S wall some blank arcading, continued in the W aisle, but not as consistently as in the N transept.‡ Above these groin-vaults is an open balcony, not a gallery with arches

* And in Westminster Hall, it seems.

‡ In the SW bay one shaft of the blank arcading is replaced by a fine C14 head. In the N transept the same was done six times, or not quite the same, as the heads are here carved out of the capitals.

to the 'nave'. There is here a change of plan, and altogether these end bays of the transepts are a headache. However, for Willis there were no headaches, and he has at least solved certain muddles at ground-level perfectly. He has pointed out that the NW and NE piers of the N and the SW and SE piers of the S transept and the wall-shafts corresponding to them W of the W and E of the E ones have been strengthened and broadened later, the NW piers to the NW, the SW piers to the SW etc., and the wall-shafts accordingly. Once one watches for this, one cannot but notice it, even without Willis's admirable little plans and illustrations. This strengthening represents a change of plan after the gallery level had been reached. The change which would make this particular strengthening necessary is that of providing towers at the corners of the transepts, and the intention to do so has already been proved. The most noticeable sign of the change of plan, however, occurs higher up. It is the breaking off of the masts below the clerestory level. This poses a different problem, and Willis does not help on it. It may be said that the masts became unnecessary if towers were to go up. The shaft midway up the gallery spandrel which now also stops where the gallery stops may imply that the intention now was to carry the gallery arcading right round and thus provide a next stage for the tower. In this case the clerestory passage would probably also have come forward. Whatever the intention, however, it was very soon given up, and the odd rhythm of the present wall-passage on the E (and W) sides shows that, when that level was reached, towers were no longer considered. In the SW bay an upper doorway, now reached by a wooden staircase, gives access to the present library. The staircase is Jacobean, with flat, cut-out balusters. The doorway itself, however, is not that which connected with the dormitory: it is clearly, like its neighbours l. and r., a window. Where then was the night-stair?

On the W side both aisle arches are blocked, the more northerly one by masonry with blank decoration continuing into the nave, which, in its zigzag at r. angles to the wall and its curious compound shafts, must be the work of, or inspired by, the masons working on the triforium at St Cross, i.e. in the 1170s or 1180s. Nothing else new in the W wall.

The NORTH TRANSEPT is essentially the same. On the E side the middle bay of the aisle is an early C14 replacement (cf. the window tracery). The rib profile is different, and the ribs start from four delightful little figures. The distribution between preserved groin-vaults and replacement rib-vaults is not quite the same, but otherwise there is nothing to report.*

Of the Norman chancel and the Norman nave we have scarcely any evidence, though one can assume that they were like the transepts. Externally, on the N side, the chancel at the very W end of the clerestory shares the r. shaft of the first window. Internally, on the N side, the chancel aisle has part of its westernmost arcade respond preserved, and there is, moreover, the stump of a strong round pier inside the Gardener Chantry. This was one of the four piers round Walkelin's apse. Outside the nave, on the cloister side, in the third bay from the W, there is a doorway, and some length of billet shows that it took the place of a Norman doorway. Of the Norman W front nothing is known for certain. In the N wall of No. 11 The Close, i.e. just SW of the present façade, is very thick Norman walling, and this has been taken to represent the S wall of a mighty W front projecting beyond the aisles to the S and N. What excavations have shown is a thick-walled square foundation in the centre and longitudinally oblong foundations l. and r., of which the standing fragment is part of the S wall. Whether this means a W tower as at Ely with side chambers or a westwork must be left open. The foundations at Old Sarum are the most similar we know. As for the interior of the nave, part of the SE respond of the arcade also survives and the arches of the gallery to the E, in both N and S aisles.

That is all. In all this work, it will be noticed, there is inside no enrichment whatever, no billet, not even a roll. Outside these motifs do occur, but also nothing beyond them. All is power at Winchester, nothing grace. The transepts (and the chapter-house front) are the most complete statement in England of the Early Norman style.

RETROCHOIR AND LADY CHAPEL

These parts were built by Bishop de Lucy, even if he did not complete them. He died in 1204, and in 1202 he established a confraternity for five years to carry on his building. As we shall see, completion took much longer. The EXTERIOR of the N and S sides of the retrochoir is of a noble design. Three bays, with a high bare ground stage and above tall blank

* The ceilings of the transepts were put in by *Garbett* in 1819.

Winchester Cathedral, retrochoir with monuments removed
(reconstruction by Sheila Gibson)

arcading, four units per bay with the middle ones a pair of lancet windows. Inside there is shafting as well, and the pair of lancets has a detached shaft between. Further E, however, the design gets as confused externally as it is in so much E.E. external work. The walls step back with two staircase turrets, octagonal at the top. Then follows the stage of the NE and SE chapels flanking the longer Lady Chapel. These bays have one large window, now Perp, and one blank E.E. unit added to it. This is the same N (S) and E. Above are two small tiers of blank arcading with trefoil heads. The number of arches is more in the top row than in the lower row. The Lady Chapel is a Late Perp remodelling. One seven-light window (three plus one plus three) to N, S, and E with a transom and much panel tracery. Blank panelling below (not on the N side). The top corbel-table of small pointed-trefoiled corbels, however, is E.E. The re-cast buttresses have crocketed gablets applied to them.

The INTERIOR of the retrochoir is extremely beautiful, but it needs a trained imagination to recognize that through the crowd of chapels and furnishings.* Three bays, the nave wider but only slightly higher than the aisles. The piers are of Purbeck marble and have four main and four subsidiary shafts with shaft-rings and capitals ranging from crockets and the most elementary stiff-leaf to more developed stiff-leaf. The W responds now stand against the C14 chancel piers. The aisles have vaults with the ribs of a profile of three fine rolls, the nave has plain single-chamfered ribs on short shafts above the Purbeck capitals. All along the aisles is blank arcading with trefoil arches and a blank elongated rounded quatrefoil in the spandrel. This arcading continues into the NE chapel and may have continued in the other chapel as well. To the S, in the W bay, is a beautiful doorway in the direction of the prior's lodging and the bishop's palace. It is cinquefoiled and has stiff-leaf sprays on arch and hood-mould. At the entrance to the three E chapels the respond shafting is gloriously generous. The NE chapel has a rib-vault like the aisles and a splendid big stiff-leaf boss. The SE chapel now has Bishop Langton's fan or rather fan-like vault (*see* p. 673). To the Lady Chapel both chapels have curious arcading with four small bare lancet openings into it (blocked on the N). In the Lady Chapel they are screened

* Miss Sheila Gibson has therefore drawn the interior disencumbered.

by a design which dates them well past Bishop de Lucy's death. There are three times twin arches with detached shafts forming a kind of wall-passage. They are normally pointed, but the super-arch repeats their outer curvature and sets a big more-than-semicircle on top so as to make the whole a trefoil top. Moreover, in the tympanum above are two trefoils and one large quatrefoil in blank plate tracery. Plate tracery of this kind appears at Winchester in the King's Great Hall in 1222–36 (*see* p. 695) and at Salisbury Cathedral around 1230. The late date for these details of the Lady Chapel need not worry us. The entrance to the chapel shows that there was indeed an interruption between de Lucy's retrochoir and this. The entrance shows a mason's muddle. The Purbeck responds do not carry on. The capitals are there, but they are pushed up higher by a short, useless shaft. In their heightened position the capitals help to carry the retrochoir 'nave' ribs. The muddle, it can be assumed, occurred because it was only then decided to heighten the retrochoir 'nave'. Its ribs, as we have seen, are indeed different from those of the aisles. The heightening was probably considered advisable because thoughts by then began to turn to the rebuilding of the Norman chancel.* The Lady Chapel can tell us no more of the E.E. period; for, as has already been said, it was remodelled late in the C15 (p. 670). The crypt (on which *see* p. 664), however, shows that the C13 Lady Chapel had the length of the present one.

NAVE

The rebuilding or, as Willis has proved, the remodelling of the Norman nave was begun at the W end by Bishop Edington and continued by William of Wykeham mostly from *c.*1394 onwards. We do not know the name of Edington's master mason; that of Wykeham was *William de Wynford*, a man of considerable status. They had first met when Wykeham was Clerk of the Works at Windsor Castle and Wynford master mason (*c.*1360). In 1363 Wykeham became Provost of Wells Cathedral, in 1365 Wynford master mason there, remaining, however, in the King's service. He was granted a pension for life by Edward III in 1372. From 1387 Wynford was in charge of Winchester College. He also worked for the royal castle and finally the cathedral. Mr Harvey tells us that in

* Against the S respond a charming bracket on a bust and with some dogtooth and a wild stiff-leaf capital.

less than two months in 1393 he dined thirteen times with Wykeham and that in 1399 the privilege was granted him by the prior of the cathedral to dine free for ever at the prior's table.

36 The FAÇADE of Winchester Cathedral is disappointing. It lacks strong enough accents to introduce to this excessive length, a length of twelve bays. The façade is no more than a section through the nave and aisles with the low-pitched Perp roofs of the latter and the high-pitched Norman roofs of the former. On the angles of the aisles pinnacles, on the angles of the nave octagonal turrets, panelled to the top. The three entrances are in a screen wall set flat in front of the façade proper and not reaching above the ground stage. The three porches have panelled sides, lierne-vaults, and four-centred arches, those of the aisles above the initial curve straight-sided. L. and r. of the nave entrance two high image niches. Top balustrade. As for the façade proper, the aisles have a four-light window each too broad for its position. These, as we shall see, are Edington's, as are the porches. The nave W window, however, must belong to Wykeham. It is of nine lights (3+3+3), the largest in the cathedral. The side parts have two transoms, the middle part has four. Balustrade and panelled gable, crowned by an image niche with pinnacles.

Turning to the SIDES OF THE NAVE, the change from Edington to Wykeham is at once patent. It occurred after the first aisle window on the S side, the second on the N. Edington's windows are of four lights with broad four-centred arches and broad arch mouldings. His buttresses are deep. Small doorway to the N, large one to the S, probably into the cloister W range. Wykeham's aisle and clerestory windows – and all the clerestory windows right from the first bay are his – are of three lights and much slenderer. His buttresses are slenderer too. Edington's aisle corner pinnacle also differs from Wykeham's slenderer ones. Pretty frieze above the clerestory windows with heads, square fleurons, etc. The S side is of course somewhat different, because of the cloister. Big detached buttresses with two flyers, built by *Sir Thomas Jackson* in 1909 and 1912* to protect the building from collapse. Panelled fronts and pinnacles. Apart from the Edington doorway, there is a second doorway in the S aisle. It led into the W range of the cloister. It is the one with the bit of surviving Norman billet. The main doorway into the S aisle

* Carved corbels by *John Skeaping* (RH).

was made in 1818. It repeats in design the doorway once leading into the E range of the cloister.

The nave INTERIOR is the most homogeneous part of the 38
cathedral. There it is, twelve bays long, without any change of plan or details, at least in the nave. It is, moreover, amply lit from the nine-light W window and the large aisle and clerestory windows. The only irregularity is the platform in the W bay of the N aisle at half its height. But even the vault below this is identical with the aisle vaults.

The system of the elevation of the nave is determined, as Willis has shown with exemplary clarity and precision, by the retention and a mere cutting back of the Norman masonry. Hence the un-Perp stoutness of the piers, counteracted successfully by many fine mouldings which multiply the verticals. The principal shaft to the nave, running uninterrupted to the vault, is clearly the Norman mast. Instead of the Norman gallery or a triforium, there is only a shallow balcony per bay. The clerestory has blank arcading l., r., and below. The arcade is framed by a broad wave moulding reaching right up to below the balcony and is here enriched by heads, fleurons, etc. In the aisles this is the same in Wykeham's work. Edington's windows have space only for panelling below. The aisles have lierne-vaults with the chief diagonal ribs preserved and a middle octagon of liernes, not at once recognized, perhaps because of the warping due to the curvature of the vaults. The nave vaults have no chief diagonal ribs and altogether a much more complicated pattern.

THE CHANGES IN LADY CHAPEL, SOUTH-EAST CHAPEL, AND CROSSING

The Lady Chapel under Bishop Courtenay was given a new E bay with the seven-light windows to N, S, and E already mentioned. The vault of the W bay was also re-done, and these two bays now have extremely intricate lierne star-vaults with small bosses. To the N a small, finely detailed doorway. The SE chapel, remodelled by Langton, seems to have a very close fan-vault, but that is not so. It is a pseudo-fan vault; for diagonal ribs are kept and prevent the conical roundness of fans – just look at the springers – and the fans are cut into harshly by ridge-ribs longitudinal and transverse. The crossing on the other hand has a proper fan-vault, though a wooden one, on the pattern of the chancel. This was put up as late as 1635 – survival or revival? It masks the arcaded lower half of the lantern.

CHANCEL

Here the INTERIOR must be given priority, as the arcades are of the first half of the C14. Four bays, Purbeck marble piers of four main and four minor shafts connected by deep continuous hollows. Moulded capitals. The details ought to be compared with those of the retrochoir to get the full significance of the change from the early C13 to the early C14. Very fine arch mouldings. Head stops and animal stops.* The upper parts belong to Bishop Fox, i.e. the early C16. Balconies with pierced quatrefoils. Then the large upper windows. The E bay cants in noticeably, indicating where the Norman ambulatory curved round. The vault is very similar to the nave vault, but it is of wood, and hence all the ribs are
42 thinner. Many bosses. They represent emblems of the Passion and coats of arms and can be dated *c.*1505. The E bay was the feretory, a raised platform behind the reredos (*see* p. 676) for the Shrine of St Swithun. On the platform the remains of steps and the bases of colonnettes. The E end of the chancel, i.e. the E end of the feretory, is of two bays, the piers not of Purbeck. Four shafts and four sunk diagonals. Arches with fillets on rolls and sunk quadrants. Hood-moulds with figures as stops. In the aisles there is panelling l., r., and below the windows, as in the nave, and the vaults also are identical with those of the nave aisles. The vaulting of these aisles was done by *Thomas Bertie*, who died in 1555. He may have been of French origin, worked at Titchfield in 1538, was in charge of the royal works at Cowes and Calshot Castles in 1539, and probably also designed or built Hurst Castle, whose first captain he became. His son married the former Duchess of Suffolk. That far could a master mason and his family get in the world.

As for the EXTERIOR, the aisles have four-light windows with a transom, the clerestory four-light windows with panel tracery. There are flying buttresses, and the pinnacles are set diagonally. Openwork panelled balustrade. The E window is of seven lights (2+3+2) and not very high. The main gable is flanked by two octagonal turrets. It is closely panelled, and l. and r. of the E window is more panelling. At the very

* The VCH points out that the details of the E side, towards the retrochoir, and the piers and arch to the N of the feretory are earlier than the rest.

W end of Fox's work it is interesting to note that a window like the others was made and placed which is almost entirely covered by the E aisle of the Norman transepts. So there was a plan to rebuild here and cut out the E aisle. We must be grateful to fate and the Reformation that nothing was done.

FURNISHINGS

Few cathedrals are as rich in furnishings as Winchester. They will be described topographically, starting E and moving W, always taking N before S.

CRYPT. In the crypt two over-lifesize stone STATUES of the C14. One comes from the niche in the gable over the W front. Where the other comes from is not known.

LADY CHAPEL. WALL PAINTINGS. Early C16, all in brown and grey. They are English in all probability, but inspired by the most Flemish parts of the Eton College frescoes of the 1480s. The Winchester scenes represent miracles of the Virgin. – COMMUNION RAIL. A typical and enjoyable piece of *c.*1635. Not balusters but openwork ovals with spurs sticking into them from all four sides without meeting. – SCREEN. At the W end screen of four-light divisions with four-centred arches and panel tracery. Seven bays, and also the loft parapet. – STAINED GLASS. In the E window some small early C16 figures. The rest by *Kempe*, who also did N and S, 1897–1900.

NORTH-EAST (GUARDIAN ANGELS') CHAPEL. WALL PAINTINGS. On the vault, *c.*1240, of very high quality. Angels in roundels. – REREDOS. Of stone, Perp, seven tall niches. Below blank panelling. – CROZIER and TIARA. They belonged to Bishop Mews, † 1706. – STAINED GLASS. In the E window a mosaic of ancient pieces. – MONUMENTS. Arnold de Gaveston, early C14. Tomb-chest front of Purbeck marble. Five crocketed ogee arches, shield below them hanging from nobbly branches. The effigy is in the retrochoir N aisle. – Richard Weston, Lord Portland, † 1634. The most progressive 57
and one of the finest monuments of that time in England. Westminster Abbey has nothing to vie with it. Recumbent bronze effigy, probably by *Le Sueur*, the head on several pillows, a staff in one hand. The surround is of white, pink, and grey marble, and entirely classical, i.e. no longer in the least Jacobean. Four entirely bare and unmoulded niches and a wide segmentally rising top. There are here two putti

holding a shield. The sides of this superstructure have scrolls starting at the top with rams' heads and short thick garlands. What there is of ornamental form tends to be doughy, of a mid C17 rather than the strapwork character. Many cherubs' heads.

SOUTH-EAST (LANGTON) CHAPEL. Elaborate PANELLING of *c.*1500, amply cusped and with openwork cresting. – REREDOS. Of stone. Seven Perp niches, not very high. Much remains of colour. – SCREEN. Of one-light divisions, with a double door. – STAINED GLASS. E window by *Kempe*, 1899. – MONUMENT. Bishop Langton † 1500. Purbeck marble tomb-chest with cusped fields. Indent of a brass on the lid.

RETROCHOIR 'NAVE'. ST SWITHUN'S SHRINE. 1962 by *Brian Thomas* and *Wilfrid Carpenter Turner*. A strangely thin, delicate piece, inspired by the Swedish style of the twenties. Black, silver, and brass. The small realistic relief tells of the backward look of the monument and of its lack of sympathy with the tougher idiom of the mid C20. – SCREEN. Or rather blank stone arcading to cover the base of the raised feretory. Nine bays of arches with nodding ogees and much crocketing. It is the only example of really florid Dec in the cathedral. – CHANDELIER. Of brass. Dated 1756. Very large and Baroque. – TILES on the floor. – MONUMENTS. Bishop de Lucy † 1204. Plain coffin-lid of Purbeck marble. – Cardinal Beaufort's Chantry Chapel. This follows after Wykeham's (*see* p. 683). He died in 1447. The chapel rises with serried high canopies to the vault. Doorways at the W end, the altar at the E end with openwork panelled sides, the upper panels large and wide open. The whole middle part is entirely open, except for a low balustrade. That is what distinguishes the chapel from the others. Large tomb-chest with recumbent stone effigy. He is wearing his cardinal's hat. The effigy is a later C17 copy, as is easily recognizable if one looks at the cartouche at his feet. The altar has a reredos of three niches. Large fan-vault above the effigy (the first at Winchester), small ones lower down over entrance bay and altar bay. – WAYNFLETE CHANTRY. Bishop Waynflete died in 1486. The chapel has the same scheme, but the main part is open only in the upper half. Lower down three arches with four-centred heads. Tomb-chest, much smaller than Beaufort's. Recumbent stone effigy. Reredos with three niches. Above the effigy complicated lierne-vault. Over the W and E bays fan-like vaults, but with a square centre panel with a rose-window motif. – Coffin-slab with a foliated cross and a Norman-French inscription. – Bishop Sumner † 1874. Recumbent white effigy.

NORTH RETROCHOIR AISLE. TILES on the floor. – MONUMENTS. Heart burial of a C13 bishop. Purbeck marble. Demi-figure in an almond-shaped surround with stiff-leaf sprays. The figure, in spite of the mandorla, is also under a nodding trefoiled arch on short shafts. – Early C13 Bishop. Purbeck marble. The head with a short, curly, archaic beard and a low tiara is under a pointed-trefoiled canopy. One hand holds a book, the other lies on his breast. – Torso of a C13 Bishop (on the floor). – Arnold de Gaveston; early C14. Angels (broken off) by his pillow, his feet against a lion. The whole figure sways in a typical early C14 way. The armour is made interesting by the occurrence of a rare piece: ailettes at his shoulders. Shield with carved quarterings. – Thomas Masson † 1559. Very characteristic Early Elizabethan tomb-chest. No figure-work, but the two inscription plates framed by a very individual and elegant guilloche.

SOUTH RETROCHOIR AISLE. STAINED GLASS. Many small C13 bits without figures, arranged as lozenge panels. They come from Salisbury Cathedral. – SCULPTURE. Ecclesia or Synagogue, *c.*1230. Headless, but even so of a 24
quality as good as anything in France. The source of inspiration is the transept porches of Chartres (Ste Modeste, Visitation). Here the flow of the folds downwards and the disturbance when they meet the ground can be matched, and even the belt with one end hanging low down. This at Winchester was of metal. The draperies show to perfection that nobility could be expressed in the C13 in drapery. The head is hardly necessary to inform us of carriage and mood. The piece was found in the Deanery porch. – TILES. A fine spread. – MONUMENT. John Clobery † 1687. By *Sir William Wilson*. Bad white statue of alabaster. One arm stretches forward a staff, the other is held akimbo.* Black columns l. and r. Big segmental top.

CHANCEL. REREDOS. Of stone; early C16. Up to above the sills of the clerestory windows. Three tiers of statues, all of 1885–99. They are grouped as follows. The l. and r. three have a recessed middle row and the l. and r. side rows set between tiers of small statuettes as on buttresses. The

* Lord Torrington in 1782 comments on 'the ridiculous, cumbersome habits of those days with . . . more sash than any modern miss'.

centre has the Crucifixion and one tier of statuettes above, one below. Great emphasis on the filigree of the canopies of the niches. – COMMUNION RAIL and STALL FRONTS. Of the 1680s. Openwork fruit, flowers, leaves, and putto heads. – SCREENS. Stone screens N and S with four-light Gothic windows, but an Early Renaissance frieze and Early Renaissance inscription tablets towards the aisles. They are dated 1525. On them the wooden TOMB-CHESTS of Anglo-Saxon kings, painted with Renaissance motifs. – PULPIT. A very strange, over-decorated piece, carrying the name of Prior Silkstede (1498–1524). It is crowded with decoration, including Silkstede's silk skein. Yet most of it cannot be genuine. The staircase e.g. must be a job of Victorian assembly. There is also the reading ledge on ribbed coving which looks suspicious. – LECTERN. A wooden eagle on a big baluster; C17. – STALLS. The date 1308 usually given the Winchester stalls suits them, but it must be remembered that the letter of that year written by Bishop Woodlock to the Bishop of Norwich only asked for *William Lyngwode*, a carpenter, to be allowed to go on serving him until he had finished the work of construction.* The back panels are of two blank lights with mostly at the top a pointed cinquefoil in a circle. There is, however, one rounded one still, and there is also just once a typical early C14 caprice: a six-cornered star made up of two triangles. In front of these back panels rise on detached exceedingly thin shafts a system of the same panels but crowned by steep crocketed gables with an openwork elongated pointed cinquefoil in. The back panels proper have in their spandrels very close and intricate foliage, and also just once a man (a falconer) and a little more often animals (e.g. a monkey playing the harp). Much of the foliage is still botanically recognizable, but is already bossy and nobbly throughout. The seats have MISERICORDS, e.g. on the N side: a man playing a pipe, a tumbler, an owl, a mock-bishop, fools, a lion, a monkey, a woman wearing a wimple, a

*Cum . . . opus sue artis iam inceperit in choro ecclesie nostrae cathedralis . . . quod absque ipsius continua presencia non posset . . . terminari, vostram sinceram amiciciam . . . corditer rogamus quatinus dicti artificis . . . absenciam habere dignemini quatenus poteritis bono modo si placet excusatam, precipientes vestris senescallis et ballinis quod eundem causa absencie sue quousque dictum opus terminaverit a festo sancti Michaelis proximo nunc futuro usque ad terminem revolutum pro secta curie vestre nullatenus inquietent. (cf. *Arch. J.*, 1927, by J. D. Atkinson and J. D. Boden).

fox with a goose. On the S side: a dog, a ram, a man with a hunting horn, a hare, a boar, monsters, seated people, etc. In the lower row on the N side a fine laughing figure. The fronts of the upper tier of seats have rather uninspired Renaissance motifs. The front row ends have a bold shape but only rather simple decoration. On the W side the stalls return, but the SCREEN is by *Scott*, 1875. – BISHOP'S THRONE. Of *c.*1820 by *Garbett*, a remarkable piece for its date. – SCULPTURE. An excellent small demi-figure of the Virgin, datable to *c.*1500, stands W of the bishop's throne. – STAINED GLASS. Many original parts of the early C15 (from the nave), the mid C15, and the early C16 in the side windows. The E window is essentially of 1852 (by *David Evans*).* – MONUMENTS. For the chests of Anglo-Saxon kings *see* above. – William Rufus (or Henry of Blois). Large black slab, along the centre raised roof-like. – Bishop Courtenay † 1492. Gothic tomb-chest, without effigy, C19, though quite possibly a copy. – Elegant Early Renaissance tomb-chest. No name or effigy. – FOX CHANTRY CHAPEL.‡ Bishop Fox died in 1528. Though he was responsible for the introduction of the *all'antica* fashion to the cathedral, there is nothing of it in his chapel. The front to the chancel aisle has much more solidity of wall (though of course pierced) than Beaufort's and Waynflete's chantries. Four bays. The lowest stage is closed in except for the doorways and a low niche with his corpse, shockingly realistically rendered. Statuettes around by *Frampton*. Above open panelling with four-centred arches and wide, strongly horizontal top cresting. No high finials any longer. That tells of a Renaissance feeling. Inside is a richly 43
cusped lierne-vault. Reredos of three niches and below them an oblong recess. Panelled W wall. To the E small vestry(?). – Opposite the Fox Chantry the GARDENER CHANTRY. Bishop Gardener died as late as 1555, and to the architectural observer the chapel tells that in a most illuminating way. The chapel is far from homogeneous. It is Gothic in parts, Early Renaissance in parts, and as early as anywhere in England High Renaissance in a few parts. The chapel front is to the N aisle not the chancel. The substructure here is entirely English mid C16, i.e. two fine long strapwork panels, very subdued in the

* What there is of original glass is enumerated in detail in Le Couteur's book on Winchester Glass.

‡ A genuine working drawing for one bay of it is preserved in the RIBA Library.

details. Between them is an oblong recess, and there – very late, but still earlier than Pilon's Henri II of France – is the bishop's decomposed corpse. Above are the same purely Gothic four-light windows as in the chancel screens, but they are framed by something between buttresses and pilasters. Then, however, follows a triglyph frieze, and that in England means inspiration from the full Cinquecento, no longer from the Early Renaissance. The charming cresting on the other hand is entirely Early Renaissance. Inside, the chapel is divided into a small E sacristy and the chapel proper. It is in the former that the stump of a Norman apse pier can be seen (*see* p. 668). Now inside the chapel the clash of two ages is most violent. The vault is panelled in square cusped panels. Looking towards the reredos one is surprised that there is not a coffered tunnel-vault instead, such as one finds them at Chambord and over Henri II's staircase in the Louvre. For
49 the reredos has fluted colonnettes, not decorated pilasters any longer. Such fluted columns appear so early only very rarely in England (Framlingham, Norfolk, † 1557 and 1564; Wing 1552). There are also shell-headed niches, and they are just as rare (Framlingham again; † 1554). At the top is a proper cornice, and below a guilloche frieze. The two remaining statuettes are full Cinquecento too and have nothing left of the Gothic. How is it then that the Gothic four-light windows and even more the tiny fan-vault in the sacristy were not felt to be painfully out of date?

NORTH CHANCEL AISLE. TILES on the floor. – STAINED GLASS. Early C16 glass in the heads of the tracery lights, also below the transoms. – CHEST LID of a reliquary given *c*.1325–30. Wood, painted with figures. Mostly in sunk panels. At the bottom the kneeling donor and his wife l. and r. of St John Baptist. In the panels Christ in Majesty, the Virgin and Child, the Coronation of the Virgin, the Crucifixion, Angels, and Saints. All painted very naïvely. – MONUMENT. Bishop North † 1820. By *Chantrey*, 1825. He kneels in profile in front of a high base. White marble, the composition almost identical with Chantrey's Bishop Barrington in Durham Cathedral, Bishop Ryder in Lichfield Cathedral, and Archbishop Stuart in Armagh Cathedral.

SOUTH CHANCEL AISLE. No tiles. – STAINED GLASS. The easternmost window has early C16 glass in its head. – The second window by *Powell*, *c*.1880, the third by *Kempe*, *c*.1900, the fourth again with some old bits. – GRILLE.

Between the chancel aisle and the transept. The pattern is of uprights from which identical scrolls branch out l. and r. all up the uprights. It is almost the same pattern as that of Queen Eleanor's tomb at Westminster Abbey and also probably late C13. It may well be by *Thomas of Leighton*.

CROSSING. The crossing is included in the choir.

NORTH TRANSEPT. Under the crossing arch is the CHAPEL OF THE HOLY SEPULCHRE, put in about 1200. It is a solid structure compared with later chantry chapels, of two bays with rib-vaults and massive buttresses to the N. A small doorway with one order of shafts carrying early stiff-leaf capitals is in the W bay. Nicely moulded arch. The ribs inside are simply single-chamfered. Those of the E bay stand on stiff-leaf corbels. L. and r. of the mid-corbel are blocked responds, and they still have Late Norman capitals of small scallops. The vault and the walls of the chapel are decorated with WALL PAINTINGS, the best of about 1230 in England. In the vault roundels with Christ, the Signs of the Evangelists, Annunciation, Nativity, and Annunciation to the Shepherds. On the E wall, below the bust of Christ, Deposition and Entombment. On the side wall Doubting Thomas, Entry into Jerusalem, Noli me tangere. In the W bay Lives of Saints. Also painting in the soffits of the arches. The style is still inspired by Byzantium. – MONUMENT. Under the E arch of the chapel. Purbeck coffin-lid with a foliated cross starting from a twist of stiff-leaf. – EAST AISLE. STAINED GLASS. Fragments in the SE window. – Carved into a pier recess shafts with a nodding ogee arch; early C14. In it MONUMENT to Charles Nayl † 1739 with an elegant if macabre still-life at the foot. – Canon B. K. Cunningham † 1944. Wooden Annunciation and small reliefs at the back. By *Alan Durst*. – Against the N wall tomb recess with ogee arch; early C14. It goes with the window above it and the northernmost E window. – NORTH AISLE. MONUMENTS. General Sir Redvers Buller † 1908. Recumbent bronze effigy by *Sir Bertram Mackennal*, 1910. – Rev. Frederic Iremonger † 1820. Recumbent effigy, very young. – WEST AISLE (Epiphany Chapel). STAINED GLASS by *Morris & Co.*; 1909. – MONUMENT. Thomas Rivers † 1731. Obelisk with six shields and palm fronds.

See p. 832

SOUTH TRANSEPT. In the 'nave' CHANDELIER. Of brass, dated 1756, big, Baroque, but with only one tier of branches. – Against the N screen WOODWORK of *c.*1700: garlands etc.

Where from? – MONUMENTS. Isaac Townsend † 1731. Free-standing oblong base with apsed ends. On it a square pedestal, and on that an urn. Smaller vases l. and r. – David Williams † 1860. By *W. Theed*. White marble, with Faith, Hope, and Charity, all three phlegmatic creatures. – BENCH. About 12 ft long. Very elementary poppy-heads with two rosettes on the end posts of the back and the knobs on the arms. This seems indeed to be of about 1200. – PANELLING. Against the S and part of the W walls. Linenfold, but with an Early Renaissance cresting. It must be of before 1524, as it has the initials of Prior Silkstede, who died in that year. – MONUMENT. Bishop Wilberforce † 1873. Effigy on a slab supported by six kneeling angels, the whole in a shrine-like building: a canopy on eight columns. The architectural style is E.E. Designed by *Sir G. G. Scott*, and very typical of his style at its most lavish. The effigy by *H. H. Armstead*. – EAST AISLE. Stone SCREENS to the two chapels. The one further N is high and elaborate. Upper tier of six tabernacles. – The other was provided by Prior Silkstede (1498–1524). Or was it only appropriated by him? For the tracery is purely reticulated, i.e. ought to be of the first two-thirds of the C14. – On the SOUTH BALCONY is a collection of SCULPTURE. It ranges from Norman capitals to figures from early C16 reredoses and is both interesting and enjoyable. The items cannot here be enumerated singly, however high the quality of some. A printed and illustrated catalogue would be welcome.

NAVE. From the E. For the ROOD SCREEN *see* chancel, above. – MONUMENT. Bishop Hoadly † 1761. By *Wilton*. Black background. Grey and white marble. Lively profile in an oval medallion against ample, still entirely Baroque,
37 drapery. – EDINGTON CHANTRY CHAPEL. Very simple, compared with its showy successors. Very important in that it shows how close Edington – he died in 1366 – still was to the Dec. Six bays of two-light openings; the doorway in the fifth. In the heads reticulation units. Simple cresting. To the aisle the doorway is extremely typical. Its jambs curve forward as they descend from the top, a motif taken over direct from the S transept at Gloucester, where it also still represented the loyalty to the Dec among the first Perp designers. The same spirit comes out in the curious solution of the four corners. No vault; the chapel is open. Recumbent effigy of alabaster. The tomb-chest is of Purbeck marble and has again instead of Perp panels the sexfoils of the past. – MONUMENT. Bishop

Browne † 1891. Recumbent alabaster effigy on an alabaster tomb-chest with statuettes. – PULPIT. Jacobean; on a substantial foot. From the New College Chapel, Oxford. – STAINED GLASS. Small fragments in the N windows; early C15. – FONT. The most famous of the black Tournai fonts in England. Square, the shape which the Purbeck fonts were to imitate on a smaller scale. Against two sides stories of St Nicholas, against the third three roundels with pairs of birds, against the fourth roundels with a quadruped flanked by single birds. On the top in two spandrels leaf, in the other two affronted birds drinking from a vase. – WYKEHAM CHANTRY CHAPEL. Here is the change from simplicity to show – from 1366 to 1404. The chapel reaches right up to the balcony. It is of three bays and wider than the piers are thick. It has therefore a canted extension to merge with the piers. In this extension, i.e. at an angle, are the two W doorways. The lower half is of three tiers of panelling, the top tier with the Perp equivalent of the reticulation unit, i.e. a unit with straight sides. Here then is another adjustment of the traditions of 1366. The upper half is entirely open, except for the two thin shafts. This prepares for Beaufort. The shafts carry arches with gables, fine and distinct gables, not the thicket of Beaufort. In fact the whole of the Wykeham design is very easily read and comprehended. Inside a cusped lierne-vault. The reredos has two tiers of five niches each with high canopies. The statuettes are by *Frampton*. The W wall is panelled but also has niches above. Tomb-chest with seven gabled panels. The bishop places his feet against three bedesmen. Two angels are at his head. – SCULPTURE. Against the W wall stand excellent bronze statues of James I and Charles I. They are by *Le Sueur* and come from *Inigo Jones*'s rood screen designed *c.*1638. What remains of the architecture of the screen is in the Museum of Archaeology at Cambridge. – STAINED GLASS. The great W window is filled very effectively by a close mosaic of small bits of ancient glass, hundreds of pieces.

NORTH AISLE. The aisles of Winchester Cathedral have almost as many monuments as those of Westminster Abbey. This report goes from E to W, but it must be said first that STAINED GLASS in small fragments in the window heads occurs in the majority of windows. Le Couteur dates them second quarter of the C15. – MONUMENT. Anne Morley † 1787. White and pink marble. Urn under a weeping willow.

– STAINED GLASS. Bay two has a whole window by *David Evans*, *c.*1850. – MONUMENTS. Matthew Combe † 1748. Urn and garlands in front of an obelisk. – Edward Cole † 1617. Big tablet without an effigy but with much bold strapwork. It is the only one of its kind in the cathedral. – Edward Montagu † 1776. Urn in front of an obelisk. Two small seated allegorical females l. and r. – Col. Morgan † 1808. By *Bacon Jun.* Small kneeling woman, flag, gun, and a pelican. – STAINED GLASS (eighth bay). By *Kempe*, Jane Austen Memorial, 1901. – MONUMENTS. Villiers Chernocke † 1779. Grey and white marble. An urn and two allegories under a large weeping willow. By *S. Walldin* of Winchester. – John Littlehales † 1810. By *Bacon Jun.* With a small relief of the Good Samaritan. – STAINED GLASS (eleventh bay) by *Kempe*, 1900.

SOUTH AISLE. Also from the E. Capt. Portal and Sir G. H. Portal † 1893 and 1894. A sensuous genius with the curvaceous lines of the Paris Salon, her breasts not bared but much noticed, holds the two medallions. Venetian semicircular pediment with lush decoration. The sculptor seems unrecorded. – STAINED GLASS. Another window by *Evans*, *c.*1850. – MONUMENTS. Sir George Prevost † 1816, by *Chantrey*. White woman seated in profile on a Grecian chair. On a scroll we read St Lucia taken / Dominica defended / Canada preserved. – Bishop Willis † 1734. By *Sir Henry Cheere*. He reclines on his sarcophagus, sitting up, with his arm on books. The sarcophagus feet are over-big claws. Reredos background with columns and a broken pediment. – Thomas Cheyney † 1760. Large oval palm-wreath and in it on pink the white figures of Hope and Truth by a sarcophagus on which a small relief of the rising from the grave. It is a fussy design but pretty all the same. – Bishop Tomline † 1827. By *R. Westmacott Jun.* Stone tomb-chest and by it a thoughtful white marble angel. – Joseph Warton, headmaster of the College. By *Flaxman*, 1801. White marble. He is seated and looks benign but searching. In front of him four eager and pretty boys. At the back Aristotle in precise profile, Homer precisely frontal – as neat as Piero della Francesca. It is one of Flaxman's most successful funerary monuments, intimate yet monumental. Against the sides two medallions. On the top acroteria and a lyre growing out of acanthus. – Henrietta Maria North † 1796. Also by *Flaxman*. White marble. Two allegorical figures standing by an urn. – STAINED GLASS. In the W window many medieval fragments.

LIBRARY. SCULPTURE. A very fine bearded head of the early C16. – STAINED GLASS. An early C16 panel. – BOOK-CASES. Late C17. From Bishop Morley's library at Farnham Castle.

THE PRECINCT

Winchester has a real close only on the S, with all the felicities of accidental placing and variety of style. On the N the boundary to the town is also marked, but by building less closely or not at all connected with the cathedral. Even so, if one speaks of precinct rather than close, they must be included.

THE CLOISTER. Most of the cloister was destroyed in 1563. What remains is this. The N doorway of the DORMITORY, reached by the wooden staircase from the S transept. This is in type exactly like Walkelin's parts. Then the PASSAGE between transept and chapter house without any interesting features, and then the CHAPTER HOUSE entrance, one of the mightiest pieces of Early Norman architecture in the land. Entrance and two bays of arcading l., two r. Sturdy round piers and big capitals of two scallops. Inside blank arcading all along the N side. Block capitals. S of the chapter house blocked Norman arches, called by Mr Carpenter Turner book cupboards. Also a C13 doorway with hood-mould on heads. The tympanum has an upcurved lower edge and was blank-cinquefoiled. Then the deanery wall takes over.

WOLVESEY PALACE. Wolvesey Palace is and always has been the bishop's palace. It was built by Henry of Blois, and of his time are the ruins along the N side of the site. The range is two rooms deep. The N part dates from *c.*1130–40, including what was the gatehouse. Norman half-arch, blocked to the N. To the S bigger pointed one-step arch. W of the gatehouse recently the beginning of a staircase has been excavated, of remarkably wide steps. Also recently, in the E third of the gatehouse, the foundations of a chapel(?) have come out, with a W as well as an E apse. They are assigned to the C10.

At r. angles to the N range and extending a full 140 ft S was the GREAT HALL. This, on the stylistic evidence of details, seems to have been built about 1170. It was on the upper floor, and the ground floor was apparently not vaulted. On the N side at the hall level is large, blank, round-headed arcading (cf. Bishops Waltham). The arches have an unusual variety of zigzag or rather triangles. One beautiful head

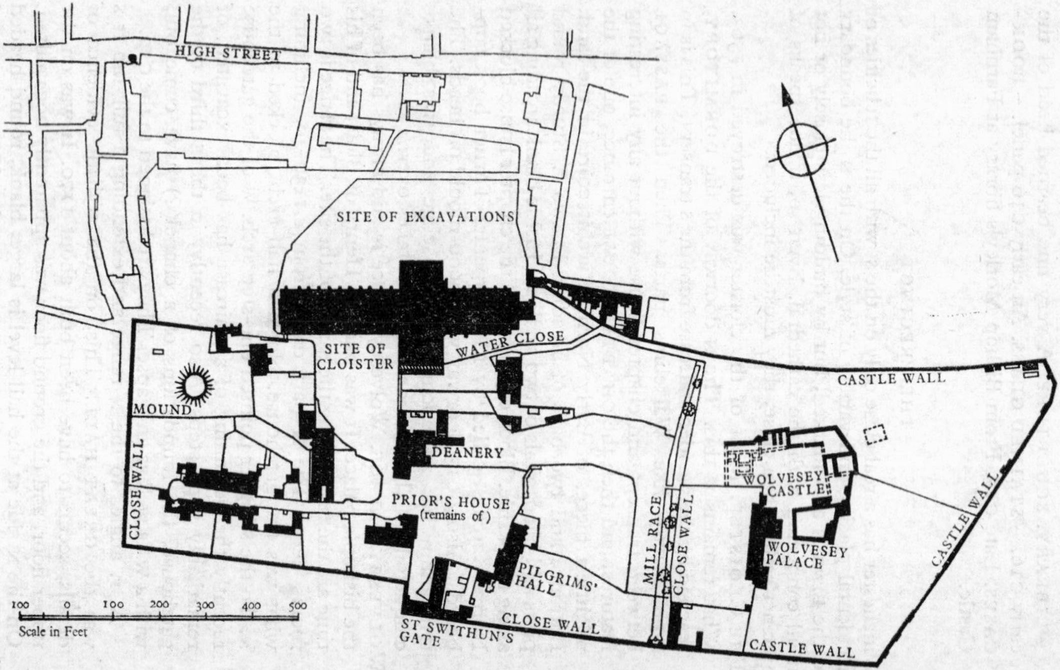

Winchester, plan of the Close

corbel remains. The hall had an upper wall-passage (like Rufus's at Westminster). Large shafted windows. To the inside pellets up the jambs. The S wall had hall windows high up, but their details have all gone.

E of the S end of the hall we are back in *c*.1130–40. It is here that the KEEP of the castle stood. Flat buttresses. Large round-headed recess to the W. S of the keep was the guard tower. On the E side it still has some ashlar facing. The wall from the guard tower to the S has herringbone flintwork, usually accepted as a sign of the C11.

The BISHOP'S HOUSE is dated 1684, i.e. it was begun a 63
year after the King's House (*see* Barracks, p. 696). Ashlar-faced, with to the W eleven bays of wooden cross-windows, each with a curved hood. Hipped roof. Carved modillions. The doorway has a broken pediment, almost semicircular and on rather rustic Ionic pilasters. To the E there is a five-bay centre with a one-bay S wing projecting two bays. This was probably intended to be repeated on the N side, but here the chapel interfered, and this was in the end left standing. The CHAPEL stands on Norman foundations, and it is possible that the Norman ground floor is still in existence; for the chapel was, as was usual for palace chapels, on the upper floor. This is not so now. The chapel is a large and lofty room, Perp in style, and probably of the C15. Five-light E window, three three-light S windows. The doorways and the WEST GALLERY belong to *c*.1684. One can assume that the entrance to the gallery is where the principal medieval entrance was. The STABLES are ashlar-faced and low, with a broad pediment. – A good deal remains of the OUTER WALLS, especially on the E and SE sides.

DEANERY. The deanery in the Middle Ages was the Prior's Lodging. It lies S of the E range of the cloister, and the earliest part of it is in axis with this. This earliest part is the so-called cloister, i.e. a porch open to the S. Three bays 26
are open, a fourth has to the S the somewhat later spiral staircase to the upper floor. The porch has three steep arches of continuous double chamfers. Inside, it is rib-vaulted with single-chamfered ribs. They rest on Purbeck wall-shafts on the N side but on detached Purbeck piers, each of a core and four detached shafts, on the S side. These piers are placed at a sufficient distance from the porch piers to allow for small connecting transverse shouldered lintels. The E wall has blank arcading of two pointed arches with a super-

rounded trefoiled arch. This motif and the single-chamfered ribs are taken from the final state of retrochoir and Lady Chapel and need not be later. The two upper storeys above the porch have windows of two and four lights of probably the first half of the C16. To the E the C13 part has buttresses originally shafted. There is also a small blocked window with a shouldered lintel. On the W of the porch and not in line with it is the C15 PRIOR'S HALL, with five buttresses to the W and tall two-light Perp windows with one transom. To the S the hall projects beyond the porch, and there was there another window facing E. But this is now blocked. The hall has kept its original timber roof on the upper floor of the present building. It has arched braces with minimum tracery and wind-braces. The braces stand on excellent head corbels. Further N the C15 masonry continues. The KITCHEN was here, with its large fireplace, and yet further N a small Norman doorway originally leading from the cloister into the E range. Lying back N a good deal and projecting boldly E is the LONG GALLERY built by Dean Clarke (1666–79). It is of brick, laid Flemish bond, and stands on an open ground floor of varied supports: columns, then an arch, and then in the centre a composition of two pilasters with bulgy brick rustication. Above this bay on the upper floor is a Perp five-light window, re-used from somewhere else, and a pediment. The windows of the gallery l. and r. are of stone with a mullion-and-transom cross. The E window is an imitation of 1807. In the gallery is a Georgian chimneypiece recently brought in and some STAINED GLASS, mostly C16 and C17, much foreign, but also some English C15 pieces. The main STAIRCASE must be mid-C17. It has flat cut-out panels instead of balusters, an early type of this motif which culminated in the late C17. – On the E of the Deanery, in its garden, lay Bishop Ken's house. This was demolished as late as 1855.

THE CLOSE. No. 1 lies on its own NE of the Deanery, SE of the cathedral. It was built in 1699, and is of chequer brick with projecting wings and hipped roof. Over the middle of the recessed centre a small pediment.

Next follows the PILGRIMS' SCHOOL, externally Georgian with a porch on short Tuscan columns, but in fact older. Not only has the staircase twisted balusters and a stucco frieze of delightful flower and fruit garlands typical of the 1680s,
34 but the N part merges with the PILGRIMS' HALL, a hall of the mid C14, memorable as having the earliest hammerbeam

roof so far identified. Two pairs only. The ends of the hammers have big, coarse faces. The roof is half-hipped to the N. Opposite the school to the W is the long range of STABLES, running S–N. This is timber-framed and must date from the early C16. Roof with tie-beams, collar-beams, queen-posts, and wind-braces. A little further S are three gabled houses with timber-framed upper parts, all facing N. They are CHEYNE COURT of the mid C15 and the PORTER'S LODGE. One gable has fine bargeboards. The back of these houses is formed by the town wall, and there are here some mullioned windows.

ST SWITHUN'S GATE is a plain archway of C15 details. Four-centred arch; two continuous chamfers. Original traceried DOORS.

No. 4 is the JUDGE'S LODGING, apparently late C17 but altered. Basically it is medieval, as one slit window, now inside, proves. Seven bays, brick, low. The centre is a three-bay projection with quoins, but the very middle bay has its own quoins of even length which are in fact half-giant-pilasters. The side parts are chequer brick and have some wooden cross-windows. The staircase is late C17 clearly. Three twisted balusters to each tread.

Nos 5–8 are DOME ALLEY, an interesting planned layout for four long but very shallow houses, two N, two S. Each pair has eight gables, and they were originally shaped. Also, whereas the N range faces S with its main façade, the other range, very reasonably, put the two main chimneystacks there. The details, such as wooden cross-windows and a broad moulded brick frieze at the foot of the gables, make a late C17 date necessary. Exceedingly fine ornamented details of the rainwater pipes.

No. 9 is ashlar-faced, of three gables, early C17. The only window in its original state is one at the back of five lights with one transom. But there are the shapes of others left. The porch looks *c.*1840, and the staircase with three balusters to the tread is Georgian.

No. 10 is the only house in the Close with substantial medieval remains. There is a vaulted room of the C13 with three bays and two naves, i.e. with two piers. They are round with round abaci. The ribs are single-chamfered. Round wall-shafts. Doorway with two slight chamfers to the S. Next to it a one-light window with a shouldered lintel (cf. the Deanery porch). More such windows in the S wing of the

L-shaped building. Above the undercroft was the STRANGERS' HALL, and of this the large blocked S window survives and the small sexfoiled window above it. The large window is interfered with by a six-light Jacobean window. Buttresses to the W.

No. 11 lies further back. It is a five-bay brick house dated 1727. Red brick, one-bay projection with doorway with broad straight hood on brackets and small scrolls l. and r. Segmental pediment at the top, but above it a gable, and this announces an older age for the house. In fact it has a splendid staircase of the 1680s with lush openwork foliage, much as in the cathedral communion rails and the works of Warden Nicholas at the College.

To the W there is no close, though the houses of Great Minster Street allow one to keep up the illusion of a precinct. It is the same on the N side. The first houses from the W really belong to The Square. But one at least has its façade towards the cathedral. Five bays, three storeys, grey headers and red dressings. Doorway with unfluted Ionic columns and a pediment. Fluted frieze. Then follows MORLEY COLLEGE, founded in 1672 as the College of Matrons, but now of 1880 (by *Colson*). The character of roof and façade was kept, though the details are characteristically 1880.

After that the WESSEX HOTEL by *Feilden & Mawson* (with *Lionel Brett*), 1961–3. This is really a triumph. It does exactly what Peter Shepheard did not do at Winchester College (*see* p. 705). It uses the C20 idiom without compromise and proves that it can stand up to the idioms of the past and even to a cathedral. The success is due to keeping the scale down to that of the other buildings in the Close and to using materials familiar to Winchester. The building is in two blocks, stressing the position at the NE corner of the precinct. The main block runs parallel with Morley College. It has a ground floor of flint with red-brick dressings and an upper floor of stone, flint, glass, and black slate. The W front is sheer except for a doorway and a long slender window over. L. and r. is flint in a brick frame below, and brick in a stone frame above. The subsidiary block is round the corner of the Close. It is built round a courtyard and has an open ground floor, the whole of this for car parking. There are only the many round pilotis supporting the four ranges. They are faced with engineering bricks and carry shallow concrete arches. Above just plain brick walls with cut-in windows. The hotel has a total of ninety-three bedrooms. Inside, between main lounge and cocktail bar, STAINED GLASS by *John Piper* and *Patrick Reyntiens*. Semi-abstract faces in square panels; ground of many shades from dark blue to black.

THE TOWN

CHURCHES

ALL SAINTS, Petersfield Road. 1890–8 by *J. L. Pearson*. Flint and brick. Nave and equal N aisle. Two W gables. A S tower has not been built. Lancets, plate and bar tracery. In the chancel high lancets; the E windows placed very high up. Wooden roofs inside. – FONT. From St Peter Chesil. Late Norman. Of the Purbeck table-top type. With shallow blank arches. – PLATE. Paten, 1658; Chalice, inscribed 1675. Both from St Peter Chesil.

ST BARTHOLOMEW, King Alfred Place, off Hyde Street. The former village church of Hyde. Low W tower with low pyramid roof. Chequer flint and stone. The church is of nave, N aisle, and chancel. The chancel was rebuilt in 1857–9 by *Colson*. The N side of the church apparently of 1879–80, with a number of cross-gables. The nave has Norman masonry and a Norman S doorway. Two orders of columns with big ornamental capitals probably of *c.*1130. Round arch with zigzag. Billet hood-mould. Tympanum with sunk triangles, all re-tooled. The N arcade is Norman too, but nearly entirely Victorian. In the nave S wall some single-light windows of *c.*1300 and a re-set E.E. PISCINA(?). The vestry has an E window, also E.E. (shafted) and also re-set. – ARCHITECTURAL FRAGMENTS from Hyde Abbey (*see* p. 716). They are to be dated *c.*1130 and come in all probability from the cloister. They are closely dependent on the capitals of the Canterbury crypt and similar also to the capitals of Reading Abbey. There are five of them, the best those with animals or symmetrical foliage trails in roundels. Also a shaft from the cathedral (S porch) and another capital and a springer stone with zigzag, leaf, and pellets. – PLATE. Chalice and Paten Cover of 1568.

CHRIST CHURCH, Christ Church Road. 1861 by *Ewan Christian*. With a SE tower and broach-spire and a polygonal apse. Wide interior. Low round marble piers with naturalistic capitals. Cinquefoiled clerestory.

ST CROSS. *See* p. 706.

ST JOHN BAPTIST, St John's Street. Broad, unbuttressed SW tower with a Perp arch to the S aisle. Most of the windows are Perp too, though the history of the church is more varied. The one exception externally is the spectacular window of the S chapel, which is late C13, of four lights, with three bar-tracery circles, two quatrefoiled, the large top one septfoiled. Next to it is the rood-stair-turret, which oddly enough has its entrance from the E. The E view of the church along the street is three-gabled. Internally there are two arcades of *c.*1200 with round piers, trumpet-scallop (just one) or its reverse, i.e. concave-fluted capitals and pointed arches. There are remains of a contemporary N aisle W window, close to the arcade and thus indicating the narrowness of the original aisle. In the widened N wall two lancet windows were discovered in 1958. In their splays are excellent C13 WALL PAINTINGS. St John Evangelist and probably another evangelist in one window with foliage ornament above, St Christopher and a Bishop in the other, also with ornament above. – FONT. Octagonal, Perp, with quatrefoils. – PULPIT. Perp, of wood, with buttress-shafts at the angles and simple panels. – SCREENS. Between chancel and chapels C14 screen, a rarity in Hampshire. Shafts with shaft-rings instead of muntins, and cusped ogee arches and cusped open spandrels. – The rood-screen is Perp and of one-light divisions. – (BENCH ENDS. Two, with poppy-heads and tracery. VCH) – CHANDELIER. Very big; dated 1791. – STAINED GLASS. In the S aisle E window many original fragments. – In the S aisle W window glass by *Evans* of Shrewsbury (TK). – PLATE. Chalice and Paten Cover of 1568. – MONUMENT. In the N chapel a much re-tooled tomb-chest with shields on which the emblems of the Passion.

ST LAURENCE, Great Minster Street. Probably C15. W tower and higher stair-turret. Little else visible outside. – STAINED GLASS. The E window looks *c.*1850. – (A part of a C13 doorway has recently come to light on the N side of the church. RH)

(ST LUKE, Battery Hill. 1960–1 by *C. W. T. Evans.*)

ST MATTHEW, Stockbridge Road, Weeke. The village church of Weeke. Low, nave and chancel and bell-turret. Most windows are C17. The S doorway, however, and the chancel arch are Norman. The doorway has a round arch, the chancel arch a pointed one with slight chamfers. – STAINED GLASS. Fragments of the C15 and later roundels in the E window. – PLATE.

The church possesses a Paten of the mid C13, still in the Romanesque tradition. Engraved rim with the inscription: Cuncta creo, virtute rego, pietate reformo, and engraved with the Lamb and Cross. Parcel-gilt. This is one of the three or four earliest patens in England. – Cup of 1705. – BRASS. William Complyn † 1498 and wife. No effigy but a St Christopher, 8½ in. high.

ST MAURICE, High Street. Pulled down, except for the tower mostly of 1842.* Set in the tower a Norman doorway with one order of shafts with block capitals and zigzag in the arch. When the site was excavated, it was found that the Norman church had an apse stilted in plan.

ST MICHAEL, Kingsgate Street. A curious building, externally now nearly all *Butterfield*, 1882–90. But the tower remains Perp. Butterfield's is geometrical tracery. What he found was a church formerly of nave with N aisle, but the N aisle removed in 1822 to create the wide area the Late Georgian churchmen demanded. The tower thus was entirely out of true. Butterfield kept the wide area but intended to build a new N aisle. However, only the E respond was built. – PLATE. Flagon, 1682; Almsdish, 1699; Paten, 1706; Chalice, 1730.

ST PAUL, St Paul's Hill. By *Colson Sen.*, who died in 1894, and *Colson Jun.* The chancel was consecrated in 1872, nave and transepts were ready in 1889, the aisles in 1902 and 1910 by *Colson Jun.* Flint, no tower. Nave and aisles, the S aisle very wide. Geometrical tracery.

ST PETER CHESIL, Chesil Street. The church lies along the street. The SE tower, tile-hung above and with pyramid roof, is of the C13 (cf. the E bell-opening with an E.E. shaft), the W windows are Dec, the rest of the windows are Perp. Inside, the S arcade turns out to belong to the early C13 (round piers, round abaci, arches with two slight chamfers). The church has recently been converted into a theatre.

ST PETER (R.C.), Jewry Street. 1926 by *F. A. Walters*. The first Catholic church at Winchester had been by *John Carter* for Dr Milner, 1792, a building much discussed. Its shell survives. The long side has a porch, then five bays in a minimum Perp and another porch. The new church is ironstone rubble and Bath stone. NE tower with higher stair-turret. Dec details. All very reactionary for 1926. Spacious interior. Set in the N side a Late Norman doorway from the chapel of the Magdalen Hospital. Two orders of shafts, trumpet-

* By *William Gover* (RH).

scallop capitals. Arch with rolls. – PLATE. Cross with the Symbols of the Evangelists; C15. (From Barton Stacey.)

ST SWITHUN. *See* Kingsgate, p. 697.

ST THOMAS AND ST CLEMENT, Southgate Street. 1845–6 by *E. W. Elmslie*, the steeple completed in 1857. St Thomas is the most ambitious Victorian church in Winchester, and it is remarkable that it should be so early; for it is 'archaeological', i.e. no longer uninformed in its Gothic motifs and their handling. S steeple with broach-spire, pinnacles on the broaches; lucarnes. Geometrical tracery, i.e. the Second Pointed which Pugin, Scott, and Ferrey and of course *The Ecclesiologist* were bringing back in those very years. It is odd that one should know so little about Elmslie. The church faces the street with its steeple and the three gables of chancel and chancel aisles. Tall nave with clerestory. The ensemble as well as the details excellent. – STAINED GLASS. Characteristic glass of *c.*1850 in the E window. Whom by? – In the S chapel by *Powell*, 1858 (designed by *Lyon*) and 1861 (designed by *Moberly*). – PLATE. Chalice of 1629; Chalice and Paten Cover of 1634; Almsdish of 1664; Paten given in 1697; Paten of 1705; Flagon of 1715.

HOLY TRINITY, North Walls. 1853–4 by *Woodyer*, an important early work, i.e. Early Victorian rather than High Victorian. Flint. Nave with aisles, chancel, and clerestory. Flèche over the E end of the nave. No external or internal division of nave and chancel. Seven-bay arcades. Dec style, in the tracery and also the piers. The arches die into broaches above the abaci. – PAINTINGS. The Stations of the Cross, by *Joseph A. Pippet*, before 1889. – STAINED GLASS. A good series by *Clayton & Bell*. – (To the SE, at the corner of North Walls and Upper Brook Street, stands the VICARAGE, an excellent design by *Woodyer*, 1864. Flint and brick, with characteristic detail in the steeply pointed windows and the dated rainwater heads. Double-height living room at first-floor level, going up into the roof like a medieval hall. NT)

CONGREGATIONAL CHURCH. *See* p. 716.

PUBLIC BUILDINGS

COUNTY HALL. 1959–60 by *C. Cowles Voysey*, *John Brandon-Jones*, *J. D. Broadbent & R. Ashton* and entirely untouched by the last thirty years of architecture. Large, of four storeys, *See* p. 832 neo-Georgian, red brick, with a cupola ending in the little Colonial-looking spire.

CASTLE AND COUNTY OFFICES. This is quite an impressive area, for Victorian and post-Victorian rather than medieval reasons. It is true that it is the site of William the Conqueror's earthworks and further C12 stone buildings, and that it still has Henry III's Great Hall, the finest medieval hall in England after Westminster Hall, if only it were not treated so shockingly by the Magistrates' Court and the Police. Yet what one sees mainly is the County Offices, two blocks, CASTLE HILL OFFICES and CASTLE AVENUE OFFICES. They are of a unified character, though differing in details from Henry VIII to Elizabeth I. Flint and Bath stone and studied asymmetries and irregularities. Their dates are as follows: Castle Hill Offices by the County Surveyor *James Robinson* and *Sir Arthur Blomfield*, completed 1895, Castle Avenue Offices, the E half by the County Surveyor *W. J. Taylor* with *Sir T. G. Jackson*, completed 1912, the W half by *Sir Herbert Baker*, completed 1932. The link between this and the Great Hall was originally of 1774, by the then Surveyor *Thomas Whitcombe*.

The motte of the Norman castle lay at the S end of the spur on which the castle stood, i.e. S of the present barracks. The castle was besieged and taken in 1216 by Prince Louis of France, the later Louis IX and Henry III's brother-in-law. Rebuilding was necessary after the French had gone, and so the GREAT HALL was built between 1222 and 1236. The master mason was called *Stephen*. It is a double cube, which is interesting: 110 by 55 by 55 feet. It is of five bays with large two-light windows with a transom, trefoil-headed lights, and a quatrefoil in plate tracery. Above these windows were originally dormers with round windows and cross-gables. But in the late C14 this arrangement was changed. The dormers were taken down, the round windows placed lower, and a straight eaves-line was made. All this is still recognizable inside. The present doorway, in the middle in a totally unmedieval way, dates from 1845. The original doorways survive where one would expect to find them, in the (E) end bays. They have one order of shafts, a depressed two-centred arch, and a hood-mould on stiff-leaf stops. On the S side the doorway is complete; on the N side there is only one jamb. To the immediate E of the S doorway is another of which at present only one jamb appears. The dais was on the W side, and part of its masonry is still there. There is also a fine doorway from the dais end, probably to the staircase up to the solar.

The doorway has one order of Purbeck shafts, and the arch starts with a vertical piece and continues depressed two-centred. Hood-mould on stiff-leaf corbels. The hall is
22 aisled. The arcade is of beautiful tall Purbeck piers, of eight attached shafts with barely noticeable shaft-rings. Round sub-bases, round abaci. Arches of one chamfer, a group of thin rolls, and another chamfer. The roof was renewed in 1873 (by *T. H. Wyatt*). Above the dais high up is a group of three stepped lancet lights. – SCULPTURE. Queen Victoria seated, by *Alfred Gilbert*, 1897, formerly in the Abbey Grounds. It is typical Gilbert, especially the fantastic openwork crown held above the queen's head. Can Winchester really not find a better place for this? – ROUND TABLE. Huge round table-top with a Tudor rose in the middle and black letter inscriptions. The Round Table is first mentioned in the first half of the C15, but was not new then. So it must have been repainted.

BARRACKS, Romsey Road. The Green Jackets Barracks adjoin the castle site and belong closely to it in so far as their site is that of Charles II's Palace designed by *Wren*, begun in 1683 and stopped in 1685. Work by then, however, had proceeded quite far, for Defoe writes that 'the front next to the city [is] carried to the roof and covered'. What was meant by that is doubtful, as the plan has a centre and two very far-projecting wings, the courtyard formed by them being open to the city, i.e. the E. The wings were stepped in plan towards the courtyard, a motif Wren had taken from Levau's Versailles, which he knew. The details represented Wren's first turn from the calm of his earlier to the Baroque drama of his later style. Lord Torrington in 1782 called it 'a miserable deserted intention of Royalty' and likely to have resulted in something 'unsightly, ill situated' and 'without beauty or retirement'. What had been built and taken over by the military was destroyed by fire in 1894. The present buildings are of *c.*1900 etc. They are quite impressive, of brick, with stone dressings. Facing the parade yard there is one block of thirty-five bays and four storeys, with a total of five pediments. The centre is all stone-faced and has a giant portico of attached Corinthian columns from the ground and r. and l. of it recessed bays with detached giant columns. A second block at r. angles is thirteen bays long. It has only one pediment, carried by giant pilasters, not columns. Opposite the first is a third block, two-storeyed only, of fifteen bays with one pediment and a cupola. Good recent buildings close to the entrance and also by the S end of the site, by *Booth, Ledeboer & Pinckheard.* Along Southgate Street is the former Garrison School. It is now stores. It is flint with brick dressings, eleven bays long, with giant segmental arches. The low brick apse added *c.* 1891. No tower.

WALLS. They largely follow the lines of the Roman wall, and contain Roman evidence, but mostly date from the C13. They were very ruinous by 1376 and repaired then and in the C15. Two gates only remain (*see* below). The best preserved stretch is along College Street.

WESTGATE. Basically C13, but the W face of the late C14. Of the C13 remains the carriageway to the E with its depressed two-centred arch and E.E. mouldings. The W side has a different moulding, a frieze of animals and fleurons above the arch, two early gunports of keyhole shape (cf. the Southampton walls) above the frieze, then two quatrefoils with shields and hood-moulds on heads, another frieze, and finally the remains of the machicolation.

KINGSGATE. C14 gateway and above it the church of ST SWITHUN with small domestic late C15 or early C16 windows. Only the E window is of three lights. The gate has two pedestrian entrances of the C18. Inside the passageway to the l. and r. are two wide bays of open wooden arcading, with four-centred arches and some elementary tracery (cf. St Cross). The church has a single-framed roof and a pretty Perp niche in the N wall. – STAINED GLASS. E window. Some of the C15, from St Peter Chesil. – PLATE. Almsplate 1713; Set 1717.

GUILDHALL. By *Jeffery & Skiller*, 1871–3. Gothic, symmetrical, with a middle tower and this as well as the angle pavilions provided with French pavilion roofs. The style is Second Pointed and evidently influenced by Godwin's Northampton Town Hall.* The long, much plainer r. extension is of 1892–3, by *J. B. Colson.* The tender for the original building was £10,313, for the extension £4,837 (GS). The main building is entered by a deep vaulted porch, but no climax follows. – CIVIC PLATE. Silver Seal, *temp.* Edward I. – Bronze Seal, 1587. – Gold Ring, 1653. – Salver, 1660. – Silver-covered Vase, 1660. – Covered Cup with two handles, 1664. – Twelve large Spoons, presented 1674. – Four silver-gilt

* For the extension to the Northampton Town Hall *Jeffery* was made joint architect in 1889.

Maces, 1722 by *Benjamin Pyne*. – Service, bought in 1762 (cost: £78 19s. 10d.). – Many Victorian pieces.

COUNTY POLICE HEADQUARTERS, Romsey Road. 1962–5 by the County Architect, *H. Benson Ansell*. A reasonable building, but placed as it is on a hill-top and having eight storeys and a big tank, it engages far more attention in the general picture of Winchester than it should have been allowed.

80 LIBRARY, Jewry Street. Built as the Corn Exchange in 1836–8. By *O. B. Carter*,* evidently a man of considerable talent and character. Yellow brick and white ashlar. Classical but with pronounced Italianate roofs, i.e. low pitches and deep eaves. Even the square turret in the middle has one. The turret is placed behind the central portico, inspired by Inigo Jones's St Paul, Covent Garden, with its Tuscan columns and its Etruscanly deep eaves to the pediment. Three-bay links with arched windows to end pavilions. Excellent internal remodelling recently by *Casson, Conder & Partners*.

WINCHESTER COLLEGE. Bishops had founded colleges before William of Wykeham. Their need, i.e. the need for educated clergy familiar especially with canon and civil law, was accepted. And colleges had taught boys as a side-line before Wykeham too. But he was the first to have a coherent idea of a system of tuition rising from school to college, and his two foundations, New College Oxford and Winchester College, were on a scale unprecedented in England and – as far as Winchester, i.e. a school, is concerned – abroad also. William had become bishop in 1366. In 1369 he bought land at Oxford for his college. It was finally built in 1380–6.

Winchester College was founded in 1382. The first stone was laid in 1387, and it was opened in 1394. It was, according to the final statutes of 1400, to have a warden, a headmaster, ten fellows, three chaplains, one usher, three chapel clerks, seventy 'poor and needy scholars', sixteen choristers, and up to ten commoners, i.e. paying scholars coming from wealthy or noble families.

It is the commoners who in the end made public schools what they were until recently. William also instituted the prefectural system which still prevails. Moreover, with his pedagogic vision went an equally original architectural vision. Down to the time of William of Wykeham schools had been small, and, if they grew, had grown any accidental way. The growth of colleges had not been more planned.

* Carter was G. E. Street's master in 1841–4 (NT).

Winchester College is planned in its layout, and New College even more so. For both the master mason was *William de Wynford* (*see* p. 671). The late C14 parts of Winchester College consist of the Outer Court with its gatehouse, the Chamber Court with its gatehouse and with Chapel and Hall at the far end, and the Cloister or Cemetery beyond. All this was complete when William died in 1404. Additions were made in the C15, and many have of course been made since. We take the buildings topographically, starting in College Street.*

The first building to make the presence of the college felt is the HEADMASTER'S HOUSE, forbidding in its C19 Gothic. It is by *G. S. Repton*, 1839–42. Knapped and squared flint. Three storeys, basically symmetrical, but with a pointed contrast between the openness of the main bay window and the closedness of a chimneybreast. Windows straight-headed with pointed, cusped lights. The back of the house is still Georgian in style.

Then follows some of the C14 college work. Few windows high up, small, oblong, and barred. OUTER GATE is of two storeys. Four-centred arch with a hollow chamfer, typical – as we shall see – of the college, and rounded edge. Above in a niche statue of the Virgin and two windows l. and r. The gateway has a fine, out-of-the-ordinary lierne-star vault with leaf bosses. The warden originally lived above Middle Gate, but in 1597 he moved into what has remained his lodging, namely the E end of the College Street frontage and the area behind. To College Street the WARDEN'S LODGINGS has buttresses. Above are arched windows of 1730, and the second floor is of brick. Round the corner to the E all is the remodelling by Warden Nicholas. This is dated 1692. Rubbed brick, sunk panels between the windows. Inside the Warden's House is a chimneypiece dated 1615 and also a chimneypiece with garlands and a staircase with twisted balusters, the latter two clearly of *c.*1695.‡

OUTER COURT is entered by the gatehouse which, on this side, has a higher stair-turret. The E side is a re-fronting of the WARDEN'S LODGINGS by *G. S. Repton*, 1832–3, and again coursed, knapped flint and windows like the headmaster's. To the W is a screen (the archway is dated 1663), but originally

* Most of the buildings are of Binstead stone.

‡ Also a large Annunciation by *Le Moyne*, painted in 1727 and given to the College for the chapel in 1729.

Outer Court went on. Simple doorways of one hollow chamfer to the N and W, where brewhouse, slaughter house, and stables were located. Most of the windows oblong, single-light, and barred, but in the W range one original larger window with a cusped head. The brewhouse was converted internally into the MOBERLY LIBRARY by *Sir Herbert Baker*, 1932–4 (NT). The S range is the most interesting. Three-storeyed MIDDLE GATE, the arch like that of the outer gatehouse. First-floor windows of two lights with a transom. Then three niches. One is empty.* In the others are the Virgin and William of Wykeham. Two one-light windows between. Tierceron-star vault inside.

Through the archway one reaches CHAMBER COURT. Middle Gate here has the same design. Three statues are preserved (badly), and there is a higher stair-turret. Round the corner lay the chambers of the scholars, the fellows, the commoners, and also headmaster, usher, chaplains, and so on. Doorways with one hollow chamfer, windows of one and two lights. Doorways and windows have hood-moulds, and their head label-stops must all be studied. In the N range W of Middle Gate (Second Master) a fine wooden Jacobean overmantel. In the SW corner is the staircase up to Hall. It is entered under an arch with broad wave and hollow mouldings which die against the imposts. At its top is a curious half-arch.
39 The arrangement on the S side is this. Chapel and Hall divide the S range between them, the Chapel on the ground floor, Hall to its W on the upper floor – all as it is at New College, though reversed. Below Hall is the original school-room. It is now called Seventh Chamber. It has small two-light windows. Originally the passage W of the chapel was part of the school-room. Hall has large two-light windows with a transom, to S as well as N. The Chapel windows are of three lights with a transom, but the E window is of seven lights. Attached to the Chapel at its NE end is the Muniment Tower, of three storeys, not high, with two-light windows. The vestry, on its ground floor, has a tierceron-star vault with bosses.

The CHAPEL is entered by an ante-chapel above which is the E bay of Hall. This has doorways to N and S. Against its W wall is *Butterfield*'s Crimean War MEMORIAL, blank wall arcading in the E.E. style; 1858. – A stone SCREEN divides antechapel from chapel. Doorway and tall two-light windows l. and r. The chapel is of six bays plus the antechapel. Fine

* But the statue, the Angel of the Annunciation, is preserved.

cusped lierne-vault* in appearance close to a fan-vault. Very thin ribs. The 'fans' stand on three heads. The room under the tower has a tierceron-star vault. – REREDOS. Of stone, *c.*1470, scrupulously restored by *Butterfield*, 1874–5. It has fifteen niches all with crocketed canopies. The middle three‡ are higher than the others and have a top cresting. The first and last are round the corners on the N and S walls, and above them is a thick fleuron frieze. – PANELLING, STALLS, and PEWS. By *Caröe*, 1913–21. – WEST GALLERY. By the same, 1908.§ – ORGAN CASES. That on the N wall by *S. E. Dykes Bower*, 1948–9, the one on the W gallery by *Caröe*. – COMMUNION RAIL. Of openwork foliage. 1680–3. By *Edward Pierce* (cf. New Hall, p. 706, and also the communion rail in the cathedral). – STALL ENDS. They, with their misericords, belong to the original work of *c.*1390–5. Of bold shapes with fleuron borders and some tracery. Heads on the arms. – MISERICORDS. Represented are e.g. (N) a dragon, a shepherd, a falcon with a mallard, the demi-figure of a man, and (S) a cripple with pieces of wood tied to hands and feet so that he can move on them, another dragon, a pelican, two goats affronted, a man with a dagger. – STAINED GLASS. The famous Jesse Window was datable to 1393, but what is there now is all by *Betton & Evans* of the years 1822–3. The original glass disappeared, but a good deal has recently returned from Ettington in Warwickshire and other places. This is now in Thurbern's Chantry (*see* below). – The side windows by *David Evans* too, 1825–8. – BRASSES. The many brasses on the floor are copies made in 1882 from earlier rubbings.‖

* Of wood.

‡ Altered by *Caröe* in 1920.

§ Caröe's work involved replacing almost all Butterfield's except the two items mentioned above. Butterfield's stalls are now at Binstead, Isle of Wight.

‖ PLATE (also domestic). Founder's Spoon, first half C15. – Founder's Ring, later C16. – Silver-gilt Cup and Cover, first half C16; the Election Cup. – Tazza, 1554. – Standing Salt, s.-g., *c.*1560. – Parcel-gilt Rosewater Dish of 1562 and its companion, a Ewer, both splendidly ornate. – Chalice and Paten Cover, 1568. – S.-g. Chalice of *c.*1610. – Two s.-g. Chalices and Paten Covers of 1611. – Rosewater Dish and Ewer of *c.*1613. – Tankard and Cover of 1614. – S.-g Steeple Cup and Cover of 1615. – Two s.-g. Flagons of 1627. – S.-g. Steeple Cup and Cover of 1632. – Parcel-gilt Tankard and Lid of 1649. – Caudle Cup of 1652. – Seven two-handled Drinking Cups of 1657. – Spool Salt of 1664. – Loving Cup and Cover of 1680. – S.-g. Almsdish of 1681. – S.-g. two-handled Porringer and Cover of 1682. – Two s.-g. Patens of 1683. – Octagonal

Warden Thurbern died in 1450. Shortly before his death the foundations had been laid for his CHANTRY CHAPEL to be added to the chapel on the S side. Building began in 1473–4, the high tower above it was started in 1476, and the structure was complete in 1485. In 1862–3 it had to be pulled down completely and rebuilt (by *Butterfield*). The chantry is of two bays and has lierne-star vaults with bosses. The arch between the two bays is panelled. The pier towards the chapel is naturally very strong, but it is much subdivided so as to counteract any appearance of massiveness. The S windows are of five and of two lights. The tower is the most prominent beacon of Winchester. It is of four stages with the bell-stage blank-panelled around the quite small bell-openings. Tall square pinnacles and yet higher stair-turret. – TAPESTRY. Two splendid Flemish pieces of *c.*1500, known as the Tapestry of the Roses. – STAINED GLASS. Much of *c.*1502, but also the recovered original glass of 1393 from the chapel E window. This is in the chantry W window. It is signed by Master *Thomas* of Oxford, who also worked at New College Oxford, and is among the best of its date in the country. – BELL. A bell, given by William of Wykeham, is in Thurbern's Chantry.

The HALL is 63 ft long and 40 ft high. It has a roof of low pitch with arched braces and tracery above them. The PANELLING was made in 1540. – The STAINED GLASS is by *Gleadowe*, 1931. – Simple SCREEN. – In the W wall the three usual doorways. The large r. one led to the staircase to

---

Chafing Stand with wooden handle of 1686. – Salver of 1703. – Two Salvers, *c.*1720. – Ten Tablespoons, 1723. – Salver, 1727. – Twenty-four silver-handled Knives, *c.*1730. – Pair of Salvers, 1746. – Two Tablespoons, 1749. – Two Gravy Spoons, 1750. – Four Tablespoons, 1752. – Tankard, 1753. – Twelve Tablespoons, 1754. – Quart Tankard, with lid, 1757. – Soup Ladle, 1760. – Two Marrow Spoons, 1760. – Cruet Stand, with five castors, 1764. – Six Salt Cellars, 1764. – Sugar Basin, with handle, 1766. – Quart Tankard, with lid, 1770. – Wine Strainer, 1778. – Four Sauce Ladles, 1788. – Bread basket, with handle, 1790. – Pair of Sauce Tureens, 1790. – Pair of Sauce Boats, 1790. – Two Salvers, 1790. – Eight Tablespoons, 1794. – Four Salt Cellars, 1799. – Four Salt Cellars, 1800. – Pair of Candlesticks, 1802. – Two pint Tankards, 1803. – Twelve Dessert Spoons, 1807. – Four Skewers, 1807. – Cruet Stand, with two silver castors and two glass cruets, 1808. – Mustard Pot, 1808. – Two Salvers, 1809. – Soup Ladle, 1809. – Ten Tablespoons, 1809. – Fish Slice, 1812. – Two Gravy Spoons, 1817. – Pair of Chalices, 1821. – Jug, with lid and spout, 1823. – Sixty Table Forks, 1823. – Twelve Dessert Forks, 1824. – Flagon, 1824. – Twenty-four Dessert Forks, 1827. – Cup, 1830. – Teapot, 1831. – Cruet Stand, with four glass bottles, 1833. – S.-g. Paten, 1833. – Twelve Dessert Spoons, 1834. – Snuff Box, 1836.

the kitchen. The other two must have led to buttery and pantry. All three have hatches. Below buttery and pantry, on the ground floor, W of Hall, is the BEER CELLAR, with one octagonal pier and ribs with long chamfers, in tierceron-stars. Against the walls the ribs stand on busts. Above buttery and pantry is the AUDIT ROOM (with a wooden SCREEN and Wessex TILES) and on the fourth floor the CHEESE ROOM. This whole block of rooms is flint-faced, whereas Hall and Chapel are ashlar. The windows on the four floors are few and not aligned. The KITCHEN lies in the W range, and has little of interest preserved. It is a square room, as kitchens usually were. Roof with wind-braces. In the kitchen lobby the Trusty Servant, a highly popular PAINTING. In its present form it is by *William Cave* and dates from 1809.

The CLOISTER adjoins the tower almost immediately. It is 132 ft square and not in axis, which is strange and connected with the shape of the available site for the whole college. It has completely bare walls to the outside, and as one enters it, one is reminded of Italy by its seclusion and the wagon roofs. The openings to what was the garth are of three lights under two-centred arches. Some panel tracery. – Of the many MONUMENTS only the following need attention. First a number of brasses, all three-quarter or demi-figures. John Erewaker † 1514, a 16 in. figure. – John Gylbert † 1514 (15½ in.). – John Taknell † 1494 (12 in.). – Edward Tatcham † 1473 (12½ in.). – Then some characteristic cartouches of † 1666, † 1674, and † 1679. – More ambitious Humphrey May † 1657 with a free-standing urn on a square base. – Dr John Cobb † 1724. Tablet with putto heads and a broken segmental pediment. – Charles Scott † 1762. Charming relief in the 'predella'. Three putti with allegorical instruments and a profile medallion.

In the middle of the Cloister lies the FROMOND CHANTRY CHAPEL. Fromond's bequest dates from 1420. The chapel is two-storeyed and largely of green Ventnor stone. The chapel proper is on the ground floor, above and much lower was (and is) a library. The chapel windows are of three and – W and E – five lights, the upper windows of two or three, with four-centred heads and transoms. All windows have head-stops. The doorway on the W side cuts into the W window. In the SW corner is the stair-turret. Eaves frieze with heads, animals, monsters, etc. Inside, as in the cathedral nave, there is panelling l., r., and below the windows. The vault is a complicated lierne-vault with bosses. – STAINED GLASS. E window from the Thurbern Chantry, i.e. of *c*.1502. – SCULPTURE. St Michael and Gabriel, by *George Frampton*, l. and r. of the altar; 1898 and 1900. – The roof of the building visible in the library rests on stone angel busts.

SCHOOL lies close to the Cloister, to the W, i.e. S of Hall. It was built in 1683–7. The cost was £2,600, of which Warden Nicholas gave more than half. It is 80 by 36 ft in size. The attribution to *Wren* has no authority. Red brick and much stone. Seven bays, the central three projecting and pedimented. Carved modillions; hipped roof. Quoins. The windows are arched with straight hoods on brackets. Very fine garlands above them. In the three middle bays they have heads in their centres. Large doorway with segmental pediment on brackets. Above, a niche with volutes and an arched hood enriched by a foliage frieze. In the niche STATUE of the founder by *C. G. Cibber*; 1692. The ceiling starts with a broad coving. In this shells, branches, palm-fronds, and shields. The ceiling proper has two simple oval panels and one thickly garlanded round panel. Facing the entrance two-bay PANELLING with a broad segmental pediment. The S side of the building has just two windows and a middle pediment. – CHANDELIER. Of brass; 1729. – TAPESTRIES. Flemish, one later C15, the other later C16.

S of the Headmaster's House and W of the W end of the Hall Range are MOBERLY COURT and Flint Court. They are by *Butterfield*, 1867–70, a remodelling of Repton's job of 1837–9 and, probably for that reason, not as eventful as Butterfield's work at Rugby and Keble. They are brick, partly chequer, partly diaper. To the N the front is of nine bays and symmetrical. The centre is an archway and a big canted bay window over. The first and last bays are higher than the rest. The W range is more utilitarian and three-storeyed throughout. The S side of the main range, i.e. FLINT COURT, is more or less symmetrical. It has two projecting wings, and in the centre a Perp cloister of three-light windows lies in front of the range proper. The W wing was later extended S. The interiors were much rebuilt by *Christian Doll* after the fire of 1947 (NT).

Extensions from 1890 have been to the S. In topographical order the first is *Sir Herbert Baker*'s WAR MEMORIAL CLOISTER of 1922–4. It is one of his best buildings. Flint and stone blocks. To the outside the walls are as closed as those of the ancient cloister. Only Baker would not have been satisfied with as discreet an entrance as the ancient one. His is larger, central, and has a gable with a Madonna by *Sir Charles Wheeler*. Inside, the cloister itself is of Tuscan columns, two deep, carrying arches. Against the walls a long inscription in flushwork and many shields and emblems by *G. Kruger Gray*. Baker liked this sort of thing. In the centre a Cross on shaft by *Alfred Turner*.

S of this is *Basil Champneys*'s MEMORIAL BUILDINGS, principally museum and art school, dated 1898, a curiously Baroque building. Brick and Bath stone. The front is of nine bays, with bays one and nine solid and with columns and window surrounds of heavy stone blocking. The centre has on the ground floor a recessed loggia with Tuscan columns two deep (Baker may have got his inspiration from this) and above them big oriels and Baroque roundels between (Grocyn, Bishop Ken, Seaton, Selborne). In the solid bays statues of the founder and Queen Victoria. To the N, lying back, a broad tower with Baroque cartouches. To the S on the upper floor three convexly projecting balconies. Nothing of architectural interest inside, but the exterior is personal, bold, and successful. This is more than one can say of the contemporary Science Building. But this is separated from the Museum by the SICK HOUSE, a building put up at a suitable distance from the rest in 1656. Brick, two gables and a smaller gable for the projecting middle porch. Mullioned windows. The SANATORIUM S of the Sick House is of 1884–93, a late work of *W. White* (NT). Then follows the SCIENCE SCHOOL. This was built in 1902–5. The architect was *Henry L. G. Hill*. It is brick with stone dressings, thirteen bays long and badly organized and detailed. (The dull and utilitarian BIOLOGY BLOCK is by *Ruthven O. Hall*, 1958. NT)

SE of College is NEW HALL, reached through *Bodley*'s small Stewart Memorial Gateway of 1885.* New Hall is by *Peter Shepheard* and was built in 1958–60. It is a curious and in many ways regrettable building. It stands on its own and so might well have been of its own time, instead of which the architect (much like Sir William Holford at Eton) lost his nerve and decided to be above all tactful. The result is not self-effacing, however. It is very noticeable, only in a pleadingly inoffensive way. Low-pitched roof. Blue brick and stone with much stress on quoins absolutely flat and window

* Not *in situ*.

surrounds. Only on the entrance side the windows have surrounds, and they are strikingly conventional. They are placed in a chequer of stone and blue brick. Porches on the W and N sides. On the S side only one row of upper windows. The self-effacement was perhaps induced by the terms of reference of the job; for the new hall was primarily meant to be
62 the receptacle for the superb WOODWORK from the Chapel, made in 1680–3. SCREEN of transparent panels, REREDOS of two pairs of Ionic columns, an open pediment and garlands, and wall PANELLING. All this had disappeared in Butterfield's restoration and was finally returned from Hursley Park. Mr Harvey is inclined to attribute it to *Pierce*, who is known to have worked for the college in the pertinent years.

Further away from the other buildings is the COMMONER GATE (South Africa Memorial) to Kingsgate Street. Stone, with polygonal turrets, in an ornate Perp, by *Frank L. Pearson*, 1902–4. Lower adjoining flint buildings. The ARMOURY is of the same date, by *John W. Little*.

Finally, in Romans Road the MUSIC SCHOOL, with a central room as its main accent. Flint and green stone. A composition of strange elements indeed. Three big round gables and an octagonal pyramid roof. The doorway has a big rounded hood too. 1903–4 by *E. S. Prior*. At the corner of Romans Road and St Cross Road is CHERNOCKE HOUSE by *Sir Charles Nicholson*, 1910–12. Flint, with gables a little sheerer and of a little lower pitch than more conventional architects might have done. Mullioned and transomed windows. The composition is asymmetrical to entrance as well as garden side. Short square tower.

KING ALFRED'S COLLEGE, Sparkford Road. By *Colson*, 1861–2. Long asymmetrical range with mullioned and transomed windows. Additions, right up to date. The Dining Hall of 1960–2 is by *Woodroffe, Buchanan & Coulter*, with its collapsed-tent roof.

COUNTY HOSPITAL. 1864–8 by *Butterfield*. Gothic. Red brick with blue diapers. The composition is of the calculated asymmetry which Butterfield had practised in a similar situation at Rugby School. The unexpected placing of traceried windows is specially telling. Later additions.

ST CROSS. St Cross Hospital was founded in 1136 by Bishop Henry of Blois, but of that time nothing is left except the S sacristy, which remains outside the composition of the church. It is rib-vaulted and reached from the S transept by a small doorway. The ribs rise from the ground on the S side. They have the same profile of a demi-roll and two half-hollows as those put up in the cathedral after 1107. There is no keystone. On the N the present transept has cut off the end of the vault. The room has a small window to the W and a blocked doorway in the E wall, where at that time there was probably the cloister. S of the sacristy is a largely later room continuing it. It is assumed that they were the N end of the W range of an original cloister.

The present church was built quite independent of it. It is a large, remarkably high, cruciform building with an aisled nave. That it was begun in the C12 and completed in the C13 is evident at once, but beyond that no documents help. Yet it would be extremely valuable for various reasons to be able to date the church of St Cross: for one thing it fills a gap in the architectural development of Winchester; for another it represents a transition fully illustrated but rarely datable in Hampshire churches (Portsmouth St Thomas, consecrations 1188, 1196). It is a matter of transition indeed, and a disorderly, illogical transition in which fully Gothic and fully Romanesque elements stand side by side or overlap.

The EXTERIOR will be examined first. The church was begun at the E end, and the chancel for that reason looks wholly Norman. Round-arched windows, circular windows in the gable, square angle turrets, and blank arcading. Only the very top has shaft-rings. The chancel aisles also have all round-arched windows, except for the curious row of pointed ones which originally went into the aisle roofs and were not meant to be seen. It will be shown presently how they came about. The aisles have doorways with zigzag, that in the angle of S aisle and S transept an odd arrangement of two zigzag half-arches meeting at a r. angle. These two entries must have led into the NW angle of the cloister. The N aisle has much more zigzag than the S aisle, and this is continued in the transepts.

The N transept still has rich zigzag in the ground-floor windows to the E, but pointed windows on the upper level. On the ground level to the W the zigzag stops and shafting takes its place – with waterleaf, may it be noted. In the S transept there is no zigzag, but there are no pointed windows yet either.

The crossing tower has Perp windows, set inside in long recesses with continuous double-chamfers, and above is an outer row of blank arcading, also with continuous double-

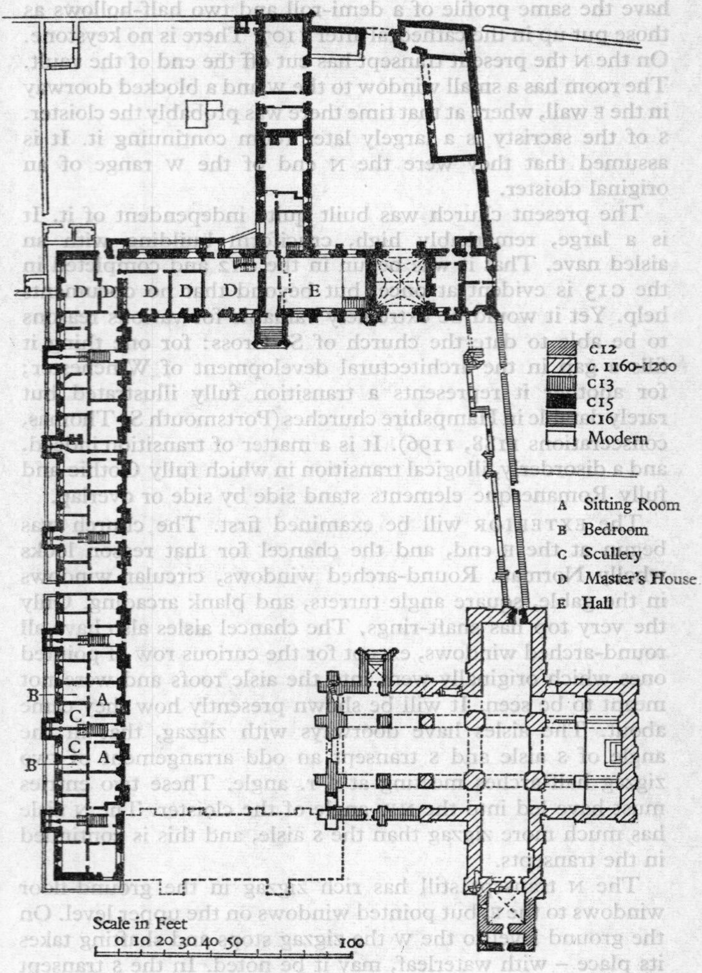

Winchester, St Cross, plan

chamfering. This must be late C13, though it is recorded that the tower was rebuilt in 1384.

The nave clerestory is of 1334–5, and so must be the W window. But the rest is the continuation of the story watched so far. The aisles still start Norman, but then turn completely E.E., and the N porch is mature E.E. Rib-vault on shafts inside. Stiff-leaf boss, though early rather than full stiff-leaf. The upper N window has trefoil-headed lights and plate tracery. Beautiful inner doorway with two orders of columns and many arch mouldings. The W doorway has a *trumeau* and trefoiled arches. The dogtooth of the arch is of a charming openwork variety. The five-light W window is Dec. In its head it has a large circle with three inscribed spherical triangles. On the S side it can be observed how even the buttresses change from the flat Norman to the deeper Gothic type with set-offs.

The story of the INTERIOR is much more intricate. Beginning again in the chancel, the first problem is what *Butterfield* did in 1864–5.* Evidently the detail on the N and S sides is all his, but were the arcades of two bays e.g. always pointed? That would mean that pointing starts inside much earlier than outside. And how early can we go with pointed arches? In the E wall the lowest windows are Norman with much zigzag all at r. angles to the wall, a decidedly Late Norman motif. Above is the oddest triforium, low, with very depressed intersecting arches, again a Norman motif. The intersections cause pointed arches, and they are the ones originally open into the aisle roofs and now appearing like real pointed arches in the external picture. The details of the triforium are bizarre, with odd compound shafts, and zigzag towards us, but also keeling of shafts. The capitals have enriched leaf and also waterleaf. Round-headed clerestory windows.

And then the vault. It is a rib-vault done in a competent French manner, even in the infilling of the cells or webs, which is managed in such a way that at the crown the courses of stones meet in a clean edge, not saw-tooth-wise. Also the vaulting-shafts start from the ground in the corners (with detached Purbeck shafts) but are cruelly corbelled off in the middle of the N and S sides. That must be *Butterfield*'s work. The vaulting ribs have partly zigzag.

The chancel aisles, built and vaulted of course before the

* Though his terrific polychromatic mural decorations have been removed (NT).

upper parts of the chancel itself could be continued, are overloaded with zigzag in windows and ribs. The problem so far is this. When can the chancel have been designed? Detached Purbeck shafts do not seem to appear before the 1170s, nor can such competent vaulting be assumed before 1175 at the very earliest (Canterbury choir). Similarly waterleaf and this kind of zigzag towards us is more likely in the 1170s than earlier. So probably the VCH's *c.*1160 is too early. As for development within the work, the overdone zigzag stands at the beginning, the French vaulting, being at top level, at the end.

20 In the crossing the arches are simply stepped, but the grouped shafts in the diagonals have shaft-rings. The transepts differ much one from the other. The openings to the chancel aisles are the same, both pointed, and that from the N transept is gratifyingly unrestored in the capitals. The triforium is continued into the transept by two lights on the S, by one only on the N side. Then this motif of the chancel stops. Also the rib-vaulting now is not prepared any longer from the ground, but starts from short vaulting-shafts, a little longer S than N. Otherwise the N transept, as we have already seen outside, continues the zigzag on the ground floor and goes pointed on the upper floor in the form of a bleak stepped wall-passage. The vaulting-ribs keep the zigzag even at that level (without bosses, where there had been bosses in the chancel). In the S transept S of the arch to the chancel aisle is a curious blank arch with a Greek-key motif and a joggled lintel under. This connected with the equally curious angle entry to the former cloister already referred to. Then follows a C13 recess, and another is in the S wall. The lower windows are all still round-headed. The rib-vault of the S transept has abandoned zigzag.

Even the nave, as far as it was built at one go with the E parts – for the sake of the stability of the crossing tower – is essentially Norman. Indeed it looks as if the French-Gothic impetus of the chancel vaulting were flagging. The first piers are round and fat, about 5 ft in diameter, and have many-fluted capitals. The arches from the transepts into the aisles again have fluted or scalloped capitals. The arcade arches of the first bay are pointed but have only two slight chamfers. The N aisle vault still has zigzag, though the S has not (just as it was in the upper transept vaults). Then, however, exactly as externally, all changes at last from transition to E.E. The second pair of piers, though still fat and round, have moulded capitals. The piers all have spurs on the bases, and the E.E. ones are of a monstrous size but uniquely dramatic. The aisle vaults now stand on totally different wall-shafts and have ribs without zigzag. Finally the W responds have stiff-leaf. So the stage of the N porch is reached.

The nave was vaulted much later. The bosses have the arms of William of Wykeham and Cardinal Beaufort. The latter, as we shall see, rebuilt the hospital.

FITTINGS. CHANCEL. SCREENS. To the E bays elaborate Perp stone screens with steep crocketed gables. Said to come from St Faith. – SHELF (SE corner), like a short tomb-chest. Arcading and top frieze. Perp. – In the W bay remains of STALLS. They must be Early Renaissance, say of *c.*1525. Profiles in medallions. Charming and excellently done tiny corbel figurines. – STAINED GLASS. In the E window Virgin, St John, St Catherine, St Swithun; late C15. – MONUMENTS. Brass to John de Campedon † 1410, nearly 6 ft long. – Brass to Richard Harward † 1493 (2 ft). – Brass to Thomas Laune † 1518 (3 ft 2 ins).

NORTH CHANCEL AISLE. PILLAR PISCINA. Base with spurs C12; top Perp. – Also two pretty Perp BRACKETS. – PAINTING. At the SE corner figure with a halo. – On the S wall figures under trefoil-headed arches; C13. – Also masonry patterns. – TILES. On the floor.

SOUTH CHANCEL AISLE. PAINTING. Flemish triptych of *c.*1520. – STALLS. More fragments from the Early Renaissance canopies. – COMMUNION RAIL. Jacobean or later. A specially ingenious pattern, not of balusters, but of openwork cruciform shapes interlocking. – TILES. On the floor.

CROSSING. SCREEN to the N transept.

NORTH TRANSEPT. BENCH ENDS with poppy-heads. – STAINED GLASS. St Gregory in an E window. Late C15.

SOUTH TRANSEPT. SCREEN to the S chapel. Restored. – PAINTING. In the E recess, C13, faded. Two rows of trefoil-headed panels. A quatrefoil above.

NAVE AND AISLES. LECTERN. With a splendid wooden eagle. What is its date and provenance? – STAINED GLASS. The W window is of 1860. – TILES in both aisles. – MONUMENTS. In the N aisle a large late C13 tomb recess. – In the S aisle Charles W. Cornwall † 1789. By *J. F. Moore*. Coloured marbles. Sarcophagus and below it the Speaker's mace. No figures.

PLATE. Two silver-gilt Patens of 1660 and 1784.

THE HOSPITAL. The premises of the hospital, as they are now, seem to have been put up in one build by Cardinal Beaufort
40 about 1445 and consist of the far-from-quadrangular quadrangle and the small entrance court to its N. N of the outer gateway is the new Master's House, built in 1899. Tudor with gables and mullioned and transomed windows. The gateway has a four-centred arch and a timber-framed gable with brick infilling. On the E and W are ranges, that on the W running against the N side of the hall range. The E range was the Hundred Men's Hall. In the W range is one original though much renewed two-light window, straight-headed, with cusped lights and a little tracery. The quadrangle is entered by a monumental gatehouse, inspired by those of the College. The archway has a four-centred arch and many continuous mouldings. In the spandrels large tracery. Above, a fine frieze with many heads. Then just one two-light window belonging to the Muniment Room and higher up three tall and slender niches, in one still the kneeling figure of the Cardinal. To the inside the gatehouse is more or less the same, except that there is only one niche and that a stair-turret rises higher than the building itself. The gateway has a tierceron-star vault with bosses. On the E of the gatehouse is the Porter's Lodge with a square stair-tower to the outside.

Adjoining the gatehouse on the W and forming the centre of the N range of the quadrangle is the hall. It is reached by a flight of steps and a porch. The porch has a two-centred arch and a lierne-vault with bosses. The label-stops of the inner doorway have excellently carved heads of a king and queen. The hall has three windows to the S, two to the N. They are of two lights with a transom. The tracery is one Perp unit, but inscribed into it is a quatrefoil in an oval – still a touch of the Dec. Plain screen inside with a gallery above. The roof timbers stand on stone angels' busts. Arched braces up to high collar-beams. Three tiers of wind-braces.* The kitchen does not lie W of the hall, as one would expect. It is – exactly as in the College – to the N, i.e. in this case in the W range of the entrance court, and the two-light window mentioned and an identical one to the W belong to it. Large fireplaces in the N wall, a hatch in the S wall. W of the hall was the Master's House. It has to the N a square bay with a traceried two-light window. Originally it was over the

* Some original STAINED GLASS in the S windows and above the door.

gateway and the porter's lodge, but from the C17, by the appropriation of brethren's lodgings, it took the position just indicated.

The long W range is all brethren's lodgings. Each house has four of them off one staircase and served by one chimney with a high octagonal stack. Each dwelling is of three rooms. All the windows are post-Reformation (one-light and two-light with a mullion). There were six staircases in this range originally.

The E range is of the early C16. It was built by Robert Sherborne and contained the infirmary and a long passage to the church. To the W the passage is a wooden cloister with very wide wooden arches. Four-centred heads and some carved tracery. A brick oriel less than halfway down.

ST JOHN'S HOSPITAL, High Street. *See* below.

GAOL, Romsey Road. 1848–50 by *Pearse*. Rendered. In the middle an archway with rustication of alternating sizes. The angle pilasters of the centre are treated in the same way. Turret; wings.

PERAMBULATION

The HIGH STREET, the *decumanus* of Roman Winchester, is still the spine of the town. The first part of the perambulation is to walk up it from E to W (on a Sunday). One can fan out N and S afterwards.

The E end of the High Street is wide, like a market place. It is dominated by the Town Hall and the STATUE of King Alfred raising one arm with a sword (1901 by *Hamo Thornycroft*). He is probably annoyed at the way in which the County Hall closes his view in the distance. Yet a little further E is ST JOHN'S HOSPITAL, the larger part on the S side, with rainwater-heads 1817, 1831, and 1833. The architect was *William Garbett*. Gatehouse of stone and grey headers. To its r., in Colebrook Street and in the courtyard, lower buildings of grey headers and red-brick dressings, also with red diapers (reversing the usual). The wing in the High Street is symmetrical with one gable. In the courtyard a gabled, tile-hung addition with white bargeboards. This must be of *c.*1880. Opposite are the medieval buildings of the hospital. Porch and to the r. CHAPEL. Six lancets to the S, at the E end three stepped lancets under one arch and a sexfoil over.* The

* PLATE. Paten of 1726; Almsdish of 1836. – Two TABLETS by *Eric Gill*; 1906 (NT).

doorway to the chapel is Perp (one hollow chamfer and one wave), and to its l. and r. are small two-light windows looking into the chapel. The doorway is reached by entering the premises through a porch, also Perp. An exit is in line on the N side. To the W extended the hospital proper, which was two-naved. This is now all merged in the bus waiting-space. One nave was for the sick, the other contained kitchen and dining hall. The great hall above, 62 by 37 ft, is now all divided. A few single-light cusped windows remain, but above the building seems now all C18, of brick. Three storeys, six bays.

In the ABBEY GROUNDS E of and behind Abbey House a TEMPLE front across the millstream, two pairs of Tuscan columns and a pediment. This, according to research done by Messrs Farmer & Dark, belonged to Abbey House and was designed by *William Pescod* in 1751 to hide the mill behind. It was originally in three parts. What now remains is only one of them. ABBEY HOUSE is a private house on its own, brick, the N front of three widely spaced bays, castellated and with angle turrets, the S front normal Georgian, five bays with a three-bay pediment.

After the town hall the High Street becomes a proper street. The first building of note, though much interfered with, is the former MARKET HOUSE, now a restaurant. It was built in 1857 and has (still) Greek Doric columns and wreaths in the frieze. No. 28, further on, has two upper bows, No. 118 (opposite) was originally a CHAPEL. It is stuccoed, has Doric pilasters, a large arched middle window, and a pediment across. It has been treated handsomely by Woolworth's. Nos 30–41 are all colonnaded, with Tuscan columns, but not uniformly. The houses themselves are largely pre-Reformation, and Nos 31, 33, 34, and 35 have original bargeboards. No. 107 (again opposite) has another pair of upper bows. Then follows another widening, but much less and only for a moment. In the widened corner is the BUTTER CROSS. It was built early in the C15, but sweepingly restored by *Scott* in 1865. Ground floor with crocketed gables and panelled angle shafts. These become pinnacles higher up, and the whole ends in a high pinnacle. Next to the Cross No. 43 (tea rooms) with a wooden front window of four ogee-headed lights, probably of the C14, and a C16 chimneypiece on the first floor. This is the site of the Norman royal palace of Winchester, and some minor walling has been identified. Then, on the N side, a splendid house, No. 105, of seven bays and three storeys. The ground floor has very pretty small pilasters carrying a thin entablature, projecting above the windows. The mid-windows on the first and second floors are arched, and it may well be that the house is older than the ground-floor decoration. No. 46 on the S side is striking and curious. It is of only three bays, but in the middle is a large arched window divided below the arch into two – not three – by one unfluted Ionic column. Grey brick. No. 101 on the N side is GOD BEGOT HOUSE, timber-framed, four-storeyed, with two front gables. The front to the High Street is too much restored to be of interest, but the long side, towards an alley, with its overhang, is still what it had been in the C16. Inside, a hall with tie-beams on arched braces and queen-posts. The internal timber-work continues in the recent building to the r. Again on the S side the former GUILDHALL (Lloyds Bank), built in 1713. The ground floor with Tuscan columns was open. Above are six windows in stone surrounds, and in the middle a STATUE of Queen Anne. Moulded stone top cornice and – the most striking thing in the High Street – the gorgeous clock bracket of wood. Squared weatherboarded tower with four-sided domed top at the W end. The scale of the guildhall makes that of BARCLAYS BANK at the corner of Jewry Street appear rather impertinent. Nine-bay neo-Georgian, brick, with pediment and cupola, 1957–9 by *W. Curtis Green, Son & Lloyd*.* It must be one of the last historicist buildings in England. Also on the N side, No. 86 has two upper bows and No. 79 a nice Late Georgian doorway. Nos 77 and 73 have early C19 façades, rendered, with upper pilasters and tripartite windows.

Up to the Westgate (*see* p. 697). In CASTLE HILL on the way to the castle (*see* p. 695) a fine Georgian house of five bays, brick, with rusticated rendered ground floor. Fine late C18 doorway in an added bay. Broken pediment on carved brackets. Beyond the Westgate the corner of the WESTGATE HOTEL, Romsey Road and Upper High Street, early C19, with upper giant pilasters, and rounded corner, as the Regency liked it. Also tripartite, pedimented windows. Next to this and the County Hall is the Plague Memorial OBELISK, put up in 1759. Off Upper High Street in NEWBURGH STREET is NEWBURGH HOUSE with its archway and vermiculated quoins patently imitated from the Old Gaol (*see* Jewry Street, below).

* Opposite this No. 57 on the S side has a charming Georgian shop-front.

Along ROMSEY ROAD on the N side WEST HAYES, built in the 1890s and converted into a school *c.*1911 by *H. L. G. Hill.* Brown stone porch with strapwork top, but l. and r. tile-hung gables and pebbledash à la Norman Shaw. Yet further out, on the S side, DAWN HOUSE by *Ernest Newton,* with his typical semicircular hood over the entrance and, towards the S, the town, and the view, a symmetrical front with two gables and two canted bay windows. Hipped roof. Built in 1907.

Having dealt with the High Street, the streets to its N can now be walked. First in JEWRY STREET No. 11a, the OLD GAOL, with a former angle pavilion, No. 12. The gaol was built in 1805 by *George Moneypenny.* It is of yellow brick, and No. 11a has five bays and three storeys. Arched first-floor windows, vermiculated quoins, pediment right across. No. 12 has vermiculated quoins too and a main window with alternatingly pitted rustication. Between the two parts is now the CONGREGATIONAL CHURCH of 1853. Yellow brick; lancets. Then on the E side Nos 35–37, early C19, with a shop-front with Tuscan columns. Further N the PRESBYTERY, Georgian, six bays and a parapet. Doorway with broken pediment on Corinthian pilasters. At the NW end of Jewry Street an early C19 range with coupled upper giant pilasters and the typical rounded corner.

See p. 832

N from Jewry Street into HYDE STREET. The HYDE BREWERY still has one range of 1821. Date in the pedimental gable. Below three bays with tight giant arches. Red brick. HYDE ABBEY HOUSE (formerly Mr Richards's Academy) is C17 with a Late Georgian façade. Doorway with broken pediment on Tuscan columns. *Soane*'s Schoolroom of 1795 is at the back and quite plain with arched windows in blank arcading. On the other side HYDE HOUSE, with its façade at r. angles to the street, a C16 stone part to the E (with one one-light window), and to the street a strange brick front of *c.*1660–70, with a big Dutch gable and a blocked doorway with Doric brick pilasters and a moulded entablature. Horizontally placed oval window in the gable. Further N No. 43, a Late Georgian house on its own, built in the country. Five bays, red brick, with parapet. Doorway with thin Tuscan columns and a broken pediment. Off at the end of KING ALFRED PLACE is the HYDE ABBEY GATEWAY, the only building that remains of Hyde Abbey, the Benedictine nunnery founded in 965 as the New Minster (*see* p. 659) and moved to Hyde in 1110. The gateway is Perp. Four-centred arch of many fine mouldings. To the outside also a much plainer pedestrian entrance. An adjoining shed has Norman masonry.

Further out a good deal, in WORTHY ROAD, is ABBOT'S BARTON FARM. Six bays to the garden. Red brick. The ground-floor windows still have their wooden crosses. On the first floor arched middle window. At the back C17 stone chimneys. A dovecote near by.

Back towards the High Street by ST PETER'S STREET. AVEBURY HOUSE is dated 1690 by the MHLG. Five bays, chequer brick. Very elegant late C18 doorcase with Tuscan columns and a fluted frieze. The ROYAL HOTEL with its wings has a plan which looks late C17. The present stuccoed exterior seems early C18. (Early C18 staircase. MHLG) No. 4 is late C17 again and has an excellent doorcase with straight hood on carved brackets and a swag in the middle of the bolection frieze. The side is of brick exposed and has raised window surrounds.

In PARCHMENT STREET there is only No. 9, with an apsed door-hood on richly carved brackets. The house was originally chequer brick. From the corner of Parchment Street and ST GEORGE'S STREET to that of Upper Brook Street new shopping by *Casson, Conder & Partners*, 1962–5, excellent in scale (three storeys) and townscaping, with all its shops behind colonnading. Pre-cast concrete framing and blue brick. Fenestration with the fashionable slit windows l. and r. of the concrete posts to separate carrying and infilling elements. *See* p. 832

Nothing in the next streets.* So now the continuation of the High Street to the E, first turning N immediately into EASTGATE STREET, where Nos 1–19 are a good stretch of early C19 frontage, starting with a rounded corner. Then across the one-arch stone BRIDGE of 1813, just S of the CITY MILL of 1744 (brick and tile-hung gables). Turn first S into CHESIL STREET. No. 1 is early C16, timber-framed, with gables and heavy diagonal braces. No. 4 has a charming C18 shop and doorway canopy wavy in plan. No. 12 is of brick, late C18, of five bays, with a specially pretty doorcase. At the back C17 chimneybreasts of chequer stone and flint. A little further on No. 54 has fine C18 wrought-iron GATES from Mildmay House in Eastgate Street.

In ST JOHN'S STREET, N of Chesil Street, a house with a stone

* Recent excavations in and around LOWER BROOK STREET have revealed much of interest about the houses and lives of ordinary people in medieval Winchester.

ground floor and an oversailing timber-framed upper floor. Higher up the BLUE BOAR, which has turned out recently (Mr Carpenter Turner) to be a most interesting C14 hall house, with longitudinal balconies, one extended in width by oversailing over the pavement.

The streets N, W, and E of the High Street having been explored, the streets to the S, i.e. round the cathedral and the college, remain. The buildings immediately N of the cathedral have already been discussed as part of the precinct (p. 690).

We start once more by St John's Hospital. In COLEBROOK STREET No. 108 is of five wide bays, the first and last with wide blank arches with elliptical tops in vermiculated rustication. A male and a female keystone head. This is probably late C18. No. 16 has its five-bay brick front at r. angles to the street. Broken pediment on Tuscan columns. No. 26 is odd. What is its date ? The early C18 or early C19 ? The centre has one arch on giant pilasters and one arched window in it. Stepped-up parapet. No. 27 seems of *c.*1700. Chequer brick and wooden cross-windows. No. 34 is Late Georgian with handsome windows under big blank faces.

Next, a good deal further W, i.e. W of the cathedral, GREAT MINSTER STREET. Charming start at the end of the passage from the High Street. A close group of attractive brick houses. More further S, and at the end No. 3, MINSTER HOUSE, early C18. Five bays, chequer brick, hipped roof. Later doorway with Tuscan columns and broken pediment. The house faces the front of the cathedral. SYMOND'S STREET more or less continues Great Minster Street. On the E side all is the precinct wall. On the W side SYMOND'S HOUSE, white, early C19, with a big Tuscan porch, and then CHRISTIE'S HOSPITAL, founded in 1607. Brick, two-storeyed, with a central gable rebuilt in the C19.

In ST SWITHIN STREET on the E part of the N side again all precinct wall. On the S side small property, attractive in scale. Further W No. 25 with a pretty doorcase and Nos 26–7, a splendid early C18 house, spoiled by its ground floor. Five bays, two storeys. Segment-headed windows. The central window, however, is round-arched, and the moulded eaves rise round it. On the l. and r. one-bay three-storey wings, i.e. a kind of towers. The style prepares us for Southgate Street. The house faces ST THOMAS'S STREET, and we must first walk down this, back to the High Street. No. 18 is a plain Georgian brick house of five bays and two and a half storeys, set back from the road. Doorway with segmental pediment on brackets, a motif of *c.*1700 this. On the other side is No. 12, also red brick and on a substantial scale: five by five bays and three storeys. Doorcase with broken pediment on Ionic demi-columns. No. 9 is long and low, of two storeys and has a specially handsome doorcase with Tuscan columns and a fluted frieze. Its STABLES were across the road, with three semi-elliptical arches, the middle one leading into the stables proper. The bays of the side ones have pediments with oval windows. Late Georgian. Nos 21 and 22 lie back behind the churchyard of the former St Thomas. No. 21 is early C18, grey headers and red dressings, with segment-headed windows, but the middle window round-arched with a raised surround. No. 2 still has mullion-and-transom-cross windows. Finally No. 24 has another doorcase with Tuscan columns and a fluted frieze. (Inside this house is a Norman vaulted undercroft of two bays with groin-vaults. VCH)

Now S again, along SOUTHGATE STREET, the street with the most ambitious houses of Winchester. They are of red brick, all of them. No. 12 is of five bays and two and a half storeys, with segment-headed windows. The centre window alone is round-arched. The doorway below has Corinthian pilasters and a segmental pediment. So that is early C18. So is the SOUTHGATE HOTEL, which actually has the date 1715. Five bays, three storeys, segment-headed windows. The middle window has brick pilasters and a segmental pediment. Doorway set against a rusticated background. Thin Roman Doric columns and a triglyph frieze. Then follows SERLE'S HOUSE, the Regimental Museum. This stands back on its 64
own and is conceived on a surprising scale. Seven bays, two and a half storeys, red brick with blue dressings. Doric giant pilasters with Baroquely swelling capitals at the angles, the angles of the centre, and round the corner on the S side. Segment-headed windows. Low ground floor. The centre projects flat but by means of quadrant curves. The parapet moves up over it and against it stands an incongruous pediment. Doorcase of 1952. The window above with a segmental pediment is of stone. Inside, a round entrance hall and behind it a good staircase, starting in one arm and returning in two. The house is probably of about 1710–20, and one would like to know who designed it. Nos 33–39 is an Early Victorian Italianate terrace. Yellow brick, three and a half storeys. The first-floor windows have triangular and segmental pediments.

Nos 43–47 are also Early Victorian. Yellow brick; three Ionic porches. Southgate Street continues into ST CROSS ROAD. At the top on the E side the ORIEL HOTEL, with a straight door-hood on carved brackets. Opposite MORRIS HOUSE, detached and lying back. Early C19, yellow brick, three bays, Tuscan porch.

From Southgate Street and St Cross Road W is an area of early C19 terraces, semi-detached houses, and villas. From Southgate Street walk E now by CANON STREET (terraces of sweet cottages and only one bigger house: HAMILTON HOUSE, of five bays and three storeys and with a pedimented doorway) to the N end of KINGSGATE STREET. Kingsgate Street is very rewarding. No. 4 has a tripartite doorway. No. 5, of *c.*1700, is of chequer brick and has raised brick surrounds with lugs to the windows. No. 73, opposite, is of the same time and has wooden cross-windows. (Good staircase. MHLG) Again of the same time Nos 8 to 9a, see the raised brickwork on the upper floor. Three pretty later doorcases, and also the most charming of the typical Winchester upper bows. No. 70 has its Georgian double-bow shop-front. No. 69 is MOBERLEY'S (a house of the college). This is dated 1571. It is of brick with blue diapers and has two gables. One original five-light mullioned window remains on the ground floor. The doorcase with Tuscan columns belonged originally to the next house. No. 15 is of five bays and two and a half storeys, later Georgian, and No. 16 is lower, but also of five bays. Doorcase with Tuscan demi-columns. Then follows the South Africa Gatehouse of the College (*see* p. 706).

KINGSGATE ROAD is the continuation of Kingsgate Street. In the garden of a house at its S end, called PRIOR'S BARTON, stands a fragment of an interesting ANGLO-SAXON CROSS assigned to the late C9. The best-preserved side has the typical wild interlace, another an equally typically high-legged quadruped. The house itself has a Late Georgian façade with two ample bows and a doorway with recessed Tuscan columns. Old parts behind. At the corner of CRIPSTEAD LANE and ST CROSS BACK STREET, a little further S, a good timber-framed house with stone chimney. In St Cross Back Street itself BROOKSIDE, early C19, with a porch of thin Greek Doric columns. Down the street a fine view of the tower of St Cross.

Back now to the top of Kingsgate Street; from here COLLEGE STREET starts. It runs along the precinct wall, and most of the houses are on the S side. Nos 13–18 must be C16 in their bones – see the overhang. No. 15 has a pretty C18 oriel. No. 12 has a pretty doorcase, No. 8 another. It is in No. 8 that Jane Austen died. No. 7 (on the N side) seems C18 (five bays, two storeys) but has to the S one window with a decorated brick surround which must be late C17. The College follows, and that is the end of the Perambulation. College Street turns S, and becomes COLLEGE WALK, and this has as its E *point de vue* St Catherine's Hill.

(On ST CATHERINE'S HILL is one of the mysterious MAZES which appear in divers places in England and must have existed in many more. They are usually turf-cut and placed on hills or downs. No-one knows what their purpose was. Some people attribute profound religious meanings to them, others think they were provided for fun at fairs. In Hampshire another maze survives on Breamore Down. The Winchester one lies E of the site of the former St Catherine's Chapel, and this, in its turn, was E of the mound of an earthwork. The chapel was cruciform and aisleless and dated from the earlier C12.)

IRON AGE HILLFORT, also on St Catherine's Hill. The fort is a roughly oval area of 23 acres defended by a single rampart and ditch with a slight counterscarp bank. The defences are inturned at the entrance on the NE. Excavation of this entrance has revealed a complicated history. In the first phase in the C3 B.C., the inturned passage was revetted with timbers and had double wooden gates behind which were two guard rooms. These guard rooms were later dismantled and the entrance area outside the gates narrowed. This structure was allowed to fall into decay until the late C2, when fresh unrest saw the remodelling of the earthworks and strengthening of the entrance. Again these modifications were allowed to decay, and the fort was finally sacked in the C1 and not reoccupied thereafter.

WINCHFIELD 7050

ST MARY. Much of the church is Norman of a singular ferocity. The coarseness of detail might tempt one to plead for early dating, but the motifs are not earlier than 1170 or so. The pieces are as follows. Broad W tower with three original windows, N, S, and W, a top part obviously of the restoration of 1850 (by *Woodyer*), and a mighty arch to the nave. This is

triple-shafted with leaf-capitals, also trumpet scallops and intersected flutes. Round arch with a slight chamfer and a roll.* The simple N doorway has similar mouldings but a pointed arch. The S doorway is a big hulking piece with extremely large, rude reeded leaves – no two capitals alike – vertical zigzag projecting diagonally, and a round arch with much zigzag.
17 The chancel arch is all re-tooled. Few stones look untouched, but the character is exactly that of the S doorway. The main responds are keeled here. The innermost soffit of the arch has a profile of two hollows to one roll. Actually the roll looks like sawn branches. Completely re-done, if they ever were original, are also the details inside the chancel windows. Externally the chancel is in order. Two N, two S windows. The N aisle with its C14-looking arcade is of 1850. – PULPIT. Dated 1634. Arched panels in two tiers. Pretty decoration, partly vegetable, partly strapwork in the panels. – BENCHES. Two, plain, the ends with a curve down from back to arm. – COMMUNION RAIL. Jacobean, of a heavy dumb-bell type. – PLATE. Chalice, 1640. – MONUMENTS. The Rt Hon. and Rev. Lord Frederick Beauclerk † 1850. By *J. G. Lough*, 1851. Faith seated on the ground. White relief.

(ELMHURST. By *E. P. Warren*, 1890–1.)

WINKLEBURY CAMP *see* BASINGSTOKE

4030

WINNALL

ST MARTIN. Rebuilt in 1858 by *William Coles* (RH), with some old materials. Nave and chancel and bellcote. Flint. Lancets, some shafted.

6040

WINSLADE

ST MARY. Built, the VCH says, in 1816, but of that nothing can be seen. The bleak W tower of yellow and red brick looks *c.*1850, and the wooden Perp tracery of the windows must be Victorian too. – STAINED GLASS. Fragments in the E window. – PLATE. Set of 1815. – MONUMENT. Tablet to William Pincke † 1694. Cartouche with flowers.

WINTON *see* BOURNEMOUTH, p. 124

*A water-colour in the church shows a tower W doorway, but there is no evidence of this ever having been there.

WOLVERTON

5050

ST CATHERINE. Built in 1717, and the best Early Georgian church in Hampshire. It has a very powerful, high and broad W tower of light red brick with alternatingly raised stone quoins, a doorway with big rustication of alternating sizes, and a top parapet. If the church appears disproportionately low in comparison, the reason is that it was only a re-casing; for inside the roof with arched braces up to high collar-beams and three tiers of wind-braces, two of them forming themselves into circles, is medieval. The casing is of red brick with blue-brick dressings, a curious, idiosyncratic combination. Curious also the shaped gable of the E wall and the stepped gables of the transepts, framing a niche. The transept, two porches, and the gables combine to create a varied outline and skyline. Unfortunately, silly Victorian brick mullions have been put into the windows. Internally the church is as original. The transepts are screened off from the crossing (as it were) by a tripartite arrangement which is, however, not at all straightforward. It consists of a narrow arch, then a wide one, and then the second narrow one turned at 45 degrees so as to allow access to pulpit and reading desk through them. Similarly inside the tower there are very long, slim blank arched niches, and the upper floor is carried on squinches. These arches with plain blocks instead of capitals and abaci are typically Queen Anne and English Baroque, i.e. Vanbrugh–Hawksmoor–Archer. – FONT. A stone baluster. – PULPIT and READING DESK. Well carved. – BOX PEWS. – COMMUNION RAIL. Excellent, of wrought iron. – SCREEN. Removed except for the end pieces. Also wrought iron. – REREDOS and chancel PANELLING. Good; with Ionic pilasters.

WOLVERTON HOUSE. Late Georgian. Rendered. Seven bays, two storeys. Porch of two pairs of unfluted Ionic columns. Balustrade.

WONSTON

4030

HOLY TRINITY. Of about 1200 the S doorway with its curiously imprecisely moulded round arch. Equally imprecise the mouldings of the chancel arch, which is, however, pointed. The responds are triple, and the capitals go from a design derived from decorated trumpet scallops just going stiff-leaf to stiff-leaf proper, mostly of tripartite, fleur-de-lis-like leaves. The church was gutted by fire in 1908 and restored by *Sir T. G. Jackson*. Due to him is the elegant N arcade of slender, finely and continuously moulded piers and arches. The W tower is Late Perp. – FONT. 1872. Elaborately neo-Perp, with close foliage panels. – STAINED GLASS. The E window clearly by *Powell*. – Other chancel windows by *Morris & Co.* as late as 1909. – PLATE. Silver-gilt Set of 1716; Silver-gilt Bowl of 1815.

OLD HOUSE, W of the church. Georgian, stuccoed. On the first floor quoins of rustication of even size. The same at the angles of the two-storeyed porch. (But behind is a late C14 hall house, running N–S, with its hall once open to the roof and screens at the S end. VCH)

NORTON MANOR HOUSE, 1 m. NNW. An eight- by six-bay brick house of *c*.1700 with hipped roof. Giant angle pilasters with brick capitals. Chimneystacks with blank arches. Attached to the long side an early C19 conservatory.

WOODCOTE MANOR *see* BRAMDEAN

WOODCOTT

4050 2 m. WNW of Litchfield

ST JAMES. Small, nave and chancel in one. Coursed knapped flint. E window with flowing tracery. All this is of 1853, though Kelly says that in 1853 the church of 1704 was restored. – PULPIT and READING DESK. They incorporate angle-posts with angels and C18 oval medallions with St Peter and St Paul and ribbons. This is certainly not English. Is it Netherlandish or French? It does not seem to be Italian. – PLATE. Chalice of 1571.

WOODCOTE HOUSE. 1910 by *Crickmay & Sons*. Neo-William-and-Mary.

5040 WOODMANCOTT

ST JAMES. 1855 by *J. Colson*. Nave and chancel and bellcote. Flint.

WOOLBURY RING *see* STOCKBRIDGE

WOOLMER LODGE *see* BRAMSHOTT

WOOLSTON *see* SOUTHAMPTON, pp. 590, 594, 595

WOOLTON HILL 4060

St Thomas. 1849 by *T. H. Wyatt*. Flint, with a thinnish NE tower with stone broach-spire. Blank lucarnes; rather an absurdity. Plate tracery, including Kentish plate tracery, another absurdity. The church is really not worthy of the architect who could do Wilton parish church. N aisle with round and octagonal piers. The arches treated in exactly the same improbable way as by Hansom at Ryde in 1844–6: the arches proper are depressed on vertical pieces, but the hood-moulds rise to form normal two-centred blank arches. – STAINED GLASS. The W window still in the style of the first half of the C19, the E window by *Kempe*, 1903. – (The VICARAGE is by *G. G. Scott Jun.*, 1875–7. NT)

WOOTTON ST LAWRENCE 5050

St Lawrence. 1864 by *J. Colson*, but without destroying certain medieval features. S doorway Norman. One order of columns with decorated scallops. In the arch one order of zigzag and one of three bands of small triangles in relief. The N arcade goes with this, i.e. is also *c.*1180. Three bays, circular piers with square abaci and trumpet-scallop capitals. Round arches with a slight chamfer. The W bay was added a little later (narrow pointed arch with a slight chamfer), probably to connect with a tower. The S arcade is of 1864, with its showy marble piers and its exuberant foliage capitals which one must be allowed to call bigger and better. The church is sizeable, of flint, and has plate and bar tracery apart from re-used C14 and C15 windows. The Victorian parts display a passion for small heads, and Rupert Gunnis has indeed found that one *Thomas Penneley* was paid in 1864 for carving eighteen heads. – PLATE. Chalice and Paten, 1624; Flagon, 1688; Almsdish and Paten, 1735; Baptismal Bowl, 1745. – MONUMENTS. Mrs Wither † 1632. Oblong slate plate under a stone pediment with coat of arms and oddly stylized garlands. – William Wither † 1733. Tablet with a long inscription and a bust on the top in front of an obelisk. – Sir Thomas Hooke † 1677, but carved in the 1750s by *Roubiliac*. Semi-reclining at perfect ease, though in armour. A beautiful piece of carving. Back panel black and white marble, round arch, and a kind of Y-tracery division. – In the churchyard stepped pyramid of granite to Mary Poynder † 1831.

Manydown House. The main front is of 1790 (brick, seven

bays, two and a half storeys, broad Tuscan porch), but according to the VCH there are in the cellar pillars which may be C14. (In one room a carved chimneypiece dated 1602.)

TANGIER HOUSE. Built and named by Sir Thomas Hooke after Charles II's marriage to Catherine of Braganza. Brick. Front of three gables, the centre one recessed. Raised brick quoins. The windows are now all sashed. Round the corner a Georgian front of five bays with a three-bay pediment.

WORTHY PARK *see* KINGS WORTHY

6050

WORTING

ST THOMAS OF CANTERBURY. 1848 by *Woodyer*. Nave and chancel. Thin shingled bell-turret with spire. Fancy Dec tracery. – The ORGAN CASE seems to be High Victorian.

WORTING HOUSE, NW of the church. Five bays, two and a half storeys, parapet. Red brick. In the middle a Venetian window. One-bay wings with a Venetian window, a tripartite lunette window over, and a pediment.

WYFORD FARM *see* PAMBER END

WYMERING *see* PORTSMOUTH, p. 468

8060

YATELEY

ST PETER. The nave was initially C11. Repairs in 1952 revealed a substantial length of N wall, a blocked window, and the NE long-and-short nave quoin (now covered up). The mutilated N doorway with billet and nailhead mouldings is C12, as is the W end of the nave, with a window now only visible from inside. The remaining nave windows are mixed. The chancel is a complete early C13 piece with three stepped E lancets and two S and three N lancets. In the N wall traces of an anchorite's cell. Nave and chancel are rendered.* The most exciting part of the church, however, is the C15 W tower. This is timber-framed and has a N, S, and W aisle like the more famous Essex timber bell towers. Posts carry the shingled bell-stage. Originally the three aisles were separated from the core by arched braces, but later straight scissor-bracing was added, resulting in a most im-

*Sensitive restoration by *Blomfield*, 1878–9. The SW vestry is by *T. B. Carter* – a pretty Perp job of 1900 (NT).

pressive thicket of timbers. The tower arch is of stone and of the same time as the timberwork. C14 S arcade of standard elements. C14 ogee-headed doorway and squint to the former anchorite's cell. – SCREEN. Largely of 1879, but parts of the C14 (two lights and an ogee-headed roundel). – TILES. Some are medieval. They were probably made at Penn (Bucks). The motifs are unusual, e.g. a kneeling figure, and stag and hounds. – CHANDELIERS. Of brass. Quite a series. Dated 1738 by Mr C. D. Stooks. – STAINED GLASS. E lancets by *Morris & Co.*, 1876. Three single figures and beautiful silvery green foliage backgrounds. – W window by *Powell*, 1885, designed by *Holiday*, influenced by Morris. – PLATE. Altar Cross medieval, probably Italian, with embossed figures; Cup of 1568; superb silver-gilt crystal Cup, English, late C16; Paten, 1710. – MONUMENTS. Brasses to William Lawerd † 1517 and wife (18 in. figures); to William Rygg † 1532 and wife (19 in.); to Elizabeth Morflett † 1558 (7 in. demi-figure). – Sir Richard Ryvves † 1671. A very impressive short black and white column with a strangely organic-looking urn on top. The whole in a recess. – Several decent C18 tablets at the W end. – Dame Betty Miles † 1834. By *William Osmond* of Salisbury. White marble. A young genius with lowered torch standing by an urn on a high base. (The cool Grecian taste compares well with the horrid Gothic tablet next to it, says NT. This is to Elizabeth Bassnett † 1844, and also by *Osmond*, i.e. after his association with Pugin.)

(CHURCH SCHOOL, ½ m. SW, on a lane facing the Common. An excellent example of 1865 in the brick and tile-hung Gothic of Street or William White. Now used as the Village Hall. NT)

YATELEY HALL, ½ m. SW. The core is a five-bay brick house with recessed centre and hipped roof. The stables are also C18, with lunette windows. Poor recent additions for the convent (NT).

(BARCLAY HOUSE, Vicarage Road, off the much spoilt village green, is a dashing Italianate villa of *c.*1835. ½ m. E on the main road are YATELEY LODGE, a medium-sized house of *c.*1820, white, with a Tuscan porch, and CORNER COTTAGE, a late C18 farmhouse with an extremely attenuated Tuscan porch. NT)

(On the main road, E of the village green, is THE PARADE, an excellent three-sided courtyard of sixteen shops (1964–5) by *Chapman Taylor Partners*. Brick cross walls, white weatherboarding. NT)

(Further E again is YATELEY PLACE, formerly Hilfield, at first sight an ordinary bogus-timber mansion, but with an indefinable dignity about it. The explanation is that the Stilwell family commissioned *G. F. Bodley*,* who hardly ever did houses, to replace a Regency Gothick house burnt in 1900. Bodley left after a row over functional requirements and *Charles Smith & Son* of Reading worked up the present design, freely altering Bodley's. NT)

(DARBY GREEN HOUSE, 1 m. E, was designed for himself in 1911 by *J. D. Coleridge*, a former assistant of Lutyens, whose early style has here influenced the use of rich red brick and timber-framed windows. Another Lutyens pupil, *A. C. Martin* (cf. Royal Military Academy Chapel, Sandhurst, Berks.), designed THRIFTSWOOD, S of Yateley Place, *c.*1910. NT)

* But one of the *Blomfields* seems more probable.

THE ISLE OF WIGHT

★

APPULDURCOMBE 5080

Appuldurcombe House was built in the first decade of the C18 by Sir Robert Worsley. It is now internally a ruin, and it does not make as good a ruin as one might hope to find. The Worsleys had been one of the leading families on the Isle of Wight ever since the early C16. Henry VIII visited Sir James Worsley at Appuldurcombe in 1538. But of the house then existing nothing is left. The present house is a total rebuilding, and it is the grandest house on the island. It is strange that the architect should not be known, and some speculation on this matter will be made when the house has been described. Colen Campbell illustrated it in *Vitruvius Britannicus* in 1725. So it was known in London circles.

In plan as well as elevations it is singular and not easily pigeonholed. It is compact, with a square centre and four oblong angle pavilions. That is the plan of Poggio Reale, as included in Serlio's treatise, which was familiar alike to English patrons and architects, and also – broadly speaking – of the Elizabethan Wollaton. It makes a strange pedigree, with no Palladio in it at all. With the new fashion of Campbell's and Lord Burlington's Palladianism Appuldurcombe has nothing to do. Nor has it with Wren, nor with Gibbs and his mixed Wrenian and Roman Carlo-Fontana style.

But this is only the plan. In elevation the corner pavilions are not higher but lower than the centre. So the dominating thing is the centre block. This is of two and a half storeys. The pavilions have only two. On the roof of the centre at the four corners are four twin chimneys, each pair connected by an arch. That is a Vanbrugh motif, and with Vanbrugh we approach at least the mood of Appuldurcombe more closely. Even the Wollaton sympathy – if such it can be called – would find an explanation in Vanbrugh.

Now the details. The house is ashlar-faced. The garden-front is accentuated by giant Corinthian pilasters throughout. The pilasters rise from the ground. The centre is of five bays with a doorway surmounted by a roundel and swags and flanked by giant columns. The top of the centre carries a balustrade. The wings are of three bays and two bays deep. They end in pediments, and on the inner sides the ground floor has niches instead of windows. All windows have raised surrounds. The entrance side was originally similar, but has no giant pilasters except at the angles. The entrance was remodelled in the 1770s by *Wyatt* for Sir Richard Worsley, who shortly after travelled extensively in Greece and Asia Minor and brought back the first of all English collections of Greek as against Roman sculpture. The new entrance is decidedly odd, with a bare front wall and doorways from l. and r. The garden side faces E, the entrance side W. To the S is a Tuscan colonnade between the wings, and this also is an addition by Wyatt. The house here has a seven-bay centre and wings only two bays wide. The principal room inside which is still recognizable in its decorative aspects is the entrance hall. It has screens of scagliola columns l. and r. and is in this form by Wyatt. Wyatt also did the subsidiary staircase, next to the main staircase. The walls of the latter are treated as though they were external walls, a device occasionally found in that group of Shropshire houses which seem connected with the Smiths of Warwick.

That brings us back to the sources of the style of Appuldurcombe. Giant pilasters from the ground are indeed a feature also characteristic of that group of buildings and of the Smiths. But it also occurs in Talman's design for Witham, and the portal has affinities with Talman too (Drayton). In addition there are the relations with Vanbrugh and – it may be added – Hawksmoor. *In fine*, it might be suggested that Appuldurcombe is a house designed not by a Talman or Smith, but by a minor provincial architect whose one great chance this was.

5080 ## ARRETON

ST GEORGE. There is first of all evidence of a remarkably long Early Norman church. Its W doorway, now leading into the tower, survives and a window above it, and also a window in the N wall of the chancel. Then, about 1200, a N aisle was added. It is of three bays and has round piers and square abaci with chamfered corners. Only one capital has decoration by many scallops. The S aisle came a little later. It has round abaci and double-chamfered arches. Whether the two long W lancets which the W tower half-covers belong to the first or the second phase cannot be said with certainty. The present W doorway, however, re-used no doubt, does go with the S aisle. And so does the clerestory of quatrefoiled circles. Then, in the late C13, a new campaign began, perhaps when in 1289 a quarrel between the abbeys of Quarr and Lyre (in France) over the church was settled. The chancel has windows with geometrical tracery, two and three lights and originally just plain, unfoiled circles above. The chancel arch is tall and wide. Also of that moment is the three-bay S chapel with the same kind of windows. The thin shafts attached to the mullions are specially attractive. The arcade has three graceful, slender round piers and double-chamfered arches. Bases and capitals are models of beauty. The bases belong to the so-called water-holding kind and are of Purbeck marble. The chapel windows are shafted inside. The S aisle was originally lower than it now is – cf. the chapel W window which now gives on to the aisle. – PULPIT. Some parts seem to be Jacobean. – SCULPTURE. In the N aisle E wall a beautiful fragment of a C13 Christ in Majesty in an elongated quatrefoil, pointed top and bottom, rounded l. and r. Can it have come from a tympanum? – PLATE. Chalice and Cover, 1566–7; Salver, 1732–3. – MONUMENTS. Brass to Henry Hawls, early C15, a 2 ft 6 in. figure, now headless. – Sir Henry Worsley Holmes † 1811. By *Sir Richard Westmacott*. A youth, like St John on Patmos, seated among rocks. From the l. comes an eagle, from the r. a female genius. – Sir Richard Fleming Worsley Holmes, drowned in 1814. Also by *Westmacott*, and even more Baroque than the other. A woman in despair, a wrecked ship on the r., a broken anchor on the l. – Sir Leonard Worsley Holmes † 1825. By *J. Haskoll*, 1829. The wife seated like a Grecian matron by a wreathed pedestal with an urn. Two children stand on the other side, mourning also. A very fine work, and one that shows of what local carvers were still capable at that time.

ARRETON MANOR. Built for Sir Humphrey Bennet on an H-plan. The front has in the middle the porch, and this carries a date 1639. The porch entrance has an arch between the segmental and the basket type. Mullioned windows. In one room an overmantel of wood said to have been taken out and bought back.

MERSTONE MANOR, 1¼ m. SW. Red brick. Mullioned and transomed windows. On the porch a steep pediment. All much re-done.

6080 BEMBRIDGE

HOLY TRINITY. 1845–6. Quite a large church. W tower with stone broach-spire. Lancet windows. N aisle and chancel also said to be of 1845–6.

The finest house in Bembridge is HILL GROVE, Ducy Avenue, ¼ m. N, and it is, at the time of writing, derelict. It is one of the best neo-classical houses on the island. Stuccoed. Three-bay front with the centre crowned by a dome. L. and r. of the doorway pairs of fluted Ionic giant pilasters set diagonally, a surprising and successful motif.

At Bembridge Point is the ROYAL SPITHEAD HOTEL, built in 1882, but looking 1850. Plain, three storeys, and dormers. Canted bay windows to sea and to entrance. Near the entrance a FOUNTAIN which looks 1880, but is 1910. The former STATION is an impressive building. Dark blue and red brick. To the outside eight blank arches and in two of the spandrels blank roundels. The building is dated 1877.

BEMBRIDGE SCHOOL. Founded in 1919 by J. Howard Whitehouse. Whitehouse was greatly influenced by Ruskin, and the school has an important Ruskin collection. Geddes also inspired him. Before settling at Bembridge he had done social work at Bournville for Cadbury's, at Toynbee Hall, and at Ancoats, the Manchester University settlement. Of the buildings the following deserve notice: Culver Cottage, designed by *Baillie Scott* in 1914–15 as a miner's cottage for Scotland and erected at Bembridge in 1920. New House is also by *Scott*, *c.*1925, but assisted and interfered with by Whitehouse. *Whitehouse* is said to have been his own architect for the gymnasium (1924–5). The refectory was done with *Neil Rock*. The chapel is by *W. A. Harvey* and *H. G. Wicks*, the architects of Bournville. It was built in 1931. The general style of Bembridge is similar to that of, say, Welwyn Garden City. Brick houses with hipped roofs. The chapel has a square W tower.

WINDMILL, ½ m. SW of the church. The only one left on the island. A Georgian tower mill complete with its sails.

OBELISK in memory of the first Earl of Yarborough (of Appuldurcombe), founder of the Royal Yacht Squadron at Cowes. 1 m. SW of the school. Erected in 1849. The obelisk is of granite in vermiculated rustication. Its lower part is stepped, and it stands on a tall square base.

BILLINGHAM MANOR *see* KINGSTON

BINSTEAD 5090

HOLY CROSS. The chancel is of the late C13, with typical Hampshire motifs, two- and three-light windows with one or three unfoiled circles. The rest is Victorian, the crazy Norman bellcote of 1844 by *Hellyer*, the N aisle of 1875. The architect was *G. T. Windyer Morris*. Of genuine Norman work there remains, re-erected in the churchyard, a Norman doorway, quite simple, and above it a beast's head and a small kneeling man. – (PANELLING. In sanctuary and chancel, from Winchester College Chapel.) – LECTERN. With openwork Victorian carving. Moses, his arms supported by two men, holds up the lectern. – SCULPTURE. Flemish scenes, Apostles and Virgin. The scenes belong together, and the other panels belong together. The date seems late C16 to early C17.

BLACKGANG *see* CHALE

BONCHURCH 5070

OLD ST BONIFACE. Nave and chancel and small square bell-turret. In the nave S wall a small lancet, in the chancel N wall another. So the church is of the C13, though most of the inside details are Perp. – WALL PAINTINGS. On the nave N wall. – SCULPTURE. A Flemish Rococo Cross of wood.

ST BONIFACE. By *Ferrey*, 1847–8. Norman, with transepts and bellcote. Quite a large church. – STAINED GLASS. Mostly by *Wailes*. – The two saints S transept W and E by *Henry Holiday*, 1878. The windows were discussed by him with Swinburne. – See p. 832 In the churchyard the egyptianizing MAUSOLEUM of the Leeson family, with dates 1864, 1867, 1872.

EAST DENE. The house in which Swinburne spent his childhood. Built *c.*1825 for Mr Surman. Stone with two front gables. The back gables with bargeboards.

BRADING 6080

ST MARY. An interesting church. Its story starts with the S doorway of *c.*1200. This prepares you for the S and N arcades of five bays, which must also be of *c.*1200. Round piers, multi-scalloped capitals, square abaci with chamfered corners, pointed arches with one slight chamfer. The N aisle W lancet belongs to this phase. The next stage of development still recognizable is remains of lancets and a N doorway in the chan-

cel. Much more prominently visible is the W tower, with a processional way through from N to S. The W, N, and S arches are of two big chamfers. The buttressing is by angle-buttresses. The tower was evidently built into the pre-existing nave. Bell-openings of two lights under one pointed arch. Battlements and a short recessed spire which may well be original; for it seems that recessed spires came in in the second half of the C13. The rest is Perp, i.e. first and foremost the Oglander Chapel with its two-bay arcade. Pier of an eight-shafts-and-eight-hollows section, four-centred arches of complex mouldings. The N arcade has a plain octagonal pier instead, but the arches are nearly the same. Perp aisle and chapel windows. – PILLAR PISCINA of the C12. – CHANDELIER, in the chancel. Of brass, dated 1798. – PLATE. Chalice and Paten, 1696; Almsdish, 1725–6. – MONUMENTS. There are so many in the church that a topographical arrangement is advisable. In the chancel: John de Cherewin † 1441. Large and once splendid incised slab with elaborate canopy in perspective. Life-size figure. – Tomb-chest with three cusped lozenges. On two are inscriptions referring to William Howlys and 1520. – In the N chapel is an almost identical tomb-chest. The inscription here refers to Helizabeth his wife. – In the N aisle at the E end Elizabeth T. A. Rollo † 1875. A little girl asleep on a mattress. Actually she died fifteen months old. – In the Oglander Chapel: Tomb-chest with shields in quatrefoils. – Tomb-chest with, against the front under four arches, a kneeling father, his sons, his wife, his daughters. The date must be *c.*1530. – Sir William Oglander † 1608. Recumbent effigy on a half-rolled-up mat. Strangely enough it is of oak. – Sir John † 1655. A very strange
58 monument and one of national importance. It is of oak and robustly carved, and it represents Sir John still on a half-rolled-up mat and still with his elbow propping up his head, a gesture out of date by 1655. But one would waive these details as simply reactionary, if it were not for the fact that his legs are crossed and that he carries a sword and a shield (with a little ornament of 1650) just as the so-called crusaders of the early C14 had done. So here is romantic historicism in retrospective admiration of the Middle Ages and, this being so, perhaps also already in the same admiration of the Elizabethan Age. – Sir Henry † 1874. Tomb-chest of marble, alabaster, and mosaic (designed by *J. C. Powell*, 1897; NT). At the front corners two small white angels (by *Henry Pegram*. A thorough and sensitive piece of Arts and Crafts Jacobean; NT).

Facing the churchyard is a gabled, timber-framed COTTAGE of perhaps the early C16. Overhang and above it closely set studs. Next to the cottage the OLD TOWN HALL. Its ground floor consists of the old (stone) lock-up and open brick arches added in the C18. The upper floor is of 1875.

The High Street consists of two-storeyed cottages and has no houses of interest. The NEW TOWN HALL is of 1902–3, by *James Newman*, small, in the Norman-Shaw tradition.

THE MALL continues in the direction of the High Street. BEECH GROVE is quite a handsome late C17 house. Five bays, two storeys. Chequer brick. Wooden cross-windows. Then, on the other side, a castellated, cemented house with two adjoining bow windows. Opposite a tall three-storey house with a hefty Tuscan porch.

ROMAN VILLA. The Roman villa was discovered and excavated in the last century. It consists of a courtyard surrounded on at least three sides by detached buildings. The main block, on the W side of the court, is composed of thirteen rooms. Structurally it would seem probable that the arrangement consisted first of a simple strip house, to which a front corridor, wings, and a back range were later added. In its final phase the block was floored with a series of fine figured mosaics depicting characters from classical mythology. The N wing appears to have started life as an aisled structure, which was later modified by the addition of a small heated bath. The S wing may also have been an aisled building, but the excavation was not sufficiently complete to be sure. The main W wing and part of the N wing are now laid open for visitors.

BRIGHSTONE

4080

ST MARY. Late C12 N arcade. Three bays, round piers, square abaci, round arches with a slight chamfer. Coarse C14 S arcade. Late Perp S chapel arcade of three bays. The piers with the four-shafts-and-four-hollows section. Four-centred arches. The exterior is mostly C19, especially the Norman N aisle, which is of 1852.* Fine late C13 chancel with four side lancets and the E window of three stepped cusped lancet lights. The W doorway of the W tower looks early C14. – FONT. Octagonal, Perp, with plain cusped little arches. – PULPIT. Jacobean. The top panels are arches in false perspective with obelisks under

*Restoration by the Rev. *Edward McAll*, according to the Rev. Basil Clarke.

them. The bottom panels have strapwork. Brackets carry a bookrest which goes all round (cf. Shalfleet). – PLATE. Silver-gilt Chalice, 1663; silver-gilt Paten, 1672.

3080

BROOK

ST MARY. 1864 by *Malling*. Steeply above the road. E.E. with a S porch tower. The porch entrance is C13 work. Strange two-bay, cross-gabled N transept, two bays wide. – PLATE. Set given in 1717.

BROOK HOUSE. C18 E front, white. Seven bays, two storeys, but formerly three. The pediment sticks up now as a sham above the centre projection. Giant angle pilasters.

4080

CALBOURNE

ALL SAINTS. A C13 church, with a few exceptions. The SW tower was rebuilt in 1752, and the Barrington Chapel was added in 1842 (by *A. F. Livesay*, who had begun restoring the church in 1836; NT). Internally this is an imitation C13 job, done with gusto. Two rib-vaulted bays, large detached blank arcading with bar tracery against the walls. The source is the Winchester Lady Chapel. Otherwise lancets externally and quatrefoiled circles in plate tracery above pairs of lancets. The S arcade is of 1842. (Small neo-Norman N porch. RH) – FONT. Octagonal, of Purbeck marble, table-top type. Against the sides flat arches and elementary geometrical patterns. – ARCHITECTURAL FRAGMENT. A big, lively stiff-leaf bracket. – MONUMENTS. Brass to a Knight, later C14, good, and 4 ft 1 in. long. The only a little disconcerting thing is that he has been put up on the wall horizontally.

WESTOVER, ¼ m. SW. Early C19, white. The main front has seven bays, over the middle there is a summary pediment, but two wide bows on the ground floor include the first and third windows of the centre. Round the corner iron verandas. Inside a nice curved staircase.

SWAINSTON, 1¼ m. NE. The house consists of two stylistically totally unconnected parts which border one on the other: grand Georgian and C12 and C13. The r. half of the S front has to the S a range of the C13 with an upper hall whose E part may have been partitioned off as a chapel, but behind it, and projecting to the E not as far, is a Late Norman part with a twin round-headed window and a polygonal shaft. The E window of the chapel is of three stepped lights with three unfoiled circles over. So the C13 part must be about 1280. The N and S windows are lancets. In the W or hall part fenestration is confusing. The Georgian part, of ashlar, looks *c.*1775–80. Nine bays, the centre recessed and with a fine Adamish screen of two columns and pediment. The side pieces have pediments. Entrance hall with two pairs of columns.

(TEMPLE, on top of a hill S of the Newport–Freshwater road. C18. With six Doric columns and pediment. MHLG)

CARISBROOKE 4080

ST MARY. Of an aisleless Early Norman nave two small upper windows have been preserved above the S arcade. This arcade, i.e. a S aisle, was then built in the late C12. It is five bays long and has circular piers with multi-scallop capitals and circular abaci. The arches are pointed and have two slight chamfers. The church was at that time no doubt lengthened. The N doorway is plain, of one order, and a little earlier than the S arcade. The S doorway goes clearly with the arcade. Trefoil-leaf capitals. Pointed arch with two slight chamfers. The church has lost its chancel. The chancel arch indicates a date *c.*1200 again. Next in order of time comes a mysterious C13 arch across the S aisle and butting rawly against one of the Norman columns. Why was it put up? Simply because a place here gave reasons for worry? In the nave on the N side two recesses, one early, the other later C13. They are connected with the fact that Carisbrooke from *c.*1155–60 to the C15 was a Benedictine priory (dependent on Lyre) and hence had a cloister. Finally the truly monumental W tower, Perp, of five stages, with a higher stair-turret. The tower was ruthlessly built with its buttresses into the nave. – FONT. 1602. The stem on fat short balusters. The bowl still with medieval mouldings. – PULPIT. 1658. With back panel and tester. The decoration much soberer than twenty or thirty years before. – PLATE. Almsdish, 1729; Chalice, Paten, and Almsdish, 1750; Chalice and Paten, 1750; two Flagons, 1753–4; two Chalices and Patens, 1756–7. – MONUMENTS. Lady Wadham, *c.*1520. Stone. Tomb-chest. Recess above with very depressed arch, cusped and subcusped, and cresting. Against the back wall six standing Saints and in their middle the kneeling Lady. A fine, unhackneyed piece, reminiscent of Sussex. – Sir William Stephens † 1697. A curiously elementarized tablet, see e.g. the flat drapery. No figures.

DOMINICAN PRIORY. 1865–6 by *Gilbert Blount*. Gothic of a conventional or scholastic kind. The chapel on the r. with its apse is balanced by a tower-like part of the living quarters on the l.

CARISBROOKE CASTLE. Carisbrooke Castle is the strongest and the only extensive castle on the Isle of Wight. The general impression is of low buildings on the hill. There are three levels, the BASTIONS built in 1587–*c.*1600 to bring the defences up to date, and, like all bastions, low, the Norman CURTAIN WALL, in the absence of towers also low, and the Norman shell KEEP on an artificial mound, lower than it originally was. The keep is at the far E end of the site. Entry is from the W. The OUTER ARCHWAY is Elizabethan. Four-centred arch, double-chamfered; pediment. Then across a bridge to the mighty GATEHOUSE. Its outer part, with round towers, is of *c.*1335–6 (expenses on the gatehouse recorded). The entry arch is four-centred, the moulding the sunk quadrant. The arch dies into the imposts. Machicolation above. The first bay inside is plainly rib-vaulted. The back part with flat side walls belongs to the C13. The whole archway has three portcullis grooves. In the inner doorway C15 DOORS. As one emerges from the C13 arch one sees l. and r. stretches of the C12 curtain wall, and in front at a distance the main domestic buildings. But before one approaches them, one ought to examine the group on the immediate r. It consists of the CHAPEL, rebuilt in 1904–5 by *Percy Goddard Stone* (RH), the leading medieval archaeologist of the Isle of Wight, but still showing the base courses of C13 buttresses, the present office, and to its W the former armoury, C16 and later. The armoury has buttresses to the E.

The main domestic buldings are basically on the standard manor-house pattern: great hall, with chamber and solar on one side – here the S – the kitchen and offices on the other. The group is much restored (1857–88) and does not at first look promising. However, the GREAT HALL is in fact of the late C12, as the one window in the E wall shows, which is a twin, with pointed lights and a shaft between them. The chimneypiece is a late C14 or C15 insertion. To the E of the S third of the hall E wall was the CHAPEL. The room now holds a staircase, but it can still be seen that it was rib-vaulted in two bays and had a four-light window and lancets N and S. It must belong to the years of Isabel, daughter of Baldwin IV, i.e. 1263–93. It is recorded that she began the chapel in 1270.

S of the chapel were GREAT CHAMBER and SOLAR. They are a late C14 rebuilding, altogether three storeys high.

N of the great hall things are confusing. The buildings here are in ruins. The screens passage was preceded by a PORCH or lobby with two C13 doorways. N of this the kitchen must have been, but the kitchen evidence now is Elizabethan. Of the late C13 is a twin window to the N, i.e. through the curtain wall. It has pointed-trefoiled lights, a transom, and ribs across the soffit. Did it belong to Isabel's new kitchen built in 1287?

The C12 CURTAIN WALL can then be followed for quite a stretch, as it rises up the steep MOTTE to the KEEP. Curtain wall and keep belong to the years after Baldwin II de Redvers' defeat at Exeter, i.e. to some time between 1136 and his death in 1155. The keep is of the type known as shell keeps. The buildings inside are of the C16, except for the gatehouse, which, like the principal gatehouse, seems to belong to *c.*1335. The doorway has three continuous chamfers, a portcullis groove, and first a rib-vault and then two transverse arches. Immediately N of the gatehouse, in the curtain wall, is a rare relic, a C12 garderobe.

For the rest of the curtain wall it is interesting to note the original, i.e. C12, angle towers, rectangular and projecting only a little, and strengthened by polygonal Elizabethan bastions, that at the SE angle dated 1601, that at the SW angle 1602.

The outer Elizabethan bastions are five in number, four at the angles and the fifth W of the main entrance. Three of them have casemates, each with gunports.

As from here one looks back at the castle, one can study the EARTHWORKS which were thrown up before the Domesday Survey. At their foot chiefly on the E but also the W side the remains of a masonry WALL of Late Roman type have been traced. They enclose an approximately rectangular area. At one point, near the NE corner, a shallow semicircular bastion can be seen, and in the middle of the E side traces of an inturned gate still survive. Since the wall pre-dates the Norman motte, a Roman date has been suggested for it, but positive dating evidence is still lacking.

A ROMAN VILLA of basilican type was discovered in the Vicarage garden and partly excavated in 1859. The remains are now largely overgrown, but part of a mosaic can still be seen. *See* p. 832

4070

CHALE

ST ANDREW. With a superb view towards the Needles. A Perp church externally. W tower with higher stair-turret. But inside a two-bay S arcade with round piers, square abacus chamfered at the corners, pointed arches with one slight chamfer. That makes it *c.*1200. The third bay is Perp. The S chapel of one bay looks earlier even than the S arcade. Round arch with one slight chamfer. – ARCHITECTURAL FRAGMENT. Below the piscina a large Perp bracket. – STAINED GLASS. Nearly all by *Kempe*, the earliest W of 1891, the rest mostly of 1897. – PLATE. Chalice and Paten, 1698.

CHALE ABBEY. The house incorporates an early C14 hall. In the N gable-end is a two-light window with an arch above the two arches of the lights. In the W wall is an ogee-headed small window. A buttressed BARN close to the house.

SOUTH VIEW, Blackgang. Above the road down from Blackgang Chine stands a ROTUNDA of rustic columns to commemorate Shakespeare. It was put up by Thomas Letts, inventor of Letts's diaries.

4090

COWES

Yacht racing started at Cowes in the second half of the C18. The term regatta turns up in 1814. In the next year the Yacht Club was founded. The climax was the Edwardian years, when e.g. the Emperor William II visited Cowes. West Cowes is a little town, East Cowes has no town character.

WEST COWES

ST MARY, next to Northwood House. 1867 by *Arthur Cates*. Large, with a clerestory, and cross-gabled aisles, but aesthetic-
79 ally insignificant – except for the astonishing W tower. This is by *John Nash* and was given by George Ward, the Lord of the Manor, in 1816, as the family mausoleum.. It is so radically Grecian that one thinks at first rather of C20 Grecian disguise for modern (of the Alfred-Messel kind) than of the early C19 Grecian. The bell-stage is one opening on each side, oblong and completely unmouided, and set in it are two short Greek Doric columns. The top parapet has four acroteria again devoid of any ornamental graces. It is so unlike Nash.

See p. 832

ST FAITH, Newport Road. 1909 by *J. Standen Adkins*. Pebble-dash like Voysey, and the battered buttresses like Voysey. Freely Gothic single-light windows. Bellcote.

ST THOMAS OF CANTERBURY (R.C.), Terminus Road. 1796 by *Thomas Gabb*. Given by Mrs Heneage. A remarkably early date for a Catholic church. It is a strange building. Yellow brick with a (ritual) W end without any windows, but an Ionic porch which may not now be *in situ*. Five windows to the (ritual) S, high and arched. The later tracery ruins them thoroughly. Spacious interior with an altar wall with two giant Doric pilasters and an arch.

HOLY TRINITY, Queens Road. The first church of the fashionable Cowes. 1832 by *Benjamin Bramble* of Portsmouth. Yellow brick, of the Commissioners' type. W tower, tall lancets (with later tracery), buttresses with clumsy tops. Apse of 1862 by *R. J. Jones*.

The narrow HIGH STREET winds along close to the shore and rises and falls too. In its S continuation, BIRMINGHAM ROAD, first BLENHEIM HOUSE with a brick front of grey headers and red dressings, two bays, two and a half storeys, the first-floor windows in blank arches on broad, short pilasters. Then the ALEXANDRA HALL, a former Wesleyan Chapel (of 1831 ?), ashlar-faced, of three bays, with a pediment all across and Gothic windows with four-centred heads. Towards the end WESTBOURNE HOUSE, of brick, two-storeyed, with angle pilasters. This, according to E. H. Gooch, was built in 1752. As for the HIGH STREET, the best houses are near the N end. The FOUNTAIN HOTEL, stuccoed, with windows with blank segmental arches, is small fry. No. 88 is an interesting and attractive house: five bays with a three-bay pediment and a Late Georgian doorway. Attached to it the shop and malthouse, the latter stretching down to the river. The upper windows towards the High Street have thick cast-iron bars in an ornamental pattern. Then ADMIRALS WHARF, modern flats by *David Stern & Partners*, *c.*1961. The ground floor is carports under shallow concrete arches. Two upper storeys. The ISLAND SAILING CLUB also has a modern building, not visible from the street. White and thin metal, e.g. a spiral staircase. It is by *Howard Lobb*, 1961, and its source is ultimately the Royal Corinthian Yacht Club at Burnham-on-Crouch, built in 1931, but that is not saying anything against Mr Lobb.

The continuation of the High Street is BATH ROAD. Here a few houses with shallow bows, i.e. the seaside tradition of the Sussex coast, but very minor here. The ROYAL YACHT SQUADRON has as its club-house Henry VIII's CASTLE, the castle opposite Calshot on the mainland. Of this remains the low semicircular platform facing the sea. The short round tower behind, though it looks as if it were part of the castle, is said not to contain any vestige of the original work any longer. The stair-turret is an C18 addition, the rest is by *Salvin*, 1856–7. The NW tower e.g. is his.

From the junction of Bath Road and the High Street MARKET HILL climbs the hill and is continued in UNION STREET. In the former CLAREMONT HOUSE, grey headers and red dressings, with a nice door-head, in the latter UNION HOUSE, with two wooden canted bay windows, and the MASONIC HALL by 'Mr *Wyatt*' (which ?), 1846 (*see Ill. London News*), three bays, giant pilasters and pediment. Off the end of Market Hill CASTLE STREET starts, and with that the 1830 as against the Late Georgian type of houses: PROVIDENCE HOUSE e.g. with big hood-moulds over the windows, still faced by Late Georgian cottages. Even more varied is QUEENS ROAD: detached houses, gabled or Italianate. As one moves further W the houses go bigger and later, EGYPT HOUSE e.g. of the 1880s, red brick, with a tower, and finally, just off BARING ROAD, the continuation of Castle Road, down a footpath, a house fully representative of 1960 in architecture. It is of 1957–8 and by *Stirling & Gowan*. One storey, symmetrical plan. White brick and glass in vertical bands mostly of exactly the same width (5 ft units). Walls and windows reach right up to the top, i.e. there are no eaves nor a roof visible. At the far, S, end of Baring Road a LODGE, early C19, with a wavy eaves frieze and a tree-trunk veranda.

But the principal house of West Cowes has not so far been mentioned: NORTHWOOD HOUSE, close to St Mary and in ample grounds. It is the Urban District Offices now, but was the house built early in the C19 for George Ward (*see* St Mary) and extensively enlarged *c*.1840. It is a house strange from outside, stranger internally, and its architectural history ought to be established. The architect (probably of 1840) was called *George J. J. Mair*.* The house consists of a nine-bay range of two storeys with a three-bay pediment. The ground floor has typically French banded rustication, and the shallow single-storey projection in the middle, with attached Tuscan columns,

*Cf. Kneller Hall, Whitton, Mddx. But Prosser says that the house was by *Nash*, and altered in 1830–1 by *William Cubitt*. The rooms, according to Prosser, were done by *Gillow*. Mr Colvin gives 1837 for Northwood House, with enlargements of 1843.

strikes one as French too. The range has a large bow in the short side round the corner. But that is not all. From the W end of the main range a wing projects, by four bays, and at its end is an aedicule with a niche which probably held the main entrance originally. If that is so, then the corridor of single vaults with skylights to each bay would be original too. It leads to a boldly Egyptian painted lobby, and next to this is an Etrurian Room with a very shallow dome and an open eye in the middle. From here the main range is reached, and that also has a mid-corridor. It takes one to the two principal rooms, one behind the portico, the other including the big bow. Moreover, a short wing also projects to the N and leads to a circular room with a coffered dome appearing prominently outside as well. It is all remarkable, but how did it hang together?

The LODGE by the church belonged to the early C19 Northwood House, then called Bellevue. It is by *Nash* and has much of the ruthlessness of the tower of St Mary. Ashlar, with a recessed portico of Tuscan columns and attic windows above.

EAST COWES

East Cowes is not a town. It is almost entirely residential, and its thrill was three major houses, of which two survive. The one that has gone – disgracefully – is *Nash*'s EAST COWES CASTLE, built as his own country house in 1798. The other two are Norris Castle and Osborne.

NORRIS CASTLE was built by *James Wyatt* in 1799 for Lord Henry Seymour. It is a splendid sight from the Solent, a romantic Norman castle, not yet archaeological (as Hopper was going to be), but as a piece of theatrical setting hard to match. Lawn plunges straight down from the castle to the sea. A big round tower at the E end with a higher stair-turret, a subsidiary square turret, and quite a long front. The house itself however is not that long. The entrance side sets it off against the service wing and then the symmetrical front of the stables. The walls are of coursed rubble, galletted. The windows are round-headed. Along the drive are the FARM BUILDINGS and the KITCHEN GARDEN, an enormous oblong 73
area surrounded by an embattled wall. The front to the drive, articulated by several accents, is entirely symmetrical. There is a castellated WEST LODGE with a round tower and a less romantic SOUTH LODGE. George IV stayed at Norris Castle

in 1819, the Duchess of Kent and Princess Victoria in 1831.

OSBORNE, *see* p. 756. That entry comprises buildings visible from YORK AVENUE which, however, belong to the Osborne Estate or the Osborne story.

ST JAMES. 1831–3 by *Nash*, rebuilt, except for the tower, by *T. Hellyer*, 1868. The W tower is slender and thin. Pointed and quatrefoil windows. Low stair-turret on the N side. The rest is E.E. with plate tracery. Unhappy interior with Italian Romanesque columns but pointed arches and foiled clerestory openings. The arcade also runs on regardless of the transepts with their prominent rose windows. – In the churchyard, just S of the tower, is the grave of John Nash.

TOWN HALL. 1896 by *James Newman*. Yellow brick, five bays. Debased Italianate and Frenchy motifs.

EAST COWES *see* COWES

FARRINGFORD *see* FRESHWATER

3080

FRESHWATER

ALL SAINTS. A very dramatic W tower. A C13 doorway and window set back below a giant arch which carries the upper part of the tower. Internally the same thing takes place, but here this giant-arched substructure is placed inside the W bay of the arcades, which are again C13. So this was a C13 W end of the church, before the tower was built. But the W bay is a lengthening of a Late Norman nave. Three bays, round piers, square abaci with a slight chamfer, pointed arches, also with a slight chamfer, i.e. *c.*1200. The transept responds are more or less the same. So the church of 1200 had aisles and transepts. Externally the predominant impression is of the late C13, i.e. of bar tracery, cf. the W wall, the aisle W bays, the S porch entrance, the chancel side windows (unencircled trefoils), and the chancel E window (three uncusped circles).* In the chancel a late C13 tomb recess which projects outside. Very crudely cusped with pierced trefoiled circles. Dogtooth in the hood-mould. – PLATE. Flagon and Paten given in 1748; Chalice and Paten given in 1745 and 1768. – MONUMENT. Brass to a Knight, late C14, the figure $34\frac{1}{2}$ in. long.

ST AGNES, Freshwater Bay, 1 m. S. 1908 by *Isaac Jones*. Low, thatched, with a bell-turret and an apse. The interior does not hold what the exterior promises.

* The chancel was extended and the aisles were rebuilt in 1873 (NT).

FARRINGFORD, 1 m. SW. Now a hotel. In spite of its connexion with Tennyson, little seems to be known about the architectural vicissitudes of the house. It is of yellow brick, and the entrance side seems to be the oldest part, say of the late C18. The porch with its bunched Gothic shafts is a typical motif. To its r. is a veranda of five stone arches. The NE addition (drawing room) looks *c.*1840. Tennyson moved in in 1853. Farringford was his permanent home till 1867. He wrote *Maud* here. When he left, he still kept the house on. (In the grounds are six cottages for visitors. They are by *Clough Williams-Ellis* and *Lionel Brett*. RH)

GATCOMBE 4080

ST OLAVE. The nave on the N side has a plain Late Norman doorway, and on the S side one lancet. Otherwise the church is Perp except for the chancel (of 1865). Solid W tower, vaulted inside with a tierceron-star vault with a large circle in the middle for the bell-ropes.* Two big Perp S windows in the nave; one N window as well. Wide nave. Above the S porch entrance a monster head that might give some people a real fright. – FONT. Octagonal bowl of Purbeck marble, with, on each side, the usual two plain flat blank pointed arches. – STAINED GLASS. Original fragments in a nave S window. – E window: exquisite *Morris* glass of 1865–6. According to Mr Sewter the Last Supper, the Marys at the Sepulchre, and the Ascension are by *Morris*, the impressive Crucifixion is by *Rossetti*, the Entombment by *Ford Madox Brown*, the Baptism and the lamb and angels in the tracery by *Burne-Jones*. – PLATE. Secular Cup of *c.*1540 with fluting on the foot and the lower part of the bowl and a band of Renaissance foliage higher up the bowl. The chalice is unique in England but similar to one at Zwolle in Holland. – Cover Paten, Elizabethan. – MONUMENTS. Early C14 effigy of a Knight. Oak. Cross-legged, the head a little out of the standard frontality. His face and the one angel by his pillow are unfortunately completely re-cut by a village craftsman. – C. Grant Seely † 1917. White recumbent effigy of the young soldier. By *Sir Thomas Brock*.

GATCOMBE HOUSE. Built in 1750 for Sir Edward Worsley.

*According to Mr Hubbuck, the vault is not ancient. It is probably by *Caröe*.

Ashlar, seven bays, three storeys, with a three-bay pediment. The middle window on the top floor is arched.

SHEAT MANOR, ½ m. SSE. Jacobean. The main front on the E-plan with gabled wings and castellated porch. Mullioned windows. An adjoining BARN has vertically placed oval windows, a sign of *c.*1675.

5080
GODSHILL

ST LAWRENCE. This is a very curious church, reminiscent of Whitwell with its two dedications under one roof. Nothing in the church is earlier than the early C14. Of that date are the lower parts of the W tower (W lancet, arch to the nave with three continuous chamfers) – the top with its eight pinnacles is C16 – the chancel E window (cusped intersecting tracery), the S chapel windows (reticulated E, cusped-Y on the S side), and also the transepts (cf. the mouldings of the arches into them). But these transepts lead off a two-naved church. The arcade of six bays – there is no structural division between nave and chancel – is Perp, late or in any case very raw. However, it must replace an early C14 arcade, or else the transepts could not be arranged like this. There was a certain amount of activity in the C17 – cf. the tracery of the four-light S aisle W window, perhaps also a nave N window, and the S transept bellcote. To the C18 belongs the remodelling of the N transept as a Worsley chapel, and the S porch entrance. The S transept has a plastered wagon roof of the C15. – COMMUNION RAIL. Later C17. – Two HELMS. – PAINTING. An eminently
41 interesting wall painting of Christ hanging from a foliated cross which is really three lush boughs of a bush, in full leaf. It looks C15 or early C16, and the vegetation is much touched up. Even so, so much naturalism in this ancient iconographic scheme is rare. – Almost as interesting is the large *Rubens* or Rubens-school painting of Daniel in the lions' den. It comes from Appuldurcombe and is a Rubens composition which we know from engravings. A replica was in the Hamilton sale of 1882 and another at Sotheby's in 1927 (Witt Library). – PLATE. Chalice and Cover, 1641–2; Chalice and Cover, 1642; Tankard and Cover, 1685 or 1694; Set of Chalice, Paten, Almsdish, and Tankard, 1739–40. – MONUMENTS. Sir John Leigh † 1529. Between chancel and N chapel and open to both. Large architectural surround. Four-centred arches, cusped and sub-cusped to N and S, tracery panelling inside, tracery

in the spandrels, big cresting with angel-busts. The effigies are of alabaster, long-faced, showing no expression at all, and indeed very English. – Sir James Worsley (of Appuldurcombe, like all the following) † 1536 and his wife † 1557. Two kneeling figures facing E. Fine architectural surround with Ionic pilasters and an unusually elegantly carved frieze. Pediment. Three putto shield-bearers. – Richard † 1565. Large standing monument without any figures – typically Early Elizabethan. The ornamental forms over-sized. Daintier decoration round the upper part. – Sir Robert † 1747 and his brother. Very large, the piece for which the family chapel was remodelled. Unsigned, but in the style of *Scheemakers*. Grand architecture with pink columns and pilasters. Frieze, pediment, and a military trophy above the latter. Grey background, and in front of it a plain sarcophagus and on it two Romanly draped busts. Outside the columns two mourning putti. – James (of Stanbury) † 1787. By *Bingley* of London. The usual mourning woman by an urn in front of an obelisk. – Sir Richard † 1805, the traveller and collector of Greek sculpture. Enormous sarcophagus on lions' claws, free-standing. On it a relief panel with bold foliage. The whole on a high base. No figures.

By the entrance to the church one of the Isle of Wight's picture-postcard motifs. Trimly thatched cottages. The village has become a show village, and not without reason. It has among other things also a stone-built SCHOOL of 1826, the WESLEYAN CHAPEL of 1838, and the pretty GRIFFIN HOTEL, symmetrical, with bargeboarded gables.

GURNARD 4090

1 m. W of West Cowes

ALL SAINTS. 1892–3 by *E. P. Loftus Brock*. Yellow and red brick. Lancets and a flèche.

HAVENSTREET 5090

4 m. NE of Arreton

ST PETER. 1852 by *Thomas Hellyer* of Ryde (RH). Nave and chancel, bellcote, lancets.

KINGSTON 4080

ST JAMES. Mostly by *R. J. Jones*, 1872 (RH). Low. Nave and chancel and bellcote. Irregular fenestration. Above the E window a corbel with a bust and stiff-leaf. – PLATE. Chalice and Paten, 1671.

KINGSTON MANOR. The front with cross-windows, the back with irregular mullioned windows. But at the back is the remarkable feature of the house: a large stone chimneybreast continued by a brick stage of five by one blank arches (as if it were by Vanbrugh) and octagonal stacks. What is the date of this? Really as late as Queen Anne, or rather about 1675?

BILLINGHAM MANOR, ½ m. NE. The less prominent part dated 1631. But about 1700 the opposite façade was made with chequer brick wall facing, two projecting wings, and raised window surrounds. Hipped roof. Round the corner, of the same date, a four-bay front. Brick with stone quoins, a moulded brick frieze above the ground floor. Two prominent windows have raised brick surrounds.

LITTLE BILLINGHAM, opposite the Manor. Also *c.*1700. Ashlar-faced. Five bays, two storeys; a pity that the original casements are not preserved.

LAKE *see* SANDOWN

LOWTHERVILLE *see* VENTNOR

MERSTONE MANOR *see* ARRETON

4080

MOTTISTONE

ST PETER AND ST PAUL. W tower small, with big battlements and a recessed spire. No external interest otherwise. Inside, rustic Perp arcades of two bays. Octagonal piers, double-chamfered arches. But the bases of the N arcade with their spurs must be of *c.*1200. The chancel arch also was initially of *c.*1200. Perp tower arch, Perp N chapel of three bays, later than the rest. Thin piers of the four-shafts-and-four-hollows section; four-centred arches.* – PULPIT. Jacobean. – PLATE. Chalice of 1576–7. – MONUMENT. Raw Elizabethan tomb-chest. It turns out to be for Jane Freake, who died in 1674.

MOTTISTONE MANOR. Dated 1567 on the porch. The house lies against the steep bank of the down and was built by Thomas Cheke of the family to which Sir John, tutor to Edward VI, Greek scholar and politician, and his sister, Sir William Cecil's first wife, belonged. The house is L-shaped,

*The canopy on slender columns in the N chapel is the memorial to the first *Lord Mottistone*, by his son, the architect. It fits well into the chapel.

but with the long and the short wing not being set at r. angles. It is an extremely attractive house, due to a certain extent to a tactful restoration in the 1920s by *Seely & Paget*.* The house has no imposed symmetry. The porch is in the angle between the two wings. The short wing is a little higher than the long one and has a dormer, while the long wing has an uninterrupted eaves-line. Consistently the higher wing has mullioned and transomed windows, the lower only low mullioned ones. It seems probable that the higher wing is entirely of 1567 but that the lower one is basically pre-Elizabethan. The VCH even calls it late C15.

NETTLESTONE 6090

THE PRIORY. The house is said to date from *c.*1790 but was altered in a neo-Georgian way about 1930–5. Of that date said to be e.g. the Clock Tower.‡ The Gothic doorway with a crocketed gable is genuine. It is supposed to have been brought over from a church in France.

NEWCHURCH 5080

ALL SAINTS. Nave and chancel in one. In the chancel three N lancets, i.e. a C13 date. The other windows are Perp. The aisle W windows are small lancets too, but the main W window has Y-tracery and a typical early C14 profile. The same also in the N transept N window. The S transept S window is Perp. The SW tower has a nicely weatherboarded upper part with quatrefoil bell-openings. That looks *c.*1800. Inside the church one finds that to the time of the chancel belonged a proper crossing with a crossing tower – cf. the one surviving E window. The arches to N, S, and E are of three slight chamfers, i.e. early C13. On the other hand the raw three-bay arcades between nave and aisles have octagonal piers and double-chamfered arches and could well be early C14. – PULPIT. Late C17 or early C18. Simply panelled, but with a big ogee-shaped tester. An angel at the top. – LECTERN. This splendid gilded Pelican with three young was the crowning top of the pulpit at Frome in Somerset. – PLATE. Chalice and Cover, inscribed 1620; Almsdish, inscribed 1737.

* Seely was later Lord Mottistone.

‡ Can it be?

4080 NEWPORT

ST THOMAS. 1854–5 by *S. W. Dawkes* of Cheltenham. A large town-church with a prominent tower, well placed between two squares. The style is Dec, still under Pugin's influence. Ornate W doorway. The aisles with separate roofs embrace the tower. Well preserved Early Victorian interior. – FONT. 1633. Small bowl, against the stem monstrously big scrolls or volutes. – PULPIT. An outstandingly good piece of 1636. It was made by the Fleming *Thomas Caper* (RH). The top panels represent the Seven Virtues, the bottom panels the Seven Liberal Arts. Brackets for the bookrest, back panels, and tester. – The READING DESK is made up of parts of the SCREEN, evidently by the same hand and of the same date. – *See* p. 833 STAINED GLASS. The E window is of *c.*1857. – PLATE. Two Chalices and Covers, 1630; two Flagons, Almsdish, and two Patens, 1696. – MONUMENTS. Sir Edward Horsey † 1582. Alabaster. Recumbent effigy on a half-rolled-up mat. Two columns, strapwork background. At the top three achievements. – Princess Elizabeth, daughter of Charles I. Given by Queen Victoria in 1856 and made by Baron *Marochetti*. White marble. She is asleep. – Prince Albert. This memorial with the head in profile is also by *Marochetti*.

ST JOHN BAPTIST, St John's Road and Drake Road. 1837, in the lancet style. The W front has a projecting centre with two big polygonal turrets. A typical example of the Commissioners' style. Small yellow stones like bricks and grey stone.

ST PAUL, Staplers Road. 1844 by *J. W. Wild*. Neo-Norman. W tower; apse. Thin arcades with thin square abaci. – STAINED GLASS. In the W window by *Kempe*, 1899. – In the E window copies of *Reynolds*'s figures in the New College windows, but in strident colours. The date is *c.*1850.

ST THOMAS OF CANTERBURY (R.C.), Pyle Street. 1791. Five by three bays, arched windows, red brick. Three-bay pediment. Deep Tuscan porch with pediment. Given by Mrs Heneage (cf. Cowes).

NONCONFORMIST CHAPELS. *See* Perambulation.

COUNTY HALL, High Street. 1938 by *Gutteridge & Gutteridge*. Neo-Georgian, with a dash of Swedish of the twenties. Not large, not prominent; undistinguished.

TOWN HALL, High Street. 1816 by *Nash*. Brick, stuccoed. Three bays, with ground-floor arches and, above, a giant portico of unfluted Ionic columns and a pediment. To the r. of the façade the Victoria Tower of 1887, with a domed cap. The façade is then continued along the High Street with an Ionic colonnade.

GUILDHALL, St James's Square. 1819 by *Nash*. Ashlar-faced. Five bays, upper Doric pilasters and a three-bay pediment. Below four open arches, the outer ones round, the inner ones segmental.

TECHNICAL INSTITUTE AND SEELY LIBRARY. 1904 by *W. Venn Gough*. Red brick, symmetrical, free Jacobean – or what?

WHITECROFT HOSPITAL, 2 m. S. Red brick with a high tower. By *B. S. Jacobs* of Hull, 1894 etc. The estimate was £47,000 (GS).

PARKHURST PRISON. Parkhurst Prison was opened in 1838. The buildings were taken over from an existing Military Hospital erected in 1799. The conversion for prison use was done by *Sir Joshua Jebb*, military engineer and prison specialist. Of 1799 still the ADMINISTRATIVE OFFICES, facing the main gate, a handsome timber-framed building with a cupola, two GATE LODGES, and a large part of a STORE, behind the administrative offices. In 1838–44 the following buildings were added by Jebb: the old CHAPEL (now Concert Hall) of trefoil shape, C HALL of cells, and the OLD KITCHEN and DINING ROOM (now used differently). The main ranges of cells are B HALL of *c.*1870, and A HALL of a slightly later date. The MAIN GATE is of 1963, but a row of STAFF HOUSES just S of it dates from *c.*1840. Some way up Horsebridge Hill (NE of the prison) are another large GATE,* some COTTAGES, and the CHAPLAIN'S HOUSE, all of 1843–4. The new ALBANY PRISON was begun in 1963. It promises to be prominent and interesting. It was designed by the *Ministry of Public Building and Works*, and will probably be occupied by the end of 1966.‡

PERAMBULATION. The centre is ST JAMES SQUARE, with the Guildhall and the MONUMENT of 1901. Pillar crowned by a Gothic tabernacle. Below three bronze angels. On the base three lions. Up the pillar grows Art Nouveau stiff-leaf. On the W side is a good Late Georgian three-bay house of three storeys, quite plain. Doorway with Tuscan columns.

From here the HIGH STREET runs W as well as E. First W. No. 97 is a fine mid C18 house of brick. Five bays, two storeys, the

*Demolished 1966.

‡I am extremely grateful to Dr R. R. Prewer for all the information in this paragraph.

parapet partly balustraded. Bays one and five project a little, and on the ground floor there are here quite elaborate pediments. HOLYROOD HALL was built as the Friends' Meeting House; Gothic, rendered. The CASTLE INN is of brick, small and low. But it is dated 1684, and it is interesting that it should already have Flemish bond. Then the BAPTIST CHAPEL of 1809, enlarged in 1872. Yellow brick. Five bays with giant Corinthian columns and a three-bay pediment. Arched doorway and windows. The façade is conservative for 1872. A little further W Pyle Street (*see* below) joins the High Street. They then continue as CARISBROOKE ROAD, and for quite a stretch on the N side runs an Early Victorian Italianate terrace.

From St James Square N, along ST JAMES STREET. The GRAMMAR SCHOOL of 1614 is at the corner of Lugley Street. It is Jacobean in general character, but the details are all renewed. In LUGLEY STREET itself to the W the MASONIC TEMPLE with a cryptic date. Red brick, with upper pilasters in an Anglo-Dutch mid C17 style. To the E No. 8 has five bays and is of grey headers and dressings. Parallel with Lugley Street to the N is CROCKER STREET. To the E the interesting MALTHOUSE of Messrs Maw. The ground floor has nine blank arches, the middle one higher. No. 62 is again of grey headers, three-storeyed, Late Georgian. A good deal further N is the hospital, former WORKHOUSE or House of Industry, built shortly after 1770. Two ranges of three were built. They are 300 and 170 ft long. The centre of what was meant to be the centre wing has a five-bay pediment. Yet further N PARKHURST PRISON (*see* p. 751). Back to St James Square and now the HIGH STREET to the E.

The BUGLE HOTEL has grey headers and red dressings. Six bays, three storeys. By the town hall QUAY STREET turns off half l. It is a wide street leading down to the quay of the Medina River. Nothing special, but an attractive general appearance. Grey and red or red and blue chequer. Several nice doorways. At the end of Quay Street across runs SEA STREET. There are warehouses here, and also a few good individual houses, especially No. 30, Early Georgian, of five bays, with segment-headed windows. Sea Street runs between Crocker Street (*see* above) and the E end of the High Street (*see* below). In the HIGH STREET Nos 19–20 has its ground floor spoiled, but the upper façade with the arched window is Early Georgian, though the doorway is later. The UNITARIAN

CHAPEL dates from 1825.* It lies back and is of three bays, red brick, with Gothic windows, but a three-bay pediment.

From the end of the High Street one can go by way of East Street to the start of PYLE STREET. No. 137 is a five-bay house of grey headers. The VICTORIA METHODIST CHURCH has an uncommonly fine façade. Plum-coloured brick, three bays, broken pediment into which a giant arch reaches up. In it a lunette window and below an arched window. Doorway with thin Greek Doric columns. This cannot be part of the original building of 1804 and probably belongs to the lengthening of 1833. No. 30 is low, of seven bays, chequer brick. Opposite, with the front into a narrow lane, GOD'S PROVIDENCE HOUSE, the best house in Newport, dated 1701. Five bays, two storeys, with a big shell-hood on uncommonly large carved brackets. The house leads to St Thomas' Square, and here the NE corner is a house of yellow brick with a rounded corner, a feature dear to Regency architects. From this corner S along Town Lane to the GATEWAY of the former plague churchyard. Erected probably in 1583, when the churchyard was consecrated. The shape of the arch is between segmental and basket. On top an ogee-shaped gable.

On in PYLE STREET. Facing St Thomas' Square an early C18 house of yellow brick, seven bays, three storeys, three-bay pediment, shifted doorway. The CATHOLIC PRESBYTERY stands at r. angles to the street. (In it a staircase with a Chinese-Chippendale handrail.)

Really outside Newport on the road to Staplers is a good Georgian house of yellow brick, four bays, with a lower three-bay addition. Two-bay pedimental gable, and in it a segmental lunette with a fan motif.

ROMAN VILLA. Discovered in 1926 between Avondale Road and Cypress Road. Of the well-known corridor type, with a small bath suite at the W end. Several of the rooms originally contained geometric mosaics. The building is open to the public.

NEWTOWN 4090

Newtown, as its name implies, was a made, not a grown town. It was, like New Alresford and some others, due to the initiative of the Bishops of Winchester, was founded in 1256 by Bishop Aymer and originally called Francheville. Names such as

*Or 1774?

Newtown, Neustadt, Villeneuve, Francheville, Villefranche, Villafranca, Castelfranco are of course all indications of made towns. Newtown was a port on the Solent. It was destroyed by the French in 1377 but hung on as a borough until the disenfranchisement of 1832.

CHAPEL OF THE HOLY GHOST. By *A. F. Livesay* of Portsea, 1835, an architect consistently interesting and surprising. Here he proves particularly knowledgeable and resourceful. What he has designed suits Bishop Aymer exactly. Three bays with lancets, tall in the general proportions. Inside three rib-vaulted bays. Stiff-leaf bosses. Much shafting of windows, and also dogtooth.

The town consists, apart from the church, of some Georgian estate cottages of three bays and, on its own, not in anything like a street, the TOWN HALL. However, the streets of the C13, two running parallel W–E, can still be traced. The date of the town hall is unknown, but it is of course Georgian, even if the stone base may be older. Brick, of four bays with a hipped roof. In one of the short sides entrance up steps to the upper hall. This side is faced with yellow mathematical tiles; on the other short side the ground-floor entrance is under a four-column wooden porch. – REGALIA. Mace, silver, parcel-gilt, late C15.

NITON

5070

ST JOHN BAPTIST. The N arcade is of round piers with square abaci chamfered at the corners and round arches. The S arcade is just a little later. The abaci are round now. Both are of *c.*1200. Again later, i.e. full C13, the S chapel with a double-chamfered arch. Also C13 the S aisle W window with a diagonally set quatrefoil in a circle. Perp W tower with battlements and a recessed short stone spire. Perp S porch with a pointed tunnel-vault and two chamfered transverse arches. – FONT. Norman, of cauldron type, with a rope moulding at the top. – MONUMENT. George Arnold † 1806. Gothic surround. Female figure with a pelican on a high base with the portrait of the deceased. He appears nearly *en face*. Signed *H. Rouw*. – (CHURCHYARD CROSS. By *Joseph Clarke*. RH)

WESTCLIFF, on the N side of the A-road. 1803. Ashlar-faced, of two storeys, with a wide middle bow.

ROYAL SANDROCK HOTEL. An C18 cottage of three bays with

two canted bay windows, and lower one-bay wings of *c.*1830. The Duchess of Kent and Princess Victoria stayed here.

MOUNT CLEVES, next to the former. 1829. White, with two slightly projecting wings. This front is emphasized by coupled giant Ionic pilasters. Round the corner a three-bay front, also with giant Ionic pilasters. Above the house a SPIRE on a square base. Was this meant as a mark for shipping?

BOWL BARROW, ½ m. NW, at the head of Bury Lane. This barrow covered an unaccompanied inhumation burial and is built on top of an earlier Neolithic occupation site.

NORTHWOOD

4090

ST JOHN BAPTIST. Norman S doorway with one order of shafts, zigzag on the arch, and a hood-mould with chip-carved small motifs. Arcades inside of four bays. Low circular piers, square chamfered abaci, pointed arches with a slight chamfer, i.e. *c.*1200. The N arcade is the earlier of the two by a little. The aisles still have the Norman narrowness. Supporting half-arches in the aisles, probably an emergency action. Victorian W tower with slated broach-spire. Nearly all the windows are Victorian too. – PULPIT. Mid C17. With back panels and tester. – PLATE. Chalice and Paten, 1722; oval Paten, 1813. – MONUMENTS. Two tablets of cartouche type, one † 1681, the other † 1798, yet both basically the same.

NUNWELL

5080

¾ m. W of Brading

When Sir John Oglander moved to Nunwell in 1607, there was probably a high stone house here. One can deduce that from the straight joint of the W side between this stone part and the part to its r. which continues round the corner in brick and has just one original mullioned window. Probably the house 'bwylt' by Sir John had this S side as its façade. The surviving bit is a wing, the front absolutely windowless, the one window referred to facing inward, i.e. E. One may assume that a second wing projected S from the E end of the S front, where there is now later C18 work with C20 Jacobean references. The centre of this preserved façade was hidden and altered about 1700 or a little later by a five-bay front of two storeys faced with red mathematical tiles. The windows originally had wooden mullion and transom crosses, as they still have on the ground floor.

The doorway has a rusticated surround with angle pilasters, starting duly from bases but then disappearing in the rustication and only re-emerging with their capitals (cf. Radley House of 1721–5 and Kingston House, both in Berkshire). The E front as it is now is a well-proportioned late C18 seven-bay front of three storeys with a canted three-bay centre. Grey headers and red dressings. In fact this late C18 façade is largely an overlay on a façade of five bays from the present N end to just S of the bay window, where there is an outer wall. Beyond this is a new room with a typical later C18 stucco ceiling. This room must replace the second Jacobean wing. – The STABLES are by *Nash*, red brick, with a pedimented centre and two projecting pedimented wings. Archways under the pediments. Many circular windows and blank windows.

OAKFIELD *see* RYDE, p. 762

5090

OSBORNE HOUSE

On the site of Osborne House stood a big plain C18 house which *The Beauties of England and Wales* call one of the most spacious ones in the island. The Duchess of Kent and Princess Victoria visited the island in 1831 (when they stayed at Norris Castle, East Cowes) and again in 1833. Three years after her accession to the throne Queen Victoria married Prince Albert. They wanted a private house, to be paid for by them and not by the Commissioners of Works and Forests, something, as she wrote to King Leopold, 'quiet and retired'. The result is the new Osborne House. They bought the estate in 1845. *Prince Albert* was his own designer, but he employed as builder and no doubt to a certain degree also as architect *Thomas Cubitt*, the famous London builder. We know nothing in detail of the partnership. Whose vision was this grand Italianate villa? Building started in 1845. The Pavilion Wing came first and was completed in 1846. The Household Wing followed and was finished in 1851. The house is of brick, rendered. In its construction iron girders were used.

84 The best view is that from the entrance, not the garden, the W, not the E view. To appreciate it, it must be remembered that the l. wing, the Durbar Wing, was added only in 1890. Until then this was an L-shaped façade, anti-symmetrical even in this. But the distaste for symmetry goes further. The centre, the so-called Pavilion Wing, which contains the state rooms

and above them the private apartments, has from l. to r. two wide bays with diamond-cut pilasters below and large Palladio windows above, then follows the porch with four Tuscan columns, and the main, three-storeyed block lying somewhat behind, and then the Flag Tower, 107 ft high, with its loggia of three arches at the top and the deep eaves of Italian villas. Finally one more bay like the first leads on to the far-projecting so-called Household Wing, which has to the entrance, i.e. the N, a perfectly even façade of eleven bays, again diamond-cut pilasters below, again the windows of Palladio's Basilica above. The Household Wing itself, in its own, main W front, is also quite symmetrical and restrained. Seven bays, three storeys, the first and last with a tripartite window on the ground floor and a balcony with statues over.

The Solent front is wider and more varied still. To reach it one passes along the N side of the Durbar Wing and then the Pavilion Wing, which here has arched ground-floor windows with vermiculated rustication. The E front of this block has a big central bow like the garden front of Buckingham Palace, i.e. an English Georgian motif. Another such motif is the canted bay window of the same block to the S. In this case from r. to l. there are two of the bays with the Palladio windows, then the plain eleven bays of the Household Wing, and then the Clock Tower, a second tower, 90 ft high. The eleven bays incidentally have on the ground floor typically Florentine rusticated surrounds to the windows.

Having now described these fronts, the question must be asked how Albert could design such a building and why he designed just such a building. His artistic talents were remarkable and universal. He wrote poetry, he composed, he painted juicily like the Belgian history-painters of the 1830s but admired the disciplined dryness of the German Nazarenes. But none of that points to the Italianate style of Osborne. If it is called Italianate, it must at once be added that it is not like any Italian *palazzo* or villa. Its source is the villas in paintings of Claude Lorraine. Albert did not create this Italianate villa style. It seems to have been the vision of Sir Charles Barry at Mount Felix, Walton-on-Thames, in 1835 etc. and at Trentham Park in 1837 etc. Here, as Professor Hitchcock recognized, are the sources for Prince Albert and Cubitt. The style caught on enormously and is reflected e.g. in the Prussia of Frederick William IV (Potsdam Pfingstberg 1849 etc., Orangery 1851 etc., Dresden Albrechtsburgen for a Prussian prince 1850 etc.), but not with the asymmetry which is the very spice of Osborne.

Close to the entrance hall is the staircase with an iron balustrade of a crowded Victorian pattern. On the wall *Dyce*'s fresco of Neptune entrusting the Command of the Sea to Britannia. This was done in 1847. Dyce was an admirer of Overbeck, the German Nazarene, and so Albert's and his sympathies coincided. The main state rooms on the ground floor are three, or rather two, as billiard room and drawing room are one. They form an L and are connected by a screen of columns. The drawing room part lies behind the big E bow. The third of the state rooms, the dining room, corresponds to the big canted bay window to the S. The ceilings in their distribution of motifs are still in the Georgian tradition, but the motifs are more crowded and intricate. On the first floor is the Queen's private suite, with her sitting room behind the bow.

The Long Corridor in the Household Wing is paved with *Minton* tiles. It has many bays for sculpture. The council chamber is five bays long and has a less closely ornamented ceiling. The Durbar Wing was carried out under the supervision of *Bhai Ram Singh* and *John Lockwood Kipling*, Rudyard Kipling's father. The walls are all covered with Indian plaster decoration, and over the fireplace with its Indian columns is a peacock as an overmantel ornament. But the ceiling rests on heavy, typically Victorian, brackets and is coffered in quite an un-Indian way.

On the collection of Victorian paintings, including a number of German ones, and on the thousands of bits and pieces of furnishing nothing can here be said. Mr John Charlton's guidebook* is admirable, but one would like a volume of several hundred pages to carry round.

The TERRACES towards the sea were made concurrently with the house, in 1847–53. The VENUS FOUNTAIN and ANDROMEDA FOUNTAIN were designed by Professor *Grüner*. The Andromeda is by *John Bell* and was bought from the exhibition of 1851. The sea allegories around are by *Theed*. Prince Albert himself took much interest in the PLANTING of the grounds.

As an entry to the KITCHEN GARDEN a Georgian doorway from the old house was re-erected. It is tripartite and set in a Victorian surround with pediment. The re-erection took place in 1848.

*Ministry of Public Building and Works, 1960.

Immediately by the sea, with its paved ESPLANADE, ⅔ m. long, is the Queen's ALCOVE, a plain little apsed structure, decorated inside in blue with a little gold and red. It dates from 1869.

Not far from here is the LANDING HOUSE of 1855, now a private house. It originally had a jetty. It is of a very original composition. The centre is an Italianate tower with far-projecting eaves. Two bays l., two bays r., and a top terrace. A curved outer staircase in two flights leads up to the house. When was it built, and how much has been added?

SWISS COTTAGE, ½ m. SE of the house. Brought from Switzerland in 1853.* Of timber, two-storeyed, with the familiar projecting balconies. The kitchen has delightful white tiles with blue spots on all walls and a shiny black range.

A second SWISS COTTAGE was built close by – in 1862 – to house the children's collections. The interior is three-naved, with timber posts and tie-beams. All timbers have scalloped chamfers.

ALBERT BARRACKS. 1860. Also close by. This is a toy earthwork-fort built by the children.

(The final excitement of this group is QUEEN VICTORIA'S BATHING MACHINE, its canopy supported by scrolly brackets. NT)

On the fringe of the estate, along York Avenue, are a number of subsidiary buildings. The present LODGE is Italianate with twin windows with arched lights. ARTHUR COTTAGE is similar. OSBORNE COTTAGE is of yellow and red brick, long and low like almshouses. The windows are segment-headed. The date is 1856–7. ALBERT COTTAGE is mostly of 1868 and again in the style of the lodge. Arthur and Albert were named after sons of Queen Victoria, Osborne Cottage was Princess Beatrice's and her husband, Prince Henry of Battenberg's. The SOVEREIGN'S ENTRANCE is a plain, rather thin archway with horizontal top. The lodges are two windows wide.

BARTON MANOR, ⅜ m. SE, was rebuilt in 1846 as a Jacobean house. It is an early example of perfect imitation. E-shaped front and in it, re-set no doubt, lancet windows from the Augustinian oratory founded on the site in 1275.

PARKHURST PRISON *see* NEWPORT

*Nicholas Taylor says: a kind of adventure playground for the royal children.

5090 QUARR ABBEY

QUARR ABBEY was founded in 1131 by Baldwin de Redvers for Savignac monks. The house, like others, soon turned Cistercian. It was dissolved in 1537. It never was a very large or important house, and the remaining ruins are singularly unenlightening. The inspection begins at an Early Victorian cottage with C13 motifs. It stands against a big barn, the drive-in bay of which has a group of genuine C13 tall stepped lancets re-set. This is one of the few aesthetically rewarding details on the site. The barn represents the W range of the cloister, i.e. the store-rooms and the rooms for the lay-brothers. To understand the rest, it must be remembered that the church stood S of the cloister. So the arch between cottage and barn may be connected with the W front of the church and the entrance from the lay-brothers' quarters. The W end of the N wall of the church anyway is recognizable. The rest is more confusing, especially as in the C18 or early C19 much must have been shifted around for picturesque reasons. What can be recognized is the kitchen entrance and something of the interior of the kitchen, in the N range, the boldly chamfered hatch between kitchen and refectory, and of the refectory one shafted jamb of the doorway and one wall-shaft of former blank arcading. Next to the doorway a cupboard recess. What took place further N? What e.g. is the meaning of the arch with a slight continuous chamfer, and of the wall standing higher near it? It has been suggested that this is part of the Abbot's Lodging. A good deal further E is a fragment of the small infirmary chapel, just a round-headed N window with continuous mouldings.

Much of the precinct walls is preserved. Licence to crenellate was given in 1365.

QUARR ABBEY. In 1907 Quarr House, a Victorian house, was sold to French Benedictines of Solesmes, and in 1908 the new buildings began to rise to its S. They were designed by *Dom Paul Bellot*, who went on living at Quarr. Later in life he moved to Canada and died there in 1943. He had been born in 1876, the son of an architect, and had studied architecture at the École des Beaux Arts in Paris. He took his diploma in 1900, but decided for a monastic life and was accepted a monk at Solesmes in 1904. He built much in Holland and also in Belgium, France, and Canada, but Quarr is his outstanding achievement. Why does he not appear in all the histories of C20 architecture? Why have those younger scholars not discovered him yet who are looking for a pedigree for 1960 Expressionism by way of 1920 Expressionism? He should appear in books in the line of descent of the early Gaudí of the Casa Vicens and then of Berlage and de Klerk and of Hoeger in Germany. But this attempt at historical placing should not reduce anyone's respect for Bellot's originality and achievement. The church was built in 1911–12. It is built of Belgian bricks, rough, unattractive bricks, bricks others would have tried to hide. It is high and long and high again, and its plan is wholly original. It consists of a short and low nave, then, a few steps up, a long choir with bare side walls, very narrow side passages (like Gaudí's corridors at the college of St Teresa at Barcelona), and ampler galleries above, and then an altar space under a high square tower. Everything is of the same brick, externally and internally. Externally the low nave looks like a Cluniac ante-church or a narthex; for it is followed by the high S tower, the low N tower, and much high bare wall between. The square tower at the E end is not as high as the S tower but mighty in its square volume and overwhelmingly blunt in its marking the E end of the whole building.

Paul Bellot was a virtuoso in brick. All is brick and all has to be done angularly; for such is the brick's nature. Instead of pointed arches triangular heads. Stepped gables for the low façade of the church and for the entrance to the abbey, cut-brick friezes and stepped patterns of all kinds. They are again curiously reminiscent of Gaudí. Inside the church, and also the chapter house and the refectory, Paul Bellot repeats one powerful motif: transverse pointed brick arches carrying the roofs, and that is a Catalan motif as well, used in religious and secular architecture and especially similar to Quarr in the Cistercian abbey of Poblet. But it is also present in such South French Cistercian buildings as Le Thoronet. But Spain altogether must have impressed Paul Bellot most; for the tremendous arches inside the E tower of the church, dazzling with 95
the arched openings pierced in the spandrels, are inspired in their crossing – two diagonal ribs and four running from the middle of one side to the middle of the next – by the Mosque at Cordova. The way in which the four immensely high narrow windows in the E wall are cut into by the ribs in the tower and the series of open arches in the spandrels is brilliant indeed and establishes Dom Paul Bellot beyond doubt as one of the pioneers of C20 Expressionism.

5090 RYDE

The population of Ryde in 1795 was 600, in 1811 1600, in 1821 nearly 3,000. Sheridan in 1834 writes: 'Within the last few years houses of very superior description have been built', both for permanent use and as 'desirable winter residences'. Sheridan gives as examples the houses of the Duke of Buckingham, Earl Spencer, Sir Richard Simeon, Lord Vernon, and others. Thus it is that, in contrast to the other seaside towns of the Isle of Wight, the first strata of preserved buildings at Ryde are Regency, in character, if not in date. The bargeboards and the Italian villa windows come only later. There is only one monumental terrace, and that neglected, as so much seems to be at Ryde, but there are scattered over most of the streets up from the Esplanade enjoyable pre-Victorian or pre-Victorian-looking houses. The tramway was laid in 1864 and became in 1880 one of the earliest electric lines in the country.

ALL SAINTS. 1868–72 by *Sir George Gilbert Scott*, the sign of a prosperity and a pride now sadly absent. Very large, in an ornate Second Pointed, with a high NE steeple and plenty of pinnacles. The steeple is an addition of 1881–2. The apsed vestry is of 1891 (by *C. Pemberton Leach*). Six-bay arcades. Naturalistic capitals carved rather mechanically. The chancel walls painted by *Clayton & Bell*. – FONT of alabaster; also ornate. – PULPIT. By *Scott*. Alabaster and marble, *c.*1870.

ST JAMES, Lind Street. Neglected at the time of writing. 1827, built as a proprietary chapel. Stone, very gimcrack, i.e. medieval without any knowledge. Thin W tower. Perp windows, i.e. with four-centred arches. Aisleless interior with galleries.

ST JOHN, High Park Road, Oakfield. 1843 by *T. Hellyer*. Aisles and transepts. Lancets and plate tracery. Bellcote. The E wall has l. and r. of the windows very tall pointed niches, no doubt for Commandments, Creed, and Lord's Prayer.

ST MARY (R.C.), High Street. 1844–6 by *Joseph Hansom*.* Additions in the 80s and 90s. The façade introduces Hansom as a rogue, a part he rarely played. The style is E.E., but the composition is wildly unbalanced. The interior is in its own way as odd; for the arcade arches are very depressed two-centred on vertical pieces, and the normal two-centred arches appear only, reaching of course much higher, as hood-moulds.

ST MICHAEL, Swanmore. By the *Rev. William Grey* under the architectural supervision of *R. J. Jones*; 1861–3. A remarkable

* So Mr Evinson tells me.

church in such a place. Big and serious. Crossing tower and lancets. It was a very ritualistic church and hence intensely controversial. The chancel was completed only in 1874. The interior is very different, brick showing, yellow, red, black, and also stone. The piers have stop-chamfers and oversized pointed trefoils. The arches die into them. The crossing arches have short shafts on scalloped brackets. The chancel is vaulted and has much Purbeck shafting and an apse. – CARVING by *Farmer & Brindley*; TILES by *Maw*, *c.*1865; STAINED GLASS mostly by *Lavers & Westlake*. *See* p. 833

ST THOMAS, St Thomas's Street. Neglected at the time of writing. 1827–8. Also a proprietary chapel. Stone. To the l. and r. of the W tower of pre-archaeological details two aisles, W gable, domestic Tudor rather than ecclesiastic Gothic. Tall windows with Perp tracery.

HOLY TRINITY, Dover Street. 1845 by *T. Hellyer*, the transepts of 1848 and 1860. SW steeple with octagonal bell-stage. Lancets and plate tracery. Apsidal chancel. Thin arcades, thin roof timbers.

CONGREGATIONAL CHURCH, George Street. Behind it, in Melville Street, a former coach-house of before 1816. Three-bay, the centre projecting with giant pilasters and a pediment. The new church is by *R. J. Jones*, 1870–2, and an architectural nightmare if ever there was one. Façade with a thin NW tower changing by exceedingly steep long slopes into an octagon and carrying a very steep spire. But behind, in extreme perspective, appears the body of the church, with seven steep cross-gables.

TOWN HALL, Lind Street. 1830. Quite big. Five bays. Classical, with an upper recessed portico of Ionic columns above a low recessed ground-floor portico of short Tuscan columns. Additions are recorded for 1864. Did they include the cupola and the whole r. hand addition?

PIER. Begun in 1813. Nearly ½ m. long.

PERAMBULATION. The natural centre is ST THOMAS'S SQUARE. From here to the W is LIND STREET, with a consistent early *ensemble*. On the N side almost at once the TURK'S HEAD, with a Tuscan colonnade with straight entablature as if it were the Paris of the rue des Colonnes, or Drury Lane. Then the town hall and opposite it a whole terrace in the Regency style, interrupted only by TOWN HALL CHAMBERS of 1853–4, with the unmistakable group of two or more small arched windows of which Loudon was so fond.

It is a typical forties motif. Upper giant pilasters. The building was originally the Assembly Rooms. Lind Street is short.

The HIGH STREET is long, but apart from the CROWN HOTEL at its very start, with Tuscan doorway between two bows, it has nothing to offer. The corners of JOHN STREET are both rounded, a motif fashionable about 1830. In John Street a characteristic Early Victorian shop and warehouse. The shop front is recessed, and twisted iron columns carry the three upper storeys, which are as sweepingly glazed as the age could do it. Then two pairs of semi-detacheds with giant pilasters and finally ANGLESEA LODGE, grander than any of its neighbours and probably of the forties. Three bays, but a palazzo scale. Arched windows (but not with Italian details) on the *piano nobile*. The porch is English in any case.

John Street is continued in QUEEN'S ROAD, where the most ambitious house in Ryde stands, RYDE SCHOOL. This was built *c.*1820 for Dr Lind. Five bays, two storeys, lower wings. The entrance is a one-storeyed portico of four Ionic columns with a pediment. The windows l. and r. are arched, and an arched window also sticks up into the broken pediment in the centre, which is in fact part of a dormer.

Now down N from St Thomas's Square, i.e. first ST THOMAS'S STREET.* To its E lies BRIGSTOCKE TERRACE, the one monumental sea-front composition on the Isle of Wight. Rendered and, at the time of writing, shabby. Twenty-eight bays, the corners with towers with Italian villa eaves. The other accents lacking in strength, e.g. tripartite windows. Built *c.*1832 by *James Sanderson*. At the foot of St Thomas's Street and facing the sea the ROYAL VICTORIA YACHT CLUB, 1846, by *W. Huntley* of Dover. Italianate, with arched windows and brackets and dormers. To the sea two high storeys. It looks fine from that side. Colonnade of Tuscan columns carrying a balcony with cast-iron railing. On the roof arms and the initials of the club. To the land a single-storey forebuilding with a porch flanked by two large rooms, all with giant Corinthian pilasters.‡ Opposite the radical turn away from Regency. A Jacobean group of brick with shaped gables,

*Off to the W along Spencer Street and into an area called PELHAMFIELD, where the NMR has illustrations of YARBOROUGH HOUSE, a three-storeyed villa of *c.*1830 with giant angle pilasters and a veranda towards the sea, and ASHBY, a Gothic cottage of *c.*1820–30 with gables and dormers and bargeboards.

‡ This forebuilding probably represents the enlargements recorded for 1864.

probably of the 1840s. Opposite again, and now 1850s, a yellow and red brick house with segment-headed windows.

So down to the ESPLANADE. In it the outstanding building is of course the High Victorian ESPLANADE HOTEL, three-storeyed, with dormers. All the details must be studied, especially round the eaves brackets. But there are also seaside bow windows on the Esplanade. The dates of building are 1845, 1860, and 1895. Further E the HOTEL CASTLE RYDE, embattled and with a short tower. Even after the hotel there are still bargeboarded gables and giant pilasters, i.e. motifs of the 1830s and 1840s. So far did Ryde stretch already.*

The main streets of Old Ryde run up the hill from the sea front. We go up UNION STREET, much interfered with by shopping developments. Some stuccoed houses of *c.*1830 remain, the best the ROYAL SQUADRON HOTEL, two bays and four storeys with pairs of giant pilasters. Attic storey of five windows with a wreath l. and another r. On the other side No. 15, a one-storeyed portico with pediment. Again opposite the ROYAL VICTORIA ARCADE, Italianate front, Doric pilasters. Original shops and lantern lighting inside. It is all an extremely attractive ensemble. Once more on the other side a whole terrace of *c.*1830, not one composition, but with giant pilasters to every house. Turn E at St Thomas's Square along Cross Street and to GEORGE STREET. First up the street to the N. Nos 75–7 have tripartite windows and flanking pilasters. No. 79, yellow brick, turns Italian-Villa, see the pairs of small arched windows. Opposite SUFFOLK TOWERS has the Italian-Villa tower. Back to the E side for Nos 85, 87, 89 – all fully Victorian, bigger, yellow and red brick, segment-headed windows, some incised decoration – 1850s perhaps. But even higher up (MORETON) there is still a bow and a honeysuckle balcony.

Now down George Street to the N. On the E side a cottage with a bow which, on the upper floor, has attached Tuscan columns. Opposite a Tuscan porch and tripartite windows. Then alas a modernistic shock of between the wars, the ROYAL OAK HOTEL, 1938–9 by *Harrison & Gilkes.*

Up again, DOVER STREET, with a few bows and a few Greek Doric porches. Turn W into Melville Street. On the S side of it VERNON SQUARE. At its NW corner a house with Greek Doric columns and a garden gate with nice overthrow. At the far end of the square VERNON HOUSE. Three bays, bowed centre,

*More in THE STRAND, off East Street, behind.

carried on Greek Doric columnns. Pediment over the centre bay. In MELVILLE STREET WYNDHAM HOUSE, more carefully detailed than usual at Ryde. Greek Doric porch, upper giant Ionic pilasters.

Of mansions outside the centre by far the most interesting is *S. S. Teulon*'s WOODLANDS VALE HOTEL in Calthorpes. The house was built in 1870–1 for Lord Calthorpe, for whom Teulon had built Elvetham on the mainland ten years before. It was not a completely new building. The back is clearly pre-Teulon. Teulon has the typical freely shaped entrance tower with a high round staircase turret, and in front of it a half-timbered porte-cochère. The entrance side is screened towards the garden and the sea by an arched yellow-and-red-brick screen. The main garden front is quite asymmetrical, but the house was not complete in 1871. Dates of additions appear on various parts: 1880, 1894, 1912. Also there may be more pre-Teulon parts in different places. Is e.g. the iron veranda in front of the drawing room earlier than 1870? The drawing room has two bays, and they differ so oddly that older parts may be the explanation. *Minton* tiles on the corridor floor.

4080

ST CATHERINE'S DOWN

1–1½m. WNW of Niton

Near the S end of the down is the C14 LIGHTHOUSE, an octagonal tower with four buttresses and an eight-sided pyramid roof making it appear just like a rocket. Eight oblong top openings. Doorway to the N, and also a roof-line. In this direction an ORATORY existed, but this is only known from excavations. Near by a circular LIGHTHOUSE was begun in 1785, but not continued, as it was found more useful to move the lighthouse to the beach. Near the N end of the down is HOY'S MONUMENT, commemorating the visit of Tsar Alexander to Britain in 1814. The monument is a column 72 ft high and has a ball on top.

6080

ST HELENS

Of the OLD CHURCH the tower stands immediately by the sea. It is finished diagonally by a brick wall. All that lies beyond has been swallowed up. The tower has C13 details.

ST HELEN, 1 m. NW. Outside the village. Built in 1831, but the chancel is of 1862. Thin W tower, pointed windows with

Y-tracery in wood. No aisles, but transepts. – STAINED GLASS. S transept S evidently by *Powell*, *c.*1910. – PLATE. Set given in 1719. – MONUMENTS. Many tablets, notable amongst them Edward Grose † 1815. Inscription, with bundled trophies l. and r. By *W. Pistall*, New Road, London. – Sir Nash Grose † 1814. Lictor's fasces instead. Unsigned.

ST HELEN'S FORT. *See* Portsmouth, p. 421.

ST LAWRENCE *5070*

ST LAWRENCE. 1878 by *Sir G. G. Scott*, and indifferent, especially internally. Nave and chancel. Double bellcote on two W buttresses. – PLATE. Chalice, C17; two Chalices and a Paten, 1804; Paten, 1825.

OLD ST LAWRENCE, Seven Sisters Road, a little higher up the hill. Small (25 by 11 by 11 ft $4\frac{1}{2}$ in.), low, with a bellcote. Irregular windows of different dates. (Chancel 1842. NT)

WOOLVERTON MANOR, $\frac{3}{8}$ m. SW of the new church. In the grounds the ruin of a two-storeyed oblong medieval building, not orientated. It is not known what it was. In one gable-end is a long lancet.

SANDOWN *5080*

Sandown began to develop later than Shanklin and Ventnor, and there is less to see even now.

CHRIST CHURCH. Built in 1845, by *Woodman* of Reading (RH), but of that nothing has remained unchanged. Additions by Woodman 1861 and by *S. E. Tomkins* 1874. SW tower. Plate tracery and windows with pointed-trefoiled heads. Chancel arcades with rich capitals, stiff-leaf and naturalistic.

ST JOHN EVANGELIST, St John's Road. 1880–1 by *Luck*. E.E. W front with lancets. Tiled roof with a flèche. Wide brick interior. Narrow aisles, short chancel. An impressive church.

GOOD SHEPHERD, Lake, $\frac{3}{4}$ m. SW. 1892 by *Temple Moore*. Dec in style, with flowing tracery. The interesting motif is that the church is two-naved, but has one chancel with two chancel arches. The piers are very up-to-date for 1890. Square, placed diagonally, with chamfered angles. The W front shows the two naves, and has a low timber-framed porch between, overlapping both.

TOWN HALL, Grafton Street. 1869. Rendered and, at the time

of writing, shabby. With three pediments on giant columns, the middle one higher and wider.

The OCEAN HOTEL is probably the best individual building. Seven bays and three storeys, stuccoed. The first and last bays are singled out by paired pilasters. In one of them the high carriageway in. The first-floor windows of the middle five bays all have pediments. All this looks *c.*1850.

(PIERHEAD PAVILION. Modernistic, *c.*1935. NT)

6090 SEAVIEW

ST PETER. 1859. By *Hellyer* (RH). Nave and aisles and chancel. No tower. A humble interior. – SCREEN. Gothic, of iron, the sort of thing Gilbert Scott used, but in this case the date is 1909.

4080 SHALFLEET

CHURCH. Of the Norman age the impressively broad and short W tower, and the S doorway. The tower has clasping buttresses and a billet frieze, the doorway two orders of columns with decorated scallop capitals and a tympanum of disciplined composition. A bearded man in a lay robe grips by their heads two affronted lions, one of their heads in profile, the other frontal. But both have long tails sprouting out into ornamental forms almost as in Steinberg drawings. The S arcade is C13. Round piers, round abaci, double-chamfered arches dying into rounded vertical continuations of the piers. The piers were lengthened by putting a long piece in above the base. This was probably done when the S windows received their highly odd tracery. The most likely date for this sort of tracery is the C17, and indeed the REREDOS of the S aisle is dated 1630. It is still essentially Gothic, not Jacobean. At that time the W window, which is C13, was re-set high up. Why so high? Were there galleries? The chancel is all C13, see the bar tracery of the windows. The mullions are round in section, always an attractive thing. Only the small foiling is not original. The chancel arch goes with the windows, but the tower arch looks just a few decades later (the capitals). The nave N windows with their wooden intersecting tracery date from 1812. – PULPIT. Early C17, with a bookrest on brackets all round. The upper set of panels has arches in false perspective. – BOX PEWS. – PLATE. Two Patens, 1594; Chalice, 1798. – MONUMENTS. A series of Georgian tablets with urns.

(Vicarage. The MHLG reports that inside part of a C14 roof remains.)

SHANKLIN 5080

The old church and the manor house lie nearly half a mile away from the C19 centre, which is the centre of Shanklin as a seaside resort. The beginnings of this development were late. In 1846 Lord Jeffery still wrote: 'The village is very small and scattery.' In 1855 there were still mostly thatched cottages and low picturesque villas. The railway reached Shanklin in 1862. The Esplanade was built about 1865. Development down there was only one row deep. Behind rose the steep cliff. The lift was ori- 2
ginally built in 1891. The present LIFT, a very sensible concrete structure, dates from 1956.

St Blasius. Rebuilt in 1859. Nave and chancel and (later) long transept. The treatment of the timbers over the crossing and of the turret is reminiscent of Lamb. – PULPIT. With four Apostles and the Virgin, small panels, of *c.*1520–30, probably Flemish. – PLATE. Chalice and Paten, 1681–2; Paten, 1719; Paten, 1807. – MONUMENT. Sarah Popham † 1808. Relief of the young girl rising to heaven.

The Manor House close to the church is of no interest, but it has a simple stone SUMMER HOUSE of the C17. The so-called Village, a group of thatched cottages, is away a little to the E.

St Saviour, Queens Road. 1869–87 by *Thomas Hellyer* of Ryde. With a NW tower which turns octagonal higher up, while the buttresses stay square and end in pinnacles. The clerestory also is deliberately exceptional (cf. Cley in Norfolk). This and all the rest E.E. Uncomfortably thin arcades. – WAR MEMORIAL ALTAR. By *Macdonald Gill*, 1921. – (The Vicarage is by *Woodyer*, *c.*1870. RH)

St Paul, Regent Street. 1875–6 by *C. L. Luck*. NW tower with rustically open wooden top stage. Long tiled roof. Nave and aisles. E apse. All stone.

Sacred Heart (R.C.), Atherly Road. 1956 by *Gilbert & Hobson*. Brick, and with motifs ranging from the Coventry seesaw windows to a parabolic entrance arch.

Town Hall. 1879 by *E. C. Cooper*. French Classical, i.e. with an upper portico of attached columns and plaques, ribbons, and other French C17 to C18 motifs. A more ambitious building than the Ventnor town hall.

DAISH'S HOTEL. This is typical of Shanklin: a small stone cottage first, with gable and bargeboards, and then, probably *c.*1870, a big three-storeyed addition.*

SHEAT MANOR *see* GATCOMBE

4080

SHORWELL

ST PETER. W tower with a recessed stone spire, renewed in the C17. Is the N chapel of *c.*1200, on the strength of the blocked round-headed doorway and the one lancet? The S doorway is a nice, simple early C13 piece. Otherwise mostly Perp. The tower is vaulted inside with a tierceron-star vault. Clumsy three-bay arcades, on the N side interrupted by the original stone PULPIT with its doorway. Two-bay chapel arcades. No division between nave and chancel. – PULPIT. *See* above. The wooden tester is dated 1620. – On the pulpit a C17 HOUR-GLASS. – FONT COVER. Handsome, Jacobean, not florid. – SCULPTURE. Small Netherlandish Early Renaissance panel of the Flagellation of Christ. – PAINTINGS. St Christopher, nave N side, mid C15. The legend of the saint takes place in small figures l. and r. In the middle his large figure wading through the water. Entertaining fishes and ships. Also the fisherman who goes back iconographically all the way to Giotto's 'Navicella'. – Last Supper, painted on board, rustically. C16, from Iceland. – PLATE. Chalice of 1569. – MONUMENTS. Richard Bethell † 1518, vicar. Brass figure, 20 in long. – Brass plate to the two wives of Barnaby Leigh † 1615 and † 1619. They stand and together hold his heart. Scrolls with inscriptions surround them. – Lady Elizabeth Leigh † 1619. Big monument without effigy. Only on the top two putti with instruments of death. Otherwise strapwork and inscriptions. – John Leigh † 1629 and his baby son. Two kneeling figures, the baby miniature, yet fully dressed and kneeling. He died at nine months. High substructure. Columns l. and r. of the kneelers. – John Leigh † 1688. Fine writing-master's flourishes: garlands l. and r.

NORTH COURT, N of the church. The manor house of the Leighs. The E front is symmetrical and has the date 1615 on the porch. One bay with cross-window, one canted bay window with mullioned and transomed windows, topped by a surfeit of obelisks, one cross-window, porch, and the same the

* Opposite, No. 1 Eastcliffe Road is an early thatched house with bargeboards.

other side. Three top gables. The last bay on the r. belongs to an extension which goes round the corner (N). This is gabled too, but the fenestration was completely changed in the early C18. Sash-windows in raised surrounds. The porch, however, is dated 1837, a removal of the main entrance from the E front. Inside, a fine spacious early C18 staircase with twisted, turned, and fluted balusters to each tread. Venetian window. The other rooms which have kept their decoration look rather 1730–40 than earlier. In one first-floor room a Jacobean overmantel of wood.

WEST COURT, ½ m. WSW. Mainly of 1579, but with Jacobean extensions. Irregular, except for one portion of the N front which is completely symmetrical. The architectural history of the house is not clear.

WOLVERTON MANOR, ⅝ m. SW. A very fine Elizabethan front on the E-plan. The end wings gabled, the porch with a flat top. The porch has a plain lozenge over the entrance, and the ground floor of the front of the r. wing has the same. The upper part of the porch is flanked by thin polygonal angle-shafts, the sides concave (cf. Clifton Maybank, now at Montacute House). The windows are original in the r. half (mullions and transoms), sashed in the l. half.

Shorwell is a village rich in charming cottages, and lying handsomely below the downs.

SWAINSTON *see* CALBOURNE

SWANMORE *see* RYDE, p. 762

THORLEY

3080

ST SWITHIN. 1871 by *W. J. Stratton.* The bellcote is a roguish piece. It sits E of the S porch on three buttresses, E, W, and S, is oblong, and has chamfered corners. The effect is demonstratively angular. The church is aisleless and has transepts, their entry arches lower than the chancel arch. The exterior is stone, the interior brick, yellow with red bands. In building the church some old material from the previous church (*see* below) was used. – FONT. Octagonal, on a strange base, called Jacobean by Kelly.

OLD CHURCH, ⅝ m. WNW. All that remains is the lower parts of the S porch tower. The strange thing is that it is buttressed not only to the outside, but also into the former nave.

THORLEY FARMHOUSE, by the old church. A perfect William-and-Mary house. Stone, two storeys, five bays, hipped roof. The wooden mullion-and-transom crosses are unfortunately not original. Oval windows l. and r. of the doorway, set vertically.

3080
TOTLAND

CHRIST CHURCH. 1875 by *Habershon & Pite*, additions of 1888 and the early C20. The original part must be the nave and chancel, now S aisle and chapel. Polygonal N vestry.

ST SAVIOUR (R.C.), ¼ m. E. 1923 by *Wilfrid Mangan*. Red brick, with a NW tower with exaggeratedly projecting eaves. Round-arched windows, i.e. Early Christian to Italian Romanesque. Internally and also externally a tiresome play with brick patterns.

5070
VENTNOR

Ventnor as a resort started later than Ryde, but earlier than Shanklin. It was James Clark's book of 1841 which drew attention to Ventnor and its mild climate. Until then there had been cottages and a few large houses, the principal being Steephill Castle (*see* below). In 1842–3 the road to Bonchurch was built. In 1844 a bill for improvements was passed. In 1848 the Esplanade was made down in the cove. Much still remains of the mid C19 character. The best individual building is the KING CHARLES HOTEL, Grove Road, which must essentially date from *c.*1850 and is quietly classical. A typical town house is Messrs Pittis's in the HIGH STREET, with a five-bay centre and gables. Another, further out, is the MANOR HOUSE, by St Catherine's church, thatched, gabled, and bargeboarded. The centre of Ventnor up the steep cliffside is intricate in its layout.

ST CATHERINE. 1837 by *R. Ebbels*, paid for by John Hambrough of Steephill Castle. The chancel followed in 1849, the S aisle in 1897. The original building had big lancets. Inside, two of the three galleries are left, in decidedly Victorian forms. – MONUMENT. Benjamin Freeman Coleman † 1838. By *R. Brown*. A big sarcophagus.

HOLY TRINITY. 1860–2 by *C. E. Giles* of Taunton. The first church of Ventnor, the health resort. The NW tower turns octagonal and very shafted E.E. higher up. In the part below a stair-turret accompanies the tower. Plate tracery. The arcades differ one from the other. The chancel ends in a five-light window with geometrical tracery. (The interior is a perfect period piece with much foliage carving and a complete scheme of STAINED GLASS by *Clayton & Bell*. – SCREEN. 1912 by *C. R. Baker-King*. NT)

ST MARGARET, Lowtherville. 1882. By *T. R. Saunders* (RH).

OUR LADY AND ST WILFRID (R.C.), Trinity Road. 1871 by *J. Clarke*, doubled in size in the early C20. – (STAINED GLASS. The W window by *O'Connor*, strong and large in scale. NT)

CONGREGATIONAL CHURCH, High Street. 1836. This is now the church hall. Plain pointed windows. The new church with bar tracery is of 1853–4 by *Raffles Brown* of Liverpool. It was enlarged in 1872.

TOWN HALL. 1877–8 by *T. R. Saunders*. Kelly says: built by a limited liability company. Unprominent. Classical with columns and arched windows.

ALBERT HALL, Victoria Street. Now Youth Centre. 1887, but in style still 1860s Gothic, in yellow and red brick. Big rose window in the façade. The whole is like a Nonconformist chapel.

(WINTER GARDENS. 1935 by *A. D. Clare*. Inspired by Bexhill, a brave attempt. NT)

SCHOOL, Albert Street. Built in 1859. Very Gothic. By *Charles Turner* (RH).

NATIONAL HOSPITAL FOR DISEASES OF THE CHEST, Steephill Road. 1868–71 by *Thomas Hellyer*. Tudor, but with a French pavilion tower. Some motifs Gothic, some Elizabethan. To the S a row of many small gables. The chapel is Gothic, Perp, with a N tower. Additions of 1885 and later. – (STAINED GLASS. By *Morris & Co.*, 1873, and by *Sir William Reynolds Stephens*, 1892. The latter is in its designer's memorable Art Nouveau style, in strong green, purple, white, and red, with bold leading – all very different from Morris. NT)

STEEPHILL CASTLE, the principal mansion of Ventnor, was built by *Sanderson* c.1828 and pulled down in 1964.

As a tailpiece to Ventnor, here is what Paxton said of Steephill Castle: 'I have visited nearly every place of note from Stockholm to Constantinople, but never have I seen anything more beautiful than this.'

WEST COURT *see* SHORWELL

WEST COWES *see* COWES

5090

WHIPPINGHAM

85 ST MILDRED. The Osborne estate church. The chancel was built in 1854–5, the rest in 1861–2. The architect was *Albert Jenkins Humbert*, architect of Sandringham and the two mausolea at Windsor. Prince Albert is said to have been in charge. It is a weird design, especially the crossing tower, square and big, E.E., with on each side a row of six blank arches with thin lancets set in, a parapet with four square pinnacles, then a kind of truncated pyramid and an eight-sided lantern and spire. Otherwise the chancel is E.E. too, but the nave and transepts are Norman, though the transepts have Early Gothic rose windows, and Norman or rather Italian Romanesque is the porch to the Royal Pew also. Aisleless nave, the crossing tower dramatically open to the upper windows. The chancel opens in six bays on a screen wall to the S into the Royal Pew, to the N into a memorial chapel. – FONT. A Greek Doric column and a small unadorned square bowl on it. Is it by *Nash*? – The new FONT is by *Princess Louise*. – SCULPTURE. In the porch W wall remains of a Norman tympanum or lintel with a tree of life and two affronted quadrupeds (with men riding on them ?). – On the E wall of the porch also short lengths of zigzag and billet. – PAINTING. *Sir John Lavery*'s The Supreme Sacrifice, popularly famous as The Angel of Mons. – PLATE. Set presented 1856; Set owned by Princess Beatrice, silver-gilt; two Candlesticks and a Cross, given by Princess Beatrice. – MONUMENTS. Memorial to Prince Albert, 1864 by *Humbert* and *W. Theed*. Elaborate Gothic surround. Inside two angels and the medallion of the deceased. – Grand-Duchess of Hesse † 1878. By *F. Theed*, 1879. Two kneeling angels holding a medallion. – Duke of Albany † 1884. Profile head in a wreath. – Prince Henry of Battenberg † 1896. Large white tomb-chest with a sword on top. The splendidly Art Nouveau metal GRILLE is by *Alfred Gilbert*, 1897. – Sir Henry Ponsonby † 1898. By Countess *Feodora Gleichen*.

ALMSHOUSES. Built in 1880 by order of Queen Victoria for retired royal servants. Warm red brick. A symmetrical group, but very varied all the same. The porches e.g. of one and eight, of two-three and six-seven, and of four-five are managed in three different ways. There are plenty of gables as well, also asymmetrical and also of different heights. Pretty glazing.

WHITECROFT HOSPITAL *see* NEWPORT

WHITWELL

5070

THE BLESSED VIRGIN AND ST RADEGUND. This was really two chapels side by side, and St Radegund ought to come first; for the chapel arch has a N respond which is Norman, with scalloped capitals. The Chapel of the Virgin was then added about 1200. Three-bay arcade, round piers, square abaci with chamfered corners, single-chamfered arches. The arch to the E of the arcade is Perp, but there appears never to have been a structural division between nave and chancel. Perp W tower with big battlements, Perp N windows, Perp S porch with a pointed tunnel-vault on two chamfered transverse arches. The interior of the church was much restored by *R. J. Jones* (Rev. Basil Clarke). – PULPIT. 1623. The top panels small with arabesques, the bottom panels with the usual short blank arches. – (STAINED GLASS. By *Lavers & Barraud*. RH)

WOLVERTON MANOR *see* SHORWELL

WOOLVERTON MANOR *see* ST LAWRENCE

WOOTTON

5090

ST EDMUND. Nave and chancel and bellcote. Norman S doorway with one order of shafts with single-scallop capitals, zigzag in the arch, and billet in the hood-mould. Outline of the N doorway as well. N chapel of one bay also C12, but later. Semicircular respond, multi-scalloped capital. Pointed arch with one chamfer and one slight chamfer. E.E. chancel with lancets and one low-side lancet. – FONT. Baluster stem, the bowl with flat leaves. – PULPIT. Jacobean, with back panel and tester. – STAINED GLASS. E by *Kempe*, 1894. – PLATE. Almsdish, 1644; silver-gilt Chalice and Paten, 1787. – MONUMENT. Mary Rockfort † 1819. By *Coade & Sealy*. The Coade stone surface is at once recognizable. The usual female by an urn. Cherub's head at the foot.

WROXALL

5070

ST JOHN. 1875–7, and poor stuff. By *T. R. Saunders* (RH). Plate tracery. The SW porch tower with its steep pyramid roof and obtrusive lucarnes is of 1911 – an almost unbelievable date.

3080

YARMOUTH

Yarmouth in the earlier Middle Ages was the most important town in the Isle of Wight. It received its first charter about 1135. In the later Middle Ages the town declined, and by *c.*1800 it had under a hundred inhabitants.

ST JAMES. W tower with an upper part with long lancets. This is by *Daniel Asher Alexander*, 1831. The rest of the church was rebuilt from 1635. Homely interior. Four-bay arcades, octagonal piers. The Holmes Chapel at the SE end is of the late C17. Brick and a fine doorcase from the church. Broad bolection moulding. Open pediment, the open sides ending in scrolls. The chapel was built for the MONUMENT to Sir Robert Holmes, Governor of the Isle of Wight from 1667 to his death. The surround and especially the columns very rustic, but the white statue accomplished. The reason is that this is a French statue appropriated by Sir Robert and provided with his own, indeed not entirely fitting, head. Contemporary iron GRILLE too.

CASTLE. This is one of the chain of castles built by Henry VIII to defend the S coast of England against France. Their immediate cause was the reconciliation of France and the Holy Roman Empire in 1538. Cowes Castle on the Isle of Wight and Calshot and Hurst Castles on the mainland also belong to this chain. Yarmouth Castle was completed about 1547. The builder was *George Mills*, but we do not know whether he was also the designer (cf. Hurst). Henry VIII's castles differ from earlier castles by being designed for the use of cannon, a re-thinking of defence first done in Italy in the C15. Towers were no longer any use. Instead there are low bastions to mount cannon. Yarmouth Castle is different from the others just named by being square and provided with only one bastion. And whereas the normal bastions of Henry VIII are rounded, that of Yarmouth is the shape of a pointed spade blade. This was an innovation of defensive design which was only coming in even on the Continent in the 1540s. The square shape is arrived at in an odd way. The whole N half is filled with earth to carry at second-floor level a platform for the heaviest guns. The sea washed the walls on the N and W sides. On the E and S sides originally was a moat. One enters from the S now, but originally the entrance was from the E. The arch here is four-centred with a double chamfer. Above are the arms of Henry VIII.

All this has no Renaissance motifs such as they were introduced at Hurst. Through the original as well as the present entry one reaches a small irregular courtyard. In the original gateway is a brick vault. Its s side is the range of living quarters of the castle, partly later C16, partly of 1632. The earlier part is the E half, which was the Master Gunner's House, the W half was tunnel-vaulted Gunners' Lodgings (one of them being now the entrance gateway) and above them the Long Room, the largest room in the castle. The original parapets are triangular in section, not rounded as e.g. at Hurst. The original gunports are arched or straight-headed and can easily be picked out.*

There is little of note at Yarmouth. THE SQUARE, N of the church, has the TOWN HALL, built in 1763 by Thomas Lord Holmes, Governor of the Isle. Brick, three bays, two storeys, the ground-floor arches originally open. Hipped roof. Several other attractive houses. The HIGH STREET, which turns off E, is not at all high. Cottages l. and r., and just one bigger house: THE TOWERS, early C19, with battlements and two towers. Further out on the road to Bouldnor THE MOUNT, a very original early C19 house of yellow brick. The entrance side is almost devoid of windows. Semicircular porch of Tuscan columns. One narrow window l., one r. A lunette window above. All the rest is decorated by blank arches in circles. Especially l. and r. of the centre there are two crazily elongated blank arches, and they seem to carry the pediment. Round the corner a five-bay front, the middle three in a wide bow, the first and last in giant blank arches.

From The Square the short QUAY STREET, and in it the GEORGE HOTEL, formerly the governor's house. Stone, seven bays, two storeys, hipped roof. Later doorway with Tuscan pilasters. But the staircase of three twisted balusters per step is original. The house must be of about 1700.‡ From the end of Quay Street THE QUAY returns S. Nice cottages – no more. E of the garden of the George Hotel is the YACHT CLUB, designed by *Aston Webb* and built in 1897 – a very pretty, quite intimate building.

YAVERLAND 6080

ST JOHN BAPTIST. Nave and chancel and bell-turret. The nave is Norman, cf. the S doorway, which has one order of columns

*For a more detailed description see the guide of the Ministry of Public Building and Works by S. E. Rigold.

‡W. C. F. G. Sheridan's *Guide to the Isle of Wight* of 1834 dates it 1671.

and a tympanum with a small chip-carved repeat pattern. Was it originally a normal tympanum, and was the middle three-quarters of the lintel cut out later? Or was it always like today? The arch has an odd motif of raised radial bars. The hood-mould has zigzag. The chancel arch is Norman too, but all new. In the nave S wall a recess which comes out externally as a projection. It has a two-light window with plate tracery, i.e. is of the later C13, and inside a big transverse arch crosses the inner splay. (N aisle and bell-turret by *Ewan Christian*, 1889. RH) – (REREDOS. By *C. E. Ponting*. Elaborate, with figures by *Frampton*. RH) – PLATE. Chalice of 1733; C18 Paten.

MANOR HOUSE. The house carries a date 1620. It is built on the H-plan, with gables and mullioned and transomed windows. The main front is symmetrical. Much restoration. (The principal staircase is original. NMR)

GLOSSARY

ABACUS: flat slab on the top of a capital (q.v.).

ABUTMENT: solid masonry placed to resist the lateral pressure of a vault.

ACANTHUS: plant with thick fleshy and scalloped leaves used as part of the decoration of a Corinthian capital (q.v.) and in some types of leaf carving.

ACHIEVEMENT OF ARMS: in heraldry, a complete display of armorial bearings.

ACROTERION: foliage-carved block on the end or top of a classical pediment.

ADDORSED: two human figures, animals, or birds, etc., placed symmetrically so that they turn their backs to each other.

AEDICULE, AEDICULA: framing of a window or door by columns and a pediment (q.v.).

AFFRONTED: two human figures, animals, or birds, etc., placed symmetrically so that they face each other.

AGGER: Latin term for the built-up foundations of Roman roads; also sometimes applied to the banks of hill-forts or other earthworks.

AMBULATORY: semicircular or polygonal aisle enclosing an apse (q.v.).

ANNULET: *see* Shaft-ring.

ANSE DE PANIER: *see* Arch, Basket.

ANTEPENDIUM: covering of the front of an altar, usually by textiles or metalwork.

ANTIS, IN: *see* Portico.

APSE: vaulted semicircular or polygonal end of a chancel or a chapel.

ARABESQUE: light and fanciful surface decoration using combinations of flowing lines, tendrils, etc., interspersed with vases, animals, etc.

ARCADE: range of arches supported on piers or columns, free-standing; or, BLIND ARCADE, the same attached to a wall.

ARCH: round-headed, i.e. semicircular; pointed, i.e. consisting of two curves, each drawn from one centre, and meeting in a point at the top; segmental, i.e. in the form of a segment;

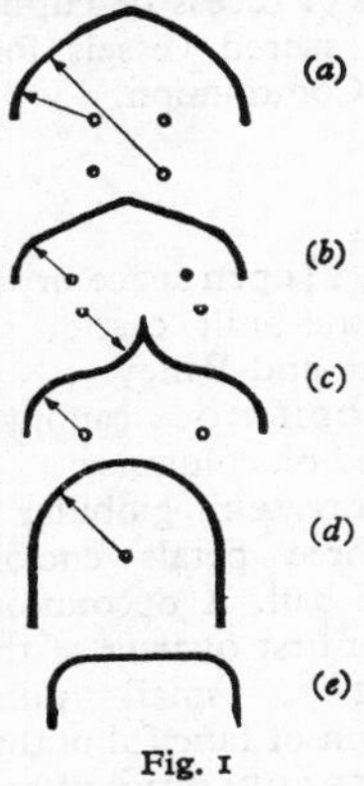

Fig. 1

pointed; four-centred (a Late Medieval form), *see* Fig. 1(*a*); Tudor (also a Late Medieval form), *see* Fig. 1(*b*); Ogee (introduced *c.* 1300 and specially popular in the C14), *see* Fig. 1(*c*); Stilted, *see* Fig. 1(*d*); Basket, with lintel connected to the jambs by concave quadrant curves, *see* Fig. 1(*e*).

ARCHITRAVE: lowest of the three main parts of the entablature (q.v.) of an order (q.v.) (*see* Fig. 12).

ARCHIVOLT: under-surface of an arch (also called Soffit).

ARRIS: sharp edge at the meeting of two surfaces.

ASHLAR: masonry of large blocks wrought to even faces and square edges.

ATLANTES: male counterparts of caryatids (q.v.).

ATRIUM: inner court of a Roman house, also open court in front of a church.

ATTACHED: *see* Engaged.

ATTIC: topmost storey of a house, if distance from floor to ceiling is less than in the others.

AUMBRY: recess or cupboard to hold sacred vessels for Mass and Communion.

BAILEY: open space or court of a stone-built castle; *see* also Motte-and-Bailey.

BALDACCHINO: canopy supported on columns.

BALLFLOWER: globular flower of three petals enclosing a small ball. A decoration used in the first quarter of the C14.

BALUSTER: small pillar or column of fanciful outline.

BALUSTRADE: series of balusters supporting a handrail or coping (q.v.).

BARBICAN: outwork defending the entrance to a castle.

BARGEBOARDS: projecting decorated boards placed against the incline of the gable of a building and hiding the horizontal roof timbers.

BARROW: *see* Bell, Bowl, Disc, Long, *and* Pond Barrow.

BASILICA: in medieval architecture an aisled church with a clerestory.

BASKET ARCH: *see* Arch (Fig. 1*e*).

BASTION: projection at the angle of a fortification.

BATTER: inclined face of a wall.

BATTLEMENT: parapet with a series of indentations or embrasures with raised portions or merlons between (also called Crenellation).

BAYS: internal compartments of a building; each divided from the other not by solid walls but by divisions only marked in the side walls (columns, pilasters, etc.) or the ceiling (beams, etc.). Also external divisions of a building by fenestration.

BAY-WINDOW: angular or curved projection of a house front with ample fenestration. If curved, also called bow-window; if on an upper floor only, also called oriel or oriel window.

BEAKER FOLK: Late New Stone Age warrior invaders from the Continent who buried their dead in round barrows and introduced the first metal tools and weapons to Britain.

BEAKHEAD: Norman ornamental motif consisting of a row of bird or beast heads with beaks biting usually into a roll moulding.

BELFRY: turret on a roof to hang bells in.

BELGAE: Aristocratic warrior bands who settled in Britain in two main waves in the C1 B.C.

In Britain their culture is termed Iron Age C.

BELL BARROW: Early Bronze Age round barrow in which the mound is separated from its encircling ditch by a flat platform or berm (q.v.).

BELLCOTE: framework on a roof to hang bells from.

BERM: level area separating ditch from bank on a hill-fort or barrow.

BILLET FRIEZE: Norman ornamental motif made up of short raised rectangles placed at regular intervals.

BIVALLATE: Of a hill-fort: defended by two concentric banks and ditches.

BLOCK CAPITAL: Romanesque capital cut from a cube by having the lower angles rounded off to the circular shaft below (also called Cushion Capital) (Fig. 2).

Fig. 2

BOND, ENGLISH or FLEMISH: *see* Brickwork.

BOSS: knob or projection usually placed to cover the intersection of ribs in a vault.

BOWL BARROW: round barrow surrounded by a quarry ditch. Introduced in Late Neolithic times, the form continued until the Saxon period.

BOW-WINDOW: *see* Bay-Window.

BOX: A small country house, e.g. a shooting box. A convenient term to describe a compact minor dwelling, e.g. a rectory.

BOX PEW: pew with a high wooden enclosure.

BRACES: *see* Roof.

BRACKET: small supporting piece of stone, etc., to carry a projecting horizontal.

BRESSUMER: beam in a timber-framed building to support the, usually projecting, superstructure.

BRICKWORK: *Header:* brick laid so that the end only appears on the face of the wall. *Stretcher:* brick laid so that the side only appears on the face of the wall. *English Bond:* method of laying bricks so that alternate courses or layers on the face of the wall are composed of headers or stretchers only (Fig. 3*a*). *Flemish Bond:* method of laying bricks so that alternate headers and stretchers appear in each course on the face of the wall (Fig. 3*b*).

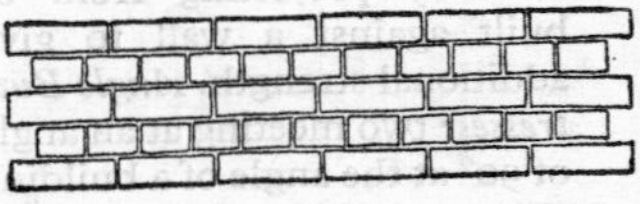

(*a*)

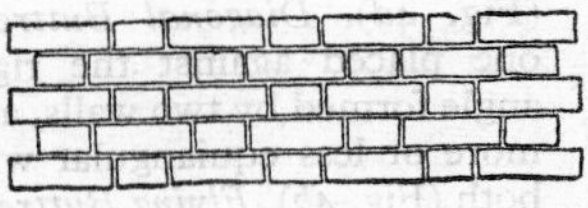

(*b*)

Fig. 3

BROACH: *see* Spire.

BROKEN PEDIMENT: *see* Pediment.

BRONZE AGE: In Britain, the period from *c.* 1600 to 600 B.C.

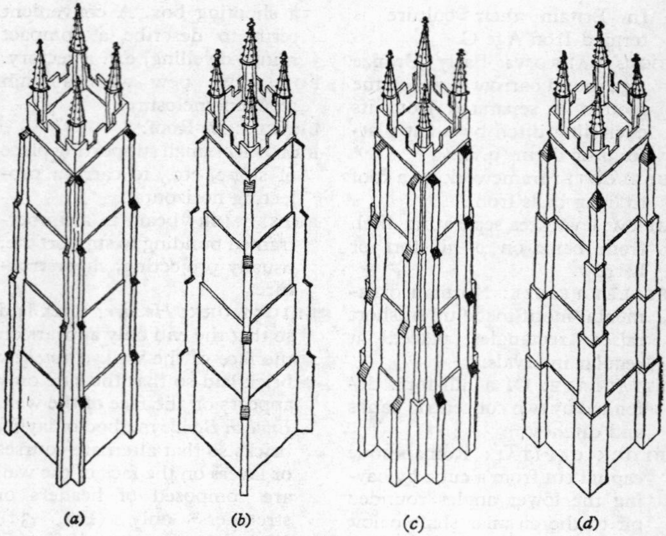

Fig. 4

BUCRANIUM: ox skull.

BUTTRESS: mass of brickwork or masonry projecting from or built against a wall to give additional strength. *Angle Buttresses:* two meeting at an angle of 90° at the angle of a building (Fig. 4*a*). *Clasping Buttress:* one which encases the angle (Fig. 4*d*). *Diagonal Buttress:* one placed against the right angle formed by two walls, and more or less equiangular with both (Fig. 4*b*). *Flying Buttress:* arch or half arch transmitting the thrust of a vault or roof from the upper part of a wall to an outer support or buttress. *Setback Buttress:* angle buttress set slightly back from the angle (Fig. 4*c*).

CABLE MOULDING: Norman moulding imitating a twisted cord.

CAIRN: a mound of stones usually covering a burial.

CAMBER: slight rise or upward curve of an otherwise horizontal structure.

CAMPANILE: isolated bell tower.

CANOPY: projection or hood over an altar, pulpit, niche, statue, etc.

CAP: in a windmill the crowning feature.

CAPITAL: head or top part of a column.

CARTOUCHE: tablet with an ornate frame, usually enclosing an inscription.

CARYATID: whole female figure

supporting an entablature or other similar member. *Termini Caryatids:* female busts or demi-figures or three-quarter figures supporting an entablature or other similar member and placed at the top of termini pilasters (q.v.). Cf. Atlantes.

CASTELLATED: decorated with battlements.

CELURE: panelled and adorned part of a wagon-roof above the rood or the altar.

CENSER: vessel for the burning of incense.

CENTERING: wooden framework used in arch and vault construction and removed when the mortar has set.

CHALICE: cup used in the Communion service or at Mass. *See also* Recusant Chalice.

CHAMBERED TOMB: burial mound of the New Stone Age having a stone-built chamber and entrance passage covered by an earthen barrow or stone cairn. The form was introduced to Britain from the Mediterranean.

CHAMFER: surface made by cutting across the square angle of a stone block, piece of wood, etc., at an angle of 45° to the other two surfaces.

CHANCEL: that part of the E end of a church in which the altar is placed, usually applied to the whole continuation of the nave E of the crossing.

CHANCEL ARCH: arch at the W end of the chancel.

CHANTRY CHAPEL: chapel attached to, or inside, a church, endowed for the saying of Masses for the soul of the founder or some other individual.

CHEVET: French term for the E end of a church (chancel, ambulatory, and radiating chapels).

CHEVRON: Norman moulding forming a zigzag.

CHOIR: that part of the church where divine service is sung.

CIBORIUM: a baldacchino.

CINQUEFOIL: *see* Foil.

CIST: stone-lined or slab-built grave. First appears in Late Neolithic times. It continued to be used in the Early Christian period.

CLAPPER BRIDGE: bridge made of large slabs of stone, some built up to make rough piers and other longer ones laid on top to make the roadway.

CLASSIC: here used to mean the moment of highest achievement of a style.

CLASSICAL: here used as the term for Greek and Roman architecture and any subsequent styles inspired by it.

CLERESTORY: upper storey of the nave walls of a church, pierced by windows.

COADE STONE: artificial (cast) stone made in the late C18 and the early C19 by Coade and Sealy in London.

COB: walling material made of mixed clay and straw.

COFFERING: decorating a ceiling with sunk square or polygonal ornamental panels.

COLLAR-BEAM: *see* Roof.

COLONNADE: range of columns.

COLONNETTE: small column.

COLUMNA ROSTRATA: column decorated with carved prows of ships to celebrate a naval victory.

COMPOSITE: *see* Order.

CONSOLE: bracket (q.v.) with a compound curved outline.

COPING: capping or covering to a wall.

CORBEL: block of stone projecting from a wall, supporting some horizontal feature.

CORBEL TABLE: series of corbels, occurring just below the roof eaves externally or internally, often seen in Norman buildings.

CORINTHIAN: *see* Orders.

CORNICE: in classical architecture the top section of the entablature (q.v.). Also for a projecting decorative feature along the top of a wall, arch, etc.

CORRIDOR VILLA: *see* Villa.

COUNTERSCARP BANK: small bank on the down-hill or outer side of a hill-fort ditch.

COURTYARD VILLA: *see* Villa.

COVE, COVING: concave undersurface in the nature of a hollow moulding but on a larger scale.

COVER PATEN: cover to a Communion cup, suitable for use as a paten or plate for the consecrated bread.

CRADLE ROOF: *see* Wagon roof.

CRENELLATION: *see* Battlement.

CREST, CRESTING: ornamental finish along the top of a screen, etc.

CRINKLE-CRANKLE WALL: undulating wall.

CROCKET, CROCKETING: decorative features placed on the sloping sides of spires, pinnacles, gables, etc., in Gothic architecture, carved in various leaf shapes and placed at regular intervals.

CROCKET CAPITAL: *see* Fig. 5. An Early Gothic form.

CROMLECH: word of Celtic origin still occasionally used of single free-standing stones ascribed to the Neolithic or Bronze Age periods.

Fig. 5

CROSSING: space at the intersection of nave, chancel, and transepts.

CROSS-WINDOWS: windows with one mullion and one transom.

CRUCK: big curved beam supporting both walls and roof of a cottage.

CRYPT: underground room usually below the E end of a church.

CUPOLA: small polygonal or circular domed turret crowning a roof.

CURTAIN WALL: connecting wall between the towers of a castle.

CUSHION CAPITAL: *see* Block Capital.

CUSP: projecting point between the foils in a foiled Gothic arch.

DADO: decorative covering of the lower part of a wall.

DAGGER: tracery motif of the Dec style. It is a lancet shape rounded or pointed at the head, pointed at the foot, and cusped inside (*see* Fig. 6).

Fig. 6

DAIS: raised platform at one end of a room.

DEC ('DECORATED'): historical division of English Gothic architecture covering the period from *c.*1290 to *c.*1350.

DEMI-COLUMNS: columns half sunk into a wall.

DIAPER WORK: surface decoration composed of square or lozenge shapes.

DISC BARROW: Bronze Age round barrow with inconspicuous central mound surrounded by bank and ditch.

DOGTOOTH: typical E.E. ornament consisting of a series of four-cornered stars placed diagonally and raised pyramidally (Fig. 7).

Fig. 7

DOMICAL VAULT: *see* Vault.

DONJON: *see* Keep.

DORIC: *see* Order.

DORMER (WINDOW): window placed vertically in the sloping plane of a roof.

DRIPSTONE: *see* Hood-mould.

DRUM: circular or polygonal vertical wall of a dome or cupola.

E.E. ('EARLY ENGLISH'): historical division of English Gothic architecture roughly covering the C13.

EASTER SEPULCHRE: recess with tomb-chest usually in the wall of a chancel, the tomb-chest to receive an effigy of Christ for Easter celebrations.

EAVES: underpart of a sloping roof overhanging a wall.

EAVES CORNICE: cornice below the eaves of a roof.

ECHINUS: Convex or projecting moulding supporting the abacus of a Greek Doric capital, sometimes bearing an egg and dart pattern.

EMBATTLED: *see* Battlement.

EMBRASURE: small opening in the wall or parapet of a fortified building, usually splayed on the inside.

ENCAUSTIC TILES: earthenware glazed and decorated tiles used for paving.

ENGAGED COLUMNS: columns attached to, or partly sunk into, a wall.

ENGLISH BOND: *see* Brickwork.

ENTABLATURE: in classical architecture the whole of the horizontal members above a column (that is architrave, frieze, and cornice) (*see* Fig. 12).

ENTASIS: very slight convex deviation from a straight line; used on Greek columns and sometimes on spires to prevent an optical illusion of concavity.

ENTRESOL: *see* Mezzanine.

EPITAPH: hanging wall monument.

ESCUTCHEON: shield for armorial bearings.

EXEDRA: the apsidal end of a room. *See* Apse.

FAN-VAULT: *see* Vault.

FERETORY: place behind the high altar where the chief shrine of a church is kept.

FESTOON: carved garland of flowers and fruit suspended at both ends.

FILLET: narrow flat band running down a shaft or along a roll moulding.

FINIAL: top of a canopy, gable, pinnacle.

FLAGON: vessel for the wine used in the Communion service.

FLAMBOYANT: properly the latest phase of French Gothic architecture where the window tracery takes on wavy undulating lines.

FLÈCHE: slender wooden spire on the centre of a roof (also called Spirelet).

FLEMISH BOND: *see* Brickwork.

FLEURON: decorative carved flower or leaf.

FLUSHWORK: decorative use of flint in conjunction with dressed stone so as to form patterns: tracery, initials, etc.

FLUTING: vertical channelling in the shaft of a column.

FLYING BUTTRESS: *see* Buttress.

FOIL: lobe formed by the cusping (q.v.) of a circle or an arch. Trefoil, quatrefoil, cinquefoil, multifoil, express the number of leaf shapes to be seen.

FOLIATED: carved with leaf shapes.

FOSSE: ditch.

FOUR-CENTRED ARCH: *see* Arch.

FRATER: refectory or dining hall of a monastery.

FRESCO: wall painting on wet plaster.

FRIEZE: middle division of a classical entablature (q.v.) (*see* Fig. 12).

FRONTAL: covering for the front of an altar.

GABLE: *Dutch gable:* A gable with curved sides crowned by a pediment, characteristic of *c.*1630–50 (Fig. 8*a*). *Shaped gable:* A gable with multi-curved sides characteristic of *c.*1600–50 (Fig. 8*b*).

(*a*)

Fig. 8]

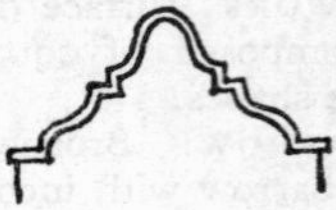

(*b*)

Fig. 8

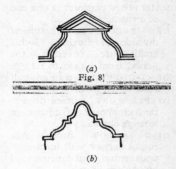

GADROONED: enriched with a series of convex ridges, the opposite of fluting.

GALILEE: chapel or vestibule usually at the W end of a church enclosing the porch. Also called Narthex (q.v.).

GALLERY: in church architecture upper storey above an aisle, opened in arches to the nave. Also called Tribune and often erroneously Triforium (q.v.).

GALLERY GRAVE: chambered tomb (q.v.) in which there is little or no differentiation between the entrance passage and the actual burial chamber(s).

GARDEROBE: lavatory or privy in a medieval building.

GARGOYLE: water spout projecting from the parapet of a wall or tower; carved into a human or animal shape.

GAZEBO: lookout tower or raised summer house in a picturesque garden.

'GEOMETRICAL': *see* Tracery.

'GIBBS SURROUND': of a doorway or window. An C18 motif consisting of a surround with alternating larger and smaller blocks of stone, quoin-wise, or intermittent large blocks, sometimes with a narrow raised band connecting them up the verticals and along the face of the arch (Fig. 9).

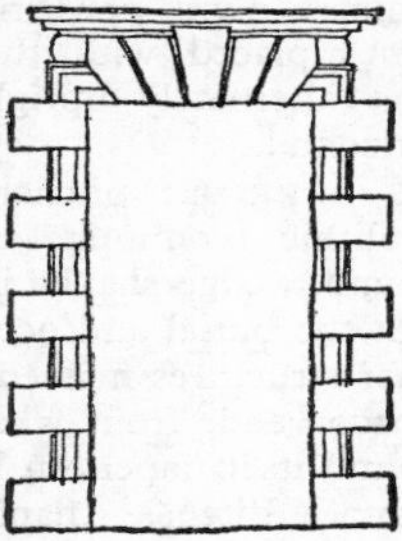

Fig. 9

GROIN: sharp edge at the meeting of two cells of a cross-vault.

GROIN-VAULT: *see* Vault.

GROTESQUE: fanciful ornamental decoration: *see* also Arabesque.

HAGIOSCOPE: *see* Squint.

HALF-TIMBERING: *see* Timber-Framing.

HALL CHURCH: church in which nave and aisles are of equal height or approximately so.

HAMMERBEAM: *see* Roof.

HANAP: large metal cup, generally made for domestic use, standing on an elaborate base and stem; with a very ornate cover frequently crowned with a little steeple.

HEADERS: *see* Brickwork.

HERRINGBONE WORK: brick, stone, or tile construction where the component blocks are laid diagonally instead of flat. Alternate courses lie in opposing directions to make a zigzag pattern up the face of the wall.

HEXASTYLE: having six detached columns.

HILL-FORT: Iron Age earthwork enclosed by a ditch and bank system; in the later part of the period the defences multiplied in size and complexity. They vary from about an acre to over 30 acres in area, and are usually built with careful regard to natural elevations or promontories.

HIPPED ROOF: *see* Roof.

HOOD-MOULD: projecting moulding above an arch or a lintel to throw off water (also called Dripstone or Label).

ICONOGRAPHY: the science of the subject matter of works of the visual arts.

IMPOST: bracket in a wall, usually formed of mouldings, on which the ends of an arch rest.

INDENT: shape chiselled out in a stone slab to receive a brass.

INGLENOOK: bench or seat built in beside a fireplace, sometimes covered by the chimneybreast, occasionally lit by small windows on each side of the fire.

INTERCOLUMNIATION: the space between columns.

IONIC: *see* Orders (Fig. 12).

IRON AGE: in Britain the period from *c.* 600 B.C. to the coming of the Romans. The term is also used for those un-Romanized native communities which survived until the Saxon incursions.

JAMB: straight side of an archway, doorway, or window.

KEEL MOULDING: moulding whose outline is in section like that of the keel of a ship.

KEEP: massive tower of a Norman castle.

KEYSTONE: middle stone in an arch or a rib-vault.

KING-POST: *see* Roof (Fig. 14).

KNOP: a knob-like thickening in the stem of a chalice.

LABEL: *see* Hood-mould.

LABEL STOP: ornamental boss at the end of a hood-mould (q.v.).

LACED WINDOWS: windows pulled visually together by strips, usually in brick of a different colour, which continue vertically the lines of the vertical parts of the window surrounds. The motif is typical of *c.* 1720.

LANCET WINDOW: slender pointed-arched window.

LANTERN: in architecture, a small circular or polygonal turret with windows all round crowning a roof (*see* Cupola) or a dome.

LANTERN CROSS: churchyard cross with lantern-shaped top usually with sculptured representations on the sides of the top.

LEAN-TO ROOF: roof with one slope only, built against a higher wall.

LESENE OR PILASTER STRIP: pilaster without base or capital.

LIERNE: *see* Vault (Fig. 21).

LINENFOLD: Tudor panelling ornamented with a conventional representation of a piece of linen laid in vertical folds. The piece is repeated in each panel.

LINTEL: horizontal beam or stone bridging an opening.

LOGGIA: recessed colonnade (q.v.).

LONG AND SHORT WORK: Saxon quoins (q.v.) consisting of stones placed with the long sides alternately upright and horizontal.

LONG BARROW: unchambered Neolithic communal burial mound, wedge-shaped in plan, with the burial and occasional other structures massed at the broader end, from which the mound itself tapers in height; quarry ditches flank the mound.

LOUVRE: opening, often with lantern (q.v.) over, in the roof of a room to let the smoke from a central hearth escape.

LOWER PALAEOLITHIC: *see* Palaeolithic.

LOZENGE: diamond shape.

LUCARNE: small opening to let light in.

LUNETTE: tympanum (q.v.) or semicircular opening.

LYCH GATE: wooden gate structure with a roof and open sides placed at the entrance to a churchyard to provide space for the reception of a coffin. The word *lych* is Saxon and means a corpse.

LYNCHET: long terraced strip of soil accumulating on the downward side of prehistoric and medieval fields due to soil creep from continuous ploughing along the contours.

MACHICOLATION: projecting gallery on brackets constructed on the outside of castle towers or walls. The gallery has holes in the floor to drop missiles through.

MAJOLICA: ornamented glazed earthenware.

MANSARD: *see* Roof.

MATHEMATICAL TILES: Small facing tiles the size of brick headers, applied to timber-framed walls to make them appear brick-built.

MEGALITHIC TOMB: stone-built burial chamber of the New Stone Age covered by an earth or stone mound. The form was introduced to Britain from the Mediterranean area.

MERLON: *see* Battlement.

MESOLITHIC: 'Middle Stone' Age; the post-glacial period of hunting and fishing communities dating in Britain from *c.* 8000 B.C. to the arrival of Neolithic communities, with which they must have considerably overlapped.

METOPE: in classical architecture of the Doric order (q.v.) the space in the frieze between the triglyphs (Fig. 12).

MEZZANINE: low storey placed between two higher ones.

MISERERE: *see* Misericord.

MISERICORD: bracket placed on the underside of a hinged choir stall seat which, when turned up, provided the occupant of the seat with a support during long periods of standing (also called Miserere).

MODILLION: small bracket of which large numbers (modillion frieze) are often placed below a cornice (q.v.) in classical architecture.

MOTTE: steep mound forming the main feature of C11 and C12 castles.

MOTTE-AND-BAILEY: post-Roman and Norman defence system consisting of an earthen mound (the motte) topped with a wooden tower eccentrically placed within a bailey (q.v.), with enclosure ditch and palisade, and with the rare addition of an internal bank.

MOUCHETTE: tracery motif in curvilinear tracery, a curved dagger (q.v.), specially popular in the early C14 (Fig. 10).

Fig. 10

MULLION: vertical post or upright dividing a window into two or more 'lights'.

MULTIVALLATE: Of a hill-fort: defended by three or more concentric banks and ditches.

MUNTIN: post as a rule moulded and part of a screen.

NAIL-HEAD: E.E. ornamental motif, consisting of small pyramids regularly repeated (Fig. 11).

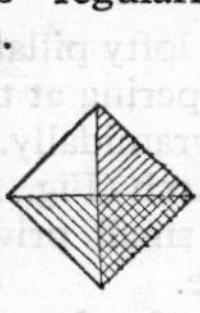

Fig. 11

NARTHEX: enclosed vestibule or covered porch at the main entrance to a church (*see* Galilee).

NEOLITHIC: 'New Stone' Age, dating in Britain from the appearance from the Continent of the first settled farming communities *c.* 3500 B.C. until the introduction of the Bronze Age.

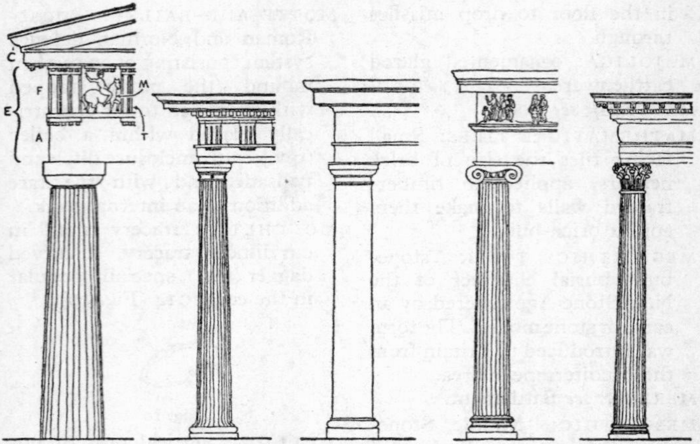

Fig. 12 – Orders of Columns (Greek Doric, Roman Doric, Tuscan Doric, Ionic, Corinthian) E, Entablature; C, Cornice; F, Frieze; A, Architrave; M, Metope; T, Triglyph.

NEWEL: central post in a circular or winding staircase; also the principal post when a flight of stairs meets a landing.

NOOK-SHAFT: shaft set in the angle of a pier or respond or wall, or the angle of the jamb of a window or doorway.

OBELISK: lofty pillar of square section tapering at the top and ending pyramidally.

OGEE: *see* Arch (Fig. 1*c*).

ORATORY: small private chapel in a house.

ORDER: (1) *of a doorway or window:* series of concentric steps receding towards the opening; (2) *in classical architecture:* column with base, shaft, capital, and entablature (q.v.) according to one of the following styles: Greek Doric, Roman Doric, Tuscan Doric, Ionic, Corinthian, Composite. The established details are very elaborate, and some specialist architectural work should be consulted for further guidance (*see* Fig. 12).

ORIEL: *see* Bay-Window.

OVERHANG: projection of the upper storey of a house.

OVERSAILING COURSES: series of stone or brick courses, each one projecting beyond the one below it.

PALAEOLITHIC: 'Old Stone' Age; the first period of human culture, commencing in the Ice Age and immediately prior to the Mesolithic; the Lower Palaeolithic is the older phase, the Upper Palaeolithic the later.

PALIMPSEST: (1) *of a brass:* where a metal plate has been re-used by turning over and engraving on the back; (2) *of a wall painting:* where one overlaps and partly obscures an earlier one.

PALLADIAN: architecture following the ideas and principles of Andrea Palladio, 1518–80.

PANTILE: tile of curved S-shaped section.

PARAPET: low wall placed to protect any spot where there is a sudden drop, for example on a bridge, quay, hillside, housetop, etc.

PARGETTING: plaster work with patterns and ornaments either in relief or engraved on it.

PARVIS: term wrongly applied to a room over a church porch. These rooms were often used as a schoolroom or as a store room.

PATEN: plate to hold the bread at Communion or Mass.

PATERA: small flat circular or oval ornament in classical architecture.

PEDIMENT: low-pitched gable used in classical, Renaissance, and neo-classical architecture above a portico and above doors, windows, etc. It may be straight-sided or curved segmentally. *Broken Pediment:* one where the centre portion of the base is left open. *Open Pediment:* one where the centre portion of the sloping sides is left out.

PENDANT: boss (q.v.) elongated so that it seems to hang down.

PENDENTIF: concave triangular spandrel used to lead from the angle of two walls to the base of a circular dome. It is constructed as part of the hemisphere over a diameter the size of the diagonal of the basic square (Fig. 13).

PERP (PERPENDICULAR): historical division of English Gothic architecture covering

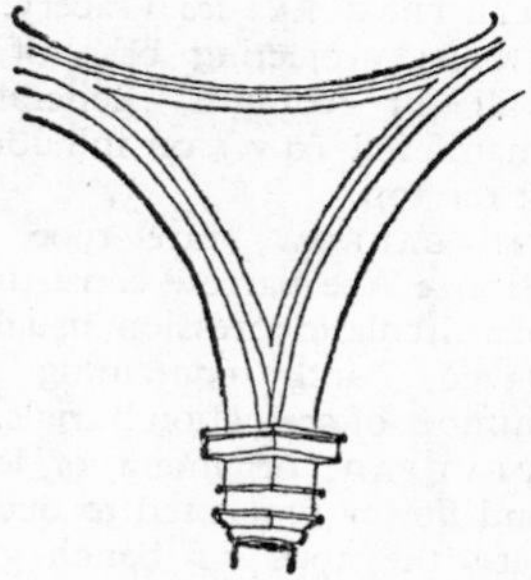

Fig. 13

the period from *c.*1335–50 to *c.*1530.

PIANO NOBILE: principal storey of a house with the reception rooms; usually the first floor.

PIAZZA: open space surrounded by buildings; in C17 and C18 England sometimes used to mean a long colonnade or loggia.

PIER: strong, solid support, frequently square in section or of composite section (compound pier).

PIETRA DURA: ornamental or scenic inlay by means of thin slabs of stone.

PILASTER: shallow pier attached to a wall. *Termini Pilasters:* pilasters with sides tapering downwards.

PILLAR PISCINA: free-standing piscina on a pillar.

PINNACLE: ornamental form crowning a spire, tower, buttress, etc., usually of steep pyramidal, conical, or some similar shape.

PISCINA: basin for washing the Communion or Mass vessels, provided with a drain. Generally set in or against the wall to the S of an altar.

PLAISANCE: summer-house, pleasure house near a mansion.

PLATE TRACERY: *see* Tracery.

PLINTH: projecting base of a wall or column, generally chamfered (q.v.) or moulded at the top.

POND BARROW: rare type of Bronze Age barrow consisting of a circular depression, usually paved, and containing a number of cremation burials.

POPPYHEAD: ornament of leaf and flower type used to decorate the tops of bench- or stall-ends.

PORTCULLIS: gate constructed to rise and fall in vertical grooves; used in gateways of castles.

PORTE COCHÈRE: porch large enough to admit wheeled vehicles.

PORTICO: centre-piece of a house or a church with classical detached or attached columns and a pediment. A portico is called *prostyle* or *in antis* according to whether it projects from or recedes into a building. In a portico *in antis* the columns range with the side walls.

POSTERN: small gateway at the back of a building.

PREDELLA: in an altarpiece the horizontal strip below the main representation, often used for a number of subsidiary representations in a row.

PRESBYTERY: the part of the church lying E of the choir. It is the part where the altar is placed.

PRINCIPAL: *see* Roof (Fig. 14).

PRIORY: monastic house whose head is a prior or prioress, not an abbot or abbess.

PROSTYLE: with free-standing columns in a row.

PULPITUM: stone screen in a major church provided to shut off the choir from the nave and also as a backing for the return choir stalls.

PULVINATED FRIEZE: frieze with a bold convex moulding.

PURLIN: *see* Roof (Figs. 14, 15).

PUTTO: small naked boy.

QUADRANGLE: inner courtyard in a large building.

QUARRY: in stained-glass work, a small diamond or square-shaped piece of glass set diagonally.

QUATREFOIL: *see* Foil.

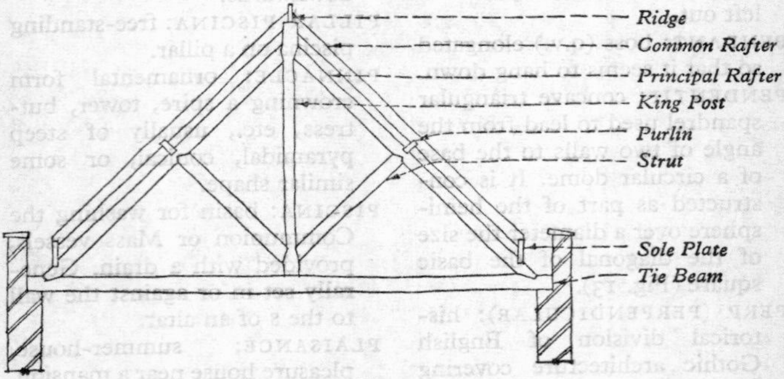

Fig. 14

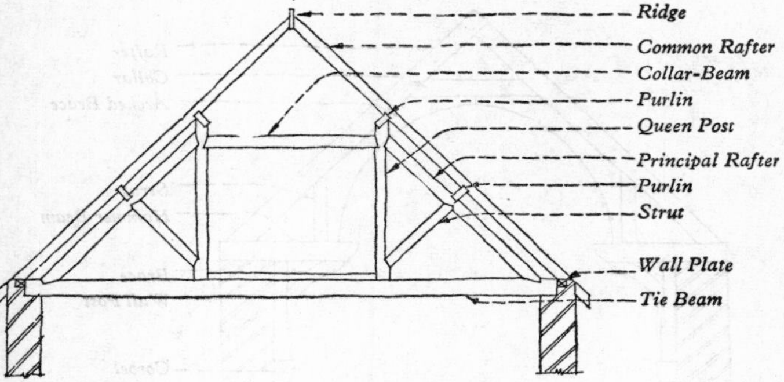

Fig. 15

QUEEN-POSTS: *see* Roof (Fig. 15).

QUOINS: dressed stones at the angles of a building. Sometimes all the stones are of the same size; more often they are alternately large and small.

RADIATING CHAPELS: chapels projecting radially from an ambulatory or an apse.

RAFTER: *see* Roof.

RAMPART: stone wall or wall of earth surrounding a castle, fortress, or fortified city.

RAMPART-WALK: path along the inner face of a rampart.

REBATE: continuous rectangular notch cut on an edge.

REBUS: pun, a play on words. The literal translation and illustration of a name for artistic and heraldic purposes (Belton = bell, tun).

RECUSANT CHALICE: chalice made after the Reformation and before Catholic Emancipation for Roman Catholic use.

REEDING: decoration with parallel convex mouldings touching one another.

REFECTORY: dining hall; *see* Frater.

RENDERING: plastering of an outer wall.

REPOUSSÉ: decoration of metal work by relief designs, formed by beating the metal from the back.

REREDOS: structure behind and above an altar.

RESPOND: half-pier bonded into a wall and carrying one end of an arch.

RETABLE: altarpiece, a picture or piece of carving, standing behind and attached to an altar.

RETICULATION: *see* Tracery (Fig. 20).

REVEAL: that part of a jamb (q.v.) which lies between the glass or door and the outer surface of the wall.

RIB-VAULT: *see* Vault.

ROCOCO: latest phase of the Baroque style, current in most Continental countries between *c.*1720 and *c.* 1760.

ROLL MOULDING: moulding of semicircular or more than semicircular section.

ROMANESQUE: that style in

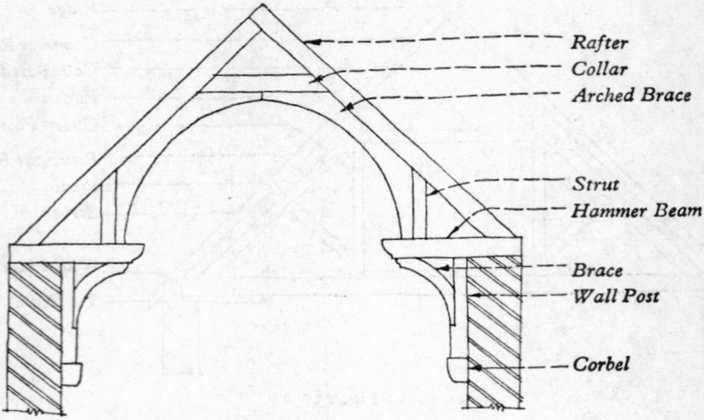

Fig. 16

architecture which was current in the C11 and C12 and preceded the Gothic style (in England often called Norman). (Some scholars extend the use of the term Romanesque back to the C10 or C9.)

ROMANO-BRITISH: A somewhat vague term applied to the period and cultural features of Britain affected by the Roman occupation of the C1–5 A.D.

ROOD: cross or crucifix.

ROOD LOFT: singing gallery on the top of the rood screen, often supported by a coving.

ROOD SCREEN: *see* Screen.

ROOD STAIRS: stairs to give access to the rood loft.

ROOF: *Single-framed:* if consisting entirely of transverse members (such as rafters with or without braces, collars, tie-beams, king-posts or queen-posts, etc.) not tied together longitudinally. *Double-framed:* if longitudinal members (such as a ridge beam and purlins) are employed. As a rule in such cases the rafters are divided into stronger principals and weaker subsidiary rafters. *Hipped:* roof with sloped instead of vertical ends. *Mansard:* roof with a double slope, the lower slope being larger and steeper than the upper. *Saddle-back:* tower roof shaped like an ordinary gabled timber roof. The following members have special names: *Rafter:* roof-timber sloping up from the wall plate to the ridge. *Principal:* principal rafter, usually corresponding to the main bay divisions of the nave or chancel below. *Wall Plate:* timber laid longitudinally on the top of a wall. *Purlin:* longitudinal member laid parallel with wall plate and ridge beam some way up the slope of the roof. *Tie-beam:* beam connecting the two slopes of a roof across at its foot, usually at the height of the wall plate, to prevent the roof from spreading. *Collar-beam:* tie-beam applied higher up the slope of the roof. *Strut:* upright timber connecting the tie-beam with the rafter above it. *King-post:* upright timber connecting a tie-beam and collar-beam with the ridge beam. *Queen-posts:* two struts placed symmetrically on a tie-beam or collar-beam. *Braces:* inclined timbers inserted to strengthen others. Usually braces connect a collar-beam with the rafters below or a tie-beam with the wall below. Braces can be straight or curved (also called arched). *Hammer-beam:* beam projecting at right angles, usually from the top of a wall, to carry arched braces or struts and arched braces (*see* Figs. 14, 15, 16).

ROSE WINDOW (or WHEEL WINDOW: circular window with patterned tracery arranged to radiate from the centre.

ROTUNDA: building circular in plan.

RUBBLE: building stones, not square or hewn, nor laid in regular courses.

RUSTICATION: *rock-faced* if the surfaces of large blocks of ashlar stone are left rough like rock; *smooth* if the ashlar blocks are smooth and separated by V-joints; *banded* if the separation by V-joints applies only to the horizontals.

SADDLEBACK: *see* Roof.

SALTIRE CROSS: equal-limbed cross placed diagonally.

SANCTUARY: (1) area around the main altar of a church (*see* Presbytery); (2) sacred site consisting of wood or stone uprights enclosed by a circular bank and ditch. Beginning in the Neolithic, they were elaborated in the succeeding Bronze Age. The best known examples are Stonehenge and Avebury.

SARCOPHAGUS: elaborately carved coffin.

SCAGLIOLA: material composed of cement and colouring matter to imitate marble.

SCALLOPED CAPITAL: development of the block capital (q.v.) in which the single semicircular surface is elaborated into a series of truncated cones (Fig. 17).

Fig. 17

SCARP: artificial cutting away of the ground to form a steep slope.

SCREEN: *Parclose screen:* screen separating a chapel from the rest of a church. *Rood screen:* screen below the rood (q.v.), usually at the W end of a chancel.

SCREENS PASSAGE: passage between the entrances to kitchen, buttery, etc., and the screen behind which lies the hall of a medieval house.

SEDILLA: seats for the priests (usually three) on the S side of the chancel of a church.

SEGMENTAL ARCH: *see* Arch.

SET-OFF: *see* Weathering.

SEXPARTITE: *see* Vault.

SGRAFFITO: pattern incised into plaster so as to expose a dark surface underneath.

SHAFT-RING: motif of the C12 and C13 consisting of a ring round a circular pier or a shaft attached to a pier.

SHEILA-NA-GIG: fertility figure, usually with legs wide open.

SILL: lower horizontal part of the frame of a window.

SLATEHANGING: the covering of walls by overlapping rows of slates, on a timber substructure.

SOFFIT: underside of an arch, lintel, etc.

SOLAR: upper living-room of a medieval house.

SOPRAPORTE: painting above the door of a room, usual in the C17 and C18.

SOUNDING BOARD: horizontal board or canopy over a pulpit. Also called Tester.

SPANDREL: triangular surface between one side of an arch, the horizontal drawn from its apex, and the vertical drawn from its springer; also the surface between two arches.

SPERE-TRUSS: roof truss on two free-standing posts to mask the division between screens passage and hall. The screen itself, where a spere-truss exists, was originally movable.

SPIRE: tall pyramidal or conical pointed erection often built on top of a tower, turret, etc. *Broach Spire:* spire which is generally octagonal in plan rising from the top or parapet of a square tower. A small inclined piece of masonry covers the vacant triangular space at each of the four angles of the square and is carried up to a point along the diagonal sides of the octagon. *Needle Spire:* thin spire rising from the centre of a tower roof, well inside the parapet.

SPIRELET: *see* Flèche.

SPLAY: chamfer, usually of the jamb of a window.

SPRINGING: level at which an arch rises from its supports.

SQUINCH: arch or system of concentric arches thrown across the angle between two walls to support a superstructure, for example a dome (Fig. 18).

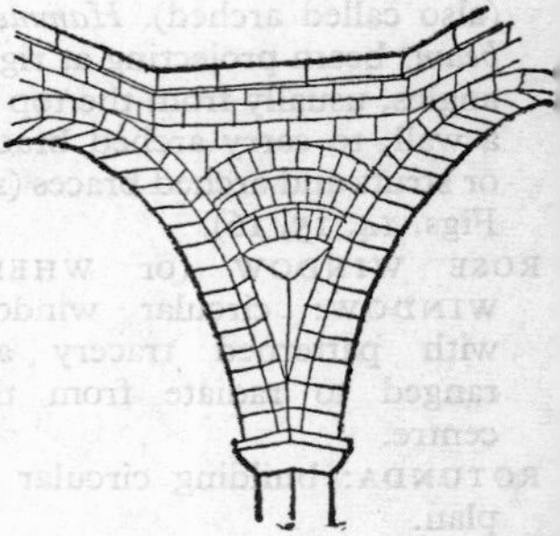

Fig. 18

SQUINT: hole cut in a wall or through a pier to allow a view of the main altar of a church from places whence it could not otherwise be seen (also called Hagioscope).

STALL: carved seat, one of a row, made of wood or stone.

STAUNCHION: upright iron or steel member.

STEEPLE: the tower of a church together with a spire, cupola, etc.

STIFF-LEAF: E.E. type of foliage of many-lobed shapes (Fig. 19).

STILTED: *see* Arch.

STOREY-POSTS: the principal posts of a timber-framed wall.

STOUP: vessel for the reception of holy water, usually placed near a door.

Fig. 19

STRAINER ARCH: arch inserted across a room to prevent the walls from leaning.

STRAPWORK: C16 decoration consisting of interlaced bands, and forms similar to fretwork or cut and bent leather.

STRETCHER: *see* Brickwork.

STRING COURSE: projecting horizontal band or moulding set in the surface of a wall.

STRUT: *see* Roof.

STUCCO: plaster work.

STUDS: the subsidiary vertical timber members of a timber-framed wall.

SWAG: festoon formed by a carved piece of cloth suspended from both ends.

TABERNACLE: richly ornamented niche or free-standing canopy. Usually contains the Holy Sacrament.

TARSIA: inlay in various woods.

TAZZA: shallow bowl on a foot.

TERMINAL FIGURES (TERMS, TERMINI): upper part of a human figure growing out of a pier, pilaster, etc., which tapers towards the base. *See also* Caryatid, Pilaster.

TERRACOTTA: burnt clay, unglazed.

TESSELLATED PAVEMENT: mosaic flooring, particularly Roman, consisting of small 'tesserae' or cubes of glass, stone, or brick.

TESSERAE: *see* Tessellated Pavement.

TESTER: *see* Sounding Board.

TETRASTYLE: having four detached columns.

THREE-DECKER PULPIT: pulpit with Clerk's Stall below and Reading Desk below the Clerk's Stall.

TIE-BEAM: *see* Roof (Figs. 14, 15).

TIERCERON: *see* Vault (Fig. 21).

TILEHANGING: *see* Slatehanging.

TIMBER-FRAMING: method of construction where walls are built of timber framework with the spaces filled in by plaster or brickwork. Sometimes the timber is covered over with plaster or boarding laid horizontally.

TOMB-CHEST: chest-shaped stone coffin, the most usual medieval form of funeral monument.

TOUCH: soft black marble quarried near Tournai.

TOURELLE: turret corbelled out from the wall.

TRACERY: intersecting ribwork in the upper part of a window, or used decoratively in blank arches, on vaults, etc. *Plate tracery: see* Fig. 20(*a*). Early form of tracery where decoratively shaped openings are cut through the solid stone infilling in a window head. *Bar tracery:* a form introduced into England *c.*1250. Intersecting ribwork made up of slender shafts, continuing the lines of the mullions of windows up to a decorative mesh in the head of the window. *Geometrical tracery: see* Fig. 20(*b*). Tracery characteristic of *c.*1250–1310 consisting chiefly of circles or foiled circles. *Y-tracery: see*

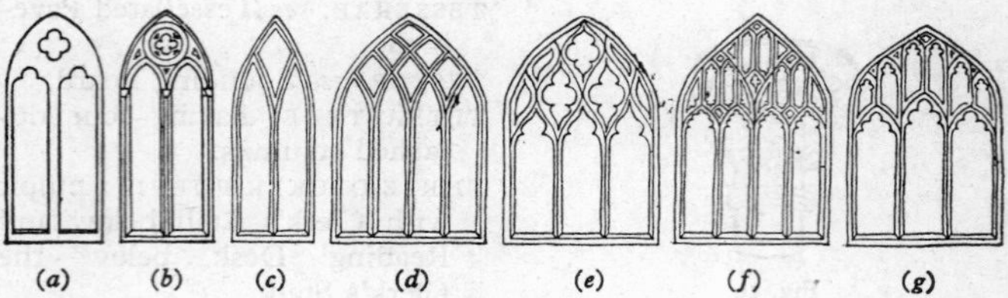

Fig. 20

Fig. 20(*c*). Tracery consisting of a mullion which branches into two forming a Y shape; typical of *c.* 1300. *Intersected tracery: see* Fig. 20(*d*). Tracery in which each mullion of a window branches out into two curved bars in such a way that every one of them is drawn with the same radius from a different centre. The result is that every light of the window is a lancet and every two, three, four, etc., lights together form a pointed arch. This treatment also is typical of *c.*1300. *Reticulated tracery: see* Fig. 20(*e*). Tracery typical of the early C14 consisting entirely of circles drawn at top and bottom into ogee shapes so that a net-like appearance results. *Panel tracery: see* Fig. 20(*f*) and (*g*). Perp tracery, which is formed of upright straight-sided panels above lights of a window.

TRANSEPT: transverse portion of a cross-shaped church.

TRANSOM: horizontal bar across the openings of a window.

TRANSVERSE ARCH: *see* Vault.

TRIBUNE: *see* Gallery.

TRICIPUT, SIGNUM TRICIPUT: sign of the Trinity expressed by three faces belonging to one head.

TRIFORIUM: arcaded wall passage or blank arcading facing the nave at the height of the aisle roof and below the clerestory (q.v.) windows. (*See* Gallery.)

TRIGLYPHS: blocks with vertical grooves separating the metopes (q.v.) in the Doric frieze (Fig. 12).

TROPHY: sculptured group of arms or armour, used as a memorial of victory.

TRUMEAU: stone mullion (q.v.) supporting the tympanum (q.v.) of a wide doorway.

TUMULUS: *see* Barrow.

TURRET: very small tower, round or polygonal in plan.

TUSCAN: *see* Order.

TYMPANUM: space between the lintel of a doorway and the arch above it.

UNDERCROFT: vaulted room, sometimes underground, below a church or chapel.

UNIVALLATE: of a hill-fort: defended by a single bank and ditch.

UPPER PALAEOLITHIC: *see* Palaeolithic.

VAULT: *Barrel-vault: see* Tunnel-vault. *Cross-vault: see* Groin-vault. *Domical vault:* square or polygonal dome ris-

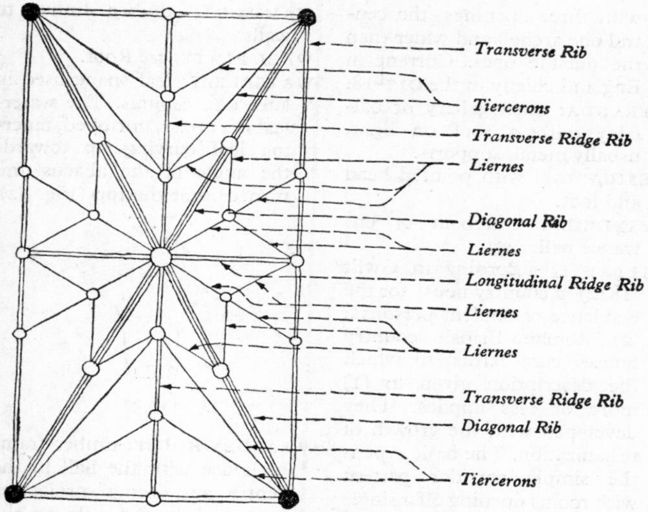

Fig. 21

ing direct on a square or polygonal bay, the curved surfaces separated by groins (q.v.). *Fan-vault:* Late Medieval vault where all ribs springing from one springer are of the same length, the same distance from the next, and the same curvature. *Groin-vault* or *Cross-vault:* vault of two tunnel-vaults of identical shape intersecting each other at r. angles. Chiefly Norman and Renaissance. *Lierne:* tertiary rib, that is, rib which does not spring either from one of the main springers or from the central boss. Introduced in the C14, continues to the C16. *Quadripartite vault:* one wherein one bay of vaulting is divided into four parts. *Rib-vault:* vault with diagonal ribs projecting along the groins. *Ridge-rib:* rib along the longitudinal or transverse ridge of a vault. Introduced in the early C13. *Sexpartite vault:* one wherein one bay of quadripartite vaulting is divided into two parts transversely so that each bay of vaulting has six parts. *Tierceron:* secondary rib, that is, rib which issues from one of the main springers or the central boss and leads to a place on a ridge-rib. Introduced in the early C13. *Transverse arch:* arch separating one bay of a vault from the next. *Tunnel-vault* or *Barrel-vault:* vault of semicircular or pointed section. Chiefly Norman and Renaissance. (*See* Fig. 21.)

VAULTING SHAFT: vertical member leading to the springer of a vault.

VENETIAN WINDOW: window

with three openings, the central one arched and wider than the outside ones. Current in England chiefly in the C17–18.

VERANDA: open gallery or balcony with a roof on light, usually metal, supports.

VESICA: oval with pointed head and foot.

VESTIBULE: anteroom or entrance hall.

VILLA: (1) according to Gwilt (1842) 'a country house for the residence of opulent persons'; (2) Romano-British country houses cum farms, to which the description given in (1) more or less applies. They developed with the growth of urbanization. The basic type is the simple corridor pattern with rooms opening off a single passage; the next stage is the addition of wings. The courtyard villa fills a square plan with subsidiary buildings and an enclosure wall with a gate facing the main corridor block.

VITRIFIED: made similar to glass.

VITRUVIAN OPENING: A door or window which diminishes towards the top, as advocated by Vitruvius, bk. IV, chapter VI.

VOLUTE: spiral scroll, one of the component parts of an Ionic column (*see* Order).

VOUSSOIR: wedge-shaped stone used in arch construction.

WAGON ROOF: roof in which by closely set rafters with arched braces the appearance of the inside of a canvas tilt over a wagon is achieved. Wagon roofs can be panelled or plastered (ceiled) or left uncovered.

WAINSCOT: timber lining to walls.

WALL PLATE: *see* Roof.

WATERLEAF: leaf shape used in later C12 capitals. The waterleaf is a broad, unribbed, tapering leaf curving up towards the angle of the abacus and turned in at the top (Fig. 22).

Fig. 22

WEALDEN HOUSE: timber-framed house with the hall in the centre and wings projecting only slightly and only on the jutting upper floor. The roof, however, runs through without a break between wings and hall, and the eaves of the hall part are therefore exceptionally deep. They are supported by diagonal, usually curved, braces starting from the short inner sides of the overhanging wings and rising parallel with the front wall of the hall towards the centre of the eaves.

WEATHERBOARDING: overlapping horizontal boards, covering a timber-framed wall.

WEATHERING: sloped horizontal surface on sills, buttresses, etc., to throw off water.

WEEPERS: small figures placed in niches along the sides of some medieval tombs (also called Mourners).

WHEEL WINDOW: *see* Rose Window.

INDEX OF PLATES

AVON TYRRELL, Exterior (*James Austin*) 93
BEAULIEU, Church, Reading Pulpit (*Hants Field Club*) 23
BEAULIEU, Spence Cottage, Exterior (*Architectural Review; photo de Burgh Galwey*) 99
BEAULIEU, Palace House (former Abbey Gatehouse), Interior (*By kind permission of Lord Montagu of Beaulieu*) 30
BEDALES, Library, Interior (*James Austin*) 94
BOARHUNT, Church, Exterior (*N.M.R.*) 9
BOURNEMOUTH, Air View (*Aero Pictorial Ltd*) 3
BOURNEMOUTH, St Stephen, Apse Vaulting (*N.M.R.*) 89
BRADING (I.o.W.), Church, Oglander Monument (*James Austin*) 58
BRAMLEY, Church, Brocas Monument (*James Austin*) 69
BRAMSHILL HOUSE, Exterior (*Country Life*) 53
BROADLANDS, Saloon (*Country Life*) 70
BURGHCLERE, Sandham Chapel, Wall Painting (*J. L. Behrend; photo M. Beck*) 96
CATHERINGTON, Church, Wall Painting (*Hants Field Club*) 31
CHILWORTH, Church, Interior (*N.M.R.*) 77
CHRISTCHURCH, Castle, Hall, Exterior (*Christopher Dalton*) 18
CHRISTCHURCH, Christchurch Priory, Fitzharris Monument (*N.M.R.*) 78
CHRISTCHURCH, Christchurch Priory, North Transept, Exterior (*Christopher Dalton*) 14
CHRISTCHURCH, Christchurch Priory, Reredos, Detail (*N.M.R.*) 32
CHRISTCHURCH, Christchurch Priory, South-East Chapel, Interior (*Christopher Dalton*) 28
COWES (I.o.W.), Norris Castle, Exterior (*N.M.R.*) 73
COWES (I.o.W.), St Mary, Tower, Exterior (*James Austin*) 79
CRANBURY PARK, Ballroom (*A. F. Kersting*) 72
EAST MEON, Church, Font (*N.M.R.*) 15
EAST STRATTON, Stratton Park, Portico (*Architectural Review; photo de Burgh Galwey*) 75
EAST TISTED, Church, Norton Monument (*Hants Field Club*) 47
ELLINGHAM, Church, Interior (*Christopher Dalton*) 52
ELVETHAM, Elvetham Hall, Exterior (*James Austin*) 87
FAREHAM, High Street (*E. G. Patience*) 4
FARNBOROUGH, Mausoleum of the Empress Eugenie, Interior (*James Austin*) 91
GODSHILL (I.o.W.), Church, Wall Painting (*James Austin*) 41
GOSPORT, Railway Station, Exterior (*Portsmouth and Sunderland Newspapers Ltd*) 82

THE GRANGE, Exterior (*N.M.R.*) 76
HALE, Church, Transept Doorway (*James Austin*) 65
HARTLEY WESPALL, Church, West End, Exterior (*Hants Field Club*) 33
HEADLEY, near Grayshott, Church, Stained Glass (*James* (*Austin*) 25
HIGHCLERE, Highclere Castle, Exterior (*Country Life*) 81
HIGHCLIFFE, Highcliffe Castle, Oriel Window on South Front (*Country Life*) 45
HOUGHTON, Houghton Lodge, Exterior (*Country Life*) 74
HURSLEY, Hursley Park, Chimneypiece (*James Austin*) 51
IBSLEY, Church, Constable Monument (*N.M.R.*) 55
IDSWORTH, Church, Wall Paintings (*N.M.R.*) 29
LAVERSTOKE, Parsonage, Exterior (*James Austin*) 86
LYNDHURST, Church, Interior (*James Austin*) 88
NETLEY, Netley Abbey, South Transept, Interior (*James Austin*) 27
NEW FOREST (*J. Allan Cash*) 1
ODIHAM, King John's Hunting Lodge, Exterior (*J. Lees-Milne*) 71
OSBORNE HOUSE (I.o.W.), Entrance Side (*John H. Stone*) 84
PETERSFIELD, Statute of William III (*Mrs B. B. Parry*) 66
PORTCHESTER, Church, West Front (*N.M.R.*) 16
PORTCHESTER, Portchester Castle, Keep (*N.M.R.*) 11
PORTCHESTER, Portchester Castle, Walls (*A. F. Kersting*) 5
PORTSMOUTH, Cathedral, Buckingham Monument (*N.M.R.*) 56
PORTSMOUTH, Cathedral, Chancel, Interior (*N.M.R.*) 19
PORTSMOUTH, Dockyard, No. 18 Store (former Ropery), Exterior (*N.M.R.*) 68
PORTSMOUTH, Dockyard, Fire Station, Exterior (*Eric de Maré; Architectural Press*) 83
PORTSMOUTH, Royal Garrison Church, Boss in the Chancel (*N.M.R.*) 21
PORTSMOUTH, St Agatha, Interior (*J. A. Hewes*) 92
QUARR ABBEY (I.o.W.), Abbey Church, Interior of East Tower (*By kind permission of the Procurator of Quarr Abbey*) 95
ROMSEY, Abbey, Capital in the Chancel Aisle (*Hants Field Club*) 13
ROMSEY, Abbey, Nave, Interior (*N.M.R.*) 12
ROMSEY, Abbey, Rood (*Hants Field Club*) 8
SHANKLIN (I.o.W.), Beach (*Reece Winstone*) 2
SHEDFIELD, New Place, Bristol Room (*Country Life*) 54
SHERBORNE ST JOHN, Church, Stained Glass (*Hants Field Club*) 44
SOUTHAMPTON, University, Nuffield Theatre (*Sir Basil Spence, Bonnington & Collins; photo Henk Snoek*) 98
SOUTHAMPTON, Walls (*N.M.R.*) 35
STRATTON PARK, *see* EAST STRATTON
SWAY, Peterson's Tower (*John Bland*) 90
TITCHFIELD, Church, Southampton Monument (*A. F. Kersting*) 50
TITCHFIELD, Titchfield Abbey, Gatehouse (*A. F. Kersting*) 48

THE VYNE, Garden Pavilion, Exterior (*A. F. Kersting*) 61
THE VYNE, Long Gallery, Chimneypiece (*N.M.R.*) 59
THE VYNE, Long Gallery, Linenfold Panelling (*N.M.R.*) 46
THE VYNE, North Portico (*N.M.R.*) 60
THE VYNE, Staircase (*N.M.R.*) 67
WARSASH, School of Navigation, Exterior (*Richard Sheppard, Robson & Partners; photo Colin Westwood*) 97
WEST COWES (I.o.W.), *see* COWES
WHIPPINGHAM (I.o.W.), Church, Exterior (*A. F. Kersting*) 85
WHITCHURCH, Church, ninth-century Gravestone (*Lady T. Cox*) 6
WINCHESTER, Castle, Great Hall, Interior (*Walter Scott, Bradford*) 22
WINCHESTER, Cathedral, Boss from Presbytery (*Rev. E. V. Tanner*) 42
WINCHESTER, Cathedral, Chapter House Entrance (*Iris Hardwick*) 10
WINCHESTER, Cathedral, Ecclesia or Synagogue (*Victoria and Albert Museum, Crown Copyright*) 24
WINCHESTER, Cathedral, Edington Chantry (*N.M.R.*) 37
WINCHESTER, Cathedral, Fox Chantry (*Rev. E. V. Tanner*) 43
WINCHESTER, Cathedral, Frieze found in Excavations (*Winchester Excavations Committee*) 7
WINCHESTER, Cathedral, Gardener Chantry (*N.M.R.*) 49
WINCHESTER, Cathedral, Monument to Lord Portland (*Hants Field Club*) 57
WINCHESTER, Cathedral, Nave, Interior (*N.M.R.*) 38
WINCHESTER, Cathedral, West Front (*Iris Hardwick*) 36
WINCHESTER, Deanery, Porch (*Country Life*) 26
WINCHESTER, Library, Exterior (*N.M.R.*) 80
WINCHESTER, Pilgrims' Hall, Interior (*Country Life*) 34
WINCHESTER, St Cross, Interior (*N.M.R.*) 20
WINCHESTER, St Cross Hospital, Hall and Gatehouse (*Rev. F. Sumner*) 40
WINCHESTER, Serle's House, Exterior (*James Austin*) 64
WINCHESTER, Winchester College, Hall and Chapel, Exterior (*Country Life*) 39
WINCHESTER, Winchester College, New Hall, Woodwork (*Country Life*) 62
WINCHESTER, Wolvesey Palace, Bishops's House, Exterior (*N.M.R.*) 63
WINCHFIELD, Church, Chancel Arch (*Reece Winstone*) 17

INDEX OF ARTISTS

Abraham, R., 284n
Adam, Robert, 291, 294
Adams (Cole) and Horner, 121
Adams, George G., 615
Adey, W. G., 150
Adkins, J. Standen, 740
Albert, Prince, 50, 756
Alexander, Daniel Asher, 776
Alexander, G., 183
Allen, H. R., 265
Allen, Lewis, 403
Allom, Thomas, 50n, 290, 291
Anrep, Boris, 341
Ansell, H. Benson (Hampshire County Architect), 93, 178, 218, 222, 278, 487, 698, 832
Ansell & Bailey, 134
Archer, Thomas, 42, 262, 263, 301
Architects' Co-partnership, 141
Armstead, H. H., 682
Ashken, Tanya, 610
Ashpitel, A., 633
Austin-Smith (J. M.) & Partners, 475
Austin-Smith, Salmon, Lord Partnership, 603n
Bacon, John, the elder, 48, 325, 413
Bacon, John, the younger, 50, 287, 574, 593, 684
Bacon, Percy, 600
Bailey & Piper, 220, 258, 446
Baily, E. H., 222
Baines, George Grenfell, 73
Baines & Son, 525
Baker, Sir Herbert, 54, 110, 695, 700, 704
Baker, T., 83
Baker-King, C. R., 773
Ball, C. W., 462
Ball, J. H., 59, 199, 242, 432, 439, 440, 639n
Barkentin & Krall, 122
Barker, A. R., 92, 595
Barker, E. H. Lingen, 121
Barnsley, Edward, 610
Barry, Sir Charles, 50, 289, 291
Barry, Charles E., 77
Barton, K., 254
Barton, Kinder & Alderson, 644
Bashford, Charles Brome, 508
Bath, Fred, 502
Bazzanti, Niccolo, 573, 593
Bedborough, Alfred, 127, 487, 594; *see also* Hinves & Bedborough
Bedford, Eric, 528
Beeston & Burmester, 301
Behnes, William, 366
Bell, John, 758
Bellot, Dom Paul, 58, 760
Benham, Thomas, 182
Benson, William, 473
Bentham, Sir Samuel, 52, 408, 411, 415
Benyon, Richard, 340
Berger, L. (Southampton City Architect), 60, 516, 524, 529, 531, 532, 555, 561, 562n, 569, 570, 584, 594, 595, 596, 598, 599, 619
Bertie, Thomas, 302, 627, 641n, 674
Betton & Evans, 701
Beverley, S., 133n
Bhai Ram Singh, 758
Billing & Son, 205
Bingley (of London), 747
Birch, George, 273
Bird, T. A., 137
Birkett, J. C., 589
Birt, A., 600
Blacking, W. H. Randoll, 126, 162, 232, 437, 466, 591

Blomfield, Sir Arthur, 56, 97, 123, 163, 198, 212, 218, 241, 242, 281, 319, 327, 352, 353n, 372, 441, 470, 471, 491, 500, 646, 695, 726n
Blomfield, (Sir Arthur) & Sons, 126, 229, 243
Blomfield, Sir Reginald, 113, 135, 286, 324, 362, 442
Blount, G. L. W., 603
Blount, Gilbert, 738
Blow, Detmar, 59, 620
Blow (Detmar) & Billerey, 311
Bodley, G. F., 118, 119, 162, 163, 207, 339, 357, 358, 705, 728
Bodley & Garner, 57, 206
Boehm, Sir J. E., 334
Bonella & Paull, 57, 486; *see also* Paull, J. S.
Bonomi, Joseph, 46, 316
Booth, Ledeboer & Pinckheard, 697
Braddell, Darcy, 51n, 332
Brain, 559
Brakspear, Sir H., 370
Bramble, Benjamin, 741
Bramhill, H., 134
Brandon, David, 206
Brandon, J. & A. R., 571
Brandon, Raphael, 644
Brannon, Philip, 559
Brett, Lionel (Lord Esher), 690, 745
Brett (Lionel) & Pollen, 392, 446, 493
Brewer, F. (of Petersfield), 271
Broadbent, F. G., 645
Brock, E. P. Loftus, 747
Brock, Sir Thomas, 745
Brooke, K. G., 656
Brown, Ford Madox, 745
Brown, F., the younger, 509
Brown (Sir John) & Henson, 374
Brown, J., 287
Brown, Lancelot ('Capability'), 144, 233, 289
Brown, Raffles, 773
Brown, Robert, 772
Brunel, Marc Isambard, 408, 415
Bryans, Herbert, 122, 283
Buckeridge, C., 280
Building Design Partnership, 73, 74, 827
Burges, William, 56, 234
Burlison & Grylls, 120, 126, 442
Burn, William, 51, 79, 308, 508, 509, 631
Burn & McVicar Anderson, 322
Burne-Jones, Sir Edward, 86, 120, 287, 327, 745
Burnet (Sir John), Tait & Partners, 831
Burrough (E.) & G. Ede, 593
Burrow, 142
Burton, Decimus, 51, 117, 252
Butler, T., 221
Butterfield, William, 54, 57, 78, 121, 135, 155, 182, 211, 287, 299, 300, 375, 431n, 434, 609, 693, 700, 701, 702, 704, 706, 709
Cacciatori, B., 192
Cachemaille-Day, N., 59n, 574, 619, 619n
Caine, Osmund, 438
Campbell Douglas & Sellars, 127
Campbell-Jones & Partners, 229
Campbell-Smith & Co., 241n
Cancellor & Hill, 367n
Caper, Thomas, 750
Capes, S. C., 140
Capronnier, J. B., 76, 103
Carew, J. E., 621
Carey, Oliver, 516, 556
Caröe, W. D., 77, 124, 480, 486, 701, 701n, 745n
Carpenter, *see* Slater & Carpenter
Carter, John, 693
Carter, Owen B., 54, 78, 366, 524, 698
Carter, Thomas, 48, 137, 486, 638
Carter, T. B., 726n
Carter, Salaman, MacIver & Upfold, 374, 610
Casolani, 78

Casson, Conder & Partners, 698, 717
Cates, Arthur, 740
Caumartin, J., 437
Cavaillé-Coll, 230
Cave, William, 703
Chamberlain, Roy, 93
Champneys, Basil, 54, 705
Chancellor, F., 92
Chantrey, Sir Francis, 50, 174, 359, 593, 625, 680, 684
Chapman Taylor Partners, 727
Chase, N., 265
Chatwin (J. A.) & Son, 121
Cheere, Sir Henry, 44, 365n, 684
Cheere, John, 44, 373
Christian, Ewan, 160, 188, 261, 269, 315, 323, 485, 691, 778, 830
Christian, J. H., 260
Christmas, John and Matthias, 37, 615
Chute, John, 43, 636, 637, 638
Cibber, C. G., 704
Clacy, J. B., 280
Clare, A. D., 773
Clark & Holland, 300
Clarke, George, 309
Clarke, Joseph, 754, 773
Claxton, Kenneth, 610
Clayton & Bell, 115, 119, 120, 123, 125, 277, 323, 327, 403, 485, 518, 567, 694, 762, 773
Clayton, Black & Petch, 458
Clutton, Henry, 51, 125, 332, 338
Coade, Mrs E., 190n, 217, 228, 273
Coade & Sealy, 775
Cockerell, C. R., 258, 259
Cockerell, F. P. 52, 185, 600
Cockerell, S. P., 258
Cockerell, S. P., Jun., 327
Coggin & Wallis, 76
Cogswell, A. E., 436, 437, 442, 443, 449; *see also* Rake & Cogswell
Coleridge, J. D., 439, 728
Coles, William, 308, 722
Collcutt, T. E., 132, 274, 319
Collins, Herbert, 586, 587, 588, 589, 597
Collmann, L. W., 51n, 333
Colson, John, 55, 86, 114, 134, 181, 195, 212, 218, 287, 287n, 313, 322, 334n, 354, 359, 365, 368, 383, 468, 473, 496, 572, 593, 612, 661, 690, 691, 693, 706, 724, 725
Colson, J. B., 693, 697
Colson (J. B.) & Nesbitt, 199
Colson & Son, 497
Comper, J. Sebastian, 594
Comper, Sir Ninian, 59, 102, 119, 120, 126, 200, 431, 439, 464, 521, 567
Conybeare, Henry, 56, 309
Cooke (of London), 228, 625
Cooper, E. C., 769
Cooper, J. C., 252
Cort, Henry, 238
Corvo, Baron, *see* Rolfe, Frederick
Cory & Ferguson, 55n, 126
Cox, Oliver, 296
Cox Sons, Buckley & Co., 124
Craig, John, 296
Crawley, J., 278, 431
Craze, Romilly B., 436, 518, 567
Creeke, Christopher Crabbe, 117, 126, 130, 131, 600
Creeke, Gifford & Oakley, 124
Crickmay, G. R., 374n
Crickmay & Sons, 724
Critchlow, R., 492, 544
Croggan, W., 190
Cross, A. W. S., 252
Cross, Max, 192
Cubitt, Thomas, 50, 756
Cubitt, William, 48n, 742n
Cubitt & Collinson, 574
Culpin (Clifford) & Partners, 235
Cutler, Joseph, 133
Cutts, J. E. K. & J. P., 230, 521
Dacombe, W. J., 828
Dance, George, the younger, 47, 183, 185, 202, 334, 649
Davies (George) & Webb, 229

Davies, John, 114
Dawber, Sir Guy, 324, 829
Dawkes, S. W., 750
Dawson, Clare, 438
Denman, Thomas, 222
Derick, J., 329
Desmaretz, L. P., 419
Destailleur, H.-A.-G.-W., 58, 230
Devey, George, 51n, 338, 369, 828, 829
Dexter & Staniland, 325
Dolby, Edwin, 286
Dolci, Carlo, 403
Doll, Christian, 704
Donaldson, T. L., 317
Donthorne, W. J., 50, 195, 292
Drake, Charles, 131
Draper, George, 599
Drew, R., 276, 280
Dromgoole, C. B., 554, 564, 565
Drysdale, George, 59, 75
Durst, Alan, 372, 681
Dyce, William, 299, 758
Dyer, F. C., 77
Dyer, J., 353n
Dykes Bower, S., 221, 435, 443, 701
Eales, F. S., 93
Earp, T. W., 119, 120, 242, 407 519
Easton, Hugh, 185, 437, 491
Ebbels, R., 772
Edis, R. W., 132, 610
Edwards, Carl, 407
Edwards, J. A., 221, 358
Elderton (of Southampton), 115
Elliott, John, 212, 520
Elliott & Mason, 571–2
Elmslie, E. W., 55, 694
Elsom (C. H.) & Partners, 337
Emes, 192
Emms, J., 510
Esher, Lord, *see* Brett, Lionel
Evans, C. W. T., 692
Evans, Charles, 620
Evans, David, 58n, 366n, 620, 679, 684, 692, 701
Evans, G., 109, 273, 295
Evans, W. Charles, 336
Evans & Fletcher, 124
Everett, 463
Evesham, Epiphanius, 624
Farmer & Brindley, 122, 763
Farmer & Dark, 60, 134, 233, 300, 328, 492
Farrar Bell, M., 468
Feibusch, Hans, 468
Feilden & Mawson, 60, 690
Ferrata, Andrea, 337
Ferrey, Benjamin, 55, 94, 117, 130, 142, 169, 170, 176, 178, 180, 181, 191, 207, 295, 480n, 616, 650, 733, 828
Ferrey, Benjamin & Edmund B., 158
Ferrey, Edmund B., 158
Field, Horace, 546
Fielding, Copley, 299
Firmin (Eric) & Partners, 229
Fisher (Carl) & Associates, 76
Fisher, Major-General Sir John, 426
Flaxman, John, 49, 90, 176, 221, 222, 327, 334, 372, 486, 615, 630, 684
Fletcher, Sir Banister, 317
Flockton, William, 286
Foden, S. O., 651
Fogerty, J., 127
Ford, Thomas, 438, 467
Foster, James, 269
Fowler, C. Hodgson, 118, 120
Fowler, Grove & Heggar, 487
Frampton, Sir George, 124, 679, 683, 704, 778
Francis, F. & H., 56, 474, 575, 652
Fraser (Ian) & Associates, 91, 93
Frederick, Sir Charles, 45, 288
Fuchs, Emil, 485
Gabb, Thomas, 741
Gaffin & Co., 651
Galloway (E. M.) & Partners, 495, 592
Garbett, William, 87, 172, 175n, 299, 661, 668n, 679, 713

Gardiner, Stephen, 60, 202
Garner, Thomas, *see* Bodley & Garner
Geddes, D., 549
Gelder, P. M. van, 49, 277, 359
Gibbons, Grinling, 40, 262
Gibbons, J. Harold, 123
Gibbs, Charles, 121
Gibbs, James, 44, 262
Gibbs, W., 83, 302
Gibson, Sir Donald, 230n
Gibson, John (architect), 547
Gibson, John (sculptor), 476
Gibson, J. S., 446n
Gilbert, Alfred, 58, 696, 774
Gilbert & Hobson, 769
Giles, Alfred, 553
Giles, C. E., 296, 370, 772
Gill, Eric, 59, 128, 192, 295, 319, 359, 437, 510, 569, 616, 620, 713n
Gill, Macdonald, 769
Gillow, Richard, 742n
Gimson, Ernest, 60, 86, 98
Giovanni da Majano, 34, 636
Gleadowe, R. M. Y., 702
Gleichen, Feodora, 774
Goddard, W. S., 55, 79
Gollins, Melvin, Ward & Partners, 392, 448
Gomme, Sir Bernard de, 39, 247, 408, 419, 422, 426, 427
Goodchild, T., 185
Goodhart-Rendel, H. S., 228, 306, 308
Goodwin, Francis, 461n, 522
Gordon & Gunton, 91, 372
Gore, Gibberd & Saunders, 101
Gough, W. Venn, 751
Gover, William, 693n
Gray, G. Kruger, 705
Green, F. S. M., 133
Green, James Baker, 131
Green, Percy, 332
Green, W. Curtis, 183
Green (W. Curtis), Son & Lloyd, 715
Greenleaves, E., 123
Greenwood, Sydney, 449
Grey, William, 492, 762, 833
Groves, J. T., 388n
Grüner, Professor L., 758
Gruning, E., 98
Guillaume, George, 150, 181, 573, 592
Guthrie, G., 648
Gutteridge & Gutteridge, 568, 574, 576, 578, 581, 583, 584, 750, 831
Guy, F. J., 454n
Habershon & Pite, 772
Habershon, W. G. & E., 111
Hack, T. S., 515, 528, 542
Hair, C. J., 544
Hakewill, 649
Halcrow (Sir William) & Partners, 328
Hall, Edmund, 413
Hall, E. Stanley, 437
Hall, Ruthven O., 705
Hamilton, Hector O., 133n
Hannaford, J., 142
Hansom, Joseph, 57, 325, 432, 649, 762
Hansom, J. S., 431
Hardman, John, 323, 354, 364, 473
Hardwick, P. C., 74, 500
Hardy, G. Haywood, 245
Hardy, James, 211, 505
Harding, James, 179, 237
Harris, J., 239
Harrison, J. P., 299, 300, 351, 472
Harrison & Gilkes, 765
Harvey & Wicks, 732
Haschenberg, Stephan von, 302
Haskoll, J., 731
Hawke, 553
Hawksmoor, Nicholas, 515, 571, 574, 581, 827
Heal, A. V., 433n
Heaton, Butler & Bayne, 119
Hellyer, Thomas, 310, 311, 440, 443, 475, 733, 744, 747, 762, 763, 768, 769, 773
Hems, Harry, 124

Henderson, Ann, 217
Hicks, W. S., 180
Hill, Henry L. G., 705, 716
Hill, William, 53, 445
Hinves, W., 568
Hinves & Bedborough, 517n, 521, 525
Hiolle, M., 338n
Hirst, Philip, 453
Hiscock, William, 174, 178, 337
Hoare, Henry, 473
Hoare (of Southsea), 439
Hodgeman, 412
Holden (Patrick) & Associates, 134
Holiday, Henry, 78, 122, 141, 215, 521, 727, 733
Holland, Henry, 46, 145, 263
Holland, W. (of Warwick), 618
Holliss, Elisabeth, 645
Home (G. Wyville) & Shirley Knight, 128
Hopper, Humphrey, 167n, 359, 501, 611
Horder, Morley, 201n
Howell, Sydney, 607
Hoyland, Douglas, 603
Hubbard Ford (H.) & Associates, 587, 654
Huckle (H. G.) & Partners, 93
Hudson, Alfred J., 443
Hugall, J. West, 502
Hughes, H., 271
Humbert, Albert Jenkins, 55, 774
Huntingdon, John, 300
Huntley, W., 764
Huskisson, Samuel, 372
Hutchinson, C. E., 76
Hutton, John, 564
I'Anson, E. B., 260
I'Anson & Son, 260
Jackson, Sir T. G., 57, 74, 76, 91, 104, 115, 119, 124, 188, 202, 209, 210, 356, 661, 672, 695, 724
Jackson & Greenen, 133, 134
Jacobs, B. S., 751
James, Captain, 246
James, John, 42, 85, 215, 216, 288, 300
Jeavons, Thomas, 221
Jebb, Sir Joshua, 751
Jeffery & Skiller, 54, 697
Jekyll, Gertrude, 194
Jewell, 496
John, Augustus, 236
Johnson, Gerard, 37, 624
Johnson, John, 56, 602
Johnson, M. W., 113
Johnson, Nicholas, 37
Jones, Inigo, 38, 683
Jones, Isaac, 744
Jones, R. J. (of Ryde), 56, 179, 741, 747, 762, 763, 775, 833
Jones, Wyn, 453
Jordan, Abraham, 242, 403
Joy, Henry, 132, 133n
Keable (Julian) & Partners, 163
Kelly, 372
Kelsall, Charles, 829
Kempe, C. E., 58, 83, 147, 163, 180, 195, 210, 229, 237, 275, 283, 293, 295, 319, 327, 339, 367, 436, 444, 485, 624, 630, 648, 675, 676, 680, 684, 725, 740, 750, 775
Kempe & Tower, 485
Kemp Welch & Pinder, 126n, 177, 510n, 617
Kendall, H. E., the younger, 51, 230
Kent, William, 291
Kilgour, Stewart, 449, 568, 569
Kimber, L. F., 243
Kinder, G. S., 524n
Kipling, John Lockwood, 758
Knight, Christopher, 60, 202
Lacey, F. W., 127
Lamb, E. B., 127, 131
Lanchester & Lodge, 233, 449
Lander, Felix, 236
Lansdowne, E. A., 274
Lavers & Barraud, 174, 372, 775
Lavers & Westlake, 463
Lavery, Sir John, 774
Law & Dunbar-Nasmith, 217

Lawrence, Frederic W., 125, 600
Lawson & Donkin, 126, 126n, 132
Lawson & Reynolds, 127
L.C.C. Architect's Department, 296
Leach, C. Pemberton, 762
Leaver, 119
Lee, John T., 440
Leggatt, R. W., 444
Leighton, Lord, 58, 327
Lelliott, C. G., 93
Le Moyne, François, 699n
Lennox, J. D., 417
Leroux, Jacob, 227, 515, 558
Le Sueur, Hubert, 40, 424, 455, 675, 683
Lethaby, W. R., 52, 86, 274, 328
Little, John W., 706
Livesay, Augustus F., 54, 55, 79, 397n, 439, 444, 449, 736, 754
Livesay, G. A. B., 600, 601
Llewelyn-Davies, Weeks & Partners, 91, 93
Lobb (Howard V.) & Partners, 596, 741
Locke, Joseph, 335
Loire, Gabriel, 518, 567
Lorimer, Sir Robert, 75, 462
Loudon, J. C., 575
Lough, J. G., 722
Louise, Princess, 774
Lucas, Colin, 153
Lucas, R. C., 166, 359, 558
Lucas, R. M., 541
Luck, C. L., 767, 769
Luder, Owen, 60, 392, 448, 458
Lunn, J. W., 122, 519
Lutyens, Sir Edwin, 52, 79, 83, 90, 312, 497, 558
Lyngwode, William, 678
Lyon, 694
Lyons, Eric, 60, 516, 545
Lyons, Israel & Ellis, 516, 543, 548, 555, 563, 568, 596
Mabey, C. H., 338n
McAll, Edward, 735n
Macartney, Sir Mervyn, 505
McCormick, Liam, 567
McCulloch, Alan G., 92
Mackennal, Sir Bertram, 620, 681
Mackenzie, A. Marshall, 300
McVicar Anderson, *see* Burn & McVicar Anderson
McWilliam, F. E., 578
Maddox (of Welbeck Street), 649
Mair, George, J. J., 48n, 742
Makins, Thomas E., 245, 277, 465
Malling, 736
Mangan, Wilfred C., 122, 567, 595, 645, 772
Manning, S., 287
Marnock, R. Morrison, 611
Marochetti, Baron C., 616, 750
Marquand, 436
Martin, A. C., 728
Martin, Pilch & Harris, 596
Martineau, E. H., 293
Massey, T. H., 231
Matcham, Frank, 460
Matthew (Robert), Johnson-Marshall & Partners, 830
Maufe, Sir Edward, 296, 319, 603
Maw, 763
Mawson, Thomas, 599n
Mayer (of Munich), 80, 94, 123, 124, 264, 271, 323, 325
Mellor, F., 447, 457, 459
Mennie, 350n
Michie, Lieutenant, 75
Micklethwaite, J. T., 443
Miles, C. T., 120, 124, 600
Millais, Sir John Everett, 176
Mills, George, 776
Milner, Victor, 136
Milner-White, Eric, 591
Ministry of Public Building & Works, 74, 222, 247, 278, 329, 429, 430, 492, 608, 751, 827, 832
Minton's, 758, 766
Mitchell, A., 336
Mitchell, W. H., 97, 593
Mitchell, William, 831

Mitchell, Son & Gutteridge, 166n, 199, 576
Moberly, 694
Moiret & Wood, 93
Moneypenny, George, 54, 716
Moore, J. F., 49, 359, 711
Moore, Temple, 91, 136, 444, 767
Morgan & Carn, 134
Morris, G. T. Windyer, 733
Morris, Hugh, 296
Morris, William, 58, 120, 327, 745
Morris & Co., 287, 323, 592, 595, 681, 724, 727, 773
Morris & Sons, 310
Mort, E. T., 317
Mostaert, Jan, 496
Mottistone, Lord, 748n; *see also* Seely & Paget
Mowbray, A. W., 648
Murphy, L. R., 568
Murray, Fairfax, 288
Mussellwhite, G. B., 217
Mylne, Robert, 488
Nash, John, 47, 53, 137, 297, 470, 740, 742n, 743, 744, 750, 751, 774
Natter, Paul, 327
Navy Works Department, 417
Nelme, Anthony, 403
Nervi, Pier Luigi, 402
Nesfield, W. Eden, 52, 145, 317n, 487
New, Anthony, 402
Newman, James, 735, 744
Newman (of Winchester), 181
Newton, Ernest, 94, 128, 633, 647, 716, 829
Newton (William G.) & Partners, 128
Nicholls, Thomas, 235
Nicholson, A. K., 126, 434, 591
Nicholson, Sir Charles, 59, 90, 124, 193, 218, 243, 332, 400, 403, 434, 443, 518, 590, 591, 706
Noble, Matthew, 487
Nollekens, Joseph, 49, 191, 241, 625, 630
Norris, James, 219
Norton, John, 553
Noyes, Eliot, 300
Nutcher, J., 156
Nye (D. E.) & Partners, 278
O'Connor, 174, 773
Oldrieve, 76
Osmond, William, 727
Owen, Jacob, 221, 225, 238, 435, 453n, 490, 495, 645n
Owen, Thomas Ellis, 204, 440, 441, 447, 453n, 459, 461, 490n, 495n, 645
Page-Johnson Design Group, 472
Pallister, L. K., 318
Papworth, J. B., 184
Parfect, J., 353n
Parken, A. H., 124
Parker, Barry, 374
Parkinson, J. T., 203
Parlby (Thomas) & Son, 408
Parsons, Karl, 439
Paull, J. S., 210; *see also* Bonella & Paull
Pearce, Edmund, 118
Pearse, 713
Pearson, F. L., 125, 706
Pearson, J. L., 56, 118, 125, 198, 316, 343, 368, 691
Pearson, Lionel, 150
Peniston, John, 137, 304
Penneley, Thomas, 725
Pegram, Henry, 734
Pescod, William, 714
Peto, Harold, 293
Phillips, H., 277
Phillips, Ronald, 123
Phillips, 243
Phipps, C. J., 460
Phipps, Paul, 146
Phyffers, Theodore, 463
Pierce, Edward, 41n, 701, 706
Pierce, Thomas, 244
Pigott (R. Mountford) & Partners, 134
Pike (Charles) & Partners, 93

Pilkington, A. J., 125
Pinckney, R. A. P., 80
Pinckney & Gott, 191, 567, 592
Pinder, R. G., 124
Pink (C. R.) & S. Fowler, 190
Piper, John, 691
Pippet, Joseph A., 694
Pistall, W., 767
Pitt, Major, 75
Plaw, John, 515
Playne & Lacey, 502
Pollen, John Hungerford, 327
Pollen, Mrs, 58, 327n
Pomeroy, F. W., 122
Ponting, C. E., 235n, 476, 494, 778
Poole, J. G., 519, 535n
Pope, S. Kelway, 546, 596
Porri (A. G.) & Partners, 93
Potter & Hare, 491, 492, 576, 581, 583, 591, 652n, 827
Powell, Alfred, 98
Powell, J. C., 734
Powells, 78, 119, 122, 142, 202, 215, 324, 327, 367, 433, 485, 572, 680, 694, 724, 727, 767
Prior, E. S., 706, 827, 829
Prynne, G. H. Fellowes, 120, 495
Pugin, A. W. N., 174, 176, 205, 519
Purser, John, 234
Pyne, Benjamin, 698
Rake, G., 645
Rake & Cogswell, 441
Randall, Terence, 436
Rawlins, J. M., 633
Raymond, G., *see* Scoles & Raymond
Redfern, Frank, 119
Regnart, Charles, 49n
Rennie, John, the younger, 246
Repton, G. S., 699
Reveley, William, 517, 524n
Revett, Nicholas, 263n
Reynolds, Bainbridge, 103, 444
Reynolds, Sir Joshua, 509n, 750
Reynolds Stephens, Sir William, 773
Reynolds & Tamblin, 130
Reyntiens, Patrick, 59, 298, 691
Rhys-Davies, Miall, 460
Richardson, Sir Albert, 648
Richardson & Gill, 831
Richmond, George, 299
Robbia, Andrea della, 403
Robert (of Romsey), 481, 482
Roberts, E., 535n
Roberts, Henry, 211
Robertson, Sir Howard, 337
Robinson, James, 695
Robinson, P. F., 141
Rock, Neil, 732
Rodin, Auguste, 527
Rogers, W. H., 575
Rolfe, Frederick (Baron Corvo), 123, 177
Roma, Spiridone, 44, 637
Romaine Walker, W. H., 325
Romaine Walker & Besant, 146
Romaine Walker & Tanner, 52, 146
Rossetti, Dante Gabriel, 745
Roubiliac, L. F., 45, 288, 725
Rouw, H., 754
Rowell, John, 638
Rubens, Sir Peter Paul, 746
Ruskin, John, 238
Ryder & Yates, 570, 599
Rysbrack, J. Michael, 45, 208, 325
St Aubyn, J. P., 500, 520
Salter & Wyatt, 92
Salviati, 296, 521
Salvin, Anthony, 343, 742
Sampson, G., 300
Samwell, William, 258
Sanderson, James, 764, 773
Saunders, T. R., 773, 775
Saunders (W. H.) & Son, 60, 134, 251, 542, 557, 558n, 559, 572
Scheemakers, Peter, 45, 508, 747
Scherrer & Hicks, 462
Schneck, 252
Schultz, R. Weir, 489
Scoles, A. J. C., 91, 431, 440
Scoles (A. J.) & G. Raymond, 141

Scott, Adrian Gilbert, 230
Scott, Sir George Gilbert, 55, 187, 288, 436, 517, 572, 647, 679, 682, 762, 767
Scott, George Gilbert, the younger, 82, 274, 355, 725
Scott, Sir Giles Gilbert, 59, 121, 576
Scott, J. Oldrid, 56, 118, 124, 304, 355n, 436, 439, 488
Scott (J. Oldrid) & Son, 120, 216, 572, 600
Scott, Lady Katherine, 411
Scott (Kenneth) Associates, 286, 827
Scott, M. H. Baillie, 266, 732
Scott, Brownrigg & Turner, 93, 286
Seal (A. J.) & Partners, 133n
Seale, G. W., 122, 327n
Searle, C. C., 81
Sedding, J. D., 52, 58, 58n, 118, 121, 122, 131, 155, 348, 349
Seely & Paget, 318, 373, 402, 749
Shankland, Graeme, 296
Sharpe, 556
Shaw, Ivor, 134
Shaw, R. Norman, 52, 57, 113, 118, 124, 125, 127, 150, 599n
Shaw, Sax, 217
Shepheard, Peter, 60, 705
Shepherd, 129
Sheppard (Richard), Robson & Partners, 60, 93, 516, 560, 580, 584, 595, 643
Sherrin, George, 230
Shickle, Alec, 229
Shout, Benjamin R., 325
Shurmur, T. M., 82
Sillock & King, 565
Sims, Ronald, 91, 93, 127, 359, 516, 564, 576, 579, 580
Skeaping, John, 672n
Skipworth, A. H., 828
Slater & Carpenter, 26, 78
Sly, Henry, 501
Smart, Henry C., 77
Smirke, Sir Robert, 313
Smirke, Sydney, 79
Smith, G. E., 255, 392, 443, 445, 447, 449, 460n
Smith, G. E. R., 518, 592
Smith, J. C., 318
Smith, Osborne, 449
Smith (Charles) & Son (of Reading), 216, 728
Smith (E. Findlay) & Ernest Bird, 830
Soane, Sir John, 47, 136, 267, 716
Soissons (Louis de), Peacock, Hodges & Robertson, 253
Soissons (Louis de), Peacock, Hodges, Robertson & Fraser, 253
South, Robert, 364
Southern, Richard, 578n
Spalding & Myers, 568
Spear, F. H., 441, 442
Spence, Sir Basil, 60, 97, 516, 578, 579, 580, 581
Spence (Sir Basil), Bonnington & Collins, 576, 831
Spencer, Stanley, 59, 150
Squire (Raglan) & Partners, 229
Stabler, Harold, 600
Stallard, A. E., 279
Stapley, Sidney, 75
Stedman, A. J., 234
Stephen (of Winchester), 695
Stern (David) & Partners, 741
Stevens, Alfred, 51n, 333
Stevens, R. A., 92
Stevens, T., 123, 127
Stirling & Gowan, 60, 742
Stokes, Leonard, 449, 519, 520, 528, 645
Stone, J., 491
Stone, Nicholas, 40, 386, 404
Stone, Percy Goddard, 738
Stone, Reynolds, 84
Stratton, W. J., 771
Street, G. E., 56, 56n, 58, 118, 119, 120, 123, 127, 198, 199, 202, 281, 293n, 316, 327, 361, 404, 405, 407, 466, 467, 468, 516, 517, 518, 519, 524n, 603, 630, 831

Stubington, James, 105, 605
Suffolk, Philip, 439
Sumner, Heywood, 59, 179, 242, 433, 433n, 601
Surman, J. B., 372
Sutcliffe, Brandt & Partners, 519
Talbot, E., 252
Talman, William, 288
Tarte, F. W. Kinnear, 361
Tatham, C. H., 655, 656
Taylor, Sir Robert, 472n
Taylor, W. J., 695
Telford, Thomas, 412n, 436
Teulon, S. S., 51, 55, 210, 211, 280, 766
Theed, F., 774
Theed, W., 50, 476, 682, 758, 774
Thicke, F. E., 490
Thomas, Brian, 676
Thomas, Cecil, 217
Thomas, R. P., 220
Thomas, 486
Thomas of Leighton, 681
Thomas (of Oxford), 31, 702
Thornycroft, Sir Hamo, 713
Tilden, Philip, 831
Tinling, G. D., 122
Tite, Sir William, 54n, 198, 222, 253, 335, 532, 554, 560, 584
Tomkins, S. E., 767
Tomlinson, R., 593
Tompsett, H., 645
Tower, W. E., 122, 443; *see also* Kempe & Tower
Traquair, Phoebe, 620
Travers, Martin, 319, 485
Trentanove, A., 176
Triggs, H. Inigo, 830
Tripp, C. N., 294
Tristram, E. W., 398
Truefitt, J., 463
Tugwell, Sidney, 121, 125, 133
Tulloch, John, 118, 197
Turner, Alfred, 705
Turner, Charles, 773
Turner, J. T., 623
Turner, Wilfrid Carpenter, 676
Tyrrell, J. E., 254, 258
Underwood, Charles, 155
Unsworth, W. F., 610
Unsworth, Son & Triggs, 610, 830
Upton, Charles, 624
Veitch, James, the younger, 338
Vellert, Dirk, 33, 637
Voysey (C. Cowles), John Brandon-Jones, J. D. Broadbent & R. Ashton, 694
Vulliamy, Lewis, 280
Wailes, William, 78, 120, 164, 299, 323, 650, 733
Walldin, S., 361, 684
Waller, 300
Walters, F. A., 260, 693
Ward, Ronald, 565
Ward (of London), 493
Ward & Hughes, 271, 474n
Warren, E. P., 97, 103, 571, 722
Waterhouse, Alfred, 51, 57, 110, 460, 556, 610, 630
Watts, Mrs G. F., 600
Webb, Sir Aston, 204, 777
Webb, Christopher, 90
Webb, Geoffrey, 434
Webb, John, 38, 44, 262, 635, 636, 637, 638
Webb, Philip, 319
Webber, E. Berry, 429, 445, 526, 527, 568
Weekes, H., 177
Weir, Helen, 217
Wellington, 7th Duke of, 294, 614
Wells, T., 339
Westlake, N. H. J., 122, 432n
Westmacott, Henry, 593
Westmacott, Richard, the elder, 220
Westmacott, Sir Richard, 49, 220, 264, 649, 731
Westmacott, Richard, the younger, 49, 141, 356, 684
Weston, Burnett & Thorne, 525
Whall, 122
Wheeler, Sir Charles, 705
Whinney, T. B., 546
Whinney, Son & Austen Hall, 133

Whistler, Rex, 342
Whitcombe, Thomas, 695
White, William, 57, 275, 319, 323, 326, 495, 506, 517, 566, 594, 618n, 705
Whitehouse, J. Howard, 732
Whittle, Jack, 296
Wicks, H. G., *see* Harvey & Wicks
Wild, J. W., 114, 517, 750
Wilkins, William, 47, 258
William de Wynford, 30, 514n, 535, 671, 699
Williams, Mrs R., 568
Williams-Ellis, Clough, 745
Williamson, Benedict, 58n, 230
Willis's, 651
Wilson, Derek, 191
Wilson, Henry, 58, 121
Wilson, Sir William, 45, 677
Wilton, J., 48, 264, 682
Wiltshire, K. F., 491n, 591
Withers, R. J., 320, 502
Wood, Richard, 633
Woodman, William, 502, 767
Woodroffe, Buchanan & Coulter, 706
Woodyer, Henry, 55, 57, 92, 179, 201, 231, 240, 242, 265, 303, 315, 329, 339, 354, 517, 519, 567, 629, 650, 694, 721, 726, 769
Woore, Edward, 439
Wornum, R. Selden, 52, 489
Worthington, Sir Hubert, 128
Wren, Sir Christopher, 41, 696, 704
Wyatt, Benjamin, 614
Wyatt, James, 47, 49, 264, 301, 730, 743
Wyatt, Lewis, 47, 261
Wyatt, Matthew Cotes, 75, 615
Wyatt, Samuel, 46, 412, 508
Wyatt, T. H., 57, 89, 128, 147, 362, 366, 648, 696, 725
Wyatt, 742
Wyatville, Sir Jeffrey, 476
Wyllie, H., 429
Wyllie, W. L., 403
Wynne, David, 439
Yates, Cook & Darbyshire, 318
Yevele, Henry, 514n, 535
Yonge, William, 78, 366, 367
Yorke, Rosenberg & Mardall, 278, 516, 557, 830

INDEX OF PLACES

Abbotts Ann, 73
Adhurst St Mary, *see* Sheet, 500
Aldershot, 15, 52, 59, 71, 73, 827
Alresford, *see* New Alresford, 17, 24, 351, *and* Old Alresford, 45, 365
Alton, 27, 35, 46n, 70, 76
Alton Abbey, *see* Medstead, 332
Alverstoke, *see* Gosport, 51, 51n, 240, 252, 256
Ampfield, 78
Amport, 26, 51, 78
Andover, 36, 53, 55, 61, 79, 827
Andwell, 22, 82
Appleshaw, 82
Appuldurcombe (I.o.W.), 41, 729
Arreton (I.o.W.), 25, 38, 49, 64, 65, 730
Ashe, 52, 58n, 82
Ashlett, *see* Fawley, 234
Ashley, 83
Ashley, *see* Ringwood, 475
Ashmansworth, 83
Ashton, *see* Bishops Waltham, 109
Avington, 42, 45, 46n, 84
Avon Castle, *see* Ringwood, 475
Avon Tyrrell, 52, 86
Awbridge, 48, 86
Baddesley, *see* North Baddesley *and* South Baddesley
Barton Stacey, 27, 87
Basing, 24, 27, 33, 34, 35, 88
Basingstoke, 15, 27, 32, 34n, 39, 53, 61, 90, 827
Bassett, *see* Southampton, 571, 581, 584, 831
Baughurst, 55, 94
Beacon Hill, *see* Burghclere, 154
Beaulieu, 21, 22, 60, 66, 94
Beaurepaire, *see* Bramley, 137
Beauworth, 97
Bedales, 60, 97
Bedhampton, 98
Bembridge (I.o.W.), 732
Bentley, 72, 100
Bentworth, 28, 36, 100
Berrydown, *see* Ashe, 52, 83
Bighton, 20, 101, 828
Billingham Manor (I.o.W.), *see* Kingston, 748
Binstead (I.o.W.), 15, 72, 733
Binstead, 20, 26, 27, 102
Bishops Sutton, 32, 103
Bishopstoke, 103
Bishops Waltham, 23, 24, 28, 35, 104
Bisterne, 109
Bitterne, *see* Southampton, 69, 589, 590, 592, 595, 596, 597
Blackfield, *see* Fawley, 234
Blackgang (I.o.W.), *see* Chale, 740
Blackmoor, 52, 57n, 110
Blackwater, *see* Hawley, 280
Blendworth, 70, 111
Boarhunt, 16, 36, 111
Boldre, 40, 52, 113
Bonchurch (I.o.W.), 55, 733, 832
Bonhams, *see* Froyle, 237
Bordon Camp, *see* Headley, 286
Boscombe, *see* Bournemouth, 56 118, 120, 121, 122, 124, 128, 131ff.
Bossington, 38, 114, 828
Botley, 15n, 53, 114
Bournemouth, 15, 51, 52, 55n, 56, 56n, 57, 58, 59, 71, 117, 827, 828
Brading (I.o.W.), 20, 32, 37, 46n, 68, 733
Bradley, 134
Braishfield, 135
Bramdean, 68, 135
Bramley, 26, 31, 32, 45, 47, 49, 136
Bramshaw, 137
Bramshill House, 37, 38, 138
Bramshott, 38, 62, 140

Bransgore, 142
Breamore, 16, 17, 38, 142
Bridgemary, *see* Rowner, 492
Brighstone (I.o.W.), 71, 735
Broadhalfpenny Down, *see* Hambledon, 272
Broadlands, 46, 52, 144
Brockenhurst, 52, 146
Brockhurst, *see* Gosport, 243, 247, 249, 253
Brook (I.o.W.), 736
Broughton, 34n, 146
Brown Candover, 32, 41n, 147
Bucklers Hard, 28, 44, 147
Bullington, 149
Bullsdown Hillfort, *see* Sherfield-on-Loddon, 502
Burghclere, 59, 149
Buriton, 154
Burley, 155
Bursledon, 58n, 155
Burton, 158
Bury, *see* Gosport, 257
Bury Hill, *see* Upper Clatford, 67, 632
Butser Hill, *see* Petersfield, 374
Calbourne (I.o.W.), 32, 71, 736
Calleva Atrebatum, *see* Silchester, 503
Calshot Castle, 29, 158
Cams Hall, *see* Fareham, 227
Carisbrooke (I.o.W.), 20, 23, 27, 33, 35, 36, 69, 71, 737, 832
Castle Malwood, *see* Minstead, 339
Catherington, 20, 27, 37, 158
Catsfield, *see* Fareham, 227
Chale (I.o.W.), 28, 71, 740
Chalton, 25, 36, 160
Chandler's Ford, 162
Charlton, 163
Chawton, 40, 163
Cheriton, 164
Chilbolton, 164
Chilcomb, 165
Chilton Candover, 19n, 165
Chilworth, 54, 165
Christchurch, 15, 18n, 19, 21, 24, 25, 26, 27, 30, 32, 33, 34, 34n, 49, 53, 64, 71, 167, 828
Church Crookham, 179
Clanfield, 56, 179
Clanville House, *see* Weyhill, 649
Clausentum, *see* Bitterne, Southampton, 69, 589, 596
Cliddesden, 180
Colbury, 180
Colden Common, 181
Coldhayes, *see* Steep, 51, 610
Coldrey House, *see* Bentley, 100
Colemore, 181
Compton, 40, 45n, 181
Copnor, *see* Portsmouth, 434, 437, 440, 463
Copythorne, 182
Corhampton, 16, 17, 182
Cosham, *see* Portsmouth, 59, 464
Cove, 54, 183
Cowes (I.o.W.), 29, 47, 48, 48n, 60, 740, 832
Cranbury Park, 47, 183
Crawley, 30, 52, 185
Crofton and Stubbington, 45, 185
Crondall, 20, 32, 33, 40, 187
Crux Easton, 45, 188
Curbridge, *see* Curdridge, 188
Curdridge, 188
Damerham, 18, 188
Danesbury Down, *see* Nether Wallop, 67, 344
Daneshill, *see* Basing, 90
Deane, 35n, 48, 189
Denmead, 190, 828
Dibden, 190
Dogmersfield, 43, 49, 55, 59, 191
Drayton, *see* Portsmouth, 466
Droxford, 35, 192
Duck's Nest Long Barrow, *see* Rockbourne, 477
Dummer, 32, 66, 195
Dunbridge, 62
Durley, 35, 195
Eaglehurst, 47n, 196
East Boldre, 197
East Cowes (I.o.W.), *see* Cowes, 47, 743

East Dean, 197
Eastleigh, 15n, 198
East Meon, 17, 19, 24, 199
Eastney, *see* Portsmouth, 428, 429, 436, 440, 443, 463
Easton, 20n, 36, 55, 201, 828
East Parley, 56n, 202
East Stratton, 47, 57, 60, 202
East Tisted, 27, 34, 36, 203
East Tytherley, 26, 36, 70, 204
East Wellow, 26, 204
East Woodhay, 45, 205, 828
East Worldham, 27, 206
Ecchinswell, 57, 206
Efford Park, *see* Milford-on-Sea, 337
Egbury Grange, *see* St Mary Bourne, 494
Eldon, *see* Upper Eldon
Eling, 45, 207
Ellingham, 39, 45, 209
Ellingham Cottage, *see* Sherfield English, 502
Ellisfield, 210
Elvetham, 51, 54, 210, 828
Embley Park, *see* East Wellow, 205
Emery Down, 211
Empshott, 36, 211
Emsworth, 54, 212
Enham Alamein, *see* Knight's Enham
Eversley, 42, 215
Ewhurst, 216
Ewshot, 216
Exbury, 216
Exton, 217
Faccombe, 217
Fair Oak, 218
Fareham, 15n, 16, 25, 32, 46, 49nn, 54, 218
Farleigh Wallop, 39n, 43, 227
Farley Chamberlayne, 37, 228
Farlington, *see* Portsmouth, 57n, 466
Farnborough, 15, 23, 26, 51, 58, 229, 829
Farringdon, 72, 230
Farringford (I.o.W.), *see* Freshwater, 745
Fawley, 19, 26, 32, 60, 231
Fir Grove, *see* Eversley, 215
Fleet, 56, 234
Fontley, *see* Funtley
Fordingbridge, 30, 235, 829
Forton, *see* Gosport, 240, 243
Fouracre, *see* West Green House, 647
Four Marks, 236
Foxcott, 236
Foxlease, *see* Lyndhurst, 44, 328
Fratton, *see* Portsmouth, 449, 463
Freefolk, *see* Laverstoke, 316
Freemantle, *see* Southampton, 57, 566
Freshwater (I.o.W.), 25, 71, 744
Froxfield, 237
Froyle, 46n, 58n, 237
Fryern Hill, *see* Chandler's Ford, 162, 163
Funtley, 238
Fyfield, 239
Gatcombe (I.o.W.), 27, 32, 58, 745
Giant's Grave, *see* Breamore, 144
Godsfield, 239
Godshill (I.o.W.), 26, 31, 33, 36, 45, 49, 746
Goleigh Manor, *see* Priors Dean, 471
Goodworth Clatford, 239
Gosport, 15n, 43, 46, 51, 51n, 53, 54n, 56, 60, 240
The Grange, 47, 258
Grange Farm, *see* Rowner, 492
Grans Barrow, *see* Rockbourne, 477
Grateley, 26, 259
Grayshott, 260
Greatham, 37, 260
Greywell, 260
Grim's Ditch, *see* Martin, 66, 330
Grove Place, *see* Nursling, 38, 361
Gurnard (I.o.W.), 747
Hackwood Park, 40, 42n, 44, 47, 261

Hale, 42, 42n, 45, 46, 48, 49, 262
Hall Place, *see* West Meon, 647
Hamble, 47, 264
Hambledon, 16, 24, 70, 269
Hannington, 16, 65, 272
Harbridge, 273
Harefield, *see* Southampton, 598
Hartford Bridge, 273
Hartley Mauditt, 19, 273
Hartley Wespall, 30, 274
Hartley Wintney, 274, 829
Haslar, *see* Gosport, 46, 240, 243, 247
Hatherden, 57, 275
Havant, 15n, 25, 48n, 49, 275
Havenstreet (I.o.W.), 747
Hawkley, 55, 280
Hawley, 280
Hayling Island, 25, 51n, 281, 829
Headbourne Worthy, 16, 17, 26, 285
Headley (nr Grayshott), 26, 286, 829
Headley (nr Kingsclere), 286
Heath End, 286
Heckfield, 58, 286
Hedge End, 287
Hengistbury Head, *see* Southbourne, 62, 65, 66, 601
Herriard, 36, 42, 287
Highclere, 36, 44, 45, 50, 56, 70, 71, 288
Highcliffe, 28, 50, 291 827, 829
High Coxlease, *see* Lyndhurst, 328
High Cross, 293
Highfield, *see* Southampton, 571, 584
Hildon Hall, *see* East Tytherley, 204
Hilsea, *see* Portsmouth, 430, 437, 442, 463
Hinton Admiral, 42, 293
Hinton Ampner, 16, 294
Hinton Daubnay, *see* Catherington, 160
Holbury, *see* Fawley, 234
Holdenhurst, 63, 64, 295
Hollington Farmhouse, *see* East Woodhay, 206
Holybourne, 295
Holywell House, 295
Hook, 296
Hook-with-Warsash, *see* Warsash, 644
Hordle, 296
Horndean, 297
Houghton, 48, 297
Hound, 59, 298
Hunton, 298
Hurn Court, 299
Hursley, 38, 42, 299
Hurstbourne Priors, 37, 42, 300
Hurstbourne Tarrant, 27, 301
Hurst Castle, 29, 302
Hyde, 303
Hyde Abbey, *see* Winchester, 18, 22, 716
Hythe, 303, 829
Ibsley, 36, 304
Ibthorpe, 305
Ibworth, 65
Idsworth, 26, 27, 51, 305
Iford, *see* Bournemouth, 125
Itchen Abbas, 41, 55, 308
Itchen Stoke, 56, 309
Kilmeston, 309
Kimpton, 32, 310
King John's Hunting Lodge, *see* Odiham, 48, 365
Kingsclere, 18n, 40, 46n, 310
Kingsclere Woodlands, 311
Kingsley, 311
King's Somborne, 52, 312
Kingston, *see* Portsmouth, 441, 463
Kingston (I.o.W.), 747
Kings Worthy, 66, 313
Kinson, 66, 313
Kitcombe House, *see* Newton Valence, 354
Knap Barrow, *see* Rockbourne, 63, 477
Knight's Enham, 46n, 314
Ladle Hill, *see* Litchfield, 65, 66, 67, 321
Lainston, 43, 314

Lake (I.o.W.), *see* Sandown, 767
Landport, *see* Portsmouth, 54, 59, 60, 432, 435, 438, 449, 458, 831
Langley, *see* Fawley, 234
Langrish, 315
Langstone, 62, 315
Lasham, 315
Laverstoke, 37, 46, 57n, 316
Leckford, 317
Lee, 317
Lee-on-the-Solent, 318
Leigh Park, *see* Havant, 275, 277, 279
Linkenholt, 319
Liphook, 319, 830
Liss, 59, 319, 830
Litchfield, 66, 320
Little Somborne, 16, 322
Littleton, 322
Lockerley, 322
Lock's Heath, 323
Longparish, 323
Longstock, 323, 830
Long Sutton, 324, 830
Loom Field, *see* Bentworth, 101
Lower Froyle, *see* Froyle, 238
Lowtherville (I.o.W.), *see* Ventnor, 773
Lymington, 15, 43, 45, 48, 64, 324
Lyndhurst, 44, 49, 57, 58, 326
Malshanger House, *see* Oakley, 29, 363
Mapledurwell, 328
Marchwood, 60, 328
Marelands, *see* Bentley, 100
Marsh Court, *see* King's Somborne, 52, 72, 312
Martin, 65, 66, 330
Martyr Worthy, 331
Marwell Hall, 48, 331
Mattingley, 30, 331
Maybush, *see* Southampton, 567, 568
Medstead, 59n, 332
Melchet Park, 51, 332
Mengham, *see* Hayling Island, 284
Meonstoke, 333
Merdon Castle, 334
Merstone Manor (I.o.W.), *see* Arreton, 731
Micheldever, 47, 49, 334, 830
Michelmersh, 34, 36, 64, 335
Midanbury, *see* Southampton, 592, 599
Midlington House, *see* Droxford, 194
Milford Lake, *see* Highclere, 50, 291
Milford-on-Sea, 25, 335, 830
Millbrook, *see* Southampton, 57, 566, 567, 568, 569
Milton, 337
Milton, *see* Portsmouth, 439, 445, 448, 463
Minley, 51, 338
Minstead, 18n, 45, 338, 830
Monk Sherborne, 339
Monxton, 339
Moordown, *see* Bournemouth, 118, 123
Moore Place Farm, *see* Bramshill House, 140
Morestead, 340
Mortimer West End, 48n, 340
Mottisfont, 20, 21, 22, 32, 36, 43, 340
Mottistone (I.o.W.), 748
Moundsmere Manor, *see* Nutley, 362
Moyles Court, *see* Ellingham, 39, 210
Mudeford, 343, 830
Nately Scures, 343
Netherton, 343
Nether Wallop, 20, 64, 67, 343
Netley, 22, 29, 52n, 53, 58n, 345
Netley Marsh, 351
Nettlestone (I.o.W.), 749
New Alresford, 17, 24, 351
Newbies, *see* Baughurst, 94
Newchurch (I.o.W.), 749
Newlands Manor, *see* Milford-on-Sea, 337
New Milton, *see* Milton, 337
Newnham, 55, 353

New Place, *see* Shedfield, 38, 52, 497
Newport (I.o.W.), 35, 36, 37, 53, 54, 750, 833
Newton Valence, 353
Newtown (nr Burghclere), 354
Newtown (nr Soberton), 354
Newtown, *see* Southampton, 520, 561
Newtown (I.o.W.), 53, 55, 753
Newtown Park, *see* South Baddesley, 46, 599
Niton (I.o.W.), 64, 754
Northam, *see* Southampton, 60, 519, 561
North Baddesley, 36, 354
North Charford Manor, *see* Breamore, 144
North End, *see* Portsmouth, 441, 446
Northerwood, *see* Lyndhurst, 328
North Foreland Lodge, *see* Sherfield-on-Loddon, 502
North Hayling, *see* Hayling Island
Northington, 49, 57, 356
North Stoneham, 35, 37, 49, 50, 357
North Waltham, 359
North Warnborough, 360
Northwood (I.o.W.), 755
Norton Manor House, *see* Wonston, 724
Nunwell (I.o.W.), 755
Nursling, 37, 38, 360
Nursted House, *see* Buriton, 155
Nutley, 362
Oakfield (I.o.W.), *see* Ryde, 762
Oakley, 29, 33, 57, 362
Odiham, 24, 29, 48, 363
Old Alresford, 45, 365
Old Ditcham Farm, *see* Buriton, 155
Old Winchester Hill, *see* Meonstoke, 333
Osborne House (I.o.W.), 50, 756
Otterbourne, 366
Overton, 24, 367
Over Wallop, 368
Ovington, 368
Owslebury, 45, 368
Pamber End, 19, 20, 22, 25, 27, 369
Park, 370
Park House, *see* Hambledon, 272
Parkhurst Prison (I.o.W.), *see* Newport, 751
Paulsgrove, *see* Portsmouth, 467
Peartree Green, *see* Southampton, 35n, 50, 589, 592, 593, 597
Pelham Place, *see* Newton Valence, 353
Pennington, 370
Penton Mewsey, 63, 65, 371
Petersfield, 19, 44, 49, 371
Peterson's Tower, *see* Sway, 617
Pitt, 375
Pittleworth Manor, *see* Bossington, 38, 114
Plaitford, 375
Pokesdown, *see* Bournemouth, 66, 118, 123, 128
Polhampton Farm, *see* Overton, 368
Portchester, 18, 19, 21, 23, 28, 28n, 40, 69, 72, 375, 830
Portsdown Hill, 70, 71, 387
Portsea, *see* Portsmouth, 40n, 393, 428, 429, 438, 456
Portsmouth, 15, 20, 24, 25, 25n, 26, 29, 32, 39, 40, 40n, 42, 43, 45, 46, 46n, 52, 53, 54, 55, 56, 57n, 59, 60, 62, 70, 71, 389, 831
Portswood, *see* Southampton, 571n, 572
Preshaw House, 470
Preston Candover, 470
Priors Dean, 40, 471
Privett, 471
Purbrook, 472, 831
Quarley, 43, 66, 472
Quarr Abbey (I.o.W.), 15, 22, 23, 58, 72, 760
Quidhampton Farmhouse, *see* Overton, 367

Ramsdell, 473
Ranville's Farmhouse, *see* Broadlands, 145
Redbridge, *see* Southampton, 566, 567n, 569, 570
Redhill, *see* Rowlands Castle, 490
Redrice House, *see* Upper Clatford, 51, 631
Remenham House, *see* Appleshaw, 82
Rhinefield Lodge, *see* Brockenhurst, 52, 146
Ringwood, 46n, 48n, 56, 474
Roche Court, 475
Rockbourne, 24, 34n, 50, 63, 476
Romsey, 17, 19, 22, 24, 25, 26, 31, 40, 49, 57, 70, 477, 831
Rookley House, *see* Little Somborne, 322
Rooksbury, *see* Wickham, 655
Rookwood Farm, *see* Denmead, 190, 828
Ropley, 488
Rosebank, *see* Silchester, 505
Rotherfield Park, *see* East Tisted, 203
Rotherwick, 30, 52, 489
Rowlands Castle, 490
Rowner, 36, 490
Rownhams, 492
Rudmore, *see* Portsmouth, 439
Ryde (I.o.W.), 50, 51, 53, 56, 57, 762, 833
St Catherine's Down (I.o.W.), 28, 71, 766
St Denys *see* Southampton, 21, 572, 584, 588n
St Helens (I.o.W.), 766
St Lawrence (I.o.W.), 767
St Leonard's Grange, *see* Bucklers Hard, 28, 149
St Margaret's, *see* Titchfield, 626
St Mary Bourne, 17, 27, 493
Sandleheath, 494
Sandown (I.o.W.), 29, 51, 71, 767
Sarisbury and Swanwick, 495
Seaview (I.o.W.), 768
Selborne, 20, 21, 34n, 62, 70, 495
Seven Barrows, *see* Litchfield, 321
Shalden, 496
Shalfleet (I.o.W.), 768
Shanklin (I.o.W.), 51, 71, 769
Shawford, 41, 496
Sheat Manor (I.o.W.), *see* Gatcombe, 746
Shedfield, 38, 52, 69, 497
Sheet, 500
Sherborne St John, 33, 33–4, 34, 35, 40, 45, 45n, 500
Sherfield English, 502
Sherfield-on-Loddon, 502
Shipton Bellinger, 502
Shirley, *see* Southampton, 566, 567, 568, 569, 570
Sholing, *see* Southampton, 590, 593
Shorwell (I.o.W.), 31, 38, 770
Silchester, 27, 35, 67, 68, 69, 503
Smannell, 57, 506
Soberton, 26, 45, 506
Soldiers Rings, *see* Damerham, 189
Somerley, 47, 508
Sopley, 509
Southampton, 15, 17, 19, 19n, 20, 21, 23, 24, 28, 30n, 32, 35n, 50, 51, 53, 54, 57, 57n, 59n, 60, 511, 831
South Baddesley, 46, 599
Southbourne, 62, 65, 66, 600, 831
South Gorley, 601
South Hayling, *see* Hayling Island
Southsea, *see* Portsmouth, 29, 426, 440, 443, 444, 445, 446, 449, 459
South Stoneham, *see* Southampton, 571, 573, 581, 827
South Tidworth, 56, 602
South Warnborough, 32, 603
Southwick, 21, 34n, 35, 45, 604
Southwick House, *see* Purbrook, 472
Sparsholt, 26, 609

Spence Cottage, *see* Beaulieu, 60, 97
Stanbridge Earls, 609
Steep, 51, 610
Steventon, 17, 29, 611
Stockbridge, 53, 54, 64, 65, 611
Stoke Charity, 26, 45, 613
Stratfield Saye, 37, 39, 45, 614
Stratfield Turgis, 616
Stratton Park, *see* East Stratton, 47, 60, 202
Stubbington, *see* Crofton and Stubbington, 185
Swainston (I.o.W.), *see* Calbourne, 24, 736
Swanmore, 54, 55, 616
Swanmore (I.o.W.), *see* Ryde, 762
Swanwick, *see* Sarisbury and Swanwick
Sway, 617
Swaythling, *see* Southampton, 571, 573, 574, 581, 583, 584, 588
Sydmonton, 617
Sydney Lodge, *see* Hamble, 47, 267
Tadley, 35, 618
Talbot Village, *see* Bournemouth, 130
Tangley, 36, 618
Testwood, 619
Thorley (I.o.W.), 771
Thorney Hill, 59, 620
Thornhill, *see* Southampton, 594, 596, 598
Thruxton, 25, 33, 34, 37, 57, 68, 620
Tichborne, 37, 621
Tidworth House, *see* South Tidworth, 602
Timsbury, 62, 622
Tipner, *see* Portsmouth, 443
Titchfield, 15n, 16, 19, 22, 25, 29, 37, 39, 50, 622, 831
Totland (I.o.W.), 772
Totton, *see* Eling, 207
Tufton, 31, 629
Tunworth, 629
Twyford, 49, 57, 630
Tylney Hall, *see* Rotherwick, 52, 489
Upham, 630
Upnately, 631
Upper Clatford, 36, 51, 631
Upper Eldon, 632
Upton Grey, 632
Venards, *see* Ibsley, 305
Venta Belgarum, *see* Winchester, 658
Ventnor (I.o.W.), 51, 71, 772
Vernham Dean, 633
Vernon Hill, *see* Bishops Waltham, 109
The Vyne, 29, 32, 33, 34, 38, 43, 44, 48, 634
Wallop House, *see* Nether Wallop, 344
Waltham Chase Mill, *see* Bishops Waltham, 109
Warblington, 16, 21, 28, 639
Warbrook House, *see* Eversley, 42, 215
Warnford, 17, 20, 24, 37, 642
Warsash, 60, 643
Waterlooville, 54, 644
Weatham Farm, *see* Liss, 320
Weeke, *see* Winchester, 26, 692
Westbourne, *see* Bournemouth, 118, 121, 127, 128
Westbury House, *see* East Meon, 199
West Court (I.o.W.), *see* Shorwell, 771
West Cowes (I.o.W.), *see* Cowes
West End, 646
West Green House, 43, 646
West Howe, *see* Bournemouth, 134
West Leigh, *see* Havant, 278
West Meon, 55, 647
Weston, *see* Southampton, 594, 596, 599
Weston Patrick, 648
West Tisted, 648

West Town, *see* Hayling Island, 284
West Tytherley, 70, 648
West Worldham, 649
Weyhill, 49, 649
Whale Island, *see* Portsmouth, 430
Wheatsheaf Inn, *see* North Waltham, 360
Wherwell, 36, 650
Whippingham (I.o.W.), 18, 48, 55, 58, 774
Whitchurch, 17, 53, 53n, 54, 650
Whitecroft Hospital (I.o.W.), *see* Newport, 751
Whitsbury, 651
Whitwell (I.o.W.), 20, 35, 775
Wickham, 15n, 24, 37, 39, 652
Widley, *see* Portsmouth, 55, 468
Wield, 32, 37, 656
Winchester, 15, 16, 17, 18, 18n, 19, 19n, 20, 21, 22, 23, 25, 26, 27, 30, 31, 32, 33, 34, 34n, 36, 36n, 38, 39, 40, 41, 41nn, 42, 44, 45, 46n, 47, 48, 49, 50, 53, 54, 55, 57, 58, 58n, 60, 64, 68, 69, 70, 72, 657, 831, 832
Winchfield, 20, 35, 721
Winklebury Camp, *see* Basingstoke, 66, 93
Winnall, 722
Winslade, 722
Winton, *see* Bournemouth, 124
Wolverton, 43, 723
Wolverton Manor (I.o.W.), *see* Shorwell, 38, 771
Wonston, 28, 723
Woodcote Manor, *see* Bramdean, 135
Woodcott, 724
Woodmancott, 724
Woolbury Ring, *see* Stockbridge, 612
Woolmer Lodge, *see* Bramshott, 141
Woolston, *see* Southampton, 57, 590, 594, 595
Woolton Hill, 57, 725
Woolverton Manor (I.o.W.), *see* St Lawrence, 767
Wootton (I.o.W.), 775
Wootton St Lawrence, 45, 725
Worthy Park, *see* Kings Worthy, 313
Worting, 726
Wroxall (I.o.W.), 775
Wyford Farm, *see* Pamber End, 370
Wymering, *see* Portsmouth, 25n, 468
Yarmouth (I.o.W.), 29, 45, 53, 776
Yateley, 30, 40, 46n, 58, 726
Yaverland (I.o.W.), 38, 777

ADDENDA

(OCTOBER 1966)

p. 15 [Introduction.] Professor Colin Buchanan's recent report on South Hampshire suggests that all these places should be joined into one single city.

p. 42 [Introduction.] *Hawksmoor* probably designed South Stoneham House, however; cf. p. 581.

p. 52 [Introduction, Bournemouth, St Clement, Vicarage.] Demolished since this was written.

p. 52 [Introduction.] Also Lutyenesque, enlivened by typically wilful touches, is *E. S. Prior*'s Greystones, Highcliffe, of 1911–12 (*see* below).

p. 74 [Aldershot.] Of the Royal Pavilion's graceful timberwork, looking oddly like C20 Scandinavia and an impressive testimony to Prince Albert's modernity, there remains an excellent LODGE on the main road (NT).

p. 76 [Aldershot.] Mr Taylor sent in the following last-minute comments: The most impressive single new building is perhaps the POWER STATION, off Thornhill Road, 1964–6 by the *Building Design Partnership*. It has a row of oblong concrete stacks and an all-glazed cabin resting on a massive substructure of rough bush-hammered concrete. Most recent of all (1965–6) is RAMILLIES PARK, off the end of Redvers Buller Road, an attractive group of timber-faced housing by *Kenneth Scott Associates* (with the *Ministry of Public Building and Works*) in the same 12M Jespersen system as at Rowner. WILLEMS PARK, a group of eight-storey maisonettes by the same architects in the same system, was begun in 1966 in Wellington Avenue.

p. 80 [Andover.] ST JOHN (R.C.), Weyhill. 1957–8 by *Potter & Hare*.

p. 90 [Basingstoke, St Michael.] ROYAL ARMS of Elizabeth I (R. L. P. Jowitt).

p. 93 [Basingstoke.] Mr Taylor's survey of New Basingstoke owes much to information given him by Mr C. G. Lelliott.

p. 101 [Bighton, All Saints.] Mr R. L. P. Jowitt tells me that a Saxon window was discovered in 1965.

p. 114 [Bossington, Bossington House.] *George Devey* did work here. Did he have a hand in the shaped gables? (NT).

p. 127 [Bournemouth.] FIRST CHURCH OF CHRIST SCIENTIST, Christchurch Road. 1926 by *W. J. Dacombe*, surprisingly good neo-Georgian, in plum-coloured brick and Ham Hill stone (NT).

p. 134 [Bournemouth.] In MEYRICK ROAD is an octagonal PILLAR BOX (cf. Gosport, p. 253; information from Mr Jowitt).

p. 177 [Christchurch Priory.] S AISLE. STAINED GLASS. Fifth window from E, good figured medallions in memory of *Benjamin Ferrey* sen., † 1847, no doubt designed by his son. Seventh from E, fragment of early C14 French glass given by Lord Stuart de Rothesay (cf. Highcliffe) (NT).

p. 177 [Christchurch Priory.] Of the PRIORY BUILDINGS a good deal of the precinct WALL survives, and also the MILL, very pretty, with later brick above medieval stone, but without telling details. The site of the cloister is occupied by PRIORY HOUSE, a plain C18 brick house with a canted bay window in the centre. Arcaded ground floor to the E wing on which is a polygonal timber enclosure to the central dormer (NT).

p. 190 [Denmead, Rookwood Farm.] This is in fact a C12 stone house, formerly with an undercroft, and with parts of the original windows remaining, altered and enlarged in timber framing in Tudor times (information from Mr J. G. Draper).

p. 202 [Easton, St Mary.] Agatha Barlow was a bishop's widow and her five daughters married five bishops (R. L. P. Jowitt).

p. 206 [East Woodhay, St Martin.] There is also an HOUR GLASS STAND, as Mr Jowitt tells me. He also draws my attention to the fact that the feet of the lady on the monument are in fact incised in the slab.

p. 211 [Elvetham, St Mary.] REREDOS. Alabaster scenes in a gilt wooden frame, 1889 by *A. H. Skipworth*, a pupil of Bodley (NT).

p. 230 [Farnborough, Farnborough Hill.] Extensions to Kendall's house were made by *Devey* before 1878 (NT).

p. 235 [Fordingbridge, St Mary.] ROYAL ARMS. Probably George I, very handsome (R. L. P. Jowitt).

p. 275 [Hartley Wintney.] At HAZELEY HEATH, 1½ m. NW, is the cottage designed for himself in 1898 by *Ernest Newton*. T-shaped, the stem old work, the cross-bar in roughcast with prominent shutters. Other residents of Hartley Wintney at that time included Lethaby, Schultz Weir, and the American historian Charles H. Moore (NT).

p. 285 [Hayling Island.] The HAYLING BILLY, a new pub, has as its sign one of the original Stroudley locomotives, used on the Hayling Island branch railway (closed in 1963). It is painted in the original colours and set up on a plinth. (Mr R. L. P. Jowitt provided this information.)

p. 286 [Headley.] HEATH LODGE is cultured neo-Georgian of *c.* 1920 by *Sir Guy Dawber*. Red brick, symmetrical weatherboarded bay windows (NT).

p. 293 [Highcliffe.] GREYSTONES, Waterford Road, is a major house by *E. S. Prior*, 1911–12. The main garden front relatively restrained, with segment-headed windows reminiscent of Webb dressed flush with the stone walls. Splendid tall chimneys. E and W loggias, the former two-storey, with round brick columns without capitals supporting the big roof slopes. Naughtiness breaks out only in the diamond-shaped dormers. Elegant hall with rough-plastered walls and an inscribed hexagon of wooden Tuscan columns. Staircase smacking of chinoiserie (NT).

p. 304 [Hythe.] KNIGHTONS. This was the home from 1841 of the eccentric neo-classical author and amateur architect *Charles Kelsall* (1782–1857). He called it the Villa Amalthea, erected behind the sea-wall nine busts on pedestals, including Homer, Pythagoras, Dryden, Milton, and Newton, some of which survive, and added a round clock-tower surmounted by a triple cross. A Latin inscription explains that the lower cross signifies Old Catholicism, the middle Protestantism, and the upper the Reformation of Both. (Information supplied by Mr David Watkin.)

p. 319 [Liphook.] LITTLE BOARHUNT is a farmhouse cosily rebuilt for himself by *H. Inigo Triggs* (of *Unsworth, Son & Triggs*), 1910–11. He wrote the standard work on *Formal Gardens in England and Scotland* (1901–2) and the garden is naturally the interesting feature here (NT).

p. 320 [Liss.] GREEN WALLS, Hill Brow, is a large modernistic flat-roofed house (with white walls) of 1933, by *E. Findlay Smith & Ernest Bird* (NT).

p. 323 [Longstock.] There is a HOUSE here designed in 1959 by *Yorke, Rosenberg & Mardall* for the late John Spedan Lewis (NT).

p. 324 [Long Sutton, Lord Wandsworth's College.] This has an admirable new copper-roofed Assembly Hall, 1965–6, by *Robert Matthew, Johnson-Marshall & Partners* (NT).

p. 335 [Micheldever, Railway Station.] The opening ceremony of the London and Southampton Railway was held here in 1840 (R. L. P. Jowitt).

p. 336 [Milford-on-Sea.] In VICTORIA ROAD is a very early PILLAR BOX. It is in the form of a fluted column and has a perpendicular letter-slit (R. L. P. Jowitt).

p. 339 [Minstead.] MALWOOD, ¼ m. NE of Castle Malwood, was designed in a vaguely Shaw style, 1883–4 by *Ewan Christian*, for Sir William Harcourt. He had first thought, more wisely, of employing Devey, but feared that, as an aristocrats' architect, Devey would not condescend to such a *bicoque*, as a house of less than £5000 – ironical in view of Devey's pioneering of the cottage style (NT).

p. 343 [Mudeford.] In the village is a PILLAR BOX in the form of a fluted column, so Mr Jowitt tells me (cf. Milford-on-Sea).

p. 386 [Portchester, St Mary.] ROYAL ARMS. Of Elizabeth I, 1577. These are the earliest royal arms in Hampshire (R. L. P. Jowitt).

p. 392 [Portsmouth.] The position will be changed radically if Portsmouth Corporation carries out the bold plans by *Sir John Burnet, Tait & Partners* for building high density housing on a broad belt of reclaimed land at the head of Langstone Harbour (NT).

p. 399 [Portsmouth Cathedral.] ROYAL ARMS of William III, an exceptionally fine piece (R. L. P. Jowitt).

p. 432 [Portsmouth, St Agatha, Landport.] In September 1966 it was announced that St Agatha is to be demolished. It was promised that the sgraffito decoration of the apse will be stored for use elsewhere.

p. 472 [Purbrook.] The VICARAGE was by *Street* (NT).

p. 485 [Romsey.] The architecture of Mrs Ashley's monument was by *Richardson & Gill* (NT).

p. 581 [Southampton University, Glen Eyre Hall.] Large extensions were begun in 1966, this time designed by *Sir Basil Spence, Bonnington & Collins*, with *Gutteridge & Gutteridge* only as executive architects. A series of linked U-shaped courtyards, carried out in storey-height units cast from moulds designed by the sculptor *William Mitchell* (NT).

p. 601 [Southbourne.] Hengistbury Head was only saved by the 1929 slump from being the site of a monster castle of the Citizen Kane type designed by *Philip Tilden* for Gordon Selfridge (Tilden's superb drawings are at the R.I.B.A.) (NT).

p. 623 [Titchfield, St Peter.] The outline of the original W gable can still be made out in the change of the texture of the stonework.

p. 661 [Saxon Winchester.] Excavations in 1966 immediately N of the W end of Winchester Cathedral revealed the W end of the C10 Old Minster. Although badly robbed, this is in the form of a W transept forming a W façade about 90 ft broad, with the nave projecting some 8 ft W of the flanking transepts. The interior of the N of these transepts contained a network of sleeper walls indicating the existence of an arched and perhaps vaulted ground floor of several bays. The floors were of opus signinum and remains of window glass were found. The whole of the C10 cathedral has now been uncovered, and its total length is approximately 180 ft, the structures found this year being those of a westwork as predicted by the late Mr Roger Quirk, but more of the type of Gernrode than Corvey. W of the W front was an extensive plaster-surfaced atrium in which a number of stone coffins were set in a regular pattern. Around and above one such robbed grave on the axis of the Saxon cathedral the Chapel of St Swithun was constructed in the Middle Ages with its altar above the grave. It seems that this grave was regarded in the Late Saxon and Norman period as the original grave of St Swithun, but the discovery of the C7 cathedral below this area, rather than further W, makes it uncertain if this were in fact the original grave of 862. The C7 cathedral will be excavated in 1967 (Martin Biddle).

p. 681 [Winchester Cathedral.] Recently, underneath the paintings of Deposition and Entombment, remains of earlier paintings of the same subjects have been found. They are, as Dr Oakeshott commented, remarkably fresh in colour, bold and effective, and stylistically related to the Winchester Bible.

p. 694 [Winchester, County Hall.] Work started in 1966 on a large extension in the style of today by *H. Benson Ansell*, County Architect (NT).

p. 716 [Winchester, Jewry Street.] No. 40 was the N wing of the old THEATRE. A bold arch embraces the whole front. Within is a Venetian window (R. L. P. Jowitt).

p. 717 [Winchester.] Opposite part of this group is a good new POST OFFICE SORTING OFFICE, by the *Ministry of Public Building and Works*, 1965–6, which sensibly keeps to the same façade rhythm, though in red brick (NT).

p. 733 [Bonchurch, St Boniface.] ROYAL ARMS. A very handsome Victorian piece (R. L. P. Jowitt).

p. 739 [Carisbrooke Castle.] The GREAT WELL, sunk *c.*1150, is 160 ft deep and has a diameter of 5 ft 3 in. It was worked by a donkey pulling round a wheel, 15 ft 6 in in diameter (R. L. P. Jowitt).

p. 740 [Cowes, St Mary.] ROYAL ARMS. Of Queen Victoria, uncommonly rich; surrounded by flags (R. L. P. Jowitt).

p. 750 [Newport, St Thomas.] ROYAL ARMS. Of Queen Victoria. Over the chancel arch. Very elaborate, with flags (R. L. P. Jowitt).

p. 763 [Ryde, St Michael, Swanmore.] The CLERGY HOUSE and SCHOOLS, also no doubt by *Grey* and *Jones*, form a group with the church. Two stone-faced wings to its E and to its S (NT).